The Bar Handbook 2014 – 2015

The Bar Handbook 2014–2015

Nicholas Bacon QC

Barrister, 4 New Square,
Member of the Bar Council Remuneration Committee, Bar Council Joint Tribunal,
Bar Council CFA Committee,
Appointed High Court Costs Assessor,
Advocacy Trainer (Inner Temple)

James Woolf

Manager of Ethics and Training at the Bar Council

Simon Garrod

Head of Regulatory Affairs at the Law Society
Formerly Deputy Director, Representation & Policy at the Bar Council

LexisNexis®

Members of the LexisNexis Group worldwide

United Kingdom	LexisNexis, a Division of Reed Elsevier (UK) Ltd, Lexis House, 30 Farringdon Street, London, EC4A 4HH, and London House, 20–22 East London Street, Edinburgh EH7 4BQ
Australia	LexisNexis Butterworths, Chatswood, New South Wales
Austria	LexisNexis Verlag ARD Orac GmbH & Co KG, Vienna
Benelux	LexisNexis Benelux, Amsterdam
Canada	LexisNexis Canada, Markham, Ontario
China	LexisNexis China, Beijing and Shanghai
France	LexisNexis SA, Paris
Germany	LexisNexis GmbH, Dusseldorf
Hong Kong	LexisNexis Hong Kong, Hong Kong
India	LexisNexis India, New Delhi
Italy	Giuffrè Editore, Milan
Japan	LexisNexis Japan, Tokyo
Malaysia	Malayan Law Journal Sdn Bhd, Kuala Lumpur
New Zealand	LexisNexis NZ Ltd, Wellington
Singapore	LexisNexis Singapore, Singapore
South Africa	LexisNexis Butterworths, Durban
USA	LexisNexis, Dayton, Ohio

Published by LexisNexis

A CIP Catalogue record for this book is available from the British Library.

ISBN 9781405787963

Typeset by Columns Design Ltd, Reading, England
Printed and bound in Great Britain by Hobbs the Printers Ltd, Brunel Road, Southampton, Hampshire SO40 3W
Visit LexisNexis at www.lexisnexis.co.uk

Foreword by the Chairman of the Bar Council

The Bar Handbook is essential reading for anyone working at, or interested in, the Bar. It provides in a single volume all of the rules, guidance and related material produced by the Bar Standards Board (BSB) and the Bar Council.

This seventh edition of *The Bar Handbook* contains an updated Code of Conduct, which is now part of the BSB's Handbook. The launch of the BSB's Handbook in January 2014 is just one instance of how the regulatory environment for the Bar is subject to continual change. At the same time, we face a challenging economic environment, reductions in the scope of, and the level of the fees paid for, legal aid, developments in the market for criminal advocacy services and an increasing use by lawyers of new and innovative practice models. In that regard, this edition contains details of changes made to the Public Access Scheme and of BARCO, the new escrow account for the Bar.

Meanwhile, despite these many changes, the Bar continues to offer not only high standards of advocacy, legal advice and professional conduct, but also value for money and flexibility. *The Bar Handbook* is intended to assist barristers to continue doing so.

Nicholas Lavender QC
Chairman of the Bar Council

July 2014

Foreword by the Chairman of the Bar Standards Board

I am once again very pleased to welcome the new edition of *The Bar Handbook* for 2014/15.

Much has happened since the publication of last year's volume.

In January 2014, the Bar Standards Board introduced the BSB Handbook; the ninth edition of the Code of Conduct is Part 2 of that Handbook which brings together all of the BSB's guidance and regulations for the first time. The Handbook represents the BSB's move towards "outcomes focused regulation" by which it is less prescriptive about how a barrister should act, instead describing the expected outcomes of compliance with the Code.

During the lifetime of this edition, the BSB will become a regulator of entities (in which barristers work) as well as of individual practitioners. The BSB is also moving towards a system of "risk-based supervision" through which it will encourage those it regulates to better manage risk. These are some of the most important changes to affect the Bar in a generation and are driven by the aim of permitting more innovative and flexible provision of barristers' services to users, in the public interest.

In promoting better regulation and high quality at the Bar, and facilitating good practice, the BSB continues to work closely with the Legal Services Board and is committed to promoting the Regulatory Objectives of the 2007 Act.

This Handbook remains the central repository of guidance and best practice for barristers and anyone interested in understanding how the Bar works; it is a crucial means also of disseminating and promoting these high standards. This is even more essential now that the regulatory ambit of the BSB is set to expand.

I commend this Handbook as an excellent point of reference which demystifies the workings of the Bar for professional and lay people alike and promotes best practice in the public interest.

Baroness Deech DBE QC(Hon)
Chairman of the Bar Standards Board

July 2014

Introduction

The annual publication of Bar Handbook has become a recording of a profession in flux in recent years. In 1975–76 the number of practising barristers was 3,730. In the following decade, this increased to more than 5,000. Now the number of practitioners is in excess of 15,000.

In the 2013 Barrister's Working Lives survey of the Bar, just under two thirds (65%) of self-employed barristers reported that they had undertaken some publicly funded work in the past year. Legal aid is still subject to almost continuous review with the Government pursuing a radical overhaul of the way in which it procures legal services. Although the Bar Council has consistently opposed the Government's proposed cuts to criminal legal aid and calls for a proper, considered review, there is little doubt that that work in publicly funded cases in 2014/15 will again present many challenges for publicly funded barristers.

Given this backdrop, the Bar continues to evolve and develop new ways of working: the number of Practitioners qualified to work through the Public Access Scheme continues to grow as barristers look for means of diversifying their practices. A significant recent development permits all barristers to become authorised to conduct litigation. Others anticipate the Bar Standards Board introduction of entity regulation towards the end of 2014 as offering further possibilities.

As ever, in an increasingly competitive market-place, barristers have had to become more professional in marketing their services. Barristers and chambers are continuing to explore other modes of delivery of their services with procurement companies and other special purpose vehicles being discussed and developed.

The regulatory context is also moving forward. At the time of going to press, the Bar Standards Board has just submitted its application to regulate new business entities. The move will allow BSB-regulated barristers to set up companies or partnerships and enable publicly funded barristers to contract directly with the Legal Aid Agency, taking control over work away from solicitors. The Legal Services Board (LSB), which has oversight over the whole regulatory structure, has 90 days to consider this proposal.

The origins of the Bar Council lie in the nineteenth century when the management of the profession rested with the four Inns of Court. Following a petition of barristers to the Attorney-General, a Bar Committee was created in 1883. In 1894, a new General Council of the Bar was established, but it was not until 1946 that a new constitution for the Bar Council set out its main objects systematically. In that year the Bar Council assumed a number of "trade union" functions, such as fee negotiation, which have become of increasing importance to the profession over the years.

As the governing body of the profession, the Bar Council seeks to discharge its representative and regulatory functions to the highest standards and always in the public interest. This benefits consumers as well as the profession.

The Bar Handbook is now in its seventh edition, building on the success of the previous six versions. It again brings together all the current guidance produced by the Bar Council and BSB in a single, convenient work of reference.

In this edition, in keeping with the "One Bar" ethos, we no longer separate employed barristers from the work of the self-employed Bar.

The Handbook does not provide "all the answers" to every query about practice at the Bar in the twenty-first century. However, it does act as a "sign-post" to other sources of guidance in areas of evolving practice. It also seeks to clarify the important distinction between the Bar Council's representative and regulatory functions. It is structured to cover all the career stages of a barrister and to offer practical information in relation to every element of practice. The Handbook will develop alongside the rapidly evolving legal services market and reflect the changing and new perspectives on practice that arise in response to future developments in the regulatory environment.

The effectiveness and strength of the Bar Council depends to a very high degree on the contributions of barristers themselves (and others) who give freely, and generously, of their time to the various committees, working groups and to the Bar Council itself. Almost all of the material reproduced in this Handbook is the result of their labours. It is to them, once again, that this Handbook is dedicated, in the hope that the collective wisdom represented in these pages will continue to add something of value to all members of the profession.

Disclaimer

At the time of writing (July 2014) every effort has been made to ensure that the content of this Handbook is accurate.

However, as with any publication seeking to encompass such a huge range of specialist and, until now, disparate material, it is inevitable that some of the contents are undergoing amendment or review at the point of publication. Readers should not therefore seek to rely on the content without satisfying themselves about the currency of the information. Nor can the information in the Handbook act as a substitute for taking advice where appropriate. The material contained in this publication is made available only for the purpose of offering guidance. It does not constitute advice nor does it offer a definitive interpretation of matters with which it is concerned.

Neither the General Council of the Bar (GCB) nor any other person working for or with the GCB in the preparation or production of this Handbook accepts any liability in law for any loss or damage howsoever caused including by any lack of care.

Acknowledgements

As the introduction of the Handbook highlights, this work represents the current collective wisdom of various Bar Council representative and regulatory Committees, the individuals serving on them, and the Executive supporting their work. All of them are owed a considerable debt of thanks for making this publication possible as well as individuals at other external organisations. However, some are worthy of particular reference for their contribution to this project:

Charlotte Hudson – Manager of the Chairman's Office, Bar Council
Dr Vanessa Davies – Director, Bar Standards Board
Paul Mosson – Head of Member Services, Bar Council
Carol Harris – BARCO Escrow Account Manager
Adrian Vincent – Head of Remuneration & Policy, Bar Council

Christian Wisskirchen – Head of International Relations, Bar Council
Smita Shah – Records Manager
Russell Wallman and Bob Gillies – QC Appointments
Jonathan Goldsmith – Secretary-General, CCBE

Status of the Guidance

Following the creation of the BSB in January 2006 and the separation of the Bar Council's regulatory and representative functions, certain Bar Council committees ceased to exist and were replaced completely or in part by new regulatory committees reporting to the BSB.

The Professional Standards Committee (PSC) was replaced by two committees, the Standards Committee – a regulatory committee reporting to the BSB and responsible for the Code of Conduct, and for issuing guidance on the application of the Code of Conduct, and the Professional Practice Committee (to be renamed the Ethics Committee) – a representative committee with the remit of issuing guidance to the Bar on issues of professional standards.

The Professional Conduct and Complaints Committee was renamed the Complaints Committee. Its remit and functions remained unchanged.

In relation to references to the Legal Services Commission (LSC), the LSC was abolished as a result of the Legal Aid, Sentencing and Punishment of Offenders (LASPO) Act 2012 and was replaced on 1 April 2013 by the Legal Aid Agency, an executive agency of the Ministry of Justice.

Contents

Table of the Bar Code of Conduct and Associated Material

Paragraph references printed in **bold** type indicate where the Code is set out in part or in full.

Table of Statutes

Paragraph references printed in **bold** type indicate where the Statute is set out in part or in full.

Table of Statutory Instruments

Paragraph references printed in **bold** type indicate where the Statutory Instrument is set out in part or in full.

Table of Cases

A

B

C

D

E

G

H

I

J

K

L

M

N

O

P

R

V

W

Part I
The Code of Conduct of the Bar of England and Wales

The Code and Legislative Background

Introduction

[1.1]

The Code of Conduct is now in its ninth edition. From January 2014, the Code was published as Part 2 of the first edition of the BSB Handbook. The Handbook aims to bring together all the BSB's guidance and regulations for the Bar in one publication for the first time, with the BSB's move towards outcomes focussed regulation, less prescriptive, with more focus and guidance on what the outcome of a rule should be, rather than attempting to define how a barrister should act in every situation.

Basic structure

[1.2]

The Handbook itself sets out and explains the new structure but basically it comprises:

Part 1 – Introduction.

Part 2 – **The Code of Conduct**: this is made up of 10 'Core Duties', the 'rules' which supplement those Duties, and the 'outcomes' which compliance with the Duties and Rules are designed to achieve. The BSB takes a 'risk-based approach to regulation' so outcomes are designed with the 'risks' that the Bar needs to manage to ensure compliance in mind.

The Code of Conduct part will also include guidance to assist interpretation. The Code is now divided into 4 sections:

(A) Application.

(B) Core Duties.

(C) Conduct Rules.

This is in turn split into subsections:

(a) You and the court.

(b) Your behaviour towards others.

(c) You and your client – including the QASA Rules.

(d) You and your regulator.

(e) You and your practice.

(D) Rules applying to specific regulated individuals

Part 3 – **Scope of Practice and Authorisation Rules**: covering requirements to practise and scope of permitted activities 'authorsied persons' are permitted to make.

Part 4 – **Qualification Rules**: covering requisite training required in order to become qualified to practise.

Part 5 – **Enforcement Regulations**: setting out procedures applied in realtion to non-compliance with the Handbook.

Part 6 – **Definitions.**

Terminology

Core duties

There are now ten Core Duties which build on rules that were in the previous Code. However, they now apply to all barristers, not just practising barristers (therefore unregistered barristers are required to comply with the Core Duties when providing legal services). They underpin the entire regulatory framework and set the mandatory standards that all BSB regulated persons are required to meet.

Outcomes

At the beginning of each section are identified outcomes, which explain the reasons behind the regulatory scheme and what it is designed to achieve. The outcomes are derived from the regulatory objectives of the Legal Services Act 2007 and the risks that must be managed if they are to be achieved. These outcomes put the rules into context and, together with the Core Duties, help barristers to determine how they should act if a specific situation is not covered by the rules or it is not clear how a rule should be applied in a specific situation. The outcomes are not themselves mandatory, but the BSB will take into account whether or not an outcome has, or might have been, adversely affected when considering how to respond to alleged breaches of the Core Duties or rules. As such, barristers should have the outcomes in mind when interpreting the rules.

Rules

The rules supplement the Core Duties and are similarly mandatory. Prescriptive rules have only been used where necessary to achieve a desired outcome. The rules provide barristers with a clear understanding of exactly what is required of them and ensure that clients and the public know what they can reasonably expect of those who provide legal services.

However, the rules are not intended to be exhaustive. In any situation where no specific rule applies, reference should be made to the Core Duties. In situations where specific rules do apply, it is still necessary to also consider the Core Duties, since compliance with the rules alone will not necessarily be sufficient to comply with the Core Duties.

Guidance

Throughout the Handbook, including Part Two – the Code of Conduct – we have presented relevant guidance alongside associated rules. The guidance serves several purposes. It may assist in the interpretation of the rules by giving further explanations and examples of how the rules apply in certain circumstances. It may draw attention to related rules. Also it may provide examples of the types of behaviour that might lead to compliance with the rules or factors that need to be considered by the regulated person if they are to act in compliance with the Core Duties and the rules and achieve the outcomes.

Scored through text

The Handbook still contains scored through text which is still subject to approval by the Legal Services Board (LSB). This text relates only to entity regulation and is provided for information. The BSB will be seeking approval from the LSB for these outstanding rules, which we expect to come into force in early 2014.

Main changes

The BSB issued accompanying information related to the new Handbook and in it, some of the main changes cited were:

Conducting litigation

Self-employed barristers will be able to apply for an extension to their practising certificate in order to conduct litigation. This is designed to relieve clients approaching Public Access barristers from having to act as a self-representing litigant and conducting certain administrative tasks themselves if they are not going through a solicitor.

Associations with others

Rules preventing self-employed barristers from sharing premises and forming associations with non-barristers have been removed. This will allow barristers to pool together risks and resources with others so long as the interests of clients are protected.

Obligation to report serious misconduct

Barristers will be required to self-report and report others in relation to 'serious misconduct' (there will be an exemption for barristers giving advice via the Bar Council ethics helpline).

Unregistered barristers

Core duties apply to all barristers including 'unregistered' if supplying legal services.

International Practice Rules

The 'international work' definition has changed to 'foreign work', 'foreign clients' and 'foreign lawyers'. Public Access rules will apply to foreign work when instructions are received directly from a lay foreign client or a lay client in England and Wales in relation to foreign work.

The Cab-rank Rule

Extended to apply to instructions for work in England and Wales coming from lawyers in Scotland, Northern Ireland and EEA member states and to non-advocacy work.

Obligation to cooperate with regulator

This is enshrined in the Core Duties. The previous duty of Heads of Chambers is replaced by chambers' obligation to appoint a member responsible for liaising with the BSB.

The BSB Handbook

Foreword

Justice and the rule of law are fundamental to our society. So is public confidence in the administration of justice.

Barristers play a central part in our legal system. The effective and efficient running of our legal system relies on barristers using their independent judgment when advising their client, presenting their clients' cases effectively, and carrying out their duty to the court and their other professional duties. The trust and confidence which the public places in barristers, and the reputation of the Bar as a whole, depend on the behaviour of all barristers continuing to merit the trust reposed in them. Barristers therefore must act with integrity, honesty and independence. In their practice they must provide a competent and professional service, keep their knowledge fully up to date, give sound advice and deal frankly and courteously with clients, colleagues and others.

When acting as an advocate or conducting litigation, the role of a barrister is to present their client's case as effectively as possible. Justice requires that people appearing before a court should have a fair hearing. This in turn means that they should be able to have their case presented by skilled advocates who will do so fearlessly, independently and in the best interests of their client. The sound administration of justice also requires that those who are acting as an advocate, or conducting litigation, always observe their duty to the court, even where this conflicts with the interests of their client.

~~Barristers are now free, if they choose to do so, to offer their services through a range of different business structures, including structures jointly managed and owned by other types of lawyers, such as solicitors, and non-lawyers. The consumer can now choose different means of access tothe services of the Bar. However, the public needs to be sure that the standards that apply will be no less rigorous and that access to justice will be safeguarded. So, this Handbook applies not only to barristers but also to alternative business structures, and other entities which are authorised by the Bar Standards Board, to their managers and owners, and to those whom they employ to provide legal services to their clients. It is important that the same high standards are maintained by all those whom the Bar Standards Board regulates.~~

(To be signed by the Chair of the BSB)

The BSB Handbook

Part I – Introduction

A GENERAL

AI The Bar Standards Board

[1.3]

I1

The *Bar Standards Board* is a specialist regulator focussing primarily on the regulation of advocacy, litigation and legal advisory services. These legal services have a close relationship to access to justice and the rule of law. Our society is based on a rule of law. Everyone needs to be able to seek expert advice on their legal rights and obligations and to have access to skilled representation in the event of a dispute or litigation. Our system of justice depends on those who provide such services acting fearlessly, independently and competently, so as to further their clients' best interests, subject always to their duty to the Court.

I2

The regulatory objectives of the *Bar Standards Board* derive from the Legal Services Act 2007 and can be summarised as follows:

1. protecting and promoting the public interest;
2. supporting the constitutional principles of the rule of law;
3. improving access to justice;
4. protecting and promoting the interests of consumers;
5. promoting competition in the provision of the services;
6. encouraging an independent, strong, diverse and effective legal profession;
7. increasing public understanding of the citizen's legal rights and duties; and
8. promoting and maintaining adherence to the following professional principles:
    a. that *authorised persons* act with independence and integrity;
    b. that *authorised persons* maintain proper standards of work;
    c. that *authorised persons* act in the best interests of their clients;
    d. that *authorised persons* comply with their duty to the court to act with independence in the interests of justice; and
    e. that the affairs of clients are kept confidential.

I3

The BSB Handbook ("*this Handbook*" or "*the Handbook*") sets out the standards that the *Bar Standards Board* requires the *persons* it regulates to comply with in order for it to be able to meet its *regulatory objectives*.

14

Although the *Handbook* is drafted with specific reference to those regulated by the BSB and for use by them, the *Handbook* should also act as a useful reference tool for all consumers of legal services regulated by the *Bar Standards Board*. In particular, the Core Duties and the outcomes set out in Part 2 of this Handbook should give consumers a useful indication of what they should expect from the *Bar Standard Board's* regulatory framework and those subject to it.

A2 Structure of the Handbook

[1.4]

15

The *Handbook* consists of the following parts:

1. Part 1 – Introduction;
2. Part 2 – The Code of Conduct –this part includes the ten Core Duties which underpin the *Bar Standards Board's* entire regulatory framework, as well as the rules which supplement those Core Duties. Compliance with both the Core Duties and the rules is mandatory. The Code of Conduct also contains details of the outcomes which compliance with the Core Duties and the rules is designed to achieve. The *Bar Standards Board's* approach to regulation is risk-focused and so these outcomes have been defined by considering the risks which the profession needs to manage if the *regulatory objectives* are to be achieved;
3. Part 3 – Scope of Practice and Authorisation Rules~~, Authorisation and Licensing Rules –~~ this part includes the requirements that must be met to become entitled to practise as a *barrister* or a *registered European lawyer* ~~and the process that must be followed in order to obtain authorisation to practise as a *BSB authorised body*.~~ It also provides a summary of the scope of activities that each type of *BSB authorised person* is permitted to undertake;
4. Part 4 – Qualification Rules –this part sets out the training which a person must complete, and other requirements which a person must satisfy, in order to be called to the Bar by an *Inn* and become qualified to practise as a *barrister*. It also includes details of the training requirements that *BSB authorised persons* are required to meet;
5. Part 5 – Enforcement Regulations – this part sets out the enforcement procedures that apply if *BSB regulated persons* and/or *relevant persons* fail to act in accordance with the requirements of this *Handbook*;
6. Part 6 – Definitions –this part defines all the italicised terms used in this *Handbook*.

16

The *Handbook* includes Core Duties, Outcomes, Guidance, Rules and Regulations. "CD" refers to Core Duties, "o" to Outcomes, "g" to Guidance, "r" to Rules and Regulations. The Regulations form the basis upon which enforcement action may be taken and are set out in Part E of this Handbook. The effect of something being classified as a Core Duty, Outcome, Guidance, Rule or Regulations is as follows:

1. Core Duties – these underpin the entire regulatory framework and set the mandatory standards that all *BSB regulated persons* are required to meet. They also define the core elements of professional conduct. Disciplinary proceedings may be taken against a *BSB regulated person* if the *Bar Standards Board* believes there has been a breach by that person of the Core Duties set out in this *Handbook* and that such action would be in accordance with the *Enforcement Policy*.

2. The Outcomes – these explain the reasons for the regulatory scheme and what it is designed to achieve. They are derived from the *regulatory objectives* as defined in the LSA and the risks which must be managed if those objectives are to be achieved. They are not themselves mandatory rules, but they are factors which *BSB regulated persons* should have in mind when considering how the Core Duties, Conduct Rules or Qualification Rules (as appropriate) should be applied in particular circumstances. The *Bar Standards Board* will take into account whether or not an Outcome has, or might have been, adversely affected when considering how to respond to alleged breaches of the Core Duties, Conduct Rules or Qualification Rules.

3. The Rules – The Rules serve three purposes:

   a. the Conduct Rules supplement the Core Duties and are mandatory. Disciplinary proceedings may be taken against a *BSB regulated person* if the *Bar Standards Board* believes there has been a breach by that person of the Conduct Rules set out in Part 2 of this *Handbook* and that it would be in accordance with the *Enforcement policy* to take such action. However, the Conduct Rules are not intended to be exhaustive. In any situation where no specific Rule applies, reference should be made to the Core Duties. In situations where specific Rules do apply, it is still necessary to consider the Core Duties, since compliance with the Rules alone will not necessarily be sufficient to comply with the Core Duties;

   b. the Rules contained within "Scope of Practice Rules" set out the requirements for authorisation and the scope of practice for different kinds of *BSB authorised person*. These rules are mandatory;

   c. the rest of Part 3 and Part 4 set out the requirements which must be met by a *relevant person* before they may undertake a specific role within those regulated by the *Bar Standards Board*. If a person fails to meet those requirements, they will not be permitted to undertake that role by the *Bar Standards Board*. Where requirements are continuing and a *BSB regulated person* fails to meet such requirements which are relevant to that *BSB regulated person*, the *Bar Standards Board* may take steps in accordance with Part 3 or Part 5 to have that *BSB regulated person* prevented from continuing within that role.

4. Guidance:

   a. Guidance serves a number of purposes:

      i. to assist in the interpretation and application of the Core Duties or Rules to which such Guidance relates.

      ii. to provide examples of the types of conduct or behaviour that the Rules are intended to encourage or which would likely indicate compliance with the relevant Rule or, conversely, which may constitute non-compliance with the Rule to which such Guidance relates.

iii. to explain how the Rule applies to a particular type of *BSB regulated person* and how that particular BSB regulated person could comply with that Rule.

iv. to act as a signpost to other rules or to guidance on the *Bar Standard's Board* website or elsewhere which may be relevant when considering the scope of the Rule.

v. in Part 3, to give further information about the process of applying for authorisation ~~and about how the *Bar Standards Board* intends to exercise its discretionary powers in relation to the authorisation of entities.~~

b. The Guidance set out in this Handbook is not the only guidance which is relevant to *BSB regulated persons*. In addition to the Guidance, the *Bar Standards Board* has published and will publish from time to time various guidance on its website which supplements this *Handbook*, including (but not limited to):

i. the *Pupillage* Handbook; and

ii. the Equality and Diversity Code Good Practice Guidelines.

c. In carrying out their obligations or meeting the requirements of this *Handbook*, *BSB regulated persons* must have regard to any relevant guidance issued by the *Bar Standards Board* which will be taken into account by the *Bar Standards Board* if there is an alleged breach of or otherwise non-compliance with of the obligations imposed on a *BSB regulated person* under this *Handbook*. Failure to comply with the guidance will not of itself be proof of such breach or non-compliance but the *BSB regulated person* will need to be able to show how the obligation has been met notwithstanding the departure from the relevant guidance.

5. Regulations – Part 5 of this *Handbook* sets out the regulations which bind the *Bar Standards Board* when it considers alleged breaches of the *Handbook* and subsequent enforcement action. These Regulations also bind the various Tribunals and panels referred to in that Part and all regulated persons who are subject to the enforcement process. When considering enforcement action under Part 5, the *Bar Standards Board's* response to any alleged breach of or non-compliance with the Core Duties or the Rules will be informed by the impact of the alleged breach or non-compliance on the achievement of the relevant Outcomes, as well by as its own *Supervision and Enforcement Policies* and any other policies published from time to time which the *Bar Standards Board* regards as relevant (taking into account the nature of the alleged breach or non-compliance).

A3 Amendments to the Handbook

[1.5]

rI1

Subject to Rules rI1 and rI2, the *Bar Standards Board* may make amendments and/or additions to this *Handbook* by resolution and any such amendments and/or additions will take effect on such date as the *Bar Standards Board* appoints or, if no such date is appointed, on the date when notice of the amendment is first published on the *Bar Standard Board's* website following approval under Schedule 4 of the Legal Services Act 2007.

rI2

The *Bar Standards Board* has no power without the unanimous consent of the *Inns* to amend or waive Rule Q4.1 or this Rule so as to permit a person who has not been called to the Bar by an Inn to practise as a barrister.

rI3

Any amendments to Section 5.C must be made in accordance with the requirements of that Section.

rI4

Amendments and additions will be published on the *Bar Standards Board's* website.

A4 Waivers

rI5

Subject to rI2, the *Bar Standards Board* shall have the power to waive or modify:

1. the duty imposed on a *BSB regulated person* to comply with the provisions of this *Handbook*; or
2. any other requirement of this *Handbook*;
3. in such circumstances and to such extent as the *Bar Standards Board* may think fit and either conditionally or unconditionally.

rI6

Any application to the *Bar Standards Board* for a waiver of any of the mandatory requirements or to extend the time within which to complete any of the mandatory requirements must be made in writing, setting out all relevant circumstances relied on and supported by all relevant documentary evidence.

B APPLICATION

[1.6]

rI7

Subject to paragraphs rI8 to rI11 below, this *Handbook* applies to the following categories of person:

1. all *barristers*, that is to say:
   a. barristers who hold a practising certificate in accordance with Section 3.C ("*practising barristers*");
   b. barristers who are undertaking either the first non-practising six months of *pupillage* or the second practising six months of *pupillage*, or a part thereof and who are registered with the *Bar Standards Board* as a *pupil* ("*pupils*"); and
   c. all other barristers who do not hold a practising certificate but who have been called to the Bar by one of the *Inns* and have not ceased to be a member of the Bar ("*unregistered barristers*");
2. European lawyers registered as such by the *Bar Council* and by an *Inn* in accordance with Section 3.D but only in connection with professional work undertaken by them in England and Wales ("*registered European lawyers*");
3. ~~entities which have been authorised or licensed by the *Bar Standards Board* in accordance with Section 3.E of this Handbook, which means *BSB authorised bodies* and *BSB licensed bodies* ("*BSB authorised bodies*");~~
4. ~~individuals who are authorised to provide *reserved legal activities* by another *Approved Regulator* where such individuals are directly or *indirectly employed* by a *BSB authorised person* ("*authorised (non-BSB) individuals*");~~
5. ~~all partners, members or directors of a partnership, limited liability partnership or company respectively where such partnership, limited liability partnership or company is a *BSB authorised body* ("*BSB regulated managers*") and, to the extent that this *Handbook* is expressed to apply to them in their capacity as such, owners of a *BSB authorised body* ("*BSB regulated owners*");~~
6. solely as regards provisions in this *Handbook* relating to disqualification from performing a *relevant activity* or *relevant activities* and not otherwise, any *non-authorised individuals* who are directly or *indirectly employed* by a *BSB authorised person*; and
7. solely as regards Section 4.B of the *Handbook*, students and *approved training organisations*.
8. and persons within paragraphs rI7.1 to rI7.5, when taken together, are referred to as "*BSB regulated persons*" throughout this *Handbook*, while persons in those categories when taken together with persons referred to in paragraph rI7.6 are referred to as "*relevant persons*". For the avoidance of doubt, students, and *approved training organisations* are neither *BSB regulated persons* nor *relevant persons*.

rI8

If you are a *BSB authorised individual* who is employed by or a *manager* of an *authorised (non-BSB) body* and is subject to the regulatory arrangements of the *Approved Regulator* of that body, and the requirements of that other *Approved Regulator* conflict with a provision within this *Handbook* then the conflicting provision within this *Handbook* shall not apply to you. You will instead be expected to comply with the requirements of that other *Approved Regulator* and, if you do so, you will not be considered to be in breach of the relevant provision of this *Handbook*.

rI9

If you are a *pupil* and are:

1. the pupil of an employed barrister (non-authorised body); or
2. ~~the pupil of a manager or employee of a BSB authorised body; or~~
3. the pupil of a manager or employee of an authorised (non-BSB) body; or
4. spending a period of external training with a BSB authorised body or an authorised (non-BSB) body;
5. this Handbook will apply to you as though you were an employee of the barrister's employer or the body concerned.

rI10

If you are a *registered European lawyer*, then, except where otherwise provided, the provisions of this *Handbook* which apply to *barristers* shall apply to you, in connection with all professional work undertaken by you in England and Wales, as if you were a *self-employed barrister* or an *employed barrister* (*non-authorised body or a manager or employee of an authorised* (*non BSB*) *body* ~~*or a manager or employee of a BSB authorised body*~~ (as the case may be) depending on the way in which you practise.

rI11

In addition to the above, each Part to this Handbook has its own application section which sets out the more detailed application of that particular Part. In the event of any inconsistency, the application section specific to the particular Part shall prevail over these general provisions.

C COMMENCEMENT AND TRANSITIONAL PROVISIONS

[1.7]

rI12

This first edition of the *Handbook* came into force on 6 January 2014 and replaced the eighth edition of the Code of Conduct including its various Annexes (which came into effect from 31st October 2004).

rI13

Subject to rI14 below, in respect of anything done or omitted to be done or otherwise arising before 6 January 2014:

1. Parts 2, 3 and 5 of this Handbook shall not apply;
2. the edition of the Code of Conduct or relevant Annexe in force at the relevant time shall apply; and
3. any reference to Part 2, Part 3 or Part 5 of this *Handbook* shall include reference to the corresponding Part of the edition of the Code of Conduct or relevant Annexe which was in force at the relevant time.

rl14

Where:

1. a matter is being dealt with under Annexe J (The Complaints Rules 2011), Annexe K (The Disciplinary Tribunals Regulations (2009) (Reissued 1 February 2012)), Annexe M (Hearings before the Visitors Rules), Annexe N (Interim Suspension Rules) or Annexe O (Fitness to Practise Rules) as at 6 January 2014; or
2. anything done or omitted to be done or otherwise arising before 6 January 2014 required referral for consideration in accordance with any of the above Annexes,

then Part 5 of this *Handbook* shall apply to all such cases and any step taken pursuant to the Annexes then applying (if any) shall be regarded, unless otherwise decided, as having been taken pursuant to the equivalent provisions of Part 5 of this *Handbook,* save that no fine in excess of £15,000 may be imposed by a *Disciplinary Tribunal* in respect of conduct before 6 January 2014 and no financial *administrative sanction* in excess of £300 may be imposed by the *PCC* in respect of conduct before 6 January 2014.

D INTERPRETATION

[1.8]

rl15

In this *Handbook*:

1. words and phrases in italics shall have the meaning given to them in Part 6;
2. any reference to the masculine shall be deemed to include the feminine and any reference to the singular shall include the plural;
3. any reference to another provision in this *Handbook* shall be a reference to that provision as amended from time to time; and
4. where references are made to an enactment, it is a reference to that enactment as amended, and includes a reference to that provision as extended or applied by or under any other enactment.

Part 2 – The Code of Conduct

Contents

[1.9]

A APPLICATION

[1.10]

rC1

Who?

1. Section 2.B (Core Duties): applies to all *BSB regulated persons* except where stated otherwise, and references to "you" and "your" in Section 2.B shall be construed accordingly.
2. Section 2.C (Conduct Rules):
   a. Applies to all *BSB regulated persons* apart from *unregistered barristers* except where stated otherwise.
   b. Rules rC3.5, rC4, rC8, rC16, rC19 and rC64 to rC70 (and associated guidance to those rules) and the guidance on Core Duties also apply to *unregistered barristers*.

References to "you" and "your" in Section 2.C shall be construed accordingly

3. Section 2.D (Specific Rules): applies to specific groups as defined in each sub-section and references to "you" and "your" shall be construed accordingly.

rC2

When?

1. Section 2.B applies when practising or otherwise providing *legal services*. In addition, CD5 and CD9 apply at all times.
2. Section 2.C applies when practising or otherwise providing *legal services*. In addition, rules rC8, rC16 and rC64 to rC70 and the associated guidance apply at all times.
3. Section 2.D applies when practising or otherwise providing *legal services*.
4. Sections 2.B, 2.C and 2.D only apply to *registered European lawyers* in connection with professional work undertaken by them in that capacity in England and Wales.

B THE CORE DUTIES

[1.11]

CD1

You must observe your duty to the *court* in the administration of justice [CD1].

CD2

You must act in the best interests of each *client* [CD2].

CD3

You must act with honesty and integrity [CD3].

CD4

You must maintain your independence [CD4].

CD5

You must not behave in a way which is likely to diminish the trust and confidence which the public places in you or in the profession [CD5].

CD6

You must keep the affairs of each *client* confidential [CD6].

CD7

You must provide a competent standard of work and service to each *client* [CD7]

CD8

You must not discriminate unlawfully against any person [CD8].

CD9

You must be open and co-operative with your regulators [CD9].

CD10

You must take reasonable steps to manage your *practice*, or carry out your role within your *practice*, competently and in such a way as to achieve compliance with your legal and regulatory obligations [CD10].

Guidance to the Core Duties

[1.12]

gC1

The Core Duties are not presented in order of precedence, subject to the following:

1. CD1 overrides any other core duty, if and to the extent the two are inconsistent. Rules rC3.5 and rC4 deal specifically with the relationship between CD1, CD2 and CD6 and you should refer to those rules and to the related Guidance;
2. in certain other circumstances set out in this Code of Conduct one Core Duty overrides another. Specifically, Rule rC16 provides that CD2 (as well as being subject to CD1) is subject to your obligations under CD3, CD4 and CD8.

gC2

Your obligation to take reasonable steps to manage your *practice,* or carry out your role within your *practice,* competently and in such a way as to achieve compliance with your legal and regulatory obligations (CD10) includes an obligation to take all reasonable steps to mitigate the effects of any breach of those legal and regulatory obligations once you become aware of the same.

C THE CONDUCT RULES

C1 You and the Court

[1.13]

Outcomes

oC1

The *court* is able to rely on information provided to it by those conducting litigation and by advocates who appear before it.

oC2

The proper administration of justice is served.

oC3

The interests of *clients* are protected to the extent compatible with outcomes oC1 and oC2 and the Core Duties.

oC4

Both those who appear before the *court* and *clients* understand clearly the extent of the duties owed to the *court* by advocates and those conducting litigation and the circumstances in which duties owed to *clients* will be overridden by the duty owed to the *court*.

oC5

The public has confidence in the administration of justice and in those who serve it.

Rules

rC3

You owe a duty to the *court* to act with independence in the interests of justice. This duty overrides any inconsistent obligations which you may have (other than obligations under the criminal law). It includes the following specific obligations which apply whether you are acting as an advocate or are otherwise involved in the conduct of litigation in whatever role (with the exception of Rule C3.1 below, which applies when acting as an advocate):

1. you must not knowingly or recklessly mislead or attempt to mislead the *court*;
2. you must not abuse your role as an advocate;
3. you must take reasonable steps to avoid wasting the *court's* time;
4. you must take reasonable steps to ensure that the *court* has before it all relevant decisions and legislative provisions;
5. you must ensure that your ability to act independently is not compromised.

rC4

Your duty to act in the best interests of each *client* is subject to your duty to the *court*.

rC5

Your duty to the *court* does not require you to act in breach of your duty to keep the affairs of each *client* confidential.

Not misleading the court

rC6

Your duty not to mislead the *court* or to permit the *court* to be misled will include the following obligations:

1. you must not:
   a. make submissions, representations or any other statement; or
   b. ask questions which suggest facts to witnesses;

   which you know, or are instructed, are untrue or misleading.
2. you must not call witnesses to give evidence or put affidavits or witness statements to the *court* which you know, or are *instructed*, are untrue or misleading, unless you make clear to the *court* the true position as known by or instructed to you.

Guidance on Rules C3 – C6 and relationship to CD1 and CD2

gC3

Rules rC3 – rC6 set out some specific aspects of your duty to the *court* (CD1). See CD1 and associated Guidance at gC1.

gC4

Knowingly misleading the *court* includes inadvertently misleading the *court* if you later realise that you have misled the *court*, and you fail to correct the position. Recklessness means being indifferent to the truth, or not caring whether something is true or false.

gC5

Your duty under Rule rC3.3 includes drawing to the attention of the *court* any decision or provision which may be adverse to the interests of your *client*. It is particularly important where you are appearing against a litigant who is not legally represented.

gC6

You are obliged by CD2 to promote and to protect your *client's* interests so far as that is consistent with the law and with your overriding duty to the *court* under CD1. Your duty to the *court* does not prevent you from putting forward your *client's* case simply because you do not believe that the facts are as your *client* states them to be (or as you, on your *client's* behalf, state them to be), as long as any positive case you put forward accords with your *instructions* and you do not mislead the *court*. Your role when acting as an advocate or conducting litigation is to present your *client's* case, and it is not for you to decide whether your *client's* case is to be believed.

gC7

For example, you are entitled and it may often be appropriate to draw to the witness's attention other evidence which appears to conflict with what the witness is saying and you are entitled to indicate that a *court* may find a particular piece of evidence difficult to accept. But if the witness maintains that the evidence is true, it should be recorded in the witness statement and you will not be misleading the *court* if you call the witness to confirm their witness statement. Equally, there may be circumstances where you call a hostile witness whose evidence you are instructed is untrue. You will not be in breach of Rule rC6 if you make the position clear to the *court*. See further the guidance at gC14

gC8

As set out in Rule rC4, your duty to the *court* does not permit or require you to disclose confidential information which you have obtained in the course of your *instructions* and which your *client* has not authorised you to disclose to the *court*. However, Rule rC6 requires you not knowingly to mislead the *court* or to permit the *court* to be misled. There may be situations where you have obligations under both these rules.

gC9

Rule rC3.5 makes it clear that your duty to act in the best interests of your *client* is subject to your duty to the *court*. For example, if your *client* were to tell you that he had committed the crime with which he was charged, in order to be able to ensure compliance with Rule rC4 on the one hand and Rule rC3 and Rule rC6 on the other:

1. you would not be entitled to disclose that information to the *court* without your *client's* consent; and
2. you would not be misleading the *court* if, after your *client* had entered a plea of 'not guilty', you were to test in cross-examination the reliability of the evidence of the prosecution witnesses and then address the jury to the effect that the prosecution had not succeeded in making them sure of your *client's* guilt.

gC10

However, you would be misleading the *court* and would therefore be in breach of Rules rC3 and rC6 if you were to set up a positive case inconsistent with the confession, as for example by:

1. suggesting to prosecution witnesses, calling your *client* or your witnesses to show; or submitting to the *jury*, that your *client* did not commit the crime; or

2. suggesting that someone else had done so; or
3. putting forward an alibi.

gC11

If there is a risk that the *court* will be misled unless you disclose confidential information which you have learned in the course of your *instructions*, you should ask the *client* for permission to disclose it to the *court*. If your *client* refuses to allow you to make the disclosure you must cease to act, and return your *instructions*: see Rules rC25 to rC27 below. In these circumstances you must not reveal the information to the *court*.

gC12

For example, if your *client* tells you that he has previous *convictions* of which the prosecution is not aware, you may not disclose this without his consent. However, in a case where mandatory sentences apply, the non-disclosure of the previous *convictions* will result in the *court* failing to pass the sentence that is required by law. In that situation, you must advise your *client* that if consent is refused to your revealing the information you will have to cease to act. In situations where mandatory sentences do not apply, and your *client* does not agree to disclose the previous *convictions*, you can continue to represent your *client* but in doing so must not say anything that misleads the *court*. This will constrain what you can say in mitigation. For example, you could not advance a positive case of previous good character knowing that there are undisclosed prior *convictions*. Moreover, if the *court* asks you a direct question you must not give an untruthful answer and therefore you would have to withdraw if, on your being asked such a question, your *client* still refuses to allow you to answer the question truthfully. You should explain this to your *client*. See further the guidance on this issue on the *Bar Standards Board's* website which can be accessed here [hyperlink].

gC13

Similarly, if you become aware that your *client* has a document which should be disclosed but has not been disclosed, you cannot continue to act unless your *client* agrees to the disclosure of the document. In these circumstances you must not reveal the existence or contents of the document to the *court*.

Not abusing your role as an advocate

rC7

Where you are acting as an advocate, your duty not to abuse your role includes the following obligations:

1. you must not make statements or ask questions merely to insult, humiliate or annoy a witness or any other person;
2. you must not make a serious allegation against a witness whom you have had an opportunity to cross-examine unless you have given that witness a chance to answer the allegation in cross-examination;
3. you must not make a serious allegation against any person, or suggest that a person is guilty of a crime with which your *client* is charged unless:

   a. you have reasonable grounds for the allegation; and

   b. the allegation is relevant to your *client's* case or the credibility of a witness; and

   c. where the allegation relates to a third party, you avoid naming them in open *court* unless this is reasonably necessary.

4. you must not put forward to the *court* a personal opinion of the facts or the law unless you are invited or required to do so by the *court* or by law.

C2 Behaving Ethically

[1.14]

Outcomes

oC6

Those ~~and entities~~ regulated by the *Bar Standards Board* maintain standards of honesty, integrity and independence, and are seen as so doing.

oC7

The proper administration of justice, access to justice and the best interests of *clients* are served.

oC8

Those ~~and entities~~ regulated by the *Bar Standards Board* do not discriminate unlawfully and take appropriate steps to prevent *discrimination* occurring in their practices.

oC9

Those ~~and entities~~ regulated by the *Bar Standards Board* and *clients* understand the obligations of honesty, integrity and independence.

Rules – Honesty, integrity and independence

rC8

You must not do anything which could reasonably be seen by the public to undermine your honesty, integrity (CD3) and independence (CD4).

rC9

Your duty to act with honesty and integrity under CD3 includes the following requirements:

1. you must not knowingly or recklessly mislead or attempt to mislead anyone;
2. you must not draft any statement of case, witness statement, affidavit or other document containing:

a. any statement of fact or contention which is not supported by your *client* or by your *instructions*;

b. any contention which you do not consider to be properly arguable;

c. any allegation of fraud, unless you have clear instructions to allege fraud and you have reasonably credible material which establishes an arguable case of fraud;

d. (in the case of a witness statement or affidavit) any statement of fact other than the evidence which you reasonably believe the witness would give if the witness were giving evidence orally;

3. you must not encourage a witness to give evidence which is misleading or untruthful;

4. you must not rehearse, practise with or coach a witness in respect of their evidence;

5. unless you have the permission of the representative for the opposing side or of the *court*, you must not communicate with any witness (including your *client*) about the case while the witness is giving evidence;

6. you must not make, or offer to make, payments to any witness which are contingent on his evidence or on the outcome of the case;

7. you must only propose, or accept, fee arrangements which are legal.

Guidance on Rules C8 and C9 and their relationship to CD1, CD2, CD3, CD4 and CD5

gC14

Your honesty, integrity and independence are fundamental. The interests of justice (CD1) and the *client's* best interests (CD2) can only be properly served, and any conflicts between the two properly resolved, if you conduct yourself honestly and maintain your independence from external pressures, as required by CD3 and CD4. You should also refer to Rule rC16 which subjects your duty to act in the best interests of your *client* (CD2) to your observance of CD3 and CD4, as well as to your duty to the *court* (CD1).

gC15

Other rules deal with specific aspects of your obligation to act in your *client's* best interests (CD2) while maintaining honesty, integrity (CD3) and independence (CD4), such as rule rC21.10 (not acting where your independence is compromised), rule rC10 (not paying or accepting *referral fees*) and rC21 (not acting in circumstances of a conflict of interest or where you risk breaching one *client's* confidentiality in favour of another's).

gC16

Rule rC3 addresses how your conduct is perceived by the public. Conduct on your part which the public may reasonably perceive as undermining your honesty, integrity or independence is likely to diminish the trust and confidence which the public places in you or in the profession, in breach of CD5. Rule rC8 is not exhaustive of the ways in which CD5 may be breached.

gC17

In addition to your obligation to only propose, or accept, fee arrangements which are legal in Rule C9.7, you must also have regard to your obligations in relation to *referral fees* in Rule rC10 and the associated guidance.

Examples of how you may be seen as compromising your independence

gC18

The following may reasonably be seen as compromising your independence in breach of Rule rC3 (whether or not the circumstances are such that Rule rC10 is also breached):

1. offering, promising or giving:
    a. any commission or referral fee (of whatever size) – note that these are in any case prohibited by Rule rC10 and associated guidance; or
    b. a gift (apart from items of modest value),

    to any client, professional client or other intermediary; or
2. lending money to any such *client*, *professional client* or other *intermediary*; or
3. accepting any money (whether as a loan or otherwise) from any *client*, *professional client* or other *intermediary*, unless it is a payment for your professional services or reimbursement of expenses or of disbursements made on behalf of the *client*;

gC19

If you are offered a gift by a current, prospective or former *client*, *professional client* or other *intermediary*, you should consider carefully whether the circumstances and size of the gift would reasonably lead others to think that your independence had been compromised. If this would be the case, you should refuse to accept the gift.

gC20

The giving or receiving of entertainment at a disproportionate level may also give rise to a similar issue and so should not be offered or accepted if it would lead others reasonably to think that your independence had been compromised.

gC21

Guidance gC18 to gC20 above is likely to be more relevant where you are a *self-employed barrister*~~, a *BSB authorised body*~~, ~~an *authorised (non-BSB) individual*, an *employed barrister (BSB authorised body)* or a *BSB regulated manager*~~. If you are a *BSB authorised individual* who is a an *employee* or *manager* of an *authorised (non-BSB) body* or you are an *employed barrister (non-authorised body)* and your *approved regulator* or *employer* (as appropriate) permits payments to which Rule rC10 applies, you may make or receive such payments only in your capacity as such and as permitted by the rules of your *approved regulator* or *employer* (as appropriate). For further information on referral fees, see the guidance at C32.

gC22

The former prohibition on *practising barristers* expressing a personal opinion in the media in relation to any future or current proceedings in which they are briefed has been removed. *Practising barristers* must, nevertheless, ensure that any comment they may make does not undermine, and is not reasonably seen as undermining, their independence. Furthermore, any such comment must not bring the profession, nor any other *barrister* into disrepute. Further guidance is available on the *Bar Standards Board's* website.

Examples of what your duty to act with honesty and integrity may require

gC23

Rule C9 sets out some specific aspects of your duty under CD3 to act with honesty and integrity. Further guidance in relation to drafting witness statements and other documents (which relates to Rule C9.2) and making allegations of fraud (which relates to Rule C9.2.c) can be found on the *Bar Standards Board's* website.

gC24

In addition to the above, where the other side is legally represented and you are conducting correspondence in respect of the particular matter, you are expected to correspond at all times with that other party's legal representative – otherwise you may be regarded as breaching CD3 or Rule rC9.

Other possible breaches of CD3 and/or CD5

gC25

A breach of Rule C9 may also constitute a breach of CD3 and/or CD5. Other conduct which is likely to be treated as a breach of CD3 and/or CD5 includes (but is not limited to):

1. subject to Guidance C26 below, breaches of Rule C8;
2. breaches of Rule C10;
3. criminal conduct, other than *minor criminal offences* (see Guidance C27);
4. seriously offensive or discreditable conduct towards third parties;
5. dishonesty;
6. unlawful *victimisation* or *harassment*; or
7. abuse of your professional position.

gC26

For the purposes of Guidance C25.7 above, referring to your status as a *barrister*, for example on professional notepaper, in a context where it is irrelevant, such as in a private dispute, may well constitute abuse of your professional position and thus involve a breach of CD3 and/or CD5.

gC27

Conduct which is not likely to be treated as a breach of Rules C8 or C9, or CD3 or CD5, includes (but is not limited to):

1. minor criminal offences;
2. your conduct in your private or personal life, unless this involves:
   a. abuse of your professional position; or
   b. committing a *criminal offence*, other than a *minor criminal offence*.

gC28

For the purpose of Guidance C27 above, *minor criminal offences* include:

1. an offence committed in the United Kingdom which is a fixed-penalty offence under the Road Traffic Offenders Act 1988; or
2. an offence committed in the United Kingdom or abroad which is dealt with by a procedure substantially similar to that for such a fixed-penalty offence; or
3. an offence whose main ingredient is the unlawful parking of a motor vehicle.

Referral Fees

rC10

You must not pay or receive *referral fees*.

Guidance on Rule C10 and its relationship to CD2, CD3, CD4 and CD5

gC29

Making or receiving payments in order to procure or reward the referral to you by an intermediary of professional *instructions* is inconsistent with your obligations under CD2 and/or CD3 and/or CD4 and may also breach CD5.

gC30

Moreover:

1. where *public* funding is in place, the *Legal Aid Agency's* Unified Contract Standard Terms explicitly prohibit contract-holders from making or receiving any payment (or any other benefit) for the referral or introduction of a *client*, whether or not the lay *client* knows of, and consents to, the payment;
2. whether in a private or publicly funded case, a *referral fee* to which the *client* has not consented may constitute a bribe and therefore a *criminal offence* under the Bribery Act 2010;
3. *referral fees* are prohibited where they relate to a claim or potential claim for damages for personal injury or death or arise out of circumstances involving personal injury or death personal injury claims: section 56 Legal Aid, Sentencing and Punishment of Offenders Act 2012;

gC31

Rule rC10 does not prohibit proper expenses that are not a reward for referring work, such as genuine and reasonable payments for:

1. clerking and administrative services (including where these are outsourced);
2. membership subscriptions to ADR bodies that appoint or recommend a person to provide *mediation*, arbitration or adjudication services; or
3. advertising and publicity, which are payable whether or not any work is referred. On the other hand, payments which purport to represent fees payable for the outsourcing of clerking or administrative or other services but which in fact are expressly or implicitly linked to, or conditional on, or vary in amount with, the receipt of instructions, are *referral fees* and are prohibited.

gC32

Further guidance is available, see BSB website.

Undertakings

rC11

You must within an agreed timescale or within a reasonable period of time comply with any undertaking you give in the course of conducting litigation.

Guidance on Rule C11

gC33

You should ensure your insurance covers you in respect of any liability incurred in giving an undertaking.

Discrimination

rC12

You must not discriminate unlawfully against, victimise or harass any other person on the grounds of race, colour, ethnic or national origin, nationality, citizenship, sex, gender re-assignment, sexual orientation, marital or civil partnership status, disability, age, religion or belief.

Guidance on Rule C12

gC34

Rules rC110 and associated guidance are also relevant to equality and diversity.

Foreign work

rC13

In connection with any *foreign work* you must comply with any applicable rule of conduct prescribed by the law or by any national or local Bar of:

1. the place where the work is or is to be performed; and
2. the place where any proceedings or matters to which the work relates are taking place or contemplated;

unless such rule is inconsistent with any requirement of the Core Duties.

rC14

If you solicit work in any jurisdiction outside England and Wales, you must not do so in a manner which would be prohibited if you were a member of the local Bar.

Guidance on Rules C13 and C14

gC35

When you are engaged in *cross border activities* within a *CCBE State* other than the UK, you must comply with the rules at 2.D5 which implement the part of the *Code of Conduct for European Lawyers* not otherwise covered by this Handbook as well as with any other applicable rules of conduct relevant to that particular *CCBE State*. It is your responsibility to inform yourself as to any applicable rules of conduct.

C3 You and Your Client

[1.15]

Outcomes

oC10

Clients receive a competent standard of work and service.

oC11

Clients' best interests are protected and promoted by those acting for them.

oC12

BSB authorised persons do not accept instructions from *clients* where there is a conflict between their own interests and the *clients'* or where there is a conflict between one or more *clients* except when permitted in this *Handbook*.

oC13

Clients know what to expect and understand the advice they are given.

oC14

Care is given to ensure that the interests of vulnerable *clients* are taken into account and their needs are met.

oC15

Clients have confidence in those who are instructed to act on their behalf.

oC16

Instructions are not accepted, refused, or returned in circumstances which adversely affect the administration of justice, access to justice or (so far as compatible with these) the best interests of the *client.*

oC17

Clients and *BSB authorised persons* ~~and *authorised (non-BSB) individuals*~~ ~~and *BSB regulated managers*~~ are clear about the circumstances in which *instructions* may not be accepted or may or must be returned.

oC18

Clients are adequately informed as to the terms on which work is to be done.

oC19

Clients understand how to bring a *complaint* and *complaints* are dealt with promptly, fairly, openly and effectively.

oC20

Clients understand who is responsible for work done for them.

Rules

Best interests of each client, provision of a competent standard of work and confidentiality

rC15

Your duty to act in the best interests of each *client* (CD2), to provide a competent standard of work and service to each *client* (CD7) and to keep the affairs of each *client* confidential (CD6) includes the following obligations:

1. you must promote fearlessly and by all proper and lawful means the *client's* best interests;
2. you must do so without regard to your own interests or to any consequences to you (which may include, for the avoidance of doubt, you being required to take reasonable steps to mitigate the effects of any breach of this *Handbook*);
3. you must do so without regard to the consequences to any other person (whether to your *professional client*, *employer* or any other person);

4. you must not permit your *professional client*, *employer* or any other person to limit your discretion as to how the interests of the *client* can best be served; and
5. you must protect the confidentiality of each *client's* affairs, except for such disclosures as are required by law or to which your *client* gives informed consent.

rC16

Your duty to act in the best interests of each *client* (CD2) is subject to your duty to the *court* (CD1) and to your obligations to act with honesty, and integrity (CD3) and to maintain your independence (CD4).

Guidance on Rules C15 and C16 and its relationship to CD2, CD6 and CD7

gC36

Your duty is to your *client*, not to your *professional client* or other *intermediary* (if any).

gC37

Rules C15 and C16 are expressed in terms of the interests of each *client*. This is because you may only accept *instructions* to act for more than one *client* if you are able to act in the best interests of each *client* as if that *client* were your only *client*, as CD2 requires of you. See further Rule C17 on the circumstances when you are obliged to advise your *client* to seek other legal representation and Rules C21.2 and C21.3 on conflicts of interest and the guidance to those rules at gC69.

gC38

CD7 requires not only that you provide a competent standard of work but also a competent standard of service to your *client*. Rule C15 is not exhaustive of what you must do to ensure your compliance with CD2 and CD7. By way of example, a competent standard of work and of service also includes:

1. treating each *client* with courtesy and consideration; and
2. seeking to advise your *client*, in terms they can understand; and
3. taking all reasonable steps to avoid incurring unnecessary expense; and
4. reading your instructions promptly. This may be important if there is a time limit or limitation period. If you fail to read your instructions promptly, it is possible that you will not be aware of the time limit until it is too late.

gC39

In order to be able to provide a competent standard of work, you should keep your professional knowledge and skills up to date, regularly take part in professional development and educational activities that maintain and further develop your competence and performance ~~and, where you are a *BSB authorised body* or a *manager* of such body, you should take reasonable steps to ensure that *managers* and *employees* within your *organisation* undertake such *training*~~. Merely complying with the minimum Continuing Professional Development requirements may not be sufficient to comply with Rule C15. You should also ensure that you comply with any specific *training* requirements of the *Bar Standards Board* before undertaking certain activities – for example, you should not attend a police station to advise a suspect or interviewee as to the handling and conduct of police interviews unless you have complied with such *training* requirements as may be imposed by the *Bar Standards Board* in respect of such work. Similarly, you should not undertake public access work without successfully completing the required training specified by the *Bar Standards Board.*

gC40

~~In addition to Guidance C38 above, a *BSB authorised body* or a *manager* of such body should ensure that work is allocated appropriately, to *managers* and/or *employees* with the appropriate knowledge and expertise to undertake such work.~~

gC41

You should remember that your *client* may not be familiar with legal proceedings and may find them difficult and stressful. You should do what you reasonably can to ensure that the *client* understands the process and what to expect from it and from you. You should also try to avoid any unnecessary distress for your *client*. This is particularly important where you are dealing with a vulnerable *client*.

gC42

The duty of confidentiality (CD6) is central to the administration of justice. *Clients* who put their confidence in their legal advisers must be able to do so in the knowledge that the information they give, or which is given on their behalf, will stay confidential. In normal circumstances, this information will be privileged and not disclosed to a *court*. CD6, rC4 and Guidance C8 and C11 to C13 provide further information.

gC43

Rule C15.5 acknowledges that your duty of confidentiality is subject to an exception if disclosure is required by law. For example, you may be obliged to disclose certain matters by the Proceeds of Crime Act 2002. Disclosure in those circumstances would not amount to a breach of CD6 or Rule C15.5. In other circumstances, you may only make disclosure of confidential information where your *client* gives informed consent to the disclosure. See the Guidance to Rule C21 at gC68 for an example of circumstances where it may be appropriate for you to seek such consent.

gC44

There may be circumstances when your duty of confidentiality to your *client* conflicts with your duty to the *court*. Rule C4 and Guidance C8 and C11 to C13 provide further information.

gC45

Similarly, there may be circumstances when your duty of confidentiality to your *client* conflicts with your duty to your regulator. Rule C64 and Guidance C92 to C93 in respect of that rule provide further information. In addition, Rule C66 may also apply.

gC46

If you are a *pupil* of, or are *devilling* work for, a *self-employed barrister*, Rule C15 applies to you as if the *client* of the *self-employed barrister* was your own *client*.

gC47

The section You and Your Practice, at 2.C5, provides for duties regarding the systems and procedures you must put in place and enforce in order to ensure compliance with Rule C15.5.

gC48

~~If you are an *authorised individual* or a *manager* working in a *BSB authorised body* your personal duty to act in the best interests of your *client* requires you to assist in the redistribution of *client* files and otherwise assisting to ensure each *client's* interests are protected in the event that the *BSB authorised body* itself is unable to do so for whatever reason (for example, insolvency).~~

rC17

Your duty to act in the best interests of each *client* (CD2) includes a duty to consider whether the *client's* best interests are served by different legal representation, and if so, to advise the *client* to that effect.

Guidance on Rule C17

gC49

Your duty to comply with Rule C17 may require you to advise your *client* that in their best interests they should be represented by:

1. a different advocate or legal representative, whether more senior or more junior than you, or with different experience from yours;
2. more than one advocate or legal representative;
3. fewer advocates or legal representatives than have been instructed; or
4. in the case where you are acting through a *professional client*, different *solicitors*.

gC50

Specific rules apply where you are acting on a public access basis, which oblige you to consider whether *solicitors* should also be instructed. As to these see the public access rules at Section 2.D2~~ and further in respect of *BSB regulated bodies* Rule S28 and the associated guidance~~.

gC51

CD2 and Rules C15 and C17 require you, subject to Rule C16, to put your *client's* interests ahead of your own and those of any other person. If you consider that your *professional client*, another *solicitor* or *intermediary*, another *barrister*, or any other person acting on behalf of your *client* has been negligent, you should ensure that your *client* is advised of this.

rC18

Your duty to provide a competent standard of work and service to each *client* (CD7) includes a duty to inform your *professional client*, or *your client* if instructed by a *client*, as far as reasonably possible in sufficient time to enable appropriate steps to be taken to protect the *client's* interests, if:

1. it becomes apparent to you that you will not be able to carry out the *instructions* within the time requested, or within a reasonable time after receipt of *instructions*; or
2. there is an appreciable risk that you may not be able to undertake the *instructions*.

Guidance on Rule C18

gC52

For further information about what you should do in the event that you have a clash of listings, please refer to our guidance which can be accessed on the *Bar Standards Board's* website.

Not misleading clients and potential clients

rC19

If you supply, or offer to supply, *legal services*, you must not mislead, or cause or permit to be misled, any person to whom you supply, or offer to supply, *legal services* about:

1. the nature and scope of the *legal services* which you are offering or agreeing to supply;
2. the terms on which the *legal services* will be supplied, who will carry out the work and the basis of charging;
3. who is legally responsible for the provision of the services;
4. whether you are entitled to supply those services and the extent to which you are regulated when providing those services and by whom; or
5. the extent to which you are covered by insurance against claims for professional negligence.

Guidance on Rule C19

Gc53

The best interests of *clients* (CD2) and public confidence in the profession (CD5) are undermined if there is a lack of clarity as to whether services are regulated, who is supplying them, on what terms, and what redress *clients* have and against whom if things go wrong. Rule C19 may potentially be infringed in a broad variety of situations. You must consider how matters will appear to the *client*.

gC54

Clients may, by way of example, be misled if *self-employed barristers* were to share premises with *solicitors* or other professionals without making sufficiently clear to *clients* that they remain separate and independent from one another and are not responsible for one another's work.

gC55

Likewise, it is likely to be necessary to make clear to *clients* that any entity established as a "ProcureCo" is not itself able to supply *reserved legal activities* and is not subject to regulation by the *Bar Standards Board.*

gC56

A set of *chambers* dealing directly with unsophisticated lay *clients* might breach Rule C19 if its branding created the appearance of an entity or *partnership* and it failed to explain that the members of *chambers* are, in fact, self-employed individuals who are not responsible for one another's work.

gC57

Knowingly or recklessly publishing advertising material which is inaccurate or likely to mislead could also result in you being in breach of Rule rC19. You should be particularly careful about making comparisons with other persons as these may often be regarded as misleading.

gC58

If you carry out public access work but are not authorised to *conduct litigation*, you would breach Rule C19 if you caused or permitted your *client* to be misled into believing that you are entitled to, or will, provide services that include the *conduct of litigation* on behalf of your *client.*

gC59

If you are a *self-employed barrister*, you would, for example, likely be regarded as having breached Rule C19 if you charged at your own hourly rate for work done by a *devil* or *pupil*. Moreover, such conduct may well breach your duty to act with honesty and integrity (CD3).

gC60

If you are an *unregistered barrister*, you would breach Rule C19 if you misled your *client* into thinking that you were providing *legal services* to them as a *barrister* or that you were subject to the same regulation as a *practising barrister*. You would also breach the rule if you implied that you were covered by insurance if you were not, or if you suggested that your *clients* could seek a remedy from the *Bar Standards Board* or the *Legal Ombudsman* if they were dissatisfied with the services you provided. You should also be aware of the rules set out in Section D5 of this Code of Conduct and the additional guidance for *unregistered barristers* available on the *Bar Standards Board* website.

gC61

Rule C19.3 is particularly relevant where you act in more than one capacity, for example as a *BSB authorised individual* as well as a manager or employee of an *authorised (non BSB) body*. This is because you should make it clear to each *client* in what capacity you are acting and, therefore, who has legal responsibility for the provision of the services.

gC62

If you are a *pupil*, you should not hold yourself out as a member of *chambers* or permit your name to appear as such. You should describe yourself as a *pupil barrister.*

gC63

A number of other rules impose positive obligations on you, in particular circumstances, to make clear your regulatory status and the basis and terms on which you are acting. See, for example, Rule C23 and gC74.

Personal responsibility

rC20

Where you are a *BSB authorised individual,* you are personally responsible for your own conduct and for your professional work. You must use your own professional judgment in relation to those matters on which you are instructed and be able to justify your decisions and actions. You must do this notwithstanding the views of your *client*, *professional client*, *employer* or any other person.

Guidance on Rule C20

gC64

It is fundamental that *BSB authorised individuals* ~~and *authorised (non-BSB) individuals*~~ are personally responsible for their own conduct and for their own professional work, whether they are acting in a self-employed or employed capacity (in the case of *BSB authorised individuals*)~~or as an *employee* or *manager* of a *BSB authorised body* (in the case of *authorised (non-BSB) individuals*)~~.

gC65

Nothing in Rule rC20 is intended to prevent you from delegating or outsourcing to any other person discrete tasks (for example, research) which such other person is well-equipped to provide. However, where such tasks are delegated or outsourced, you remain personally responsible for such work. Further, in circumstances where such tasks are being outsourced, Rule C87 which deals with outsourcing, must be complied with.

gC66

You are responsible for the service provided by all those who represent you in your dealings with your *client*, including your clerks or any other *employees* or agents.

gC67

~~Nothing in this rule or guidance prevents a *BSB authorised body* from contracting on the basis that any civil liability for the services provided by a *BSB regulated individual* lies with the *BSB authorised body* and the *BSB regulated individual* is not to be liable. However, any such stipulation as to civil liability does not affect the regulatory obligations of the *BSB regulated individual* including (but not limited to) that of being personally responsible under Rule rC20 for the professional judgments made.~~

gC68

See, further, guidance to Rule C19, as regards work by *pupils* and *devils* Rule C15, gC124 and Rule C85 (on outsourcing).

Accepting instructions

rC21

You must not accept *instructions* to act in a particular matter if:

1. due to any existing or previous *instructions* you are not able to fulfil your obligation to act in the best interests of the prospective *client*; or
2. there is a conflict of interest between your own personal interests and the interests of the prospective *client* in respect of the particular matter; or
3. there is a conflict of interest between the prospective *client* and one or more of your former or existing *clients* in respect of the particular matter unless all of the *clients* who have an interest in the particular matter give their informed consent to your acting in such circumstances; or
4. there is a real risk that information confidential to another former or existing *client*, or any other person to whom you owe duties of confidence, may be relevant to the matter, such that if, obliged to maintain confidentiality, you could not act in the best interests of the prospective *client*, and the former or existing *client* or person to whom you owe that duty does not give informed consent to disclosure of that confidential information; or
5. your instructions seek to limit your ordinary authority or discretion in the conduct of proceedings in *court*; or
6. your instructions require you to act other than in accordance with law or with the provisions of this *Handbook*; or
7. you are not authorised and/or otherwise accredited to perform the work required by the relevant *instruction*; or
8. you are not competent to handle the particular matter or otherwise do not have enough experience to handle the matter; or
9. you do not have enough time to deal with the particular matter, unless the circumstances are such that it would nevertheless be in the *client's* best interests for you to accept; or
10. there is a real prospect that you are not going to be able to maintain your independence.

Guidance on Rule C21

gC69

Rules C21.2, C21.3 and C21.4 are intended to reflect the law on conflict of interests and confidentiality and what is required of you by your duty to act in the *client's* best interests (CD2), independently (CD4), and maintaining *client* confidentiality (CD6). You are prohibited from acting where there is a conflict of interest between your own personal interests and the interests of a prospective *client*. However, where there is a conflict of interest between an existing *client* or *clients* and a prospective *client* or *clients* or two or more prospective *clients*, you may be entitled to accept instructions or to continue to act on a particular matter where you have fully disclosed to the relevant *clients* and prospective *clients* (as appropriate) the extent and nature of the conflict; they have each provided their informed consent to you acting; and you are able to act in the best interests of each *client* and independently as required by CD2 and CD4.

gC70

Examples of where you may be required to refuse to accept *instructions* in accordance with Rule C21.7 include:

1. where the *instructions* relate to the provision of litigation services and you have not been authorised to *conduct litigation* in accordance with the requirements of this *Handbook*; and
2. where the matter involves *criminal advocacy* and you are not ~~(or, where you are a *BSB authorised body*, none of your *managers* or *employees* are)~~ accredited at the correct *QASA level* to undertake such work in accordance with the Quality Assurance Scheme for Advocates Rules set out at 2.C3; and
3. where the matter would require you to conduct correspondence with parties other than your *client* (in the form of letters, faxes, emails or the like), you do not have adequate systems, experience or resources for managing appropriately such correspondence and/or you do not have adequate insurance in place in accordance with Rule rC75 which covers, amongst other things, any loss suffered by the *client* as a result of the conduct of such correspondence.

gC71

Competency and experience under Rule C21.8 includes your ability to work with vulnerable *clients*.

gC72

Rule C21.9 recognises that there may be exceptional circumstances when *instructions* are delivered so late that no suitable, competent advocate would have adequate time to prepare. In those cases you are not required to refuse *instructions* as it will be in the *client's* best interests that you accept. Indeed, if you are obliged under the cab rank rule to accept the *instructions,* you must do so.

gC73

Rule C21.10 is an aspect of your broader obligation to maintain your independence (CD4). Your ability to perform your duty to the *court* (CD1) and act in the best interests of your *client* (CD2) may be put at risk if you act in circumstances where your independence is compromised. Examples of when you may not be able to maintain your independence include appearing as an advocate in a matter in which you are likely to be called as a witness (unless the matter on which you are likely to be called as a witness is peripheral or minor in the context of the litigation as a whole and is unlikely to lead to your involvement in the matter being challenged at a later date).

gC74

Where the *instructions* relate to public access or licensed access work and you are a self-employed barrister you will also need to have regard to the relevant rules at 2.D2. ~~If you a BSB authorised body, you should have regard to the guidance to Rule S28.~~

Defining terms or basis on which instructions are accepted

rC22

Where you first accept *instructions* to act in a matter:

1. you must, subject to Rule C23, confirm in writing acceptance of the *instructions* and the terms and/or basis on which you will be acting, including the basis of charging;
2. where your instructions are from a *professional client*, the confirmation required by rC22.1 must be sent to the *professional client;*
3. where your instructions are from a *client*, the confirmation required by rC22.1 must be sent to the *client*.

rC23

In the event that, following your acceptance of the *instructions* in accordance with Rule rC22, the scope of the *instructions* is varied by the relevant *client* (including where the *client* instructs you on additional aspects relating to the same matter), you are not required to confirm again in writing acceptance of the instructions or the terms and/or basis upon which you will be acting. In these circumstances, you will be deemed to have accepted the instructions when you begin the work, on the same terms or basis as before, unless otherwise specified.

rC24

You must comply with the requirements set out in Rules C22 and C23 before doing the work unless that is not reasonably practicable, in which case you should do so as soon as reasonably practicable.

Guidance to Rules C22 to C24

gC75

Compliance with the requirement in Rule rC22 to set out the terms and/or basis upon which you will be acting may be achieved by including a reference or link to the relevant terms in your written communication of acceptance. You may, for example, refer the *client* or *professional client* (as the case may be) to the terms of service set out on your website or to standard terms of service set out on the *Bar Council's* website. Where you agree to do your work on terms and conditions that have been proposed to you by the *client* or by the *professional client*, you should confirm in writing that that is the basis on which your work is done. Where there are competing sets of terms and conditions, which terms have been agreed and are the basis of your retainer will be a matter to be determined in accordance with the law of contract.

gC76

Your obligation under Rule rC23 is to ensure that the basis on which you act has been defined, which does not necessarily mean governed by your own contractual terms. In circumstances where Rule rC23 applies, you should take particular care to ensure that the *client* is clear about the basis for charging for any variation to the work where it may be unclear. You must also ensure that you comply with the requirements of the Provision of Services Regulations 2009. See further Rule C19 (not misleading *clients* or prospective *clients*) and the guidance to that rule at gC52 to gC62.

gC77

If you are a *self-employed barrister* a clerk may confirm on your behalf your acceptance of *instructions* in accordance with Rules C22 and C23 above.

gC78

When accepting *instructions*, you must also ensure that you comply with the *complaints* handling rules set out in Section 2.D.

gC79

When accepting instructions in accordance with Rule C22, confirmation by email will satisfy any requirement for written acceptance.

gC80

You may have been instructed in relation to a discrete and finite task, such as to provide an opinion on a particular issue, or to provide ongoing services, for example, to conduct particular litigation. Your confirmation of acceptance of instructions under Rule C22 should make clear the scope of the *instructions* you are accepting, whether by cross-referring to the *instructions*, where these are in writing or by summarising your understanding of the scope of work you are instructed to undertake.

gC81

Disputes about costs are one of the most frequent complaints. The provision of clear information before work starts is the best way of avoiding such complaints. *The Legal Ombudsman* has produced a useful guide "An Ombudsman's view of good costs service" which can be found there.

gC82

Where the *instructions* relate to public access or licensed access work and you are a self-employed barrister, you will also need to have regard to the relevant rules at 2.D2 ~~If you a BSB authorised body, you should have regard to the guidance to Rule S23.~~

Returning instructions

rC25

Where you have accepted *instructions* to act but one or more of the circumstances set out in Rules C21.1 to C21.10 above then arises, you must cease to act and return your *instructions* promptly. In addition, you must cease to act and return your *instructions* if:

1. in a case funded by the *Legal Aid Agency* as part of the Community Legal Service or Criminal Defence Service it has become apparent to you that this funding has been wrongly obtained by false or inaccurate information and action to remedy the situation is not immediately taken by your *client*; or
2. the *client* refuses to authorise you to make some disclosure to the *court* which your duty to the *court* requires you to make; or
3. you become aware during the course of a case of the existence of a document which should have been but has not been disclosed, and the *client* fails to disclose it or fails to permit you to disclose it, contrary to your advice.

rC26

You may cease to act on a matter on which you are instructed and return your *instructions* if:

1. your professional conduct is being called into question; or
2. the *client* consents; or
3. you are a *self-employed barrister* and:
    a. despite all reasonable efforts to prevent it, a hearing becomes fixed for a date on which you have already entered in your professional diary that you will not be available; or
    b. illness, injury, pregnancy, childbirth, a bereavement or a similar matter makes you unable reasonably to perform the services required in the *instructions*; or
    c. you are unavoidably required to attend on jury service;
4. ~~you are a *BSB authorised body* and the only appropriate *authorised individual(s)* are unable to continue acting on the particular matter due to one or more of the grounds referred to at Rules C26.3.a to C26.3.c above occurring;~~
5. you do not receive payment when due in accordance with terms agreed, subject to Rule C26.7 (if you are conducting litigation) and in any other case subject to your giving reasonable notice requiring the non-payment to be remedied and making it clear to the *client* in that notice that failure to remedy

the non-payment may result in you ceasing to act and returning your *instructions* in respect of the particular matter; or

6. you become aware of confidential or privileged information or documents of another person which relate to the matter on which you are instructed; or
7. if you are conducting litigation, and your *client* does not consent to your ceasing to act, your application to come off the record has been granted; or
8. there is some other substantial reason for doing so (subject to Rules C27 to C29 below).

Guidance on Rule C26

gC83

In deciding whether to cease to act and to return existing instructions in accordance with Rule C26, you should, where possible and subject to your overriding duty to the *court*, ensure that the *client* is not adversely affected because there is not enough time to engage other adequate legal assistance.

gC84

If you are working on a referral basis and your *professional client* withdraws, you are no longer instructed and cannot continue to act unless appointed by the *court*, or you otherwise receive new instructions. For these purposes working on a "referral basis " means where a *professional client* instructs a *BSB authorised individual* to provide *legal services* on behalf of one of that *professional client's* own clients;

gC85

You should not rely on Rule C26.3 to break an engagement to supply legal services so that you can attend or fulfil a non-professional engagement of any kind other than those indicated in Rule C26.3.

gC86

When considering whether or not you are required to return instructions in accordance with Rule rC26.6 you should have regard to relevant case law including *Ablitt v Mills & Reeve (a firm)* (1995) Times, 25 October and *English and American Insurance Co Ltd v Herbert Smith & Co* [1988] FSR 232, [1987] NLJ Rep 148.

gC87

If a fundamental change is made to the basis of your remuneration, you should treat such a change as though your original instructions have been withdrawn by the *client* and replaced by an offer of new *instructions* on different terms. Accordingly:

1. *you must decide whether you are obliged by Rule C29 to accept the new instructions;*
2. if you are obliged under Rule C29 to accept the new *instructions*, you must do so;
3. if you are not obliged to accept the new *instructions*, you may decline them;
4. if you decline to accept the new *instructions* in such circumstances, you are not to be regarded as returning your *instructions*, nor as withdrawing from the

matter, nor as ceasing to act, for the purposes of Rules C25 to C26, because the previous *instructions* have been withdrawn by the *client*.

rC27

Notwithstanding the provisions of Rules C25 and C26, you must not:

1. cease to act or return *instructions* without either:
   a. obtaining your *client's* consent; or
   b. clearly explaining to your *client* or your *professional client* the reasons for doing so; or
2. return instructions to another person without the consent of your *client* or your *professional client*.

Requirement not to discriminate

rC28

You must not withhold your services or permit your services to be withheld:

1. on the ground that the nature of the case is objectionable to you or to any section of *the public*;
2. on the ground that the conduct, opinions or beliefs of the prospective *client* are unacceptable to you or to any section of *the public*;
3. on any ground relating to the source of any financial support which may properly be given to the prospective *client* for the proceedings in question.

Guidance on Rule C28

gC88

As a matter of general law you have an obligation not to discriminate unlawfully as to those to whom you make your services available on any of the statutorily prohibited grounds such as gender or race. See https://www.barstandardsboard.org.uk/about-bar-standards-board/equality-and-diversity/equality-and-diversity-rules-of-the-code-of-conduct/ for guidance as to your obligations in respect of equality and diversity. This rule of conduct is concerned with a broader obligation not to withhold your services on grounds that are inherently inconsistent with your role in upholding access to justice and the rule of law and therefore in this rule "discriminate" is used in this broader sense. This obligation applies whether or not the *client* is a member of any protected group for the purposes of the Equality Act 2010. For example, you must not withhold services on the ground that any financial support which may properly be given to the prospective *client* for the proceedings in question will be available as part of the Community Legal Service or Criminal Defence Service.

The 'Cab-rank' rule

rC29

If you receive *instructions* from a *professional client*, and you are:

1. a self-employed barrister instructed by a professional client~~; or~~

~~2. an authorised individual working within a BSB authorised body; or~~

~~3. a BSB authorised body and the instructions seek the services of a named authorised individual working for you,~~

and the *instructions* are appropriate taking into account the experience, seniority~~ or~~ and field of practice of yourself ~~or (as appropriate) of the named *authorised individual*~~ you must, subject to Rule C30 below, accept the *instructions* addressed specifically to you, irrespective of:

a. the identity of the *client*;

b. the nature of the case to which the *instructions* relate;

c. whether the *client* is paying privately or is publicly funded; and

d. any belief or opinion which you may have formed as to the character, reputation, cause, conduct, guilt or innocence of the *client*.

rC30

The cab rank Rule C29 does not apply if:

1. you are required to refuse to accept the *instructions* pursuant to Rule C21; or

2. accepting the *instructions* would require you or the named *authorised individual* to do something other than in the course of their ordinary working time or to cancel a commitment already in their diary; or

3. the potential liability for professional negligence in respect of the particular matter could exceed the level of professional indemnity insurance which is reasonably available and likely to be available in the market for you to accept; or

4. you are a Queen's Counsel, and the acceptance of the *instructions* would require you to act without a junior in circumstances where you reasonably consider that the interests of the *client* require that a junior should also be instructed; or

5. accepting the *instructions* would require you to do any *foreign work*; or

6. accepting the *instructions* would require you to act for a *foreign lawyer* (other than a *European lawyer,* a lawyer from a country that is a member of EFTA, a *solicitor* or *barrister* of Northern Ireland or a *solicitor* or advocate under the law of Scotland); or

7. the *professional client:*

   a. is not accepting liability for your fees; or

   b. is named on the List of Defaulting Solicitors; or

   c. is instructing you as a lay *client* and not in their capacity as a professional *client*; or

8. you have not been offered a proper fee for your services (except that you shall not be entitled to refuse to accept *instructions* on this ground if you have not made or responded to any fee proposal within a reasonable time after receiving the *instructions*); or

9. except where you are to be paid directly by (i) the *Legal Aid Agency* as part of the Community Legal Service or the Criminal Defence Service or (ii) the Crown Prosecution Service:
    a. your fees have not been agreed (except that you shall not be entitled to refuse to accept *instructions* on this ground if you have not taken reasonable steps to agree fees within a reasonable time after receiving the *instructions*);
    b. having required your fees to be paid before you accept the *instructions*, those fees have not been paid;
    c. accepting the *instructions* would require you to act other than on (A) the Standard Contractual Terms for the Supply of Legal Services by Barristers to Authorised Persons 2012 as published on the *Bar Standards Board's* website; or (B) if you publish standard terms of work, on those standard terms of work.

Guidance on Rule C29 and C30

gC89

Rule C30 means that you would not be required to accept *instructions* to, for example, *conduct litigation* or attend a police station in circumstances where you do not normally undertake such work or, in the case of litigation, are not authorised to undertake such work.

gC90

In determining whether or not a fee is proper for the purposes of Rule C30.2, regard shall be had to the following:

1. the complexity length and difficulty of the case;
2. your ability, experience and seniority; and
3. the expenses which you will incur.

gC91

Further, you may refuse to accept instructions on the basis that the fee is not proper if the instructions are on the basis that you will do the work under a *conditional fee agreement*.

Quality Assurance Scheme for Advocates Rules

Scope of QASA

rC31

Subject to Rule C32, you must not undertake *criminal advocacy* unless you have *provisional accreditation* or *full accreditation* in accordance with these *QASA Rules* and with the *QASA Handbook*.

rC32

Barristers who do not have provisional accreditation or full accreditation under the QASA are permitted to undertake criminal advocacy:

1. in hearings which primarily involve advocacy which is outside of the definition of *criminal advocacy*; or
2. if they have been instructed specifically as a result of their specialism in work outside of the definition of *criminal advocacy*.

rC33

You shall only undertake *criminal advocacy* in hearings which you are satisfied fall within the *QASA level* at which you are accredited, or any *QASA level* below the same, unless you are satisfied that you are competent to accept instructions for a case at a higher *QASA level* strictly in accordance with the criteria prescribed in the *QASA Handbook*.

Provisional accreditation

rC34

If you are granted *provisional accreditation*, you must apply to convert this to *full accreditation* within 12 or 24 months of the date on which your *provisional accreditation* was granted.

Full accreditation

rC35

If you are granted *full accreditation*, it will be valid for 5 years from the date on which it was granted.

General provisions relating to applications for registration, progression or re-accreditation

rC36

You may apply for *registration*, *progression* or *re-accreditation* under these *QASA Rules*. In support of an application you shall submit such information as may be prescribed by the *QASA*. This will include:

1. completing the relevant application form supplied by the *Bar Standards Board* and submitting it to the *Bar Standards Board*;
2. submitting such information in support of the application as may be prescribed by the *QASA*. This will include all of the *criminal advocacy evaluation forms* that you have obtained; and
3. paying the appropriate fee in the amount determined in accordance with the *Bar Standards Board's* published fees policy.

rC37

An application will only have been made once the *Bar Standards Board* has received the application form completed in full, together with all information required in support of the application and confirmation from you in the form of a declaration that the information contained within, or submitted in support of, the application is full and accurate.

rC38

You are personally responsible for the contents of your application and any information submitted to the *Bar Standards Board* by you or on your behalf, and you must not submit (or cause or permit to be submitted on your behalf) information to the *Bar Standards Board* which you do not believe is full and accurate.

rC39

On receipt of an application, the *Bar Standards Board* shall decide whether to grant or refuse the application, and shall notify you accordingly, giving reasons for any decision to refuse the application. This decision will take effect when it has been communicated to the *barrister* concerned.

rC40

Before reaching a decision on the application, the *Bar Standards Board* may appoint an *independent assessor* to conduct an assessment of your competence to conduct *criminal advocacy* at the relevant *QASA level.*

Registration for QASA

rC41

In order to be accredited under *QASA barristers* must first apply for *registration*. In support of an application you shall submit such information as may be prescribed by the *QASA*.

QASA Level 1

1, If you apply for *registration* at *QASA level* 1 and your application is successful, you will be awarded *full accreditation* at *QASA level* 1.

QASA Levels 2 to 4

2. If you apply for *registration* at *QASA levels* 2, 3 or 4 and your application is successful, you will be awarded *Provisional accreditation* which will be valid for 24 months.

3. You must apply to convert your provisional *accreditation* to *full accreditation* within 24 months.

4. You must be assessed in your first effective criminal trials at your *QASA level* and submit the prescribed number of completed *criminal advocacy evaluation forms* confirming that you are competent in accordance with the competence framework detailed in the *QASA Handbook* .

5. Your application must include all completed *criminal advocacy* evaluation forms obtained by you in *effective trials.*

6. If your application is successful you will be awarded *full accreditation.*

7. Subject to Rule C41.8, if your application for *full accreditation* is unsuccessful, you shall be granted *provisional accreditation* at the *QASA level* below and shall be required to apply to convert this to *full accreditation* at that lower *QASA level* in accordance with Rules C41.3 to C41.5.

8. If your application for *full accreditation* at *QASA level* 2 is unsuccessful, you shall be granted *accreditation* at *QASA level* 1.

Barristers not undertaking trials

9. If you do not intend to undertake criminal trials you may apply for *registration* at *QASA level* 2. If your application is successful, you will be awarded *provisional accreditation*. You must be assessed via an *approved assessment organisation* within 24 months.

10. If your application for *full accreditation* is successful you shall be awarded *full accreditation* and will be permitted to undertake non-trial hearings up to *QASA level* 3 and trials at *QASA level* 1.

11. Once you have *full accreditation*, if you wish to undertake trials at *QASA level* 2 you must inform the BSB of your intention and comply with Rules C42.2 to Rules C42.5.

Barristers who took silk between 2010 and 2013

12. If you took silk between 2010 and 2013 inclusive you can register through the modified entry arrangements set out in paragraph 2.38 of the *QASA Handbook* .

Progression

rC42

If you have *full accreditation*, you may apply for *accreditation* at the next higher *QASA level* to your current *QASA level*:

1. Progression to QASA level 2.

2. If you wish to progress to *QASA level 2* you must first obtain *provisional accreditation* at *QASA level 2* by notifying the Bar Standards Board of your intention to progress.

3. Your *provisional accreditation* will be valid for 24 months. In order to convert this to *full accreditation* you must be assessed in your first effective criminal trials at *QASA level 2* and submit the prescribed number of completed *criminal advocacy evaluation forms* confirming that you are competent in *QASA level 2* trials in accordance with the competence framework detailed in the *QASA Handbook.*

4. Your application must include all completed *criminal advocacy evaluation forms* obtained by you in *effective trials.*

5. Where your application is successful, you shall be granted *full accreditation* at *QASA level 2*, which is valid for 5 years from the date of issue.

Progression to QASA level 3 and 4

Stage 1

6. You must first apply for *provisional accreditation* at the next higher *QASA level* to your current *QASA level*. In order to apply for *provisional accreditation*, you must submit the prescribed number of *criminal advocacy evaluation forms* confirming that you are very competent at your current *QASA level* in accordance with the competence framework detailed in the *QASA Handbook* .

7. Your application must include all completed *criminal advocacy evaluation forms* obtained by you in *effective trials*. These should be obtained within a 12 month period.

8. If your application is successful you will be awarded *provisional accreditation*.

Stage 2

9. Your *provisional accreditation* will be valid for 12 months. You must apply to convert your *provisional accreditation* to *full accreditation* before your *provisional accreditation* expires.

10. You must be assessed in your first effective criminal trials at your new *QASA level* and submit the prescribed number of completed *criminal advocacy evaluation forms* confirming that you are competent in accordance with the competence framework detailed in the *QASA Handbook*.

11. Your application must include all completed *criminal advocacy evaluation forms* obtained by you in *effective trials*.

12. If your application is successful you will be awarded *full accreditation*.

13. If your application for *full accreditation* is unsuccessful, you may continue to conduct *criminal advocacy* at your current *QASA level* until the expiry of your current accreditation.

Re-accreditation

rC43

You must apply for *re-accreditation* at the *QASA level* at which you are accredited within five years from the date on which your *full accreditation* was granted.

rC44

You shall submit, in support of an application for *re-accreditation*, evidence to demonstrate your competence to conduct *criminal advocacy* at the *QASA level* at which you are accredited, comprising:

1. if you are accredited at *QASA level* 1, evidence of the assessed continuing professional development undertaken by you in the field of advocacy in the period since you were accredited at *QASA level* 1 or, if you have previously been re-*accredited* at that *QASA level*, since your most recent *re-accreditation*;

2. if you are *accredited* at *QASA level* 2, 3 or 4, the number of *criminal advocacy evaluation forms prescribed by the QASA*. Your application must include all completed *criminal advocacy evaluation forms* obtained by you in consecutive *effective trials* in the 24 months preceding the application.

rC45

If your application is successful you will be awarded *full accreditation* for a period of 5 years.

rC46

Subject to Rules C47, if your application for *re-accreditation* is unsuccessful, you shall be granted *provisional accreditation* at the *QASA level* below and shall be required to apply to convert this to *full accreditation* at that lower *QASA level* in accordance with Rules C41.3 to C41.5.

rC47

If your application for *re-accreditation* at *QASA level* 2 is unsuccessful, you shall be granted accreditation at *QASA level* 1.

Lapse of accreditation

rC48

Subject to Rule C50, your *provisional accreditation* will lapse if you do not apply for *full accreditation* before it expires.

rC49

Subject to Rule C50, your *full accreditation* will lapse if you do not apply for *re-accreditation* within 5 years of the date on which you were awarded *full accreditation.*

rC50

If the BSB has received an application within the period of *accreditation*, the accreditation will not lapse whilst a decision is pending.

rC51

If your *accreditation* lapses, you may not undertake *criminal advocacy* in accordance with Rule 2.

Applications for variation

rC52

Where your individual circumstances result in you encountering difficulties in obtaining completed *criminal advocacy evaluation forms* within the specified period, then you may apply to the *Bar Standards Board* for an extension of time to comply with the requirements; or

rC53

Where your individual circumstances result in you encountering difficulties in obtaining completed *criminal advocacy evaluation forms*, then you may apply to the *Bar Standards Board* for your competence to conduct *criminal advocacy* to be assessed by an *independent assessor*, and you may submit the results of the assessment in support of your application for *registration*, *re-accreditation* or *progression* in the place of one *criminal advocacy* evaluation form.

Managing underperformance

rC54

The *Bar Standards Board* may receive *criminal advocacy evaluation forms* raising concerns regarding your competence to conduct *criminal advocacy* at any time.

rC55

Where concerns regarding your competence to conduct *criminal advocacy* are brought to the attention of the *Bar Standards Board*, either during the course of its consideration of an application brought by you under these Rules, or as a result of concerns raised under Rule rC54, it may decide to do one or more of the following:

1. appoint an *independent assessor* to conduct an assessment of your *criminal advocacy*;
2. recommend that you undertake, at your own cost, such training for such period as it may specify;
3. revoke your *accreditation* at your current *QASA level*; and/or
4. refer you for consideration of your health or conduct under the Fitness to Practise Rules or the Complaints Rules, as it considers appropriate,

and shall notify you accordingly, giving reasons for its decision.

rC56

Where your *accreditation* has been revoked, you shall be granted *provisional accreditation* at the *QASA level* below and shall be required to apply to convert this to *full accreditation* in accordance with Rules C41.3 to C41.5.

rC57

Where you have applied for *registration* or *re-accreditation* at *QASA level* 1, and your application has been refused, you will not be entitled to accept any instructions to conduct *criminal advocacy*, and the *Bar Standards Board* may recommend that you undertake training in accordance with Rule C55.2 before you re-apply for *registration* or *re-accreditation* as appropriate.

rC58

Where you have undertaken training under Rule C55.2, the *Bar Standards Board* shall, at the end of the specified period, assess whether you have satisfactorily completed the training before reaching a decision in relation to any further steps that it may consider appropriate to take in accordance with Rule C55.

Appeals

rC59

You may appeal to the *Bar Standards Board* against any decision reached by it under these rules. Appeals must be made in accordance with the published *Bar Standards Board QASA* Appeals Policy.

Commencement and transitional arrangements

rC60

Subject to Rule C63, the *QASA Rules* commence on 30 September 2013.

Registration of barristers currently undertaking criminal advocacy

rC61

Barristers currently undertaking *criminal advocacy* are required to apply for *registration* under the *QASA Scheme* in accordance with the phased implementation programme as set out at paragraphs 2.11 to 2.13 of the *QASA Handbook.*

rC62

The dates for *registration* will depend upon the primary circuit in which you practise. This will be the circuit in which you undertake *criminal advocacy* more frequently than in any other circuit.

1. If you primarily practise in the Midland or Western Circuit, you must register for *QASA* from 30 September 2013 and before the first occasion on which you undertake *criminal advocacy* after 7 March 2014.
2. If you primarily practise in the South Eastern Circuit, you must register for *QASA* from 10 March 2014 and before the first occasion on which you undertake *criminal advocacy* after 13 June 2014.
3. If you primarily practise in the Northern, North Eastern or Wales and Chester Circuit, you must register for *QASA* from 30 June 2014 and before the first occasion on which you undertake *criminal advocacy* after 3 October 2014.

rC63

Subject to Rules C63.1, C63.2 and Rule C31 commences for all advocates from 4 October 2014.

1. Rule C31 will commence for those advocates who primarily practise in the Midland or Western Circuit from 10 March 2014. Any advocate who undertakes *criminal advocacy* in these circuits without *accreditation* must be able to prove to the *Bar Standards Board* that they practise primarily in another circuit.
2. Rule C31 will commence for those advocates who primarily practise in the South Eastern Circuit from 14 June 2014. Any advocate who undertakes

criminal advocacy in this circuit without *accreditation* must be able to prove to the *Bar Standards Board* that they practise primarily in the Northern, North Eastern or Wales and Chester Circuit.

C4 You and Your Regulator

[1.16]

Outcomes

oC21

BSB regulated persons are effectively regulated.

oC22

The public have confidence in the proper regulation of *persons* regulated by the *Bar Standards Board.*

oC23

The *Bar Standards Board* has the information that it needs in order to be able to assess risks and regulate effectively and in accordance with the *regulatory objectives.*

Rules

Provision of information to the Bar Standards Board

rC64

You must:

1. promptly provide all such information to the *Bar Standards Board* as it may, for the purpose of its regulatory functions, from time to time require of you, and notify it of any material changes to that information; and
2. comply in due time with any decision or sentence imposed by the *Bar Standards Board*, a *Disciplinary Tribunal*, the *Visitors*, an *interim panel*, a *review panel*, an *appeal panel* or a *medical panel.*

Guidance to Rule C64

gC92

Your obligations under Rule C64 include, for example, responding promptly to any request from the *Bar Standards Board* for comments or information relating to any matter whether or not the matter relates to you, or to another *BSB regulated person.*

gC93

The documents that you may be required to disclose pursuant to Rule C64 may include *client* information that is subject to legal privilege. It has been recognised in

R (on the application of Morgan Grenfell & Co Ltd) v Special Comr of Income Tax [2002] UKHL 21, [2003] 1 AC 563, [2002] 3 All ER 1 that the disclosure of a *client's* privileged information to a legal regulator does not infringe the *client's* right to privilege. This is because the information is not being sought for the purposes of making it public or to be used against the person entitled to the privilege. Note the difference where you are being required to report serious misconduct by others. In those circumstances, where legal professional privilege applies, this will override the requirement to report serious misconduct by another.

Duty to Report Certain Matters to the Bar Standards Board

rC65

You must report promptly to the *Bar Standards Board* if:

1. you are charged with an *indictable offence*; in the jurisdiction of England and Wales or with a *criminal offence* of comparable seriousness in any other jurisdiction;
2. you are convicted of, or accept a caution, for any *criminal offence*, in any jurisdiction, other than a *minor criminal offence*;
3. you (or an entity of which you are a *manager*) to your knowledge are the subject of any disciplinary or other regulatory or enforcement action by another *Approved Regulator* or other regulator, including being the subject of disciplinary proceedings;
4. you are a *manager* of an *non-BSB authorised body* which is the subject of an intervention by the *approved regulator* of that body;
5. you are a *registered European lawyer* and:
   a. to your knowledge any investigation into your conduct is commenced by your *home regulator*; or
   b. any finding of professional misconduct is made by your *home regulator*; or
   c. your authorisation in your *home state* to pursue professional activities under your *home professional title* is withdrawn or *suspended*; or
   d. you are charged with a disciplinary offence.
6. any of the following occur:

a. bankruptcy proceedings are initiated in respect of or against you;

b. *director's disqualification* proceedings are initiated against you;

c. a *bankruptcy order* or *director's disqualification order* is made against you;

d. you have made a composition or arrangement with, or granted a trust deed for, your creditors;

~~e. winding up proceedings are initiated in respect of or against you~~

~~f. you have had an administrator, administrative receiver, receiver or liquidator appointed in respect of you;~~

~~g. administration proceedings are initiated in respect of or against you;~~

7. you have otherwise committed serious misconduct;

8. you become authorised to *practise* by another *approved regulator.*

Guidance to Rule C65

gC94

In circumstances where you have committed serious misconduct you should take all reasonable steps to mitigate the effects of such serious misconduct.

Reporting Serious Misconduct by others

rC66

Subject to your duty to keep the affairs of each *client* confidential and subject also to Rules C67 and C68, you must report to the *Bar Standards Board* if you have reasonable grounds to believe that there has been serious misconduct by a *barrister* or a *registered European lawyer*~~, a *BSB authorised body*, a *BSB regulated manager* or an *authorised (non-BSB) individual* who is working as a *manager* or an *employee* of a *BSB authorised body*~~.

rC67

You must never make, or threaten to make, a report under Rule C66 without a genuine and reasonably held belief that Rule C66 applies.

rC68

You are not under a duty to report serious misconduct by others if:

1. you become aware of the facts giving rise to the belief that there has serious misconduct from matters that are in the public domain and the circumstances are such that you reasonably consider it likely that the facts will have come to the attention of the *Bar Standards Board*; or
2. you are aware that the relevant person that committed the serious misconduct has already reported the serious misconduct to the *Bar Standards Board*; or
3. the events which led to you becoming aware of that other person's serious misconduct are subject to their legal professional privilege; or
4. you become aware of such serious misconduct as a result of your work on the *Bar Council's* ethical enquiry service.

rC69

You must not victimise anyone for making in good faith a report under Rule C66.

Guidance on Rules C65.7 to C68

gC95

It is in the public interest that the *Bar Standards Board*, as an *Approved Regulator*, is made aware of, and is able to investigate, potential instances of serious misconduct. The purpose of Rules C65.7 to C69, therefore, is to assist the *Bar Standards Board* in undertaking this regulatory function.

gC96

Serious misconduct includes, without being limited to:

1. dishonesty (CD3);
2. assault or harassment (CD3 and/or CD5 and/or CD8);
3. seeking to gain access without consent to *instructions* or other confidential information relating to the opposing party's case (CD3 and/or CD5); or
4. seeking to gain access without consent to confidential information relating to another member of *chambers*, member of staff or *pupil* (CD3 and/or CD5);
5. encouraging a witness to give evidence which is untruthful or misleading (CD1 and/or CD3);
6. knowingly or recklessly misleading, or attempting to mislead, the *court* or an opponent (CD1 and/or CD3); or
7. being drunk or under the influence of drugs in *court* (CD2 and/or CD7); or
8. failure by a *barrister* to report promptly to the *Bar Standards Board* pursuant to rC66 above;
9. a breach by a *barrister* of rC70 below.

gC97

If you believe (or suspect) that there has been serious misconduct, then the first step is to carefully consider all of the circumstances. The circumstances include:

1. whether that person's *instructions* or other confidential matters might have a bearing on the assessment of their conduct;
2. whether that person has been offered an opportunity to explain their conduct, and if not, why not;
3. any explanation which has been or could be offered for that person's conduct;
4. whether the matter has been raised, or will be raised, in the litigation in which it occurred, and if not, why not.

gC98

Having considered all of the circumstances, the duty to report arises if you have reasonable grounds to believe there has been serious misconduct. This will be so where, having given due consideration to the circumstances, including the matters identified at Guidance C97, you have material before you which as it stands establishes a reasonably credible case of serious misconduct. Your duty under Rule C66 is then to report the potential instance of serious misconduct so that the *Bar Standards Board* can investigate whether or not there has in fact been misconduct.

gC99

Circumstances which may give rise to the exception from the general requirement to report serious misconduct set out in Rule rC68.1 include for example where misconduct has been widely reported in the national media. In these circumstances it would not be in the public interest for every *BSB regulated person* to have an obligation to report such serious misconduct.

gC100

In Rule C68.4 "work on the *Bar Council's* ethical enquiry service" means:

1. dealing with queries from *BSB regulated persons* who contact the ethical enquiry service operated by the *Bar Council* for the purposes of providing advice to those *persons*; and
2. either providing advice to *BSB regulated persons* in the course of working for the ethical enquiry service or to any individual working for the ethical enquiry service where (i) you are identified on the list of *BSB regulated persons* maintained by the *Bar Council* as being permitted to provide such advice (the "approved list"); and (ii) the advice which you are being asked to provide to the individual working for the ethical enquiry service arises from a query which originated from their work for that service; and
3. providing advice to *BSB regulated persons* where any individual working for ethical enquiry service arranges for you to give such advice and you are on the approved list.

gC101

Rule C68.4 has been carved out of the general requirement to report serious misconduct of others because it is not in the public interest that the duty to report misconduct should constrain *BSB authorised persons* appointed by or on behalf of the *Bar Council* to offer ethical advice to others from doing so or inhibit *BSB regulated persons* needing advice from seeking it. Consequently, *BSB authorised persons* appointed by or on behalf of the *Bar Council* to offer ethical advice to *BSB regulated persons* through the *Bar Council's* ethical enquiry service will not be under a duty to report information received by them in confidence from persons seeking such advice, subject only to the requirements of the general law. However, in circumstances where Rule rC68.3applies, the relevant *BSB authorised person* will still be expected to encourage the relevant *BSB regulated person* who has committed serious misconduct to disclose such serious misconduct to the *Bar Standards Board* in accordance with Rule C65.7.

gC102

~~Misconduct which falls short of serious misconduct should, where applicable, be reported to your *HOLP* so that they can keep a record of non-compliance in accordance with Rule C96.4.~~

Access to Premises

rC70

You must permit the *Bar Council*, or the *Bar Standards Board*, or any person appointed by them, reasonable access, on request, to inspect:

1. any premises from which you provide, or are believed to provide, *legal services* ; and

2. any documents or records relating to those premises and your *practice*~~, or *BSB authorised body*~~,

and the *Bar Council*, *Bar Standards Board*, or any person appointed by them, shall be entitled to take copies of such documents or records as may be required by them for the purposes of their functions.

Co-operation with the Legal Ombudsman

rC71

You must give the *Legal Ombudsman* all reasonable assistance requested of you, in connection with the investigation, consideration, and determination, of *complaints* made under the Ombudsman scheme.

Ceasing to practise

rC72

Once you are aware that you (if you are a *self-employed barrister*) ~~or a *BSB authorised body*) or the *BSB authorised body* within which you work (if you are an authorised individual or *manager* of such *BSB authorised body*)~~ will cease to practise, you shall effect the orderly wind-down of activities, including:

1. informing the *Bar Standards Board* and providing them with a contact address;
2. notifying those *clients* for whom you have current matters and liaising with them in respect of the arrangements that they would like to be put in place in respect of those matters;
3. providing such information to the *Bar Standards Board* in respect of your *practice* and your proposed arrangements in respect of the winding down of your activities as the *Bar Standards Board* may require.

C5 You and Your Practice

[1.17]

Outcomes

oC24

Your *practice* is run competently in a way that achieves compliance with the Core Duties and your other obligations under this *Handbook*. Your *employees*, *pupils* and trainees understand, and do, what is required of them in order that you meet your obligations under this *Handbook*.

oC25

Clients are clear about the extent to which your services are regulated and by whom, and who is responsible for providing those services.

Rules

C5.1 GENERAL

Client money

rC73

Except where you are acting in your capacity as a *manager* of an *authorised (non-BSB) body*, you must not receive, control or handle *client money* apart from what the client pays you for your services.

rC74

If you make use of a third party payment service for making payments to or from or on behalf of your *client* you must:

1. Ensure that the service you use will not result in your receiving, controlling or handling *client money;* and
2. Only use the service for payments to or from or on behalf of your *client* that are made in respect of legal services, such as fees, disbursements or settlement monies; and
3. Take reasonable steps to check that making use of the service is consistent with your duty to act competently and in your *client's* best interests.

rC75

The *Bar Standards Board* may give notice under this rule that (effective from the date of that notice) you may only use third party payment services approved by the *Bar Standards Board* or which satisfy criteria set by the *Bar Standards Board.*

Guidance on Rules C73 and C74

gC103

The prohibition in Rule C73 applies to you and to anyone acting on your behalf, including any "ProcureCo" being a company established as a vehicle to enable the provision of *legal services* but does not in itself supply or provide those *legal services.* Rule C73 prohibits you from holding *client money* or other *client* assets yourself, or through any agent, third party or nominee.

gC104

Receiving, controlling or handling *client money* includes entering into any arrangement which gives you de facto control over the use and/or destination of funds provided by or for the benefit of your *client* or intended by another party to be transmitted to your *client*, whether or not those funds are beneficially owned by your client and whether or not held in an account of yours.

gC105

The circumstances in which you will have de facto control within the meaning of Rule C73 include when you can cause money to be transferred from a balance standing to the credit of your *client* without that *client's* consent to such a withdrawal. For large withdrawals, explicit consent should usually be required. However, the client's consent may be deemed to be given if:

1. the *client* has given informed consent to an arrangement which enables withdrawals to be made after the *client* has received an invoice; and
2. the *client* has not objected to the withdrawal within a pre-agreed reasonable period (which should not normally be less than one week from receipt of the invoice).

gC106

A fixed fee paid in advance is not *client money* for the purposes of Rule C73.

gC107

If you agree with a *client*, who can reasonably be expected to understand the implications of such an agreement, that (1) your fee for any work will be charged according to the time spent on it, but (2) you will be paid a fixed fee in advance for it, and (3), when the work has been done, you will pay the *client* any difference between that fixed fee and the fee which has actually been earned, and (4) you will not hold the difference between the fixed fee and the fee which has been earned on trust for the *client*, that difference will not be *client money*. Such fees may be considered as *client money* if you cannot demonstrate that the agreement was made in advance and on clear terms. You should also consider carefully whether such an arrangement is in the client's interest and that the client fully understands the implications. Further guidance on this issue is published on the *Bar Standards Board's* website.

gC108

Acting in the following ways may demonstrate compliance with Rules C73, C74 and C75:

gC109

Checking that any third party payment service you may use is not structured in such a way that the service provider is holding, as your agent, money to which the *client* is beneficially entitled. If this is so you will be in breach of Rule C73.

gC110

Considering whether your *client* will be safe in using the third party payment service as a means of transmitting or receiving funds. The steps you should take in order to satisfy yourself will depend on what would be expected in all the circumstances of a reasonably competent legal adviser acting in their *client's* best interests. However, you are unlikely to demonstrate that you have acted competently and in your *client's* best interests if you have not:

1. ensured that the payment service is authorised or regulated as a payment service by the *Financial Conduct Authority* (*FCA*) and taken reasonable steps to satisfy yourself that it is in good standing with the FCA;

2. if the payment service is classified as a small payment institution, ensured that it has arrangements to safeguard *clients*' funds or adequate insurance arrangements;
3. ensured that the payment service segregates *client* money from its own funds;
4. satisfied yourself that the terms of the service are such as to ensure that any money paid in by or on behalf of the *client* can only be paid out with the *client's* consent;
5. informed your *client* that moneys held by the payment service provider are not covered by the *Financial Services Compensation Scheme.*

gC111

Unless you are reasonably satisfied that it is safe for your client to use the third party payment service (see rC74.3, gC109 and gC110 above), advising your *client* against using the third party payment service and not making use of it yourself.

gC112

The *Bar Standards Board* has not yet given notice under Rule C75.

Insurance

rC76

You must:

1. ensure that you have insurance (taking into account the nature of your practice) which covers all the *legal services* you supply to *the public;* and
2. if you are a *BSB authorised person* ~~or *BSB authorised body* or a manager of a *BSB authorised body*~~, then in the event that the *Bar Standards Board,* by any notice it may from time to time issue under this Rule rC75, stipulates a minimum level of insurance and/or minimum terms for the insurance which must be taken out by *BSB authorised persons*, you must ensure that you have or put in place within the time specified in such notice, insurance meeting such requirements as apply to you.

rC77

Where you are acting as a *self-employed barrister*, you must be a member *of BMIF*, unless:

1. you are a *pupil* who is covered by his *pupil supervisor's* insurance; or
2. you were called to the *Bar* under Rule Q94, in which case you must either be insured with *BMIF* or be covered by insurance against claims for professional negligence arising out of the supply of your services in England and Wales in such amount and on such terms as are currently required by the *Bar Standards Board*, and have delivered to the *Bar Standards Board* a copy of the current insurance policy, or the current certificate of insurance, issued by the insurer.

rC78

If you are a member *of BMIF*, you must:

1. pay promptly the insurance premium required by *BMIF*; and
2. supply promptly such information as *BMIF* may from time to time require pursuant to its rules.

Guidance on Rules C75 to C77

gC113

~~Where you are working in a *BSB authorised body*, you will satisfy the requirements of Rule rC76.1 so long as the *BSB authorised body* has taken out insurance, which covers your activities.~~

gC114

Any notice issued under Rule C75 will be posted on the *Bar Standards Board's* website and may also be publicised by such other means as the *Bar Standards Board* may judge appropriate.

gC115

Where you are working in an *authorised (non-BSB) body*, the rules of the *approved regulator* of that body will determine what insurance the *authorised (non-BSB) body* must have.

gC116

Where you are working as an *employed barrister (non-authorised body)*, the rule does not require you to have your own insurance if you provide *legal services* only to your *employer*. If you supply *legal services* to other people (to the extent permitted by the *Scope of Practice*~~*, Authorisation and Licensing Rules*~~ set out at Section S.B you should consider whether you need insurance yourself having regard to the arrangements made by your *employer* for insuring against claims made in respect of your services. If your *employer* already has adequate insurance for this purpose, you need not take out any insurance of your own. You should ensure that your *employer's* policy covers you, for example, for any pro-bono work you may do.

gC117

Where you are a *registered European lawyer*, the rule does not require you to have your own insurance if:

1. you provide to the *Bar Standards Board* evidence to show that you are covered by insurance taken out or a guarantee provided in accordance with the rules of your *home State*; and
2. the *Bar Standards Board* is satisfied that such insurance or guarantee is fully equivalent in terms of conditions and extent of cover to the cover required pursuant to Rule C76. However, where the *Bar Standards Board* is satisfied that the equivalence is only partial, the *Bar Standards Board* may require you to arrange additional insurance or an additional guarantee to cover the

elements which are not already covered by the insurance or guarantee contracted by you in accordance with the rules of your *home state.*

Associations with others

rC79

You may not do anything, practising in *an association*, which you are otherwise prohibited from doing.

rC80

Where you are in *an association* on more than a one-off basis, you must notify the *Bar Standards Board* that you are in *an association*, and provide such details of that association as are required by the *Bar Standards Board.*

rC81

If you have a material commercial interest in an organisation to which you plan to refer a *client*, you must:

1. tell the *client* in writing about your interest in that organisation before you refer the *client*; and
2. keep a record of your referrals to any such organisation for review by the *Bar Standards Board* on request.

rC82

If you have a material commercial interest in an organisation which is proposing to refer a matter to you, you must:

1. tell the *client* in writing about your interest in that organisation before you accept such *instructions*;
2. make a clear agreement with that organisation or other public statement about how relevant issues, such as conflicts of interest, will be dealt with; and
3. keep a record of referrals received from any such organisation for review by the *Bar Standards Board* on reasonable request.

rC83

If you refer a *client* to a third party which is not a *BSB authorised person* or an *authorised (non-BSB) person*, you must take reasonable steps to ensure that the *client* is not wrongly led to believe that the third party is subject to regulation by the *Bar Standards Board* or by another *approved regulator.*

rC84

You must not have a material commercial interest in any organisation which gives the impression of being, or may be reasonably perceived as being, subject to the regulation of the *Bar Standards Board* or of another *approved regulator*, in circumstances where it is not so regulated.

rC85

A material commercial interest for the purposes of Rules C78 to C84 is an interest which an objective observer with knowledge of the salient facts would reasonably consider might potentially influence your judgment.

Guidance on Rules C78 to C84 and CD5

gC118

You may not use an association with the purpose of, or in order to evade rules which would otherwise apply to you. You may not do anything, practising in *an association*, which you are individually prohibited from doing.

gC119

You will bring yourself and your profession into disrepute (CD5) if you are personally involved in arrangements which breach the restrictions imposed by the Legal Services Act 2007 on those who can provide reserved legal activities. For example, you must not remain a member of any "ProcureCo" arrangement where you know or are reckless as to whether the ProcureCo is itself carrying on reserved legal activities without a licence or where you have failed to take reasonable steps to ensure this is not so before joining or continuing your involvement with the Procureco.

gC120

The purpose of Rules C78 to C84 is to ensure that *clients* and members of *the public* are not confused by any such association. In particular, the public should be clear who is responsible for doing work, and about the extent to which that person is regulated in doing it: see Rules C77 and C80.

gC121

This *Handbook* applies in full whether or not you are practising in an association. You are particularly reminded of the need to ensure that, notwithstanding any such association, you continue to comply with Rules C8, C9, C10, C12, C15, C19, C20, C28, C73, C75, C79, C82 and C86 (and, where relevant C80, C81, C83 and C74) and [Rule 12 of section E].

gC122

References to "organisation" in Rules C81 and C82 include ~~BSB authorised bodies and~~ *authorised* (*non-BSB*) *bodies*, as well as non-authorised bodies. So, if you have an interest, as owner, or manager, in any such body, your relationship with any such organisation is caught by these rules.

gC123

These rules do not permit you to accept *instructions* from a third party in any case where that would give rise to a potential conflict of interest contrary to CD2 or any relevant part of Rule C79.

gC124

You should only refer a *client* to an organisation in which you have a material commercial interest if it is in the *client's* best interest to be referred to that organisation. This is one aspect of what is required of you by CD2. Your obligations of honesty and integrity, in CD3, require you to be open with *clients* about any interest you have in, or arrangement you have with, any organisation to which you properly refer the *client*, or from which the *client* is referred to you. It is inherently unlikely that a general referral arrangement obliging you (whether or not you have an interest in such organisation) to refer to that organisation, without the option to refer elsewhere if the *client's* circumstances make that more appropriate, could be justified as being in the best interests of each individual *client* (CD2) and it may well also be contrary to your obligations of honesty and integrity (CD3) and compromise your independence (CD4).

gC125

The *Bar Standards Board* may require you to provide copies of any protocols that you may have in order to ensure compliance with these rules.

gC126

Your obligations under CD5 require you not to act in an *association* with a person where, merely by being associated with such person, you may reasonably be considered as bringing the profession into disrepute or otherwise diminishing the trust that the public places in you and your profession.

gC127

Members of *chambers* are not in partnership but are independent of one another and are not responsible for the conduct of other members. However, each individual member of *chambers* is responsible for his own conduct and the constitution of *chambers* enables, or should enable, each individual member of *chambers* to take steps to terminate another person's membership in specified circumstances. Rule C78 does not require you to sever connection with a member of *chambers* solely because to your knowledge he or she is found to breach this *Handbook*, provided that he or she is not disbarred and complies with such sanctions as may be imposed for such breach; however, your *chambers* constitution should be drafted so as to allow you to exclude from *chambers* a member whose conduct is reasonably considered such as to diminish the trust the public places in you and your profession and you should take such steps as are reasonably available to you under your constitution to exclude any such member.

Outsourcing

rC86

Where you outsource to a third party any support services that are critical to the delivery of any *legal services* in respect of which you are instructed:

1. any outsourcing does not alter your obligations to your *client*;
2. you remain responsible for compliance with your obligations under this *Handbook* in respect of the *legal services*;

3. you must ensure that such outsourcing is subject to contractual arrangements which ensure that such third party:

    a. is subject to confidentiality obligations similar to the confidentiality obligations placed on you in accordance with this *Handbook*;

    b. complies with any other obligations set out in this Code of Conduct which may be relevant to or affected by such outsourcing;

    c. processes any personal data in accordance with your *instructions* and, for the avoidance of doubt, as though it were a data controller under the Data Protection Act; and

    d. is required to allow the *Bar Standards Board* or its agent to obtain information from, inspect the records (including electronic records) of, or enter the premises of such third party in relation to the outsourced activities or functions.

Guidance on Rule C86

gC128

Rule C86 applies to the outsourcing of clerking services.

gC129

Rule C86 does not apply where the *client* enters into a separate agreement with the third party for the services in question.

gC130

Rule C86 does not apply where you are instructing a *pupil* or a *devil* to undertake work on your behalf. Instead rC15 will apply in those circumstances.

gC131

Notwithstanding Rule C86.3.c you are still likely to remain the data controller of the personal data in question. Therefore, Rule C86.3.c does not relieve you of your obligations to comply with the Data Protection Act in respect of such data.

C5.2 Administration and conduction of self-employed practice

rC88

You must take reasonable steps to ensure that:

1. your practice is efficiently and properly administered having regard to the nature of your practice; and
2. proper records of your practice are kept.

Guidance on Rule C87

gC132

Please refer to the *Bar Standards Board* website [hyperlink here] for further guidance about what constitutes proper records for the purposes of Rule C87.2.

rC88

You must:

1. ensure that adequate records supporting the fees charged or claimed in a case are kept at least until the later of the following:
   a. your fees have been paid; and
   b. any determination or assessment of costs in the case has been completed and the time for lodging an appeal against that assessment or determination has expired without any such appeal being lodged, or any such appeal has been finally determined;
2. provide your *client* with such records or details of the work you have done as may reasonably be required for the purposes of verifying your charges.

C5.3 ADMINISTRATION OF CHAMBERS

rC89

Taking into account the provisions of Rule C90, you must take reasonable steps to ensure that:

1. your *chambers* is administered competently and efficiently;
2. your *chambers* has appointed an individual or individuals to liaise with the *Bar Standards Board* in respect of any regulatory requirements and has notified the *Bar Standards Board*;
3. your *chambers* does not employ any person who has been disqualified from being employed by an authorised person or a *licensed body* by another *approved regulator* pursuant to its or their powers as such and such disqualification is continuing in force;
4. proper arrangements are made in your *chambers* for dealing with *pupils* and pupillage;
5. proper arrangements are made in *chambers* for the management of conflicts of interest and for ensuring the confidentiality of *clients*' affairs;
6. all non-authorised persons working in your *chambers* (irrespective of the identity of their *employer*):
   a. are competent to carry out their duties;
   b. carry out their duties in a correct and efficient manner;
   c. are made clearly aware of such provisions of this *Handbook* as may affect or be relevant to the performance of their duties;

d. do nothing which causes or substantially contributes to a breach of this *Handbook* by any *BSB authorised individual* ~~or *authorised (non-BSB) individual* within *Chambers*~~,

and all *complaints* against them are dealt with in accordance with the *complaints rules*;

7. all *registered European lawyers* and all *foreign lawyers* in your *chambers* comply with this *Handbook* insofar as applicable to them;

8. appropriate risk management procedures are in place and are being complied with; and

9. there are systems in place to check that:

   a. all persons practising from your *chambers* whether they are members of the *chambers* or not have insurance in place in accordance with Rules C75 to C77 above (other than any *pupil* who is covered under his *pupil supervisor's* insurance); and

   b. every *BSB authorised individual* practising from your *chambers* has a current *practising certificate* ~~and every other *authorised (non-BSB) individual* providing *reserved legal activities* is currently authorised by their *Approved Regulator*~~.

rC90

For the purposes of Rule C89 the steps which it is reasonable for you to take will depend on all the circumstances, which include, but are not limited to:

1. the arrangements in place in your *chambers* for the management of *chambers*;
2. any role which you play in those arrangements; and
3. the independence of individual members of *chambers* from one another.

Guidance on Rule C88 and C89

gC133

Your duty under Rule C89.4 to have proper arrangements in place for dealing with pupils includes ensuring:

1. that all *pupillage* vacancies are advertised in the manner prescribed by the *Pupillage* Funding and Advertising Rules (C113 to C118);
2. that arrangements are made for the funding of *pupils* by *chambers* which comply with the *Pupillage* Funding and Advertising Rules (C113 to C118);

gC134

Your duty under Rule C89.5 to have proper arrangements in place for ensuring the confidentiality of each *client's* affairs includes:

1. putting in place and enforcing adequate procedures for the purpose of protecting confidential information;
2. complying with data protection obligations imposed by law;

3. taking reasonable steps to ensure that anyone who has access to such information or data in the course of their work for you complies with these obligations; and
4. taking into account any further guidance on confidentiality which is available on the *Bar Standards Board's* website.

gC135

In order to ensure compliance with Rule C89.6.d, you may want to consider incorporating an obligation along these lines in all new employment contracts entered into after the date of this *Handbook*.

gC136

For further guidance on what may constitute appropriate risk management procedures in accordance with Rule C89.8 please refer to the further guidance published by the *Bar Standards Board*.

gC137

Rule C90.3 means that you should consider, in particular, the obligation of each individual members of *chambers* to act in the best interests of his or her own *client* (CD2) and to preserve the confidentiality of his or her own *client's* affairs (CD6), in circumstances where other members of *chambers* are free (and, indeed, may be obliged by the cab rank rule (C29) to act for *clients* with conflicting interests.

~~*C5.4 ADMINISTRATION OF BSB AUTHORISED BODIES*~~

~~Duties of the BSB authorised body, authorised (non-BSB) individuals and BSB regulated managers.~~

~~**rC91**~~

~~If you are a *BSB authorised body*, you must ensure that (or, if you are a *BSB regulated individual* working within such *BSB authorised body*, you must use reasonable endeavours (taking into account the provisions of Rule C37) to procure that the *BSB authorised body* ensures that):~~

~~1.~~ ~~the *BSB authorised body* has at all times a person appointed by it to act as its *HOLP*, who shall be a *manager*;~~

~~2.~~ ~~the *BSB authorised body* has at all times a person appointed by it to act as its *HOFA*; and~~

~~3.~~ ~~subject to rC91, the *BSB authorised body* does not appoint any individual to act as a *HOLP* or a *HOFA*, or to be a *manager* or *employee* of that *BSB authorised body*, in circumstances where that individual has been disqualified from being appointed to act as a *HOLP* or a *HOFA* or from being a *manager* or employed by an *authorised person* (as appropriate) by the *Bar Standards Board* or another *Approved Regulator* pursuant to its or their powers as such and such disqualification is continuing in force.~~

~~**rC92**~~

~~Rule C91.3 shall not apply where the *BSB authorised body* obtains the express written consent of the *Bar Standards Board* to the appointment of a person who has been disqualified before he is appointed.~~

~~rC93~~

~~If you are a *manager* or *employee*, you must not do anything to cause (or substantially to contribute to) a breach by the *BSB authorised body* or by any *BSB authorised individual* in it of their duties under this *Handbook*.~~

~~rC94~~

~~If you are a *BSB authorised body*, you must at all times have (or, if you are a *BSB regulated individual* working in such *BSB authorised body*, you must use reasonable endeavours (taking into account the provisions of Rule rC95. to procure that the *BSB authorised body* shall have) suitable arrangements to ensure that:~~

~~1.~~ ~~the *managers* and other *BSB regulated individuals* working as *employees* of the *BSB authorised body* comply with the *Bar Standards Board's* regulatory arrangements as they apply to them, as required under section 176 of the *LSA*;~~

~~2.~~ ~~all *employees*:~~

- ~~a.~~ ~~are competent to carry out their duties;~~
- ~~b.~~ ~~carry out their duties correctly and efficiently;~~
- ~~c.~~ ~~are made clearly aware of such provisions of this *Handbook* as may affect or be relevant to the performance of their duties; and~~
- ~~d.~~ ~~do nothing which causes or substantially contributes to, a breach of this *Handbook* by the *BSB authorised body* or any of the *BSB regulated individuals* employed by it;~~

~~3.~~ ~~the *BSB authorised body* is administered competently and efficiently, is properly staffed and keeps proper records of its practice;~~

~~4.~~ ~~*pupils* and *pupillages* are dealt with properly;~~

~~5.~~ ~~conflicts of interest are managed appropriately and that the confidentiality of *clients'* affairs is maintained at all times;~~

~~6.~~ ~~all *registered European lawyers* and all *foreign lawyers* employed by or working for you comply with this *Handbook* insofar as it applies to them;~~

~~7.~~ ~~every *BSB authorised individual* employed by, or working for, the BSB authorised body has a current *practising certificate* (except where a *barrister* is working as an *unregistered barrister*, in which case there must be appropriate systems to ensure that they are complying with the provisions of this *Handbook* which apply to *unregistered barristers*) and every other *authorised (non-BSB) individual* providing *reserved legal activities* is currently authorised by their *Approved Regulator*; and~~

~~8.~~ ~~adequate records supporting the fees charged or claimed in a case are kept at least until the later of the following:~~

- ~~a.~~ ~~your fees have been paid; and~~
- ~~b.~~ ~~any determination or assessment of costs in the case has been~~

completed and the time for lodging an appeal against that assessment or determination has expired without any such appeal being lodged, or any such appeal has been finally determined;

9. your *client* is provided with such records or details of the work you have done as may reasonably be required for the purpose of verifying your charges;

10. appropriate procedures are in place requiring all *managers* and *employees* to work with the *HOLP* with a view to ensuring that the *HOLP* is able to comply with his obligations under Rule C96;

11. appropriate risk management procedures are in place and are being complied with; and

12. appropriate financial management procedures are in place and are being complied with.

rC95

For the purposes of Rule C91 and C94 the steps which it is reasonable for you to take will depend on all the circumstances, which include, but are not limited to:

1. the arrangements in place in your *BSB authorised body* for the management of it; and

2. any role which you play in those arrangements.

Guidance to Rules C91 to C94

gC138

Section 90 of the *LSA* places obligations on *non-authorised individuals* who are *employees* and *managers* of *licensed bodies*, as well as on *non-authorised individuals* who hold an ownership interest in such a *licensed body* (whether by means of a shareholding or voting powers in respect of the same) to do nothing which causes, or substantially contributes to a breach by the *licensed body* or by its *employees* or *managers,* of this *Handbook*. Rule C91 extends this obligation to *BSB legal services bodies.*

gC139

Your duty under Rule C94.4 to have proper arrangements for dealing with pupils includes ensuring:

1. that all pupillage vacancies are advertised in the manner prescribed by the Pupillage Funding and Advertising Rules (C113 to C118);

2. that arrangements are made for the funding of *pupils* by *chambers* which comply with the Pupillage Funding and Advertising Rules (C113 to C118).

Duties of the HOLP/HOFA

rC96

If you are a *HOLP*, in addition to complying with the more general duties placed on the *BSB authorised body* and on the *BSB regulated individuals* employed by it, you must:

1. take all reasonable steps to ensure compliance with the terms of your *BSB authorised body's* authorisation;
2. take all reasonable steps to ensure that the *BSB authorised body* and its *employees* and *managers* comply with the duties imposed by section 176 of the *LSA*;
3. take all reasonable steps to ensure that *non-authorised individuals* subject to the duty imposed by section 90 of the *LSA* comply with that duty;
4. keep a record of all incidents of non-compliance with the Core Duties and this *Handbook* of which you become aware and to report such incidents to the Bar Standards Board as soon as reasonably practicable (where such failures are material in nature) or otherwise on request by the *Bar Standards Board* or during the next monitoring visit or review by the *Bar Standards Board*.

rC97

If you are a *HOFA*, in addition to complying with the more general duties placed on the *BSB authorised body* and its *BSB regulated individuals*, you must ensure compliance with Rules C73 and C74.

New managers/HOLP/HOFA

rC98

A BSB *authorised body* must not take on a new *manager*, *HOLP* or *HOFA* without first submitting an application to the *Bar Standards Board* for approval in accordance with the requirements of Section S.D.

D. RULES APPLYING TO SPECIFIC GROUPS OF REGULATED PERSONS

D1. Self-employed Barristers, Chambers and BSB Authorised Bodies

[1.18]

Outcomes

oC26

Clients know that they can make a *complaint* if dissatisfied, and know how to do so.

oC27

Complaints are dealt with promptly and the *client* is kept informed about the process.

oC28

Self-employed barristers, *chambers* and *BSB authorised bodies* run their practices without *discrimination*.

oC29

Pupils are treated fairly and all vacancies for *pupillages* are advertised openly.

Rules

D1.1 COMPLAINTS RULES

Provision of information to clients

rC99

You must notify *clients* in writing when you are *instructed*, or, if that is if not practicable, at the next appropriate opportunity:

1. of their right to make a *complaint*, including their right to complain to the *Legal Ombudsman* (if they have such a right), how, and to whom, they can complain, and of any time limits for making a *complaint*;
2. if you are doing referral work, that the lay *client* may complain directly to *chambers* ~~or the *BSB authorised body*~~ without going through *solicitors*.

rC100

If you are doing public access, or *licensed access* work using an *intermediary*, the *intermediary* must similarly be informed.

rC101

If you are doing referral work, you do not need to give a *professional client* the information set out in Rules C99.1 and C99.2, in a separate, specific letter. It is enough to provide it in the ordinary terms of reference letter (or equivalent letter) which you send when you accept *instructions* in accordance with Rule C21.

rC102

If you do not send a letter of engagement to a lay *client* in which this information can be included, a specific letter must be sent to him giving him the information set out at Rules C99.1 and C99.2.

rc103

Chambers' websites and literature must display information about the *chambers'* complaints procedure. A *BSB's authorised body's* website and literature must carry information about that *BSB authorised body's* Complaints Procedure.

Response to complaints

Rc104

All *complaints* must be acknowledged promptly. When you acknowledge a *complaint*, you must give the complainant:

1. the name of the person who will deal with the *complaint* and a description of that person's role in *chambers* ~~or in the *BSB authorised body* (as appropriate)~~;
2. a copy of the *chambers*' complaints procedure ~~or the *BSB authorised body's* Complaints Procedure (as appropriate)~~;
3. the date by which the complainant will next hear from *chambers* ~~or the *BSB authorised body* (as appropriate)~~.

rC105

When *chambers* has dealt with the *complaint*, complainants must be told in writing of their right to complain to the *Legal Ombudsman* (where applicable), of the time limit for doing so, and how to contact him.

Documents and Record Keeping

rC106

All communications and documents relating to *complaints* must be kept confidential. They must be disclosed only so far as is necessary for:

1. the investigation and resolution of the *complaint*;
2. internal review in order to of improve *chambers*' handling of complaints;
3. complying with requests from the *Bar Standards Board* in the exercise of its monitoring and/or auditing functions.

rC107

The disclosure to the *Bar Standards Board* of internal documents relating to the handling of the *complaint* (such as the minutes of any meeting held to discuss a particular *complaint*) for the further resolution or investigation of the *complaint* is not required.

rC108

A record must be kept of each *complaint*, of all steps taken in response to it, and of the outcome of the *complaint*. Copies of all correspondence, including electronic mail, and all other documents generated in response to the *complaint* must also be kept. The records and copies should be kept for 6 years from resolution of the *complaint*.

rC109

The person responsible for the administration of the procedure must report at least annually to ~~either~~:

~~1.~~ ~~the *HOLP*; or~~

2. the appropriate member/committee of *chambers*,

on the number of *complaints* received, on the subject areas of the *complaints* and on the outcomes. The *complaints* should be reviewed for trends and possible *training* issues.

D1.2 EQUALITY AND DIVERSITY

rC110

You must take reasonable steps to ensure that in relation to your *chambers ~~or BSB authorised body~~*:

1. there is in force a written statement of policy on equality and diversity; and
2. there is in force a written plan implementing that policy;
3. the following requirements are complied with:

   Equality and Diversity Officer

   a. chambers ~~or BSB authorised body~~ has at least one Equality and Diversity Officer;

   Training

   b. except in unforeseen and exceptional circumstances, the person with lead responsibility for any *selection panel* and at least one member of any *selection panel* (who may be the same person) has received recent and appropriate *training* in fair recruitment and selection processes;

   c. save in exceptional circumstances, every member of all *selection panels* has been trained in fair recruitment and selection processes;

   Fair and Objective Criteria

   d. recruitment and selection processes use objective and fair criteria;

   Equality monitoring

   e. your chambers ~~or BSB authorised body:~~

      i. conducts a *regular review* of its policy on equality and diversity and of its implementation in order to ensure that it complies with the requirements of this Rule rC110; and

      ii. takes any appropriate *remedial action* identified in the light of that review;

   f. subject to Rule rC110.3.h *chambers ~~or BSB authorised body~~* regularly reviews:

      i. the number and percentages of its *workforce* from different groups; and

      ii. applications to become a member of its *workforce*; and

      iii. in the case of *chambers*, the *allocation of unassigned work*,

   g. the reviews referred to in Rule C110.3.f above include:

      i. collecting and analysing data broken down by race, disability and gender;

      ii. *investigating* the reasons for any disparities in that data; and

      iii. taking appropriate *remedial action*;

   h. the requirement to collect the information referred to in Rule C110.3.f does not apply to the extent that the people referred to in Rule C110.3.f.i and Rule C110.3.f.ii refuse to disclose it.

Fair access to work

i. if you are a *self-employed barrister*, the affairs of your *chambers* are conducted in a manner which is fair and equitable for all members of *chambers*, *pupils* and/or *employees* (as appropriate). This includes, but is not limited to, the fair distribution of work opportunities among *pupils* and members of *chambers*;

Harassment

j. *chambers* ~~or *BSB authorised body*~~ has a written anti-*harassment* policy which, as a minimum:

   i. states that *harassment* will not be tolerated or condoned and that ~~*managers*,~~ *employees*, members of *chambers*, *pupils* and others temporarily in your *chambers* ~~*or BSB authorised body*~~ such as mini-pupils have a right to complain if it occurs;

   ii. sets out how the policy will be communicated;

   iii. sets out the procedure for dealing with *complaints* of *harassment*;

Parental leave

k. *chambers*–has a *parental leave* policy which, in the case of a *chambers*, must cover as a minimum:

   i. the right of a member of *chambers* to return to *chambers* after a specified period (which must be at least one year) of parental or adoption leave;

   ii. the extent to which a member of *chambers* is or is not required to contribute to *chambers*' rent and expenses during *parental leave*;

   iii. the method of calculation of any waiver, reduction or reimbursement of *chambers*' rent and expenses during *parental leave*;

   iv. where any element of rent is paid on a flat rate basis, the *chambers* policy must as a minimum provide that *chambers* will offer members taking a period of *parental leave*, or leave following adoption, a minimum of 6 months free of *chambers*' rent;

   v. the procedure for dealing with grievances under the policy;

   vi. *chambers*' commitment to regularly review the effectiveness of the policy;

Flexible Working

l. *chambers* ~~or *BSB authorised body*~~ has a flexible working policy which covers the right of a member of *chambers*~~, *manager*~~ or *employee* (as the case may be) to take a career break, to work part-time, to work flexible hours, or to work from home, so as to enable him to manage his *family responsibilities* or disability without giving up work;

Reasonable Adjustments Policy

m. *chambers ~~or BSB authorised body~~* has a reasonable adjustments policy aimed at supporting disabled *clients*, its *workforce* and others including temporary visitors;

Appointment of Diversity Data Officer

n. *chambers ~~or BSB authorised body~~* has a Diversity Data Officer;

o. *chambers ~~or BSB authorised body~~* must provide the name and contact details of the Diversity Data Officer to the *Bar Standards Board* and must notify the *Bar Standards Board* of any change to the identity of the Diversity Data Officer, as soon as reasonably practicable;

Responsibilities of Diversity Data Officer

p. The Diversity Data Officer shall comply with the requirements in relation to the collection, processing and publication of *diversity data* set out in the paragraphs rC110.3.q to .t below;

Collection and Publication of Diversity Data

q. The Diversity Data Officer shall invite the members of the *workforce* to provide *diversity data* in respect of themselves to the Diversity Data Officer using the model questionnaire at Annex C of the BSB Guidance on these Rules;

r. The Diversity Data Officer shall ensure that such data is anonymised and that an accurate and updated summary of it is published on *chambers' ~~or BSB authorised body's~~* website every three years. If *chambers ~~or the BSB authorised body~~* does not have a website, the Diversity Data Officer shall make such data available to the public on request;

s. The published summary of anonymised data shall:

   i. exclude *diversity data* relating to the characteristics of sexual orientation and religion or belief, unless there is consent from each of the members of the *workforce;* and

   ii. exclude diversity data in relation to any characteristic where there is a real risk that individuals could be identified, unless all affected individuals consent; and

   iii. subject to the foregoing, include anonymised data in relation to each characteristic, categorised by reference to the job title and seniority of the *workforce.*

the Diversity Data Officer shall:

   i. ensure that *chambers ~~or BSB authorised body~~* has in place a written policy statement on the collection, publication, retention and destruction of *diversity data* which shall include an explanation that the provision of *diversity data* is voluntary;

   ii. notify the *workforce* of the contents of the written policy statement; and

   iii. ask for explicit consent from the *workforce* to the provision and processing of their *diversity data* in accordance with the written policy statement and these rules, in advance of collecting their *diversity data.*

rC111

For the purposes of Rule C110 above, the steps which it is reasonable for you to take will depend on all the circumstances, which include, but are not limited to:

1. the arrangements in place in your chambers ~~or BSB authorised body~~ for the management of chambers ~~or the BSB authorised body~~; and
2. any role which you play in those arrangements.

rC112

For the purposes Rule C110 above "allocation of unassigned work" includes, but is not limited to work allocated to:

1. *pupils*;
2. *barristers* of fewer than four years' *standing*; and
3. barristers returning from parental leave;

Guidance to Rule C110 and Rule C111

gC140

Rule C110 places a personal obligation on all *self-employed barristers*, however they practise, ~~and on the *managers* of BSB authorised bodies, as well as on the entity itself,~~ to take reasonable steps to ensure that they have appropriate policies which are enforced.

gC141

In relation to Rule C110, if you are a Head of *chambers* ~~or a *HOLP*~~ it is likely to be reasonable for you to ensure that you have the policies required by Rule C110, that an *Equality and Diversity Officer* is appointed to monitor compliance, and that any breaches are appropriately punished. If you are a member of a *chambers* you are expected to use the means available to you under your constitution to take reasonable steps to ensure there are policies and that they are enforced. ~~If you are a *manager of a BSB authorised body*, you are expected to take reasonable steps to ensure that there are policies and that they are enforced.~~

gC142

For the purpose of Rule C110 training means any course of study covering all the following areas:

a. Fair and effective selection & avoiding unconscious methods of discrimination.

b. Attraction and advertising.

c. Application processes.

d. Shortlisting skills.

e. Interviewing skills.

f. Assessment and making a selection decision.

g. Monitoring and evaluation.

gC143

Training may be undertaken in any of the following ways:

a. Classroom sessions.

b. Online sessions.

c. Private study of relevant materials and guidance.

d. Completion of CPD covering fair recruitment and selection processes.

gC144

The purpose of Rule C110.3.d is to ensure that *applicants* with relevant characteristics are not refused *employment* because of such characteristics. In order to ensure compliance with this rule, therefore, it is anticipated that the *Equality and Diversity Officer* will compile and retain data about the relevant characteristics of all *applicants* for the purposes of reviewing the data in order to see whether there are any apparent disparities in recruitment.

gC145

For the purpose of Rule C110 "regular review", means as often as is necessary in order to ensure effective monitoring and review takes place. In respect of data on pupils it is likely to be considered reasonable that "regularly" should mean annually. In respect of ~~managers of a *BSB authorised body*~~ or tenants, it is likely to be considered reasonable that "regularly" should mean every three years unless the numbers change to such a degree as to make more frequent monitoring appropriate.

gC146

For the purposes of Rule C110, "remedial action" means any action aimed at removing or reducing the disadvantage experienced by particular relevant groups. Remedial action cannot, however, include positive discrimination in favour of members of relevant groups.

gC147

Rule C110.3.f.iii places an obligation on *practices* to take reasonable steps to ensure the work opportunities are shared fairly among its *workforce*. In the case of *chambers*, this obligation includes work which has not been allocated by the solicitor to a named *barrister*. It includes fairness in presenting to solicitors names for consideration and fairness in opportunities to attract future named work (for example, fairness in arrangements for marketing). These obligations apply even if individual members of *chambers* ~~incorporate their practices, or~~ use a "ProcureCo" to obtain or distribute work, as long as their relationship between each other remains one of independent service providers competing for the same work while sharing clerking arrangements and costs.

gC148

Rule C110.3.k.iv sets out the minimum requirements which must be included in a parental and adoption leave policy if any element of rent is paid on a flat rate. If rent is paid on any other basis, then the policy should be drafted so as not to put any *self-employed barrister* in a worse position than he would have been in if any element of the rent were paid on a flat rate.

gC149

For the purposes of Rule C110 above investigation means, considering the reasons for disparities in data such as:

1. Under or overrepresentation of particular groups e.g. men, women, different ethnic groups or disabled people;
2. Absence of particular groups e.g. men, women, different ethnic groups or disabled people;
3. Success rates of particular groups;
4. In the case of *chambers,* over or under allocation of unassigned work to particular groups.

gC150

These rules are supplemented by the equality and diversity good practice guidelines ("*The Guidelines*"). These describe the legal and regulatory requirements relating to equality and diversity and provide guidance on how they should be applied in *chambers* ~~and in *BSB authorised bodies*~~. If you are a *self-employed barrister*~~, a *BSB authorised body*, or a *manager of a BSB authorised body*~~, you should seek to comply with *the Guidelines* as well as with the rules as set out above.

gC151

The Guidelines are also relevant to all *pupil supervisors* and *authorised training organisations*. These will be expected to show how they comply with *the Guidelines* as a condition of authorisation.

gC152

Although *the Guidelines* do not apply directly to *BSB authorised persons* working as *employed barristers* (non-authorised bodies) or *employed barristers (authorised non-BSB body)*, they provide helpful guidance which you are encouraged to take into account in your practice.

D1.3 PUPILLAGE FUNDING

Funding

rC113

The members of a set of *chambers* ~~or *the BSB authorised body*~~ must pay to each non-practising *pupil* (as appropriate), by the end of each month of the non-practising six months of his *pupillage* no less than:

1. the *specified amount*; and
2. such further sum as may be necessary to reimburse expenses reasonably incurred by the *pupil* on:

3. travel for the purposes of his *pupillage* during that month; and
4. attendance during that month at courses which he is required to attend as part of his *pupillage*.

rC114

The members of a set of *chambers*~~, or the *BSB authorised body*,~~ must pay to each practising *pupil* by the end of each month of the practising six months of his *pupillage* no less than:

1. the *specified amount*; plus
2. such further sum as may be necessary to reimburse expenses reasonably incurred by the *pupil* on:
   a. travel for the purposes of his *pupillage* during that month; and
   b. attendance during that month at courses which he is required to attend as part of his *pupillage*; less
   c. such amount, if any, as the *pupil* may receive during that month from his *practice* as a *barrister*; and less
   d. such amounts, if any, as the *pupil* may have received during the preceding months of his practising *pupillage* from his *practice* as a *barrister*, save to the extent that the amount paid to the *pupil* in respect of any such month was less than the total of the sums provided for in sub-paragraphs rC114.2.a and .b above.

rC115

The members of a set of *chambers*~~, or the *BSB authorised body*,~~ may not seek or accept repayment from a *chambers pupil* ~~or an *entity pupil*~~ of any of the sums required to be paid under Rules C113 and C114 above, whether before or after he ceases to be a *chambers pupil* ~~or an *entity pupil*~~, save in the case of misconduct on his part.

rC116

If you are a *self-employed barrister*, you must pay any *chambers pupil* for any work done for you which because of its value to you warrants payment, unless the *pupil* is receiving an award or remuneration which is paid on terms that it is in lieu of payment for any individual item of work.

Application

rC117

The requirements set out in Rules C113 to C116 above:

1. do not apply in the case of *pupils* who were granted exemption from the *vocational stage* of *training* under Rule Q73;
2. do not apply in the case of *pupils* who are doing a period of *pupillage* in a set of *chambers*~~, or in a *BSB authorised body*,~~ as part of a *training* programme offered by another organisation which is authorised by the *Bar Standards Board* to take *pupils*;

3. do not apply in the case of *pupils* who have completed both the non-practising and the practising six months of *pupillage*;
4. save as provided in Rule C117.3 above, do not apply in respect of any period after a *pupil* ceases, for whatever reason, to be a *chambers pupil* ~~or an entity *pupil*~~; and
5. may be waived in part or in whole by the *Pupillage* Funding Committee of the BSB.

rC118

For the purposes of these requirements:

1. "*chambers pupil*" means, in respect of any set of *chambers*, a *pupil* doing the non-practising or practising six months of *pupillage* with a *pupil supervisor*, or *pupil supervisors*, who is or are a member, or members, of that set of *chambers*;
2. ~~"entity *pupil*" means, in respect of a *BSB authorised body*, a *pupil* doing the non-practising or practising six months of *pupillage* with a *pupil*-master or *pupil*-masters who are *managers* or *employees* of such *BSB authorised body*;~~
3. "non-practising *pupil*" means a *chambers pupil* ~~or an entity *pupil*~~ doing the non-practising six months of *pupillage*;
4. "practising *pupil*" means a *chambers pupil* ~~or an entity *pupil*~~ doing the practising six months of *pupillage*;
5. "month" means calendar month starting on the same day of the month as that on which the *pupil* began the non-practising, or practising, six months *pupillage*, as the case may be;
6. any payment made to a *pupil* by a *barrister* pursuant to Rule rC5 above shall constitute an amount received by the *pupil* from his *practice* as a *barrister*; and
7. the following travel by a *pupil* shall not constitute travel for the purposes of his *pupillage*:
   a. travel between his home and *chambers* ~~or, for an entity *pupil*, his place of work~~; and
   b. travel for the purposes of his *practice* as a *barrister*.

D2 Barristers undertaking Public Access and Licensed Access Work

[1.19]

Outcomes

oC30

Barristers undertaking public access or licensed access work have the necessary skills and experience required to do work on that basis.

oC31

Barristers undertaking public access or licensed access work maintain appropriate records in respect of such work.

oC32

Clients only instruct via public access when it is in their interests to do so and they fully understand what is expected of them.

Rules

D2.1 PUBLIC ACCESS RULES

rC119

These rules apply to *barristers* instructed by or on behalf of a lay *client* (other than a *licensed access client*) who has not also instructed a *solicitor* or other *professional client* (public access clients). Guidance on public access rules is available on the *Bar Standards Board website.*

rC120

Before accepting any *public access instructions* from or on behalf of a *public access client*, a *barrister* must:

1. be properly qualified by having been issued with a full *practising certificate*, by having satisfactorily completed the appropriate public access training, and by registering with the *Bar Council* as a public access practitioner;
2. if a barrister was already registered with the *Bar Council* to undertake public access work on [insert date] then he must undertake any additional training required by the *Bar Standards Board* within 24 months of that date or cease to undertake public access work;
3. take such steps as are reasonably necessary to ascertain whether it would be in the best interests of the *client* or in the interests of justice for *the* public access client to instruct a *solicitor* or other *professional client*; and
4. take such steps as are reasonably necessary to ensure that the *client* is able to make an informed decision about whether to apply for legal aid or whether to proceed with public access.

rC121

A barrister with less than three *years' standing* who has completed the necessary training must:

1. Have a *barrister* who is a qualified person within Rule S17.ii and has registered with the *Bar Council* as a public access practitioner readily available to provide guidance to the barrister;
2. Maintain a log of public access cases they have dealt with, including any issues or problems which have arisen;
3. Seek appropriate feedback from their public access *clients* on the service provided;
4. Make this log available, on request, to the *Bar Standards Board* for review.

rC122

A *barrister* may not accept direct *instructions* from or on behalf of a public access *client* in or in connection with any matter of proceedings in which, in all the circumstances, it would be in the best interests of the public access *client* or in the interests of justice for the public access *client* to instruct a *solicitor* or other *professional client.*

rC123

In any case where a *barrister* is not prohibited from accepting *instructions*, the *barrister* must at all times consider the developing circumstances of the case, and whether at any stage it is in the best interests of the public access *client* or in the interests of justice for the public access *client* to instruct a *solicitor* or other *professional client.* If, after accepting direct *instructions* from a public access *client* a *barrister* forms the view that circumstances are such that it would be in the best interests of the public access *client*, or in the interests of justice for the public access *client* to instruct a *solicitor* or other *professional client* the *barrister* must:

1. inform the public access *client* of his view; and
2. withdraw from the case in accordance with the provisions of Rules C25 and C26 and associated guidance unless the *client* instructs a *solicitor* or other *professional client* to act in the case.

rC124

A *barrister* must have regard to guidance published from time to time by the *Bar Standards Board* in considering whether to accept and in carrying out any *public access instructions*.

rC125

A *barrister* who accepts *public access instructions* must forthwith notify his public access *client* in writing, and in clear and readily understandable terms, of:

1. the work which the *barrister* has agreed to perform;
2. the fact that in performing his work the *barrister* will be subject to the requirements of Parts 2 and 3 of this *Handbook* and, in particular, Rules C25 and C26.
3. unless authorised to *conduct litigation* by the *Bar Standards Board,* the fact that the *barrister* cannot be expected to perform the functions of a *solicitor* or other authorised litigator and in particular to fulfil limitation obligations, disclosure obligations and other obligations arising out of or related to the *conduct of litigation*;
4. the fact that the *barrister* is a sole practitioner, is not a *member* of a firm and does not take on any arranging role;
5. in any case where the *barrister* has been instructed by an *intermediary*:
    a. the fact that the *barrister* is independent of and has no liability for the *intermediary*; and
    b. the fact that the *intermediary* is the agent of the lay *client* and not the agent of the *barrister*;

6. the fact that the *barrister* may be prevented from completing the work by reason of his professional duties or conflicting professional obligations, and what the *client* can expect of the *barrister* in such a situation;
7. the fees which the *barrister* proposes to charge for that work, or the basis on which his fee will be calculated;
8. the *barrister's* contact arrangements; and
9. the information about the *barrister's* complaints procedure required by E1 of this Part 2.

rC126

Save in exceptional circumstances, a *barrister* will have complied with Rule C125 above if he has written promptly to the public access *client* in the terms of the model letter provided on the *Bar Standards Board* website.

rC127

In any case where a *barrister* has been instructed by an *intermediary*, he must give the notice required by Rule C123 above both:

1. directly to the public access *client*; and
2. to the *intermediary*.

rC128

A *barrister* who accepts *public access instructions* must keep a case record which sets out:

1. the date of receipt of the *instructions*, the name of the lay *client*, the name of the case, and any requirements of the *client* as to time limits;
2. the date on which the *instructions* were accepted;
3. the dates of subsequent *instructions*, of the despatch of advices and other written work, of conferences and of telephone conversations;
4. when agreed, the fee.

rC129

A *barrister* who accepts *public access instructions* must either himself retain or take reasonable steps to ensure that the lay *client* will retain for at least seven years after the date of the last item of work done:

1. copies of all *instructions* (including supplemental *instructions*);
2. copies of all advices given and documents drafted or approved;
3. the originals, copies or a list of all documents enclosed with any *instructions*;
4. notes of all conferences and of all advice given on the telephone.

rc130

A *barrister* who has accepted *public access instructions* may undertake correspondence where it is ancillary to permitted work, and in accordance with the guidance published by the *Bar Standards Board.*

Rc131

Save where otherwise agreed:

1. a *barrister* shall be entitled to copy all documents received from his lay *client*, and to retain such copies permanently;
2. a *barrister* shall return all documents received from his lay *client* on demand, whether or not the *barrister* has been paid for any work done for the lay *client*;
3. a *barrister* shall not be required to deliver to his lay *client* any documents drafted by the *barrister* in advance of receiving payment from the lay *client* for all work done for that *client*;
4. a *barrister* who has accepted *public access instructions* in any civil matter may take a proof of evidence from his *client* in that matter.

D2.2 LICENSED ACCESS RULES

rC132

Subject to these rules and to compliance with the Code of Conduct (and to the *Scope of Practice, Authorisation and Licensing Rules*) a *barrister* in self-employed *practice* may accept *instructions* from a *licensed access client* in circumstances authorised in relation to that *client* by the Licensed Access Recognition Regulations whether that *client* is acting for himself or another.

rC133

These rules apply to every matter in which a *barrister* in self-employed *practice* is instructed by a *licensed access client* save that Rules C134.2, C136, C137 and C139 do not apply to any matter in which a *licensed access client* is deemed to be a *licensed access client* by reason only of paragraph 7 or paragraph 8 of the Licensed Access Recognition Regulations.

rC134

A barrister is only entitled to accept instructions from a licensed access client if at the time of giving instructions the licensed access client:

1. is identified; and
2. sends the *barrister* a copy of the Licence issued by the *Bar Standards Board.*

rC135

A barrister must not accept any instructions from a licensed access client:

1. unless the *barrister* and his *chambers* are able to provide the services required of them by that *licensed access client*;

2. if the *barrister* considers it in the interests of the lay *client* or the interests of justice that a *solicitor* or other authorised litigator or some other appropriate *intermediary* (as the case may be) be instructed either together with or in place of the *barrister.*

rC136

A *barrister* who accepts instructions from a *licensed access client* otherwise than on the terms of the *Licensed Access Terms of Work*:

1. must first agree in writing the terms upon which he has agreed to do the work and the basis upon which he is to be paid;
2. must keep a copy of the agreement in writing with the *licensed access client* setting out the terms upon which he has agreed to do the work and the basis upon which he is to be paid.

rC137

A *barrister* who accepts *instructions* from a *licensed access client*:

1. must promptly send the *licensed access client*:
2. a statement in writing that the *instructions* have been accepted (as the case may be) (1) on the standard terms previously agreed in writing with that *licensed access client* or (2) on the terms of the *Licensed Access Terms of Work* (and thereafter if requested a copy of the *Licensed Access Terms of Work*); or
3. if he has accepted *instructions* otherwise than on such standard terms or on the terms of the *Licensed Access Terms of Work*, a copy of the agreement in writing with the *licensed access client* setting out the terms upon which he has agreed to do the work and the basis upon which he is to be paid;
4. unless he has accepted *instructions* on the terms of the *Licensed Access Terms of Work* or on terms which incorporate the following particulars must at the same time advise the *licensed access client* in writing of:
   a. the effect of rC21 as it relevantly applies in the circumstances;
   b. unless authorised by the *Bar Standards Board* to *conduct litigation*, the fact that the *barrister* cannot be expected to perform the functions of a *solicitor* or other authorised litigator and in particular to fulfil limitation obligations disclosure obligations and other obligations arising out of or related to the *conduct of litigation*;
   c. the fact that circumstances may require the *client* to retain a *solicitor* or other authorised litigator at short notice and possibly during the case.

rC138

If at any stage a *barrister* who is instructed by a *licensed access client* considers it in the interests of the lay *client* or the interests of justice that a *solicitor* or other authorised litigator or some other appropriate *intermediary* (as the case may be) be instructed either together with or in place of the *barrister*.

1. the *barrister* must forthwith advise the *licensed access client* in writing to instruct a *solicitor* or other authorised litigator or other appropriate *intermediary* (as the case may be); and
2. unless a *solicitor* or other authorised litigator or other appropriate *intermediary* (as the case may be) is instructed as soon as reasonably practicable thereafter the *barrister* must cease to act and must return any *instructions*.

rC139

If at any stage a *barrister* who is instructed by a *licensed access client* considers that there are substantial grounds for believing that the *licensed access client* has in some significant respect failed to comply either with the terms of the Licence granted by the *Bar Standards Board* or (where applicable) with the terms of the *Licensed Access Terms of Work* the *barrister* must forthwith report the facts to the *Bar Standards Board*.

rC140

A *barrister* who accepts *instructions* from a *licensed access client* must keep a case record (whether on card or computer) which sets out:

1. the date of receipt of the *instructions*, the name of the *licensed access client*, the name of the case, and any requirements of the *licensed access client* as to time limits;
2. the date on which the *instructions* were accepted;
3. the dates of subsequent *instructions*, of the despatch of advices and other written work, of conferences and of telephone conversations;
4. when agreed, the fee.

rC141

A *barrister* who accepts *instructions* from a *licensed access client* must either himself retain or take reasonable steps to ensure that the *licensed access client* will retain for six years after the date of the last item of work done:

1. copies of *instructions* (including supplemental *instructions*);
2. copies of all advices given and documents drafted or approved;
3. a list of all documents enclosed with any *instructions*;
4. notes of all conferences and of all advice given on the telephone.

D3 Registered European Lawyers

[1.20]

Outcomes

oC33

Clients are not confused about the qualifications and status of *registered European lawyers*.

Rules

rC142

If you are a *registered European lawyer* and not a *barrister*, you must not hold yourself out to be a *barrister.*

rC143

You must in connection with all professional work undertaken in England and Wales as a *registered European lawyer*:

1. use your *home professional title*;
2. indicate the name of your *home professional body* or the *court* before which you are entitled to practise in that *Member State*; and
3. indicate that you are registered with the *Bar Standards Board* as a *European lawyer.*

D4 Unregistered Barristers

[1.21]

Outcomes

oC34

Clients who receive *legal services* from *unregistered barristers* are aware that such *unregistered barristers* are not subject to the same regulatory safeguards that would apply if they instructed a *practising barrister.*

Rules

rC144

If you are an *unregistered barrister* and you supply *legal services* (other than as provided for in Rule C145) to any inexperienced *client* then, before supplying such services:

1. you must explain to the *client* that:
    a. (unless you are supplying *legal services* pursuant to Rule S12) you are not acting as a *barrister*;
    b. you are not subject to those parts of the Code of Conduct and other provisions of this *Handbook* which apply only to *BSB authorised persons*;
    c. the *Bar Standards Board* will only consider *complaints* about you which concern the Core Duties or those parts of the Code of Conduct and other provisions of this *Handbook* which apply to you;
    d. (unless you are covered by professional indemnity insurance) you are not covered by professional indemnity insurance;
    e. they have the right to make a *complaint*, how they can complain, to

whom, of any time limits for making a *complaint* but that they have no right to complain to the *Legal Ombudsman* about the services you supply;

2. you must get written confirmation from the *client* that you have given this explanation.

For the purposes of this Rule C144, an inexperienced *client* includes any individual or other person who would, if you were a *BSB authorised person*, have a right to bring a *complaint* pursuant to the Legal Ombudsman Scheme Rules.

Guidance on Rule C144

gC153

For the purposes of determining whether Rule C144 applies, the people who would be entitled to complain to the *Legal Ombudsman* if you were a *BSB authorised person* are:

1. an individual; or
2. a business or enterprise that was a micro-enterprise within the meaning of Article 1 and Article 2(1) and (3) of the Annex to Commission Recommendation 2003/361/EC (broadly a business or enterprise with fewer than 10 employees and turnover or assets not exceeding €2 million), when it referred the *complaint* to you; or
3. a charity with an annual income net of tax of less than £1 million at the time at which the complainant refers the *complaint* to you; or
4. a club, association or organisation, the affairs of which are managed by its members or a committee of its members, with an annual income net of tax of less than £1 million at the time at which the complainant refers the *complaint* to you; or
5. a trustee of a trust with an asset value of less than £1 million at the time at which the complainant refers the *complaint* to you; or
6. a personal representative or beneficiary of the estate of a person who, before he or she died, had not referred the complaint to the *Legal Ombudsman*.

rC145

rC144 does not apply to you if you supply *legal services*:

1. as an employee or manager of an authorised body;
2. as an *employee* or *manager* of a body subject to regulation by a professional body or regulator;
3. as provided for in Section S.B9 (*Legal Advice Centres*);
4. pursuant to an authorisation that you have obtained from another *approved regulator*; or
5. in accordance with Rules S13 and S14.

Guidance on Rule C145

gC154

Guidance on the disclosures which unregistered barristers should consider making to *clients* covered by Rule C145, and other *clients* who are not inexperienced *clients*, to ensure that they comply with Rule C19 and do not mislead those *clients* is available on BSB website.

D5 Cross-Border Activities within the European Union and the European Economic Area

[1.22]

Outcomes

oC35

BSB regulated persons who undertake cross-border activities comply with the terms of the Code of Conduct for European Lawyers.

Rules

rC146

If you are a *BSB regulated person* undertaking *cross-border activities* then, in addition to complying with the other provisions of this *Handbook* which apply to you, you must also comply with Rules C147 to C158 below.

Guidance on Rule C146

gC155

Where the *cross-border activities* constitute *foreign work* (in other words, limb (a) of the definition of *cross-border activities*), you should note, in particular, Rules C13 and C14 and the associated guidance.

gC156

The purpose of this section D5 is to implement those provisions of the *Code of Conduct for European Lawyers* which are not otherwise covered by the *Handbook*. If a provision of the *Code of Conduct for European Lawyers* has not been included here then the equivalent provisions of *Handbook* need to be complied with in respect of all *cross-border activities* (including where they place a higher burden on the *BSB regulated person* than the *Code of Conduct for European Lawyers* itself which is the case, for example, in respect of the handling of *client* money (Rule C73 and C74)).

Incompatible Occupations

rC147

If you act in legal proceedings or proceedings before public authorities in a *CCBE State* other than the *UK*, you must, in that *CCBE State*, observe the rules regarding incompatible occupations as they are applied to lawyers of that *CCBE State*.

rC148

If you are established in a *CCBE State* other than the *UK* and you wish to participate directly in commercial or other activities not connected with the practice of the law in that *CCBE State*, you must respect the rules regarding forbidden or incompatible occupations as they are applied to lawyers of that *CCBE State*.

Fee Sharing with Non-Lawyers

rC149

You must not share your fees with a person situated in a *CCBE State* other than the *UK* who is not a lawyer except where otherwise permitted by the terms of this *Handbook* or Rule C150 below.

rC150

Rule C149 shall not preclude you from paying a fee, commission or other compensation to a deceased lawyer's heirs or to a retired lawyer in respect of taking over the deceased or retired lawyer's practice.

Co-operation among Lawyers of Different Member States

rC151

If you are approached by a lawyer of a *CCBE State* other than the UK to undertake work which you are not competent to undertake, you must assist that lawyer to obtain the information necessary to find and instruct a lawyer capable of providing the service asked for.

rC152

When co-operating with a lawyer of a *CCBE State* other than the UK you must take into account the differences which may exist between your respective legal systems and the professional organisations, competencies and obligations of lawyers in your respective states.

Correspondence between lawyers in different CCBE States

rC153

If you want to send to a lawyer in a *CCBE State* other than the UK a communication which you wish to remain "confidential" or "without prejudice", you must, before sending the communication, clearly express your intention in order to avoid misunderstanding, and ask if the lawyer is able to accept the communication on that basis.

rC154

If you are the intended recipient of a communication from a lawyer in another *CCBE State* which is stated to be "confidential" or "without prejudice", but which you are unable to accept on the basis intended by that lawyer, you must inform that lawyer accordingly without delay.

Responsibility for Fees

rC155

If in the course of practice you instruct a lawyer of a *CCBE State* other than the UK to provide *legal services* on your behalf, you must pay the fees, costs and outlays which are properly incurred by that lawyer (even where the *client* is insolvent) unless:

1. you were simply introducing the *client* to him and the lawyer of the *CCBE State* other than the UK has since had a direct contractual relationship with the *client*; or
2. you have expressly disclaimed that responsibility at the outset, or at a later date you have expressly disclaimed responsibility for any fees incurred after that date; or
3. the lawyer of the *CCBE State* other than the UK is, in the particular matter, practising as a lawyer in England or Wales (whether authorised by the *BSB* or any other *Approved Regulator*).

Disputes Amongst Lawyers in Different Member States

rC156

If you consider that a lawyer in a *CCBE State* other than the UK has acted in breach of a rule of professional conduct you must draw the breach to the other lawyer's attention.

rC157

If any personal dispute of a professional nature arises between you and a lawyer in a *CCBE State* other than the UK you must first try to settle it in a friendly way.

rC158

You must not commence any form of proceedings against a lawyer in a *CCBE State* other than the UK on matters referred to in Rules C156 or C157 without first informing the *Bar Council* and the other lawyer's bar or law society in order to allow them an opportunity to assist in resolving the matter.

Part 3 – Scope of Practice and Authorisation ~~and Licensing~~ Rules

Contents

[1.23]

A APPLICATION

[1.24]

rS1

Section 3.B applies to all *BSB regulated persons* and "You" and "Your" should be construed accordingly. It provides that you must not carry on any *reserved legal activity* or practise as a *barrister* unless you are authorised to do so, and explains the different capacities within which you may work if you are so authorised and any limitations on the scope of your *practice*. It also explains the further requirements which you must follow if you intend to work in more than one capacity.

rS2

Section 3.C applies to *barristers* and *registered European lawyers* and sets out the basis on which they may apply for a *practising certificate* which will entitle them to practise within England and Wales.

rS3

Section 3.D applies to *European lawyers and provides details about how to apply to* become a *registered European lawyer* in England and Wales, thus entitling them to apply for a *practising certificate* in accordance with the provisions of 3.B.

~~rS4~~

~~Section 3.E applies to all entities wishing to be regulated by the BSB and sets out the basis upon which entities may be:~~

1. ~~authorised to practise as a BSB *legal* services body; or~~
2. ~~licensed to practise as a *BSB licensed body*.~~

~~rS5~~

~~Section 3.F applies to all BSB authorised bodies. It contains the continuing compliance requirements which apply to them.~~

B SCOPE OF PRACTICE RULES

B1 No practise without authorisation

[1.25]

rS6

You must not carry on any *reserved legal activity* unless you are entitled to do so under the *LSA*.

Guidance to Rule S6

gS1

You are not entitled to carry on any *reserved legal activity*, whether on your own behalf or acting as a *manager* or *employee*, unless you are either authorised or exempt in respect of that *reserved legal activity*. Where you are a *manager* or *employee* of a *person* who, as part of his *practice*, supplies services to *the public* or to a section of *the public* (with or without a view to profit), which consist of, or include, the carrying on of *reserved legal activities*, that *person* must also be entitled to carry on that *reserved legal activity* under the *LSA*. Authorisation in accordance with this Part 3 permits you to carry on the *reserved legal activities* specified in your authorisation.

rS7

You must not permit any third party who is not authorised to provide *reserved legal activities* to provide such *reserved legal activities* on your behalf.

rS8

If:

1. you are an individual and do not have a *practising certificate*; or
2. ~~you are an entity and you have not been authorised or licensed to provide *reserved legal activities* in accordance with Section 3.E,~~

   then:

   a. you may not practise as a *barrister* or a *registered European lawyer* ~~or as a *BSB authorised body*~~ (as appropriate); and

b. you are not authorised by the *Bar Standards Board* to carry on any *reserved legal activity*.

rS9

For the purposes of this *Handbook*, you practise as a *barrister* or a *registered European lawyer*, ~~or a *BSB authorised body*~~ if you are supplying *legal services* and:

1. you are an individual and you hold a *practising certificate*; or
2. you hold yourself out as a *barrister* or a *registered European lawyer* (as appropriate) or
3. ~~you are an entity and you have been authorised or licensed to provide *reserved legal activities* in accordance with Section3.E; or~~
4. you act as a *manager* of, or have an ownership interest in, an *authorised (non-BSB) body* and as such you are required by the rules of that body's *Approved Regulator* to hold a *practising certificate* issued by the *Bar Council* (as the case may be).

rS10

For the purposes of this Section 3.B1 any reference to the supply of *legal services* includes an offer to supply such services.

rS11

Rule 9.1 above does not apply to you if you are a *pupil* in the non-practising six months of *pupillage* if and insofar as you accept a noting brief with the permission of your *pupil-supervisor* or head of *chambers* ~~or *HOLP*~~.

rS12

If you are an *unregistered barrister* or *registered European lawyer* but do not hold a *practising certificate* and you supply *legal services* in the manner provided for in Rules S13, S14 and S15 below, then you shall not, by reason of supplying those services:

1. be treated for the purposes of this Section B of Part 3 as *practising barrister* or a *registered European lawyer*; or
2. be subject to the rules in Part 2 of this *Handbook* or the rules in this Section 3.B which apply to *practising barristers*.

rS13

Rule 12 applies to you if and insofar as:

1. you are practising as a *foreign lawyer*; and
2. you do not:
    a. give advice on *English Law*; or
    b. supply *legal services* in connection with any proceedings or contemplated proceedings in England and Wales (other than as an expert witness on foreign law).

rS14

Rule 12 applies to you if:

1. you are authorised and currently permitted to carry on reserved legal activities by another *Approved Regulator*; and
2. you hold yourself out as a *barrister* or a *registered European lawyer* (as appropriate~~) other than as a *manager* or *employee* of a *BSB authorised body*~~; and
3. when supplying *legal services* to any *person* or *employer* for the first time, you inform them clearly in writing at the earliest opportunity that you are not practising as a *barrister* or a *registered European lawyer.*

rS15

Rule 12 applies to you provided that:

1. you supplied *legal services* prior to 31 March 2012 pursuant to paragraph 206.1 or 206.2 of the 8th Edition of the Code; and
2. if you supply any *legal services* in England and Wales, you were called to the *Bar* before 31 July 2000; and
3. before 31 March in each year, and promptly after any change in the details previously supplied to the *Bar Council* (acting by the *Bar Standards Board*), you provide in writing to the *Bar Council* (acting by the *Bar Standards Board*), details of the current address(es) with telephone number(s) of the office or premises from which you do so, and:
   a. if you are employed, the name, address, telephone number and nature of the *practice* of your *employer*; or
   b. if you are an *employee* or *manager* of, or you have an ownership interest in, an *authorised body*, the name, address, email address, telephone number and the name of the *authorised body* and its *Approved Regulator*; and
4. unless you only offer services to your *employer* or to the *authorised body* of which you are a *manager* or an *employee* or which you have an ownership interest in, you are (or, if you are supplying *legal services* to *clients* of your *employer* or *authorised body* of which you are an *owner*, *manager* or an *employee*, your *employer* or such body is) currently insured in accordance with the requirements of Rule C76r and you comply with the requirements of Section 2.D5.

B2 Provision of reserved legal activities and of legal services

[1.26]

rS16

You may only carry on *reserved legal activities* or supply other *legal services* in the following capacities:

1. as a *self-employed barrister*, subject to the limitations imposed by Section 3.B3;
2. ~~as a *BSB authorised body*, subject to the limitations imposed by Section 3.B4;~~

~~3. as a *manager* of a *BSB authorised body* or as an *employed barrister (BSB authorised body)*, subject to the limitations imposed by Section 3.B5;~~

4. as a *manager* of an *authorised* (*non-BSB*) *body* or as an *employed barrister* (*authorised non-BSB body*), subject to the limitations imposed by Section 3.B6;
5. as an *employed barrister* (*non authorised body*), subject to the limitations imposed by Section 3.B7; or
6. as a *registered European lawyer* in any of the above capacities, in which case the equivalent limitations that would have applied if you were practising as a *barrister* shall apply to your *practice* as a *registered European lawyer.*

rS17

Where you carry on *reserved legal activities* in one of the capacities set out at Rule S16, so as to be subject to regulation by the *Bar Standards Board* in respect of those *reserved legal activities*, any other *legal services* you may supply in that same capacity will also be subject to regulation by the *Bar Standards Board*, even if unreserved.

rS18

You may only *practise* or be involved with the supply of *legal services* (whether *reserved legal activities* or otherwise) in more than one of the capacities listed in Rule 16 after:

1. having obtained an amended *practising certificate* from the *Bar Standards Board* which recognises the capacities in respect of which you are intending to practise; and
2. having agreed with each *employer* or *authorised body* with which you are involved a protocol that enables you to avoid or resolve any conflict of interests or duties arising from your *practice* and/or involvement in those capacities,

and provided always that you do not work in more than one capacity in relation to the same case or issue for the same *client,* at the same time.

rS19

If you are a *pupil* who has completed or been exempted from the non-practising six months of *pupillage*, you may only supply *legal services* to *the public* or exercise any right which you have by reason of being a *barrister,* if you have the permission of your *pupil-supervisor,* or head of *chambers* ~~or *HOLP*~~ (as appropriate).

rS20

Subject to Rule 21, if you are a *barrister* of less than three *years' standing*, you may:

1. only supply *legal services* to *the public* or exercise any *right of audience* by virtue of authorisation by the *Bar Standards Board*; or
2. only *conduct litigation* by virtue of authorisation by the *Bar Standards Board*,

   if your principal place of *practice* (or if you are *practising* in a dual capacity, each of your principal places of *practice*) is either:

a. a *chambers* or an annex of *chambers* which is also the principal place of *practice* of a relevant qualified *person* who is readily available to provide guidance to you; or

b. an office of an organisation of which an *employee, partner, manager* or *director* is a relevant qualified *person* who is readily available to provide guidance to you.

rS21

If you are an *employed barrister (non-authorised body)* and you are only providing *legal services*, exercising a *right of audience* or conducting litigation for those *persons* listed at Rule S39.2 to S39.6, then the place of *practice* from which you perform such duties is only required to be an office of an organisation of which an *employee, partner, manager* or *director* is a relevant qualified *person* who is readily available to provide guidance to you if you are of less than one year's standing.

rS22

In Rule S20 and Rule S21 above, the references to "qualified *person*" mean the following:

Supply of legal services to the public – qualified person

1. Where you are a *barrister* intending to supply *legal services* to the *public*, a *person* shall be a qualified *person* for the purpose of Rule S20 if he:

   a. has been entitled to *practise* and has *practised* as a *barrister* (other than as a *pupil* who has not completed *pupillage* in accordance with the *Bar Training Regulations*) or as a *person* authorised by another *Approved Regulator* for a period (which need not have been as a *person* authorised by the same *Approved Regulator*) for at least six years in the previous eight years; and

   b. for the previous two years has made such *practice* his primary occupation; and

   c. is not acting as a qualified *person* in relation to more than two other people; and

   d. has not been designated by the *Bar Standards Board* as unsuitable to be a qualified *person*.

The exercise of a right of audience – qualified person

2. Where:

   a. you are a *barrister* exercising a *right of audience* in England and Wales, a *person* is a qualified *person* for the purpose of Rule S20 if he:

      i. has been entitled to *practise* and has *practised* as a *barrister* (other than as a *pupil* who has not completed *pupillage* in accordance with the *Bar Training Regulations*) or as a *person* authorised by another *Approved Regulator* for a period (which need not have been as a *person* authorised by the same *Approved Regulator*) for at least six years in the previous eight years; and

ii. for the previous two years:

(1) has made such *practice* his primary occupation; and

(2) has been entitled to exercise a *right of audience* before every *court* in relation to all proceedings; and

iii. is not acting as a qualified *person* in relation to more than two other people; and

iv. has not been designated by the *Bar Standards Board* as unsuitable to be a qualified *person*; or

b. you are a *barrister* exercising a *right of audience* in a *Member State* other than the United Kingdom pursuant to the *Establishment Directive*, or in Scotland or Northern Ireland pursuant to the European Communities (Lawyer's Practice) Regulations 2000, a *person* shall be a qualified *person* for the purposes of Rule S20 if he:

i. has been designated by the *Bar Standards Board* as possessing qualifications and experience in that state or country which are equivalent to the qualifications and experience required by Rule S22.3(a)(i) and S22.3(a)(ii) above; and

ii. is not acting as a qualified *person* in relation to more than two other people; and

iii. has not been designated by the *Bar Standards Board* as unsuitable to be a qualified *person*.

The exercise of a right to conduct litigation – qualified person

3. Where:

a. you are a *barrister* exercising a *right to conduct litigation* in England and Wales, a *person* is a qualified *person* for the purpose of Rule S20 if he:

i. has been entitled to *practise* and has *practised* as a *barrister* (other than as a *pupil* who has not completed *pupillage* in accordance with the *Bar Training Regulations*) or as a *person* authorised by another *Approved Regulator* for a period (which need not have been as a *person* authorised by the same *Approved Regulator*) for at least six years in the previous eight years; and

ii. for the previous two years has made such *practice* his primary occupation; and

iii. is entitled to *conduct litigation* before every *court* in relation to all proceedings; and

iv. is not acting as a qualified *person* in relation to more than two other people; and

v. has not been designated by the *Bar Standards Board* as unsuitable to be a qualified *person*; or

b. you are a *barrister* exercising a *right to conduct litigation* in a *Member State* other than the United Kingdom pursuant to the *Establishment Directive*, or in Scotland or Northern Ireland pursuant to the European Communities (Lawyer's Practice) Regulations 2000, a *person* is a qualified *person* for the purposes of Rules S20 and S21 if he:

i. has been designated by the *Bar Standards Board* as having qualifications and experience in that state or country which are equivalent to the qualifications and experience required by Rule S22.3(a)(i) and S22.3(a)(ii) above; and

ii. is not acting as a qualified *person* in relation to more than two other people; and

iii. has not been designated by the *Bar Standards Board* as unsuitable to be a qualified *person*.

Guidance to Rules 20 and 22

gS2

If you are a *practising barrister* of less than three *years' standing* and you are authorised to *conduct litigation*, you will need to work with a qualified *person* who is authorised to do litigation as well as with someone who meets the criteria for being a qualified *person* for the purpose of providing services to *the public* and exercising *rights of audience*. This may be, but is not necessarily, the same *person*.

B3 Scope of Practice as a Self-Employed Barrister

[1.27]

rS23

Rules S24 and S25 below apply to you where you are acting in your capacity as a self-*employed barrister*, whether or not you are acting for a fee.

rS24

You may only supply *legal services* if you are appointed or instructed by the *court* or instructed:

1. by a professional *client* (who may be an *employee* of the *client*); or
2. by a *licensed access client*, in which case you must comply with the *licensed access rules*; or
3. by or on behalf of any other *client*, provided that:
    a. the matter is public access instructions and:
        i. you are entitled to provide public access work and the *instructions* are relevant to such entitlement; and
        ii. you have notified the *Bar Standards Board* that you are willing to accept *instructions* from lay *clients*; and
        iii. you comply with the *public access rules*; or
    b. the matter relates to the *conduct of litigation* and
        i. you have a litigation extension to your *practising certificate*; and
        ii. you have notified the *Bar Standards Board* that you are willing to accept *instructions* from lay *clients*.

Guidance to Rule 24

gS3

References to professional *client* in Rule S24.1 include *foreign lawyers* and references to *client* in Rule S24.3 include *foreign clients.*

gS4

If you are instructed by a *foreign lawyer* to provide advocacy services in relation to *court proceedings in England and Wales, you should advise the foreign lawyer of any limitation on the services you can provide. In particular, if conduct of litigation will be required, and you are not authorised to conduct litigation or have not been instructed to do so, you should advise the foreign lawyer to take appropriate steps to instruct a person authorised to conduct litigation and, if requested, assist the foreign lawyer to do so. If it appears to you that the foreign lawyer is not taking reasonable steps to instruct someone authorised to conduct litigation, then you should consider whether to return your instructions under rules C25 and C26.*

rS25

Subject to Rule S26, you must not in the course of your *practice* undertake the management, administration or general conduct of a *client's* affairs.

rS26

Nothing in Rule S25 prevents you from undertaking the management, administration or general conduct of a client's affairs where such work is *foreign work* performed by you at or from an office outside England and Wales which you have established or joined primarily for the purposes of carrying out that particular *foreign work* or *foreign work* in general.

~~B4 Scope of Practice as a BSB authorised body~~

[1.28]

~~**rS27**~~

~~Rules S28 and S29 apply to you where you are acting in your capacity as a *BSB authorised body.*~~

~~**rS28**~~

~~You may only supply *legal services* if you are appointed or instructed by the *court* or instructed:~~

1. ~~by a professional *client* (who may be an *employee* of the *client*);~~
2. ~~by a *licensed access client*, in which case you must comply with the *licensed access rules*; or~~
3. ~~by or on behalf of any other *client*, provided that:~~
    a. ~~at least one manager or employee is either authorised to conduct litigation or is entitled to undertake public access work; and~~

~~b. you have notified the *Bar Standards Board* that you are willing to accept *instructions* from lay *clients*.~~

~~*Guidance to Rule S28*~~

~~**gS5**~~

~~References to professional client in Rule S28.1 include foreign lawyers and references to client in Rule S28.3 include foreign clients.~~

~~**gS6**~~

~~If you are instructed to provide advocacy services in relation to *court* proceedings in England and Wales by a *foreign lawyer* or other professional *client* who does not have a *right to conduct litigation* pursuant to Rule S28.1 and you are not authorised to *conduct litigation* yourself or you are otherwise not instructed to conduct the litigation in the particular matter, then you must:~~

1. ~~advise the *foreign lawyer* to take appropriate steps to instruct a *solicitor* or other authorised litigator to conduct the litigation and, if requested, take reasonable steps to assist the *foreign lawyer* to do so;~~
2. ~~cease to act and return your *instructions* if it appears to you that the *foreign lawyer* is not taking reasonable steps to instruct a *solicitor* or other authorised litigator to conduct the litigation; and~~
3. ~~not appear in *court* unless a *solicitor* or other authorised litigator has been instructed to conduct the litigation.~~

~~**gS7**~~

~~The public access and licensed access rules do not apply to *BSB authorised bodies* as their circumstances will vary considerably. Nevertheless those rules provide guidance on best practice. If you are a *BSB authorised body*, you will also need to have regard to relevant provisions in the Code of Conduct (Part 2 of this Handbook), especially C17, C21.vii, C21.viii and C22 You will therefore need to consider whether:~~

1. ~~You have the necessary skills and experience to do the work, including, where relevant, the ability to work with a vulnerable client.~~
2. ~~The employees who will be dealing with the *client* are either authorised to *conduct litigation* or entitled to do public access work or have had other relevant training and experience.~~
3. ~~It would be in the best interests of the client or of the interests of justice for the client to instruct a solicitor or other professional client if you are not able to provide such services.~~
4. ~~If the matter involves the *conduct of litigation* and you are not able or instructed to *conduct litigation*, whether the *client* will be able to undertake the tasks that you cannot perform for him.~~
5. ~~The *client* is clear about the services which you will and will not provide and any limitations on what you can do, and what will be expected of him.~~

6. ~~If you are not able to act in legal aid cases, the *client* is in a position to take an informed decision as to whether to seek legal aid or proceed with public access.~~

~~gS8~~

~~You will also need to ensure that you keep proper records.~~

~~rS29~~

~~Subject to Rule S30, you must not in the course of your *practice* undertake the management, administration or general conduct of a *client's* affairs.~~

~~rS30~~

~~Nothing in Rule S29 prevents you from undertaking the management, administration or general conduct of a client's affairs where such work is foreign work performed by you at or from an office outside England and Wales which you have established or joined primarily for the purposes of carrying out that particular foreign work or foreign work in general.~~

~~B5 Scope of Practice as a manager of a BSB authorised body or as an employed barrister (BSB authorised body)~~

[1.29]

~~rS31~~

~~Rules S32 and S33 below apply to you where you are acting in your capacity as a *manager* of a *BSB authorised body* or as an *employed barrister (BSB authorised body)*.~~

~~rS32~~

~~You may only supply *legal services* to the following *persons*:~~

1. ~~the BSB authorised body; or~~
2. ~~any employee, director, or company secretary of the BSB authorised body, in a matter arising out of or relating to that person's employment;~~
3. ~~any client of the BSB authorised body;~~
4. ~~if you supply legal services at a Legal Advice Centre, clients of the Legal Advice Centre; or~~
5. ~~if you supply legal services free of charge, members of the public.~~

~~rS33~~

~~Subject to Rule S34, you must not in the course of your *practice* undertake the management, administration or general conduct of a *client's* affairs.~~

~~rS34~~

~~Nothing in Rule S33 prevents you from undertaking the management, administration or general conduct of a client's affairs where such work is foreign work~~

~~performed by you at or from an office outside England and Wales which you have established or joined primarily for the purposes of carrying out that particular foreign work or foreign work in general.~~

B6 Scope of Practice as a manager of an authorised (non-BSB) body or as an employed barrister (authorised non-BSB body)

[1.30]

rS35

Rules S36 and S37 apply to you where you are acting in your capacity as a *manager* of an *authorised (non-BSB) body* or as an *employed barrister (authorised non-BSB body)*

rS36

You may only supply *legal services* to the following *persons*:

1. the *authorised (non-BSB) body*;
2. any *employee*, *director* or company secretary of the *authorised (non-BSB) body* in a matter arising out of or relating to that *person's employment*;
3. any *client* of the *authorised (non-BSB) body*;
4. if you provide *legal services* at a *Legal Advice Centre*, *clients* of the *Legal Advice Centre*; or
5. if you supply *legal services* free of charge, members of the public.

rS37

You must comply with the rules of the *Approved Regulator* or *licensing authority* of the *authorised (non-BSB) body*.

B7 Scope of Practice as an employed barrister (non authorised body)

[1.31]

rS38

Rule S39 applies to you where you are acting in your capacity as an *employed barrister (non authorised body)*.

rS39

Subject to s. 15(4) of the Legal Services Act 2007, you may only supply *legal services* to the following *persons*:

1. your *employer*;
2. any *employee*, *director* or company secretary of your *employer* in a matter arising out of or relating to that *person's employment*;
3. if your *employer* is a public authority (including the Crown or a Government department or agency or a local authority), another public authority on

behalf of which your *employer* has made arrangements under statute or otherwise to supply any *legal services* or to perform any of that other public authority's functions as agent or otherwise;

4. if you are employed by or in a Government department or agency, any Minister or Officer of the Crown;
5. if you are employed by a *trade association*, any individual member of the association;
6. if you are, or are performing the functions of, a *Justices' clerk*, the Justices whom you serve;
7. if you are employed by the *Legal Aid Agency*, members of the public;
8. if you are employed by or at a *Legal Advice Centre*, *clients* of the *Legal Advice Centre*;
9. if you supply *legal services* free of charge, members of the public; or
10. if your *employer* is a *foreign lawyer* and the *legal services* consist of foreign work, any *client* of your *employer*.

B8 Scope of Practice of a Barrister called to undertake a particular case

[1.32]

rS40

If you are called to the *Bar* under rQ98 of the *Bar Training Regulations* (temporary membership of the *Bar*), you may not *practise* as a *barrister* other than to conduct the case or cases specified in the certificate referred to in rQ99.

B9 Legal Advice Centres

[1.33]

rS41

You may supply *legal services* at a *Legal Advice Centre* on a voluntary or part time basis and, if you do so, you will be treated for the purposes of this *Handbook* as if you were employed by the *Legal Advice Centre*.

rS42

If you supply *legal services* at a *Legal Advice Centre* to *clients* of a *Legal Advice Centre* in accordance with Rule 41:

1. you must not in any circumstances receive either directly or indirectly any fee or reward for the supply of any *legal services* to any *client* of the *Legal Advice Centre* other than a salary paid by the *Legal Advice Centre*;
2. you must ensure that any fees in respect of *legal services* supplied by you to any *client* of the *Legal Advice Centre* accrue and are paid to the *Legal Advice Centre*, or to the Access to Justice Foundation or other such charity as prescribed by order made by the Lord Chancellor under s.194(8) of the Legal Services Act 2007; and

3. you must not have any financial interest in the *Legal Advice Centre*.

Guidance to Rules 41 and 42

gS9

You may provide *legal services* at a *Legal Advice Centre* on an unpaid basis irrespective of the capacity in which you normally work.

gS10

If you are a *self-employed barrister*, you do not need to inform the Bar Standards Board that you are also working for a *Legal Advice Centre*.

gS11

Transitional arrangements under the *LSA* allow *Legal Advice Centres* to provide *reserved legal activities* without being authorised. When this transitional period comes to an end, the rules relating to providing services at *Legal Advice Centres* will be reviewed.

B10 Barristers Authorised by other Approved Regulators

[1.34]

rS43

If you are authorised by another *Approved Regulator* to carry on a *reserved legal activity* and currently permitted to *practise* by that *Approved Regulator*, you must not *practise* as a *barrister* and you are not eligible for a *practising certificate*.

C PRACTISING CERTIFICATE RULES

C1 Eligibility for Practising Certificates and Litigation Extensions

[1.35]

rS44

In this Section 3.C, references to "you" and "your" are references to *barristers* and *registered European lawyers* who are intending to apply for authorisation to *practise* as a *barrister* or a *registered European lawyer* (as the case may be) or who are otherwise intending to apply for a *litigation extension* to their existing *practising certificate*.

rS45

You are eligible for a *practising certificate* if:

1. you are a *barrister* or *registered European lawyer* and you are not currently *suspended* from *practice* and have not been disbarred; and
2. you meet the requirements of Rules S46.1, S46.2, S46.3 or S46.4; and

3. [either :

   ~~a. within the last 5 years either (i) you have held a *practising certificate*; or (ii) you have satisfactorily completed (or have been exempted from the requirement to complete) either the non-practising period of 6 months of pupilage or 12 months of pupilage; or~~

   ~~b. if not, you have complied with such training requirements as may be imposed by the *Bar Standards Board*.~~]

   ~~The above does not come into effect until 1 April 2015.~~

rS46

You are eligible for:

1. a full practising certificate if either:

   a. you have satisfactorily completed 12 months *pupillage*; or

   b. you have been exempted from the requirement to complete 12 months of *pupillage*; or

   c. on 30 July 2000, you were entitled to exercise full *rights of audience* by reason of being a *barrister*; or

   d. you were called to the *Bar* before 1 January 2002 and:

      i. you notified the *Bar Council* that you wished to exercise a *right of audience* before every *court* and in relation to all proceedings; and

      ii. you have complied with such training requirements as the *Bar Council* or the *Bar Standards Board* may require or you have been informed by the *Bar Council* or the *Bar Standards Board* that you do not need to comply with any such further requirements;

   in each case, before 31 March 2012;

2. a *provisional practising certificate* if you have satisfactorily completed (or have been exempted from the requirement to complete) the non-practising period of 6 months of *pupillage* and at the time when you apply for a *practising certificate* you are registered as a *Pupil*;

3. a *limited practising certificate* if you were called to the *Bar* before 1 January 2002 but you are not otherwise eligible for a *full practising certificate* in accordance with Rule S46.1 above; or

4. a *registered European lawyer's practising certificate* if you are a *registered European lawyer*.

rS47

You are eligible for a litigation extension:

1. where you have or are due to be granted a *practising certificate* (other than a *provisional practising certificate*); and

2. where you are:

a. more than three *years' standing*; or

b. less than three *years' standing*, but your principal place of *practice* (or if you are *practising* in a dual capacity, each of your principal places of *practice*) is either:

i. a *chambers* or an annex of *chambers* which is also the principal place of *practice* of a qualified *person* (as that term is defined in Rule S22.3) who is readily available to provide guidance to you; or

ii. an office of an organisation of which an *employee*, *partner*, *manager* or *director* is a qualified *person* (as that term is defined in Rule S22.3) who is readily available to provide guidance to you;

3. you have the relevant administrative systems in place to be able to provide *legal services* direct to *clients* and to administer the *conduct of litigation*; and

4. you have the procedural knowledge to enable you to *conduct litigation* competently.

Guidance to Rule 47.3

gS12

You should refer to the more detailed guidance published by the *Bar Standards Board* from time to time. This gives which provides more information about the evidence you may be asked for to show that you have procedural knowledge to enable you to *conduct litigation* competently.

C2 Applications for Practising Certificates and Litigation Extensions by Barristers and Registered European Lawyers

[1.36]

rS48

You may apply for a *practising certificate* by:

1. completing the relevant application form supplied by the *Bar Council* (acting by the *Bar Standards Board*) and submitting it to the *Bar Council* (acting by the *Bar Standards Board*); and

2. submitting such information in support of the application as may be prescribed by the *Bar Council* (acting by the *Bar Standards Board*); and

3. paying (or undertaking to pay in a manner determined by the *Bar Council*) the appropriate *practising certificate fee* in the amount determined in accordance with Rule 50 (subject to any reduction pursuant to Rule S53).

rS49

You may apply for a litigation extension to a *practising certificate* (other than a *provisional practising certificate*) by:

1. completing the relevant application form supplied by the *Bar Council* (acting by the *Bar Standards Board*) and submitting it to the *Bar Council* (acting by the *Bar Standards Board*); and
2. confirming that you meet the relevant requirements of Rule S47.1;
3. paying (or undertaking to pay in a manner determined by the *Bar Council*) the *application fee* (if any) and the *litigation extension fee*;
4. confirming, in such form as the *Bar Standards Board* may require from time to time, that you have the relevant administrative systems in place to be able to provide *legal services* direct to *clients* and to administer the *conduct of litigation* in accordance with Rule S47.3; and
5. confirming, in such form as the *Bar Standards Board* may require from time to time, that you have the procedural knowledge to enable you to *conduct litigation* competently in accordance with Rule S47.4.

rS50

An application will only have been made under either Rule S48 or S49 once the *Bar Council* (acting by the *Bar Standards Board*) has received, in respect of the relevant application, the application form in full, together with the *application fee* (if any), *the practising certificate fee, the litigation extension fee* (or an undertaking to pay such fees in a manner determined by the *Bar Council*), all the information required in support of the application and confirmation from you, in the form of a declaration, that the information contained in, or submitted in support of, the application is full and accurate.

rS51

On receipt of the application, the *Bar Council* (acting by the *Bar Standards Board*) may require, from you or a third party ~~(including, for the avoidance of doubt, any *BSB authorised body*)~~, such additional information, documents or references as it considers appropriate to the consideration of your application.

rS52

You are *person*ally responsible for the contents of your application and any information submitted to the *Bar Council* (acting by the *Bar Standards Board*) by you or on your behalf and you must not submit (or cause or permit to be submitted on your behalf) information to the *Bar Council* (acting by the *Bar Standards Board*) which you do not believe is full and accurate.

rS53

When applying for a *practising certificate* you may apply to the *Bar Council* for a reduction in the *practising certificate fee payable by you* if your gross fee income or salary is less than such amount as the *Bar Council* may decide from time to time. Such an application must be submitted by completing the form supplied for that purpose by the *Bar Council.*

C3 Practising Certificate Fees and Litigation Extension Fees

[1.37]

rS54

The *practising certificate fee* shall be the amount or amounts prescribed in the Schedule of *Practising Certificate* Fees issued by the *Bar Council* from time to time, and any reference in these Rules to the "*appropriate practising certificate fee*" or the "*practising certificate fee payable by you*" refers to the *practising certificate fee* payable by you pursuant to that Schedule, having regard , amongst other things, to:

1. the different annual *practising certificate fees* which may be prescribed by the *Bar Council* for different categories of *barristers*, e.g. for Queen's Counsel and junior counsel, for *barristers* of different levels of seniority, and/or for *barristers practising* in different capacities and/or according to different levels of income (i.e. *self-employed barristers*, *employed barristers*, *managers* or *employees* of authorised bodies or *barristers practising* with dual capacity);
2. any reductions in the annual *practising certificate fees* which may be permitted by the *Bar Council* in the case of *practising certificates* which are valid for only part of a *practising certificate year*;
3. any discounts from the annual *practising certificate fee* which may be permitted by the *Bar Council* in the event of payment by specified methods;
4. any reduction in, or rebate from, the annual *practising certificate fee* which may be permitted by the *Bar Council* on the grounds of low income, change of category or otherwise; and
5. any surcharge or surcharges to the annual *practising certificate fee* which may be prescribed by the *Bar Council* in the event of an application for renewal of a *practising certificate* being made after the end of the *practising certificate year.*

rS55

The litigation extension fee shall be the amount or amounts prescribed by the Bar Council from time to time, and in these Rules the "appropriate litigation extension fee" or the "litigation extension fee payable by you" is the litigation extension fee payable by you having regard to, among other things:

1. any reductions in the annual *litigation extension fees* which may be permitted by the *Bar Council* in the case of *litigation extensions* which are valid for only part of a *practising certificate year*;
2. any discounts from the annual *litigation extension fee* which may be permitted by the *Bar Council* in the event of payment by specified methods;
3. any reduction in, or rebate from, the annual *litigation extension fee* which may be permitted by the *Bar Council* on the grounds of low income, change of category, or otherwise; and
4. any surcharge or surcharges to the annual *litigation extension fee* which may be prescribed by the *Bar Council* in the event of an application for a *litigation extension* being made at a time different from the time of your application for a *practising certificate.*

rS56

If you have given an undertaking to pay the *practising certificate fee* or *the litigation extension fee*, you must comply with that undertaking in accordance with its terms.

C4 Issue of Practising Certificates and Litigation Extensions

[1.38]

rS57

The Bar Council (acting by the Bar Standards Board) shall not issue a practising certificate to a barrister or registered European lawyer:

1. who is not eligible for a *practising certificate*, or for a *practising certificate* of the relevant type; or
2. who has not applied for a *practising certificate*; or
3. who has not paid or not otherwise undertaken to pay in a manner determined by the Bar Council, the appropriate *practising certificate fee*; or
4. who is not insured against claims for professional negligence as provided for in Rule S71.

rS58

The Bar Council (acting by the Bar Standards Board) shall not grant a litigation extension to a barrister or registered European lawyer:

1. in circumstances where the Bar Council (acting by the Bar Standards Board) is not satisfied that the requirements of *litigation extension* are met; or
2. who has not applied for a *litigation extension*; or
3. who has not paid or not otherwise undertaken to pay in a manner determined by the Bar Council, the appropriate *application fee* (if any) and the *litigation extension fee*.

rS59

The *Bar Council* (acting by the *Bar Standards Board*) may refuse to issue a *practising certificate* or to grant a *litigation extension*, or may revoke a *practising certificate* or a *litigation extension* in accordance with Section 3.C5, if it is satisfied that the information submitted in support of the application for the *practising certificate* or *litigation extension* (as the case may be) is (or was when submitted) incomplete, inaccurate or incapable of verification, or that the relevant *barrister* or *registered European lawyer*:

1. does not hold adequate insurance in accordance with Rule C78;
2. has failed and continues to fail to pay the *appropriate practising certificate fee* or *litigation extension fee* when due;
3. would be, or is, *practising* in breach of the provisions of Section 3.B; or
4. has not complied with any of the requirements of the Continuing Professional Development Regulations applicable to him.

rS60

When the Bar Council (acting by the Bar Standards Board) issues a practising certificate or a litigation extension, it shall:

1. inform the relevant *barrister* or *registered European lawyer* of that fact; and
2. in the case of a *practising certificate*, publish that fact, together with the name and *practising address* of the *barrister* and *registered European lawyer* and the other details specified in Rule S61 in the register on the *Bar Standards Board*'s website; or
3. in the case of a litigation extension:
    a. issue a revised and updated *practising certificate* to incorporate an express reference to such litigation extension in accordance with Rule S66; and
    b. amend the register maintained on the Bar Standards Board's website to show that the relevant *barrister* or *registered European lawyer* (as the case may be) is now authorised to *conduct litigation*.

rS61

A practising certificate must state:

1. the name of the barrister or registered European lawyer (as the case may be);
2. the period for which the practising certificate is valid;
3. the reserved legal activities which the barrister or registered European lawyer (as the case may be) to whom it is issued is thereby authorised to carry on;
4. the capacity (or capacities) in which the barrister or registered European lawyer (as the case may be) practises; and
5. whether the barrister or registered European lawyer (as the case may be) is registered with the Bar Council as a Public Access practitioner.

rS62

A *practising certificate* may be valid for a *practising certificate year* or part thereof and for one month after the end of the *practising certificate year.*

rS63

A *full practising certificate* shall authorise a *barrister* to exercise a *right of audience* before every *court* in relation to all proceedings.

rS64

A *provisional practising certificate* shall authorise a *pupil* in his second six to exercise a *right of audience* before every *court* in relation to all proceedings.

rS65

A *limited practising certificate* shall not authorise a *barrister* to exercise a *right of audience*, save that it shall authorise a *barrister* to exercise any *right of audience* which he had by reason of being a *barrister* and was entitled to exercise on 30 July 2000.

rS66

A *practising certificate* shall authorise a *barrister* to *conduct litigation* in relation to every *court* and all proceedings if the *practising certificate* specifies a *litigation extension*.

rS67

Every *practising certificate* issued to a *barrister* shall authorise the *barrister*:

1. to undertake:
   a. *reserved instrument activities*;
   b. *probate activities*;
   c. *the administration of oaths*; and
   d. *immigration work*.

rS68

A registered European lawyer's practising certificate shall authorise a registered European lawyer to carry on the same reserved legal activities as a full practising certificate issued to a barrister, save that:

1. a *registered European lawyer* is only authorised to exercise a *right of audience* or *conduct litigation* in proceedings which can lawfully only be provided by a *solicitor*, *barrister* or other qualified *person*, if he acts in conjunction with a *solicitor* or *barrister* authorised to *practise* before the *court*, tribunal or public authority concerned and who could lawfully exercise that right; and
2. a *registered European lawyer* is not authorised to prepare for remuneration any instrument creating or transferring an interest in land unless he has a *home professional title* obtained in Denmark, the Republic of Ireland, Finland, Sweden, Iceland, Liechtenstein, Norway, the Czech Republic, Cyprus, Hungary or Slovakia.

C5 Amendment and Revocation of Practising Certificates and Litigation Extensions

[1.39]

rS69

You must inform the *Bar Council* (acting by the *Bar Standards Board*) as soon as reasonably practicable, and in any event within 28 days, if any of the information submitted in support of your *practising certificate* application form or *litigation extension* application form:

1. was incomplete or inaccurate when the application form was submitted; or

2. changes before the expiry of your *practising certificate*.

rS70

If you wish to:

1. change the capacity in which you *practise* (e.g. if you change from being an *employed barrister* or a *manager* or *employee* of ~~a *BSB authorised body* or~~ an *authorised (non-BSB) body* to a *self-employed barrister*, or vice versa, or if you commence or cease *practice* in a dual capacity); or

2. cease to be authorised to *conduct litigation*,

   before the expiry of your *practising certificate*, you must:

   a. notify the *Bar Council* (acting by the *Bar Standards Board*) of such requested amendment to your *practising certificate*; and

   b. submit to the *Bar Council* (acting by the *Bar Standards Board*) such further information as the *Bar Council* (acting by the *Bar Standards Board*) may reasonably require in order for them to be able to determine whether or not to grant such proposed amendment to your *practising certificate*; and

   c. within 14 days of demand by the *Bar Council* pay to the *Bar Council* the amount (if any) by which the *annual practising certificate fee* which would apply to you in respect of your amended *practising certificate* exceeds the *annual practising certificate fee* which you have already paid (or undertaken to pay) to the *Bar Council*. In the event that the revised annual *practising certificate fee* is less than the amount originally paid to the *Bar Council* (acting by the *Bar Standards Board*) or in circumstances where you wish to cease to be authorised to *conduct litigation*, the *Bar Council* (acting by the *Bar Standards Board*) is not under any obligation to refund any part of the annual *practising certificate fee* or *litigation extension fee* already paid although it may in its absolute discretion elect to do so in the circumstances contemplated by the Schedule of *Practising Certificate* Fees issued by the *Bar Council* from time to time.

rS71

The *Bar Council* (acting by the *Bar Standards Board*) may amend a *practising certificate* if it is satisfied that any of the information contained in the relevant application form was inaccurate or incomplete or has changed, but may not amend a *practising certificate* (except in response to a request from the *barrister or a registered European lawyer*) without first:

1. giving written notice to the *barrister or registered European lawyer* of the grounds on which the *practising certificate* may be amended; and

2. giving the *barrister or registered European lawyer* a reasonable opportunity to make representations.

rS72

The *Bar Council* (acting by the *Bar Standards Board*) shall endorse a *practising certificate* to reflect any qualification restriction or condition imposed on the *barrister* or *registered European lawyer* by the *Bar Council* (acting by the *Bar Standards Board*) or by a *Disciplinary Tribunal, Interim Suspension or Disqualification Panel, Fitness to Practise Panel* or the *Visitors to the Inns of Court.*

rS73

The *Bar Council* (acting by the *Bar Standards Board*):

1. shall revoke a practising certificate:
   a. if the *barrister* becomes authorised to practise by another *approved regulator;*
   b. if the *barrister or registered European lawyer* is disbarred or *suspended* from *practice* as a *barrister* or *registered European lawyer* whether on an interim basis under section D of Part 5 or otherwise under section B of Part 5;
   c. if the *barrister* or *registered European lawyer* has notified the *Bar Council* or the *Bar Standards Board* that he no longer wishes to have a *practising certificate*; and
2. may revoke a practising certificate:
   a. in the circumstances set out in Rule S59; or
   b. if the *barrister or registered European lawyer* has given an undertaking to pay the appropriate *practising certificate fee* and fails to comply with that undertaking in accordance with its terms,

   but in either case only after:
      i. giving written notice to the relevant *barrister or registered European lawyer* of the grounds on which the *practising certificate* may be revoked; and
      ii. giving the relevant *barrister or registered European lawyer* a reasonable opportunity to make representations.

rS74

The Bar Council (acting by the Bar Standards Board):

1. shall revoke a litigation extension if the barrister or registered European lawyer has notified the Bar Council or the Bar Standards Board that he no longer wishes to have the litigation extension; and
2. may revoke a litigation extension:
   a. in the circumstances set out in Rule S59; or
   b. if the *barrister or registered European lawyer* has given an undertaking to pay the appropriate *litigation extension fee* and fails to comply with that undertaking in accordance with its terms,

   but in either case only after:

i. giving written notice to the relevant *barrister or registered European lawyer* of the grounds on which the *litigation extension* may be revoked; and

ii. giving the relevant *barrister or registered European lawyer* a reasonable opportunity to make representations.

C6 Applications for Review

[1.40]

rS75

If you contend that the *Bar Council* (acting by the *Bar Standards Board*) has:

1. wrongly failed or refused to issue or amend a *practising certificate*; or
2. wrongly amended or revoked a *practising certificate*; or
3. wrongly failed or refused to issue a *litigation extension*; or
4. wrongly revoked a *litigation extension*,

in each case in accordance with this Section 3.C, then you may lodge an application for review with the *Qualifications Committee* using the form supplied for that purpose by the *Bar Standards Board*. For the avoidance of doubt, this Section 3.C6 does not apply to any amendment or revocation of a *practising certificate* or *litigation extension* made by order of a *Disciplinary Tribunal, Interim Suspension or Disqualification Panel, Fitness to Practise Panel* or the *Visitors to the Inns of Court*.

rS76

The decision of the *Bar Council* (acting by the *Bar Standards Board*) shall take effect notwithstanding any application for review being submitted in accordance with Rule 75. However, the *Bar Council* (acting by the *Bar Standards Board*) may, in its absolute discretion, issue a temporary *practising certificate* or *litigation extension* to a *barrister* or *registered European lawyer* who has lodged an application for review.

rS77

If the Qualifications Committee finds that the Bar Council (acting by the Bar Standards Board):

1. has wrongly failed or refused to issue a *practising certificate*, then the *Bar Council* (acting by the *Bar Standards Board*) must issue such *practising certificate* as ought to have been issued; or
2. has wrongly failed or refused to amend a *practising certificate*, then the *Bar Council* (acting by the *Bar Standards Board*) must make such amendment to the *practising certificate* as ought to have been made; or
3. has wrongly amended a *practising certificate*, then the *Bar Council* (acting by the *Bar Standards Board*) must cancel the amendment; or
4. has wrongly revoked a *practising certificate*, then the *Bar Council* (acting by the *Bar Standards Board*) must re-issue the *practising certificate*; or

5. has wrongly failed or refused to grant a *litigation extension*, then the *Bar Council* (acting by the *Bar Standards Board*) must grant such *litigation extension* as ought to have been granted; or
6. has wrongly revoked a *litigation extension*, then the *Bar Council* (acting by the *Bar Standards Board*) must re-grant the *litigation extension*.

D THE REGISTRATION OF EUROPEAN LAWYERS' RULES

[1.41]

rS78I

f you are a *European lawyer* and wish to *practise* on a permanent basis in England and Wales under a *home professional title*, you may apply to the *Bar Standards Board* to be registered as a *registered European lawyer.*

rS79

An application for registration must be made in such form as may be prescribed by the *Bar Standards Board* and be accompanied by:

1. a certificate, not more than three months old at the date of receipt of the application by the *Bar Standards Board*, that you are registered with the competent authority in a *Member State* as a lawyer qualified to *practise* in that *Member State* under a *Member State* professional title;
2. a declaration that:
   a. you have not on the grounds of misconduct or of the commission of a *criminal offence* been prohibited from practising in your *Member State* and are not currently *suspended* from so practising;
   b. no *bankruptcy order* or *directors disqualification order* has been made against you and you have not entered into an individual voluntary arrangement with your creditors;
   c. you are not aware of any other circumstances relevant to your fitness to *practise* under your *home professional title* in England and Wales; and
   d. you are not registered with the Law Society of England and Wales, of Scotland or of Northern Ireland; and
3. the prescribed fee.

rS80

Provided that it is satisfied that the application complies with the requirements of Rule S79, the *Bar Standards Board* will:

1. register you as a registered European lawyer; and
2. so inform you and the competent authority in your Member State which has issued the certificate referred to in Rule S79.1.

rS81

The *Bar Standards Board* will:

1. remove a *registered European lawyer* from the register:
   a. pursuant to a sentence of a *Disciplinary Tribunal*; or
   b. if the *registered European lawyer* ceases to be a *European lawyer*;
2. suspend a *registered European lawyer* from the register:
   a. pursuant to a sentence of either a *Disciplinary Tribunal* or an *Interim Suspension Panel*; or
   b. if the *registered European lawyer's* authorisation in his *home State* to pursue professional activities under his *home professional title* is *suspended*; and

in each case, notify the European lawyer's home professional body:

c. of his removal or suspension from the register; and
d. of any criminal *conviction* or *bankruptcy order* of which it becomes aware against a *registered European lawyer*.

~~E ENTITY APPLICATION AND AUTHORISATION~~

~~E1 Eligibility for Authorisation to Practise as a BSB authorised body~~

[1.42]

~~rS82~~

~~In this Section 3.E, "you" and "your" refer to the *partnership, LLP* or *company* which is applying for, or has applied for (in accordance with this Section 3.E), authorisation or (if a *licensable body*) a licence to *practise* as a *BSB authorised body*, and references in these Rules to "authorisation to *practise*" mean the grant by the *Bar Council* as *Approved Regulator* or *licensing authority* of an authorisation or a licence (as the case may be) under this Section 3.E (distinguishing between the two only where the context so requires).~~

~~rS83~~

~~To be eligible for authorisation to *practise* as a *BSB authorised body*, you:~~

1. ~~must ensure at all times that any obligations imposed from time to time on the *BSB authorised body*, its *managers, owners* or *employees* by or under the *Bar Standards Board's* regulatory arrangements, including its rules and disciplinary arrangements, are complied with;~~
2. ~~must ensure at all times that any other statutory obligations imposed on the *BSB authorised body*, its *managers, owners* or *employees*, in relation to the *activities* it carries on, are complied with;~~
3. ~~must confirm that you will have in place, at all times, individuals appointed to act as a *HOLP* (who must also be a *manager*) and a *HOFA* of the *BSB authorised body*;~~
4. ~~must confirm that you have or will have appropriate insurance arrangements in place at all times in accordance with Rule C76 and you must be able to provide evidence of those insurance arrangements if required to do so by the *Bar Standards Board*;~~

5. must confirm that, in connection with your proposed *practice*, you will not directly or indirectly hold *client money* in accordance with Rule C71 or have someone else hold *client money* on your behalf other than in those circumstances permitted by Rule C72;

6. must confirm that no individual that has been appointed or will be appointed as a *HOLP, HOFA, manager* or *employee* of the *BSB authorised body* is disqualified from acting as such by the *Bar Standards Board* or any *Approved Regulator* pursuant to section 99 of the *LSA* or otherwise as a result of its regulatory arrangements;

7. must confirm that you will at all times have a *practising address* in England or Wales;

8. must confirm that:

   a. if you are an *LLP*, you are incorporated and registered in England and Wales, Scotland or Northern Ireland under the Limited Liability Partnerships Act 2000;

   b. if you are a *Company*, you are:

      i. incorporated and registered in England and Wales, Scotland or Northern Ireland under Parts 1 and 2 of the Companies Act 2006; or

      ii. incorporated in an *Establishment Directive* state and registered as an overseas company under Part 34 of the Companies Act 2006; or

      iii. incorporated and registered in an *Establishment Directive* state as a societas Europaea,

9. must confirm that at least one *manager* or *employee* is an *authorised individual* in respect of each *reserved legal activity* which you wish to provide;

10. must confirm that you will pay annual fees as and when they become due.

rS84

In addition to the requirements set out at Rule 83:

1. to be eligible for authorisation to *practise* as a BSB legal services body:

   a. all of the managers of the partnership, LLP or company (as the case may be) must be BSB authorised individuals or authorised (non-BSB) individuals; and

   b. all of the owners (whether or not the ownership interest is material) of the partnership, LLP or company (as the case may be) must be BSB authorised individuals or authorised (non-BSB) individuals;

2. to be licensed to practise as a BSB licensed body:

   a. the body must be a *licensable body*, as defined by section 72 of the *LSA* but must also meet the eligibility requirements set out at Rule S83; and

   b. all of the non-authorised *owners* in the *partnership*, *LLP* or *company* (as

~~the case may be) must be approved by the *Bar Standards Board* as being able to hold such interest taking into account the relevant *suitability criteria*.~~

~~rS85~~

~~In the event that you meet the eligibility criteria set out in Rule S83, you may submit an application in accordance with Section 3.E2 and the *Bar Standards Board* will review that application in accordance with Section 3.E3 and 3.E4 to determine whether or not to authorise you or to grant you a licence (as appropriate) to *practise* as a *BSB authorised body*.~~

~~rS86~~

~~In the event that the *Bar Standards Board* determines that you should be authorised or licensed (as appropriate) to *practise* as a *BSB authorised body* then it may either:~~

~~1.~~ ~~authorise you to *practise* as a BSB *legal* services body in the event that you also meet the eligibility criteria set out in Rule S84.1 and you have applied to be authorised as such in your relevant application form; or~~

~~2.~~ ~~license you to *practise* as a *BSB licensed body*, in the event that you also meet the eligibility criteria set out in Rule S84.2 and you have applied to be authorised as such in your relevant application form.~~

~~rS87~~

~~Such authorisation or licence (as appropriate) will entitle you:~~

~~1.~~ ~~to exercise a *right of audience* before every *court* in relation to all proceedings;~~

~~2.~~ ~~to carry on:~~

   ~~a.~~ ~~reserved instrument activities;~~

   ~~b.~~ ~~probate activities;~~

   ~~c.~~ ~~the administration of oaths;~~

~~3.~~ ~~to do immigration work; and~~

~~4.~~ ~~if you have been granted a litigation extension, to conduct litigation.~~

~~Guidance on Rules S82 to S85~~

~~gS13~~

~~Single person entities are permitted under these arrangements. Therefore, a BSB legal services body may (subject to any structural requirements imposed by general law for the particular type of entity) comprise just one barrister who is both the owner and manager of that entity.~~

~~gS14~~

These are mandatory eligibility requirements. The *Bar Standards Board* has a discretion to take other factors into account in deciding whether an *applicant body* is one which it would be appropriate for it to regulate (see Section 3.E3 and 3.E4 below).

E2 Applications for Authorisation

[1.43]

Application to be authorised or licensed as a BSB authorised body

rS88

To apply for authorisation to *practise* as a *BSB authorised body*, you must:

1. complete the application form supplied by the *Bar Standards Board* and submit it to the *Bar Standards Board*; and
2. submit such other information, documents and references in support of the application as may be required by the application form or by the *Bar Standards Board* from time to time; and
3. pay the *application fee* in the amount determined in accordance with Rule S94 and the *authorisation fee* for the first year.

Application for a litigation extension

rS89

To apply for a *litigation extension* you must:

1. make this clear on your application form submitted in accordance with Rule S88 (where appropriate) or otherwise submit the relevant application form made available by the Bar Standard Board on its website for this purpose; and
2. pay (or undertake to pay in a manner prescribed by the Bar Standards Board) the *application fee* (if any) and the relevant *litigation extension fee* in the amount determined in accordance with Rule S94; and
3. provide such other information to the *Bar Standards Board* as it may require in order to satisfy itself that:
   (a) you have the relevant administrative systems in place to be able to provide *legal services* direct to *clients* and to administer the *conduct of litigation*; and
   (b) you have a sufficient number of *persons* who are authorised to *conduct litigation* and to provide guidance to any *managers* or *employees* that may be involved in assisting in the *conduct of litigation* who are not themselves authorised and that you have an adequate number of qualified *persons* to provide guidance to any *persons* authorised to *conduct litigation* who are of less than three *years' standing*.

Guidance on Rules S88 and S89

gS15

~~In the event that your application is rejected, the *authorisation fee* and/or *litigation fee* (as appropriate) will be reimbursed to you but the *application fee(s)* shall be retained by the Bar Standards Board.~~

~~gS16~~

~~a qualified *person* referred to in Rule S89.3 shall be defined in accordance with Rule S22.3.~~

~~*Approval applications for any new HOLPs, HOFAs, owners and/or managers*~~

~~rS90~~

~~If, following authorisation or the grant of a licence (as appropriate), a *BSB authorised body* wishes to appoint a new *HOLP*, *HOFA*, *owner* or *manager*, the *BSB authorised body* must:~~

1. ~~notify the *Bar Standards Board* of such a proposed appointment before it is made; and~~
2. ~~make an application to the *Bar Standards Board* for approval of the new *HOLP*, *HOFA*, *owner* or *manager* (as appropriate); and~~
3. ~~pay any fees set by the *Bar Standards Board* in respect of such approval applications.~~

~~*Application Process*~~

~~rS91~~

~~An application for authorisation and/or a *litigation extension* is only made once the *Bar Standards Board* has received the application form in full, together with the appropriate fees, all the information required in support of the application and confirmation from you in the form of a declaration that the information contained in, or submitted in support of, the application is full and accurate.~~

~~rS92~~

~~On receipt of the application, the *Bar Standards Board* may require, from you or from a third party, such additional information, documents or references as it considers appropriate to the consideration of your application.~~

~~rS93~~

~~You are responsible for the contents of your application and any information submitted to the *Bar Standards Board* by you, or on your behalf, and you must not submit (or cause or permit to be submitted on your behalf) information to the *Bar Standards Board* which you do not believe is full and accurate.~~

~~rS94~~

~~The *application fee* and the *litigation extension fee* shall be the amount or amounts prescribed by the *Bar Standards Board* from time to time. The *authorisation fee* and~~

~~*litigation fee* shall also be payable and shall be the amount or amounts prescribed by the *Bar Standards Board* from time to time.~~

~~*Guidance on Rules S91 to S93*~~

~~gS17~~

~~Application forms and guidance notes for completion can be found on the *Bar Standard Board's* website.~~

~~gS18~~

~~Once you have submitted an application, if you fail to disclose to the *Bar Standards Board* any information of which you later become aware and which you would have been required to supply if it had been known by you at the time of the original application the Bar Standards Board may refuse your application in accordance with rS101.6~~

~~gS19~~

~~Details of the relevant *application fee, litigation extension fee, authorisation fee and litigation fee* can be found on the *Bar Standards Board's* website.~~

~~E3 Decision Process~~

[1.44]

~~rS95~~

~~Subject to Rules S96 and S97, the *Bar Standards Board* must make a decision in respect of each valid and complete application within the *decision period*.~~

~~rS96~~

~~In the event that the *Bar Standards Board* is not able to reach a decision within the *decision period*, it must notify you and must confirm to you the latest date by which you will have received a response to your application from the *Bar Standards Board*.~~

~~rS97~~

~~The *Bar Standards Board* may issue more than one notice to extend the *decision period* except that:~~

1. ~~any notice to extend must always be issued before the *decision period* expires on the first occasion, and before any such extended *decision period* expires on any second and subsequent occasions; and~~
2. ~~no notice to extend can result in the total *decision period* exceeding more than 9 months.~~

~~rS98~~

~~During its consideration of your application form, the *Bar Standards Board* may identify further information or documentation which it needs in order to be able to~~

reach its decision. If this is the case, you must provide such additional information or documentation as soon as possible after you receive the relevant request from the *Bar Standards Board*. Any delay in providing this information shall further entitle the *Bar Standards Board* to issue an extension notice in accordance with Rule 96 and 97 (as the case may be) or to treat the application as having been withdrawn.

E4 Issues to be Considered by the Bar Standards Board

[1.45]

Applications for authorisation or the grant of a licence

rS99

In circumstances where the mandatory conditions in Rules S83 and S84 have been met, the *Bar Standards Board* must then consider whether to exercise its discretion to grant the authorisation or licence (as appropriate). In exercising this discretion, the *Bar Standards Board* will consider whether the entity is one which it would be appropriate for the *Bar Standards Board* to regulate, taking into account its analysis of the risks posed by you, the *regulatory objectives* of the *LSA* and the Entity Regulation Policy Statement of the *Bar Standards Board* as published from time to time.

rS100

In circumstances where the mandatory conditions set out at Rules S83 and S84 have not been met, the *Bar Standards Board* must refuse to grant the authorisation or licence (as appropriate).

Guidance

gS20

In exercising its discretion whether to grant the authorisation or license the *Bar Standards Board* will have regard to its current Entity Regulation Policy Statement.

rS101

Where the *Bar Standards Board* concludes that you are an entity which it is appropriate for it to regulate the *Bar Standards Board* may nonetheless in its discretion refuse your application for authorisation if:

1. it is not satisfied that your *managers* and *owners* meet the relevant *suitability criteria* which apply to *managers* and *owners* of *BSB authorised bodies*;
2. it is not satisfied that your *managers* and *owners* are suitable as a group to operate or control a *practice* providing services regulated by the *Bar Standards Board*;
3. if it is not satisfied that your proposed *HOLP* and *HOFA* meet the relevant *suitability criteria*;
4. it is not satisfied that your management or governance arrangements are adequate to safeguard the *regulatory objectives* of the *LSA* or the policy objectives of the *Bar Standards* Board as set out in the Entity Regulation Policy Statement;

5. it is not satisfied that, if the authorisation is granted, you will comply with the *Bar Standards Board's* regulatory arrangements including this *Handbook* and any conditions imposed on the authorisation;

6. you have provided inaccurate or misleading information in your application or in response to any requests by the *Bar Standards Board* for information;

7. you have failed to notify the *Bar Standards Board* of any changes in the information provided in the application;

8. you have applied for authorisation to become a *BSB legal services body* and the *Bar Standards Board* has concluded that it may require the intervention powers allocated to it in respect of *licensed bodies* under the *LSA* in respect of you; or

9. for any other reason, the *Bar Standards Board* considers that it would be inappropriate for the *Bar Standards Board* to grant authorisation to you, having regard to its analysis of the risk posed by you, the regulatory objectives of the LSA or the Entity Regulation Policy Statement of the Bar Standards Board.

Guidance to Rule S101

gS21

In circumstances where the *Bar Standards Board* rejects your application on the basis of Rule 101, you will have the opportunity to make the necessary adjustments to your composition and to re-apply to become a *BSB authorised body* or a *BSB licensed body* (as appropriate).

Applications for authorisation to conduct litigation

rS102

If the *Bar Standards Board* is unable to satisfy itself that the *BSB authorised body* meets the requirements set out in Rule 89, it can refuse to grant the litigation extension.

Approval applications for any new HOLPs, HOFAs, owners and/or managers

rS103

The *Bar Standards Board* must consider any approval applications for any new *HOLPs, HOFAs, owners* and/or *managers* made in accordance with Rule 90 and must determine any application by deciding whether the relevant individual meets the *suitability criteria* which apply relevant to such a proposed appointment.

E5 Suitability Criteria in respect of HOLPs, HOFAs, owners and managers

[1.46]

rS104

The *Bar Standards Board* must conclude that an individual does not meet the suitability criteria to undertake the role of a *HOLP* if:

1. he is not an authorised individual;
2. he is disqualified from acting as a HOLP by the Bar Standards Board or an Approved Regulator pursuant to section 99 of the LSA or otherwise as a result of its regulatory arrangements; or
3. It determines that the individual is not able effectively to carry out the duties imposed on a HOLP by section 91 of the LSA.

rS105

The *Bar Standards Board* may conclude that an individual does not meet the suitability criteria to undertake the role of a *HOLP* if any of the circumstances listed in Rule 110 apply to the individual designated as the *HOLP*.

rS106

The *Bar Standards Board* must conclude that an individual does not meet the suitability criteria for acting as a *HOFA* if:

1. he is disqualified from acting as a *HOFA* by the *Bar Standards Board* or by an *Approved Regulator* pursuant to section 99 of the *LSA* or otherwise as a result of its regulatory arrangements; or
2. the *Bar Standards Board* determines that he is not able effectively to carry out the duties imposed on a *HOFA* by section 92 of the *LSA*.

rS107

The *Bar Standards Board* may conclude that an individual does not meet the suitability criteria for acting as a *HOFA* if any of the circumstances listed in Rule S110 apply to him.

rS108

If an *owner* is also a *non-authorised individual*, the *Bar Standards Board* must approve him as an *owner*. The *Bar Standards Board* shall approve a *non-authorised individual* to be an *owner of BSB licensed body* if:

1. he is also a *manager* and approved as such; and
2. his holding of an ownership interest does not compromise the *regulatory objectives*; and
3. his holding of an ownership interest does not compromise compliance with

the duties imposed pursuant to section 176 of the *LSA* by the *licensed body* or by any authorised individuals who are to be *employees* or *managers* of that *licensed body*; and

4. he otherwise meets the *suitability criteria* to hold that ownership interest taking into account:

    a. his probity and financial position;

    b. whether he is disqualified pursuant to section 100(1) of *LSA* or included in the list maintained by the *Legal Services Board* pursuant to paragraph 51 of Schedule 13 of the *LSA*; and

    c. his *associates*; and

    d. the *suitability criteria* in Rule S110 which apply to *managers* and *employees*.

rS109

If a *manager* is a *non-authorised individual*, the *Bar Standards Board* must approve him as a *manager*. The *Bar Standards Board* must approve a *non-authorised individual* to be a *manager* of a *BSB licensed body* if he meets the *suitability criteria* to hold that interest taking into account:

1. his probity;
2. whether he is disqualified pursuant to section 100(1) of the *LSA* or included in the list maintained by the *Legal Services Board* pursuant to paragraph 51 of Schedule 13 of the *LSA*; and
3. the *suitability criteria* in Rule S110 which apply to *managers* and *employees*.

rS110

The *Bar Standards Board* may reject an application if it is not satisfied that:

1. an individual identified in an application for authorisation or the grant of a licence as a proposed *owner, manager, HOLP* or *HOFA* of the relevant *applicant body*; or
2. any individual identified as a replacement *owner, manager, HOLP* or *HOFA*,

    meets the *suitability criteria* to act as an *owner, manager, HOLP* or *HOFA* of a *BSB authorised body*. Reasons why the *Bar Standards Board* may conclude that an individual does not meet the *suitability criteria* include where an individual:

3. has been committed to prison in civil or criminal proceedings;
4. has been disqualified from being a *director*;
5. has been removed from the office of charity trustee or trustee for a charity by an order under section 72(1)(d) of the Charities Act 1993;
6. is an undischarged bankrupt;
7. has been adjudged bankrupt and discharged;
8. has entered into an individual voluntary arrangement or a *partnership* voluntary arrangement under the Insolvency Act 1986;

9. has been a *manager* of an *authorised body* or a *BSB authorised body* which has entered into a voluntary arrangement under the Insolvency Act 1986;

10. has been a *director* of a *company* or a *member* of an *LLP* (as defined by section 4 of the Limited Liability Partnerships Act 2000) which has been the subject of a winding up order, an administration order or administrative receivership; or has entered into a voluntary arrangement under the Insolvency Act 1986; or has been otherwise wound up or put into administration in circumstances of insolvency;

11. lacks capacity (within the meaning of the Mental Capacity Act 2005) and powers under sections 15 to 20 or section 48 of that Act are exercisable in relation to that individual;

12. is the subject of an outstanding judgment or judgments involving the payment of money;

13. is currently charged with an *indictable offence*, or has been convicted of an *indictable offence*, any offence of dishonesty, or any offence under the Financial Services and Markets Act 2000, the Immigration and Asylum Act 1999 or the Compensation Act 2006;

14. has been disqualified from being appointed to act as a *HOLP* or a *HOFA* or from being a *manager* or employed by a *licensed body* (as appropriate) by the *Bar Standards Board* or another *Approved Regulator* pursuant to its or their powers under section 99 of the *LSA* or otherwise as a result of its regulatory arrangements;

15. has been the subject in another jurisdiction of circumstances equivalent to those listed in Rules S110.1 to S110.14;

16. has an investigation or disciplinary proceedings pending against them and/or has professional conduct findings against them either under the disciplinary scheme for *barristers* or otherwise; or

17. has been involved in other conduct which calls into question his or her honesty, integrity, or respect for the law.

E6 Notification of the Authorisation Decision

[1.47]

rS111

The *Bar Standards Board* will notify you of its decision in writing within the *decision period* or by such later date as may have been notified to the *applicant body* in accordance with Rules 96 or 97. In the event that the *Bar Standards Board* decides to refuse to grant the application, it must give the reasons for such refusal.

E7 Terms of Authorisation

[1.48]

rS112

Any authorisation given by the *Bar Standards Board* to a *BSB legal services body* , and the terms of any licence granted by the *Bar Standards Board* to a *BSB licensed body* in accordance with this Section 3.E must specify:

1. ~~the activities which are *reserved legal activities* and which the *BSB authorised body* is authorised to carry on by virtue of the authorisation or the licence (as the case may be); and~~
2. ~~any conditions subject to which the authorisation or the licence (as the case may be) is given (which may include those in Rule S114).~~

~~rS113~~

~~Authorisations and licences must, in all cases, be given on the conditions that:~~

1. ~~any obligation which may from time to time be imposed on you (or your *managers, employees*, or *owners*) by the *Bar Standards Board* is complied with; and~~
2. ~~any other obligation imposed on you (or your *managers, employees* or *owners*) by or under the *LSA* or any other enactment is complied with.~~

rS114

~~In addition to the provisions in Rule S113, an authorisation or a licence may be given subject to such other terms as the *Bar Standards Board* considers appropriate including terms as to:~~

1. ~~the *non-reserved activities* which you may or may not carry on; and/or~~
2. ~~in the case of *licensed bodies*:~~
   a. ~~the nature of any interest held by a non-authorised *owner* provided always that the *Bar Standards Board* complies with its obligations under paragraph 17 of Schedule 13 to the *LSA*; and/or~~
   b. ~~any limitations on the shareholdings or voting controls which may be held by non-authorised *owners* in accordance with paragraph 33 of Schedule 13 to the *LSA*.~~

~~E8 Duration of the Authorisation/Licence granted~~

[1.49]

~~rS115~~

~~Except where indicated otherwise in the authorisation or licence, any authorisation or licence granted in accordance with this Section 3.E will be of unlimited duration except that the authorisation or licence:~~

1. ~~shall cease to have effect on the occurrence of any of the following:~~
   a. ~~if you have your authorisation/licence withdrawn in accordance with Rule S117; or~~
   b. ~~if you obtain authorisation/licence from an *Approved Regulator* or *licensing authority*;~~
2. ~~may cease to have effect on the occurrence of any of the following:~~
   a. ~~if you fail to provide the relevant monitoring information or fail to pay any relevant fees in circumstances where the *Bar Standards Board*~~

has notified you (i) that such information or payment is required within a particular time; and (ii) that failure to provide such information or payment within that time may result in the withdrawal of your authorisation or licence being withdrawn in accordance with this Rule S115; or

b. if you fail to replace your *HOLP/HOFA* in accordance with the requirements of this *Handbook*.

E9 Modification of an authorisation/licence

[1.50]

rS116

In addition to any powers which the Bar Standards Board may have in accordance with Part 5, the *Bar Standards Board* may modify the terms of an authorisation or licence granted by it:

1. if you apply to the *Bar Standards Board* for the terms of such authorisation or licence (as the case may be) to be modified; or
2. if it is satisfied that any of the information contained in the relevant application form was inaccurate or incomplete or has changed; or
3. if such modification is required in accordance with the provisions of this *Handbook*; or
4. where the *Bar Standards Board* reasonably considers that such modification is appropriate and in accordance with the *regulatory objectives* under the *LSA* or the policy objectives of the *Bar Standards Board*,

   but, in the circumstances set out in Rules S116.2 to S116.4 above, shall only be entitled to do so after:

   a. giving notice to *you* in writing of the modifications which the *Bar Standards Board* is intending to make to your authorisation or licence (as the case may be); and

   b. giving you a reasonable opportunity to make representations about such proposed modifications.

E10 Revocation or suspension of an authorisation/licence

[1.51]

rS117

In addition to any powers which the Bar Standards Board may have in accordance with Part 5, the *Bar Standards Board* may:

1. revoke an authorisation or licence granted by it:

   a. subject to Section 3.F, in the event that you no longer comply with the mandatory requirements set out in Rules S83 and S84; or

   b. if your circumstances have changed in relation to the issues considered by the *Bar Standards Board* in Section 3.E4; or

c. if revocation otherwise appears appropriate taking into account the *regulatory objectives* of the *Bar Standards Board*; or

2. suspend an authorisation or licence granted by it to give it an opportunity to investigate whether or not your authorisation or licence should be revoked in accordance with Rule S117,

but in either case only after:

a. giving written notice to the relevant *BSB authorised body* of the grounds on which the authorisation or licence may be revoked; and

b. giving the relevant *BSB authorised body* a reasonable opportunity to make representations.

E11 Applications for Review

[1.52]

rS118

If you consider that the *Bar Standards Board* has (other than pursuant to [Section 5]):

1. wrongly refused an application for authorisation or licence; or
2. wrongly imposed a term or condition on an authorisation or licence; or
3. wrongly modified the terms of your authorisation or licence; or
4. wrongly refused to modify the terms of your authorisation or licence; or
5. wrongly revoked or *suspended* your authorisation or licence; or
6. wrongly done any of these things in relation to a litigation extension to your authorisation or licence; or
7. failed to provide to you notice of a decision in accordance with this Section 3.E,

then you may lodge an application for review of that decision with the *Qualifications Committee* using the form supplied for that purpose by the *Bar Standards Board*. Such application for review will only have been made once the *Bar Standards Board* has received the relevant fee in respect of such application for review.

rS119

Any individual:

1. designated to act as a *HOLP* or a *HOFA*; or
2. identified as a non-authorised *owner* or *manager* of the *applicant body*,

who considers that the *Bar Standards Board* has wrongly concluded that he does not meet the *suitability criteria* which apply to his proposed position in the entity, may lodge an application for a review of that decision with the *Qualifications Committee* using the form supplied for that purpose by the *Bar Standards Board*. Alternatively, you may lodge an application for review on his behalf whether or not he has asked you to. In either case, such an application for a review will only have been made once the *Bar Standards Board* has received the relevant fee for it.

~~rS120~~

~~Any application for a review of the decision must be made within 28 days from the date when the decision is notified to you.~~

~~rS121~~

~~The decision of the *Bar Standards Board* will take effect notwithstanding the making of any application for a review in accordance with Rule S118 or S119. However, the *Bar Standards Board* may, in its absolute discretion, issue a temporary authorisation, licence or litigation extension to a *BSB authorised body* which has lodged an application for a review in accordance with this Section 3.E11.~~

~~rS122~~

~~If the *Qualifications Committee* finds that the *Bar Standards Board*:~~

~~1.~~ ~~has wrongly failed or refused to grant an authorisation or licence,; or~~

~~2.~~ ~~has wrongly imposed a term or condition on an authorisation or licence;~~

~~then in each case the *Bar Standards Board* must issue such authorisation or licence as ought to have been issued.~~

~~rS123~~

~~If the Qualifications Committee finds that the Bar Standards Board:~~

~~1.~~ ~~finds that the *Bar Standards Board* has wrongly modified an authorisation or licence; or~~

~~2.~~ ~~finds that the *Bar Standards Board* has wrongly refused to modify an authorisation or licence,~~

~~then in each case the *Bar Standards Board* shall make such modification to the authorisation or licence as ought to have been made.~~

~~rS124~~

~~If the *Qualifications Committee* finds that the *Bar Standards Board* has wrongly revoked or *suspended* an authorisation or licence, then the *Bar Standards Board* shall re-issue such authorisation or licence.~~

~~1.~~ ~~If the *Qualifications Committee* finds that the *Bar Standards Board* has wrongly done any of the things described in S122 or S123 in relation to your *litigation extension*, then the *Bar Council* (acting by the *Bar Standards Board*) shall grant such *litigation extension* as ought to have been granted.~~

~~rS125~~

~~If the *Qualifications Committee* finds that the *Bar Standards Board* has wrongly concluded that an individual does not meet the *suitability criteria* relevant to his proposed position, the *Bar Standards Board* shall amend its decision and confirm that he does meet the *suitability criteria* which apply to his proposed position.~~

rS126

If, after such a review, you or the relevant individual(s) (as the case may be) do not agree with the decision of the Qualification Committee you or the relevant individual(s) may appeal to the *First Tier Tribunal*

This will require secondary legislation and confirmation that the First Tier Tribunal's jurisdiction could be expanded to conclude such appeals in the case of *BSB legal services bodies.* against the *Qualification Committee's* decision.

rS127

Any appeal to the First Tier Tribunal against a decision of the Qualification Committee must be lodged within 28 days from the date that the decision is notified to you.

E12 Register

[1.53]

rS128

The *Bar Standards Board* must keep a public register containing the names and places of *practice* of all *BSB authorised bodies* (together with details of the *reserved legal activities* which such *BSB authorised bodies* are able to undertake) as well as details of any bodies which have in the past been granted authorisation or obtained a licence from the *Bar Standards Board* but where such licence and/or authorisation is no longer current.

rS129

If an authorisation or licence is, at any time, *suspended* or made subject to conditions, this must be noted on the register of *BSB authorised bodies* by the *Bar Standards Board.*

F CONTINUING COMPLIANCE WITH THE AUTHORISATION AND LICENSING REQUIREMENTS

F1 Non-compliance with the mandatory conditions

[1.54]

rS130

If, at any time, and for whatever reason, you fail to meet the mandatory conditions in Rules S83 and S84 which apply to the type of *BSB authorised body* which you are, then you must notify the *Bar Standards Board* of your failure to comply with the mandatory conditions within seven days of your failure to comply and, at the same time, you must submit your proposals for rectifying that non-compliance which, for the avoidance of doubt, must include your proposed timetable for rectifying them. If *Bar Standards Board* considers that your proposals for rectifying them are not sufficient, the *Bar Standards Board* may issue a notice suspending or revoking your authorisation or licence (as appropriate) in accordance with Section 3.E10.

Guidance

gS22

Examples of non-compliance include:

1. where your last remaining *authorised person*:
   a. dies; or
   b. abandons, retires or resigns from the *practice*; or
2. where you are a *BSB legal services body* a *non-authorised individual* is appointed as a *manager* of or otherwise acquires an ownership interest in such a *practice*, or where you are a *licensable body* and a *non-authorised individual* who is not a *manager* becomes an *owner* (for example on inheriting the interest from a *manager* who dies);
3. where you cease to have available at least one *employee* who is authorised to carry on a particular reserved activity which you are authorised to provide. Examples of situations where an individual should be considered to be unavailable to a *BSB authorised body* include where:
   a. he is committed to prison;
   b. he is unable to attend to the *practice* because of incapacity caused by illness, accident or age;
   c. he becomes and continues to who lack capacity under Part 1 of the Mental Capacity Act 2005;
   d. he is made subject to a condition on his *practising certificate* or registration which would be breached if he continues to be an *owner* and/or *manager* of the body; or
   e. he is no longer authorised to perform the particular *reserved legal activity*.
4. you cease to have a *HOLP* or a *HOFA* appointed;
5. your *HOLP*, *HOFA*, any *manager* or *owner* ceases to meet the relevant *suitability criteria*; or
6. where you are a *licensed body*, your last remaining *owner* and/or *manager* who is a *non-authorised individual* dies or otherwise leaves the *practice*.

gS23

Examples of proposals that you may submit in order to rectify such non-compliance include:

1. In the case of Guidance S22.1, that you are seeking to appoint a different *authorised person* to be an *owner* and/or a *manager* of a *BSB authorised body*;
2. In the case of Guidance S22.2, confirmation that you will take the necessary steps to rectify your status, whether by submitting an application to the *Bar Standards Board* for authorisation to *practise* as a *licensed body* and/or for approval of the *non-authorised individual* as a *manager* or by ensuring that the

~~*non-authorised person* divests himself of his interest as soon as is reasonably practicable, or by seeking a licence from another *licensing authority*, as the case may be [but note Guidance S24];~~

~~3.~~ ~~in the case of Guidance S22.4, that you are seeking to appoint a replacement *HOLP* or *HOFA* (as appropriate) in accordance with the relevant procedure in Rule S90;~~

~~4.~~ ~~in the case of Guidance S22.5, that you are taking the necessary steps to exclude the *relevant* individual from the *practice* and, where necessary, you are taking steps to replace him; and~~

~~5.~~ ~~in the case of Guidance S22.6, you confirm whether or not you are likely to appoint a replacement *non-authorised individual* or, if not, whether you will be seeking authorisation from the *Bar Standards Board* to *practise* as a *BSB legal services body.*~~

~~gS24~~

~~In respect of Guidance S23.2, it may be the case that a *non-authorised individual* obtains an ownership interest in a *BSB authorised body* following the death of a *barrister* or a *non-authorised person*. Similarly, a *non-authorised person* who has not been approved pursuant to the *suitability criteria* may acquire an ownership in a interest *licensed body*. In these cases, it may be that the *BSB authorised body* will not need to apply for authorisation to *practise* as a *licensed body* or for approval of such *non-authorised individual* (as appropriate) if the *BSB authorised body* instead satisfies the *Bar Standards Board* that it is taking steps to ensure that such *non-authorised individual* divests himself of his interest as soon as is reasonably practicable (for example, on completion of the relevant probate).~~

~~F2 Temporary emergency approvals for HOLPs and HOFAs~~

[1.55]

~~rS131~~

~~If a *BSB authorised body* ceases to have a *HOLP* or *HOFA* whose designation has been approved by the *Bar Standards Board*, the *BSB authorised body* must immediately and in any event within seven days:~~

~~1.~~ ~~notify the Bar Standards Board;~~

~~2.~~ ~~designate another manager or employee to replace its previous HOLP or HOFA, as appropriate; and~~

~~3.~~ ~~make an application to the Bar Standards Board for temporary approval of the new HOLP or HOFA, as appropriate.~~

~~rS132~~

~~The *Bar Standards Board* may grant a temporary approval under this Section 3.F2 if on the face of the application and any other information immediately before the *Bar Standards Board*, there is no evidence suggesting that the new *HOLP* or *HOFA* is not suitable to carry out the duties imposed on them under this *Handbook*.~~

~~**rS133**~~

~~If granted temporary approval under Rule S132 for its designation of a new *HOLP* or *HOFA*, the *authorised body* must:~~

~~1.~~ ~~designate a permanent *HOLP* or *HOFA*, as appropriate; and~~

~~2.~~ ~~submit a substantive application for approval of that designation in accordance with Rule S90;~~

~~before the expiry of the temporary approval or any extension of that approval by the *Bar Standards Board*, otherwise the *Bar Standards Board* may be entitled to suspend or revoke the authorisation or licence in accordance with Section 3.E10.~~

Part 4 – Qualification Rules

Contents

[1.56]

A APPLICATION

[1.57]

rQ1

Section 4.B applies to all *persons* who wish to be called to the *Bar* and to become qualified to practise as a *barrister*, to *pupil supervisors* and to *approved training organisations*.

rQ2

Section 4.C applies to all *practising barristers*

B BAR TRAINING RULES

B1 Purpose of the Bar Training Rules

[1.58]

Outcomes

oQ1

To ensure that any *person* who qualifies to *practise* as a *barrister* is a fit and proper *person*, and competent to do so.

Rules

rQ3

To be called to the *Bar* by an *Inn* a *person* must:

1. be a member of that *Inn*;
2. complete (or be exempted from):
   a. the Academic Stage, and
   b. the *Vocational stage*

   of training; and
3. fulfil any applicable requirement to attend *qualifying sessions*.

rQ4

To become qualified to *practise* as a *barrister* a *person* must:

1. be called to the *Bar* by an *Inn*;
2. complete (or be exempted from) the Professional Stage of training; and
3. satisfy such further requirements as are set out in Part 3 of this *Handbook*.

rQ5

The *Bar Standards Board* may charge such fees as it prescribes for dealing with applications, conducting assessments or examinations and issuing certificates under this Section 4.B.

rQ6

Any function or power which under this Section 4.B is exercisable by the *Bar Standards Board* may be delegated (and sub-delegated) to any committee, body or *person* to the extent permitted by the standing orders of the *Bar Standards Board*.

B2 Admissions to an Inn of Court

[1.59]

Eligibility for Admission

rQ7

To be eligible for *admission to an Inn* under this Section 4.B a *person* must:

1. have the necessary educational qualifications; and
2. be a fit and proper *person* to become a *practising barrister.*

rQ8

A *person* has the necessary educational qualifications to be admitted to an *Inn* if that *person*:

1. is reading for a qualifying law degree; or
2. is attending (or has been accepted for and is about to attend) a Conversion Course; or
3. has completed (or been exempted under Section 4.B7 from) the Academic Stage of training.

rQ9

A *person* is a fit and proper *person* to become a *practising barrister* if:

1. there is no reason to expect that that *person*, if admitted to an *Inn,* will engage in conduct which is dishonest or which otherwise makes that *person* unfit to become a *practising barrister*; and
2. that *person* does not suffer from serious incapacity due to mental disorder (within the meaning of the Mental Health Act 1983), addiction to alcohol or drugs or any other condition which makes that *person* unfit to become a *practising barrister.*

rQ10

In the case of an applicant who is authorised to *practise* by another *Approved Regulator* or who is a *Qualified European Lawyer*, a *certificate of good standing* is to be treated as conclusive evidence that the applicant is a fit and proper *person* to become a practising *barrister.*

rQ11

A *person* whose application for *admission to an Inn* has been rejected on the ground that that *person* is not a fit and proper *person* to become a practising *barrister* or who has been expelled from an *Inn* because of a disciplinary offence may not apply for *admission to an Inn* unless a period of at least five years (or such other period as the *Bar Standards Board* may determine in the particular case) has elapsed from the date of such rejection or expulsion.

Application Procedure

rQ12

To apply for *admission to an Inn* a *person* ("the applicant") must submit to the Inn:

1. a duly completed and signed application including an *admission declaration* in the form prescribed by the *Bar Standards Board* from time to time;
2. two certificates of good character which comply with the requirements in rQ13 below or, if the applicant is a *qualified lawyer*, a *certificate of good standing*, which (in either case) was issued within the previous three months; and
3. the fee prescribed by the Inn.

Certificates of Good Character

rQ13

A certificate of good character must contain the information specified by the *Bar Standards Board* from time to time and be provided by a professional *person* or *person* of standing in the community who:

1. has known the applicant for at least one year;
2. does not have a close family or personal relationship with the applicant; and
3. has read the *admission declaration* submitted by the applicant under Rule Q12.1.

Decision to Admit or Refuse Admission

rQ14

Before deciding whether to admit the applicant, the *Inn* may make any further enquiries or require the applicant to provide any further information that it considers relevant.

rQ15

The *Inn* must admit the applicant if the applicant:

1. is eligible for *admission to an Inn* and has given the undertaking on the *admission declaration* to commence the *Vocational stage* within five years of *admission to an Inn* and complete that Stage within ten years of admission; and
2. has complied with Rule Q12,

otherwise the *Inn* must reject the application and inform the applicant of its reasons for doing so.

rQ16

If the applicant falls within Rule Q17, the *Inn* must refer the question whether the applicant is a fit and proper *person* to become a *practising barrister* to the Inns' Conduct Committee to decide and must notify the applicant that it has done so.

rQ17

An applicant falls within this Rule Q17 if:

1. the applicant has been convicted of a *Criminal offence* (or is the subject of *pending Criminal Proceedings*); or
2. the applicant has been convicted of a disciplinary offence by a professional or regulatory body (or is the subject of pending proceedings for such an offence); or
3. the applicant has been the subject of a *Bankruptcy Order* or *director's disqualification order* or has entered into an individual voluntary arrangement with creditors; or
4. the applicant has previously been refused admission to or expelled from an *Inn*; or
5. there is any other circumstance which in the opinion of the *Inn* calls into question the applicant's fitness to become a *practising barrister.*

rQ18

When the Inns' Conduct Committee is asked to decide whether the applicant is a fit and proper *person* to become a *practising barrister*, it must send a report of its decision and the reasons for the decision to the applicant and to the Inn.

rQ19

If the Inns' Conduct Committee decides that the applicant is not a fit and proper *person* to become a *practising barrister* or if the *Inn* rejects an application for admission for any other reason, the applicant may request a review of the decision under Section 4.B10, provided that the request is made in writing to the *Bar Standards Board* within one month of the date when notice of the decision was given.

rQ20

If on a review under Section 4.B10 the *Bar Standards Board* is satisfied that the applicant is eligible for *admission to an Inn* and has complied with Rule Q12, the *Inn* must admit the applicant.

B3 The Academic Stage

[1.60]

rQ21

A *person* completes the Academic Stage of training by:

1. obtaining a qualifying law degree; or
2. obtaining a qualifying degree and successfully completing a Conversion Course.

rQ22

For the purpose of Rule Q21.1 a qualifying law degree is a qualifying degree approved by the *Bar Standards Board* which includes a course of study of the *foundations of legal knowledge*.

rQ23

For the purpose of Rule Q21.2 a qualifying degree is:

1. a degree of the required standard awarded by a *University* in the United Kingdom following a course of study of the minimum period; or
2. a degree awarded by a *University* or establishment of equivalent level outside the United Kingdom which the *Bar Standards Board* accepts as equivalent to a degree satisfying the requirements of Rule Q23.1.

and a *person* obtains a qualifying degree on being adjudged to have successfully completed the academic requirements of the degree irrespective of when the degree is actually conferred.

rQ24

For the purpose of Rule Q23.1, unless the *Bar Standards Board* on an application showing good grounds permits otherwise, the required standard is first or second class honours.

rQ25

A Conversion Course is a course approved by the *Bar Standards Board* which includes study of the *foundations of legal knowledge*.

rQ26

For the purpose of Rules Q22 and Q25, *foundations of legal knowledge* means those subjects the study of which is prescribed by the *Bar Standards Board* for the purposes of obtaining a qualifying law degree and for inclusion in any Graduate Conversion Course, and which currently comprise:

1. Obligations I (Contract).
2. Obligations II (Tort).
3. Criminal Law.
4. Public Law.
5. Property Law.
6. Equity & The Law of Trusts.
7. Foundations of EU Law.

B4 The Vocational Stage

[1.61]

rQ27

A *person* starts the *vocational stage* of training on starting to attend at a *Bar Professional Training Course*, and completes the *vocational stage* on being certified by the course provider that he has successfully completed a *Bar Professional Training Course*.

rQ28

Before starting the *vocational stage*, a *person* must:

1. have completed (or been exempted under Section 4.B7 from) the Academic Stage; and
2. have successfully completed the *Bar Course Aptitude Test* which is set by the *Bar Standards Board* from time to time; and
3. be a member of an *Inn* of Court.

rQ29

A *person* may not start the *vocational stage* more than five years after completing the Academic Stage except with the permission of the *Bar Standards Board* and after complying with any condition which *the Bar Standards Board* may impose.

B5 The Professional Stage

[1.62]

rQ30

A *person* starts the professional stage of training when he starts *pupillage* in accordance with this Section 4.B5 and completes the professional stage by:

1. satisfactorily completing 12 months of *pupillage* and such further training as may be required by the *Bar Standards Board*; and
2. being issued with a *full qualification certificate*.

rQ31

Before starting the professional stage, a *person* must have completed (or been exempted under Section 4.B7 from) the *vocational stage*.

rQ32

A *person* may not start the Professional Stage more than five years after completing the *vocational stage* except with the permission of the *Bar Standards Board* and after complying with any condition which the *Bar Standards Board* may impose.

Pupillage

rQ33

Pupillage is divided into two parts:

1. a non-practising period of six months; and
2. a practising period of six months.

rQ34

Except with the written permission of the *Bar Standards Board*, the non-practising period of *pupillage* must be done :

1. in a *Member State* of the European Union; and
2. in a continuous period of six months.

rQ35

Except with the written permission of the *Bar Standards Board*, the practising period of *pupillage* must:

1. start within 12 months after completion of the non-practising period;
2. be done in a *Member State*; and
3. be completed within an overall period of nine months.

rQ36

Any period of *pupillage* must provide training which is adequate and which complies with such criteria as may be published by the *Bar Standards Board*.

rQ37

Except as provided in Rule Q60, any period of *pupillage* must be done :

1. in an approved training organisation; and
2. with a barrister who is a registered pupil supervisor.

rQ38

During any period of *pupillage* the *pupil* must;

1. be diligent in receiving the instruction given; and
2. observe all legal and professional obligations of confidence.

Approved training organisations

rQ39

The *Bar Standards Board* may authorise any organisation as an *approved training organisation* subject to such terms as the *Bar Standards Board* may from time to time determine.

rQ40

The *Bar Standards Board* may withdraw approval from an *approved training organisation* if it considers after investigation:

1. that *pupillage* training provided by the organisation is or has been seriously deficient; or
2. that the organisation has not made proper arrangements for dealing with pupils and *pupillage* in accordance with the Code of Conduct.

rQ41

The *Bar Standards Board* will give notice in writing:

1. in the case of a decision to refuse to designate an organisation as an *approved training organisation*, to that organisation; and
2. in the case of a decision to withdraw approval from an *approved training organisation*, to:
    a. that organisation;
    b. any *person* who is undertaking or has agreed to undertake a *pupillage* in that organisation; and
    c. the *Inn* of which any such *person* is a member.

rQ42

Any *person* or organisation to whom the *Bar Standards Board* is required to give notice of a decision under Rule Q41 may ask for a review of the decision under Section 4.B10, provided that the request is made in writing to the *Bar Standards Board* within one month of the date when notice of the decision was given.

rQ43

If the *Bar Standards Board* withdraws approval from an *approved training organisation*, the organisation may not claim repayment of any *pupillage* award or other sum paid to any *pupil* or prospective *pupil*.

Acting as a Pupil Supervisor

rQ44

A barrister may act as a pupil supervisor if the barrister:

1. is on the register of approved *pupil supervisors* kept by the *Bar Standards Board*;

2. has a current practising certificate; and
3. has regularly practised as a *barrister* during the previous two years.

Registration as a Pupil Supervisor

rQ45

The *Bar Standards Board* may enter a *barrister* on the register of approved *pupil supervisors* if the *barrister* is approved by an *Inn* of which the *barrister* is a member.

rQ46

The *Bar Standards Board* may refuse to enter a *barrister* on the register of approved *pupil supervisors* if the *Bar Standards Board* finds that the *barrister* is unsuitable for any reason to act as a *pupil supervisor.*

rQ47

If the *Bar Standards Board* refuses to enter a *barrister* on the register of approved *pupil supervisors*, it will notify the *barrister* and the *Inn* which approved the *barrister* as a *pupil supervisor* of its decision and of the reasons for it.

rQ48

An Inn must approve a barrister as a pupil supervisor if:

1. the barrister has a current practising certificate;
2. the Inn is satisfied that the barrister has the necessary experience and is otherwise suitable to act as a pupil supervisor; and
3. the barrister has submitted an application in accordance with Rule Q50.

RQ49

To have the necessary experience to act as a *pupil supervisor* a *barrister* should normally:

1. have practised in the United Kingdom or another *Member State* as a *barrister* (other than as a *pupil* who has not completed *pupillage* in accordance with this Section 4.B5) or as a *person* authorised to exercise a *right of audience* or to *conduct litigation* by another *Approved Regulator* for a period for at least six years in the previous eight years; and
2. for the previous two years have regularly practised as a *barrister* and been entitled to exercise a *right of audience* before every *court* in England and Wales in relation to all proceedings.

Application Procedure to become a Pupil Supervisor

rQ50

A *barrister* who wishes to be entered on the register of approved *pupil supervisors* must submit to the *Inn* an application in the form currently prescribed by the *Bar Standards Board*. The application must be supported:

1. by an independent *person* who is a High Court Judge or Circuit Judge, a Leader of a Circuit, a Deputy High Court Judge, a Recorder, a Queen's Counsel, a Master of the Bench of an Inn, Treasury Counsel or a *person* of comparable standing who is able to comment from *person*al knowledge on the applicant's suitability to act as a *pupil supervisor*, and
2. Subject to Rule Q50.3 below,
3.
   a. in the case of a *self-employed barrister*, by the applicant's Head of *chambers*, or
   b. in the case of an employed *barrister*, by a more senior lawyer employed in the same organisation and who has direct knowledge of the work of the applicant;
4. If the applicant is a Head of *chambers*, or there is no more senior lawyer employed in the same organisation with the required knowledge, or for any other reason the support of the *person* referred to in Rule Q50.2 is not available, by a second *person* falling within Rule Q50.1 above.

Training of Pupil Supervisors

rQ51

The *Bar Standards Board*, in consultation with the Inns, may and will normally require *pupil supervisors* to undertake training before they may be entered or after they have been entered on the register of approved *pupil supervisors*.

Removal from the Register of Pupil Supervisors

rQ52

The *Bar Standards Board* may remove a *barrister*'s name from the register of approved *pupil supervisors* if the *barrister*:

1. ceases to practise as a *barrister* or is *suspended* from *practice* as a *barrister*; or
2. requests the *Bar Standards Board* in writing to be removed from the register; or
3. fails to complete any training required under Rule Q51; or
4. is found by the *Bar Standards Board* to be unsuitable for any reason to act as a *pupil supervisor*; or
5. has not acted as a *pupil supervisor* for the previous five years.

rQ53

If the *Bar Standards Board* decides that a *barrister*'s name should be removed from the register of approved *pupil supervisors*, it will notify the *barrister* and the *Inn* which approved the *barrister* as a *pupil supervisor* of its decision and of the reasons for it.

Duties of Pupil Supervisors

rQ54

A *pupil supervisor* must when responsible for supervising any pupil:

1. take all reasonable steps to provide the *pupil* with adequate tuition, supervision and experience;
2. have regard to any *pupillage* guidelines issued by the *Bar Standards Board* and to the Equality Code for the Bar; and
3. ensure that the *pupil* prepares for and attends any further training required by the *Bar Standards Board* such as advocacy training provided by the *pupil*'s Circuit or Inn.

rQ55

A *pupil supervisor* may not be responsible for supervising more than one *pupil* at a time except with the approval in writing of the *Bar Standards Board*.

Complaints about Pupil Supervisors

rQ56

If any complaint or other matter which appears to affect the suitability of a *barrister* to continue to act as a *pupil supervisor* comes to the notice of the *Inn* which approved the *barrister*, the *Inn* must inform the *Bar Standards Board* of the matter.

rQ57

If any complaint or other matter which appears to affect the suitability of a *barrister* to continue to act as a *pupil supervisor* comes to the notice of the *Bar Standards Board*, the *Bar Standards Board* will investigate the matter.

rQ58

After such an investigation, the *Bar Standards Board* may:

1. dismiss any complaint; or
2. take no action; or
3. if in its opinion the matter is such as to require informal treatment, draw it to the *barrister*'s attention in writing and if thought desirable direct the *barrister* to attend upon a nominated *person* for advice; or
4. if in its opinion the conduct disclosed shows that the *barrister* is unsuitable to act as a *pupil supervisor*, remove the name of the *barrister* from the register of approved *pupil supervisors*.

rQ59

A *barrister* whose application to be approved as a *pupil supervisor* is rejected or whose name is removed from the register of approved *pupil supervisors* may ask for a review of the decision under Section 4.B10, provided that the request is made in writing to the *Bar Standards Board* within one month of the date when notice of the decision was given.

External Training

rQ60

With the written permission of the *Bar Standards Board*, part or all of the practising period of *pupillage* may be satisfied by training:

1. with a *solicitor*, judge or other suitably *qualified lawyer* who is not a registered *pupil supervisor*; and/or
2. in an organisation which is not an *approved training organisation* but which, in the opinion of the *Bar Standards Board*, provides suitable training and experience.

Advertising

rQ61

Subject to Rule C114, all vacancies for *pupillage* must be advertised on a website designated by the *Bar Council* and the following information must be provided:

1. In respect of *chambers*:
   a. the name and address of *chambers*;
   b. the number of tenants;
   c. a brief statement of the work done by *Chambers*, e.g., "predominantly criminal";
   d. the number of *pupillage* vacancies;
   e. the level of award;
   f. the procedure for applying;
   g. the minimum educational or other qualifications required;
   h. the closing date for applications;
   i. the date by which the decisions will be made;
2. ~~in respect of entities:~~
   ~~a. the name and address of the *BSB authorised body*;~~
   ~~b. the number of *barristers* employed by that entity;~~
   ~~c. a brief statement of the work done by the entity, eg, "predominantly criminal";~~
   ~~d. the number of *pupillage* vacancies;~~
   ~~e. the level of award;~~
   ~~f. the procedure for application;~~
   ~~g. the minimum educational or other qualifications required;~~

~~h. the closing date for applications;~~

the date by which the decisions will be made.

Registration of Pupillage

rQ62

Before starting any period of *pupillage* (including any period of external training) a *person* must apply to the *Bar Standards Board* for registration of the *pupillage* by submitting an application in the form prescribed by the *Bar Standards Board.*

rQ63

The *Bar Standards Board* will register the *pupillage* if it is satisfied that the application has been duly completed and that the *pupillage* complies with this Section 4.B5.

rQ64

If a *person* applies to the *Bar Standards Board* for registration of a *pupillage* after the *pupillage* has started, the *pupillage* will be treated as having started on the date the application is received, unless the *Bar Standards Board* permits otherwise.

rQ65

If the *Bar Standards Board* refuses to register a *pupillage*, it will inform the *pupil* in writing of its decision and of the reasons for it.

rQ66

If the *Bar Standards Board* refuses to register a *pupillage*, the *pupil* may ask for a review of the decision under Section 4.B10, provided that the request is made in writing to the *Bar Standards Board* within one month of the date when notice of the decision was given.

rQ67

If any of the information provided in an application for registration of a *pupillage* changes before the *pupillage* has been completed, the *pupil* must promptly notify the *Bar Standards Board* in writing of the change.

Qualification Certificates

rQ68

On completion of the non-practising period of *pupillage*, the *Bar Standards Board* will issue the *pupil* with a *provisional qualification certificate* provided that the *pupil* has been called to the *Bar* under Section 4.B9 and the *Bar Standards Board* is satisfied:

1. that the *pupil* has satisfactorily completed the non-practising period of *pupillage* and any further training required under Rule Q30.1; and
2. that the *pupillage* is registered and complied with this Section 4.B5.

rQ69

When the pupil completes the practising period of pupillage, the Bar Standards Board will issue him with a full qualification certificate, if the pupil has a provisional qualification certificate and the Bar Standards Board is satisfied:

1. that the *pupil* has satisfactorily completed the practising period of *pupillage* and any further training required under Rule Q30.1; and
2. that the *pupillage* is registered, and has complied with this Section 4.B5.

rQ70

For the purpose of this Section 4.B5, a *pupil* is to be treated as having satisfactorily completed a period of *pupillage* if the *pupil*:

1. has been diligent in receiving the instruction given; and
2. has achieved the minimum level of competence required of a *pupil* at the end of the relevant period.

rQ71

The *Bar Standards Board* may accept as evidence that a *pupil* has satisfactorily completed any period of *pupillage* a certificate to this effect from the *pupil supervisor* (or the *person* responsible for external training) with whom the *pupil* has completed that period.

rQ72

If a *pupil supervisor* is unable or unwilling to provide a certificate that a *pupil* has satisfactorily completed a period of *pupillage*, the *Bar Standards Board* may accept such a certificate signed by the Head of *chambers* or *person* in charge of *pupillage* in the training organisation where the *pupillage* has been done if the certificate contains a satisfactory explanation of why the *pupil supervisor* has not signed it.

rQ73

If the *Bar Standards Board* is not satisfied:

1. that the *pupil* has satisfactorily completed a period of *pupillage*, and/or
2. that the *pupillage* is registered and complied with this Section 4.B5;

the *Bar Standards Board* may specify further training which the *pupil* must satisfactorily complete before the *Bar Standards Board* will issue the *pupil* with a *provisional qualification certificate* or a *full qualification certificate* (as the case may be).

rQ74

If the *Bar Standards Board* refuses to issue a *provisional qualification certificate* or a *full qualification certificate*, the *pupil* may ask for a review of the decision under Section 4.B10, provided that the request is made in writing to the *Bar Standards Board* within one month of the date when notice of the decision was given.

B6 Qualifying Sessions

[1.63]

rQ75

In this Part 4.B6 a qualifying session means an event (or part of an event) of an educational and collegiate nature arranged by or on behalf of an Inn;

rQ76

Subject to Rules Q77 and Q78, a *person* who is admitted to an *Inn* must attend 12 *qualifying sessions* during a period of no more than five years ending on the date on which that *person* is called to the Bar.

rQ77

An *Inn* may on an application showing such exceptional grounds as satisfy criteria agreed by all four Inns waive or modify the requirement to attend *qualifying sessions.*

rQ78

Each *Inn* is responsible, in cooperation with the other Inns, for:

1. ensuring that suitable *qualifying sessions* are available for its members; and
2. deciding what requirements must be satisfied for a *person* to be credited with attendance at one or more qualifying session*s*; and
3. agreeing criteria which specify the grounds on which the requirement to attend qualifying sessions may be waived or modified.

B7 Exemptions from Training Requirements

[1.64]

rQ79

The *Bar Standards Board* may grant exemptions from part or all of:

1. the Academic Stage,
2. the *vocational stage*, and/or
3. the Professional Stage,

of training.

rQ80

In exercising its discretion whether to grant an exemption from part or all of any Stage of training, the *Bar Standards Board* will determine whether the relevant knowledge and experience of the applicant make it unnecessary for the applicant to do such training.

rQ81

An exemption from part or all of any Stage of training may be granted unconditionally or subject to conditions, which may include in an appropriate case:

1. a requirement to do training instead of the training prescribed by this Section 4.B; and/or
2. a condition that the applicant must pass a *Bar* Transfer Test.

rQ82

Where the *Bar Standards Board* exempts a *person* from the Vocational or Professional Stage of training, it may also:

1. grant exemption in whole or in part from the requirement to attend *qualifying sessions*; and
2. specify the period within which any requirement to attend *qualifying sessions* must be fulfilled, which may be a period ending after the *person* concerned has been called to the *Bar* and in the case of a Specially Qualified Applicant is usually a period of three years during which the applicant must attend six *qualifying sessions* unless special circumstances apply.

Applications

rQ83

An application for exemption under this Section must be in such form as may be prescribed by the *Bar Standards Board* and contain or be accompanied by the following:

1. details of the applicant's educational and professional qualifications and experience;
2. evidence (where applicable) that the applicant is or has been entitled to exercise rights of audience before any court, specifying the rights concerned and the basis of the applicant's entitlement to exercise such rights;
3. any other representations or evidence on which the applicant wishes to rely in support of the application;
4. verified English translations of every document relied on which is not in the English language; and
5. the prescribed fee.

rQ84

Before deciding whether to grant any exemption under this Section, the *Bar Standards Board* may make any further enquiries or require the applicant to provide any further information that it considers relevant.

rQ85

A *person* whose application for exemption is rejected may ask for a review of the decision under Section 4.B10, provided that the request is made in writing to the *Bar Standards Board* within one month of the date when notice of the decision was given.

Full Exemption

rQ86

If the *Bar Standards Board* is satisfied that an applicant falls within Rule Q87, the *Bar Standards Board* will:

1. exempt the applicant from any Stage of training prescribed by this Section 4.B which the applicant has not fulfilled;
2. issue the applicant with a *full qualification certificate*; and
3. authorise the applicant to practise as a *barrister* on his being admitted to an *Inn* and called to the *Bar* under Section 4.B9 subject to complying with the Code of Conduct.

rQ87

The following categories of *person* fall within this Rule rQ87:

1. a *person* who has been granted rights of audience by an *authorised body* and is entitled to exercise those rights in relation to all proceedings in all courts of England and Wales;
2. subject to Rule Q88, a *person* who has been granted rights of audience by an *authorised body* and is entitled to exercise those rights in relation to either all proceedings in the High Court or all proceedings in the Crown Court of England and Wales (but not both);
3. a *barrister* of Northern Ireland who has successfully completed *pupillage* in accordance with the rules of the *Bar* of Northern Ireland;
4. subject to Rule Q89, a *Qualified European Lawyer.*

rQ88

The *Bar Standards Board* may exceptionally require an applicant who falls within Rule Q87.2 to do part or all of the practising six months of *pupillage* if it considers this necessary having regard in particular to the knowledge, professional experience and intended future *practice* of the applicant.

rQ89

Subject to Rules Q91 to Q95, the *Bar Standards Board* may require a *Qualified European Lawyer* to pass a *Bar Transfer Test* if the *Bar Standards Board* determines that:

1. the matters covered by the education and training of the applicant differ substantially from those covered by the Academic, Vocational and Professional Stages of training; and

2. the knowledge acquired by the applicant in the course of his professional experience does not fully cover this substantial difference.

Registered European Lawyers

rQ90

The Rules governing registration as a *Registered European Lawyer* in Section 3.D of this *Handbook*.

rQ91

The *Bar Standards Board* may not require an applicant who is a *Registered European Lawyer* and who falls within Rule Q93 or Q94 to pass a *Bar Transfer Test* unless it considers that the applicant is unfit to *practise* as a *barrister*.

rQ92

In considering whether to require an applicant who falls within Rule Q94 to pass a *Bar Transfer Test,* the *Bar Standards Board* must:

1. take into account the professional activities the applicant has pursued while a *Registered European Lawyer* and any knowledge and professional experience gained of, and any training received in, the law of any part of the United Kingdom and of the rules of professional conduct of the Bar; and
2. assess and verify at an interview the applicant's effective and regular pursuit of professional activities and capacity to continue the activities pursued.

rQ93

To fall within this Rule Q93 an applicant must have:

1. for a period of at least three years been a *Registered European Lawyer*; and
2. for a period of at least three years effectively and regularly pursued in England and Wales under a Home Professional Title professional activities in the law of England and Wales.

rQ94

To fall within this Rule Q94 an applicant must have:

1. for a period of at least three years been a *Registered European Lawyer*; and
2. for a period of at least three years effectively and regularly pursued in England and Wales professional activities under a Home Professional Title; and
3. for a period of less than three years effectively and regularly pursued in England and Wales under a Home Professional Title professional activities in the law of England and Wales.

rQ95

For the purpose of this Section 4.B17, activities are to be regarded as effectively and regularly pursued if they are actually exercised without any interruptions other than those resulting from the events of everyday life.

Partial Exemption

rQ96

If the *Bar Standards Board* is satisfied that an applicant falls within Rule Q96, the *Bar Standards Board* will:

1. exempt the applicant from the Academic Stage and the *vocational stage* and, if the *Bar Standards Board* thinks fit, from part or all of the Professional Stage of training; and
2. if the applicant is exempted from the whole of the non-practising six months of *pupillage*, issue the applicant with a *provisional qualification certificate*.

rQ97

The following categories of *person* fall within this Rule Q96:

1. a *person* who has been granted rights of audience by another Approved Regulator and is entitled to exercise those rights in relation to any class of proceedings in any of the *Senior Courts* or all proceedings in county courts or magistrates' courts in England and Wales;
2. a *Qualified Foreign Lawyer* who has for a period of at least three years regularly exercised full rights of audience in courts which administer law substantially similar to the common law of England and Wales;
3. a teacher of the law of England and Wales of experience and academic distinction.

Temporary Call to the Bar of Qualified Foreign Lawyers

rQ98

A *Qualified Foreign Lawyer* ("the applicant") who falls within Rule Q96.2 is entitled to be admitted to an *Inn* and called to the *Bar* on a temporary basis for the purpose of appearing as counsel in a particular case before a *court* of England and Wales without being required to satisfy any other requirements of this Section 4.B if the applicant has:

1. obtained from the *Bar Standards Board* and submitted to an *Inn* a *Temporary Qualification Certificate* specifying the case for the purposes of which the applicant is authorised to be called to the Bar;
2. duly completed and signed a *call declaration* in the form prescribed by the *Bar Standards Board* from time to time; and
3. paid the fee prescribed by the Inn.

rQ99

The *Bar Standards Board* will issue a Temporary Qualification Certificate if the applicant submits to the *Bar Standards Board*:

1. evidence which establishes that the applicant is a *Qualified European Lawyer* or falls within Rule Q96.2;
2. a *certificate of good standing*; and
3. evidence which establishes that a Professional *Client* wishes to instruct the applicant to appear as counsel in the case or cases for the purposes of which the applicant seeks temporary *call* to the Bar.

rQ100

Admission to an Inn and *call* to the *Bar* under Rule Q97 take effect when the applicant is given notice in writing by the *Inn* that the applicant has been admitted to the *Inn* and called to the *Bar* under Rule Q97 and automatically cease to have effect on conclusion of the case or cases specified in the applicant's Temporary Qualification Certificate.

B8 Conduct of Students

[1.65]

rQ101

References in this Section to "the Inn" are to any *Inn* of which the *student* concerned is a member.

rQ102

A *student* must observe any regulations about to conduct and discipline made by the Inn.

rQ103

If a student:

1. becomes the subject of *pending Criminal Proceedings* or is convicted of a *Criminal offence*, or
2. becomes the subject of pending disciplinary proceedings or is convicted of a disciplinary offence by a professional or regulatory body, or
3. is the subject of a *Bankruptcy Order* or *directors disqualification order* or enters into an individual voluntary arrangement with creditors, or
4. is found guilty by the course provider of cheating or other misconduct on a *Bar Professional Training Course*,

the *student* must immediately notify the *Inn* in writing.

rQ104

This Rule Q104 applies where notification is given or a *complaint* or report is made or it appears to an *Inn* from information given in the *student*'s *call declaration* or otherwise that a *student* of the *Inn* has or may have:

1. made any false statement or acted in breach of any undertaking given in the *student*'s *admission declaration* or *call declaration*; or
2. while a *student*:
   a. committed any breach of any regulations made by the *Inn* concerning the conduct and discipline of its members; or
   b. been convicted of a *Criminal offence*; or
   c. been convicted of a disciplinary offence by a professional or regulatory body; or
   d. been the subject of a *Bankruptcy Order* or *directors disqualification order* or entered into an individual voluntary arrangement with creditors; or
   e. been found guilty by the course provider of cheating or other misconduct on a *Bar Professional Training Course* (and has not successfully appealed against that finding); or
   f. otherwise been guilty of any conduct discreditable to a member of an Inn.

rQ105

Where Rule Q104 applies, the Inn:

1. may make any enquiries or require the *student* to provide such information as it may think fit; and
2. must consider whether the matter is a *serious matter*.

rQ106

If the *Inn* decides that the matter is not a *serious matter*, the *Inn* may deal with the matter under its internal disciplinary procedure and at the conclusion of that procedure may:

1. dismiss any complaint; or
2. decide to take no action; or
3. advise the *student* as to future conduct; or
4. reprimand the *student*; or
5. ban the *student* for a specified period from using some or all of the Inn's facilities.

rQ107

A *student* may appeal from a decision of an *Inn* under its internal disciplinary procedure to the Inns' Conduct Committee.

rQ108

If at any stage the *Inn* decides that the matter is a *serious matter*, the *Inn* must refer the matter to the Inns' Conduct Committee for determination. After determining the matter, the Inns' Conduct Committee must send a report of its findings and reasons to the *student* and to the Inn.

rQ109

If the Inns' Conduct Committee (or the *Bar Standards Board* on a review under Section 4.B11) finds a *serious matter* proved, it may:

1. advise the *student* as to future conduct; or
2. reprimand the *student*; or
3. order that the *student*'s *call* to the *Bar* be postponed for a specfied period; or
4. direct that the *student* be expelled from the *Inn* (in which case the *Inn* must expel the *student*).

rQ110

If the Inns' Conduct Committee finds a *serious matter* proved, the *student* may ask for a review under Section 4.B9 of the decision of the Inns' Conduct Committee, provided that the request is made in writing to the *Bar Standards Board* within one month of the date when notice of the decision was given.

rQ111

Where Rule Q104 applies, the *student* is not entitled to be called to the Bar:

1. until the *Inn* has decided that the matter is not a *serious matter*; or
2. if the *Inn* decides that the matter is a *serious matter*, until the matter has been determined; or
3. if the Inns' Conduct Committee (or the *Bar Standards Board* following a review under Section 4.B9) orders that the *student*'s *call* to the *Bar* be postponed for a specified period, until that period has expired.

B9 Call to the Bar

[1.66]

Requirements for Call

rQ112

Subject to Rules Q111, Q113 and, Q117 a *person* is entitled to be called to the *Bar* by an *Inn* of which that *person* is a member if that *person* has:

1. completed or been exempted from the *vocational stage* of training in accordance with this Section 4.B;
2. complied with any applicable requirement to attend *qualifying sessions*;

3. submitted to the *Inn* a duly completed and signed a *call declaration* in the form prescribed by the *Bar Standards Board* from time to time; and
4. paid the fee prescribed by the Inn.

rQ113

Before deciding whether a *person* who has complied with Rule Q112 ("the candidate") is entitled to be called to the Bar, the Inn:

1. may make any enquiries or require the candidate to provide any further information that it considers relevant;
2. must consider whether Rule Q113 applies; and
3. if Rule Q113 applies, must give effect to Rule Q111.

rQ114

If the *Inn* decides that the candidate is not entitled to be called to the Bar, the *Inn* must inform the candidate of its decision and of the reasons for it.

rQ115

If the *Inn* decides that the candidate is not entitled to be called to the Bar, the candidate may request a review of the decision under Section 4.B10, provided that the request is made in writing to the *Bar Standards Board* within one month of the date when notice of the decision was given by the Inn.

rQ116

If on a review under Section 4.B10 the *Bar Standards Board* decides that the candidate is entitled to be called to the Bar, the *Inn* must *call* the candidate to the Bar.

rQ117

Where it is alleged that the *call declaration* made by a *barrister* on *call* is false in any material respect or that the *barrister* has engaged before *call* in conduct which is dishonest or otherwise discreditable to a *barrister* and which was not, before *call*, fairly disclosed in writing to the Benchers of the *Inn* calling him or where any undertaking given by a *barrister* on *call* to the *Bar* is breached in any material respect that shall be treated as an allegation of a breach of this *Handbook* and will be subject to the provisions of Part 5.

Call Days and Procedure

rQ118

Calls to the *Bar* will take place on such days as may be authorised from time to time by the Inns' Council.

rQ119

A candidate must be called to the *Bar* in *person* unless given written permission by the *Inn* to be absent from the *call* ceremony.

B10 Review and Appeals

[1.67]

rQ120

Where provision is made under this Section 4.B for a review by the *Bar Standards Board* of a decision, any request for such a review must be accompanied by:

1. a copy of any notice of the decision and the reasons for it received by the *person* or organisation requesting the review ("the applicant");
2. where the decision is a decision of an *Inn* or of the Inns' Conduct Committee, copies of all documents submitted or received by the applicant which were before the *Inn* or the Inns' Conduct Committee (as the case may be);
3. any further representations and evidence which the applicant wishes the *Bar Standards Board* to take into account; and
4. the prescribed fee.

rQ121

Where the decision under review is a decision of an *Inn* or of the Inns' Conduct Committee, the *Bar Standards Board* will invite the *Inn* or the Inns' Conduct Committee (as the case may be) to comment on any further representations and evidence which the applicant submits under Rule Q120.3.

rQ122

On a review under this Section the *Bar Standards Board*:

1. may affirm the decision under review or substitute any other decision which could have been made on the original application;
2. may in an appropriate case reimburse the fee paid under Rule Q120.4; and
3. will inform the applicant and any other interested *person* of its decision and the reasons for it.

rQ123

Where under this Section 4.B provision is made for a review by the *Bar Standards Board* of a decision, no appeal may be made to *the Visitors to the Inns of Court* unless such a review has taken place.

rQ124

Subject to Rule Q123, a *person* or organisation who is adversely affected by a decision of the *Bar Standards Board* may appeal to *the Visitors to the Inns of Court* against the decision, in accordance with the *Hearings before the Visitors Rules.*

B11 Powers of the Inns

[1.68]

Inns' Conduct Committee

rQ125

Subject to this Section 4.B, the Inns' Conduct Committee shall have power to carry out the functions specified in the Inns' Conduct Committee Rules.

rQ126

The Inns' Conduct Committee Rules must be approved by the *Bar Standards Board* and any amendment to those rules will take effect on:

1. the date when the amendment is approved by the *Bar Standards Board*; or
2. such later date as the *Bar Standards Board* appoints.

rQ127

The *Bar Standards Board* may:

1. issue guidance which the Inns' Conduct Committee must follow in carrying out its functions; and
2. ask for information about the performance of those functions which the Inns' Conduct Committee must provide to the *Bar Standards Board*.

Other Powers

rQ128

Subject to the approval of the *Bar Standards Board*, an *Inn* may charge such fees as it prescribes for dealing with applications and calling *persons* to the *Bar* under this Section 4.B.

rQ129

Any function or power which under this Section 4.B is exercisable by an *Inn* or by the Inns' Conduct Committee may be delegated (and sub-delegated) to any committee, body or *person* to the extent permitted by the standing orders of the *Inn* or the Inns' Conduct Committee Rules (as the case may be).

C The CPD Rules

[1.69]

The Mandatory Continuing Professional Development Requirements

rQ130

For the purpose of this Section 4.C:

1. "calendar year" means a period of one year starting on 1 January in the year in question;
2. the "mandatory requirements" are those in Rules Q131 to Q136 below.
3. a "*pupillage* year" is any calendar year in which a *barrister* is at any time a *pupil*.

rQ131

Any practising *barrister* who, as at 1 October 2001, had started but not completed the period of three years referred to in the Continuing Education Scheme Rules at Annex Q to the Sixth Edition of the Code of Conduct must complete a minimum of 42 hours of continuing professional development during his first three years of *practice*.

Guidance on Rule Q131

gQ1

Rule Q131 is intended to apply only in those limited circumstances where a *barrister* started *practice* before 1 October 2001 but after the New Practitioners Programme ("NPP") first came into force, left *practice* before completing the NPP, but has since returned. Rule rQ131 requires them to finish their NPP during whatever is left of their first three years of *practice*.

rQ132

Any practising *barrister* who starts *practice* on or after 1 October 2001 must during the first three calendar years in which the *barrister* holds a practising certificate after any *pupillage* year complete a minimum of 45 hours of continuing professional development.

rQ133

Subject to Rule rQ134, any *barrister*:

1. must, if he holds a practising certificate or certificates throughout the whole of any calendar year, complete a minimum of 12 hours of continuing professional development during that period; and
2. must, if he holds a *practising certificate* or certificate for part only of a calendar year, complete one hour of continuing professional development during that calendar year for each month for which he holds a *practising certificate*.

rQ134

Rule Q133 does not apply:

1. in the case of a *barrister* to whom Rule Q131 applies, to any calendar year forming or containing part of the period of 3 years referred to in Rule rQ131; or
2. in the case of a *barrister* to whom Rule Q132 applies, during any *pupillage* year or during the first three calendar years in which the *barrister* holds a *practising certificate*.

rQ135

Any *practising barrister* must submit details of the continuing professional development he has done to the *Bar Standards Board* in the form prescribed, and at the time specified, by the *Bar Standards Board.*

rQ136

The *Bar Standards Board* may, by resolution, specify the nature, content and format of courses and other activities which may be done by *barristers* (or by any category of *barristers*) in order to satisfy the mandatory requirements.

rQ137

The *Bar Standards Board* may, by resolution and after consultation with the Inns, Circuits and other providers as appropriate, increase the minimum number of hours of continuing professional development which must be completed in order to satisfy any of the mandatory requirements.

Part 5 – Enforcement Regulations

Contents

[1.70]

A THE COMPLAINTS REGULATIONS

A1 Powers and Functions of the PCC

[1.71]

rE1

The membership of the *PCC* shall be as prescribed by the Standing Orders of the *Bar Standards Board* from time to time.

rE2

The powers of the *PCC* shall be as set out in this Part 5, and shall include (but not be limited to) the power:

1. to consider *complaints* made by *persons* other than the *Bar Standards Board*;
2. to raise *complaints* on behalf of the *Bar Standards Board*, and to withdraw such *complaints*;

3. to determine whether any *complaint*:

   a. discloses a potential breach of the *Handbook*; and/or

   b. discloses a potential case of *professional misconduct*; and/or

   c. potentially satisfies the *disqualification condition*,

   and if so to deal with it in accordance with this Section 5.A;

4. to direct the investigation of *complaints*;

5. to seek, in appropriate cases, to resolve *complaints* using the *determination by consent procedure*;

6. to bring and prosecute charges of *professional misconduct* or make an application for *disqualification* before *Disciplinary Tribunals* (as provided by Section 5. B);

7. to seek an immediate interim suspension or immediate *disqualification order* in accordance with Section 5.D of this *Handbook*;

8. to seek an interim suspension or disqualification order in accordance with Section 5.D of this Handbook;

9. to refer *practising barristers* to a Fitness to Practise panel in accordance with Section 5.E of this *Handbook*;

10. to refer to *disciplinary tribunals* any *legal aid complaint* relating to the conduct of a *BSB regulated person* and to be responsible for prosecuting any such charges or *legal aid complaints* before such *disciplinary tribunals*;

11. to refer any *complaint* for supervisory action by the *supervision team*;

12. to take such other actions in relation to *complaints* or infringements of the *handbook* as are permitted by this Section 5.A;

13. to impose, or direct the imposition, of an *administrative sanction* in accordance with the provisions of rE37.3 below;

14. to make recommendations on matters of professional conduct to the *Bar Standards Board* or to any of its committees, as the *PCC* may think appropriate; and

15. to make rulings on matters of professional conduct in accordance with the *determination by consent procedure*.

rE3

The *PCC* and the Chairman of the *PCC* shall each have the power to authorise any *person*, group or body to fulfill any function or exercise any power given to them by this Section 5.A. Any authorisations given under rE3 must be in writing and may be either or both retrospective and prospective, and either or both general and for a particular purpose.

rE4

Save in respect of the matters dealt with at rE29.2 (time limits for making a *complaint*), the *PCC* or the Chairman of the *PCC* shall have the power to extend any time limits prescribed by this Section 5.A, in their absolute discretion, whenever it appears to be appropriate to do so.

rE5

In determining which of its powers under this Section 5.A to use the *PCC* will take into account all the circumstances, including:

1. the *enforcement strategy* and any other published *Bar Standards Board* policy that appears to the PCC to be relevant; and
2. any other factor relevant to the issue including whether it is appropriate, sufficient, proportionate and effective, in the public interest, to proceed in that manner.

rE6

The *PCC* may at any time postpone consideration of a *complaint*, whether to permit further investigation of the *complaint* to be made, or during the currency of related legal proceedings, or for any other reason it sees fit.

rE7

The *PCC* may at any time seek information or assistance, orally or in writing, as it thinks fit, from any *person*, group or body.

rE8

If at any time the *PCC* decides in accordance with this Section 5.A:

1. to refer a *complaint* to another *person* or body for consideration; or
2. to dismiss or take no further action on a *complaint*; or
3. to postpone consideration of a *complaint*;

it must give written reasons for that decision, and provide those reasons to the *relevant person* against whom the *complaint* was made and (where the *complaint* was made by a *person* other than the *Bar Standards Board*) the complainant.

rE9

Any *complaint* received from a *person* other than the *Bar Standards Board* shall first be dealt with by the *PCC* in accordance with Section 5.A2 and, where relevant, shall then be considered by the *PCC* in accordance with Section 5.A3 below.

rE10

Any *complaint* raised by the *Bar Standards Board* itself shall be considered by the *PCC* in accordance with Section 5.A3 below.

A2 Initial Procedure to be followed by the PCC when dealing with complaints received from persons other than the Bar Standards Board

[1.72]

Referral of complaints to other persons or to the supervision team

rE11

When it receives a *complaint*, the *PCC* must first consider whether it is appropriate to refer the *complaint* to another *person* or to the *supervision team*, accordance with rE13 to rE28 below. If at any time the *PCC* decides to refer a *complaint* to another *person* or body for consideration or to the *supervision team* it must give written reasons for that decision, and provide such reasons to the *relevant person* against whom the *complaint* was made and the complainant.

rE12

The PCC's decision under rE11 is final and no one has the right to appeal against it.

Reference to the Legal Ombudsman

rE13

If a *complaint* is made by or on behalf of a *client* of a *BSB regulated person* (excluding for the purposes of this rE13 only, unregistered barristers) against that *BSB regulated person* ~~(or, in the case of a *BSB authorised body*, such a *complaint* is made against any individual working as an *employee* or *manager* of such *BSB authorised body*)~~, the *PCC* must refer such *complaint* without further consideration to the *Legal Ombudsman*, or will signpost the complainant to the *Legal Ombudsman* and must in the case of a referral notify the complainant of the referral, unless it is clear on the face of the *complaint* that the matter falls outside the jurisdiction of the *Legal Ombudsman*.

rE14

If a *complaint* is made by or on behalf of a *client* of an *unregistered barrister* against that *unregistered barrister*, the PCC may refer such complaint to the Legal Ombudsman if it is satisfied that the Legal Ombudsman may have jurisdiction in relation to such complaint, and the PCC shall notify the complainant of the referral.

rE15

For the avoidance of doubt, such a referral does not prevent the immediate operation of the *Interim Suspension* and Disqualification *Regulations* or the *Fitness to Practise Regulations*, where appropriate.

rE16

When a *complaint* is referred, or referred back, to the *Bar Standards Board* by the *Legal Ombudsman*, rE29 and following, below, apply.

Reference to chambers/~~BSB authorised bodies~~

rE17

If it appears to the *PCC* that a *complaint* against a *relevant person* (which is not a *complaint* made by or on behalf of *BSB regulated person's client* against that *BSB regulated person*) may appropriately be resolved by:

1. *chambers* (where the *complaint* is against a *self-employed barrister* who is a member of, or other *relevant person* who is working at, such *chambers* at the relevant time); ~~or~~

~~2.~~ ~~*a BSB authorised body* (where the *complaint* is against a *BSB authorised body* or the *complaint* is against *a relevant person* acting in their capacity as a *manager* or *employee* of such *BSB authorised body* at the relevant time),~~

3. the *PCC* may refer the *complaint* to the *chambers* ~~or *BSB authorised body*~~ for investigation and resolution. For the avoidance of doubt, where a *complaint* is made against an *employed barrister* (*authorised non-BSB body*) or an *employed barrister* (*non-authorised body*), the provisions of rE28 apply.

rE18

When deciding whether to refer a *complaint* in accordance with rE16 above, the *PCC* must take into account all the circumstances, including the factors referred to at rE4 above, and the relationship (if any) between the complainant and the relevant *chambers*/~~*BSB authorised body*~~ and whether such a relationship continues.

rE19

The *PCC* must consider whether the *complaint* should be dismissed on the grounds that it has not been made within the period identified in rE29.2 below before it decides whether to refer the *complaint* to the relevant *chambers* /~~*BSB authorised body*~~ in accordance with rE17 above.

rE20

Where a *complaint* is referred to the relevant *chambers*/~~*BSB authorised body*~~ in accordance with rE17 above, the PCC will send any information held by it relating to the *complaint* to the head of *chambers* or to the *person* nominated by the *chambers* as being responsible for such issues (in the case of a referral to *chambers*) ~~or to the *HOLP* (in the case of a referral to a *BSB authorised body*)~~.

rE21

Following a referral to a *chambers*/~~*BSB authorised body*~~ in accordance with rE17 above, the *PCC* must inform the complainant of the complainant's rights under rE22.2 below.

rE22

If:

1. the *PCC* considers that progress made by the *chambers/~~BSB authorised body~~* in investigating and resolving the *complaint*, or the outcome of such an investigation, is unsatisfactory; or
2. a complainant informs the *PCC* that he is dissatisfied with the progress or outcome of the *chambers/~~BSB authorised body's~~* investigation, giving reasons for such dissatisfaction,

then the *PCC* must consider the *complaint* in accordance with rE29 and following below.

Reference where BSB regulated individual acting in judicial or quasi-judicial capacity

rE23

If it appears to the *PCC* that the *complaint* arises out of a *relevant person's* actions in a part-time or temporary judicial or quasi-judicial capacity, it must act as follows:

1. if it appears to the *PCC* that the *complaint* would otherwise fall to be dismissed under this Section 5.A, the *PCC* must dismiss it; or
2. if it appears to the *PCC* that the *complaint* would otherwise not fall to be dismissed, the *PCC* must refer the *complaint* without further consideration to the Office of Judical Complaints and/or *person* or body responsible for the appointment of the *relevant person* to the judicial or quasi-judicial office concerned (whether the Lord Chancellor, a Minister of the Crown or other *person* or body as appropriate) ("the appropriate body"), requesting the appropriate body to notify the *PCC* when the *complaint* has been dealt with and of any action taken by it. Where the appropriate body is a *person* other than the Lord Chancellor or a Minister of the Crown, and where the *PCC* considers it inappropriate to refer the *complaint* to the appropriate body, or where the appropriate body refuses to deal with a *complaint*, the *PCC* must consider the *complaint* and, subject to rE25 below, direct it to be proceeded with in accordance with rE29 and following below.

rE24

If the appropriate body, having dealt with a *complaint*, believes that it may be appropriate for it to be considered further by the *Bar Standards Board*, the *appropriate body may*, subject to rE25 below, refer the matter back to the *Bar Standards Board* and, following such referral, the *PCC* may reconsider the *complaint* and may, if it sees fit, direct it to be proceeded with in accordance with rE29 and following below.

rE25

No such reference to the *Bar Standards Board* as is mentioned in rE24 above by the appropriate body shall be acted upon by the *PCC*, nor shall the *PCC* exercise the powers under the last sentence of rE23.2 above, in respect of a *complaint* relating to anything said or done by the *BSB regulated individual* in the exercise of his judicial functions or affecting the independence of the *BSB regulated person* in his judicial or quasi-judicial capacity.

Reference to the Lord Chancellor or appropriate body

rE26

If it appears to the *PCC* that the *complaint* relates to the conduct of a *BSB regulated individual* who, since the events giving rise to the *complaint* took place, has been appointed to and continues to hold full-time judicial office and has ceased *practice*, the *PCC* shall not consider the *complaint* further and must inform the complainant that his *complaint* should be directed to the Lord Chancellor or the Office of Judical Complaints or to such other *person* or appropriate body with responsibility for addressing complaints about judges.

Reference to the supervision team

rE27

If it appears to the *PCC* that a *complaint* received in respect of a *relevant person* relates to a matter which might more appropriately be dealt with by the *supervision team* rather than investigation in accordance with rE29 onwards, it may refer the *complaint* to the *supervision team*. If, the *supervision team* then concludes that the *complaint* is best dealt with more formally by the *PCC* in accordance with rE29 onwards, then the *supervision team* may refer the *complaint* back to the *PCC*. The *PCC* must then deal with the *complaint* in accordance with rE29 and following below.

Reference to any other person

rE28

If it appears to the *PCC* that a *complaint* received in respect of a *relevant person* relates to a matter which might more appropriately be dealt with by an *Inn*, Circuit, *employer* or any other professional or regulatory body (including, for the avoidance of doubt, any other *approved regulator*), it may refer the *complaint* to such other body. If, having referred a *complaint* to another body under rE28, the *PCC* subsequently considers that the *complaint* has not been dealt with by that other body within a reasonable time or fully or satisfactorily, the *PCC* may in its discretion then choose to consider the *complaint* in accordance with rE11 above and/or rE29 and following below.

PCC's powers before investigation of complaints

rE29

In determining whether a *complaint* raised by a person other than the *Bar Standards Board* potentially discloses a breach of the *Handbook*, a potential case of *professional misconduct* or a breach of the *Handbook* satisfying the *disqualification condition*, and whether, if it does, it is apt for further consideration, the *PCC* must first consider:

1. whether the *complaint* concerns a *relevant person*; and
2. whether the *complaint* has been made:
    a. within twelve months of the conduct of which *complaint* is made, or
    b. where a complainant has indicated to the *PCC* his dissatisfaction with

the outcome of a chambers~~/BSB authorised body's~~ investigation in accordance with rE22 above, within three months of the end of the investigation by chambers~~/BSB authorised body~~, whichever is the later; and

in either case, where the conduct of which a *complaint* is made is (or was) continuing or consisted of a series of related acts or omissions, the conduct must for the purposes of this rule be treated as having taken place at the time when the continuing conduct ceased or at the date of of the last of any such acts or omissions.

rE30

Where the *PCC* decides that the *complaint* does not relate to a *relevant person* or that it relates to a *non-authorised person* in circumstances where the nature of the *complaint* is unlikely to satisfy the *disqualification condition*, it must dismiss the *complaint.*

rE31

Where the *PCC* decides that the *complaint* has not been made within the period identified in rE29.2 above it must dismiss the *complaint* unless it decides that further consideration of the complaint is justified in the public interest, having regard to the *regulatory objectives.*

rE32

Where the *PCC* has not dismissed a *complaint* in accordance with rE30 or rE31 above, the *PCC* must next consider, having regard to the *enforcement strategy*, whether further consideration of the *complaint* is justified. If the *PCC* considers that:

1. the *complaint* for any reason lacks substance; or
2. the *complaint* cannot be properly or fairly investigated; or
3. the *complaint* or its consequences are insufficiently serious to justify further action; or
4. for any other reason the *complaint* is not apt for further consideration,

then the *PCC* must dismiss the *complaint*, although it may also elect in such circumstances to refer the matter for to the *supervision team* in accordance with rE27 above (except that the *supervision team* can not refer the matter back to the *PCC* unless and until further evidence comes to light such that the matter would warrant further consideration by the *PCC*). The *PCC* must give written reasons for referring the matter to the *supervision team.*

rE33

If a *complaint* is not dismissed by the *PCC* after its initial consideration, it must be investigated and dealt with in the manner set out in Section 5.A3 below and the complainant and *barrister* must be informed, in writing, that such an investigation is to take place.

A3 Procedure for dealing with complaints to be handled by the PCC – general

[1.73]

Investigation of complaints

rE34

The investigation of *complaints* must be conducted by the Professional Conduct Department under the direction of the *PCC*.

rE35

When an investigation into a *complaint* is complete, the *PCC* must exercise the powers given to it by rE36 and following below.

Additional potential breaches of the Handbook

rE36

If in the course of its investigation or consideration of a *complaint* ("*the original complaint*") the *PCC* considers that there is any matter other than that originally complained of which might give rise to a potential breach of this *Handbook*, and/or a potential case of *professional misconduct*, and/or potentially satisfy the *disqualification condition*, the *PCC* may raise a *complaint* about that matter on behalf of the *Bar Standards Board* ("*the new complaint*").

1. Then, unless the new matter falls within rE36.2 below:
   a. *the new complaint* must be investigated in the manner set out in rE34 and following above;
   b. the *PCC* must not consider whether there is a *realistic prospect of a finding of professional misconduct* or a *realistic prospect of the disqualification condition being satisfied* in respect of *the new complaint* unless and until the *relevant person* has been given the opportunity to comment in writing on the matter complained of in *the new complaint*. The *PCC* must take any comments made by the *relevant person* into account when it decides whether there is a *realistic prospect of a finding of professional misconduct* or a *realistic prospect that the disqualification condition will be satisfied* in respect of *the new complaint*;
   c. the *PCC* may defer further consideration of *the original complaint* until the *the new complaint* has been investigated.
2. No further investigation or opportunity to respond is required where the subject matter of *the new complaint* has already been investigated in the course of investigations into *the original complaint* and the *relevant person* has already been given an opportunity to comment thereon.

PCC consideration of complaints

rE37

When any investigation is complete, the *PCC* must consider the *complaint*, together with the results of any investigation thereof, and may conclude (having regard to the *enforcement strategy* and any other published *Bar Standards Board* policy that appears to the *PCC* to be relevant) in respect of *complaints* made against a *relevant person* (but subject always to rE37 and rE40 below):

1. that the conduct did not constitute a breach of the *Handbook*, in which case the *PCC* must dismiss the *complaint* and rE43 to rE45 apply; or
2. that the conduct did constitute a breach of the *Handbook* (on the balance of probabilities) but that, in all the circumstances, no further action should be taken in respect of the breach in which case rE46 to rE49 apply; or
3. that the conduct did constitute a breach of the *Handbook* (on the balance of probabilities) and that that breach should be dealt with by an *administrative sanction* in which case rE50 to rE55 apply; or
4. that the conduct may constitute a breach of the *Handbook*; and (ii) if such breach were to be proved, that an *administrative sanction* pursuant to rE37.3 would not be appropriate in all the circumstances, in which case rE38, rE41, rE42 and rE56 to rE66 apply; or
5. that the subject matter of the *complaint* against a BSB *regulated person* involves a *conviction* for an offence of dishonesty or deception, in which case the *PCC* must direct that the *complaint* should form the subject matter of a charge before a *Disciplinary Tribunal* in which case rE42 and rE56 to rE66 shall apply.

rE38

Where the *PCC* has concluded that rE37.4 is applicable, it must refer the *complaint* to a *Disciplinary Tribunal*, subject to rE40, provided that no complaint shall be referred unless the *PCC* is satisfied that:

1. there is a *realistic prospect of a finding of professional misconduct being made* or there is a *realistic prospect of the disqualification condition being satisfied*; and
2. that it is in the public interest, having regard to the *regulatory objectives* to pursue disciplinary proceedings.

rE39

For the avoidance of doubt, where the *relevant person* is a *non-authorised individual* the *PCC* may not impose an *administrative sanction* or make a referral to a Disciplinary Tribunal on charges of *professional misconduct*. The *PCC* may only decide to dismiss the *complaint*, take no further action or make an application to the *Disciplinary Tribunal* that the *non-authorised individual* be subject to a disqualification order.

rE40

The *PCC* must not conclude that any conduct alleged by an external complainant did constitute a breach of the *Handbook* (on the balance of probabilities) if the *relevant person* has not had a reasonable opportunity to respond in writing to the allegation on which the the *complaint* is based unless the matter has already been investigated by the *Legal Ombudsman*. For the avoidance of doubt, complaints referred to the *PCC* by the *supervision team* are not caught by this requirement.

rE41

Where the *PCC* is minded to refer the matter to a *Disciplinary Tribunal* for determination it may, in appropriate cases and with the consent of the *defendant*, instead direct that the *complaint* be subject to the *determination by consent procedure* (under Section 5.A4 below).

rE42

Where the *BSB regulated person* referred to a *Discplinary Tribunal* is a *registered European Lawyer*, the *PCC* shall:

1. inform the professional body of which the registered **European lawyer** is a member in his home *Member State*;
2. offer the professional body the opportunity to make representations to the *Disciplinary Tribunal* to which the complaint has been referred or (where the *determination by consent procedure* is used) to the *PCC*; and
3. inform the professional body of findings made by the Discplinary Tribunal, the *PCC* or any other *Bar Standards Board* Panel.

A4 Possible outcomes of an investigation of a complaint under Section 5.A3

[1.74]

Dismissal

rE43

Where a decision to dismiss a *complaint* in accordance with rE37.1 is being taken at a meeting of the *PCC* and not by some other person, group or body authorised in accordance with rE3 of this Section 5.A, the majority of the *lay members* present at the meeting must consent to such dismissal.

rE44

Where the *PCC* takes the decision to dismiss a *complaint*, but the *BSB regulated person's* conduct is nevertheless such as to give cause for concern, the *PCC* may in those circumstances, and either before or after any disposal of the *complaint*, do any or both of the following:

1. draw to the *BSB regulated person's* attention in writing the *PCC's* concerns;
2. advise him as to his future conduct either in writing or by directing him to attend on the Chairman of the *PCC* or on some other *person* nominated by the *PCC*, to receive such advice.

rE45

Any decision by the *PCC* to dismiss a *complaint* must only be disclosed in accordance with rE92 and rE93.

No further action

rE46

Where the *PCC* decides to take *no further action* in respect of a *complaint* in accordance with rE37.2, the *PCC* shall write to the relevant *BSB regulated person*:

1. notifying him of the provisions of the *Handbook* which the *PCC* has concluded were breached by him and that the *PCC* has decided in this instance to take no further action; and
2. informing him of the consequences of its decision (including that the decision will be formally recorded and will be disclosable to third parties, where relevant, that it will be notified to the *supervision team* and, where relevant in accordance with rE47, that it will be notified to the *Barrister's Inn*); and
3. confirming that if the *BSB regulated person* objects to the decision taken by the *PCC* that he may ask for that the matter to be referred for resolution by a *Disciplinary Tribunal* in accordance with rE49; and
4. where the *PCC* considers it appropriate in all the circumstances, advising him on to his future conduct either in writing or by directing him to attend on the Chairman of the *PCC* or on some other *person* nominated by the *PCC*, to receive such advice.

rE47

If, when deciding to take no further action on a *complaint* in respect of a *Barrister*, the *PCC* nonetheless considers that the circumstances of the *complaint* are relevant to the *Barrister's* position as a *pupil supervisor*, it may notify the *Barrister's Inn* of its concern in such manner as it sees fit.

rE48

Any decision by the *PCC* to take no further action will be formally recorded, will be disclosable to certain third parties (in accordance with the *Bar Standards Board's* policy on publication and disclosure) and may, where appropriate, be referred to the *supervision team* for continuing monitoring and supervision, but will not be made public.

rE49

The *BSB regulated person* shall have the right to object to a decision of the *PCC* to take no further action in accordance with Section 5.A5 by asking for that the matter to be referred for resolution by a *Disciplinary Tribunal*.

Administrative fines and warnings

rE50

Pursuant to rE37.3 above, the *PCC* may impose an *administrative sanction* on a *BSB regulated person* only where:

1. there is sufficient evidence on the balance of probabilities of a breach of the *Handbook* by that *person*; and
2. the *PCC* considers that to impose an *administrative sanction* is a proportionate and sufficient in the public interest.

rE51

In determining the level of *administrative sanction* to be imposed, the *PCC* must have due regard to the *enforcement strategy* and may have regard to such other matters as the *Bar Standards Board* may consider relevant from time to time.

rE52

The maximum level of a fine which can be imposed by the *PCC* under rE51 is:

1. £1,000 (one thousand pounds) where the fine is to be imposed on a *BSB regulated individual*; ~~and~~
2. ~~£1,500 (one thousand and five hundred pounds) where the fine is to be imposed on a *BSB authorised body*.~~

rE53

Any decision by the *PCC* to impose an administrative fine or warning will be formally recorded and may, where appropriate, be referred to the *supervision team* for continuing monitoring and supervision but will not be disclosed to any third parties except in accordance with rE92 and rE93.

rE54

Any failure by the *BSB regulated person* to pay the administrative fine within the relevant time is likely to be treated as *professional misconduct* and shall entitle the *PCC* to refer the matter to a full *Disciplinary Tribunal* for disposal.

rE55

The *BSB regulated person* may appeal a decision of the *PCC* to impose an *administrative sanction* in accordance with Section 5.A5.

Disciplinary charges

rE56

If the *PCC* directs under rE37.5 or rE38 above that a *complaint* shall form the subject matter of a charge of *professional misconduct* before a *Disciplinary Tribunal* and/or that an application should be made to a *Disciplinary Tribunal* for a *disqualification order*, the following rules apply.

rE57

At the same time as the *PCC* directs that a *complaint* shall form the subject matter of a disciplinary charge and/or *disqualification application* before a *Disciplinary Tribunal*, the *PCC* must also decide whether a three-person panel or a five-person panel is to be constituted.

rE58

Where the direction is made pursuant to rE37.5 (*complaint* involving *conviction* for dishonesty or deception), the *PCC* must direct that a five-person panel is to be constituted.

rE59

In all other cases, in deciding whether to direct the constitution of a three-person or a five-person panel, the *PCC* shall consider the sanction which it considers is likely to be imposed on the *relevant person* if the charge or application is proved, having regard to:

1. any applicable sentencing policy and guidelines issued by the *Bar Standards Board* and/or the *Council of the Inns of Court* from time to time; and
2. the previous disciplinary record of the *relevant person*; and
3. any deferred sentence which would be activated if the *relevant person* were to be found guilty of the charges alleged.

rE60

The *PCC*:

1. shall direct that a five-*person* panel is to be constituted if the *PCC* considers that:
   a. the *BSB authorised individual* would be likely to be disbarred or *suspended* from *practice* for more than twelve months; or
   b. that the *relevant person* would be likely to be *disqualified* indefinitely or for a defined term of more than twelve months; ~~or~~
   ~~c.~~ ~~that the *BSB authorised body* would be likely to have its authorisation or licence revoked or *suspended* for a period of more than twelve months;~~
2. may refer to a five *person* panel where it considers it desirable to have a broader range of expertise available, having regard to the subject matter of the complaint.

   Otherwise, the *PCC* must direct that a three-*person* panel is to be constituted

rE61

The *PCC* must inform the *BSB regulated person* and the complainant (if any) of the direction that it has made pursuant to rE57. No one may appeal against the decision taken by the *PCC* under that **RULE** (and those following).

rE62

Where the *PCC* directs that a three-person panel is to be constituted, the *PCC* may, if it thinks fit, recommend that a Judge rather than a QC be appointed to act as Chairman of the Panel, giving reasons for any such recommendation.

rE63

The *PCC* may :

1. refer to the same *Disciplinary Tribunal* any charges and/or *disqualification* applications which the *PCC* considers may conveniently be dealt with together;
2. refer any additional charges or *disqualification* applications relating to the same *BSB regulated person* to the *Disciplinary Tribunal* which is dealing with the original disciplinary charge or *disqualification* application (as the case may be), even if the additional charge or application, by itself, may be regarded as insufficiently serious to merit disposal by a *Disciplinary Tribunal* of that level.

rE64

The *PCC*:

1. may direct that the prosecution of the charges be expedited if it considers that one or more of the following conditions is satisfied:
   a. the facts of the *complaint* are unlikely to be disputed (for example because it involves a criminal *conviction*); or
   b. witnesses are unlikely to be called for the hearing; or
   c. the case should be resolved urgently; or
   d. there is some other good reason for expedition; and
2. must direct that the prosecution of the charges be expedited if the *defendant* has requested an expedited hearing under Section 5.D.

rE65

When the *PCC* has directed that a *complaint* shall form the subject matter of a charge or application before a *Disciplinary Tribunal*, the *PCC* must be responsible for bringing the charge or application on behalf of the *Bar Standards Board* and prosecuting that charge before such *Disciplinary Tribunal*. If so:

1. the *PCC* may arrange for the appointment of counsel to settle the charge and to present the case before the *Disciplinary Tribunal*; and
2. any charges shall be brought in the name and on behalf of the *Bar Standards Board*.

rE66

Section 5.B applies in respect of the procedure to be followed by the *Disciplinary Tribunal*.

A5 Determination by consent

[1.75]

rE67

A *complaint* which the *PCC* is otherwise intending to refer to the *Disciplinary Tribunal* in accordance with rE38 above may, with the consent of the *relevant person* against whom the *complaint* is made, be finally determined by the *PCC*. This is referred to as the "*determination by consent procedure*".

rE68

The circumstances in which the *determination by consent procedure* is to be used, and how it is to be used, are set out below.

rE69

The *PCC* must, in deciding whether to make a *complaint* subject to the *determination by consent procedure*, consider all the circumstances. The *PCC* may make the *complaint* subject to the *determination by consent procedure* only if:

1. the *relevant person* submits to the jurisdiction of the *PCC*; and
2. the *PCC* considers that:
    a. there is a realistic prospect of a finding of professional misconduct being made or there is *a realistic prospect of the disqualification condition being satisfied* in respect of the complaint; and
    b. there are no substantial disputes of fact which can only fairly be resolved by oral evidence being taken; and
    c. there are no exceptional circumstances which would warrant no further action being taken on the complaint or the *complaint* being dismissed; and
    d. having regard to the *regulatory objectives*, it is in the public interest to resolve the *complaint* under the *determination by consent procedure*; and
    e. the potential professional misconduct or disqualification condition, if proved, combined with:
        i. the *relevant person's* previous disciplinary history, and
        ii. any deferred sentences which would be activated if the breach or breaches were proved,

    do not appear to be such as to warrant a period of suspension or disbarment, ~~the withdrawal of an *authorisation* or *licence* (as appropriate)~~ or the imposition of a *disqualification order* (or equivalent by another *Approved Regulator*).

rE70

The *determination by consent procedure* will be conducted in accordance with such procedures as the *PCC* may prescribe from time to time.

rE71

The *PCC* may terminate the *determination by consent procedure* at any time if it no longer considers that the requirements of rE69 are satisfied, or for any other good reason.

rE72

If the *determination by consent procedure* ends other than by a finding and sentence to which the *relevant person* consents, then the *complaint* may be referred to a full *Disciplinary Tribunal*.

rE73

The *PCC* must publish any finding and sentence resulting from the *determination by consent procedure* to the same extent as such publication would have taken place on a finding and sentence by a *Disciplinary Tribunal*, as provided for in the *Disciplinary Tribunal* Regulations.

rE74

If the *relevant person* accepts a *determination by consent*, no one may appeal against it.

rE75

In determining what sanction, if any, to impose under the *determination by consent procedure*, the *PCC* shall have regard to the relevant *enforcement strategy* and to any sentencing policy or guidelines issued by the *Bar Standards Board* and/or by the *Council of the Inns of Court* from time to time.

rE76

The *PCC* may impose on a *relevant person* against whom a charge of *professional misconduct* has been found proved under the *determination by consent procedure* any one or more the following sanctions:

1. An order to pay a fine to the *Bar Standards Board* (the amount of such fine to be determined in accordance with the relevant fines policy);
2. ~~the imposition of any conditions on his licence or authorisation (where appropriate);~~
3. a reprimand by the *PCC* or an order to attend on a nominated *person* to be reprimanded;
4. advice by the *PCC* as to his future conduct or an order to attend on a nominated *person* to be given advice as to his future conduct;
5. an order to complete ~~(or, in the case of a BSB authorised body, an order to procure that any relevant managers or employees complete)~~ continuing professional development of such nature and duration as the *PCC* shall direct and to provide satisfactory proof of compliance with this order to the *PCC*.

rE77

Where the *PCC* has imposed a fine, the confirmation letter to the *relevant person* must indicate that the *relevant person* must pay the fine within 28 days of the date when that letter is received, subject to any representations that the relevant *person* needs extra time to pay. Any application to pay a fine in instalments is to be decided in his discretion by the Chairman of the *PCC*.

rE78

Any failure by the *BSB regulated person* to pay a fine within the relevant timescale is likely to be treated as *professional misconduct* and will entitle the *PCC* to refer the matter to a full *Disciplinary Tribunal* for disposal.

rE79

Where a sanction imposed by the *PCC* includes a fine, that element of the sentence may be directed by the *PCC* to have deferred effect. A sentence may be deferred for a period which is no less than six months and no more than two years long (the "*period of deferral*").

rE80

A deferred sentence is liable be activated where the *relevant person* is later found (whether during the *period of deferral* or afterwards) to have committed *professional misconduct* during the *period of deferral*.

rE81

Where the *PCC* finds that there has been *professional misconduct* during the *period of deferral*, it must (at the same time as imposing sentence for the *professional misconduct*) activate the sentence which had been deferred, save in exceptional circumstances.

rE82

For the avoidance of doubt, the *PCC* may (where the conditions for activation of a deferred sentence are satisfied) activate a deferred sentence imposed by a *Disciplinary Tribunal*, so long as the total sanction imposed does not exceed the powers of the *PCC* set out in rE76 above.

rE83

The *PCC* may not make an award of costs when dealing with a complaint under the determination by consent procedure.

A6 Appeals

[1.76]

BSB regulated person's right to appeal from a decision to take no further action or from a decision to impose an administrative sanction

rE84

A *BSB regulated person* has a right to appeal from a decision to impose an *administrative sanction*. That appeal is to an *appeal panel* constituted under the auspices of the *Council of the Inns of Court* in the same composition as a three-*person* panel constituted under rE133 of the *Disciplinary Tribunal* Regulations.

rE85

An appeal, if made, shall be made by the *BSB regulated person* sending to the Chairman of the *PCC* a notice identifying the decision of the *PCC* appealed against, the decision the *BSB regulated person* contends for, the grounds of such appeal and a statement whether the *BSB regulated person* requires his appeal to be disposed of at an oral hearing. If the *BSB regulated person* does not expressly request an oral hearing, the appeal will be dealt with by a review of the papers. The appeal is a review of the original decision, not a re-hearing.

rE86

The notice must be accompanied by such sum as may be prescribed by the *Bar Standards Board* from time to time, such sum being payable to the *Bar Standards Board* to defray expenses.

rE87

Where the appeal is to be dealt with at an oral hearing then:

1. at least 5 working days before the time set for the appeal, the *PCC* will provide each member of the *appeal panel* and the *BSB regulated person* with a paginated bundle of the correspondence and other documents on its files relating to the original decision; and
2. the *BSB regulated person* may be represented at the hearing.

rE88

The *appeal panel* must decide whether to set aside or to vary the original decision.

rE89

If the *appeal panel* allows the appeal in whole or in part, the *appeal panel* may direct that any administrative fine or appeal fee already paid by the *BSB regulated person* be refunded either in whole or in part: but the *appeal panel* has no power to award costs.

A7 Reopening or reconsidering complaints which have been disposed of

[1.77]

rE90

The *PCC* may reopen or reconsider a complaint which has been disposed of, unless it has been disposed of by a Disciplinary Tribunal:

1. where new evidence becomes available to the *PCC* which leads it to conclude that it should do so, or
2. for some other good reason.

rE91

Following such reopening or reconsideration, the *PCC* may take any further or different action it thinks fit, as if any earlier decision had not been made, provided that if the complaint has already been referred to a *Disciplinary Tribunal* and charges have been served on the *defendant* or the application has been served on the *respondent* (as the case may be) then the *PCC*'s may only instruct counsel for the *Bar Standards Board* to:

1. offer no evidence on a charge or application, or
2. apply to the *Directions Judge* for:
    a. the making of amendments to the charge or application; or
    b. leave to bring additional charges or applications.

A8 Confidentiality

[1.78]

rE92

The *Bar Standards Board* must keep *complaints* confidential. The *Bar Standards Board* must not disclose the fact that a *complaint* has been made or details of the *complaint,* or of its disposal save as specified in this Section 5.A8 or as otherwise required by law.

rE93

Disclosure may be made:

1. for the purpose of investigating the *complaint*; or
2. for the purpose of keeping the complainant and the relevant *person* informed of the progress of the *complaint*; or
3. for the purpose of publicising any forthcoming public hearing of charges arising from the *complaint*; or
4. where the complainant and the relevant *person* consent; or
5. for the purposes of rE42 of this Section 5.A; or

6. where the publication of a finding is required by the provisions of the *Disciplinary Tribunals* Regulations or the *Disqualification* Panel Regulations; or
7. subject to rE94, in response to a request from the selection panel or a member of its secretariat in respect of an application by a *barrister* for silk; or from any body responsible for the appointment of judges in respect of an application for judicial appointment; or from some other body or the *authorised individual* for a *certificate of good standing* in respect of a *barrister*; or from one of the Inns of Court in respect of an application from a *barrister* to become a *pupil supervisor*; or
8. for the purposes of providing examples of the types of behaviour that may constitute breaches of the *Handbook* either externally or internally within the *Bar Standards Board*, provided that where disclosure occurs in these circumstances although details of the individual complaints may be published, any relevant party's identities will remain anonymous; or
9. with the approval of the *PCC*, for any other good reason.

rE94

Where a disclosure is made pursuant to rE93.7 above, if any *complaint* has been made against the *barrister* concerned which has not been disposed of by the *PCC* under these Rules, or dismissed by any *Disciplinary Tribunal* or by any other body to which it may have referred by the *PCC*, the *Bar Standards Board* shall simply indicate that a *complaint* has been received which has not been dismissed.

rE95

Where any finding of professional misconduct has been made (whether by a Disciplinary Tribunal, the Visitors, or the *PCC* in the course of a determination by consent), the *Bar Standards Board* and/or the Council of the Inns of Court must publish on the relevant website(s) the name of the BSB regulated person against whom that finding was made, the nature of that finding, the sentence imposed and any other information about the finding and sentencing which the Bar Standards Board considers it is in the interests of the public to publish, unless the body making the finding directs otherwise.

rE96

Where any *disqualification order* has been made (whether by a *Disciplinary Tribunal* or *the Visitors*), *the Bar Standards Board* and/or *the Council of the Inns of Court* shall publish on the relevant website(s) the name of the relevant *person* against whom the order has been made and its terms.

rE97

Where any interim suspension or interim *disqualification order* has been made or interim conditions imposed, the *Bar Standards Board* must publish on the *Bar Standards Board's* website the name of the *relevant person* against whom the order has been made and its terms.

A9 Interpretation

[1.79]

rE98

In these *Complaints Regulations* all italicised terms shall be interpreted in accordance with the defintions in Part 4.

rE99

If a *barrister* is a member of more than one Inn, references in these Regulations to his *Inn* shall mean the *Inn* by which he was called, unless he is a Bencher in which case his *Inn* shall mean the *Inn* of which he is a Bencher.

A10 Commencement

[1.80]

rE100

This Section 5.A shall come into force in accordance with the provisions of Part 1 of this *Handbook*.

B THE DISCIPLINARY TRIBUNALS REGULATIONS

B1 Arrangement of Regulations

[1.81]

These *Disciplinary Tribunal* Regulations are organised as follows:

- Definitions
- Service of Charges and/or Applications
- Documents to be served on the defendant
- Directions etc
- Setting the date, appointing a tribunal and issuing a Convening Order
- The *Disciplinary Tribunal*
- Provision of documents to the *Disciplinary Tribunal*
- Procedure at the hearing
- Decision of a court or tribunal
- Absence of defendant
- Recording of proceedings
- Amendment of charge(s) and/or application(s)
- Adjournment
- The finding

- The sentence
- Sentence of suspension from practice ~~or from authorisation or licensing~~
- Power to order that a sentence has deferred effect
- Power to activate a deferred sentence
- Wording of the sentence when defendant not present
- Report of finding and sentence
- Appeal to the Visitors
- Appeal: sum payable
- Action to be taken by the Inn (in circumstances where a Barrister has been sentenced to be disbarred or suspended)
- Action to be taken by the Council of the Inns of Court (in all other circumstances)
- Publication of finding and sentence
- Suspension/withdrawal of practising rights pending the hearing of any appeal
- Costs
- Miscellaneous
- Exclusion from providing representation funded by the Legal Aid Agency – Application for termination
- Citation, commencement and revocation
- Annex 1: Sentencing powers against Barristers
- ~~Annex 2: Sentencing powers against BSB legal services bodies~~
- ~~Annex 3: Sentencing powers against licensed bodies~~
- Annex 4: Sentencing powers against registered European Lawyers
- Annex 5: Sentencing powers against all other BSB regulated persons
- Annex 6: Standard Directions

B2 The Regulations

[1.82]

Service of Charges and/or Applications

rE101

Once the *PCC* has decided to refer a matter to a *Disciplinary Tribunal* in accordance with Section 5.A, the *Bar Standards Board* must appoint a *person* or *persons* to represent the *Bar Standards Board* in respect of the charge(s) and or application(s).

rE102

The *BSB Representative*, once appointed, must ensure that a copy of the charge(s) and/or application(s) is served on the relevant *defendant(s)*, together with a copy of these Regulations not later than 10 weeks (or 5 weeks if the *PCC* has directed that the prosecution of the charges be expedited) after the date on which by the *PCC* decides to refer the matter to a *Disciplinary Tribunal.*

rE103

The *BSB Representative* must at the same time ensure that copies of the charge(s) and/or application(s) are sent to the *President.*

Documents to be served on the defendant

rE104

As soon as practicable after the issue of the charges and/or applications to the *defendant(s)*, the *BSB representative* must give the *defendant(s)*:

1. a copy of the evidence of any witness intended to be called in support of any charge(s) or application(s) (which, for the avoidance of doubt, may be a formal witness statement or an informal document such as a letter or attendance note); and
2. a copy of any other documents intended to be relied on by the *BSB Representative*; and
3. either:
    a. the *standard directions* which, subject to rE107, automatically apply to the case and must include such timetable as may be considered reasonable by the *BSB representative*, having regard to the facts of that case; or
    b. the *standard directions*, together with any proposed amendments to the *standard directions* that the *BSB representative* considers reasonable; and
4. details of any *special directions* for which the *BSB Representative* proposes, in default of agreement, to apply for (which may include, but are not limited to):
    a. any of the matters listed at rE107.2 below; or
    b. an application for leave to amend and/or add charges and/or applications.

rE105

If the documents referred to in rE104.1 and/or rE104.2 are not sent to the *defendant(s)* within 28 days of the service of the charges on *the defendant(s)* in accordance with rE102 above, then the *BSB representative* must provide to the *defendant(s)* within that period:

1. details of the *evidence* that is still being sought; and
2. details of when it is believed that it will be practicable to supply that evidence to the *defendant(s)*.

rE106

Nothing in rE104 or rE105 above shall prevent a *Disciplinary Tribunal* from receiving the evidence of a witness which has not been served on the *defendant(s)* in accordance with s rE104 or rE105, or of a document not included in the list of documents referred to at rE104.2 above, provided that the Tribunal is of the opinion either that this does not materially prejudice the *defendant(s)*, or that the evidence is accepted on such terms as are necessary to ensure that no such prejudice occurs.

Directions etc

rE107

Within 21 days, after they receive the *standard directions* (or, where relevant, the special direction of which the *BSB Representative* has given notice in accordance with rE104.4) the *defendant(s)* must:

1. provide to the *BSB representative* written submissions explaining why the *standard directions* and, where relevant, any special directions of which the *BSB representative* gave notice under rE104.4 above, should be amended, withdrawn or added to; and
2. confirm whether they intend, if no of agreement is reached, to make any of the following applications for special directions, namely:
   a. an application to sever the charges and/or applications;
   b. an application to strike out the charges and/or applications which relate to the *defendant* who makes the application;
   c. an application to stay the proceedings;
   d. an application about the admissibility of documents;
   e. an application for disclosure of documents in accordance with rE116.2c;
   f. an application to extend or abridge any relevant time limits;
   g. an application to adjourn the substantive hearing;
   h. an application for the hearing to be held in private;
   i. an application for separate hearings or an application that proceedings pending against separate *defendants* be dealt with at the same hearing; or
   j. any other application for special directions [which the *defendant* considers reasonable, having regard to the facts of the case].

rE108

If, in a case where the *BSB representative* has not suggested any amendments to *the standard directions* pursuant to rE104.3b above or proposed any special directions in accordance with rE104.4 above, a *defendant* does not provide the information referred to in rE107.1 within the relevant twenty one day period, the *defendant* will be deemed to have accepted the *standard directions* and they shall be deemed to apply to the particular matter, save and in so far as they may have been modified on the application of any other *defendant* to the same proceedings which was made within the relevant twenty one day period. The *BSB representative* must forthwith serve on *the President* any directions which are deemed to apply to the matter in accordance with this rE108.

rE109

If, in a case where the *BSB representative* has suggested amendments to the *standard directions* pursuant to rE104.3b above and/or has proposed some special directions in accordance with rE104.4 above, a *defendant* does not provide the information referred to in rE107.1 within the relevant twenty one day period, the *BSB representative* must invite *the President* to appoint a *Directions Judge* in accordance with rE113 below and, once a *Directions judge* has been appointed, the *BSB representative* must apply to him to endorse the proposed amendments to the *standard directions* or the proposed special directions (as appropriate), in accordance with the procedure in rE114 to rE123 below.

rE110

Within fourteen days of the date when he receives any written submissions from a *defendant* in accordance with rE107.1 and/or rE107.2 above, the *BSB representative* must consider them and must during that fourteen day period:

1. inform the *defendant(s)* of those changes to the *standard directions* or the special directions (as appropriate) which he is able to agree; and
2. seek to agree with the *defendant(s)* such other changes to the *standard directions* or the special directions (as appropriate) as may be acceptable to all parties.

rE111

Where the parties, pursuant to rE110 above, agree the directions and special directions which are to apply to the case, those directions will apply to the case and the *BSB representative* must forthwith serve those directions on *the President.*

rE112

If, after the end of the fourteen day period referred to in rE110 above the parties have not agreed any of the *standard directions* or special directions (as appropriate) the *BSB representative* must send to the *President* the following (where relevant):

1. a copy of the *standard directions* and/or special directions which have been agreed;
2. any written submissions received from the *defendant(s)* in accordance with rE107.1;
3. any notice from the *defendant(s)* that they may be intending to make an application referred to at rE107.2; and
4. the *BSB Representative's* response to any such request(s) and/or submissions.

rE113

When the *President* has received the documents referred to in rE112 above, the *President* must designate a Judge or Queen's Counsel ("the *Directions judge*") to exercise the powers and functions conferred on the *Directions Judge* in the following Regulations the *Directions Judge* must not be the *person* who Chairs the *Disciplinary Tribunal*, once convened subject to rE218.

rE114

The *President* must ensure that copies of the charge(s) or application(s), together with the documentation referred to at rE112 above, are sent to the *Directions Judge* once he has been designated.

rE115

When he receives the relevant documents, the *Directions Judge* must consider any submissions about directions In an appropriate case, the *Directions Judge* may decide that an oral directions hearing is necessary.

rE116

If the *Directions Judge* considers that no oral hearing is necessary, then:

1. he must make an order setting out those directions which are to apply in the case taking into account all the relevant circumstances, including any written submissions of the parties and his own findings; and
2. he may consider and decide any other issues which may be necessary including but not limited to:
    a. how any of the applications referred to at rE104.4 and/or rE107.2 are to be dealt with;
    b. what documents are to be admitted ;
    c. what documents which are in the *Bar Standards Board's* possession or control, and/or documents which later come into the possession of the *Bar Standards Board*, and which may support a defence or undermine the *Bar Standards Board's* case should be disclosed;
    d. what facts should be made the subject of admissions;
    e. the provision of a statement that the *defendant* has been duly served (in accordance with rE215 of these Regulations) with the documents required by rE102 and rE104;
    f. the extension or abridgement of any time limit governing the proceedings;
    g. fixing the date for the hearing;
    h. such other matters as he consider are expedient for the efficient conduct of the hearing.

rE117

If the *Directions Judge* considers that an oral hearing is necessary, the *Directions Judge* must give written notice to the *BSB representative* and the *defendant(s)* that an oral hearing is to be held for the purpose of giving directions and taking such other steps as he considers suitable for the clarification of the issues before the tribunal and generally for the just and expeditious handling of the proceedings. The *Directions Judge* shall also provide the *BSB representative* and the *defendant(s)* with a time estimate for the oral directions hearing.

rE118

Within 7 days of receiving the notice referred to in rE117 above the *BSB representative* and the *defendant(s)* must notify the *President* and the other party of their and, where relevant, their Counsel's available dates and times during the six week period immediately after the date of that notice.

rE119

The *President* must try to find a date and time within that six week period which are convenient for all parties. If that is not possible, the *Directions Judge* must fix a date and time for the oral directions hearing within that six week period and must notify the *BSB representative* and the *defendant(s)* of that date and time.

rE120

At the hearing when convened the *Directions Judge* may deal with, amongst other things, all of the issues referred to at rE116 above.

rE121

A Clerk must take a note of the proceedings at any oral directions hearing and must draw up a record of the directions given and/or any admissions made at it.

rE122

After the oral directions hearing (or, if one was not required, after the review of the papers by the *Directions Judge*) the *President* must ensure that copies of the directions order are served on the *BSB representative* and on the *defendant(s)*.

rE123

The directions order served by the *President* under rE122 is be final, and there is no appeal against it.

Setting the date, appointing a tribunal and issuing a convening order

rE124

This regulation applies where, after the deemed acceptance, later agreement, of directions, or the service of a directions order by *the President*, the date of the hearing has not been fixed. Where this Regulation applies, each party must submit details of its availability for the substantive hearing to the *Council of the Inns of Court* in accordance with the directions. After he receives such details, or, where no such details are provided, once the time for providing such details has expired, the *President* must fix, the date of the substantive hearing having regard to the availability of the parties (if provided) and the need for the prompt determination of any charges and/or application(s) made against the *defendant(s)*, in accordance with the provisions of these Regulations. *The President* must also inform all parties of the date fixed for the hearing as soon as reasonably practicable after he has fixed the date.

rE125

On:

1. the deemed acceptance or later agreement of *the standard directions* by the parties; or receipt of the directions order from the *President*; or

2. where the date of the hearing has not been fixed in the directions referred to in rE125.1 above, the fixing of the date of the hearing in accordance with rE124 above,

the President must, in all cases,

a. appoint an appropriate *Disciplinary Tribunal* to sit on the relevant date(s), taking into account the requirements of these Regulations;

b. appoint a *person* or *persons* to act as Clerk or Clerks to the *Disciplinary Tribunals* to perform the functions specified in these Regulations and such other functions as the *President, Directions Judge* or the Chairman of any Tribunal may direct. No *person* who has been engaged in the investigation of a *complaint* or application against a *defendant* in accordance with the relevant procedure or otherwise shall act as Clerk of proceedings under these Regulations arising out of that *complaint*;

c. not less than fourteen days before the date of the substantive hearing, serve an order on the *defendant(s)* ("the *convening order*") specifying:

i. the name of the *defendant(s)* to the proceedings and such other information as may be relevant to the *defendant(s)*, for example:

(1) where any *defendant* is a *barrister*, details of the *barrister's* Inn, his date of *call* and (if appropriate) the date of his appointment as Queen's Counsel, and details of whether or not the *barrister* was acting as a *self-employed barrister* or an *employed barrister* (and, in the latter case, details of his *employer*~~, including whether or not it is a *BSB authorised body*~~) and if the *barrister* was acting as a *HOLP* or *manager* of an *authorised body*, identifying this fact and identifying the *authorised body* ~~and whether or not it is a *BSB authorised body*~~;

~~(2) where any *defendant* is a *BSB authorised body*, details of the date when that body was so authorised or licensed with a summary of the number of *barristers* and other individuals working within that *BSB authorised body*;~~ and

~~(3) where any *defendant* is another type of *BSB regulated person*, details of whether or not the *BSB regulated person* is an *authorised (non-BSB) person* or is otherwise subject to regulation by any other regulator and, if so, the identity of that regulator, and the role of that individual, including whether he was acting as a *HOLP, HOFA, manager* or *employee* of an *authorised body* and identifying that *authorised body* and its Approved Regulator;~~

(4) where any *defendant* is a *non-authorised individual* employed by a *BSB authorised person*, details of the role of by that individual and identifying the *BSB authorised person* who directly or indirectly employs the *defendant*;

(ii) the date and time of the sitting of the *Disciplinary Tribunal* at which it is proposed the charge(s) and/or application(s) should be heard; and

(iii) the names and status (that is, as Chairman, as *lay member*, as *barrister* or other) of those *persons* who it is proposed should constitute the *Disciplinary Tribunal* to hear the case; and

(iv) the name of the Clerk,

and send copies of that *Convening Order* to the nominated members of the *Disciplinary Tribunal*, the BSB Respresentative, and the Clerk. In the Order the attention of the *defendant(s)* will be drawn to:

d. their right to represent themselves or be represented by counsel, with or without instructing a *solicitor*, as they shall think fit; and

e. their right to inspect and be given copies of documents referred to in the list served pursuant to rE104 above; and

f. their right (without prejudice to their right to appear and take part in the proceedings) to deliver a written answer to the charge(s) and/or application(s) if they think fit.

rE126

The *defendant(s)* may, when they receive the *Convening Order*, give notice to the *President* objecting to any one or more of the proposed members of the *Disciplinary Tribunal*. He must give this notice as soon as is reasonably practicable and must specify the grounds for his objection.

rE127

When the *President* receives such an objection, he must, if satisfied that it is justified (but subject to rE128), exercise the power conferred on him by rE139 to nominate a substitute member or members of the Tribunal, and must notify the *defendant(s)* accordingly. When they receive that notification, the *defendant(s)* may object to any substitute member or members, in the same way as they may object under rE126 above.

rE128

No objection to any member of the Tribunal may be made, or if made, may be upheld, on the grounds only that he knows, or might have known, about a previous application to *disqualify*, or a charge of *professional misconduct*, or of breach of proper professional standards, or a charge consisting of *a legal aid complaint*, against the *defendant(s)*, or any finding on any such application or charge, or any sentence imposed on the *defendant(s)* in connection with any such application or charge.

rE129

The Convening Order must inform the *defendant(s)* of the rights conferred by rE126.

The Disciplinary Tribunal

Hearing in private

rE130

The hearing before a *Disciplinary Tribunal* must be in public, unless it has been directed that it is not to be held in public, and that direction has not been over-ruled by the tribunal.

Composition of Disciplinary Tribunals

rE131

A *Disciplinary Tribunal* must consist of either three persons or five persons.

rE132

A five-person panel must include the following *persons* nominated by the *President*:

1. as chairman, a Judge; and
2. at least one *lay member*; and
3. at least one *practising barrister* of not less than seven years' standing.

rE133

A three-person panel shall include the following *persons* nominated by *the President*:

1. as chairman, a Queen's Counsel or a Judge; and
2. one *lay member*; and
3. one *practising barrister of not less than seven years' standing.*

rE134

In deciding who will sit on the panel the *President* must have regard to the nature of the charge(s) and/or application(s) being determined and to the identity of the *defendant*(s) against whom the charges have been made. When constituting the panel, as well as taking into account the requirements of rE132 and rE133 above and rE135 below, the *President* must also have regard to (but shall not be bound by) any recommendations by the *PCC*, which may include a recommendation that a Judge rather than a Queen's Counsel be appointed to act as Chairman of a three-person panel.

rE135

A *person* must not be nominated to serve on a *Disciplinary Tribunal* if they:

1. are a member of the *Bar Council* or of any of its committees; or
2. are a member of the *Bar Standards Board* or of any of its committees; or
3. was a member of the *Bar Standards Board* or of any of its committees at any time when the matter was being considered by the *Bar Standards Board.*

rE136

The President may publish qualifications or other requirements made for those appointed to serve on a *Disciplinary Tribunal* and those appointed to be Clerks.

rE137

For the purposes of rE132 and rE133, a Judge includes:

1. a puisne judge of the High Court;
2. a judge of the Court of Appeal;
3. a Circuit judge;
4. a Recorder who has been authorised to sit as a judge of the High Court under section 9(1) of the Supreme Court Act 1981;
5. a deputy judge of the High Court appointed under section 9(4) of the Supreme Court Act 1981; and
6. a *person* who has been a judge of the Court of Appeal, or a puisne judge of the High Court, or a Circuit Judge, provided that he remains permitted by virtue of section 9 of the Supreme Court Act 1981 to be requested to act as a judge of the High Court, or is eligible for appointment as a deputy Circuit judge under section 24 of the Courts Act 1971.

rE138

If a vacancy in the *Disciplinary Tribunal* arises before the substantive hearing of the charge, the *President* must choose another member of the relevant class to fill that vacancy.

rE139

At any time before the substantive hearing of the charge starts, the *President* may cancel any or all of the nominations made pursuant to these Regulations, and make such alternative nominations as, in the exercise of his discretion, he deems necessary or expedient, provided always that *the President* notifies the *defendant(s)* of the identity of such substitutes as soon as is reasonably practicable after he has chosen them. The *defendant(s)* may object to such substitute members in the same way as they may object under rE126.

rE140

The proceedings of a five-person panel will not be invalidated on the sole ground that after the *Convening Order* has been issued (in accordance with rE125 above), one or more of the members becomes unable to act or is *disqualified* from acting, provided that:

1. the chairman and at least one *lay member* are still able to act and are present throughout the substantive hearing; and
2. the number of members present throughout the substantive hearing of the charge is not reduced below three.

rE141

A member of a *Disciplinary Tribunal* who has been absent for any time during a sitting shall take no further part in the proceedings.

Provision of documents to the Disciplinary Tribunal

rE142

There shall be provided to each member of the *Disciplinary Tribunal* before the start of the substantive hearing copies of the following documents:

1. the *convening order*;
2. the charge(s) and/or application(s) and any particulars of them;
3. any documents which the *BSB representative* or the *defendant(s)* propose to rely on, unless a direction has been made that copies of such documents be withheld;
4. any written answer to the charge(s) and/or application(s) submitted by or on behalf of the *defendant(s)*;
5. such other documents as have been agreed or directed to be laid before the Tribunal before the start of the hearing; and
6. the *standard directions* (as amended by the parties) and any agreed special directions, or failing such agreement, the directions order served by the *President* pursuant to rE122.

Procedure at the hearing

rE143

The Tribunal must apply the criminal standard of proof when deciding charges of *professional misconduct* and in deciding whether the *disqualification condition* has been established.

rE144

The rules of natural justice apply to proceedings of a *Disciplinary Tribunal*. Subject to those, the Tribunal may:

1. (subject to rE145 below) admit any evidence, whether oral or written, whether given in *person*, or over the telephone, or by video link, or by such other means as the Tribunal may deem appropriate, whether direct or hearsay, and whether or not it would be admissible in a *court* of law;
2. give such directions with regard to the conduct of, and procedure at, the hearing, and, with regard to the admission of evidence at the hearing, as it considers appropriate for securing that a *defendant* has a proper opportunity of answering the charge(s) and/or application(s) made against him, or otherwise as shall be just;
3. exclude any hearsay evidence if it is not satisfied that reasonable steps have been taken to obtain direct evidence of the facts sought to be proved by the hearsay evidence.

rE145

Any party may refer to the fact (if relevant) that the *determination by consent* procedure was used before the *complaint* was referred as a charge before a *Disciplinary Tribunal*. However, no reference may be made to the substance of the procedure (including, without limitation, any reference to the contents of any report produced in the course of such procedure, or to the circumstances in which the *determination by consent* procedure ended), unless and until the *defendant* refers to the substance of the procedure in the course of presenting his case, or when he is being sentenced, once the facts have been found.

Decision of a court or tribunal

rE146

In proceedings before a *Disciplinary Tribunal* which involve the decision of a *court* or tribunal in previous proceedings to which the *defendant* was a party, the following rules shall apply:

1. a copy of the certificate of *conviction* relating to the offence shall be conclusive proof that the *defendant* committed the offence;
2. any *court* record of the findings of fact upon which the *conviction* was based (which may include any document prepared by the sentencing judge or a transcript of the relevant proceedings) shall be proof of those facts, unless proved to be inaccurate;
3. the finding and sentence of any tribunal in or outside England and Wales exercising a professional disciplinary jurisdiction may be proved by producing an official copy of the finding and sentence and the findings of fact upon which that finding or sentence was based shall be proof of those facts, unless proved to be inaccurate; and
4. the judgment of any civil *court* may be proved by producing an official copy of the judgment, and the findings of fact upon which that judgment was based shall be proof of those facts, unless proved to be inaccurate.

rE147

In proceedings before a *Disciplinary Tribunal* which involve the decision of a *court* or tribunal in previous proceedings to which the *defendant* was not a party, the provisions of rE146 do not apply.

Absence of Defendant

rE148

If a *Disciplinary Tribunal* is satisfied that the relevant procedure has been complied with and the *defendant* has been duly served (in accordance with rE216 of these Regulations) with the documents required by rE102, rE104, and rE125.2c (as appropriate) but that *defendant* has not attended at the time and place appointed for the hearing, the Tribunal may nevertheless proceed to hear and determine the charge(s) or application(s) relating to that *defendant* if it considers it just to do so, subject to compliance with rE180.1 in respect of that *defendant* if the *Disciplinary Tribunal* finds any charge or application proved.

rE149

If the relevant procedure has not been complied with, but a *Disciplinary Tribunal* is satisfied that it has not been practicable to comply with it, the Tribunal may hear and determine the charge(s) or application(s) in the absence of that *defendant*, if it considers it just to do so, subject to compliance with rE180.2 in respect of that *defendant* if the *Disciplinary Tribunal* finds any charge or application proved.

rE150

If the procedure under rE149 has been followed, the *defendant* may apply to the *Directions judge* for an order that there should be a new hearing before a fresh *Disciplinary Tribunal*.

Recording of proceedings

rE151

The Clerk must arrange for a record of the proceedings before a *Disciplinary Tribunal* to be made, eitherby a shorthand writer, or by a recording machine.

Amendment and addition of charge(s) and/or application(s)

rE152

A *Disciplinary Tribunal* may at any time before or during the hearing direct the charge(s) and/or application(s) against any *defendant* to be amended, or that new charge(s) and/or application(s) be added, provided that:

1. that the Tribunal is satisfied that no *defendant* will by reason of such an amendment or addition suffer any substantial prejudice in the conduct of his defence; and
2. that the Tribunal will, if so requested by a *defendant*, adjourn for such time as is reasonably necessary to enable that *defendant* to meet the charge(s) or application(s) as so amended in respect of him.

Adjournment

rE153

Subject to the provisions of rE154, the *Disciplinary Tribunal* must sit from day to day until it has made a finding and, if any charge or application is found proved, until sentence has been pronounced.

rE154

A *Disciplinary Tribunal* may, if the Tribunal decides an adjournment is necessary for any reason, adjourn the hearing for such period or periods as it may decide.

The finding

rE155

At the end of the hearing, the *Disciplinary Tribunal* must record in writing its finding(s) on each charge or application, and its reasons. That record must be signed by the chairman and by all members of the Tribunal. If the members of the *Disciplinary Tribunal* do not agree on any charge or application, the finding to be recorded on that charge or application must be that of the majority. If the members of the *Disciplinary Tribunal* are equally divided on any charge or application, then, as the burden of proof is on the *Bar Standards Board*, the finding to be recorded on that charge or application must be that which is the most favourable to the *defendant*. The chairman of the *Disciplinary Tribunal* must then announce the *Disciplinary Tribunal*'s finding on the charge(s) or application(s), and state whether each such finding was unanimous or by a majority.

rE156

In any case where the *Disciplinary Tribunal* dismisses the charge(s) and/or application(s), it may give advice to the *defendant* about his future conduct

The sentence

rE157

If the *Disciplinary Tribunal* finds any of the charges or applications proved against a *defendant*, it may hear evidence of any previous *disqualification order*, or finding of *professional misconduct*, or of breach of proper professional standards by the *Bar Standards Board*, or by any other regulator, or any finding on a charge consisting of a *legal aid complaint* against that *defendant*, or of the outcome of any previous *determination by consent procedure*. After hearing any representations by or on behalf of the *defendant(s)*, the *Disciplinary Tribunal* must decide what sentence to impose on a *defendant*, taking into account the *sentencing guidelines*, must record its sentence in writing, together with its reasons. If the members of the Tribunal do not agree on the sentence to be imposed on a *defendant*, the sentence to be recorded must be that decided by the majority. If the members of the *Disciplinary Tribunal* are equally divided on the sentence to be imposed on a *defendant*, the sentence to be recorded must be that which is the most favourable to the *defendant*. The chairman of the *Disciplinary Tribunal* must then announce the *Disciplinary Tribunal*'s decision on sentence and state whether the decision was unanimous or by a majority.

rE158

Subject to rE159 below:

1. a *defendant* against whom a charge of *professional misconduct* has been found proved may be sentenced by the *Disciplinary Tribunal* as follows:

    a. in the case of *barristers*, in accordance with Annex 1 to these Regulations;

    ~~b. in the case of a *BSB legal services body*, in accordance with Annex 2 to these Regulations;~~

c. ~~in the case of a *licensed body*, in accordance with Annex 3 to these Regulations;~~

d. in the case of *registered European lawyers*, in accordance with Annex 2 to these Regulations;

e. in the case of all other *BSB regulated persons*, in accordance with Annex 3 to these Regulations;

2. in the case of a defendant who is a relevant person in respect of whom the Disciplinary Tribunal finds the disqualification condition to be established, the Disciplinary Tribunal may make a Disqualification Order if the Disciplinary Tribunal considers that the making of such a Disqualification Order is a proportionate sanction and is in the public interest (there being no other available sentence in respect of a relevant person who is a non-authorised individual directly or indirectly employed by a BSB authorised person).

rE159

In any case where a charge of *professional misconduct* has been found proved, the *Disciplinary Tribunal* may decide that no further action should be taken against the *defendant*.

rE160

A three-*person* panel must not:

1. disbar a *barrister* or suspend a *barrister's practising certificate* for a period longer than twelve months; or

~~2. revoke the authorisation or licence (as appropriate) of a *BSB authorised body* or suspend it for a period longer than twelve months; or~~

3. remove a registered European lawyer from the register of European lawyers; or

4. impose a sentence of suspension on any *BSB regulated person* for a prescribed period longer than twelve months; or

5. impose a *Disqualification Order* for more than twelve months.

This Regulation does not prevent a three-*person* panel making an order in accordance with rE161 below.

rE161

In the event that a three-*person* panel considers that a case before it merits (in conjunction with any deferred sentence) the imposition on a *defendant* of any of the sentences referred to in rE160 above or the three-*person* panel otherwise considers that the case of a particular *defendant* is complex enough to warrant sentencing by a five-*person* panel:

1. the three-*person* panel must refer the case to a five-*person* panel for it to sentence that *defendant* (but may proceed to sentence any other *defendants* to the proceedings in respect of whom this rE161 does not apply);

2. the three-*person* panel must, in order to help the five-*person* panel, prepare a statement of the facts as found (and, where relevant, the sentences passed on

any other *defendants* to the proceedings). The *defendant* cannot challenge the facts found by the three-person panel; and

3. the three-person panel must direct within what period of time the sentencing hearing before the five-*person* panel is to be held and make appropriate directions for the parites to provide the *President* with their dates of availability.

rE162

Following a referral by a three-person panel under rE161, the five-*person* panel must be constituted in accordance with rE132. The *defendant* must be informed as soon as practicable of the names and status (that is, as Chairman, as *lay member*, as *barrister* or other) of those *persons* who it is proposed will constitute the five-*person* panel. The *defendant* may, when he is so informed, give notice to *the President* objecting to any one or more of the proposed members of the panel. That notice must be given as soon as is reasonably practicable, must specify the ground of objection, and must be dealt with in accordance with rE127 and rE128.

rE163

The *President* must fix the date for the sentencing hearing and in so doing shall have regard to the availability of the parties, save that *the President* may disregard the availability of any party where that party has failed to provide any, or any reasonable dates of availability. As soon as is reasonably practicable after he has fixed the sentencing hearing, the *President* must inform all the parties of that date .

rE164

If the five-person panel is satisfied that the requirements of rE162 and rE163 above have been complied with, and the *defendant* has not attended at the time and place appointed for the sentencing hearing, the five-person panel may nonetheless sentence the *defendant*, provided that it complies with rE180.3.

rE165

If the five-person panel is satisfied that it has not been practicable to comply with the requirements of rE162 and rE163, above, and the *defendant* has not attended at the time and place appointed for the sentencing hearing, the five-*person* panel may nonetheless sentence the *defendant*, provided that it complies with rE180.4.

rE166

If the procedure under rE165 has been followed, the *defendant* may apply to the *Directions Judge* for an order that there should be a new sentencing hearing before a fresh five-person panel.

rE167

Sections 41 and 42 of the Administration of Justice Act 1985 (as substituted by Section 33 of the Legal Aid Act 1988 and as amended by Schedule 4 to the Access to Justice Act 1999) confer certain powers (relating to the reduction or cancellation of fees otherwise payable by the *Legal Aid Agency* in connection with services provided as part of the Community Legal Service or Criminal Defence Service and to the exclusion from providing representation funded by the *Legal Aid Agency* as part of the Community Legal Service or Criminal Defence Service) on a *Disciplinary Tribunal* in the cases to which those Sections apply). Accordingly:

1. any *Disciplinary Tribunal* which hears a charge consisting of a *legal aid complaint* relating to the conduct of a *defendant* who is a *barrister* may if it thinks fit (and whether or not it sentences the *defendant* in accordance with rE158.1 in respect of any conduct arising out of the same *legal aid complaint*) order that any such fees as are referred to in Section 41(2) of the Act of 1985 shall be reduced or cancelled;
2. where a *Disciplinary Tribunal* hears a charge of *professional misconduct* against a *defendant* who is a *barrister* it may (in addition to, or instead of, sentencing that *defendant* in accordance with rE158.1) order that he be excluded from providing representation funded by the *Legal Aid Agency* as part of the Community Legal Service, or Criminal Defence Service, either temporarily, or for a specified period, if it determines that there is a good reason to exclude him arising from (i) his conduct in connection with any such services as are mentioned in Section 40(1) of the Act of 1985; or (ii) his professional conduct generally.

rE168

Whether or not a *Disciplinary Tribunal* finds any charge or application proved against a *barrister* who is a *pupil supervisor*, if the *Disciplinary Tribunal* considers that the circumstances of the *complaint* are relevant to the *defendant* in his capacity as a *pupil supervisor*, it may notify the *defendant's Inn* of those concerns in such manner as it sees fit.

rE169

If a *barrister* is a member of more than one *Inn*, each *Inn* of which he is a member must be mentioned in the sentence imposed on him.

Sentence of suspension from practice ~~or from authorisation or licensing~~ or imposition of conditions

rE170

For the purposes of rE171 to rE173:

1. The effect of a sentence of suspension for a *BSB authorised individual* is that:
   a. the *defendant's practising certificate* is *suspended* for the period of the suspension;
   b. any and all enjoyment of all rights and privileges as a member of the *Inn(s)* of which he is a member are *suspended* for the period of the suspension; and
   c. the *defendant* is prohibited from practising as a *barrister*, or holding himself out as being a *barrister* when providing *legal services* or as otherwise being authorised by the *Bar Standards Board* to provide *reserved legal activities* or when describing himself as a *Barrister* in providing services other than *legal services* (whether or not for reward) unless he discloses the suspension);

2. the effect of a sentence of suspension for a *registered European lawyer* shall mean that the *defendant* is *suspended* from the *register of European lawyers* maintained by the *Bar Standards Board* and is, for so long as he remains *suspended*:

   a. prohibited from holding himself out as registered with the *Bar Standards Board*; and;

   b. not authorised to *practice*.

~~3. The effect of a sentence of suspension for a *BSB authorised body* shall mean that the body's authorisation or licence is *suspended* for the period of the suspension such that the *defendant* is not an *authorised person* for that period;~~

4. The effect of a sentence on a *BSB authorised individual* or a *registered European lawyer* requiring completion of continuing professional development shall be in addition to the mandatory requirements set out in the continuing professional development rules at Part 4 of this *Handbook*.

rE171

The period for which a sentence of suspension from *practice* is expressed to run may be:

1. a fixed period; or
2. until the *defendant* has complied with any conditions specified in the order imposing the sentence of suspension.

rE172

Conditions may be imposed on a *barrister's practising certificate* ~~or on the authorisation or licence of a *BSB authorised body*~~:

1. without its being *suspended*; or
2. to take effect on a *barrister's practising certificate* ~~or on the authorisation or licence of a *BSB authorised body*~~ when a period of suspension ends.

rE173

Conditions may (depending on the circumstances) include conditions limiting the scope of the *defendant's practice* (after the end of any suspension, if relevant) to such part as the *Disciplinary Tribunal* may determine, either indefinitely or for a defined period; and/or imposing requirements that the *defendant*~~, or in the case of a *BSB authorised body*, its *managers* or *employees*,~~ undergo such further *training* as the *Disciplinary Tribunal* may determine; and/or prohibiting the *defendant* from accepting or carrying out any *public access instructions*; and/or such other matters as the Tribunal may consider appropriate for the purpose of protecting *the public* and/or preventing a repetition of the conduct in question.

Power to order that a sentence has deferred effect

rE174

Where a sentence imposed by a *Disciplinary Tribunal* includes a fine, condition and/or a suspension from *practice*, the *Disciplinary Tribunal* may direct that those elements of the sentence are to have deferred effect.

rE175

A sentence may be directed to have deferred effect for a minimum of six months or a maximum of two years (the "*period of deferral*").

Power to activate a deferred sentence

rE176

A deferred sentence must be activated if the *defendant* is later found (whether during the period of suspension. or afterwards) to have committed *professional misconduct* during the *period of deferral.*

rE177

Where a *Disciplinary Tribunal* finds that there has been *professional misconduct* during the *period of deferral*, it shall (at the same time as imposing sentence for the *professional misconduct*) activate the sentence which had been deferred, unless there are exceptional circumstances.

rE178

A *Disciplinary Tribunal* may (where the conditions for activation of a deferred sentence are satisfied) activate a sentence which has been deferred when imposed by the *PCC* pursuant to the *determination by consent* procedure.

rE179

Where a deferred sentence is activated pursuant to this Regulation, the sentence must then be pronounced, and any action as may be required to give effect to the sentence must be taken, in accordance with rE189 to rE197 below.

Wording of the sentence when defendant not present

rE180

If a *defendant* has not been present throughout the proceedings, the sentence in respect of that *defendant* must include one or more of the following statements:

1. if the relevant procedure under rE148 has been complied with, that the finding and sentence were made in the absence of the *defendant* in accordance with rE148;
2. if the procedure under rE149 has been complied with, that the finding and the sentence were made in the absence of the *defendant* and that he has the

right to apply to the *Directions Judge* for an order that there should be a new hearing before a fresh *Disciplinary Tribunal*;

3. if the relevant procedure under rE163 has been complied with, that the sentence was made in the absence of the *defendant* in accordance with rE164;

4. if the procedure under rE165 has been complied with, that the sentence was made in the absence of the *defendant* and that he may apply to the *Directions Judge* for an order that there should be a new hearing before a fresh *Disciplinary Tribunal.*

Report of Finding and Sentence

rE181

As soon as is practicable after the end of the proceedings of a *Disciplinary Tribunal*, the chairman must prepare a report in writing of the finding(s) on the charges of *professional misconduct* and/or on any applications, and the reasons for those findings and the sentence, if any. At the discretion of the chairman, the report may also refer to matters which, in the light of the evidence given to the *Disciplinary Tribunal*, appear to require investigation or comment. He must send copies of the report to:

1. the defendant;
2. the Director of the *Bar Standards Board*;
3. the Treasurers of the *defendant's Inn* of *Call* and of any other *Inns* of which he is a member.

rE182

He must also send copies of the report to:

1. those of the following whom he deems, in his absolute discretion, to be appropriate taking into account the circumstances:
   a. the Lord Chancellor;
   b. the Lord Chief Justice;
   c. the Attorney General;
   d. the Director of Public Prosecutions;
   e. the Chairman of the *Bar Council*; and
   f. the Chairman of the *PCC*; and
2. in cases where one or more charges of *professional misconduct* have been found proved and any such charge constitutes, or arises out of, a *legal aid complaint*, and/or the sentence includes an order under rE167, the *Legal Aid Agency*.

Appeal to the Visitors

rE183

In cases where one or more charges of *professional misconduct* have been proved, and/or a *disqualification order* has been made, an appeal may be lodged with *the Visitors* in accordance with the *Hearings Before the Visitors* rules 2010:

1. by the *defendant* against *conviction* and/or sentence;
2. with the consent of the Chairman of the *Bar Standards Board* or the Chairman of the *PCC*, by the *Bar Standards Board* against sentence on any of the grounds in rE185 below.

rE184

In any case where any charge of *professional misconduct* or application to *disqualify* has been dismissed, the *Bar Standards Board* may (with the consent of the Chairman of the *Bar Standards Board* or of the Chairman of the *PCC*) lodge an appeal with *the Visitors*, in accordance with the *Hearings Before the Visitors* Rules 2010, on any of the grounds in rE185 below.

rE185

The *Bar Standards Board* may only lodge an appeal (against sentence or dismissal) where the *Bar Standards Board* considers the *Disciplinary Tribunal* has:

1. taken into account irrelevant considerations;
2. failed to take into account relevant considerations;
3. reached a decision that is wrong in law; and/or
4. reached a decision which no reasonable Tribunal could properly have reached.

rE186

Where a *defendant* lodges an appeal against a disbarment, *Disqualification order* ~~or the revocation of a licence or authorisation~~, he may at the same time lodge with *the Visitors* an appeal against any requirement imposed pursuant to rE203 to rE205 as appropriate.

rE187

A complainant (other than the *Bar Standards Board*) has no right of appeal.

Appeal: sum payable

rE188

Where an appeal is lodged with *the Visitors* by the *defendant*, the Notice of Appeal must be accompanied by the sum of £250 (or such other amount as may be specified by the *Bar Standards Board* from time to time), payable to the *Bar Standards Board*, to defray its expenses, such sum to be refunded in the discretion of *the Visitors* in the event of an appeal which is successful wholly or in part.

Action to be taken by the Inn (in circumstances where a barrister has been sentenced to be disbarred or suspended)

rE189

When the Treasurer of the *defendant's Inn* of *Call* receives a report prepared in accordance with rE181, he must, not fewer than 21 days after the end of the

Tribunal's proceedings (or, where the *defendant* has given notice of appeal to *the Visitors* against the finding and/or sentence, once the time for appeal to *the Visitors* has expired and any appeal to *the Visitors* has been disposed of) pronounce the sentence decided on by the Tribunal, and take such further action as may be required to carry the sentence into effect. The Treasurer must inform the *persons* specified in rE181 of the date on which the sentence is to take effect, (which must be no later than two working days after the date when that sentence is pronounced).

rE190

Similar action must be taken by the Treasurer of any other *Inn* of which the *defendant* is a member, in conjunction with the Treasurer of the *defendant's Inn* of Call.

rE191

In any case in which the *defendant* has given notice of appeal to *the Visitors* against the finding and/or sentence of the Tribunal on the charges of *professional misconduct*, no action referred to in rE189 and rE190 may be taken until the appeal has been heard by *the Visitors*, or otherwise disposed of without a hearing.

rE192

Where, pursuant to rE203, a Tribunal has required the *Bar Standards Board* to suspend the *defendant's practising certificate* or not to issue a *practising certificate* to the *defendant* pending an appeal ("the Interim Measure"), the Treasurer must direct that any period of suspension to which the *defendant* has been sentenced will be deemed to have taken effect on the date on which the Interim Measure came into effect, or on the date on which the *defendant* would otherwise have been eligible to be issued with a *practising certificate*, whichever is later.

Action to be taken by the Council of the Inns of Court (in all other circumstances)

rE193

If the *Disciplinary Tribunal* has imposed a sentence (other than disbarring or suspending a *barrister* see rE189 to rE192, above), the *Council of the Inns of Court*, when it receives the report prepared in accordance with rE181, must, not fewer than 21 days after the end of the Tribunal's proceedings, pronounce the sentence decided on by the Tribunal, and take such further action as may be required to carry that sentence into effect. The *Council of the Inns of Court* shall inform the *persons* specified in rE181 of the date on which the sentence is to take effect. That date must be no later than two clear days after the date when the sentence is pronounced.

rE194

In any case in which a *BSB regulated person* has given notice of appeal to *the Visitors* against the finding and/or sentence of the Tribunal on the charges of *professional misconduct*, no action referred to in rE193 may be taken until the appeal has been heard by *the Visitors*, or otherwise disposed of without a hearing.

rE195

The *Council of the Inns of Court* must take all such steps as may be necessary or expedient to give effect to any requirement made by the Tribunal pursuant to rE189 above.

Action to be taken by the Bar Council/Bar Standards Board

rE196

Subject to rE197, below, after the sentence has been pronounced in accordance with rE189, above, the *Bar Council/Bar Standards Board* must, as appropriate, in accordance with the finding and/or sentence of the Tribunal:

1. remove the relevant *BSB authorised individual's practising certificate, litigation extension* and/or right to undertake public access work (as appropriate);
2. ~~impose conditions on the relevant *BSB authorised person's* authorisation and/or licence (as appropriate);~~
3. either include a note on the *Bar Standards Board's* register of *BSB authorised persons* that the *BSB authorised person* is *disqualified*, *suspended* ~~or is otherwise subject to certain conditions on the terms of his authorisation/licence~~ or that the *relevant person* is the subject of a *disqualification order*,

except that in any case in which a *BSB regulated person* has given notice of appeal to *the Visitors* against the finding and/or sentence of the Tribunal on the charges of *professional misconduct*, no action referred to in this rE196 may be taken until the appeal has been heard by *the Visitors* or otherwise disposed of without a hearing.

rE197

Where the finding and/or sentence of the Tribunal is that the *BSB authorised person* should be subject to an immediate suspension ~~and/or immediate imposition of conditions~~ in accordance with rE202 below, the *Bar Council/Bar Standards Board* must immediately:

1. remove the relevant *BSB authorised individual's practising certificate, litigation extension* and/or right to do public access work (as appropriate),
2. ~~impose conditions on the relevant *BSB authorised person's* authorisation and/or licence (as appropriate);~~
3. either include a note on the *Bar Standards Board's* register of *BSB authorised persons* that the *BSB authorised person* is *suspended* ~~or is otherwise subject to certain conditions on the terms of his authorisation/licence~~,

the actions of the *Bar Council/Bar Standards Board* must not be deferred even if the *BSB regulated person* has given notice of appeal to *the Visitors* against the finding and/or sentence of the Tribunal on the charges of *professional misconduct*.

rE198

The Bar Standards Board and/or the Council of the Inns of Court also:

1. must publish the finding and sentence of the Tribunal on the relevant

website(s) within fourteen (14) days of the date when the Tribunal's proceedings end, unless the Chairman of the Tribunal directs that publication shall be delayed until *the President* has published the finding under rE198; and

2. may where charges have been dismissed publish the decision of the Tribunal on their websites at any time provided that in this case all details of the relevant parties involved in the hearing are anonymised.

Publication of finding and sentence

rE199

The following procedures apply to the publication of the finding and sentence of a *Disciplinary Tribunal*:

1. When the Tribunal has found that one or more charges of *professional misconduct* are proved, then, as soon as it has heard from the Inn. or from the *Council of the Inns of Court* (as the case may be), of the date that any sentence is to take effect, *the President* must publish those charges, the sentence, and the date when that sentence is to take effect.
2. When the Tribunal has found that the *disqualification condition* is established and has made a *Disqualification order*, as soon as it has heard from the *Council of the Inns of Court* on what date that order is to take effect, *the President* must publish the findings on which that order was based, the terms of the *Disqualification Order*, and the date when that order is to take effect.
3. When the Tribunal has found that any charge of *professional misconduct* has not been proved *the President* must not publish that charge, or the finding unless the *defendant* asks him to subject to rE197.2.

rE200

When publishing any finding, sentence or decision in accordance with rE198, *the President* must communicate it in writing to:

1. the *defendant*;
2. the Chairman of the *Bar Standards Board*;
3. the *defendant*'s head of *chambers*, *HOLP*, or *employer* (as appropriate);
4. in the case of a *registered European lawyer*, his *home professional body*;
5. the Treasurers of the *defendant*'s *Inn* of *Call* and of any other Inns of which he is a member;
6. other *Approved Regulators* and the *LSB*; and
7. one or more press agencies or other publications.
8. the following *persons* only where *the President* deems, in his absolute discretion, to be appropriate, taking into account the circumstances:
    a. the Lord Chancellor;
    b. the Lord Chief Justice;
    c. the Attorney General;
    d. the Director of Public Prosecutions;

e. the Chairman of the Bar Council;

Suspension/withdrawal of practising rights pending the hearing of any appeal

rE201

rE202 to rE209 below apply to any *defendant* who:

1. Is a a *barrister*, who has been sentenced to be disbarred or to be *suspended* or to be prohibited from accepting or doing any public access work or *instructions* for more than one year;
2. Is a *BSB authorised individual*, who has been sentenced to be *disqualified* or to be *suspended* for more than one year;
3. ~~is a *BSB authorised body*, which has been sentenced to have its authorisation or licence revoked or *suspended* for more than one year; or~~
4. is a *BSB authorised person*, who has been sentenced to have conditions placed on his *practising certificate*~~, authorisation or licence (as appropriate)~~ prohibiting him from accepting any *public access instructions* or *conducting anylitigation* or for more than one year.

rE202

Where rE201 applies the Tribunal must seek representations from the *defendant* and from the *BSB representative* on the appropriateness or otherwise of taking action under rE203 below.

rE203

Having heard any representations under rE201 above, the Tribunal must (unless in the circumstances of the case it appears to the Tribunal to be inappropriate to do so), either:

1. in relation to rE201 and rE201.2, require the *defendant* to suspend his *practice* immediately, in which case the Bar Standards Board must suspend that *defendant*'s *practising certificate* with immediate effect; or
2. in relation to rE201.3, decide that the condition prohibiting the *defendant* from accepting *public access instructions* or conducting any litigation, shall take effect immediately; or
3. where the *defendant* has been sentenced to be disbarred or to be *suspended*, and where that *defendant* does not currently hold a *practising certificate*, require the Bar Standards Board not to issue any *practising certificate* to him.

rE204

If the Tribunal decides that it would be inappropriate to require immediate suspension or immediate imposition of conditions (as the case may be) it may nonetheless require the *defendant* to suspend his *practice* or to impose conditions, from such date as the Tribunal may specify.

rE205

Where the *defendant* is permitted to continue to practise for any period before being *suspended* under rE204, the Tribunal may require the *Bar Standards Board* to impose such terms on the *defendant's practice* as the Tribunal deems necessary to protect *the public* until the suspension comes into effect.

rE206

Where an order is made in respect of a *defendant* under rE203 above and that *defendant* considers that, due to a change in the circumstances, it would be appropriate for that order to be varied, he may apply to *the President* in writing for it to be varied.

rE207

When *the President* receives an application made pursuant to rE206 above, he must refer it to the Chairman and to one of the *lay members* of the Tribunal which originally made the order.

rE208

Any application made pursuant to rE206 above must be sent by the applicant, on the day that it is made, to the *PCC* and the *PCC* may make such representations as they think fit on that application to those to whom the application has been referred by *the President*.

rE209

The *persons* to whom an application made pursuant to rE206 above is referred may vary or confirm the order in relation to which the application has been made.

~~rE210~~

~~References in rE206 to the *Bar Standards Board* shall be treated as referring to such body as may from time to time have the power to issue or suspend *practising certificates* or to impose conditions on *practising certificates* and the authorisations and licences of *BSB authorised bodies*.~~

Costs

rE211

A *Disciplinary Tribunal* may make such Orders for costs, whether against or in favour of a *defendant*, as it shall think fit.

rE212

It makes such an Order a *Disciplinary Tribunal* must either itself decide the amount of such costs or appoint a suitably qualified *person* to do so on its behalf.

rE213

Any costs ordered to be paid by or to a *defendant* must be paid to or by the *Bar Standards Board*.

rE214

All costs incurred by the *PCC* preparatory to the hearing before the Tribunal must be borne by the *Bar Standards Board*.

Miscellaneous

Representation of complainant's interests

rE215

The *BSB representative* must keep the complainant (if any) informed of the progress of the *complaint*.

Service of documents

rE216

Any documents required to be served on a *defendant* in connection with proceedings under these Regulations shall be deemed to have been validly served:

1. If sent by registered post, or recorded delivery post, or receipted hand delivery to:

   a. in the case of a *BSB authorised individual*, the address notified by him pursuant to the requirements of Part 2 of this *Handbook* (or any provisions amending or replacingit) as his *practising address*; or

   ~~b.~~ ~~in the case of a *BSB regulated person* or *non-authorised individual* acting as a *manager* or *employee* of a *BSB authorised body*, the address provided by the *BSB authorised body* as his home address or, in the absence of such information, the address of the relevant *BSB authorised body* notified pursuant to the requirements of Part 2 of this *Handbook*; or~~

   c. ~~in either case,~~ an address to which the *defendant* may has asked in writing that such documents be sent; or

   d. in the absence of any of the above, to his last known address ~~or; in the case of a *BSB regulated person* or *non-authorised individual* acting as a *manager* or *employee* of a *BSB authorised body*, the last known address of the relevant *BSB authorised body*,~~

and such service shall be deemed to have been made on the second working day after the date of posting or on the next working day after receipted hand delivery;

2. If served by e-mail, where:

   a. the *defendant's* e-mail address is known to the *Bar Standards Board*; and

   b. the *defendant* has asked for or agreed to service by e-mail, or it is not possible to serve by other means;

and such service shall be deemed to have been made on the second working day after the date the e-mail is sent;

c. if actually served;

d. if served in any way which may be directed by the *Directions judge* or the Chairman of the *Disciplinary Tribunal*.

rE217

For the purpose of this regulation "receipted hand delivery" means by a delivery by hand which is acknowledged by a receipt signed by the *defendant* or by a relevant representative of the *defendant* (including, for example, his clerk~~, a *manager* or *employee* of the *BSB authorised body* at which he works~~).

Delegation

rE218

The powers and functions conferred by these Regulations on a *Directions judge* may be exercised by any other Judge or Queen's Counsel nominated by *the President*, including the Judge designated in the *convening order* as Chairman of the Tribunal appointed to hear and determine the charge or charges against the *defendant*, if the *Directions judge* is unable to act due to absence, or to any other reason.

rE219

Any duty or function or step which, pursuant to the provisions of these regulations, is to be discharged or carried out by *the President* may, if he is unable to act due to absence or to any other reason, be discharged or carried out by any other member of the *Council of the Inns of Court*, the Treasurer of any Inn, or by any other *person* nominated in writing by *the President* for any specific purpose.

rE220

Anything required by these Regulations to be done or any discretion required to be exercised by, and any notice required to be given to, *the President* may be done or exercised by, or given to, any *person* authorised by *the President* (either prospectively or retrospectively and either generally or for a particular purpose) subject to rE218.

Other

rE221

When the Treasurer of an *Inn* is a Royal Bencher, references in these Regulations to the Treasurer shall be read as references to his deputy.

Exclusion from providing representation funded by the Legal Aid Agency – Application for termination

rE222

A *defendant* who has been excluded from legal aid work under Section 42 of the Administration of Justice Act 1985 may apply for an order ending his exclusion from providing representation funded by the *Legal Aid Agency* as part of the Community Legal Service or Criminal Defence Service in accordance with this rE222 and rE223 below.

rE223

Any such application must be in writing and addressed to *the President.*

rE224

The President may dismiss the application, or may decide that the *defendant's* exclusion from providing representation funded by the *Legal Aid Agency* as part of the Community Legal Service or Criminal Defence Service be ended forthwith, or on a specified future date.

rE225

The President must notify his decision in writing to all those *persons* who received copies of the report of the *Disciplinary Tribunal* which ordered that the *defendant* be excluded from providing such representation.

rE226

When the Treasurer of the applicant's *Inn* of Call, and of any other *Inn* of which he is a member, receives any such report, he shall take action equivalent to that which he took in respect of the report of the *Disciplinary Tribunal* which sentenced the *defendant* to be excluded from providing representation funded by the *Legal Aid Agency* as part of the Community Legal Service or Criminal Defence Service.

rE227

The procedures about the publication of the decision of *the President* on any such application as is referred to in this Regulation are those which applied to the publication of the finding and sentence by which the applicant was excluded from providing representation funded by the *Legal Aid Agency* as part of the Community Legal Service or Criminal Defence Service.

rE228

The President may make such order for costs as he thinks fit and rE211 to rE214 apply with all necessary modifications.

Interpretation

rE229

In Section 5.B2 all italicsed terms shall be interpreted in accordance with the defintions in Part 4.

B3 Citation and commencement

[1.83]

rE230

These Regulations may be cited as "The *Disciplinary Tribunal* Regulations".

rE231

These Regulations come into force in accordance with the provisions of Part 1 of this *Handbook.*

B4 Annexes to the Disciplinary Tribunals Regulations

[1.84]

ANNEX 1 – SENTENCING POWERS AGAINST BARRISTERS

When a charge of professional misconduct has been found proved against a barrister[1] by a Disciplinary Tribunal, the Disciplinary Tribunal may decide:

1. to disbar him;
2. to suspend his *practising certificate* and suspend hsi rights and privileges as a member of his *Inn* for a prescribed period (either unconditionally or subject to conditions);
3. not to renew his practising certificate;
4. to impose conditions on his *practising certificate*;
5. be prohibited, either indefinitely or for a prescribed period and either unconditionally or subject to conditions, from accepting or carrying out any *public access instructions*;
6. to remove or to suspend his authorisation to *conduct litigation* or to impose conditions on it;
7. to order him to pay a fine of up to £50,000 to the *Bar Standards Board* ~~(or up to £50,000,000 if the charges relate to his time as an *employee* or *manager* of a *licensed body*)~~;
8. to order him to complete continuing professional development of such nature and duration as the Tribunal may direct, whether outstanding or additional requirements, and to provide satisfactory proof of compliance with this order to the *supervision team*;
9. to order him to be reprimanded by the Treasurer of his Inn;
10. to order him to be reprimanded by the Tribunal;
11. to give him advice about his future conduct;
12. to order him to attend on a nominated *person* to be reprimanded; or
13. to order him to attend on a nominated *person* to be given advice about his future conduct.

1 If an application to disqualify the *Barrister* from acting as *HOLP*, manager or employee of an *authorised person* is made in the same proceedings, the Disciplinary Tribunal may also disqualify the *Barrister* in accordance with the provisions of Annex 6.

~~ANNEX 2 – SENTENCING POWERS AGAINST BSB LEGAL SERVICES BODIES~~

~~If a *Disciplinary Tribunal* finds a charge of *professional misconduct* proved against a *BSB legal services body*, the *Disciplinary Tribunal* may decide to:~~

~~1.~~ ~~remove its authorisation to practise as a *BSB legal services body;*~~

~~2.~~ ~~impose conditions on its authorisation to practise as a *BSB legal services body;*~~

~~3.~~ ~~suspend its authorisation to *practise* for a prescribed period (either unconditionally or subject to conditions);~~

~~4.~~ ~~re-classify it as a *licensed body* (either unconditionally or with conditions imposed on its licence to practise as a *licensed body*);~~

~~5.~~ ~~withdraw, or suspend its authorisation to *conduct litigation* or to impose conditions on it;~~

~~6.~~ ~~order a fine of up to £250,000 to the *Bar Standards Board*;~~

~~7.~~ ~~order that its *managers* or *employees* complete continuing professional development of such nature and duration as the Tribunal may direct and to provide satisfactory proof of compliance with this order to the *supervision team*;~~

~~8.~~ ~~reprimand it;~~

~~9.~~ ~~give it advice about its future conduct; or~~

~~10.~~ ~~order it to attend (by its *HOLP* or other *person* identified in the order) on a nominated *person* to be given advice about its future conduct.~~

~~ANNEX 3 – SENTENCING POWERS AGAINST LICENSED BODIES~~

~~If a *Disciplinary Tribunal* finds a charge of *professional misconduct* proved, against a *licensed body* the *Disciplinary Tribunal* may decide to:~~

~~1.~~ ~~revoke its licence to practise revoked;~~

~~2.~~ ~~suspend its licence to practise for a prescribed period (either unconditionally or subject to conditions);~~

~~3.~~ ~~impose conditions on its licence to practise;~~

~~4.~~ ~~withdraw or suspend its *right to conduct litigation* or to impose conditions on it;~~

~~5.~~ ~~order it to pay a fine of up to £250,000,000 to the *Bar Standards Board*;~~

~~6.~~ ~~order it to ensure that its *managers* or *employees* complete continuing professional development of such nature and duration as the Tribunal shall direct and to provide satisfactory proof of compliance with this order to the *supervision team*;~~

~~7.~~ ~~reprimand it;~~

~~8.~~ ~~give advice to it about its future conduct; or~~

9. ~~order it to attend (by its *HOLP* or other *person* identified in the order) on a nominated *person* to be given advice about its future conduct.~~

ANNEX 4 – SENTENCING POWERS AGAINST REGISTERED EUROPEAN LAWYERS

If a *Disciplinary Tribunal* finds a charge of *professional misconduct* proved against a *registered European lawyer*, the *Disciplinary Tribunal* may decide to:

1. remove him from the register of European lawyers;
2. suspend him from the *register of European lawyers* for a prescribed period (either unconditionally or subject to conditions);
3. impose a condition on him prohibiting him, either indefinitely or for a prescribed period and either unconditionally or subject to conditions, from accepting or carrying out any *public access instructions*;
4. order him to pay a fine of up to £50,000 to the *Bar Standards Board* (or of up to £50,000,000 if, the charges relate to his time as an *employee* or *manager* of a *licensed body*);
5. order him to complete continuing professional development of such nature and duration as the Tribunal shall direct, whether outstanding or additional requirements, and to provide satisfactory proof of compliance with this order to the *supervision team*;
6. reprimand him;
7. give him advice about his future conduct;
8. order him to attend on a nominated *person* to be reprimanded; or
9. order him to attend on a nominated *person* to be given advice about his future conduct.

ANNEX 5 – SENTENCING POWERS AGAINST ALL OTHER BSB REGULATED PERSONS

If a *Disciplinary Tribunal* finds a charge of *professional misconduct* proved against any other *BSB regulated person*,[1] the *Disciplinary Tribunal* may decide to:

1. order him to pay a fine of up to £50,000 to the *Bar Standards Board* (or up to £50,000,000 if the charges relate to their time as an *employee* or *manager* of a *licensed body*);
2. reprimand him;
3. give him advice about his future conduct;
4. order him to attend on a nominated *person* to be reprimanded;
5. order him to attend on a nominated *person* to be given advice about his future conduct.

1 If an application to disqualify is made in the same proceedings, the Disciplinary Tribunal may also disqualify a *BSB regulated person* in accordance with these Regulations.

ANNEX 6 – STANDARD DIRECTIONS

Pursuant to the *Disciplinary Tribunal* Regulations:

1. The hearing will be in public;
2. That by [ ] the *defendant* is required to specify:
   a. whether he admits the charges;
   b. whether any of the facts relied on by the *Bar Standards Board* and set out in the documents provided pursuant to rE104 are admitted;
3. That the *defendant* provide by [ ] a list of the documents, rely and of the witnesses, on which and on whom he intends to rely, and copies of any witness statemens on which he intends to rely;
4. That on or before [ ] both the *BSB representative* and the *defendant* serve written notice of the witnesses (if any) whom they require the other party to tender for cross-examination;
5. That the *defendant* provide to the *Bar Standards Board* at least fourteen days before the date fixed for the substantive hearing [ ] copies of any defence bundle already provided pursuant to direction (3) above for circulation to the Tribunal members;
6. That the estimated length duration of the hearing is [ ] days/hours;
7. That the substantive hearing shall take place on [ ];

OR

8. By [ ] all parties l provide *the President* with dates when they are available for the substantive hearing, failing which *the President* may fix the hearing without reference to the availability of any party;
9. Any skeleton argument to be relied on at the hearing be served on *the President* and on the other parties at least 48 hours before the time fixed for the hearing.
10. That there be liberty for the parties to agree in writing to vary these directions;
11. That there be liberty to apply to the *Directions judge* for further directions.

C THE HEARINGS BEFORE THE VISITORS RULES

CI The Rules

[1.85]

We, the Judges of Her Majesty's High Court of Justice, in the exercise of our powers as Visitors to the Inns of Court, hereby make the following rules for the purpose of appeals to *the Visitors* from *Disciplinary Tribunals* of the *Council of the Inns of Court* and certain other appeals to *the Visitors*:

rE232

Service of Documents

1. Where pursuant to these Rules any document is to be served on any of the *persons* specified in the first column of Table 1 in the Annexe to these Rules, that document shall be served on that *person* by sending it to the *person* specified and the address specified in the second column of that table against the *person* to be served.

2. Such documents shall be served

   a. by recorded delivery post, or

   b. by hand delivery, if a written confirmation of receipt is obtained, or

   c. (save where any fee is payable on the service of a document) by fax or other electronic means in accordance with rE232.4 below.

32. Where, in accordance with Table 1, the address for service on a *respondent* is his last known address, service by first class post shall constitute good service.

4. Where a document is to be served by fax or other electronic means, the party who is to be served must previously have indicated in writing to the party serving:

   a. that the party to be served is willing to accept service by fax or other electronic means; and

   b. the fax number, e-mail address or other electronic identification to which it must be sent.

5. Documents shall be deemed to be served on the date set out in Table 2 in the Schedule to these Rules.

6. For the purpose of this rule, a "written confirmation of receipt" means a receipt signed by or on behalf of the intended recipient.

rE233

Notice of Intention to Appeal

1. Written notice of intention to appeal against the *relevant decision* must be served by the *appellant* on the Clerk to *the Visitors* within the period of 21 days beginning with the date of the *relevant decision* or within such further time as may be allowed by the *Directions judge*.

2. A copy of the notice of intention to appeal should also be served by the *appellant* on the *respondent* and (when the appeal is against a decision of a *Disciplinary Tribunal*) on the *Council of the Inns of Court*.

3. When serving a notice of intention to appeal, an *appellant* (other than the BSB) shall give notice of a current address at which service is to be made on the *appellant*.

4. An *appellant* (other than the BSB) must ensure that the Clerk to *the Visitors* is informed of any change to the *appellant*'s address.

rE234

Directions Judge

1. The Lord Chief Justice shall nominate judges of the High Court or the Court of Appeal to exercise the functions conferred by this Rule.

2. No *person* shall act as a *Directions judge* in relation to any appeal if they were a member of any committee of the BSB at any time when the matter was being considered by that committee.

3. A *Directions Judge* shall consider the course of any appeal and may at any time prior to the appointment of a panel to hear the appeal give such directions and take such steps as appear to him to be necessary or desirable for the purpose of securing the just, expeditious and economical disposal of the appeal.

4. Any applications to be heard by a *Directions Judge* must be served on the Clerk to *the Visitors*.

5. Any applications to the *Directions Judge* will be heard on paper and without an oral hearing, unless there is good reason for an oral hearing.

6. The directions that may be given and the steps that may be taken by the *Directions Judge* may relate to (but shall not be limited to) the following matters:

   a. the anticipated duration of the hearing (which shall not, absent good reason, exceed one day);

   b. the variation of any timetable specified in these Rules;

   c. further procedural steps that should be taken before the hearing;

   d. the failure by either party to comply with any timetable specified in these Rules or directed by him;

   e. the adjournment of the hearing; and

   f. where (in the case of an appeal against a decision of a *Disciplinary Tribunal*) the sentence of the original *Disciplinary Tribunal* has been pronounced, whether it should be stayed pending the outcome of the appeal.

7. The *Directions Judge* may, on application made by the *appellant* (which must be served on the BSB at the time of making the application) and after giving the BSB the opportunity to respond to the application, vary or set aside an order made against the *appellant* under Regulations [30(3) or (4)] of the *Disciplinary Tribunal* Regulations 2009 (Code of Conduct of the Bar Council of England and Wales 8th Edition) on such terms and subject to such conditions (if any) as he considers appropriate.

8. If, at any time, the *Directions Judge* concludes that a party has failed to comply with any obligation imposed by, or timetable specified in, these Rules or directed by him in exercise of his functions and powers (as the case may be), he may also

   a. make a final order for compliance by the party in default;

   b. direct that that party may not serve a *petition* or *answer*;

c. dismiss or strike out the *petition* or *answer* of that party;

d. order that any further step that appears to him to be necessary or desirable in order to provide for a fair and expeditious hearing of the matter be undertaken within a specified period;

e. direct an expedited hearing where the party in default has been prohibited from serving an *answer* or the *answer* has been struck out.

rE235

No appeal from Directions Judge

There shall be no appeal against an order of the *Directions Judge*.

rE236

Service of Petition

1. A written *petition* of appeal containing the information required by rE238. 1below must be served by the *appellant* on the *persons* specified in rE236.2 below within the period of 42 days beginning with the date of the *relevant decision* or within such further time as may be allowed by the Lord Chief Justice or the *Directions Judge*.

2. The *persons* to be served are

   a. the Clerk to *the Visitors*; and

   b. the *respondent*.

3. Service of the *petition* will be valid only if

   a. the *petition* is served on both *persons* identified in rE236.2 above, and

   b. where the *appellant* is a *defendant*,

   c. the *petition* served on the Clerk to *the Visitors* is accompanied by any fee payable in accordance with rE237.1 below, or by an application pursuant to rE237.2, and

   d. a copy of such fee or such application is served on the BSB.

4. If an application for an extension of the period of 42 days specified in rE236.1 above is made, the *Directions Judge* may, if he sees fit, extend the period within which the *petition* must be served.

rE237

Fees

1. Where an appeal is lodged with *the Visitors* by the *defendant*, the *petition* must (subject to the provisions of this rule) be accompanied by the sum of £250 payable to the BSB to defray expenses, such sum to be refunded in the discretion of *the Visitors* in the event of an appeal which is successful wholly or in part.

2. Where payment of the sum required by rE237.1 above would cause undue hardship to the *appellant*, the *appellant* may apply to the *Directions Judge* for an order reducing the amount payable.

3. If the *Directions Judge* is satisfied that payment of the sum required by rE237.1 above would cause undue hardship to the *appellant*, he shall:

   a. direct that some lesser (or nil) amount be paid; and

   b. (where applicable) direct by when such amount be paid.

rE238

Petition of Appeal

1. Where the appeal is against a decision of a *Disciplinary Tribunal*, the *petition* shall state whether the appeal is against the findings or sentence of the *Disciplinary Tribunal*, or both, and shall contain the following particulars:

   a. the charges;

   b. a summary of the facts on which the charges were based;

   c. the findings of the *Disciplinary Tribunal*;

   d. the sentence;

   e. any finding against which the *appellant* appeals (if any);

   f. the grounds for appeal, including for each matter appealed against the specific evidence on which the *appellant* will place reliance;

   g. the relief sought; and

   h. if the hearing is estimated to last longer than one day, an estimate of the time required for the hearing and the reasons for that estimation.

2. In the case of an appeal against sentence the *petition* may also refer to:

   a. any factors which it is contended make the sentence unduly severe (or lenient) in relation to the *appellant*'s (or the *defendant*'s) record; and

   b. sentences in other similar cases.

3. Where the appeal is against a Qualification Decision, the *petition* shall contain the following particulars:

   a. the decision, on review, of the BSB against which the appeal is being made;

   b. a summary of the facts giving rise to that decision;

   c. the grounds for appeal; and

   d. the relief sought.

4. Subject to rE240.5, the *appellant* may not, without the permission of the *Directions Judge*, support the appeal on a ground not relied upon before the body which took the *relevant decision*.

rE239

Service of other documents

1. Subject to rE239.2 below, the *appellant* against a decision of a *Disciplinary Tribunal* shall, at the same time as serving the *petition*, serve on the Clerk to

the Visitors the number of copies specified in rE239.4 below of the transcript of the proceedings before the *Disciplinary Tribunal* whose decision is being appealed.

2. If any transcript to be served pursuant to rE239.1 above is not available when the *petition* is served, the copies of that transcript shall be served on the Clerk to *the Visitors* as soon as practicable thereafter.

3. Not less than 14 days before the date set for the hearing of an appeal

    a. a copy of every document intended to be produced at the hearing by any party shall be served by that party on every other party; and

    b. the number of copies of any such document specified in rE239.4 below shall be served on the Clerk to *the Visitors*.

4. The number of copies required to be served on the Clerk to *the Visitors* is

    a. if the appeal is of a type falling within rE241.2 below, three copies; and

    b. in any other case, two copies.

rE240

Answer

1. The *respondent* may (or, if so directed by the *Directions Judge*, shall) serve on the Clerk to *the Visitors* an *answer* to the *petition* within the period of 28 days starting with the date on which the *petition* is served or on which the transcript of the lower hearing is provided pursuant to rE239.2 (whichever is the later) or such further time as may be allowed by the *Directions Judge*.

2. Where an *answer* is served pursuant to rE240.1 the *respondent* shall also serve forthwith a copy of that *answer* on the *appellant*.

3. The *answer* shall follow the form of the *petition* and shall state which points in the *petition* are accepted and which are rejected.

4. If, in the view of the *person* serving an *answer*, the hearing is likely to last longer than one day, the *answer* shall include an estimation of the time required for the hearing and the reasons for that estimation.

5. The BSB may, in any *answer* it serves in respect of an appeal against a decision of a *Disciplinary Tribunal*, refer to any factors which it is contended make the sentence unduly lenient in relation to the *appellant*'s record or to sentences in other cases.

rE241

Appointment of panel to hear appeal

1. When a *petition* is served upon the Clerk to *the Visitors* (whether or not served in time), and after the period for service of any *answer* in accordance with rE240.1 above has elapsed, the Lord Chief Justice shall nominate the *persons* who are to hear the appeal.

2. An appeal against a decision of a *Disciplinary Tribunal* presided over by a Judge of the High Court shall be heard by a panel comprised of

a. a Judge of the Court of Appeal;

b. a Queen's Counsel; and

c. a *lay representative*.

3. Subject to rE241.4 below, an appeal that is not of a type mentioned in rE241.2 and is an appeal against a decision of a *Disciplinary Tribunal* shall be heard by a panel comprised of:

a. a Judge of the High Court;

b. a *Barrister* (who, where the *defendant* is a Queen's Counsel, shall himself be a Queen's Counsel); and

c. a *lay representative*.

4. An appeal that is not of a type mentioned in rE241.2 and that is an appeal against a decision of a *Disciplinary Tribunal* may be heard by a Judge of the High Court or of the Court of Appeal sitting alone, if the Lord Chief Justice or the *Directions Judge* directs that the appeal relates solely to a point of law and is appropriate to be heard by a judge sitting alone.

5. Any other appeal shall be heard by a Judge of the High Court or the Court of Appeal.

6. No *person* shall be nominated to serve on a panel if they:

a. are a member of the *Bar Council* or of any of its committees; or

b. are a member of the BSB or of any of its committees; or

c. were a member of any committee of the BSB at any time when the matter was being considered by that committee.

rE242

Date of Hearing

1. Unless the *Directions Judge* orders otherwise, the time allocated for the hearing of an appeal shall be one day.

2. The appeal shall be listed by the Clerk to *the Visitors* for a hearing on the first available date after the expiry of a period of four weeks beginning with the date of service on the Clerk to *the Visitors* of the *answer* (or, where no *answer* is served, beginning with the last date for service of the *answer* under rE240.1 above).

3. A notice of the hearing of the appeal shall be served on the *appellant* and on the *respondent* at least 14 days before the date fixed for hearing of the appeal.

rE243

Procedure at hearing

1. Subject to the following paragraphs of this Rule, *the Visitors* may give any directions with regard to the conduct of, and procedure at, a hearing of an appeal they consider appropriate.

2. *The Visitors* may give such directions before or during the hearing.

3. The hearing shall be held in public unless either party has made an

application that the hearing shall not be in public and the public interest does not require that it shall be held in public.

4. A hearing may proceed in the absence of an *appellant* (or *defendant*), but not in the absence of a representative of the BSB.

5. No witness may be called at the hearing without the consent of *the Visitors*.

6. Evidence that was not before the *Disciplinary Tribunal* whose decision is being appealed may be given at the hearing only in exceptional circumstances and with the consent of *the Visitors*.

7. Grounds of appeal based on issues that were not relied upon before the body making the *relevant decision* may be relied upon only with the permission of the *Directions Judge* in accordance with rE238.4 above or, in exceptional circumstances, with the consent of *the Visitors*.

8. An *appellant* or *defendant* (as the case may be) may only challenge before *the Visitors* a decision of a court of law on which the *relevant decision* was based in exceptional circumstances and with the consent of *the Visitors*.

9. The proceedings of *the Visitors* shall continue to be valid notwithstanding that one or more of the members of the panel becomes unable to continue or is or becomes *disqualified* from continuing to act, if the remaining members of the panel include a judge (other than a retired judge) and a *lay representative*.

10. A full record shall be made of the hearing.

11. A transcription of the audio recording shall be provided upon request to either party to the hearing but at his own expense.

rE244

Findings of the Visitors

1. The findings of *the Visitors* shall be pronounced in a single decision. The decision shall state whether it has been reached unanimously or by a majority.

2. The findings may be pronounced in public or in private but should normally be pronounced in public unless a party to the hearing requests otherwise and the public interest does not require that the findings be pronounced in public.

3. In respect of an appeal against a decision of a *Disciplinary Tribunal*, *the Visitors* may:

    a. dismiss the appeal;

    b. allow an appeal in whole or in part;

    c. confirm or vary an order of the *Disciplinary Tribunal* whose decision is being appealed;

    d. order a re-hearing on such terms as they may deem appropriate in the circumstances;

    e. in the case of an appeal brought by the BSB against a decision of a *Disciplinary Tribunal*, issue a declaration, but only where this will have no consequences whatsoever for the *defendant*.

4. In respect of an appeal against a Qualification Decision, *the Visitors* may:
   a. allow an appeal in whole or in part;
   b. confirm or vary the decision of the BSB;
   c. order the BSB to reconsider its decision on such terms as the panel appointed to hear the panel may determine to be appropriate in the circumstances.
5. *The Visitors* shall give reasons for their decision. These reasons may be given orally or in writing.
6. *The Visitors* may order, in the event of an appeal against a decision of a *Disciplinary Tribunal* by the *defendant* which is successful wholly or in part, a refund to the *appellant* of any sum paid to the BSB in accordance with rE237.1 above.
7. There is no appeal against a decision of *the Visitors*.

rE245

Barrister's Exclusion from providing representation funded by the Legal Aid Agency as part of the Community Legal Service or Criminal Defence Service

1. These Rules shall apply in relation to an appeal against an order of the *Disciplinary Tribunal* that a *Barrister*'s exclusion from providing representation funded by the *Legal Aid Agency* as part of the Community Legal Service or Criminal Defence Service pursuant to section 42(3) of the Administration of Justice Act 1985 (as substituted by Section 33 of the Legal Aid Act 1988 and amended by section 24, Schedule 4, ss 32 and 35 of the Access to Justice Act 1999) is not to be terminated, subject to the following modifications set out in the following paragraphs of this rule.
2. The *petition* shall contain the following particulars
   a. the date of the order of the *Disciplinary Tribunal* that excluded the *appellant* from providing representation funded by the *Legal Aid Agency* as part of the Community Legal Service or Criminal Defence Service;
   b. the charges in respect of which that order was made;
   c. a summary of the facts on which those charges were based;
   d. the findings of the *Disciplinary Tribunal*;
   e. the findings against which the appeal is brought; and
   f. the grounds for appeal.
3. An order of the *Disciplinary Tribunal* to terminate a *Barrister*'s exclusion from providing representation funded by the *Legal Aid Agency* as part of the Community Legal Service or Criminal Defence Service only from a date that is subsequent to that order shall, for the purposes of any appeal, be treated as an order that the *Barrister*'s exclusion from such work is not to be terminated.

rE246

Costs

1. *The Visitors* may make such order for costs of the appeal as they consider appropriate.
2. Any order for costs made may include an order for payment of the cost of any transcript required for the purposes of the appeal.

rE247

Transition

Where any appeal has been commenced before 1 September 2010 but has not been completed by that date, these rules shall apply to that appeal from that date but any steps that have been taken in relation to that appeal pursuant to any provision of the Hearings Before *the Visitors* Rules 2005 shall be regarded as having been taken pursuant to the equivalent provisions of these Rules.

rE248

Revocation

The Hearings before *the Visitors* Rules 2005 are hereby revoked.

rE249

Citation and Commencement

These rules may be cited as the Hearings before *the Visitors* Rules 2010 and shall come into effect on 1 September 2010.

rE250

Interpretation

1. The Interpretation Act 1978 shall apply in relation to the interpretation of these Rules as it applies to the interpretation of an Act of Parliament.
2. These Rules shall be interpreted in accordance with Part 6.
3. Where a *Disciplinary Tribunal* has made a finding and imposed sentence in two separate decisions, whether in accordance with [regulation 19(5)] of the *Disciplinary Tribunal* Regulations 2009 (Code of Conduct of the Bar Council of England and Wales 8th Edition) or otherwise, the date of the *relevant decision* shall be deemed to be the date of the later decision.
4. Where the *relevant decision* is a decision, on review, under [Part X of the *Bar* Training Regulations], the date of the *relevant decision* shall be deemed to be the date upon which notice of the decision was sent by the BSB to the *person* affected by the decision.
5. Any term defined in this Section 5.C shall carry the same meaning as it does in Part 6 of this *Handbook*.
6. The powers conferred upon the Lord Chief Justice by these Rules can be

exercised on his behalf by a Judge of the Court of Appeal or a Judge of the High Court who is selected by him to act in this capacity. This delegation does not prevent the Lord Chief Justice from exercising these powers.

7. In these Rules a period of time expressed as a number of days shall be computed as clear days.

On behalf of the Judges of Her Majesty's

High Court of Justice

Lord Chief Justice

President of the Queen's Bench Division

President of the Family Division

The Chancellor of the High Court

C2 Annexes to the Hearings Before the Visitors Rules

[1.86]

ANNEX 7 – ADDRESSEE AND PLACE FOR SERVICE OF DOCUMENTS

Person to be served	**Addressee and place of service**
The Clerk to the Visitors	Addressed to the Clerk to the Visitors at the Royal Courts of Justice, Strand, London WC2A 2LL.
The Council of the Inns of Court	Addressed to the President of the Council of the Inns of Court, c/o The Honourable Society of the Inner Temple, c/o 10 Fleet Street, London EC4Y 1AU.
The BSB	*In respect of a decision of a Disciplinary Tribunal*: Addressed to the Secretary to the Complaints Committee of the BSB at 289–293 High Holborn, London WC1V 7HZ. *In respect of a Qualification Decision*: Addressed to the Secretary to the Qualifications Committee of the BSB at 289–293 High Holborn, London WC1V 7HZ.
An *appellant* other than the BSB	Addressed to him at the address specified by him pursuant to rE233.3.

A *defendant*	Addressed to him at – (a)the address notified by him pursuant to [paragraphs 202(d) or 206.1(a)(i) of the Code of Conduct of the *Bar* of England and Wales 8th Editon] (or any provisions amending or replacing those paragraphs); (b)if he has specified in writing an address to which documents may be sent, that address; or (c)where no address has been notified pursuant to the provisions mentioned in paragraph (a) above or specified as mentioned in paragraph (b) above, to his last known address.

ANNEX 8 – DEEMED DATE OF SERVICE OF DOCUMENTS

Method of service	**Deemed date of service of document**
First-class post	The second day after it was posted, left with, delivered to or collected by the relevant service provider provided that day is a business day; or if not, the next business day after that day.
Hand delivery	If the document is served *person*ally before 4.30 pm on a business day, on that day; or in any other case, on the next business day after that day.
Recorded delivery	If it is delivered to or left at the permitted address on a business day before 4.30 pm, on that day; or in any other case, on the next business day after that day.
Fax	If the transmission of the fax is completed on a business day before 4.30 pm, on that day; or in any other case, on the next business day after the day on which it was transmitted.
E-mail or other electronic transmission	If the e-mail or other electronic transmission is sent on a business day before 4.30p.m., on that day; or in any other case, on the next business day after the day on which it was sent.

D THE INTERIM SUSPENSION AND DISQUALIFICATION REGULATIONS

D1 Application

[1.87]

rE251

This Section 5.D prescribes the manner in which the BSB may seek to take interim action to:

1. suspend a *BSB authorised person* (excluding, for the avoidance of doubt, any *unregistered barrister*); or

2. *disqualify* any *relevant person* from acting as an ~~a *HOLP* or a *HOFA* or from working as a *manager* or~~ *employee* of a *BSB authorised person*;

   subject to the criteria outlined at rE257 and rE258 below, and pending consideration by a *Disciplinary Tribunal* under Section 5.B.

rE252

In addition to the above, this Section 5.D sets out the basis upon which the *PCC* may impose an immediate interim suspension or *disqualification* on any *relevant person* subject to the criteria outlined at rE259 to rE261 below, and pending consideration by an *interim panel* in accordance with this Section 5.D.

rE253

Anything required by this Section 5.D to be done or any discretion required to be exercised by, and any notice required to be given to, the *President* may be done or exercised, or given to, any *person* authorised by the *President* (either prospectively or retrospectively and either generally or for a particular purpose).

D2 The Regulations

[1.88]

Composition of panels

rE254

An *interim panel* shall consist of three members nominated by the *President* being a Chairman (who shall be a Queen's Counsel) and two others, of whom at least one must be a *lay member*. Provided that:

1. the proceedings of an *interim panel* shall be valid notwithstanding that one of the members becomes unable to act or is *disqualified* from acting, so long as the number of members present throughout the substantive hearing is not reduced below two and continues to include the Chairman and one *lay member*;
2. no *person* shall be appointed to serve on a panel if s/he:
   a. is a member of the *Bar* Council or of any of its committees; or
   b. is a member of the *Bar Standards Board* or of any of its committees; or
   c. was a member of the *Bar Standards Board* or any of its committees at any time when the matter was being considered by the *Bar Standards Board*.

rE255

A *review panel* shall consist of three members nominated by *the President* being a Chairman (who shall be a Queen's Counsel) and two others, of whom at least one must be a *lay member*. Provided that:

1. the proceedings of a *review panel* shall be valid notwithstanding that one of

the members becomes unable to act or is *disqualified* from acting, so long as the number of members present throughout the substantive hearing is not reduced below two and continues to include the Chairman and one *lay member*;

2. no *person* shall be appointed to serve on a panel if s/he:

   a. is a member of the *Bar Council* or of any of its committees; or

   b. is a member of the *Bar Standards Board* or of any of its committees; or

   c. was a member of the *Bar Standards Board* or any of its committees at any time when the matter was being considered by the *Bar Standards Board*;

3. no individual who is intended to sit on the *review panel* shall have sat on either the *interim panel* or the *appeal panel* considering the same matter.

rE256

An *appeal panel* shall consist of three members nominated by *the President* being:

1. two Queen's Counsel, each of whom is entitled to sit as a Recorder or a Deputy High Court Judge or who has been Queen's Counsel for at least ten years. Unless the *appeal panel* otherwise decides, the senior *barrister* member will be the Chairman of the *appeal panel*; and

2. a *lay member.*

   Provided that:

   a. the proceedings of an *appeal panel* shall be valid notwithstanding that one of the members, becomes unable to act or is *disqualified* from acting, so long as the number of members present throughout the substantive hearing is not reduced below two and continues to include the Chairman and the *lay member*;

   b. no *person* shall be appointed to serve on an *appeal panel* if s/he:

      i. is a member of the *Bar* Council or of any of its committees; or

      ii. is a member of the *Bar Standards Board* or of any of its committees; or

      iii. was a member of the *Bar Standards Board* or any of its committees at any time when the matter was being considered by the *Bar Standards Board*;

3. no individual who is intended to sit on the *appeal panel* shall have sat on either the *interim panel* or the *review panel* considering the same matter.

Referral to an interim panel

rE257

On receipt of a *complaint* or any other information, the *PCC* may refer a *defendant* to an *interim panel* if:

1. subject to rE258:

a. the *defendant* has been convicted of, or charged with, a *criminal offence* in any jurisdiction other than a *minor criminal offence*; or

b. the *defendant* has been convicted by another *Approved Regulator*, for which they have been sentenced to a period of suspension or termination of the right to practise; or

~~c. the *defendant* is a *BSB licensed body* and has been intervened into by the *Bar Standards Board*; or~~

~~d. the *defendant* is a *BSB legal services body* and the *grounds for intervention* would have been met in relation to it had the *BSB legal services body* been a *BSB licensed body*; or~~

e. the referral is necessary to protect the interests of *clients* (or former or potential *clients*); and

2. the *PCC* decides having regard to the *regulatory objectives* that pursuing an interim suspension or an interim *disqualification order* is appropriate in all the circumstances.

rE258

No matter shall be referred to an *interim panel* on any of the grounds of referral set out in rE257.1.a to rE257.1.b unless the *PCC* considers that, whether singly or collectively, the relevant grounds of referral would warrant, in the case of a *BSB authorised person*, a charge of *professional misconduct* and referral to a *Disciplinary Tribunal*, or, in the case of a *relevant person*, an application to a *Disciplinary Tribunal* for *disqualification* (in each case such referral or application to be made in accordance with Section 5.B).

rE259

If the *PCC* refers a *defendant* to an *interim panel* under rE257, the *PCC* (or the Chair on its behalf) shall go on to consider whether or not the *defendant* should be subject to an immediate interim suspension or *disqualification* under rE261 pending disposal by the *interim panel*.

rE260

An immediate interim suspension or *disqualification* may only be imposed if the *PCC* is satisfied that such a course of action is justified having considered the risk posed to the *public* if such interim suspension or *disqualification* were not implemented and having regard to the *regulatory objectives*.

rE261

Any immediate interim suspension or *disqualification* imposed by the *PCC* shall:

1. take immediate effect;
2. be notified in writing by the *PCC* to the *defendant*;
3. remain in force until the earlier of:

   a. such time as an *interim panel* has considered the matter; or

b. the date falling four weeks after the date on which the immediate interim suspension or *disqualification* is originally imposed;

4. where relevant, result in the removal of the relevant *BSB authorised individual's practising certificate, litigation extension* and/or right to undertake public access work (as appropriate);

5. ~~where relevant, result in the imposition of conditions on the relevant *BSB authorised person's* authorisation and/or licence (as appropriate)~~

6. be published on the *Bar Standards Board's* website; and

7. be annotated on the *Bar Standards Board's* register of *BSB authorised persons* which is to be maintained by the *Bar Standards Board* in accordance with S123r or be included on the *Bar* Standards Board's register of individuals that are the subject of a *disqualification order* (as appropriate).

Guidance

gE1

If an immediate interim suspension or *disqualification* has been imposed by the *PCC* it must be considered by an *interim panel* within four weeks of the date that that the immediate interim suspension or *disqualification* is originally imposed. If it is not considered by an *interim panel* within that period, it shall automatically fall away and no further period of interim suspension or *disqualification* may be imposed on the *defendant* until the matter is considered by an *interim panel.*

gE2

If, subsequent to the imposition of an immediate suspension or *disqualification* under rE260, the *relevant person* agrees to provide to the *PCC* an undertaking in written terms in accordance with the provisions of rE263.4 below which is satisfactory to the *PCC* and which is subject to such conditions and for such period as the *PCC* may agree, the *PCC* may elect to remove or qualify the immediate interim suspension or *disqualification* pending the disposal of any charges or application by a *Disciplinary Tribunal.* For the avoidance of doubt, in these circumstances the referral to the *interim panel* shall also be withdrawn in accordance with the provisions of rE264 below.

Procedure after referral to an Interim Panel and, where relevant, the decision to impose an immediate interim suspension or disqualification

rE262

As soon as practicable after the *PCC* has made a decision to refer a *defendant* to an *interim panel*, the *Bar Standards Board* shall write to the *President* notifying him of the decision and informing him about whether or not an immediate interim suspension or *disqualification* has also been imposed on such *defendant.*

rE263

As soon as practicable after receipt of the notice referred to in rE262, the *President* shall write to the *defendant* notifying him of the decision, together with a copy of these *Enforcement Regulations*, and briefly setting out the details that have caused the referral to the *interim panel.* The letter of notification shall:

1. where relevant, inform the *defendant* that he is the subject of an immediate interim suspension or *disqualification* (as appropriate) together with a summary of the consequences of that decision;

2. lay down a fixed time and date (normally not less than fourteen and not more than twenty-one days from the date of the letter) for the hearing to take place. One alternative shall be given;

3. invite the *defendant* to accept one or other of the dates proposed or to provide a written representation to the *President*, which should be copied to the Chairman of the *PCC*, objecting to both dates with reasons and providing two further alternative dates which shall be not more than:

   a. four weeks after the date of the imposition of the immediate interim suspension or *disqualification*, where relevant; or

   b. in all other cases, twenty-one days from the date of the letter of notification;

   Any such representation must be received by the *President* not more than ten days from the date of the letter of notification. The *President* shall consider any such representation together with any representations from the Chairman of the *PCC*, and either confirm one of the original dates or re-fix the hearing. If no such representation is received within ten days of the date of the letter of notification the hearing shall take place at the time and date first fixed pursuant to rE263.2 above. The *President's* decision, which shall be notified in writing to the *defendant* by the *President*, shall be final. Once fixed, a hearing date shall be vacated only in exceptional circumstances and with the agreement of the *President*:

4. inform the *defendant* that he may by letter to the Chairman of the *PCC* undertake, pending the disposal of any charge(s) or application(s) by a *Disciplinary Tribunal*:

   a. to be immediately *suspended* or *disqualified* (in which case the consequences set out at rE261.4 to rE261.6 would apply);

   b. not to accept or carry out any *public access instructions*; and/or

   c. to inform his professional and/or lay *clients* about any *convictions*, charges or other matters leading to a referral, in written terms satisfactory to the Chairman of the *PCC;*

   and summarising the consequences of the *defendant* electing to make such an undertaking (which for the avoidance of doubt, may include those set out at rE261.4 to rE261.6 above);

5. shall inform the *defendant* that he is entitled to make representations in writing or orally, by himself or by others on his behalf; and

6. shall inform the *defendant* that he is entitled to request an expedited hearing of any charges of *professional misconduct* or applications for *disqualification orders* by a *Disciplinary Tribunal.*

rE264

If a *defendant* sends a letter in accordance with rE263.3 above which is satisfactory to the Chairman of the *PCC*, the Chairman shall accept the undertaking contained in the letter in lieu of the *interim panel* imposing any period of interim suspension or interim *disqualification* pending the disposal by a *Disciplinary Tribunal* of any charges of *professional misconduct* or applications for a *disqualification order* (as the case may be).

Procedure and powers of interim panels

rE265

At any hearing of an *interim panel* the proceedings shall be governed by the rules of natural justice, subject to which:

1. the procedure shall be informal, the details being at the discretion of the Chairman of the *interim panel*;
2. the *defendant* shall be entitled to make representations in writing or orally, by himself or by another on his behalf, as to;
   a. why a period of interim suspension or interim *disqualification* should not be imposed; or
   b. why the *interim panel* should not direct the *defendant* to notify his professional *clients* and/or lay *clients* about any *convictions*, charges or other matters leading to a referral; or
   c. any further or alternative direction which the *interim panel* is empowered to make in relation to the *defendant* under rE36.3 below;

   pending the disposal of any charges or applications by a *Disciplinary Tribunal*;
3. no witnesses may be called without the prior consent of the Chairman of the Panel and without the submission of a proof of evidence;
4. the attendance of the *defendant* shall be required. Should he nevertheless fail to attend, the hearing may proceed in his absence subject to the *interim panel* being satisfied that this course is appropriate. Should the *interim panel* not be so satisfied, it shall have the power to adjourn the hearing;
5. the hearing shall not be in public unless so requested by the *defendant* and a record shall be taken electronically; and
6. if the *interim panel* decides an adjournment is necessary for any reason, it may adjourn the hearing for such period and to such time and place, and upon such terms, as it may think fit.

rE266

If the members of the *interim panel* are not unanimous as to any decision, the decision made shall be that of the majority of them. If the members of the *interim panel* are equally divided the decision shall be that which is most favourable to the *defendant*.

rE267

At the conclusion of the hearing the *interim panel*:

1. may decide not to impose any period of interim suspension, interim *disqualification* or other order;
2. may impose a period of interim suspension or interim *disqualification* (in each

case, either unconditionally or subject to conditions) pending the hearing before a *Disciplinary Tribunal*, provided that no interim suspension or interim *disqualification* may be imposed unless the *interim panel* considers that:

a. were a *Disciplinary Tribunal* to find a related charge of *professional misconduct* proven, it would be likely to impose a sentence of disbarment (with respect to *barrister defendants*), a sentence of suspension (with respect to *barrister defendants* or *registered European lawyer defendants* ~~or *BSB authorised body defendants*~~), ~~revocation of the licence or authorisation (with respect to *BSB authorised body defendants*)~~ or a *disqualification order* (with respect to *relevant person defendants*); and

b. such interim suspension or interim *disqualification* is in the public interest;

3. in lieu of imposing a period of interim suspension or interim *disqualification*, the *interim panel* may either:

a. where the *defendant* is a *BSB authorised person*, direct the *defendant* to carry out his or its future activities in accordance with such interim conditions on the *defendant's* authorisation ~~or licence~~ as the *interim panel* may think fit pending final disposal of the charges or application against him or them; or

b. where the *defendant* is a ~~*manager or*~~ *employee* of a *BSB authorised person*, direct such *person* (after affording the *BSB authorised person* an opportunity to be heard) to take such steps in relation to the *defendant* as the *interim panel* may think fit, which may include limits on the type of work the *defendant* is to be permitted to do, or requirements as to his supervision or training, pending final disposal of the charges or application against him;

c. accept from the *defendant* an undertaking in written terms satisfactory to the *interim panel* (and subject to such conditions and for such period as the *interim panel* may agree):

i. to be immediately *suspended* or *disqualified*; or

ii. not to accept or carry out any *public access instructions* or to *conduct litigation*; or

iii. to inform his professional and lay *clients* about any *convictions*, charges or other matters leading to a referral;

pending the disposal of any charges or application by a *Disciplinary Tribunal* provided always that the *defendant* accepts that the following consequences may arise as a result of such undertaking being provided depending on the nature of the undertaking being provided:

(1) the removal of the relevant *BSB authorised individual's practising certificate*, *litigation extension* and/or right to undertake *public access* work (as appropriate);

~~(2) the imposition of conditions on the relevant *BSB authorised person's* authorisation and/or licence (as appropriate)~~;

(3) publication of the details of such interim suspension ~~or *disqualification*~~ on the *Bar Standards Board's* website; and

(4) either the inclusion of a note on the *Bar Standards Board's*

register of *BSB authorised persons* to the effect that such *BSB authorised person* is temporarily *suspended* from *practice* ~~or the inclusion of the details of such interim *disqualification* on the *Bar* Standards Board's register of individuals that are the subject of a *disqualification order*~~;

4. shall set down in writing signed by the Chairman of the *interim panel* the decision of the *interim panel* and the terms of any period of interim suspension, interim *disqualification* or interim condition imposed under these *Interim Suspension and Disqualification Regulations* or accepted (in the form of an undertaking) under rE267.3.c above.

   a. Where the *defendant* is a *BSB authorised individual*, the imposition of any period of suspension shall be recorded as follows:

      "That ....be suspended from *practice* as a .... and from enjoyment of all rights and privileges as a member of the Honourable Society of ....and be prohibited from holding himself out as being a .... for a period expiring on [the .... day of ..../[insert applicable condition/event on which expiry is contingent] or such earlier date as a *Disciplinary Tribunal* shall have disposed of any charges that have caused the interim suspension or such *Disciplinary Tribunal* may otherwise direct." (Note: If the Panel decides that the suspension should apply to only part of the *defendant's practice* or shall be subject to conditions, such part or such conditions (as the case may be) shall be recorded);

   b. ~~Where the *defendant* is a *BSB authorised body*, the imposition of any period of suspension shall be recorded as follows:~~

      ~~"That .... have its BSB licence/authorisation *suspended* for a period expiring on [the ...... day of ..../[insert applicable condition/event on which expiry is contingent] or such earlier date as a *Disciplinary Tribunal* shall have disposed of any charges that have caused the interim suspension or such *Disciplinary Tribunal* may otherwise direct." (Note: If the Panel decides that the suspension should apply to only part of the *defendant's practice* or shall be subject to conditions, such part or such conditions (as the case may be) shall be recorded);~~

   c. Where the *defendant* is a *relevant person*, the imposition of any period of *disqualification* shall be recorded as follows:

      "That .... be disqualified from [specify here the relevant capacities in respect of which the order applies, which may be some or all of: ~~acting as a HOLP, HOFA or manager of any BSB authorised body or~~ being an employee of any BSB authorised person] and that any BSB regulated person is prohibited from permitting the defendant to work in any such capacity for a period expiring on [the .... day of................../[insert applicable condition/event on which expiry is contingent] or such earlier date as a Disciplinary Tribunal shall have disposed of any charges that have caused the interim disqualification or such Disciplinary Tribunal may otherwise direct";

5. shall, if a period of interim suspension ~~or interim *disqualification*~~ or an interim condition is imposed or a written undertaking is accepted under these *Interim Suspension and Disqualification Rules*:

a. inform the *defendant* of his right to request a *review panel* to review the matter as provided in rE268 below;

b. inform the *defendant* of his right of appeal as provided in rE272 below;

c. inform the *defendant* that he is entitled to request an expedited hearing of any charges or applications by a *Disciplinary Tribunal* and, if so requested, the Chairman of the Panel may so direct;

6. may, if it has not already been referred to a *Disciplinary Tribunal*, refer the matter to a *Disciplinary Tribunal*.

Review

rE268

In the event of a significant change in circumstances or other good reason the *defendant* may at any time while on interim suspension, interim *disqualification* or subject to interim conditions make a request in writing to *the President* for a *review panel* to be convened to review the matter.

rE269

The letter must set out the details of any alleged change in circumstances or good reason. On receipt of such a letter the *President* may seek representations from the Chairman of the *PCC* and may in his discretion convene a *review panel* or refuse the request. In either case *the President* shall notify the *defendant* in writing of the decision. If the *President* decides to convene a *review panel* the procedure to be followed for fixing the time and date of the hearing shall be as set out in rE263.2 and rE263.3.

rE270

The proceedings before a *review panel* shall be by way of a rehearing and the provisions of rE265 above shall apply as if for references therein to the *interim panel* and the Chairman of the *interim panel* there were substituted references respectively to the *review panel* and the Chairman of the *review panel*.

rE271

Unless in the meantime the hearing before a *Disciplinary Tribunal* of any charges or applications arising from and/or related to the referral to an *interim panel* has commenced, a hearing by a *review panel* convened pursuant to rE268 above shall take place at the time and date fixed. Such hearing shall be a rehearing of the matter by the *review panel* which may reconsider the matter as if there had been no previous hearing.

rE272

If the hearing before a *Disciplinary Tribunal* of any charges or applications arising from and/or related to the referral to an *interim panel* has commenced before the date fixed for a rehearing by a *review panel*, the date fixed for the rehearing shall be vacated and any interim suspension, interim *disqualification* or interim conditions made or undertaking accepted by the *interim panel* shall continue until such charges or applications have been disposed of by the *Disciplinary Tribunal.*

Appeals

rE273

A *defendant* may by letter served on the *President* and on the Chair of the *PCC* not more than fourteen days after the date of the *relevant decision* of an *interim panel* give notice of his wish to appeal against the decision.

rE274

As soon as practicable after receipt of a letter in accordance with rE273 above the *President* shall convene an *appeal panel* and write to the *defendant* notifying him of a fixed time and date (normally not less than fourteen and not more than twenty-one days from the date of receipt of the letter) for the hearing to take place. The *defendant* may make a written representation, addressed to the Chairman of the proposed *appeal panel*, objecting to the date with reasons and providing two further alternative dates. Any such representation must be received by the Chairman of the *appeal panel* not more than fourteen days from the date of the letter of notification. The Chairman shall consider any such representation and either confirm the original date or re-fix the hearing. If no such representation is received within fourteen days of the date of the letter of notification the hearing shall take place at the time and date originally notified to the *defendant.* The Chairman's decision, which shall be notified in writing to the *defendant* shall be final. Once fixed, a hearing date shall be vacated only in exceptional circumstances and with the agreement of the Chairman of the *appeal panel.*

rE275

The proceedings before an *appeal panel* shall be by way of a rehearing and the provisions of rE265 above shall apply as if for references therein to the *interim panel* and the Chairman of the *interim panel* there were substituted references respectively to the *appeal panel* and the Chairman of the *appeal panel.*

rE276

At the conclusion of the hearing the *appeal panel*:

1. may remove the period of interim suspension or interim *disqualification* and/or any interim conditions imposed under this Section 5.D;
2. may confirm the period of interim suspension or interim *disqualification* or impose further or alternative interim conditions, or substitute such shorter period (either unconditionally or subject to conditions) as may be thought fit;
3. in lieu of confirming or imposing a period of interim suspension or interim *disqualification* or imposing interim conditions, may accept from the *defendant* in terms satisfactory to the Chairman of the Panel an undertaking in writing to continue to be *suspended, disqualified* and/or to submit to such conditions and for such period as the *appeal panel* may agree, pending the disposal of any charges by a *Disciplinary Tribunal*;

4. shall set down in writing signed by the Chairman of the *appeal panel* the decision of the *appeal panel* and the terms of any interim suspension, interim *disqualification* or interim conditions confirmed or imposed under rE276.2 above or undertaking accepted under rE276.3 above;

5. may, if it has not already been referred to a *Disciplinary Tribunal*, refer the matter to a *Disciplinary Tribunal*;

If the members of the *appeal panel* are not unanimous as to the decision, the decision made shall be that of the majority of them. If the members of the *appeal panel* are equally divided, the decision shall be that which is most favourable to the *defendant*. Any period of interim suspension or interim *disqualification* or interim conditions having been set, which is confirmed or imposed, shall be recorded as set out in rE276.4 above.

rE277

A pending appeal to an *appeal panel* shall not operate as a stay of any period of interim suspension or interim *disqualification* or interim conditions having been set or the terms of any direction or undertaking which is/are the subject of the appeal.

rE278

There shall be no right of appeal from the decision of an *appeal panel*.

Suspension or disqualification ceases to have effect

rE279

Unless a *Disciplinary Tribunal* shall otherwise direct, any period of interim suspension or *disqualification* and any interim conditions imposed by the *interim panel* or *appeal panel* under this Section 5.D shall cease and the *defendant* shall cease to be bound by the terms of any direction made or undertaking accepted by a *interim panel* or an *appeal panel* immediately upon:

1. a *Disciplinary Tribunal* dismissing or making an order disposing of all charges of *professional misconduct* or applications for *disqualification* based on the referral from the *interim panel* or the *PCC* (as appropriate);

2. any appeal by the *defendant* against the *conviction* or all the *conviction(s)* which had caused the referral to a *interim panel* being successful;

3. the acquittal of the *defendant* of the criminal charge or (as the case may be) all of the criminal charges which had caused the referral to a *interim panel*;

4. the criminal charge or (as the case may be) all of the criminal charges which had caused the referral to an *interim panel* being withdrawn.

Costs

rE280

An *interim panel*, *review panel* and an *appeal panel* shall have no power to award costs.

Report and Publication of Decisions

rE281

As soon as practicable after the conclusion of an *interim panel* hearing or an *appeal panel* hearing, the *President* shall confirm the decision to the *defendant* in writing.

rE282

In any case where a period of interim suspension or interim *disqualification* is imposed or an interim condition is imposed under this Section 5.D or a direction is made requiring notification to lay and/or professional *clients* or an undertaking from a *defendant* is accepted, the *President* shall communicate brief details in writing of the fact that the *defendant* is on an interim basis *suspended*, *disqualified* and/or subject to conditions (as the case may be) to:

1. the defendant;
2. the Chairman of the Bar Standards Board;
3. the defendant's head of chambers, HOLP, or employer (as appropriate);
4. in the case of a registered European lawyer, his home professional body;
5. the Treasurers of the defendant's Inn of Call and of any other Inns of which he is a member;
6. other Approved Regulators and the LSB; and
7. those of the following whom he deems, in his absolute discretion, to be appropriate taking into account the particular circumstances:
    a. the Lord Chancellor;
    b. the Lord Chief Justice;
    c. the Attorney General;
    d. the Director of Public Prosecutions;
    e. the Chairman of the Bar Council;
    f. the Leaders of the six circuits;
    g. the Chairman of the *PCC*; and
    h. such one or more press agencies or other publications, as the Chairman of the *PCC* may direct.

rE283

The *Bar Standards Board* shall keep a record of those who are subject to suspension orders or *disqualification orders* or conditions imposed on their authorisation made under the procedures in this *Handbook* and shall publish details of any interim suspension, interim *disqualification* or interim conditions on its website and in such of its registers as it considers appropriate, for as long as they remain in effect.

Service of documents

rE284

Any documents required to be served on a *defendant* arising out of or in connection with proceedings under these Regulations shall be deemed to have been validly served:

1. If sent by registered post, or recorded delivery post, or receipted hand delivery to:

   a. in the case of a *BSB authorised individual*, the address notified by such *defendant* pursuant to the requirements of Part 2 of this *Handbook* (or any provisions amending or replacing the same) as being his *practising address*; or

   ~~b.~~ ~~in the case of a *BSB regulated person* or *non-authorised individual* acting as a *manager* or *employee* of a *BSB authorised body*, the address provided by the *BSB authorised body* as being his home address or, in the absence of such information, the address of the relevant *BSB authorised body* notified pursuant to the requirements of Part 2 of this *Handbook*~~; or

   c. in either case, an address to which the *defendant* may request in writing that such documents be sent; or

   d. in the absence of any of the above, to his last known address ~~or; in the case of a *BSB regulated person* or *non-authorised individual* acting as a *manager* or *employee* of a *BSB authorised body*, the last known address of the relevant *BSB authorised body*~~;

   and such service shall be deemed to have been made on the second day after it was posted, left with, delivered to or collected by the relevant service provider, (provided that that day is a business day, or, if not, the next business day after that day) or on the next working day after receipted hand delivery;

2. If served by e-mail, where:

   a. the *defendant's* e-mail address is known to the *Bar Standards Board*; and

   b. the *defendant* has requested or agreed to service by e-mail, or it is not possible to serve by other means;

   and such service shall be deemed to have been made on the second working day after the date of sending the e-mail;

3. if actually served;

4. if served in any way which may be directed by the *President* of the *Council of the Inns of Court*.

rE285

For the purpose of this regulation "receipted hand delivery" means by a delivery by hand which is acknowledged by a receipt signed by the *defendant* or a relevant representative of such *defendant* (including, for example, his clerk ~~and a *manager* or *employee* of the *BSB authorised body* at which he works~~).

D3 Interpretation

[1.89]

rE286

In this Section 5.D unless the context otherwise requires all italicized terms shall be defined and all terms shall be interpreted in accordance with the definitions in Part 6.

D4 Commencement

[1.90]

rE287

These rules shall come into force in accordance with the provisions of Part 1 of this *Handbook*.

E THE FITNESS TO PRACTISE REGULATIONS

E1 Preliminaries

[1.91]

These Regulations, commencing 6 January 2014, are made by the *Bar Standards Board*, in liaison with the *Council of the Inns of Court*, under section 21 (regulatory arrangements) Legal Services Act 2007, under authority delegated by the General Council of the Bar as the Approved Regulator of the Bar under Part 1 of Schedule 4 to the Legal Services Act 2007, and with the approval of the *Legal Services Board* under Paragraph 19 of Schedule 4 to the Legal Services Act 2007.

Commencement and application

rE288

These Regulations will come into effect on 6 January 2014 and shall apply to all cases referred to a *Fitness to Practise Panel* or *an Appeal Panel* prior to that date under the Regulations then applying, and any step taken in relation to any *Fitness to Practise Panel* or *Appeal Panel* pursuant to those Regulations shall be regarded as having been taken pursuant to the equivalent provisions of these Regulations.

rE289

Anything required by these Regulations to be done or any discretion required to be exercised by, and any notice required to be given to, the *President* of the Council of the Inns of Court or the *PCC*, may be done or exercised by, or given to, any *person* or body authorised by the *President* or by the *PCC* as the case may be (either prospectively or retrospectively and either generally or for a particular purpose).

Definitions

rE290

Any term defined in Definitions Section of the Handbook shall carry the same meaning in these Regulations. For the purpose of the Fitness to Practise Regulations, "Individual" means any "BSB authorised individual".

E2 Constitution of Panels

[1.92]

rE291

The *President* shall constitute *Fitness to Practise Panels* and *Appeal Panels* (Panels) to exercise the functions afforded to those Panels under these Regulations, in accordance with the provisions set out Schedule 1.

E3 The Fitness to Practise Procedure

[1.93]

Referral to a Fitness to Practise Panel

rE292

Where the *PCC* receives information suggesting that an *Individual* is *unfit to practise*, the matter shall be considered under Regulation E294.

rE293

The *PCC* may carry out any investigation, appropriate to the consideration of whether the *Individual* may be *unfit to practise*, prior to consideration of any referral under Regulation E295.

rE294

Where the *PCC* receives information under Regulation E292, the Chair of the *PCC* shall, subject to Regulation 6, as soon as reasonably practicable, write to the *Individual* concerned:

1. notifying him or her that information has been received which appears to raise a question of whether he or she is *unfit to practise*; and,
2. providing him or her with copies of any information received under Regulation 5 or obtained under Regulation E293.

rE295

Where the *PCC*, following receipt of information under Regulation E292 or during its consideration of a complaint of professional misconduct under the *Complaints Regulations*, considers that an *Individual* may be *unfit to practise*, it shall refer the matter to a *Fitness to Practise Panel* for determination (Regulation E298).

rE296

No decision to refer shall be taken under Regulation E295 without the *Individual* having been provided with a reasonable opportunity (as to the circumstance) to make representations on the matter.

rE297

In reaching a decision under Regulation E295, the *PCC* shall take into account any information received under Regulation E292 or obtained under Regulation E293, and any representations submitted by the *Individual.*

Preliminary Hearings

rE298

As soon as reasonably practicable after referral of a matter by the *PCC* to a *Fitness to Practise Panel*, the Chair of the Panel shall send a notice in writing of the referral to the *Individual* which shall:

1. contain a summary of the case and the reasons why it has been referred to a *Fitness to Practise Panel*;
2. inform the *Individual* of the time and date for a preliminary hearing before the Panel;
3. inform the *Individual* of his or her right to attend and be represented at the preliminary hearing, and to produce evidence at the preliminary hearing, in accordance with Regulations E324.2 and E324.3 below;
4. inform the *Individual* of the Panel's powers at a preliminary hearing under Regulations E299 and rE302 to rE305 below; and,
5. inform the *Individual* of his or her right to appeal under Regulation E317 below.

Directions

rE299

At a preliminary hearing, the *Fitness to Practise Panel* may give directions for the full hearing before the Panel, which may include that:

1. the *Individual*, within a specified period of time, submit to a relevant medical examination to be carried out by a *Medical Examiner* nominated by the Panel;
2. the *PCC* instruct a *Medical Examiner* to conduct such examination and to provide a report setting out an opinion as to whether the *Individual* is *unfit to practise* and as to any other matters as may be specified by the Panel;
3. the *Individual* authorise disclosure to the *PCC* and the *Medical Examiner*, of such of his or her relevant medical records as may be reasonably required for the purposes of the medical examination and subsequent report; and,
4. the *PCC* carry out such other investigations or seek such advice or assistance as the Panel considers appropriate to the matters for consideration at the full

hearing, and where it gives a direction under Paragraph .1 or .3 above, it shall inform the *Individual* that failure to comply with the direction may be taken into account by the Panel in accordance with Regulation E308.2

Medical Examinations

rE300

Where a *Medical Examiner* is nominated by a Panel under Regulation E299.1 or E309.2.a, the *Medical Examiner* shall:

1. within the period specified by the Panel, undertake a relevant medical examination of the *Individual* in accordance with any directions from the Panel;
2. prepare a report which shall express an opinion as to:
    a. whether the *Individual* has a physical or mental condition;
    b. whether the *Individual* is fit to practise either generally or on a restricted basis; and
    c. any other matters which he or she has been instructed to address, in accordance with any directions of the Panel; and
3. where requested by the *PCC* to do so, attend a hearing to present his or her findings.

rE301

An *Individual's* medical records and any report prepared by a *Medical Examiner* under these Regulations shall not be used for any other purpose than is provided for in these Regulations and shall not be disclosed to any other *person* or body without the consent in writing of the *Individual.*

Interim Restrictions

rE302

At a preliminary hearing, a *Fitness to Practise Panel* may, where it is satisfied that it is necessary to protect the public, is otherwise in the public interest or is in the *Individual's* own interests to do so, direct that the *Individual* is subject to an interim *restriction*.

rE303

An interim *restriction* may be imposed subject to such conditions as the Panel may consider appropriate, and shall have effect pending the determination of the matter at a full hearing before the *Fitness to Practise Panel* for a specified period, which shall not, save in exceptional circumstances, exceed 3 months.

rE304

In lieu of imposing an interim *restriction* under Regulation E302 above, the Panel may accept from the *Individual* an undertaking in writing on terms satisfactory to the Panel:

1. agreeing to an immediate interim restriction for such period as may be agreed; or,
2. as to the Individual's conduct or behaviour pending the conclusion of the full hearing.

rE305

Where it has directed an interim *restriction* under Regulation E302 or accepted undertakings under Regulation E304, a Panel may, at any point during the period of an interim restriction:

1. at the request of the Chair of the *PCC*, or at the request of the *PCC* or of the Individual, direct that the interim *restriction* or undertaking be reviewed at a further hearing of the Panel, on such date as the Panel shall specify, or on an unspecified date provided that the *Individual* is served with no less than 14 days' notice in writing of the hearing;
2. at the request of the *Individual*, direct an expedited full hearing of the *Fitness to Practise Panel*;

   and, shall:

   a. inform the *Individual* of his or her right to request a *Fitness to Practise Panel* to review the interim *restriction* or undertaking under Regulation E313 below;

   b. inform the *Individual* of his or her right of appeal under Regulation E317 below.

rE306

The Chair of the Panel shall record, in writing, the decision of the Panel, together with its reasons and the terms of any direction made, interim *restriction* imposed or undertakings accepted.

Full Hearings before a Fitness to Practise Panel

rE307

As soon as reasonably practicable after receipt of any report prepared by a *Medical Examiner* or, where no report has been prepared, the *PCC* considers that the case is ready for hearing, the Chair of the Panel shall send a notice in writing of hearing to the *Individual* which shall:

1. contain a summary of the case and a copy of the report, where applicable;
2. inform the *Individual* of the time and date of the full hearing;
3. inform the *Individual* of his or her right to attend and be represented at the hearing, and to produce evidence at the hearing, in accordance with Regulations E324.2 and .3 below;
4. inform the *Individual* of the Panel's powers at a full hearing under Regulations E308 to E310 below; and,
5. inform the *Individual* of his or her right to appeal under Regulation E317 below.

Decisions of a Fitness to Practise Panel

rE308

At a full hearing, the *Fitness to Practise Panel* shall decide whether the *Individual* is *unfit to practise* and, in reaching its decision, shall be entitled to take into account:

1. the *Individual's* current physical or mental condition, any continuing or episodic condition experienced by the *Individual*, or any condition experienced by the *Individual* which, although currently in remission, may be expected to cause impairment if it recurs; and
2. any failure by the *Individual* to comply with a direction to undergo a relevant medical examination made under Regulation E300.1.

rE309

Where a *Fitness to Practise Panel* has decided that an *Individual* is *unfit to practise*, the Panel may direct:

1. that the *Individual* be subject to a *restriction* which may be subject to such conditions as the Panel may consider appropriate, and which may be imposed indefinitely or for such period, not exceeding six months, as shall be specified in the direction;
2. that the *Individual's* right to continue to practise, or to resume practice after any period of *restriction* shall be subject to such conditions as the Panel may think fit, including that the *Individual*:
   a. submit for regular examination before one or more *Medical Examiners* nominated by the Panel,
   b. authorise disclosure to the *PCC* and the *Medical Examiner* such of his or her medical records as may be reasonably required for the purposes of the medical examination and subsequent report,
   c. is reviewed by a registered medical practitioner and shall follow the treatment they recommend in respect of any physical or mental condition, which the Panel consider may be a cause of the Individual being unfit to practice.

rE310

In lieu of imposing any direction under Regulation E309 above, the Panel may accept from the *Individual* one or more undertakings in writing in which the *Individual* agrees to such period of *restriction*, or such conditions, as the Panel would otherwise have imposed.

rE311

Where it has made a direction under Regulation E309 or agreed undertakings under Regulation E310, the Panel shall inform the *Individual*:

1. of his or her right to request a *Fitness to Practise Panel* to review any direction made, or undertakings agreed, under Regulation E313 below;

2. of his or her right of appeal under Regulation E317 below; and

3. that a failure to comply with the direction or undertakings would be likely to result in a charge of professional misconduct being brought against the *Individual* before a Disciplinary Tribunal.

rE312

The Chair of the Panel shall record, in writing, the decision of the Panel, together with its reasons and the terms of any direction made or undertakings accepted.

E4 Reviews and Appeals

[1.94]

Review of decisions made by a Fitness to Practise Panel

rE313

At any time during which an *Individual* is subject to a period of *restriction* or conditions, directed or undertaken pursuant to these Regulations, the Chair of the *PCC* may, of his or her own motion, or at the request of the *PCC* or of the *Individual*, refer the matter to be reviewed before a *Fitness to Practise Panel*, where he or she considers there has been a significant change in the *Individual 's* circumstances or that there is some other good reason for a review to be undertaken.

rE314

Where a case has been referred to a *Fitness to Practise Panel* for a review hearing under Regulation E313, Regulations E298 to E312 and E324 shall apply, save that the Chair of the Panel and the *Individual* may agree in writing that no preliminary hearing shall be held.

rE315

At the conclusion of a review hearing, the *Fitness to Practise Panel* may:

1. confirm or revoke the direction made or undertakings agreed;

2. extend or vary (or further extend or vary) the period for which the direction has effect, or agree with the *Individual* concerned an extension or variation of the period for which an undertaking has been agreed;

3. replace the direction or undertakings, exercising any of the powers of a *Fitness to Practise Panel* under Regulations E302, E304, E309 or E310 above.

rE316

Where a case has been referred to a *Fitness to Practise Panel* for a review hearing under Regulation 26 above and the review hearing cannot be concluded before the expiry of any period of *restriction* imposed under Regulation E302 or E309.1, or agreed under Regulation E304.1 or E310, the Panel may extend the *restriction* for such period as it considers necessary to allow for the conclusion of the review hearing.

Appeals before an Appeal Panel

rE317

An *Individual* may appeal a decision of a *Fitness to Practise Panel* to impose, extend, vary or replace a period of *restriction* by notifying the *President* in writing that he or she wishes to do so, no more than 14 days after the date of the decision subject to appeal.

rE318

As soon as reasonably practicable after receipt of an appeal under Regulation E317, the Chair of the *Appeal Panel* shall send a notice in writing of the appeal hearing to the *Individual*, which shall:

1. inform the *Individual* of the time and date of the appeal hearing;
2. ~~inform the *Individual* of his or her right to attend and be represented at the hearing, and to produce evidence at the hearing, in accordance with Regulations E324.2 and .3 below; and~~
3. inform the *Individual* of the Panel's powers under Regulation E320 below.

rE319

A pending appeal to an *Appeal Panel* shall not operate as a stay of the decision subject to appeal.

Decisions of an Appeal Panel

rE320

At the conclusion of an appeal hearing, the *Appeal Panel* may:

1. allow the appeal;
2. confirm the decision that is subject to appeal;
3. exercise any of the powers of a *Fitness to Practise Panel* under Regulations E309 or E310 above;

rE321

The *Appeal Panel* shall inform the *Individual*:

1. of his or her right to request a *Fitness to Practise Panel* to review any direction made, or undertakings agreed, under Regulation E313 above; and
2. that failure to comply with a *restriction* or condition imposed under Regulation E320.3 above would be likely to result in a charge of professional misconduct being brought before a *Disciplinary Tribunal*.

rE322

The Chair of the Panel shall record, in writing, the decision of the Panel, together with its reasons, and the terms of any *restriction* imposed or undertakings accepted.

rE323

There shall be no right of appeal from a decision of an *Appeal Panel.*

E5 Conduct of Fitness to Practise and Review Panel Hearings

[1.95]

Procedure before a Panel

rE324

At any hearing before a *Fitness to Practise* or *Appeal Panel*, the proceedings shall be governed by the rules of natural justice, subject to which:

1. the procedure shall be informal, the details being at the discretion of the Chair of the Panel;
2. the *Individual* shall attend the hearing and may be represented by another member of the bar or a solicitor, save that where the *Individual* does not attend and is not represented, the hearing may nevertheless proceed if the Panel is satisfied that it is appropriate to do so and that all reasonable efforts have been made to serve the *Individual* with notice in writing of the hearing in accordance with these Regulations;
3. the *Individual* may, on his or her own behalf or through his or her representative:
    a. make representations in writing or orally,
    b. produce evidence, provided (but subject to the discretion of the Chair) that a proof of such evidence has been submitted no less than 24 hours prior to the hearing, and
    c. put questions to any *Medical Examiner* whose report is in evidence before the Panel;
4. the hearing shall be in private, unless the *Individual* requests a public hearing, and shall be recorded electronically;
5. decisions shall be taken by simple majority;
6. where the votes are equal the issue shall be decided, at a hearing before a *Fitness to Practise Panel*, in the *Individual 's* favour and, in an appeal case, against the *Individual.*

rE325

If at any time it appears to a Panel that it would be appropriate to do so, the Panel may refer the case to the *PCC* for consideration of whether to refer any matter for a hearing before a *Disciplinary Tribunal.*

rE326

Where it considers it necessary, a Panel may appoint a practising barrister or solicitor to assist it on any question of law or interpretation of these Regulations, by providing an independent advice either orally or in writing, such advice to be tendered in the presence of the parties, or, where the parties are not present at the hearing, copied to the parties as soon as reasonably practicable.

rE327

A Panel shall have no power to award costs.

rE328

The proceedings before an *Appeal Panel* shall be by way of a rehearing.

rE329

At any review hearing before a *Fitness to Practise Panel* or appeal hearing before an *Appeal Panel,* copies of the report of any expert or any proof of evidence referred to at any previous hearing of the Panel in respect of the same case may be referred to by the Panel.

rE330

In the arrangements that it makes to perform its functions, and in undertaking its functions, in particular, in reaching any decision concerning an *Individual's* fitness to practise, a Panel shall:

1. take into account its duties to make reasonable adjustments which arise under the Equality Act 2010; and
2. have due regard to the need to:
   a. eliminate unlawful discrimination and other conduct prohibited by the Equality Act 2010, and
   b. advance equality of opportunity and foster good relations between *persons* who share a relevant protected characteristic as set out in Section 149 of the Equality Act 2010 and those who do not.

Postponement, adjournment and cancellation

rE331

Before the opening of any hearing in which notice has been served in writing in accordance with these Regulations, the Chair of the Panel may, of his or her own motion or on the application of the *PCC* or the *Individual*, postpone the hearing until such time and date as he or she thinks fit.

rE332

Where any hearing under these Regulations has commenced, the Panel considering the matter may, at any stage in the proceedings, whether of its own motion or on the application of the *PCC* or the *Individual*, adjourn the hearing until such time and date as it thinks fit.

rE333

No hearing shall be postponed or adjourned under Regulations E335 or E336 unless the *Individual* has been given reasonable opportunity to make representations on the matter.

rE334

Where a hearing has been postponed or adjourned, the parties shall be notified as soon as reasonably practicable of the time, of the date and place at which the hearing is to take place or to resume.

rE335

Where notice of hearing has been served in writing under these Regulations, the Chair of the Panel may, on application of the *PCC* or the *Individual*, cancel the hearing where the Chair considers that there are no reasonable grounds for questioning whether the *Individual* is *unfit to practise.*

Notice and publication of Decisions

rE336

Where a decision has been taken by *Fitness to Practise Panel* or an *Appeal Panel* under these Regulations, the Chair of the Panel shall, as soon as reasonably practicable, serve notice in writing of the decision on the *Individual* concerned.

rE337

Where a decision is taken at a full hearing of a *Fitness to Practise Panel* or at an *Appeal Panel* hearing, unless the decision is to take no action and the *Individual* is permitted to continue to practise without *restriction*, the Chair shall provide notice in writing of the decision to any *person* to whom he or she considers it to be in the public interest to do so.

Service of documents

rE338

Regulation rE216 of the Disciplinary Tribunals Regulations (section 5B) shall apply for the purposes of the service of any notices or documents under these Regulations save that, for the reference in Regulation rE216.2.d to the "*Directions Judge* or the Chairman of the *Disciplinary Tribunal*", there shall be substituted the "Chair of the Panel".

rE339

Where a Panel directs that an *Individual's* ability to practise be subject to *restrictions,* conditions or agreed undertakings, the *President* shall always communicate brief details of the decision, in writing to:

1. the *Individual*;
2. the Chair of the PCC;

3. the Director of the *Bar Standards Board*;
4. the Barrister's Head of Chambers, where relevant;
5. the Treasurers of the Barrister's Inn of Call and of any other Inns of which he is a member, where relevant; and
6. other regulators, where relevant.

rE340

The following shall have details of the decision of the Panel communicated to them in writing, at the discretion of the *President*:

1. the Chair of the *Bar Council*;
2. the Lord Chancellor;
3. the Lord Chief Justice;
4. the Attorney General;
5. the Director of Public Prosecutions; and,
6. the Leaders of the six circuits.

Schedule 1: Constitution of Fitness to Practise and Appeal Panels

1. The *President* shall appoint and maintain:
   (a) a list of barristers and lay persons eligible to be members of Fitness to Practise Panel;
   (b) a list of barristers and lay persons eligible to be members of an Appeal Panel; and,
   (c) from the lists at (a) and (b), lists of Queen's Counsel eligible to act as Chairs of a Fitness to Practise Panel and an Appeal Panel respectively.
2. The *President* shall remove from the lists at Paragraph 1 *persons*:
   (a) whose term of appointment has come to an end, unless that term is renewed;
   (b) who resign from the relevant list by giving notice in writing to that effect to the *President*; or
   (c) who in the opinion of the *President* have ceased to be eligible for appointment.
3. The *President* shall appoint, and ensure that arrangements are in place to be able to access suitably qualified *medical members* to sit on Fitness to Practise and Appeal Panels.
4. A *Fitness to Practise Panel* shall consist of five members selected by the *President* from the list of *persons* under Paragraph 1(a) and in line with the arrangements arising from paragraph 3, being:
   (a) a Chair whose name appears on the relevant list at Paragraph 1(c);
   (b) two practising barristers;
   (c) a *medical member*; and

(d) a *lay member.*

5. An *Appeal Panel* shall consist of four members selected by the *President* from the list of *persons* under Paragraph 1(b) and in line with paragraph 3, being:

(a) two practising barristers, including a Chair whose name appears on the relevant list at Paragraph 1(c), and who shall, unless the *Appeal Panel* decide otherwise, be the most senior of the barrister members;

(b) a *medical member*; and

(c) a *lay member.*

6. No *person* shall be selected to sit on a *Fitness to Practise Panel* or an *Appeal Panel* if:

(a) they are a member of the *PCC* or of the *PCC* or any of its other Committees; or

(b) they were a member of the *PCC* when the matter being dealt with by the Panel was considered by the *PCC.*

7. No *person* shall sit on a *Fitness to Practise Panel* or an *Appeal Panel* for the hearing of a case that they have previously considered or adjudicated upon in any other capacity.

8. The proceedings of a *Fitness to Practise Panel* or an *Appeal Panel* shall be valid notwithstanding that one or more members of the Panel become unable to sit or disqualified from sitting on the Panel, or are replaced by another member from the appropriate list or by the arrangement at paragraph 3, subject to there being a minimum of three Members which shall include a Chair from the relevant list held under Paragraph 1(c), a *medical member* and a *lay member.*

9. The validity of the proceedings of a Panel shall not be affected by any defect in the appointment of a member.

~~F INTERVENTIONS AND DIVESTITURE~~

~~F1 Interventions~~

[1.96]

~~rE320~~

~~The *Bar Standards Board* has the statutory power under Schedule 14 of the Legal Services Act 2007 to intervene into a *BSB licensed body.*~~

~~rE321~~

~~The *Bar Standards Board* may authorise an intervention into a *BSB licensed body* where:~~

~~1.~~ ~~in relation to the *BSB licensed body*, one or more of the intervention conditions (as such term is defined in the Legal Services Act 2007) is satisfied; or~~

~~2.~~ ~~the licence granted to the *BSB licensed body* has expired and has not been renewed or replaced by the *Bar Standards Board.*~~

~~rE322~~

~~In circumstances where the *Bar Standards Board* authorises an intervention under rE321 above, such intervention shall be carried out in accordance with the provisions of the Legal Services Act 2007.~~

~~F2. Divestiture~~

[1.97]

~~rE323~~

~~The *Bar Standards Board* has the statutory power under Schedule 13 of the Legal Services Act 2007 to make an application for divestiture in relation to a *non-authorised person* and a *BSB licensed body*.~~

~~rE324~~

~~The *Bar Standards Board* may make an application for divestiture if the divestiture condition (as such term is defined in the Legal Services Act 2007) is satisfied in relation to such *non-authorised person* and a *BSB licensed body* (as the case may be).~~

~~rE325~~

~~In circumstances where the *Bar Standards Board* elects to make an application for divestiture under rE114 above, such application shall be carried out in accordance with the provisions of the Legal Services Act 2007.~~

Part 6 – Definitions

[1.98]

In this Handbook, the following words and phrases have the meaning set out below:

~~accreditation~~	~~means for the purpose of the *QASA Rules* the status required under the QASA to be permitted to undertake criminal advocacy in the courts of England and Wales "accredited" shall be construed accordingly~~
admission to an Inn	includes readmission of a former member who has ceased (whether as a result of disbarment or otherwise) to be a member of the *Inn*
admission declaration	means the declaration referred to in Q12 in Part 4
administration of oaths	has the same meaning as set out in paragraph 8 of Schedule 2 to the *LSA*
administrative sanction	means the imposition of an administrative warning, fixed penalty fine or other administrative fine up to the prescribed maximum, or any combination of the above in accordance with Section 5.A
answer	in Part 5, means any document served in accordance with Rule E240

appeal panel	in Section 5.A means an appeal panel constituted in accordance with paragraph rE84, to perform the functions set out in regulations E88 and E89 of that Section 5.A in Section 5.D means an appeal panel constituted in accordance with paragraph 6 of that Section V.D, to perform the functions set out in paragraphs rE276 and rE277 of that Section 5.D
appellant	in Part 5 means an appellant wishing to appeal to the visitors against a *relevant decision*
~~applicant body~~	~~in Part 3, means a licensable body, or a *BSB legal services body* which makes an application to the *Bar Standards Board* for authorisation in accordance with the *Scope of Practice, Authorisation and Licensing Rules* in Part 3~~
application fee	means the amount payable by a *person* seeking to be authorised by the *BSB* to carry out any *reserved legal services* or seeking to extend an existing authorisation
~~approved assessment organisation~~	~~means an organisation approved by the *Joint Advocacy Group* to assess the competence of advocates to conduct *criminal advocacy* against the *statement of standards*~~
approved regulator	means any body specified as an approved regulator in paragraph 1 of Schedule 4 of the *LSA* or designated as an approved regulator by an order under paragraph 17 of that Schedule
approved training organisation	means any body or organisation (including *chambers*) which has been approved by the *Bar Standards Board* for the purpose of providing professional *training* under Section 4.B5

~~associates~~	~~has the meaning given in paragraph 5 to Schedule 13 of the *LSA* namely:~~ ~~(i)"associate", in relation to a *person* ("A") and:~~ ~~(a) a shareholding in a body ("S"); or~~ ~~(b) an entitlement to exercise or control the exercise of voting power in a body ("V");~~ ~~means a *person* listed in sub-paragraph (ii).~~ ~~(ii)The *persons* are:~~ ~~(a) the spouse or civil *partner* of A;~~ ~~(b) a child or stepchild of A (if under 18);~~ ~~(c) the trustee of any settlement under which A has a life interest in possession (in Scotland a life interest);~~ ~~(d) an undertaking of which A is a director;~~ ~~(e) an employee of A;~~ ~~(f) a *partner* of A (except, where S or V is a *partner*ship in which A is a *partner*, another *partner* in S or V);~~ ~~(g) if A is an undertaking:~~ ~~(I) a *director* of A;~~ ~~(II) a subsidiary undertaking of A; or~~ ~~(III) a *director* or *employee* of such a subsidiary undertaking;~~ ~~(h) if A has with any other *person* an agreement or arrangement with respect to the acquisition, holding or disposal of shares or other interests in S or V (whether or not they are interests within the meaning of section 72(3) of the *LSA*), that other *person*; or~~ ~~(i) if A has with any other *person* an agreement or arrangement under which they undertake to act together in exercising their voting power in relation to S or V, that *person*~~
an association	means where: *BSB* authorised individuals are *practising* as a chambers; or *BSB* authorised *person*s are sharing premises and/or costs and/or using a common vehicle for obtaining or distributing work with any *person* other than a *BSB regulated person*, in a manner which does not require the *association* to be authorised as an entity under the *Legal Services Act 2007*
~~authorisation fee~~	~~means the fee prescribed from time to time by the *Bar Standards Board* in accordance with Rule S90~~
authorised body	means ~~*BSB authorised bodies* and~~ *authorised* (*non-BSB*) *bodies*
authorised individual	means *BSB authorised individuals* ~~and *authorised (non-BSB) individuals*~~
authorised (non-BSB) body	means a *partner*ship, *LLP* or company authorised or licensed by another *approved regulator* to undertake *reserved legal activities*

~~authorised (non-BSB) individual~~	~~means an individual that is authorised to provide reserved legal activities by another *approved regulator* where such an individual is working as a *manager* or an *employee* of a *BSB authorised body*~~
authorised (non-BSB) person	means an *authorised* (*non-BSB*) *body* ~~or an *authorised* (*non-BSB*) *individual* (as the case may be)~~
authorised person	has the meaning set out in section 18(1) of the *LSA*
bankruptcy order	includes a bankruptcy order made pursuant to the Insolvency Act 1986 and any similar order made in any jurisdiction in the world
Bar	means the Bar of England and Wales
Bar Council	means The General Council of the Bar as constituted from time to time or a committee thereof
Bar Professional Training Course	means a course which has been approved by the *Bar Standards Board* as providing vocational *training* of appropriate content and quality to satisfy the requirements of the *Vocational Stage*
Bar Standards Board	means the board established to exercise and oversee the regulatory functions of the *Bar Council*
Bar Transfer Test	means an examination administered by the *Bar Standards Board* which: (a) is designed to assess whether a *person* has the professional knowledge (including knowledge of the rules of professional conduct) required in order to practise as a *barrister* in England and Wales; and (b) covers subjects not already covered by the education and training of the *person* concerned, the knowledge of which is essential for such *practice*
barrister	has the meaning given in s. 207 of the *LSA* and includes *practising barristers*; *pupils*; and *unregistered barristers*
BMIF	means Bar Mutual Indemnity Fund Limited
~~BSB authorised body~~	~~means *BSB legal services bodies* and *BSB licensed bodies*~~; "BSB authorised bodies" shall be construed accordingly
BSB authorised individuals	means all individuals authorised by the *Bar Standards Board* to carry on *reserved legal activities* including: (*a*) *practising barristers*; (*b*) second six *pupils*; (*c*) *registered European lawyers*
BSB authorised persons	means ~~BSB authorised bodies and~~ BSB authorised individuals
~~BSB legal services body~~	~~means a body authorised by the *Bar Standards Board* in accordance with Section 3.E other than a *BSB licensed body*;~~ ~~"BSB legal services bodies" shall be construed accordingly~~

~~BSB licensed body~~	~~means *partnerships*, *LLPs* and companies that have been and continue to be licensed to act as *a licensed body* by the *Bar Standards Board* in accordance with Section 3.E; (Note that this term is used only where it is necessary to distinguish between BSB licensed bodies and other BSB authorised *persons*. Otherwise, BSB licensed bodies are within the definition of BSB authorised bodies)~~
BSB regulated individuals	means *BSB authorised individuals*, ~~authorised (non-BSB) individuals employed by BSB authorised bodies and BSB regulated *managers*~~
~~BSB regulated managers~~	~~means all *partners*, *members* or directors of a *partnership*, limited liability *partnership* or company respectively where such *partnership*, limited liability *partnership* or company is a BSB authorised body~~
BSB regulated persons	means, as stated by paragraph rI7: *barristers* (including, for the avoidance of doubt, *unregistered barristers*); *registered European lawyers*; ~~*BSB authorised bodies*;~~ ~~*authorised (non-BSB) individuals*; and~~ ~~*BSB regulated managers*~~
BSB Representative	means a *person* or *persons* appointed by the *Bar Standards Board* in accordance with Regulation E103 following a referral of a matter by the *PCC* to a *Disciplinary Tribunal*
call	means call to the *Bar* in accordance with the *Bar* Training Rules
call declaration	means the Declaration referred to in Rule Q112.iii
CCBE	means The Council of Bars and Law Societies of Europe
CCBE State	means any state whose legal profession is a full member, an associate member or an observer member of the *CCBE*

Certificate of Good Standing	means: in relation to a *person* authorised by another *Approved Regulator* or by a *Qualified Foreign Lawyer*, a certificate issued by the *Approved Regulator* or the professional body or other authority responsible for regulating the profession of which the *person* concerned is a member attesting that the *person* concerned: is of good character; has not been the subject of a *Bankruptcy Order* or Directors Disqualification Order nor entered into an individual voluntary arrangement with creditors; and has not been prohibited and is not currently suspended from *practising* on account of serious professional misconduct or the commission of a criminal offence; in relation to a *Qualified European Lawyer*, evidence of the kind referred to in Regulation 9(2) of the European Qualification Regulations, that the *person* concerned: is of good character; has not been the subject of a *Bankruptcy Order* or *Directors Disqualification Order* nor entered into an individual voluntary arrangement with creditors; and has not been prohibited and is not currently suspended from *practising* on account of serious *professional misconduct* or the commission of a *criminal offence*
chambers	means a place at or from which one or more *self-employed barristers* carry on their *practices* and also refers where the context so requires to all the *barristers* (excluding *pupils*) who for the time being carry on their *practices* at or from that place
client	means, the *person* for whom you act and, where the context permits, includes prospective and former clients;
client money	means (a) money, securities or other assets beneficially owned by a *client*; or (b) money, securities or other assets provided by, or for the benefit of, your *client* or intended by another party to be transmitted to your *client*, But excludes: (c) a fixed fee paid in advance; or (d) a payment made in settlement of an accrued debt; or (e) money which belongs to your *employer*.
Code of Conduct for European Lawyers	means the code of conduct adopted by the *CCBE* (as may be amended from time to time) applying to all lawyers undertaking *cross border activities* in a *CCBE State*
Company	has the same meaning as in section 1 of the Companies Act 2006

complaint	means, for the purposes of Part 2, a complaint by a client about the standard of service received that is addressed either to the *Legal Ombudsman* or the chambers or the *BSB authorised person* and, for the purposes of Part 5, an allegation by any *person* or by the *Bar Standards Board* of its own motion of *professional misconduct* or a breach of the rules of this *Handbook* and includes a *legal aid complaint*
Complaints Regulations	means the rules set out at section 5.A
conditional fee agreement	means a conditional fee agreement as defined in Section 58 of the Courts and Legal Services Act 1990
conduct litigation or conduct of litigation	has the same meaning as set out in paragraph 4 of Schedule 2 to the *LSA*. Conducting litigation shall be construed accordingly
Convening Order	means the Order described in Rule E126
conviction	means a criminal conviction for an *indictable offence*
Council of the Inns of Court (COIC)	means the Council of the Inns of Court and its successors including any entity or part through which it exercises its functions
court	means any court or tribunal or any other *person* or body whether sitting in public or in private before whom a *barrister* appears or may appear as an advocate
~~criminal advocacy~~	~~means advocacy in all hearings arising out of a police-led or Serious Fraud Office-led investigation and prosecuted in the criminal courts by the Crown Prosecution Service or the Serious Fraud Office but does not include hearings arising out of Parts 2, 5 or 8 of the Proceeds of Crime Act 2002~~
~~criminal advocacy evaluation form~~	~~means a form completed by a judge to record the competence of a barrister to conduct *criminal advocacy* against the *statement of standards*~~
criminal offence	means any offence, wherever committed, under the criminal law of any jurisdiction (including an offence the conviction for which is a spent conviction within the meaning of the Rehabilitation of Offenders Act 1974) except: (a) an offence for which liability is capable of being discharged by payment of a fixed penalty; and (b) an offence which has as its main ingredient the unlawful parking of a vehicle
pending criminal proceedings	are pending if a *person*: (a) is currently charged with, or (b) is on bail or in detention or custody (or has failed to surrender to custody) in connection with, any *criminal offence*

Cross border activities	means: (a) the undertaking by a *BSB authorised person* of foreign work in a *CCBE State* other than the *UK*, whether or not the *BSB authorised person* is physically present in that *CCBE State*; and (b) any professional contact by a *BSB authorised person* with a lawyer of a *CCBE State* other than the *UK*
~~decision period~~	~~for the purposes of applications for authorisation in Part 3 means:~~ ~~in respect of an application for authorisation or licensing, the period of 6 months;~~ ~~in respect of a standalone application for authorisation to conduct litigation, the period of 3 months; and~~ ~~in respect of an application for approval of a *manager, owner, HOLP or HOFA*, the period of 1 month,~~ ~~in each case, commencing on the last date on which the *Bar Standards Board* receives any of the documentation, information or payments required to be submitted with such application~~
defendant	in Section 5.B means the *relevant person* who is the subject of the disciplinary charge or charges brought before a *Disciplinary Tribunal* and/or of a disqualification application made to the *Disciplinary Tribunal* under the *Complaints Regulations* and in Section 5.D means the *relevant person* against whom the *Bar Standards Board* is considering taking interim action in accordance with Section 5.D;
Definitions Section	means Part 4 of the *Handbook*
determination by consent procedure	means the procedure set out in Regulation E67
devilling	means where a *self-employed barrister* ("A") arranges for another *barrister* ("B") in the same *chambers* to carry out work for A on the basis that A will be responsible for the payment of B's remuneration for such work and will be responsible to the client for the work as if it were his own. "devil" and "devils" will be construed accordingly
Directions Judge	means a Judge or Queen's Council designated by the *President*
Director	means a *director* of a company, and includes the director of ~~a *BSB authorised body* or~~ an *authorised* (*non-BSB*) *body* which is a company, and in relation to a societas Europaea includes: in a two-tier system, a member of the management organ and a member of the supervisory organ; in a one-tier system, a member of the administrative organ

directors disqualification order	includes a disqualification order made by a court, or disqualification undertaking accepted by the secretary of state, pursuant to the Company Directors Disqualification Act 1986 and any similar order made or undertaking given in any jurisdiction in the world
Disciplinary Tribunal	means a Tribunal convened pursuant to E130 of the Disciplinary Tribunal Regulations to consider an allegation of *professional misconduct* against a *BSB regulated person* (for which the sanctions may include disqualification, where Part 5 so provides) and/or to consider an application for *disqualification* against a relevant *person*
discrimination	has the same meaning as in chapter 2 of the Equality Act 2010
disqualification condition	means that, in their capacity ~~as a *HOLP, HOFA, manager or employee of a BSB authorised body* or~~ as an employee of a *BSB authorised person* ~~(as the case may be)~~, the *relevant person* has (intentionally or through neglect): (if a *BSB regulated person*) breached a relevant duty to which the *BSB regulated person* is subject under this handbook or under applicable rules of another approved regulator; or (if either a *BSB regulated person* or a *non-authorised individual* employed by a *BSB authorised person*) caused, or substantially contributed to, a *BSB regulated person* breaching a relevant duty to which the *BSB regulated person* is subject under this handbook or under applicable rules of another *approved regulator*; and in either case, that it is undesirable that the *relevant person* should engage in the relevant activity in respect of which the disqualification order is made
disqualification order	means an order: made by the *PCC* under the *Determination by Consent procedure* or made by a *Disciplinary Tribunal* in disposing of a disciplinary charge or disqualification application referred to it by the *PCC*; and made on the basis that the *disqualification condition* is satisfied in respect of the relevant *person* who is the subject of the *disqualification order*; and either indefinitely or for a stated period, disqualifying a relevant *person* from one or more relevant activities and prohibiting any *BSB authorised person* from appointing them or directly or indirectly employing them in respect of such relevant activities, namely acting ~~as a *HOLP, HOFA, manager or employee of a BSB authorised body* or~~ as an employee of a *BSB authorised individual* ~~(as the case may be)~~

disqualify or disqualification	means the power of the *Bar Standards Board*, pursuant to Section 5.B, to disqualify a *relevant person* from performing one or more of the *relevant activities* where the *disqualification condition* is satisfied, which power when exercised on an interim basis shall be exercised in accordance with Section 5.D;
diversity data	Means information relating to the following characteristics in respect of an individual: Age Disability Gender reassignment Pregnancy and maternity Race (including ethnic or national origins, colour or nationality Religion or belief (including lack of belief) Sex Sexual orientation Marriage and civil partnership
~~effective trial~~	~~means a trial that allows for the assessment of a *barrister* against standards 1–4 as set out in the *statement of standards*~~
employed barrister	means: an employed *barrister* (*authorised non-BSB body*); or ~~an employed *barrister* (*BSB authorised body*); or~~ an employed *barrister* (*non authorised body*)
employed barrister (authorised non-BSB body)	means a *practising barrister* who is employed by an authorised (non-BSB) body either: under a contract of employment; or under a written contract for services which is for a determinate period (subject to any provision for earlier termination on notice), who supplies *legal services* as a *barrister* in the course of his employment
~~employed barrister (BSB authorised body)~~	~~means a *practising barrister* who is employed by a *BSB authorised body* either:~~ ~~under a contract of employment; or~~ ~~under a written contract for services which is for a determinate period (subject to any provision for earlier termination on notice),~~ ~~who supplies *legal services* as a *barrister* in the course of his *employment*~~

employed barrister (non-authorised body)	means a *practising barrister* who is employed: other than by an authorised body; either: (i) under a contract of *employment*; or (ii) under a written contract for services which is for a determinate period (subject to any provision for earlier termination on notice); or (iii) by virtue of an office under the Crown or in the institutions of the European Union; and who supplies *legal services* as a *barrister* in the course of his *employment*
employees	means: *non-authorised individuals* who are directly and *indirectly employed* by *BSB authorised persons*; ~~and~~ ~~*authorised (non-BSB) individuals* who are *indirectly employed* by *BSB authorised persons*~~
employer	means *persons* by whom employed *barristers* (non-authorised bodies) are directly or *indirectly employed* including any holding subsidiary or associated company, corporate body or firm of that *person*
employment	means direct or *indirect employment*
enforcement strategy	means the strategy on enforcement from time to time published by the *Bar Standards Board*, in effect as at the date the complaint is made to the *Bar Standards Board* or raised by the *Bar Standards Board* of its own motion under Part 5
Enforcement Regulations	means the supervision and enforcement regulations set out at Part 5
English law	includes international law and the law of the European Communities
Equality and Diversity Officer	means the individual appointed as such by the *chambers* or the *BSB authorised body* (as appropriate), one of whose responsibilities is to ensure compliance with the Equality and Diversity set out at rules C110-C111
Establishment Directive	means Directive 98/5/EC of the European Parliament and of the Council of February 1998 to facilitate *practice* of the profession of lawyer on a permanent basis in a *Member State* other than that in which the qualification was obtained
European lawyer	means a *person* who is a national of a *Member State* and who is authorised in any *Member State* to pursue professional activities under any of the professional titles appearing in article 2(2) of the European Communities (Lawyer's *Practice*) Order 1999, but who is not any of the following: a *solicitor* or *barrister* of England and Wales or Northern Ireland; or a *solicitor* or advocate under the law of Scotland

European Qualifications Regulations	means the European Communities (Recognition of Professional Qualifications) Regulations 2007
family responsibilities	includes caring responsibilities for older, young, or disabled dependants or relatives
foreign client	means a lay *client* who has his centre of main interests outside England and Wales, or who reasonably appears as having that characteristic
foreign lawyer	is a *person* who is a member, and entitled to *practice* as such, of a legal profession regulated within a jurisdiction outside England and Wales and who is not an *authorised person* for the purposes of the *LSA*
foreign work	means *legal services* of whatsoever nature relating to: court or other legal proceedings taking place or contemplated to take place outside England and Wales; or if no court or other legal proceedings are taking place or contemplated, any matter or contemplated matter not subject to the law of England and Wales
~~full accreditation~~	~~means accreditation that permits a *barrister* to undertake *criminal advocacy* in the courts in England and Wales for a period of up to five years~~
full practising certificate	means, in accordance with Rule S63r, a *practising* certificate which entitles a *barrister* to exercise a *right of audience* before every *court* in relation to all proceedings
Full Qualification Certificate	means a certificate issued by the *Bar Standards Board* under Rule Q68 or Rule Q86 on satisfactory completion of, or exemption from, the *Professional Stage*
Handbook	means this Handbook
harassment	has the same meaning as in section 26 of the Equality Act 2010
Hearings before the Visitors	means an appeal hearing constituted under Section 3.V
~~HOFA~~	~~means a Head of Finance and Administration within the meaning of paragraph 13(2) of Schedule 11 to the *LSA*~~
~~HOLP~~	~~means a Head of Legal Practice within the meaning of paragraph 11(2) of Schedule 11 to the *LSA*~~
home regulator	means the body in a *Member State* which authorises a European lawyer to pursue professional activities under any of the professional titles appearing in article 2(2) of the European Communities (Lawyer's *Practice*) Order 1999 and, if he is authorised in more than one *Member State*, it shall mean any such body

home professional title	means, in relation to a European lawyer, the professional title or any of the professional titles specified in relation to his *home State* in article 2(2) of the European Communities (Lawyer's *Practice*) Order 1999 under which he is authorised in his *home State* to pursue professional activities
home State	means the *Member State* in which a European lawyer acquired the authorisation to pursue professional activities under his home professional title and, if he is authorised in more than one *Member State*, it shall mean any such *Member State*
immigration work	means the provision of immigration advice and immigration services, as defined in section 82 of the Immigration and Asylum Act 1999
~~independent assessor~~	~~means a person appointed by the *Joint Advocacy Group* to attend court to assess the competence of a *barrister* to conduct *criminal advocacy* against the *statement of standards*~~
indictable offence	has the same meaning as in Schedule 1 of the Interpretation Act 1978, namely "an offence which, if committed by an adult is triable on indictment whether it is exclusively so triable or triable either way"
indirectly employed	means employment by a *non-authorised person* that in turn is owned or controlled by one or more BSB authorised *persons* and indirect employment shall be construed accordingly
Inn	means one of the four Inns of Court, namely, the Honourable Societies of Lincoln's Inn, Inner Temple, Middle Temple and Gray's Inn. "*Inns*" should be construed accordingly
instructions	means *instructions* or directions in whatever form (including a brief to appear as an advocate before a Court) given to a *practising barrister* ~~or a BSB authorised body~~ to supply legal services whether in a contentious or in a non-contentious matter and "instructed" shall have a corresponding meaning
interim panel	means an *interim panel* constituted in accordance with paragraph rE254, to perform the functions set out in paragraphs rE265 to rE267 of Section 5.D
intermediary	means any *person* by whom a *self-employed barrister* or *authorised body* is instructed on behalf of a *client* excluding a *professional client* who is not also the *client* save for an *intermediary* in the context of a *referral fee* which includes a *professional client*
~~Joint Advocacy Group~~	~~means the group established by the *Bar Standards Board*, the Solicitors' Regulation Authority and ILEX Professional Standards, in order to oversee the quality assurance and accreditation of *criminal advocacy*~~

Justices' clerk	means a serving Justices' clerk or assistant Justices' clerk, appointed under the Courts Act 2003
lay member	means a lay *person* appointed to be a member of the *Bar Standards Board* or one of its regulatory committees
lay representative	means either a lay *person* appointed by the President of the Council of the Inns of Court to serve on Disciplinary Tribunals, Interim Suspension Panels and Appeal Panels therefrom, and *Medical Panels* and Review Panels therefrom; or a lay *person* appointed by the Lord Chief Justice to serve on Hearings before the Visitors
legal aid complaint	has the same meaning as in section 40 of the Administration of Justice Act 1985
Legal Advice Centre	means a centre operated by a charitable or similar non-commercial organisation at which legal services are habitually provided to members of the public without charge (or for a nominal charge) to the client and: which employs or has the services of one or more *solicitors* conducting work pursuant to rule 4.16 of the SRA *Practice* Framework Rules 2011; or which has been and remains designated by the *Bar Standards Board* as suitable for the employment or attendance of *barristers* subject to such conditions as may be imposed by the *Bar Standards Board* in relation to insurance or any other matter whatsoever
Legal Ombudsman	means scheme administered by the Office for Legal Complaints under Part 6 of the *LSA*
legal services	includes legal advice representation and drafting or settling any statement of case witness statement affidavit or other legal document but does not include: sitting as a judge or arbitrator or acting as a mediator; lecturing in or teaching law or writing or editing law books articles or reports; examining newspapers, periodicals, books, scripts and other publications for libel, breach of copyright, contempt of court and the like; communicating to or in the press or other media; giving advice on legal matters free to a friend or relative or acting as unpaid or honorary legal adviser to any charitable benevolent or philanthropic institution; in relation to a *barrister* who is a non-executive director of a company or a trustee or governor of a charitable benevolent or philanthropic institution or a trustee of any private trust, giving to the other directors trustees or governors the benefit of his learning and experience on matters of general legal principle applicable to the affairs of the company institution or trust; (Note that *legal activities* are more broadly defined)

Legal Services Board or LSB	means the independent body established under the *LSA* to be the over-arching regulator for the legal profession as a whole
Legal Aid Agency	is the executive agency established under Legal Aid Sentencing and Punishment of Offenders Act 2012 to manage and administer the legal aid system
licensed access client	means a *person* or organisation approved as such by the *Bar Standards Board* in accordance with the Licensed Access Recognition Regulations
licensed access rules	means the rules on Licensed Access set out at rC132
~~licensable body~~	~~Has the same meaning as set out in s. 72 *LSA* namely:~~ ~~(1) A body ("B") is a licensable body if a *non-authorised person*–~~ ~~(a) is a *manager* of B, or~~ ~~(b) has an interest in B.~~ ~~(2) A body ("B") is also a licensable body if–~~ ~~(a) another body ("A") is a *manager* of B, or has an interest in B, and~~ ~~(b) *non-authorised persons* are entitled to exercise, or control the exercise of, at least 10% of the voting rights in A.~~ ~~(3) For the purposes of this Act, a *person* has an interest in a body if–~~ ~~(a) the *person* holds shares in the body, or~~ ~~(b) the *person* is entitled to exercise, or control the exercise of, voting rights in the body.~~ ~~(4) A body may be licensable by virtue of both subsection (1) and subsection (2).~~ ~~(5) For the purposes of this Act, a *non-authorised person* has an indirect interest in a licensable body if the body is licensable by virtue of subsection (2) and the *non-authorised person* is entitled to exercise, or control the exercise of, voting rights in A.~~ ~~(6) "shares" means–~~ ~~(a) in relation to a body with a share capital, allotted shares (within the meaning of the Companies Acts);~~ ~~(b) in relation to a body with capital but no share capital, rights to share in the capital of the body;~~ ~~(c) in relation to a body without capital, interests–~~ ~~(i) conferring any right to share in the profits, or liability to contribute to the losses, of the body, or~~ ~~(ii) giving rise to an obligation to contribute to the debts or expenses of the body in the event of a winding up;~~ ~~and references to the holding of shares, or to a shareholding, are to be construed accordingly~~
licensed body	a licensable body which has been granted a licence by ~~the *Bar Standards Board* or other~~ licensing authority to undertake *reserved legal activities*

licensing authority	means an *approved regulator* which is designated as a licensing authority under Part 1 of Schedule 10 to the *LSA,* and whose licensing rules have been approved for the purposes of the *LSA*
limited practising certificate	in accordance with rS65, a limited *practising* certificate authorises a *barrister* to exercise any right of audience that they had on 30 July 2000 as a result of them being a *barrister*
litigation extension fee	means the amount payable by a *BSB authorised person* which has a litigation extension
~~LLP~~	~~means a limited liability *partnership* formed by being incorporated under the Limited Liability *Partnerships* Act 2000~~
LSA	means the *Legal Services Act 2007* (as amended)
manager	has the same meaning as set out in s. 207 *LSA* namely: a member of an *LLP*; a director of a company; a *partner* in a *partnership*; or in relation to any other body, a member of its governing body
~~material interest~~	~~has the same meaning as in paragraph 3 of Schedule 13 to the *LSA* namely:~~ ~~a *person* holds a *material interest* in a body ("B") if the *person*:~~ ~~holds at least 10% of the shares in B,~~ ~~is able to exercise significant influence over the management of B by virtue of the *person*'s shareholding in B,~~ ~~holds at least 10% of the shares in a parent undertaking ("P") of B,~~ ~~is able to exercise significant influence over the management of P by virtue of the *person*'s shareholding in P,~~ ~~is entitled to exercise, or control the exercise of, voting power in B which, if it consists of voting rights, constitutes at least 10% of the voting rights in B,~~ ~~is able to exercise significant influence over the management of B by virtue of the *person*'s entitlement to exercise, or control the exercise of, voting rights in B,~~ ~~is entitled to exercise, or control the exercise of, voting power in P which, if it consists of voting rights, constitutes at least 10% of the voting rights in P, or~~ ~~is able to exercise significant influence over the management of P by virtue of the *person*'s entitlement to exercise, or control the exercise of, voting rights in P.~~ ~~and for the purposes of this definition "*person*" means-~~ ~~the *person*,~~ ~~any of the *person*'s associates, or~~ ~~the *person* and any of the *person*'s associates taken together~~

mediation	means the process whereby the parties to a dispute appoint a neutral *person* (mediator) to assist them in the resolution of their dispute
medical expert	means a *medical expert* appointed by the President for the purpose of serving on Medical and Review Panels
Medical Panel	means a panel constituted under Section 5.E;
Member State	means a state which is a member of the European Union
minor criminal offence	includes: an offence committed in the United Kingdom which is a fixed-penalty offence under the Road Traffic Offenders Act 1988; an offence committed in the United Kingdom or abroad which is dealt with by a procedure substantially similar to that for such a fixed-penalty offence; an offence whose main ingredient is the unlawful parking of a motor vehicle
non-authorised body	any body that is not an authorised body
non-authorised individual	means any individual who is not a BSB authorised individual ~~or an authorised (non-BSB) individual~~ but who is directly or *indirectly employed* by a Chambers~~,~~ ~~*BSB legal services body* and/or a *licensed body*, *or a BSB authorised person*~~
non-authorised person	means: (a) non-authorised bodies; and (*b*) *non-authorised individuals*
non-reserved activities	means any activities other than reserved legal activities
notarial activities	has the same meaning as set out in paragraph 7 of Schedule 2 to the *LSA*
~~Owner~~	~~means:~~ ~~in relation to a BSB authorised body that is a company or an *LLP* (or an applicant to become such a body), any *person* who holds a *material interest* in that company or *LLP*;~~ ~~in relation to a *BSB authorised body* that is a *partnership* (or an applicant to become such a body), any *partner* of that *partnership* who holds a *material interest* in that *partnership*~~
parental leave	means leave taken by the main carer of a child preceding or following birth or adoption. This could be the mother, father or adoptive parent of either sex
partner	means a *person* who is or is held out as a *partner* in an unincorporated firm
partnership	means an unincorporated *partnership*, and includes any unincorporated firm in which *persons* are or are held out as *partners*, but does not include an *LLP*

PCC	means the Professional Conduct Committee and its successors in title from time to time
period of deferral	has the meaning set out in Regulation E79
person	includes a body of *persons* (corporate or unincorporated)
petition	In Part 5 means the petition of appeal served pursuant to Rule E236.1
practice	means the activities, including business related activities, in that capacity, of: a *practising barrister*; a *barrister* exercising a *right of audience* in a *Member State* other than the United Kingdom pursuant to the *Establishment Directive*, or the European Communities (Lawyer's *Practice*) Regulations 2000; ~~a BSB authorised body;~~ ~~a *manager of a BSB authorised body or a BSB licensed body;*~~ ~~an employee of a *BSB authorised body* or *a BSB licensed body;*~~ "practise", "*practising*" and "*practised*" should be construed accordingly
practising address	means an address from which the services which consist of or include the carrying on of *reserved legal activities* are being provided
practising barrister	Means a *barrister* who practices as a barrister as defined in rule S9
practising certificate	means a *full practising certificate*, a *provisional practising certificate*, a *limited practising certificate*, or an *European lawyer's practising certificate* or a temporary *practising* certificate issued by the *Bar Council*
practising certificate fee	means the amount payable for a *practising certificate* each year, such amount to be calculated by reference to the Schedule of *Practising* Certificate Fees issued by the *Bar Council* from time to time, together with the provisions of Section 3.C
practising certificate year	means the period from 1 April in any calendar year to 31 March in the next calendar year
the President	means the President of the Council of the *Inns* of Court
probate activities	has the same meaning as set out in paragraph 6 of Schedule 2 to the *LSA*

professional client	means in relation to giving *instructions* to a BSB authorised *person*: any *person* authorised by another *approved regulator or licensing authority*; an employed *barrister* or registered European lawyer; any *practising barrister* or registered European lawyer acting on his own behalf; a foreign lawyer; a Scottish or Northern Irish *Solicitor*; or the representative of any body (such as a Legal Advice Centre or Pro Bono or Free Representation Unit) which arranges for the supply of legal services to the public without a fee, and which has been and remains designated by the *Bar Standards Board* (subject to such conditions as may be imposed by the *Bar Council* or *Bar Standards Board* in relation to insurance or any other matter whatsoever) as suitable for the instruction of *barristers*, and which instructs a *barrister* to supply legal services without a fee; any member of a profession who is acting on behalf of their own *client*
professional misconduct	means a breach of this Handbook by a *BSB regulated person* which the *PCC* does not consider appropriate for disposal by way of no further action or the imposition of *administrative sanctions*, pursuant to Section 5.A
professional principles	has the same meaning as set out in s 1(3) *LSA* namely: (a) that authorised *person*s should act with independence and integrity, (b) that authorised *persons* should maintain proper standards of work, (c) that authorised *person*s should act in the best interests of their clients, (d) that *person*s who exercise before any court a right of audience, or conduct litigation in relation to proceedings in any court, by virtue of being authorised *persons* should comply with their duty to the court to act with independence in the interests of justice, and (e) that the affairs of clients should be kept confidential
progression	means for the purposes of the *QASA Rules* the process by which a *barrister* can increase their level under the QASA;
provisional accreditation	means for the purposes of the *QASA Rules* accreditation that permits a *barrister* to undertake *criminal advocacy* in the courts in England and Wales for a period of up to 12 or 24 months, but which requires further steps to be taken to obtain *full accreditation*
provisional practising certificate	In accordance with rule rS66 a *provisional practising certificate* authorises a *pupil* in his second six to exercise a *right of audience* before every *court* in relation to all proceedings

Provisional Qualification Certificate	means a certificate issued by the *Bar Standards Board* under Q68 or Q96 following satisfactory completion of, or exemption from, the non-*practising* six months of *pupil*age
public access client	a *client* (other than a *licensed access client*) that instructs a *barrister* directly on their behalf
public access instructions	means *instructions* given to a *barrister* by or on behalf of a public access client, in accordance with Rules C119–C130
pupil	means an individual who is undertaking either the first non-*practising* six months of *pupillage* or the second *practising* six months of *pupillage*, or a part thereof and who is registered with the *Bar Standards Board* as a *pupil*
pupil supervisor	an individual, qualified *barrister* who has been approved as a *pupil* supervisor by his or her *Inn* of Court, and in accordance with the Bar Training Regulations
pupillage	means a period of professional training under Section 4.B5 and includes a period of external training for which permission has been given by the *Bar Standards Board* under rQ45
Qualifications Committee	means the Qualifications Committee of the *Bar Standards Board* or its successor
Qualification Regulations	means the rules on qualification set out at Part 4
qualified European lawyer	means a *person* who is a national of a *Relevant State* and who either: (a) holds a diploma required in a *Relevant State* for the *practice* of a legal profession regulated by that State which diploma satisfies the requirements of Regulation 22(1)(a) of the European Qualification Regulations; or (b) satisfies the requirements of Regulation 22(1)(b) of the European Qualification Regulations
qualified foreign lawyer	means a *person* who is a member of a legal profession regulated in a jurisdiction outside England and Wales and entitled to *practise* as such
qualified lawyer	means a *person* who is authorised to *practise* by another *Approved Regulator*, a *Qualified European Lawyer* or a *Qualified Foreign Lawyer*
the Quality Assurance Committee	means the *Quality Assurance Committee* of the *Bar Standards Board* or its successor
QASA	means the Quality Assurance Scheme for Advocates developed by the *Joint Advocacy Group* and set out in the *QASA Rules* and *QASA Handbook*
Quality Assurance Scheme for Advocates Rules (QASA Rules)	means the rules set out in rC31 to rC63 of the *Handbook*, "QASA Rules" shall be construed accordingly

QASA Handbook	means the Handbook for the Quality Assurance Scheme for Advocates (crime) developed by the *Joint Advocacy Group* and published from time to time
QASA level	means one of the four QASA levels. Advocates will be accredited at one of these levels and this will correspond to the level of hearings that they can undertake
re-accreditation	means for the purposes of the *QASA Rules* the process by which a *barrister* demonstrates their competence and renews their accreditation at their existing level for a further five years, "re-accredited" shall be construed accordingly
a realistic prospect of a finding of professional misconduct being made	means that the *PCC* considers, on the information then available to it and having regard to the evidence which it regards as likely to be available at any tribunal or final determination of a complaint, that it is more likely than not that a finding of *professional misconduct* will be made
a realistic prospect of the disqualification condition being satisfied	means that the *PCC* considers, on the information then available to it and having regard to the evidence which it regards as likely to be available at any tribunal or final determination of a complaint, that it is more likely than not that it shall be determined that the *disqualification condition* has been satisfied
referral fee	means any payment or other consideration made in return for the referral of professional *instructions* by an *intermediary,* For the avoidance of doubt, a payment for the provision of a particular service or for some other reason, and not for the provision or referral of professional *instructions* is not a *referral fee* for the purposes of this definition
register of European lawyers	means the register of European lawyers maintained by the *Bar Standards Board* under regulation 15 of the European Communities (Lawyer's *Practice*) Regulations 2000 (SI 2000/1119)
registered European lawyer	means a European lawyer registered as such by the *Bar Council* and by an *Inn* in accordance with Section 3.D

Registered European lawyer's practising certificate	means, in accordance with rS68, a *practising certificate* which entitles a registered European lawyer to carry on the same reserved legal activities as a full *practising certificate* issued to a *barrister,* save that: a registered European lawyer is only authorised to exercise a right of audience or a right to conduct litigation if he acts in conjunction with a *solicitor* or *barrister* who is entitled to practise before the court, tribunal or public authority concerned and who could lawfully exercise that right; and a registered European lawyer is not authorised to prepare for remuneration any instrument creating or transferring an interest in land unless he has a home professional title obtained in Denmark, the Republic of Ireland, Finland, Sweden, Iceland, Liechtenstein, Norway, the Czech Republic, Cyprus, Hungary or Slovakia
registration	means for the purposes of the *QASA Rules* the process by which *barristers* enter the *QASA*
regulatory objectives	has the meaning given to it by section 1 of the *LSA* and consists of the following objectives: protecting and promoting the public interest; supporting the constitutional principles of the rule of law; improving access to justice; protecting and promoting the interests of consumers; promoting competition in the provision of the services; encouraging an independent, strong, diverse and effective legal profession; increasing public understanding of the citizen's legal rights and duties; and promoting and maintaining adherence to the professional principles
relevant activity	means acting as ~~a *HOLP, HOFA, manager* or employee of a *BSB authorised body* or as~~ an employee of a *BSB authorised individual* ~~(as the case may be)~~
relevant breach	in Parts 5.A and 5.B means a breach of the Code of Conduct amounting to *professional misconduct*
relevant decision	means: a decision of a *Disciplinary Tribunal*; or a decision, on review, by the *BSB* under Part X of the Bar Training Regulations (where the Bar Training Regulations provide for an appeal to the Visitors against such a decision), herein a "Qualification Decision"

relevant persons	means: *persons* who were *BSB regulated persons* at the time of the conduct complained of (including, for the purposes of Part 5 of the Handbook only, *persons* who would have fallen within the definition of *BSB regulated persons* but for the fact that, at the time of the conduct complained of, they had their authorisation ~~or licence~~ suspended or revoked, or were subject to a sentence of suspension or disbarment, or were subject to a disqualification order (as the case may be) that has subsequently been overturned on appeal); and *non-authorised persons* who are directly or *indirectly employed* by a *BSB authorised person* or who were so employed at the time of the conduct complained of
Relevant State	means a *Member State*, Iceland, Norway, Liechtenstein or Switzerland
reserved instrument activities	has the same meaning as set out in paragraph 5 of Schedule 2 to the *LSA*
reserved legal activity	means: the exercise of a right of audience; the *conduct of litigation*; reserved instrument activities; *probate activities*; *notarial activities*; and the administration of oaths; "reserved activities" shall be construed accordingly
respondent	In Part 5 means the *person* with an interest in upholding a *relevant decision*, being: (a) in the case of an appeal by the *BSB* against a decision of a *Disciplinary Tribunal*, the defendant; (b) in all other cases, the *BSB*
review panel	In Section 5.D, means a review panel constituted in accordance with rE255 of that Section V.D, to perform the functions set out in paragraphs rE270 to rE272 of that Section 5.D
right of audience	has the same meaning as set out in paragraph 3 of Schedule 2 to the *LSA*
right to conduct litigation	refer to *conduct of litigation* above
Scope of Practice, Authorisation and Licensing Rules	means the rules set out at Part 3 of this *Handbook*

selection panel	any panel formally tasked with the final decision on recruitment or selection or promotion (as the case may be) of *pupils*, assessed mini-pupils, tenants, clerks, or staff, or, in the context of a *BSB authorised body*, any panel formally tasked with the final decision on recruitment or selection or promotion (as the case may be) of *pupils*, assessed mini-pupils, *managers* or employees of that *BSB authorised body*
self-employed barrister	means a *practising barrister* who is self-employed
Senior Courts	means the Senior Courts of England and Wales, namely, the Court of Appeal, the High Court of Justice and the Crown Court
serious matter	For the purpose of Section 4.B8, a matter is a serious matter if it: falls within Rule Q104.1 or Rules Q104.2.b to .f; or in the opinion of the *Inn* otherwise calls into question whether the *Student* is a fit and proper *person* to become a *practising barrister*
solicitor	means a *solicitor* of the Supreme Court of England and Wales
specified amount	means in respect of a *pupil*, the amount payable to a *pupil* in their non-*practising* period or their *practising* period (as appropriate), such amount being specified by the *Bar Standards Board* from time to time
the standard directions	mean the standard directions set out at Annex 6 to Section 5.B (as such Annex may be amended or updated by the *Bar Standards Board* from time to time)
statement of standards	means for the purposes of the *QASA Rules* the standards against which the competence of advocates will be assessed for the purposes of *registration*, *progression* and *re-accreditation*
suitability criteria	means: in respect of a *HOLP*, the criteria set out at Rules S104, S105 and S110; in respect of a *HOFA*, the criteria set out at Rules S106, S107 and S110; in respect of *owners*, the criteria set out at Rule S108 and S110; and in respect of *managers*, the criteria set out at Rule S109 and S110
Supervision Team	means the Supervision Team of the *Bar Standards Board*

suspended or suspension	means to suspend the *practising* certificate, ~~licence or authorisation~~ of a *BSB authorised person*, either generally or in respect of any separate authorisation that *person* may have to *conduct litigation* or to carry out public access work (and which includes, in the case of a *barrister*, the fact that he is suspended from *practice* and from the rights and privileges as a member of his *Inn*) which power when exercised on an interim basis shall be exercised in accordance with Section 5.D
trade association	means a body of *persons* (whether incorporated or not) which is formed for the purpose of furthering the trade interests of its members or of *persons* represented by its members, and does not include any association formed primarily for the purpose of securing legal assistance for its members
Temporary Qualification Certificate	means a certificate issued by the *Bar Standards Board* under Rule Q100 authorising a Qualified Foreign Lawyer to be admitted to temporary membership of an *Inn* and called to the *Bar* for the purpose of appearing as counsel in a particular case or cases before a court or courts of England and Wales
unfit to practise	when used to describe a *barrister* means that he is incapacitated by reason of ill health and: the *barrister* is suffering from serious incapacity due to his physical or mental condition (including any addiction); and as a result the *barrister*'s fitness to practise is seriously impaired; and his *suspension* or the imposition of conditions is necessary for the protection of the public
university	means an institution which makes available educational services under a name which includes the word "university" and in the case of an institution to which section 39(1) of the Higher Education Act 1998 applies which is authorised or has approval to include that word in that name as mentioned in that subsection
unregistered barrister	means an individual who does not hold a *practising* certificate but who has been called to the *Bar* by one of the *Inns* and has not ceased to be a member of the *Bar*
UK	means United Kingdom
victimisation	has the same meaning as in section 27 of the Equality Act 2010
the Visitors	means the panel nominated to hear an appeal pursuant to Rule E244.1 or, in the case of an appeal within Rule E244.3 to E244.5 the single judge nominated to hear the appeal
vocational stage	has the meaning set out in rQ27

workforce	means: in the case of a *Chambers*, the staff, *barristers*, *pupils* and assessed mini-pupils; and ~~in the case of a *BSB authorised body*, the *employees*, *managers*, *pupils* and assessed mini-pupils~~
Years' standing	Means that a *barrister* shall be treated as being of a particular number of years' standing if they: have been entitled to practise and have practised as a *Barrister* (other than as a *pupil* who has not completed *pupillage* in accordance with the *Bar Training Regulations*) or as a *person* authorised by another *Approved Regulator*; have made such *practice* their primary occupation; and have been entitled to exercise a *right of audience* or to *conduct litigation* before every *court* in relation to all proceedings, for a period (which need not be continuous and need not have been as a *person* authorised by the same *Approved Regulator*) of at least that number of years

Part II
Qualifying as a Barrister and Entering Practice

Section I: Qualification

Introduction

[2.1]

Before embarking on a legal career it is important to have a clear understanding of the stages of training which lead to becoming a barrister and possible obstacles that you may have to overcome. If you are convinced that life at the practising Bar really is for you, you will need a great deal of tenacity and commitment in terms of both time and resources. For those who succeed, a career at the Bar can be immensely rewarding, not only financially but also in terms of job satisfaction: barristers face a very wide variety of challenges and no two days in practice will be the same.

This section of the Bar Handbook should give you a better idea of whether you feel you have what it takes to become a barrister, and will outline the stages of training barristers must complete as well as the sources of help and advice available.

To qualify as a barrister there are four main stages you must complete:

(1) The academic stage;

(2) The vocational stage;

(3) Pupillage;

(4) Completion of compulsory continuing education courses.

Academic Stage

[2.1a]

The Academic Stage is designed to ensure that the student has a basic body of legal knowledge, which may be assumed and built upon at the Vocational Stage (BPTC). Neither entry to a law degree or the CPE/GDL, nor successful completion thereof, will guarantee progress onto the Bar Professional Training Course for intending Barristers.

The standard requirement for completion of the Academic Stage is a 2:2 UK Honours degree or its equivalent; this applies to law and non-law degrees alike. Under the Bar Training Regulations, professional qualifications may not be accepted in lieu of this requirement. The Bar Training Regulations are set out below.

In addition to the 2:2 minimum requirement, students must study the foundations of legal knowledge, which now form the Academic Stage of Legal Education and which are compulsory for professional exemption purposes where students are seeking to enter the Vocational Stage of Legal Education and Training.

The foundation subjects are:

(a) Public Law (including Constitutional Law, Administrative Law and Human Rights).

(b) Law of the European Union.

(c) Criminal Law.

(d) Obligations (including Contract, Restitution and Tort).

(e) Property Law.

(f) Equity and the Law of Trusts.

In addition, students will also be expected to have appropriate expertise in Legal Research Skills, the English Legal System and Another Area of Legal Study.

The current version of the Bar Training Regulations is set out below.

The Bar Training Regulations

[2.2]

Part I – Introduction

1. These Regulations set out training which a person must complete, and other requirements which a person must satisfy, in order to be called to the Bar by an Inn and become qualified to practise as a barrister.

2. To be called to the Bar by an Inn a person must:

   (a) be a member of that Inn;

   (b) complete (or be exempted from)

      (i) the Academic Stage, and

      (ii) the Vocational Stage of training; and

(c) fulfil any applicable requirement to attend Qualifying Sessions.

3. To become qualified to practise as a barrister a person must:

(a) be called to the Bar by an Inn;

(b) complete (or be exempted from) the Professional Stage of training; and

(c) satisfy such further requirements as are set out in the Code of Conduct.

3A. The general objective of these Regulations is to ensure that any person who becomes qualified to practise as a barrister is a fit and proper person and competent to do so.

3B. Where these Regulations confer upon the Board a discretion to be exercised either in individual cases or generally (by the publication of criteria or otherwise), such discretion shall be exercised in a manner likely to promote the general objective of these Regulations.

3C. The Board shall publish from time to time a general statement of the minimum level of competence reasonably to be expected of a barrister when first qualified to practise.

Part II – Admission to Inns of Court

Eligibility for Admission

4. To be eligible for admission to an Inn under these Regulations a person must:

(a) have the necessary educational qualifications; and

(b) be a fit and proper person to become a practising barrister.

5. A person has the necessary educational qualifications to be admitted to an Inn if that person:

(a) is reading for a Qualifying Law Degree; or

(b) is attending (or has been accepted for and is about to attend) a Conversion Course; or

(c) has completed (or been exempted under Part VII of these Regulations from) the Academic Stage of training.

6. A person is a fit and proper person to become a practising barrister if:

(a) there is no reason to expect that that person, if admitted to an Inn, will engage in conduct which is dishonest or which otherwise makes that person unfit to become a practising barrister; and

(b) that person does not suffer from serious incapacity due to mental disorder (within the meaning of the Mental Health Act 1983), addiction to alcohol or drugs or any other condition which makes that person unfit to become a practising barrister.

7. In the case of an applicant who is authorised to practice by another approved regulator or a Qualified European Lawyer, a Certificate of Good Standing is

to be treated as conclusive evidence that the applicant is a fit and proper person to become a practising barrister.

8. A person whose application for admission to an Inn has been rejected on the ground that that person is not a fit and proper person to become a practicing barrister or who has been expelled from an Inn because of a disciplinary offence may not apply for admission to an Inn unless a period of at least five years (or such other period as the Board may determine in the particular case) has elapsed from the date of such rejection or expulsion.

Application Procedure

9. To apply for admission to an Inn a person ("the applicant") must submit to the Inn:

   (a) a duly completed and signed application including an Admission Declaration in the form set out in Schedule A;

   (b) two Certificates of Good Character or, if the applicant is a Qualified Lawyer, a Certificate of Good Standing, which (in either case) was issued within the previous three months; and

   (c) the fee prescribed by the Inn.

Certificates of Good Character

10. A Certificate of Good Character must contain the information specified in Schedule B and be provided by a professional person or person of standing in the community who:

   (a) has known the applicant for at least one year;

   (b) does not have a close family or personal relationship with the applicant; and

   (c) has read the Admission Declaration submitted by the applicant under Regulation 9(a).

Decision to Admit or Refuse Admission

11. Before deciding whether to admit the applicant, the Inn may make any further enquiries or require the applicant to provide any further information that it considers relevant.

12. The Inn must admit the applicant if the applicant:

   (a) is eligible for admission to an Inn and has given the undertaking on the admission declaration (Schedule A) to commence the Vocational Stage within five years of admission to an Inn and complete that Stage within ten years of admission; and

   (b) has complied with Regulation 9.

   Otherwise the Inn must reject the application and inform the applicant of its reasons for doing so.

13. If the applicant falls within Regulation 14, the Inn must refer the question whether the applicant is a fit and proper person to become a practicing barrister to the Inns' Conduct Committee to decide and must notify the applicant that it has done so.

14. An applicant falls within this Regulation if:

(a) the applicant has been convicted of a Criminal Offence (or is the subject of pending Criminal Proceedings); or

(b) the applicant has been convicted of a disciplinary offence by a professional or regulatory body (or is the subject of pending proceedings for such an offence); or

(c) the applicant has been the subject of a Bankruptcy Order or Directors Disqualification Order or has entered into an individual voluntary arrangement with creditors; or

(d) the applicant has previously been refused admission to or expelled from an Inn; or

(e) there is any other circumstance which in the opinion of the Inn calls into question the applicant's fitness to become a practising barrister.

15. When the Inns' Conduct Committee is asked to decide whether the applicant is a fit and proper person to become a practising barrister, it must send a report of its decision and the reasons for the decision to the applicant and to the Inn.

16. If the Inns' Conduct Committee decides that the applicant is not a fit and proper person to become a practising barrister or if the Inn rejects an application for admission for any other reason, the applicant may request a review of the decision under Part X of these Regulations, provided that the request is made in writing to the Board within one month of the date when notice of the decision was given.

17. If on a review under Part X the Board is satisfied that the applicant is eligible for admission to an Inn and has complied with Regulation 9, the Inn must admit the applicant.

Part III – The Academic Stage

18. A person completes the Academic Stage of training by:

(a) obtaining a Qualifying Law Degree; or

(b) obtaining a Qualifying Degree and successfully completing a Conversion Course.

19. A Qualifying Law Degree is a Qualifying Degree approved by the Board which includes a course of study of the Foundations of Legal Knowledge.

20. A Qualifying Degree is:

(a) a degree of the required standard awarded by a University in the United Kingdom following a course of study of the minimum period; or

(b) a degree awarded by a University or establishment of equivalent level outside the United Kingdom which the Board accepts as equivalent to a degree satisfying the requirements of paragraph (a).

21. For the purpose of Regulation 20(a), unless the Board on an application showing good grounds permits otherwise:

(a) the required standard is first or second class honours.

22. A Conversion Course is a course approved by the Board which includes study of the Foundations of Legal Knowledge.

23. For the purpose of Regulation 18, a person obtains a Qualifying Degree on being adjudged to have successfully completed the academic requirements of the degree irrespective of when the degree is actually conferred.

Part IV – The Vocational Stage

24. A person commences the Vocational Stage of training on commencing attendance at a Bar Professional Training Course and completes the Vocational Stage on being certified by the course provider as having successfully completed a Bar Professional Training Course.

25. Before commencing the Vocational Stage, a person must:

    (a) have completed (or been exempted under Part VII of these Regulations from) the Academic Stage; and

    (b) be a member of an Inn of Court.

26. A person may not commence the Vocational Stage more than five years after completing the Academic Stage except with the permission of the Board and after complying with any condition which the Board may impose.

Part V – The Professional Stage

27. A person commences the Professional Stage of training on commencing pupillage in accordance with these Regulations and completes the Professional Stage by:

    (a) satisfactorily completing 12 months of pupillage and such further training as may be required by the Board; and

    (b) being issued with a Full Qualification Certificate.

28. Before commencing the Professional Stage, a person must have completed (or been exempted under Part VII of these Regulations from) the Vocational Stage.

29. A person may not commence the Professional Stage more than five years after completing the Vocational Stage except with the permission of the Board and after complying with any condition which the Board may impose.

Pupillage

30. Pupillage is divided into two parts:

    (a) a non-practising period of six months; and

    (b) a practising period of six months.

31. Except with the written permission of the Board, the non-practising period of pupillage must be undertaken:

    (a) in a Member State of the European Union; and

    (b) in a continuous period of six months.

32. Except with the written permission of the Board, the practising period of pupillage must:

    (a) commence within 12 months after completion of the non-practising period;

    (b) be undertaken in a Member State; and

    (c) be completed within an overall period of nine months.

33. Any period of pupillage must provide training which is adequate and which complies with such criteria as may be published by the Board.

34. Except as provided in Regulation 42, any period of pupillage must be undertaken:

    (a) in an Approved Training Organisation; and

    (b) with a barrister who is a registered pupil supervisor.

35. Schedule C to these Regulations sets out rules applicable to pupil supervisors.

36. During any period of pupillage the pupil must;

    (a) be diligent in receiving the instruction given; and

    (b) observe all legal and professional obligations of confidence.

Approved Training Organisations

37. The Board may authorise any organisation as an Approved Training Organisation subject to such terms as the Board may from time to time determine.

38. The Board may withdraw approval from an Approved Training Organisation if it considers following investigation:

    (a) that pupillage training provided by the organisation is or has been seriously deficient; or

    (b) that the organisation has not made proper arrangements for dealing with pupils and pupillage in accordance with the Code of Conduct.

39. The Board will give notice in writing:

    (a) in the case of a decision to refuse to designate an organisation as an Approved Training Organisation, to that organisation; and

    (b) in the case of a decision to withdraw approval from an Approved Training Organisation, to:

        (i) that organisation;

        (ii) any person who is undertaking or has agreed to undertake a pupillage in that organisation; and

        (iii) the Inn of which any such person is a member.

40. Any person or organisation to whom the Board is required to give notice of a decision under Regulation 39 may request a review of the decision under Part X of these Regulations, provided that the request is made in writing to the Board within one month of the date when notice of the decision was given.

41. If the Board withdraws approval from an Approved Training Organisation, the organisation may not claim repayment of any pupillage award or other sum paid to any pupil or prospective pupil.

External Training

42. With the written permission of the Board, part or all of the practising period of pupillage may be satisfied by training:

 (a) with a solicitor, judge or other suitably qualified lawyer who is not a registered pupil supervisor; and/or

 (b) in an organisation which is not an Approved Training Organisation but which, in the opinion of the Board, provides suitable training and experience.

Registration of Pupillage

43. Before commencing any period of pupillage (including any period of external training) a person must apply to the Board for registration of the pupillage by submitting an application in the form prescribed by the Board.

44. The Board will register the pupillage if it is satisfied that the application has been duly completed and that the pupillage complies with these Regulations.

45. If a person applies to the Board for registration of a pupillage after the pupillage has commenced, the pupillage will be treated as having commenced on the date of receipt of the application, unless the Board permits otherwise.

46. If the Board refuses to register a pupillage, it will inform the pupil in writing of its decision and the reasons for it.

47. If the Board refuses to register a pupillage, the pupil may request a review of the decision under Part X of these Regulations, provided that the request is made in writing to the Board within one month of the date when notice of the decision was given.

48. If any of the information provided in an application for registration of a pupillage changes before the pupillage has been completed, the pupil must promptly notify the Board in writing of the change.

Qualification Certificates

49. On completion of the non-practising period of pupillage, the Board will issue the pupil with a Provisional Qualification Certificate provided that the pupil has been called to the Bar under Part IX of these Regulations and the Board is satisfied:

 (a) that the pupil has satisfactorily completed the non-practising period of pupillage and any further training required under Regulation 27(a); and

 (b) that the pupillage is registered and complied with these Regulations.

50. On completion of the practising period of pupillage, the Board will issue the pupil with a Full Qualification Certificate if the pupil has a Provisional Qualification Certificate and the Board is satisfied:

(a) that the pupil has satisfactorily completed the practising period of pupillage and any further training required under Regulation 27(a); and

(b) that the pupillage is registered and complied with these Regulations.

51. For the purpose of these Regulations, a pupil is to be treated as having satisfactorily completed a period of pupillage if the pupil:

(a) has been diligent in receiving the instruction given; and

(b) has achieved the minimum level of competence required of a pupil at the end of the relevant period.

52. The Board may accept as evidence that a pupil has satisfactorily completed any period of pupillage a certificate to this effect from the pupil supervisor (or person responsible for external training) with whom the pupil has completed that period.

53. If a pupil supervisor is unable or unwilling to provide a certificate that a pupil has satisfactorily completed a period of pupillage, the Board may accept such a certificate signed by the Head of Chambers or person in charge of pupilage in the training organisation where the pupillage has been undertaken if the certificate contains a satisfactory explanation of why the pupil supervisor has not signed it.

54. If the Board is not satisfied:

(a) that the pupil has satisfactorily completed a period of pupillage, and/or

(b) that the pupillage is registered and complied with these Regulations, the Board may specify further training which the pupil must satisfactorily complete before the Board will issue the pupil with a Provisional Qualification Certificate or a Full Qualification Certificate (as the case may be).

55. If the Board refuses to issue a Provisional Qualification Certificate or a Full Qualification Certificate, the pupil may request a review of the decision under Part X of these Regulations, provided that the request is made in writing to the Board within one month of the date when notice of the decision was given.

Part VI – Qualifying Sessions

56. Subject to Regulations 57 and 62, a person who is admitted to an Inn must attend 12 Qualifying Sessions during a period of no more than five years ending on the date on which that person is called to the Bar.

57. An Inn may on an application showing such exceptional grounds as satisfy criteria agreed by all four Inns waive or modify the requirement to attend Qualifying Sessions.

58. Each Inn is responsible, in cooperation with the other Inns, for:

(a) ensuring that suitable Qualifying Sessions are available for its members; and

(b) deciding what requirements must be satisfied for a person to be credited with attendance at one or more Qualifying Sessions; and

(c) agreeing criteria which specify the grounds on which the requirement to attend Qualifying Sessions may be waived or modified.

Part VII – Exemptions from Training Requirements

59. The Board may grant exemptions from part or all of:

(a) the Academic Stage,

(b) the Vocational Stage, and/or

(c) the Professional Stage, of training.

60. In exercising any discretion whether to grant an exemption from part or all of any Stage of training, the Board will determine whether the relevant knowledge and experience of the applicant make it unnecessary for the applicant to undertake such training.

61. An exemption from part or all of any Stage of training may be granted unconditionally or subject to conditions, which may include in an appropriate case:

(a) a requirement to undertake training in substitution for training prescribed by these Regulations; and/or

(b) a condition that the applicant must pass a Bar Transfer Test.

62. Where the Board exempts a person from the Vocational or Professional Stage of training, it may also:

(a) grant exemption in whole or in part from the requirement to attend Qualifying Sessions; and

(b) specify the period within which any requirement to attend Qualifying Sessions must be fulfilled, which may be a period ending after the person concerned has been called to the Bar and in the case of a Specially Qualified Applicant is usually a period of three years during which the Applicant must attend six Qualifying Sessions unless special circumstances apply.

Applications

63. An application for exemption under this Part must be in such form as may be prescribed by the Board and contain or be accompanied by the following:

(a) details of the applicant's educational and professional qualifications and experience;

(b) evidence (where applicable) that the applicant is or has been entitled to exercise rights of audience before any court, specifying the rights concerned and the basis of the applicant's entitlement to exercise such rights;

(c) any other representations or evidence on which the applicant wishes to rely in support of the application;

(d) verified English translations of every document relied on which is not in the English language; and

(e) the prescribed fee.

64. Before deciding whether to grant any exemption under this Part, the Board may make any further enquiries or require the applicant to provide any further information that it considers relevant.

65. A person whose application for exemption is rejected may request a review of the decision under Part X of these Regulations, provided that the request is made in writing to the Board within one month of the date when notice of the decision was given.

Full Exemption

66. If the Board is satisfied that an applicant falls within Regulation 67, the Board will:

(a) exempt the applicant from any Stage of training prescribed by these Regulations which the applicant has not fulfilled;

(b) issue the applicant with a Full Qualification Certificate; and

(c) authorise the applicant to practise as a barrister upon being admitted to an Inn and called to the Bar under Part IX of these Regulations subject to complying with the Code of Conduct.

67. The following categories of person fall within this Regulation:

(a) a person who has been authorised to exercise rights of audience by another approved regulator and is entitled to exercise those rights in relation to all proceedings in all courts of England and Wales;

(b) subject to Regulation 68, a person who has been authorised to exercise rights of audience by another approved regulator and is entitled to exercise those rights in relation to either all proceedings in the High Court or all proceedings in the Crown Court of England and Wales (but not both);

(c) a barrister of Northern Ireland who has successfully completed pupilage in accordance with the rules of the Bar of Northern Ireland;

(d) subject to Regulation 69, a Qualified European Lawyer.

68. The Board may exceptionally require an applicant who falls within Regulation 67(b) to undertake part or all of the practising six months of pupillage if it considers this necessary having regard in particular to the knowledge, professional experience and intended future practice of the applicant.

69. Subject to Regulations 71 to 75, the Board may require a Qualified European Lawyer to pass a Bar Transfer Test if the Board determines that:

(a) the matters covered by the education and training of the applicant differ substantially from those covered by the Academic, Vocational and Professional Stages of training; and

(b) the knowledge acquired by the applicant in the course of the applicant's professional experience does not fully cover this substantial difference.

Registered European Lawyers

70. The rules governing registration as a Registered European Lawyer are set out in Annexe B to the Code of Conduct.

71. The Board may not require an applicant who is a Registered European Lawyer and who falls within Regulation 73 or 74 to pass a Bar Transfer Test unless it considers that the applicant is unfit to practise as a barrister.

72. In considering whether to require an applicant who falls within Regulation 74 to pass a Bar Transfer Test, the Board must:

(a) take into account the professional activities the applicant has pursued while a Registered European Lawyer and any knowledge and professional experience gained of, and any training received in, the law of any part of the United Kingdom and of the rules of professional conduct of the Bar; and

(b) assess and verify at an interview the applicant's effective and regular pursuit of professional activities and capacity to continue the activities pursued.

73. To fall within this Regulation an applicant must have:

(a) for a period of at least three years been a Registered European Lawyer; and

(b) for a period of at least three years effectively and regularly pursued in England and Wales under a Home Professional Title professional activities in the law of England and Wales.

74. To fall within this Regulation an applicant must have:

(a) for a period of at least three years been a Registered European Lawyer; and

(b) for a period of at least three years effectively and regularly pursued in England and Wales professional activities under a Home Professional Title; and

(c) for a period of less than three years effectively and regularly pursued in England and Wales under a Home Professional Title professional activities in the law of England and Wales.

75. For the purpose of these Regulations, activities are to be regarded as effectively and regularly pursued if they are actually exercised without any interruptions other than those resulting from the events of everyday life.

Partial Exemption

76. If the Board is satisfied that an applicant falls within Regulation 77, the Board will:

(a) exempt the applicant from the Academic Stage and the Vocational Stage and, if the Board thinks fit, from part or all of the Professional Stage of training; and

(b) if the applicant is exempted from the whole of the non-practising six months of pupillage, issue the applicant with a Provisional Qualification Certificate.

77. The following categories of person fall within this Regulation:

(a) a person who has been authorised to exercise rights of audience by another approved regulator and is entitled to exercise those rights in relation to any class of proceedings in any of the Senior Courts or all proceedings in county courts or magistrates' courts in England and Wales;

(b) a Qualified Foreign Lawyer who has for a period of at least three years regularly exercised full rights of audience in courts which administer law substantially similar to the common law of England and Wales;

(c) a teacher of the law of England and Wales of experience and academic distinction.

Temporary Call to the Bar of Qualified Foreign Lawyers

78. A Qualified Foreign Lawyer ("the applicant") who falls within Regulation 77(b) is entitled to be admitted to an Inn and called to the Bar on a temporary basis for the purpose of appearing as counsel in a particular case before a court of England and Wales without being required to satisfy any other requirements of these Regulations if the applicant has:

(a) obtained from the Board and submitted to an Inn a Temporary Qualification Certificate specifying the case for the purposes of which the applicant is authorised to be called to the Bar;

(b) duly completed and signed a Call Declaration in the form set out in Schedule E; and

(c) paid the fee prescribed by the Inn.

79. The Board will issue a Temporary Qualification Certificate if the applicant submits to the Board:

(a) evidence which establishes that the applicant is a Qualified European Lawyer or falls within Regulation 77(b);

(b) a Certificate of Good Standing; and

(c) evidence which establishes that a Professional Client wishes to instruct the applicant to appear as counsel in the case or cases for the purposes of which the applicant seeks temporary call to the Bar.

80. Admission to an Inn and call to the Bar under Regulation 78 take effect when the applicant is given notice in writing by the Inn that the applicant has been admitted to the Inn and called to the Bar under that Regulation and automatically cease to have effect on conclusion of the case or cases specified in the applicant's Temporary Qualification Certificate.

Part VIII – Conduct of Students

81. References in this Part to "the Inn" are to any Inn of which the Student concerned is a member.

82. A Student must observe any regulations as to conduct and discipline made by the Inn.

83. If a Student:

(a) becomes the subject of pending Criminal Proceedings or is convicted of a Criminal Offence, or

(b) becomes the subject of pending disciplinary proceedings or is convicted of a disciplinary offence by a professional or regulatory body, or

(c) is the subject of a Bankruptcy Order or Directors Disqualification Order or enters into an individual voluntary arrangement with creditors, or

(d) is found guilty by the course provider of cheating or other misconduct on a Professional Training Course,

the Student must immediately notify the Inn in writing.

84. This Regulation applies where notification is given or a complaint or report is made or it appears to an Inn from information given in the Student's Call Declaration or otherwise that a Student of the Inn has or may have:

(a) made any false statement or acted in breach of any undertaking given in the Student's Admission Declaration or Call Declaration; or

(b) while a Student:

(i) committed any breach of any regulations made by the Inn concerning the conduct and discipline of its members; or

(ii) been convicted of a Criminal Offence; or

(iii) been convicted of a disciplinary offence by a professional or regulatory body; or

(iv) been the subject of a Bankruptcy Order or Directors Disqualification Order or entered into an individual voluntary arrangement with creditors; or

(v) been found guilty by the course provider of cheating or other misconduct on a Professional Training Course (and has not successfully appealed against that finding); or

(vi) otherwise been guilty of any conduct discreditable to a member of an Inn.

85. Where Regulation 84 applies, the Inn:

(a) may make any enquiries or require the Student to provide such information as it may think fit; and

(b) must consider whether the matter is a Serious Matter.

86. For the purpose of these Regulations, a matter is a Serious Matter if it:

(a) falls within Regulation 84(a) or (b)(ii)–(v); or

(b) in the opinion of the Inn otherwise calls into question whether the Student is a fit and proper person to become a practising barrister.

87. If the Inn decides that the matter is not a Serious Matter, the Inn may deal with the matter under its internal disciplinary procedure and at the conclusion of that procedure may:

(a) dismiss any complaint; or

(b) decide to take no action; or

(c) advise the Student as to future conduct; or

(d) reprimand the Student; or

(e) ban the Student for a specified period from using some or all of the Inn's facilities.

87A. A Student may appeal from a decision of an Inn under its internal disciplinary procedure to the Inns' Conduct Committee.

88. If at any stage the Inn decides that the matter is a Serious Matter, the Inn must refer the matter to the Inns' Conduct Committee for determination. After determining the matter, the Inns' Conduct Committee must send a report of its findings and reasons to the Student and to the Inn.

89. If the Inns' Conduct Committee (or the Board on a review under Part X of these Regulations) finds a Serious Matter proved, it may:

(a) advise the Student as to future conduct; or

(b) reprimand the Student; or

(c) order that the Student's call to the Bar be postponed for a specified period; or

(d) direct that the Student be expelled from the Inn (in which case the Inn must expel the Student).

90. If the Inns' Conduct Committee finds a Serious Matter proved, the Student may request a review under Part X of these Regulations of the decision of the Inns' Conduct Committee, provided that the request is made in writing to the Board within one month of the date when notice of the decision was given.

91. Where Regulation 84 applies, the Student is not entitled to be called to the Bar:

(a) until the Inn has decided that the matter is not a Serious Matter; or

(b) if the Inn decides that the matter is a Serious Matter, until the matter has been determined; or

(c) if the Inns' Conduct Committee (or the Board following a review under Part X) orders that the Student's call to the Bar be postponed for a specified period, until that period has expired.

Part IX – Call to the Bar

Requirements for Call

92. Subject to Regulations 91 and 93, a person is entitled to be called to the Bar by an Inn of which that person is a member if that person has:

(a) completed or been exempted from the Vocational Stage of training in accordance with these Regulations;

(b) complied with any applicable requirement to attend Qualifying Sessions;

(c) submitted to the Inn a duly completed and signed a Call Declaration in the form set out in Schedule D; and

(d) paid the fee prescribed by the Inn.

93. Before deciding whether a person who has complied with Regulation 92 ("the candidate") is entitled to be called to the Bar, the Inn:

(a) may make any enquiries or require the candidate to provide any further information that it considers relevant;

(b) must consider whether Regulation 84 applies; and

(c) if Regulation 84 applies, must give effect to Regulation 91.

94. If the Inn decides that the candidate is not entitled to be called to the Bar, the Inn must inform the candidate of its decision and of the reasons for it.

95. If the Inn decides that the candidate is not entitled to be called to the Bar, the candidate may request a review of the decision under Part X of these Regulations, provided that the request is made in writing to the Board within one month of the date when notice of the decision was given by the Inn.

96. If on a review under Part X the Board decides that the candidate is entitled to be called to the Bar, the Inn must call the candidate to the Bar.

Call Days and Procedure

97. Calls to the Bar will take place on such days as may be authorised from time to time by the Inns' Council.

98. A candidate must be called to the Bar in person unless given written permission by the Inn to be absent from the call ceremony.

Part X – Review and Appeals

99. Where provision is made under these Regulations for a review by the Board of a decision, any request for such a review must be accompanied by:

(a) a copy of any notice of the decision and the reasons for it received by the person or organisation requesting the review ("the applicant");

(b) where the decision is a decision of an Inn or of the Inns' Conduct Committee, copies of all documents submitted or received by the applicant which were before the Inn or the Inns' Conduct Committee (as the case may be);

(c) any further representations and evidence which the applicant wishes the Board to take into account; and

(d) the prescribed fee.

100. Where the decision under review is a decision of an Inn or of the Inns' Conduct Committee, the Board will invite the Inn or the Inns' Conduct Committee (as the case may be) to comment on any further representations and evidence which the applicant submits under Regulation 99(c).

101. On a review under this Part the Board:

(a) may affirm the decision under review or substitute any other decision which could have been made on the original application;

(b) may in an appropriate case reimburse the fee paid under Regulation 99(d); and

(c) will inform the applicant and any other interested person of its decision and the reasons for it.

102. Where under these Regulations provision is made for a review by the Board of a decision, no appeal may be made to the Visitors to the Inns of Court unless such a review has taken place.

103. Subject to Regulation 102, a person or organisation who is adversely affected by a decision of the Board may appeal against the decision to the Visitors to the Inns of Court in accordance with the Hearings before the Visitors Rules.

Part XI – Powers

Amendment

104. Subject to Regulations 105 and 106, the Board may amend these Regulations and any such amendment will take effect on such date as the Board appoints or, if no such date is appointed, on the later of:

(a) the date when notice of the amendment is first published on the Board's website; and

(b) if the amendment requires approval under Schedule 4 of the Courts and Legal Services Act 1990, the date when such approval is given.

105. Before making any amendment to these Regulations under Regulation 104, the Board must consult and take account of any representations duly made by:

(a) the Inns; and

(b) such other bodies or persons as the Board considers it reasonable to consult in relation to the proposed amendment.

106. The Board has no power without the unanimous consent of the Inns to amend or waive Regulation 3(a) or this Regulation so as to permit a person who has not been called to the Bar by an Inn to practise as a barrister.

Inns' Conduct Committee

107. Subject to these Regulations, the Inns' Conduct Committee shall have power to carry out the functions specified in the Inns' Conduct Committee Rules.

108. The Inns' Conduct Committee Rules must be approved by the Board and any amendment to those Rules will take effect on:

(a) the date when the amendment is approved by the Board; or

(b) such later date as the Board appoints.

109. The Board may:

(a) issue guidance which the Inns' Conduct Committee must follow in carrying out its functions; and

(b) request information relating to the performance of those functions which the Inns' Conduct Committee must provide to the Board.

Other Powers

110. Subject to Regulation 106, the Board may in any particular case waive or modify any requirement of these Regulations either unconditionally or subject to conditions.

111. The Board may charge such fees as it prescribes for dealing with applications, conducting assessments or examinations and issuing certificates under these Regulations.

112. Subject to the approval of the Board, an Inn may charge such fees as it prescribes for dealing with applications and calling persons to the Bar under these Regulations.

113. Any function or power which under these Regulations is exercisable by the Board or by an Inn or by the Inns' Conduct Committee may be delegated (and sub-delegated) to any committee, body or person to the extent permitted by the standing orders of the Board or the Inn or the Inns' Conduct Committee Rules (as the case may be).

Part XII – Definitions

114. In these Regulations, the following terms have the following meanings:

"Admission" to an Inn includes readmission of a former member who has ceased (whether as a result of disbarment or otherwise) to be a member of the Inn.

"Admission Declaration" means the Declaration referred to in Regulation 9(a).

"Approved Regulator" has the same meaning as in section 20(2) of the Legal Services Act 2007.

"Approved Training Organisation" means a chambers, company, firm or other organisation which has been approved by the Board for the purpose of providing professional training under Part V of these Regulations.

"Bar Transfer Test" means an examination administered by the Board which:

(a) is designed to assess whether a person has the professional knowledge (including knowledge of the rules of professional conduct) required in order to practise as a barrister in England and Wales; and

(b) covers subjects not already covered by the education and training of the person concerned, the knowledge of which is essential for such practice.

"Bankruptcy Order" includes a bankruptcy order made pursuant to the Insolvency Act 1986 and any similar order made in any jurisdiction in the world.

"Barrister" means a person who has been called to the Bar by an Inn and who has not been disbarred by the Inn or otherwise ceased to be a barrister.

"Bar Professional Training Course" means a course which has been approved by the Board as providing vocational training of appropriate content and quality to satisfy the requirements of the Vocational Stage.

"Board" means the Bar Standards Board, which is responsible for exercising the regulatory functions of the General Council of the Bar of England and

Wales, and any committee, body or person to whom the Bar Standards Board has delegated the exercise of a relevant power under these Regulations.

"Call Declaration" means the Declaration referred to in Regulation 92(c).

"Call to the Bar" means the formal act by which a person is awarded the degree of barrister by an Inn.

"Certificate of Good Character" means a certificate which complies with the requirements of Regulation 10.

"Certificate of Good Standing" means:

(a) in relation to a person who has been authorised to practice by another approved regulator or Qualified Foreign Lawyer, a certificate issued by the approved regulator or professional body or other authority responsible for regulating the profession of which the person concerned is a member attesting that the person concerned:

  (i) is of good character;

  (ii) has not been the subject of a Bankruptcy Order or Directors Disqualification Order nor entered into an individual voluntary arrangement with creditors; and

  (iii) has not been prohibited and is not currently suspended from practising on account of serious professional misconduct or the commission of a criminal offence;

(b) in relation to a Qualified European Lawyer, evidence of the kind referred to in Regulation 9(2) of the European Qualification Regulations, that the person concerned:

  (i) is of good character;

  (ii) has not been the subject of a Bankruptcy Order or Directors Disqualification Order nor entered into an individual voluntary arrangement with creditors; and

  (iii) has not been prohibited and is not currently suspended from practising on account of serious professional misconduct or the commission of a criminal offence.

"Code of Conduct" means the Code of Conduct of the Bar of England and Wales.

"Complaints Rules" means the rules at Annexe J to the Code of Conduct.

"Conversion Course" is defined in Regulation 22.

"Criminal Offence" means any offence, wherever committed, under the criminal law of any jurisdiction (including an offence the conviction for which is a spent conviction within the meaning of the Rehabilitation of Offenders Act 1974) except:

(a) an offence for which liability is capable of being discharged by payment of a fixed penalty; and

(b) an offence which has as its main ingredient the unlawful parking of a vehicle.

"Criminal Proceedings" are pending if a person:

(a) is currently charged with, or

(b) is on bail or in detention or custody (or has failed to surrender to custody) in connection with, any Criminal Offence.

"Directors Disqualification Order" includes a disqualification order made by a court, or disqualification undertaking accepted by the secretary of state, pursuant to the Company Directors Disqualification Act 1986 and any similar order made or undertaking given in any jurisdiction in the world.

"European Lawyer" means a person who is a national of a Relevant State and who is authorised in any Relevant State to pursue professional activities under any of the professional titles appearing in Regulation 2(4) of the European Communities (Lawyer's Practice) Regulations 2000, but who (subject to Regulation 2(3) of those Regulations) is not:

(a) a solicitor or barrister of England and Wales or Northern Ireland; or

(b) a solicitor or advocate under the law of Scotland.

"European Qualification Regulations" means the European Communities (Recognition of Professional Qualifications) Regulations 2007.

"Foundations of Legal Knowledge" means those subjects the study of which is prescribed by the Board for the purpose of obtaining a Qualifying Law Degree and for inclusion in any Graduate Conversion Course, and which currently comprise:

(i) Obligations I (Contract)

(ii) Obligations II (Tort)

(iii) Criminal Law

(iv) Public Law

(v) Property Law

(vi) Equity & The Law of Trusts

(vii) Foundations of EU Law

"Full Qualification Certificate" means a certificate issued by the Board under Regulation 50 or 66 on satisfactory completion of, or exemption from, the Professional Stage.

"Home Professional Title" means, in relation to a European Lawyer, any of the professional titles specified in relation to the Home State in Regulation 2(4) of the European Communities (Lawyer's Practice) Regulations 2000 under which the European Lawyer is authorised in the Home State to pursue professional activities.

"Home State" means, in relation to a European Lawyer, any State specified in Regulation 2(4) of the European Communities (Lawyer's Practice) Regulations 2000 in which a European Lawyer acquired authorisation to pursue professional activities.

"Inn" means one of the four Inns of Court, namely, the Honourable Societies of Lincoln's Inn, Inner Temple, Middle Temple and Gray's Inn.

"Inns' Council" means the Council of the Inns of Court.

"Inns' Conduct Committee" means a Committee constituted by the four Inns for the purpose of deciding in accordance with the Inns' Conduct Committee Rules issues relating to admission to an Inn and to the conduct of Students.

"Inns' Conduct Committee Rules" means rules made by the Inns and approved by the Board which govern the composition and operation of the Inns' Conduct Committee.

"Member State" means a state which is a member of the European Communities.

"Practise as a barrister" has the meaning given in paragraph 201 of the Code of Conduct.

"Professional Client" has the meaning given in Part X of the Code of Conduct.

"Provisional Qualification Certificate" means a certificate issued by the Board under Regulation 49 or 76 following satisfactory completion of, or exemption from, the non-practising six months of pupillage.

"Pupillage" means a period of professional training under Part V of these Regulations and includes a period of external training for which permission has been given by the Board under Regulation 40.

"Qualified European Lawyer" means a person who is a national of a Relevant State and who either:

(a) holds a diploma required in a Relevant State for the practice of a legal profession regulated by that State which diploma satisfies the requirements of Regulation 22(1)(a) of the European Qualification Regulations; or

(b) satisfies the requirements of Regulation 22(1)(b) of the European Qualification Regulations.

"Qualified Foreign Lawyer" means a person who is a member of a legal profession regulated in a jurisdiction outside England and Wales and entitled to practise as such.

"Qualified Lawyer" means a person who has been authorised to practice by another approved regulator, a Qualified European Lawyer or a Qualified Foreign Lawyer;

"Qualifying Degree" is defined in Regulation 20.

"Qualifying Law Degree" is defined in Regulation 19.

"Qualifying Session" means an event (or part of an event) of an educational and collegiate nature arranged by or on behalf of an Inn.

"Registered European Lawyer" means a European Lawyer registered as such by the Board and by an Inn pursuant to Annexe B of the Code of Conduct.

"Relevant State" means a Member State, Iceland, Norway, Liechtenstein or Switzerland.

"Senior Courts" means the Senior Courts of England and Wales, namely, the Court of Appeal, the High Court of Justice and the Crown Court.

"Serious Matter" is defined in Regulation 86.

"Solicitor" means a solicitor of the Supreme Court of England and Wales.

"Student" means a person who has been admitted to an Inn under these Regulations and remains a member of the Inn but has not been called to the Bar.

"Temporary Qualification Certificate" means a certificate issued by the Board under Regulation 79 authorising a Qualified Foreign Lawyer to be admitted to temporary membership of an Inn and called to the Bar for the purpose of appearing as counsel in a particular case or cases before a court or courts of England and Wales.

"University" means an institution which makes available educational services under a name which includes the word "university" and in the case of an institution to which section 39(1) of the Higher Education Act 1998 applies which is authorised or has approval to include that word in that name as mentioned in that subsection.

115. In these Regulations, unless the contrary intention appears:

(a) words in the singular include the plural and words in the plural include the singular;

(b) any reference to any Act of Parliament or statutory instrument which has been repealed and re-enacted in relevant part, with or without modification, is to be construed as a reference to the provision re-enacted.

116. Any notice under these Regulations shall be deemed to have been given two working days after the notice was sent.

Part XIII – Commencement and Transitional Provisions

117. These Regulations came into force on 1 September 2009.

118. Except as stated in Regulations 119 to 121, these Regulations replace the Consolidated Regulations of the Inns of Court and the General Council of the Bar.

119. In respect of anything done or omitted to be done or otherwise arising before 1 September 2009:

(a) these Regulations will not apply; and

(b) the Consolidated Regulations in force at the relevant time will apply.

120. Any application made, and any investigation or process begun, before 1 September 2009 under the Consolidated Regulations then in force which on 1 September 2009 had not been determined or completed will be determined or completed as if these Regulations had not come into effect.

121. Where a provision of these Regulations corresponds, with or without modification, to a provision of the Consolidated Regulations which was in force before that date, anything done under such provision of the Consolidated Regulations will have effect as if done under these Regulations.

Schedule A

[2.3]

Admission declaration (Regulation 9)

To the Masters of the Bench of the Honourable Society of.................................

I, (full names[1])...

of (home address)...

....

Email.. Tel:..

for the purpose of obtaining admission as a member of the Inn do hereby **declare and undertake** as follows:

1. My present occupation is ....

2.

(a) I have never been convicted of any criminal offence[2] nor are there any proceedings pending[3] against me anywhere in respect of any criminal offence.

(b) I have never been convicted of a disciplinary offence by a professional or regulatory body nor are there any disciplinary proceedings pending against me anywhere in respect of any such offence.

(c) I have never had any bankruptcy order[4] or directors disqualification order[5] made against me nor entered into an individual voluntary arrangement with creditors.

(d) I have not previously been refused admission to or expelled from an Inn.

(e) I do not suffer from serious incapacity due to mental disorder (within the meaning of the Mental Health Act 1983) nor addiction to alcohol or drugs, nor from any other condition which might impair my fitness to become a practising barrister[6].

If any of the statements in paragraph 2 above is incorrect in any respect, please delete the statement as appropriate.

3. Except as disclosed below, I am not aware of any matter which might reasonably be thought to call into question my fitness to become a practising barrister[7].

If you delete any of the statements in paragraph 2 above or there is any other matter which might reasonably be thought to call into question your fitness to become a practising barrister, please give details in the box below – use a continuation sheet if necessary and attach supporting documents. (**If giving details of a criminal conviction, please ensure you specify the sentence**.)

PART II QUALIFYING AS A BARRISTER AND ENTERING PRACTICE

Please indicate whether the following statement applies to you:

4. I am a disabled person within the meaning of the Equality Act 2010 and would like to discuss with the Inn what, if any, reasonable adjustments need to be made to enable me to participate in all aspects of the Inn's activities.

5. If requested by the Inn, I undertake to apply or to assist the Inn in applying to the Criminal Records Bureau for disclosure about me.

6. I undertake that I will inform the Inn immediately if any statement made in this Declaration ceases to be true before I have been admitted to the Inn and while I am an applicant for admission to the Inn.

7. I undertake that while I am a Student member of the Inn:

   (a) I will comply with such regulations as are made by the Inn concerning the conduct and discipline of its Students[8];

   (b) If and in so far as they apply to me, I will comply with Bar Training Regulations and with the Code of Conduct of the Bar;

   (c) I will promptly inform the Under Treasurer (or Sub-Treasurer) of the Inn in writing if:

      (i) there are proceedings pending against me in respect of a criminal offence or I am convicted of a criminal offence; or

      (ii) there are disciplinary proceedings pending against me or I am convicted of a disciplinary offence by a professional or regulatory body; or

      (iii) I have a bankruptcy order or director's disqualification order made against me or enter into an individual voluntary arrangement with creditors; or

      (iv) I am found guilty by the course provider of cheating or other misconduct on a Bar Professional Training Course.

8. I have read and understood the terms of the further Declaration which I will be required to sign before I can be called to the Bar.

9. I will inform the Inn of any change to my name or address.

10. I will commence the Vocational Stage within five years of admission to the Inn and complete that Stage within ten years of admission on the understanding that if I fail to comply with either of those requirements my membership of the Inn will cease on the expiration of either period.

Dated..

Signature..

1 Give your name as shown on your passport.
2 For this purpose a "criminal offence" means any offence, wherever and whenever committed, under the criminal law of any jurisdiction except: (i) an offence for which liability is capable of being discharged by payment of a fixed penalty; and (ii) an offence which has as its main ingredient the unlawful parking of a vehicle. Any conviction which is spent within the meaning of the Rehabilitation of Offenders Act 1974 is nevertheless required to be disclosed by virtue of the Rehabilitation of Offenders Act 1974 (Exceptions) Order 1975.
3 Proceedings are pending if (i) you are currently charged with, or (ii) you are on bail or in detention or custody (or have failed to surrender to custody) in connection with, any criminal offence.
4 A "bankruptcy order" includes a bankruptcy order made pursuant to the Insolvency Act 1986 and any similar order made in any jurisdiction in the world.
5 A "directors disqualification order" includes a disqualification order made by a court, or disqualification undertaking accepted by the Secretary of State, pursuant to the Company Directors Disqualification Act 1986 and any similar order or undertaking made or given in any jurisdiction in the world.
6 If you are a disabled person within the meaning of the Equality Act 2010 and are unable to make this declaration, then on application to the Inn consideration will be given as to whether reasonable adjustments can be made.
7 This includes any incident or behaviour which if known to the Inn might cause your application to be considered more carefully. If in doubt, disclose the incident/behaviour. Two examples are given by way of illustration but not as limitations on disclosure: (i) Receipt of a police caution; (ii) a Court injunction or Anti-Social Behaviour Order restricting your conduct.
8 Copies of the Disciplinary Rules and other regulations of the Inn are available for inspection in the Treasury Office.

Schedule B

[2.4]

Certificate of Good Character (Regulation 10)

I,(name)... (job title)[1]..

of (address[2])..

....

Email:... Tel:.....................................

certify that I have known (name of applicant) ....

of (address of applicant) ....

....

for .... year(s) and that I have had the following opportunities of judging his/her character:

....

....

I believe the applicant to be of good character and am not aware of any fact about the applicant which gives me any reason to expect that, if admitted to any of the Inns of Court, he/she will engage in any conduct which is dishonest or which otherwise renders him/her unfit to become a practising barrister.

I do not have a close family or personal relationship with the applicant.

I have read the Admission Declaration signed by applicant and dated .... and believe the information given in it to be true.

Dated.. Signature..

1 The maker of the certificate must be a professional person or person of standing in the community.
2 Please give your work address and the name of the organisation (if any) by which you are employed.

Schedule C

[2.5]

Pupil Supervisors (Regulation 35)

Acting as a Pupil Supervisor

1. A barrister may act as a pupil supervisor if the barrister:

   (a) is on the register of approved pupil supervisors kept by the Board;

   (b) has a current practising certificate; and

   (c) has regularly practised as a barrister during the previous two years.

Registration as a Pupil Supervisor

2. The Board may enter a barrister on the register of approved pupil supervisors if the barrister is approved by an Inn of which the barrister is a member.

2A. The Board may refuse to enter a barrister on the register of approved pupil supervisors if the Board finds that the barrister is unsuitable for any reason to act as a pupil supervisor.

2B. If the Board refuses to enter a barrister on the register of approved pupil supervisors, it will notify the barrister and the Inn which approved the barrister as a pupil supervisor of its decision and of the reasons for it.

3. An Inn must approve a barrister as a pupil supervisor if:

   (a) the barrister has a current practising certificate;

   (b) the Inn is satisfied that the barrister has the necessary experience and is otherwise suitable to act as a pupil supervisor; and

   (c) the barrister has submitted an application in accordance with paragraph 5.

4. To have the necessary experience to act as a pupil supervisor a barrister should normally:

   (a) have practised in the United Kingdom or another Member State as a barrister (other than as a pupil who has not completed pupillage in accordance with these Regulations) or has been authorised to practice by another approved regulator for a period (which need not have been continuous and need not have been authorised to practice by the same approved regulator) of at least six years in the previous eight years; and

(b) for the previous two years have regularly practised as a barrister and been entitled to exercise a right of audience before every court in England and Wales in relation to all proceedings.

Application Procedure

5. A barrister who wishes to be entered on the register of approved pupil supervisors must submit to the Inn an application in the form currently prescribed by the Board. The application must be supported:

(a) By an independent person who is a High Court Judge or Circuit Judge, a Leader of a Circuit, a Deputy High Court Judge, a Recorder, a Queen's Counsel, a Master of the Bench of an Inn, Treasury Counsel or a person of comparable standing who is able to comment from personal knowledge on the applicant's suitability to act as a pupil supervisor; and

(b) Subject to sub-paragraph (c) below,

(i) in the case of a self-employed barrister, by the applicant's Head of Chambers, or

(ii) in the case of an employed barrister, by a more senior lawyer employed in the same organisation and who has direct knowledge of the work of the applicant;

(c) If the applicant is a Head of Chambers, or there is no more senior lawyer employed in the same organisation with the required knowledge, or for any other reason the support of the person referred to in sub-paragraph (b) is not available, by a second person falling within sub-paragraph (a) above.

Training of Pupil Supervisors

6. The Board, in consultation with the Inns, may and will normally require pupil supervisors to undertake training before they may be entered or after they have been entered on the register of approved pupil supervisors.

Removal from the Register of Pupil Supervisors

7. The Board may remove a barrister's name from the register of approved pupil supervisors if the barrister:

(a) ceases to practise as a barrister or is suspended from practice as a barrister; or

(b) requests the Board in writing to be removed from the register; or

(c) fails to complete any training required under paragraph 6; or

(d) is found by the Board to be unsuitable for any reason to act as a pupil supervisor; or

(e) has not acted as a pupil supervisor for the previous five years.

8. If the Board decides that a barrister's name should be removed from the register of approved pupil supervisors, it will notify the barrister and the Inn which approved the barrister as a pupil supervisor of its decision and of the reasons for it.

Duties of Pupil Supervisors

9. A pupil supervisor must when responsible for supervising any pupil:

   (a) take all reasonable steps to provide the pupil with adequate tuition, supervision and experience;

   (b) have regard to any pupillage guidelines issued by the Board and to the Equality Code for the Bar; and

   (c) ensure that the pupil prepares for and attends any further training required by the Board such as advocacy training provided by the pupil's Circuit or Inn.

10. A pupil supervisor may not be responsible for supervising more than one pupil at a time except with the approval in writing of the Board.

Complaints

11. If any complaint or other matter which appears to affect the suitability of a barrister to continue to act as a pupil supervisor comes to the notice of the Inn which approved the barrister, the Inn must inform the Board of the matter.

12. If any complaint or other matter which appears to affect the suitability of a barrister to continue to act as a pupil supervisor comes to the notice of the Board, the Board will investigate the matter.

13. Following such an investigation, the Board may:

   (a) dismiss any complaint; or

   (b) take no action; or

   (c) if in its opinion the matter is such as to require informal treatment, draw it to the barrister's attention in writing and, if thought desirable, direct the barrister to attend upon a nominated person for advice; or

   (d) if in its opinion the conduct disclosed shows that the barrister is unsuitable to act as a pupil supervisor, remove the name of the barrister from the register of approved pupil supervisors.

Review

14. A barrister whose application to be approved as a pupil supervisor is rejected or whose the Board refuses to enter on the register of approved pupil supervisors or whose name is removed from the register of approved pupil supervisors may request a review of the decision under Part X of these Regulations, provided that the request is made in writing to the Board within one month of the date when notice of the decision was given.

Schedule D

[2.5a]

Call Declaration (Regulation 92)

To the Masters of the Bench of the Honourable Society of ....

I, (full names)

....

of (address)

....

....

Email:.. Tel:...

for the purpose of being Called to the Bar do hereby **declare and undertake** as follows:

1. I confirm that the declaration which I made for the purpose of obtaining admission to this Inn was true in every respect when I made it.
2. Since I made that admission declaration:
   (a) I have not been convicted of any criminal offence[1] (nor been the subject of any pending proceedings[2] for such an offence);
   (b) I have not been convicted of a disciplinary offence by a professional or regulatory body (nor been the subject of any pending proceedings for such an offence);
   (c) I have not been the subject of any bankruptcy order[3] or directors disqualification order[4] nor have I entered into an individual voluntary arrangement with creditors;
3. I do not suffer from serious incapacity due to mental disorder (within the meaning of the Mental Health Act 1983) nor addiction to alcohol or drugs, nor from any other condition which might impair my fitness to become a practising barrister.[5]

If any of the statements in paragraphs 1 to 3 above is incorrect in any respect, please delete the statement as appropriate.

4. Except as disclosed below, I am not aware of any circumstance which has occurred while I have been a Student member of the Inn which might reasonably be thought to call into question my fitness to become a practising barrister.[6]

If you delete any of the statements in paragraphs 1 to 3 above or there is any other circumstance has occurred while you have been a Student which might reasonably be thought to call into question your fitness to become a practising barrister, please give details in the box below – use

PART II QUALIFYING AS A BARRISTER AND ENTERING PRACTICE

a continuation sheet if necessary and attach supporting documents. (***If giving details of a criminal conviction, please ensure you specify the sentence.***)

5. If called to the Bar I will, unless otherwise authorised, attend .... Qualifying Sessions within a period of .... months immediately following my call.[7]

6. So long as I remain a barrister, I will comply with the Code of Conduct of the Bar of England and Wales.

7. I understand that if this declaration is found to have been false in any material respect, or if I breach any undertaking given in it in any material respect, then that will constitute professional misconduct.

Dated .... Signature ....

1 For this purpose a "criminal offence" means any offence, wherever and whenever committed, under the criminal law of any jurisdiction except (i) an offence for which liability is capable of being discharged by payment of a fixed penalty; and (ii) an offence which has as its main ingredient the unlawful parking of a vehicle. Any conviction which is spent within the meaning of the Rehabilitation of Offenders Act 1974 is nevertheless required to be disclosed by virtue of the Rehabilitation of Offenders Act 1974 (Exceptions) Order 1975.

2 Proceedings are pending if (i) you are currently charged with, or (ii) you are on bail or in detention or custody (or have failed to surrender to custody) in connection with, any criminal offence.

3 A "bankruptcy order" includes a bankruptcy order made pursuant to the Insolvency Act 1986 and any similar order made in any jurisdiction in the world.

4 A "directors disqualification order" includes a disqualification order made by a court, or disqualification undertaking accepted by the secretary of state, pursuant to the Company Directors Disqualification Act 1986 and any similar order or undertaking made or given in any jurisdiction in the world.

5 If you are a disabled person within the meaning of the Disability Discrimination Act 1995 and 2005 and are unable to make this declaration, then on application to the Inn consideration will be given as to whether reasonable adjustments can be made.

6 This includes any incident or behaviour which if known to the Inn might cause your application to be considered more carefully. If in doubt, disclose the incident/behaviour. Two examples are given by way of illustration but not as limitations on disclosure:

(a) Receipt of a police caution.

(b) A Court injunction or Anti-Social Behaviour Order restricting your conduct.

7 This paragraph should be deleted unless you are required to attend any Qualifying Sessions after call.

Schedule E

[2.5b]

Declaration for Temporary Admission and Call of a Qualified Foreign Lawyer (Regulation 78)

To the Masters of the Bench of the Honourable Society of ....

I, (full names)

....

of (address)

....

.... Tel: ....

for the purpose of being admitted as a member of the Inn and Called to the Bar on a temporary basis do hereby DECLARE AND UNDERTAKE as follows:

1. I am a member of[1] ....

2. The information which I have provided in support of my application to be admitted as a member of the Inn and Called to the Bar is true in every respect.

3. So long as I remain a barrister, I will comply with the Code of Conduct of the Bar of England and Wales.

4. I will not at any time hold myself out or allow myself to be held out as a barrister nor will I exercise any right that I have by reason of being a barrister other than in connection with the case or cases which I have been authorised by the Bar Standards Board to conduct as a barrister.

5. I understand that I will automatically cease to be a barrister and a member of the Inn on conclusion of the case or cases which I have been authorised by the Bar Standards Board to conduct as a barrister.

6. I understand that if this declaration is found to have been false in any material respect, or if I breach any undertaking given in it in any material respect, then that will constitute professional misconduct.

Dated .... Signature ....

1 Specify the legal profession regulated in a jurisdiction outside England and Wales of which you are a member.

Vocational Training

[2.6]

The Vocational Stage is the next part of training after the academic stage and this takes the form of the Bar Professional Training Course

What is the Vocational Stage?

Course Format and Assessment

The purpose of the BPTC (Bar Professional Training Course) is to ensure that students intending to become barristers acquire the skills, knowledge of procedure and evidence, attitudes and competence to prepare them, in particular, for the more specialised training in the twelve months of pupillage. The full-time Bar Professional Training Course (BPTC) runs for one academic year; the part-time course for two years. All students are required to be admitted to an Inn of Court before registration on the Bar Professional Training Course.

Course Content

The main skills taught on the BPTC are:

- Case Work Skills;
- Legal Research;
- General written skills;
- Opinion-writing (that is, giving written advice);
- Interpersonal Skills;
- Conference Skills (interviewing clients);
- Negotiation; and
- Advocacy (court or tribunal appearances).

The main areas of knowledge taught on the Bar Professional Training Course are:

- Civil Litigation & remedies;
- Criminal Litigation & sentencing;
- Evidence;
- Professional Ethics; and
- Two optional subjects, selected from a choice of at least six.

Assessment

Assessment takes several forms and may differ from institution to institution. Key areas of knowledge are often assessed through multiple choice tests. Written skills are evaluated by means of written papers, while advocacy, negotiation and conference skills may be appraised by videoed performance of practical exercises.

Quality Assurance of the BPTC

Each BPTC provider has been subject to validation by the Bar Standards Board. Validation ensures that the BPTC they offer satisfies the vocational stage of training for the Bar. Approval will only be granted if the course outcomes, content and resources comply with the specification set out by the Bar Council in the Wood Report. This report was used to form the basis of the current Bar Professional Training Course Handbook, which is set out below.

Bar Professional Training Course Handbook 2013–2014

Part A – The Curriculum and its delivery

[2.7]

A1 Introduction

1.1 **Structure and rationale of this document**

This Handbook is the official reference document for the BPTC academic Year 2013–2014. It is intended for:

- Regulators of the profession setting the standards and requirements of the course.
- Those wishing to offer an educational course leading to the professional qualification.
- Those wishing to train as barristers, their sponsors and supporters.
- Clients and members of the lay public interested in the standards required for the education of barristers.
- Educators in related professions, seeking an explicit statement of the philosophy and the detailed framework for the education of barristers at the Vocational Stage of training.

1.2 **Aims, objectives and ethos of the BPTC**

1.2.1 Professional and educational values

The Bar of England and Wales [Bar] is a demanding profession. Barristers must demonstrate the qualities and standards of professional practice that justify the responsibility and trust placed in them by members of the public and by other qualified professionals from whom work is referred. They also play a vital role in the administration of justice.

The public is entitled to expect standards of excellence from barristers in the execution of their duties and the BSB is committed to promoting excellence and quality within the profession and to ensuring that those who qualify as barristers have the right level of skills and knowledge to provide services to the public, including employers The Inns of Court have a vital role in pastoral care during the BPTC and beyond; play an important role in admitting students before they go on to Bar professional training, and also in providing training. However, the BSB is the regulator of training for the Bar, and regulates in accordance with its own Code of Conduct and rules and regulations as well as pursuant to the Legal Services Act 2007.

The purpose of the BPTC is to enable students, building on their knowledge, to acquire and develop the skills, knowledge and values to become effective members of the Bar. As part of the continuum of training, from the academic stage through to pupillage and continuing professional development of practising barristers, it acts as the bridge between the academic study of law and the practice of law, moving the student from the classroom to the courtroom. It is, therefore, different in its culture and the nature of its demands from those of the academic stage of training, the Qualifying Law Degree or Common Professional Examination. The BPTC must reflect the requirements of this stage of training in terms of the standards to be met by those who provide the course, and the standards that are to be attained by students before they can be recognised as having successfully completed the course.

1.2.2 Aims and objectives

(a) The overarching aims of the BPTC are:

- to prepare students of the Inns of Court for pupillage at the Bar of England and Wales;
- to enable students of the Inns from overseas jurisdictions to acquire the skills required for pupillage at the Bar of England and Wales, thereby assisting them to undertake further training or practice in their home jurisdiction.

(b) Specific objectives of the course are to:

- bridge the gap between the academic study of law and the practice of law;
- provide the foundation for the development of excellence in advocacy;
- inculcate a professional and ethical approach to practice as a barrister;
- prepare students for practice in a diverse society;
- prepare students for the further training to be given in pupillage;
- equip students to perform competently in matters which they are likely to encounter during pupillage;
- lay the foundation for future practice, whether in chambers or as an employed barrister; and
- encourage students to take responsibility for their own professional development.

1.2.3 Ethos

A career at the Bar requires a mixture of sound temperament and talent. As highlighted in the Bar Council of England and Wales' Final Report of the Working Party on Entry to the Bar (November 2007), these include a combination of honesty, courage, commitment, common sense, and perseverance as well as analytical skills, intellect, persuasiveness,discipline, good judgment and fluency (p 18 at 22). The ethos of the BPTC is to nurture and develop to a high level these existing attributes in candidates.

1.3 **Principles of delivery of the BPTC**

1.3.1 The ethos of the course requires a method of delivery that:

- provides students with opportunities for learning by doing, and requires students to apply their knowledge in practical work;
- requires students to play an active role in the course and to take responsibility for their own learning;
- requires students to reflect on their own learning;
- seeks to inculcate a professional approach to work and to develop in students a respect for the principles of professional ethics; and
- seeks to provide students with an informed view of a barrister's working life.

1.4 **Principles of Accreditation of Bar Professional Training Courses**

1.4.1 Statutory Obligation

The BSB has a statutory obligation to maintain and enhance standards in respect of the education and training of those seeking to practise as barristers. In relation to the vocational stage, it is considered that this can best be achieved by accrediting rather than franchising institutions to run the course. Freedom permitted to institutions by accrediting courses within the requirements of the BPTC Course Specification (rather than requiring delivery of a completely detailed predetermined 'package') is aimed to enhance commitment among course teams and encourage appropriate creativity and diversity between courses. Certain aspects, such as centralised testing for admission and final assessment in some subject areas (aimed at achieving continuity of entry and exit standards) will inevitably put some restrictions on provision. However, provided an institution satisfies the BSB that the course it offers is appropriately resourced and enables students to achieve the outcomes specified, a degree of autonomy and flexibility is devolved to Providers of the BPTC. The BSB aims to work with Providers in a spirit of partnership and co-operation. This approach is believed to be the most effective in assuring the quality of delivery of the BPTC and in stimulating its development and enhancement.

1.4.2 Principles

(1) Autonomy

A validation approach to the accreditation process respects the autonomy of the Provider to organise the administration, delivery, assessment and resourcing of the BPTC, as is consistent with satisfying the aims and objectives as specified above, and in line with the requirements designed to ensure that any person qualifying will meet the requirement of readiness for pupillage.

(2) Accountability

In order to ensure that the minimum standards are being satisfied and to safeguard the benefits of autonomy, Providers are required to be accountable to the Bar Standards Board for the way in which the course is organised and delivered and for ensuring that there are appropriate mechanisms for collating and analysing course information, ensuring the quality of the course, and for dealing with student concerns, complaints and appeals.

(3) Evidence

Providers are required to supply information and evidence to the satisfaction of the Bar Standards Board of how and where the course requirements are satisfied. This must include evidence that course content is being delivered, assessed and resourced according to specification, and that the defined standards are being met. In addition, details will also be required for example about the involvement of practitioners with the course; pro- bono opportunities; staffing and staff development; the delivery of the knowledge and skills areas, and professional conduct issues (including contact hours allocated to each skill and knowledge area). Evidence will also be sought concerning the method of assessment utilised to verify the attainment of outcomes by students, to the appropriate standard or level.

(4) Delivery

Institutions are required to be able to explain and justify the organisation and method of delivery of the BPTC, including, for example, the details of the structure of the course, the teaching and learning methodologies used, and the nature and scheduling of formative and summative assessment. Any variations from the course specification or subsequent good practice guidelines will need to be justified.

5 Good Practice

It will also be the aim of the BSB, through the accreditation and subsequent monitoring and review processes not only to assure but to maintain and enhance standards of the BPTC. In addition, the process aims to encourage, identify and disseminate good practice in order to contribute to the continuous improvement of the BPTC as a whole, within the current specified threshold requirements.

1.4.3 Validation of academic awards

The validation of a course as leading to an academic award of a Higher Education Institution [HEI] with degree awarding powers is a matter for the HEI. The formal approval of an academic award for a course may be combined as an event with the BSB accreditation process, but for accreditation of BPTCs the event will be managed by the BSB.

A2 The Curriculum Framework

A2.1 **Framework for the BPTC**

2.1.1 The BPTC curriculum is made up of the following main elements:

(1) Professional ethics and conduct

(2) The knowledge areas:

- Civil litigation, evidence and remedies
- Criminal litigation, evidence and sentencing
- Professional Ethics

(3) The skills areas:

- Advocacy

- Opinion Writing
- Drafting
- Conferencing
- Resolution of Disputes out of Court (including Negotiation, Mediation and Arbitration)

(4) The options:

The above areas will also incorporate writing skills, casework skills, fact management, legal research, management and interpersonal skills.

2.1.2 Overall approach to delivery of the BPTC framework

The BPTC curriculum (including course content, delivery and assessment) is specified in the sections which follow. Specified requirements must be demonstrated as having been met at accreditation and maintained thereafter. Formal requirements are in some areas distinguished from guidance that is indicative and represents the Bar Standards Board's view of best practice. All requirements must be met, and any departure from good practice expressed in the guidance must be explained and justified, including the appropriate distribution of contact and self-study time across the duration of the course.

In emphasising the practical focus of the course, Providers must ensure that students have a sound understanding of the way in which civil and criminal proceedings develop from commencement to trials, of the centrality of the trial to an understanding of procedural and evidential rules, and of the overall structure of a trial. The practical application of knowledge of law and legal procedure within the development and practice of the skills are regarded as part of the successful performance of the skill.

The BPTC must be delivered as a discrete course, and students must not be co-taught with others on different programmes with different study aims, (e.g., the LLB (Hons.) degree course of study or Legal Practice Course. (NB see section B1.3 for special arrangements for 'Exempting Degrees').

The knowledge areas should initially be delivered separately, primarily by means of small group sessions, although large group sessions may be utilised. Small group sessions should be centred upon the exploration of a prepared problem or case. As the course progresses, the knowledge areas should be increasingly integrated into the practice of the skills.

The specifications included in this handbook for individual subjects, their content, delivery and assessment are definitive for accreditation purposes.

2.1.3 Summary of BPTC curriculum content, delivery and assessment framework, with required weightings shown by indicative correlation with percentage based and credit rated systems [in summary: Advocacy weighted 25% – the remainder weighted equally for the purposes of assessment].

	Subject	**Minimum assessment requirements**	**% of course**	**Indicative CATS[1] credits**
Section A2.2.1	Advocacy	⋆ one assessment with oral plus written components (33.33%) 9% of total BPTC grade. The two components may be aggregated. ⋆ two further oral assessments (examination–inchief; cross examination) (33.33% and 33.33%) 8% each of total BPTC grade. Both assessments must be passed. (3 assessments to have equal weighting)	25%	30 credits

Section A2.2.2	Civil Litigation, Evidence and Remedies	* one closed book examination of 3 hours, comprising Part A multiple choice questions, set centrally, marked centrally and electronically plus Part B short answer questions, set centrally and marked locally. Both parts must be passed	10%	12 credits
Section A2.2.3	Criminal Litigation, Evidence and Sentencing	* one closed book examination of 3 hours, comprising Part A multiple choice questions, set centrally, marked centrally and electronically plus Part B short answer questions, set centrally and marked locally. Both parts must be passed	10%	12 credits

Section A2.2.4	Professional Ethics	* one closed book examination of 2 hours comprising Part A MCQs, set centrally, marked centrally and electronically, plus Part B SAQs, set centrally and marked locally. Both parts must be passed	5%	6 credits
Section A2.2.5	Opinion Writing	* one formal time-constrained examination (materials may be used) (100%).	10%	12 credits
Section A2.2.6	Drafting	* one formal time-constrained examination (materials may be used) (100%).	10%	12 credits
Section A2.2.7	Conference Skills	* one oral assessment (100%).	5%	6 credits
Section A2.2.8	Resolution of Disputes out of Court	* one formal examination consisting of Multiple Choice questions and short answer questions (100%)	5%	6 credits

Section A2.2.9	Option 1	* one assessment (can be written or oral assessment) (100%).	10%	12 credits
Section A2.2.9	Option 2	* one assessment (can be written or oral assessment) (100%)	10%	12 credits
	Totals	12 (including 3 centrally set)	100%	120 credits

Note: In addition to the above curriculum and assessment framework, an induction must be provided covering legal research methods. Basic management skills, opportunities for Court visits and pro bono (FRU) work may also be included but these are not assessed (see section 2.2.10).

2.1.4 Overall Standards, level descriptors and Competencies for the BPTC:

(1) In order to maintain standards, it is required that the BPTC must be delivered as a course of 120 credits lasting a minimum of one academic year, in line with the descriptors below that specify the core competencies required of graduates of the course. The descriptors specifically relate to the professional qualification of the BPTC, and aim to ensure that barristers provide professional service of the highest standard to their clients.

Typically, students who have successfully completed the course will:

- be able to be a fluent and articulate advocate, whether orally or in writing, and adapt their submissions or questioning as may be required by circumstances;
- be able to critically evaluate arguments, assumptions, abstract concepts and data in order to deal with complex issues systematically, make sound judgments and demonstrate skill in identifying solutions and tackling and solving problems, clearly communicating their conclusions;
- demonstrate the qualities and skills necessary for future employment at the Bar, with the ability to act autonomously in planning and implementing tasks at a professional level;
- demonstrate self-direction, initiative, personal responsibility and decision making in complex situations, and the necessary independent learning abilities required to undertake appropriate further professional training and development, and continue to advance their knowledge and develop new skills to a high level.

Students successfully completing the BPTC must have demonstrated:

- that they have met the minimum required competency standards set forth for Level 1 Advocates under the Quality Assessment Scheme for Advocates (Crime) [QASA];
- a high level ability to (i) persuade orally and in written argument using cogent legal and factual analysis; (ii) develop reasoned argument; and (iii) deploy forensic skills with evidence (both written and oral);
- a systematic understanding of relevant knowledge and ethical principles in law and practice; together with a comprehensive understanding of techniques applicable to practice at the Bar;
- expertise in the application of legal knowledge in the interests of the client, together with a practical understanding of how established technical skills are used in relation to the interpretation of knowledge in the discipline;
- conceptual understanding that enables the student to collect and analyse relevant information; evaluate current developments and advanced theory in law and practice, and acquire in-depth knowledge of written material, law reports, journals and articles in applicable areas of study;
- knowledge and understanding of the ethical values (including equality and diversity issues, and duty to the client and to the court), and the skills and underpinning knowledge necessary to assess and manage cases without supervision;
- the ability to utilise and develop their knowledge and understanding of the principles underpinning their professional practice;
- the ability and competence to undertake case analysis, research, conferences, opinion writing, drafting, negotiation and advocacy with/without supervision;
- the ability to apply analytical and critical reasoning in a manner sufficient for someone commencing pupillage.

(2) Staff and students should use the descriptors for the BPTC (as above) to determine the aspects of practice that have reached the required standards and which need to be developed. Internal and External Examiners must be satisfied that a student has fulfilled all descriptors within these areas in order to be deemed to be performing at the required level.

(3) The descriptors above broadly relate to the The Quality Assurance Agency for Higher Education [QAA] level descriptors for postgraduate study. However, whether a Provider awards a higher education qualification (for example a postgraduate diploma, normally 120 credits at Level 7, or as an interim award in progression to a Master's degree) is a matter for the awarding body and the QAA.[2]

2.1.5 **Generic grading descriptors for 'Exit Standards' for each individual assessment.**

These should be used in conjunction with level descriptors as in 2.1.4 above:

Grading	Descriptor	% scale for all assessments including ALL MCQs	Code
Outstanding	Additionally to Very Competent, demonstrates very high level knowledge and skills – with imagination, originality or flair, based on proficiency in all the learning outcomes, and providing realistic professional advice or performance. Work is comprehensively and very well researched, and argued	85–100%	O

Very Competent	Additionally to Competent, demonstrates high level awareness and understanding of the knowledge and skills required, such as the ability to identify and debate critical issues or problems, ability to solve non-routine problems, ability to adapt and apply ideas to new situations, and ability to invent and evaluate new ideas to a standard of competence such that a client could reasonably expect to rely on	70–84%	VC

Competent	Work is satisfactory and accurate with few errors or omissions, and is of a standard that demonstrates an ability to perform the sort of tasks appropriate to pupillage. Has attained the specified outcomes of the course (in terms of knowledge of fundamental concepts and performance of skills). Demonstrates sufficient quality to be considered satisfactory and competent in terms of fitness to progress to the pupillage stage of training. Able, with the additional training and supervision in pupillage, to represent lay clients/members of the public	60–69%	C
Not Competent	Does not satisfy the threshold requirements of the course. Work is inarticulate and of poor standard, faulty and badly expressed. The candidate is not capable of producing work on which a prospective client could rely	0–59%	NC

NB The term 'fail' may be used to designate a situation where a student does not satisfy the threshold requirements for an assessment and/or for the course as a whole, ***and*** the maximum number of re-sit opportunities have been exhausted.

2.1.6 Overall grades for the course

Students successfully completing the course will be awarded an overall grade, in line with the grades for individual assessments – i.e. Outstanding, Very Competent or Competent.

(1) To gain the overall grade of 'Outstanding' a candidate must have passed all assessments at the first attempt and must achieve either an overall mark of 85% or above, ***or*** six or more grades in the outstanding category.

(2) To gain the overall grade of 'Very Competent' a candidate must have failed no more than one assessment at the first attempt and must achieve either an overall mark 70% ***or*** eight or more grades in the very competent or outstanding categories.

(3) To gain the overall grade of 'Competent' a candidate must pass each assessment subject to the rules governing the opportunity to re-sit (see B4 4.11 below).

The above course, grade and overall descriptors must be made clear to students.

(Note: *The term 'assessment' as used above refers to a 'sit' in a subject. Hence a student failing the same subject twice will not be able to obtain an overall grade of Very Competent*)

1 According to nationally recognised Credit Accumulation and Transfer Systems (for which see http://www.seec-office.org.uk/credit.htm).

2 The QAA Level Descriptors are defined in the QAA Framework for Higher Education Qualification http://www.qaa.ac.uk/academicinfrastructure/FHEQ/

A2.2 **Core subject areas**

2.2.1 Advocacy

(a) Description/rationale:

This section aims to prepare students for the practice of advocacy which they should be capable of conducting during pupillage and thereafter, as a barrister. It aims to provide the skills necessary to prepare, present and respond to a case or legal argument before a court or other tribunal.

(b) Aims and objectives (knowledge and skills):

This section seeks to:

- provide the skills necessary to prepare, manage, present and/or respond to a case or legal argument, both orally and in writing, before a court or other tribunal, whether formal or informal;
- provide, at an initial level, the essential skills for a persuasive modern advocate, as defined by the Dutton[1] criteria:

  (i) the ability to persuade orally;

(ii) the ability to persuade in written argument;

(iii) cogent legal and factual analysis;

(iv) the ability to develop reasoned argument;

(v) forensic skills with evidence (both written and oral); and

(vi) all of the foregoing undertaken to high ethical standards,

- prepare students for the advocacy training methods to which they will be exposed in pupillage and thereafter;
- introduce students to the advocacy training methods approved by the Advocacy Training Council [ATC], by training students in accordance with those methods as modified according to additional guidance provided by the BSB (that follow in section G below);
- provide knowledge and understanding of the manner in which legal submissions should bE made and responded to;
- provide knowledge and understanding of relevant equality and diversity issues in advocacy;
- ensure that successful students meet the minimum required competency standards set forth for Level 1 Advocates under QASA as they may be stated from time to time.

1 Report of Bar Council Working Party, chaired by Timothy Dutton QC, published October 2002.

(c) Intended learning outcomes:

By the end of this unit, following the study of Advocacy, the student will be able to:

(1) prepare a case effectively, understanding the relevant law, facts and principles, observing the rules of professional conduct and planning the advocacy task in question;

(2) demonstrate basic advocacy skills in a range of civil and criminal scenarios, in applications and in trial(s), and before a range of tribunals;

(3) prepare and deliver each of the following:

(i) an opening speech;

(ii) a closing speech;

(iii) an unopposed submission; and

(iv) an opposed submission.

(4) examine, cross-examine and re-examine witnesses.

(5) meet the minimum required competency standards set forth for Level 1 Advocates under QASA.

(d) Teaching and learning strategies:

The format and progression of sessions must be appropriate to the skill being taught, so that when taken as a whole and in conjunction with other course activity, a coherent framework is provided for the development of the skills of advocacy. The first skill taught should be the making of unopposed submissions, followed by opposed submissions. Legal submissions may be dealt with by means of mooting. Witness handling should be dealt with in the latter part of the course.

Most, if not all, sessions should be recorded on DVD for future discussion and feedback (where the assessment is formative) and for marking and moderation purposes (where the assessment is summative).

(e) Assessment:

Each student must undertake at least 12 advocacy exercises under the supervision of a tutor; of which 75% may be formative whilst 25% must be summative. *ATC methods of training (ie the Hampel Method) must be used but this may be modified in accordance with the guidance provided. The Hampel Method must be used in the final stages of advocacy teaching (ie by the completion of advocacy training during the course, students must be taught by means of and be experienced in the Hampel Method)*.

The diet of advocacy assessments must contain the following elements:

- submission of written argument;
- advancing and responding to legal, factual and procedural submissions; knowledge and application of legal principle;
- witness handling, including examination in chief, cross examination and re-examination;
- dealing with interventions from the bench.

Of the (minimum) 12 exercises, at least three must be formally assessed as follows: One formal assessment must have an oral plus skeleton argument. There must be two further oral assessments (of examination-in-chief; cross examination). All three summative assessments must receive the specified weighting (see 2.1.3).

(f) QASA Level 1 Competency Generic Standards and Performance Indicators:

Providers must ensure that upon successful completion of Advocacy, students shall meet the QASA generic standards [Generic Standards] as well as the more specific detailed performance indicators [Performance Indicators] competency standards for a Level 1 Advocate who will be undertaking work in the Magistrates Court.

The Generic Standards and the Performance Indicators are available at: http://www.barstandardsboard.org.uk/media/1418468/annex_b_qasa_handbook.pdf:

Standard 1 Has demonstrated the appropriate level of knowledge, experience and skill required for accepting the case

1.1 Familiar with law and practice at this level.

1.2 Knowledge of procedure and law is up-to-date.

1.3 Demonstrated skills and experience necessary for this level of advocacy.

Standard 2 Was properly prepared

2.1 Had a clear strategy for the case.

2.2 Demonstrated an awareness of both client's and opponent's case and identified issues.

2.3 Familiar with facts of the case.

2.4 Understood the relevant law and procedure for the matter in hand

Standard 3 Presented clear and succinct written and oral submission

3.1 Drafted clear Skeleton Arguments which:

3.1.1 Show clarity of purpose and expression.

3.1.2 Are the appropriate length.

3.1.3 Have a logical structure and identify the issues.

3.1.4 Make appropriate reference to authorities and documentary reference to external materials.

3.2 Made relevant and succinct submissions by reference to appropriate authority:

ORGANISATION

3.2.1 Demonstrated a clear aim (i.e. sets out what the court is being asked to do and the source of the power to do it).

3.2.2 Employed a logical structure (beginning, middle and end).

3.2.3 Correct application of relevant authority to relevant facts and legal principles.

3.2.4 Was concise

INTER-ACTION WITH TRIBUNAL/DEALING WITH OPPONENT'S ARGUMENTS

3.2.9 Dealt with court's questions/concerns promptly.

3.2.10 Dealt with opponent's points in an effective way.

3.3 Used materials appropriately:

3.3.1 Appropriate use of materials and appropriate use of authorities.

3.3.2 Managed documents effectively.

3.4 Communicates clearly and audibly:

3.4.1 Was audible.

3.4.2 Used clear and simple language.

3.4.3 Used language adapted to a tribunal.

3.4.4 Used appropriate eye contact.

3.4.5 Was persuasive.

3.5 Maintains appropriate pace throughout the course of the trial.

3.5.1 Appropriate pace adopted.

3.6 Non-verbal Communication.

3.6.1 Body Language does not undermine or distract from advocate's performance.

Standard 4 Conducts focussed questioning

4.1 Conducted appropriate Examination-in-chief:

4.1.1 Observed restrictions and directions on questioning.

4.1.2 Able to question effectively.

4.1.3 Was aware of the tribunal.

4.1.4 Avoided leading questions in matters that remain in dispute.

FORM OF QUESTIONS

4.1.8 Questions to witness are clear and understandable.

4.1.9 Used short, simple questions, one point at a time.

DELIVERY

4.1.12 Was audible.

QUESTIONING STRATEGY

4.1.16 Questioning strategy relevant to the issues.

4.1.17 Avoided introducing irrelevant material.

4.2 Conducted appropriate cross-examination.

4.2.1 Observed restrictions and directions on questioning.

4.2.2 Able to question effectively.

4.2.3 Was aware of the tribunal.

FORM OF QUESTIONS

4.2.5 Questions to witnesses are clear and understandable.

4.2.6 Used closed and concise questions.

4.2.7 Used short, simple questions, one point at a time.

DELIVERY

4.2.13 Was audible

QUESTIONING STRATEGY

4.2.16 Questioning strategy relevant to the issues.

4.2.17 Avoided introducing irrelevant material.

4.2.18 Made challenges necessary to put advocate's case.

4.2.19 Avoided inadvertently attacking the witness's character (if this had implications for bad character evidence).

Standard 5 Was professional at all times and sensitive to equality and diversity principles

5.1 Established professional relationships in court.

5.2 Observed professional etiquette and ethics in relation to the client, third parties and the court.

INTEGRITY

5.3 Observed professional duties.

5.4 Observed duty to act with independence.

5.5 Advised the court of adverse authorities and, where they arise, procedural irregularities.

5.6 Assisted the court with the proper administration of justice.

EQUALITY AND DIVERSITY

5.7 Had a demonstrable understanding of equality and diversity principles.

5.8 Recognised the needs and circumstances of others and acted accordingly.

5.9 Treated clients, colleagues and parties fairly and did not discriminate against them.

Standard 6 Provided a proper contribution to case management

6.1 Advocate's conduct did not hinder case progression.

6.2 Had considered appropriate directions and was able to assist the court.

6.3 Complied with appropriate procedural rules and judicial direction.

6.4 Was aware of the requirements regarding disclosure in the case and how they affect the client's case.

6.5 Provided appropriate disclosure of evidence.

6.6 Kept or ensured that the court was kept promptly informed of any timings problems/delays.

6.7 Complied with court imposed timetables.

Standard 7 Handled vulnerable, uncooperative and expert witnesses appropriately

7.1 Gave clear guidance to own witnesses

7.2 Dealt appropriately with vulnerable witnesses

7.3 Dealt effectively with uncooperative witnesses

7.4 Used and challenged expert evidence effectively

7.5 Complied with all obligations and good practice in respect of victims and witnesses

Standard 8 Understood and assisted court on sentencing.

8.1 Made appropriate factual representations to the court on sentencing.

8.2 Understood court's sentencing power and power to commit for sentence.

8.3 Made a coherent and persuasive plea in mitigation

8.4 Applied relevant law and facts.

8.5 Took appropriate steps to ensure that relevant legal materials necessary for sentencing were before the court.

Standard 9 Working with others

9.1 Assisted client in decision making (if observed or able to infer from advocacy):

9.1.1 Any advice given to a client was clear and accurate.

9.1.2 Accurately identified the relevant factual, legal, evidential and/or procedural issues.

9.1.7 Took all reasonable steps to help the lay client understand the process.

9.1.8 Used language that was appropriate to the person being advised.

9.1.9 Ensured the decision making process was adequately recorded.

9.1.10 Kept an appropriate record of information obtained, steps taken, advice given and decisions taken.

(g) Guidance on use of the Hampel method at BPTC level

General

(1) The six stages of the Hampel Method (Headnote – Playback – Reason – Remedy – Demonstration – Replay) may be adapted at BPTC level.

(2) Scope is allowed for continued innovation and improvement in the way that the BPTC Providers construct their advocacy programmes over the duration of the BPTC.

Modification of the method on the BPTC

(3) The demands of teaching to the BPTC syllabus (with particular advocacy issues being taught on a week-by-week basis) mean that some adaptation of the Hampel Method is acceptable. For example, exercises may be designed to ensure the identified 'headline' and 'reason' will be pertinent to that week's core skill.

(4) At the BPTC stage, teaching can be primarily focused on the instruction and reinforcement stages of teaching. More praise and encouragement than that normally allowed by Hampel Method should be given to students during the early part of the transition from the academic to the professional/vocational stage.

(5) In addition, wider feedback (more than a single headline) may be provided from tutors in the course of their reviews. For example (where appropriate), additional areas for improvement may be identified. Areas may also be identified where improvement has been achieved, so that it is made clearer to students which aspects they are getting right.

(6) However, the application of the Hampel Method is expected (ie required by the BSB) before the end of the course. That is, by the end of the course BPTC students must have been trained in accordance with the Hampel Method so that they are properly prepared when they come to the compulsory advocacy course in the first six months of their pupillage.

(7) The 'milestones' by which BPTC students should be taught using 'pure' Hampel (for example after the formative assessments) are not specifically defined, owing to the variations in delivery between BPTC courses. Further recommendations may however be made by the ATC to the BSB.

BPTC advocacy tutors

(8) Only tutors who have been accredited by the BSB on the recommendation of the ATC may teach advocacy to BPTC students. For the purpose of accreditation, tutors must be fully acquainted with and competent in teaching according to the Hampel Method. They are required to demonstrate proficiency in the application of the Hampel Method to the ATC.

(9) In spite of the fact that the Hampel Method may be modified for delivery of teaching on the BPTC, BPTC advocacy tutors must be able to demonstrate proficiency in the Method. They must have sufficient practical experience as advocates in order to be able to identify an appropriate headline, and to offer a relevant remedy and demonstration. There must be no change in the experience and expertise (standards) of BPTC Advocacy tutors.

(10) The accreditation process for tutors cannot focus on determining whether they are equipped with diagnostic skills and the ability to improve the performance of BPTC students. Knowledge of and expertise in the Hampel Method remains essential.

(11) Candidates for accreditation will still be required to demonstrate the ability to provide a fluent Hampel 'demonstration' of how a student's performance might be improved before requiring a 'playback'. If this is not demonstrated then an essential skill for tutors would remain untested.

(12) The ATC has emphasised that mere training in and facility with the Hampel method is insufficient to guarantee accreditation. Candidates must have the necessary diagnostic skills and remedial expertise, as well as being well trained in the stages of the Method. Tutors must also be able to deliver an effective demonstration.

(13) The ATC no longer provides training immediately prior to the test. Supplementary questions have also been devised to confirm that candidates are able to identify the problem in the performance of the student which most called for improvement. Further details of the assessment process, criteria, procedures and forms used are available from the ATC.

Reading/reference list

Providers should draw on a balanced selection of student text books dealing with advocacy which are currently available.

2.2.2 Civil litigation, evidence and remedies

(a) Description/rationale:

This part of the course aims to provide knowledge, understanding and the ability to apply and evaluate the key areas of civil litigation and evidence. It will cover practice procedure and evidence in civil claims from compliance with pre-action protocols through to appeals, with particular emphasis on the common types of work done at the junior Civil Bar.

(b) Aims and objectives (knowledge and skills):

This section seeks to:

- provide a sound understanding of the organisation of the High and County Courts, the overriding objective of the Civil Procedure Rules, the impact of the Human Rights Act on civil claims and various types of claims (small claim, fast track and multi-track), pre-action protocols and limitation;
- explain the rules for commencing proceedings and the rules and procedures relating to multiple causes of action, multiple parties and additional claims;
- explain statements of case and the rules for amendment and requesting further information;
- explain the rules and procedure relevant to track allocation, case management and directions;
- explain the principles and procedure for obtaining judgment without trial;
- explain the procedure for making interim applications and in particular applying for an interim injunction, freezing injunction and search order, interim payment and security for costs;
- explain the law, principles and procedure regulating the disclosure and inspection of documents;
- provide knowledge and understanding of striking out, stays and discontinuance and offers to settle;
- explain the law and practice relating to the admission of types of evidence in civil trials, and preparation for trial;
- explain costs, funding and the implications of Community Legal Service funding;
- explain the procedure for appealing and for claiming judicial review and for making references to the ECJ;
- explain the rules and principles relating to judgments and orders;
- develop skills in applying the different methods of enforcing money and other judgments.

(c) Intended learning outcomes:

By the end of this unit the student will be able to:

(1) demonstrate a sound understanding of the organisation of the High Court and the County Courts;

(2) demonstrate a sound understanding of the procedures that must be observed in the High Court and County Court;

(3) demonstrate a sound understanding of the how claims are commenced and of limitation and case management;

(4) demonstrate a sound understanding of the manner in which parties are required to set out and verify the factual basis of their respective cases in statements of case;

(5) understand the procedure in cases involving three or more parties including a sound knowledge of the rules and procedures relating to multiple causes of action and multiple parties and additional claims;

(6) understand the procedures relating to disclosure and inspection of documents;

(7) demonstrate a sound understanding of requests for further information, how to respond to a request for further information and the rules on amendment of statements of case;

(8) have a sound understanding of the law and procedure relating to applications for interim injunctions both prohibitory and mandatory;

(9) demonstrate a sound understanding of freezing and search orders, sanctions, striking out, stays and discontinuance, interim payments and security for costs;

(10) be able effectively to consider interim applications;

(11) be able to demonstrate a sound understanding of default, summary and other judgments;

(12) demonstrate a sound understanding of the principles and procedures in respect of Part 36 offers to settle;

(13) demonstrate a sound understanding of the law and practice relating to the admission of evidence in civil trials;

(14) have a sound understanding of preparations necessary for trial;

(15) understand and distinguish between different bases of assessment of costs, funding and the impact of Community Legal Service funding;

(16) demonstrate a sound understanding of practice relating to drawing up judgments and orders;

(17) gain a sound working knowledge of the different methods of enforcing money and other judgments;

(18) have a sound understanding of the principles and procedures governing civil appeals and to be able to understand and advise on the procedure for claiming judicial review and for making references to the ECJ.

(d) Teaching & learning strategies:

Small group sessions should be centred upon the exploration of prepared problems or case studies. Large Group sessions may also be used.

(e) Assessment:

The knowledge areas are assessed through discrete papers (but also pervasively through the skills assessments). The precise form of assessment is subject to the conditions set out in the Assessment Framework (A2.1.3). Summative assessment must take the form of one closed book examination, 3 hours long, comprising Part A MCQ questions, set centrally, marked centrally and electronically, plus Part B SAQs, set centrally and marked locally (with equal weighting). Students are required to pass in each part. Assessment will be such that a broad range of the syllabus is assessed and that any part of it may be assessed. No indication must be given to students as to which parts of the syllabus will or will not be assessed. Students must be given the opportunity to attempt, and receive feedback on, formative (mock) assessments so as to provide appropriate preparation for summative (final) assessments. It is for Providers to demonstrate how this requirement has been met.

Note:

The CEB, acting through its Chief Examiners, will issue clarification from time to time of any changes in substantive law, rules of procedure, or Codes of Practice as they affect the assessment of the centrally set assessments in Civil Litigation, Evidence and Remedies It is incumbent upon students and Providers to refer to the CEB page of the BSB website for updates and further guidance on a regular basis

The CEB page of the BSB may be found at:

http://www.barstandardsboard.org.uk/qualifying-as-a-barrister/

(f) Required content for the centrally set assessment in civil litigation and evidence:

(1) **Organisational matters**

- the organisation of the High Court (in outline);
- the organisation of the County Courts (in outline);
- the allocation of business between the High and County Courts (in outline);
- the allocation of business between tracks;
- the overriding objective of the Civil Procedure Rules; and
- the impact of the Human Rights Act on civil claims.

(2) **Pre-action protocols**

- the list of specific pre-action protocols;
- the principles relating to pre-action conduct under the Personal Injury pre-action protocol (in outline);
- the details of pre-action conduct where no specific protocol applies; and
- the consequences of non-compliance with pre-action protocols.

(3) **Limitation**

- rules on calculating limitation (accrual and when time stops running);
- limitation periods in tort, latent damage cases, personal injuries, fatal accidents, contract, recovery of land, judicial review and contribution claims. Also the provisions of the Limitation Act 1980, ss 14, 14A, 14B and 33; and
- Limitation Act 1980 provisions dealing with persons under a disability, fraud, concealment and mistake.

(4) **Commencing proceedings**

- when the Part 7 procedure is appropriate and how Part 7 claims are commenced;
- when the Part 8 procedure is appropriate and how Part 8 claims are commenced;
- how court documents are brought to the notice of other parties;
- the principles governing the validity and renewal of claim forms;
- the procedures for bringing and settling proceedings by or against: children and persons suffering from mental incapacity; and
- the procedures for bringing proceedings by or against: sole traders, partnerships, LLPs and registered companies; charities and trusts; deceased persons and bankrupts.

(5) **Proceedings involving three or more parties and multiple causes of action**

- multiple causes of action and multiple parties;
- additional claims, including in particular:
  - (i) the various types of claims that can be raised in such proceedings;
  - (ii) the management of additional claims; and
  - (iii) the effect on additional claims of the main proceedings being determined without trial.

(6) **Statements of case**

- the manner in which parties are required to set out and verify the factual basis of their respective cases in statements of case; and
- the methods by which parties may respond to statements of case, defences, replies, counterclaims;
- [not the Drafting of statements of case, for which see section 2.2.6].

(7) **Remedies (general)**

- the cost of pursuing a remedy;
- whether a self-help remedy is available;
- whether alternative forms of resolving a dispute are available;
- the capacity of the defendant to pay damages if awarded;
- whether a range of remedies should be pursued;
- whether interim remedies should be pursued; and
- applicable time limits.

(8) **Contract**

- the general principles underlying damages for breach of contract, including limitations on compensatory damages;
- the availability of equitable remedies, including specific performance, injunctions, rescission and rectification;
- remedies for misrepresentation;
- the law and practice in respect of interest on judgment debts pursuant to contract or statute (Judgments Act 1838; County Court (Interest on Judgment Debts) Order 1991; Late Payment of Commercial Debts (Interest) Act 1998).

(9) **Tort**

- the general principles underlying the amount of damages, the calculation of quantum, the reduction of damages, aggravated and exemplary damages and the availability of injunctions;
- the principles according to which damages are quantified, the process by which a court would arrive at a final figure, and the practical steps to be taken in advising on quantum in cases of personal injury;
- the impact of Social Security payments on the assessment of damages ;
- the law and practice in respect of interest on damages in claims for personal injury.

(10) **Amendment**

- permission/consent to amend: when required, and how permission is sought;
- principles governing applications for permission to amend;
- principles governing amendments introducing new causes of action after the expiry of limitation;
- principles governing amendments adding or substituting parties after the expiry of limitation;
- amendments affecting accrued limitation rights; and
- costs consequences of amending.

(11) **Further information**

- when it may be appropriate to make a request for further information;
- the principles on which requests for further information may be administered or are allowed; and
- how to respond to a request for further information.

(12) **Interim applications**

- with notice and without notice applications;
- documentation required in interim applications;
- calculating periods of notice in interim applications; and

- duty of full and frank disclosure in without notice applications.

(13) **Judgment without trial**

- default judgments, including calculating time for entry of default judgment, procedure, whether permission is required, and the principles applied on applications to set aside; and
- summary judgments, including the procedure, who may apply, the test to be applied, conditional orders, the principles applied on applications for summary judgment, how the test applies where there are counterclaims and set-offs and the cheque rule.

(14) **Case management**

- the allocation of business between the small claims track, the fast track and the multi-track;
- the procedure at case management conferences;
- typical directions in small claims track, fast track and multi-track claims; and
- the impact of costs and the role of costs budgets in case management.

(15) **Disclosure and inspection of documents**

- the law, principles and procedure regulating disclosure and inspection of documents;
- the principles and procedure relating to specific disclosure;
- collateral use of disclosed documents;
- *Norwich Pharmacal* orders (*Norwich Pharmacal Co v Customs and Excise Comrs* [1974] AC 133) [1973] 2 All ER 943, HL;
- pre-action disclosure under SCA 1981 s.33 (2) and CPR 31.16 and disclosure against nonparties under SCA 1981 s.34 (2) and CPR 31.17.

(16) **Sanctions, striking out, stays and discontinuance**

- identification of whether, in any given case, an application should be made for sanctions or to strike out;
- the procedure for applying for sanctions, to strike out and for relief from sanctions, and the principles applied by the court; and
- applications for stays pending consent to medical examination and the effect of stays; and
- discontinuing and the costs consequences of discontinuing.

(17) **Interim payments and security for costs**

- the principles and procedure relating to applications for interim payments;

- grounds for applying for interim payments, to include cases with more than one defendant and effect of set-offs and counterclaims;
- amount to be ordered by way of interim payment, including the effect of set-offs and counterclaims;
- procedure on applications for security for costs;
- applying for security for costs on the grounds of residence outside the jurisdiction and against impecunious companies; and
- the approach to the discretion to order security for costs in these cases,
- the Court's power to make orders subject to conditions.

(18) **Interim injunctions**

- the procedure for applying for an interim injunction;
- *American Cyanamid* principles;
- the principles governing the following exceptions and variations to *American Cyanamid*: applications for mandatory interim injunctions, interim injunctions that finally dispose of the case, cases where there is no arguable defence, restraint of trade cases, defamation claims and cases involving freedom of expression and privacy;
- how those principles apply in the particular circumstances; and
- the meaning and effect of the usual undertakings and cross-undertakings given in interim injunction cases.

(19) **[not used]**

(20) **Offers to settle**

- the requirements in making offers to settle under Part 36;
- calculation of the relevant period;
- consequences of accepting offers to settle under Part 36;
- withdrawing, reducing and increasing offers to settle;
- consequences of failing to obtain judgment which is more advantageous than an offer to settle;
- secrecy relating to offers to settle, and the consequences of breach.

(21) **Trial**

- the use of witness summonses;
- skeleton arguments;
- the procedure on the trial of civil cases, including trial timetables, the order of speeches, calling and examining witnesses; and

- judgment and submissions on orders for costs and permission to appeal.

(22) **Costs, funding and community legal service**

- the nature of private funding, qualified one-way costs shifting, damages based agreements, before the event insurance, and public funding;
- the difference between funding and costs orders;
- the different methods of assessing costs (summary and detailed assessment) and when each is appropriate;
- the different bases on which costs are assessed (standard and indemnity);
- the various interim costs orders and their effects;
- the situations where costs orders do not follow the event;
- the likely effect on the order for costs where:
  - (i) a party achieves only partial success,
  - (ii) there is a joinder of defendants and the claimant succeeds against some but not all of them,
  - (iii) one or more parties is publicly funded,
- the effects of state funding and the statutory charge on civil litigation and counsel's duty to the Legal-Aid Agency; and
- the power of the courts to make a costs order in favour of the Access to Justice Foundation in a pro bono case (CPR 44. 3C).

(23) **Judgments and orders**

- who, generally, is responsible for drawing up a judgment/order, together with exceptions to the general rule;
- the consequences where a party fails to draw up and file a judgment/order within the time permitted;
- the time for payment of a money judgment;
- penal notices in interim injunction orders;
- Tomlin orders; and
- the form of orders requiring an act to be done.

(24) **Enforcement of judgments**

- the different methods of enforcing money and other judgments (in outline); and
- which method or combination of methods is appropriate to the particular circumstances of the judgment debtor in question.

[NB This topic will be assessed at the level of junior counsel advising a client on enforcement immediately after a fast track trial.]

(25) **Judicial review**

- the requirements and principles for obtaining permission to claim judicial review; and
- the availability of remedies of quashing order, mandatory order, prohibiting order, injunction and declaration in judicial review claims.

(26) **Appeals**

- the principles and procedures governing civil appeals in England and Wales (excluding appeals to the Supreme Court), comprising permission to appeal, routes of appeal, time for appealing, appellant's notice and grounds on which an appeal may succeed, fresh evidence in appeals, respondent's notice, and skeleton arguments.

(27) **Civil evidence**

All the following rules are to be considered in the context of civil claims on the fast track and multi-track.

- burden and standard of proof [but not presumptions or judicial notice];
- competence and compellability of witnesses;
- the law and practice relating to the admission of hearsay evidence in civil trials;
- the practice and procedure relating to the preparation and exchange of witnesses statements;
- the principles underlying the general exclusionary rule in relation to evidence of opinion and the main exceptions to that rule;
- the special rules relating to the opinion of experts, comprising the definition of an expert, the form of experts' reports, disclosure of reports and literature, use of secondary facts, ultimate issues, and the requirements for permission to use expert evidence and to call experts;
- the principles relating to legal professional privilege, privilege against self-incrimination, without prejudice communications and public interest immunity in civil cases, and exceptions to these rules;
- waiver of privilege;
- evidence rules governing examination-in-chief and cross-examination, comprising: leading and non-leading questions; cross-examination as to credit, the rule of finality, and exceptions to that rule, hostile and unfavourable witnesses; and use of previous consistent and inconsistent evidence;
- previous judgments, comprising *res judicata*, abuse of process and the CEA 1968, s 11; and
- character evidence.

Reading/Reference List:

Books

Providers must use:

- *Civil Procedure* (Sweet & Maxwell), known as 'The White Book' (2012), must be used as the primary text.
- Providers should draw on a balanced selection of books in addition to The White Book dealing with Civil Litigation, Evidence and Remedies which are currently available.
- *Blackstone's Civil Practice* (OUP) (2012) (Main Book and Supplements).
- *Practical Approach to Civil Procedure*, 15th ed., S Sime (OUP) (2012).
- *The Bar Handbook 2014-2015*, Simon Garrod and Nicholas Bacon QC, in association with the Bar Council and BSB, 2012 (LexisNexis).
- *The Civil Court Practice 2011* ('the Green Book'), Editor-in-Chief: The Rt Hon Lord Neuberger of Abbotsbury, March 2011 (Lexis-Nexis) [NB this is not a substitute for the use of the White Book].

2.2.3 Criminal litigation, evidence and sentencing

A **Description/rationale:**

Building on criminal law courses of the Qualifying Law Degree, this area will familiarise students with current procedures relating to arrests, pre-trial issues, summary and jury trials, sentencing and appeals. It will also consider the more important evidential rules that apply to criminal cases.

B **Aims and objectives (knowledge and skills):**

This section aims to provide students with details of the law relating to:

- criminal arrest and the various modes of trial and sentencing;
- the roles of the Youth Court, adult Magistrates', Crown and appellate Courts;
- jury trials;
- evidential rules relating to criminal cases;
- sentencing powers of the various courts;
- appeal procedures.

C **Intended learning outcomes:**

On successful completion, the students should be able to demonstrate a *sound understanding of the criminal process as a whole and how cases progress through the system*. In addition the students should be able to demonstrate a sound understanding and knowledge of the following specific topics:

(1) the processes related to police investigation and arrest;

(2) the law and practice relating to bail in criminal cases;

(3) mode of trial, committal, the procedures for sending indictable only cases to the Crown Court and the transfer of cases involving complex fraud and child victims and witnesses;

(4) plea and other pre-trial issues in the Magistrates' Court;

(5) disclosure of unused material;

(6) the conduct of summary trials;

(7) the rules relating to indictments, arraignment and conducting pre-trial hearings in the Crown Court;

(8) the conduct of jury trials;

(9) the main evidential rules relating to criminal trials;

(10) the principles, procedures and types of sentence in criminal cases;

(11) the procedures for dealing with youth cases;

(12) the law and practice of appeals in criminal cases.

D **Teaching & learning strategies:**

Small group sessions should be centred upon the exploration of a prepared problem or case. Large Group sessions may also be used.

E **Assessment:**

The knowledge areas are assessed through separate papers (but also pervasively through the skills assessments). The precise form of assessment is subject to the conditions set out in the Assessment Framework (A2.1.3). Summative assessment must take the form of one closed book examination 3 hours long, comprising Part A MCT questions, set centrally, marked centrally and electronically, plus Part B SAQs, set centrally and marked locally. There must be a pass in each part. Assessment will be such that a broad range of the syllabus is assessed and that any part of it may be assessed. No indication must be given to students as to which parts of the syllabus will or will not be assessed. Students must be given the opportunity to attempt, and receive feedback on, formative (mock) assessments so as to provide appropriate preparation for summative (final) Assessments. It is for Providers to demonstrate how this requirement has been met.

Note:

The CEB, acting through its Chief Examiners, will issue clarification from time to time of any changes in substantive law, rules of procedure, or Codes of Practice as they affect the assessment of the centrally set assessments in Criminal Litigation, Evidence and Sentencing It is incumbent upon students and Providers to refer to the CEB page of the BSB website for updates and further guidance on a regular basis.

The CEB page of the BSB may be found at:

http://www.barstandardsboard.org.uk/qualifying-as-a-barrister/bar-professional-trainingcourse/bptc-syllabus-and-centralised-examinations/

F **Indicative content/teaching schedule:**

Unless otherwise indicated (that is, where a topic requires an outline only) at the end of the course the students should be able to demonstrate that they have reached the required standard, as set out in paragraph C above, in all of the individual content areas specified below.

Section 1: Overview

(1) **Overview of criminal procedure**

- the classification of offences (indictable, either-way and summary);
- the court structure in England and Wales;
- how a criminal case progresses through the system (outline of the progress of the three categories of criminal offence, with respect to adults and of offences of varying seriousness with respect to youths);
- the funding of criminal cases (a detailed knowledge is not required, but students should have an understanding of the general structure of funding arrangements);
- the importance and application of the Criminal Procedure rules 2005, in particular the overriding objective and the case management functions of the court (other parts of the rules may be relevant to individual topics; where this is the case they are specifically referred to below).

Section 2: Criminal investigations, commencement of proceedings and pre-trial issues

(2) **Preliminaries to prosecution:**

- the structure of the codes of conduct issued under the Police and Criminal Evidence Act 1984 (PACE) and their importance to criminal investigations (outline only);
- the provisions of Code C.10 (cautions and special warnings) and Code C.11 (interviews);
- the provisions of Code D.3 (identification by witnesses);
- the different powers of search and arrest;
- the role of the Crown Prosecution Service;
- the different forms of commencing criminal proceedings.

(3) **Bail and remands**

- the difference between adjournments and remands;
- time limits applicable to defendants remanded in custody;
- the general right to bail under the Bail Act 1976 and the occasions when it does not apply;
- the grounds and reasons for refusing bail;
- bail conditions that can be applied and under what circumstances;
- the practice and procedure on appeal to the Crown Court against a decision to refuse bail in the Magistrates' Court;
- the grounds upon which the prosecution can appeal to the Crown court against a decision to grant bail;
- dealing with defendants who have failed to surrender to bail or breached their bail conditions.

(4) **Plea in the Magistrates' Court, mode of trial, committal, sending and transfers**

- the rules relating to the provision of advance information;
- preliminary hearings in the Magistrates' Court (outline only required);
- pleas generally in the Magistrates' Court, including equivocal pleas;
- the factors which the defendant should be aware of in deciding whether to elect Crown Court trial;
- the approach taken by the magistrates to the question whether or not to accept jurisdiction;
- plea before venue and mode of trial, including the special rules for criminal damage cases;
- committal for sentence;
- the committal of either-way offences to the Crown Court for trial;
- sending indictable only offences to the Crown Court;
- the transfer of complex fraud cases and cases involving child victims and witnesses (outline only);
- the committal/sending of linked summary only cases and the procedure for dealing with them in the Crown Court.

(5) **Disclosure of unused material and defence statements**

- the investigator's duty to retain unused material;
- the prosecutor's duty of disclosure;
- the test for determining whether unused material should be disclosed by the prosecution, including the requirement of continuous review;
- time limits for prosecution disclosure;
- applications to compel the prosecution to disclose;
- defence duties of disclosure;
- the requirements relating to the contents of a defence statement;
- the consequences of defence failures in the disclosure process;
- public interest immunity and public policy;
- third party disclosure.

(6) **Indictments**

- the time limits for preferring a bill of indictment;
- the structure and format of an indictment;
- the format of a count;
- counts which can lawfully be joined on an indictment;
- the rules relating to duplicity, specimen counts and overloading of indictments;
- the joinder of defendants on an indictment;

- applications to sever the indictment;
- the consequences of misjoinder;
- applications to amend indictments;
- applications to stay and quash indictments;
- voluntary bills of indictment (outline only).

(7) **Preliminaries to trial in the Crown Court**

- the plea and case management hearing in the Crown Court and its importance to case management;
- arraignment;
- special pleas, autrefois acquit and convict (outline only);
- pleas to alternative counts, offering no evidence and leaving counts to lie on file;
- preliminary and pre-trial hearings in complex and serious and sensitive cases, including the powers of dismissal of transferred and sent cases.

Section 3: Procedural and evidential issues relating to criminal trials

(8) **Summary trial procedure**

- the circumstances in which the Magistrates can proceed in the absence of the defendant;
- abuse of process in the Magistrates' Court (outline only);
- the procedural steps in a summary trial, including reading statements and formal admissions;
- submission of no case to answer;
- order of speeches;
- verdicts;
- costs after trial (outline only);
- the role of the Magistrates' Legal Advisor in the trial (outline only).

(9) **Jury trial procedure**

- judge only trials (outline only);
- proceeding in the absence of the defendant;
- abuse of process in the Crown Court (outline only);
- the law and practice relating to juries, including the circumstances when individual jurors or the whole jury can be discharged;
- procedural steps in a jury trial, including submissions of no case to answer, formal admissions and reading statements;
- dealing with points of law during the trial, including the procedure for determining the admissibility of evidence;
- speeches;
- the content of summing up;

- verdicts, including majority verdicts and conviction of a lesser offence;
- costs after trial (outline only).

(10) **Preliminary evidential matters**

- the basic terminology of evidence;
- facts in issue;
- relevance;
- admissibility, including the discretionary power to exclude under s 78 and the common law powers to exclude evidence;
- weight;
- tribunals of fact and law;
- presumptions (outline only).

(11) **Burden and standard of proof**

- the distinction between the legal burden and the evidential burden of proof;
- the general rule concerning the incidence of the burden of proof in criminal cases and the exceptions to it;
- the standard of proof required in criminal cases when the legal burden rests on the prosecution;
- the standard of proof required when the legal burden rests on the defence.

(12) **Preliminary issues relating to witnesses**

- competence and compellability;
- oaths and affirmations;
- the principles and procedure for the issue of a witness summons and warrant of arrest (outline only).

(13) **The rules relating to the examination of witnesses**

- examination in chief: form of questioning, memory refreshing, the use of previous consistent statements, hostile witnesses;
- Cross-examination: form of questioning, previous inconsistent statements, restrictions on cross-examination, including finality on collateral matters;
- re-examination: form of questions;
- the special measures available to vulnerable witnesses and witnesses in fear of testifying.

(14) **Hearsay evidence**

- the definition of hearsay under the Criminal Justice Act 2003;
- the difference between hearsay and original evidence;
- the difference between hearsay and real evidence;
- general restriction on the admissibility of hearsay evidence;

- the gateways to admissibility under the Criminal Justice Act 2003;
- how to make applications to adduce hearsay evidence and the procedural requirements for making such applications under the Criminal Procedure Rules;
- how to apply to exclude hearsay evidence and what safeguards are set out in the Criminal justice Act 2003;
- procedural requirements relating to applications to exclude under the Criminal Procedure Rules.

(15) **Character evidence**

- the definition of bad character under the Criminal Justice Act 2003;
- the gateways for admissibility of non-defendant bad character;
- the gateways for admissibility of defendant bad character;
- how to make applications to adduce bad character evidence and the procedural requirements for such applications under the Criminal Procedure rules;
- how to make applications to exclude bad character evidence and the grounds upon which such evidence can be excluded;
- the tactical use of character evidence;
- proving convictions under ss73–75 of PACE;
- good character directions.

(16) **Confessions and unlawfully obtained evidence**

- the definition of confessions under PACE;
- the principles governing the admissibility of confessions, including reference to the effect of breaches of the Codes issued under PACE;
- the admissibility of evidence obtained as a result of inadmissible confessions;
- how to make or challenge applications to exclude confessions during the course of the trial;
- the principles governing the exclusion of other prosecution evidence under s 78 of PACE;
- common categories of evidence that are the subject of applications to exclude under s 78 of PACE;
- how to make or challenge applications to exclude to evidence under s 78 of PACE.

(17) **Inferences from the defendant's silence and other conduct**

- the evidential significance of the defendant's lies and what directions should be given to the jury;
- the principles that apply to and the potential consequences of the defendant's failure to mention facts when questioned: s 34 of the Criminal Justice and Public Order Act 1994;
- the principles that apply to and the potential consequences of the

defendant's failure to account for objects, substances and marks: s 36 of the Criminal Justice and Public Order Act 1994;

- the principles that apply to and the potential consequences of the defendant's failure to account for his presence at the scene of a crime: s 37 of the Criminal Justice and Public Order Act 1994;
- the principles that apply to and the potential consequences of the defendant's failure to testify in his own defence during the trial: s 35 of the Criminal Justice and Public Order Act 1994, including the advice that should be given to a defendant about this issue.

(18) **Identification evidence and other issues relating to corroboration**

- the special need for caution required in identification cases;
- the circumstances in which the judge may withdraw an identification case from the jury;
- the nature and content of a "Turnbull" warning;
- the grounds on which the judge might exclude identification evidence (consideration of Code D.3 of PACE will also be required);
- how to make or challenge applications to exclude identification evidence;
- the circumstances in which the judge might warn the jury about "suspect" evidence as set out in the case of *R v Makanjuola* [1995] 3 All ER 730, [1995] 1 WLR 1348, CA.

(19) **Opinion evidence and experts**

- the general prohibition on the use of opinion evidence in criminal cases;
- the exception to this rule in relation to expert evidence;
- the definition of an expert;
- the scope and limits of expert evidence in the trial;
- the procedural requirements for the introduction of expert evidence under the Criminal Procedure Rules.

(20) **Privilege**

- the privilege against self-incrimination;
- the principles that apply to legal professional privilege, including waiver of privilege.

Section 4: Cases involving youths

(21) **Youth courts**

- the categorisation of youths into "child" and "young person" and its legal consequences;
- the diversion of youths from the criminal justice system by the use of reprimands and warnings etc (outline only);
- the procedure in the Youth Court and how it differs from the adult court;
- the circumstances in which a youth will appear in the adult

Magistrates' Court and in the Crown Court, including *brief* reference to how the dangerous offender provisions apply to youths;

- the sentences available to the Youth Court.

Section 5: Sentencing

(22) **Sentencing principles**

- the sentencing powers of the Magistrates' Court and the Crown Court (including, their power to sentence youths);
- the sentencing procedure in the Magistrates' Court;
- the sentencing procedure in the Crown Court, including committals for sentence,
- determining the facts of the offence, including Newton hearings, the use of a basis of plea and pre-sentence reports;
- indications as to sentence;
- the role of prosecuting counsel in sentence;
- the purposes of sentence;
- the principles relevant to the assessment of seriousness;
- common aggravating and mitigating features of cases, including discount for a guilty plea;
- custody and community sentence thresholds;
- the purpose of the Sentencing Guidelines Council and how it issues guidance for the courts, including the importance of Court of Appeal guideline cases.

(23) **Non-custodial sentences**

- the principles for the imposition of absolute and conditional discharges;
- the principles relevant to the imposition of a fine, including the consequences of default;
- the principles for the imposition of a community sentence, including the objectives of such sentences;
- the main types of community sentences available to the courts;
- the consequences of breach of a community sentence;
- binding over orders (outline only).

(24) **Custodial sentences**

- the requirements before a custodial sentence can be passed;
- concurrent and consecutive sentences, including the totality principle;
- suspended sentences;
- mandatory and minimum sentences;
- principles applicable in determining the length of custodial sentences;
- provisions as to early release and time spent on remand (outline only).

(25) **Ancillary orders and costs on conviction**

- costs on conviction (outline only);
- compensation;
- forfeiture and deprivation orders;
- endorsement of driving licences and disqualification (outline only);
- registration of sex offenders;
- confiscation under the Proceeds of Crime Act 2002 (brief outline only).

(26) **The dangerous offender provisions**

- how to identify specified offences;
- the principles involved in the assessment of dangerousness;
- the nature of and conditions for the imposition of life sentences, imprisonment for public protection and extended sentences under the dangerous offender provisions.

Section 6: Appeals

(27) **Appeals from the Magistrates' Court**

- the power of the Magistrates to rectify mistakes;
- the general right of appeal from the Magistrates' court to the Crown Court;
- the procedure in the Crown Court for dealing with the appeal, including the constitution of the court;
- the powers of the Crown Court on appeal, including the power to increase sentence;
- appeal to the High Court by case stated (outline only);
- appeal to the High Court by judicial review (outline only).

(28) **Appeals from the Crown Court**

- the power of the Crown Court to rectify mistakes as to sentence;
- the right to appeal to the Court of Appeal (CA);
- the requirement to obtain leave to appeal to the CA;
- the more common grounds that can give rise to appeal against conviction and sentence;
- the procedural requirements for applying for leave under the Criminal Procedure Rules, including the practical steps that counsel should take when advising and preparing grounds of appeal;
- renewal of application before full court after a refusal by single judge;
- the power of the Court to make a loss of time direction;
- the rules concerning the CA hearing fresh evidence during the appeal;
- the principles and procedure the CA will adopt when determining appeals against conviction and sentence;

- consequences of a conviction being quashed, including ordering re-trials;
- Attorney General's references on points of law and references of unduly lenient sentences;
- Prosecution appeals against trial judge rulings;
- The Criminal Cases Review Commission (brief outline only);
- appeals to the Supreme Court (outline only).

Reading/reference lst:

Law reports

Criminal Appeal Reports (1908-)

Criminal Appeal Reports (Sentencing) (1979-)

Criminal Law Review (1954-)

Justice of the Peace Reports (1903-) – at least a 5 year backrun

Road Traffic Law Reports (1970-)

Practitioner works

Archbold's Criminal Pleading and Practice (Sweet & Maxwell, annual)

Archbold's Magistrates' Court Criminal Practice (Sweet and Maxwell, annual)

Blackstone's Criminal Practice (Oxford University Press, annual)

Thomas, DA (ed), *Current Sentencing Practice* (including the Sentencing Referencer), (Sweet & Maxwell)

Stones' Justices' Manual, (Butterworth Law, annual)

Electronic sources

The Stationary Office: www.opsi.gov.uk

The Judicial Studies Board: www.jsboard.co.uk

The Sentencing Guidelines Council: www.sentencing-guidelines.gov.uk

The criminal justice system online: www.cjsonline.gov.uk

The Crown Prosecution Service: www.cps.gov.uk

Finding tools

Anthony and Berryman: Magistrates' Court Guide (Butterworth Law, annual)

Morrish and Mclean: Crown court index (Sweet and Maxwell)

Criminal Law Week (1997-)

2.2.4 Professional Ethics

(a) **Description/rationale:**

This unit, taught as a discrete topic, highlights the core professional values which underpin practice at the Bar of England and Wales. It aims to instil and build up in students the essential qualities of ethical behaviour at the Bar by nurturing and developing to a high level these existing attributes in students. Encompassing more than the knowledge and formalities outlined in the Professional Code of Conduct, this will furnish far reaching and fundamental knowledge of ethics that underlies practice at the Bar.

(b) **Aims and objectives (knowledge and skills):**

This section seeks to:

- inculcate the fundamental concepts of professional and ethical values required of a practising barrister at the Bar of England and Wales;
- provide knowledge and understanding of the philosophical issues and purposes underpinning ethical behaviour, including the concept of duty in professional life both to the client and to the rule of law;
- provide in depth knowledge and understanding of the requirements of the Code of Conduct and the Equality code.

(c) **Intended learning outcomes:**

By the end of this unit the student will be able to:

(1) understand and appreciate the core professional values which underpin practice at the Bar of England and Wales, particularly the additional moral responsibilities held by the profession (over and above the population in general) due to decision-making roles, functions and authority which are key to practice at the Bar;

(2) correctly identify issues of professional ethics and conduct which appear in given situations as likely to arise in a barrister's practice (eg conflict of interest);

(3) demonstrate a sound working knowledge of the provisions of the Code of Conduct of the Bar of England and Wales, including the equality and diversity rules, and demonstrate existing and future adherence to that Code;

(4) demonstrate the capacity to provide a professional and responsible approach to clients who place trust in the profession on the basis that the service provided will be of benefit;

(5) display a professional and responsible approach to the course, staff and other students, and to observe the Code of Practice in order to prevent exploitation of clients and preserve the integrity of the profession, maintaining the public's trust and ensuring continuance of the provision of service.

(d) **Teaching & learning strategies:**

Professional ethics must be taught as a separate unit, seriously and in-depth. Case studies (highlighting practical dilemmas) and practical examples should be used. All teaching and learning must be designed to enable students to appreciate the core principles which underpin the Code of Conduct. Providers must ensure the participation of experienced practitioners in the design and delivery of professional ethics issues within the course. Professional ethics issues should be included in group discussions and other course activities, so that Providers can demonstrate that professional ethics pervade all aspects of their course.

(e) **Assessment:**

Students must be assessed and be judged competent in professional ethics and conduct, and they should, on a regular basis, be required to make explicit use of the Code in timetabled lessons. The tutor notes accompanying these lessons should clearly indicate the nature of the issue(s) and possible responses. The precise form of assessment is subject to the conditions set out in the Assessment Framework (A2.1.3). Formative-only exercises may be used. Summative assessment must take the form of one closed book examination, 2 hours long, comprising Part A, MCT questions, set centrally, marked centrally and electronically, plus Part B SAQs, set centrally and marked locally. There must be a pass in each part. Assessment will be such that a broad range of the syllabus is assessed and that any part of it may be assessed. No indication must be given to students as to which parts of the syllabus will or will not be assessed.

Students must be given the opportunity to attempt, and receive feedback on, formative (mock) assessments so as to provide appropriate preparation for summative (final) assessments. It is for Providers to demonstrate how this requirement has been met.

Note:

The CEB, acting through its Chief Examiners, will issue clarification from time to time of any changes in substantive law, rules of procedure, or Codes of Practice as they affect the assessment of the centrally set assessments in Professional Ethics. It is incumbent upon students and Providers to refer to the CEB page of the BSB website for updates and further guidance on a regular basis.

The CEB page of the BSB may be found at: http://www.barstandardsboard.org.uk/qualifying-as-a-barrister/bar-professional-trainingcourse/bptc-syllabus-and-centralised-examinations/

Students may wish to maintain, during their year of study, a reflective journal on ethical issues which relates in particular to their courtroom observation. This is advisable, but not a requirement.

(f) **Indicative content/teaching schedule:**

(1) Ethical issues at the Bar:

- core professional values which underpin practice at the Bar of England and Wales (what is meant by ethics and why it matters; the ethics according to which barristers work in England and Wales);
- the equality rules of the Code of Conduct;
- core principles underpinning the Code of Conduct and Bar Council guidance including:
  - (i) the principle of professional independence;
  - (ii) the principle of integrity;
  - (iii) the principle of duty to the court;
  - (iv) the principle of loyalty to the lay client;

(v) an understanding of the problems and perception of conflict of interest;

(vi) the principle of non-discrimination on grounds of gender, race, ethnicity or sexual orientation;

(vii) commitments to maintaining the highest professional standards of work, to the proper and efficient administration of justice and to the Rule of Law.

- issues of professional ethics and conduct which appear in given situations likely to arise in a barrister's practice (including requirements as to the client's identity, the proper keeping of records, and knowledge and awareness of money laundering regulation);
- the 'Cab Rank Rule' and its importance;
- provisions of the Code of Conduct of the Bar of England and Wales (in given situations) – instilling the ability to follow the spirit of the Code in situations where there is no provision that is directly applicable;
- reconciling the different duties owed to a professional client, lay client, the court, and the Legal Services Commission:

  (i) duties to the Lay Client including performance in and out of court, privilege and confidentiality issues;

  (ii) duty to the court – not misleading the court, dealing with clients' previous convictions, pleading fraud;
- means of handling relationships with other people: opponents and colleagues; the tribunal; judiciary; instructing solicitors; clients (both lay and expert); court clerks; dealing with witnesses;
- consideration of dishonest conduct and conduct likely to diminish public confidence in the legal profession;
- choosing the course of action which is consistent with the provisions and principles of the Code; where to find guidance if/when needed.

(2) Personal attributes and skills

- professional and responsible approaches to the profession, to the course and to their obligations to staff and other students;
- approach to equality issues, including non-discrimination on grounds of gender, race, disability, age, sexual orientation or religious belief; awareness of equality issues; need for 'reasonable adjustment' where appropriate;
- the Complaints procedure and penalties for infringement of the Code of Conduct (what happens if things go wrong and how to minimise the risk; and
- awareness of penalties for academic offences on the BPTC.

Reading/reference list:

Code of Conduct of the Bar of England and Wales (latest edition) (The Code of Conduct incorporated new equality rules on 1 September 2012 including a number of new requirements for self-employed barristers)

Boon, A & Levin, J: *The Ethics and Conduct of Lawyers in England and Wales* (Hart)

A balanced selection of textbooks on professional ethics and client care

BSB Guidelines on the Equality and Diversity Provisions of the Code of Conduct

BSB Guidance on the Bar Standard Board's Diversity Data Collection Rules

JSB Equal Treatment Bench Book

2.2.5 Opinion writing

(a) **Description/rationale:**

The aim of this part of the course is to develop the student's skill in opinion writing; that is, providing written advice to the instructing solicitor and lay client. Providing written advice in the forms of opinions is an important part of professional activity. Opinions must be practical, reliable, clear and well-presented.

(b) **Aims and objectives:**

The unit aims to:

- take students from the academic sphere (in which legal essays are expected to discuss legal principles and difficulties with some depth of research) into the professional sphere in which they hope to prosper in competition with other skilled professionals, in assisting clients with particular legal problems;
- develop students' skill by teaching them:
  - (i) that they must understand the client's problem and do their best (subject always to ethical considerations) to provide a practical solution to the problem;
  - (ii) that they must understand the facts, distinguishing between those which are undisputed and those which are likely to be in dispute, and distinguishing the relevant from the irrelevant (a process which interacts with analysis of the applicable law);
  - (iii) they must have a sound knowledge of the applicable law, analysing the problem so as to give reliable and realistic advice on its solution;
  - (iv) their advice must be clear, practical and as definite as possible;
  - (v) in giving written advice they must eliminate mistakes in spelling and grammar, cultivate a clear and concise prose style, and present the opinion in a professional format.
- enable students to identify clients' needs through a thorough grasp of the facts, the law and the relevant procedures;
- develop in students the skill of analytical reasoning.

(c) **Intended learning outcomes:**

By the end of this unit the student will be able to:

- identify and address the needs and objectives of the client and seek (subject always to ethical considerations) to provide a practical solution to the client's problems;
- accurately identify and show a thorough grasp of all the material facts, the relevant law, the real issues, the relevant procedure, parties and evidence, distinguishing one issue from another; and asking;
- identify and ask for further information/evidence, when necessary;
- give clear, sound, practical advice on the matters raised in the instructions and advise on any practical steps to be taken:
  - (i) where appropriate, advise on the need for expert evidence, on quantum of damages, and on any limitation aspects;
  - (ii) and generally give realistic and practical advice as to steps to be taken, including further inquiries or investigations, compliance with pre-action protocols, and other protocols necessary to take the matter forward.
- in addition, opinions must:
  - (i) cover everything that needs to be covered, be fully reasoned and follow a clear line of reasoning;
  - (ii) answer all questions put in instructions;
  - (iii) use a clear and appropriate structure, dealing with each issue in a logical order and separating issues into paragraphs in a sensible way, dealing with one issue at a time and giving each its due weight and significance;
  - (iv) be signed and dated, properly headed and laid out, making sensible use of sub-headings where appropriate, and written in a style appropriate to an Opinion;
  - (v) be in clear grammatical English, correctly spelt, appropriately punctuated and written fluently and concisely in appropriate language;
  - (vi) follow a logical order, distinguishing between different topics with appropriate subheadings;
  - (vii) be as short as is consistent with advising properly on all aspects of the matter.

(d) **Teaching and learning strategies:**

Knowledge and understanding gained in Civil and Criminal areas should be utilised for opinion writing as well as their being taught as a discrete subject.

(e) **Assessment:**

Assessment must consist, as a minimum, of one formal unseen time-constrained invigilated examination (where 'open book' materials may be used as specified in advance).

In addition, at least five opinions covering a broad range of scenarios should be undertaken by students as formative exercises. Each exercise must require the application of legal research and legal knowledge, and on each of the six occasions, the student must receive individual feedback from the tutor. Poor English, grammar and syntax must be penalised.

(f) **Indicative content/teaching schedule:**

(1) Overview:

- needs and objectives of the client; solution of the client's problems;
- identification of material facts, relevant law, real issues, relevant procedure and evidence; distinction between issues;
- specialised language and grammar;
- headings, sub-headings, lay out and style; lines of reasoning;
- structure, order, weight and significance; conciseness and length;
- practical approach, as opposed to academic discussion of the law;
- addressing questions expressly or implicitly raised in the instructions by expressing clear conclusions where appropriate, alternatively explaining why there can be no clear conclusions;
- explanation of legal and factual alternatives, and setting out of conclusions, with full advice;
- identifying the need for relevant further information/ evidence, explaining where appropriate why the further information is needed;
- providing clear, identifiable, appropriate, sound, practical advice on the matters raised in the instructions.

Reading/reference list:

A balanced selection of textbooks on opinion writing.

2.2.6 Drafting

(a) **Description/rationale:**

The aim of this unit/section is to equip the student with a critical knowledge, understanding and the conceptual and analytical skills necessary to draft a variety of documents including, inter alia, Claim Forms, Statements of Case and Witness Statements, Indictment, Grounds and Advice on Appeal in a criminal case.

(b) **Aims and objectives (knowledge and skills):**

This unit will:

- examine the nature, function and value of pleadings and learn to draft a full range of pleadings and other documents from simple to complex in civil and criminal proceedings using precedent appropriately;

- explain and demonstrate how to analyse critically a range of legal issues (claims, Witness Statements, Indictments, Grounds of Appeal and Advice on Appeal in a criminal case and settlement agreements);
- develop practical skills in drafting do that documents are properly presented and structured in clear grammatical and correct English.

(c) **Intended learning outcomes:**

By the end of this unit the student will be able to:

- demonstrate a sound understanding of the nature, function and value of pleadings;
- draft a full range of pleadings and other documents from simple to complex in civil and criminal proceedings using precedent appropriately (for example Particulars of Claim in a Claim Form; Any Statement of Case; Order; Witness Statement; Indictment; Grounds of Appeal and Advice on Appeal in a criminal case. Part 8 Claim Form; compromise agreement);
- draft documents that are written in clear grammatical English, correctly spelt and appropriately punctuated, and in a style that is fluent and concise, and appropriate to the document;
- draft documents that are well structured, with proper headings and laid out, neat on the page, and containing all necessary formalities;
- produce work that is accurate and contains correct figures and sums;
- produce drafts that are precise and unambiguous, in terms that are appropriate, in compliance with the requirements of practice, sound in law, settled in the appropriate court and drafted to achieve the objectives agreed with the client;
- analyse and set out the material facts and tell a clear story, identifying the material issues and omitting all immaterial matters;
- accurately state the client's case, and identify the relief sought.

(d) **Teaching and learning strategies:**

Teaching may make use of large and/or small group sessions. Following each practice exercise students must receive individual feedback from the tutor.

(e) **Indicative content/teaching schedule:**

(1) General drafting:

- claim form with Particulars of Claim;
- Statement of Case;
- order;
- witness statement;
- indictment;
- grounds of appeal and advice on appeal in a criminal case;
- Part 8 Claim Form;
- settlement/compromise agreement.

(2) Style and terminology

- stating the client's case, and identify the relief sought;
- application of material facts, clarity and identifying material issues (omitting all immaterial matters);
- requirements of practice, relevant law, and court procedures;
- relation structurally to other documents and consistency with accompanying advice;
- use of precedents;
- drafting, terminology;
- accurate and correct use of figures and sums;
- grammatical English, correctly spelt and appropriately punctuated;
- language and style appropriate to the document;
- headings and lay out, formalities and structure.

(3) Remedies (general)

- whether a range of remedies should be pursued; and
- applicable time limits.

(4) Contract

- pleading and responding to the correct heads of damages for breach of contract, including limitations on compensatory damages;
- pleading quantum in accordance with the correct legal principles and consistently with the evidence;
- the availability of equitable remedies, including specific performance, injunctions, rescission and rectification;
- remedies for misrepresentation;
- pleading claims for interest pursuant to contract or statute (Judgments Act 1838; Late Payment of Commercial Debts (Interest) Act 1998).

(5) Tort

- pleading and responding to the correct heads of damages, the calculation of quantum, the reduction of damages, aggravated and exemplary damages and the availability of injunctions; and
- quantifying damages in cases of personal injury;
- pleading interest on damages in claims for personal injury.

(f) **Assessment:**

Formal assessment must be by means of one formal unseen time constrained invigilated examination (where open book materials may be used as specified in advance). From Academic Year 2013–14, candidates may be provided with an option to undertake their Opinion Writing and Drafting assessments on computers, as long as security requirements are met, and a policy is in place to deal with issues in the event of software failure.

In addition, at least five practice drafting exercises covering a broad range of legal issues should be undertaken by students as formative exercises. Each exercise must require the application of legal research and legal knowledge. On each of the six occasions in each skill the student must receive individual feedback from the tutor. Poor English, grammar and syntax will be penalised.

[NB see section B3.2.3 on language issues.]

Reading/reference list:

Written skills

Providers should draw on a balanced selection books dealing with drafting which are currently available including:

Encyclopedias and loose-leaf works

Butterworths Civil Court Precedents (2012)

Encyclopedia of Forms & Precedents (LexisNexis Butterworths) (2012)

The Litigation Practice (Sweet & Maxwell) (2012)

Practical Civil Courts Precedents (Sweet & Maxwell) (2012)

Books

Atkins Court Forms (2012)

Blackstone's Civil Practice (OUP) (2012)

Bullen, E., Leake, S.M, Jacob, Sir J.I.H, Bullen, *Leake and Jacob's Precedents of Pleadings* (Sweet & Maxwell) (2011)

Civil Procedure (Sweet & Maxwell)

Bar Manual: Drafting l, CLS, (OUP) (16th ed., 2012)

Pleadings Without Tears, W Rose & R Eastman (OUP) (8th ed., 2012)

2.2.7 Conference skills

(a) **Description/rationale:**

The aim of this part of the course is to provide students with knowledge and understanding of the theory underpinning the application of the skills of a conference, making them sensitive to issues of client care, and emphasising the importance of an associated awareness of professional ethics.

(b) **Aims and objectives (knowledge and skills):**

This section/unit seeks to:

- provide students with knowledge and understanding of the theory underpinning the application of the skills of a conference;
- make students sensitive to issues of client care;
- make students aware of professional ethics and conduct issues that may arise within the context of a conference (including issues regarding ethnicity, gender, sexual orientation, age, disability etc).

(c) **Intended learning outcomes:**

By the end of this unit the student will be able to:

(1) demonstrate an understanding of the objectives of a conference and the factual, legal, procedural and evidential issues that should be raised in a conference;

(2) conduct the conference in a structured and efficient way, follow an agenda as far as possible and cover all relevant issues in a logical sequence;

(3) communicate effectively with the client and advise the client as appropriate.

(d) **Teaching and learning strategies:**

Students must be given the opportunity to practise conducting a conference on at least four occasions across a broad range of scenarios involving lay and professional clients. Each of the four conferences must be observed by a tutor and the tutor must provide feedback to the student.

Each conference should, wherever possible, be video/DVD recorded.

Following each conference exercise, students should be offered the opportunity to reflect on the conduct of the exercise and to review their own performance, including how, with hindsight, they might have done it differently.

There should, if possible, be participation by members of the public, as 'clients' or observers to provide additional feedback.

(e) **Assessment:**

There must be a minimum of one formal oral assessment, although additional formative assessment should be utilised, as indicated above (ie at least 3 additional 'formative- only' opportunities).

(f) **Indicative content/teaching schedule:**

(1) General Conference skills

- demonstrating an understanding of the objectives of a conference;
- demonstrating an understanding of the factual, legal, procedural and evidential issues that should be raised in a conference;
- conducting the conference in a structured and efficient way, following an agenda as far as possible and covering all relevant issues in a logical sequence;
- communicating effectively with the client and responding appropriately to the client's concerns and questions by putting the client at ease and using appropriate language;
- advising the client appropriately by explaining the legal, procedural and evidential issues in clear and unambiguous language;
- demonstrating an understanding of the need to observe professional ethics when conducting and concluding a conference.

(2) Conducting a conference with a client

- ensuring the client understands the objectives of the conference;
- listening to what the client says;
- permitting the client to raise concerns;
- listening to the client in a non-judgmental manner, empathising with and reassuring the client when appropriate;
- clarifying the relevant gaps and any ambiguities;
- selecting and using appropriate questioning techniques;
- eliciting the information required to advise the client;
- demonstrating a clear understanding of the client's account of the case/facts.

(3) Advising

- setting out the strengths and weaknesses of the case;
- advising on the consequences of any course of action taken;
- advising on what further action should be taken;
- ensuring the client understands what has been discussed;
- obtaining the client's full instructions;
- adhering to the instructions;
- avoiding invention/fabrication of facts;
- avoiding misleading the client as to the facts or the law;
- explaining fully and frankly when required;
- observation of the rules of professional conduct.

(4) Interpersonal skills/diversity

- having due regard for the client's cultural, ethnic, social and economic background, together with the impact this might have on their situation and view of their case (and in order to avoid stereotyped assumptions being made);
- possessing and exercising sensitivity to the client's predicament and state of mind (as caused by anxiety, distress, or anger).

Reading/reference list:

Providers should draw on a balanced selection of books dealing with conference skills currently available including:

Bar Manual: Conference Skills (16th ed., 2012) by M Soanes (OUP)

2.2.8 Resolution of disputes out of court

(a) **Description/rationale:**

This section/part of the course aims to provide knowledge and understanding of the various alternative methods of dispute resolution which fall outside the usual judicial process before courts or tribunals and may be exercised prior to a possible court hearing, or at any time during the litigation process, or prior to appeal, including mediation, negotiation, arbitration, early neutral evaluation, expert determination, and other alternative dispute resolution processes. It focuses on the advisory, representational and advocacy skills required of barristers in such processes with particular attention to mediation. It explains the theory underpinning the application of the skills of such processes, including the range of tactics and strategies for use in mediation, negotiation and other techniques, and their use in the context of professional ethics and conduct.

(b) **Aims and objectives:**

This section seeks to:

- provide knowledge and understanding of the theory and processes underpinning the range of methods of dispute resolution that lie outside the normal judicial processes, invluding negotiation, mediation (through a neutral third party), arbitration, collaborative law and conciliation and the practical skills required to advise upon, prepare for and represent parties at all stages of these processes;
- provide an understanding (leading to the use of) the skills needed in a range of tactics and strategies for use as basic tools in negotiation and mediation;
- make students aware of the key elements of mediation (but not with the intention of training them as mediators) and the role of the mediation advocate or representative;
- make students aware of the links to case analysis and professional ethics and conduct issues that may arise within the context of mediation, negotiation or other forms of dispute resolution;
- give students a basic understanding of the barrister's role in mediation and the skills required to be effective on behalf of their clients and encourage them to develop such skills.

(c) **Intended learning outcomes:**

By the end of this unit the student will be able to:

(1) demonstrate an understanding of the importance of the range of methods of dispute resolution outside process in court, and an ability to select cases appropriate for each process together with an understanding of the appropriate stage at which to engage in each process;

(2) demonstrate an awareness and basic knowledge of the process and practice of mediation, including some of the techniques adopted by mediators, so as to be able effectively to advise professional and lay clients about, prepare them for, and represent them at mediation;

(3) have a working knowledge of the law and practice of arbitration and expert determination and other methods of dispute resolution;

(4) be able to select strategies and methods for conducting a negotiation or representing the client at a mediation that will further the client's best interests including giving advice as to the steps that need to be taken and the preparations in terms of documents, evidence and where necessary invoking the aid of the court to assist the process;

(5) understand and demonstrate the skills needed in order to conduct a negotiation in their client's best interests;

(6) apply factual and legal issues in a case that is otherwise being resolved, in an effective way;

(7) demonstrate an understanding of the need to observe professional ethics when conducting and concluding alternative methods of dispute resolution;

(8) demonstrate a basic level of mediation advocacy skills.

(d) Teaching and learning strategies:

Formal lectures/large group sessions are normally used for knowledge delivery. Demonstrations by experienced practitioners should also be incorporated. Students may be given the opportunity to practise conducting a negotiation and mediation with fellow students across a broad range of scenarios. These should be observed by a tutor, should ideally be recorded on video/DVD and used for discussion/feedback provided to students involved or observing.

The mediation awareness and mediation advocacy training should be a minimum of eight to ten hours either over two days or in modular form over a longer period and include at least one mock mediation session.

The process should include opportunities for students to demonstrate the mediation advocacy skills they have learned by means of participation in 'mock' mediation. The mock mediation session should be inter-active, with pauses to allow for moderated question and answer sessions.

Opportunities for role play may be included as a formative exercise, as part of the teaching methodology.

(e) Assessment:

There must be a minimum of one formal examination totalling 100% of assessment for this topic, to include reference to and coverage of the necessary skills involved. Opportunities for role play may be included as a formative exercise, but these should not count towards summative assessment.

The written examinations should ideally involve providing students with a series of hypothetical cases and scenarios and asking them practical and ethical questions.

(f) Indicative content/teaching schedule:

(1) General dispute resolution skills

- the importance of mediation, arbitration and negotiation as means of settling a case;
- the importance of planning alternative ways of resolving a case;
- the importance of giving clear, accurate, advice to a client about the potential advantages and disadvantages of ADR processes such as mediation;
- selecting strategies and methods for involvement in mediation or conducting a negotiation that furthers the client's best interests;

- the observation of professional ethics when involved in these processes.

(2) Planning

- identifying factual and legal issues and how they relate to each other;
- identifying the objectives of the client and of the other side;
- identifying any conflict in the objectives of both sides and identify means of resolving such conflicts;
- prioritising objectives and controlling clients' expectations;
- identifying the strengths and weaknesses of each side;
- counteracting the perceived weakness of his/her own case, undermining the strengths of the other side's case, and exploiting weaknesses of the other side's case;
- identifying the best alternative to a negotiated settlement ('BATNA') and bottom line as appropriate;
- identifying and dealing with practical issues such as choice of appropriate mediator, venue, documentation, and parties attending and authority to settle;
- identifying the requisite contents of the pre-mediation agreement.

(3) Conducting

- choosing and implementing a strategy or strategies for achieving the realistic objectives of the client;
- modifying and/or changing the chosen strategy or strategies as appropriate;
- constructing and working within a structure that allows the negotiation, mediation or other dispute resolution process, to proceed in a clear, logical and coherent fashion;
- creating an environment that is 'safe' and conducive to settlement;
- presenting arguments clearly and in a confident and persuasive manner;
- where appropriate presenting the case in a favourable light by emphasising its strengths and mitigating its weaknesses and in a way that is likely to achieve its desired ends;
- picking up points made by the opponent and replying in a way that progresses the client's case;
- advising upon offers and concessions where it is in the client's best interests to do so;
- seeking to protect the client's position against the arguments of the opponent and responding in a way that is likely to achieve the desired ends;

- demonstrating an understanding of the need throughout to observe professional ethics;
- ensuring that the written heads of agreement or settlement agreement is clear, unambiguous and enforceable, and fully complies with the wishes and intent of the parties.

(4) Compromise

- principles and procedures governing consent and Tomlin Orders.

Reading/reference list:

Providers should draw on a balanced selection of books dealing with ReDOC which are currently available including:

A Practical Approach to Alternative Dispute Resolution, S Blake, J Browne and S Sime (2012, OUP)

ADR: Principles and Practice, H Brown and A Marriott (2012, Sweet & Maxwell).

Mediation Handbook: A Practical Guide, M Mantle (2011, Dundee)

A2.3 **Options (specialised subject areas)**

2.3.1 General requirements

General requirements relating to the options are as follows:

(1) All new option proposals must be presented to the BPTC Sub-Committee for approval at least 1 year before the commencement of the academic year in which the new option is proposed to be taught. "For example, for a new option to commence academic year 2014/2015, the proposed option content and learning outcomes should be sent to the BSB and BPTC Sub-Committee before the start of the 2013/2014 academic year (i.e. before about September 2013)."

(2) Flexibility is permitted to Providers (subject to validation), so booklists rather than details of course content are provided.

(3) There should be a minimum number of six options offered (no more than two may be offered as 'double options' to ensure choice).

(4) The options must offer a broad range of areas from which the students may make their choice.

(5) Students must choose two single options or one double option.

(6) Taught single options should be delivered over no less than sixteen hours contact time. All other options, such as clinical options and double options should be equivalent in the nature of the contact time provided.

(7) No less than 50% of the duration of the option must be directed to the practice of skill(s(learnt in the core of the course.

(8) Options must build upon the development of the skills delivered in the core of the course.

(9) Options must be taught with a view to professional practice.

(10) The assessment of the options must include a skills exercise, which may be formative. Summative assessment must be a minimum of one written or oral assessment (materials may be used).

(11) Options may be delivered during terms two and three, or three only, but must not be delivered in term one (during the first 10 weeks of the course) with the exception of a Pro Bono/Law Clinic option.

NB Providers will be expected, at accreditation/review, to provide details, for example of the intended learning outcomes, for each option. Owing to the wide range of options which, subject to approval by the BSB, may be offered by Providers, the following list focuses on a selection of the most popular and is indicative of the range of different types of related publications that an institution will be expected to hold. For serial publications, Providers will be expected to possess complete or substantially complete sets covering at least the last 10 years issues. Items marked thus [*] indicate that paper format is essential; electronic optional [may be subject to change].

Law Reports

A selection from:

Administrative Law Reports (1989-)

Butterworths Local Government Law Reports (1999-)

Crown Office Digest (1988-)

Knights Local Government Reports (1902–1998) continued as Butterworths Local Government

Reports (1999-)

Law Journals

Public Law (1956-)

Statute Law Review (1980-)

Encyclopedias and loose-leaf works

Encyclopedia of Local Government Law (Sweet & Maxwell)

2.3.3 Advanced arbitration

Law reports

Arbitration Law Reports (2001-)

Lloyd's Arbitration Reports (1985–1992)

Law journals

A selection from:

Arbitration International (1985-)

International Arbitration Law Review (1997-)

Practitioner works

International Handbook on Commercial Arbitration (Kluwer)

Merkin, R. *Arbitration Law.* (Informa Publishing Group)

Mustill, Sir M.J. & Boyd, S. *Commercial Arbitration* (LexisNexis)

2.3.4 Company law

Law reports

A selection from:

All England Law Reports Commercial Cases (1999-)

British Company Cases (1990-), formerly British Company Law Cases (1983–1989)

Business Law Reports (2006-)

Butterworths Company Law Cases (1978-)

Commercial Cases (1896–1941)

Lloyd's Law Reports (1919-)

Law journals

A selection from:

Company Lawyer (1980-)

Industrial Law Journal (1972-)

Journal of Business Law (1975-)

Lloyd's Maritime and Commercial Law Quarterly (1974-)

Encyclopedias and loose-leaf works

A selection from:

British Company Law & Practice (Sweet & Maxwell)

British Company Law Library (Sweet & Maxwell)

Butterworths Corporate Law Service (LexisNexis)

Gore-Brown on Companies (Jordans)

Palmer's Company Law (Sweet & Maxwell)

Thomas, R. *Company Law in Europe* (LexisNexis)

2.3.5 Competition law

Law journals

Journal of Business Law (1975-)

Encyclopedias and loose-leaf works

Butterworths Competition Law Service (LexisNexis)

Encyclopedia of Competition Law (Sweet & Maxwell)

Books

A balanced selection of textbooks.

2.3.6 Employment Law

Law reports

A selection from:

Employment Law Reports (2000-)

Industrial Cases Reports (1972-)

Industrial Relations Law Reports (1972-)

Industrial Tribunal Reports (1966–1978)

Knights Industrial and Commercial Reports (1966–1975)

Restrictive Practices Cases (1957–1972)

Law journals

A selection from:

Equal Opportunities Review (1985-)

European Industrial Relations Review (1974-)

IDS Employment Law Brief (2005-), formerly IDS Brief, Employment Law and Practice (1972–2005)

Industrial Law Journal (1972-)

Industrial Relations Legal Information Bulletin (1973–1992) continued as Industrial Relations Law Bulletin

Industrial Relations Law Bulletin (1993-)

Industrial Relations Review and Report (1971–1994) continued as IRS Employment Review

IRS Employment Review (1995–2007)

Encyclopedias and loose-leaf works

A selection from:

Encyclopedia of Employment Law (Sweet & Maxwell)

Harvey on Industrial Relations and Employment Law (LexisNexis)

2.3.7 Family law

Law reports

Butterworths Family Court Reporter (2000-), formerly Family Court Reporter

(1987–1999)

Family Law (1971-)

Family Law Reports (1980-)

Law journals

A selection from:

Child and Family Law Quarterly (1995-) (Formerly Journal of Child Law, 1988–1995)

Childright: Journal of Child Law (1983-)

Journal of Child Law (1988–1995) continued as Child and Family Law Quarterly

Journal of Social Welfare and Family Law (1978-)

Family Law (1971 –)

Family Court Practice (the Red Book)

Encyclopedias and loose-leaf works

A selection from:

Butterworths Family Law Service (LexisNexis)

Children: Law and Practice (Hersham and McFarlane)

Clarke Hall & Morrison on Children (LexisNexis)

Family Law Practice (annual issue)

Matrimonial Property and Finance (Duckworth)

Rayden and Jackson on Divorce and Family Matters

2.3.8 Housing law

Law reports

Housing Law Reports (1976-)

Law journals

Legal Action (1972-)

Encyclopedias and loose-leaf works

A selection from:

Arden, A. & Partington, M., *Housing Law* (Sweet & Maxwell)

Encyclopedia of Housing Law & Practice (Sweet & Maxwell)

Housing Law & Precedents (Sweet & Maxwell)

2.3.9 Landlord and tenant

Law reports

A selection from:

Estates Gazette Law Reports (1902-)

Estates Gazette Case Summaries (1988-)

Estates Times Legal Supplement (1986-)

Property, Planning and Compensation Reports (1950-)

Law journals

Conveyancer and Property Lawyer (1936-)

Estates Times (1968-)

Encyclopedias, loose-leaf works and practice books

A selection from:

Emmet & Farrand on Title (Sweet & Maxwell)

Hill & Redman's Law of Landlord & Tenant (LexisNexis)

Woodfall, W., *The Law of Landlord and Tenant* (Sweet & Maxwell)

2.3.10 Planning law

Law reports

A selection from:

Estates Gazette Planning Law Reports (1987-)

Journal of Planning and Environment Law (1948-)

Planning Appeals Decisions (1985-)

Property, Planning and Compensation Reports (1950-)

Law journals

Journal of Planning and Environment Law (1948-)

Encyclopedias and loose-leaf works

A selection from:

Butterworths Planning Law Service (LexisNexis)

Encyclopedia of Environmental Law (Sweet & Maxwell)

Encyclopedia of Environmental Health Law & Practice (Sweet & Maxwell)

Encyclopedia of Planning Law & Practice (Sweet & Maxwell)

Garner's Environmental Law (LexisNexis)

Sweet & Maxwell's Planning Law, Practice & Precedents (Sweet & Maxwell)

2.3.11 Sale of goods and consumer law

Law reports

Butterworths Trading Law Cases (1984-)

Trading Law (includes Trading Law Reports) (1984-)

Law journals

Consumer Law Journal (1993-)

Encyclopedias and loose-leaf works

A selection from:

Butterworths Trading and Consumer Law (LexisNexis)

Encyclopedia of Consumer Credit Law (Sweet & Maxwell)

Encyclopedia of Consumer Law (Sweet & Maxwell)

Howell., *Law of Weights and Measures* (LexisNexis)

Miller, C.J., *Product Liability and Safety Encyclopaedia* (LexisNexis)

2.3.12 Taxation

Law reports

A selection from:

British Tax Cases (1982-)

Reports of Tax Cases (1875-)

Simon's Tax Cases (1972-)

Value Added Tax Tribunal Reports (1973-)

Law journals

British Tax Review (1979-)

Encyclopedias and loose-leaf works

A selection from:

British Tax Service (LexisNexis)

CCH British Tax Library (CCH Publishing)

De Voil Indirect Tax Service (LexisNexis)

Foster's Inheritance Tax (LexisNexis)

Simon's Direct Tax Service (LexisNexis)

Sumption, A. Capital Gains Tax (LexisNexis)

2.3.13 Pro Bono work as an option

Pro Bono work may be included as an option (with assessment by means of a self- reflective journall). See also **2.4.3** below.

A2.4 **Additional areas**

2.4.1 General

Additional subject areas and activities may be included in the course, as described in this section, but they are not assessed. Information on these topics should be covered at induction or subsequently. For example, orientation and general introductions to accommodation, library and IT provision etc should be provided as part of induction. Further and more detailed information about methods of Legal Research, Pro Bono opportunities, Court visits, Forensic Accounting, management skills and other subject areas may be provided as part of induction and/or at a subsequent point in the course. The areas should not be assessed but made available to students.

2.4.2 Legal research methods

(1) Legal research methods should normally be dealt with as part of induction for students, or otherwise early in the course, in order to furnish the student with the necessary skills to follow a line of investigation and explore the necessary contexts of a case (using both paper-based and online resources), effectively building on prior experience to underpin the various knowledge and skills areas

(2) Induction into legal research methods should:

- enable students to approach methods of legal research in a practical rather than academic manner;
- enable students to be selective, precise and efficient in the identification and utilisation of resources so that students will be able to:

  (i) analyse issues raised by the case, identifying questions of law that need to be investigated and answered;

  (ii) analyse and discuss the arguments presented and judgments delivered in cases reported in the law reports;

  (iii) demonstrate an understanding of the structure of legal literature and the media through which it is made available;

(iv) make effective use of a law library (using both paper based and IT resources), keeping up to date with developments;

(v) examine facts in detail, look at all the possible interpretations, identify which facts are in dispute and which information is missing/needed, how the facts can be linked together to prove a case and construct a persuasive argument;

(vi) use and interpret legal citations and abbreviations, and correctly reference material used.

(3) Steps should be taken (at induction and/or in subsequent sessions) to ensure that students are familiar and able to work with the following:

- Legal research methods:

  (i) analysis of the issues raised by the case and identification of which questions of law have to be answered;

  (ii) development of relevant keywords;

  (iii) the structure of legal literature and the media through which it is made available;

  (iv) use of a law library and the catalogues and indexes it contains;

  (v) use of IT skills to locate and retrieve relevant information;

  (vi) selection of relevant original material, commentary, opinion and guidance;

  (vii) use of indexes within legal materials to find relevant information;

  (viii) use and interpretation of legal citations and abbreviations;

  (ix) currency of information and being up to date with legal developments generally;

  (x) organisation of the written response into a logical structure with concise and accurate summary/paraphrase of relevant material;

  (xi) application of the law to the facts of the problem so as to produce satisfactory answers to the problem posed;

  (xii) provision of clear advice as a result of legal investigation and research;

  (xiii) acknowledgement/referencing of all sources and materials cited;

  (xiv) devising a research trail to show how the answers have been reached;

  (xv) use of IT skills to present the results of research.

- Fact management/case analysis:

(i) presentation of data in a variety of ways;

(ii) gaps, ambiguities and contradictions in information, and their identification;

(iii) prioritising the objectives of the client in terms of practical outcomes and legal remedies;

(iv) placing information in context;

(v) identifying and prioritising the facts and legal issues raised;

(vi) selecting possible solutions to the client's problem;

(vii) recognising the interaction between law and fact;

(viii) assessing the strengths and weaknesses of a case;

(ix) organising information in a variety of ways to aid understanding, prove propositions of law, and assist at trial;

(x) distinguishing between relevant and irrelevant facts; and between fact and inference;

(xi) constructing an argument from the facts to support the client's case by developing a theory of the case and/or by selecting a theme or themes to fit that theory;

(xii) evaluation of issues in response to new information and in the light of tactical considerations.

Recommended reading:

Providers should draw on a balanced selection of student text books dealing with legal research skills which are currently available.

2.4.3 Pro Bono opportunities

Providers are required to ensure there are opportunities for students to undertake suitable Pro Bono (or FRU) work. The BSB recognizes the immense value of such opportunities and experience, and the contribution such activity may make to the overall learning experience. However, it is not compulsory for students to undertake such work. Pro Bono work may be included as an option, with assessment by means of a self-reflective journal. See **2.3.13** above.

2.4.4 Court visits and Personal Development Files

Students are encouraged to attend court to observe cases for full or half days and Providers may wish to assist or support students' attendance at court. A reflective report (Personal Development Portfolio) may be compiled by the student but is not compulsory and will not be assessed.

Recording details of the case(s) observed in court, with consideration of procedures and events and evaluation of how they informed learning on the BPTC, can be very valuable for students (considered in relation to the formal tuition on the course), but is not a requirement. Students may be briefed and debriefed on the cases they observe and, ideally, have the opportunity to be addressed by the judge or counsel.

2.4.5 Management and 'soft' skills

(1) Providers are at liberty to include management skills related to leadership, team-working, communication, people management, client care and skills for dealing with the public. These may well permeate other areas of the course, but the separate delivery of management skills appropriate to practice at the Bar (as a self employed practitioner or as a member of the Employed Bar) is not a requirement.

Providers may also want to incorporate consideration of the ability of barristers to supply legal services to the public, e.g., public access scheme.

Consideration of the significant recent change that barristers are now permitted to practise as managers or employees of Alternative Business Structures (ABSs) and the implications therein for practice management is an area ripe for exploration.

(2) Forensic accounting (i.e., guidance in the use of financial information and accounts, both corporate and individual) will normally be covered at the Pupillage stage. The inclusion of such management skills is therefore not a compulsory element of the BPTC, should not be assessed separately, and must not contribute to the overall grade for the course.

A3 Teaching and Learning

3.1 **Principles of teaching and learning**

(1) A number of principles underlie the requirements for the delivery of the Bar Professional Training Course content as outlined in section A2 above.

(2) Courses approved by the BSB must conform in terms of aims and objectives, course content and standards to the requirements as specified. The delivery and assessment of the intended learning outcomes may be achieved in a variety of ways, but certain requirements for the delivery of the course are mandatory and are specified in the sections which follow.

3.2 **Teaching and learning strategy**

It is acknowledged that each Provider will have their own departmental and institutional strategies for teaching and learning. However, it is important that, for delivery of the BPTC, strategies for delivery are in line with BSB requirements as outlined in this document. A copy of the teaching strategy for the course must be provided at accreditation and when any course is reviewed.

3.3 **Structure and mode of delivery of the BPTC**

(1) The preponderance of teaching must be delivered by small group lessons.

(2) Small group sessions must be designed for delivery to no more than 12 students.

(3) Teaching and learning must focus on what happens in practice.

(4) Providers must demonstrate the appropriateness of their chosen teaching methodologies for delivery of their chosen approach to content, throughout the course.

(5) The following must be considered in determining how the course is to be delivered:

- contact hours;
- the learning outcomes for the session in which the particular skill, knowledge or values is delivered or assessed;
- the stage of the course at which the lesson is to be delivered;
- the nature of the pre-session preparation required of students;
- the nature of any learning activities to be conducted in the lesson;
- the number of practice sessions that the student is to be afforded.

3.4 **Details of delivery**

3.4.1 General

The curriculum is presented in this Handbook according to units or modules, and must be assessed according to the schedule provided (A 2.1.3); it is acceptable for delivery to take place integrating knowledge and skills within broad Civil and Criminal areas. Assessment must be as specified.

The skills must be introduced through discrete lessons. Thereafter, they must be developed through small group lessons, workshops, practice sessions, formative assessments and other course activities.

Providers must demonstrate that the format of teaching sessions on the course is appropriate to the skill being taught and that, when taken as a whole and in conjunction with other course activity, these provide a coherent framework for progression and the development of skills.

Providers must be able to demonstrate that the development and practice of the skills is done in the context of the application of legal knowledge, and with regard to what happens in practice. At all stages it must be emphasised that the training is designed to enable the students to render a professional service to members of the public.

3.4.2 Small group sessions

The majority of teaching must take place in small group sessions of 12 students or fewer.

3.4.3 Large group sessions

Large groups are defined as those comprising more than 12 students and range from combined group teaching in multiples of 12 or lectures to the whole cohort.

Providers must be able to justify the inclusion of large group sessions within the course, both collectively and for individual sessions. The Bar Standards Board would require strong justification for any ratio of large to small group sessions that favoured large group sessions at more than 25% of contact hours. Justification for large group sessions may include:

- introducing and providing an overview of a new area;
- elucidating difficult issues;
- providing demonstrations;
- providing a synthesis or summary of learning and testing understanding;
- providing a forum for debate after small group sessions.

Wherever possible large group sessions should be interactive, encourage questions and answers from the floor and make full use of visual aids.

Large group sessions should not be used merely to deliver or dictate material that is available in a similar format in commercially available texts or that otherwise is available or could be delivered in printed form.

3.4.4 Practical work/sessions for the delivery of skills and competencies

Students must be provided with at least the following opportunities to practise and receive feedback on each skill in small group sessions across a range of scenarios likely to be encountered by a barrister in the early years of practice:

Advocacy:	the equivalent of twelve 15-minute practice exercises (of which three formally assessed)
Conferencing:	4 complete, tutor observed conferences (of which one formally assessed)
Opinion Writing:	6 assignments (of which one formally assessed)
Drafting:	6 assignments (of which one formally assessed)

Students must on occasion practise oral skills in unfamiliar student groupings.

Students must be provided with training in the skills necessary to support peer review, self-evaluation, and reflective learning.

Providers must ensure that students routinely receive feedback on their practice of each skill, consistent with the learning outcomes set for the session in which the practice took place.

Providers must ensure that students receive formal individual tutor feedback following at least one formative assessment before each summative assessment.

Students must be provided with exemplars of good practice in respect of each skill.

The range of scenarios used for skills practice should reflect the learning outcomes and ensure an appropriate mix of civil and criminal work. Providers should use the scenarios to integrate pervasive themes such as Ethics which should permeate all courses (although also taught and assessed as a separate unit).

3.4.5 Legal research and casework skills

Fact management/case analysis and legal research methods are the fundamental enabling skills of the specialist advocate, and students need to be judged competent in legal research methods. They must be given due prominence in the course and be closely integrated with other skills. Fact management and legal research must be introduced in discrete induction or training sessions, even though they are not separately assessed. (see section A2.4.1 for a list of areas that will need to be covered at induction, through subsequent sessions or by self direction by students).

Candidates' skills in such areas will be reflected in their written and advocacy work. Providers must demonstrate how the skills of fact management and legal research pervade their course (in addition to the training sessions) and include fact management skills in the assessment criteria for the assessed skills.

For delivery of information about legal research methods, Providers are advised to use a range of sessions, as part of induction or delivered subsequently. It is important that this should be in relation to student needs, given that, owing to variations in undergraduate courses, some students may commence the BPTC with different levels of skills and experience in the field. Where some may need a great deal of support, others may well need less.

3.4.6 Use of learning resources

Course materials include not only those prepared for or used in teaching and assessment, but also documentation such as student handbooks and other explanatory documents intended for student use. Students shall be expected to make frequent and regular use of an appropriate variety of practitioner and original source material.

Where Providers rely on commercially published teaching manuals, they must demonstrate how Learning resources requirements are achieved within their course, and also be able to demonstrate their appropriateness to the session or activity in which they are used.

The course materials used by Providers must reflect the need to prepare students for practice in a culturally diverse society.

3.4.7 Part-time, distance and supported learning

It is expected that appropriate use will be made by Providers of Virtual Learning Environments (VLEs) in order to support student learning, as well as for use as a means of communication with students (e.g. Blackboard, WebCT or in-house packages). This may in particular be helpful if Providers wish to deliver the knowledge areas in a manner in which distance and supported learning is appropriate.

Where the BPTC is validated for delivery in part-time mode, the use of electronic or paper-based additional study material and guidance for students is essential and will be carefully considered at validation. Although the BSB supports in principle the need to make the course available in parttime and/or supported learning mode (in order to enable access), the need for the practical skills areas to be delivered in 'live' situations, means that a full distance learning mode is unlikely to be a successful way of delivering the BPTC and part-time day/evening or block teaching must be included in all part time courses.

3.4.8 Diversity and equality in teaching and learning

Providers must ensure that all students have equality of opportunity both in admission to the course, whilst undertaking the course, and in terms of their final assessments. The BSB sees its role as one of working in partnership with Providers with a focus on fostering a culture in which equality and diversity can be encouraged and supported. As such, should Providers have questions with respect to equality and diversity issues and how to address such issues in the preparation, administration, teaching and assessing of their respective course, they are encouraged to contact the BSB for guidance.

A4 Assessment and Progression

4.1 **Arrangements for assessment**

4.1.1 The knowledge areas are assessed through discrete papers and pervasively through the skills assessments. The precise form of the final examination papers is determined centrally while it is for Providers to determine the pervasive elements subject to the conditions set out in the Assessment Framework (section A2.1.3). However, assessment must be such that any part of the syllabus may be assessed and that a broad range of the syllabus is assessed. No indication will be given to students as to which parts of the syllabus will or will not be assessed.

4.1.2 The BPTC assessment regulations of each of the validated institutions shall conform to the assessment framework set out in A2.1.3, providing assessments and calculating overall performance in accordance with those requirements. Students shall be assessed in accordance with the assessment regulations in force at the time of their first registration on the course. In addition, students shall be assessed in accordance with the regulations and methods published by the institution at which they are registered. Students must consent in writing to any changes to the assessment regulations made after their registration.

4.1.3 As part of assessment, the minimum attendance requirement of 90% must be met. This should usually be calculated on a termly basis (see B4.11.3 for details). Students should be able to demonstrate, if required, fulfilment of the attendance requirement, i.e. that he or she has maintained full attendance or that where classes have been missed, evidence has been provided of mitigating circumstances accepted by the Provider, and the missed outcomes covered in the student's own time.

4.1.4 All candidates must thus engage in at least the minimum number of supervised skills practice opportunities required by the BSB and made available during the course. Evidence might include videotapes of performance and tutor feedback, or written feedback sheets, in the oral skills, and submitted drafts with written feedback in the written skills. Students are encouraged to maintain a file of their experiences, which can demonstrate coverage of as wide a range of the outcomes as practicable. This may also include the student's own notes and completion of a reflective and analytical report covering court visits undertaken. This is regarded as a useful exercise but is not compulsory.

4.2 **Centralised assessment**

The following papers, each comprising a SAQ section and an MCQ section, are set on behalf of the BSB by the CEB:

- Civil Litigation, Evidence and Remedies.
- Criminal Litigation, Evidence and Sentencing.
- Professional Ethics.

Students at all BPTC Providers will attempt the examinations in the knowledge subjects (comprising both an SAQ and MCQ element) on the same day at the same time (dates to be determined by the BSB and published at the start of the academic year). SAQs will be marked locally by Providers and multiple choice questions will be marked electronically at the BSB. The Central Examinations Board will then sample and take an overview of marks across all Providers, making any adjustments that are deemed necessary. Confirmed marks for the centralised subjects will then be returned to Providers and combined with marks for other parts of the course to give an overall BPTC score for each student.

The CEB is concerned only with overall consistency in the three specified knowledge subjects and at no time will it be involved in discussing the marks of individual students, or in discussing an individual student's mitigating circumstances. Providers will continue to operate local processes for issues pertaining to individual students (e.g. extenuating circumstances and academic misconduct).

4.3 **Forms of assessment**

4.3.1 Coursework (in-course assessment)

Procedures for the submission of coursework will be in accordance with institutional procedures. Care must be taken to ensure there is no 'bunching' of assignments and that scheduling of assessments/deadlines is appropriate.

4.3.2 Recorded 'performance' assessment

Skills assessments should wherever possible be recorded (by video or DVD) to facilitate feedback and discussion of performance.

4.3.3 Formal time-constrained examinations

Formal time-constrained examinations must be conducted in accordance with the regulations for examinations B4.5.

4.4 **External examiners and external moderators**

4.4.1 In order to ensure that assessment is fair to candidates and that there is comparability of assessment across Providers, a system of External Examiners is also in place. External Examiners moderate the assessments and student performance in the areas to which they are allocated in particular Providers. They do not mark individual papers, other than in exceptional circumstances. For details see Part B Regulations (section B4.8).

4.5 **Referrals and re-sits**

The facility should be made available for candidates failing assessments to retrieve or make good that failure. Regulations governing this process, together with any limitations are given in section 4.11 of Part B Regulations.

4.6 **Academic offences and plagiarism**

Procedures are in place to deal with academic offences that may occur as part of the Assessment process. Details are provided in Part B, Regulations, section B6, together with information about the related appeals process. The

BSB takes academic offences very seriously and students must be warned by Providers that any such transgressions by students will clearly impact on the appropriateness of their behaviour in terms of professional ethics and conduct.

Transgressions or 'convictions' for academic offences (including plagiarism) by students will be reported to the Inn of Court of which they are a member and can result in the exercise of a disciplinary procedure that may lead to expulsion from membership of the Inn of Court.

A5 Resources

5.1 **Staffing**

5.1.1 Staff:student ratio

The current staff to student ratio (SSR) is set at 1:12.5 for the first 125 validated student places. Thereafter, a full-time equivalent member of staff must be appointed for every group, or part group, of 16 students. A part-time student should be calculated as 0.5 of a full-time equivalent student (FTE) when calculating the staff student ratio.

There must be a sufficient proportion of full-time staff who are entirely or largely dedicated to the BPTC in accordance with specified SSRs above. Any staff drawn from undergraduate teaching must be fully inducted to the ethos of the BPTC. Utilisation of a large number of fractional staff (below 0.25 full-time equivalent) will require specific justification.

5.1.2 Support staff

In addition to the course team there must be:

- a dedicated course administrator;
- an on-site IT/AV technician (need not be dedicated to the BPTC but support must be adequate);
- a professionally qualified law librarian responsible for maintaining the BPTC book stock and services;
- sufficient library staff trained to support the BPTC.

5.1.3 Staffing requirements

(1) In order to teach and assess advocacy, staff must be accredited by the BSB on the recommendation of the ATC. Prior to seeking accreditation, they must have received adequate in-house training in the principles and application of the Hampel Method of advocacy teaching.

Staff appointed for the teaching and assessment of advocacy must be accredited at the date of being first employed to teach advocacy on the BVC/BTPC. In exceptional circumstances (for example where an appointment is made at short notice due to the sudden departure of an existing member of staff, or to cover for illness or maternity leave etc) staff who are not accredited must gain accreditation within ten weeks of having first started to teach advocacy.

During this ten week period unaccredited staff may teach but not assess advocacy, and must be monitored and receive guidance and support from a nominated accredited advocacy trainer.

Where a candidate fails to be recommended for accreditation, he or she will receive written feedback on their performance from the ATC examiners, and may seek accreditation on another occasion. Such candidates may not teach or assess advocacy until such time as they do become recommended for BSB accreditation by the ATC.

Note: *Additional guidance on the process is provided by the ATC. There will be no exemptions to the above policy, since it is difficult to define the circumstances under which a trainer has qualified, and to distinguish between the standards of accreditation in other countries. It is unlikely to be onerous for those accredited in other jurisdictions to undergo the BSB/ATC accreditation process as a form of staff development, which is likely to be beneficial in any circumstances.*

(2) Each full-time member of the BPTC team must undertake at least 5 days of staff development each year. The course leader will decide what is considered legitimate staff development. In the case of staff members who no longer practise as barristers, it should include time spent with practising barristers whose practices cover the subject(s) being taught by the staff member (see 5.1.4 below for details). The monitoring panel will review the course leader's decisions. Proportionate training must be undertaken by staff on fractional appointments to a minimum of one day per year.

5.1.4 Staff development activities

Staff development may exceptionally be carried over for up to three years where an individual member of staff plans to, or has taken part in, an approved, extensive staff development activity. But, in such a case, the member of staff would be expected to complete at least one day of staff development in each of the intervening years.

Under normal circumstances the staff development activities should address (over a given period of time):

- delivery skills;
- professional practice experience;
- changes in the law and legal process;
- the ability to relate to a cultural and ethnically diverse student body (achieved, for example, by training normally expected to be provided in a Higher Education Institution);
- facility with IT equipment and software;
- management skills;
- engagement in developments in education within the wider academic community.

Examples of activities that would fulfil these requirements are:

- enrolment on a teaching qualification;
- in-house designed and delivered courses;
- externally delivered courses;
- conferences (Bar, BPTC, LPC, ALT, SLS etc);

- professional practice as a door tenant or on a release basis;
- marshalling;
- engagement in external working parties and projects;
- delivering legal training to other professional bodies e.g. the police and solicitors.

The above list is not intended to be complete or exclusive. However, the spirit of the requirement is that the development needs of staff are identified honestly (during appraisal and review) and that staff are exposed to a range of development activities from which their involvement on the BPTC will benefit. In this regard it would be usual to see staff engage in professional updating and delivery skills courses on a regular basis. A notional budget of at least £500 per staff member per annum should be agreed.

5.2 **Rooms and accommodation**

5.2.1 General requirements

(1) Accommodation must be appropriate to professional training in specification and presentation.

(2) Institutions will be expected to ensure that all reasonable adjustments are made to accommodate disabled candidates, and in accordance with current legislation on disability and equality [see also section on assessment below].

(3) Lecture theatres must contain modern presentational tools (eg video or DVD, PowerPoint, CD-ROM, Internet, OHP). The acoustics and sight lines of the lecture theatre must be satisfactory. The layout should facilitate an interactive approach to teaching in large group sessions and the seating ideally should be raked.

5.2.2 Seminar rooms

- Seminar rooms must be of sufficient size to conduct oral skills in groups of twelve comfortably.
- Furnishings and the size and nature of the room must be sufficiently flexible to be able to conduct advocacy exercises that facilitate behaviour in court (stance, voice projection, position of court officers, witnesses, defendants etc) and in the judge's chambers, with other students being well sighted to observe comfortably.
- Court room furniture, whether demountable or permanent, must be available in a sufficient number of seminar rooms to enable advocacy exercises to take place in a court room setting regularly.
- A permanent mock court room must be available.
- A video/DVD camera/player and TV must be available in each room.
- Core practitioner works must be readily available for reference within seminar rooms.

5.2.3 Collaborative study

There must be a common, social or base room to provide a place for study and discussion. The room must have access to refreshment facilities.

5.3 **Library**

5.3.1 Library Facilities and services

Each Provider shall have a dedicated law library. Where this is part of an undergraduate provision or is not close to and readily accessible to BPTC accommodation, a practitioners' library must be provided that houses the reference material as listed in this document and meets the other specifications set out below and elsewhere in this paper relevant to the provision of a library.

The law library should meet the essential criteria for law library provision outlined in *the Statement of Standards and Indicative List* (2003) published by the Society of Legal Scholars (or its current version), available at http://www.legalscholars.ac.uk/documents/standards2003.pdf. This sets out the standards that a law library established for educational purposes should provide to meet the resource needs of staff and students. The *Statement* is wide-ranging in scope and covers management, liaison and staffing issues, services to students, space and physical facilities, the content of printed collections and electronic database provision.

The library provision as a whole should be to a practitioner level, with an appropriate range of practitioner works (treatises, encyclopedias, precedents) for all areas of legal practice taught on the course, and consistent with the principles set out in the *Statement of Standards and Indicative List*. The provision of general sources must be over and above that provided for use by undergraduates but, on condition that sufficient multiple copies are provided, these may be shared with students following other courses of study. With regard to BPTC-specific material also, Providers must include texts for the study of professional ethics and practice, the knowledge subjects, the skills areas and option courses which must be over and above those provided for use by undergraduates but, on condition that sufficient multiple copies are provided these may be shared with students following other courses of study.

The collection of the law library should be held in a format, or combination of formats, that best serves the needs of its users and teaching requirements. A suitable balance between printed and electronic formats must be maintained so that students are able to make use of both paper-based and electronic legal research resources. A range of different types of publication must also be offered, which must include law reports, law journals, encyclopedias and loose-leaf works, other practitioner works and finding tools.

Collections must be kept up-to-date with loose-leaf works regularly updated. The latest editions of textbooks must be purchased. Sufficient multiple copies must be provided, and alternative and specialist works must be available where the syllabus requires.

The library must be open in term time for at least 11 hours a day from Monday to Friday inclusive, 7 hours on Saturdays and on Sundays where practicable. Opening times must adequately address the support needs of part-time students.

The library must provide study spaces at a ratio of 1 study space to 3 students (FTE). This ratio excludes spaces for use with PCs unless there is adequate space around the PC for workbooks to be laid flat.

The library must provide a book loan service. Adequate printing and photocopying facilities must be provided at a reasonable price.

5.3.2 Budget

Since pupil barristers should be able to display equal competence in the use of paper and electronic research sources, Providers should ensure that their policies for access to research sources and the provision of library collections reflect this requirement. Providers must also ensure that, in the allocation of time to training and practice in legal research methods, a reasonable balance is maintained between the two formats. This will need to be demonstrated at approval, and during monitoring and review.

The library budget must be set at a level sufficient to provide the resources needed in order to meet the requirements set out in the *Statement of Standards* referred to above and any additional course requirements set out in this document. It must for example take into account the need for both printed and electronic formats of some material in order to meet the requirements that pupil barristers be able to display equivalent competence in paper and electronic research.

Annual expenditure must keep pace with current prices for materials and with developments in course provision, teaching needs and professional legal practice. The annual budget is exclusive of capital expenditure for set-up costs; back runs of material, staff books and copies of manuals to students. The sufficiency of the budget will need to be demonstrated as approval, and during monitoring and review.

5.3.3 List of library holdings for the BPTC

The lists included with each subject area in Part A2.2 give the titles of required and/or recommended texts and materials in paper and electronic format. Reference works listed in this Handbook are those institutions should provide, unless a particular title is marked "holding optional" in the list.

5.4 **Information technology**

5.4.1 Hardware

The following specifications must be met:

- Providers must meet a ratio of one IBM compatible PC to every five students.
- An appropriate number of printers must be provided.
- CPUs and the operating system must be to current or immediately previous industry standard.
- 95% of PCs must be networked and capable of supporting the software outlined below.
- Wireless network technology must be available and operational over a substantial part of the study areas in the library and in any seminar rooms frequently used by students for personal or group study purposes.

5.4.2 Software

The following software should be available to staff and students:

- a word processing package to current or immediately previous industry standard;
- a keyboard skills package to current or immediately previous industry standard;
- a spreadsheet package to current or immediately previous industry standard;
- a presentation package, such as PowerPoint;
- full internet access with an up to date internet browser;
- a substantial range of legal research databases providing access to statutes, law reports, law encyclopedias and practitioner works;
- off-site access to legal research databases, virtual learning environments (VLEs) and, ideally, the personal accounts of students containing word processing software and files;
- an e-mail service;
- a network/web site for use by the BPTC.

Providers will be expected to be using virtual learning environments (VLEs) for the delivery of at least a part of the course.

5.4.3 Training

Providers will be required to provide IT skills support classes for students.

5.4.4 Audio-visual

In addition to the audio-visual equipment mentioned under accommodation and the technical support mentioned under staffing, institutions must provide sufficient audio-visual recording and playback equipment and appropriate accommodation to enable students to practise their oral skills (through self study or in informal groupings) outside of class time.

A6 Student Support

6.1 **Information to students and student handbooks**

6.1.1 Providers will be expected to act in accordance with the Charter for Higher Education, and the requirements of the Quality Assurance Agency for Higher Education. Providers will be required to publish a student charter (or equivalent) setting out the rights and duties of staff and students.

6.1.2 Prior to admission, Providers are advised to make applicants aware of what will be expected of them on the course and how they should prepare. Information should include reference to the formal admissions requirements, attendance requirement and the standard of English language required.

6.1.3 In addition to information about entry requirements and the standard of the course, information must also be provided about careers, expectations and possibilities, in terms of the numbers of pupillages available nationally, and the success rates. A 'Health warning' about the risks of entering the profession should be given to all students and statistical information should be prominently displayed in on-line and paper material. Destinations (including pupillages) of graduates should be included, normally for the previous three years.

6.1.4 On enrolment, every student must be provided with a copy of the course handbook containing, inter alia, staffing list, accommodation and learning resources (dedicated and shared) , the course structure, course timetable, assessment timetable, course regulations, assessment regulations, equality policy and appeals procedure.

6.2 **Admissions advice**

The formal admissions requirements must be met before the course commences (see Regulations section B3). Providers should have in place a transparent system for scoring candidates' application to the BPTC. [Examples of good practice can be supplied.]

6.3 **Attendance**

6.3.1 Providers must include within the student charter details of the attendance requirement that sets out what is expected of students. This must make clear the interactive and participative demands of the course and, in this respect, their obligations to the learning experience of their fellow students. See Attendance Rule section B4.11.3.

6.3.2 Each applicant must be made aware of the Bar Standards Board's attendance requirement and each student must agree to abide by that requirement. The attendance requirement must state that full attendance on the course is expected but that, with reasons acceptable for the purposes of any internal mitigating circumstances procedure, the student may be absent for up to 10% of classes or other timetabled activities. Students who fall between 80%-89% attendance may exceptionally be allowed these absences, where there are documented medical or other circumstances and missed work has been made up. A student falling below 80% attendance should be failed on the basis that it is not possible to meet the learning outcomes or to demonstrate that they have been met through assessment (B4.11.3).

6.3.3 Students who fall below the attendance requirement for reasons that would not normally be accepted as mitigating circumstances should be considered on an individual basis and warned accordingly if they are at risk of failure due to non attendance. Such activities as attending minipupillages, Moots, events of Inns of Court, pro bono work, pupillage interviews etc may be allowed as mitigating circumstances if in moderation (see B4.11.3.3).

6.4 **Academic advice**

Students must have a designated tutor for academic advice, and must be provided as appropriate with advice and guidance on:

- study skills (note taking, essay writing etc);
- examinations technique;
- correct forms of referencing;
- contacting staff;
- withdrawal, deferral;
- appeals.

6.5 **Pastoral support**

Provision must be made for student counselling services. Each student must have access to a counsellor for pastoral purposes if needed (this may be the same as for academic support).

6.6 **Support Services for Disabled Students**

Procedures must be put in place to identify and evaluate the support requirements of any disabled student. Prior to enrolment, the Provider must agree a learning contract with any student that may require specialised learning support services, and with disabled students requiring reasonable adjustments. Such contracts must set out the duties and obligations of both the Provider and the student concerned.

6.7 **Student services, including Students Union**

Students must have access to the normal range of recreational and social facilities appropriate for those undertaking postgraduate study. Access to formal advice outside of the Provider's counselling services (such as a Student Union would supply in the event of academic offences, complaints or disciplinary procedures) should also be made available.

6.8 **Careers**

A careers service must be provided to students studying on the BPTC, making them aware od opportunities and means for progression at the Bar, and elsewhere.

6.9 **Work Based Learning – placements and Pro Bono**

Opportunities for placements, for example Pro Bono work, must be made available to students (see also A2.4.3 and A2.3.13).

6.10 **Student involvement in Quality Assurance**

Provision must be made to collect students' views on the course through questionnaires and for student representation on the course committee or similar body. There must be student involvement in Quality Assurance Processes, including:

- representation on committees;
- opportunities to provide formal and informal feedback on the course and/or aspects of it;
- use of student questionnaires.

6.11 **Health and Safety**

There must be adherence to all standard Health and Safety requirements, according to the legal requirements for educational institutions.

Part B – Academic Regulations

[2.8]

Note: The BPTC is governed by the Bar Training Regulations as approved on 1 September 2012 (which supersede the previous Consolidated Regulations of the Inns of Court and General Council of the Bar). Sections of the Bar Training Regulations relevant to the BPTC are included as Appendix A. The material which follows below summarises and supplements those regulations. The making of an application by a Provider, or of enrolment on an approved course by a student, implies acceptance of these regulations.

B1 General Regulations for the BPTC

1.1 **Overall standard**

The Bar Professional Training Course must be designed and delivered in accordance with the BPTC specification, to the level as defined in A2.1.4 above. The BPTC must be delivered as a discrete course, and students must not be co-taught with others on different programmes with different study aims.

1.2 **Academic awards and professional qualifications**

Accreditation for the award of the professional qualification is the responsibility of the Bar Standards Board as regulator. The requirements for the BPTC are specified as a means of determining both the level and duration of the course, but the granting of an academic award within the Framework for Higher Education Qualifications is within the remit of the awarding institution (or University) with Degree Awarding Powers. It is expected that the course will be delivered at postgraduate level.

It is anticipated that only very exceptionally would a candidate attain the academic award but not the professional qualification, for example where a disciplinary matter resulted in expulsion from Inn membership.

1.3 **Credit framework**

In addition to the professional qualification, Providers may wish to deliver the course in such a way as to be recognised as a postgraduate diploma, equivalent to 120 CATS credits at postgraduate level (Level M or level 7, formerly known as level 4) according to the QAA Framework for Higher Education Qualifications. The facility to 'top up' such an award to a Master's degree (180 credits) following suitable additional study is similarly outside the remit of the BSB, but is viewed positively. It is of interest to the BSB to know whether such an option is offered, even though there will be no BSB involvement in the validation of the academic award.

An 'exempting degree' may combine the academic stage of training with the BPTC.

1.4 **Duration of course**

1.4.1 The course shall begin no earlier than the third full week of September each year in accordance with normal arrangements for the academic year at the providing HEI. It must be of at least 30 weeks' duration, excluding vacations. The course may be delivered in any of the three following modes:

- Full-time over one academic year.
- Part-time over two academic years.
- Integrated as an extension to a qualifying law degree, to a total of 4 academic years.

1.4.2 Providers must demonstrate a minimum notional study time of 1200 hours, i.e. 3 x 10 week terms or 2 x 15 week semesters. The course must commence not earlier than the third week of September each year, in order to fit in with the normal pattern of the Academic Year. "Notional study time" includes all scheduled lessons and associated course activity, placement days or weeks, revision time and assessments, and private study time calculated as appropriate to the task for which the student is preparing.

1.5 **Structure of the course**

1.5.1 It is expected that teaching on the full-time and integrated degree modes will take place on at least four out of five days of the working week.

1.5.2 The course must be structured so as to ensure the completion of the 'inductiom' components of the course at an early stage (e g guidance on legal research methods).

1.5.3 The 'knowledge areas' of Civil Litigation and Criminal Litigation should also be 'front loaded' on the course, and may be delivered in supported or online mode, if justified and approved at validation. Knowledge areas should not, however, be taught in isolation. The focus in the latter part of the course should be on the skills elements with, in particular, a significant proportion allocated to the teaching of skills, particularly Advocacy. The options may be taught in the final phase or term. There must be a significant proportion of final assessment in the last weeks of the course, in order to take into account the 'exit velocity' of students.

B2 Regulations for Approval, Monitoring and Review

NB this section covers the regulatory aspects of approval, monitoring and review. Details of procedures are included in Section C of this handbook.

2.1 **Regulations for the approval of courses**

[this section should be read in conjunction with the procedures in Part C2]

2.1.1 Approval of new Bar Professional Training Courses

All new courses must be approved both internally by the University/Provider and externally by the Bar Standards Board. Accreditation by the BSB will ensure that: the course is consistent with the BSB's mission and objectives; it meets the BSB's requirements; standards are appropriate to the professional qualification; the documentation is in accordance with requirements; the resources (staffing, library and IT) are satisfactory; and the quality and standards of teaching are maintained and will be enhanced where possible.

2.1.2 Changes to approved courses and approval of new modules/options

Changes to existing provision will also be subject to approval, the level of scrutiny being dependent on the amount and nature of the change. All individual new units/modules or components of courses leading to the BPTC qualification must be approved internally by the University/Provider in accordance with internal approval processes. The level of scrutiny by the BSB will depend on the nature of the new proposal and/or additions or changes to the existing course.

- ***Minor modifications***, such as updating of bibliographies, timing of assessments or, other small changes not affecting the aims and outcomes of the course may be made without affecting its accreditation. Such changes should be dealt with through the normal internal monitoring processes.

- ***Significant changes***, such as changes in assessment methods or weightings, addition or subtraction of units, or changes that may affect the aims and objectives of the course must be notified to the BSB, accompanied by evidence of internal approval through the Provider's own mechanisms. This process must be completed before the change is implemented. Approval cannot be granted retrospectively.
- ***Major changes***, such as major content or structural changes, significant increase in numbers, the addition of a part-time mode, delivery on an alternative or additional site, or a collaborative arrangement of any kind will require re-accreditation. Part-time courses will only be approved where the Provider already delivers the course full time. 'Serial franchising' of the course (i e delegation to a third party) will not be permitted.

2.1.3 Requirements for accreditation

A proposal will only be accepted by the BSB if it conforms to all BSB regulations and procedures. The process of accreditation will be based on consideration of the rationale, aims and objectives of the course, a review or critical appraisal of any former, existing or related provision, scrutiny of available documentation, and a visit by a panel to consider the proposal, after which a report will be produced. Where advanced information or advertising of a proposed course is undertaken, where this is not approved first, the course must be advertised as 'subject to accreditation'. Costs of accreditation visits will be met by the Provider.

2.1.4 Time limits for approval

Courses will normally be accredited for three years in the first instance, after which review and/or reaccreditation must take place. Continued approval will always be subject to satisfactory monitoring of the course. A shorter period of approval or limit to the number of intakes may be imposed if concerns are identified.

2.1.5 Conditional approval

Approval may be subject to certain conditions being met. All conditions must be fulfilled, and confirmed by the BSB as having been fulfilled satisfactorily before delivery of the course can commence.

2.1.6 Infringement of conditions and 'triggered' visits

Where conditions have not been met, or where there is infringement of conditions (e g student numbers, unacceptable operation of Examination Boards), then it is possible that an additional procedure, such as a special visit, may take place as necessary. Costs of such visits will be met by the Provider.

2.1.7 Appeals against accreditation decisions

In the event of a proposal not being approved by the BSB, further discussion should take place between the potential Provider that has made the appeal, and the Chair of the BSB, the Chair of the Education & Training Committee and members of the accreditation panel. The decision of the BSB will be final.

2.1.8 Withdrawal of approval/course closure

Withdrawal of approval of a course may occur if there is evidence that it no longer meets minimum standards required or is no longer viable (for example if it no longer forms part of the strategic or business plan of the Provider). Withdrawal/termination of a course may also be instigated by a Provider that decides to close a course for similar reasons. In no case will approval be withdrawn without discussion with the Provider and those concerned. Where a course closes, then special care must be taken of students on the course and support provided so they can finish their studies as appropriate. This may mean assistance with arrangements to complete the course elsewhere, or possibly financial compensation by the Provider. The care and support of any students on the course to be closed should always be a primary consideration.

2.1.9 Information requirements for accreditation

Documentation must be provided according to the guidance in Part C2. BSB requirements are designed to align with internal requirements so as to avoid repetition and/or duplication of effort. A self evaluation or review of former or related provision will need to be produced specially, as well as the rationale as to why a licence should be granted to deliver the BPTC, and accreditation given to the course specified. In summary, the formal submission must include the specification for the course (and title of any award), the aims and objectives; details of how the course framework is to be structured, delivered and assessed; the resources available; and the duration and mode of study. For details see Part C2.

2.1.10 Courses delivered on additional sites

Courses delivered on secondary sites will require special scrutiny, including a site visit (see procedures in section C2.9.1).

2.1.11 Courses offered in partnership with other institutions

Courses delivered through collaborative partnerships will require special scrutiny including a site visit and discussion of the management and quality assurance relations and structures at the partner institutions, and the mechanisms for oversight of the course by the HEI (see procedures in section C2.9.1).

2.2 **Regulations for the monitoring and review of courses**

[this section should be read in conjunction with the procedures in Part C3]

2.2.1 Internal monitoring

All courses must be subject to extensive internal monitoring on an annual basis. Providers will also be required to allow free access each year to the course for inspection and review purposes by the Bar Standards Board's Education Standards Department, review/visiting panels and External Examiners. The Annual Monitoring process by Providers must be based on rigorous self-critical analysis of the previous year's performance, to be carried out following the completion of the academic year (in line also with QAA guidance). Consideration should be given to individual units, as well as the course as a whole. Pass and progression rates of students, and feedback from students, employers and other stakeholders should also be taken into account. An Annual Monitoring Report (AMR) must be drawn up, including an action plan to address areas in need of improvement. AMRs must be carefully considered and discussed according to Providers' internal systems in time for submission to the BSB by 30 November of each academic year.

2.2.2 Monitoring/review by the BSB

In addition to the internal annual monitoring process, all courses will be subject to monitoring/review by the BSB. This may take the form of either regular monitoring visits (generally one day) or triggered visits (where a cause for concern has been identified.

Reviews are used to ensure that provision is up to date, fit for purpose and well resourced –and to consider the cumulative effect of the internal annual monitoring process over a period of time. The monitoring process is based on the provision of a self-critical analysis, with accompanying documentation, to be considered and discussed at an event with a monitoring panel involving both internal and external assessors and subject specialists. For guidance on procedures see Part C3.

B3 Admission Regulations

[NB see Appendix A, with the relevant extract of the Bar Training Regulations]

3.1 **Entry requirements (principles)**

3.1.1 **The BPTC Provider and the Bar Standards Board**: The admission of an individual applicant to the Bar Professional Training Course is managed by the BPTC Provider but subject to fulfilment of the entry requirements to the BPTC as required by the Bar Standards Board, and there being a presumption that the applicant will be able to complete the course successfully and have the potential to progress eventually to practise at the Bar.

3.1.2 **BPTC Online System**: Applications to the BPTC must be made via the BPTC Online clearing system.

3.1.3 **Minimum Requirements for Admission**: Providers must abide by the minimum requirements for admission to the BPTC, as set down and amended from time to time by the Bar Standards Board.

3.1.4 **Admissions Policy**: Providers must operate an admissions policy that is fair, based on merit, and nondiscriminatoru. Applications from 'non-standard' entrants from all sections of society (regardless of race, gender, disability, age or religion/belief) should be welcomed as long as requirements are met.

3.1.5 Entry requirements are summarised as follows:

- Completion of the Academic Stage (Qualifying Law Degree or non-Law Degree).
- Common Professional Examination /Graduate Diploma in Law).
- Membership of an Inn of Court.
- Proficiency in the English Language.
- A pass in the BPTC Aptitude Test (for entry from September 2013).

3.1.6 **Course Failure**: Students who have failed the course may take it again from the beginning (subject to acceptance on a course by a Provider and the student having passed the BCAT).

3.2 **Entry requirements (details)**

Detailed below are the specified entry requirements for the Bar Professional Training Course.

3.2.1 Completion of the Academic Stage of Training (see Training Regulations)

In order to complete the Academic Stage through a QLD for the purpose of qualifying as a barrister, a student must:

(i) hold a degree that is recognised as a QLD by the Joint Academic Stage Board;

(ii) have been awarded the degree at or above the minimum standard;

(iii) have completed the degree within the designated time-limits;

(iv) have passed all of the foundation subjects at the required level;

(v) not have exceeded the maximum number of attempts at any one foundation subject;

(vi) have completed the whole degree at one institution, or, if not, have done so within the Credit Transfer rules; and

(vii) not have reached the time after which a QLD is considered to be 'stale'.

In order to complete the Academic Stage through the CPE or GDL, a student must:

(i) be eligible to undertake the CPE/GDL in accordance with the rules and regulations of the BSB;

(ii) complete a CPE/GDL course that has been validated by the Joint Academic Stage Board;

(iii) complete the CPE/GDL course within the designated time-limits;

(iv) pass all Foundation subjects plus one other area of legal study, except where exemptions have been granted;

(v) not exceed the maximum number of attempts at any one Foundation subject;

(vi) complete the whole of the CPE/GDL (other than subjects for which exemptions have been granted) at one institution; and

(vii) not have reached the time after which the CPE/GDL is considered to be "stale".

Further details of each of these requirements and the most recent regulations relating to the Academic Stage can be found in the Academic Stage Book at http://www.barstandardsboard.org.uk/qualifying-as-a-barrister/academic-stage/

3.2.2 Membership of an Inn of Court

(a) Before commencing the BPTC, a person must have been admitted to an Inn of Court.

(b) As with the requirement for completion of the Academic Stage of training, the process of obtaining membership of an Inn must similarly be fully completed before commencement of the BPTC. Applications must normally be made by 31 May each year. The process of application for membership of an Inn may take a considerable period of time and a candidate admitted to the Bar Professional Training Course who has not obtained membership of an Inn before the course commences will not be able to enrol or, having enrolled, will be asked to leave (or otherwise not have their BPTC qualification recognised professionally by the BSB).

Inns fees, or a portion thereof, are normally refundable if the candidate wishes for good reason not to apply or take up, or to withdraw from, a place on the BPTC. If the Provider accepts that the fees are properly refundable, Inns admission fees will also normally be refunded.

(c) Where membership of an Inn is withdrawn for disciplinary or other reasons then the student must withdraw from the BPTC with immediate effect. It should be noted that there is currently no requirement for a CRB check for applicants to the BPTC. The Inns of Court currently rely on self declaration. Where a candidate has reason to believe that their application for Inn membership may not be straightforward (e g where they have a criminal conviction that they must declare), the candidate must allow for the extra time that consideration of their case may take and apply to the Inn well in advance of the deadline.

3.2.3 English language requirement

Please always check BSB website for most current information reproduced below: www.barstandardsboard.org.uk/.../2011**_english_language_rule_**updated.doc

(a) One of the entry requirements for the BPTC is that students are fluent in English. Applicants for the BPTC should therefore be able to demonstrate that their oral and written English language ability is at least equivalent to:

(i) a minimum score of 7.5 in each section of the IELTS academic test;

(ii) a minimum score of 28 in each part of the internet based TOEFL test; or

(iii) a minimum score of 73 in each part of the Pearson Test of English (academic).

(b) On entry to the course students will be required to sign a statement that they are aware that this standard is required of all students who enter the BPTC, and that they consider that they have met it. For those with any doubt as to the level of their English skills, they are strongly advised to undertake one of the above tests before enrolling on the course.

(c) Certificates issued by a test provider verifying the score achieved by a candidate in one of the above tests must be current and valid by reference to the rules of that test provider as at the date the candidate commences the BPTC.

(d) Subsequent to being admitted to the BPTC, should the BPTC Provider consider that a student's language ability is unsatisfactory or there is question as to whether any aspect of it is at the required level, the BPTC Provider will require the student to take one of the above language tests at any stage in the course (at the student's cost) and achieve the required score. This right is unrestricted regardless of the students' first language.

(e) For the avoidance of doubt, those who are required to sit one of the above tests by a BPTC Provider must achieve the requisite score required above for each section or part of the English language test, e.g., a minimum score of 7.5 in each section of the IELTS academic test, a minimum score of 28 in each part of the internet based TOEFL test; or a minimum score of 73 in each part of the Pearson Test of English (academic) **in the same sitting**.

(f) Should the student then fail to achieve a required minimum score in one of the tests specified above, the provider may require the student to:

(i) withdraw from the course; or

(ii) intermit and improve their score prior to being re-admitted to the course in a subsequent year. This will be dependent on how much of the course has been undertaken.

(g) In all cases the student is wholly liable for any costs incurred.

(h) The BSB believes that compliance with one of the standards identified above is the absolute minimum necessary to successfully complete the Bar Professional Training Course.

(i) Note that the Inns of Court and Providers may also impose entry requirements in addition to those requested by the BSB.

3.2.4 BPTC Aptitude Test

As a requirement for entry to the BPTC commencing September 2013, the BSB will require all BPTC applicants to take the Bar Course Aptitude Test (BCAT) and to achieve a pass. The BCAT is administered by Pearson Vue for the BSB; full details can be found here: (weblink) http://www.pearsonvue.co.uk/Pages/default.aspx

NB where any of the above specified entry requirements (3.2.1 – 3.2.4) have not been completed and evidenced in full, any offer letter by a Provider must clearly indicate that the offer is conditional upon the requirements (e.g. revival of stale qualifications) being completed **prior to the commencement of the course**.

3.3 **Admission with 'advanced standing' or AP(E)L**

There is no admission with advanced standing to the BPTC. The course must be undertaken in its entirety. However, exemptions may be granted to those who are, or have been, practising in other jurisdictions (e g overseas) or as solicitors. Such persons may undertake the Bar Transfer Test for entry into pupillage. This is designed for this purpose as a means for qualifying to undertake pupillage (see Training Regulations paragraph 61f.)

3.4 **Study mode and admission requirements**

3.4.1 Mode of study (full-time, part-time, distance learning etc) does not modify the regulations regarding admission. These regulations apply equally and uniformly to full-time and part-time study, to 'conventionally' taught courses and courses delivered through open, flexible, work-based or distance learning.

3.4.2 Students may be allowed to change the mode of study in the light of their changing academic, personal or professional circumstances if the Provider is able to offer the alternative study mode for that course, and if the proposed change is consistent with the aims and outcomes of the BPTC being met in full.

3.5 Changes of course to another Provider

3.5.1 Students may, at the discretion of the Provider, transfer to another Provider subject to:

- the availability of a 'vacant' place on the proposed course, and
- the agreement of the Course Directors of both current and future/proposed courses, and
- the change being proposed at an appropriate stage in the new course, and
- successful resolution of financial matters.

3.5.2 Sufficient time must remain between the agreement of the change and entry to the new course for the student to be able to fulfil the learning objectives according to the proposed new course, and to demonstrate that they have been fulfilled. The Inn of which the student is a member must be informed.

3.6 **Authentication of entry qualifications**

3.6.1 The Provider must seek evidence of personal, professional and educational experiences that indicate ability to meet the demands of the course. Students are required to provide proof that they hold the qualifications that they claim in seeking admission to a given course of study. Such documentation must be verified by Providers.

3.6.2 Any student who:

- does not comply with any reasonable request to provide such proof;
- makes a false claim in respect of application for admission;
- presents false or fraudulent evidence of qualifications; or
- engages another person to impersonate him or her, or themselves impersonates another person in connection with an application for admission or in providing evidence of qualifications

is liable to exclusion. The facts must be reported to the relevant Inn of Court in every such case, in order for the Inn to assess whether the candidate is a fit and proper person to practise as a barrister.

3.7 **Interviewing of prospective students**

The interviewing of prospective candidates, in order to determine suitability, is considered by the BSB as desirable, but it is not a requirement. Especially where there are more applicants than places, Providers may devise and apply additional selection criteria.

3.8 **Securing pupillage before commencing the BPTC**

The securing of pupillage before undertaking the BPTC is considered by the BSB as desirable but is not a requirement. [It should be noted that, due to changes made by the SRA, holders of the BVC/BPTC will not be entitled in the future to take the Qualified Lawyers Transfer Test (QLTT) to qualify as solicitors. The exemption previously allowed to holders of the BVC will no longer apply, since Call to the Bar does not indicate qualified lawyer/ entitlement to practice status].

3.9 **Students with disabilities**

In terms of the Equality Act 2010 and other relevant legislation 'reasonable adjustment' should be made for candidates with disabilities, including adjustments for assessment. The BSB should be consulted where there are any special difficulties. Disabled students should be advised of any difficulties they may face, given the content and nature of the course. Note also that in certain circumstances it may possibly not be in a student's best interests to undertake the course.

3.10 **Registration information (as required by BSB and Inns of Court)**

3.10.1 It is a requirement of the Bar Standards Board and the Inns of Court that a student may not enrol on the BPTC unless he or she is a member of an Inn of Court. Consequently, both the Inns and Bar Standards Board request that the data is provided to both parties simultaneously according to the agreed Protocol set out below. This data will be used in conjunction with the BSB Register of the profession.

3.10.2 A draft list of all students who have enrolled must be provided within 10 working days of the start of term. A final list of all students who have enrolled on the course indicating any students who have since left the course should be provided by 15 October or the next working day. Where a course does not commence until after this date, then information must be provided within 10 working days of the commencement of term.

3.10.3 Each list must present students in alphabetical order by surname, and should include all first and middle names together with a gender and/or professional title (Mr, Ms, Dr etc), and the Inn of Court of which he/she is a member. An indication of whether the student is home or overseas domiciled should be given. The details must be provided in electronic form in a table in Excel. Information required: Surname, first/second names, Inn, Mode of study, home/overseas:

Surname	First name	Second name	Title	Inn	Mode of study	Home/ overseas	Additional notes
Smith	Philip	John	Mr	Middle Temple	PT	O/S	
Brown	Samantha		Ms	Lincoln's Inn	FT	H/S	Joined Inn 2002
Mohammed	Ali	Ahmed	Prof	Gray's Inn	FT	H/S	

3.10.4 Any student who leaves the BPTC after the October list has been issued must be notified to the relevant Inn of Court and Bar Standards Board as and when they leave.

This requirement may be amended slightly according to a development of the BPTC Online system, but this cannot be confirmed at the time this Handbook went to print.

B4 Assessment Regulations for the BPTC

4.1 General principles

4.1.1 The purpose of assessment is to allow students to demonstrate that they have fulfilled the course objectives (and achieved the standard required for the award).

4.1.2 The process of assessment must be clear, precise, valid and reliable.

4.1.3 Assessment must be carried out with rigour and fairness by examiners who are impartial, and who are competent to make judgments about the performance of individual students in relation both to the cohort and to students on other comparable courses. The particular role of the examiners is to ensure that the standard of the course is maintained and that each individual student receives fair treatment.

4.1.4 Each individual course will have its own description and assessment requirements, within the specified framework. Students must be informed at the commencement of the course of the material covered within each course and its assessment requirements (both formative and summative), including weightings.

4.1.5 The medium of assessment shall be in English. Written assessments may be provided in Welsh if requested by candidates. The requirements of the Welsh Language Act are recognised but candidates who can only satisfy the assessment requirements in Welsh will not be competent to practise at the Bar of England and Wales.

4.1.6 Assessment of the BPTC must include an element of formal time-constrained examinations. Any instances of where this may not be appropriate for a particular candidate must be discussed with the BSB.

4.1.7 The maximum proportion of MCTs permitted for the assessment of any individual course (including those assessed centrally) is 50%. The maximum proportion of MCTs permitted for the assessment of the BPTC as a whole is 40%.

4.1.8 Provision will be made for centrally set final examinations in Civil Litigation, Criminal Litigation and Professional Ethics for candidates first enrolled on course from Academic Year 2011–12. This will be compulsory for all BPTC students.

4.2 Processes

4.2.1 Detailed arrangements must be specified for the operation of the assessment process, including the scheduling and amount of assessment, security, first and second marking, and moderation and arrangements for Examination Boards.

4.2.2 Assessment grades must be recorded accurately and systematically by suitably trained academic and/or administrative staff, with arrangements made for the aggregation of marks and grades. Students' achievement must be recorded and their progress monitored for the duration of the course, including notification of failure of components and/or their being at risk of failing the course (for example through non adherence to the attendance rule, see B4.11.3).

4.2.3 Decisions (ie provisional grades for in-course assessment) should be notified to students as soon as possible after assessments, but it should be noted that all grades are provisional until moderated by External Examiners and confirmed at Examination Boards. End of course assessment grades and final overall course grades must not be notified to students until they have been confirmed at the final Examination Board with External Examiners present.

4.2.4 It must be made clear to students where assessment is summative (ie the marks will count towards the grading of the final award) or where it is 'formative' only. Appropriate feedback must be provided to students on their assessment, so as to promote learning and ensure improvement.

4.2.5 All staff involved in assessment must receive appropriate training and development, for example mentoring for new staff, or practitioner staff new to teaching, and ongoing staff development for others.

4.2.6 Anonymity of assessment should be in place where practicable (eg for examinations).

4.2.7 Oral examinations should be used for the skills areas as appropriate.

4.2.8 Provision must be made for retrieval of initial failure where appropriate. One opportunity to re-sit each failed assessment is allowed in any subject, regardless of and not subject to any minimum grade being achieved on the remainder of the course. Where there are documented and accepted mitigating circumstances, a re-sit examination may be taken as 'first sit' and thus not count as the single permitted re-sit opportunity. Candidates who fail 50% or more of the course (by weighting rather than by number of modules) on first sitting may forfeit the right to be referred, that is they will be recorded as a fail. This must be confirmed at the Examination Board when BSB external Examiners are present).

4.3 **Assessment details**

Details of assessment must be provided and must:

(1) state the overall basis on which students will be assessed in relation to the overarching aims and intended outcomes of the course and in accordance with the assessment framework (A2.1.3);

(2) state the specific requirements for individual assessments as they occur at different points in the course (with criteria for the marking and grading of assessments A2.1.5);

(3) provide an appropriate balance between course work, practical work and formal examinations. It may be specified that all components of an assessment must be passed to demonstrate that all outcomes have been met;

(4) specify which assessments are formative only; that is the grades do not count in the overall grade for the course, for example in mock and practice assessments;

(5) adhere to regulations concerning the drafting of questions and assignments;

(6) adhere to the criteria for the recommendation of the qualification/ level of qualification (eg Outstanding/Very Competent/Competent/ Not Competent);

(7) make clear to students that no compensation for failure in assessment is permitted;

(8) provide details concerning how initial failure may be made good (including the limit to the number of attempts at re-sit to one only – unless there are documented and accepted mitigating circumstances).

4.4 **Responsibilities of students**

4.4.1 Students must make themselves available for examination and assessment, and present their work as required by the Provider.

4.4.2 Where a student fails to attend an examination or to submit work on time without good reason (supported by evidence, eg a medical certificate) then the student will be deemed to have failed that assessment.

4.4.3 Work must be legible and comprehensible and word processed or written in ink.

4.4.4 Students must provide details of any special circumstances which may affect their work (such as Mitigating Circumstances, see B4.11.5 below). These must be communicated as soon as possible and normally in advance of the date of the examination, or due date for coursework. Special circumstances may not subsequently be invoked as 'insurance claims' following poor performance, nor as excuses for academic offences. Long standing conditions are dealt with separately (see B4.11.6.2). Providers have local protocols for dealing with Mitigating Circumstances.

4.4.5 If students are found to have cheated or attempted to gain an unfair advantage then they may be deemed to have failed in terms of the academic offences procedure (see B6 below), and a decision may be taken as to whether the student may be reassessed and/or continue with their studies. Where a student is found to have cheated or behaved improperly in any assessment, that fact must be reported to the relevant Inn as soon as it is known to the Provider. The student must report the matter in his or her Call declaration (Training Regulations paragraph 4), but if it is left until the student identifies it in the Call declaration, for practical purposes that is too late for the Inn to take effective action before the scheduled Call date. The inns must be in a position to decide on a person's fitness for Call.

4.4.6 The Provider is responsible for making information accessible to students regarding the timing, nature and location of assessment/reassessment but responsibility to attend lies with the student.

4.5 **Examinations**

4.5.1 Timing and location of examinations

Students are required to attend for examinations and other assessments in locations specified by the Provider. The time and place of formal time-constrained examinations must be specified in advance by the Provider, giving due warning to candidates. A calendar of examinations must be drawn up and published to students well in advance. An accurate register of students eligible to take the examination must be made. Where a disabled student has particular access needs in relation to an assessment centre, it is the responsibility of the provider to ensure that locations are accessible for such students.

4.5.2 Format and duration of examinations

Examinations may take a variety of forms, which may include permitting access to specified equipment or material (i e 'seen' or 'unseen' examinations). The kind of examination, and also the duration, must have been approved at validation and should not be varied (unless the change is notified to the BSB and approved). The length of an examination may vary. Some forms of examinations (e g Multiple Choice) may be shorter in duration. Centrally set examinations will be managed by the BSB.

4.5.3 Drafting of course work and examination papers

Tutors with responsibility for specified areas of the course must finalise examination and assignment questions anticipating the time required for internal checking and moderating as well as review by External Examiners. Papers must undergo internal checking and moderating to ensure that questions are clear and unambiguous, that they are a valid means of assessing that outcomes have been met, that they are properly edited and that external advice is sought if needed. The same assessment questions must not be reused within a three-year period. All assessments must be approved by External Examiners. Papers must then be kept in a secure place until required, for secure delivery to the place of the examination. Questions for examinations and referral or re-sit examinations must be drafted at the same time and must be similar (to ensure fairness) but not repeated/identical.

4.5.4 Conduct of examinations

Examinations must be carried out in accordance with institutional procedures that adhere to the QAA UK Quality Code for Higher Education, Chapter B6, on the assessment of students. (Institutions must ensure that assessment is conducted with rigour, probity and fairness and with due regard for security.) Examinations should be invigilated by members of staff who must be made aware of their responsibilities and provided with appropriate guidance on how to ensure that necessary arrangements are made, check attendance lists, 'patrol' from time to time, and deal with irregularities, e.g. late arrivals etc. Invigilators must be able and alert to detect the use of any unfair means or cheating. Examinations for centrally set subjects will follow similar protocols and maybe subject to specific arrangements as determined by the BSB.

4.5.5 Cheating in examinations

If a student is suspected of cheating in an examination (e g using notes, overlooking etc) then the invigilator should, acting according to institutional guidance, move the student and/or remove the material in question, sign the script at the point, note the time and details on the report, but allow the candidate to continue. Students suspected of communicating should first be warned and the moved if the situation recurs, with the time noted. If cheating or indiscipline of any kind disturbs other students then the offender should be removed from the room. Such incidents must be reported to the relevant Inn as appropriate (see B6 below).

4.6 **Marking and moderation of examinations and coursework**

4.6.1 When submitting work for assessment, students are expected to comply with instructions, including the assessment criteria set for module assessments. They should also take cognisance of the generic grading descriptors (A2.1.5). If candidates do not comply with instructions, e.g., by exceeding the word limit, then a penalty may be imposed. Work submitted late without special permission due to Extenuating Circumstances (applied for in advance) should not normally be marked. An extension should not be granted beyond the time when work is due to be returned to other students.

4.6.2 Moderation of marks (ie by other internal examiners) is not necessary for every single piece of assessed work. However, work should be sampled by a second internal marker, who should pay particular attention to the top and bottom ends of the scale, and borderlines. This should preferably take place with the second internal marker unaware of the grade awarded by the first marker. If serious disagreement occurs between internal markers then a third marker may be consulted. The External Examiner, appointed by the BSB, may be consulted but may not act as a third marker. An External Examiner's view on academic judgement is final.

4.6.3 Coursework scripts should be annotated with feedback to students (indicating errors, highlighting areas for improvement and showing how this may be achieved) and returned within three weeks. Since examination scripts are not returned to students there is no need for formative feedback. However an indication of the reason for a high/low mark can be helpful for the external examiner or moderator.

4.6.4 Oral presentations can be double marked by appropriate sampling, by a second marker in attendance, or by the use of video/DVD. Examination scripts have no formative function and are therefore not returned to students.

4.6.5 Samples/copies of both course work and examination papers (top/middle/bottom and borderline) should be retained for 3 years in case they are needed for scrutiny by BSB External Examiners. Examination papers should be retained and made accessible to students for reference purposes, except for case studies that are reused. Students should be advised to retain work at least until they have been assessed for the qualifications.

4.6.6 Sections 4.6.1–4.6.5 above are only applicable to the marking and moderation of noncentralised examinations and coursework.

4.7 Examination boards

4.7.1 Appointment

A board of examiners (Board or Examinations Board) must be appointed for every BPTC Provider in order to ensure fairness to students. The Board must be chaired by a senior academic who is not involved with the BPTC or responsible for delivery of the course and must include the director/leader responsible for the course itself. It should also if possible include a representative of the Provider's academic quality unit/department. The board must include at least one BSB appointed External Examiner, without which it will not be regarded as quorate by the BSB. An administrator or secretary must be present to record the final grades and awards.

4.7.2 Consideration of results

The BSB gives no discretion to the boards of examiners to amend the grades of students in the llight of circumstances affecting performance (i.e. marks may not be raised as a result of special circumstances) or for any other reason. This is to help achieve consistency between individual Provider Boards, equality of treatment to students at different institutions and to ensure that the principle of the demonstration of minimum competence is rigorously observed to protect the public. It follows that no discretion or rounding up is possible, even where there are extenuating circumstances. In addition, there is no reason for rounding up to be allowed simply because the overall mark for the course is finally very marginal. However, for overall grades (not grades of individual assessments), a 'rounding up' of borderline aggregate grades may be permissible (specifically the raising of a 69.95 – 69.99 to 70 and similar for other borderlines).

4.7.3 Release of mark to students

No results may be recommended for conferment of the professional qualification other than by a properly constituted Examinations Board. Hence course work grades may only be released (as provisional) to students after they have been confirmed by External Examiners, and grades of end-of-course assessments or final results must not be released to students until moderated by External Examiners and confirmed at the Examinations Board. The final decision for any professional qualification rests with the BSB.

4.7.4 Individual grades and overall profiles

An Examinations Board is authorised to consider students' individual grades and overall profiles in accordance with the approved assessment regulations for the course (see A2.1.5 for grading of individual assessments and A2.1.6 for overall grades for the course). The qualification will be awarded to candidates who in the judgment of the Examination Board have fulfilled the objectives and achieved the specified standard. Boards must determine the action to be taken where a student fails to complete some or the entire course or where extenuating circumstances have affected a student's performance.

4.7.5 Meetings of Examinations Boards

The appointed secretary to the Examinations Board (working with the Chair of the Board and the course leader/director) is responsible for organising the Board, notifying the date, and providing the following documentation:

- a detailed agenda, including: note of apologies; consideration of minutes of the last meeting; consideration of extenuating circumstances as appropriate; consideration of any applications of the Red Light Rule or the Attendance Rule; approval of results with discussion of borderlines; oral reports of External Examiners on standards and any other issues; date of next meeting;
- the BSB and Provider assessment regulations;
- examination papers and project titles or briefs;
- the marking schemes used;

- the full draft mark sheet showing marks for the course, individual units and individual profiles of each student;
- information about how sample and double marking and moderating was carried out;
- an analysis of the statistics;
- any additional information, for example any extenuating circumstances or any examination or invigilation irregularities.

4.8 **External examiners**

4.8.1 Principles

(1) The BSB appoints (and pays for) External Examiners who are involved with both quality (monitoring of provision) and standards (as set and attained by students). The system of External Examiners should operate broadly in accordance with The UK Quality Code for Higher Education Chapter B7: External examining and *Higher Education Academy: A Handbook for External Examining.*

(2) External Examiners are appointed to each individual subject area at each Provider, the number appointed being proportional to the numbers of students on the course or in a specific subject area. The view of the majority of the External Examiners shall prevail on any matters of principle at an Examination Board.

(3) BSB appointed External Examiners may also be used by institutions to fulfil QAA requirements for External Examining and the verification of their academic awards. This is not, however, of direct concern to the BSB.

4.8.2 Rights and responsibilities of External Examiners

The primary responsibilities of External Examiners are:

- to ensure that the objectives of the BPTC are met;
- to verify that the standards of the BPTC, as indicated by students' attainment in assessment, have been set and maintained at the correct level by Providers;
- to ensure that the appropriate assessment regulations are correctly followed;
- to ensure that justice is done to all students; and
- to act as members of Examination Boards.

In order to carry out these responsibilities, the External Examiners for the BPTC must, individually or collectively:

(1) be able to judge students impartially on the basis of the work submitted for assessment without being influenced by previous association with the course, the staff or any of the students;

(2) be competent in assessing students' knowledge and skills at higher education level, expert in the field of study concerned, impartial in judgment and able to calibrate the performance of students with that of their peers on other BPTC courses;

(3) approve the form and content of proposed assessment tasks that count

towards the qualification. External Examiners will normally approve all proposed assessments (ie examination papers as well as coursework and other, eg oral, assessments) before implementation. This is in order to ensure that all students will be assessed against the aims and objectives of the course syllabus and have reached the required standard;

(4) scrutinise the work done by a sample of students (including Outstandings, borderlines and failures), in order to ensure that the students are correctly placed in relation to the national standards of the BPTC. It may be necessary for examiners to see a sample of referral work to ensure the equivalence of standards of marking (ie that re-sits are not graded more leniently).

Referral work is marked as pass/fail only, the grade being capped at a bare pass.

(5) have the right to moderate the marks awarded by internal examiners, and adjust the overall range of grades if warranted. Examiners moderate, they do not mark, and hence should not adjust individual grades but rather ensure that, where marking is too strict or too generous, the whole cohort will be adjusted accordingly.

(6) attend the meeting of the Board of Examiners, ensuring that recommendations have been reached according to the BPTC requirements and participating as required in any reviews of decisions about individual students' performance.

(7) report back to the Provider and to the BSB on the effectiveness of the assessments and any lessons to be drawn from them (see External Examiner Interim Report pro-forma at Appendix B and Final Report pro-forma at Appendix C).

(8) report immediately to the Head of Education Standards at the BSB on any matters of serious concern arising from the assessments which might put at risk the standard of the BPTC.

(9) External Examiners are responsible for considering and having the final ruling in consultation with the BSB, if needed, on any case where the 'Red Light Rule' is put into practice (see B 4.11.2).

(10) External Examiners are responsible for considering and having the final ruling in consultation with the BSB, if needed, on any case where the 'Attendance Rule' is put into practice (see B 4.11.3).

(11) The External Examiner must plan their duties with the Provider around their own commitments and workloads so that they are able to manage the role on behalf of the BSB.

(12) All Boards of Examiners must be organised in accordance with the QAA UK Quality Code for Higher Education Chapter B6: Assessment of students. See also Understanding assessment: its role in safeguarding academic standards and quality in higher education, Second edition, published by the QAA (September 2012). A formal agenda, plus the course assessment regulations, marking scheme used by the internal examiners, and the full draft mark sheet including a profile of the marks awarded to each student in each piece of assessed work (both final marks and marks for each question) must be

provided for the External Examiner. Analysis of the mean and standard deviation of the marks in each assessment and any recommendations on decisions should also be available.

External Examiners for areas with centrally set examinations.

Examiners for:

- Civil Litigation, Evidence and Remedies
- Criminal Litigation, Evidence and Sentencing
- Professional Ethics

have slightly adjusted roles in that they will not be involved in the approval of draft papers or in confirming the final marks for the subject areas, as these functions will be performed by the Central Examination Board (CEB). They will however perform a vital function in moderating local marking of SAQs and in alerting the CEB to any issues that may merit their special attention.

4.8.3 The appointment of External Examiners

(1) All External Examiner appointments must be approved by the BPTC Sub-Committee. Responsibility for nominations for examiners lies with the Education Department of the BSB but may be determined in consultation with Providers. A board of examiners which does not include an approved External Examiner is not authorised to assess students for the BPTC or to recommend the attainment of the professional qualification.

(2) External Examiner nominations must be submitted (via a self-nomination form and a current curriculum vitae) to the BSB Education & Training Department for the approval procedure so that they may be appointed before the start of the academic year in time to take up their duties. Appointments will be made using the criteria below (B4.8.4). All examiners who moderate Advocacy must be ATC accredited. An examiner's normal term of office will be one which allows the examiner to be involved in the assessment of four successive cohorts of full time students (normally 4 years), extendable for one more year.

(3) External Examiners should not normally hold more than the equivalent of two substantial examining appointments at the same time including appointments other than for the BPTC (see below, criteria for appointment).

(4) In order to maintain their independence, External Examiners should not concurrently act as consultants to the Course team on its design, or be members of a panel established to review the course they examine. However, they are encouraged to support course teams by identifying areas for enhancement and improvement. External Examiners should not have had any significant connection within the last five years with the institution where they are to examine.

(5) The Course Director at each Provider must make arrangements for new External Examiners to be briefed as soon as possible after appointment. Each External Examiner should receive the necessary

material including the Course Specification Requirements and Guidance (BPTC Handbook), the Provider's definitive document (including staff roles and responsibilities) or student handbook plus supplementary material; relevant teaching materials; a copy of the assessment regulations and assessment schedule for the course, including the dates when scripts will be available for scrutiny and the dates set for meetings of the Board of Examiners. Briefing of External Examiners should include the provision of previous External Examiner reports and statistical material on the performance of the cohorts for which the examiner has responsibility (see Appendix D for External Examiner schedule and checklist).

(6) An agreement will be made between the BSB and each External Examiner, specifying the subjects or units for which he/she is to be responsible. The BSB has designed the external examiner fee to take into account a variety of factors such as, core or optional subjects, centrally set assessments, size of the Provider and the number of sites. All external examiners will be notified of the final fee in the contract. The BSB shall have the right to terminate the appointment of an external examiner at any time and with good reason. An external examiner who wishes to resign their appointment must give the BSB three months' notice in writing.

(7) All summative assessment questions must be sent to External Examiners in advance for approval. This includes formal examinations (with the exception of the centrally set examinations), course work and details of oral assessments.

4.8.4 Criteria for Appointment

(1) External Examiners for the BPTC must:

- have relevant knowledge and experience of the area of the course for which he/she is appointed as examiner;
- have previous experience of assessing students on the BPTC and/or;
- have professional expertise in the subject area for which they are examiner;
- maintain their independence from the Provider and course team;
- not hold more than one other External Examinership in another higher education institution;
- be familiar with the practices established in the higher education community of the UK;
- have appropriate practitioner experience;
- be impartial in judgment and not have previous close involvement with the Provider or its staff which might compromise objectivity.

* For those External Examiners who work directly at another Provider and teach on the BPTC, the issue of the perception of impartiality and independence must be demonstrated with a high level of professionalism and integrity. Providers should not recommend any colleague for an External

Examiner role with whom they have previously been connected. The independence of the External Examiner role is crucial for the maintenance of the quality assurance process. Any staff member who feels that their independence may be compromised should inform the BSB.

Where an External Examiner is appointed who is employed in professional practice but is not directly familiar with higher education, then such experience must be present amongst the External Examiner team as a whole appointed to the course.

For additional guidance on the criteria for appointing External Examiners for the BPTC, reference should be made to the UK Quality Code for Higher Education Chapter B7: External examining and *Higher Education Academy: A Handbook for External Examining*.

(2) To ensure independence of External Examiners, there should not be:

- more than one examiner from the same institution in the team of External Examiners;
- reciprocal external examining between BPTC courses;
- replacement of a retiring External Examiner by another from the same institution.

4.8.5 External Examiners' reports

(1) External Examiners are required to submit two reports annually by 28 February and 31 August respectively, to the Education Department of the BSB. Receipt of each report (for which pro-formas are available at Appendix B and C) is a necessary pre-condition for payment of the examiner's fee. In these reports, the External Examiner should report on the conduct of the assessments just concluded and on issues related to assessment, including:

- the overall performance of the students;
- the strengths and weaknesses of students;
- the quality of knowledge and skills (both general and subject specific) demonstrated by the students;
- the structure, organisation, design and marking of all assessments;
- the quality of teaching;
- any implications which the experience of conducting the assessments may have for the curriculum, syllabus, teaching methods and resources of the course;
- any other recommendations arising from the assessments.

(2) The purpose of the report is to enable the BSB to judge whether the course is meeting its stated objectives and to satisfy itself that any necessary improvements are made, either immediately or at the next review as appropriate.

(3) A report will be made annually to the Education & Training Committee (via the BPTC Sub-Committee) on the issues raised by the External Examiners in their reports, highlighting in particular any common matters of concern and any examples of good or bad

practice which warrant institutional attention. Copies of the External Examiners' reports will be supplied to Providers for consideration and a response to each External Examiner's report must be made by the Provider. The reports form an intrinsic part of the annual monitoring processes, and the standing of the course in the eyes of its External Examiners is an important part of the evidence which Providers should consider in evaluating their courses annually. External Examiner reports are also extensively used in the review visits undertaken by the BSB.

(4) Providers must respond in full to each External Examiner's report, copied to the BSB, indicating how any points raised will be addressed; these issues should also be followed up in the Annual Monitoring Report.

4.9 **Decisions of the Examination Board**

Cohort results for centrally set subjects will be confirmed by the CEB before being remitted to Provider Examination Boards where they will be combined with results for other parts of the course to give overall results for individual students.

4.9.1 Finalisation

After the Provider's Board's decisions are finalised the results must be signed off by the Chair. Action must be noted against any decisions for referral or deferrals (where there are extenuating circumstances). The minutes must record all decisions and actions as well as the names of those present, time and date. The list of successful candidates must be notified to the BSB. Under no circumstances should results be given to students until a duly constituted Board of Examiners has confirmed them. Results should be notified to students in writing normally within one week after the Examination Board.

4.9.2 Referrals/deferrals

Referrals or deferrals should be notified and discussion should take place including reference to the means by which failure may be retrieved (if applicable) and how further advice may be sought in order for the student to be considered for eventual completion of the course.

4.10 **Failure, non attempts and reassessment**

4.10.1 General principles

(1) Provision must be made for a student to make good an initial failure (or to demonstrate a competency not yet demonstrated), and a Board of Examiners which decides to refer a student must specify which elements must be retaken and when this reassessment shall take place. A student may be required either:

- to retake an assessment in order to gain a pass in a unit; or
- to retake an entire unit.

(2) Failure in any assessment gives the right to one further opportunity to retake the failed assessment(s). With the exception of ReDOC where the requirement to pass both parts is not specified, if there are two parts to a single assessment then it must be retaken as a whole even if only one part is failed. No aggregation of marks is permitted in assessments based on this principle. A maximum of a total of two

attempts shall therefore be permitted for any single assessment, excepting where documented and accepted extenuating circumstances (see below B4.11.5) have caused an attempt to be assessed 'as if for the first time'. Where the course has been failed due to marginal failure in one resit only [at 57 – 59.9%, or due to failure to pass both sections but with a mark of 57% or above for the subject] or due to a red light fail in one resit only, then one further resit in that failed assessment will be permitted. Since eligibility for such a second resit depends upon the rest of the course having been passed, no candidate may take a second resit in any subject unless and until they have passed all of their subjects.

(3) When a full time candidate commences the BPTC in September of a specific academic year their anticipated completion date is within that academic year. For these purposes an academic year comprises the cycle of first sit assessments and referred or deferred assessments immediately following the first sit assessments. By way of example, a full time candidate who commences in September 2010 would normally complete the course in either July 2011 or September/October 2011. For this candidate the two year time limit would therefore be two year after the end of the 10/11 cycle, i.e. September/October 2013. The time limit for a part time candidate who commences in September 2010 will be three years therefore they should complete the BPTC by September or October 2014). Even in cases where there are documented and accepted extenuating circumstances, the course must be completed within a maximum of two years of the expected completion date [or three years for part time students] (NB in the event of long term illness or disability, a candidate would normally withdraw their registration and suspend study and/or start again ab initio or resume at a specified point.)

(4) Where an assessment has been failed on two occasions, then the candidate shall be recorded as having failed the course. Where there are extenuating circumstances, and a 'first sit' has been allowed, then the number of attempts will be considered accordingly, but no more than two attempts (not affected by extenuating circumstances) will be allowed, excepting in circumstances detailed in 4.10.1.2 above. A candidate who fails the course in its entirety in this way will be permitted subsequently to apply for and retake the course (if the application is successful) *ab initio* at the same or a different Provider.

(5) A student may not retake an assessment in order to improve upon a mark which is already above the pass level.

(6) A student who does not complete referral work by the specified time limit must be assessed as Not Competent.

(7) Opportunities for re-sits should be provided during August/September following the June examinations. Re-sit dates for centrally set subjects take place in August and are specified at the start of each year. **Where an assignment or course is retaken then the mark or grade will be capped at the minimum pass mark**. All attempts must be recorded on the student's transcript.

(8) Candidates passing all elements of the BPTC on first attempt will normally be Called to the Bar in the Trinity (July and October) Call.

Those who have not passed everything on first attempt will normally be Called to the Bar at the Michaelmas Call (November) or later.

(9) Requirements for reassessment must be equivalent (but not the same as) those for the initial assessment.

(10) A student who withdraws, or is required to withdraw, from the course may incur financial loss, but this is a matter between the Provider and the student. Where there are special reasons for withdrawal, e g serious mitigating circumstances, then a student may intermit, and resume study at a later date. It is expected that Providers will be sympathetic to special, serious cases. The BSB should be consulted for advice if necessary.

(11) Whether a Provider will give support to students undertaking re-sits (with or without extra financial charges) must be made clear to students in advance. Resits will normally be undertaken at the Provider location, but they may exceptionally be taken at overseas locations, arranged under the auspices of the local British Council, if notified at least 6 weeks in advance. All additional expenses must be met by the candidates.

(12) If an individual candidate assessment is mislaid, marks cannot be awarded or interpolated, whether on the basis of the candidate academic profile or otherwise.

4.10.2 The Red Light Rule

(1) Principles

The Red Light Rule has been put in place in order to ensure that a candidate gaining an average overall pass can still be failed or referred if an essential (or 'must pass') element was failed. Inadequate demonstration of knowledge and comprehension, or inadequate case analysis and preparation should result in the candidate being failed in that assessment, irrespective of the marks achieved in the different components of the assessment. The Red Light Rule only applies to skills subjects. The Red Light Rule does not operate to restrict the number of attempts, this is governed by Part B – Regulations 4.10.1.

(2) Application

The rule must be applied where legal or other analysis by the student is so clearly incorrect that it would:

- put the client(s) interests at risk, and/or
- put the [potential] barrister at risk of liability for negligence.

A case of this 'fatal flaw' type cannot be addressed by the weighting of assessments since such mistakes might be unpredictable. A 'fatal flaw' is normally defined, for these purposes, as an error of law or procedure. However, an Ethics issue in a skills assessment may also be regarded for consideration as a 'fatal flaw.'

(3) Examples of where the Red Light Rule should be applied are as follows:

- A personal injury claim where counsel advises that the claim is statute barred because the three years since the date of the accident have expired (has failed to consider the date of knowledge and or an application under section 33).

- A contract claim where counsel fails to advise that the claim cannot be brought because the breach of contract was over six years from the date of the advice.
- Giving inaccurate advice in conference, for example advising a client to settle a civil claim where they have a perfectly good defence, eg on limitation.
- In advocacy, failing to challenge inadmissible evidence that might lead a client to be convicted.
- In negotiation, making a concession contrary to specific instructions.
- Insufficiently clear use of the English language which could result in the client's interests being put at risk or the barrister being at risk of liability for negligence.
- Serious professional misconduct that would result in action by the BSB.

4.10.3 The Attendance Rule

(1) The 'Attendance Rule' states that students are *expected* to attend all sessions (100%) and *must* attend 90% of sessions of the BPTC in order to achieve a pass grade. Attendance is defined as including classes and other timetabled activities. It can exceptionally include rescheduled classes when the student is unable to attend their scheduled class for good reasons (in accordance with 4.10.3.3) if written verification is provided and accepted, and an alternative class is attended by arrangement with the Provider. Further, if a student has not prepared for class, is more than 10 minutes late, or fails to participate fully in that class, then this can also be counted as non-attendance. Attendance should be calculated on a termly basis, in order for warnings to be provided where a candidate is at risk of falling below the requirement for the course. Attendance during the induction process is essential and permission not to attend induction and the first weeks of study will only exceptionally be granted.

(2) Application of the Attendance Rule

100% attendance - This is the normal expectation.

Attendance between 90% & 99% - The student may be absent for up to 10% of the course with reasons acceptable for the purposes of any internal mitigating circumstances procedure. Students must be able to demonstrate that they have made up any missed work. Both circumstances and additional work can be verified by the Provider.

Attendance between 80% and 89% - Students may exceptionally be allowed absences in excess of the 10%, where there are exceptional documented medical or other circumstances and missed work has been made up. Full details of the case must be referred to the External Examiner with advice from the Examination Board, for a decision. The Examiner must be satisfied that the intended learning outcomes of the course have been met in full. Any appeals should follow normal appeals processes but the BSB and External Examiner must be informed.

Attendance below 80% - The student must be failed, on the grounds that with less than 80% attendance it will not be possible to meet the learning outcomes, nor to demonstrate that they have been met, through assessment.

(3) Additional points

- The following may be taken into consideration as mitigating circumstances: pro bono work, attending moots, mini pupillages, pupillage interviews, jury service, religious observances etc, although these exceptions must be applied sensibly, for instance a person could not miss four weeks whilst attending four mini pupillages. Mini pupillages are important for the student but should preferably be undertaken prior to the start of the BPTC or during vacation. They should not cause students to miss important formal training.
- Inns events, such as Qualifying Sessions may also be taken into account. Note that Providers outside London should pay for travel and make a contribution towards accommodation if needed for students attending events in London, as appropriate.
- Where serious documented and accepted mitigating circumstances have occurred so as to cause attendance to fall below 80% (such as serious long term illness or accident) then the student should be advised to defer and resume study the following year.
- Deferring a place (for one year) that has been offered and accepted may be permitted if there are good (documented) reasons for doing so and as long as prior qualifications have not gone stale in the meantime. Deferring a place (i.e. starting the course) for two years may only exceptionally be permitted, and any additional requirements (e.g. the BCAT) must be met.
- Students who fall below 90% attendance may be required to intermit or leave the course (in both cases, financial considerations are a matter between the student and the Provider).

4.10.4 Compensation for failure

Under no circumstances may a student's overall performance on the course compensate for partial failure in an assessment for the BPTC. All components of the course must be taken and passed satisfactorily.

4.10.5 Mitigating and other circumstances

(1) Where a student provides evidence of mitigating circumstances that have, in the opinion of the board of examiners, affected his or her performance in one or more assessments, or prevented the undertaking of an assessment, then the board of examiners has the discretion to disregard the result and offer the student the opportunity to sit the assessment(s) as a first attempt of that sitting.

(2) If it is established that there are valid reasons for poor performance or that a student's absence was due to illness or other cause for which acceptable evidence has been provided, then those circumstances may be considered in determining the decision of the Examination Board. This must be in accordance with the Institutional procedures of the Providing Institution for the consideration of mitigating circumstances, as audited by the QAA.

(3) A student whose case is accepted as having been affected by mitigating circumstances should have the right to be re-assessed as if for the first time (ie with no penalty or restriction on the mark that may be obtained).

(4) In order to prevent the proliferation of 'insurance claims' for special circumstances, where a candidate has effectively declared himself or herself 'fit to sit' then a subsequent declaration of special circumstances will not normally be accepted. One exception might be where a candidate is suddenly taken seriously ill during the course of an examination.

(5) If the Board (and the BSB External Examiner) is not satisfied that the student has presented a valid case then the student will not be offered the chance to re-sit as if for the first time.

(6) Disabled students (ie those with long term disabilities) must be considered separately (see below, B4.11.7).

(7) Aegrotat qualifications should not be granted for the BPTC. They may only exceptionally be offered where there is no prospect of the student completing the requirements due to serious, life-threatening or terminal illness, and as long as there is evidence that performance has been at the standard in question. A posthumous award may be made and accepted on the deceased student's behalf where there is evidence of performance at the standard in question. The BSB must be consulted.

4.10.6 Consideration of mitigating circumstances

(1) Extenuating Circumstances must be formally reported by students in accordance with any institutional procedures, as acceptable to the QAA and the ARC Reference Document on Academic Appeals and Extenuating Circumstances for University Practitioners (2011). This must be at the time of the event (for example by telephone on the day of an examination) or as soon as possible afterwards, and accompanied by formal documented evidence as far as possible, such as a medical certificate (i.e. this must not wait until after results have been confirmed). Pleas for extenuating circumstances should not normally be considered retrospectively, i.e. after a poor grade has been obtained or as an excuse for academic misconduct. The date of the extenuating circumstances in relation to the timing of the assessment will always be checked by Examination Boards. Circumstances should thus be dealt with prior to final Examination Boards, the intervening period being used to allow for the provision of further evidence if appropriate. If further evidence is requested at the Examination Board, then this may cause delay for the final decision,

however with the agreement of the Exam Board Chair's Action may be taken so that the results can be agreed. There should be an appeals procedure in place.

(2) Ongoing circumstances such as a long term physical disability, a visual or hearing impairment, dyslexia, a heart condition etc should be discussed and planned for prior to the start of the course and special arrangements or facilities negotiated and agreed in advance, eg extra time for dyslexia (see B4.11.7).

(3) Extenuating Circumstances which affect coursework will normally be dealt with by the granting of an extension until a later date. This should not exceed the date of return of work with feedback to other students.

(4) Circumstances arising during the last weeks of the term/semester need a different treatment, especially if the ability to undertake an examination is affected. The following should be taken into consideration:

- whether the circumstances were outside the student's control (ie not of their own choosing);
- how significant the effect of that circumstance would be;
- how relevant the circumstances were to the assessment, for example proximity in time, which must be carefully recorded and considered;
- whether independent and reliable evidence is provided about the circumstance. Medical certification of a condition affecting the student would normally be accepted.

(5) A non-exhaustive list of examples of circumstances that could have seriously affected performance and could not have been remedied in the time available and would normally justify special consideration include:

- bereavement – death of close relative/significant other (of a nature which, in an employment context, would have led to an absence in accordance with the compassionate leave regulations);
- serious short term illness or accident (of a nature which, in an employment context, would have led to an absence on sick leave);
- evidence of a long term health condition worsening;
- significant adverse personal/family circumstances;
- other significant exceptional factors for which there is evidence of stress caused.

(6) A non-exhaustive list of circumstances that would not normally be acceptable include:

- the illness of a distant relative;
- financial problems or difficulties with housing;

- inadequate arrangements for baby-sitters, child-minders or other domestic or work situations;
- foreseeable transport difficulties, road works or private transport break downs;
- computer problems such as disc corruption, photocopying or printing problems;
- problems with handing in work by the given deadline;
- claims that students were unaware of dates or times of submission of work;
- any claim not supported by reliable evidence (e.g. a letter from a 'flatmate');
- alleged statement of a medical condition without reasonable evidence (medical or otherwise) to support it;
- alleged medical circumstances outside the relevant assessment period or learning period for which appropriate adjustments for extenuating circumstances have already been made;
- alleged medical condition supported by 'retrospective' medical evidence – that is, evidence that is not (contemporaneous) in existence at the same time as the illness, e.g. a doctor's note which states that the student was seen (after the illness occurred) and declared that they had been ill previously;
- if there is a reasonable case that circumstances relied on were foreseeable or preventable;
- long term health condition for which the student is already receiving reasonable or appropriate adjustments;
- minor illness or ailment, which in a work situation would be unlikely to lead to absence from work;
- holidays;
- poor practice e.g. no back up of electronic documents;
- confusion over time, date or location of the examination on the part of the candidate when this has been clearly notified, and not posed any problem to other students;
- late disclosure of circumstances on the basis that students 'felt unable – did not feel comfortable' confiding in a staff member about their extenuating circumstances;
- examination stress.

(7) A student whose claim for Extenuating Circumstances is accepted will normally be recommended to be reassessed with no academic penalty (i.e. mark not restricted to a threshold pass). There is no provision for raising marks of borderline fail students who have extenuating circumstances accepted. Where a course is to be repeated then fees may be waived where there are accepted extenuating circumstances, but this will be at the discretion of the Provider.

4.10.7 Assessment of disabled students

(1) Academic assessment practices must ensure that disabled students are given the opportunity to demonstrate the achievement of learning outcomes and competence standards. If a disabled student is unable, to be taught and/or assessed in the usual way, then the Provider should negotiate and agree to any necessary 'reasonable adjustments' e.g. additional support or a varied method of assessment as appropriate. If known, this should be arranged before enrolment.

(2) The need to ensure that course objectives are met and that the student should be assessed in a manner which is fair both to them and the other students (neither advantaged nor disadvantaged) must be borne in mind.

(3) It is the student's responsibility to ensure that the Provider is made aware of the disability and written evidence (normally medical) must be provided. Advice should be sought from relevant medical agencies if necessary.

(4) Disabled students may be permitted extra facilities, particularly in examinations – for example extra time (e.g. students with dyslexia), technological aids (dictaphone, computer, larger fonts etc), breaks in examinations (physically disabled students, impaired manual dexterity), an amanuensis or scribe (visually impaired students, or unable to write e.g. limb disability), or a reader (for visually impaired). In some cases it may be necessary for assessments to be adapted or modified in order for a disabled student to be assessed in an equivalent way to non disabled students (e.g. alternative to presentation for speech impairment).Any such adjustments should be agreed to by the relevant External Examiner. [NB some of the above may also apply to temporary impairments, e.g. broken limb].

(5) Such conditions must be notified at or before the commencement of study, ahead of registration. Any additional facilities or considerations can thus be agreed well in advance, unlike consideration of Extenuating Circumstances which occur on a short term basis by definition.

B5 Appeals against Assessment Decisions

5.1 **Appeals policy**

5.1.1 Each Provider must have a published appeals procedure, which facilitates the proper conduct of the investigation and resolution by the institution of students' appeals. In accordance with the QAA Code of Practice, the Provider must deal openly and fairly with students who wish to appeal against assessment decisions. They must not penalise students for making an appeal, nor note this on their academic record.

5.1.2 Appeals must be made by students within a specified time limit, and according to institutional guidance and procedures.

5.1.3 Since all grades are subject to internal marking and moderation systems and are confirmed by a Board of Examiners, appeals based solely on disagreement with the academic judgment of the staff making the assessment should not normally be considered by Providers.

5.1.4 Appeals systems will typically consist of an informal stage where, for example, a query is made as to why a lower grade than expected was awarded. Such queries should be resolved locally if possible with the relevant member of staff.

5.1.5 Where a query is not resolved through an informal process (for example if a student can show that not all evidence was taken into account) then a formal request should be made for the case to be considered by the Examination Board. Formal appeals against Examination Board decisions are normally only possible where performance was affected by ill health or other extenuating circumstances not declared at the time (for good reason), where regulations were not followed correctly, where an administrative error occurred, or where decisions were not in accordance with natural justice and fairness. Such cases should be subject to the Provider's systems as acceptable to the QAA. In cases where the internal systems recommend a remark, then that is permitted, but there is no appeal to the BSB. (See Appendix L for Centralised Examinations) Typically the final appeal will be made to the Vice Chancellor or Head of Institution or special Review Board whose decision is final. Once the final appeal stage has been decided at a Provider, if the student remains dissatisfied, he or she may be able to submit their appeal to the OIA whose website is available at: http://www.oiahe.org.uk.

5.1.6 The Provider should seek advice from the BSB if necessary and, in turn, monitor their own procedures and the scale, range and outcomes of academic appeals.

5.1.7 Where a case is referred to an Inn, the Inn will not attempt to go behind the findings of the Provider or the Office of the Independent Adjudicator [see www.oia.ac.uk]. However, in deciding the appropriate punishment (expulsion, delay of call etc) the Inn will require a full set of documentation. The Provider's conclusions and sanctions should not bind the Inn as to the appropriate outcome. The Inns' Conduct Committee exists in order to achieve consistency which may be lost if the decision of a Provider as to sanctions or 'sentence' must always prevail, with regard to the Inn. This will include copies of the scripts if plagiarism or collusion has been proved, statements by the marker, and the reports and findings of any previous appeals.

B6 Academic Misconduct

6.1 **Principles**

6.1.1 A student commits an academic offence if it is demonstrated that (on a balance of probabilities) he or she has used unfair means in order to obtain an advantage in carrying out an assessment or other academic work through cheating, plagiarism or fabrication of information. Academic offences will be reported to the student's Inn and may result in termination of membership of the Inn, and termination of study on the BPTC.

6.1.2 Those who undertake the BPTC aspire to attain the professional qualification of barrister. Any student who copies the work of another and presents it as his or her own work, thereby jeopardises their personal integrity and is likely to lose their reputation for honesty, putting into doubt their fitness to practise as a barrister. For this reason, any offence of dishonesty (cheating, plagiarism or misrepresentation) is a matter of concern in a potential barrister and will not only be dealt with by the Provider but must also immediately be reported to the student's Inn. This will normally lead to a referral by the Inn to the Inns' Conduct Committee to ensure consistency and equality of treatment. A judgment can be made in relation to whether or not that student remains a fit and proper person to be called to the Bar.

6.1.3 Provider procedures for dealing with offences should be in line with and as approved by the QAA. Action and penalties taken will depend on the class of offence and the degree of falsehood which may be significant, serious or grave.

6.1.4 Examples of misconduct include cheating in an examination or test that contributes to a summative grade by:

- copying or attempting to copy from work of other candidates;
- bringing unauthorised materials into the examination;
- referring to unauthorised materials during the examination;
- obtaining, or attempting to obtain, help from others in the examination;
- obtaining help in an examination by use of a mobile phone, text, pager or other device;
- any form of impersonation;
- providing, or attempting to provide, help in an examination;
- any arrangement to break, avoid or subvert the regulations;
- fabrication of data in any form of assessment;
- plagiarism from published or unpublished sources, including collusion (see next section);
- attempting to obtain examination papers or questions by computer hacking or other dishonest means.

6.2 **Plagiarism**

6.2.1 Plagiarism is defined as 'copying or attempting to copy from any other source (published or unpublished, and including the work of a fellow student or another person) in an unauthorised manner and attempting to present that work as if it were the student's own in order to obtain an unfair advantage'.

6.2.2 Work presented for assessment is expected to be the student's own and while quotations from recognised sources are usually acceptable, this must be clearly acknowledged and a reference given for the source.

6.2.3 Collusion, whereby a second student or person knowingly supplies work with consent is also defined as plagiarism. Supplier and receiver may be equally guilty. In those circumstances where one student entrusts a second student with their work and the second copies or attempts to copy the first student's work, both students may be held responsible.

6.2.4 Steps must be taken by Providers to prevent plagiarism and academic offences (particularly copying from the internet), for example by basing assessment on specialised topics or case studies; requiring working plans, drafts and notes to be submitted; warning students that electronic devices may be used to check for plagiarism; warning that vivas (oral examinations) may be required to check that work is the student's own; warning students of penalties (eg noting the offence on their academic record or transcript; failing or expulsion in extreme cases; or in ineligibility for professional qualifications).

6.2.5 It is recognised that acts of plagiarism, fabrication and cheating may vary in the degree of seriousness, for example, ranging from:

Type A

- a first offence (may be less serious);
- the reproduction of small amounts of texts, not properly referenced/without attribution.

Type B

- the reproduction of large amounts of texts, not properly referenced/without attribution;
- use of another student's work with or without his/her knowledge;
- collaboration or collusion, knowingly or unknowingly;
- a second or subsequent offence.

Type C

- the reproduction of very large amounts of texts, not properly referenced/without attribution, at any level, with intent to deceive or fraudulently obtain the qualification

Type B and Type C will all be considered to be very serious in terms of the requirements of the profession and must always be reported to the student's Inn.

6.2.6 Procedures

(1) Procedures as detailed above, as required by the BSB and the Inns of Court are paramount. In addition, Institutional procedures for dealing with academic offences must also be in line with the QAA Code of Practice and in accordance with procedures in place, and approved by the QAA, at the awarding institution. Typically, for example, where an academic offence is suspected in an examination (eg cheating by using unauthorised books or notes in an examination), then details and evidence must be recorded and unless a satisfactory response is received, the institutional procedures should be implemented.

(2) Where an academic offence is suspected in-course work (eg plagiarism, fabrication) the matter should be reported to the Course Director providing details of the alleged offence and evidence for it (such as a passage quoted verbatim or paraphrased without proper acknowledgement).

(3) If a student is suspected of cheating or plagiarism, the allegation should be put to the student in a formal meeting with the Course Director; the student must be given the opportunity to answer the allegations. If academic misconduct is admitted, the procedures outlined in s6.2.6.4 apply. If the offence is not admitted, the Provider must arrange a formal hearing as soon as possible. At that hearing, the relevant evidence must be considered and a decision made as to whether academic misconduct has been committed. If the hearing

establishes that any form of academic misconduct has been committed, the procedures outlined in s 6.2.6.4 apply.

(4) Once the student's misconduct has been established, whether by admission or after a hearing, the Provider must decide on an appropriate sanction, addressing the academic misconduct. It is a matter for the Provider what that sanction should be. If the student accepts the decision, the procedures outlined in s6.2.6.5 apply. If the student appeals the decision, the Provider must inform the student's Inn of the facts of the case, the sanctions imposed, and the fact that an appeal is pending. If the appeal establishes the student's innocence, his or her Inn must be informed immediately. If the decision stands after the provider's appeal process has been exhausted, the procedures outlined in s 6.2.6.5 apply.

(5) Once the student's academic misconduct has been established, the Provider must inform the student's Inn of the facts of the case and the sanction imposed. The Inn must then refer the case to the Inns Conduct Committee (ICC). The ICC will consider the facts of the case and determine whether to impose a further sanction in relation to Call to the Bar and Inn membership thereby addressing the issue of integrity and fitness to practise. It is a matter for the ICC what that sanction, if any, should be.

6.3 **Appeals against academic misconduct**

There must be a system of appeals against Academic misconduct, in accordance with institutional procedures. Such appeals may only be made on the grounds that Extenuating Circumstances, that may have affected the student's behaviour, were not taken into account, or that new evidence may be presented that was not previously available. Appeals may not be made on the basis of continued denial of guilt. The appeals process will normally be referred to an Academic Misconduct Committee or to the Head of Institution or his/her nominee.

B7 Student Code of Conduct

7.1 **General requirements**

7.1.1 It is expected that all Providers will have in place a Student Code of Conduct together with Student Disciplinary procedures to deal with infringement of the Code. The Bar Training Regulations must also be adhered to (see extract in Appendix A).

7.1.2 In accordance with the aims and philosophy of the BPTC, as outlined above (section A1) , BPTC students are expected to conduct themselves with due regard for their responsibilities as adults and members of the academic community, and with regard for the good name and reputation of the Bar.

7.1.3 Individual codes of conduct as implemented by Providers for BPTC students are expected to cover such areas as:

- engaging in any behaviour that prevents, obstructs or disrupts teaching, learning, research, administrative activity or recreational, and social activities;
- acting in a way likely to cause injury to or impair the health of others;
- assaulting, engaging in harassment or discriminatory behaviour

(eg sexual or racial harassment), or otherwise insulting other students or staff, or, for example, engaging in any other sexist or racist or other manner liable to give offence;

- acting in a violent, indecent, or threatening manner, or insubordinate behaviour;
- misusing or damaging premises or property;
- committing a breach of the regulations (for example by committing an academic offence);
- being found guilty of any criminal offence, or engaging in fraud, deceit, deception or dishonesty;
- failing to adhere to any institutional Code of Practice, for example relating to the usage of Library, Learning resources and IT;
- failing to comply with a previous sanction or penalty imposed; or
- behaving in a way that brings the Provider, BSB or the Bar into disrepute.

7.1.4 Such infringements of the Code of Conduct must be rigorously investigated on a case by case basis. The Provider must take appropriate action which may include, but is not limited to warning, suspension, exclusion, expulsion, transfer, remediation or termination.

7.1.5 A student may lose the right to continue with the BPTC if enrolment has not been completed by the due date, if he or she is not in good financial standing with the Provider (eg fees are owed), if the outcome of an academic offence is that they should not continue, if he/she has brought the BPTC into disrepute, or if there are circumstances that may affect the health or welfare of other students or staff.

7.1.6 Student Disciplinary Procedures must be in place to deal with any breach of the Code of Conduct. This will be a serious matter and any student subjected to the procedure will be dealt with by the relevant Inn of Court. The BSB must be informed. The system should normally consist of stages, for example Preliminary Investigation, Formal Hearing, Final Hearing, and possibly appeal to the Head of Institution, Vice Chancellor, and/or the Inn of Court. The BSB must be kept informed.

B8 Complaints

8.1 Policy

8.1.1 It is acknowledged that problems do occur and in such cases a complaint may be made. The Provider should deal openly, fairly and effectively with any comment or complaint about its services, and offer an appropriate remedy to anyone who is adversely affected by a service which fails to meet specified standards.

8.1.2 A complaints procedure (in line with the requirements of the QAA) must therefore be in place that can be used in relation to any service that does not appear to be up to the required standard. It may be used by students, prospective students or other interested parties. The Provider should not penalise anyone in any way for making a complaint about services provided.

8.1.3 Complaints must be investigated as fairly, openly and as quickly as possible.

Procedures must be in place, and publicised to students. Complaints made to the BSB will be referred to the relevant Provider.

8.1.4 If a student or other person wishes to comment or make a suggestion about improving the course or a related service, it can be done informally by raising it with those concerned or otherwise providing feedback (for example, the library, IT etc). Suggestion boxes are also helpful and feedback, suggestions, or complaints at this level should be considered carefully by Providers.

8.1.5 The student's Inn will also have a legitimate interest in pursuing a complaint, for example on behalf of a student member in relation to the quality of provision made for a particular student or for students generally at that Provider.

8.2 **Procedures**

8.2.1 If there is a general comment relating to the course, it may first be raised informally, through the staff student liaison committee or through a student representative. If a student wants personal and specific redress on a particular issue, this is defined as a complaint. Wherever possible, efforts should be made to resolve a complaint at the local point where it arose, with the members of staff concerned.

8.2.2 If a complaint cannot be resolved informally, then the institutional procedures should pertain, normally involving the detailing of the complaint in writing, followed by formal consideration of the evidence etc, whether anyone else was affected, or saw what happened, and the response or redress sought.

8.2.3 It will normally be the complainant's responsibility to provide all the relevant evidence that supports the complaint. The complaint must be properly investigated, normally in a staged process at various levels if satisfaction is not obtained. The final stage normally involves an independent external person.

8.2.4 Advice can be provided by the BSB, who may also be notified by the student if a cause for complaint against a Provider arises. Such students are normally advised to follow the complaints procedure of the Institution. The highest authority is the Office of the Independent Adjudicator (www.oiahe.org.uk/).The student may submit to the OIA if and only if they have exhausted all of their Provider's procedures for redress and are still not satisfied with the outcome achieved. The scheme of the OIA must be scrupulously complied with in terms of meeting deadlines associated with the types of complaints they will review.

Part C – Quality Assurance Procedures

[2.9]

NB Quality Assurance procedures are designed to fit in with institutional procedures for validation, monitoring and review. It is expected that common documentation should be used wherever possible.

C1 Quality Assurance Principles and Processes

1.1 Quality and Standards: principles

In accordance with the mission and strategic objectives of the Bar Standards Board, to promote excellence and quality within the profession and ensure that those who qualify as barristers have the right level of skills and knowledge to provide services to the public, including employers, quality assurance of the BPTC is based on the following principles:

- that, as regulator, the BSB is responsible for determining the aims, content, outcomes, and methods of delivery and assessment of the BPTC;
- that each Provider, however, also bears responsibility for ensuring that all BPTC requirements are met in the delivery of the course;
- that there is always room for improvement with regard to the quality of the BPTC, such that the BSB will seek to ensure continuous enhancement of the BPTC, as well as performing a 'quality control' function, in order to improve both design and performance;
- that judgments about quality should be made by suitably experienced and trained academics and professionals.

1.2 Key terms and definitions

In accordance with practice in the Higher Education sector worldwide, key terms are used in the following way:

Quality (of student experience)*: refers to what is done or provided to ensure that students are enabled to meet the learning outcomes and standards of the BPTC*

Standards (to be attained by students)*: are predetermined, explicit levels of achievement to be attained by students in order to justify progression or awards and qualifications*

Quality Standards (for delivery of the course)*: must be met as specified*

Quality Assurance*: refers to the planned and systematic mechanisms that are in place in order to ensure that given requirements are met and responsibilities properly discharged*

Quality Enhancement*: focuses on systems for improvement; learning from experience; nurturing, disseminating and exchanging good practice*

1.3 Quality Assurance: processes

In order to ensure that the quality of provision and standards of awards are maintained, and to assist with improvements and developments, the following processes are implemented in the course of the accreditation (approval), monitoring and review of the BPTC:

A *Validation/accreditation of the BPTC*

Accreditation (or reaccreditation) of Bar Professional Training Courses is subject to a rigorous process of validation by the BSB, in cooperation with the (existing or potential) Provider. Every new course must be approved by the BSB in order to be recognised for professional accreditation.

Accreditation procedures are detailed in section C2 below. It is expected that any new proposal will have already been subjected to internal scrutiny, and that final accreditation procedures will be combined with institutional (re)approval processes. The accreditation process will be managed by the BSB Education Department who should be contacted for further information.

B *Procedures for approval of changes to courses*

Any changes to Bar Professional Training Courses must be notified to the BSB, and re-approval processes may be required, depending on the degree of change.

C *Annual monitoring*

Providers of the BPTC are required to submit an Annual Monitoring Report (AMR) by the end of November each year, with information on the previous year's activity (with evidence from a variety of sources including examiners, academic staff, and students, and statistical information), as well as a self-evaluation of activity. A formal action plan is required to be developed and must be fully addressed.

D *Monitoring visits*

A system of periodic review, with an emphasis on quality management is in place. Regular visits take place in the form either of monitoring visits or visits triggered by a specific event or cause for concern. Visiting panels comprise legal academic and practitioner representative as well as members of the BSB secretariat and relevant committee member. They have available to them a wide range of information including the External Examiners' reports and the Providers' annual reports. Meetings with senior staff, teaching staff and students typically take place on all visits; panels also have an opportunity to see learning resources including library facilities.

E *Triggered visits*

A special 'triggered' visit may take place where cause for concern has been identified, such as falling standards, over-recruitment or deficiencies in facilities. Details will be organised on a needs basis. Additional costs may be incurred.

F *External Examiners*

G *External Moderators*

See B4 section 4.8.

H *Student feedback*

Students should participate in academic approval, monitoring and review decisions through questionnaires relating to specific courses. Provision must also be made for students to provide feedback through the use of focus groups and to have input into quality assurance through student representation on formal committees. Periodically students will be asked to complete a BSB survey in relation to their experience on the BPTC.

I *Staff feedback and development*

Opportunities should be provided for staff involved in the BPTC (management, teaching and support staff) to have input into the delivery of the BPTC at each Provider. Staff groups provide support and help to ensure uniformity and the exchange of good practice. Peer observation of teaching, and a system of staff appraisal (and details of staff development) are also required, in order to contribute to the maintenance of standards and the nurturing, development and dissemination of good practice.

J *The BPTC Sub-Committee of the BSB*

The BPTC Sub-Committee oversees all matters relating to the BPTC and reports to the Bar Standards Board's Education and Training Committee. Each year, overall reports on the external examining and annual monitoring processes are produced for consideration by the Education and Training Committee, and the Committee also receives all reports of monitoring visits. Any proposals arising from the reports will be actioned as appropriate.

K *BPTC Providers' Group Meetings*

Regular meetings with representatives of the Providers take place at the BSB office, approximately five times yearly. They involve the course leaders and directors from each of the BPTC Providers and are managed by the Education Standards team. The meetings provide a valuable forum to disseminate information, and discuss and debate initiatives.

L *The BPTC Conference*

A two day conference is held annually, usually in July. The BPTC course teams, External Examiners, advisers, Bar Standards Board staff, practising barristers and members of the judiciary, and, increasingly, members of the wider academic community, attend. The conference deals with issues affecting the quality of the BPTC and wider initiatives for development and enhancement.

M *User/Employer feedback*

Care is taken (in the processes of validation, monitoring and review as described above) to ensure that feedback is obtained from professionals, employers and other interested parties as appropriate, as 'users' of the graduates of the BPTC.

N *Additional procedures*

Additional scrutiny and special procedures will be drawn up as necessary and specified for use where arrangements for additional sites or for collaboration are proposed.

1.4 **Relation between internal and external procedures**

It is the intention that BSB Quality Assurance Procedures and requirements interface with institutional procedures, rather than requiring the replication or duplication of effort on the part of Providers. Documentation required for approval, monitoring and review is designed to be in line with the requirements of the HEI or private Provider, and in accordance with that normally required of institutions by the QAA. Where audit and review is carried out by the QAA with positive outcomes, then the BSB will normally have confidence in the Provider so far as such areas as general quality assurance mechanisms, general resources, and student support etc are concerned. Documentation for students, for approval, annual monitoring reports, External Examiner reports etc will normally be similar to QAA and/or internal requirements.

1.5 **The Quality AA**

The BSB is mindful of activity carried out by the QAA in reviewing and auditing provision in UK Higher Education (http://www.qaa.ac.uk/AssuringStandardsAndQuality/qualitycode/Pages/default.aspx). However, the accreditation of the Professional Qualification of the BPTC is the statutory duty and responsibility of the BSB. The quality control and quality assurance specifically of the BPTC as a professional qualification is also a matter for the BSB as regulator of education and training for the Bar. It is acknowledged that the BPTC has in the past frequently been delivered in HEIs as a postgraduate diploma (consisting of a minimum of 120 credits at postgraduate level) with the facility made available by some Providers for students subsequently to "top up" to a Master's award.

C2 Approval and Accreditation of Courses

2.1 **Aims and objectives**

2.1.1 The overall aim of course accreditation, validation and review is to ensure that BPTC students have a high quality educational and academic experience (directed to preparing students for practice as members of the Bar), by assessing the quality and standards of the course as it is to be (or is being) delivered. The approval process also stimulates development by requiring Providers to evaluate their courses, in the context of the thinking and practices of others.

2.1.2 Objectives

Validation of any course must ensure that:

(1) the course as proposed and defined according to the Provider's specification has been thoroughly thought out and adequately documented, and is consistent with the BSB's official BPTC course specification;

(2) the course meets the BSB's requirements for the professional qualification, its content matches the stated rationale, and the standards that will be achieved are appropriate in terms of the specified descriptors;

(3) the course and its documentation are in accordance with the requirements of the BSB;

(4) the staff and physical resources available, and the environment within which the course is offered, are satisfactory;

(5) the quality of teaching and standards of assessment in the subject are maintained and, where possible, will be enhanced.

2.1.3 Expressions of interest

An expression of interest in providing the BPTC must first be made by a potential Provider, using the appropriate form, available from the Education Department. Costs of the accreditation process will be met by the proposer (details are available separately).

2.2 **Procedures and information requirements for new courses (documentation)**

2.2.1 The documentary requirements of the accreditation process must be as concise as is consistent with clarity for the external audience/panel members. Firstly a formal expression of interest must be made to the BSB, outlining the proposal. Once this has been agreed then the procedures for accreditation can be put into place.

2.2.2 For accreditation of a new BPTC, material can be presented either as a Definitive Course Document (DCD) or it may be focused on the production of information for students. Student handbooks with overall course and unit/module specifications may form the basis of a submission, supplemented by additional information such as a review of related provision, the rationale for the proposed course, analysis of student demand, details of resources, accommodation and facilities, (library and IT) as well as details of staffing (staff CVs), so that appropriate academic consideration of the proposal may be made.

2.2.3 Where a proposal relates to existing, previous or similar provision, then a critical review of a former or related course must be provided, together with analysis of admission, progression, retention and destination statistics.

2.2.4 Documentation should be presented in three parts as follows:

A Student Handbook, containing information about:

- aims, objectives and philosophy of the proposal – rationale for tendering to provide the BPTC;
- the specific course objectives, structure and regulations as it is to be delivered at the Provider;
- admissions criteria and details of the management of the process;
- details of the course structure/syllabus and content (ie the Programme Specification as required by the QAA and descriptors for each unit/module/area);
- details of the intended learning outcomes;
- teaching and learning strategies;
- teaching methods;
- assessments and assessment regulations; schedule and criteria for assessment for each element/unit (with information about progression, withdrawal, failure, mitigating circumstances etc);
- progression regulations (including information about re-sit and referral procedures);
- individual unit/module content (summaries);

- details of any special requirements (eg projects, portfolios) if appropriate;
- information about exactly how the skills and competencies are to be attained by students and assessed;
- details of work placements/experience/Pro Bono opportunities as appropriate;
- details of equal opportunities, diversity processes;
- arrangements for student support arrangements (academic and pastoral) with cross references to student services and careers support);
- information or cross references concerning complaints/appeals procedures and procedures for dealing with academic offences and other disciplinary matters;
- concise summaries/information about staff involved in the course;
- details of mechanisms for student representation, feedback and input into QA systems.

B **Critical self-evaluation, including details of:**

- rationale and demand (the context of the course in terms of institutional, departmental strategies and mission – and of regional and national demand and provision);
- critical review/self-evaluation in terms of relation to existing provision and previous monitoring, review and external comments and responses.

C **Supplementary information** (**not appropriate for inclusion in student handbooks**)

- resources information (indicating approval/guarantee by relevant Academic Planning/Resources Committee), particularly any major items of equipment and/or any specialist accommodation to be devoted to the course; as well as library, computing and other provision, as agreed;
- copies of any existing or previous contract (if appropriate);
- staffing (full CVs including qualifications, teaching/practitioner experience and dates)*, evidence of practice, scholarly activity and research if applicable, staff development strategies, and details of any posts to be filled;
- quality assurance arrangements, including the constitution and operation of the course, how this fits in with institutional procedures,* the name(s) and position(s) of the manager(s),* and the constitution and terms of reference of any committees/examinations board*;
- teaching, learning and assessment strategies; sample teaching materials*;
- any special supporting arrangements eg for projects, work placements etc as appropriate*.

NB *Documentation marked thus [*] above may be made available on the day of the accreditation event (in a 'base room) rather than sent in advance*

2.3 **Validation/accreditation reports**

2.3.1 The accreditation process demonstrates the BSB's public accountability for the standards achieved by the BPTC, so reports will be produced on the validation of all Bar Professional Training Courses leading to the professional qualification. The report will provide a clear indication of discussion and conclusions to an external audience with evidence and analysis sufficient to explain the panel's conclusions and any conditions of approval and any recommendations. These will be produced by the Education & Training Department of the BSB. It is expected that internal reports will be available that relate to earlier internal scrutiny processes by Providers.

2.3.2 Reports of all final stage accreditation events should be circulated to panel members for confirmation and to the BPTC course director to check for factual accuracy. Reports must be formally approved by the BPTC Sub-Committee, received by the Education & Training Committee of the BSB, and reported to the BSB itself.

2.3.3 Accreditation reports must record the date(s) and place(s) of the meeting(s) of the visiting panel; membership of the panel (showing members' names and occupations); members of the course team and other contributors; any conditions which must be fulfilled (together with the datesby when they should be met); and any recommendations for changes or future developments desirable in order to enhance the quality of the course, and/or any matters to which particular attention should be given at annual monitoring. The BPTC Sub-Committee will ensure that accreditation conditions are met before a course starts.

2.4 **Procedures and timetable of events for accreditation**

2.4.1 Procedures for conducting and arranging accreditation events (including appointment of panels, chairs and officers) must be strictly followed. Occasionally, a different (or 'lighter') level of scrutiny may be acceptable, depending on whether a proposal is based on largely existing provision or on a significant amount of new material.

2.4.2 After an expression of interest in providing the BPTC has been made, a planning meeting may be held and a preliminary assessment given as to the quality of the proposal, the Provider's support for it and confirmation of the availability of all the necessary resources to operate the BPTC successfully. If this first stage is successful, the second, BSB-organised stage will be implemented. It is following this stage, that the final 'yes/no' decision is made (subject to confirmation by the BSB) as to whether the course will be allowed to run.

2.4.3 New proposals must normally be notified to the Education Department of the BSB by the commencement of the academic year in which the process of accreditation is to take place. That is, two years before the proposed commencement of the new course (allowing for one year for the recruitment process). Further proposals may come forward later, if approved, but no validations (eg for an additional mode) will normally take place after May each year for recruitment the following October. Any later than this does not allow time for a response to be made and circulated, and for conditions to be demonstrated as having been met. Accreditation events will not take place automatically following an expression of interest and formal submission of documentation, but only where the submitted material is of sufficient quality.

Commencement of the academic year prior to the academic year in which recruitment is to take place (eg October 2012 for a 2013 recruitment for a 2014 start)	Expressions of interest to be submitted to the Education Department of the BSB
Approximately four-six months before the BSB accreditation event	Liaison to take place between the Education Department and the Provider to determine schedule of events and date by which documentation is due
Approximately two-four months before the accreditation event	The Education Department will appoint and contact panel members, who will be appropriately briefed. Arrangements for venue, refreshments, accommodation etc will be made
At least two months before the accreditation event	An internal approval event (at the Provider) should preferably take place, a report should be produced and the teaching team should respond as appropriate
Two weeks before the accreditation event	Sufficient copies of the accreditation documents should be made for all participants of the accreditation event, for circulation with event programme to the panel [NB. If documents are not received 14 days before the event, it will be postponed/cancelled]
Within one month after the event	Unconfirmed report sent to the panel for agreement
Within two months after the event	Report sent to Course Director for response and checking for factual accuracy
By a set/agreed deadline (normally about two months)	Course team provides written response to any conditions/recommendations. The response will be circulated and the panel and comments invited. Approval may be confirmed or a supplementary response (and further visit) sought
Once conditions are satisfactorily met	Letter of confirmation of approval is sent out together with contract (with confirmed report)
Three months after final approval	Definitive documentation (hard copy and electronic) must be supplied to the Education Department

2.5 Information and guidance for validation panel members

2.5.1 The process

The Accreditation event will normally take the form of a one day event involving discussions between the course team and a panel appointed by the BSB. The panel may consist of 4–6 persons with appropriate expertise such as:

- A senior practitioner/senior member of the BSB or Secretariat as Chair (to focus on the overall proposal and Quality management systems in place).
- A senior practitioner (to focus on curriculum/content).
- A senior legal academic, member of another BPTC Provider, or practitioner (to focus on Teaching, Learning and Assessment issues).
- A lay member, where possible (to focus on Student support).
- A member with appropriate learning resources expertise.
- A member of staff from the Education Department to act as officer to the panel.
- A member of the University/Institution may attend as an observer and in order to fulfil University requirements if appropriate.

2.5.2 Panel members

Panel members must have undergone briefing/training before they are able to participate. They will be able to contribute in different ways, with some having experience and expertise in curriculum design, delivery and management, and others having more specific subject knowledge. Prior to the event, panel members will be supplied with the submission documentation (as detailed above), together with notes of any earlier planning or internal meetings, and any other relevant documentation. The event will normally begin with a private (or 'closed') meeting of the panel at which members will decide on the issues which they wish to discuss with the management and course team. During the event it should normally be possible for panel members to meet students on the existing or a related course where this is in place. There will not normally be any teaching observation, or scrutiny of student work, but sample teaching material may be required to be available. A well equipped base room is helpful to visitors/panel members, including PC/laptop and internet connection, printing facilities, and stationery).

2.5.3 The role of panel members

Panel members should read the submission documentation carefully (bearing in mind the purposes and objectives of accreditation) and also the criteria given below. Panel members should rotate between institutions if engaged on multiple occasions. The role of panel member is an important one and the documents and discussions will help the panel to decide if a proposal is satisfactory, and whether it should go forward in its current form, or with modifications, or not at all.

Before the event, panel members must:

- familiarise themselves with the purposes and procedures for accreditation

- carefully read the documentation supplied
- note any strengths and areas of excellence
- note areas which may require clarification or discussion
- note any possible shortcomings, omissions or deficiencies, or any other matters which should be discussed with the team during the event

Subject specialists should scrutinise the course content, in the context of the course specification requirements. They should ensure that it is up to date and at the appropriate level. Areas that might appear to need clarification or improvement may be redeemed by a convincing team discussion on the day. If this is the case, documentation should normally be revised and improved to match the quality of the team's responses. Conversely, good documentation may occasionally appear as the work of one member of the team alone, and the team may appear less strong. This should also be tested.

2.5.4 The accreditation event

The event will be chaired by a senior practitioner, member of the BSB or Secretariat. All panel members must be independent of the Provider making the proposal. At the first closed meeting, panel members will be asked to give preliminary judgments about the proposal, voicing any concerns but also commenting on any examples of good practice. An agenda for meeting(s) with the senior management and team will then be drawn up.

At the meeting with the team, the panel should allow team members to explain their proposal and to clarify any areas on which further discussion is needed. The panel should allow the team to explain or provide further detail by using a constructive and collegial approach identifying aspects of good practice as well as areas of concern. Where there are issues, it may be necessary to attach conditions to approval, and/or to provide recommendations. A response must be provided and conditions must always be met before a course is allowed to run. If panel members have strong doubts as to the team's readiness to run the course, they may reject the proposal, or refer it back for further development.

If possible, panel members should meet a group of students on a similar or related course. The meeting should not be too formal as it provides the opportunity to find out about the students' experiences, what they think of the institution, the learning environment, the teaching and assessment methods and the resources.

At the end of the event there will be a private meeting of all the panel members to make a final, appropriate, decision which must reflect the consensus of all panel members. Courses will not be approved where panel members have serious reservations. General feedback will be provided orally to the team at the end of the event, but decisions may be deferred until all those tendering to deliver the course have been considered, and/or until the visiting panel has reported to the BPTC Sub-Committee.

2.5.5 The report

A report of each event will be compiled by the visiting panel members, according to each section for which he or she is responsible. A pro-forma for the report is available at Appendix F. The report will be compiled and edited by the Education Standards team, suitable for publication on the web (once finalised).

2.5.6 After the event

Panel members will be asked to comment on the draft report of the event and will normally be involved if further action takes place (for example, more information may be supplied or the team may respond to issues raised).

2.6 **Criteria for accreditation (checklist for panel and team members)**

A Course will be successfully approved if the panel is confident in the proposal itself and in the ability of the course team to deliver it satisfactorily. These are the fundamental criteria for success.

Proposals must be academically sound and well documented, and based on a good self critical evaluation by the course team. Areas to be considered include:

2.6.1 Rationale and demand

The rationale behind the proposal to deliver the BPTC must be sound and in line with the Institution's mission and strategic plan. Management support must be demonstrated, with evidence of demand and need (possibly local or regional, but not confined to that). A review of existing or related provision should be used to demonstrate this. Details will be sought about the proposed fee to be charged, how it is arrived at, and the criteria that would be applied in increasing fees.

2.6.2 Aims, objectives and philosophy of the BPTC

Adherence to the aims and objectives of the BPTC must be demonstrated, consistent with the BSB framework for the course.

2.6.3 Resources

The specific physical and human resource requirements of the course must be detailed and evidence provided of how resources (eg facilities, library, IT) will be funded. This must include purchasing plans, particularly for new proposals.

2.6.4 Staffing and staff development

Details must be provided of suitably qualified staff who are to run the course. These may be curricula vitae of staff to be involved or job/position specifications where they are not yet appointed. This can be difficult since staff may not be appointed before approval is given – but approval cannot be given until information is provided about staff who are to deliver the course. Staff must be able to run the course to the level as specified, and relevant developmental and practitioner activity should be undertaken (collectively) by staff. Plans for the continuing development of staff should also be laid out. Involvement of local practitioners is essential.

2.6.5 Equality and diversity

The course must promote the development of all students to their full potential, and provide equal opportunities for the range of student intake – fairly, and without discrimination on grounds of age, disability, gender reassignment, pregnancy and maternity, race, religion or belief, sex, sexual orientation or marriage and civil partnership. The Equality Act 2010 must be scrupulously followed in all aspects of the delivery of the BPTC.

2.6.6 Admission criteria and regulations

Admission to the BPTC must comply with the BSB admission regulations. It must be securely demonstrated that all admissions requirements will be met by students before they are admitted onto the course (see Admissions Regulations, Part B, section B3).

2.6.7 Course structure and content

The course structure must be clearly stated, consistent with the BPTC framework as specified by the BSB. The content, and methods of teaching, learning and assessment, must be demonstrated as appropriate, at the right level, and up-to-date.

2.6.8 Skills

The delivery of specified professional skills (as opposed to knowledge) must be identified for the course, in line with the BSB framework.

2.6.9 Teaching and learning methods

There must be effective and varied teaching and learning methodologies which should relate to the aims and objectives of the course.

2.6.10 Assessment strategy and assessment methods

There must be an effective assessment strategy, in line with the regulations and requirements for the BPTC. This must ensure assessment at the right level whilst allowing for variety. Individual assessments must be very clearly stated and must provide effective measurements of performance, with an acceptable student workload. Evidence must be provided of verification of the students' own work in assessment (such as by the use of time-constrained examinations). It must be clear what a student has to achieve to progress through each part and achieve the professional qualification (see A4 Assessment information and B4 Assessment Regulations).

2.6.11 Content of individual units

Panel members (particularly those with specific subject expertise) will check that the content of each individual unit/area is appropriate in terms of aims and objectives, level, standards, learning outcomes, assessments, transferable skills and competencies, and reading lists.

2.6.12 Project, work placements, work-based and independent learning

Where placements are a formal part of a BPTC, details must be provided of the aims, methods of supervision and assessment methods to be used.

2.6.13 Student Support

Details must be provided of academic, general and special support to be provided for students.

2.6.14 Quality Assurance

The proposal must demonstrate how the Institution's monitoring and evaluation procedures will be implemented, how these fit in with BSB procedures and how the team will respond to QA processes and maintain standards.

2.7 **The outcome of an accreditation event**

2.7.1 The outcome of an accreditation event will be a recommendation to the BSB, which will be one of the following:

(1) Unqualified approval (possibly with recommendations).

(2) Approval subject to conditions, for example that specific amendments are made (conditions must be met by a specified date, usually before the commencement of the course).

(3) Approval, but for a limited number of intakes only, with indications of developments that must occur if the course is to receive any longer or fuller approval.

(4) A decision that the panel should consider revised documentation before being able to give its approval, but without the necessity for another meeting of the panel.

(5) A decision not to approve at the present time, but to reconvene the panel at a later, specified date to reconsider the proposal after stipulated changes have been made.

(6) Rejection, possibly accompanied by a recommendation concerning the timing of any future submission. This will be accompanied by a clear statement of the reasons why the panel does not feel able to approve the proposal, and by further dialogue and discussion.

2.7.2 The broad views of the panel will normally be notified to the course management orally at the end of the event in a short report feed-back session. Final decisions may be postponed until the full accreditation process for the new course has been completed. If it is felt that the panel has not given them full opportunity to justify their proposal, or that the panel's decision is unjustified, they may appeal against that decision (see Regulations B2.1.7).

2.8 **Procedures following an Accreditation event**

An unconfirmed report of the event will be produced normally within one month of the meeting. This draft will be sent to the panel members for agreement. The agreed report will then be formally sent to the Institution to provide a formal response within a specified time interval. Any response will be circulated to panel members. If panel members are not content with a response made to conditions, further action may be required. Students cannot be recruited before full approval at a time when all conditions have been met. The final confirmed report will be sent to the BPTC Sub-Committee and the Education & Training Committee. A final definitive set of documentation (eg student handbook and other material) will be kept by the Education Department of the BSB.

2.9 **Amendments/changes to Courses**

2.9.1 Changes to a BPTC

To make amendments to a course (where a full revalidation is not needed) the following steps should be taken:

(1) A full report must be written on the changes, providing the rationale for every change. The report should give:

- full details of the proposed change;

- the rationale for the amendment;
- the amended section of the course;
- full details of new/amended sections;
- any additional documentation which helps to clarify the purpose of the amendments (e g records of internal processes governing change).

(2) The amendment procedure should be conducted prior to the students' enrolment on the changed course, since changes may not be made while students are undertaking the study. The proposal, along with the necessary documentation, must be submitted for approval to the BSB. Note that minor changes need not be notified but the BSB must be consulted where there is any doubt.

(3) For major changes, for example the addition of a part-time mode, delivery on a different or additional site, or in partnership with another organisation, then a full visit will be required (see Regulations B2.1.2). Part-time courses will only be approved where the Provider already delivers the course full time.

C3 Annual Course Monitoring by Providers

The annual monitoring guidance is currently under review and a new approach is being piloted this year.

C4 Monitoring of the BPTC

4.1 **Principles, aims and objectives of monitoring**

4.1.1 General

The overall aim of the review process is to secure for students a high quality of educational and academic experience. Its most important function is to assess the quality and standards of provision of the BPTC, by considering the academic management, content, teaching, learning, assessment and support for the BPTC. It will be particularly important as the new BPTC is rolled out in a range of Providers, and will help to ensure that standards are met, that there is consistency across provision, and adequate support and resources. It is expected that careful scrutiny will be necessary in the early period of the new course, but that, gradually, where there is confidence a more 'hands-off' approach maybe taken. This will be based on a risk management approach, with a lighter touch where there is confidence in a Provider, but including mechanisms for 'triggered' visits if and when causes for concern arise. The review process also provides a mechanism for quality enhancement and the identification and exchange of good practice.

4.1.2 Principles

The main principles of the monitoring process are that:

- it is based on self-evaluation;
- it uses existing documentation and materials as much as possible;
- it relates closely to Providers' existing quality management structures;

- it focuses on objectivity, peer review and an external perspective.

4.1.3 Aims

The general over arching aims of the monitoring process are:

- to enable the BSB to satisfy itself that the BPTC is being appropriately delivered to the right standard and that students are attaining the correct level of achievement, before being assessed as competent;
- to consider the cumulative effect of the processes of approval, validation and annual monitoring by Providers;
- to provide a mechanism for the identification, nurturing and dissemination of good quality management practices across the HEI.

4.1.4 Objectives

The evaluation/monitoring process provides the opportunity:

- to ensure that the BPTC is being delivered to the agreed specifications and standards as laid down by the BSB, and to provide assurance that appropriate standards are being set and maintained;
- to review how Providers are managing academic quality and standards and fulfilling their responsibilities for delivering the BPTC;
- to evaluate the study experience of students, through feedback from the students;
- to ensure that the human and physical resources available and the environment within which the course is offered are satisfactory;
- to ensure that the quality of teaching and standards of assessment in the subject are maintained;
- to ensure that appropriate support is provided for students, and the quality of the student experience is appropriate for the achievement of the aims and outcomes of the course;
- to encourage the enhancement of the quality of the course and share good practice amongst the Providers of the BPTC as a whole;
- to disseminate to the public accessible information about provision by means of reports (placed on the BSB website).

4.2 Procedures and information requirements for monitoring visits

4.2.1 Monitoring visits are based on a process of self-evaluation undertaken by the course team/Provider being reviewed.

4.2.2 The necessary documentation will therefore consist of a formal, written self-critical assessment, which must in turn refer to a range of other evidence provided. Apart from the critical review statement, all material should be existing rather than new. For example, details of provision, annual course monitoring reports, examiners' reports, strategic statements/plans and policies, the accreditation report, details of external activities and scholarship, any external reports, details of staff induction, mentoring and peer observation, student induction, statistical indicators, and details of academic support services. Providers are advised to ensure that papers on all these topics are routinely collected and stored.

4.2.3 Courses to be reviewed will be identified in a provisional rolling schedule and notified in advance to Providers. A monitoring panel will be set up for each review, who will visit the course in order to review the provision, undertake discussion with staff and students and make conditions and/or recommendations for continuing approval and improvement. An agenda of matters to be discussed will be drawn up, based on the self-critical statement and previous action plans. This agenda will be discussed at an event by the formally constituted panel. The monitoring visit will normally take the form of a one-day visit but the length of a visit may vary and is at the discretion of the BSB. The panel will scrutinise the supporting documentation, and meet members of staff and (in some cases) technical support staff and student representatives. The length of visits may vary and the balance of meetings and teaching observations may be varied as necessary.

4.2.4 Following the visit, a written report will be agreed by the panel and presented to the BPTC Sub-Committee and the Education & Training Committee for consideration. Checking that recommendations and observations have been addressed ('closing the loop') will be carried out through the cycle of monitoring and reporting. An update or response should be provided by the course director subsequently showing how any conditions or recommendations identified have been addressed. A panel may wish to see a report or response on issues requiring immediate attention within a defined time limit. 'Conditions' are unlikely to be set in the same way as at accreditation unless there is a serious issue. One year will be the maximum allowed for any Provider to address any matters identified as 'unsatisfactory' and to respond on the implementation of recommendations, although shorter timescales may also be set.

4.3 **Monitoring Panels and membership**

An agenda for the visit will be discussed monitoring event by a formally constituted panel. The panel will scrutinise the supporting documentation, and meet members of staff (including support staff) and student representatives from the subject area in question.

Panels should normally comprise:

- a senior practitioner/senior member of the BSB or Secretariat as Chair (and to focus on Quality management systems);
- a senior practitioner (to focus on curriculum/content and structure);
- a senior legal academic, member of another BPTC Provider, or practitioner (to focus on Teaching, Learning and Assessment issues);
- a member with appropriate learning resources expertise;
- a member of staff from the Education Department to act as officer to the panel.

4.4 **Timetable/schedule of events for the process**

It is important that a careful timetable or schedule of events, with responsibilities allocated, is determined in line with the following:

At least six months before the monitoring visit	Course and timing of visit identified in consultation with the Provider
At least five months before the monitoring visit	Date agreed for the event
Four months before the visit	Planning meeting/discussion to take place with those involved to determine details of meetings, panel membership, and documentation requirements
Two months before the visit	Panel members to be contacted with confirmed date of the visit. 'Housekeeping arrangements' (accommodation etc) for the visit and panel members to be determined
At least three weeks before the visit	Sufficient copies of the advanced documentation should be sent to panel members, together with a list of participants and draft programme
The visit	Proceeds according to the draft agenda
Within one month after the event	Unconfirmed report sent to the panel for agreement
Within two months after the event	Report sent to Course Director for response and checking for factual accuracy
Within three months after the event	Report received from the Provider with response and factual corrections in track changes
By the end of the academic year	Report and response considered by the BPTC Sub-Committee, the Education & Training Committee and published online
Within one year maximum (sooner if specified)	Action taken on any recommendations will be monitored

4.5 **Timetable/schedule for the Monitoring event**

(1) Outline programmes for monitoring events are provided in Appendix E. The programme will be negotiated for each event individually in consultation between the Education Department and the Course Director, according to the availability of staff, observations, tours of resources etc.

The visit may be extended beyond one day if considered necessary. A well equipped base room is helpful to visitors/panel members, including PC/laptop and internet connection, sufficient sets of teaching materials and schedules if observation is to take place, printing facilities, and stationery.

(2) Meetings should be arranged at convenient times, in accordance with the programme outline. This should include, as a minimum, meetings with management, teaching staff and students. The following are

indicative of areas that will normally be discussed, depending on what appears to be particularly relevant to the provision and in relation to matters raised in annual monitoring reports and External Examiner reports:

Meeting with Management

- Course management and resourcing
- Quality assurance arrangements; response to previous reports etc
- Physical resources e.g. accommodation, library
- Learning resources e.g. IT library services
- Staffing & staff development
- Student services and welfare, including equality policies and disabled access arrangements
- Likely developments

Meeting with students

- Induction, workload, level and challenge of the course
- Clarity of information, student handbooks, teaching materials, case studies and the aims and objectives of each class
- Understanding of teaching methods, methods of assessment, and criteria for assessment
- Appropriateness of the teaching and assessment timetable
- Number/range of opportunities to practise skills
- Quality and timeliness of feedback received on coursework and progress (written and oral)
- Operation of the personal tutor system, academic and pastoral
- Quality of resources and equipment – accommodation, IT, library etc
- Participation in QA – feedback, issues and action taken; awareness of procedures
- Personal tutor system and careers advice
- Special activities and events (involvement of local practitioners)
- Aspects of the course they have found most difficult and most enjoyable

Meeting with teaching staff

- Recruitment and selection
- Course materials
- Teaching and learning methods
- Assessment methods
- Any other issues raise by External Examiners in their reports

- Any issues arising out of the meeting with students
- Notable achievements and areas of best practice.

Additional meetings should be held with library, learning resources, student support and careers staff as appropriate, or representatives from these areas may be present in the meeting with management. The purpose of the visit should be made clear to students, and assurances provided of student anonymity. There will normally be sampling of student work, some formal teaching observation, and a short tour of resources/facilities; particularly if there have been changes since the last visit.

4.6 Details of documentation required for the visit

Good quality documentation supplied in advance is essential, so that the review panel can give due consideration to the provision.

Documentation to be provided in advance:

(1) A formal, written self-evaluation document (SED) compiled by the subject leader and team, and about 10 pages long, detailing the rationale for the provision and the main aims and objectives. Evidence must be provided that the standard of the BPTC is set at the correct level; that the intellectual challenge is sufficiently demanding; that there is a high quality of learning environment; and that the teaching, learning and assessment methods used are effective. Evidence should also be provided that, through staff development activities underpinning the curriculum, syllabuses are being kept up to date with developments in the subject and professional practice.

Additional material to be provided in advance (can be presented as appendices to the SED:

(1) outline of the structure of the course, together with course statement, plans and policies (including admissions policies and procedures);

(2) definitive course documentation (a DCD or a student handbook plus additional information) giving details of each knowledge and skills area by method of delivery (indicating contact and study hours);

(3) statistical information relating to student intake and progression data;

(4) External Examiner reports for the previous 3 years;

(5) approval/accreditation reports, and reports of previous BSB visits (up to 3 years) as appropriate;

(6) a short summary of staff, with a note on each member, mentioning qualifications, main teaching activity and involvement in practice (full CVs should be provided during the visit but it is helpful for panel members to have a brief summary of staff in advance);

(7) a summary of resources, including a description of major items of equipment and specialist accommodation; library, computing and other relevant supporting provision.

Documentation to be made available on the day of the review event (in a 'base room')

(1) the previous 3 years' Annual Monitoring Reports (including action plans and responses);

(2) relevant committee minutes and reports (course teams, staff student liaison meetings, quality assurance meetings);

(3) course documentation, course manuals, textbooks etc as given to each student;

(4) further details of individual units or subject areas, including timetables, lesson plans and tutor notes for the course, including details of assessment instruments and procedures, assessment criteria and marking schemes;

(5) lesson plans, tutor notes and sample teaching materials for the period of the visit (ie materials relating to any observations to be undertaken);

(6) details of staffing with CVs of all members contributing to the course, whether full-time or part-time, full-time equivalent contribution to the BPTC, staff development undertaken and dates, whether an accredited advocacy tutor, years of practice experience, whether currently in practice (and if so to what extent), professional updating and teaching qualifications if any;

(7) equality and diversity policy and reasonable adjustments policy;

(8) staff development policies and strategies, including details of staff induction, mentoring and peer observation, and staff development/career review;

(9) details of student induction and support; appeals and complaints procedures;

(10) statistical indicators of trends (entry profiles, staff-student ratios, progression and output data, examination results, pass rates, destinations, student questionnaires etc);

(11) information on support services including learning resources, registry functions etc;

(12) financial statements setting out income from the BPTC and expenditure on it.

4.7 **Guidance on the compilation of the self evaluation document**

4.7.1 The Self-evaluation Document (SED) should be no longer than 10 pages plus appendices. Following a short introduction, it should begin by stating the aims and objectives of the department and courses. This needs to be written analytically, so it is not sufficient simply to describe the teaching and learning activities. There should be an indication of how Quality Assurance procedures have been used to identify areas which need to be addressed and indicate what action has been taken as a result. Evidence of continuous effective self assessment (eg annual monitoring gaining feedback from students, peer observation) which leads to an improved learning experience for students as well as increased opportunities for staff will be highly rated. The document should be well structured and logical. Clarity and coherence are essential and it should relate to annual monitoring and evaluation processes, showing how and why things operate in the way they do. Attention should be drawn to evidence to support statements (eg cross references to appendices).

4.7.2 An outline framework is suggested below (which may be used for headings):

(1) Introduction: educational aims of the provision: statement of aims and objectives, summary of plans and policies and strategies for any future development.

(2) Curriculum/course management: summary of the course including any changes made or imminent; evaluation of appropriateness of courses to the BPTC aims and intended learning outcomes.

(3) Summary of institutional quality assurance: eg discussion of action plans, how change has been achieved as a result of annual monitoring or feedback.

(4) Standards: discussion of standards, showing that the standard of the BPTC is at the correct level, and that the level of intellectual challenge is appropriate, in accordance with the course specification.

(5) Quality of student experience and teaching and learning opportunities: evidence of the provision of a high quality of learning environment and student support, and of the effectiveness of the teaching, learning and assessment methods used in relation to aims, objectives and learning outcomes.

(6) Student data and progression: analysis, drawing on statistics of student admission, retention and progression rates, and commentary as appropriate (see Statistics Protocol, as in section C3.4).

(7) Staffing: Staffing (including changes and developments); staff development, practice and other activity. A summary of staff (ie 4–5 lines on each showing teaching/research responsibilities) can be helpful (it is also helpful if full CVs are available in the base room).

(8) Resources: Information on resources and facilities, and critical review of this provision, including any updating/developments.

(9) Externality and benchmarking: confirmation that national expectations are being met.

(10) Conclusions: Summary discussion of strengths, good practice and any special distinguishing features, and of areas identified as requiring improvement.

4.8 **Guidance for participants in monitoring visit**

4.8.1 The main role of panel members is to consider the submission in terms of aims and objectives of the review process as specified above, with particular emphasis on the quality of the student experience and the standards of awards. Key themes for discussion will be to consider whether the framework as specified is being adhered to; the quality of teaching and learning; effectiveness of assessment; quality enhancement (including staff development and good practice); support for students and the overall quality of the student experience. Care should be taken to ensure there is adequate evidence to check and support critical judgments. Good, as well as less commendable, areas of practice should be highlighted. Leading questions to students should be avoided and consideration should be made of the sensitivity of a review situation. External panel members will be invited to comment on subject specific matters such as the curriculum. Teaching observation and viewing of student work may be undertaken.

4.8.2 Panel members should read the submission documentation carefully. When accepting the invitation to take part in a monitoring visit, they are taking on an important role and face interesting and challenging situations. The submission documentation and the meetings which make up the event should help the visiting panel to decide whether provision is of satisfactory quality, and meets acceptable standards for awards.

4.8.3 The panel should allow staff to explain and justify their proposals and to clarify any areas on which further discussion appears necessary. They must be rigorous but adopt a constructive approach in the spirit of dialogue and discussion. Panel members will usually meet a group of students enrolled on the BPTC in order to give them the opportunity to find out about the students' experiences and what they think about the learning environment, the teaching and assessment methods, the resources and the quality of administration. What the students say may prompt further questions for the course team, and may well throw light on answers already given by the staff.

4.9 **Criteria for Monitoring visit**

The following areas should be considered in particular:

4.9.1 Rationale and demand. This must be sound and should meet strategic plans and the institutional mission statement.

4.9.2 Resources. The physical and human resource requirements of the provision should be identified with information about how they are provided.

4.9.3 Staffing, research and staff development. Staff should be adequate for the delivery of the course, and there should be evidence of staff development, professional practice and scholarly activity to underpin the provision. Evidence of peer observation, and staff appraisal/review should be provided.

4.9.4 Aims, objectives and philosophy of course. Clear, coherent and attainable aims and objectives should be expressed, consistent with those of the BSB.

4.9.5 Equality. Delivery of the BPTC should demonstrate an appreciation of the BSB policies on equality and diversity and promote the development all students to their full potential.

4.9.6 Admission criteria and regulations. Strict adherence to BSB entry requirements for the BPTC must be demonstrated. Any additional entry requirements or selection criteria should be stated and justified.

4.9.7 Course structure. The course structures should be clearly stated and consistent with stated aims and objectives of the BSB. The content must be well-organised, appropriate, at the right level, and up to date.

4.9.8 Skills. Emphasis on skills, particularly Advocacy, must be reflected in the course as appropriate.

4.9.9 Teaching and learning methods. There should be an effective and varied process which should relate to the aims and objectives of the BPTC. The process should ensure delivery of the course at the right level.

4.9.10 Assessment. There should be an effective assessment strategy, which adheres to BSB Assessment regulations and requirements, and ensures assessment at the right level whilst allowing for variety. Individual assessments must be clearly defined and must provide effective measurements of performance and assessment, with correct weighting and an acceptable and balanced overall student workload. Assessment should be related to the specified outcomes as well as to the overall aims and objectives. The importance of verification of the students' own work in assessment (such as by the use of time constrained examinations) should be considered.

4.9.11 Assessment and progression. Consideration will be given to how students progress through the Course and obtain a pass in accordance with the regulations, particularly concerning re-sits.

4.9.12 Content. Review panel members with specific subject expertise will check that the content of courses is appropriate in terms of aims and objectives, level, standards, learning outcomes, assessments, transferable skills and competencies, reading lists etc.

4.9.13 Work placements and additional activities. Where applicable, the use of work placements and other forms of practical legal experience provided will be considered, particularly in terms of methods of supervision and assessment (if applicable).

4.9.14 Students. Information about general or special support to be provided for students will be considered. Evidence of a student representation and feedback system should be provided, including use of questionnaires, discussion groups, student representatives and participation in committees. Evidence of student feedback having been addressed, leading to improvement is also helpful.

4.9.15 Quality Assurance. The material provided should demonstrate overall how monitoring and evaluation procedures will be applied in order to respond to QA processes and maintain standards.

4.10 **Class observation**

The panel should try to observe as many classes during the visit as is practicable, including a range of classes and teaching methods. It should be borne in mind that the presence of a panel member to observe the class may be disruptive or likely to have an effect on the teaching process.

Additional guidance on class observation is provided in Appendix I. A class report should be written up by the panel member after each observation.

4.11 **After the event**

A written report of the event will be produced, first in draft form, including a summary of strengths and areas identified as in need of improvement. Observations and recommendations and observations by the panel will be made. Conditions for continuing approval may be specified. Panel members will be asked to comment on the draft report of the event and will also be involved if a written response is provided to conditions and recommendations set by the panel. Checking that recommendations and observations have been addressed will be carried out through the Education Department and subsequent reporting.

The report will be presented under the following headings:

- Course management and quality assurance
- Course structure and content
- Teaching and learning (including summary of class observations)
- Assessment

- Learning resources (accommodation, library, IT)
- Staffing and staff development
- Student support

C5 Triggered Visits

5.1 **Principles**

5.1.1 A 'triggered visit' may prove necessary where concerns have arisen, outside the normal scheduling of monitoring, review and visiting. The sorts of circumstances which may cause a triggered visit to be necessary include:

- Over-recruitment in excess of approved numbers by a Provider
- Serious under-recruitment, such that it would impact on the student experience
- Receipt of serious complaints about a Provider (eg by students)
- Concern that standards are at risk
- Financial or other issues

5.1.2 The process may well have an effect on any subsequent re-accreditation exercise, and there may be specific conditions attached to the continuation of the course. Recommendations will also be made. Costs of triggered visits are to be met by the Providers.

5.2 **Process**

5.2.1 Panel composition

For a triggered visit, the panel will be comprised of staff of the Bar Standards Board, with the addition of at least one practitioner and one committee member. The reason for the visit must be made clear to the Provider, and opportunities will be given to respond before the visit is arranged.

This may eliminate the need for an actual visit.

5.2.2 Documentation

Documents relating to the matter under investigation must be provided, as specified.

5.2.3 The visit

A programme will be drawn up for the one-day visit, including meetings with relevant persons involved in the issue that has been the cause for concern. The one-day visit will therefore normally include a meeting with senior management, and those with direct involvement or responsibility for the matter under discussion. Meetings with staff and students may not be required, unless relevant.

5.2.4 Matters to be discussed

Discussion will normally be limited to the issue of concern that has resulted in the need for a visit, although additional areas may also be covered. Sampling of student work, teaching observation and viewing of resources will only occur if these are germane to the matter at issue (e.g. overrecruitment would impact on resources).

5.2.5 Outcome/report

A report will be produced after a triggered visit highlighting the findings of the panel and any action needed. If the matter is serious then the Education and Training Committee and/or the BSB will be notified immediately. A response will be requested, as well as evidence that the required action has been completed (within any specified timescale). The report will be used as a reference point for any subsequent visit.

[2.10]–[2.11d]

Once running, all BPTC courses will be monitored through visits by the BPTC Sub Committee, of the Education & Training Committee. This group inspect the quality of provision and delivery, in conjunction with the Bar Standards Board's External Examiners who assure the standards of assessment.

Institutions Validated to run the BPTC

[2.11e]

BPP Law School
68–70 Red Lion Street
London WC1R 4NY
Tel: 020 7430 2304
http://www.bpp.com/law/bvc_pages/bvc_ft.htm

BPP Law School – Leeds
Whitehall
2 Whitehall Quays
Leeds LS1 4HR
Tel: 0113 386 8250
http://www.bpp.com/law/bvc_pages/bvc_ft.htm

Cardiff Law School
Centre for Professional Legal Studies
Law Building, Museum Avenue
Cardiff CF10 3AX
Tel: 029 2087 4964
http://www.law.cf.ac.uk/cpls/

The College of Law
14 Store Street
London WC1E 7DE
Tel: 0800 289 997
http://www.college-of-law.co.uk/prospective_students/content2-354.html

The College of Law – Birmingham
133 Great Hampton Street
Birmingham B18 6AQ
Tel: 0800 015 9519
http://www.college-of-law.co.uk/prospective_students/content2-354.html

The City Law School (formerly Inns of Court School of Law)
4 Gray's Inn Place
Gray's Inn
London WC1R 5DX
Tel: 020 7404 5787
http://www.city.ac.uk/law/icsl.html

Kaplan Law School
Palace House
3 Cathedral Street
London
SE1 9DE
020 7367 6400
http://www.kaplanlawschool.org.uk

Manchester Metropolitan University
School of Law,
All Saints West,
Lower Ormond Street,
Manchester M15 6HB
Tel: 0161 247 3053
http://www.law.mmu.ac.uk/postgrad/bvc/content.php

Nottingham Law School
Belgrave Centre
Chaucer Street
Nottingham NG1 5LP
Tel: 0115 848 2888
http://www.ntu.ac.uk/nls/professional_courses/bvc/5881gp.html

The University of Northumbria at Newcastle
School of Law
Sutherland Building
Northumberland Road
Newcastle Upon Tyne NE1 8ST
Tel: 0191 227 3939
http://northumbria.ac.uk/sd/academic/law/llm/llmopp/?view=Standard

University of the West of England at Bristol
Faculty of Law
Frenchay Campus
Coldharbour Lane
Bristol BS16 1QY
Tel: 0117 965 6261 x3769
http://bilp.uwe.ac.uk/bvc/default.asp

How to apply for the BPTC

[2.11f]

Applications for a place on the BPTC must be made through the Bar Standards Board's central applications system; BPTC Online. As the name suggests, BPTC Online is an internet based system. To make an application visit www.barprofessionaltraining.org.uk

Please note that once your application is submitted, the BPTC Providers make the decision on whether you will be offered a place, not the BSB. You should contact the Provider with queries regarding your application unless it is a technical matter.

BPTC places

There is heavy competition for places on the BPTC. In the region of 2500 candidates apply for approximately 1800 places each year. You will find specific place allocation for each BPTC Provider within the Course Contact Information document.

BPTC provider information

All the information applicants require about a specific BPTC Provider is at www.barstandardsboard.org.uk.

Submitting your chosen provider

Applicants should note that all applications submitted in the first round will be considered at the same time after the closing date. It is important that if you wish to be considered for the second round, you ensure you make **ALL** choices in the first round. Failure to do this will mean that your application will **ONLY** be considered in the first round. If you are then unsuccessful within the first round, your application will be discarded and you will no longer be considered for a place on the BPTC for that current year.

BPTC Online timetable

Applicants are strongly advised to submit your application as early as possible. The online application process timetable is:

- 4 November 2013: The system opens for applicants for September 2014 (9.00am).
- 9 January 2014: Closing date for first round applications (2.00pm).
- 6 February 2014: System reopens for new applications into the clearing round (9.00am).
- 5 March 2014: Offers start to be released from first round applications (9.00am).
- 2 April 2014: Acceptance deadline for first round offers (2.00pm).
- 15 April 2014: New clearing round applications and unsuccessful first round applications are released to Providers (2.00pm).

In order to ensure the security of their place on BPTC, students must log in and accept their place through BPTC Online in both the first and the clearing rounds.

Joining an Inn

[2.11g]

Information on how and why you should join an Inn, and what benefits they can offer.

The Inns of Court

Anyone wishing to train for the Bar must join one of the four Inns of Court. They are:

- Lincoln's Inn
- Inner Temple
- Middle Temple
- Gray's Inn

What is their purpose?

The Inns alone have the power to call a student to the Bar. Only those called to the Bar are able to exercise rights of audience in the superior courts of England and Wales as barristers.

What do they provide?

The Inns are principally non-academic societies which provide collegiate and educational activities and support for barristers and student barristers. They all provide the use of a library, lunching and dining facilities, common rooms and gardens.

They also provide a number of grants and scholarships for the various stages on the way to becoming a barrister. Please contact your Inn for details of the closing date for CPE scholarships. Closing date for BPTC scholarships is the first Friday in November for the BPTC in the following academic year.

As well as awards and scholarships, the Inns are able to offer advice to their student members, for example, assistance with completing CVs and application forms for the BPTC and for pupillage. Mock interviews are also available, as are the arrangement of marshalling schemes. Check with the student officers of the Inns for details.

When should you become an Inn member?

Admission to an Inn is required before registration on the BPTC, although many undergraduates join before this stage in order to participate in activities, use the library, or start their qualifying sessions. Students are reminded that they must join an Inn by 31st May of the year their BPTC is due to commence.

Qualifying units

Students are required to complete 12 qualifying units in order to be called to the Bar. These units, also known as qualifying sessions can be defined as "educational and collegiate activities arranged by or on behalf of the Inn(s)" for the purpose of preparing junior barristers for practice. These sessions used to be known as 'dining sessions', traditionally focused on dining with senior practitioners, which also provided networking opportunities and sharing of best practice. It is more common now for these sessions to have relevant talks and training workshops.

Qualifying sessions can be achieved through a number of different ways:

Attendance at

- Weekends either in the Inn or at a residential centre such as Cumberland Lodge.
- Education Days (primarily for out of London students).
- Education Dinners (with lectures or talks).
- Domus Dinners (when students and seniors dine together).
- Social Dinners (such as Grand Night or student guest nights or dinners at the providers).

The weekends count as 3 units, the days count as 2 units and dinners and Call Night count as 1 unit.

BPTC Students are reminded that qualifying session dinners are held both in London and in the provinces, as are various guest lectures throughout the year.

London students starting the BPTC are invited to attend the Introductory Party for London Students (held by all four Inns jointly). The introductory weekends for out of London students take place on different dates, check with your Inn.

These all count towards your qualifying units. See the Inns' websites for full details and to book places. Details of other events which can count as qualifying units are also available from their websites.

Advocacy training

Each Inn also runs advocacy training courses for their pupils. These vary in format and length and combine advocacy training with lecturers on particular areas of law or forensic skills.

Additionally, each Inn has student societies and supports involvement in debating activities which range from internal events to inter-Inn, national and international competitions. The students organise their own social events through their Inns' student association and some Inns also support sporting societies.

Some of these training sessions count as qualifying units.

Dates for Inns' sessions for students

Please contact your Inns for details of forthcoming sessions for students.

Contacting the Inns:

Lincoln's Inn
Students' Department
Treasury Office
Lincoln's Inn
London WC2A 3TL
Tel: 0207 405 1393

Inner Temple
Education & Training Department
Treasurer's Office
Inner Temple
London EC4Y 7HL
Tel: 0207 797 8208

Middle Temple
Students' Department
Treasury Office
Middle Temple
London EC4Y 9AT
Tel: 0207 427 4800

Gray's Inn
Education Department
8 South Square
Gray's Inn
London WC1R 5ET
Tel: 0207 458 7900

Pupillage

[2.12]

This section summarises the essential ingredients of Pupillage. The Pupillage Handbook at para **[2.18]** below sets out a more detailed exposition of Pupillage and what is to be expected from Pupillage.

Brief outline of Pupillage

[2.13]

Pupillage is the final stage of the route to qualification at the Bar, in which the pupil gains practical training under the supervision of an experienced barrister. Pupillage is divided into two parts: the non-practising six months (also known as the first six) and the practising six months (also known as the second six).

Pupillage advertising requirements

[2.14]

All pupillage providers must advertise all pupillage vacancies on the designated website www.pupillages.com. For further information regarding pupillage applications, please visit www.pupillages.com.

Pupillage funding requirements

[2.15]

All pupils must be paid no less than £10,000pa, which is £833.33 per month plus reasonable travel expenses where applicable.

The Pupillage Funding & Advertising Panel of the Qualifications Committee has the authority to allow exceptions, which must be applied for on the relevant application form and which are decided on a case-by-case basis.

Mini Pupillage

[2.16]

Mini-pupillage is a short period of work experience (usually one or two weeks) in a set of chambers. Some chambers require applicants to undertake an assessed mini-pupillage as part of the recruitment process, and others use it as one of their selection criteria. All applicants to the Bar are advised to undertake at least one mini-pupillage as spending time in this way within chambers will provide an invaluable insight into life at the Bar and may provide some useful advice to assist in finding pupillage. The Pupillage and Awards Handbook provides details of which chambers offer mini-pupillages, as does the chambers entry on the Pupillage Portal website. You should apply direct to chambers enclosing a copy of your CV and specifying the dates you are available. The Inns' Student Officers can also provide advice on obtaining a mini-pupillage.

Where to find Pupillage information

[2.17]

Competition for places is very intense. Therefore, applicants are advised to make sure that they are suited to a career at the Bar by visiting court, talking to people in the legal profession and undertaking work experience in solicitors' offices or barristers' chambers (see also Mini Pupillage paragraph on this page). Applicants should also ensure that they have thoroughly researched the chambers/pupillage training organisations to which they have applied. If you would like further information on pupillage figures please refer to our statistics section.

The Pupillage and Awards Handbook is an indispensable guide containing details of all organisations offering pupillage in the forthcoming year and comprehensive information about pupillage awards. This Handbook accompanies the Pupillage Portal website and allows you to view pupillage vacancies offline. The handbook is available from the annual National Pupillage Fair at the start of each March. If you would like to receive a copy of the Pupillage and Awards Handbook please refer to the Bar Council's website. The Inns of Court will also be able to advise on matters relating to pupillages.

Pupillage Handbook

[2.17a]

Following the report that was prepared by the Wood Working Group, the BSB has incorporated all the information relating to pupillage matters in one single document. This is the Pupillage Handbook. This document is designed to be used by pupils, pupil supervisors and all other interested parties. All the information a pupil will require is contained within the Pupillage Handbook.

Immigration support for non-European Economic Area (EEA) pupils and mini pupils

[2.17b]

Under the UK Border Agency's points based system, all non-EEA individuals who intend to enter the UK to undertake pupillage or mini pupillage should obtain their leave to enter under Tier 5 (Government Approved Exchange), having first successfully applied to the Bar Council for a Certificate of Sponsorship. Please visit the Bar Council website for more information.

The Pupillage Handbook

1. The regulatory framework for pupillage

[2.18]–[2.35]

1.1 The aims and objectives of Pupillage

Pupillage is the final stage on the route to qualification as a practising barrister, in which practical training is undertaken supervised by an experienced member of the Bar. Those who successfully complete pupillage according to the specified standards, together with the compulsory continuing education courses, will be granted a full qualification certificate.

The BSB is committed to ensuring that pupillages are of the highest quality, in terms of both the individual learning experience and the overall training environment. Therefore, in order to ensure that standards for the provision of training are met, all chambers and other Approved Training Organisations (ATOs) that take pupils must be approved by the BSB before they may take pupils. In addition, chambers and other ATOs are also monitored by the BSB in a number of ways. In particular, pupils have the opportunity to provide feedback about the quality of their pupillage learning experience.

In line with the principles expressed in the Bar Training Regulations (BTRs), the aims of the Pupillage stage of training are:

- to prepare pupils (who have been Called to the Bar) for practice at the Bar of England and Wales;
- to develop further the knowledge, skills and competencies gained at the Vocational stage of training so that pupils can be assessed as competent in the practice of law;
- to provide further development of excellence in advocacy;
- to further develop a high level professional and ethical approach to practice as a barrister, in accordance with the Code of Conduct;
- to establish the skills and competencies necessary for practice, whether in chambers or as an employed barrister;
- to equip pupils to perform competently in matters in which they are likely to be briefed during the early years of practice, and to provide skills and experience to enable them to deal with more complex matters as they develop;
- to ensure that pupils are able to take responsibility for their own professional development;
- to prepare pupils for practice in a culturally diverse society;
- to enable members of the Bar from overseas jurisdictions to acquire the skills required for practice at the Bar of England and Wales, thereby assisting them to undertake further training or practice in their home jurisdiction.

1.2 Principles of regulation of pupillage by the BSB

Pupillage is the final stage of training for practice at the Bar and, following satisfactory completion, a barrister is entitled to provide legal services and exercise a right of audience in all courts. Recruitment to pupillage is therefore an activity which is of vital importance both to applicants and for the long term health and vitality of the Bar.

1.3 The Bar Training Regulations

The Legal Services Act 2007 provides an overall framework for the regulation of the legal profession. The BSB derives its authority from the Inns of Court. Previously, the 'Consolidated Regulations of the Inns of Court' were published jointly by all four Inns, in order (among other things) to specify the training which a student had to complete in order to become a barrister.

More recently, the Inns agreed that the Bar Council would be wholly responsible for making rules of conduct which apply to barristers and will have primary responsibility for areas of education and training (including pupillage). From 2006, all the regulatory powers of the Bar Council including this one were delegated to the BSB.

1.4 The Code of Conduct

The Code of Conduct is currently under review. The new Code of Conduct will be replaced as the BSB Handbook. Upon approval, Barristers will be required to adhere to the core duties and rules stated in this document. Please see the Bar Standards Board website for further information.

1.5 The Equality and Diversity Requirements of the Code of Conduct

The current Equality and Diversity requirements of the Code are to be found on the Bar Standards Board website. The rules and accompanying guidance documents may be downloaded from the website.

All barristers, especially those involved in pupillage should make themselves familiar with the Equality and Diversity rules and ensure they are compliant.

The rules that are particularly pertinent to pupillage are as follows:

- 305.1 – the general prohibition on discrimination;
- 408.2(b) & (c) – the rules relating to the training of selection panels;
- 408.2(d) the requirement that chambers uses fair and objective criteria;
- 408.2(e) diversity monitoring requirements;
- 408.2(f) fair access to work rule;
- 408.2(g) the anti- harassment policy requirement.

Those involved in pupillage should also note that the Bar Council has developed a Fair Recruitment Guide for the Bar which may be downloaded from the Bar Council website.

2. Overview

2.1 The professional stage of training

BTR3: To become qualified to practise as a barrister a person must:(a) be called to the bar by an Inn (b) complete or be exempted from the Professional stage of training and (c) satisfy such further requirements as are set out in the Code of Conduct.

There is an important distinction between being a barrister and practising as a barrister. A person may become, and remain, a barrister without undertaking pupillage as the BTRs allow a student to be called to the Bar after completing the Vocational Stage and without having commenced pupillage. However, in order to become qualified to practise as a barrister, a person must complete (or be exempted from) the Professional Stage of training (into which pupillage has been subsumed) and satisfy such further requirements as are set out in the Code of Conduct (the Code). A person practises as a barrister if either he/she holds him/herself out as a barrister or exercises a right that he/she has by reason of being a barrister, in connection with the supply of legal services.

BTR 3C empowers the BSB to specify the level of competence expected of a barrister.

BTR3C: The Board shall publish from time to time a general statement of the minimum level of competence reasonably to be expected of a barrister when first qualified to practise

The BSB is therefore authorised to make any changes that it thinks fit to any of the requirements and regulations relating to the pupillage stage of training, subject to the need to obtain the approval of the LSB where necessary.

This is also made explicit in BTR33.

BTR 33: Any period of pupillage must provide training which is adequate and which complies with such criteria as may be published by the Board.

The BSB is authorised to set additional regulations, or provide additional detail, relating to the pupillage stage of training, the approval of ATOs and the approval of supervisors. The following sections therefore deal in particular with the requirements for the approval of chambers and other ATOs in providing pupillage placements; the training and accreditation process required of pupil supervisors; the overall framework and content of training at the pupillage stage; and the standards and competencies to be demonstrably attained by pupils.

2.2 Overall structure and duration of pupillage

BTR 30: Pupillage is divided into two parts: (a) a non-practising period of six months; and (b) a practising period of six months.

The BTRs require that a person who intends to practise as a barrister must complete at least 12 months pupillage. Pupillage should thus be divided into the first non-practising six months and the second practising six months.

Non-Practising six. The non-practising six must be undertaken in an Approved Training Organisation. The non-practising six must be undertaken in a continuous period of six months (unless undertaken part time). Pupils do not have to have been called to commence the nonpractising six months, provided that they have successfully passed the Bar Vocational Course / Bar Professional Training Course.

Practising six. The practising period of pupillage must commence no later than twelve months after the non-practising period of pupillage has been completed. It must be undertaken in a continuous period of six months or with only such intervals (each not exceeding one month) as to ensure that the practising six months is completed within an overall period of nine months.

Pupillage should normally be organised on a twelve months' basis. Although a twelve months' pupillage is arranged as 'first six' and 'second six', subdivisions of time may occur, for example in Chambers where it has become normal practice to 'rotate' pupils through two or more placements. This practice exposes pupils to a wider range of experience and leads to a more rounded assessment of their performance (see also 14.9 for duration of pupillage and part time pupillages).

For details of the content and structure of training (i.e. curriculum and competencies and how these are to be taught/supervised, learned and assessed); see Chapters 8–11 of this Handbook.

2.3 Bar Training Regulations governing pupillage

BTR 34 Except as provided in Regulation 42, any period of pupillage must be undertaken: (a) in an Approved Training Organisation; and (b) with a barrister who is a registered pupil supervisor.

Pupillage must be undertaken both with a registered pupil supervisor and in an ATO.

Applications for accreditation as a pupil supervisor are made to a barrister's own Inn of Court, under the procedures set out in BTR Schedule C. Approved pupil supervisors are registered with the BSB on the recommendation of the relevant Inn. For details of requirements for approval as a supervisor, see Chapter 4. Applications for authorisation as an ATO are made to the Qualifications Committee of the BSB. For details of requirements for approval as an ATO, see Chapter 3 below.

2.4 Duties of institutions involved with pupillage

(1) The Bar Standards Board

The BSB is authorised by the Bar Council, in compliance with the Legal Services Act 2007, to determine all matters of policy affecting the education, training and discipline of barristers, and to perform various administrative and regulatory functions relating to pupillage. These include:

- maintaining registers of pupils and their supervisors;
- issuing provisional and full qualification certificates to pupils;[1]
- overseeing the training offered to pupils and laying down standards of performance;
- monitoring of pupillage offered by pupillage providers;
- advising pupils on regulatory matters;
- maintaining a register of satisfactory completion of compulsory continuing education courses;
- regulating the conduct of members of the profession and taking appropriate action in respect of pupil supervisors and pupils who are in breach of their obligations under the BTRs or the Code.

1 The Bar Council is responsible for issuing practising certificates to those who are entitled to practise as barristers. From 1 January 2010 it has been a criminal offence to practise as a barrister without a practising certificate (in accordance with the Legal Services Act 2007). Therefore practising pupils are now issued with practising certificates.

(2) The Inns of Court

All pupils must be a member of one of the four Inns of Court before commencing pupillage, although they may commence the non-practising six before they have been Called to the Bar. The Inns have a number of functions relating to pupillage. They deliver the compulsory courses (Pupillage Advocacy Training and the Practice Management Course) for pupils in London, provide various library facilities and administrative services, and are a focus for activities such as moots, lectures and social events. Each Inn's Education Officer can provide pupils with advice and assistance regarding all aspects of pupillage, and who will support pupils in the pursuit of a complaint or grievance. The Inns assess pupils on the compulsory courses and are also involved in monitoring the overall standard of pupillages. Except in exceptional circumstances, the Advocacy Course should be completed in the first six months of pupillage. Failure to pass the assessment means that the pupil cannot proceed to a second six.

(3) The Circuits

Many practising barristers work from chambers and organisations that are closely linked with one of the six Circuits (Northern, North Eastern, Wales and Chester, Midland, South Eastern, Western) into which the administration and organisation of the court system of England and Wales is divided. A significant number of these locations offer pupillages, and for pupils in these chambers and organisations, the Circuits will share or replace some of the duties of the Inns in relation to pupillage. Each Circuit organises a compulsory continuing education programme for pupils, comprising Advocacy Training and the Practice Management Course.

They also offer a range of educational and social opportunities for pupils and barristers and may, depending on the Circuit, offer some administrative or other facilities to members.

Circuits also carry out some monitoring of pupillage (in conjunction with the Inns and the BSB).

(4) Chambers and other ATOs

Organisations, including sets of chambers, may be authorised by the BSB to offer first and/or second six pupillages, provided that there are one or more registered pupil supervisors who are eligible to take pupils and the organisation can meet the other requirements laid down by the BSB.

The Head of Chambers is ultimately responsible for pupils in chambers, and is required by the Code of Conduct to take all reasonable steps to ensure that proper arrangements are made for dealing with pupils and pupillage and that matters are conducted in a manner which is fair and equitable for all barristers and pupils. A Director of Pupil Training, normally the Chair ofthe Pupillage

Committee, should however be appointed to oversee pupillage arrangements in chambers on a day to day basis.

Other ATOs (in the Employed Sector) authorised by the BSB to take pupils must appoint a Director of Pupil Training (preferably a practising barrister) who will take overall responsibility for pupils and pupillage arrangements within the organisation. At the Employed Bar, the personnel or human resources department should also be able to provide any information that pupils need about the terms and conditions of their employment.

Heads of Chambers and Directors of Pupil Training are responsible initially for ensuring that appropriate pupillage documentation is prepared setting out the chambers' or ATOs' policy in relation to the BSB's requirements and recommendations.[1]

1 The role of Director of Pupil Training has been a BSB requirement from 1 September 2010, or as soon after as practicable for these arrangements to be made (subject to any necessary change in the BTRs or Code).

Even if a pupil aims to practise as an employed barrister on completion of pupillage, it is still important to understand how sets of chambers and clerking arrangements work. ATOs at the Employed Bar are therefore encouraged to arrange placements or exchange schemes with sets of chambers to give pupils the opportunity to experience self-employed practice.

(5) Specialist Bar Associations

As the law has become more complex, barristers increasingly specialise in particular areas of work. A number of Specialist Bar Associations (SBAs) exist to provide support, training and representation for their members. Many SBAs provide guidance on the specialist training which pupils attached to their members ought to receive. Indicative content of specialist areas of training for the Bar are provided separately on the BSB website, in order to facilitate their individual updating by the relevant SBA (see also Chapter 10 below).

3. Accreditation as an Approved Training Organisation

BTR37: The Board may authorise any organisation as an Approved Training Organisation subject to such terms as the Board may from time to time determine.

3.1 Accreditation as an Approved Training Organisation (ATO)

As specified in the BTRs (BTR37 cited above) chambers and other organisations must formally apply to the BSB to be accredited as an Approved Training Organisation. The system of formal accreditation applies equally to chambers and other organisations (for example, those which employ practising barristers) and has been in place since the inception of the BSB in 2006. However, all chambers having at least one pupil in place at 1 September 2006 were approved by virtue of this fact (in a 'grandparenting' process exempting those already involved in this activity from the new procedures). Such organisations were therefore deemed to have been authorised, without needing to make an application.

3.2 Approval of supervisors within an ATO

Not only do chambers and other Approved Training Organisations need approval to take pupils, supervisors must also be approved as individuals to supervise and assess pupils. An ATO will not be approved if adequate supervision is not provided and accessible. For information relating to supervision, see Chapter 4 below.

3.3 Application procedure

Formal applications for ATO status must be made to the BSB by chambers or other organisations who wish to offer pupillages. Applicants should also demonstrate that standards for ATOs have been met. Applications must be made in writing on the appropriate and current application form, which is available from the BSB (online or hard copy) and must be accompanied by the appropriate application fee. Applications made other than in accordance with current procedures and using the current application form will not be considered.

Detailed guidance of the procedures are available on the BSB website, but are summarised below. Applications are normally dealt with on paper only and it is the responsibility of the applicant to ensure that all supporting evidence is submitted.

3.4 Information and documentation required

The application should be submitted with supporting documentation. The BSB regards it as good practice to present information in the form of a Pupillage Policy Document which should demonstrate the following:

- The requirements and standards normally required of an ATO are met.
- Each proposed pupil will be supervised, on a regular basis, by a registered pupil supervisor (See BTRs Schedule C, reproduced here as Appendix B).
- Each pupil will have regular contact with at least one other solicitor or barrister with at least three years' experience of practice.
- At least one of the lawyers mentioned above is entitled to exercise a right of audience before every Court in relation to all proceedings and has been so entitled for at least three years.
- A Director of Pupil Training is in place in the ATO with overall responsibility for pupillage. Provided that the director is aware of the responsibilities involved, and has undergone the same training as a supervisor, that person does not have to be an accredited pupil supervisor him/herself. The Director of Pupil Training can be the Head of Chambers, another senior practitioner within the organisation, or a senior administrator.
- The proposed pupillage programme satisfactorily covers all of the outcomes and specified standards and competencies to be attained by pupils.
- The organisation undertakes to provide training in accordance with guidance issued from time to time by the Bar Standards Board.

3.5 The Pupillage Policy Document

The Pupillage Policy Document should also include details of:

- The number and type of pupillages on offer.
- Recruitment of pupils, and how this adheres to BSB requirements.
- The roles and duties of pupils, demonstrating adherence to BSB requirements.
- The roles and duties of pupil supervisors, demonstrating adherence to requirements.
- The general pattern of pupillage (e.g. whether served with more than one supervisor).
- Funding/salary arrangements and the finance available to pupils (including details of any guaranteed earnings or loan schemes).
- Payment for travelling expenses and compulsory courses.
- The programme/checklist(s) to be used during pupillage. The ways in which mandatory competencies are to be attained by pupils must be demonstrated, as well as simply the completion of a list of tasks.
- The method for fairly distributing work amongst working pupils.
- Procedures for providing pupils with an objective assessment of their progress at regular intervals during pupillage.
- Chambers/organisation's complaints and grievance procedures.
- Equality and Diversity policy and other policies required by the equality rules of the Code.
- General policy as to recruitment of tenants/employed barristers and those not taken on as tenants/employed barristers.
- Details of registered pupil supervisors and other lawyers in the organisation.

The BSB may request further information or documentation if considered necessary.

Additional factors such as Investors in People status may be taken into account.

3.6 Changes to approved placements

Once approval has been granted, any material change (e.g. change in location, change in resources, departure of supervisor) must be notified to the BSB. This may result in the need for further details to be provided, or possibly a meeting or visit or discussion.

3.7 Time limits and conditional approval

Approval will normally be without time limit, but approval may be conditional upon certain additional requirements being met. These will be specified, together with a time limit for meeting conditions and addressing recommendations. The BSB reserves the right to carry out a visit to an ATO at the point of its seeking approval, where issues arise (or for random sampling purposes, either as part of general chambers monitoring, or for the purpose of monitoring and sampling pupillage arrangements).

3.8 Appeals against approval decisions

Where an application for authorisation as an ATO is refused by the BSB, an appeal may be made (see BTR40), provided that the request is made in writing to the Board within one month of the date when notice of the decision was given. Appeals are dealt with on paper only.

Further details are available from the BSB.

3.9 Infringement of conditions and 'triggered' visits

Where the BSB has cause for concern, a paper-based review and/or a 'triggered visit' to an ATO may take place. The need for a 'triggered visit' will normally happen when one or more requirements of the BTRs and/or the Code of Conduct have been infringed, such as:

- where there is evidence that a pupillage has not been properly advertised;
- where there is evidence that a pupillage has not been properly funded;
- where there is evidence that training is inadequate;
- where there is evidence that a code requirement may have been breached;
- where there is evidence that improprieties have taken place.

Information about sample or 'triggered' visits is provided in Chapter 16.

3.10 Withdrawal of approval of ATO status

BTR 38: The Board may withdraw approval from an Approved Training Organisation if it considers, following investigation: (a) that pupillage training provided by the organisation is or has been seriously deficient, or (b) that the organisation has not made proper arrangements for dealing with pupils and pupillage in accordance with the Code of Conduct.

Accredited status as an ATO to provide pupillage training may be withdrawn if the requirements of the BTRs and/or the Code of Conduct are not being met: see BTR 38.

Formal notice will be provided.

BTR 39 The Board will give notice in writing (a) in the case of a decision to refuse to designate an organisation as an Approved Training Organisation, to that organisation; and (b) in the case of a decision to withdraw approval from an Approved Trainig Organisation to: (i) that organisation; (ii) any person who is undertaking or has agreed to undertake a pupillage in that organisation; and (iii) the Inn of which any such person is a member.

Under BTR 40, an organisation may request the BSB to review a decision to withdraw approval, provided that the request is made in writing to the Board within one month of the date when notice of the decision was given. Details of the appeals procedure will be made available when a request is received. ATO status is normally retained pending the appeal.

Note: Where, for any reason, an ATO and/or supervisor finds themselves no longer in a position to supervise a pupillage to completion (e.g. for reasons of the dissolution of Chambers/ATO, departure of supervisor etc, then the ATO and supervisor are jointly responsible to honour the pupillage and assist the pupil thereby left unsupported to attempt where possible to find alternative provision (sometimes known as a 'rescue pupillage'. A waiver from funding/advertising may well need to be sought and both the ATO and the supervisor should assist with this.

4. Supervision of pupils

BTR35 and Schedule C

- A barrister may act as a pupil supervisor if the barrister: is on the register of approved pupil supervisors kept by the Board; has a current practising certificate; and has regularly practised as a barrister during the previous two years.
- The Board may enter a barrister on the register of approved pupil supervisors if the barrister is approved by an Inn of which the barrister is a member.
- An Inn must approve a barrister as a pupil supervisor if:
  (1) the barrister has a current practising certificate;
  (2) the Inn is satisfied that the barrister has the necessary experience and is otherwise suitable to act as a pupil supervisor; and
  (3) the barrister has submitted an application in accordance with paragraph 5.

4.1 Eligibility as pupil supervisor

The BSB may enter a barrister on the register of approved pupil supervisors (BTR Schedule C, para 2) if the barrister is approved by an Inn of which the barrister is a member. Inns must approve a barrister as a pupil supervisor if they fulfil the requirements of Schedule C, para 3.

The Inn will then make a recommendation for approval to the BSB as the final point of approval of a supervisor.

BTR Schedule C para 5 (see Appendix B to this Handbook) sets out the rules regarding eligibility to be registered as and to act as a pupil supervisor which are *summarised* below, viz, a barrister will be eligible to be a pupil supervisor if he/she fulfils all of the following:

- has a current practising certificate;
- has the necessary experience and is otherwise suitable to act as a pupil supervisor;
- has submitted an application in accordance with requirements of the application procedure (supported as required);
- has normally practised in the United Kingdom or another Member State as a barrister or as a member of another Authorised Body for a period of at least six years in the previous eight years;
- has, for the previous two years, regularly practised as a barrister and been entitled to exercise a right of audience before every court in England and Wales in relation to all proceedings;
- has undergone pupil supervisor training as provided by his/her Inn (Schedule C, para 6);

- is consequently entered on the register of approved pupil supervisors maintained by the BSB.

In addition to the eligibility requirements summarised above, BTRs Schedule C para 9 requires that a pupil supervisor must, when responsible for supervising any pupil: take all reasonable steps to provide the pupil with adequate tuition, supervision and experience; have regard to any pupillage guidelines issued by the BSB and to the Equality rules of the Code of Conduct ; and ensure that the pupil prepares for and attends any further training required by the BSB such as advocacy training provided by the pupil's Circuit or Inn.

Once registered with the BSB, a pupil supervisor may take a pupil if his/her chambers or employer is registered as an ATO. Pupil supervisors may only supervise one pupil at a time unless they have the special permission of the BSB (BTR Schedule C, para 10).

Although pupil supervisors in self-employed practice used to be removed from the register of approved pupil supervisors on becoming a QC under the BTRs the former restriction no longer applies. QCs will nevertheless consider whether their practice will provide the most suitable training for a pupil.

4.2 Suitability, standards and principles for pupil supervisors: good practice

In addition to the requirements stated above, it is considered desirable and good practice that pupil supervisors should:

- have up to date knowledge of the core competencies and their relevant specialist curriculum applicable to pupils, remaining aware of changes and developments in relevant legal practice;
- have understanding of the learning experience, be able to assess learning needs of pupils and hence identify their own teaching/supervisory objectives;
- be competent to conduct one-to-one reviews and feedback sessions;
- understand and be able to put into practice the process of assessment and have the ability to use formative assessment and feedback for the benefit of the pupil;
- be familiar with and understand professional values set out in documents such as the Code of Conduct;
- understand developments relevant to the context of pupillage training, such as issues affecting training under the Legal Services Act 2007, the operation of the Legal Services Board (LSB), the operation of the BSB, and the effect of other relevant legislation;
- be able to use appropriate technology;
- be aware of equality rules of the Code of Conduct and relevant legislation (such as the Equality Act 2010), promoting equality and valuing diversity and be able to apply them as a supervisor;
- be able to devote sufficient time to the role;
- ensure there is a sufficient volume of work available for training;

- possess enthusiasm and a personal commitment to supervising his/her pupil;
- be sensitive and responsive to the needs of his/her pupil;
- be willing to develop individually as practitioner and supervisor;
- be aware of the need for and operation of quality assurance and enhancement processes for professional practice.

4.3 Procedures for accreditation as pupil supervisor

In order to become a pupil supervisor, the barrister needs to contact his/her own Inn and complete the necessary application form from that Inn. The Inn will check that the barrister fulfils the criteria, seek references and then inform the barrister that he/she needs to attend a training and accreditation session for pupil supervisors. Inns and Circuits run the training sessions and most attend the session provided by their own Inn. Prospective supervisors may however attend sessions run by an Inn which is not their own, or by a Circuit (of which they may not need to be a member). In such cases the host provider will confirm attendance with the barrister's own Inn. Sessions are run four-five times per year. See section 4.4.5 for details of what is covered by the training sessions.

Once the barrister has had his/her application approved, attended the training session for pupil supervisors, and been considered as having successfully completed the training, he/she will be recommended by the Inn to be placed on the register of accredited pupil supervisors held by his/her own Inn and the BSB. The Register will also record each pupil supervised by the supervisor and the start and end date of each such period of supervision.

All those involved in the supervision of pupils need to undergo training, although some may sometimes assume the role of being an additional supervisor for a short period of time, for example in a particular specialist area. In such cases, the Director of Pupil Training has an over arching role to oversee pupillage arrangements in chambers on a day to day basis.

4.4 Training of supervisors by the Inns of Court and Circuits

4.4.1 Aims of supervisor training

The overarching aims of pupil supervisor training are to:

- prepare those members of the profession who are suitably qualified and committed to contribute to the development of the profession to nurture, develop and supervise pupils in order that they might become competent practitioners at the Bar of England and Wales, and be worthy of a full practising certificate;
- enable practitioners effectively to engage in training of pupils, as both supervisor and assessor, so that pupils may attain the skills and competencies of pupillage as identified;
- enable practitioners to support their pupils, academically, professionally and personally (as adviser/mentor);
- remind practitioners of the formal obligations on pupils and supervisors and the structures relating to supervising pupils.

4.4.2 Outcomes of supervisor training

The specific objectives of pupil supervisor training are presented as outcomes below (in accordance with the aims and objectives of pupillage). Hence, by the end of the training, the intended outcomes are that supervisors will be enabled to:

- understand (and be confident in) their key role as supervisor, and hence their key role in upholding standards and as 'guardian' of the practising certificate;
- prepare pupils for practice at the Bar of England and Wales, whether at the Self Employed Bar or at the Employed Bar;
- develop further the knowledge, skills and competencies gained by pupils on the Bar Professional training Course (BPTC) and Inns' and Circuits' advocacy training courses in order that pupils can be assessed as competent in the practice of law and thereby gain a practising certificate;
- assist pupils in further development of their advocacy skills, both written and oral;
- inculcate in pupils a robust professional and ethical approach to practice as a barrister, in accordance with the Code of Conduct;
- prepare pupils for practice in a culturally diverse society;
- prepare pupils for independent practice (whether at the self-employed Bar or at the Employed Bar);
- furnish pupils with skills and competencies necessary for practice, whether in chambers or as an employed barrister;
- encourage pupils to take responsibility for their own professional development;
- provide the necessary support for pupils, academically, professionally and as mentor/advisor;
- undertake competent assessment of their pupils;
- understand the process of issuing the practising certificate;
- equip pupils to perform competently in matters in which they are likely to be briefed during the early years of practice.

4.4.3 Supervising, teaching and learning

Learning will be largely pupil-centred but it is important for supervisors to be aware of the differences between supervising (guiding) and teaching (delivering and/or facilitating knowledge acquisition). Although supervisor 'contact time' with pupils will vary according to the nature of the placement, the portfolio of the supervisor, the type of chambers and general availability, a minimum amount of contact time should be timetabled. There should, as a minimum, be:

- a formal induction session lasting not less than 1–2 hours at the beginning of each six month period;
- regular feedback sessions (monthly as a minimum, but at least weekly is recommended as good practice);

- a formal appraisal session lasting not less than 1–2 hours at the end of each six months;
- additional formal assessment meetings, as appropriate to go over specific pieces of work (particularly in the wirting of skeleton arguments);
- additional appraisal meetings where possible;
- at least one opportunity for observation by the supervisor (e.g. in advocacy).

For further guidance on good practice, see Chapter 14 below.

4.4.4 Assessment

Supervisors must be fully aware of their equally important role as 'assessor', although assessment of pupils will vary according to the nature of the work undertaken. In certain situations, the majority of work will be written, whilst in others attendance at Court will predominate. Assessment of pupils will therefore vary accordingly (see Chapter 9).

4.4.5 Indicative content to be covered in supervisor training

The Inns of Court and Circuits are autonomous bodies so a detailed framework for Supervisor training prior to recommendation for accreditation by the BSB is not specified. However the BSB will wish to ensure that best practice is maintained through Inns and Circuits and will maintain a broad oversight of standards. It is expected that the following will be covered:

1. ***An interactive 'ice breaker' session*** to discuss the aims and philosophy of pupillage and reasons for engaging in supervision.
2. ***Regulations and the BSB*** - based on the framework and requirements detailed in this Handbook (also available online and on CD ROM).
3. ***Roles and responsibilities*** – the role as trainer/manager should be explained by an experienced pupil supervisor, particularly the way that 'supervision' differs from 'teaching' and how various teaching, supervising and learning styles can contribute to the overall process.
4. ***Induction*** – areas to be covered (physically as well as theoretically) should be explained (see Chapter 14, para 14.2 below).
5. ***Standards and competencies*** – this should be based on the need to emphasise the generic core standards and competencies that must be attained by all pupils before they are signed off (i.e. not simply the checklist of tasks to be completed).
6. ***Curriculum*** – this should cover (without going into excessive detail) the ways in which subjects and checklists can be used for specialised areas.
7. ***Compulsory courses and Advocacy*** – again the needs and requirements should be emphasised, but with a particular emphasis on advocacy and how supervisors may assist in, and share responsibility for, ensuring that the standard of written and oral advocacy is at the correct level. Attention should be drawn to the Dutton3 and other current criteria, e.g. by the ATC. The role of the ATC should be emphasised and how the Hampel method is used in training. ATC

representation would be helpful in such sessions, if this is possible. Pupil supervisors should also be encouraged to attend ATC training, although this is not essential.

8. ***Review and monitoring of pupils*** – this section could be divided into how to teach/supervise and give good feedback; and how to review pupils' work effectively.

9. ***Appraisal*** – formal appraisal, at the end of each six should be discussed and distinguished from 'feedback' in general (proformas are available – see Appendix H). Such a process may well already be in place at the Employed Bar.

10. ***Assessment*** – the role of the supervisor in assessing the pupil as competent and worthy of a practising certificate should be emphasised, including exactly how supervisors should assess against the checklists (assignments completed) and competencies.

11. ***Ethics and the Code of Conduct*** – without going into detail, reference can be made to some key sections, with some examples. An emphasis on ethics and client care is needed.

12. ***Provision of opportunities*** – an emphasis can be made here on the need to ensure that pupils are given sufficient opportunities for work and learning, and that this is fairly apportioned.

13. ***Equality & Diversity*** – the rules and guidance documentation should be circulated in advance.

14. ***Paperwork requirements*** – a short session should cover the procedures and documentation, such as registration, certification etc, and including funding, payment and cash flow issues. Information on sick leave, holidays, special circumstances should be included. Such information could probably consist of references to this Handbook.

15. ***Discussion session*** – this could be a considerable element of the training, focussing on case studies to provide potential supervisors with the knowledge and skills to deal with operational dilemmas and difficult or unusual situations (testing the application of material in the general sections).

16. ***Plenary question and answer session***

The above outline for training is indicative and not definitive. Sections may be combined, and/or consist of drawing attention to places where guidance is provided on various matters in the Handbook. Training should be of at least 4–5 hours' duration including breaks. Attendance at all sessions is required for accreditation. Those who need to refresh their training may attend the latter discussion part only but attendance at the entire training would be preferable.

4.5 Accreditation, reaccreditation and de-accreditation of supervisors

Accreditation of pupil supervisors

Once training has been completed, then those who have completed the training will be first registered/approved by their Inn and then recommended for registration/approval with the BSB. The latter is likely to follow. Those approved in principle by their Inn should preferably undertake training within six months.Those who have completed the training and have been registered/approved by their Inn will be recommended for registration/approval by the BSB. The latter is likely to follow.

Accreditation of those who provide training for supervisors

Managed through the Inns' and Circuits' Education Committees, there is currently no requirement for training and accreditation of those who train supervisors. They are selected by the Inns according to experience and expertise. This may be reviewed in the future.

Re-accreditation of supervisors

Accreditation will be valid for five years as a maximum, whether or not the supervisor has supervised a pupil. Where a person has not supervised for five years then accreditation will lapse and training must be repeated. Pupil supervisors will thus be removed from the register if they do not take a pupil for more than five years, but they may retrain (ab initio) unless there is anything to prohibit this. Where a person has not supervised (i.e. not supervised a pupil for at least three months in that period) for three years, then 'refresher' training must be undertaken. This will normally consist of the second part of standard training (i.e. discussion of case studies and plenary question and answer session) although the introductory and formal session may be attended if wished.[1]

Removal from the register of pupil supervisors

BTRs Schedule C1, para 7 The Board may remove a barrister's name from the register of approved pupil supervisors if the barrister: ceases to practise as a barrister or is suspended from practice as a barrister; or requests the Board in writing to be removed from the register; or fails to complete any training required under paragraph 6; or is found by the Board to be unsuitable for any reason to act as a pupil supervisor; or has not acted as a pupil supervisor for the previous five years.

If the Board decides that a barrister should be removed from the register of approved pupil supervisors, it will notify the barrister and the relevant Inn (Schedule C para 8). It should be noted that Disciplinary Tribunals have the power to refer pupil supervisors to their Inn, whether or not charges are proved against them, if the circumstances of the complaint are relevant to the Barrister's capacity to act as pupil supervisor: Disciplinary Tribunal Regulations 19(11).

This may not lead to removal from the register but it should be borne in mind. A barrister whose application to be approved as a pupil supervisor is rejected or whose name is removed from the register of approved pupil supervisors may request a review of that decision (see Schedule C para 14).

1 This new requirement, as approved by the BSB, will be introduced as soon as practicably possible.

4.6 Roles and responsibilities of organisations and supervisors

It is important for roles of ATOs, supervisors and pupils to be clearly understood by all parties, to ensure that supervisor(s) and pupils are fully aware of the extent of one another's responsibilities, while the supervisor must advise and support, there is a point at which responsibility lies with the pupil and it is important that both understand the supervisor's contribution to supporting the pupil and where the supervisor's responsibilities end.

Roles and responsibilities of the ATO

BTR 37: The Board will designate an organisation as an Approved Training Organisation if it is satisfied: (a) that one or more registered pupil supervisors who are available to provide pupillage training practise in the organisation; and (b) that the organisation has made proper arrangements for dealing with pupils and pupillage in accordance with the Code of Conduct.

Work that pupils will see and do during pupillage will vary according to the chambers or organisation where he/she is based and the variety in the individual practice of the pupil supervisor. In accordance with BTR 37(b) above, all ATOs must ensure that a pupil obtains:

- Adequate supervision.
- Adequate resources to enable the timely completion of pupillage.
- An understanding and appreciation of the operation in practice of the rules of conduct and etiquette at the Bar.
- Sufficient practical experience of advocacy to be able to prepare and present a case competently.
- Sufficient practical experience of conferences and negotiation to be able to undertake the same competently.
- Sufficient practical experience in the undertaking of legal research and the preparation of drafts and opinions to be able to undertake the same competently.

Roles and responsibilities of pupil supervisors

BTRs Schedule C1, para 9: duties of pupil supervisors: A pupil supervisor must when responsible for supervising any pupil: take all reasonable steps to provide the pupil with adequate tuition, supervision and experience; have regard to any pupillage guidelines issued by the Board and to the Equality Code for the Bar; and ensure that the pupil prepares for and attends any further training required by the Board such as advocacy training provided by the pupil's Circuit or Inn.

Pupil supervisors must therefore (in order to fulfil the above):

- Provide/organise induction for pupils (in conjunction with the ATO).
- Establish and maintain regular contact with the pupil, ensuring his/her accessibility when advice is needed.
- Ensure resources are in place (in conjunction with the ATO).
- Provide learning opportunities for the pupil.
- Provide timely, effective and constructive guidance, advice and feedback on the pupil's work.
- Act as assessor of the pupil's work.
- Ensure outcomes of core areas are met and competencies attained to the required standard.
- Instil professional ethics and conduct, ensuring that the pupil is aware of the need to exercise probity and conduct him/herself according to ethical principles (and of the implications of misconduct).

- Ensure that compulsory courses are undertaken and passed.
- Ensure the pupil is initially registered, and signed off after the first six in order to be able to obtain a practising certificate.
- Ensure the pupil is covered through his/her own insurance when providing legal advice.
- Comply with other rules or guidelines relating to pupillage issued by the BSB.

In addition, pupil supervisors should (as a matter of good practice):

- Act as mentor/advisor/counsellor to pupils (as well as supervisor).
- Ensure outcomes of selected/optional specialist areas are met.
- Perform appraisal of pupils (in addition to feedback) as appropriate in order to monitor the pupil's overall progress.
- Support the pupil also in non-professional/academic areas, e.g. where some counselling might be needed (or ensure that such support is available).
- Deal with any other issues arising (e.g. conduct, complaints, special circumstances).
- Assist in placing the pupil if he/she is unable to continue supervision for any reason.
- Ensure that the pupil is aware of other sources of advice (e.g. Inns, BSB), including careers guidance, health and safety and equality policies.
- Maintain the necessary supervisory expertise, including the appropriate skills, to perform the role satisfactorily, supported by relevant continuing professional development opportunities.

5. Applications and admission and registration of pupils

5.1 Advertising requirements

All vacancies for pupillages must be advertised .To this end and to ensure fairness, a website designated by the Bar Council is in place: Pupillage Gateway (www.pupillagegateway.com). Pupillage Gateway Approve Training Organisations can subscribe to Pupillage Gateway and use the system to conduct their recruitment process.

5.1.1 The advertisement must contain all information required in accordance with the Code of Conduct, Annex R. To reduce the risk of receiving applications from candidates who do not fully understand the type of practice which chambers conduct, or the selection criteria which will be applied, advertisements should give a full account of the type of work done and the qualities (positive and negative) which will be especially relevant in the selection process.

ATOs should state, if possible, whether they give consideration to applicants applying before undertaking the Bar Course. Also whether they will cover expenses for candidates to attend for interview.

5.1.2 Waivers from advertising requirements

Waivers from advertising requirements will only be granted in exceptional circumstances. Each case will be considered on an individual basis on its own merits. The relevant form must be used where an application is sought for a waiver from pupillage advertising requirement. A formal application must be made to the BSB, by the ATO. The Pupillage Funding and Advertising Panel of the BSB Qualifications Committee deals with these applications. Details of procedures are provided on the Bar Standards Board website.

5.2 Registration of pupillages

All pupillages must be registered with the BSB on the appropriate registration form before pupillage is commenced (see website, as above). Periods of pupillage undertaken prior to registration will not be recognised. The Supplementary Information Survey must be submitted at the same time. Periods of time spent in chambers before registration will not count towards pupillage. Registration forms must be returned to the Training Compliance Assistant in the Standards & Quality Section of the BSB.

Where possible, registration forms should be returned two weeks prior to commencement of pupillage. The name of the designated pupil supervisor and a specific commencement date must be stated. It is therefore advisable that such arrangements are made in advance.

Registration will be confirmed by email from the BSB. If confirmation is not received then pupils should contact the BSB.

5.3 Changes in pupillage

The BSB keeps records of all pupillages and any change during pupillage must be notified, using the prescribed form (see Appendix F). The periods of time involved must be noted.

There is no specified maximum amount of time that a supervisor may be absent or unavailable (e.g. overseas or ill) before an alternative supervisor must be appointed. However, it is the duty of the supervisor to ensure that the BSB is contacted for advice (when a material change occurs) so that special provision can be made where necessary. Detailed information must be provided, signed off by the Head of Chambers or other person authorised by the Head of Chambers in the case of a pupillage in chambers. For a pupillage in employment, it should be signed by a person authorised by the employer, normally the Director of Pupil Training.

5.4 Pupillage contract

The BSB recommends that ATOs draw up a contract before the commencement of pupillage, between the ATO and the individual pupil, laying out in detail what the ATO policies and procedures are during pupillage as well as the grounds on which pupillage might be terminated.

5.5 Other ways of completing pupillage (reductions, external training, part time)

BTR 59: The Board may grant exemptions from part or all of: the Academic Stage, the Vocational Stage, and/or the Professional Stage of Training.

It is possible for reductions and exemptions of pupillage to be granted by the BSB, in accordance with BTR 59.

Further information and guidance is available separately on the following:

- ***External Training*** – undertaking training outside England and Wales
- ***Reductions in Pupillage*** – due to time spent working in a legal environment
- ***Qualified Legal Practitioners*** – for applicants who are qualified as solicitors, Northern Irish Barristers, Scottish advocates, common law practitioners or legal academics
- ***Deferred pupillages*** – to consider the circumstances where pupillages may be deferred
- ***Part time pupillages-*** the BSB is of the view that, where appropriate, efforts should be made to make part time pupillages available

Please consult the BSB website or contact the Qualifications Department of the BSB.

6. Recruitment and selection for pupillage

6.1 Principles of recruitment and selection

ATOs must approach the recruitment of those wishing to practise at the Bar of England and Wales in a responsible and reasonable way and thereby ensure fairness to applicants and a secure future not only for themselves but also for the profession.

Key principles in recruitment are as follows:

- That methods of selection and recruitment must be accessible, fair and just (for information about online and other applications systems, as well as advertising requirements, see Appendix C).
- That the Bar is strengthened and enriched by recruiting practitioners from all sections of society.
- That ATOs must take into account relevant legislation and the Equality & Diversity rules of the Code of Conduct for the Bar.
- That good equality practices should permeate the whole recruitment and selection process.
- That the academic (and other, personal) demands being faced by potential applicants should be respected, in terms of availability for interview.
- That the financial predicament of many applicants should be taken into account.

6.2 Promotional activities

It is recognised that ATOs have a legitimate interest in promoting themselves amongst those who may be interested in joining them. This may take the form of preparation and distribution of printed and electronic materials, the funding of prizes and competitions and the hosting of social events.

The BSB recommends that ATOs keep their promotional activities under review and, in determining priorities, take into account the importance of promoting themselves amongst the widest possible number of potential entrants to the profession. Where an ATO intends to visit a University (or other Higher Education Institution, private College etc), they should advise the institution's careers service in advance. If possible, invitation to attend any event should be extended to students in any neighbouring Universities or HEIs. Promotional activities directed at first or second year undergraduates should focus on careers at the Bar generally as well as a particular ATO or area of specialism.

6.3 Mini pupillages and work experience

A mini pupillage is often the first experience a person will have of the Bar. ATOs should therefore seek to ensure that the opportunities to take a mini pupillage are made available as widely as possible. Mini pupillages are not regulated by the BSB although the Code of Conduct requires some diversity monitoring of assessed mini-pupillages and fair recruitment training for selection panels responsible for the recruitment of assessed mini-pupils.

Where the completion of an assessed mini-pupillage is made a condition for obtaining pupillage itself (effectively the first part of the selection and recruitment process), ATOs must advertise its mini-pupillages and comply with the Equality & Diversity rules of the Code when selecting individuals for a mini-pupillage. A list of mini pupillages offered and details of the recruitment process must be maintained (for three years) and made available to the BSB on request.

The distinction should be made between a formal mini pupillage and 'work experience' opportunities that do not and will not count formally towards pupillage. The BSB encourages ATOs to consider taking positive action to make mini pupillage and work experience opportunities available to groups that are under-represented at the Bar.

6.4 Selection procedures and criteria

(1) ATOs must formally agree and set out selection procedures and criteria. When developing their selection procedures, ATOs should have regard to any relevant guidance issued by the Bar Standards Board and in particular to the Equality & Diversity rules of the Code of Conduct for the Bar. (See para 408.2 Code of Conduct).

(2) All pupils should be selected through the same selection procedure. Special provision may be made for the selection of those with exemptions and reductions or waivers.

(3)Where an ATO is not a member of the Pupillage Portal system, it is recommended that it develops and uses an application form which draws out the ways in which candidates fulfil the criteria for selection, rather than asking for the submission of a curriculum vitae alone. Good practice includes the use of written exercise(s) which can draw out analytical skills and written communication. Such exercises should however be equally accessible to those who may not yet have undertaken a law degree, or those at various stages of their legal studies if such candidates are to be considered.

(4) Decisions on applications must be taken by more than one member of the ATO. All selections must be made against written objective and explicit selection criteria.

(5) Selection procedures in commercial organisations will also have regard to corporate policies.

6.5 Interviews

(1) Wherever possible, ATOs should not hold interviews at times when potential applicants may be involved in final preparation for and sitting examinations at an institution of higher education.

(2) Where interviews or other parts of the selection process take place during term time, ATOs should treat sympathetically any request for an alternative date made by the applicant for academic or other good reasons.

(3) The conduct of interviews must accord with the Equality rules of the Code for the Bar and the BSB encourages adherence to the Bar Council's Fair Recruitment Guide in all aspects of recruitment.

(4) ATOs must ensure that the fair recruitment training rules (408. 2(b)&(c)of the Code of Conduct are complied with. Guidance on appropriate courses may be obtained from the Bar Council equality and diversity team on 020 7611 1320.

(5) Where persons invited to interview live some distance from the ATO, it should give serious consideration to paying or making a contribution towards their travel expenses, and make clear any policy on this.

(6) ATOs must make reasonable adjustments for disabled candidates at interview.

(7) Where possible, ATOs should advise applicants at interview when they are likely to reach a decision on their pupillage applications.

(8) ATOs should also ensure that application forms are well drafted and not obscure or unclear in any way. Where possible, all applications should be acknowledged and candidates should be notified of outcomes, for example if they are unsuccessful or if, for example, pupillage is no longer to be offered. The provision of feedback to unsuccessful candidates is also regarded as good practice and the process, which is generally very demanding and stressful to candidates, should always be conducted with efficiency and courtesy.

6.6 Equality and diversity issues in recruitment

(1) The legislative framework

The Equality Act 2010 ("the Act") consolidates and replaces the numerous Acts and Regulations which previously dealt with equalities law. It recognises the following as 'protected characteristics': age, disability, gender reassignment, marriage and civil partnership, race, religion or belief, sex and sexual orientation. Barristers and clerks are bound by specific provisions relating to the Bar in section 47 of the Act which prohibits discrimination against pupils, tenants and would-be pupils and tenants, and requires barristers to make reasonable adjustments. The positive action provisions in section 159 of the Act apply specifically to pupillage and tenancy recruitment. Chambers as trade organisations are under a duty not to discriminate, harass or victimise; the duty to make reasonable adjustments also applies to chambers as trade organisations. Section 60 of the Act prohibits pre-selection questions of applicants (including for pupillage or tenancy) about their health or disability save in very narrow circumstances. The Act also clarifies that protection from discrimination because of a perceived characteristic or because of association extends to all protected characteristics except marriage and civil partnership and pregnancy and maternity.

As employers, chambers are subject to the provisions in Part 5 Chapter 1 of the Act prohibiting direct and indirect discrimination, harassment and victimisation, and are subject to the duty to make reasonable adjustments. As service providers, chambers are covered by Part 3 of the Act.

(2) The Code of Conduct

Para 305.1 of the Code states that: 'a barrister must not in his professional practice, discriminate unlawfully against victimise or harass any other person on the grounds of race, colour, ethnic or national origin, nationality, citizenship, sex, gender re-assignment, sexual orientation, marital or civil partnership status, disability, age, religion or belief or pregnancy and maternity.'

As stated above the equality rules of the Code of Conduct are contained at paragraph 408.2 and apply to all self employed barristers. The rules and supporting guidance documents, which cover interpretation and application of the rules and data protection considerations, may be downloaded from the BSB website.

(3) Queries on equality and diversity

Queries or complaints regarding equality issues can be discussed in confidence with the Bar Council Equality team, on 020 7242 0082. Advice is available on options and/or course of action, as well as concerning specialist organisations that may be able to provide representation or other assistance if pupils wish to pursue a grievance. Various organisations that may be of assistance are listed in Appendix J.

6.7 Offers and acceptances

(1)The offer of a pupillage and its acceptance by the person to whom it is made will give rise to a legally binding contract for education and training.[1] Offers of pupillage may be made by ATOs through Pupillage Portal (if a member) or otherwise if not included in Pupillage Portal A record should be kept of decisions taken, with reasons. Unsuccessful candidates should be given feedback if possible, and when this is asked for. An example of a contract is available from the BSB on request.

1 *Edmunds v Lawson* [2000] QB 501, [2000] 2 WLR 1091, CA.

(2) The offer of a pupillage must contain the date of commencement, details of supervision arrangements, the details of the award to be made to the pupil and such other information as the Bar Standards Board may, from time to time, require. The name of the supervisor should be provided, but the pupil should otherwise be told a reasonable time before the pupillage begins who his or her first supervisor will be (so that a meeting can be arranged before pupillage begins).

(3) Except with the prior approval of the Bar Standards Board, no offer of a pupillage may be made without including a provision for the payment of an award at the level prescribed by the Bar Standards Board.

(4) All offers must remain open for at least 14 days. An applicant should respond as quickly as possible to any offer of pupillage which is made. Applicants should not accumulate offers and may not retain more than two offers for more than seven days, whether the online system is used or not. An applicant who accepts an offer of pupillage should withdraw all other applications for pupillage and make no further applications.

(5) For pupillage providers in the Pupillage Portal system, the closing date for applications is normally the end of April.

(6) In the case of Pupillage Portal applications, no offers may be made before the date/time specified by the Portal Timetable.

(7) All pupillages must be registered with the BSB before commencement.

7. Funding and financial matters

7.1 Funding of pupillage

(1) All pupillages must be funded in accordance with the Code, Annex R, paras 1–2.

Code of Conduct, Annex R

(1) The members of a set of chambers must pay to each non-practising chambers pupil by the end of each month of the non-practising six months of his pupillage no less than: (a) £1,000 plus (b) such further sum as may be necessary to reimburse expenses reasonably incurred by the pupil on: (i) travel for the purposes of his pupillage during that month; and (ii) attendance during that month at courses which he is required to attend as part of his pupillage.

(2) The members of a set of chambers must pay to each practising chambers pupil by the end of each month of the practising six months of his pupillage no less than: (a) £1,000; plus (b) such further sum as may be necessary to reimburse expenses reasonably incurred by the pupil on: (i) travel for the purposes of his pupillage during that month; and (ii) attendance during that month at courses which he is required to attend as part of his pupillage; less (c) such amount, if any, as the pupil may receive during that month from his practice as a barrister; and less (d) such amounts, if any, as the pupil may have received during the preceding months of his practising pupillage from his practice as a barrister, save to the extent that the amount paid to the pupil in respect of any such month was less than the total of the sums provided for in sub-paragraphs (a) and (b) above.

(3) The members of a set of chambers may not seek or accept repayment from a chambers pupil of any of the sums required to be paid under paragraphs 1 and 2 above, whether before or after he ceases to be a chambers pupil, save in the case of misconduct on his part.

7.2 Waivers from pupillage funding requirements

(1) The Code (Annex R, paras 1–3) requires that all ATOs fund their pupils in line with the minimum funding requirements prescribed in the Code. The requirement to fund pupils lies with the ATO, and an ATO must apply for a waiver from the Pupillage Funding Regulations to the Qualifications Committee of the BSB if it does not or cannot fund a particular pupil. It is not possible for a pupil to enter into an agreement with chambers to undertake an unfunded pupillage or for pupils themselves to apply for a waiver from the pupillage funding requirements.

(2) A pupil or prospective pupil cannot apply for a waiver. It is not acceptable for a pupil to undertake an unfunded pupillage in a set of chambers which is prepared to take on a pupil but cannot provide funding. Even if no funding is required by the pupil (due to assets or a loan) an application for a waiver must still be made, and may not necessarily be granted. Where pupillage is at the Employed Bar, then a salary will be in place, so the concept of a waiver from funding will not pertain. Waivers from advertising will need different considerations and evidence will normally need to be provided concerning the rationale for not advertising and information about how a fair recruitment process was undertaken at an earlier stage. Waivers from funding requirements will only be granted in exceptional circumstances. Each case will be considered individually on its own merits.

The relevant form must be used where an application is sought for a waiver from pupillage funding. A formal application must be made to the BSB, by the ATO, not the pupil in question (if there is one). The Pupillage Funding and Advertising Panel of the Qualifications Committee of the BSB deals with these applications. Details of these procedures can be found on the Bar Standards Board website.

(3) International students

International students sometimes wish to complete pupillage in England and Wales and may not require funding, due to sponsorship from their home jurisdictions. Such arrangements promote a desirable spread of good practice throughout the common law world. However, there is a need to ensure that any such proposal would not detract from the system of providing pupillages by means of fair and open competition, and funded accordingly, to prospective members of the Bar of England and Wales. Otherwise, in the event of a nonreturn overseas, the fairness of the system may be impaired. Exceptionally, it may be possible for slightly different arrangements to be put in place for overseas candidates in such circumstances. There are merits and disadvantages of a shorter type of placement for overseas candidates. But, with no assessment or formal 'signing off' being considered, this type of training does not have the same status as pupillage and does not formally count towards pupillage. Waivers may be applied for but the BSB will guard against abuses of the system and waivers will only be exercised in the most exceptional circumstances.

7.3 Financial matters (fees, funding, taxation and expenses)

As part of the compulsory training in pupillage, attendance at the Practie Management Course is required. A qualified accountant usually give presentation on financial matters that relate to pupils and barristers. It is important to attent this session in order to familiarise yourself with tax and National Insurance.

(1) Council tax

Pupils are not automatically exempted from council tax as they do not meet the definitions of a student or apprentice set out in the Council Tax. However, they may be eligible for Council Tax Benefit if they are on a low income and have savings of less than £16,000. Further details may be obtained from the local Department of Work and Pensions' Council Tax office at the pupil's local authority. Further information about tax and insurance/national insurance issues is provided as part of the compulsory Practice Management Course, provided by Inns and Circuits.

(2) Payment of travel expenses to pupils

As mentioned above, ATOs are expected to pay travel expenses for pupils in certain circumstances. This is particularly important where there is extensive travel but limited fees. It is not as necessary where funding or fees are very extensive. It can be helpful and good practice for ATOs to:

- pay a monthly sum in advance to cover travel costs;
- reimburse pupils next day after they return from court (on submission of form for travel expenses);
- pay the predicted cost of travel prior to pupils going to a court away from their place of work (e.g. London) with any difference reimbursed promptly on return from court;
- fund a London travel card (if London based);
- ask pupils in advance of commencement of pupillage to determine what financial assistance is likely to be needed.

(3) Insurance

Pupils are covered by their pupil supervisor's Bar Mutual Indemnity Fund (BMIF) insurance, or their employer's insurance for work performed during pupillage. Once pupillage ceases however, they must apply immediately to the BMIF for their own cover for legal services offered in self-employed practice. If a pupil enters employed practice he/she should ensure that they are covered by the employer's insurance. Failure to take out insurance is a breach of the Code and will be referred to the Complaints Committee. Some Employers self insure which is acceptable.

(4) Chambers awards

If a pupil has an award, he/she needs to establish what the exact terms of the award are. The pupil supervisor should be able to provide all the relevant details including: how and when the award is to be paid, whether a minimum income is guaranteed in the practising six months, whether the pupil is expected to repay any of the award, and what happens if a pupil leaves before completing pupillage.

(5) Inns awards

The Inns tend to focus their funding on the CPE/Diploma in Law and the BVC/BPTC. However, there are still some awards available for the pupillage year. Further information is available from the Students' Officers at each of the Inns or from the Inns' websites.

8. Standards and the curriculum framework

8.1 Overall framework for pupillage

It is required that the Pupillage stage of training must normally be of one calendar year's duration, 'satisfactorily' completed.

BTR 27: A person ... completes the Professional Stage by: satisfactorily completing 12 months of pupillage and such further training as may be required by the Board In addition, in order to maintain standards, the minimum level of competence must be demonstrated.

BTR 3C: The Board shall publish from time to time a general statement of the minimum level of competence reasonably to be expected of a barrister when first qualified to practise.

Paragraphs 276–280 of the Report of the Review of Pupillage (May 2010) focus on the issue of what is 'satisfactory' in pupillage, and what precisely level of competence should be attained in order to satisfy the BSB. The standard to be achieved and the criteria for assessment are therefore set out in this Chapter, together with the defined standards to be attained by pupils.

8.2 Generic standards

"The standard of performance which a pupil's work must achieve is the standard at which the work (whether it is oral advocacy or written work of any description) professionally addresses all the points raised, and is capable of rendering a real and valuable service to the client."[1]

In a professional environment the value and quality of work is always assessed according to its worth to the client. Since the thrust of the reforms to the BPTC was to cement the Vocational Stage with the Professional Stage (i.e. pupillage), the natural consequence is that the standards of assessment to be applied to the work of pupils should equally be clientoriented.

Advice given in conference or in writing must be clear, accurate, comprehensible and constructive. It must address all the issues which the client faces. Where documents are submitted to court (statements of case, indictments, application notices of various kinds, witness statements, notices of appeal, skeleton arguments, written submissions) these must accurately and fairly represent the client's case, and also gain the respect of the court. Oral advocacy is of overriding importance, and must be measured against the client's interests and needs. The advocate must be able to present the best possible case for the client in an attractive, persuasive and clear manner. All the points in the case must be properly and professionally dealt with.

Training must be focussed on the core knowledge, skills and competencies as specified; they directly relate to the eligibility for a practising certificate. The detailed requirements aim to ensure that barristers provide professional service of the highest standard to their clients.

Pupil supervisors must be satisfied that a pupil has met all descriptors as defined in order to be deemed to be performing at the required level in a particular area.

1 Wood Review of Pupillage, Recommendation 54.

8.3 Standards for advocacy

The required advocacy skills are in accordance with ATC and other requirements. Attention is also drawn to the Dutton criteria and the website of the ATC. This should be consulted for criteria for advocacy training, best practice and common mistakes: http://www.advocacytrainingcouncil.org/index.php.

8.4 Roles and responsibilities of pupils

BTR 36: During any period of pupillage the pupil must; (a) be diligent in receiving the instruction given; and (b) observe all legal and professional obligations of confidence.

The Code specifies:

> **801:** A barrister who is a pupil must: (a) comply with Part V of the Bar Training Regulations; (b) apply himself full time to his pupillage save that a pupil may with the permission of his pupil-supervisor or head of chambers take part time work which does not in their opinion materially interfere with his pupillage; (c) preserve the confidentiality of every client's affairs and accordingly paragraph 702 applies to him in the same way as it does to his pupil-supervisor and to every person whom he accompanies to Court or whose papers he sees.
>
> **802:** A barrister who is a pupil may supply legal services as a barrister and exercise a right of audience which he has by reason of being a barrister provided that (a) he has completed or been exempted from the non-practising six months of pupillage; and (b) he has the permission of his pupil-supervisor or head of chambers; provided that such a barrister may during the non-practising six months of pupillage with the permission of his pupil-supervisor or head of chambers accept a noting brief.
>
> Pupils must therefore:
>
> - Act appropriately on feedback provided by the supervisor(s).
> - Act appropriately to assessment and appraisal of his/her work.
> - Take steps to ensure that the outcomes of core and specialist areas are met and that competencies are attained to the required standard.
> - Undertake additional compulsory courses as required.
> - Complete any remedial/additional work as required.
> - Behave at all times in accordance with professional ethics and conduct.

- Preserve the confidentiality of every client's affairs, including clients of the pupil supervisor and other barristers with whom they work.
- Not attempt to exercise rights of audience during the non-practising period of pupillage. A noting brief may be undertaken.
- Prepare documentation to assist the supervisor in the completion of documentation for signing off after first six:
  - — Ensure the initial registration of pupillage.
  - — Notify the BSB Standards & Quality Section of any material changes in pupillage arrangements (e.g. a change in pupil supervisor, a change in start or end dates of pupillage).
  - — Ensure they have met the required standards/ competencies and that outcomes have been met as defined in core and specialist units. The completion of checklists and work diaries are helpful in ensuring that the suggested range of core tasks are completed (especially for the non practising period of pupillage).
  - — Make sure they have completed the pupillage advocacy course as part of the non-practising period of pupillage. If a pupil does not satisfactorily complete the pupillage advocacy course, he/she will not be issued with a provisional qualification certificate (and practising certificate) and so will not be eligible to commence the practising period of pupillage, until the course has been completed.
  - — Make sure his/her pupil supervisor signs the certificate of satisfactory completion of the non-practising period of pupillage and submit it at once to the BSB.
  - — Register the practising period of pupillage (if he/she did not register the whole pupillage at the beginning of the non-practising period).
- Exercise rights of audience during the practising period of pupillage only with the permission of his/her pupil supervisor or Head of Chambers and having received notification from the BSB that they are eligible to do so.
- Prepare documentation to assist the supervisor in the completion of documentation for signing off after the second six:
  - — Complete any additional checklist for the practising period of pupillage.
  - — Make sure his/her pupil supervisor signs the certificate of satisfactory completion of the practising period of pupillage and submit it at once to the BSB.
  - — On completion of pupillage, keep the Bar Council's Records Office and his/her Inn notified of current

status (e.g. tenant, squatter, third six pupil, employed or not in practice) and contact details.

— Register as self employed (with the Tax Office) as soon as possible after commencing the second six pupillage [NB does not apply to the Employed Bar].

- Comply with any other rules or guidelines relating to pupillage issued by the Bar Standards Board.

9. The assessment process

9.1 General principles

Pupils will benefit from:

- the drawing up of a formal work plan for each phase of pupillage; and
- being formally and systematically assessed at regular intervals (every 1–3 months) during their pupillage.

This will enable them to understand their progress and what difficulties, if any, they face in terms of successful completion of pupillage and tenancy selection.

Many ATOs already follow such a procedure, with formal work plans devised for pupils, followed by formal assessment at regular intervals. Whilst formal assessment and grading of pupils' work is not an absolute requirement, it is considered that some form of assessment is considered to have a useful function. It is suggested that all ATOs put such a procedure in place.

For information on the assessment of core areas see Chapter 10; for assessment of specialist areas, see section 10.5 and the specialist checklists available on the BSB website. For assessment of compulsory courses see Chapter 11 and additional information provided by the ATC.

9.2 Assessment and feedback

Although there is no formal specification for examinations or written or oral assessment, it is important that some forms of assessment take place. This can and often does take the form of written pieces of work being assessed by the supervisor and/or others, which is noted as good practice.

'Assessment' is defined in this context by the BSB as 'a structured measurement of the pupil's progress against standards'. Feedback should follow.

'Feedback' is defined as the regular comments on a pupil's work which the supervisor provides in order to improve performance against the standards and competencies. Feedback is also about reinforcing good practice and work as well as identifying areas for improvement.

Persons other than the supervisor may also participate in the evaluation of pupils' performance, for example, clerks, solicitors, members of the judiciary, clients etc. This should normally be categorised as 'feedback' rather than formal assessment – although it may ultimately have a bearing on the latter.

9.3 Monitoring progress during pupillage

Apart from formal assessment, monitoring and evaluation of progress during pupillage is an important element of the pupillage stage of training. Whilst it is mandatory that some form of monitoring of progress takes place, the nature of this is at the discretion of the ATO and supervisor(s).

9.4 Appraisal

It is recommended that formal appraisal, in addition to regular feedback and informal monitoring of progress takes place during pupillage. Whilst it is regarded as good practice that some form of periodic appraisal takes place, the nature of this is at the discretion of the ATO and supervisor(s).

9.5 Assessment of competence: checklists

In order to determine, at the end of the period of pupillage whether the competencies as defined have been met, the standards and competencies carefully considered.

Checklists are to be used for the purpose of verifying that outcomes and competencies have been met. Pupil supervisors and others involved in formal supervision, the Pupillage Training Principal Director of Training and Head of Chambers are all required to countersign checklists completed by pupils to demonstrate that they have covered all areas of training to the required standard. All pupils must ensure that a copy of their completed checklist is submitted to the BSB together with a certificate of satisfactory completion of the second six pupillage. The pupil supervisor is responsible for ensuring the correct paperwork is completed. Records of checklists of pupils must be retained by ATOs for a period of three years following completion.

If any sections have not been signed off as completed, then an explanation must be provided.

9.6 Referrals and 'remedial work

Where omissions and shortcomings are identified, then steps must be taken to overcome any deficiency. These should be identified as early as possible through feedback (and also by appraisal of pupils, see section 14.5) so that corrections can be made before the end of the period of training, rather than resulting in the problem of a supervisor feeling unable to sign off pupillage as having been satisfactorily completed to the required standard. Each checklist should identify any major omissions and note what action the pupil proposes to take in order to remedy them. The adequacy of the steps being taken depends to some extent on which part of the checklist the pupil has been unable to complete and for what reason (e.g. time constraints, inability to meet the required standards etc).

9.7 Failure and reassessment or repeat of pupillage

Where it is not considered that the defined standards and competencies have been met, then the pupil supervisor must not sign off the pupil as having completed either the first six or second six (as appropriate). Discussion must take place so that the pupil is aware of precisely what shortcomings are evident and how these might be rectified. The Head of Chambers and Director of Pupil Training (or Pupillage Training Principal must be kept informed. The BSB must also be kept informed, specifically at the point of signing off a pupil, or if there are issues related to failure of a compulsory course (general problems in performance should not all be notified).

It is expected that, with systems of feedback, monitoring of progress and formal appraisal meetings, issues will be identified and corrected before the six month periods are completed.

Where a pupil is not signed off by his/her supervisor, opportunities may be provided for additional or remedial work in order to enable the pupil to attain the required level of competency, but there is no obligation for this to be provided by chambers or by any other ATO.

Note: Cheating and plagiarism at the pupillage stage of training are rare but sadly not unknown. Pupils should be aware that any form of plagiarism or cheating on the compulsory courses or in exercises required by an ATO (for example, the reuse or plagiarism of another current or previous pupil's written work – e.g. skeleton arguments – submitted for an exercise) will be treated extremely seriously indeed. This will be reported to the pupil's Inn and may be a reason (or contributory reason) for disciplinary action and/or termination of pupillage.

9.8 Appeals against assessment decisions

For appeals, in the event of a pupil not being signed off by his/her supervisor as having satisfactorily completed the pupillage stage of training, see 12.5.

10. Core and specialist knowledge and skills

Overview

The BSB requires all pupils to achieve specified standards and competencies in four core skills:

- Conduct and etiquette.
- Advocacy.
- Conferences and Negotiations.
- Drafting, paperwork and Legal Research.

The core skills are summarised in sections 10.1 – 10.4 below. A note on specialist areas is provided in 10.5. Checklists of tasks that should normally be completed for each core area are provided in Appendix D.

Use of the defined standards and Pupillage Checklists

The primary purpose of the checklist is to provide guidance to pupils and pupil supervisors about the range of tasks that are normally expected to be covered and/or completed during the pupillage stage of training. The levels to which such tasks are to be completed are defined in Chapter 8 where the descriptors of the standards and competencies to be attained by pupils are defined.

Copies of completed checklists must be submitted to the BSB on completion of the second six months' pupillage together with the Certificate of Satisfactory Completion. A full Qualification Certificate confirming completion of pupillage will not be issued until this has been satisfactorily completed and received. Pupils and ATOs should keep copies of the checklist and certificate of satisfactory completion for a period of at least three years. Completed checklists may form the basis of the monitoring process. Checklists 1–4 are for use with the four core skills.

In addition, a further specialist checklist must be submitted reflecting the area of work in which the pupil has been trained, as prepared by the relevant specialist Bar

Association or by the ATO itself (examples of 'bespoke' checklists are available from the BSB). Alternatively, ATOs and supervisors may also produce their own checklists specific to those pupillages that they offer/supervise. These must relate to the common core and be submitted to the Bar Standards Board for approval before being put into use. Significant changes to existing checklists should also be submitted to the BSB for approval.

10.1 Conduct and etiquette

This aims to ensure that pupils have a thorough understanding and appreciation of the operation in practice of rules of conduct and etiquette at the Bar and achieve a working knowledge and understanding of the Code of Conduct and the written standards for the conduct of professional work.

Please refer to the checklists (in Appendix D) for details of the tasks, knowledge and understanding that pupils are expected to have acquired before completing pupillage.

10.2 Advocacy

This aims to enable the pupil to develop and practise the skills necessary to be an effective advocate in oral or written advocacy.

A pupil must attend the advocacy course provided by his or her Inn or Circuit in the first six months. These courses provide the opportunity for pupils to practise oral advocacy under instruction. They can only be effective if pupils have prepared adequately and pupil supervisors are asked to ensure that pupils take the need to prepare very seriously and that they are given sufficient time to do so. Many chambers run their own advocacy courses in addition to those provided by the Inns. The same considerations should apply to the pupil's participation in those courses.

The pupil must maintain a record of relevant work done/issues considered, demonstrating where the outcomes detailed above have been met. Cross-reference should be made to the relevant checklist. Formal, graded, assessment by the supervisor will not be expected in this area, but the pupil will be formally assessed by means of the Compulsory Advocacy course to be undertaken through his/her Inn of Court (see Chapter 11). A formal discussion session should take place at the end of each six months. Written feedback should be provided as appropriate. The pupil supervisor should initial and date the last column of the relevant checklist of work done, when it is considered that the topic has been adequately covered, and to a satisfactory level of competence.

10.3 Conferences and negotiations

This aims to develop the skills of pupils in the area of conference and negotiation, so that pupil may be raised to a standard where he or she can competently conduct a conference or negotiation on behalf of a client.

This will be largely student-centred but pupils must be supervised closely as they develop conference and negotiation skills. Necessarily, this will largely be by observation and discussion with the pupil supervisor but pupil supervisors should not overlook the importance of instructing the pupil in respect of preparation for conferences and negotiations and the making and retaining of a full and accurate note of all conferences. Pupils must be as actively involved as possible.

The pupil must maintain a record of relevant work done/issues considered, demonstrating where the outcomes have been met. Formal assessment of written work may not be expected in this area but oral and written feedback must be provided. A formal discussion session should take place at the end of each six months. Cross-reference should be made to the relevant checklist and the pupil supervisor should initial and date the last column of the relevant checklist of work done, when it is considered that the topic has been adequately covered, and to a satisfactory level of competence, having regard to the objectives as set out.

10.4 Drafting, paperwork and legal research

This aims to enable pupils to develop the necessary writing and drafting skills by producing and obtaining feedback on written examples of work.

At the same time, legal research skills, developed from those in place on the Bar Course, will be enhanced, in order to ensure that pupils can correctly apply all sources of information.

It is of the greatest importance that pupils practise and develop the necessary skills by producing practical work and receiving constructive feedback on that work by their pupil supervisor. Simply observing the work of their pupil supervisor is not enough. Feedback on a pupil's work should be given as soon as possible by a pupil supervisor whilst the work is still fresh in the mind of the pupil. By the conclusion of pupillage a pupil should have demonstrated the appropriate degree of competence in each of the relevant skills/all areas of written work. The development of research skills will be largely pupil-centred, but it is important that help and direction is provided by the supervisor as appropriate. A pupil should be assisted as necessary to learn how to locate and employ all relevant sources of information.

It is of the greatest importance that research skills are practised and developed and that feedback is provided. Written work that is produced must be submitted for assessment and written feedback should be provided by the supervisor. An actual grade may or may not be provided. Assessment of writing and research skills may take place in the form of assessment of written pieces of work where elements of research will be evaluated as an integral part. It is important for supervisors to convey to pupils an idea of where they are without being too discouraging in the early stages. The pupil must maintain a record of relevant work done/issues considered, demonstrating where the outcomes detailed above have been met.

Cross-reference should be made to the relevant checklist (see Appendix D). The pupil supervisor should initial and date the last column of the relevant checklist of work done, when it is considered that the topic has been adequately covered, and to a satisfactory level of competence, having regard to the objective set out above.

10.5 Optional and specialist knowledge and skills

All core areas must be covered by all pupils (although clearly some specific items in the core checklist are relevant only to criminal or civil work, as the case may be). In addition, a considerable proportion of time and effort will be spent on specialist areas. Pupil supervisors must accordingly provide their pupils with a fifth, specialist, checklist, either from those available as listed below, or 'bespoke' (subject to approval by the BSB).

Training in specialist areas will clearly vary according to the set or employed position/department. The actual time spent on specialist areas should remain flexible. Whilst some pupils prefer to specialise at an early stage, others may prefer to widen their experience in different areas. Some variation or rotation between supervisors, even for short periods is recommended. It is also recommended as good practice for those with pupillages in the Employed Bar to spend some time in chambers if this can be arranged.

Specifications for checklists and indicative content, material and standards to be covered in Specialist areas are not (at present) included in this Handbook but provided separately – to enable Specialist Bar Associations and others to update them separately and periodically as appropriate. Theses checklists can be found on the Bar Standards Board website. Checklists are designed to help pupils meet their obligations under the Code and the BTRs. Items marked with an asterisk are those which the SBAs consider essential to cover during pupillage. Outcomes must have been met but it is not essential for the pupil to have covered every item on the checklist of tasks (a good range should have been covered).

There are checklists currently available for the following specialist areas:

- Administrative law.
- Chancery law and practice.
- Commercial and admiralty law.
- CPS.
- Criminal law.
- Employment law.
- Family law.
- General common law.
- Immigration law.
- Local government and planning law.
- Personal injury law.
- Revenue law.
- Technology and construction law.

If none of the specialist checklists is appropriate, ATOs or supervisors must draw up their own specification to take into account the nature of their work and the type of pupillage that is provided. These must be approved by the BSB (on an individual basis, in advance). Where the work of a pupil supervisor is highly specialised, consideration should be given to broadening the experience of the pupil, for example by secondment to others with a more general practice or marshalling. Additional supervisors must be approved if the pupil is attached for one month or more. If an ATO is unable to provide training for any essential elements set out in the checklist(s), then steps must be taken to ensure that these elements will otherwise be covered. There may be overlap between the core and specialist checklists so completion of checklists may rely on cross-referencing to save duplication of effort.

11. Compulsory courses

Overview

In accordance with BTR 33 the BSB specifies that during pupillage all pupils must attend certain compulsory courses to build on training received at the BVC/BPTC stage.

BTR 33: Any period of pupillage must provide training which is adequate and which complies with such criteria as may be published by the Board

The compulsory courses supplement training received in an ATO or from supervisors:

- the Pupillage Advocacy Training course;
- the Practice Management Course.

These courses are provided by the Inns and Circuits who provide details on how and when the courses are run. Pupils normally attend the courses of their own Inn or Circuit, although they may be allowed to attend those of another Inn or Circuit by special arrangement. Pupils are not entitled to obtain a full qualification certificate or commence practice until, following formal assessment, they have satisfactorily completed the compulsory pupillage courses. The pupillage advocacy course must be completed as part of the non-practising period of pupillage. A pupil who has not yet satisfactorily completed the pupillage advocacy course will not normally be issued with a provisional qualification certificate and so will not be eligible to commence the practising period of pupillage until the course has been completed.

Pupils must also undertake the Practice Management Course, and they are strongly advised to do so during the non-practising period during pupillage. A pupil who has not yet satisfactorily completed the Practice Management course may not be issued with a full qualification certificate and so will not be eligible to commence practice as a barrister until the course has been completed.

11.1 Advocacy course

(1) Inns and Circuits

Formal advocacy courses that pupils must undertake are provided by the Inns and Circuits. These are additional to the advocacy training and practice that generally occurs during pupillage. Details of advocacy courses (location, date and availability etc) can be obtained from the relevant Inn and/or Circuit. Courses consist of a minimum of 12 hours advocacy training, in the following four compulsory elements (based on the Dutton criteria, Appendix M):

- skeleton arguments;
- oral submissions;
- examination-in-chief;
- cross-examination.

(2) Preparation

Pupils must be afforded adequate time to prepare for compulsory advocacy training. Given that pupils are required to undertake and successfully complete this training in order to acquire a provisional qualification certificate, preparation is obviously an important issue. Concerns have been expressed in the past by the Advocacy Training Council that there is an on-going issue of uneven preparation time for pupils. Pupils sometimes arrive at courses unprepared, having been given no time off by their pupil supervisor in advance of the course. Pupils' advocacy performance is formally assessed, so it is critical that adequate time for preparation is allowed. As far as possible, all pupils should start from a common starting point and be given an equal chance of satisfactorily completing the advocacy training requirement laid down by the Board. The ATC has recommended that pupils are given (at least) a day off in advance of a compulsory and assessed advocacy training assessment to allow them to prepare. The BSB supports this approach and attention of both Pupil Supervisors and Heads of Chambers is therefore drawn to this requirement.

(3) Assessment on compulsory courses

The compulsory advocacy course provides the compulsory assessment component of pupillage. When undertaking Advocacy Training, pupils are formally assessed during each training providers' advocacy training programme, according to set criteria (based on the concept of work being worthy of providing a service to a client). Criteria are published on the ATC website at: http://www.advocacytraining council.org/.

11.2 Practice Management Course

The Practice Management Course (formerly known as the 'Advice to Counsel' course) is run by the Inns, and the Circuits, from whom further details may be obtained. It is important for the course to be undertaken early on in Pupillage so it should preferably be delivered by October each year. The Practice Management Courses thus vary slightly but the following core elements should ideally be covered by all providers:

- Ethics.
- Equality and diversity.
- Work of the Bar Council and the BSB.
- Circuits and messes.
- Complaints and professional discipline.
- Professional finances – tax, VAT (including registering for VAT), pensions, record-keeping etc.
- Professional indemnity insurance and common sources of claims.
- Services available to the Bar.
- Chambers' organisation.
- Barristers and their clerks.

- Barristers and instructing solicitors.
- Barristers and lay clients.
- Court etiquette and dress.
- Doing a noting brief (the only activity permitted).
- Money laundering legislation.
- Data protection.
- Registration and certification of pupillage.
- The role of pupil supervisors.
- Checklists for pupils.
- Pupils' expenses and how to claim them.
- Practice management and marketing.
- The employed Bar.
- The "third six".
- The FRU.
- CPD and the SBAs.

Note: More detail on the above outline will be provided in due course, in discussion with the Inns and Circuits.

11.3 Delivery of compulsory courses

Practice may vary as to how and when the courses are delivered, for example during the working week, or split over a number of evenings and/or a residential or non-residential weekend. Elements (e.g. Advocacy and Practice Management) may be combined. The Advocacy Course is delivered by experienced practitioners and sitting and retired judges. The Practice Management Courses are delivered by a mixture of practitioners, barristers' clerks and chambers' managers, accountants and financial advisers, solicitors, and officers of the Bar Council, the BSB and the Bar Mutual Indemnity Fund.

11.4 Forensic accounting

The Forensic Accounting Course can be undertaken during pupillage or in the first three years of practice. It is generally felt that the earlier this course is undertaken, the better. The course is divided into three areas of practice, namely Civil, Crime and Family. Barristers must decide which programme they should attend. Day 1 covers Finance and Accounting principles and is of relevance to all delegates. Day 2 covers an overview of Forensic Accounting in the morning (which is relevant to all three programmes) and case studies in the afternoon which are relevant to one of the three areas of law. There is also a pre-course e-learning module. The two-day course provides delegates with practical guidance in the use of financial information and accounts (both corporate and individual). The course qualifies for 20 hours and is currently provided by BPP Professional Education on a fixed term basis. See http://www.bppprofessionaldevelopment.com/forensicbar/ for further information. This course is being reconsidered as part of the ongoing review of CPD.

11.5 Additional internal training

Some Chambers and other ATOs (e.g. GLS, CPS) may provide additional training for their pupils. This may be made compulsory for pupils training in these organisations, but the provision of supplementary in house training courses is not required by the BSB, as long as the standards and competencies of pupillage can otherwise be met.

11.6 Plagiarism and cheating

Cheating (including plagiarism) is extremely rare in the pupillage stage of training. However, pupils should be aware that any form of cheating on the compulsory courses (e.g. plagiarism of the work of a current or former pupil) will be treated extremely seriously indeed. It may be, or may be linked to, grounds for termination of pupillage.

12. Certification and practice

12.1 Accepting instructions

BTR 49: On completion of the non-practising period of pupillage, the Board will issue the pupil with a Provisional Qualification Certificate provided that the pupil has been called to the Bar under Part IX of these Regulations Pupils may do a noting brief in the first six months, provided that he or she has the permission of their pupil supervisor or (*in absentia*) the Head of Chambers. Pupils may be paid for doing a noting brief during this period.

BTR 50: On completion of the practising period of pupillage, the Board will issue the pupil with a Full Qualification Certificate if the pupil has a Provisional Qualification Certificate and the Board is satisfied: that the pupil has satisfactorily completed the practising period of pupillage and any further training required under Regulation 27(a); and that the pupillage is registered and complied with these Regulations.

Note: This has now been updated in accordance with the Legal Services Act 2007. From January 2010 it has been a criminal offence to practise as a barrister without a practising certificate (in accordance with the Legal Services Act 2007). Therefore practising pupils are now issued with practising certificates. See above, section 2.1.

12.2 Insurance

Unless alternative arrangements have (exceptionally) been made, pupils are covered by their pupil supervisor's insurance until they receive a full qualification certificate. Barristers offering legal services in self-employed practice must take out their own insurance with the Bar Mutual Indemnity. Employed barristers should ensure that their employer has any appropriate professional indemnity insurance for themselves and to also cover pupils. Central government, for example, does not have specific insurance because it bears its own risk.

12.3 Certification of pupillage: first six

At the end of the first six months, a pupil who has satisfactorily completed this phase of training (that is, has met the outcomes and demonstrated the competencies specified for the first six months) will be signed off by his/her supervisor (and others as appropriate) as having successfully completed the first six to the standards described in Chapter 8. On completion of their first six pupillage, pupils have to submit a duly completed Certificate of Satisfactory Completion of Pupillage form to the BSB (see Appendix E).

The process of signing off also entails the completion of the relevant checklists for compulsory and specialist areas as appropriate (as described in Chapter 10). It is the responsibility of the pupil to self certify completion of the different sections, but the onus lies with the supervisor-assessor to confirm that training has been completed to the required standard. Once satisfactory completion of the first six is confirmed and has been submitted to the Standards & Quality Section of the BSB, then a Provisional Qualification Certificate will be issued and, providing the pupil has a practising period of pupillage, the pupil will be eligible for a practising certificate.

12.4 Certification of pupillage: second six

At the end of the second six months, a pupil who has satisfactorily completed this stage of training and has met the outcomes and demonstrated the competencies specified for the second six months will be signed off by his/her supervisor (and others as appropriate, see Certificate of Completion, Appendix E) as having successfully completed the second six to the standards as defined. On completion of their second six pupillage, pupils have to submit another Certificate of Satisfactory Completion of Pupillage to the BSB, together with a copy of the completed checklists. It is up to the pupil to self certify completion of the different sections, but the supervisor-assessor must confirm that standards have been met. The pupil supervisor (and others as appropriate) should sign the certificate of completion of the second six. On the basis of satisfactory completion of the second six pupillage, pupils are issued with a Full Qualification Certificate, after which a full Practising Certificate can be obtained from the Bar Council where appropriate.

Note: A Full Qualification Certificate is not a practising certificate. It only certifies completion of pupillage. A Provisional Qualification Certificate only certifies completion of the first six. These certificates have no practising rights attached to them. The full qualification certificate is the one-off certificate issued to show that someone has completed all the qualification requirements, in pupillage. A Practising Certificate is an annual certificate that shows that a barrister is authorised to practise in a particular year. The fact that a barrister has completed pupillage and been issued with a Full Qualification Certificate, does not necessarily mean that he/she will be entitled to a practising certificate. For the requirements for holding a practising certificate see the Bar Council website.

12.5 Pupil supervisors' obligations in signing off pupillage

(1) Every pupil supervisor must be aware of the obligation, at the end of each period of pupillage, to provide a certificate of completion of pupillage so the BSB can issue a Provisional or Full Qualification Certificate complying with BTR 49 and 50. If a pupil supervisor fails to certify a pupil where it is proper to do so (i.e. if the pupil has completed his or her pupillage satisfactorily) it is a breach of the guidelines set out in the Code of Conduct. On the other hand, it is also a breach of the Code if a supervisor fails to take his/her role seriously and inappropriately signs off a pupil. Pupil supervisors must not certify a pupil who fails to reach the required standards.

(2) If the pupil supervisor is unavailable to sign a certificate for completion of the first six, then the Head of Chambers or the Pupillage Training Principal Director of Pupil Training may sign the certificate – provided that he or she provides reasons why the pupil supervisor was unable to sign the certificate, and is him or herself satisfied that requirements and outcomes have been met. The certificate for completion of the second six must be signed by at least two people if the pupil supervisor is unavailable i.e. by both the Head of Chambers and the Pupillage Training Principal/ Director of Pupil Training or another supervisor.

12.6 Appeals against non certification

(1) Where a Certificate of completion is not provided for any reason then an appeal may be made to the BSB:

BTR 55: If the Board refuses to issue a Provisional Qualification Certificate or a Full Qualification Certificate, the pupil may request a review of the decision under Part X of these Regulations, provided that the request is made in writing to the Board within one month of the date when notice of the decision was given.

(2) Mindful of their duties and responsibilities not to sign off a pupil if he/she fails to meet the required standards, the pupil supervisor may decline to sign the certificate on the grounds that he/she is not satisfied that the pupillage has been satisfactorily completed. An appeal may be made against such a decision. Details are available from the BSB. The decision of the Qualifications Committee will be final. However, it may be possible to negotiate a remedial programme with the ATO in order to enable a pupil to meet the required level. There is no obligation on the ATO to do this.

Note: This situation may develop into a complaint, either by the pupil against the ATO or by the ATO against the pupil, where there is reason to consider that there has been an infringement of the Code of Conduct.

13. Resources

13.1 Resource requirements

Details of resources that must be provided by ATOs are outlined in the Guidelines for ATO applications. The guidelines are available on the BSB website.

13.2 Good practice

In addition to mandatory requirements, the provision of the following for pupils is regarded as good practice:

- Own workspace, dedicated PC or laptop, own phone extension, email address and facilities.
- Access to chambers or an Institutional Library, including access to Law reports etc. Rules relating to the use of the library, LEXIS, the Internet and so on must be clear to pupils who should follow them scrupulously.
- Pupils are also entitled to use the Inns' libraries of which they are a member.

- Access to facilities on Circuits may also be provided.
- Office Space – Pupils should usually share a room with their Pupil Supervisor so that they can benefit from observing their routine and professional practice.
- Secretarial services, computing facilities, photocopying, post, telephone – The extent of provision may vary but the ATO must meet the requirements for ATOs. There should be procedures in existence regarding the use of secretarial services, computing facilities and the photocopier and whether pupils need to ask permission to use them or keep any records of their use.

Arrangements for private use of the above should be made clear to pupils. Arrangements for making or receiving private telephone calls, or sending or receiving letters or emails, or using the internet through the premises should be agreed in advance.

14. Support and advice for pupils

14.1 General issues

The mandatory requirements for pupillage provision are enhanced by good practice. This is summarised in this section, presented in the form of 'support and advice' for pupils. It is important that pupils obtain as much information as possible (and at an early stage) about what is expected of them. They should be provided with a full copy of the chambers' or organisation's pupillage policy document or equivalent documentation.

Matters itemised below are to be regarded as obligatory where the word *must* is used and as good practice where *should* is used instead.

14.2 Induction

A comprehensive induction session should be provided, of about 1–2 hours' duration. The following points should be covered in induction (i.e. on the first day or during the first week), as good practice, but many will require continuing discussion as well:

General

- Time must be taken by the supervisor to hold discussion with the pupil about the supervisor's and organisation's practice and the pupillage generally.
- The pupil supervisor must ensure that the pupil is provided with, and retains, the appropriate Handbook, checklists and policy documents.
- There must be an opportunity to discuss what is expected of the pupil during pupillage.
- Time must be taken to talk the pupil through this Handbook – especially the aims and objectives of pupillage, the roles and responsibilities of supervisors, and the roles and responsibilities of pupils.

People

- The pupil must be introduced to the Head of Chambers, and other members of chambers as appropriate – or equivalents in the Employed Bar.

- Arrangements for rotation to other supervisors must be clear (if applicable).
- Procedures for taking on work for members of the ATO other than the pupil's designated supervisor must be clear.
- The pupil must be introduced to clerks, secretarial staff and other persons within the organisation associated with pupillage.
- Pupils should be provided with an outline of the executive structure of chambers/the organisation, including relevant roles/responsibilities, e.g. the pupillage committee.
- Forms of address to be used (formally and informally) should be made clear.
- Pupils should be informed of the role of other individuals in their pupillage training.
- Pupils should be made aware if and when other pupils are to start pupillages.
- The pupil should be provided with a mentor (at a similar level).

General behaviour etc

- Pupils should be informed about etiquette (towards members, clerks, staff, solicitors, court staff and clients, or Head of Department, colleagues etc at the Employed Bar).
- Pupils should be informed about dress conventions in the ATO.

Work

- The importance of confidentiality must be stressed.
- Timing for feedback and formal appraisal must be clear from the outset.
- Procedures and conduct in conferences (e.g. preparation, participation and follow up) must be clear.
- Procedure and conduct for court appearance must be clear.
- Pupils must be encouraged to ask questions.
- Pupils must be informed about presentation requirements for paperwork.
- It is important for the pupil to know about the nature of work dealt with by the pupil supervisor and the type of work in which they will be involved.
- Pupils should be informed about how their work will be planned, monitored and how feedback will be provided.
- Pupils should be informed how competencies are to be demonstrated as met.
- Pupils should be informed of the means for frank and early discussion when things go wrong/need improvement or when an actual mistake is made.
- Pupils should be informed about procedure for taking work home (if applicable).

- Pupils should be informed at induction that their work will be seen by members of the organisation in addition to the supervisor.
- Work distribution amongst pupils should be explained (and monitored to ensure fairness), in relation to chambers' policies on work distribution.

Additional educational opportunities and requirements

- Procedures for attending compulsory courses must be clear.
- In house training by the chambers/organisation must be explained (if provided).
- Procedures for undertaking FRU, pro bono or voluntary work should be explained.
- Opportunities for non-compulsory lectures and courses should be identified.

HR and financial matters etc

- Expected working hours must be made clear.
- The mechanisms for payment of pupillage awards must be clear. These should be paid on time.
- The handling of remuneration for work done (additional to pupillage award) must be made clear. This should be paid promptly or other 'cash flow' arrangements made.
- Expenses and incidentals to be borne by the ATO (e.g. course costs, travel, photocopying, stationery) must be made clear. It should be ensured that incidentals expenses met by members of chambers are met promptly.
- Clerks' fees and payment must be clarified.
- Arrangements for the pupil when the supervisor is working from home should be made clear.
- Arrangements for sick leave should be made clear.
- Holiday entitlement should be explained, and the procedure for booking this.
- Compliance with professional indemnity insurance requirements should be checked, insofar as they affect the pupil.

***Working environment** (**see also 14.8**)*

- Pupils should be informed of the geography/layout of the building(s).
- Pupils should be informed about seating arrangements and places for cases/personal effects.
- Pupils should be informed of security issues, such as the procedure on daily arrival and departure from the premises (e.g. via clerks' room; checking diary entries etc).
- Pupils should be fully briefed about health and safety issues, or related rules (e.g. smoking).

Use of equipment (professional and private)

- It must be made clear how telephone and email facilities are to be used (professional or private).
- The availability of secretarial support must be made clear.
- Availability of other administrative assistance e.g. from Clerks and staff should be made clear.
- Information should be provided on use of photocopiers, and printing facilities.
- Information should be provided on availability of computing/network facilities.
- Availability/access to books, electronic sources and borrowing facilities should be clear.

Policies

- The pupil must be provided with a copy of chambers' Equality & Diversity policy and other chambers' equality related policies (such as the antiharassment policy and reasonable adjustments policy).
- It must be ensured that promised timing and method for appraisal and for decision about second/third six months pupillage and tenancy are met, or any unavoidable delays explained.
- Attention must be drawn to the Code of Conduct, and steps taken to ensure the pupil has read it and discussed any points arising.
- The pupil must be informed of the complaints and grievance procedures, as well as the BSB complaints system.
- Discussion of professional ethics should take place and be encouraged.

Other activities

- Pupils should be provided with opportunities to meet and mix with colleagues socially.
- The desirability of membership of the Circuit and SBAs should be discussed.
- Active participation in the pupil's Inn's activities should be encouraged.

Appraisal for tenancy/permanent position

- The timing and mechanics for tenancy/permanent position interviews must be made clear.
- The timing and method for decisions on second/third six and tenancy must be explained, and how decisions will be communicated.
- Information about careers and help available to secure further pupillage or employment may be indicated.

14.3 General obligations and functions in supervision

The formal roles and responsibilities of pupils, supervisors and ATOs are specified in Chapters 4, 8 and 9.

Note – Completely non-educational tasks should of course be banned. Inordinate requests by supervisors or other members of chambers to pupils to do routine work (e.g. excessive photocopying, coffee making etc, or running shopping errands and so on) are inappropriate.

14.4 Court and other work

(1) Court work: non-practising pupils

Pupils are not permitted to supply legal services as a barrister or exercise rights of audience as a barrister during the first six except that they may, with the permission of the pupil-supervisor or Head of Chambers accept a noting brief.

Pupils should expect to see as much of their supervisor's court work as possible. If his or her practice involves extensive travelling on Circuit, pupils should try to establish early on whether or not they are expected to attend such cases and whether they will be offered any additional funds to cover the expenses. On days when a pupil supervisor is working some distance away, he or she may arrange for the pupil to accompany another member of chambers or leave them to do paperwork in chambers.

Chambers vary in the extent to which pupils are encouraged to attend court with other members of chambers, but it is particularly important that pupils see court work done by junior members of chambers in order to prepare them for court appearances in the practising six months. Pupils should consult with their pupil supervisor about the opportunities that are available for seeing such work.

Pupils will gain most benefit from observing court work if they are able to read the papers and discuss them before or after the court appearance, and it is always useful to prepare a skeleton submission or draft questions that should be asked. If a pupil attends court with his/her pupil supervisor, they should not offer an opinion regarding the case to the client. Any views should be discussed with the pupil supervisor alone.

(2) Court work: practising pupils

Pupils are entitled to supply legal services as a barrister and exercise a right of audience as a barrister provided that they have completed (or been exempted from) the non-practising six months of pupillage and they have the permission of their pupil supervisor or Head of Chambers.

Pupils must carefully check the location of the court and arrive at least 30 minutes before their case is due to be heard. Pupils should check any details about which they are unsure with the pupil supervisor (for example, whether or not they need to be robed for a hearing, or the correct form of address for a particular tribunal). Pupils should also ensure that they are familiar with the established procedures in their chambers/organisation for the issuing and handling of briefs. They will usually be expected to contact clerks at the end of the case in order to be informed whether they are needed elsewhere. Pupils will also need to keep the instructing solicitor informed of the progress of the case.

Although pupils will be doing work of their own during the practising six months, this is still part of pupillage training. Before doing a case of their own, pupils should consult with their pupil supervisor, who can be expected to provide advice and guidance. When not undertaking their own work, pupils will be expected to attend court or conferences with their pupil supervisor and continue to assist with their paperwork as part of training.

In relation to court appearances, the pupil supervisor should provide assistance before a pupil goes into court and also provide an opportunity for discussion afterwards. Ideally, the supervisor should observe the pupil's performance in court on at least one occasion, or observe the pupil undertaking a minor task in one of his or her own cases, for example, taking a small point in a conference, speaking to a solicitor on the telephone or making a small uncontested application such as costs. This will assist both supervisor and pupil to identify strengths and/or weaknesses in performance.

If a pupil is undertaking pupillage in a set of chambers or an organisation where there are limited opportunities to take on advocacy work of their own, they should discuss with the pupil supervisor how sufficient practical experience of advocacy can be otherwise obtained. This can be done, for example, through a placement at another set of chambers or undertaking FRU or other pro bono work.

(3) Conferences

Pupils and supervisors should discuss in advance what is expected from pupils in a conference. It is usually the case that a pupil should not speak at all during the conference unless he/she is specifically invited to contribute. Pupils will gain most benefit from the conference if they ensure that they have read the case papers in advance and if they have the opportunity to discuss them before or afterwards. The pupil should take a full note of the conference, particularly the advice given by Counsel and any instructions given by the client.

14.5 Appraisal (guidance and good practice for formal appraisal)

(1) General aims

Many chambers and training organisations have one or more formal reviews to monitor the work pupils have done over the course of their pupillage. Even if they do not have such a system, it can be helpful to carry out appraisal at the midpoint of each period of pupillage. If there are any difficulties or areas in which improvement is needed, this will give pupils the opportunity to address them during the remaining period of their pupillage. The review can also be used to monitor progress in completing the checklist and to identify any gaps in training.

ATOs may already have a system in place for conducting regular appraisals with pupils. If not, such systems may be introduced, along the lines of the summary below. Suggested forms are available for the purpose of guidance. These exemplars may be adapted, or existing proformas may be used.

The appraisal process is an opportunity to give structured and objective feedback to a pupil which should lead to improved performance. It is also an opportunity to obtain feedback from pupils about how they see their roles, the work they have done and the way in which they are being supervised. The appraisal is expected to achieve a range of objectives, including:

- reviewing an individual's performance over the previous few months;
- setting objectives for future performance;
- identifying pupil's strengths and areas for development;
- encouraging a pupil to improve their performance where this is necessary;
- enabling pupil supervisors to provide feedback to pupils.

Pupils should provide the major contribution. To enable the appraisal to be productive, the pupil must have time to reflect and analyse the circumstances prevailing, before the appraisal takes place. Pupil supervisors should ensure that they have regular meetings with pupils throughout the year and in particular after the appraisal to discuss progress and follow up any action that should have been taken.

(2) Preparation

Care should be taken to ensure that the pupil fully understands the appraisal process before the actual interview. They should also have a realistic view of their own performance ascertained through self-appraisal prior to the main appraisal interview (by completing the appraisal preparation form, although this is not compulsory).

A record of the previous performance appraisal(s) can provide valuable data and can serve as a useful reminder. However, caution should be exercised if the previous review was completed by a different person, whilst he/she was in a different role. The appraisal is not an opportunity to reiterate disciplinary messages or to enact formal procedures; these issues should be dealt with separately.

(3) The role of the pupil: self evaluation

The supervisor should encourage the pupil to prepare for the interview by completing a copy of the appraisal preparation form. This is a good way of ensuring the pupil is ready for the interview, has a reasonable understanding of what to expect and obtains a structured approach to self-reflection. It also provides an opportunity for a pre-appraisal briefing.

A sample proforma for self appraisal is available on request. The pupil should be able to speak freely about his/her pupillage, including the following:

- the contents of his/her current roles and duties;
- the supervisor's role and contribution to the overall objectives of pupillage;
- strengths and weaknesses in relation to the skills, knowledge, abilities and qualities necessary to perform the duties required;

- the resources available to help complete the work;
- motivation, confidence and interest in the tasks assigned to the pupil;
- performance against previously agreed objectives;
- opportunities for improvement;
- ideas for future objectives;
- training and development;
- the effectiveness of training previously received (where appropriate);
- the managerial style of their pupil supervisor;
- relationships with colleagues/members of chambers.

(4) The role of the appraiser

The supervisor/appraiser should play several roles:

- Judge/assessor – giving feedback on the pupil's past performance.
- Helper – helping the pupil to plan their future development.
- Partner – working together to plan goals and targets for the next period.

The supervisor should take the lead role objectively, drawing on real evidence of performance levels. The supervisor should be aware of their personality characteristics which may affect the appraisal interview. They should give praise where it is justified, and clarify and summarise the plans that are agreed.

The pupil may wish to use the appraisal to discuss personal problems. In such situations there may be a requirement for a counselling interview, separate from the appraisal itself.

(5) Following up the appraisal interview.

Following or during the interview, the supervisor should complete the appraisal form. The completed form should be shared with the pupil who should sign the form, having been given the opportunity to make comments. The main points of any discussions which require followup action should be noted separately, listing the action(s) which have been agreed. The complete form should then be forwarded to the Head of Pupillage Committee in the ATO (sealed and marked 'confidential') and a copy also provided to the individual. The supervisor and pupil are jointly responsible for ensuring that agreed action is carried out.

(6) Poor performance

Where poor performance is identified, or any areas that need improvement, these should be discussed in full and remedies sought. It is important for any problems to be recognised early on, and rectified, before the point of not signing off a pupil is reached. For example, poor attendance or poor time-keeping should be flagged up before they become a serious issue.

Poor professional performance will need to be discussed in detail with measures identified to resolve the problem if possible. Employed Bar organisations will have Human Resources Departments to advise on such situations and how to implement capability procedures if these become necessary. Advice may be sought from the BSB, depending on whether the issue is one of professional practice or performance, or related to a formal complaint. See section 9.8 for regulations on assessment and appeals against assessment decisions.

14.6 Record keeping

(1) Checklists

The checklists can be used to plan the training that pupils receive during pupillage, to check that they are experiencing an adequate range of work and to review progress during pupillage.

Once checklist(s) to be used during pupillage have been identified, pupils must ensure that they are familiar with them. If a checklist does not meet particular requirements, it can be discussed with the pupil supervisor how it might be amended. Bespoke checklists require BSB approval before they can be adopted.

It is not expected that pupils will be able to cover all the items in the specialist section of the checklist, particularly if they are based on Circuit. However, any items that are identified as being essential should be covered in the first six months and a good range of the other items should be covered. Pupils should identify in the appropriate section of the checklist anything that has not been covered and indicate how the gap in training can be remedied.

Pupils and supervisors will need to discuss how checklists will be used, but pupils must refer to the checklist regularly throughout pupillage, providing as much information as possible in the commentary section. The checklists will be used by the pupil supervisor to review progress and also during BSB monitoring of pupillage in chambers. They may also be useful evidence for chambers in considering tenancy applications.

(2) Work diary

Pupil supervisors should encourage pupils to keep a work diary during pupillage to record work done and the amount of time spent on it (with cross references to outcomes, core competencies and 'tasks' as specified in the checklists). It is considered good practice for pupils to keep diaries or portfolios of all work undertaken and go through the checklist every three months filling in the relevant details of their experience. This is reviewed with their pupil supervisor and plans are made to address any gaps, and will enable the pupil supervisor to check when a particular assignment/task was undertaken, what exactly was done, who the pupil worked with/for, and how long it took the pupil to complete the work. It will also assist in the accurate completion of the checklist, which in turn aids the supervisor in certifying the satisfactory completion of pupillage. Keeping a work diary is also useful if a pupil applies for another pupillage or tenancy. This is so that completion of all requirements can not only be met but can be demonstrated as having been met.

Not only does it provide an accurate record of experience, it also demonstrates organisational abilities that will be useful in practice.

(3) Work portfolio

Filing (or otherwise retaining) copies of paperwork produced is good practice from the start of professional life. An index of the names of the cases and the date when the work was done filed in chronological order is helpful to review earlier cases and precedents. The pupil will then be able to look back at work done before in similar cases, and be able to re-use legal research. The pupil will also be able to develop his/her own precedents. The ability for a pupil to review their own work side by side with the pupil supervisor's, or that of someone else in chambers with whom they have worked, is an excellent way for a pupil to become self-critical and develop good paperwork skills.

If a pupil applies for a tenancy in chambers, they may be asked to submit work for consideration, so good record keeping is essential. Client confidentiality must be maintained by blocking out identifying information.

(4) Paperwork

Although pupils will have had experience of paperwork on the Bar Course, they will require assistance in making the transition to dealing with real cases and real circumstances.

Individual pupil supervisors may well vary in the nature and extent of the feedback that they give on paperwork, but pupils should always feel able to ask for more detailed comments on work if they are not sure where they have gone wrong. It is equally important for a pupil supervisor to identify what a pupil is doing well, so they can build on their strengths.

Pupils should expect to read their supervisor's opinions and draft pleadings and to have the opportunity of discussing these with him/her. It is a good idea to keep records of such work in order to build up a library of precedents. Practice in drafting pleadings and writing opinions is an important part of most pupillages and the supervisor should discuss the pupil's attempts and provide regular feedback on progress. The accuracy and speed of work are important factors.

(5) Data protection

The Data Protection Act 1998 came into force on 1 March 2000. Barristers working in chambers are required to register under the Act if they use a computer for processing of personal data. Whilst first six pupils are considered to be processing data on behalf of a supervisor, second six pupils will be doing their own data processing and must register.

Pupils can register online via the Office of the Information Commissioner website at http://www.ico.gov.uk/ or by phoning the notification helpline (0303 123 1113). The cost of notification is currently £35 per year. It is a criminal offence not to register if there is a requirement to do so under the Act.

14.7 Conduct and etiquette

All pupillages should involve training in professional conduct and etiquette. Part one of each checklist/specification identifies the core issues that should be addressed. Pupils should familiarise themselves with the Code of Conduct in the first six months of pupillage and ensure that they are prepared for dealing with common ethical dilemmas that may arise in the second six. If issues arise in practice, pupils should, wherever possible, consult with their pupil supervisor about the appropriate course of action. They may also contact the Bar Council's Professional Practice Section if there are any specific queries (There is a hotline number available for advice: 020 7611 1307).

14.8 The working environment

(1) Chambers

The way that sets of chambers are administered varies according to size, the area of practice and the extent to which information technology is used. In smaller sets, members of chambers will carry out administrative functions themselves. Pupils should learn as much as possible about how chambers are administered, in order both to maximise efficiency during pupillage and to provide insight into issues that may be dealt with as a tenant. It is particularly important that pupils understand the role and function of barristers' clerks. A clerk usually maintains diaries of work, liaises with courts, solicitors and other chambers, fixes and recovers fees and promotes barristers and the Chambers as a whole.

Most clerks are members of the Institute of Barristers' Clerks and have a variety of qualifications and experience. The most senior clerks will have significant responsibilities including booking instructions and hearings, negotiating fees, and managing and developing the practices of individual barristers and the set of chambers as a whole. Some chambers have now replaced senior clerks with salaried practice managers or chief executives.

In the non-practising six months, pupils should aim to develop a good working relationship with the clerks in preparation for when they will be working on their own account. The clerks may also be able to let pupils know if other members of chambers, particularly the junior tenants, are appearing in any cases that the pupil supervisor might feel it would be useful for a pupil to attend. The clerks should be kept informed of pupils' movements if they need to leave chambers, and be provided with home/mobile telephone numbers and any other contact numbers in case they need to get in touch with pupils outside office hours. Pupils must also let the clerk(s), as well as their supervisor, know if they are not able to come into chambers for any reason.

During the practising six months, pupils will need to establish whether they are required to pay clerks' fees. Chambers vary in their requirements, but pupils must be clearly informed whether or not clerks' fees are payable and, if so, on what basis, before they receive any instructions on their own account. Pupils may also be required to contribute towards photocopying and other administrative costs, but they should not be asked to pay any rent. Pupils should establish what work is available for practising pupils, and how and when it is distributed. The equality rules of the Code require that the allocation of unassigned work is monitored by diversity characteristics and further require that pupils are given fair and equal access to the opportunities available in chambers. It is vital during this period of pupillage that pupils keep clerks informed of their whereabouts and also warn them of any commitments that may affect their availability.

(2) Other organisations (employed bar)

The way that ATOs in the Employed Bar operate will vary enormously, according to size, number of staff, and areas of practice. All relevant information should be provided to pupils, including 'clerking' of administrative tasks, secretarial support etc. Practice managers and office administrators may be used but, in smaller organisations, some barristers will carry out many administrative functions themselves. During pupillage it is useful for pupils to learn as much as possible about how the organisation is administered, in order to maximise efficiency and provide insight into issues that will need to be dealt with if permanent employment follows.

It can be helpful, for pupils at the employed Bar to have a period of time/secondment to Chambers, where they may learn how chambers operate and the function of barristers' clerks.

At the Employed Bar support should similarly be provided (e.g. by salaried practice managers) on booking instructions and hearings, negotiating fees, and managing and developing the practices of individuals. In the non-practising six months, pupils should keep their own appointments diaries up to date, as well as checking the diary of their supervisor so that they know what conferences and court hearings are coming up. The clerks (or managers) should be kept informed of pupils' movements if they need to leave the premises, and be provided with home/mobile telephone numbers and any other contact numbers in case they need to get in touch with pupils outside office hours. Pupils must also let relevant managers, as well as their supervisor know if they are not able to come in for any reason.

During the practising six months, pupils must be clearly informed of any fees that are payable and, if so, on what basis, before they receive any instructions on their own account. Chambers must ensure that a review of the distribution of unallocated work is undertaken to ensure pupils are given fair and equal access to the opportunities available. It is vital during this period of pupillage that pupils keep relevant staff informed of their whereabouts and also warn colleagues of any commitments that may affect their availability.

14.9 Duration, hours, leave and sick leave

(1) Duration of pupillage

As stated in Chapter 8, the duration of pupillage must be a minimum of twelve calendar months (unless a reduction in pupillage has been approved). Pupils should not move to another ATO (to complete their 12 months and/or to commence a 'third six') before this period is completed since they will be at risk of not being signed off. Similarly ATOs should not accept pupils on these terms until they have been signed off as having successfully completed pupillage in the ATO which agreed to provide the twelve month pupillage.

(2) Hours of work and holiday entitlement

The Code of Conduct requires pupils to apply themselves full-time to pupillage, which requires a minimum of 35 hours per week. Arrangements for part time pupillage are however encouraged by the BSB. The pupil supervisor will usually specify the minimum periods of time in which a pupil is expected to be in chambers or office, and pupils may be expected to work additional hours as required.

The European Working Time Directive will apply to pupils at the Employed Bar. It has not been established that it applies to the self-employed Bar but it may be taken as a guide to good practice, at least in relation to holidays (e.g. pupils are entitled to a minimum of four weeks' leave per annum (ie 20 working days, not including Bank Holidays) and pupils should take no more than two weeks leave in each period of pupillage. Longer breaks are not normally possible during pupillage). Pupils will need to apply to the BSB for dispensation from the regulations if they want or need to take longer breaks during pupillage.

(3) Illness and other extenuating circumstances

It should be made clear to pupils what the policies and procedures are in relation to sick leave. If a pupil has an excessive number of days' sick leave (at discretion of the supervisor) in any six month period of pupillage, the pupillage should be extended by the period of absence.

Pupils must notify the Standards & Quality Section of the new date, as notification of a material change in pupillage arrangements. Other extenuating circumstances (such as personal problems, bereavement) may be taken into account in determining reasonable absence and/or the need for extension of pupillage. Maternity/paternity leave arrangements should follow chambers' parental leave policy (a requirement of the Code of Conduct) and individual parental leave arrangements should be discussed with the supervisor.

(4) Disabled pupils

'Reasonable adjustments' may be necessary for some disabled pupils. These may apply to physical working conditions (e.g. access to buildings, specialised IT support or equipment).

Advice can be provided by the Bar Council Equality and Diversity team on 020 76111320.

14.10 Part time work, pro bono and voluntary work

(1) Part time work

Pupils may take part time work with the permission of the pupil supervisor, provided that it will not materially interfere with training. Pupils may be able to obtain part time work that has some relevance to work as a barrister, for example, teaching, lecturing or libel reading for the press.

Relevant opportunities are advertised on the notice boards in the Inns and in Bar News, Counsel magazine and in the national press.

(2) Pro Bono and voluntary work

Pupils may also be interested in undertaking voluntary work for organisations such as Justice or Liberty or undertaking pro bono work for the Free Representation Unit (FRU), a Law Centre or Citizen's Advice Bureau. They will need to ensure that they comply with the Code of Conduct in respect of any voluntary work that is undertaken. In the non-practising six, a pupil can act as a legal adviser or offer legal services for any organisation provided that he/she does not, in connection with the supply of such services, hold him/herself out as a barrister or exercise any rights that he/she has as a barrister. For example, a pupil could not describe him/herself as a barrister on any printed material, advertising, publicity or noticeboard; or describe him/herself as a barrister to any client or prospective client; or wear robes etc. In the second six, a pupil may supply legal services at a designated Legal Advice Centre on a voluntary basis provided they do not receive any fee or reward for services and do not have any financial interest.

Free Representation Unit

The Free Representation Unit is a registered charity that provides legal representation for individuals at tribunals where legal aid is unavailable and those individuals cannot afford to pay for representation. FRU offers representation at a range of tribunals including Employment Tribunals, the Employment Appeal Tribunal, Criminal Injuries Compensation Boards, Immigration Adjudication Hearings, Medical Appeal Tribunals, Disability Appeal Tribunals and Social Security Appeal Tribunals, and Social Security Commissioners. Before a pupil becomes a registered representative and can take on cases, he/she must attend the FRU training course, second an experienced representative and write two opinions. For further information contact FRU (www.freerepresentationunit.org.uk).

Law Centres

Law Centres offer members of the public free legal advice on areas such as employment, immigration, housing and welfare benefits. Volunteers are often needed to help with evening advice sessions and may be asked to help with casework by doing research, writing letters and making telephone calls. A full list of Law Centres together with their telephone numbers is available from the Law Centres Federation at 293–299 Kentish Town Road, London, NW5 2TJ, website: www.lawcentres.org.uk

Citizens Advice Bureau

The Citizens Advice Bureau Service offers free, independent and confidential advice to members of the public on problems such as debt and consumer issues, benefits, housing, legal matters, employment, and immigration. Advisers can help fill out forms, write letters, negotiate with creditors and represent clients at court or tribunal. There are 700 Bureaux in England, Wales and Northern Ireland, with more than 20,000 volunteers working in the Service. Pupils can find out more about volunteering from local CABs or from the National Association's website at www.nacab.org.uk.

14.11 Careers and progression to tenancy employed barrister positions

(1) Career development loans

The banks offer various schemes for career development loans, which may be considered.

(2) Devilling

The Code of Conduct requires a barrister to pay a pupil for any work done for him or her which because of its value to him or her warrants payment, unless the terms of the pupillage award is arranged such that it is in lieu of payment for any individual item of work. Any earnings from devilling are taxable as professional receipts.

(3) Careers and progression to tenancy/employed practice

A career in self-employed practice

The Pupillage Policy Document will state what the policies and procedures are for recruitment following the completion of pupillage. Pupils should seek the advice of the pupil supervisor about the likelihood of a vacancy and whether and how they should make an application. It is important to consider what alternatives might be available to pupils if an application is not successful. If a pupil is made an offer at another set of chambers, and a decision must be made on this, the pupil should make their pupil supervisor aware of their need to be told where they stand as early as possible.

Where pupillage is undertaken in an organisation other than chambers they should familiarise themselves with the relevant recruitment procedures. The organisation might have particular procedures for its own pupils/trainees and their Pupillage Policy Document will provide information about this. Pupils may wish to discuss with their supervisor what other employment options may be available in case he/she is not offered a permanent position in the organisation.

A career in employed practice

For information about careers at the employed Bar contact the Bar Association for Local Government and the Public Service (BALGPS) or the Bar Association for Commerce, Finance and Industry (BACFI), contact details are to be found in Appendix J. Pupils may also contact the Employed Barristers Committee at the Bar Council for further details about a career at the Employed Bar.

Judicial assistants scheme

Barristers who have completed 12 months' pupillage are eligible to apply for full time and part time appointments for one, two or three law terms as assistant to Lords Justices on appeals and applications in the civil division at the Royal Courts of Justice. Candidates are required to have demonstrated a very high intellectual ability. Advertisements are placed in the *Times* and in *Counsel* magazine in January and June each year and further information is available from the Courts Service website at www.hmcourts-service.gov.uk .

Other employment opportunities

Barristers have very good employment prospects outside the self-employed and employed bar. Many of the advertisements that appear in the legal press seek lawyers from either branch of the profession, and legal recruitment agencies will consider applications from barristers.

(4) Continuing Professional Development

The compulsory pupillage courses are the first stage of Continuing Professional Development (CPD) that is required of all practising barristers throughout their careers. All new practitioners are required to undertake a minimum of 45 hours of accredited CPD, including nine hours of advocacy training and three hours of ethics by the end of the first three years of practice. On completion of the 45 hours of accredited continuing professional development barristers are required to undertake 12 hours of continuing professional development per year throughout their careers. CPD hours cannot be accrued whilst in pupillage. Further information on CPD is available on the BSB website

15. Complaints and grievances

15.1 General Principles

The BSB requires all ATOs to have complaints and grievance procedures in place for pupils (para 403.2(d) of the Code and Annex S to the Code). The overarching aim should be to resolve grievances both fairly and as soon as possible, through discussion, at the point at which they occur.

15.2 Grievance procedures

It is important that, if a pupil/supervisor relationship is not working well, alternative independent sources of advice are available to the pupil. By mutual agreement between the pupil and the ATO, and where permitted by the terms of any sponsorship agreement, supervisory responsibilities can be changed, at the request of either the pupil or a supervisor:

- Each ATO that takes pupils should have a written grievance procedure, which must be brought to the attention of each pupil at the beginning of the pupillage.
- Pupils should be able to raise matters concerning pupillage with a member of chambers or other lawyer in the ATO other than their pupil supervisor. That person should be identified in the grievance procedure (e.g. Head of Chambers, Director of Pupil Training, three person committee etc, responsible for internal resolution of a dispute). The grievance procedure should also set out clearly what needs to be done in order to invoke the procedure and how the procedure operates.
- Ultimately the pupil should be able to take a complaint either to the Head of Chambers or Pupillage Training Principal/Director of Pupil Training or to a three-person committee appointed for the purpose of hearing complaints pursuant to the grievance procedure. The method of final appeal should be identified in the grievance procedure.

15.3 Advice and guidance

(1) Internal

It is a primary responsibility of the pupil supervisor to give appropriate advice, support anD guidance and pupils should approach their supervisor with any concerns that they may have.

If a pupil feels they cannot do so, other members of chambers (particularly junior tenants) or other lawyers in the ATO, may be able to help either informally or through the Pupillage Committee. Sometimes a pupil might simply wish to discuss alternative courses of action (including with other pupils). If a pupil feels they cannot approach their pupil supervisor, they should contact the Pupillage Training Principal Director of Pupil Training or the Human Resources Department of the organisation for advice and assistance. Organisations should have a complaints and grievances procedure for employees to which pupils can refer. Some ATOs, recognising the dilemma faced by a pupil wishing to pursue a grievance, have appointed person(s) to deal with such internal complaints. They should deal with the issue and ensure that the pupil's prospects are not jeopardised by the mere fact of a complaint having been made. A further option, within chambers, is to approach the Head of Chambers who is required by the Code to ensure that pupils are being treated properly and fairly. It is important that pupils (and others) keep contemporaneous notes of incident(s) that may cause a pupil to think that he/she has been treated unfairly or in a discriminatory fashion. This will provide useful evidence to assist if a dispute arises.

(2) External

Sometimes a pupil is unable or unwilling to have the matter dealt with internally and ultimately it must be for the pupil to decide which course of action is the most appropriate. It may also be inappropriate for the complaint to be dealt with internally, depending on the circumstances.

Various sources of advice and information are available that can assist pupils in making such a decision. Many matters can and should be resolved in-house and, to assist with this, the BSB, the Bar Council and the Inns have developed various formal and informal procedures for helping to resolve grievances. There is no single external body which is empowered or required to take responsibility to intervene in problem situations with a view to resolve them or preventing them from escalating. The following outside sources of help and advice are available:

- The BSB's Pupillage Officer, who may refer matters to Complaints and/or the relevant BSB Committee (Tel: 0202 611 1444).
- The Bar Council's Helpline (Tel: 0207 611 1430) The Bar Council has a Pupillage panel of practising barristers who will investigate confidential and non confidential complaints.
- The Bar Council Equality & Diversity helpline (Tel: 020 7611 1310).
- The Education Officer in the pupil's Inn of Court (see Appendix J).

A pupil is often in a difficult position when he/she wishes to complain but feels that the making of a complaint may prejudice their continued pupillage and/or any tenancy decision. Many pupils do not wish to identify their pupil supervisor or set of chambers. Any pupil in such a position is encouraged in the first instance to talk confidentially to the BSB Pupillage Officer or to their Inn's Education Officer. Complaints about supervisors may however be pursued formally through the BSB's Complaints system.

Where a pupil does not feel able to pursue a complaint during pupillage, the BSB would still welcome any feedback via the questionnaires that are distributed at the end of each period of pupillage. All such information is treated in the strictest confidence. Where discussion and mediation (as suggested above) is not successful, then a formal complaint may need to be pursued, in accordance with the Code.

15.4 Non completion

Where a pupil has been refused a certificate of satisfactory completion of pupillage by his/her supervisor/ATO then he/she should consult BTR55 and Part X, and also the criteria and guidelines for an application to the Qualifications Committee for a review under Part X of the BTRs. The Qualifications Committee does not normally permit the oral hearing of an appeal.

This situation may relate or be linked to a complaint or grievance of one form or another.

15.5 Complaints against pupils (disciplinary and other offences)

Complaints and grievances against pupils are rare. Any formal complaints against pupils concerning their professional practice, ethics etc should be pursued through the BSB's Complaints system. Any resulting disciplinary action would involve the BSB. The Inn of Court of which the pupil is a member plays no formal part in the disciplinary system except via the Council of the Inns of Court (COIC) which arranges tribunals. An individual Inn would have a role in pronouncing any findings of a disciplinary tribunal.

16. Quality Assurance procedures

16.1 Quality Assurance principles and processes

Procedures for Quality Assurance relate to:

- the approval, monitoring and review of ATOs;
- the training and accreditation of pupil supervisors; and
- the monitoring of pupillage arrangements (including evidence of feedback on performance).

Systems and procedures have been in place but are currently being further developed for the sample monitoring of pupillage (either in chambers or at the Employed Bar), and for 'triggered' visits where investigation of poor practice is justified.

Systems are also being developed for the wider monitoring of chambers, and the use of sample or triggered visits to chambers in order to ensure adherence to the regulations as well as the identification, nurturing and exchange of good practice.

16.2 Monitoring of pupillage in ATOs

The BSB is committed to ensuring that all pupillages meet the highest standards and runs a monitoring of pupillage scheme to ensure that the quality of the training environment provided by ATOs is kept under review. ATOs that take pupils are monitored and, as part of this process, pupils will be given the opportunity to give feedback on pupillage by means of a confidential questionnaire distributed with the provisional and full qualification certificates. A sample of pupils may be invited to participate in an interview about their experiences of pupillage and a sample of Approved Training Organisations may be visited each year.

The monitoring scheme that is being developed aims to improve the overall quality of pupillages through the promotion of good practice and is not, therefore, an appropriate mechanism for resolving specific problems, grievances or complaints arising in the course of an individual pupillage. Such problems might vary from not obtaining proper supervision or sufficient feedback, or being asked to do excessive or inappropriate tasks, possibly due to being the victim of discrimination, harassment or other serious misconduct.

Monitoring and review of ATOs will take place from time to time on a rotating basis in order to identify areas for improvement and also areas of good practice for dissemination and improvement of training in general – not resulting from any particular cause for concern.

Appendix A – Bar Training Regulations [excerpt]

[2.36]

PART V – THE PROFESSIONAL STAGE

27. A person commences the Professional Stage of training on commencing pupillage in accordance with these Regulations and completes the Professional Stage by:

    (a) satisfactorily completing 12 months of pupillage and such further training as may be required by the Board; and

    (b) being issued with a Full Qualification Certificate.

28. Before commencing the Professional Stage, a person must have completed (or been exempted under Part VII of these Regulations from) the Vocational Stage.

29. A person may not commence the Professional Stage more than five years after completing the Vocational Stage except with the permission of the Board and after complying with any condition which the Board may impose.

Pupillage

30. Pupillage is divided into two parts:

    (a) a non-practising period of six months; and

    (b) a practising period of six months.

31. Except with the written permission of the Board, the non-practising period of pupillage must be undertaken:

    (a) in England and Wales; and

    (b) in a continuous period of six months.

32. Except with the written permission of the Board, the practising period of pupillage must:

    (a) commence within 12 months after completion of the non-practising period;

    (b) be undertaken in a Member State; and

    (c) be completed within an overall period of nine months.

33. Any period of pupillage must provide training which is adequate and which complies with such criteria as may be published by the Board.

34. Except as provided in Regulation 42, any period of pupillage must be undertaken:

    (a) in an Approved Training Organisation; and

    (b) with a barrister who is a registered pupil supervisor.

35. Schedule C to these Regulations sets out rules applicable to pupil supervisors.

36. During any period of pupillage the pupil must;

    (a) be diligent in receiving the instruction given; and

    (b) observe all legal and professional obligations of confidence.

Approved Training Organisations

37. The Board will designate an organisation as an Approved Training Organisation if it is satisfied:

    (a) that one or more registered pupil supervisors who are available to provide pupillage training practise in the organisation; and

    (b) that the organisation has made proper arrangements for dealing with pupils and pupillage in accordance with the Code of Conduct.

38. The Board may withdraw approval from an Approved Training Organisation if it considers following investigation:

    (a) that pupillage training provided by the organisation is or has been seriously deficient; or

    (b) that the organisation has not made proper arrangements for dealing with pupils and pupillage in accordance with the Code of Conduct.

39. The Board will give notice in writing:

    (a) in the case of a decision to refuse to designate an organisation as an Approved Training Organisation, to that organisation; and

    (b) in the case of a decision to withdraw approval from an Approved Training Organisation, to:

        (i) that organisation;

        (ii) any person who is undertaking or has agreed to undertake a pupillage in that organisation; and

        (iii) the Inn of which any such person is a member.

40. Any person or organisation to whom the Board is required to give notice of a decision under Regulation 39 may request a review of the decision under Part X of these Regulations, provided that the request is made in writing to the Board within one month of the date when notice of the decision was given.

41. If the Board withdraws approval from an Approved Training Organisation, the organisation may not claim repayment of any pupillage award or other sum paid to any pupil or prospective pupil.

External Training

42. With the written permission of the Board, part or all of the practising period of pupillage may be satisfied by training:

    (a) with a solicitor, judge or other suitably qualified lawyer who is not a registered pupil supervisor; and/or

    (b) in an organisation which is not an Approved Training Organisation but which, in the opinion of the Board, provides suitable training and experience.

Registration of Pupillage

43. Before commencing any period of pupillage (including any period of external training) a person must apply to the Board for registration of the pupillage by submitting an application in the form prescribed by the Board.

44. The Board will register the pupillage if it is satisfied that the application has been duly completed and that the pupillage complies with these Regulations.

45. If a person applies to the Board for registration of a pupillage after the pupillage has commenced, the pupillage will be treated as having commenced on the date of receipt of the application, unless the Board permits otherwise.

46. If the Board refuses to register a pupillage, it will inform the pupil in writing of its decision and the reasons for it.

47. If the Board refuses to register a pupillage, the pupil may request a review of the decision under Part X of these Regulations, provided that the request is made in writing to the Board within one month of the date when notice of the decision was given.

48. If any of the information provided in an application for registration of a pupillage changes before the pupillage has been completed, the pupil must promptly notify the Board in writing of the change.

Qualification Certificates

49. On completion of the non-practising period of pupillage, the Board will issue the pupil with a Provisional Qualification Certificate provided that the pupil has been called to the Bar under Part IX of these Regulations and the Board is satisfied:

    (a) that the pupil has satisfactorily completed the non-practising period of pupillage and any further training required under Regulation 27(a); and

    (b) that the pupillage is registered and complied with these Regulations.

50. On completion of the practising period of pupillage, the Board will issue the pupil with a Full Qualification Certificate if the pupil has a Provisional Qualification Certificate and the Board is satisfied:

    (a) that the pupil has satisfactorily completed the practising period of pupillage and any further training required under Regulation 27(a); and

    (b) that the pupillage is registered and complied with these Regulations.

51. For the purpose of these Regulations, a pupil is to be treated as having satisfactorily completed a period of pupillage if the pupil:

    (a) has been diligent in receiving the instruction given; and

    (b) has achieved the minimum level of competence required of a pupil at the end of the relevant period.

52. The Board may accept as evidence that a pupil has satisfactorily completed any period of pupillage a certificate to this effect from the pupil supervisor (or person responsible for external training) with whom the pupil has completed that period.

53. If a pupil supervisor is unable or unwilling to provide a certificate that a pupil has satisfactorily completed a period of pupillage, the Board may accept such a certificate signed by the Head of Chambers or person in charge of pupillage in the training organisation where the pupillage has been undertaken if the certificate contains a satisfactory explanation of why the pupil supervisor has not signed it.

54. If the Board is not satisfied:

    (a) that the pupil has satisfactorily completed a period of pupillage, and/or

    (b) that the pupillage is registered and complied with these Regulations,

    the Board may specify further training which the pupil must satisfactorily complete before the Board will issue the pupil with a Provisional Qualification Certificate or a Full Qualification Certificate (as the case may be).

55. If the Board refuses to issue a Provisional Qualification Certificate or a Full Qualification Certificate, the pupil may request a review of the decision

under Part X of these Regulations, provided that the request is made in writing to the Board within one month of the date when notice of the decision was given.

Appendix B – Bar Training Regulations [excerpt]

[2.37]–[2.38]

SCHEDULE C – Pupil Supervisors (Regulation 35)

Acting as a Pupil Supervisor

1. A barrister may act as a pupil supervisor if the barrister:

   a. is on the register of approved pupil supervisors kept by the Board;

   b. has a current practising certificate; and

   c. has regularly practised as a barrister during the previous two years.

Registration as a Pupil Supervisor

2. The Board may enter a barrister on the register of approved pupil supervisors if the barrister is approved by an Inn of which the barrister is a member.

3. An Inn must approve a barrister as a pupil supervisor if:

   a. the barrister has a current practising certificate;

   b. the Inn is satisfied that the barrister has the necessary experience and is otherwise suitable to act as a pupil supervisor; and

   c. the barrister has submitted an application in accordance with paragraph 5.

4. To have the necessary experience to act as a pupil supervisor a barrister should normally:

   a. have practised in the United Kingdom or another Member State as a barrister (other than as a pupil who has not completed pupillage in accordance with these Regulations) or as a member of another Authorised Body for a period (which need not have been continuous and need not have been as a member of the same Authorised Body) of at least six years in the previous eight years; and

   b. for the previous two years have regularly practised as a barrister and been entitled to exercise a right of audience before every court in England and Wales in relation to all proceedings.

Application Procedure

5. A barrister who wishes to be entered on the register of approved pupil supervisors must submit to the Inn an application in the form currently prescribed by the Board. The application must be supported:

a. By an independent person who is a High Court Judge or Circuit Judge, a Leader of a Circuit, a Deputy High Court Judge, a Recorder, a Queen's Counsel, a Master of the Bench of an Inn, Treasury Counsel or a person of comparable standing who is able to comment from personal knowledge on the applicant's suitability to act as a pupil supervisor; and

b. Subject to sub-paragraph (c) below,

   i. in the case of a self-employed barrister, by the applicant's Head of Chambers, or

   ii. in the case of an employed barrister, by a more senior lawyer employed in the same organisation and who has direct knowledge of the work of the applicant;

c. If the applicant is a Head of Chambers, or there is no more senior lawyer employed in the same organisation with the required knowledge, or for any other reason the support of the person referred to in sub-paragraph (b) is not available, by a second person falling within sub-paragraph (a) above.

Training of Pupil Supervisors

6. The Board, in consultation with the Inns, may and will normally require pupil supervisors to undertake training before they may be entered or after they have been entered on the register of approved pupil supervisors.

Removal from the Register of Pupil Supervisors

7. The Board may remove a barrister's name from the register of approved pupil supervisors if the barrister:

   a. ceases to practise as a barrister or is suspended from practice as a barrister; or

   b. requests the Board in writing to be removed from the register; or

   c. fails to complete any training required under paragraph 6; or

   d. is found by the Board to be unsuitable for any reason to act as a pupil supervisor; or

   e. has not acted as a pupil supervisor for the previous five years.

8. If the Board decides that a barrister's name should be removed from the register of approved pupil supervisors, it will notify the barrister and the Inn which approved the barrister as a pupil supervisor of its decision and of the reasons for it.

Duties of Pupil Supervisors

9. A pupil supervisor must when responsible for supervising any pupil:

   a. take all reasonable steps to provide the pupil with adequate tuition, supervision and experience;

   b. have regard to any pupillage guidelines issued by the Board and to the Equality Code for the Bar; and c ensure that the pupil prepares for and attends any further training required by the Board such as advocacy training provided by the pupil's Circuit or Inn.

10. A pupil supervisor may not be responsible for supervising more than one pupil at a time except with the approval in writing of the Board.

Complaints

11. If any complaint or other matter which appears to affect the suitability of a barrister to continue to act as a pupil supervisor comes to the notice of the Inn which approved the barrister, the Inn must inform the Board of the matter.

12. If any complaint or other matter which appears to affect the suitability of a barrister to continue to act as a pupil supervisor comes to the notice of the Board, the Board will investigate the matter.

13. Following such an investigation, the Board may:

    a. dismiss any complaint; or

    b. take no action; or

    c. if in its opinion the matter is such as to require informal treatment, draw it to the barrister's attention in writing and, if thought desirable, direct the barrister to attend upon a nominated person for advice; or

    d. if in its opinion the conduct disclosed shows that the barrister is unsuitable to act as a pupil supervisor, remove the name of the barrister from the register of approved pupil supervisors.

Review

14. A barrister whose application to be approved as a pupil supervisor is rejected or whose name is removed from the register of approved pupil supervisors may request a review of the decision under Part X of these Regulations, provided that the request is made in writing to the Board within one month of the date when notice of the decision was given.

Appendix C – Code of Conduct, Annex R

[2.39]

The Pupillage Funding and Advertising Requirements

Funding

1. The members of a set of chambers must pay to each non-practising chambers pupil by the end of each month of the non-practising six months of his pupillage no less than:

    (a) £1,000.; plus

(b) such further sum as may be necessary to reimburse expenses reasonably incurred by the pupil on:

(i) travel for the purposes of his pupillage during that month; and

(ii) attendance during that month at courses which he is required to attend as part of his pupillage.

2. The members of a set of chambers must pay to each practising chambers pupil by the end of each month of the practising six months of his pupillage no less than:

(a) £1,000; plus

(b) such further sum as may be necessary to reimburse expenses reasonably incurred by the pupil on:

(i) travel for the purposes of his pupillage during that month; and

(ii) attendance during that month at courses which he is required to attend as part of his pupillage; less

(c) such amount, if any, as the pupil may receive during that month from his practice as a barrister; and less

(d) such amounts, if any, as the pupil may have received during the preceding months of his practising pupillage from his practice as a barrister, save to the extent that the amount paid to the pupil in respect of any such month was less than the total of the sums provided for in sub-paragraphs (a) and (b) above.

3. The members of a set of chambers may not seek or accept repayment from a chambers pupil of any of the sums required to be paid under paragraphs 1 and 2 above, whether before or after he ceases to be a chambers pupil, save in the case of misconduct on his part.

Advertising

4. All vacancies for pupillages must be advertised on a website designated by the Bar Council and the following information must be provided:

(a) The name and address of chambers.

(b) The number of tenants.

(c) A brief statement of the work undertaken by chambers e.g. "predominately criminal".

(d) The number of pupillage vacancies.

(e) The level of award.

(f) The procedure for application.

(g) The minimum educational or other qualification required.

(h) The date of closure for the receipt of applications.

(i) The date by which the decisions on the filling of vacancies will be made.

Application

5. The requirements set out in paragraphs 1 to 4 above:

(a) apply in the case of pupillages commencing on or after 1st January 2003;

(b) do not apply in the case of pupils who were granted exemption from the Vocational Stage of training under Regulation 59 of the Bar Training Regulations;

(c) do not apply in the case of pupils who are undertaking a period of pupillage in a set of chambers as part of a pupillage training programme offered by another organisation that is authorised by the Bar Council to take pupils;

(d) do not apply in the case of pupils who have completed both the non-practising and the practising six months of pupillage;

(e) save as provided in paragraph 3 above, do not apply in respect of any period after a pupil ceases, for whatever reason, to be a chambers pupil; and

(f) may be waived in part or in whole by the Pupillage Funding Committee.

6. For the purposes of these requirements:

(a) "chambers pupil" means, in respect of any set of chambers, a pupil undertaking the non-practising or practising six months of pupillage with a pupil-master or pupil-masters who is or are a member or members of that set of chambers;

(b) "non-practising chambers pupil" means a chambers pupil undertaking the non-practising six months of pupillage;

(c) "practising chambers pupil" means a chambers pupil undertaking the practising six months of pupillage;

(d) "month" means calendar month commencing on the same day of the month as that on which the pupil commenced the non-practising or practising six months pupillage, as the case may be;

(e) any payment made to a pupil by a barrister pursuant to paragraph 805 of the Code of Conduct shall constitute an amount received by the pupil from his practice as a barrister; and

(f) the following travel by a pupil shall not constitute travel for the purposes of his pupillage:

(i) travel between his home and chambers; and

(ii) travel for the purposes of his practice as a barrister.

Appendix D – Checklists for core areas

[2.40]–[2.44]

Pupillage Checklist, 2011–12 (First Six/Second Six)

Name of Pupil	
Name of Pupil Supervisor	
Name and Address of Approved Training Organisation where pupillage was undertaken	
Dates of Pupillage	

Declaration by Pupil	
I certify that I have completed the items set out in this checklist	
Signed: (Pupil)	Date:

Declaration by Supervisor(s)	
I have read the checklist and discussed its completion with the above pupil. I confirm that to the best of my knowledge and belief it has been completed accurately and satisfactorily in terms of the standards and competencies as defined in the Pupillage Handbook.	
Signed: (Pupil Supervisor)	Date:
Signed: (Head of Chambers)	Date:
Signed: (Director of Pupil Training)	Date:
Signed: (Additional Supervisor – for ......)	Date:
Signed: (Additional Supervisor – for ......)	Date:

NB: *Copies of completed checklists must be sent to the Bar Standards Board on completion of pupillage together with the Certificate of Completion of the Practising Six months of pupillage*

Section 1 : Conduct and Etiquette *A pupil should gain an understanding and appreciation of the operation in practice of rules of conduct and etiquette at the bar and achieve a working knowledge and understanding of the code of conduct and the written standards for the conduct of professional work. Many of these points may have been covered during the Bar Course or in the courses on Ethics run by the Inns of Court but issues of conduct and etiquette are of fundamental importance and require emphasis. Whenever a point of conduct or etiquette arises in practice the opportunity should be taken to consider the point with the pupil. For many of the following matters, a discussion between pupil and pupil supervisor will suffice.* *Pupil supervisors should initial and date the last column as indication that they consider the topic has been adequately addressed to the required standard.*		
1.	**In the case of a barrister in self employed practice, understanding of all aspects of the cab rank rule in practice** (**Part V1**)[1]**, including:**	Satisfactory
1.1	the duty not to withhold services save on proper grounds.	
1.2	the duty not to take on work beyond competence or for which there is insufficient time and opportunity to prepare.	
1.3	the duty not to take on work which may cause a conflict of interest to arise or which may jeopardise the confidentiality of information belonging to another client or former client	

1 References to parts or paragraphs are to the Code of Conduct

2.	**In the case of an employed barrister, to understand the restrictions on the supply of legal services**

3.	**Understand the relationship between counsel and instructing solicitors, including:**	
3.1	the importance of prompt response to instructions	
3.2	the dividing line between decisions in the running of the case that (i) should and (ii) should not be made without first consulting the client and the instructing solicitor	
3.3	duties in the event that two hearing dates clash	
3.4	appropriate practice when attending at court in the absence of a solicitor or representative (*para. 706*)	

4.	**Understanding the duty to avoid conflicts of interest including:**	
4.1	the overriding duty to the court; (*para. 302*)	
4.2	the duties to the lay client and professional client respectively; (*para. 303; 703*)	
4.3	duties when publicly funded; (*para. 304*)	

PART II QUALIFYING AS A BARRISTER AND ENTERING PRACTICE

4.4	when conflicts arise or may arise between two lay clients for whom a barrister is acting or is instructed to act jointly; (*para. 603*)	
4.5	the several duties that may arise to the client, the court and to opponents if a pupil comes into possession of relevant information which he/she is instructed or requested not to disclose. (*para. 608*)	
4.6	the circumstances when it may, or will, be necessary to withdraw from a case. (*para. 608*)	

5.	**Understanding the rules and practices relating to confidentiality (para. 702) including:**	
5.1	the status of clients' privileged communications	
5.2	duties in the event of obtaining confidential information belonging to other parties (*para. 608*)	
5.3	duty to the client in respect of any relevant information coming into the barrister's possession (whether or not confidentially).	
5.4	duty to ensure the preservation of client confidentiality including appropriate practice in relation to reading papers or conducting conversations in public places (*para. 702*)	

6.	**Understanding the courtesies conventionally extended to other members of the Bar including those observed:**	
6.1	On receiving instruction in a matter in which other counsel has previously acted	
6.2	On strike-out, or wasted costs applications	

7.	**Understanding the responsibilities and duties when being led including:**	
7.1	the likely division of responsibilities;	
7.2	the junior's paperwork tasks.	

8.	**Understanding what action to take and what consequences may arise if:**	
8.1	a complaint is made against a barrister	
8.2	a barrister is asked to give a witness statement or provide evidence	
8.3	a barrister is asked to withdraw from a case	
8.4	a wasted costs order is sought against a barrister	
8.5	a barrister is late for court or for a conference	

9.	**Understanding obligations in relation to practice management including:**	
9.1	the duty to have a current practising certificate (*para. 202*)	
9.2	the duty to keep or ensure that accurate practice records are kept (*para.403*)	
9.3	the duty to comply with any continuing professional development requirements (*para. 202*)	
9.4	the duty to be insured with BMIF against claims for professional negligence (*para. 204*)	
9.5	the restrictions on advertising and publicity (*para. 710*).	

10.	**Understanding the duty of ensuring that practice is competently administered, and the importance of maintaining:**	
10.1	completion of Practice Management Course	
10.2	sufficient records to support and explain details of fees claimed	
10.3	proper financial records	
10.4	a proper record of hours worked and work done	
10.5	completion of Forensic Accounting Course (must be completed during pupillage or by the end of the first three years of practice)	

Pupil's record of work done or work diary references	
Signed (pupil):	Date:

Pupil Supervisor's comments

Signed (supervisor): Date:

Section 2: Advocacy

A fundamental objective of pupillage is that the pupil should develop and practise the skills necessary to be an effective advocate. In addition to the basic techniques of oral advocacy, these skills include legal research, fact management and written presentations in particular skeleton arguments. The pupil must develop the ability to bring all these skills together (if necessary under pressure or at short notice) and be able to deploy them efficiently and effectively.

The development of Advocacy skills will depend, to a significant extent, on observation by the pupil but the pupil supervisor should discuss both the basic techniques of oral advocacy and any specific points that might arise in a particular case, so that the pupil may observe intelligently, and derive benefit from observations made. Pupil supervisors are encouraged to arrange for pupils to attend as wide a range of courts and tribunals as possible (if necessary with other members of chambers) having regard to the type of work that the pupil is likely to take on in the early years of practice. If the opportunity to attend a particular type of court does not arise in the course of a pupillage (e.g. an appellant court), the pupil supervisor should discuss any particular aspects of advocacy that the pupil should consider in respect of such a court and in the case of a first six month pupil encourage the pupil to make good the omission during the subsequent period of pupillage. During the second six months, if a pupil is doing his or her own work, a pupil supervisor should exercise supervision over the pupil's preparation and take time to evaluate the process.

In addition, the pupil must attend the advocacy course provided by his or her Inn or Circuit in the first six months. These courses provide the opportunity for pupils to practise oral advocacy under instruction. They can only be effective if pupils have prepared adequately and pupil supervisors must ensure that pupils are given sufficient time to prepare and approach the task very seriously.

Pupil-supervisors should initial and date the last column when they consider their pupil has achieved a satisfactory standard having regard to the objective set out for this checklist.

1.	**General**	**Satisfactory**
1.1	Become familiar with the proper modes of address in court and in chambers	
1.2	Become familiar with the proper use and mode of citation of authorities in court	
1.3	Obtain through observation and discussion an understanding of proper conduct towards: (i) the tribunal and court staff; (ii) the lay client, and others attending court with the client; (iii) the instructing solicitor; (iv) witnesses (including expert witnesses); (v) other parties and their representatives; (vi) litigants in person and lay advisers.	
1.4	Obtain through observation and discussion an understanding of proper conduct towards the press and other media (*para. 709*)	
1.5	Be aware of counsel's responsibilities when dealing with a litigant in person or unrepresented defendant.	

1.6 Fully understand Counsel's professional duties when conducting proceedings in court (*see Code of Conduct, especially para 708*). This includes a clear understanding of the purpose as well as the limitations on examination-in-chief, cross-examination and re-examination, particularly where there are statutory restrictions such as the sexual history of a complainant, hearsay and previous bad character.	
1.7 Completion of Advocacy Compulsory Course (during first six)	

2. Applications	
2.1 Develop the skills of preparation for oral advocacy on applications.	
2.2 Practise and develop the preparation of the appropriate paperwork to support oral argument on applications, eg[1]: (i) Skeleton arguments; (ii) Chronologies; (iii) Case Summaries; (iv) Minutes of order; (v) Bad Character and Hearsay applications and responses to same; (vi) Applications under S.41 of the Youth Justice and Criminal Evidence Act, 1999 relating to a complainant's sexual history.	
2.3 Develop by observation (and where possible practise) the skills of narrative advocacy in respect of applications generally, case management and other directions hearings.	

1 These are examples – some will not apply to those doing a civil only pupillage.

3. Trials – witness handling	
3.1 Develop the skills of preparation for examination in chief and cross examination.	
3.2 Develop by observation (and where possible practise) the skills of examination in chief and cross examination.	
3.3 Understand proper conduct in relation to witnesses (paras. 705; 707 and the written standards for the conduct of professional work).	
3.4 Understand the proper role of independent and expert witnesses.	

3.5 Consider the special considerations which apply when dealing with children, vulnerable or intimidated witnesses, in particular, what special measures may be appropriate to assist such witnesses and the type of questions that are appropriate in an individual case	

4. Trials and other final hearings – Narrative advocacy	
4.1 Practise and develop the skills of preparation for narrative advocacy in trials and other final hearings. 4.2 Practise and develop the preparation of the appropriate paperwork necessary to support oral argument, e g[1]: (i) Skeleton arguments; (ii) Chronologies; (iii) Case Summaries; (iv) Bad Character and Hearsay applications (v) Applications under S.41 YJ&CEA, 1999 4.3 Develop by observation (and where possible practise) the skills of narrative advocacy in trials and other final hearings.	

1 These are examples – some will not apply to those doing a civil only pupillage.

5. Appeals	
5.1 Develop the skills of preparation for oral advocacy on appeal in particular the preparation for use on an appeal of skeleton arguments. 5.2 Develop by observation (and where possible practise) the skills of appellate advocacy.	

Pupil's record of work done or work diary references	
Signed (pupil):	Date:

Pupil Supervisor's comments	
Signed (supervisor):	Date:

Section 3: Conferences and Negotiations
Pupils must develop conference and negotiation skills. This is likely to be largely by observation and discussion with the pupil supervisor. Pupils should be instructed with regard to the preparation for conferences and negotiations, including the making and retaining of a full and accurate note of all conferences. Even where participation is based on observation, pupils should be as actively involved as possible. The objective should be to raise the pupil to a standard where he or she can competently conduct a conference or negotiation.
If a particular topic described below does not arise during a pupillage (for example negotiating with a litigant in person) a pupil supervisor should discuss with the pupil the sort of difficulties and pitfalls that can arise in such a situation and how to avoid them. The record of work done should, where possible, cross-refer to the relevant points below. Pupil-supervisors should initial and date the last column when they consider their pupil has achieved a satisfactory standard having regard to the objective set out for this checklist.

1.	**Conferences**	**Satisfactory**
1.1	Discussion of skills needed in conferences (including potential difficulties and pitfalls that can arise and how to avoid them)	
1.2	Active involvement in preparation for a conference session	
1.3	Observation of conference sessions (actual participation may take place but is not a requirement)	
1.4	Experience through observation of the conduct of conferences with:	
	1. Solicitors and clients;	
	2. Solicitors only;	
	3. Counsel only.	
1.5	Experience through observation of the conduct of telephone conferences.	

2.	**Negotiations**	
2.1	Discussion of skills needed in negotiation (including potential difficulties and pitfalls that can arise and how to avoid them)	
2.2	Active involvement in preparation for a negotiation session	
2.3	Obtaining through observation and discussion and understanding of the conduct of negotiations in particular:	
	(i) dealing with an opponent;	
	(ii) dealing with the client and advising on settlement;	
	(iii) any special considerations that apply when conducting negotiations in the absence of the instructing solicitor.	

2.4 Understanding of any special considerations which may arise in relation to negotiations with litigants in person.	

Pupil's record of work done or work diary references
Signed (pupil): Date:

Pupil Supervisor's comments	
Signed (supervisor):	Date:

Section 4: Drafting, Paperwork and Legal Research

A pupil must be able to locate and utilise relevant sources of information, both primary (case and statute law and citation indexes) and secondary (textbooks, digests, encyclopaedias and legal journals) and to use the information so acquired appropriately in opinion writing, pleading, drafting and case preparation.

It is of the greatest importance that pupils practise and develop the necessary skills by producing practical work and receiving constructive feedback on that work from their pupil supervisor. Simply observing the work of the pupil supervisor is insufficient. Feedback on a pupil's work should be given as soon as possible by the pupil supervisor whilst the work is still fresh in the mind of the pupil. Pupils must have demonstrated the appropriate degree of competence in the skills set out below. Non-litigation drafting is of equal importance but since the type of work is likely to vary, reference should be made in Section 5, on the specialist area. Paperwork in criminal matters may be dealt with specifically in the Criminal checklist.

The record of work done should, where possible, cross-refer to the relevant sections and sub sections below. Pupil-supervisors should initial and date the last column when they consider their pupil has achieved a satisfactory standard having regard to the defined skills and competencies.

1.	**Opinions and Advice**	**Satisfactory**
1.1	Develop and practise the skill of preparing accurate and concise Opinions and other Advice, written in plain English, and demonstrating the following abilities: (i) To identify relevant facts from the papers and identify sources as appropriate;	

(ii) To identify and explain the relevant legal issues;	
(iii) To apply the relevant law to the relevant facts and to draw appropriate conclusions and give appropriate advice.	

2.	**Letters**	
2.1	Develop and practise the necessary skills: (i) for drafting letters written in accordance with pre-action protocols or similar. (ii) for drafting Part 36 Offers or similar.	

3.	**Pleadings**	
3.1	Practise and develop the skill of pleading – in particular preparation of: • Statements of Case, i.e. Particulars of Claim, Defence and Reply. • Requests for and provision of further information.	
3.2	Consider and understand the requirements of the Code of Conduct in relation to pleading and in particular to allegations of fraud (*paragraph 704*).	
3.3	Request and provide further information	

4.	**Witness Statements and Affidavits**	
4.1	Understand the ethical considerations in drafting statements of fact for witnesses in civil actions (*paragraph 704 and the Guidance on Preparation of Witness Statements dated 16 January 2001*).	
4.2	Understand the ethical considerations concerning contact with witnesses and taking statements in relation to criminal cases (*paragraph 704 and Written Standards for the Conduct of Professional Work para 6*).	
4.3	Practise and develop the skill of drafting in appropriate language, using concise and accurate statements of fact.	

5.	**Orders**	
5.1	Develop and practise the ability to draft orders, including Tomlin form and other consent orders.	

6.	**Non litigation drafting**	
6.1	This should be covered as it is of equal importance but, as the type of work varies, substantial reference should be made on the appropriate specialist checklist.	

7.	**Paperwork in criminal matters**	
7.1	This should be covered as appropriate (see Criminal Checklist)	

8.	**Cross references and research**	
8.1	Build on research work carried out on the Bar Course, further to cover: • Case Law • Statute law • Citation indexes • Secondary sources as appropriate and depending on area of specialism: text books, digests, encyclopaedias and legal journals.	

Pupil's record of work done or work diary references
Signed (pupil): Date:

Pupil Supervisor's comments   Signed (supervisor): Date:

Section 5: Specialist Areas *All pupils should additionally gain an understanding and experience of work in the specialist area practised by the pupil supervisor and the Approved Training Organisation where the pupillage is being undertaken.* *This checklist may be completed by cross reference to the other checklists and vice versa.*
The specialist section of the checklist adopted by the Approved Training Organisation must be adhered to and the relevant checklist completed and submitted together with the checklists for the core areas. There are currently thirteen sample checklists that have been prepared by the Specialist Bar Associations in each of the following areas:
• Administrative • Chancery • Commercial and Admiralty • Criminal • Family • Crown Prosecution Service • Employed Commercial • General Commercial • Intellectual Property • Local Government and Planning • Personal Injury • Revenue

- Technology and Construction
- Immigration

Checklists for the above specialist areas are available on the BSB website (http://www.barstandardsboard.org.uk/Educationandtraining/whatispupillage/pupillagechecklists/checklistsdownload/). They are provided independently in this way, so as to allow for periodic updating as appropriate by the relevant Specialist Bar Association.
ATOs and supervisors may also develop their own checklists subject to approval by the Bar Standards Board. Applications should be submitted at least one month before the pupillage commences.

Appendix E – Certificates of satisfactory completion (first six/second six)

[2.45]

CERTIFICATE OF SATISFACTORY COMPLETION OF PUPILLAGE (FIRST SIX)

I[1], (name) ....

of (chambers/employer)...

being registered by the Bar Standards Board as an approved pupil supervisor.

hereby certify that my pupil (name) ....

called to the Bar by (Inn) ....

on (month)... (year)..

has satisfactorily completed a period of[2] .... months non-practising pupillage (first six) between the following dates:

from.. to.......................................

has completed the compulsory pupillage advocacy course during this period:[3]

and completed the relevant parts of the pupillage check list conscientiously throughout this period of pupillage.

Signed.. dated.......................................

NOTES

1 The pupil supervisor at the conclusion of the first six should complete this form, after consulting with any other supervisor throughout this period of pupillage. If the pupil supervisor is not available to sign this certificate, another person acceptable to the Bar Standards Board (e.g. Head of

Chambers, Director of Pupil Training) may sign it, provided that the certificate confirms who the pupil supervisor was and why they have not signed the certificate for the relevant period.

2 Where a pupillage has been reduced by the Qualifications Committee, the certificate should be amended accordingly.

3 The pupillage advocacy course must be completed by the end of the non-practising (first six) period of pupillage.

Upon completion of the first six, pupils are issued with a provisional qualification certificate (PQC), which confirms completion of the first six. The PQC does not have any practising rights.

Please contact the Bar Standards Board if further guidance is needed in completing this form.

Meeting your needs

We can provide our literature in different formats, such as Braille, large print or on audio tape or compact disc. If you would like this form in a different format, please contact us on 020 7611 1444.

This certificate should be submitted to:

Rachel Reeves, Bar Standards Board, 289–293 High Holborn London, WC1V 7HZ, DX 240 LDE. We encourage pupils to email a scanned copy of this certificate, please email: pupillagerecords@barstandardsboard.org.uk

Bar Standards Board
September 2013

CERTIFICATE OF SATISFACTORY COMPLETION OF PUPILLAGE (SECOND SIX)

We of[1] (chambers/employer) ....

being registered by the Bar Standards Board as an approved training organisation with approved pupil supervisor(s) or having been approved by the Qualifications Committee as a supervisor of external training.[2]

hereby certify that our pupil (name) ....

called to the Bar by (Inn)................................ on (month).................. (year) ....

has satisfactorily completed a period of[3]........... months practising pupillage (second six) between the following dates:

from.. to ....

Our pupil has completed the compulsory pupillage courses required by the Bar Standards Board under Regulation 27(a) of the Bar Training Regulations. We have read and discussed the completion of the check list with the above pupil. We confirm that to the best of our knowledge and belief it has been completed accurately and satisfactorily in terms of the standards and competencies as defined in the pupillage handbook.[4]

Pupil supervisor... dated ....

from... to ....

Pupil supervisor... dated ....

from... to ....

Pupil supervisor... dated ....

from... to ....

Pupil supervisor... dated ....

from... to ....

Head of Chambers... dated..

Director of Pupil Training...................................... dated..

NOTES

1 This form should be completed by **each** pupil supervisor involved in the practising period of pupillage (second six), the Head of Chambers and the Director of Pupil Training. If this form cannot be signed by all, the form should indicate who is unable to sign the form and why they are not available. The form **must** be completed by a minimum of two members of

the approved training organisation, one of whom must be the Head of Chambers or Director of Pupillage Training.

2 All periods of external training must have been approved in advance by the Qualifications Committee.

3 Where a pupillage has been reduced by the Qualifications Committee, the certificate should be amended accordingly.

4 The completed pupillage check list must be returned with this certificate.

Please contact the Bar Standards Board if further guidance is needed in completing this form.

Meeting your needs

We can provide our literature in different formats, such as Braille, large print or on audio tape or compact disc. If you would like this form in a different format, please contact us on 020 7611 1444.

This certificate should be submitted to:

Rachel Reeves, Bar Standards Board, 289–293 High Holborn London, WC1V 7HZ, DX 240 LDE. We encourage pupils to email a scanned copy of this certificate, please email: pupillagerecords@barstandardsboard.org.uk

Bar Standards Board
September 2013

Appendix F

[2.46]–[2.47]

Notification of a material change in Pupillage or external training arrangements

Personal details

Surname……………………………………………………………………………………

Other names…………………………………………………………………………………

Title (e.g. Mr, Mrs, Ms)……………………………………………………………………

Date of birth…………………………………………………………………………………

Address………………………………………………………………………………………

……………………………………………………………………………………………………

Telephone……………………………………………………………………………………

Email address…………………………………………………………………………………

Pupillage details

Name and address of ATO / external training / organisation.................................

....

....

Telephone..

Details of material change[1]

Commencement date of new arrangements[2] ....

Details of material change:

Pupil's declaration

I confirm that the details given are correct and agree to notify the Bar Standards Board of any further material change in my pupillage arrangements.

I consent to my personal data being processed for the purpose of registration of my pupillage and in accordance with the Bar Council's Privacy Statement.[3]

I understand that my Chambers/employer may view my details (as provided in this form) online.[4]

Signed..
....

Date..

Declaration of pupillage provider[5]

I confirm that the arrangements set out above have been agreed through the appropriate procedures in my chambers/with my employer.

Signed..

Name..

Position...

Date..

Please return completed form to:

Rachel Reeves/Karen Bayley,

Bar Standards Board, 289–293 High Holborn, London WC1V 7HZ, DX 240 LDE

Fax: 020 7831 9217, Email: pupillagerecords@barstandardsboard.org.uk

1 A material change includes a change of home or pupillage or training address, a change of pupil supervisor, a change to the date of the commencement and/or proposed end date of pupillage or external training or a change in location due to a pupillage secondment. Advice should be sought from the Bar Standards Board if there is uncertainty as to whether other changes are material.

2 Under the Bar Training Regulations, the "non-practising" period of pupillage must be a continuous period of six months. The "practising" period of pupillage must be commenced not later than twelve months after the completion of the "nonpractising" period. The "practising" period of pupillage must be completed within the overall period of nine months. Permission must be obtained from the Qualifications Committee to waive any of these requirements.

3 See www.barstandardsboard.org.uk/footer-items/privacy-statement/

4 The Bar Council has will be launched an online portal for all members of the Bar, to update their details, pay their practising certificate fee etc. Chambers and employers are able to view their members/employees.

5 This declaration must be signed by the Head of Chambers or other person authorised by the Head of Chambers in the case of a pupillage.

Appendix G

[2.48]

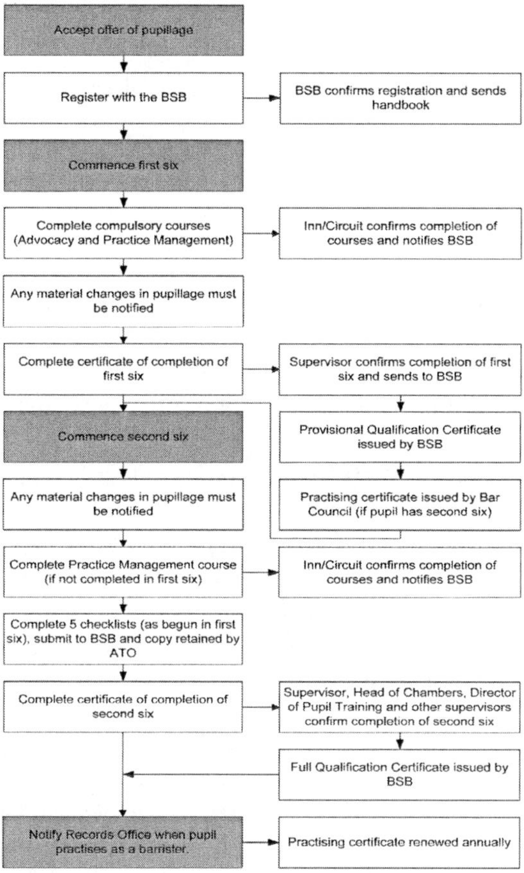

Appendix H

[2.49]

Forms and templates (available from the BSB)

- ATO Authorisation – Application Form
- Application for waiver from funding
- Application for waiver from advertising
- Application to register Pupillage
- Notification of change in pupillage

- Templates for record keeping by pupils
- Appraisal preparation form
- Appraisal form
- Pupil assessment record
- Certificate of satisfactory completion of first six pupillage
- Certificate of satisfactory completion of second six pupillage
- Example of Pupillage contract

Additional guidance and forms are available relating to Dispensations and Waivers from Pupillage Requirements (as dealt with by the Qualifications Committee):

- **External Training –** all or part of the practising six months of pupillage may be satisfied by a form of external training (time spent with a solicitor, marshalling, secondment etc)
- **Reductions in pupillage –** based on relevant experience, usually considered in relation to 'external training'
- **Breaks in and late commencement of pupillage –** e.g. maternity, medical
- **Applications from Qualified Foreign Lawyers under BTR59 –** usually required to pass some or all of the Bar Transfer Test and to undertake a period of pupillage
- **Application for admission to the Bar as a European Lawyer –** normally need to take all or part of the Bar transfer test but exemptions may be possible
- **Application for registration as a Registered European Lawyer and applications by Registered European Lawyers for membership of the Bar –** normally eligible without undertaking any further examinations or pupillage
- **Application for admission to the Bar as a distinguished Law Teacher under BTR59 –** exceptionally granted for candidates of very high academic distinction – some parts of the Bar Transfer test and/or pupillage may be required
- **Application for Temporary Membership of the Bar under BTR78 –** In respect of specific case/s only and to allow applicants to appear in court for specific cases only – no pupillage requirement
- **Qualified Solicitors –** exemptions from pupillage and the Bar Transfer test are automatic for solicitors with higher rights of audience in both civil and criminal proceedings; exemptions may be granted to other applicants
- **Non-Graduate Mature Students –** Applications for by persons who do not meet the normal minimum academic degree requirement for entry to the Bar must meet specified criteria. Normal Pupillage requirements apply
- **BTR59 Applications –** Regulation 59 of the Bar Training Regulations allows the Qualifications Committee to grant exemption from any requirement(s) of the Regulations. A wide variety of applications are made under these regulations, ranging from the very minor to full waiver from all requirements for admission to the Bar.

Appendix I – Glossary and abbreviations

[2.50]

ALBA	Administrative Law Bar Association
Assessment	is defined in this context by the BSB as 'a structured measurement of the pupil's progress against standards'. Feedback should follow.
Assessment Points	The occasions when an assessment, usually summative, takes place.
ATO	Approved Training Organisation. A set of chambers or any other organisation may only take pupils if it is authorised by the Bar Standards Board as an Approved Training Organisation (see BTRs, Part V – The Professional Stage, paragraph 37 – 41). The term 'Approved Training Organisation' (or 'ATO') is therefore used throughout this documentation to refer to both chambers and other organisations that are authorised to take pupils.
BACFI	Bar Association for Commerce, Finance & Industry
BALGPS	Bar Association for Local Government and the Public Service
BEG	Bar European Group
BPTC	Bar Professional Training Course (from September 2010)
BSB	Bar Standards Board
BTRs	Bar Training Regulations, effective from 1 September 2009
BVC	Bar Vocational Course (phased out after academic year 2009–10)
ChBA	Chancery Bar Association
CBA	Criminal Bar Association
COIC	Council of the Inns of Court
COMBAR	Commercial Bar Association
CPS	Criminal Prosecution Service
CR	The Consolidated Regulations of the Inns of Court. Superseded by the BTRs from 1 September 2009.
DDA	Disabilities Discrimination Act
Diversity Training	promotion through teaching and course materials of awareness of and sensitivity to issues of race, gender, sexual orientation, religion and disability. Required.
ELBA	Employment Law Bar Association
EWTD	European Working Time Directive

Feedback	is defined as the regular comments on a pupil's work which the supervisor provides in order to improve performance against the standards and competencies. Feedback is also about reinforcing good practice and work as well as indentifying areas of improvement.
FLBA	Family Law Bar Association
Final assessment	End of stage assessment
Formative assessment	Mock or practice assessment upon which individual feedback in preparation for the summative assessment is given.
FQC	Full Qualification Certificate (after which, on payment, a full Practising Certificate may be obtained)
GLS	Government Legal Service
HEFCE	Higher Education Funding Council for England
HEI	Higher Education Institution (i.e. a University, HEFCE funded College or private institution with degree awarding powers)
Inns Rules	Inns' own regulations, supplementary to the BSB
IPBA	Intellectual Property Bar Association
LCLCBA	London Common Law and Commercial Bar Association
Learning Resources	Collective term for Information Technology Audio-visual equipment Accommodation Library Facilities Book stock
Matrices	Documents demonstrating where knowledge or competencies are covered within the training
MCCBA	Midland Chancery and Commercial Bar Association
MCQs	Multiple Choice Questions
MCT	Multiple Choice Test
NCBA	Northern Chancery and Bar Association
NCCBA	Northern Circuit Commercial Bar Association
OLPAS	Online Pupillage Application System replaced by the Pupillage Portal system in 2009.
PBM	Parliamentary Bar
PIBA	Personal Injuries Bar Association
PEBA	Planning and Environment Bar Association
PNBA	Property Bar Association
PQC	Provisional Qualification Certificate (colloquially known as the Provisional Practising Certificate)
PTO	Pupillage Training Organisation (former name). Approved provider of pupillage training, which may be a chambers or other approved institution (e.g. CPS, GLS or commercial organisation). Now known as ATO (see ATO above) from 1 September 2009.

Pupillage Portal	The current online recruitment process for pupils/pupillage in place from 2009 (and replacing OLPAS, for which see)
QAA	Quality Assurance Agency for Higher Education
QAA	Quality Assurance for Advocates (joint BSB/SRA/ILEX project)
RBA	Revenue Bar Association
SBA	Specialist Bar Association
Seen assessment	A seen paper, in the case of a written assessment, must be taken away and completed by a specified date. In the context of oral assessments, 'seen' means a paper or case study that students can take away and prepare prior to the assessment.
Socratic Teaching	The drawing out of information and approaches through debate facilitated by the tutor/supervisor rather than led by the tutor
Summative assessment	Assessment that may count towards a final assessment or grading
TECBAR	Technology and Construction Bar Association
WCCBA	Western Chancery and Commercial Bar Association

Appendix J – Useful contacts and addresses

[2.51]

Bar Standards Board – 289–293 High Holborn, London WC1V 7HZ (0207 611 1444)

Bar Standards Board – 289–293 High Holborn, London WC1V 7HZ (0207 611 1444)

Chair of the BSB	Baroness Ruth Deech
Director of the BSB	Dr Vanessa Davies
Chair, Education & Training Committee	Professor Andrew Sanders
Chair, Qualifications Committee	Robert Behrens
Chair, Pupillage Sub Committee	Samuel Stein QC
Head of Education Standards	Dr Valerie Shrimplin
Pupillage Officer	Andrea Clerk (aclerk@barstandardsboard.org.uk)
Pupillage Assistant	Claire Hogg (chogg@barstandardsboard.org.uk)
Manager, Qualification Regulations	Joanne Dixon (jdixon@barstandardsboard.org.uk)
Training Regulations (external, reductions)	Pauline Smith (psmith@barstandardsboard.org.uk)

Training Compliance Officer	Rachel Reeves (rreeves@barstandardsboard.org.uk)

Inns of Court

Lincoln's Inn	The Treasury Office, Lincoln's Inn, London WC2A 3LT www.lincolnsinn.org.uk, Tel: 020 7693 5130 Deputy Under Treasurer Education: Joanna Robinson
Inner Temple	Treasury Office, Inner Temple, London EC4Y 7HL www.innertemple.org.uk, Tel: 020 7797 8171 Deputy Under Treasurer Education: Fiona Fulton
Middle Temple	The Treasury, 2 Plowden Buildings, Temple, London EC4Y 9AT www.middletemple.org.uk, Tel: 020 74274800 Deputy Under Treasurer Education: Christa Richmond
Gray's Inn	The Treasury, 8 South Square, Gray's Inn, London WC1R 5EU www.graysinn.org.uk, Tel: 020 7458 7900 Deputy Under Treasurer Education: Quinn Clarke

Circuits

South Eastern Circuit	www.southeastcircuit.org.uk
Midland Circuit	www.midlandcircuit.co.uk
Northern Circuit	www.northerncircuit.org.uk
North Eastern Circuit	www.northeasterncircuit.co.uk
Western Circuit	www.westerncircuit.org.uk
Wales and Chester Circuit	www.walesandchestercircuit.org.uk

Specialist Bar Associations

Administrative Law Bar Association	www.adminlaw.org.uk
Bar European Group	www.bareuropeangroup.org.uk
Chancery Bar Association	www.chba.org.uk
Commercial Bar Association	www.combar.com
Criminal Bar Association	www.criminalbar.com
Employment Law Bar Association	www.elba.org.uk
Family Law Bar Association	www.flba.co.uk
Intellectual Property Bar Association	www.ipba.co.uk

London Common Law & Commercial Bar Association	www.lclcba.com
Midland Chancery & Commercial Bar Association	Refer to www.barcouncil.org.uk
Northern Chancery Bar Association	www.nchba.co.uk
Northern Circuit Commercial Bar Association	www.nccba.org.uk
Parliamentary Bar Mess	Refer to www.barcouncil.org.uk
Personal Injuries Bar Association	www.piba.org.uk
Planning & Environmental Bar Association	www.peba.info
Professional Negligence Bar Association	www.pnba.co.uk
Property Bar Association	www.propertybar.org.uk
Revenue Bar Association	www.revenue-bar.org
Technology and Construction Bar Association	www.tecbar.org
Western Chancery & Commercial Bar Association	Refer to www.barcouncil.org.uk

Other Associations and contacts

The Law Society	www.lawsociety.org.uk
Solicitors Regulation Authority	www.sra.org.uk
Law Centres Federation	www.lawcentres.org.uk
BMIF	Telephone: 020 7621 0405
Free Representation Unit (FRU)	www.freerepresentationunit.org.uk
Bar Association for Local Government & the Public Service	www.balgps.org.uk
Bar Association for Commerce, Finance & Industry	www.bacfi.org
Association of Women Barristers	www.womenbarristers.co.uk
Society of Asian Lawyers	www.societyofasianlawyers.com
Bar Lesbian and Gay Group	www.blagg.org
Society of Black Lawyers	www.blacklawyer.org

Transferring to the Bar

Transfer to the Bar from other Legal Roles

Qualified foreign lawyers

[2.52]

A "Qualified Foreign Lawyer" means a person who is a member of a legal profession regulated in a jurisdiction outside England and Wales and entitled to practise as such.

When applying to transfer to the Bar you will need to provide:

- Evidence that you are of good character and repute, such as a Certificate of the Senior Judge, Attorney General or Senior Law Officer of the Superior Court in which you have practised, showing that: for a period of not less than three years you have regularly exercised rights of audience in that court (identifying the period(s)) and you are a fit and proper person to be Called to the Bar.
- A certificate to show that you have not been prohibited from practising in the jurisdiction in which you are qualified on the ground of commission of a criminal offence or professional misconduct and are not currently suspended from practising on such grounds.
- Evidence of all academic and professional qualifications. All applications must be supported by either the original or a certified copy of your examination certificates. Applications with overseas qualifications must also include an official English translation of their certificates and results.
- Any other evidence which you wish to supply in support of your application (e.g. references).
- Current application fee of £440 (cheque made payable to "The General Council of the Bar").

Solicitors

[2.53]

If you are a solicitor admitted and enrolled in England & Wales or Northern Ireland you can apply for a relaxation of the usual requirements for Call to the Bar and entry into practice.

When applying to transfer to the Bar you will need to provide us with:

- Original Certificate of Good Standing issued by the Law Society of England and Wales or the Law Society of Northern Ireland.
- Original Certificate of Higher Court Rights (where appropriate).
- Any other evidence which you wish to supply in support of your application (e.g. references).
- Current application fee of £440 (cheque made payable to "The General Council of the Bar").

Temporary call

[2.54]

If you need to appear in court in England and Wales to conduct a specific case (or cases) only you may apply for temporary call.

If you are applying for temporary call you will need to provide us with:

- Evidence to establish that you are of good character and repute, such as a Certificate of the Senior Judge, Attorney General or Senior Law Officer of the Superior Court in which you have practised showing that: for a period of not less than three years you have regularly exercised rights of audience in that court (identifying the period(s) and you are a fit and proper person to be Called to the Bar.
- A certificate that you have not been prohibited from practising in the jurisdiction in which the applicant is qualified on the ground of commission of a criminal offence or professional misconduct and are not currently suspended from practising on such grounds
- Evidence of all academic and professional qualifications.
- All applications must be supported by either the original or a certified copy of your examination certificates. Applications with overseas qualifications must also include an official English translation of their certificates and results.
- Any other evidence which you wish to supply in support of your application (e.g. references).
- Current application fee of £440 (cheque made payable to "The General Council of the Bar").

Legal Academics

[2.55]–[2.64]

If you are a teacher of the law of England and Wales you can apply for relaxation of the usual requirements for Call to the Bar and entry into practice.

When applying for admission to the Bar you will need to provide us with:

- References from at least one senior legal academic, such as a Head of Department or Vice Chancellor, and from at least one senior member of the Bar and/or judiciary.
- Any other evidence which you wish to supply in support of your application (e.g. references).
- Current application fee of £440 (cheque made payable to "The General Council of the Bar").

Pupillage Frequently Asked Questions

Commencing Pupillage

When can I start pupillage?

[2.65]–[2.66]

You can start pupillage as soon as you have successfully completed the Bar Vocational Course (BVC) or Bar Professional Training Course (BPTC). If you have taken resits you must wait until you have passed them before commencing pupillage.

If you are exempted under section 4.B7 of the Bar Standards Board Handbook, you can commence pupillage after passing the Bar Transfer Test, or after being exempted from that test.

Is there a time limit for starting pupillage?

Yes. If you commenced the vocational stage of training on or after 1 September 1998, you must start pupillage within five years of passing the BVC/BPTC (or the Bar Transfer Test, as the case may be). The time-limit for starting pupillage can be extended by the Bar Standards Board in individual cases if there are sufficient grounds. An application must be made on a prescribed application form and will be considered by the Qualifications Committee. The form can be downloaded from the BSB website or obtained from the Training Regulations Administrator.

Can I start pupillage before being called?

Yes. Provided you have passed the BVC/BPTC you may undertake the first six months of pupillage, in whole or in part, before being Called. However the whole of the second six months (including any periods of external training) must be served after Call.

What else do I need to do before starting pupillage?

You must register your pupillage with the Bar Standards Board on the appropriate registration form before you commence pupillage. Any periods of time spent in chambers before registration will not count towards your pupillage. Registration forms should be returned to the Pupillage Compliance Section of the Bar Standards Board.

Time requirements

How long am I required to spend in pupillage?

Twelve calendar months (unless your pupillage has been reduced by the Qualifications Committee). If you commence pupillage on 1 October 2011 you would complete your first six on 31 March 2012, commence your second six on 1 April 2012 and complete the twelve months on 30 September 2012.

What is the difference between the first (non-practising) and second six months (practising)?

The first six months are non-practising, that is, you may not accept professional instructions during that period (except for noting briefs: see below). During the second six months, you may accept instructions on your own account provided that you have the permission of your pupil supervisor or head of chambers and hold a provisional practising certificate. From January 2010, it became a criminal offence to practise as a barrister without a practising certificate (in accordance with the Legal Services Act 2007). Once satisfactory completion of the first six is confirmed, the Pupillage Compliance Section will issue pupils with a Provisional Qualification Certificate and a provisional practising certificate (provided they have registered a practising period of pupillage).

Can I take on part-time work during pupillage?

You may take part time work with the permission of your pupil supervisor, provided that, in his or her opinion, it will not materially interfere with your training.

Can I take holiday during pupillage?

The BSB guidelines state that all pupils should be permitted to take four weeks holidays during their pupillage. Policies may vary as to whether this includes bank holidays, the period between Christmas and New Year etc. If you are taking any longer period of leave, you will need to obtain permission from the Qualifications Committee and an extension of the overall period so as to compensate for the breaks. Please contact the Training Regulations Assistant for further information about making an application.

Where can I undertake pupillage?

Except with the written permission of the Board, the non-practising period of pupillage must be undertaken in a Member State of the European Union. Except with the written permission of the Board, the practising period of pupillage must be undertaken in a Member State. Any period of pupillage must be undertaken in an Approved Training Organisation and with a barrister who is a registered pupil supervisor.

Can I do pupillage in a jurisdiction outside the European Union?

The Qualifications Committee has the discretion to recognise such other form(s) of training as satisfying all or part of the practising period of pupillage as it considers appropriate having regard to the particular circumstances of the person concerned.

This may include pupillage in another jurisdiction. You will need to make an application for permission to undertake external training on the appropriate form.

External training

Do I need approval to undertake external training?

You need the prior approval of the Qualifications Committee for any period of external training. You can download an application form from the BSB website or contact the Training Regulations Assistant.

Does external training count towards pupillage?

External training may only count towards the practising six months and must be undertaken after Call.

Accepting instructions

When can I start to accept instructions?

During the second six months, provided that you have the permission of your pupil supervisor or the head of chambers, and that you have been issued with a provisional practising certificate by the Bar Standards Board.

Can I do a noting brief in the first six months?

Yes, provided that you have the permission of your pupil supervisor or head of chambers.

Can I be paid for doing a noting brief?

Yes, pupils can be paid for doing a noting brief.

When do I need to take out my own insurance?

You are covered by your pupil supervisor's insurance until you receive a full Practising Certificate. Third six pupils may continue to be covered by their pupil supervisor's insurance provided that the pupil supervisor does not have another pupil (or if he/she does, has obtained permission from the Qualifications Committee to take more than one pupil at a time). A barrister who is squatting in chambers must take out their own insurance with the Bar Mutual Indemnity Fund as they are offering services as an independent practitioner. Employed barristers should be covered by their employers insurance.

Certification of pupillage

What do I need to do at the end of the first six months (non-practising period)?

At the end of the first six months your pupil supervisor must sign a Certificate of Satisfactory Completion of Pupillage (First Six). The Certificate is available on the BSB website. This should be submitted to the Pupillage Compliance Section of the BSB. At this stage, it is not necessary to submit the relevant checklists. However, the pupil and pupil supervisor should hold regular meetings to ensure items and competency levels within the checklist are being met. Pupils should have also attended the Advocacy Course, provided by the Inns and Circuits, by the end of their non-practising six months. It is strongly advised that pupils should attend the Practice Management Course during their non-practising period of pupillage.

What do I do at the end of the second six months (practising period)?

At the end of the second six months each pupil supervisor involved in the practising period of pupillage must sign the Certificate of Satisfactory Completion of Pupillage (Second Six). The Head of Chambers or the Director of Pupil Training must also sign the Certificate. The Certificate is available on the BSB website. This should be submitted to the Pupillage Compliance Section of the BSB along with the pupils completed checklists. The Practice Management Course must be satisfactorily completed by the end of the practising six. A Pupil will not be issued with a full qualification certificate unless the course has been completed.

Reduction in pupillage

I have spent a number of years working in a legal environment, can I obtain a reduction in the length of pupillage?

If there are sufficient grounds, you may apply for a reduction in the length of pupillage. The grounds for such an application must be the completion of some substantial training and/or experience that can be realistically equated to service of pupillage.

How do I apply for a reduction in the length of pupillage?

The application must be made on a prescribed application form and will be considered by the Qualifications Committee. The form can be downloaded from the BSB website or obtained from the Training Regulations Administrator.

Will a reduction of pupillage count against the first or second six months?

Normally any reduction of pupillage will only count against the second six months.

Miscellaneous

How often do pupils "fail"?

Due to the intense competition for pupillage, it is quite unusual for a pupil to "fail" any component of their pupillage training. Standards are however more carefully defined in the Pupillage Handbook and signing off a pupil must relate to these standards, rather than simply as "time served" or "tasks completed" by pupils. Where pupils have been unsuccessful, this is most often on Inns' training courses (problems with advocacy or skeleton arguments being the most common). If a pupil is supported by the ATO, Inn and/or circuit, repeats are normally possible and the situation may be retrieved.

Continuing Professional Development ("CPD")

[2.67]

All barristers are required to complete CPD hours and maintain their record cards. Barristers no longer have to return their CPD cards to the BSB, however the BSB will conduct random spot-checks of barristers' CPD records cards.

In the first three years' of practice, newly qualified practitioners are required to complete 45 hours of CPD, including at least nine hours of Advocacy Training and three hours of Ethics (the "New Practitioners' Programme"). After the first three years of practice, barristers are required to undertake 12 hours of CPD each year (the "Established Practitioners' Programme").

Following a change in the rules the following key points must be noted.

- Barristers no longer have to return their CPD cards to the BSB.
- All barristers must still undertake their CPD hours and keep their record cards.
- The BSB has started conducting random spot-checks of barristers' CPD cards.

Background

The BSB has started conducting random spot-checks of barristers' CPD record cards. This is to ensure that barristers keep their record cards updated and undertake their set number of CPD hours.

This is a key move towards smarter regulation, saving time and money. It said by the BSB that this will also protect the public more effectively by focussing on the minority of barristers not keeping their training up-to-date. Prior to this change, the BSB required all practising members of the Bar to submit their record cards annually to the BSB for monitoring checks. Plans to introduce spot checking were first announced in November 2013 and the BSB started the process in May 2014.

Evidence

Those selected for spot-checking will be asked for evidence of completion of their CPD hours and their record card. The BSB is accepting a wide range of evidence and barristers are encouraged to provide their own examples, which could include:

- Certificate of attendance or;
- letter from University if taking or teaching a course;
- course materials or course invoices;
- test results if applicable; and
- booking confirmation or other correspondence with course provider.

For many barristers, the provision of evidence has not presented any practical difficulties. According to the BSB a barrister would not be considered non-compliant solely because they have not retained evidence. Instead, the CPD assessment team will take a proactive approach to contacting course providers to verify attendance if barristers have been unable to provide evidence themselves. In the case of CPD activities where it is impossible to verify completion – for example, with certain online courses – the BSB would accept a barrister's declaration of completion. Any barristers who have been selected for spot-checking and are concerned about potential difficulties providing evidence can get in touch with the BSB CPD team via cpdrecords@barstandardsboard.org.uk.

Selection

Potentially, any practising barrister undertaking CPD through the Established Practitioner Programme could be contacted for spot-checking. Barristers who completed the final year of New Practitioners Programme in 2013 could also be contacted for spot-checking.

Barristers who have failed to complete their required CPD hours will be considered by the BSB on a case by case basis. In most cases they will need to complete their remaining hours, within a set time frame. Those who are persistently non-compliant will ultimately face enforcement action.

Comprehensive guidance is produced by the Bar Standards Board in relation to CPD. The text of the Compliance with CPD Regulations "A General Guide to CPD" is set out below. see para **[2.69]** below.

Compliance with CPD Regulations "A General Guide to CPD"

[2.68]

The Bar Standards Board has published "*A General Guide to CPD*", the text of which is reproduced below.

CPD requirements

[2.69]

All practising members of the Bar are subject to the continuing professional development regulations. Compliance is an obligation of the Bar Handbook (Part 4, section C, The CPD Rules).

In the first three years of practice, newly qualified practitioners are required to complete 45 hours of continuing professional development (CPD), including at least 9 hours of advocacy training and 3 hours of ethics training (the 'New Practitioners' Programme'). All hours must be accredited by the Bar Standards Board.

Following completion of the 'NPP', barristers are required to undertake a minimum of 12 hours of CPD each calendar year (the 'Established Practitioners' Programme'). A minimum 4 of the required 12 hours must be activities which have been accredited by the Bar Standards Board; accreditation awarded by other professional bodies or institutions will not be accepted as accredited CPD by the Bar Standards Board.

The Bar's CPD regime is run on a calendar year basis.

CPD definition

[2.70]

CPD is work undertaken over and above the normal commitments of barristers with a view to such work developing their skills, knowledge and professional standards in areas relevant to their present or proposed area of practice, and in order to keep themselves up to date and maintain the highest standards of professional practice.

How to calculate CPD hours

- CPD hours, either accredited or unaccredited, are the hours spent in either seminars or lectures, added up and rounded down to the nearest half an hour. ***CPD courses, seminars, lectures or any other form of training event are treated as separate events. The hours for each event are rounded down to the nearest half an hour individually; practitioners are unable to add all courses together with a view to rounding the total down.***
- Registration and/or refreshment breaks and lunchtime must not be included in this calculation.

Accredited hours

Accredited hours can be obtained through attendance/speaking at courses, conferences, lectures or seminars that have been approved by the Bar Standards Board's CPD Accreditation department and been awarded accredited CPD hours.

NB: An SRA/Law Society accredited course is not automatically accredited by the Bar Standards Board.

Attendance at accredited CPD courses

- It is a barrister's responsibility to check if a training event has been accredited by the Bar Standards Board. Where there is doubt, a barrister is able to check with the Bar Standards Board's CPD Accreditation department.
- Barristers must sign the registration document supplied by the provider at the end of the course to claim CPD hours.
- Only courses registered with the CPD Office are considered as accredited.
- Applications for accreditation must be sent to the Bar Standards Board *at least two weeks* in advance of the course being held.

Undertaking university courses

- To claim hours for undertaking a university course, including LLMs, the barrister must obtain from the university a letter confirming (i) the nature and content of the course, (ii) the number of hours that the barrister has undertaken as part of the course, and (iii) that the barrister has complied with all the course requirements to date.
- If it is not a law course, it must be a course directly relevant to the barrister's present or proposed area of practice.

Training events

- Barristers may claim CPD hours for preparing and delivering a training event. Barristers may apply for one-off CPD accreditation – refer to page 8.
- A person is unable to claim for preparing a training event if they do not present it.
- A person who presented a training event, but did not produce the training material/speaker notes themselves, is eligible to claim hours for their own preparation.

Calculation of CPD hours

The rules for calculating CPD for presenting and preparing for a training event are, as follows:

- Barristers may claim CPD hours for preparing and delivering a training event, which may be accredited or unaccredited. Barristers may apply for one-off CPD accreditation – refer to page 8. Time spent attending the remaining part of a training event given by a co-presenter may be claimed in the normal way.

- The basic principle is that the number of CPD hours that may be claimed is the sum of (a) the duration of the presentation actually given by the barrister, and (b) an equal time that is deemed for the preparation of that event.
- It is acknowledged that the deemed preparation time is likely to undervalue the actual time taken. To mitigate this adverse consequence somewhat, the number of CPD hours that may be claimed should be the sum of the presentation and deemed preparation timings, and then rounded down to the nearest ½ hour unit, save that the minimum total shall not be less than ½ hour.
- A barrister cannot claim for repeat delivery of a training event in any one CPD year.
- A barrister who prepares a training event for another may claim only the deemed preparation time in the CPD year in which the training event was actually given. If the event was never given, then no preparation time may be claimed.
- A barrister who presents a training event prepared by another may still claim both the presentation and the deemed preparation timings.

Examples:

- 1 barrister gives a 1 hour training event. 2 CPD hours may be claimed: 1 for the presentation, and 1 for the deemed preparation.
- 2 barristers equally give a 1 hour training event. Each may claim 1½ CPD hours: ½ hour for the presentation and ½ hour for the deemed preparation and ½ hour for attending the other barrister's presentation.
- 3 barristers equally give a 1½ hour training event. Each may claim 2 CPD hours: ½ hour for the presentation and ½ hour for the deemed preparation and 1 hour for attending the other barristers' presentations.
- 4 barristers equally give a 1½ hour training event. Each may claim 1½ CPD hours: 22½ minutes for the presentation and 22½ minutes for the deemed preparation (which after addition to give 45 minutes is then rounded down to give ½ hour) and 67½ minutes for attending the other barristers' presentations (which is then rounded down to 1 hour).
- 4 barristers equally give a 4 hours training event. Each may claim 5 CPD hours: 1 hour for the presentation and 1 hour for the deemed preparation and 3 hours for attending the other barristers' presentations.
- 4 barristers equally give a 1 hour training event. Each may claim 1 CPD hour: 15 minutes for the presentation and 15 minutes for the deemed preparation (which after addition to give 30 minutes results in ½ hour) and 45 minutes for attending the other barristers' presentations (which is then rounded down to ½ hour).
- 6 barristers equally give a 1 hour training event. Each may claim 1 CPD hour: 10 minutes for the presentation and 10 minutes for the deemed preparation (which after addition to give 20 minutes is then deemed by the

saving provision still to merit ½ hour) and 50 minutes for attending the other barristers' presentations (which is then rounded down to ½ hour).

Repeat courses or training events

- Unless they have good reasons for doing so, barristers cannot claim hours for attending or undertaking a course or training event with the same or substantially the same content as another course or training event in respect of which CPD hours are claimed in the same calendar year or have been claimed in the previous calendar year.

Online courses/Podcasts

- There are a number of online course/podcast providers, a list of which is available from the CPD Office.
- An online test must be completed before the provider allocates CPD hours.
- To claim these hours you must attach the completed certification form produced at the end of the course to your record card.

DVDs, Videos and CD Roms

- DVDs and CD Roms etc must be obtained from a Bar Standards Board approved producer of legal programmes or an accredited CPD provider who record their events.
- Please add details of the above to your CPD Record card. You must include the number of CPD hours (length), the title and the provider.

Other accredited activities

- Courses run by the Crown Prosecution Service, the Judicial College and the Ministry of Justice are automatically accredited by the Bar Standards Board, subject to the rules which govern CPD for the Bar of England & Wales.
- Pupil supervisor training up to 3 CPD hours
- Practitioners can claim 1 CPD hour per active month of service as a Judicial Assistant.*

NB: *Active month of service is considered to be anything that exceeds ½ a month in the event that less than 1 month is completed.

Unaccredited

Unaccredited hours can be obtained by attending any course, lecture, conference or seminar, which has not been registered with the CPD Office but is directly relevant to he barrister's area of practice or intended area of practice. Unaccredited hours are designed to give increased flexibility to the CPD that a barrister can undertake and need only be added to a person's record card for the claim to be made.

NB: Those subject to the New Practitioners Programme cannot claim CPD hours for attendance at unaccredited events, or completion of unaccredited activities, but may be able to apply for one-off accreditation. Please refer to the 'One-off accreditation' section of this document for more information.

Those subject to the Established Practitioners Programme are able to claim a maximum of 8 unaccredited CPD hours in one calendar year.

Presenting an unaccredited lecture

- The rules are the same as for accredited lectures; with the distinction that the hours claimed will be unaccredited.

Teaching on university courses

- A Barrister is able to claim CPD hours for teaching on LLBs, LLMs, the CPE, BPTC, LPC or Diplomas in Law.
- Barristers are able to claim hours for teaching law on degree courses, which are not wholly about law if it is relevant to their practice and provided that the level is at least equivalent to an undergraduate law degree.
- To receive accredited hours for this work a barrister must obtain from the university a letter confirming the number of hours that they teach. The letter must be kept together with the completed CPD record card.

Advocacy training, mock trials and moots

- In relation to advocacy training (including at mock trials), delegates can claim the following: (a) the time spent attending advocacy training, and (b) additional preparation time as follows: up to a third of the length of the course.
- Advocacy Trainers can claim the following: (a) the time they spend providing the advocacy training, and (b) in relation to preparation, up to a third of the time they spend providing the advocacy training (e.g. up to an hour for a 3 hour exercise).
- Those acting as judges or witnesses in relation to advocacy training can claim the following: (a) the time they spend acting as judges or witnesses, and (b) in relation to preparation, up to a quarter of the time they spend acting as judges or witnesses (e.g. up to an hour for a 4 hour exercise).
- Preparation of advocacy training cannot be claimed if a person does not deliver the training.
- Moots can count for up to a maximum of 2 CPD hours a year.
- School moots, mock trials or tribunals do not count.

Writing

- Legal writing or editing can count for a maximum of 4 unaccredited CPD hours per calendar year.
- Writing or editing the following can count for these hours: law books, law articles, practice notes for publication, consultation papers, examination question papers, law update papers, legal dissertations and legal reports.

- A person is able to claim the hours it takes to write the article/book etc. up to this maximum.
- The hours must be claimed in the year of publication.
- Papers for moots can only count for 2 hours.
- Reviewing legal books does not attract CPD hours.

NB: Those subject to the New Practitioners Programme cannot claim CPD hours for the writing of legal articles.

Other activities

- Attending unaccredited courses directly relevant to practice as a barrister.
- This can include lectures and seminars given by Solicitors' firms and organisations not accredited by the Bar Standards Board to provide CPD hours.

One-off accreditation

- If a barrister wishes to attend an event that has not been accredited by the Bar Standards Board, they can apply for one-off accreditation.
- To do so they must send details of the event including the specific date(s) on which the event will take place, any itinerary or programme, subject matters to be covered, specific title of events, name(s) of speaker(s) and the contact details of the event organiser(s).
- This should be sent to Elizabeth Prats at the Bar Standards Board, Education Standards Department at least two weeks in advance of the event taking place.
- There is an application fee of £45 per event for consideration. Organisations which are not accredited by the Bar Standards Board are limited to 1 application for one-off accreditation per annum. There is no restriction on the number of applications a practitioner can submit to the Bar Standards Board. Payment can be satisfied by cheque, bank transfer (BACS) or debit/credit card. Cheques should be made payable to 'The Bar Standards Board'. There is a 2.5% handling fee for all card payments.

Other rules

- Barristers working part time, if they hold a practising certificate, are subject to the same rules as those working on a full time basis.
- Barristers practising abroad, if they hold a practising certificate, are subject to the same rules as those practising in England and Wales.
- Practitioners subject to the Established Practitioners Programme are not able to carry CPD hours over from one year to the next.

Cannot count for CPD hours

Personal Development:

- Personal stress management.
- Personal/time management courses.
- Personal presentation skills.
- Voice coaching.
- Mentoring or appraisal schemes.
- Listening to radio programmes.
- Subscription to periodicals.
- Reading.
- Networking skills.
- Marketing skills.
- Life coaching skills.
- Career development courses.
- Leadership/general management skills.

Other:

- Practice management courses.
- Acting as an External Examiner.
- Shadowing a Judge.
- Pro-bono work.
- Work at a Citizen's Advice Bureau.
- Bar in the community scheme.
- Working as a member of a review panel.
- Acting as a Pupil Master (mini-pupillages included).
- Sitting as a Recorder.
- Sitting as a Justice of the Peace.
- Marking work for University courses, including the BPTC.
- Sitting on a Tribunal or other part time Judicial office.
- The 'Speakers for Schools' programme.
- Annual General Meetings.
- Careers Talks.
- Attendance at a launch for any form of legal materials.
- Teaching on BTECs or ILEX level 1–3 courses.
- After-dinner speeches, tours, receptions and court visits.

What to do if you work for a solicitor's firm

- Please obtain from your employer a copy of your electronic CPD record card (most solicitors firms keep these) and attach this to your CPD record card for record keeping.

- If your firm does not keep such a record for you, you must complete the standard form.

What to do if you are not going to practise for the whole year

- If you are going on maternity/paternity leave, taking a career break or having a break in practice for any other reason which will prevent you from completing your CPD requirements then you might wish to consider suspending your practising certificate, which would, in turn, suspend your CPD requirements. If you do not suspend your practising certificate then you must apply for a waiver from the CPD requirements. The application form can be obtained from the Qualifications department.
- If you have not completed your CPD requirements by the deadline stipulated by the Bar Standards Board or you are aware that you will not complete your hours in the required time, you must apply for an extension of time. The application form can be obtained from the Qualifications department.
- It may be of benefit to download and read the Bar Standards Board's guidance on CPD requirements when taking parental leave. The document can be downloaded via: https://www.barstandardsboard.org.uk/about-bar-standards-board/equality-and-diversity/
- Extension/waiver forms can also be downloaded from the Bar Standards Board website.

Frequently asked questions

(Q) *I've found a course I would like to attend? How can I find out if it has been accredited?*

(A) Contact the Bar Standards Board's CPD Accreditation department and ask whether or not a course has been accredited. You can do this by telephone or via email.

(Q) *Where can I find details of accredited courses?*

(A) A number of courses are listed on our website: http://www.barstandardsboard.org.uk/regulatory-requirements/for-barristers/continuing-professional-development/cpd-courses/

Please note; this list is not comprehensive, as some approved providers do not advertise online.

(Q) *I've lost my Record Card? How do I get another one?*

(A) http://www.barstandardsboard.org.uk/regulatory-requirements/for-barristers/continuing-professional-development/

(Q) *Do I need to return a signed, completed CPD record card to the Bar Standards Board?*

(A) No. As of January 2014, practising barristers are not required to return a signed CPD record card to the Bar Standards Board. Instead, barristers are required to retain a comprehensive CPD record, including any documents which verify completion of training, for two years, should they be selected for monitoring as part of the BSB's wider supervision strategy. This policy change relates to barristers' 2013 CPD requirement and all future CPD requirements.

CPD Departments at the Bar Standards Board/Contacts Department	Name	Job Title
Supervision of CPD	Sarah Hellier	CPD administration assistant
CPD Accreditation	Elizabeth Prats	Continuing Education Officer
CPD Accreditation	Ruth Beaumont	Continuing Education Assistant
Qualifications	Pauline Smith	Training Regulations Officer
Qualifications	Raxa Tailor	Administration Assistant

Annex A

[2.71]

NEW PRACTITIONERS' PROGRAMME

CPD RECORD

Name:		For Year Ended:	
Address:		Area of Practice:	
(In full)		Email (if available):	

DATE	COURSE PROVIDER	COURSE TITLE	NUMBER OF HOURS	SPEAKER (IF SO HOW LONG FOR)	NOTES

I certify that I have completed the courses listed above and that they are accredited and relevant to my present or proposed area of practice.

Signed.. **Date**.............................

PLEASE RETAIN A COPY OF YOUR OWN RECORD CARD

Please retain a copy of your record card so that if, in future, you are chosen to be spot checked you can then supply us with the information we need.

New practitioners' programme

- Must be completed within the first three years of practice.
- The three-year period is treated as beginning from the 1 January following commencement of practice (either 'third six', squatting, tenancy or a position as an employed barrister.
- Barristers are able to accrue CPD hours from the date they commenced practice.
- Consists of 45 hours CPD of which at least 9 hours must be advocacy training and at least 3 hours must be ethics.
- All CPD requirements for the new practitioners' programme must be satisfied through accredited activities.
- CPD hours are the hours spent in either seminars or lectures, added up and rounded down to the nearest half an hour.
- The forensic accountancy course is an additional requirement of the new practitioners' programme for those who did not complete it during pupillage.

Accredited activities

- Undertaking courses, lectures, seminars or conferences accredited by the Bar Standards Board for CPD purposes.
- Delivering a course, lecture or seminar accredited by the Bar Standards Board for CPD purposes. This can include legal courses such as diplomas, MA's, the BVC, LLB's and LLM's.
- Credit cannot be obtained for a repeat delivery of an event in the same calendar year.

Administration

- Barristers subject to the CPD regulations are required to retain a copy of their CPD record card so that if, in future, they are chosen to be spot checked they can then supply us with the information we need.
- Barristers not complying with minimum requirements will be referred to the Complaints Committee.
- Applications for waivers, extensions of time are dealt with by the Qualifications Committee.

Further Information and Guidance

- The Bar Standards Board will be maintaining an online list of courses which have been accredited for CPD purposes on the website at www.barstandardsboard.org.uk.
- Supervision Department (cpdrecords@barstandardsboard.org.uk) can assist with queries relating to individuals' CPD requirements.
- Liz Prats, Continuing Education Officer, (lprats@barstandardsboard.org.uk) can assist with queries relating to courses and accreditation.

- Both the Supervision Department and Liz are based at the Bar Standards Board, 289–293 High Holborn, London, WC1V 7HZ, Tel: 020 7611 1444; Fax: 020 7831 9217.

Annex B

[2.72]–[2.75]

ESTABLISHED PRACTITIONERS' PROGRAMME

CPD RECORD

Name:		For Year Ended:	
Address:		Area of Practice:	
(In full)		Email (if available):	

DATE	DETAILS OF CPD ACTIVITY UNDERTAKEN AND PROVIDER OF THE ACTIVITY	NUMBER OF HOURS	ACCREDITED (Y/N)	SPEAKER (IF YES HOW LONG FOR)	ANY COMMENTS ON THIS ACTIVITY *

I certify that I have completed no fewer than 12 hours of Continuing Professional Development (CPD), at least 4 hours of which are accredited activities. Further that these hours are relevant to my present or proposed area of practice.

Signed... **Date**.............................

PLEASE RETAIN A COPY OF YOUR OWN RECORD CARD

Please retain a copy of your record card so that if, in future, you are chosen to be spot checked you can then supply us with the information we need.

* This section can be used to let us know your opinion on any courses that you have attended. All feedback will be treated with the utmost confidence.

Guidance on filling in the form

- Please include in the notes if the event has been one-off accredited by the Bar Standards Board, ie: you made an application for accreditation.
- Incomplete dates will not be accepted. The full date e.g. 10 June 2012 is necessary.
- The details of the organisers of each CPD event that you attend are essential. Incomplete data will not be accepted. Law Society reference numbers are also not acceptable.
- If you are claiming hours for delivering a lecture please make it clear how long the lecture lasted for.
- CPD hours, either accredited or unaccredited, are the hours spent in either seminars or lectures, added up and rounded down to the nearest half an hour.
- If you require more space than the form permits, please photocopy this sheet or download a record card at www.barstandardsboard.org.uk

Established practitioners' programme

- Consists of 12 hours CPD per CPD year.
- The CPD year is the same as the calendar year (ie 1 January to 31 December).
- A barrister who is subject to the established practitioners' programme for less than a whole year must complete 1 CPD hour for each month or part month that they hold a practising certificate.
- At least 4 hours CPD in each year must be satisfied through accredited activities.

Accredited activities

- Undertaking courses, lectures, seminars or conferences accredited by the Bar Standards Board for CPD purposes.
- Delivering a course, lecture or seminar accredited by the Bar Standards Board for CPD purposes. This can include legal courses such as diplomas, MA's, the BVC, LLB's and LLM's.
- Credit cannot be obtained for a repeat delivery of an event in the same calendar year.
- Barristers cannot claim hours for attending/undertaking a course or training event with the same content as another course or training event where CPD hours are claimed in the same calendar year or have been claimed in the previous calendar year.
- If claiming CPD hours for the completion of online courses the confirmation printout from the provider must be attached to the completed record card.

Other CPD activities (unaccredited)

- Attending or contributing to unaccredited courses directly relevant to practice as a barrister, this can include lectures and seminars given by solicitors firms and organisations not accredited by the Bar Standards Board to provide CPD.

- Writing law books, articles or practice notes for publication (up to a maximum of 4 CPD hours per calendar year). CPD hours must be claimed in the year of publication.
- Moots up to a maximum of 2 hours a year.
- Other activities approved in advance by the Bar Standards Board.
- Please see 'A General Guide to CPD' for more information.

Administration

- Barristers subject to the CPD regulations are required to retain their CPD record card so that, if in future, they are chosen to be spot checked they can then supply us with the information we need.
- Barristers not complying with minimum requirements will be referred to the Complaints Committee.
- Applications for waivers and extensions of time to be dealt with by the Qualifications Committee.

Further information and guidance

- The Bar Standards Board maintains an online list of courses which have been accredited for CPD purposes on the website at www.barstandardsboard.org.uk
- Supervision Department (cpdrecords@barstandardsboard.org.uk) can assist with queries relating to individuals' CPD requirements.
- Liz Prats, Continuing Education Officer, (lprats@barstandardsboard.org.uk) can assist with queries relating to courses and accreditation.
- Both the Supervision Department and Liz are based at the Bar Standards Board, 289–293 High Holborn, London, WC1V 7HZ; Tel: 020 7611 1444; Fax: 020 7831 9217.

The Practising Certificate & Authorisation to Practise

[2.76]

The Code of Conduct requires every practising barrister to have a valid annual practising certificate.

Authorisation to Practise

The BSB has adopted a more structured approach to barristers' registration, which is called Authorisation to Practise.

The new rules modernise the authorisation process and bring the arrangements into compliance with the Legal Services Act 2007.

During the new process, barristers will be asked to:

- verify their current contact details;
- verify their practising status and entitlement to exercise reserved legal activities;
- confirm whether they have completed the requisite amount of continuing professional development (CPD) activity;
- declare that they have obtained and paid for adequate indemnity insurance;
- pay their practising certificate fee, and
- sign a declaration of truth, which is designed to ensure understanding of the process and new system.

The renewal will be completed via a quick and easy online system, known as Barrister Connect. Barristers may log into this system at https://www.barristerconnect.org.uk/login/. Guidance in relation to the log in process may be found at the BSB website at http://www.barstandardsboard.org.uk/media/1408895/barrister_connect_guidance_-_may_2012_gg.pdf .

The BSB has produced the 'Policy & Guidance' paper below setting out the new regime and 2012/13 fees.

Practising Certificate: Guidance for barristers – conducting litigation

[2.77]

The BSB now allows both self-employed and employed barristers to apply to be authorised to conduct litigation. There are three ways in which barristers can be authorised to conduct litigation:

(1) self-employed and employed barristers can apply for an extension of their practising certificate by meeting the requirements of rS47 of the Scope of Practice Rules in the BSB Handbook (this process has been in place since 22 January 2014);

(2) employed barristers previously authorised to conduct litigation under Annexe I of the old Code of Conduct (8th Edn.) will retain their authorisation, provided that they remain in employed practice; or

(3) by being independently entitled to conduct litigation by virtue of primary legislation.

Barristers authorised by the BSB to conduct litigation

You may apply for an extension to your practising certificate to conduct litigation by virtue of rS47. Please note that you may not do this as part of the authorisation to practise process – detailed guidance for those seeking to secure an extension to their practising certificate is available on the BSB website: https://www.barstandardsboard.org.uk/regulatory-requirements/for-barristers/authorisation-to-conduct-litigation/.

If you have been authorised to conduct litigation but have not been entitled to exercise full rights of audience for at least three years (during which you have made practice as a barrister or other authorised person your primary occupation) or you have not been granted a waiver from this requirement by the BSB in respect of a qualified person for litigation then:[1]

- if you are a self-employed barrister, your principal place of practice must be a chambers or an annex of chambers which is also the principal place of practice of a relevant qualified person, who is readily available to provide guidance in relation to your work when you are conducting litigation;
- if you are an employed barrister, your principal place of practice must be an office of an organisation of which an employee, partner, manager or director is a relevant qualified person who is readily available to provide guidance in relation to your work when you are conducting litigation.

If you are employed by a non-authorised body and are providing legal services only to your employer and those listed at rS39.2 to rS39.6 in the BSB Handbook then the requirement to work with a relevant qualified person applies only if you have not been entitled to exercise full rights of audience in the manner described above for one year.

A qualified person (litigation) must be a person who:[2]

- has been entitled to practise and has practised as a barrister (other than as a pupil who has not completed pupillage in accordance with the Bar Training Regulations) or as a person authorised by another Approved Regulator for a period (which need not have been as a person authorised by the same Approved Regulator) for at least six years in the previous eight years; and
- for the previous two years has made such practice his primary occupation; and
- is entitled to conduct litigation before every court in relation to all proceedings;
- is not acting as a qualified person in relation to more than two other people; and
- has not been designated by the BSB as unsuitable to be a qualified person.

1 rS20 and rS21, BSB Handbook.
2 rS22.3, BSB Handbook.

Barristers entitled to conduct litigation by virtue of legislation

Barristers employed in central government roles (including Crown Prosecutors) may be entitled to exercise rights to conduct litigation without the need for authorisation from the BSB. This exemption from the requirement to seek authorisation from the BSB is by virtue of primary legislation. Unless otherwise empowered to do so by primary legislation a barrister falling into this category may not undertake litigation outside of their employment without first securing BSB authorisation to do so.

Crown Prosecutors

All barristers employed by the Crown Prosecution Service (CPS) who have been appointed as Crown Prosecutors do not need further authorisation from the BSB to conduct litigation work within that role. This exemption applies because barristers employed in this capacity act in accordance with the exercise of powers under the direction of the DPP in accordance with the Prosecution of Offences Act 1985. Crown Prosecutors are not entitled to undertake litigation outside of their role with the CPS without first securing BSB authorisation to do so.

Other Government barristers

Employed government barristers have a right to conduct litigation as part of their employment by Treasury Solicitors, any government department, or any public body which performs functions on behalf of the Crown. This exemption applies because of historical and current legislation.

It is important to note that the right to conduct litigation, unless otherwise specified by primary legislation, is restricted to the barrister's employment. If an employed barrister wanted to undertake litigation outside of their employment, for example on a pro bono basis or for a law centre, they must seek authorisation from the BSB to do so.

Practising Certificate: Guidance for applying for a practicing certificate and the Authorisation to Practice (ATP) process

[2.78]

How applications are dealt with

Applications are considered and determined by the Records Department, who will process your application and confirm that you are authorised to practise, advise you that further information is required, or refuse your application for a practising certificate. If your application is refused, you will be informed of the reasons for refusal and provided with details of how this decision can be reviewed.

All applications will be processed within seven working days.

Practising certificates

If your application is successful, your practising certificate will be available to download from your Barrister Connect account.

If you need assistance completing this form or have a query about your practising certificate fee, please contact the Records Department on 020 7242 0934 or email Records@BarCouncil.org.uk

Lines are open 09:00–17:00 Monday to Friday. Calls may be monitored for training and quality assurance purposes.

Ethical Enquiries Service

If you are unsure whether or not the work you are undertaking requires you to hold a practising certificate then please contact the Ethical Enquiries Service on 020 7611 1307 or email Ethics@BarCouncil.org.uk

Applying for an extension or exemption from the CPD requirements

If you have not completed your CPD requirements and need to apply for an extension of time or exemption from the requirements, you can download an application form from the Bar Standards Board website, please refer to: regulatory requirements for barristers, extensions and waivers.

Please call the BSB's Qualifications Section on 020 7611 1444 or email Pauline Smith at PSmith@BarStandardsBoard.org.uk

Checking whether you have any outstanding CPD requirements

If you are returning to practice and are unsure whether you have any outstanding CPD requirements, please call the CPD Compliance Team on 020 7611 1444 or email CPDRecords@BarStandardsBoard.org.uk

Useful information

What should I do if I no longer require my practising certificate?

You do not need to return this application form, but you must notify the Records Department by completing the unregistered barristers form and sending this to:

Records Department

Bar Council

289–293 High Holborn

London WC1V 7HZ

DX 240 LDE

Or fax your form to 020 7831 9217 or email it to Records@BarCouncil.org.uk

What should I do if I am unsure whether the work I am undertaking requires a practising certificate?

Please contact Ethical Enquiries Service on 020 7611 1307 or email Ethics@BarCouncil.org.uk

Please refer to the BSB's 'Guidance for Unregistered Barristers (Barristers without Practising Certificates) – Supplying Legal Services and Holding Out', which is available here: https://www.barstandardsboard.org.uk/regulatory-requirements/bsb-handbook/code-guidance/.

What do I do if I have changed my name?

To change your name on our records, you must firstly notify your Inn of Court by sending a certified copy of a deed poll or certified copy of your marriage certificate. Once your Inn of Court has amended their records, please inform the Records Department, who will be able to update their records.

Where to send the form

Please send your form and fee to:

Records Department

The Bar Council

289–293 High Holborn

London WC1V 7HZ

DX 240 LDE.

Or fax it to 020 7831 9217 or email it to Records@BarCouncil.org.uk.

Contact the Records Department on 020 7242 0934 to make payment.

The deadline for the form and the fee is 21 March 2014 (to allow six working days to process your application).

Barristers who are returning to practice part way through the practising certificate year must be authorised to practise before exercising any reserved legal activities.

Section 1 – Your personal details

Membership number

Every barrister has a unique individual member number. Please enter these details if you know your membership number.

Section 2 – Practising details and entitlement to exercise reserved legal activities

Chambers' details

The full contact details of your main chambers should be entered here.

Commencement date

This form will be used for renewal applications and those who are returning to practice.

- if your application is for a renewal and you have not moved chambers please indicate "yes";
- if your application is for a renewal and you have moved chambers or changed the capacity in which you practise, please enter the date when the new arrangements commenced. Notification of any change of status must be within 28 days; and
- if you are returning to practice, please enter the date when you will recommence practice. You must be authorised to practise before exercising any reserved legal activities.

Practising as a sole practitioner

If you are about to commence practice as a sole practitioner please refer to the BSB's guidance on 'Becoming a Sole Practitioner', which is available here: https://www.barstandardsboard.org.uk/code-guidance/becoming-a-sole-practitioner/.

Your employer's details

The full contact details of your main employer should be entered here.

Commencement date

This form will be used for renewal applications and those who are returning to practice.

- If your application is for a renewal and you have not moved employer please indicate 'yes'

- If your application is for a renewal and you have moved employer or changed the capacity in which you practise, please enter the date when the new arrangements commenced. Notification of any change of status must be within 28 days.
- If you are returning to practice, please enter the date when you will recommence practice. You must be authorised to practise before exercising any reserved legal activities.

Please confirm whether your employer is an authorised body

An Authorised body is a body that has been authorised by another approved regulator to undertake reserved legal activities.

A Licensed body is a body licensed by a licensing authority, other than the BSB, under Part 5 of the Legal Services Act 2007. Licensed bodies are a new type of law firm also called alternative business structures. For example, a licensed body could be a firm with non-lawyer managers, a company taken over by a non-lawyer enterprise, a company floated on the stock exchange, or a firm which provides both legal services and non-legal services. An alternative business structure will need to be licensed by a licensing authority.

Manager or employee

A manager of an authorised body is a person who is a partner in a partnership, a member of an LLP, as a director of a company, or (in relation to any other body) is a member of its governing body.

Entitlement to exercise full rights of audience, and provide services to the public

If you have not been entitled to exercise full rights of audience for at least three years (during which you have made practice as a barrister or other authorised person your primary occupation) or you have not been granted a waiver from this requirement by the BSB in respect of a qualified person for rights of audience and/or supplying legal services to the public then:

- If you are a self-employed barrister, your principal place of practice must be a chambers or an annex of chambers which is also the principal place of practice of a relevant qualified person, who is readily available to provide guidance in relation to your work when you are providing services to the public or exercising a right of audience
- If you are an employed barrister, your principal place of practice must be an office or an organisation of which an employee, partner, manager or director is a relevant qualified person who is readily available to provide guidance in relation to your work when you are providing services to the public or exercising a right of audience.

If you are employed by a non-authorised body and are providing legal services only to your employer and those listed at rS39.2 to rS39.6 in the Handbook then the requirement to work with a relevant qualified person applies only if you have not been entitled to exercise full rights of audience in the manner described above for one year.

If you have previously provided details of your 'qualified person' and have now changed 'qualified person', please enter their name and the date of this change.

A qualified person (supplying legal services to the public) must be a person who:

- has been entitled to practise and has practised as a barrister (other than as a pupil who has not completed pupillage in accordance with the Bar Training Regulations) or as a person authorised by another Approved Regulator for a period (which need not have been as a person authorised by the same Approved Regulator) for at least six years in the previous eight years;
- for the previous two years has made such *practice* his primary occupation;
- is not acting as a qualified *person* in relation to more than two other people; and
- has not been designated by the BSB as unsuitable to be a qualified *person*.

A qualified person (Rights of Audience) must meet the requirements above but must additionally for the previous two years have been entitled to exercise a right of audience before every court in relation to all proceedings. The same person may act as a qualified person in relation to both rights of audience and supplying legal services to the public.

If you are a barrister exercising a right of audience in a Member State other than the United Kingdom pursuant to the Establishment Directive, or in Scotland or Northern Ireland pursuant to the European Communities (Lawyer's Practice) Regulations 2000, a person shall be a qualified person (rights of audience) for the purposes of rS20 if he has been designated by the BSB as possessing qualifications and experience in that state or country which are equivalent to the qualifications and experience required by rS22.3.a.i and rS22.3.a.ii, is not acting as a qualified person in relation to more than two other people and has not been designated by the BSB as unsuitable to be a qualified person.

Employed barristers: additional guidance

Employed barristers are permitted to offer legal services to a number of individuals in the course of their employment, depending on whether they are employed in an authorised body (for example a solicitors' firm) or non-authorised body (for example acting as in-house counsel).

If you are employed in an authorised body, you may supply legal services to:

- the authorised body;
- any employee, director or company secretary of the authorised body in a matter arising out of or relating to that person 's employment;
- any client of the authorised (non-BSB) body;
- if you provide legal services at a Legal Advice Centre, clients of the Legal Advice Centre; or

- if you supply legal services free of charge, members of the public.

If you are employed by a non-authorised body, you may supply legal services to:

- your employer;
- any employee, director or company secretary of your employer in a matter arising out of or relating to that person's employment;
- if your employer is a public authority (including the Crown or a Government department or agency or a local authority), another public authority on behalf of which your employer has made arrangements under statute or otherwise to supply any legal services or to perform any of that other public authority's functions as agent or otherwise;
- if you are employed by or in a Government department or agency, any Minister or Officer of the Crown;
- if you are employed by a trade association, any individual member of the association;
- if you are, or are performing the functions of, a Justices' clerk, the Justices whom you serve;
- if you are employed by the Legal Aid Agency, members of the public;
- if you are employed by or at a Legal Advice Centre, clients of the Legal Advice Centre;
- if you supply legal services free of charge, members of the public; or
- if your employer is a foreign lawyer and the legal services consist of foreign work, any client of your employer.

If any of the legal work that you do is for clients of your employer then you are providing services to the public. If you are doing this, or exercising rights of audience, you must ensure that you comply with the requirement to work with a qualified person if required to do so by the BSB Handbook (see above).

Dual practice questions

Under rS18 of the Scope of Practice Rules in the BSB Handbook a barrister may practise or be involved with the supply of legal services in more than one capacity only after having:

- obtained a practising certificate from the BSB which recognises the capacities in respect of which you are intending to practise; and
- agreed a protocol with each employer or authorised body with which you are involved to avoid or resolve and conflicts of interests. If you have not agreed this, you will be unable to proceed with your application until this has been agreed. A copy of any such protocol must be provided to the BSB on request.

You must never work in more than one capacity in relation to the same case or issue for the same client, at the same time. rC21.3, rC81 and rC82 of the Code of Conduct in the BSB Handbook impose requirements that barristers who wish to practice in more than one capacity should pay particular attention to.

Please also refer to the BSB's 'Guidance on Practice in Authorised Bodies', which is available here: https://www.barstandardsboard.org.uk/media/1392073/guidance_on_practise_in_authorised_bodies_-_feb_2012.pdf.

You are required to confirm your main practising address for correspondence purposes.

If in your employment you do not intend to hold yourself out as a barrister or exercise any reserved legal activities, which include exercising rights of audience, conducting litigation, reserved instrument activities, probate activities and the administration of oaths, you do not need a practising certificate to practise in a dual capacity and should apply for a practising certificate to practise in a self-employed capacity.

Please note that you will still be 'practising as a barrister' when providing legal services in an employed capacity and must observe relevant provisions of the Handbook.

Conducting litigation

The BSB now allows both self-employed and employed barristers to apply to be authorised to conduct litigation. There are three ways in which barristers can be authorised to conduct litigation:

(1) self-employed and employed barristers can apply for an extension of their practising certificate by meeting the requirements of rS47 of the Code of Conduct (this process has been in place since 22 January 2014);

(2) employed barristers previously authorised to conduct litigation under Annexe I of the old Code of Conduct (8th Edn.) will retain their authorisation, provided that they remain in employed practice; or

(3) by being independently entitled to conduct litigation by virtue of primary legislation.

Barristers authorised by the BSB to conduct litigation

You may apply for an extension to your practising certificate to conduct litigation by virtue of rS47. Please note that you may not do this as part of the authorisation to practise process – detailed guidance for those seeking to secure an extension to their practising certificate is available on the BSB website: https://www.barstandardsboard.org.uk/regulatory-requirements/for-barristers/authorisation-to-conduct-litigation/.

If you have been authorised to conduct litigation but have not been entitled to exercise full rights of audience for at least three years (during which you have made practice as a barrister or other authorised person your primary occupation) or you have not been granted a waiver from this requirement by the BSB in respect of a qualified person for litigation then:

- if you are a self-employed barrister, your principal place of practice must be a chambers or an annex of chambers which is also the principal place of practice of a relevant qualified person, who is readily available to provide guidance in relation to your work when you are conducting litigation;

- if you are an employed barrister, your principal place of practice must be an office of an organisation of which an employee, partner, manager or director is a relevant qualified person who is readily available to provide guidance in relation to your work when you are conducting litigation.
- if you are employed by a non-authorised body and are providing legal services only to your employer and those listed at rS39.2 to rS39.6 in the Handbook then the requirement to work with a relevant qualified person applies only if you have not been entitled to exercise full rights of audience in the manner described above for one year.

A qualified person (litigation) must be a person who:

- has been entitled to practise and has practised as a barrister (other than as a pupil who has not completed pupillage in accordance with the Bar Training Regulations) or as a person authorised by another Approved Regulator for a period (which need not have been as a person authorised by the same Approved Regulator) for at least six years in the previous eight years; and
- for the previous two years has made such practice his primary occupation; and
- is entitled to conduct litigation before every court in relation to all proceedings;
- is not acting as a qualified person in relation to more than two other people; and
- has not been designated by the BSB as unsuitable to be a qualified person.

Barristers entitled to conduct litigation by virtue of legislation

Barristers employed in central government roles (including Crown Prosecutors) may be entitled to exercise rights to conduct litigation without the need for authorisation from the BSB. This exemption from the requirement to seek authorisation from the BSB is by virtue of primary legislation. Unless otherwise empowered to do so by primary legislation a barrister falling into this category may not undertake litigation outside of their employment without first securing BSB authorisation to do so.

Crown Prosecutors

All barristers employed by the Crown Prosecution Service (CPS) who have been appointed as Crown Prosecutors do not need further authorisation from the BSB to conduct litigation work within that role. This exemption applies because barristers employed in this capacity act in accordance with the exercise of powers under the direction of the DPP in accordance with the Prosecution of Offences Act 1985. Crown Prosecutors are not entitled to undertake litigation outside of their role with the CPS without first securing BSB authorisation to do so.

Other Government barristers

Employed government barristers have a right to conduct litigation as part of their employment by Treasury Solicitors, any government department, or any public body which performs functions on behalf of the Crown. This exemption applies because of historical and current legislation.

It is important to note that the right to conduct litigation, unless otherwise specified by primary legislation, is restricted to the barrister's employment. If an employed barrister wanted to undertake litigation outside of their employment, for example on a pro bono basis or for a law centre, they must seek authorisation from the BSB to do so.

Section 3 – Continuing Professional Development (CPD)

You will be asked to confirm whether you are up to date with your CPD requirements as required under Section C of the Qualification Rules in the BSB Handbook. If you have not completed your required CPD hours from 2012 or 2013, you will not be refused authorisation. However, you will be asked to list what action you have taken or are taking to remedy the situation. You may also be referred to the BSB's Supervision Department.

The CPD year runs from 1 January to 31 December. The question on the form relates to the completed CPD period up to 31 December 2013 or if you are returning to practice, the last time you held a practising certificate, as the CPD declaration is retrospective.

If you have not been in practice for a period of time prior to this application and chose to suspend your CPD requirements and are unsure of whether you have any outstanding CPD requirements, please call 020 7611 1444 for advice or email CPDRecords@BarStandardsBoard.org.uk.

Section 4 – Insurance

You are required to complete an insurance declaration confirming that you have and will maintain insurance as required under the Code of Conduct in the BSB Handbook.

If you are a self-employed barrister (or a self-employed registered European lawyer) providing legal services to the public, you must be insured on the terms provided by the Bar Council (under rC76.2 of the Code of Conduct in the BSB Handbook). Holding a practising certificate is not enough: before starting or offering to provide legal services to the public, you must obtain and maintain insurance. For a definition of legal services please refer to the BSB Handbook. Please note that the Bar Council will check its records against the records of BMIF to verify individual declarations where barristers should be entered as members of BMIF.

Registered European lawyers are not required to have their own insurance if:

- you provide to the BSB evidence to show that you are covered by insurance taken out or a guarantee provided in accordance with the rules of your home state; and
- the BSB is satisfied that such insurance or guarantee is fully equivalent in terms of conditions and extent of cover to the cover required pursuant to Rule C76. However, where the BSB is satisfied that the equivalence is only partial, the BSB may require you to arrange additional insurance or an

additional guarantee to cover the elements which are not already covered by the insurance or guarantee contracted by you in accordance with the rules of your home state.

If you are an employed barrister providing legal services to the public, you must be insured on the terms prescribed by the BSB or the appropriate Approved Regulator if working in an authorised body.

If you are a Government barrister you are not required under the Code of Conduct in the BSB Handbook to have insurance.

If you are an employed barrister who provides legal services to your employer only you are not required under the Code of Conduct in the BSB Handbook to have insurance. It may however, be prudent for you to confirm with your employer that they have insurance in place to cover your actions, for which you may be personally liable.

If you provide legal services pro-bono, you should ensure that you are adequately covered by insurance either under your own insurance policy or under a policy taken out by the organisation for which you are working when providing such services.

If you are a self-employed barrister performing foreign work outside England and Wales you are exempt from the requirement to enter as a member of BMIF, however you must ensure that you are insured on the terms required by law or by the rules of the Bar in the place where you are practising.

If in doubt you should refer to the Code of Conduct in the BSB Handbook and such other guidance as is available on both the BSB and Bar Council websites.

Section 5 – Payment of the PCF and Bar Representation Fee (BRF)

The 'Schedule of Practising Certificate Fees'- policy and guidance 2014–15' sets out the fee, waivers and the different ways to pay.

Please contact the Records Department on 020 7242 0934 for advice on your practising fee for 2014/15.

Please note that applications will not be processed unless they include the correct fee.

You can pay the full amount by cheque or credit/debit card.

Paying by debit or credit card

We accept Visa, Visa Debit (Delta), Visa Electron, MasterCard and UK Maestro.

Please contact the Records Office on 020 7242 0934 to arrange payment. If you have paid your fee over the telephone, you will not be authorised to practise until you have returned your completed application form and received notification of your authorisation.

Will I receive a receipt for the fee and form?

You will receive a receipt for your debit or credit card payments. In all other cases, the practising certificate will be a receipt of successful completion of the process.

Section 6 – Communication preferences

Payment of the compulsory PCF and BRF will automatically opt-in to the options outlined in the form. You are able to tick the boxes to opt-out of these preferences.

If you have not paid your BRF you are able to opt-in to receive details about products and offers from the Member Services Team.

Section 7 – Declaration of truth

The declaration of truth must be completed in all cases and for all applications, it is designed to ensure that you understand the new process and system and specifically that further information may be requested in support of your application.

Knowingly or recklessly giving the Bar Council information which is false or misleading, or failure to inform the Bar Council of materially significant information of which you are aware, may lead to disciplinary action being taken against you.

If the form is not signed, your authorisation will not be granted.

You are expected to have checked the accuracy of the information given in the form before signing. The declaration relates to the whole form.

The Bar Standards Board has issued some policy and guidance for the ATP process in 2014/15. It is set out below:

Schedule of Authorisation to Practise (ATP) process 2014/15

Policy and guidance

[2.79]

Authorisation to Practise (ATP) process

The Bar Standards Board (BSB) has modernised the authorisation process for the annual renewal of practising certificates to bring arrangements into compliance with the Legal Services Act 2007 (the Act). Section 13(2) requires individuals wishing to provide reserved legal activities as barristers to be authorised by their approved regulator.

Under section 14 of the Act, it is a criminal offence for a barrister to carry on a reserved legal activity unless they are authorised to do so by a practising certificate.

The Practising Certificate Rules (Section C of the Scope of Practice Rules in the BSB Handbook) set out the eligibility conditions for obtaining a practising certificate, the application process, the authorisations granted by practising certificates, and the arrangements for the review of contested decisions.

Making an application

For those barristers who require a practising certificate, the authorisation process requires an individual to:

- update your insurance information;
- sign a declaration of truth;
- verify that you have completed the requisite hours of Continuing Professional Development (CPD) (or indicate why you are not up to date with your CPD requirements); and
- update your personal details.

In order to grant authorisation and in accordance with rS51 of the Scope of Practice Rules, the Bar Council may request additional information to support an individual's application, this could be evidence of insurance, completion of CPD, low income etc.

rS57 of the Scope of Practice Rules outlines the circumstances in which the Bar Council (acting by the Bar Standards Board) *shall not* issue a practising certificate. rS59 outlines the circumstances in which the Bar Council (acting by the Bar Standards Board) *may* refuse to issue a practising certificate, or *may* revoke a practising certificate in accordance with Section 5 of the Practising Certificate Rules. rS73 outlines the circumstances in which the Bar Council (acting by the Bar Standards Board) *shall* revoke a practising certificate.

The decision as to whether to issue or revoke a practising certificate will usually be made by the Records Manager. Generally, when the Bar Council (acting by the Bar Standards Board) revokes a practising certificate, it is on the basis that circumstances have changed since the practising certificate was initially issued. Barristers will be able to apply to the BSB's Qualifications Committee for a review if they believe that their application for a practising certificate has been wrongly refused, or that their practising certificate has been wrongly revoked. In some circumstances a temporary certificate may be issued.

Upon refusing or revoking your practising certificate, the Records Department should have sent you the details of how to apply to the BSB's Qualifications Committee for a review of this decision. If you have not received these details, please contact the Bar Standards Board on 020 7611 1444.

How to apply

Applying for authorisation is now an online process, you must log into Barrister Connect to complete the process.

Exceptions will be made for those who have a disability, if this applies to you, please call the Records Department on 020 7242 0934 or email Records@BarCouncil.org.uk.

Your Barrister Connect account

The ATP process is a requirement of the Legal Services Act 2007 and is a significant safeguard for the public, ensuring that only appropriate persons are authorised to undertake reserved legal activities. It is therefore important that barristers take personal responsibility for meeting the ongoing requirements for authorisation and confirming that the information submitted is correct.

From 10 February 2014, all barristers will be required personally to participate in the process by logging into Barrister Connect and completing the registration process online. You will still be able to delegate the payment of your Practising Certificate Fee (PCF), if you so choose, to your chambers or employer.

You will be sent a letter and email with your Barrister Connect user number. If you are unable to remember your password, please click on the forgotten password link on the home page of the website. An email will then be sent to your registered email address in order that this may be re-set.

Please remember to check the delegation of your PCF payment if you have changed chambers or employers.

If you are creating an online account for the first time please call the Records Department on 020 7242 0934 or email Records@BarCouncil.org.uk.

Barristers are entirely responsible for the contents of their respective application and for any supporting documentation. They are also entirely responsible for the payment of their PCF, even when delegated permission has been granted to chambers or an employer to make the payment.

Application deadline and defaulters

The deadline for renewal of practising certificates for 2014–15 is **Monday 31 March 2014**.

All those who require a practising certificate and have not completed the process by 1 April 2014 will be liable to pay a surcharge of 20% of the PCF.

Those that do not complete the authorisation process by 30 April 2014, will not be listed on the BSB Barristers' Register and will not be authorised to practise. Any barrister believed to be practising without a certificate will be reported to the BSB, who will take such action as is considered appropriate.

As offering reserved legal services without a practising certificate is both a criminal offence as well as being a breach of the Code of Conduct in the BSB Handbook, the Bar Council will contact respective Heads of Chambers or employer to alert them of any individuals potentially in breach.

All individuals returning to practise part way through the practising certificate year must be authorised to practise before exercising any reserved legal activities.

Fees payable

The fees payable include those that are defined by the LSB in accordance with section 51 of the Act and those that support the representation activities of the profession undertaken by the Bar Council. Lower fees may be payable by those in defined groups as described below.

The PCF funds the Bar Council expenditure that falls within the 'permitted purposes' as defined by the LSB in accordance with section 51 of the Act and the rules made there under.

Under these rules, the Bar Council has consulted on its budget and PCF proposals with the profession and has received approval of both from LSB. A copy of the consultation paper for the 2014/15 budget is on the Bar Council's website: www.barcouncil.org.uk/media/243499/bar_council_budget_proposals_2014–15.pdf

At the end of each year the Bar Council publishes its annual report 'Representing the Bar' and, together with the Bar Standards Board, issues the joint Financial Statements, which contains an audited analysis of how this fee is used in accordance with the permitted purposes as defined in section 51 of the Legal Services Act 2007.

The LSB and OLC levy is collected by the Bar Council and remitted to LSB and OLC to fund their activities in accordance with section 51 of the Act.

Legal Services Board (LSB) and Legal Ombudsman (LeO) levies

The Bar Council has a statutory obligation to collect a share of the operating costs of both the LSB and LeO. The annual cost of the Bar Council's share for the running costs has consistently been of the order of £850,000 after the start-up period. In 2013/2014 the levy was reduced significantly allowing some over recovery from the previous year to be used. The total sum to be raised in 2014/2015 is £525,000 (£332,000 in 13/14) and this increase ensures that the combination of levy raised and retained funds will be just sufficient to meet the expected charges for the current year.

The Bar Representation Fee (BRF)

From this year the Members' Services Fee (MSF) becomes the Bar Representation Fee (BRF) in order more accurately to reflect the vital activities of the Bar Council that it supports, all of which are necessary to represent you and act as an effective professional body.

The voluntary BRF funds work which promotes the interests of the Bar to support your practices and promotes effective access to justice. The BRF helps to fund our lobbying and media activities, the issuing of remuneration guidance and representing the Bar domestically and internationally among other essential activities. We need your support to continue this important work, and to rise to the challenges ahead for the profession.

By paying the fee, you will also have access to a range of high quality goods and services that should, over the course of the year, save you considerably more than the fee itself.

The Pro bono levy

Every member of the Bar is asked to include a donation of £30 towards the running costs of the Bar Pro Bono Unit, through which the Bar makes a vital contribution in the public interest. Please remove the tick in the appropriate box in Barrister Connect if you do not wish to donate.

With the money raised through the 2013 renewal process, and in a year that saw a 39% increase in cases, the Bar Pro Bono Unit was able to employ an additional member of staff and enhance their IT system.

Levies withdrawn

The Staff Defined Pension Scheme Levy charged from 2010 to 2013 has been withdrawn following cost reductions put into place within the Bar Council.

Statutory fees

Self Employed fees

Core Fee£		**LSB/OLC Levy**
QC	1,202	58 (42)
Junior (13 years' Call and over)	813	40 (29)
Junior (eight to 12 years' Call)	417	19 (14)
Junior (five to seven years' Call)	222	11 (8)
Junior (three to four years' Call)	80	4 (3)
Junior (one to two years' Call)	80	4 (3)

Employed Bar

Core Fee £		**LSB/OLC Levy**
QC	877	58 (42)
Junior (13 years' Call and over)	615	40 (29)
Junior (eight to 12 years' Call)	340	19 (14)
Junior (five to seven years' Call)	183	11 (8)

Junior (three to four years' Call)	80	4 (3)
Junior (one to two years' Call)	80	4 (3)

Voluntary fees

All fees for 2014/2015 remain unchanged from those for 2013/2014.

14. The Fee due depends on the seniority of the barrister (the number of years' since Call). **Self Employed and Employed Bar**

BRF	**Pro Bono**	
QC	150	30
Junior (13 years' Call and over)	100	30
Junior (eight to 12 years' Call)	100	30
Junior (five to seven years' Call)	100	30
Junior (three to four years' Call)	100	30
Junior (one to two years' Call)	50	30

Reduced fees for relatively low income

A reduced fee structure will apply for self-employed and employed barristers, of five years' Call and over, whose gross annual income from practice in the 12 months preceding the fee due date is less than £40,000 and £30,000 respectively.

The concession allows an individual in the top three bands to apply online to pay the Core fee element of the PCF applicable to the band below that which would normally apply e.g. a junior in the eight to 12 years Call band can apply to pay those rates for the Core fee that apply to a junior in the five to seven years Call band. Those in receipt of a low income waiver do not qualify for any further discount.

For those in the five to seven years' Call band the Core Fee is reduced to £141 for the Self Employed Bar and £107 for the Employed Bar and for those in the one to four years' Call band there is no reduction.

There is no low-income waiver on the LSB/LeO levies. There is no low income waiver on the BRF.

Any individual who is working exclusively for a charity will be entitled to pay no more than the full rate for the Core fee that is applicable to those in the five to seven years' Call band.

An example of how the waivers work is given below:

Self-employed Core fee £	Core fee reduced rate £		LSB/LeO levy (no waiver) £
QC	1,202	813	58
Junior (13 years Call and over)	813	417	40
Junior (eight to 12 years Call)	417	222	19
Junior (five to seven years Call)	222	141	11

Employed

Core Fee £	Core Fee reduced rate £		LSB/LeO levy (no waiver) £
QC	877	615	58
Junior (13 years Call and over)	615	340	40
Junior (eight to 12 years Call)	340	183	19
Junior (five to seven years Call)	183	107	11

Applications for a reduction on grounds of low income should be made online. The Bar Council will check the applications and if so requested, proof of income or salary will be required.

How to pay

Fee payment should be made online, through one of a number of different methods. Please note that, consequent upon the introduction of the new Practising Certificate Rules and associated authorisation process, there is no instalment payment facility.

- Debit/credit card (Visa, Visa Debit (Delta), Visa Electron, MasterCard and UK Maestro are all accepted).
- Chambers or employer block payment.

Chambers or employer block payment

Individuals wishing to be part of their chambers' or employer's block payment arrangements must first create an individual online account and complete the registration process online. They must then delegate the payment of the relevant fee to their chambers or employer.

Barristers are entirely responsible for the contents of their respective application and for any supporting documentation. They are also entirely responsible for the payment of their fee, even when delegated permission has been granted to chambers or an employer to complete the payment.

The deadline for block authorisation is **14 March 2014.**

Discounts for block payment

A 2.5% discount is available on both the whole of the PCF as well as the BRF where a set of chambers (but not sole practitioner) or employer makes a single block payment on behalf of five or more of its barristers. A set of chambers or employer that makes a block payment for 100 or more barristers will receive a discount of 5%. Individuals who receive a low-income waiver are not eligible for the block payment discount.

Ceasing to practise or changing status – refunds and additional charges

The Records Department must be given notification of any change of status in writing or via the online account **within 28 days**.

Any such change that generates an entitlement to a refund or incurs an additional charge will be subject to the following policy which is that provided that notification of the change has taken place within 28-days, any refund due will be applied as of the date of the change.

In the event that notification is made later than 28 days, the refund will apply from the date of notification rather than the date of change. Whereas, any additional fee due will always be applied as at the date of the change regardless of date of notification.

The Bar Council will pay any refund, usually by bank transfer, within 14 days of notification of the change and equally requires any additional charge to be paid within 14 days of the request for payment.

A barrister who changes from self-employed to employed, or vice versa, will be either refunded or charged the pro rata difference in the Core Fee.

Any barrister who changes their status to unregistered (formerly known as non-practising) will receive a pro rata refund of the Core Fee element of the PCF, plus the BRF if they cease to practise in the first three months of the practising certificate year. No refund will be issued for the levies, as they relate to a statutory obligation.

While it is the policy of the Bar Council's Equality and Diversity Committee to encourage a practitioner taking maternity leave or additional paternity leave to maintain a practising certificate, an exception will be made to the foregoing for those who wish to suspend their practising certificates during maternity leave or additional paternity leave. Individuals on maternity leave or additional paternity leave, regardless of date, will on request be granted a pro rata refund, of the Core Fee element of the PCF and also the BRF. No refund will be issued for the levies.

Returning to practise

An individual who either returns to, or commences practise after, 1 April 2014 will be charged a pro rata proportion of the Core Fee plus the levies in full. Such individuals may also be eligible to apply for a low income waiver.

Individuals who have cease to practise and/or are retired who wish briefly to return to practice for a day case or something similar, must pay pro rata the appropriate Core Fee for the entire month or months into which the practising dates fall plus the levies in full.

Privacy policy

Once you have set up your online account you will be able to access or amend your personal details part at any time. The Bar Council's 'Privacy policy' (www.barcouncil.org.uk/privacy-statement/) details how personal data will be used.

Practising Certificate Rules

[2.79a]

rS44 In this Section 3.C, references to "you" and "your" are references to *barristers* and *registered European lawyers* who are intending to apply for authorisation to *practise* as a *barrister* or a *registered European lawyer* (as the case may be) or who are otherwise intending to apply for a *litigation extension* to their existing practising certificate.

rS45 You are eligible for a *practising certificate* if:

1. you are a barrister or registered European lawyer and you are not currently suspended from practice and have not been disbarred; and
2. you meet the requirements of Rules S46.1, S46.2, S46.3 or S46.4; and
3. [either :
   a. within the last 5 years either (i) you have held a *practising certificate*; or (ii) you have satisfactorily completed (or have been exempted from the requirement to complete) either the non-practising period of 6 months of pupilage or 12 months of pupilage; or
   b. if not, you have complied with such training requirements as may be imposed by the *Bar Standards Board*].

rS46 You are eligible for:

1. a full practising certificate if either:
   a. you have satisfactorily completed 12 months *pupillage*; or
   b. you have been exempted from the requirement to complete 12 months of *pupillage*; or
   c. on 30 July 2000, you were entitled to exercise full *rights of audience* by reason of being a *barrister*; or
   d. you were called to the *Bar* before 1 January 2002 and:
      i. you notified the *Bar Council* that you wished to exercise a *right of audience* before every *court* and in relation to all proceedings; and
      ii. you have complied with such training requirements as

the *Bar Council* or the *Bar Standards Board* may require or you have been informed by the *Bar Council* or the *Bar Standards Board* that you do not need to comply with any such further requirements;

in each case, before 31 March 2012;

2. a *provisional practising certificate* if you have satisfactorily completed (or have been exempted from the requirement to complete) the non-practising period of 6 months of *pupillage* and at the time when you apply for a *practising certificate* you are registered as a *Pupil*;

3. a *limited practising certificate* if you were called to the *Bar* before 1 January 2002 but you are not otherwise eligible for a *full practising certificate* in accordance with Rule S46.1 above; or

4. a *registered European lawyer's practising certificate* if you are a *registered European lawyer.*

rS47 You are eligible for a litigation extension:

1. where you have or are due to be granted a *practising certificate* (other than a *provisional practising certificate*); and

2. where you are:

   a. more than three *years' standing*; or

   b. less than three *years' standing*, but your principal place of *practice* (or if you are *practising* in a dual capacity, each of your principal places of *practice*) is either:

      i a *chambers* or an annex of *chambers* which is also the principal place of *practice* of a qualified *person* (as that term is defined in Rule S22.3) who is readily available to provide guidance to you; or

      ii an office of an organisation of which an *employee, partner, manager* or *director* is a qualified *person* (as that term is defined in Rule S22.3) who is readily available to provide guidance to you;

3. you have the relevant administrative systems in place to be able to provide *legal services* direct to *clients* and to administer the *conduct of litigation*; and

4. you have the procedural knowledge to enable you to *conduct litigation* competently.

rS48 You may apply for a *practising certificate* by:

1. completing the relevant application form supplied by the *Bar Council* (acting by the *Bar Standards Board*) and submitting it to the *Bar Council* (acting by the *Bar Standards Board*); and

2. submitting such information in support of the application as may be prescribed by the *Bar Council* (acting by the *Bar Standards Board*); and

3. paying (or undertaking to pay in a manner determined by the *Bar Council*) the appropriate *practising certificate fee* in the amount determined in accordance with Rule S50 (subject to any reduction pursuant to Rule S53).

rS49 You may apply for a litigation extension to a *practising certificate* (other than a *provisional practising certificate*) by:

1. completing the relevant application form supplied by the *Bar Council* (acting by the *Bar Standards Board*) and submitting it to the *Bar Council* (acting by the *Bar Standards Board*); and
2. confirming that you meet the relevant requirements of Rule S47.1;
3. paying (or undertaking to pay in a manner determined by the *Bar Council*) the *application fee* (if any) and the *litigation extension fee*;
4. confirming, in such form as the *Bar Standards Board* may require from time to time, that you have the relevant administrative systems in place to be able to provide *legal services* direct to *clients* and to administer the *conduct of litigation* in accordance with Rule S47.3; and
5. confirming, in such form as the *Bar Standards Board* may require from time to time, that you have the procedural knowledge to enable you to *conduct litigation* competently in accordance with Rule S47.4.

rS50 An application will only have been made under either Rule S48 or S49 once the *Bar Council* (acting by the *Bar Standards Board*) has received, in respect of the relevant application, the application form in full, together with the *application fee* (if any), *the practising certificate fee, the litigation extension fee* (or an undertaking to pay such fees in a manner determined by the *Bar Council*), all the information required in support of the application and confirmation from you, in the form of a declaration, that the information contained in, or submitted in support of, the application is full and accurate.

rS51 On receipt of the application, the *Bar Council* (acting by the *Bar Standards Board*) may require, from you or a third party (including, for the avoidance of doubt, any *BSB authorised body*), such additional information, documents or references as it considers appropriate to the consideration of your application.

rS52 You are *person*ally responsible for the contents of your application and any information submitted to the *Bar Council* (acting by the *Bar Standards Board*) by you or on your behalf and you must not submit (or cause or permit to be submitted on your behalf) information to the *Bar Council* (acting by the *Bar Standards Board*) which you do not believe is full and accurate.

rS53 When applying for a *practising certificate* you may apply to the *Bar Council* for a reduction in the *practising certificate fee payable by you* if your gross fee income or salary is less than such amount as the *Bar Council* may decide from time to time. Such an application must be submitted by completing the form supplied for that purpose by the *Bar Council* which can be found through Barrister Connect.

rS54 The *practising certificate fee* shall be the amount or amounts prescribed in the Schedule of *Practising Certificate* Fees issued by the *Bar Council* from time to time, and any reference in these Rules to the "*appropriate practising certificate fee*" or the "*practising certificate fee payable by you*" refers to the *practising certificate fee* payable by you pursuant to that Schedule, having regard , amongst other things, to:

1. the different annual *practising certificate fees* which may be prescribed by the *Bar Council* for different categories of *barristers*, e.g. for Queen's Counsel and junior counsel, for *barristers* of different levels of

seniority, and/or for *barristers practising* in different capacities and/or according to different levels of income (i.e. *self-employed barristers*, *employed barristers*, *managers* or *employees* of authorised bodies or *barristers practising* with dual capacity);

2. any reductions in the annual *practising certificate fees* which may be permitted by the *Bar Council* in the case of *practising certificates* which are valid for only part of a *practising certificate year*;

3. any discounts from the annual *practising certificate fee* which may be permitted by the *Bar Council* in the event of payment by specified methods;

4. any reduction in, or rebate from, the annual *practising certificate fee* which may be permitted by the *Bar Council* on the grounds of low income, change of category or otherwise; and

5. any surcharge or surcharges to the annual *practising certificate fee* which may be prescribed by the *Bar Council* in the event of an application for renewal of a *practising certificate* being made after the end of the *practising certificate year*.

rS55 The *litigation extension fee* shall be the amount or amounts prescribed by the *Bar Council* from time to time, and in these Rules the "*appropriate litigation extension fee*" or the "*litigation extension fee payable by you*" is the *litigation extension fee* payable by you having regard to, among other things:

1. any reductions in the annual *litigation extension fees* which may be permitted by the *Bar Council* in the case of *litigation extensions* which are valid for only part of a *practising certificate year*;

2. any discounts from the annual *litigation extension fee* which may be permitted by the *Bar Council* in the event of payment by specified methods;

3. any reduction in, or rebate from, the annual *litigation extension fee* which may be permitted by the *Bar Council* on the grounds of low income, change of category, or otherwise; and

4. any surcharge or surcharges to the annual *litigation extension fee* which may be prescribed by the *Bar Council* in the event of an application for a *litigation extension* being made at a time different from the time of your application for a *practising certificate*.

rS56 If you have given an undertaking to pay the *practising certificate fee* or *the litigation extension fee*, you must comply with that undertaking in accordance with its terms.

rS57 The *Bar Council* (acting by the *Bar Standards Board*) shall not issue a *practising certificate* to a *barrister* or *registered European lawyer*:

1. who is not eligible for a *practising certificate*, or for a *practising certificate* of the relevant type; or

2. who has not applied for a *practising certificate*; or

3. who has not paid or not otherwise undertaken to pay in a manner determined by the Bar Council, the appropriate *practising certificate fee*; or

4. who is not insured against claims for professional negligence as provided for in Rule S71.

rS58 The Bar Council (acting by the Bar Standards Board) shall not grant a litigation extension to a barrister or registered European lawyer:

1. in circumstances where the Bar Council (acting by the Bar Standards Board) is not satisfied that the requirements of *litigation extension* are met; or

2. who has not applied for a *litigation extension*; or

3. who has not paid or not otherwise undertaken to pay in a manner determined by the Bar Council, the appropriate *application fee* (if any) and the *litigation extension fee*.

rS59 The *Bar Council* (acting by the *Bar Standards Board*) may refuse to issue a *practising certificate* or to grant a *litigation extension*, or may revoke a *practising certificate* or a *litigation extension* in accordance with Section 3.C5, if it is satisfied that the information submitted in support of the application for the *practising certificate* or *litigation extension* (as the case may be) is (or was when submitted) incomplete, inaccurate or incapable of verification, or that the relevant *barrister* or *registered European lawyer*:

1. does not hold adequate insurance in accordance with Rule C78;

2. has failed and continues to fail to pay the *appropriate practising certificate fee* or *litigation extension fee* when due;

3. would be, or is, *practising* in breach of the provisions of Section 3.B; or

4. has not complied with any of the requirements of the Continuing Professional Development Regulations applicable to him.

rS60 When the Bar Council (acting by the Bar Standards Board) issues a practising certificate or a litigation extension, it shall:

1. inform the relevant *barrister* or *registered European lawyer* of that fact; and

2. in the case of a *practising certificate*, publish that fact, together with the name and *practising address* of the *barrister* and *registered European lawyer* and the other details specified in Rule S61 in the register on the *Bar Standards Board*'s website; or

3. in the case of a litigation extension:

   a. issue a revised and updated *practising certificate* to incorporate an express reference to such litigation extension in accordance with Rule S66; and

   b. amend the register maintained on the Bar Standards Board's website to show that the relevant *barrister* or *registered European lawyer* (as the case may be) is now authorised to conduct litigation.

rS61 A practising certificate must state:

1. the name of the *barrister or registered European lawyer* (as the case may be);

2. the period for which the *practising certificate* is valid;

3. the *reserved legal activities* which the *barrister or registered European lawyer* (as the case may be) to whom it is issued is thereby authorised to carry on;

4. the capacity (or capacities) in which the *barrister or registered European lawyer* (as the case may be) practises; and

5. whether the *barrister or registered European lawyer* (as the case may be) is registered with the *Bar Council* as a *Public Access* practitioner.

rS62 A *practising certificate* may be valid for a *practising certificate year* or part thereof and for one month after the end of the *practising certificate year.*

rS63 A *full practising certificate* shall authorise a *barrister* to exercise a *right of audience* before every *court* in relation to all proceedings.

rS64 A *provisional practising certificate* shall authorise a *pupil* in his second six to exercise a *right of audience* before every *court* in relation to all proceedings.

rS65 A *limited practising certificate* shall not authorise a *barrister* to exercise a *right of audience*, save that it shall authorise a *barrister* to exercise any *right of audience* which he had by reason of being a *barrister* and was entitled to exercise on 30 July 2000.

rS66 A *practising certificate* shall authorise a *barrister* to *conduct litigation* in relation to every *court* and all proceedings if the *practising certificate* specifies a *litigation extension.*

rS67 Every *practising certificate* issued to a *barrister* shall authorise the *barrister*:

1. to undertake:

   a. reserved instrument activities;

   b. probate activities;

   c. the administration of oaths; and

   d. immigration work.

rS68 A registered European lawyer's practising certificate shall authorise a registered European lawyer to carry on the same reserved legal activities as a full practising certificate issued to a barrister, save that:

1. a registered European lawyer is only authorised to exercise a right of audience or conduct litigation in proceedings which can lawfully only be provided by a solicitor, barrister or other qualified person, if he acts in conjunction with a solicitor or barrister authorised to practise before the court, tribunal or public authority concerned and who could lawfully exercise that right; and

2. a registered European lawyer is not authorised to prepare for remuneration any instrument creating or transferring an interest in land unless he has a home professional title obtained in Denmark, the Republic of Ireland, Finland, Sweden, Iceland, Liechtenstein, Norway, the Czech Republic, Cyprus, Hungary or Slovakia.

rS69 You must inform the *Bar Council* (acting by the *Bar Standards Board*) as soon as reasonably practicable, and in any event within 28 days, if any of the information submitted in support of your *practising certificate* application form or *litigation extension* application form:

1. was incomplete or inaccurate when the application form was submitted; or

2. changes before the expiry of your *practising certificate.*

rS70 If you wish to:

1. change the capacity in which you *practise* (e.g. if you change from being an *employed barrister* or a *manager* or *employee* of a *BSB authorised body* or an *authorised (non-BSB) body* to a *selfemployed barrister*, or vice versa, or if you commence or cease *practice* in a dual capacity); or

2. cease to be authorised to *conduct litigation*, before the expiry of your *practising certificate*, you must:

   a. notify the *Bar Council* (acting by the *Bar Standards Board*) of such requested amendment to your *practising certificate*; and

   b. submit to the *Bar Council* (acting by the *Bar Standards Board*) such further information as the *Bar Council* (acting by the *Bar Standards Board*) may reasonably require in order for them to be able to determine whether or not to grant such proposed amendment to your *practising certificate*; and

   c. within 14 days of demand by the *Bar Council* pay to the *Bar Council* the amount (if any) by which the *annual practising certificate fee* which would apply to you in respect of your amended *practising certificate* exceeds the *annual practising certificate fee* which you have already paid (or undertaken to pay) to the *Bar Council.* In the event that the revised annual *practising certificate fee* is less than the amount originally paid to the *Bar Council* (acting by the *Bar Standards Board*) or in circumstances where you wish to cease to be authorised to *conduct litigation*, the *Bar Council* (acting by the *Bar Standards Board*) is not under any obligation to refund any part of the annual *practising certificate fee* or *litigation extension fee* already paid although it may in its absolute discretion elect to do so in the circumstances contemplated by the Schedule of *Practising Certificate* Fees issued by the *Bar Council* from time to time.

rS71 The *Bar Council* (acting by the *Bar Standards Board*) may amend a *practising certificate* if it is satisfied that any of the information contained in the relevant application form was inaccurate or incomplete or has changed, but may not amend a *practising certificate* (except in response to a request from the *barrister or a registered European lawyer*) without first:

1. giving written notice to the *barrister or registered European lawyer* of the grounds on which the *practising certificate* may be amended; and

2. giving the *barrister or registered European lawyer* a reasonable opportunity to make representations.

rS72 The Bar Council (acting by the Bar Standards Board) shall endorse a practising certificate to reflect any qualification restriction or condition imposed on the barrister or registered European lawyer by the Bar Council (acting by the Bar Standards Board) or by a Disciplinary Tribunal, Interim Suspension or Disqualification Panel, Fitness to Practise Panel or the Visitors to the Inns of Court.

rS73 The Bar Council (acting by the Bar Standards Board):

1. shall revoke a practising certificate:

   a. if the *barrister* becomes authorised to practise by another *approved regulator*;

   b. if the *barrister or registered European lawyer* is disbarred or *suspended* from *practice* as a *barrister* or *registered European lawyer* whether on an interim basis under section D of Part 5 or otherwise under section B of Part 5;

   c. if the *barrister* or *registered European lawyer* has notified the *Bar Council* or the *Bar Standards Board* that he no longer wishes to have a *practising certificate*; and

2. may revoke a practising certificate:

   a in the circumstances set out in Rule S59; or

   b if the *barrister or registered European lawyer* has given an undertaking to pay the appropriate *practising certificate fee* and fails to comply with that undertaking in accordance with its terms, but in either case only after:

      i. giving written notice to the relevant *barrister or registered European lawyer* of the grounds on which the *practising certificate* may be revoked; and

      ii. giving the relevant *barrister or registered European lawyer* a reasonable opportunity to make representations.

rS74 The Bar Council (acting by the Bar Standards Board):

1. shall revoke a litigation extension if the barrister or registered European lawyer has notified the Bar Council or the Bar Standards Board that he no longer wishes to have the litigation extension; and

2. may revoke a litigation extension:

   a. in the circumstances set out in Rule S59; or

   b. if the *barrister or registered European lawyer* has given an undertaking to pay the appropriate *litigation extension fee* and fails to comply with that undertaking in accordance with its terms, but in either case only after:

      i. giving written notice to the relevant *barrister or registered European lawyer* of the grounds on which the *litigation extension* may be revoked; and

      ii. giving the relevant *barrister or registered European lawyer* a reasonable opportunity to make representations.

C6. Applications for review

rS75 If you contend that the *Bar Council* (acting by the *Bar Standards Board*) has:

1. wrongly failed or refused to issue or amend a *practising certificate*; or
2. wrongly amended or revoked a *practising certificate*; or
3. wrongly failed or refused to issue a *litigation extension*; or
4. wrongly revoked a *litigation extension*,

in each case in accordance with this Section 3.C, then you may lodge an application for review with the *Qualifications Committee* using the form supplied for that purpose by the *Bar Standards Board which* can be found here https://www.barstandardsboard.org.uk/qualifying-as-a-barrister/forms-andguidelines/bar-training-waivers-and-exemption-forms/. For the avoidance of doubt, this Section 3.C6 does not apply to any amendment or revocation of a *practising certificate* or *litigation extension* made by order of a *Disciplinary Tribunal, Interim Suspension or Disqualification Panel, Fitness to Practise Panel* or the *Visitors to the Inns of Court.*

PART II QUALIFYING AS A BARRISTER AND ENTERING PRACTICE

rS76 The decision of the *Bar Council* (acting by the *Bar Standards Board*) shall take effect notwithstanding any application for review being submitted in accordance with Rule S75. However, the *Bar Council* (acting by the *Bar Standards Board*) may, in its absolute discretion, issue a temporary *practising certificate* or *litigation extension* to a *barrister* or *registered European lawyer* who has lodged an application for review.

rS77 If the Qualifications Committee finds that the Bar Council (acting by the Bar Standards Board):

1. has wrongly failed or refused to issue a *practising certificate*, then the *Bar Council* (acting by the *Bar Standards Board*) must issue such *practising certificate* as ought to have been issued; or
2. has wrongly failed or refused to amend a *practising certificate*, then the *Bar Council* (acting by the *Bar Standards Board*) must make such amendment to the *practising certificate* as ought to have been made; or
3. has wrongly amended a *practising certificate*, then the *Bar Council* (acting by the *Bar Standards Board*) must cancel the amendment; or
4. has wrongly revoked a *practising certificate*, then the *Bar Council* (acting by the *Bar Standards Board*) must re-issue the *practising certificate*; or
5. has wrongly failed or refused to grant a *litigation extension*, then the *Bar Council* (acting by the *Bar Standards Board*) must grant such *litigation extension* as ought to have been granted; or
6. has wrongly revoked a *litigation extension*, then the *Bar Council* (acting by the *Bar Standards* Board) must re-grant the litigation extension.

Unregistered Barristers (Barristers Without Practising Certificates) – Supplying Legal Services and Holding Out

[2.79b]

The Bar Standards Board has issued specific guidance to barristers without practising certifications as to the rules relating to holding out. The Guidance is set out below:

1. Who is this guidance for?

This guidance relates to "unregistered barristers", or barristers without practising certificates, who wish to provide legal services to employers or to the public, whether such barristers are employed or self-employed. It also addresses restrictions on "holding out" as a barrister in connection with the supply of legal services.

It is now a criminal offence for a barrister without a practising certificate to provide legal services which are Reserved Legal Activities under the Legal Services Act 2007. This guidance provides advice on what legal services may be provided by a barrister without a practising certificate and on the rules which must be followed when doing so.

Core duties 5 and 9 of the BSB Handbook apply to unregistered barristers at all times. The other Core Duties apply when supplying legal services, as do certain other rules (see below).

The main Outcome this guidance relates to is Outcome C34 in the BSB Handbook:

> "Clients who receive legal services from unregistered barristers are aware that such unregistered barristers are not subject to the same regulatory safeguards that would apply if they instructed a practising barrister."

2. Introduction

There are many barristers who do not have a practising certificate either by choice or because they do not qualify for a practising certificate.

Such barristers are now called "Unregistered Barristers" because they are not on the public register of barristers who have practising certificates. It is important to note that the term "non-practising barrister" which has been used in the past should no longer be used as it can cause confusion since some barristers without practising certificates do provide legal services and are, in effect, practising as lawyers.

Many unregistered barristers will have chosen careers other than the law or may be retired and are therefore not covered by this guidance unless they provide any legal services.

Even though the rules which apply only to practising barristers do not apply to them, all unregistered barristers remain members of the profession and members of their Inn and are expected to conduct themselves in an appropriate manner. In this context, they remain subject to certain Core Duties and Conduct Rules at all times. If they provide legal services, they must comply with all the Core Duties and they have a responsibility not to mislead anyone about their status. These are new requirements introduced by the Handbook. This guidance will assist those barristers to comply with their obligations contained in the BSB Handbook.

3. What are legal services and reserved legal activities?

Rule s6 in the BSB Handbook determines that you must not carry on any reserved legal activity unless you are entitled to do so under the Legal Services Act.

Under the Legal Services Act certain legal services are reserved to those who are authorised to provide them. For barristers, only those who have practising certificates are authorised persons. Such services are known as 'reserved legal activities'1 *which* are as follows:

- the exercise of a right of audience;
- the conduct of litigation;
- reserved instrument activities;
- probate activities;
- notarial activities2 and
- the administration of oaths.

As it is now a criminal offence to carry out a reserved legal activity without a practising certificate, it is important that unregistered barristers are clear that they are not permitted to carry out these services. In particular, the administration of oaths, which formerly could be performed by any barrister, is now reserved for those with practising certificates. Advocacy is not a reserved legal activity unless it involves the exercise of a right of audience. Thus, advocacy before an arbitrator or other tribunal where rights of audience are not required is not a reserved legal activity.

If you are also a solicitor, or regulated by another approved regulator you may be authorised to carry out reserved legal activities in that capacity. Guidance for those barristers who are dual qualified can be found at paragraph 8.6 below.

As an unregistered barrister, you can provide any legal services that are not reserved legal activities. However there are some important rules in the BSB Handbook which you need to follow in doing so.

Legal services are defined in the definitions section of the Handbook as follows:

> "[Legal services] includes legal advice representation and drafting or settling any statement of case witness statement affidavit or other legal document but does not include:
>
> (a) sitting as a judge or arbitrator or acting as a mediator, early neutral evaluation, expert determination and adjudications;
>
> (b) lecturing in or teaching law or writing or editing law books articles or reports;
>
> (c) examining newspapers, periodicals, books, scripts and other publications for libel, breach of copyright, contempt of court and the like;
>
> (d) communicating to or in the press or other media;
>
> (e) giving advice on legal matters free to a friend or relative or acting as unpaid or honorary legal adviser to any charitable benevolent or philanthropic institution;
>
> (f) in relation to a barrister who is a non-executive director of a company or a trustee or governor of a charitable benevolent or philanthropic institution or a trustee of any private trust, giving to the other directors trustees or governors the benefit of his learning

PART II
QUALIFYING AS A
BARRISTER AND
ENTERING PRACTICE

and experience on matters of general legal principle applicable to the affairs of the company institution or trust."

4. Holding out as a barrister

Rule s8 provides that you must not practise as a barrister unless you have a practising certificate, and rule s9 defines practising as a barrister as including holding yourself out as a barrister while providing legal services. The restriction on 'holding out' prevents barristers who do not have a practising certificate but who are supplying or offering to supply legal services from using the title 'barrister' or otherwise conveying the impression that they are practising as barristers. It is not possible to provide a comprehensive list of the circumstances which might amount to holding out but it is hoped that the following examples will give an idea of what is prohibited.

- Describing oneself as a barrister in any printed material used in connection with the provision of legal services: in particular in advertising or publicity, on a card or letterhead, or on premises.
- Describing oneself as a barrister to clients or prospective clients.
- Describing oneself to clients or prospective clients as a non-practising barrister or barrister-at-law (titles which have been allowed in the past but not in recent years).
- Indicating to opposing parties or their representatives (e.g. in correspondence) that one is a barrister.
- Describing oneself as a barrister or (when supplying services to the public) as "counsel", wearing robes, or sitting in a place reserved for counsel, in court.
- Using other descriptions in connection with supplying, or offering to supply, legal services which imply that the individual is a barrister (e.g. membership of an Inn of Court).

(These examples are not exhaustive.)

The restriction on holding out only applies in the context of legal services. If you have been called to the Bar, there is no restriction on referring to yourself as a barrister if it is not in connection with the supply of legal services.

It should also be noted that for a BVC or BPTC graduate to mention that he/she is a holder of this qualification, is not considered as holding out as a barrister.

5. What job title can I hold; what can I/my employer put on a business card/letterhead/website etc.?

The fundamental principle is that you must not mislead or allow anyone else to mislead any person to whom you or your employer supply or offer to supply *legal services*.

You can use the title "barrister" when **not** providing *legal services.* See paragraph 3 for activities which are not regarded as *legal services* ("non-legal" services). However, you must be careful not to mislead third parties as to your status as a barrister. This would apply particularly if you were also providing *legal services* to the same people to whom you provide "non-legal" services.

It is important that you/your employer do not use the title barrister, unregistered barrister or non-practising barrister on business cards, promotional material, letter-heads, and business names. If you are employed whether by a regulated or unregulated firm, you should make sure that your employer does not use any of these titles in connection with you in its printed material or on its website.

You can use the titles "lawyer" or "legal adviser". If you are self-employed, or work for an unregulated employer, you should not use the title "counsel". However, if you provide legal services only to your employer you may use titles commonly used in companies, such as legal counsel, general counsel, corporate counsel. You may also use the description "of Counsel" if you work for an employer which is an authorised person under the Legal Services Act.

In a curriculum vitae, you can state that you qualified as a barrister.

You can refer to yourself as a BVC/BPTC graduate.

If you are a QC but do not have a practising certificate, you may continue to use the title but if you are providing *legal services* you must explain that you are not practising as a barrister.

6. Why do special rules apply to unregistered barristers who supply legal services?

Legal services, other than reserved legal activities, can be supplied by anyone and are not subject to any special statutory regulation. It would therefore be disproportionate to impose regulatory requirements on unregistered barristers who supply such services just because they are barristers, except where there would otherwise be a clear risk to their potential clients. The risk that needs to be managed is that most potential clients are not aware of the different categories of barrister and will tend to assume that the same regulatory requirements and protections apply to all barristers. Barristers with practising certificates are subject to important requirements, such as having insurance and keeping their professional knowledge up-to-date, which do not apply to unregistered barristers. Some of their clients also have the right to complain to the Legal Ombudsman. These are important safeguards for clients, who may assume that they will apply whenever they seek legal services from someone they know or believe to be a barrister. The rules discussed below are intended to manage this risk while still allowing unregistered barristers to provide unreserved legal services.

7. What rules and duties apply to you as an unregistered barrister providing legal services?

When you are providing legal services all the Core Duties in the BSB Handbook apply to you (see Rules C1.2 and C2.1–2.2). The Core Duties are:

- CD1: You must observe your duty to the court in the administration of justice.

- CD2: You must act in the best interests of each client.
- CD3: You must act with honesty and integrity.
- CD4: You must maintain your independence.
- CD5: You must not behave in a way which is likely to diminish the trust and confidence which the public places in you or in the profession.
- CD6: You must keep the affairs of each client confidential.
- CD7: You must provide a competent standard of work and service to each client.
- CD8: You must not discriminate unlawfully against any person.
- CD9: You must be open and co-operative with your regulators.
- CD10: You must take reasonable steps to manage your practice, or carry out your role within your practice, competently and in such a way as to achieve compliance with your legal and regulatory obligations.

Even when you are not providing legal services, Core Duties 5 and 9 apply to you.

The Conduct rules (and associated guidance) which apply to unregistered barristers at all times are as follows:

- Rule c8: Your duty not to do anything which could be seen to undermine your honesty, integrity and independence.
- Rule c16: Your duty to your client is subject to your duty to the court, and your obligations to act with honesty and integrity, and to maintain your independence.
- Rules c64–70: Duties in relation to provision of information to the BSB and co-operation with the BSB. These duties include the new duty to report serious misconduct by other barristers (see separate guidance).

In addition, the following Conduct Rules and associated guidance apply when providing legal services:

- Rules c4 and c5: your duty to your client is subject to your duty to the court, and your duty to the court does not require you to breach your duty to keep the affairs of your client confidential.
- Rule c19: not misleading clients.
- Rules c144 and 145 – rules relating to information which unregistered barristers must give to inexperienced clients.

Rule c19 is a new rule which applies to all barristers. It provides that **you must not mislead** anyone to whom you supply or offer to supply *legal services*. For unregistered barristers this means:

- You must not use the title "barrister" in connection with the supply of or offer to supply *legal services*. This is known as "holding out" and is explained further in section 4. Similarly, you should not use the description "unregistered barrister" when supplying or offering to supply *legal services* except to the very limited extent discussed in paragraph 8 below and subject to explaining what the term means. Barristers who were registered under paragraph 206 of the previous Code may continue to use the title "barrister", but must comply with the terms of rule s15.

- You must not mislead clients or employers about:
  - your status;
  - the extent to which you are regulated;
  - the services you can supply; and
  - your insurance cover.

In order to comply with the obligation not to mislead clients or employers, you will need to consider what information you should give them about your status as discussed further in paragraph 8 below. In certain circumstances, the Handbook prescribes the information you must give (see below).

Rules c144–145 set out the information which must be provided by unregistered barristers when providing legal services to an inexperienced client (see paragraph 8.4 below)

8. Information to be given by unregistered barristers to employers, clients or prospective clients

This section describes what information you may, or in some cases **must**, give to those with whom you deal. Keep in mind the purpose of giving the information as discussed in paragraph 6 above. Check which of the following applies to you. When you provide the explanation required by rule c144 or suggested by this guidance, the BSB would not normally consider this as constituting holding yourself out as a barrister.

8.1 I provide legal services only to my employer

You may describe yourself orally as an unregistered barrister or a barrister without a practising certificate, to your employer, colleagues and any third parties with whom you deal and you should explain what this means if there is any risk of anyone being misled. You may also state on a CV that you have been called to the Bar.

8.2 I work for a regulated professional body and provide services to clients

This applies to unregistered barristers working for solicitors firms, other bodies which are authorised under the Legal Services Act such as licensed conveyancers, or other regulated professional firms such as accountants or Patent Agents.

You may describe yourself to your employer and colleagues as an unregistered barrister or a barrister without a practising certificate and you should explain what this means if there is any risk of anyone being misled. You should **not** describe yourself as a barrister or unregistered barrister to clients of your employer but if you are asked whether you are a barrister or if it becomes known that you are, you may say that you are an unregistered barrister and explain what this means. You should seek to ensure that any publicity put out by your employer does not describe you as a barrister. You must also comply with any regulatory requirements of the professional body which regulates your employer.

8.3 I am self-employed and I provide unreserved legal services to experienced business clients

This applies to those barristers dealing with larger businesses or firms which can be expected to make informed judgments about sourcing legal services.

You may not advertise or refer to yourself as a barrister but in tendering for work you may state to a prospective client that you are an unregistered barrister provided that you explain to the client what this means. If you are in any doubt, a written statement should be provided along the same lines as that detailed in paragraph 8.4 below. Whilst we strongly advise all barristers providing legal services to carry professional indemnity insurance, if you decide not to insure then you should so advise clients or prospective clients.

8.4 I am self-employed and supply unreserved legal services to inexperienced clients, such as individuals, small companies and charities.

If you supply legal services to inexperienced clients, rule c144 applies to you. Inexperienced clients are defined as including individuals and small organisations which would be entitled under the Legal Ombudsman Scheme Rules to make a complaint to the Legal Ombudsman if you were a practising barrister.4 As you are not practising as a barrister your clients have no redress under this scheme so you are required to make your status very clear to them. But other clients, for example slightly larger organisations which only occasionally require legal services, may also be inexperienced. If you are in any doubt as to whether your client has sufficient experience to understand the implications of instructing an unregistered barrister instead of a practising barrister, then you should give them the written statement detailed in this paragraph.

Where rule c144 applies, you **must** explain to your client:

- that you are not acting as a barrister;
- that you are not subject to certain Conduct Rules applying to practising barristers and the Bar Standards Board cannot consider complaints against you in relation to these rules but only in relation to the rules which do apply to you;
- if you are not covered by professional indemnity insurance you must say so;
- that your client has no right to complain to the Legal Ombudsman.

Your client must also confirm in writing that they have received this explanation.

A suggested form of statement is contained in Annex 1.

These requirements do not apply to legal services provided when working for a Legal Advice Centre5 as defined in the Code, or if you are authorised to provide reserved legal activities by another Approved Regulator6 (see paragraph 8.6 below). They do however apply if you were formerly registered under rule 206 of the previous version of the Code. You may also wish to refer to the definition of legal services in paragraph 3 above in deciding whether you are providing legal services.

8.5 I am employed by an unregulated organisation which provides unreserved legal services to the public

The same requirements apply as if you were self-employed depending on whether the client is an experienced large business or an inexperienced client such as an individual or small business. You should follow the guidance in paragraph 8.3 or 8.4 above as appropriate. It is your responsibility and not your employer's to see that the relevant information is given and you should advise your employer of the rules so that they do not hold you out as a barrister.

Barristers who do not hold practising certificates (including first six pupils) are permitted to provide free legal advice to clients of a legal advice centre, providing they do not hold themselves out as barristers and do not undertake or offer to undertake any reserved legal services.

8.6 I am authorised to carry out legal services by another Approved Regulator

Under the LSA, only Approved Regulators can authorise the carrying out of reserved legal activities (see above). The following Approved Regulators can currently authorise the conduct of litigation and/or exercise of rights of audience: the Law Society (acting by the Solicitors Regulation Authority), the Chartered Institute of Legal Executives, the Chartered Institute of Patent Agents and the Institute of Trade Mark Attorneys.

Rule s43 determines that, if you are authorised by another Approved Regulator to carry on a reserved legal activity and currently permitted to practise by that Approved Regulator, you must not practise as a barrister and you are not eligible for a practising certificate. If you are practising as a person authorised by one of the other Approved Regulators, you may hold yourself out as a barrister in addition to your other qualification, provided that you comply with Rule s14. This Rule requires that, in these circumstances, if you hold yourself out as a barrister or a registered European lawyer, when supplying legal services to any person or employer for the first time, you must inform them clearly in writing at the earliest opportunity that you are not practising as a barrister or a registered European lawyer.

9. What are the rules for pupils?

In your first six, as you do not have a practising certificate, you cannot supply legal services as a practising barrister but you can accept a noting brief with permission of your pupil supervisor or head of Chambers. You may describe yourself as a pupil barrister in that capacity. If you provide unreserved legal services in any other capacity, for example if providing pro bono advice, you should not describe yourself as a barrister or a pupil barrister and should follow the rules and guidance for unregistered barristers.

In your second six, when you have a provisional practising certificate, you may provide legal services in accordance with Rule S19. You may describe yourself as a pupil barrister and you should ensure that the client understands your status.

10. Further help and advice

It is recognised that the rules are complex. Further advice and information is available from the BSB on 020 7611 1444 or call the Bar Council Ethical Services (020 7611 1307) for advice.

Guidance on Practising Certificates for Pupils and Newly Qualified Barristers

[2.79c]

The BSB has issued specific advice for Pupils and newly qualified barristers in relation to these new arrangements and they are set out below.

This guidance is intended to provide information regarding the need for pupils and newly qualified barristers to hold practising certificates, as part of the new Authorisation to Practise regime that has been brought in as a result of the Legal Services Act 2007 ("the Act").

Background

Under the Act, barristers are only legally entitled to undertake a reserved legal activity if they have been authorised to do so by the Bar Standards Board ("BSB") (see s 20(6) of the Act). Pursuant to s 14 of the Act, it is a criminal offence to undertake a reserved legal activity when not authorised. The punishment for such a conviction is imprisonment for up to two years and/or a fine. As a result of the Act, the Bar Standards Board has introduced an Authorisation to Practise regime to ensure that it is clear what reserved legal activities those entitled to practise as barristers are authorised to undertake.

What are 'reserved legal activities'?

Pursuant to s 12 (also see Schedule 2) of the Act, the reserved legal activities are:

- the exercise of a right of audience;
- the conduct of litigation;
- reserved instrument activities;
- probate activities;
- notarial activities; and
- the administration of oaths.

Giving legal advice (orally or written) that is outside the six reserved legal activities is not restricted by the Act. However, you are still regulated by the Code of Conduct when undertaking non-reserved legal activities.

What is the effect of Authorisation to Practise on pupils?

The Bar's Code of Conduct allows pupils who have completed the non-practising period of pupillage to practise as a pupil barrister. As this is likely to involve the exercise of reserved legal activities, practising pupils must hold a practising certificate. In line with the Authorisation to Practice process as of 1 April 2012 pupils will be issued with a Provisional Practising Certificate.

What does this mean for pupils?

The BSB will issue a Provisional Practising Certificate to those who have done the following:

- completed a first six;
- submitted to the BSB a satisfactorily completed certificate verifying completion of the first six; and
- registered a second six with the BSB (*N.B: Please note that if you are undertaking your second six by undertaking external training, you will not be issued with a Provisional Practising Certificate as pupils undertaking external training are not entitled to exercise reserved legal activities*).

Until you have done so, you will not be able to obtain a Provisional Practising Certificate and therefore will not be able to exercise any reserved legal activities, including rights of audience, as part of your second six.

The BSB will issue a Provisional Practising Certificate to those who have done the following:

- completed a first six;
- submitted to the BSB a satisfactorily completed certificate verifying completion of the first six; and
- registered a second six with the BSB.

Until you have done so, you will not be able to obtain a Provisional Practising Certificate and therefore will not be able to exercise any reserved legal activities, including rights of audience, as part of your second six.

There is likely to be a short delay between completion of your first six and when you are able to exercise a right of audience as part of your second six. In order to reduce the delay, we urge you to submit to the BSB the requisite certificate signed by your pupil supervisor as soon as possible on successful completion of your first six. We would advise that you submit your certificate one week in advance, if your pupil supervisor is happy to sign your certificate in advance of your completion of first six. Your certificate will still need to indicate the full dates of your first six.

If your pupil supervisor is unavailable to sign your certificate, you can ask your Head of Chambers/Director of Pupil Training to sign it, so long as they indicate on your form who your pupil supervisor was for the relevant period. Additionally, you can email us a scanned copy of the signed form or fax it to us to prevent any potential delays in the post. The relevant contact details are listed at the end of this guidance

Once received, the BSB will process your forms as a matter of priority. If the information provided is satisfactory, we will send you an e-mail (provided that we have your e-mail address) to confirm that you are now authorised to exercise reserved legal activities. We will then pass your details to the Bar Council's Records Office so that you can be issued with a Provisional Practising Certificate. You will still receive a Provisional Qualification Certificate which will certify that you have completed your first six; however, the Provisional Qualification Certificate does not authorise you to practise.

In order to prevent delay due to our internal administration processes, the confirmation e-mail that will be sent to you will say that you are entitled to exercise reserved legal activities from either the date and time of the e-mail or the commencement date of your second six – you do not need to wait until you have received a physical Provisional Practising Certificate. We hope that these arrangements will keep the delay to a minimum – it is therefore important that you ensure that we have an up-to-date e-mail address for you.

We urge you to ensure that your pupil supervisor and clerks are aware of these requirements, as it means that you will not be able to exercise reserved legal activities as part of your second six until you have been advised that you are authorised to do so.

A Practising Certificate that comes into effect from April of one particular calendar year remains valid until 31 March of the following year. If your second six extends beyond this date, you will be issued with a further Provisional Practising Certificate for the following calendar year automatically.

It is important to note the restrictions that apply to second six pupils practising under a Provisional Practising Certificate.

Paragraph 802 of the Code only allows second six pupils to supply legal services as a pupil barrister and exercise reserved legal activities if they have the permission of their pupil-supervisor or head of chambers. Therefore, although the Practising Certificate that is issued to you may remain valid until a date after the proposed completion date of your second six, it will only authorise you to practise so long as you remain a pupil practising with the permission of your pupil supervisor or head of chambers.

See the guidance below for information about what to do when you finish your second six.

What does this mean for newly qualified barristers?

On completion of your second six, you will need to promptly submit to the BSB a certificate signed by each pupil supervisor in your second six, the Head of Chambers and Director of Pupil Training confirming that you have satisfactorily completed your second six, along with your checklist and a completed Notification of Status form. If the form cannot be signed by all, the form should indicate who is unable to sign and why they are not available. If any of your pupil supervisors are unavailable to sign, the form should still indicate the dates of their supervision. The form must be completed by a minimum of two members of the approved training organisation, one of which must be the Head of Chambers or Director of Pupil Training.

After you have submitted the requisite forms to us, we will send you a Full Qualification Certificate which will certify that you have completed your second six. In order to commence practice after your second six, you must return a completed Notification of Status form confirming that you have commenced practice and providing your practice address. If you do not return the Notification of Status form, you may be in breach of paragraph 202(d) of the Code of Conduct, which states that a barrister may practise only if he has provided in writing details of his current practice address and telephone number.

Provided you have submitted to the BSB the requisite certificate confirming satisfactory completion of your second six, returned a Notification of Status form indicating that you are practising and applied to the Records Office for a Full Practising Certificate; you will be entitled to commence practice as a barrister. Please note that as of 1 April 2012 on completion of 2nd six, pupils are required to notify the Records Office of any change of status or details within 28 days.

The Provisional Practising Certificate that was issued to you whilst you were undertaking your second six will only be valid for the entirety of your second six. Upon completion of second six, you will be required to obtain a Full Practising Certificate from the Records Office.

Before your Full Practising Certificate expires, you will be sent annual notices to renew your Full Practising Certificate and you will be informed of the requisite fee to pay in order to do so.

What does this mean for pupil supervisors?

All pupil supervisors should be aware of the changes arising from the Legal Services Act and Authorisation to Practise. Pupil supervisors should be aware that until a pupil has complied with the requirements explained in this guidance and been issued with a Provisional Practising Certificate, the pupil will not be legally entitled to exercise reserved legal activities. It is important that you inform the clerks of these requirements so that they do not book a hearing for a pupil who has not yet been authorised to exercise reserved legal activities.

Who do I contact with questions?

If you have any questions about these requirements, or need to submit any certification forms, please contact:

Pupillage Compliance Team
Bar Standards Board, 289–293 High Holborn
London WC1V 7HZ
DX 240 LDE
E-mail: pupillagerecords@barstandardsboard.org.uk
Tel: 020 7611 1444
Fax: 020 7831 9217

QASA

What is QASA?

[2.80]

QASA is a joint scheme being developed by the BSB, the Solicitors Regulation Authority and ILEX Professional Standards. The Scheme will regulate the quality of all advocates appearing in the criminal courts in England and Wales, whether they are barristers, solicitors, or legal executives. The Scheme will apply to all advocates, whether they are self-employed or employed, and whether they are acting for the prosecution or defence.

The Scheme will systematically assess and assure the quality of criminal advocacy in the courts in England and Wales and will ensure that the performance of all advocates is measured against the same set of standards, regardless of an advocate's previous education and training.

Reference should be made to the QASA Handbook for Criminal Advocates September 2013: https://www.barstandardsboard.org.uk/media/1531917/qasa_handbook.pdf

QASA – Key Steps

(1) *Establish whether the scheme applies to you:*

[2.81]

QASA only applies to criminal advocacy:

"Criminal advocacy" means advocacy in all hearings arising out of a police-led or Serious Fraud Office-led investigation and prosecuted in the criminal courts by the Crown Prosecution Service or the Serious Fraud Office but does not include hearings arising out of Parts 2, 5 or 8 of the Proceeds of Crime Act 2002

(2) *Determine when you need to register for QASA:*

QASA will be phased in by circuit areas. The dates for registration will depend upon the primary circuit in which you practise. This will be the circuit in which you undertake criminal advocacy more frequently than in any other circuit.

The registration dates for each circuit area are:

Circuits	**Start**	**Close**
Midland and Western	30 September 13	30 May 14
South Eastern	31 May 14	3 October 14
Northern, North Eastern and Wales and Chester	4 October 14	31 December 14

You must be registered in order to undertake criminal advocacy.

You can register after the window closes (for example if you return to practise or begin criminal practise) as long as you do not undertake criminal advocacy until you have registered.

(3) *Decide the level at which you should register:*

Under QASA all criminal advocates will be accredited at a level between 1 and 4, which relate to the level of hearings that they are competent to appear in.

In order to determine the level that you should register at, you should review the trials that you have appeared in over the last two years against the QASA Levels Table (see Part 3 of the QASA Handbook). As you may have undertaken work at a range of the levels, you will need to decide the level you feel most competent performing at.

If you require any help deciding which level to register at call 020 7611 1479. The helpline is open 9:30am – 5pm Monday to Friday, and will be open on Thursdays from 5 -7pm at a later date.

(4) *Register for QASA through Barrister Connect:*

Registering for QASA only takes 10 minutes. Simply go to https://www.barristerconnect.org.uk/login/ and follow the on screen instructions. A detailed "How to" guide with screen shots will be available shortly to assist with this process.

Silks appointed in 2010 or later and those who register at level 1 will receive full accreditation following registration and do not have to complete stages 5 and 6 below.

(5) *Seek assessment in your first two trials at your level:*

Once you have registered at your chosen level through Barrister Connect you will receive provisional accreditation at that level. You must convert this to full accreditation through seeking assessment in the first two trials that you undertake at your level.

In order to be assessed, you must print a Criminal Advocacy Evaluation Form and fill in the details at the top. You must provide the judge with your CAEF at the start of the trial.

The judge will complete the CAEF and return it direct to the BSB. The BSB will then upload the CAEF to Barrister Connect and send an email to inform you that it is available for you to view.

If you do not undertake trials you can be assessed at an assessment centre as detailed in the QASA Handbook (page 10).

(6) *Apply for accreditation:*

Once you have been assessed in the first two trials at your level you can apply to convert your provisional accreditation to full accreditation. This application is made through Barrister Connect.

If your assessments include "not competent" marks, you may obtain one further assessment and then apply for accreditation on the basis of the three completed CAEFs.

The BSB will apply a grading matrix to decide whether to approve an application. Details on the matrix are available in Part 4 of the QASA Handbook.

You have 24 months to convert your provisional accreditation to full accreditation. Advocates who are unable to be assessed in two trials within 24 months (whether this is due to long running trials or lack of trial opportunities) can apply for an extension of time.

Full accreditation is valid for five years.

Quality Assurance Scheme for Advocates Rules

Interpretation

[2.82]

1. In these Rules:

"Accreditation" means the status required under the Scheme to be permitted to undertake criminal advocacy in the courts of England and Wales;

"Approved assessment organisation" means an organisation approved by the Joint Advocacy Group to assess the competence of advocates to conduct criminal advocacy against the Statement of Standards;

"Criminal advocacy" means advocacy in all hearings arising out of a police-led or Serious Fraud Office-led investigation and prosecuted in the criminal courts by the Crown Prosecution Service or the Serious Fraud Office but does not include hearings arising out of Parts 2, 5 or 8 of the Proceeds of Crime Act 2002;

"Criminal advocacy evaluation form" means a form completed by a judge to record the competence of a barrister to conduct criminal advocacy against the Statement of Standards;

"Effective trial "means a trial that allows for the assessment of a barrister against standards 1–4 as set out in the Statement of Standards;

"Full accreditation" means accreditation that permits a barrister to undertake criminal advocacy in the courts in England and Wales for a period of up to five years;

"Independent assessor" means a person appointed by the Joint Advocacy Group to attend court to assess the competence of a barrister to conduct criminal advocacy against the Statement of Standards;

"Joint Advocacy Group" means the group established by the Bar Standards Board, the Solicitors' Regulation Authority and ILEX Professional Standards, in order to oversee the quality assurance and accreditation of criminal advocacy;

"Level" means one of the four QASA levels. Advocates will be accredited at one of these levels and this will correspond to the level of hearings that they can undertake.

"Prescribed" means as set out in the QASA Handbook and the QASA Rules;

"Progression" means the process by which a barrister can increase their level under the Scheme;

"Provisional accreditation" means accreditation that permits a barrister to undertake criminal advocacy in the courts in England and Wales for a period of up to 12 or 24 months, but which requires further steps to be taken to obtain full accreditation;

"Re-accreditation" means the process by which a barrister demonstrates their competence and renews their accreditation at their existing level for a further five years;

"Registration" means the process by which barristers enter QASA;

"Statement of Standards" means the standards against which the competence of advocates will be assessed for the purposes of registration, progression and re-accreditation.

Scope of the scheme

2. Subject to Rule 3, you must not undertake criminal advocacy unless you have provisional accreditation or full accreditation in accordance with these Rules and with the QASA Handbook.

3. Barristers who do not have provisional or full accreditation under the Scheme are permitted to undertake criminal advocacy:

   3.1 in hearings which primarily involve advocacy which is outside of the definition of criminal advocacy in rule 1 above; or

   3.2 if they have been instructed specifically as a result of their specialism in work outside of the definition of criminal advocacy.

4. You shall only undertake criminal advocacy in hearings which you are satisfied fall within the level at which you are accredited, or any level below the same, unless you are satisfied that you are competent to accept instructions for a case at a higher level strictly in accordance with the criteria prescribed in the QASA Handbook.

Provisional accreditation

5. If you are granted provisional accreditation, you must apply to convert this to full accreditation within 12 or 24 months of the date on which your provisional accreditation was granted.

Full accreditation

6. If you are granted full accreditation, it will be valid for 5 years from the date on which it was granted.

General provisions relating to applications for registration, progression or re-accreditation

7. You may apply for registration, progression or re-accreditation under these Rules. In support of an application you shall submit such information as may be prescribed. This will include:

   7.1 completing the relevant application form supplied by the Bar Standards Board and submitting it to the Bar Standards Board;

   7.2 submitting such information in support of the application as may be prescribed. This will include all of the criminal advocacy evaluation forms that you have obtained; and

   7.3 paying the appropriate fee in the amount determined in accordance with the Bar Standards Board's published fees policy.

8. An application will only have been made once the Bar Standards Board has received the application form completed in full, together with all information required in support of the application and confirmation from you in the form of a declaration that the information contained within, or submitted in support of, the application is full and accurate.

9. You are personally responsible for the contents of your application and any information submitted to the Bar Standards Board by you or on your behalf, and you must not submit (or cause or permit to be submitted on your behalf) information to the Bar Standards Board which you do not believe is full and accurate.

10. On receipt of an application, the Bar Standards Board shall decide whether to grant or refuse the application, and shall notify you accordingly, giving reasons for any decision to refuse the application. This decision will take effect when it has been communicated to the barrister concerned.

11. Before reaching a decision on the application, the Bar Standards Board may appoint an independent assessor to conduct an assessment of your competence to conduct criminal advocacy at the relevant level.

Registration for QASA

12. In order to be accredited under QASA barristers must first apply for registration. In support of an application you shall submit such information as may be prescribed.

Level 1

12.1 If you apply for registration at level 1 and your application is successful, you will be awarded full accreditation at level 1.

Levels 2 to 4

12.2 If you apply for registration at levels 2, 3 or 4 and your application is successful, you will be awarded provisional accreditation which will be valid for 24 months.

12.3 You must apply to convert your provisional accreditation to full accreditation within 24 months.

12.4 You must be assessed in your first effective criminal trials at your level and submit the prescribed number of completed criminal advocacy evaluation forms confirming that you are competent in accordance with the competence framework detailed in the QASA Handbook.

12.5 Your application must include all completed criminal advocacy evaluation forms obtained in effective trials.

12.6 If your application is successful you will be awarded full accreditation.

12.7 Subject to rule 12.8, if your application for full accreditation is unsuccessful, you shall be granted provisional accreditation at the level below and shall be required to apply to convert this to full accreditation at that lower level in accordance with Rules 12.3 to 12.5.

12.8 If your application for full accreditation at level 2 is unsuccessful, you shall be granted accreditation at level 1.

Barristers not undertaking trials

12.9 If you do not intend to undertake criminal trials you may apply for registration at Level 2. If your application is successful, you will be awarded provisional accreditation. You must be assessed via an approved assessment organisation within 24 months.

12.10 If your application for full accreditation is successful you shall be awarded full accreditation and will be permitted to undertake non-trial hearings up to level 3 and trials at level 1.

12.11 Once you have full accreditation, if you wish to undertake trials at level 2 you must inform the BSB of your intention and comply with rules 13.1 to 13.4.

Barristers who took silk between 2010 and 2013

12.12 If you took silk between 2010 and 2013 inclusive you can register through the modified entry arrangements set out in paragraph 2.38 of the QASA Handbook.

Progression

13. If you have full accreditation, you may apply for accreditation at the next higher level to your current level.

Progression to level 2

13.1 If you wish to progress to Level 2 you must first obtain provisional accreditation at Level 2 by notifying the BSB of your intention to progress.

13.2 Your provisional accreditation will be valid for 24 months. In order to convert this to full accreditation you must be assessed in your first effective criminal trials at level 2 and submit the prescribed number of completed criminal advocacy evaluation forms confirming that you are competent in Level 2 trials in accordance with the competence framework detailed in the QASA Handbook.

13.3 Your application must include all completed criminal advocacy evaluation forms obtained in effective trials.

13.4 Where your application is successful, you shall be granted full accreditation at Level 2, which is valid for 5 years from the date of issue.

Progression to Level 3 and 4

Stage 1

13.5 You must first apply for provisional accreditation at the next higher level to your current level. In order to apply for provisional accreditation, you must submit the prescribed number of criminal advocacy evaluation forms confirming that you are very competent at your current level in accordance with the competence framework detailed in the QASA Handbook.

13.6 Your application must include all completed criminal advocacy evaluation forms obtained in effective trials. These should be obtained within a 12 month period.

13.7 If your application is successful you will be awarded provisional accreditation.

Stage 2

13.8 Your provisional accreditation will be valid for 12 months. You must apply to convert your provisional accreditation to full accreditation before your provisional accreditation expires.

13.9 You must be assessed in your first effective criminal trials at your new level and submit the prescribed number of completed criminal advocacy evaluation forms confirming that you are competent in accordance with the competence framework detailed in the QASA Handbook.

13.10 Your application must include all completed criminal advocacy evaluation forms obtained in effective trials.

13.11 If your application is successful you will be awarded full accreditation.

13.12 If your application for full accreditation is unsuccessful, you may continue to conduct criminal advocacy at your current level until the expiry of your current accreditation.

Re-accreditation

14. You must apply for re-accreditation at the level at which you are accredited within five years from the date on which your full accreditation was granted.

15. You shall submit, in support of an application for re-accreditation, evidence to demonstrate your competence to conduct criminal advocacy at the level at which you are accredited, comprising:

    15.1 if you are accredited at Level 1, evidence of the assessed continuing professional development undertaken by you in the field of advocacy in the period since you were accredited at Level 1 or, if you have previously been re-accredited at that level, since your most recent re-accreditation;

    15.2 if you are accredited at Level 2, 3 or 4, the prescribed number of criminal advocacy evaluation forms. Your application must include all completed criminal advocacy evaluation forms obtained in consecutive effective trials in the 24 months preceding the application.

16. If your application is successful you will be awarded full accreditation for a period of 5 years.

17. Subject to rule 18, if your application for re-accreditation is unsuccessful, you shall be granted provisional accreditation at the level below and shall be required to apply to convert this to full accreditation at that lower level in accordance with Rules 12.3 to 12.5.

18. If your application for re-accreditation at level 2 is unsuccessful, you shall be granted accreditation at level 1.

Lapse of accreditation

19. Subject to rule 21, your provisional accreditation will lapse if you do not apply for full accreditation before it expires.

20. Subject to rule 21, your full accreditation will lapse if you do not apply for re-accreditation within 5 years of the date on which you were awarded full accreditation.

21. If the BSB has received an application within the period of accreditation, the accreditation will not lapse whilst a decision is pending.

22. If your accreditation lapses, you may not undertake criminal advocacy in accordance with Rule 2.

Applications for variation

23. Where your individual circumstances result in you encountering difficulties in obtaining completed criminal advocacy evaluation forms within the specified period, then you may apply to the Bar Standards Board for an extension of time to comply with the requirements; or

24. Where your individual circumstances result in you encountering difficulties in obtaining completed criminal advocacy evaluation forms, then you may apply to the Bar Standards Board for your competence to conduct criminal advocacy to be assessed by an independent assessor, and you may submit the results of the assessment in support of your application for registration, re-accreditation or progression in the place of one criminal advocacy evaluation form.

Managing underperformance

25. The Bar Standards Board may receive criminal advocacy evaluation forms raising concerns regarding your competence to conduct criminal advocacy at any time.

26. Where concerns regarding your competence to conduct criminal advocacy are brought to the attention of the Bar Standards Board, either during the course of its consideration of an application brought by you under these Rules, or as a result of concerns raised under Rule 25, it may decide to do one or more of the following:

    26.1 appoint an independent assessor to conduct an assessment of your criminal advocacy;

    26.2 recommend that you undertake, at your own cost, such training for such period as it may specify;

    26.3 revoke your accreditation at your current level; and/or

    26.4 refer you for consideration of your health or conduct under the Fitness to Practise Rules or the Complaints Rules, as it considers appropriate,

    and shall notify you accordingly, giving reasons for its decision.

27. Where your accreditation has been revoked, you shall be granted provisional accreditation at the level below and shall be required to apply to convert this to full accreditation in accordance with Rules 12.3 to 12.5.

28. Where you have applied for registration or re-accreditation at Level 1, and your application has been refused, you will not be entitled to accept any instructions to conduct criminal advocacy, and the Bar Standards Board may recommend that you undertake training in accordance with Rule 26.2 before you re-apply for registration or re-accreditation as appropriate.

29. Where you have undertaken training under Rule 26.2, the Bar Standards Board shall, at the end of the specified period, assess whether you have satisfactorily completed the training before reaching a decision in relation to any further steps that it may consider appropriate to take in accordance with Rule 26.

Appeals

30. You may appeal to the Bar Standards Board against any decision reached by it under these rules. Appeals must be made in accordance with the published BSB QASA Appeals policy.

Commencement and transitional arrangements

31. Subject to rule 34, these rules commence on 30 September 2013.

Registration of barristers currently undertaking criminal advocacy

32. Barristers currently undertaking criminal advocacy are required to apply for registration under the Scheme in accordance with the phased implementation programme as set out at paragraphs 2.11 to 2.13 of the QASA Handbook.

33. The dates for registration will depend upon the primary circuit in which you practise. This will be the circuit in which you undertake criminal advocacy more frequently than in any other circuit.

    33.1 If you primarily practise in the Midland or Western Circuit, you must register for QASA from 30 September 2013 and before the first occasion on which you undertake criminal advocacy after 7 March 2014.

    33.2 If you primarily practise in the South Eastern Circuit, you must register for QASA from 10 March 2014 and before the first occasion on which you undertake criminal advocacy after 13 June 2014.

    33.3 If you primarily practise in the Northern, North Eastern or Wales and Chester Circuit, you must register for QASA from 30 June 2014 and before the first occasion on which you undertake criminal advocacy after 3 October 2014.

34. Subject to rules 34.1 and 34.2, rule 2 commences for all advocates from 4 October 2014.

    34.1 Rule 2 will commence for those advocates who primarily practise in the Midland or Western Circuit from 10 March 2014. Any advocate who undertakes criminal advocacy in these circuits without accreditation must be able to prove to the BSB that they practise primarily in another circuit.

    34.2 Rule 2 will commence for those advocates who primarily practise in the South Eastern Circuit from 14 June 2014. Any advocate who undertakes criminal advocacy in this circuit without accreditation must be able to prove to the BSB that they practise primarily in the Northern, North Eastern or Wales and Chester Circuit.

BSB QASA Appeals Policy

[2.83]

1. You may appeal to the Bar Standards Board against any decision reached by it to:

    1.1 refuse your application for accreditation, re-accreditation or progression; or

    1.2 revoke your accreditation at your current level,

2. You may not appeal against the content of an individual assessment conducted by a judge and recorded through a criminal advocacy evaluation form.

3. You may bring an appeal to the Bar Standards Board by serving notice in writing on the Board within 21 days from the date of the notice of the relevant decision.

4. A notice of appeal shall confirm:

   4.1 the decision appealed against;

   4.2 the grounds of appeal; and shall be accompanied by a fee of £200.

5. An appeal may only be brought on the grounds that:

   5.1 the decision reached was unreasonable; and/or

   5.2 there was a procedural error in the assessment or decision-making process and that you suffered disadvantage as a result which was sufficient to have materially affected the decision.

Procedure for considering appeals

6. An adjudicator will be appointed to consider an appeal. The adjudicator will be drawn from a Panel appointed by the Bar Standards Board.

7. An appeal shall be considered on the papers at a meeting, in private, unless the adjudicator, at their discretion, decides that a hearing in person is required.

8. Where a hearing in person is required, the adjudicator shall, no less than 28 days before the date of the meeting or hearing at which the appeal is to be determined, serve notice on you, specifying the date, time and venue of the meeting or hearing.

   Notice shall be served on you in accordance with Rule 32(1)(a)-(c) of the Disciplinary Tribunal Regulations 2009.

9. The adjudicator may admit any evidence which they considers fair and relevant to the appeal, whether or not such evidence would be admissible in a court of law, save that no person is to give oral evidence at a hearing unless the adjudicator considers such evidence is desirable to enable them to discharge their functions.

10. The appeal shall be by way of a re-hearing.

11. The adjudicator may at any time, whether of their own motion or upon the application of a party, adjourn the proceedings until such time and date as they think fit.

12. You may be required to attend at an appeal hearing and you can be represented, however, in those circumstances, where you are neither present or represented, the adjudicator may nevertheless proceed to consider and determine the appeal if they are satisfied that all reasonable efforts have been made to serve you with notice of the hearing.

13. The adjudicator may:

    13.1 dismiss the appeal;

    13.2 allow the appeal in whole or part;

13.3 substitute for the decision appealed against any other decision that it is open to the Bar Standards Board to make under the QASA rules; or

13.4 remit the decision to the Bar Standards Board for reconsideration on such terms as the adjudicator considers to be appropriate in the circumstances.

14. The adjudicator may order, in the event of a successful appeal, a refund of any appeal fee paid to the Bar Standards Board.

15. The adjudicator shall give notice of their decision in writing, together with reasons for the decision. This decision cannot be appealed.

Professional Indemnity Insurance

Bar Mutual Indemnity Fund Administrative Notes

[2.84]

Every self-employed barrister (other than a pupil who is covered under his pupil-master's insurance) must be entered as a member with Bar Mutual Indemnity Fund ("BMIF"). This is a requirement of paragraph 402.1 of the Code. Further information and forms etc is available at : http://www.barmutual.co.uk/

The following text summarises the important aspects of the requirements of professional indemnity insurance and gives some practical guidance on securing insurance. First, reproduced below are the "Administrative Notes" for the scheme produced by the BMIF.

1. Business Sequence

(*a*) *Application for Membership and Insurance, or Renewal of Cover*

[2.85]

Two documents provide the key to arranging the necessary insurance:

(i) A new barrister should complete the form entitled "Application for Membership and Insurance" (see 3 and 4 below).

(ii) A form entitled "Renewal of Cover" is printed for each barrister who is already a Member of BMIF. The forms for all the members of Chambers are sent to you in one envelope with this set of notes in mid-January, and BMIF is most grateful to you for distributing them. Please note the return date for renewal documents – 14 days from the date of receipt and by 25th February at the latest since contributions are due to be paid by 1st April.

During the renewal period you will receive lists showing which of the barristers in your Chambers have not returned their renewal forms together with premium debited details. Barristers who do not return their renewal forms at the proper time may be reported to their Head of Chambers and to the Bar Council.

Please contact the Managers urgently:

- if a barrister is missed out. He/she should not complete the form intended for new barristers, but the spare Renewal form sent with this pack can be photocopied as necessary – **or download from www.barmutual.co.uk**.
- if a barrister is unable to complete the Renewal form for any reason.

(b) Renewal online

It is now possible for members to renew online via www.barmutual.com. Each renewal form has a unique sixteen digit number on it and this should be entered along with the member's Bar Council membership number (obtainable from the Bar Council on 020 7242 0934). A member should enter the renewal details, review what level of cover to take and elect to pay via cheque/bank transfer, via instalments or by debit or credit card.

(c) Calculation of Contributions

The Managers use the information supplied to calculate the contribution to be paid in accordance with the Rating Schedule and then send a debit note for the amount to be paid, direct to each barrister. All barristers, even when their income exceeds the "cap" (remaining at £1m this year) are requested to complete the Gross Fee Income box (Box 1 on the Renewal form) with a specific figure so that the Managers may gauge the effect of the "cap".

(d) Method of Payment

The tear-off section of a debit note or statement of account should be used as a remittance advice. Cheques should be made payable to Bar Mutual Indemnity Fund Limited. If Chambers is paying collectively with a Chambers' cheque, please ensure the Chambers' number is written on the reverse of the cheque, and attach a list of the Members whose contributions are included in the cheque.

If members (or chambers) wish to settle their premiums direct by bank transfer or the internet – BMIF's bank details are:

National Westminster Bank plc
Sort Code: 50 00 00
Account No: 15427625

Please ensure that membership numbers are quoted with any payments.

BMIF has made arrangements for payments to be made via six monthly direct debit installments. Please note that a credit agreement is entered into between each barrister and Premium Credit Limited ("PCL"); if a barrister wishes to use this method of payment the relevant box should be ticked on the Renewal of Cover form and the appropriate document will be issued. For those members who have already signed a credit agreement with PCL, this means of payment will continue unless BMIF is advised otherwise.

(e) Chambers' Statements

From time to time, you will receive Chambers' statements listing the amount of each barrister's contribution, whether it has been paid and the limit of his/her cover. This will help you and your Head of Chambers to keep track of the insurance position of your Chambers.

(f) *Interest*

If a contribution is not paid by the due date, interest is chargeable at a rate of 1% per month (minimum £10) on the sum debited, without further notice. A statement will be sent and if payment is not made the barrister will be reported to his/her Head of Chambers and to the Bar Council.

2. Pupils

[2.86]

A pupil is covered by his/her pupil master's insurance policy.

3. Insuring for the First Time

[2.87]

Use the Application for Membership and Insurance form (please photocopy as required) – or download from www.barmutual.co.uk.

The new barrister should complete the form and return it to the Managers before he/she joins Chambers. A barrister within three years of call with a Gross Fee Income equal to or less than £15,000 is eligible for a reduction in the cost if Chambers requires him to buy an optional higher level of cover.

4. Squatters, Academics and Law Reporters

[2.88]

Barristers going into practice, other than as tenants, must nevertheless make their own arrangements for insurance with BMIF as soon as their pupillage ends. The Head of Chambers has an obligation to ensure they are properly insured.

Special arrangements apply for academics and door tenants. Please contact the Managers in each case. As a general guide, all those members of the Bar who are offering any form of legal services to the public, as barristers in independent practice, with a Practising Certificate, need to be insured with BMIF.

Law Reporters have been exempted by the Bar Council from the requirement to insure with BMIF.

5. Moving Chambers

[2.89]

Use the Barrister Movement form to notify BMIF of the date of joining/leaving Chambers (please photocopy as required) or email info@barmutual.co.uk. For a new joiner request his/her original Cover Note and photocopy it for your file.

6. Returning from Maternity Leave

[2.90]

Where a Member has left practice temporarily or reduced the amount of time given to practise by reason of pregnancy or childbirth or in order to care for the Member's own children below school age, the Member shall be entitled to the same limit of basic cover as the Member had previously been provided with, whatever the Member's Basic Contribution, without payment of any Optional Contribution.

7. Long Term Illness

[2.91]

Members returning to practice after long term illness should contact the Managers.

8. Retiring from Practice at the Bar

[2.92]

Please inform BMIF if a member has ceased to practise. Please provide the date the member was marked as non-practising by the Bar Council and also a correspondence address. Use the Barrister Retirement form to inform BMIF of the barrister's date of retirement (please photocopy as required or download from www.barmutual.co.uk) or telephone or email info@barmutual.co.uk.

(a) Every retiring barrister will be **given** (ie without charge) £500,000 cover for a minimum of six years. Thereafter, unless and until they decide otherwise, the cover will continue indefinitely.

(b) If a barrister opts to maintain the highest level of cover provided by BMIF in his previous three years' of practice then, assuming he is buying more than £500,000 cover, the contribution for cover up to £2,500,000 will be 75% of the average annual contribution over the last three years. That cover will last for a six year period, following which the barrister will automatically receive £500,000 of cover which will continue indefinitely, unless and unti the Directors decide otherwise. If a barrister requires higher cover on expiry of the six year period such cover is available in three-year tranches at a cost of 20% of the pemium paid for the first six years' cover.

9. Death

[2.93]

Please notify the Managers of the death of any practising or retired barrister as soon as practicable. There is no charge for six years' run-off cover at the limit pertaining at the time of death (up to £2,500,000) and the barrister's estate will be protected by the Fund in the same way as the barrister was before death.

10. Cover

[2.94]

(a) **Levels of Cover**

The barrister's basic contribution, which cannot be reduced, entitles him/her to a **Basic Limit of Cover** (please refer to Table 2 of the Rating Schedule).

If **optional cover** is required, the cost will be shown on the debit note and the barrister may then decide whether to accept the quotation. The levels of cover available and the extra cost are shown in Table 3 of the Rating Schedule.

The Bar Mutual will not be providing additional cover of £2,500,000 in excess of £2,500,000 but members are encouraged to give serious consideration to purchasing cover in excess of £2.5m In order to assist barristers in obtaining this cover BMIF has agreed with two brokers – TLO and SBJ – that BMIF will send details of a barrister's fee income, areas of practice and claims history to either of these firms to that the barrister does not need to complete a separate proposal form disclosing this information. If a barrister would like BMIF to act in this way he should indicate to which broker BMIF is authorised to send details by ticking either box 2 8B and/or 9B. The broker will then make contact direct.

(b) **Increase of Cover**

Use the Increase of Cover form to inform BMIF of any mid-year requirement for higher limits of cover (please photocopy as required). Please telephone the Managers to ascertain the cost. Any such increase in cover cannot be retrospective and the declaration regarding claims on the form is particularly important. Members should be aware that the policy works on a claims-made basis. Thus the date upon which a claim is made is the relevant date for determining the relevant level of cover.

(c) **"The Insured Practice"**

You should note that the BMIF Terms of Cover automatically include cover for those barristers acting as Arbitrators, Umpires or Mediators. Barristers who do not wish to have this cover should not declare any income for this part of their practice and leave the Arbitrator/Umpire/Mediator box in section 3 of the Renewal form blank.

(d) **Cover for practise as a Foreign or European Lawyer**

Members wishing to extend their cover for foreign practice should tick the box on the Renewal of Cover form. The box should be ticked ONLY if a barrister is (1) qualified to practise in another system of law and (2) wishes to apply for cover for that practice in that other system. A separate application form will then be issued.

There is NO need to apply for separate cover in another common law jurisdiction as a Practising Barrister or Registered European Lawyer if the member's qualification as such enables him to practise in that jurisdiction (subject to any formal local requirements in that jurisdiction as to call or certification). Those members who have already applied for Foreign Cover will automatically receive a separate Renewal Form.

11. Claims

[2.95]

In the event of a claim being made against a barrister, or of any intimation received from any person of any intention to make a claim against him/her, the barrister should inform BMIF in writing as soon as possible.A barrister may wish to inform the Managers if he/she becomes aware of circumstances which might lead to a claim being made.

Excess

In the event of a finding of professional misconduct a deductible of £350 will be payable. A deductible of £350 will also be applied in the case of successful wasted costs applications.

12. Public Access and Licensed Access Work

[2.96]

Members accepting work from public or licensed access should declare the percentage of their fees earned from these types of work in boxes 6 and 7.

13. BMIF Board of Directors

[2.97]

Justin Fenwick QC (Chairman)
Richard Anelay QC
Stephen Arthur
Michael Brindle
Gregory Denton-Cox
Colin Edelman QC
Charles Flint QC
Catherine Gibaud
Alexandra Healy
Leigh-Ann Mulcahy QC
David Railton QC
Colin Reese QC
Rajey Shetty
Sharif Shivji
Christopher Symons QC
David Wolfson

14. Managers

[2.98]

Ahmed Salim
Redvers Cunningham
Peregrine Massey

Claims:	*Underwriting & Membership:*
Ahmed Salim	Sarah Jacobs
Miranda Levey	Milli Chatha
Jessica Mance	
Adrian Mee	Joy Lake
David Simpson	

Disciplinary Cover

[2.99]

From 1 April 2007 Bar Mutual Indemnity Fund's (BMIF) cover was extended to include costs and expenses incurred with BMIF's consent in defending disciplinary proceedings.

Barristers in receipt of a formal complaint are strongly urged to make immediate use of the available support before preparing any response (for which a maximum of three weeks is usually given in the first instance).

The Managers dealing with complaints against members of the Bar are all legally qualified. It is envisaged that they would assist with advice and in carrying out the necessary investigations. Only exceptionally would solicitors be instructed. However, the Managers will instruct counsel both for specialist advice and/or if it is necessary to act as advocates in hearings.

Cover

Prior to April 1 2007 the costs of defending disciplinary proceedings were only paid by BMIF as part of the basic cover if in the view of the Managers the outcome of the disciplinary proceedings had a potential impact on a claim for a civil liability that was covered under the BMIF Rules.

With effect from April 1 2007 the BMIF Rules were changed to provide cover for the costs of responding to a complaint and, in the event that the Conduct and Complaints Committee decides that disciplinary proceedings should be instigated, providing appropriate representation at the hearing.

The extension of the Bar Mutual cover is set out at clause 1.3 of the Terms of Cover (September 2010 Edition), which provides as follows: "Bar Mutual shall indemnify the Insured against Defence Costs".

Defence Costs are defined as: Any costs or expenses incurred with the prior consent of Bar Mutual in any of the following situations:

(i) As regards a Circumstance notified under sub-clause 5.1(i):

  (a) in the investigation, defence and settlement of a potential Claim;

  (b) in the investigation or defence of potential Disciplinary Proceedings;

(ii) in the defence or settlement of any Claim;

(iii) in the conduct of any proceedings for indemnity, contribution or recovery relating to a Claim;

(iv) in the defence of any Disciplinary Proceedings.

Exclusions

Certain matters are excluded from the indemnity set out at clause 1.3 of the Terms of Cover. They are set out at clause 3 of the Terms Of Cover.

3.1 Any liability of Bar Mutual under these Terms of Cover for the following shall be excluded:

(i) Claims or Disciplinary Proceedings for bodily injury or death unless arising out of the provision of Legal Services to a client by the Insured.

(ii) Claims or Disciplinary Proceedings for loss of or physical damage to property unless:

(a) the property is property in the care of the Insured in connection with, but is not occupied or used by him for the purposes of, the Insured Practice, or

(b) the loss or physical damage arose out of the provision of Legal Services to a client by the Insured.

(iii) Claims or Disciplinary Proceedings against which the Insured is entitled to be indemnified under any other insurance, but only to the extent that he is entitled to be and is so indemnified.

(iv) Claims or Disciplinary Proceedings against which the Insured is entitled to be indemnified under any other insurance, but only to the extent that he is entitled to be and is so indemnified.

(v) Claims or Disciplinary Proceedings arising out of any breach of any duty owed by the Insured as an employer to an employee, or as owner or occupier of any property.

(vi) Claims or Disciplinary Proceedings in respect of debts incurred by the Insured.

(vii) Claims or Disciplinary Proceedings in respect of any loss or damage directly or indirectly caused by ionising radiations or contamination by radioactivity from any nuclear fuel or from any nuclear waste from the combustion of nuclear fuel, or the radioactive, toxic, explosive or other hazardous properties of any explosive nuclear assembly or nuclear assembly or nuclear component thereof.

(viii) Claims or Disciplinary Proceedings arising out of any dispute between present or former members, pupils or Clerks or Chambers in respect of matters relating to or in any way connected with ownership, occupation, possession, management or administration of the Chambers or of any property used in or for the purposes of the Chambers or the Insured Practice.

(ix) Claims or Disciplinary Proceedings in respect of any liability arising directly or indirectly out of any association (including partnership) entered into with any lawyer (whether as permitted under the Overseas Practice Rules in the Code of Conduct or otherwise), save to the extent that in the opinion of the

Directors such liability results from the personal act or omission of the Insured and would otherwise fall within the provisions of these Terms of Cover.

(x) Claims or Disciplinary Proceedings in respect of any liability arising directly or indirectly out of any association (including partnership) entered into with any lawyer (whether as permitted under the Overseas Practice Rules in the Code of Conduct or otherwise), save to the extent that in the opinion of the Directors such liability results from the personal act or omission of the Insured and would otherwise fall within the provisions of these Terms of Cover.

(xi) Claims or Disciplinary Proceedings arising out of or in any way in connection with the supply of Legal Services as a Foreign Lawyer or European Lawyer, save to the extent specified in the Cover Note or any endorsement thereto.

(xii) Claims or Disciplinary Proceedings arising out of or in any way in connection with the provision of Legal Services in a system of law and/or jurisdiction in which the Insured is not authorised to provide Legal Services by:

(a) the Bar Council or any successor regulator to it; or

(b) any competent professional body; or

(c) any judicial or other body;

(xiii) Claims or Disciplinary Proceedings against a Registered European Lawyer arising out of or in any way in connection with the provision of Legal Services as a European Lawyer before he became a Registered European Lawyer, save to the extent specified in the Cover Note or any endorsement thereto.

(xiv) Claims or Disciplinary Proceedings arising out of or in any way connected with failure to comply with the Continuing Professional Development Regulations, the Practising Certificate Regulations, paragraph 204(b) of the Code of Conduct, paragraph 402.1 of the Code of Conduct or paragraph 402.2 of the Code of Conduct, including Disciplinary Proceedings for failing to respond to Disciplinary Proceedings for any of the foregoing.

(xv) Claims or Disciplinary Proceeding arising out of any criminal offence committed or allegedly committed by the Insured or out of an enquiry conducted by Her Majesty's Revenue and Customs into the Insured's tax or VAT affairs.

In relation to these exclusions, the Directors retain the power to sanction the funding of a defence. This power is contained in at clause 1.4 of the Terms of Cover. It is only in exceptional cases that the Directors will cover what is otherwise excluded. If a member wishes to make a request for support, he should give full written details of the basis upon which it is made, to the Directors, through the Managers.

Role of the Managers

Bar Mutual is a mutual set up by barristers for barristers and is not a commercial insurance company. Accordingly, the Managers are available to give advice on any issue, even if the subject matter is excluded from cover. They will also be able to provide contact details for BCAS and LCLCBA, where pro bono support may be available.

If the subject matter of the complaint is not excluded by virtue of Rule 10.1.2, legal costs incurred by a member will be recoverable only if they are incurred with the approval of the BMIF. Accordingly, it is important that the Managers are advised of the complaint at an early stage.

Immediate Action to be Taken

The importance of the initial response to the complaint cannot be over-emphasised. In many instances an appropriate response may persuade either the Complaints Commissioner or the Conduct and Complaints Committee to dismiss the complaint. Equally an inadequate or inappropriate response may make it more likely that the matter will be escalated to the Conduct and Complaints Committee who may decide that the complaint should be made the subject of disciplinary proceedings.

If it is not practical to respond to a complaint within the three week time limit laid down by the Bar Standards Board, an extension of time will normally be granted in response to a reasoned request. An extension should be applied for as soon as it is recognised that it will be required.

Contact Details

For further information and to notify Bar Mutual of a disciplinary complaint please contact the Managers of BMIF: 90 Fenchurch Street, London EC3M 4ST. Telephone: 020 7621 0405, Facsimile: 020 7283 5988

BMIF Forms

[2.100]

The following documents, produced by the Bar Mutual Indemnity Fund Limited, are set out below: Application for Membership and Insurance; Renewal of Cover Form; Renewal Form – Explanatory Notes; Allocation to Areas of Practice; Application Form for Increase in Cover; Notice of a Barrister's Moving; and Notice of a Barrister's Retirement.

BMIF Application Form

[2.101]

BAR MUTUAL

Bar Mutual Indemnity Fund Limited
90 Fenchurch Street
London EC3M 4ST
DX: CDE621
T +44 (0)20 7621 0405
F +44 (0)20 7283 5988
info@barmutual.co.uk
www.barmutual.co.uk

Application for Membership and Insurance

Please complete the form overleaf and return to:

Bar Mutual Indemnity Fund Limited
90 Fenchurch Street
London EC3M 4ST

DX: CDE621

This application form relates to your membership of Bar Mutual Indemnity Fund Limited and your professional indemnity cover for the current policy year, which ends 31st March.

A deductible of £350 will be applied in the event of a finding of professional misconduct and also in the case of successful wasted costs applications.

BAR MUTUAL IS MANAGED BY **THOMAS MILLER**

Bar Mutual Indemnity Fund Limited
Registered in England No. 2182018. Registered office as above
Authorised and regulated by the Financial Service Authority
Managers Bar Mutual Management Company
Registered in England No.2183269. Registered office as above
AF011009

1. Chambers Membership Number | _ _ _ _ / _ _ _ _
Bar Mutual will complete these boxes

2. Bar Council Membership Number | _ _ _ _ _
If unknown, please contact the Records Office on 020 7242 0934

3. Surname (Mr/Mrs/Miss/Ms)

4. First Name(s)

5. Address of Chambers

6. Head of Chambers

7. Inn

8. Year of Call

9. Date practice to commence | _ _ / _ _ / _ _ _ _

Please give the date you started practice in the chambers whether as a tenant or as a squatter, i.e. when you lost the protection of your pupil master's policy

10. If you intend to practice from Chambers at which there is no other practising barrister, please tick here. ☐

11. Total cover required.

Members will automatically receive basic cover of £500,000 as provided in the Code of Conduct. If you need a higher limit of cover, please tick the appropriate box below. The extra cost will be shown on your debit note and you may then decide whether to accept the quotation at a higher limit.

£500,000 automatically given	☐	£1,000,000	☐	£1,500,000	☐
£2,000,000	☐	£2,500,000	☐		

Additional cover £2,500,000 in excess of £2,500,000 ☐

I apply to become a member and agree to abide by the Rules of the Bar Mutual Indemnity Fund Limited. I declare that the information contained on this form is correct to the best of my knowledge and belief. I have notified the Managers or enclose notice herewith of any claims made against me or any intimation received from any person of any intention to make a claim against me.

Signed: ______________________ Date: __________

AF011009

BMIF Renewal of Cover Form 2014/15

[2.102]

BAR MUTUAL

Bar Mutual Indemnity Fund Limited
90 Fenchurch Street
London EC3M 4ST
DX: CDE621
T +44 (0)20 7621 0405
F +44 (0)20 7283 5988
info@barmutual.co.uk
www.barmutual.co.uk

Renewal of Cover for 2014/2015

Membership No:

2014

Dear Member

Please complete this form and submit it to the Managers.

If you are returning to practice please enter the date that your Practising Certificate has been re-activated from.

I apply to renew my insurance with Bar Mutual Indemnity Fund Limited. I declare that the information contained in this form is correct to the best of my knowledge and belief. I have notified the Managers, or enclose notice herewith, of any claims made against me or any intimation received from any person of any intention to make a claim against me.

If I have ticked box 2.8B and/or 9B I hereby authorise Bar Mutual to release to the brokers indicated details of my fee income, areas of practice and claims history, solely to enable them to obtain quotations from underwriters on my behalf.

Signed: Dated:

BAR MUTUAL
IS MANAGED
BY **THOMAS**
MILLER

Bar Mutual Indemnity Fund Limited. Registered in England No.2182018. Registered office as above.
Authorised by the Prudential Regulation Authority and regulated by the Financial Conduct Authority and Prudential Regulation Authority.
Managers: Bar Mutual Management Company.
Registered in England No.2183269. Registered office as above

1. **Gross fees received in the last calendar year (excluding VAT)**[1] £ | | A

2. **Indicate the limit of cover required**[2]

£500,000		2B	£1,000,000		3B	£1,500,000		4B
£2,000,000		5B	£2,500,000		6B			

You are encouraged to give serious consideration to purchasing cover in excess of £2.5m. The following brokers can assist you in this regard. If you would like us to send them the information they require to provide you with a quote, please tick the relevant boxes.

Vernon Taylor at TLO Insurance Services	020 7839 0472		8B
Robin Wilson at Lonmar Global Risks Ltd (formerly SBJ Ltd)	020 7204 3625		9B

3. Enter the percentage of your Gross Fee Income received from each area of practice, and the percentage of that income received from the Crown.[3] See enclosed table for assistance in allocating your fees to the correct area of practice. **Please use whole numbers - not decimals.**

AREA OF PRACTICE	% GFI	% Crown	CODE	AREA OF PRACTICE	% GFI	% Crown	CODE
Admiralty			C	Construction			R
Commercial[3D]			D	Parliamentary & Local Govt.			S
Financial Services[3E]			E	Intellectual Property			T
Criminal			FC	Planning			U
Professional Discipline			FD	Competition			V
Defamation			G	Chancery – Contentious			XC
Employment			H	Chancery – Non-Contentious			XD
European			I	Personal Injury [3YC]			YC
Family – Children			J	Professional Negligence [3YD]			YD
Family – Other			K	Other Common Law [3YE]			YE
Immigration			L	Arbitrator, Umpire, Mediator[3O]			O
Insolvency			M	Other : please specify [3Z]			Z
International Law			N	**REVENUE** [3R]			
L&T Non-Residential			PC	Crown			WD
L&T Residential			PD	Non-Crown – Contentious			WE
Licensing			Q	Non-Crown – Non-Contentious			WF

Percentage of total fees which is derived from International Practice [3I]		/

4. If you are interested in paying your premium in instalments, please tick[4] | | +

5. If you wish to apply for cover for practice as a Foreign or European Lawyer, please tick[5]. If you already have this cover, a separate renewal form will be issued to you | | *

6. If you undertake Public Access work, please indicate percentage of fees derived from this work in the last calendar year | | $

7. If you undertake Licensed Access work (Direct Professional Access and/or BarDIRECT), please indicate percentage of fees derived from this work in the last calendar year | | ^

BMIF Renewal Form Notes

[2.103]

BAR MUTUAL

Bar Mutual Indemnity Fund Limited
90 Fenchurch Street
London EC3M 4ST
DX: CDE621
T +44 (0)20 7621 0405
F +44 (0)20 7283 5988
info@barmutual.co.uk
www.barmutual.co.uk

Renewal Form – Explanatory Notes

Section 1 : Gross Fee Income

Your basic contribution for 2014/2015 is determined, as in previous years, by applying varying rates to the income derived from each area of practice. Please write in the first box on the form the total fees you received (your Gross Fee Income) from practice at the Bar (without VAT), during the last calendar year or as declared in your VAT returns for that year. A specific figure should be entered in the box, not, for example, "max". Please do not enter fees derived from work for which Bar Mutual does not offer cover.

Section 2 : Limit of Cover

Your limit of cover depends on the amount of your basic contribution and increases in steps. By paying an Optional Contribution, you may purchase cover up to a limit higher than that to which your Basic Contribution entitles you. For further information please view the Rating Schedule on Bar Mutual's website. If you would like to specify a higher minimum limit of cover, please tick the appropriate box 3B - 6B.

The Bar Mutual does not provide cover in excess of £2,500,000. You are strongly encouraged to give serious consideration to purchasing such cover. In order to assist barristers in obtaining higher cover, Bar Mutual has agreed with two brokers – TLO and LONMAR - that Bar Mutual will send details of a barrister's fee income, areas of practice and claims history to one or more of these firms. If you would like Bar Mutual to act for you in this way, please indicate to which broker(s) Bar Mutual is authorised to send details by ticking box 2, 8B and/or 9B. The broker(s) will then contact you direct.

In the event of a finding of professional misconduct, a deductible of £350 will be payable. A deductible of £350 will also be applied in the case of successful wasted costs applications.

Section 3 : Practice Profile

In this section, please break down your fees received into the most relevent areas of practice from the list and show the results as percentages in the column headed "% GFI" (gross fee income). The total should be 100%. **Please use whole numbers and do not use decimals.**

In the next column headed "% Crown", please record as a percentage *of the percentage declared against each individual area of practice, how much of your income in that area derives from instructions given* on behalf of the Crown by, for example, the Treasury Solicitor or any Central Government Department, including the Crown Prosecution Service and HMRC, where the client is the Crown or one of its manifestations. This does not include instructions on behalf of other national organisations nor on behalf of local government.

For example, if you have declared 25% of your Gross Fee Income against a particular area of practice, and all of that income derives from the Crown, enter 100% in the next column.

BAR MUTUAL IS MANAGED BY THOMAS MILLER

Bar Mutual Indemnity Fund Limited. Registered in England No.2182018. Registered office as above.
Authorised by the Prudential Regulation Authority and regulated by the Financial Conduct Authority and Prudential Regulation Authority.
Managers: Bar Mutual Management Company.
Registered in England No.2183269. Registered office as above.
RFN01022014

BAR MUTUAL

Your Clerk has a table which serves as a guide to the allocation of most types of work to the areas of practice and this is also available on the downloads section of the website. Without being exhaustive, it addresses the considerable uncertainty which still exists, particularly in those areas where enquiries to the Managers have been recorded in the past. The Managers are, of course, available to assist in cases of doubt. The following notes may further assist you.

3D Commercial – Fees in respect of work relating to civil and commercial proceedings in which fraud is alleged should be categorised as Commercial, **unless** the fraud allegations concern faked or exaggerated injuries or losses in personal injury proceedings. Fees for the latter type of work should continue to be categorised as Personal Injury.

3E Financial Services means advice given in relation to the Financial Services Act other than in the course of criminal proceedings which may very well be given in an otherwise commercial matter.

3R Revenue - Please split your revenue work between the three boxes (WD, WE and WF), clearly indicating the percentage received from Crown instructions, from Non-Crown instructions in contentious matters and from Non-Crown instructions in non-contentious matters.

If you have advised or drafted documents where the sole or predominant object of the matter is to mitigate liability to pay any tax (which includes any form of duty or levy imposed by any level of government), **the fees received for this work should be declared as Revenue: Non-Crown: Non-Contentious**. Examples of such work are:

- Instructions to chancery counsel to advise on and/or settle a will or deed of variation or trust instrument, where the sole or predominant objective of the client is to reduce liability for capital gains tax or inheritance tax;

- Instructions to company or commerical counsel to advise on and/or draft documentation for a possible corporate (or corporate group) reconstruction, merger or reorganisation, where the sole or predominant objective is to reduce liability for capital gains tax or corporation tax.

If you have advised on any matter in which one of the issues falling within the scope of your instructions concerns liability to pay any tax (which includes any form of duty or levy imposed by any level of government), **the fees received for this work must be apportioned between the appropriate Revenue: Non-Crown area of practice (depending on whether the matter is Contentious or Non-Contentious) and the other area of practice.** Examples of such work are:

- Advice on tax issues arising in ancilliary relief proceedings;

- Advice on stamp duty land tax issues in real estate or landlord and tenant matters (whether contentious or non-contentious);

- Advice on liability for income tax in employment matters.

Revenue: Non-Crown – Division between Contentious and Non-Contentious

Fees received in respect of the following work must be declared as **Revenue: Non-Crown - Contentious**

- All work related to advice on, preparation and progress of litigation against HMRC in relation to tax, including an appeal or application to either of the Tax Tribunals or any of the appellate courts, a reference to the European Court of Justice, and proceedings by way of judicial review. For the avoidance of doubt, this includes advice given to professional clients about the possibility of challenging HMRC's treatment of a past transaction prior to the identification of the lay clients in whose name any such challenge may be brought;

BAR MUTUAL

- Giving advice to a taxpayer in relation to the tax implications of transactions or events or profits or gains for periods or years of assessment which are past, and in relation to the tax treatment of which HMRC have indicated a contrary view to that put forward by the taxpayer; including the settlement of correspondence on behalf of the taxpayer, and the entering into negotiations with HMRC.

Fees received in respect of all other Revenue: Non Crown work must be declared as
Revenue: Non-Crown - Non-Contentious.

3YC 3YD & 3YE Common Law (Other) is divided into three.

"Personal Injury" work includes all income derived from cases in which damages for personal injury, fatal injury or illness are being claimed. Thus income from any case in which there is a claim for damages for personal injury should be declared against this area. *This includes claims for medical negligence even though there is a separate category for professional negligence.*

However, where a case involves a claim, for instance, against a solicitor for professional negligence, the income should be declared under the "Professional Negligence" area, even though the underlying matter may be related to personal injury. "Professional Negligence" therefore includes all cases where a professional is being sued for negligence or breach of duty other than medical negligence, and irrespective of the court in which the proceedings are brought or contemplated.

The remaining "Other Common Law" area includes all common law work which is not specifically addressed in this section or properly to be declared against another area of practice. The ratings for all three areas remain the same.

3O The Bar Mutual Terms of Cover automatically include cover for barristers acting as Arbitrators, Umpires or Mediators. If you do not wish to have this cover please do not declare any income for this part of your practice in Box 1 and leave this box empty. If, however, you want cover but have not earnt any fees from this area during the calender year – simply place a tick in the box.

3Z If you are unable to allocate fee income to any of the areas of practice, please use this space but describe the work from which the income is derived. The Managers will then try to allocate the income to the appropriate area of practice. If this is not possible you should be aware that the rate for this "area" is 2%.

3/ Please indicate the percentage of your total fees which arises from any form of international work in respect of which fees are not subject to VAT. This information is for Bar Council statistical purposes and not for rating and the Bar Council will be supplied with a summary only, thereby preserving individual confidentiality.

Section 4 : Payment of premium by instalments

Bar Mutual has arrangements for payments to be made via six monthly instalments by means of direct debit. Please note that each barrister will need to enter into a credit agreement with Premium Credit Limited and there will be an additional charge for this facility. For those members who have already elected to pay by this method, their credit agreement will continue unless Bar Mutual and PCL are advised otherwise.

Section 5 : Cover for practise as a Foreign or European Lawyer

Please tick this box ONLY if you are (1) qualified to practise in another system of law and (2) wish to apply for cover for your practice in that other system. You will then receive a separate application form. Those members who have already applied for Foreign Cover will be sent a further renewal form to complete.

BAR MUTUAL

You do NOT need to apply for separate cover in another common law jurisdiction as a Practising Barrister or Registered European Lawyer if your qualification as such enables you to practise in that jurisdiction (subject to any formal local requirements in that jurisdiction as to call or certification).

Sections 6 and 7 : Public and Licensed Access Work

If you have received fees via Public or Licensed Access Work (Licensed Access combines "BarDIRECT" and "Direct Professional Access") please enter the percentage of those fees in the relevant boxes.

BMIF Areas of Practice

[2.104]

BAR MUTUAL

Bar Mutual Indemnity Fund Limited
90 Fenchurch Street
London EC3M 4ST
DX: CDE621
T +44 (0)20 7621 0405
F +44 (0)20 7283 5988
info@barmutual.co.uk
www.barmutual.co.uk

Allocation to Areas of Practice

The following table is designed to give further guidance on the allocation of fee income to areas of practice. These guidelines are not intended to be exclusive, nor will the allocation in the table always be appropriate for every individual case which falls within the general description in the right hand column. The appropriate test is the underlying subject matter of the work from which the income is derived, and not the court or other forum for proceedings, although this may assist in identifying the appropriate allocation. The identity of the client is not relevant (save for the purposes of the column on the renewal form headed ("% CROWN").

Please do not hesitate to consult the Managers for specific guidance in the case of any doubt as to the appropriate allocation.

	AREA OF PRACTICE	INCLUDES
C	ADMIRALTY	
D	COMMERCIAL	Aviation Carriage of goods Commodities Financial contracts Industrial contracts Information Technology / Computers Insurance/reinsurance Media Satellite and telecommunications Shipping
E	FINANCIAL SERVICES	
F	CRIME	Coroners' inquests Extradition Fraud Race relations Trading standards
FX	PROFESSIONAL DISCIPLINE	Disciplinary tribunals
G	DEFAMATION	
H	EMPLOYMENT	Contracts and entitlements Discrimination Dismissal Health and safety at work Industrial law / trade unions
I	EUROPEAN	EU law
J	FAMILY – CHILDREN	Care orders Custody
K	FAMILY – OTHER	Ancillary relief Divorce/cohabitation break-up
L	IMMIGRATION	Deportation
M	INSOLVENCY	Directors' disqualification
N	INTERNATIONAL	Public international law

BAR MUTUAL IS MANAGED BY **THOMAS MILLER**

Bar Mutual Indemnity Fund Limited. Registered in England No.2182018. Registered office as above.
Authorised by the Prudential Regulation Authority and regulated by the Financial Conduct Authority and Prudential Regulation Authority.
Managers: Bar Mutual Management Company.
Registered in England No.2183269. Registered office as above.
1 of 2 / AoP01022014

PART II QUALIFYING AS A BARRISTER AND ENTERING PRACTICE

BAR MUTUAL

PC PD	LANDLORD & TENANT (NON-RESIDENTIAL) or LANDLORD & TENANT (RESIDENTIAL) as appropriate	Agricultural leases Commercial leases Determination Domestic leases Forfeiture Leasehold enfranchisement Rent review	
Q	LICENSING		
R	CONSTRUCTION	Building disputes	Construction law
S	PARLIAMENTARY AND LOCAL GOVERNMENT	Administrative law Constitutional law Education law Homelessness Local authority Local government Judicial review Parliamentary	Public inquiries Public law Rights/duties of Local Authorities re: Housing policy Social security Health
T	INTELLECTUAL PROPERTY	Patents and copyright Performing rights	Registered designs Trademarks
U	PLANNING		
V	COMPETITION	Competition law Monopolies/mergers	
W	REVENUE Crown Non-Crown – Contentious Non-Crown – Non-Contentious as appropriate	Capital gains tax Income tax Inheritance tax VAT Restitution claims against HMRC	
XC XD	CHANCERY CONTENTIOUS (ie litigation) or CHANCERY NON-CONTENTIOUS as appropriate	Boundary disputes Charities Company Easement/covenants Mineral rights Partnership Wills, probate, trusts	
YC	PERSONAL INJURY	Fatal injury Industrial disease	Medical negligence Personal injury
YD	PROFESSIONAL NEGLIGENCE	Accountants Architects Barristers	Solicitors Surveyors
YE	OTHER COMMON LAW	Actions against the police Consumer contracts Consumer credit Costs litigation/Law of Costs Domestic insurance Negligence - (other than professional) Private nuisance Public nuisance Road accidents (non-injury)	
O	ARBITRATOR OR UMPIRE OR MEDIATOR	Acting as Arbitrator, Umpire or Mediator Chair of enquiry Inspector, examiner	

Please note - "OTHER"

Whilst Bar Mutual will try to allocate any declarations under "other" to the appropriate area, if this is not possible please note that the applicable rating here is 2.0%.

February 2014

2 of 2 / AoP01022014

BMIF Application Form for Increase in Cover

[2.105]

BAR MUTUAL

Bar Mutual Indemnity Fund Limited
90 Fenchurch Street
London EC3M 4ST
DX: CDE621
T +44 (0)20 7621 0405
F +44 (0)20 7283 5988
info@barmutual.co.uk
www.barmutual.co.uk

Application for Increase of Cover

Name: Membership No.:

Chambers' Address:

Present limit of cover: £

I wish my Limit of Cover to be increased to: £

With effect from (date):

I have notified the Managers, or enclose notice herewith, of any claims made against me or any intimation received from any person of any intention to make a claim against me.

Signed: Dated:

Please return your completed form to 'The Managers' at the above address or fax number, or by email to info@barmutual.co.uk

BAR MUTUAL
IS MANAGED
BY **THOMAS MILLER**

BMIF Notice of a Barrister's Moving

[2.106]

BAR MUTUAL

Bar Mutual Indemnity Fund Limited
90 Fenchurch Street
London EC3M 4ST
DX: CDE621
T +44 (0)20 7621 0405
F +44 (0)20 7283 5988
info@barmutual.co.uk
www.barmutual.co.uk

Notice of a Barrister's Moving

Name: Membership No.:

Chambers barrister is leaving:

Address:

Head of Chambers:

Date of move:

Chambers the barrister is joining:

Address:

Head of Chambers:

New Chambers telephone number:

Signed: Dated:

Please return your completed form to 'The Managers' at the above address or fax number, or by email to info@barmutual.co.uk

BAR MUTUAL IS MANAGED BY **THOMAS MILLER**

Bar Mutual Indemnity Fund Limited. Registered in England No.2182018. Registered office as above.
Bar Mutual Indemnity Fund Limited is Authorised and Regulated by the Financial Services Authority.
Managers: Bar Mutual Management Company. Registered in England No.2183269. Registered office as above.
NBM010610

BMIF Notice of a Barrister's Retirement

[2.107]

BAR MUTUAL

Bar Mutual Indemnity Fund Limited
90 Fenchurch Street
London EC3M 4ST
DX: CDE621
T +44 (0)20 7621 0405
F +44 (0)20 7283 5988
info@barmutual.co.uk
www.barmutual.co.uk

Notice of a Barrister's Retirement

Name: Membership No.:

Chambers:

Address:

Address for correspondence:

Date of retirement:

Signed: Dated:

Please return your completed form to 'The Managers' at the above address or fax number, or by email to info@barmutual.co.uk

BAR MUTUAL IS MANAGED BY **THOMAS MILLER**

Bar Mutual Indemnity Fund Limited. Registered in England No.2182018. Registered office as above.
Bar Mutual Indemnity Fund Limited is Authorised and Regulated by the Financial Services Authority.
Managers: Bar Mutual Management Company. Registered in England No.2183269. Registered office as above.
NBR010610

BMIF Rating Schedule 2014/2015

[2.107a]

BAR MUTUAL

Bar Mutual Indemnity Fund Limited
90 Fenchurch Street
London EC3M 4ST
DX: CDE621
T +44 (0)20 7621 0405
F +44 (0)20 7283 5988
info@barmutual.co.uk
www.barmutual.co.uk

Rating Schedule 2014/2015

TABLE 1

The following rates are applied to the income declared in each area of practice to assess Basic Contributions:

Areas of Practice	Rate
Crime	0.15%
Family – Children	0.15%
Arbitrator, Umpire or Mediator	0.25%
Immigration	0.25%
International Law	0.25%
Parliamentary & Local Government	0.25%
Professional Discipline	0.25%
Admiralty	0.50%
European	0.50%
Insolvency	0.50%
Intellectual Property	0.50%
Competition	0.50%
Revenue – Crown	0.50%
Employment	0.70%
Licensing	0.70%
Commercial	0.90%
Construction	0.90%
Family – Other	0.90%
Financial Services	0.90%
Planning	0.90%
Revenue – Non-Crown Instructions – Contentious	**0.90%**
Landlord & Tenant – Residential	1.50%
Personal Injury	1.50%
Professional Negligence	1.50%
Other Common Law	1.50%
Foreign Law	1.50%
Other	2.00%
Chancery – Contentious	2.00%
Chancery – Non-contentious	2.00%
Defamation	2.00%
Landlord & Tenant – Non-residential	2.00%
Revenue – Non-Crown Instructions – Non-Contentious	**6.00%**

BAR MUTUAL
IS MANAGED
BY **THOMAS**
MILLER

Bar Mutual Indemnity Fund Limited, Registered in England No.2182018. Registered office as above.
Authorised by the Prudential Regulation Authority and regulated by the Financial Conduct Authority and Prudential Regulation Authority.
1 of 2 / RS01022014

BAR MUTUAL

There are two rating changes this year, both in respect of Revenue work. Revenue – Non-Crown – Contentious has decreased from 1.50% to 0.9% and Revenue – Non-Crown – Non-Contentious has increased from 5.5% to 6.0%.

The deferral remains at 20%. The minimum premium has increased to £110 plus insurance premium tax. The income cap remains £1m.

TABLE 2

Limit of Cover is determined by the amount of the Basic Contribution, as follows:

Basic Contribution	Limit of Cover
£100 - £399	£500,000
£400 - £599	£1,000,000
£600 - £799	£1,500,000
£800 - £999	£2,000,000
£1,000 plus	£2,500,000

TABLE 3

A Member may, by payment of an Optional Contribution, purchase cover up to a limit higher than that to which his Basic Contribution entitles him or her. For a Member wishing so to do, the cost of increasing the limit of cover to the next band of cover will be the fixed sum referred to in the table below or the difference between the barrister's Basic Contribution and the minimum premium for that band, whichever is the lesser, with each additional band of cover being charged at the relevant fixed sum.

Cover Required	Extra Premium
£500,000	£100
£1,000,000	£100
£1,500,000	£100
£2,000,000	£100
£2,500,000	*

* BMIF is not providing cover in excess of £2,500,000 – but will forward Members' forms onto TLO and/or Lonmar who will be able to provide quotes.

2 of 2 / RS01022014

PART II QUALIFYING AS A BARRISTER AND ENTERING PRACTICE

Section 2: Where can I get Further Support?

The Four Inns, the Circuits and the Specialist Bar Associations

[2.108]

Having joined Chambers as a new pupil there remains a wealth of further sources and resources to call upon for general assistance in the preparation of becoming a barrister. Clearly, the pupil's Pupil Master will be the first port of call, but beyond that the Bar offers a wide range of extra-curricular activities, support and education and advice through:

(a) The Inns of Court;

(b) the Circuits, and

(c) The Specialist Bar Associations.

Inns of Court

[2.109]

There are four Inns of Court: Lincoln's Inn, Middle Temple, Inner Temple and Gray's Inn.

The Inns provide support for barristers and student barristers through a range of educational activities, lunching and dining facilities, access to common rooms and gardens, and provision of various grants and scholarships.

One of the key functions of the Inns is their responsibility for calling barristers to the Bar. Anyone wishing to train for the Bar must join one of the Inns and it is the Inns alone which have the power to call a student to the Bar. Alongside this responsibility, the Inns also have a role in administering disciplinary tribunals to deal with more serious complaints against barristers.

Students need to join an Inn before commencing the BVC. The closing date for applications to all four of the Inns is 31 May of the year you intend to start.

Other Careers Advice

[2.110]

The Inns also offer students a range of other services including Pupillage Advice, Mentoring Schemes, Mock Interviews Programmes, Mini-Pupillages and Court Pupillages.

Once in Pupillage, the Inns offer training programmes in support of the professional requirement of the Bar Council by which all pupils have to undergo a total of 12 hours of advocacy training in order to obtain a practising certificate and in support of barristers' obligations for continuing professional development.

Further Information

[2.111]

Further information may be obtained direct from the Inns themselves:

Lincoln's Inn:

The Treasury Office
Lincoln's Inn
London WC2A 3TL

Tel: 020 7405 1393
Fax: 020 7831 1839

http://www.lincolnsinn.org.uk/

Middle Temple:

Treasury Office
Middle Temple Lane
London EC4Y 9AT

Tel: 020 7427 4800
Fax: 020 7427 4801

http://www.middletemple.org.uk/

Inner Temple:

Treasury Office
Inner Temple
London EC4Y 7HL

Tel: 020 7797 8250
Fax: 020 7797

http://www.innertemple.org.uk/

Gray's Inn:

Treasury Office
8 South Square
London WC1R 5ET

Tel: 020 7458 7800
Fax: 020 7458 7801

http://www.graysinn.info/

The Circuits

[2.112]

England and Wales is divided into regions or "Circuits" for the purposes of the administration of justice. The Circuit system, which is overseen by the Ministry of Justice, has a long history.

The "Circuits" also form the basis for administration of the Bar in England and Wales. The Circuit Bars provide important sources of support, advice and representation for barristers practising in those areas. They provide a range of services to the members in their respective geographical areas, maintain lines of communication with all parts of the legal system, including the court administration, and are represented on the Bar Council through the Circuit Leaders. They liaise closely with the local court service, Crown Prosecution Service and other bodies as well as providing important training and social events for barristers.

In addition, the Bar of England and Wales has established the European Circuit of the Bar of England and Wales. The European Circuit aims to bring together barristers working in Europe, whether in chambers or employed by European institutions or companies, barristers of England and Wales whose practice includes work in European and international law, and members of other European bars who are practising in the UK under the provisions of the EU Establishment and Services Directive.

Specialist Bar Associations

[2.113]

For the pupil in his second six and for the newly appointed tenant of chambers an interest is likely to be taken at an early stage in a particular specialism. The following is a list of the Specialist Bar Associations that will be able to provide help and assistance, continuing education and development in the barrister's chosen field. Barristers can be members of more than one Association at any given time.

Administrative Law Bar Association

[2.114]

Members provide specialist advice to public bodies on their duties and powers and act as specialist advocates for and against public authorities, including the government[1].

1 Further information can be obtained from the Administrative Law Bar Association website: http://www.adminlaw.org.uk/

Bar Association for Commerce, Finance and Industry

[2.115]

BACFI[1] represents the interests of employed barristers providing legal services in a commercial environment and also "non-practising" barristers. Members also include self-employed barristers, students, overseas lawyers working in the UK and retired barristers.

1 Further information can be obtained from the BACFI website: http://www.bacfi.org/

Bar Association for Local Government and the Public Service

[2.116]

The Bar Association for Local Government and the Public Service[1] seeks to serve and protect the best interests of all barristers employed in local government and the public service. The Association is a direct successor of the Society of Local Government Barristers, which had been in existence since about 1945, and of the Bar Association for Local Government, which had been formed in 1977. Membership (currently about 100 members) is open to all barristers and bar students employed in the public sector (including those in the civil service and in the armed forces).

1 Further information can be obtained from the Bar Association for Local Government and the Public Service website: http://www.balgps.org.uk/

Bar European Group

[2.117]

The Bar European Group[1] is the Specialist Bar Association for European Community Law and European Human Rights Law. Membership includes all specialist Community law barristers, advising and appearing before the Luxembourg Court and the Commission.

1 Further information can be obtained from the Bar European Group website: http://www.bareuropeangroup.com/

Chancery Bar Association

[2.118]

Work includes property, trust and connected tax matters; litigation, drafting, and advice covering a wide field of property, business and commercial disputes; also revenue or patent work[1].

1 Further information can be obtained from the Chancery Bar Association website: http://www.chba.org.uk/

Commercial Bar Association

[2.119]

Members practise in the Commercial Court and in Commercial matters in other Tribunals and abroad. The Commercial Bar Association[1] ("COMBAR") was founded in July 1989 to represent and promote the interests of commercial barristers serving the specialist needs of international commerce, including international commercial litigation and arbitration. Its membership comprises leading commercial chambers and individual practitioners at the Commercial Bar whose expertise extends across the fields of banking, mergers and acquisitions, insurance, reinsurance, financial services, shipping and international trade, commodity transactions, professional negligence, competition law, insolvency, European Community matters and private and public international law.

COMBAR represents its members on the Bar Council, liaises with other Specialist Bar Associations on matters of common interest, comments on proposed legislation affecting the commercial field, contributes to the debate concerning the reform of the English civil justice system and offers a continuing programme of lectures and seminars and links with International Bar Associations. An annual directory is published in January. COMBAR actively encourages close working links with lawyers practising in other jurisdictions, particularly in Europe, North American the Commonwealth and the Far East.

1 Further information can be obtained from the COMBAR website: http://www.combar.com/

Criminal Bar Association

[2.120]

The Criminal Bar Association[1] exists to represent the views of the practising members of the Criminal Bar in England and Wales. Members cover all criminal cases plus extradition and human rights.

1 Further information can be obtained from the Criminal Bar Association website: http://www.criminalbar.com/

Employment Law Bar Association

[2.121]

A forum of consultation for barristers who work in employment law, the Employment Law Bar Association ("ELBA") was formed in 1994 and represents and supports UK barristers working in employment law[1].

In addition to acting as a forum for its members to be consulted by the government and other organisations, ELBA supports its members through regular meetings, dinners and other services.

1 Further information can be obtained from the ELBA website: http://www.elba.org.uk/

Family Law Bar Association

[2.122]

The Family Law Bar Association[1] ("FLBA") is a large and thriving Association with nearly 2,000 barrister members. It holds regular conferences, meeting and social events throughout the country, frequently in partnership with the Solicitors Family Law Association and often organised through its active regional membership which has permanent representatives in all the main Bar and Court Centres.

Since 1992, it has published annually 'At a Glance', a highly successful ready reckoner containing essential material and tables for use in financial cases. It has also been associated with the publication and computer program on the Child Support Acts, Child's Pay.

The Association produces a newsletter, Family Affairs, to keep members up to date and informed about events around the country and the more important changes in the law. It is circulated to every member and to the judiciary who hear family cases.

The Association plays an important consultative role with the Lord Chancellor's Department, the Law Commission and in all other areas of family law reform and practice..

1 Further information can be obtained from the FLBA website: http://www.flba.co.uk/

Intellectual Property Association

[2.123]

The Intellectual Property Bar Association[1] ('IPBA'), formerly called the Patent Bar Association, is the specialist Bar Association for barristers practising intellectual property law (intellectual property is a generic term which includes patents, registered trade marks, passing off, copyright, registered and unregistered design rights, performers' rights, trade secrets and breach of confidence).

Members of the IPBA carry out work in the whole range of intellectual property litigation, namely: patents, trade marks, copyright, registered and unregistered design rights, passing off and confidential information. Members of the IPBA also commonly advise in technically based commercial litigation and on areas of European law, especially regarding competition. Many members of the IPBA also have scientific qualifications.

1 Further information can be obtained from the IPBA website: http://www.ipba.co.uk/

London Common Law and Commercial Bar Association

[2.124]

London Common Law and Commercial Bar Association ("LCLCBA") members practise in common law, commercial, parliamentary, intellectual property, revenue, planning or rating matters.

1 Further information can be obtained from the LCLCBA website: http://www.lclcba.com/

The Parliamentary Bar Mess

[2.125]

The Parliamentary Bar Mess is an association of barristers who, as part of their practice at the Bar, specialise in the conduct of private and hybrid bill proceedings before Select Committees of both Houses of Parliament. Members are instructed normally (but not exclusively) by Parliamentary Agents either to act on behalf of the promoter of a bill or on behalf of petitioners against it.

Personal Injuries Bar Association

[2.126]

Personal Injuries Bar Association[1] is the specialist bar association for barristers who practise in the field of personal injuries.

1 Further information can be obtained from the Personal Injuries Bar Association website: http://www.piba.org.uk/

Planning and Environmental Bar Association

[2.127]

The Association[1] aims to provide a professional organisation for barristers in independent practice in the field of local government, Planning and Environmental law; to represent their views as and when appropiate within the framework for the government of the Bar of England and Wales; to provide opportunities to meet and discuss matters of interest to those barristers; and to do anything which may be conductive to or to facilitate such objectives.

1 Further information can be obtained from the Planning and Environmental Bar Association website: http://www.peba.info/

Professional Negligence Bar Association

[2.128]

Members cover medical, financial, construction and legal professional negligence[1].

1 Further information can be obtained from the Planning and Environmental Bar Association website: http://www.pnba.co.uk/

Property Bar Association

[2.129]

The Property Bar Association[1] is the professional body for Barristers in England & Wales who are able to certify in writing that not less than half of the matters that they deal with concern property or property-related work.

1 Further information can be obtained from the Property Bar Association website: http://www.propertybar.org.uk/

Revenue Bar Association

[2.130]

Members of the Revenue Bar Association[1] offer advice in relation to all taxes and advocacy in tax disputes.

1 Further information can be obtained from the Revenue Bar Association website: http://www.revenue-bar.org/

Technology and Construction Bar Association

[2.131]

The Technology and Construction Bar Association ("TECBAR")[1] is the specialist Bar Association for employed or self-employed barristers who practise in the London or provincial Technology and Construction Court or before adjudicators, arbitrators and other tribunals.

1 Further information can be obtained from the TECBAR website: http://www.tecbar.org/

Part III
In Practice

Section 1: Accepting Instructions
General Principles

Acceptance of Instructions and the 'Cab-rank rule'[1]

[3.1]

The fundamental principle enshrined in the Cab-rank rule is that a barrister who receives instructions from a professional client and the instructions are appropriate taking into account the experience, seniority and/or field of practice then subject to the exceptions below the barrister must accept the instructions irrespective of:

(a) the identity of the *client*;

(b) the nature of the case to which the *instructions* relate;

(c) whether the *client* is paying privately or is publicly funded; and

(d) any belief or opinion which you may have formed as to the character, reputation, cause, conduct, guilt or innocence of the *client*.

1 See rC29 of the Handbook para **[1.18]** above.

Exceptions to the Cab-rank Principle

[3.2]

The cab rank Rule C29 does not apply if:

(1) you are required to refuse to accept the *instructions* pursuant to Rule C21 (see below); or

(2) accepting the *instructions* would require you or the named *authorised individual* to do something other than in the course of their ordinary working time or to cancel a commitment already in their diary; or

(3) the potential liability for professional negligence in respect of the particular matter could exceed the level of professional indemnity insurance which is reasonably available and likely to be available in the market for you to accept; or

(4) you are a Queen's Counsel, and the acceptance of the *instructions* would require you to act without a junior in circumstances where you reasonably consider that the interests of the *client* require that a junior should also be instructed; or

(5) accepting the *instructions* would require you to do any *foreign work*; or

(6) accepting the *instructions* would require you to act for a *foreign lawyer* (other than a *European lawyer,* a lawyer from a country that is a member of EFTA, a *solicitor* or *barrister* of Northern Ireland or a *solicitor* or advocate under the law of Scotland); or

(7) the professional client:

 (a) is not accepting liability for your fees; or

 (b) is named on the List of Defaulting Solicitors; or

 (c) is instructing you as a lay *client* and not in their capacity as a professional *client*; or

(8) you have not been offered a proper fee for your services (except that you shall not be entitled to refuse to accept *instructions* on this ground if you have not made or responded to any fee proposal within a reasonable time after receiving the *instructions*); or

(9) except where you are to be paid directly by (i) the *Legal Aid Agency* as part of the Community Legal Service or the Criminal Defence Service or (ii) the Crown Prosecution Service:

 (a) your fees have not been agreed (except that you shall not be entitled to refuse to accept *instructions* on this ground if you have not taken reasonable steps to agree fees within a reasonable time after receiving the *instructions*);

 (b) having required your fees to be paid before you accept the *instructions*, those fees have not been paid;

 (c) accepting the *instructions* would require you to act other than on (A) the Standard Contractual Terms for the Supply of Legal Services by Barristers to Authorised Persons 2012 as published on the *Bar Council's* website; or (B) if you publish standard terms of work, on those standard terms of work.

Rule C21 – accepting instructions

You must not accept *instructions* to act in a particular matter if:

(1) due to any existing or previous *instructions* you are not able to fulfil your obligation to act in the best interests of the prospective *client*; or

(2) there is a conflict of interest between your own personal interests and the interests of the prospective *client* in respect of the particular matter; or

(3) there is a conflict of interest between the prospective *client* and one or more of your former or existing *clients* in respect of the particular matter unless all of the *clients* who have an interest in the particular matter give their informed consent to your acting in such circumstances; or

(4) there is a real risk that information confidential to another former or existing *client*, or any other person to whom you owe duties of confidence, may be relevant to the matter, such that if, obliged to maintain confidentiality, you could not act in the best interests of the prospective *client,* and the former or existing *client* or person to whom you owe that duty does not give informed consent to disclosure of that confidential information; or

(5) your instructions seek to limit your ordinary authority or discretion in the conduct of proceedings in *court*; or

(6) your instructions require you to act other than in accordance with law or with the provisions of this *Handbook*; or

(7) you are not authorised and/or otherwise accredited to perform the work required by the relevant *instruction*; or

(8) you are not competent to handle the particular matter or otherwise do not have enough experience to handle the matter; or

(9) you do not have enough time to deal with the particular matter, unless the circumstances are such that it would nevertheless be in the *client's* best interests for you to accept; or

(10) there is a real prospect that you are not going to be able to maintain your independence.

Acceptance of Instructions in Criminal Cases

Refusing work on the basis of fees

[3.3]

The purpose of the following guidance is to draw barristers' attention to issues relating to refusal or wok by members of the criminal Bar on grounds relating to fees. It applies to all self-employed criminal barristers. It was issued by the Professional Practice Committee in September 2005 but revised in January 2014. Please note that this is not "guidance" for the purposes of the BSB Handbook 16.4.

Professional Practice Committee Guidance

[3.4]–[3.9]

General approach

1. If you are a self-employed barrister, then the "Cab-rank" rule (BSB Handbook rC29) obliges you to accept instructions if they are appropriate taking into account your experience, seniority and field of practice, subject to the exceptions in the BSB Handbook rC30.
2. Accordingly, unless one of the exceptions in the BSB Handbook rC30 applies, you must accept instructions if the BSB Handbook rC29 requires you to do so.
3. Similarly, the BSB Handbook rC28 requires you not to withhold services or permit your services to be withheld (e.g. by your clerk) on various grounds relating to the nature of the case, the client or the source of financial support. As regards the last of those grounds, the BSB Handbook rC28.3 prohibits you from doing this on any ground relating to the source of any financial support which may properly be given to the prospective client for the proceedings in question, and the BSB Handbook gC88 makes clear that this includes a refusal on the ground that support may be given to the prospective client as part of the Community Legal Service or Criminal Defence Service.
4. One of the exceptions to the Cab Rank rule is where you have not been offered a proper fee for the required services (BSB Handbook rC30.8), although this exception does not apply if you have not made or responded to any fee proposal within a reasonable time after receiving the instructions. A prompt decision is necessary.
5. The BSB Handbook gC90 provides that, in determining whether or not a fee is proper for the purposes of the BSB Handbook rC30.2, regard shall be had to the following:

   (a) the complexity, length and difficulty of the case;

   (b) your ability, experience and seniority; and

(c) the expenses which you will incur.

6. With effect from 6th January 2014, the BSB Handbook no longer deems any fee to be, or not to be, a proper fee.

7. In deciding in any particular case whether a fee is "proper", you must consider two questions:

   (a) whether you in good faith regards the fee as proper; and

   (B) if in good faith you do not regard the fee as proper, whether you are acting reasonably and justifiably in reaching that decision.

8. Whether a fee is proper will vary from case to case.

9. If you are considering refusing instructions in a type of case for which the fees payable have actually been reduced since you last accepted a case of that type, then you are unlikely to be vulnerable without more to an allegation that you are in breach of the BSB Handbook in declining affected work after that date. But you will need to consider whether the reduced fees are proper fees.

10. On the other hand, if you are considering refusing instructions in a type of case for which the fees payable have not been reduced since you last accepted a case of that type, then it will obviously be less easy to demonstrate that an unreduced fee is not a proper fee. The tests set out above must be applied carefully in each case before you make a decision to refuse such work in any particular case.

Return of instructions/brief that you have already accepted where fees are later reduced

11. Where you have already accepted a brief or instructions, and the fee rates payable to you are reduced subsequently, then you will need to consider BSB Handbook rC26 to rC28. These lay down when you can, and when you cannot, return instructions which have already been accepted. More widely, in deciding what approach to take, you will need to focus on the BSB Handbook CD1 (duty to the court in the administration of justice), CD3 (to act with honesty and integrity) and CD5 (not behaving in a way which is likely to diminish the trust and confidence which the public places in you or in the profession).

12. If what has happened is that the basis on which you are to be paid has been changed fundamentally since you accepted the instructions, then the BSB Handbook gC87 will be of particular relevance. This provides as follows:

    "If a fundamental change is made to the basis of your remuneration, you should treat such a change as though your original instructions have been withdrawn by the client and replaced by an offer of new instructions on different terms."

13. The BSB Handbook gC87.1–87.3 goes on to explain that you must then judge the offer of new instructions afresh in accordance with the BSB Handbook. Thus, if the fee is not a proper fee for the purposes of the BSB Handbook rC30.8 (as explained above), then you may decline to accept the brief, subject to the qualification identified in paragraphs 15 to 18 below.

14. The BSB Handbook gC87.4 also states that in declining to accept the "new" instructions in those circumstances, you will not be regarded as returning the instructions, as withdrawing from the case, or as ceasing to act, for the purposes of the BSB Handbook rC25 and rC26 (the rules ordinarily governing such matters). It explains that this is because the previous instructions have been withdrawn by the client.

Qualifications on the current BSB guidance

15. Although paragraphs 11 to 14 above reflect the existing guidance in the BSB Handbook, they now need to be qualified.

16. In its policy statement published on 25 November 2013 in relation to Very High Cost Cases in crime, the Bar Standards Board said this, with reference to the guidance on which those paragraphs are based:

    "… the BSB is minded to review this guidance, in order to ensure that the public interest is adequately protected in circumstances where the person whom the barrister represents is not himself responsible for adversely altering the basis of the barrister's engagement and where exercising any right to withdraw would be disproportionate in view of the degree of prejudice to that person and/or to the administration of justice."

    In particular, it will be clear from the discussion of the BSB's approach to VHCCs, above, that a critical element is the fact that transitional arrangements are in place which protect the interests of consumers and the administration of justice. In relation to other types of legally aided cases, where no such transitional arrangements have been proposed, there will be a risk to consumers and the administration of justice if barristers were to treat themselves as free to withdraw from an ongoing case regardless of how serious and disruptive the consequences may be for the client and for others involved in the trial, for example, withdrawing mid-trial. The BSB believes that it may be in the public interest to require barristers in these situations to consider a number of factors and assess the proportionality of ceasing to act, in order to protect the interests of consumers and the wider regulatory objectives. The BSB is therefore urgently considering revised guidance on the rules relating to withdrawal of instructions, clarifying the relationship of those rules to the rules defining a barrister's obligations to the client and the court. In the meantime, barristers are reminded that they must reconcile any right to withdraw, because of a change in terms effected by the Ministry of Justice, with their professional obligations towards the individual whom they represent, who is not responsible for that change. The BSB will consult fully in the New Year on the updated guidance. That consultation will not take place until after the launch of the new Handbook on 6 January."

17. The Bar Council will respond to any such consultation; but in the meantime, you should take account of this statement by the BSB, particularly the passage we have underlined, in considering what the Core Duties require of you, and in reaching any decision to return instructions in a situation to which the statement applies.

18. If and when any revised guidance is published by the BSB, then that will supersede the current guidance, and paragraphs 12 to 14 above may no longer be accurate.

The position of pupils and pupil supervisors

19. In the context of the above guidance, you are reminded that:

    (a) A barrister who is a pupil supervisor with a pupil must not allow any decisions with regard to the acceptance of new instructions to affect or disrupt the pupillage training which the pupil supervisor is obliged to give.

    (b) Whatever decisions may be taken, the pupil supervisor remains under an obligation to ensure that the pupil receives the required training so that the pupil can in turn apply themselves diligently to the pupillage and properly complete the checklist and of course the pupillage.

    (c) Similarly, all members of Chambers will be obliged to ensure that, if any pupil supervisor in chambers makes a decision to refuse work, arrangements are in place which allow pupils to be properly trained. This flows from the obligation on all members of Chambers to take reasonable steps to ensure that proper arrangements are made in their Chambers for dealing with pupils and pupillage (BSB Handbook rC89.4). The steps required by each member of Chambers will depend on the circumstances, including the internal arrangements within Chambers (BSB Handbook rC90). You should also note that one of the outcomes provided for under the Code is that all pupils must be treated fairly (oC29).

    (d) Pupils have a legitimate right to proper training irrespective of any such decisions which a pupil supervisor may take, and that right should be fully recognised and respected, regardless of any steps which may be taken over the acceptance or refusal of work.

20. The respective duties of pupils and pupil supervisors are set out in the BSB Handbook rQ38 and rQ54 respectively.

Important notice

This document has been prepared by the Bar Council to assist barristers on matters of professional conduct and ethics. It is not "guidance" for the purposes of the BSB Handbook I6.4, and neither the BSB nor a disciplinary tribunal nor the Legal Ombudsman is bound by any views or advice expressed in it. It does not comprise – and cannot be relied on as giving – legal advice. It has been prepared in good faith, but neither the Bar Council nor any of the individuals responsible for or involved in its preparation accept any responsibility or liability for anything done in reliance on it. For fuller information as to the status and effect of this document, please refer to the professional practice and ethics section of the Bar Council's website.

Very High Cost Cases — Guidance

[3.10]

Guidance has been issued in two guises in connection with the acceptance of instructions in Very High Cost Cases (VHCC's). The first set of guidance is principally concerned with the application of the Cab Rank rule to VHCCs. The Cab Rank rule does not apply. The second set of guidance addresses the effect of VHCC contracts and/or the absence of a contract and its effect on the barrister's standing as regards acceptance of VHCCs. Both sets of guidance are set out below.

The Bar Council receives a number of enquiries from barristers arising out of the Very High Cost Cases regime in criminal matters. This guidance should cover most of the difficulties that arise.

General

You should bear in mind the following general points:

The Cab-rank Rule does not apply to VHCCs, unless the fee and the arrangements are appropriate for the entire case.

Having entered a VHCC there are no occasions on which it will be proper to withdraw from the agreement simply because of a dispute over the time that is allowed to undertake particular work and very few occasions on which it will be proper to delay work while a dispute is being resolved.

The relevant passages of the Code of Conduct are set out below with regard to the acceptance of work:

> **604**. Subject to paragraph 601 a barrister in independent practice is not obliged to accept instructions:
>
> (b) other than at a fee which is proper having regard to:
>
> (i) the complexity length and difficulty of the case;
>
> (ii) his ability experience and seniority; and
>
> (iii) the expenses which he will incur;
>
> and any instructions in a matter funded by the Legal Services Commission as part of the Community Legal Service or the Criminal Defence Service for which the amount or rate of the barrister's remuneration is prescribed by regulation or subject to assessment shall for this purpose unless the Bar Council or the Bar in general meeting otherwise determines (either in a particular case or in any class or classes of case or generally) be deemed to be at a proper professional fee;.

The effect of this is that barristers are not required to accept work under the VHCC regime.

The effect of paragraphs 608(a) and 603(b) is that barristers must withdraw:

> "If having regard to his other professional commitments he will be unable to do or will not have adequate time and opportunity to Prepare that which he is required to do;" (para 603(b).

The fact that a fee is unlikely to cover the *full* amount of time a barrister will spend on a case does not trigger this situation and there is no other part of the Code which requires a barrister to withdraw in the circumstances envisaged by this note.

Barristers are permitted to withdraw under the following circumstances:

> **609**. Subject to paragraph 610 a barrister may withdraw from a case where he is satisfied that:
>
> (a) his instructions have been withdrawn;
>
> (b) his professional conduct is being impugned;
>
> (c) advice which he has given in accordance with paragraph 607 or 703 has not been heeded; or
>
> (d) there is some other substantial reason for so doing."

In our view a disagreement about fees or the time to be allowed does not amount to "some other substantial reason".

Accepting a Case

When entering into negotiations over a contract, it is crucial that you should be satisfied that the overall case plan and the first stage are satisfactory. in particular, you will be bound to follow the overall case plan and you will find it difficult to obtain extensions or alterations to it at a later stage. Once you have signed the contract you are, in effect, committed to the entire case.

Cases which become VHCCs

Where a case has been privately funded but the client subsequently decides to seek legal aid, a barrister is not required to continue with the case unless he or she is satisfied with the terms of the contract. In these circumstances, it is good practice to:

set a realistic deadline for agreement of the contract leaving, if possible, sufficient time for the solicitor to seek new counsel so that the client is not prejudiced;

if agreement cannot be reached, the solicitor should be informed that you are not prepared to work under the new proposed fees and, if the solicitor is not prepared to underwrite the original agreement, will withdraw;

if agreement is not forthcoming within a reasonable length of time you should return the papers.

Where, however, the case is an ex post facto case which has been called in by the VHCC unit, there will be very little scope for withdrawal. Although, the primary duty is on the solicitor to notify cases to the unit, barristers also have a duty to do so and if the size of the case is such that you could be deemed to be on notice that it should have been reported to the unit, then you should do so. Withdrawal is only likely to be possible in cases of manifest bad faith by the solicitor (for example he assures you that the case has been reported when it has not).

Difficulties during the Case

Frequently, there are disputes over the amount of time that it is appropriate to allow to particular stages or pieces of work. There is an appeal from the decision of the Legal Services Commission case Manager. in these circumstances, your professional duty is to undertake as much work as you considers necessary in your client's interest. You are not professionally entitled to reduce the work you do to fit the hours that are permitted; the fact there is a disagreement over the hours for which you are to be paid is not sufficient to enable you to withdraw. If there is a disagreement over the length of hours, you should take this matter to the appeal panel and feel free to obtain support from the trial judge or from other sources as necessary. in extreme cases, the decision of the panel may be reviewable. Ultimately, however, it must be recognised that the function of the unit and the appeal panel is to establish how many hours' work it is reasonable to expect the taxpayer to support, not how many hours work the individual barrister needs to do. Regrettably, the Bar Council does not have the resources to take a view on the reasonableness of individual cases.

The single exception to this arises where, under the regulations or the terms of the contract, it is clear that a particular piece of work will not be paid for at all unless prior authorisation is sought. in such circumstances, we believe it is professionally proper for you not to undertake that piece of work until agreement has been obtained. If the time needed to obtain such consent is likely to delay a hearing or progress of a case, then it would be proper to inform the judge of this and to seek the necessary adjournments to enable agreement to be reached. Ultimately, however, if the unit does not agree that the work needs to be done and an appeal is unsuccessful, then if you believe that your client's interests require the work to be done, then you should do it.

The Bar Council recognises that these arrangements represent onerous terms for barristers who sign up to them. It repeats that it is a matter for each barrister's commercial judgment to decide whether or not to agree such terms in each individual case. It is very keen to hear of cases where, in counsel's view, manifestly inadequate hours are allowed by the VHCC unit and barristers are urged to report these cases to the Criminal Bar Association or the Remuneration Committee of the Bar Council.

Very High Cost Cases — Obligations under the Code of Conduct

Very High Cost Cases From The Chairman Of The Professional Practice Committee

February 13, 2008

[3.11]

In light of the recent proposed changes to the VHCC Panel Scheme, I will summarise the Professional Practice Committee's understanding of barristers' obligations under the Code of Conduct.

1. If barristers sign the new contract then they will owe an obligation to accept such instructions as are offered under this scheme subject to the normal application of the "cab rank" rule. The suitability of the fee will already have been accepted in advance by signing the contract. The only addition to the normal criteria will be "distant travel". In all other respects, nothing in the January clarification issued by the Legal Services Commission appears to go beyond the normal application of the "cab rank" rule. I reproduce below the relevant parts of Richard Collins' letter of January 17, 2008 so that you can make your own judgment.

2. Breach of contract by any barrister could give rise to a valid complaint of Professional Misconduct.

3. If barristers do not sign the new contract, it appears that they will now be eligible to be offered VHCC work where no panel member is available to accept the instructions. The fees for this work will be a matter of negotiation between the individual panel solicitor and the individual barrister subject to a ceiling of that which will be paid to the solicitor by the LSC for such services, namely the maximum open to be received by the appropriate panel advocate designated in the Representation Order for those particular instructions within the designated category.

4. The view of the PPC is that it will be a matter for the barrister who has not signed the general contract as to whether or not he accepts those instructions. If counsel is offered a VHCC at the "capped" rate or below it, and forms the view that this is not "a fee which is proper having regard to the complexity length and difficulty of the case", then under paragraph 604 of the Code it may be declined because the fee is not "prescribed by regulation or subject to assessment" within the meaning of that paragraph. Likewise, where cases are taken out of Graduated Fee and into VHCC the same will apply.

5. Where counsel who have not signed the general contract are offered individual instructions in a particular case, I would advise them (in the absence of any contract between them and the LSC or the instructing solicitor) to ensure that the precise terms of every aspect of the funding (including travel) are set out clearly and unequivocally in writing and agreed by both parties and by the solicitor and the relevant official of the Legal Services Commission/High Cost Case Unit to avoid disputes later on.

6. There is reference in Mr Collins' letter of January 17, 2008 to "capacity". For the avoidance of doubt, I wish to emphasise that declining instructions because of lack of capacity to undertake the instructions is not an option under the Code, it is an obligation. Failure to observe this provision could lead to Complaints initiated by the Legal Services Commission, the Court, opposing or co-defending advocates, the lay client or the Bar Standards Board itself.

7. The importance of understanding Code obligations is emphasised by Mr Collins' observation in his letter to the Chairman of the Bar dated February 10, 2008 where he says that, in the light of recent events, advocates who have signed the contract may receive more work than they might reasonably have expected and in the correspondence as a whole making it clear that non-panel advocates may be approached to undertake VHCC work

at rates to be negotiated with instructing solicitor up to the maximum permitted level for the applicable category but with no prescribed minimum figure.

Extract from Mr Collins' Letter of January 17, 2008

[3.12]–[3.13]

"...the LSC has decided that it would be helpful to provide further clarification on the following issues.

Contractual obligation to accept cases; there appears to be concern that the LSC will oblige Advocates to take any case that Panel Members may offer them. Whilst the purpose of the panel is to ensure that clients have adequate access to appropriate legal advice, the LSC does not require Advocates to accept each and every case where a Panel Member (PM) may wish to instruct them. The LSC accepts that for various individual reasons, (capacity, competence or other reasonable concerns such as unreasonable travel etc.), advocates may need to feel it necessary to turn down instructions. This is no different from the current situation and LSC does not intend to alter this.

The Distant travel rules. There is no compulsion on individual advocates to accept cases that are classified as "distant". The acceptance of such cases is entirely voluntarily. The LSC noted the difficulties that may be placed on individual advocates if teams were restricted to a choice of advocates on their lists and as a result of this the LSC permitted teams to access the combined list of all advocates to cover eventualities concerned with availability and distant clients. This change was implemented as a result of consultation with the Professions and their representative bodies and was specifically designed to ensure that teams and individuals would not be compelled to accept distant cases.

We believe that it is possible in the majority of cases to determine any travel implications at an early stage and indeed it is our experience that most defence teams are not fully formed until after notification. I believe it is reasonable to suggest that counsel may make an informed choice of whether or not to accept a "distant case" and if unsure as to whether they may be remunerated, their case manager may clarify the situation with the CCU before this decision is taken. In the circumstances where a change of venue occurs that cannot be predicted and is outside the control of individuals then this will be considered as an exceptional circumstance.

I do not believe there is any difference between the distant travel rules between the AGFS and the VHCC Panel scheme with respect to the ability of an advocate to demonstrate exceptional circumstances by which they may claim distant travel. It may be argued that the VHCC is more generous in some circumstances allowing for up to 2hrs / 50miles each way travel without the requirement to get any prior authority..."

Prosecuting Counsel Acceptance of Instructions

[3.14]–[3.20]

All barristers instructed by the CPS must familiarise themselves with the "CPS Instructions for Prosecuting Advocates". Those instructions are expected to be applied by all barristers instructed by the CPS. Advocates must be aware of all work that is expected to be undertaken having accepted instructions from the CPS. The instructions contain invaluable guidance and advice on the range of likely issues and complications that are likely to face a prosecuting advocate. Guidance on dealing with court procedure, sentencing, disclosure, the media, confiscation, witnesses, DNA, is juxtaposed with common difficulties faced by advocates dealing with particular offences such as rape and serious sexual offences, racially and religiously aggravated offences and domestic violence related offences. A copy of the CPS Instructions for Prosecuting Advocates can be obtained from the Bar Council or the CPS direct.

The "CPS Bar Framework of Principles for Prosecution Advocates" ("the Framework") in the Crown Court contains specific agreed "Key Principles" to be applied on the instruction of advocates. The most relevant passages from the Framework are set out below[1].

1 A full copy of the Framework can be obtained from the Bar Council.

Accepting Instructions in Two Cases Simultaneously

[3.21]

A common issue that arises concerns the acceptance of instructions in more than one case to be heard simultaneously on the same day. It may be that a case overruns leaving the barrister with two cases to attend rather than just one. Similarly, not infrequently a barrister may only be required to attend certain aspects of a hearing leaving him available to appear at another hearing in a different case taking place on the same day. The Bar Council has provided some invaluable guidance on the correct approach that a barrister should take to such predicaments. The following guidance was re issued by the Professional Practice Committee in January 2014.

Guidance On Accepting Instructions In Two Cases Simultaneously

[3.22]

1. There are occasions when you may be involved in two cases with overlapping hearings:

   (a) This may occur where the first case has overrun.

   (b) It may also occur where you are involved in a long trial which only requires attendance in respect of certain aspects of the trial, leaving you free at other times in the course of the trial to be involved with other cases.

2. Such scenarios have the potential to engage the BSB Handbook Core Duties to: observe you duty to the court in the administration of justice; act in the best interests of each client; not behave in a way which is likely to diminish the trust and confidence of the public; and provide a competent standard of work and service to each client (CD1, 2, 5 and 7). BSB Handbook rC17 provides that the duty to act in the best interests of each client includes a duty to consider whether the client's best interests are served by different legal representation, and if so, to advise the client to that effect: see gC49. BSB Handbook rC18 provides that the duty to provide a competent standard of work includes a duty to inform the professional client or client as far as reasonably possible in sufficient time to enable appropriate steps to be taken to protect the client's interests, if there is an appreciable risk that the barrister may not be able to undertake the instructions.

3. The practices referred to in paragraph 1 above are not, *per se*, contrary to the BSB Handbook, so long as you have the agreement of both your lay and professional clients where any overlap can be anticipated. It is impossible to assess with accuracy the length of any but the shortest of trials and the overrunning of a trial may lead to a client not being represented by the client's barrister of choice, even where that barrister has acted responsibly in relation to the acceptance of the brief. Furthermore as leading counsel, you

should consider at each stage of a trial whether your presence is required or whether costs could reasonably be saved by your not attending.

4. However, the following points need to be borne in mind:

(a) You should be very cautious about accepting work which you know has been fixed for hearing at the same time as a case previously accepted, or which will overlap with the first case. The BSB Handbook rC21 provides that you must not accept instructions to act: if due to any existing or previous instructions they are not able to fulfil their obligation to act in the best interests of the prospective client; or they do not have enough time to deal with the particular matter, unless the circumstances are such that it would still be in the client's best interests to accept. Where you are offered instructions in a case which you know will clash with another case already accepted and the cases are both listed to be heard in the near future, then it is very unlikely that it would be in the best interests of the prospective client to accept the new instructions. Where the listing is sufficiently far into the future for there to be a reasonable prospect that the expected clash will not materialise, a barrister ought to consider at least the following matters before deciding whether or not to accept the new instructions:

(i) The professional and lay client in the second case must be told about the clash to allow them to make an informed decision as to whether to retain you or not. In order for a decision to be informed, you will need to assist in providing a timetable to allow for a sensible review of your availability as the trial date approaches.

(ii) It is your responsibility to keep the position under review and, if there is an appreciable risk that you will be unable to do both cases, then the professional client or the client need to be informed as far as reasonably possible in sufficient time to enable appropriate steps to be taken to protect the client's interests, such as the instruction of a new barrister in sufficient time to avoid prejudice to the lay client: see the BSB Handbook rC18. You must be careful to guard against an over-optimistic professional or lay client who wants to "hang on" long past a time which would be found by a reasonable person to be safe, and make sure they advise the client if their best interests are served by different legal representation: BSB Handbook rC17.

(iii) In choosing which case to retain, you must determine which case it is most important to attend. Where applicable, the following matters should be taken into account: (1) criminal cases take precedence over civil; (2) a part-heard case takes precedence over a new matter; and (3) a case for which a fixed date has been obtained takes precedence over a "floater". Other relevant factors include the amount of work that the barrister has done on the case, the length of time that the barrister has been instructed on each case, each case's complexity and difficulty and, perhaps most importantly, which lay client will be most prejudiced by someone else taking the case over at short notice.

(b) Subject to the points made at paragraph 4(a) above, you should ensure that you have allowed a realistic gap between cases fixed for trial so as to allow for a case overrunning. This may be impractical in respect of short cases which have been assigned to a warned list without a fixed date. However, even in these circumstances, you should remain vigilant to avoid a clash and should ensure that the clerks remain in regular contact with the list office as to the progress of cases in the warned list. As with all matters of listing, without the cooperation of the courts, especially the List Office, it is very difficult for you to ensure that there are not clashes between cases.

(c) Even in circumstances where you feel able to leave the case in the hands of junior or leading counsel instructed with you during a time when the evidence does not directly affect counsel's client, you should consider very carefully whether it is in the best interests of the client to leave the case to do other work. In publicly funded cases you should give proper weight to the consideration that a funding certificate has been given for two counsel because the case is thought to merit the services of two counsel. If you have your lay and professional client's permission to absent yourself to conduct other work, you should be satisfied that you will have time to prepare for that other work without undermining the service provided to your client.

(d) You would lay yourself open to serious allegations if you charged for attendance in two cases at the same time. There may be exceptional circumstances where your active attendance is required in two different courts on the same day. In these circumstances you could not be criticised for obtaining a fee for attendance at both hearings, so long as the time attended in each court is correctly recorded and provided such payments are permitted by regulation.

Important Notice

This document has been prepared by the Bar Council to assist barristers on matters of professional conduct and ethics. It is not "guidance" for the purposes of the BSB Handbook I6.4, and neither the BSB nor a disciplinary tribunal nor the Legal Ombudsman is bound by any views or advice expressed in it. It does not comprise – and cannot be relied on as giving – legal advice. It has been prepared in good faith, but neither the Bar Council nor any of the individuals responsible for or involved in its preparation accept any responsibility or liability for anything done in reliance on it. For fuller information as to the status and effect of this document, please refer to the professional practice and ethics section of the Bar Council's website.

Accepting Instructions in Public Access Work – Guidance for Barristers

[3.23]

The Bar Standards Board has produced guidance for barristers wishing to undertake public access work. From 6 January 2014 the Bar should refer to the New Handbook for rules and guidance on their conduct as barristers. The Bar Council has produced extensive guidance for the Bar in relation to public access work. The guidance was issued in April 2013 and is reproduced below.

Scope of this guidance

[3.24]

1. A barrister may accept instructions directly from or on behalf of a member of public, also known as a lay client (the "client") (rS24 of the Scope of Practice section of the BSB Handbook). This is known as public access. In carrying out public access work a barrister must comply with the BSB Handbook and in particular the Public Access Rules which are at rC119-rC131 of the Code of Conduct section.

2. This document gives guidance on the interpretation of the Handbook and good practice. You should have regard to it in considering whether to accept and in carrying out public access instructions in accordance with the rules set out in the Handbook.

Qualification requirements

[3.25]

3. Before you may accept public access instructions, you must:

    (1) hold a full practising certificate. If you have less than three years' standing you must have a qualified person readily available to you to provide guidance, if necessary (see paragraph 5 below);

    (2) have undertaken and satisfactorily completed a Bar Standards Board approved training course. Details of such courses can be obtained from the BSB website;

    (3) notify the Bar Council of your intention to undertake such work; and

    (4) have insurance cover as required by the Handbook. BMIF cover satisfies this requirement.

Additional requirements for barristers with less than three years' standing

[3.25a]

4. The prohibition on barristers with less than three years' standing undertaking public access work has been removed. However there are two additional requirements with which a barrister under three years' standing must comply.

5. You must have a qualified person available to provide guidance. A person shall be a "qualified person" for these purposes if they are public access accredited and have:

   (a) been entitled to practise and have practised as a barrister or have been authorised to practise by another approved regulator for a period (which need not have been as a person authorised by the same approved regulator) of at least six years in the previous eight years;

   (b) made such practice their primary occupation for the previous two years; and

   (c) been entitled to exercise a right of audience before every Court in relation to all proceedings.

6. You are also required to:

   (a) keep a log of the public access cases you have dealt with and record any issues or problems that have arisen; and

   (b) where possible and appropriate, seek feedback from public access clients.

7. A pro forma for logging cases is attached at Annex A. The purpose of this requirement is twofold:

   (a) its primary purpose is as a tool to assist you to reflect upon and learn from your practice, (in this connection a barrister will need to consider whether seeking feedback from a client involved in an unsuccessful criminal case would be appropriate); and

   (b) to assist the Bar Standards Board in assessing whether the removal of the prohibition has introduced any unacceptable risk in to the process. Therefore the BSB will sample a selection of these logs to gauge the impact of the rule change.

Nature and scope of public access work

[3.26]

8. A barrister may accept public access instructions in any area of practice. You are reminded that rC21.8 of the Handbook prohibits you from accepting instructions if you lack sufficient experience or competence to handle the matter. In a public access case you should remember that dealing directly with a client may be more difficult or demanding than acting for a professional client and you must be able to handle those demands.

9. Public access does not widen the types of work a barrister may do. You are performing the same functions as you would if you were instructed by a solicitor. Examples of the type of work you may do for a public access client are:

- advocacy;
- drafting documents;
- advising in writing or in conference;
- representation in alternative dispute resolution (ADR) such as mediation or arbitration;
- negotiating on behalf of your client;
- investigating and collecting evidence. You should however have regard to the BSB's 'Guidance on Self-Employed Practice', which is published on the BSB's website and provides guidance on investigating or collecting evidence and taking witness statements. In particular, you must not conduct a case in court if you have previously investigated or collected evidence in the case unless you reasonably believe that the investigation and collection of that evidence is unlikely to be challenged;
- corresconding on behalf of your client. You may send letters on your Chambers' letterhead or faxes or emails. However, you must only conduct correspondence if you are satisfied it is in your client's best interests to do so and you have adequate systems, experience and resources for managing the correspondence (see rC130 and relevant guidance at gC24 and gC71). Bear in mind that solicitors' offices have systems for logging incoming and outgoing correspondence and dealing with urgent letters in the absence of the fee earner which your Chambers may not be able to offer.

General restrictions

(A) Restriction on conducting litigation

[3.27]

10. Public access does not put barristers on a par with solicitors. A key difference is that solicitors may conduct litigation on behalf of their client. A barrister in independent practice does not have the right to conduct litigation unless authorised by the BSB to do so. If you conduct litigation without authorisation you are not only breaching the Handbook but also committing a criminal offence under the Legal Services Act 2007.

11. The Legal Services Act 2007 defines the conduct of litigation as:

    a. the issuing of proceedings before any court in England and Wales;

    b. the commencement, prosecution and defence of such proceedings; and

    c. the performance of any ancillary functions in relation to such proceedings (such as entering appearances to actions).

12. The BSB takes the view that the following fall within this definition and therefore **you should refuse to do them if you are not authorised to conduct litigation**:

    a. issuing proceedings or applications;

    b. acknowledging service of proceedings;

    c. giving your address as the address for service;

    d. filing documents at court or serving documents on another party; and

    e. issuing notices of appeal.

13. You may advise your client on how to take any of these steps. For example you may advise on the procedure for lodging an appeal and you may of course draft the grounds of appeal. However the steps in question must be taken by the client as a litigant in person if you are not authorised to do them. Normally public access clients who are litigants in person will be expected to be able to perform the activities usually undertaken by an authorised litigator with little or no prompting. If this is not the case you must consider whether it is proper to act on a public access basis (see paragraphs 21 to 25 below). This consideration is particularly relevant when dealing with vulnerable clients. 'Vulnerable clients' is interpreted widely and may include clients who have English as a second language, who have mental or physical impairments or who are otherwise vulnerable e g because of their age, caring responsibilities or immigration status.

14. Certain activities at first blush look like they might fall within the definition of conducting litigation but in fact do not. This is generally because it is work that barristers have traditionally done when instructed by solicitors. The following are therefore **permissible if you are not authorised to conduct litigation**:

    - Lodging documents for hearings. It is proper for you or your clerk to lodge certain types of documents for hearings, provided that they are ancillary to your role as an advocate. Barristers often draft the case summary, chronology, list of issues or position statement. There is nothing wrong with clerks or barristers lodging these sort of documents. However, it is likely that lodging a full trial bundle will amount to conducting litigation.

    - Skeleton arguments. Exchanging skeletons with an opponent or sending skeletons and bundles of authorities to the court is allowed. In a criminal case defence barristers often hand a defence case statement to the Crown or the court and this would also be permitted if instructed directly.

    - Covering applications to fix trial dates. Clerks regularly fix trial dates to ensure that the date is convenient for counsel instructed. This is permissible whether instructed by a solicitor and therefore also when instructed directly. Clerks making representations to the Masters in relation to hearing dates is permissible for the same reasons.

    - Court orders. Liaising with the other side or the court over the preparation of an order is something barristers often do and is allowed. Clerks regularly deal with the sealing of court orders and so this, too, is permitted.

- Discharging a duty or a courtesy to the court. For example a letter or e-mail to a judge explaining an absence from court or providing dates to avoid or corrections to a draft judgment.
- Signing a statement of truth. A statement of truth may be signed by a legal representative, which is defined as including a barrister (Civil Procedure Rules Part 2.3). Therefore you may sign a statement of truth on behalf of your client (*O'Connor v BSB* [2012] All ER (D) 108 (Aug) Visitors to the Inns of Court, August 17, unrep.). However you should ensure that the provisions of the Civil Procedure Rules are complied with before you do so, in particular Part 22 PD paragraph 3.8.

(B) Code of Conduct restrictions

[3.28]

15. The following are expressly prohibited by the Code of Conduct:
    - Receiving or handling clients' money, except as payment for fees. The prohibition against holding clients' money means that a barrister cannot make disbursements on behalf of a client, for example by paying court fees or witnesses' expenses.(rC73-rC75, BSB Handbook).
    - Undertaking the general management, administration or conduct of a client's affairs (rS25, BSB Handbook).

Public funding (legal aid)

[3.29]

16. In each case, before a barrister accepts a public access instruction, it is a Code of Conduct requirement to:

    "Take such steps as are reasonably necessary to ensure that the client is able to make an informed decision about whether to apply for legal aid or whether to proceed with public access." (rC120.4, BSB Handbook)

17. If a client qualifies for legal aid it may be, and often will be, in their best interests to instruct a solicitor on a public funding basis. There may however be some situations where the client will prefer to instruct a barrister on public access – for example if their legal aid contributions would be higher than instructing a barrister without a solicitor, or they want to instruct a more senior barrister, such as a QC, than they would be entitled to on legal aid.

18. It is important that the client makes an informed choice about public funding. In many cases it will be obvious from the nature of the case, or the nature of the client, that public funding is unlikely to be available. However in other cases you may take the view that it would be in the best interests of the client to explore their eligibility for legal aid. In those cases, you are likely to want to discuss this with them when you first meet and draw their attention to where they can find out more about legal aid and get help to assess their eligibility. Before accepting an instruction you will want to discuss this matter with the client to ensure that they understand the position

regarding legal aid, have made an informed decision and that proceeding on a public access basis will be in their best interests.

19. Information about public funding is available to clients in the guidance for clients, which is available on the BSB's website at: https://www.barstandardsboard.org.uk/regulatory-requirements/bsb-handbook/code-guidance/.

20. The model client care letter (see paragraph 33 below) explains that a barrister cannot be instructed directly on a legal aid basis, gives details of how the client can find out if they are eligible for public funding and the basis on which you can advise and represent them. Writing to your client in the terms set out in the model client care letter can therefore help to demonstrate that you have covered this matter with them.

Interests of the client and interests of justice

[3.30]

21. You cannot accept public access instructions if you form the view that it is either in the best interests of your client or in the interests of justice for the client to instruct a solicitor or other professional client (rC120.3, BSB Handbook). This is a continuing duty which you must keep under review during the course of a case.

22. This decision is likely to depend both on the complexity of the case, the capability of the client and whether you are authorised to conduct litigation e g a well-resourced client, such as a large corporation, may be able to handle very complex litigation.

23. In making this assessment you are likely to reach one of three views:

- The level of the case and the likely work involved is within the client's capabilities and there is no obvious reason why a solicitor or other professional client should be instructed.
- The case is of such complexity or has reached a stage that it is not in the client's interests or the interests of justice to instruct a barrister without a solicitor or other professional client. Having reached such a view you can no longer act on a public access basis. You would be able to act if instructed by a solicitor (or other professional client) and you can make recommendations as to who could act.
- The case may well become complex and may involve work which the client cannot do, but you do not consider that a solicitor or other professional client needs to be instructed yet.

24. In every case you must make your client aware at the outset that there may be circumstances in which you will have to recommend that a solicitor (or other professional client) is instructed, and that you will have to withdraw if that advice is not heeded. There is a paragraph in the model client care letter (see paragraph 33 below) setting this out.

25. It is essential that barristers should consider at every point at which they are instructed whether a client needs to instruct a solicitor and to advise as soon as it becomes clear that this is the case. This is of particular importance where limitation periods are involved or where hearings are imminent. Barristers

failing to do this may find themselves at risk of actions in negligence, findings of inadequate professional service by the Office of the Legal Ombudsman, or professional misconduct charges by the BSB.

Relationship with client

(A) *Initial contact*

[3.31]

26. It is likely that initial contact will be by a telephone call or email between the client and yourself or your clerk, or the receipt of written instructions in Chambers. You are required to keep a record of the date that instructions were received, the name of the client, the name of the case and any requirement of the client as to time limits (rC128). As you will also need to send a client care letter you will need the client's address.

27. You may take the view that a preliminary meeting is required. This may be necessary to comply with the requirements of the Money Laundering Regulations (see paragraphs 72 to 75 below). If so, you should write to the client summarising those regulations and setting out what is required in order to satisfy the identification requirements. A preliminary meeting may be helpful to decide whether you will accept the instructions. It is open to you to accept instructions for the limited purpose of reading papers and advising whether you are able to perform substantive professional work; in such a situation it is open to you to make an arrangement that you are paid a fee for doing so. If you decide to charge for the preliminary meeting, a client care letter should be sent to the client in the usual way, setting out the charge for the advice and any other work done and making it clear that you do not agree to do more in the first instance than assess whether or not you can assist the client. In many cases, you may consider that it is good client care not to charge for a preliminary meeting.

(B) *Identifying and representing vulnerable clients*

[3.32]

28. There are a number of factors which may make a client vulnerable and which may have implications for how you manage their case. Some of these factors may be obvious, for example a client may be very young or may not be able to speak English. Issues related to the protected characteristics listed in the Equality Act 2010 which may make a client vulnerable include:

Race:

- Clients with English as a second, third or non-existent language.
- Asylum seeking or refugee clients who may have mental health issues such as post-traumatic stress conditions related to treatment (e.g. torture or persecution) in their home country.
- Immigration clients who may have been separated from their families or who are new to the UK, may be unfamiliar with the UK legal system and who may have difficulties carrying out litigation work.

Gender:

- Clients with caring responsibilities for young or disabled children, particularly lone parents who may have difficulties in undertaking tasks such as serving documentation at court.
- Clients with caring responsibilities for older dependents, in particular lone carers.
- Lone parents who may have access to less financial resources than other clients.
- Sensitivity of men or women in relation to one to one meetings with the opposite sex – if this is necessary or in relation to questioning/discussion of intimate subjects.

Disability:

- Clients with physical impairments which may impact upon their ability to undertake physical aspects of litigation.
- Clients with physical or mental health issues which may impact upon their ability to undertake litigation activities.
- Clients with learning disabilities.
- Clients who are heavily reliant on carers to manage their day to day activities.

Age:

- Very young clients.
- Clients who for reasons relating to their age (particularly older clients) may find the physical aspects of litigation difficult.
- Clients who for reasons relating to their age have difficulties associated with memory loss and/or confusion.

Pregnancy/maternity:

- Heavily pregnant or new mothers who may find the physical aspects of conducting litigation difficult.
- New mothers with post natal health issues affecting physical mobility or mental health (e.g. post natal depression).

Gender re-assignment:

- Clients undergoing transition (which may involve frequent visits to hospital or other medical appointments).

Religion or belief:

- Clients whose religious beliefs make it difficult for them to undertake litigation activities on particular days or at particular times.

29. Other relevant factors to consider in relation to the vulnerability of a client include:

- Limited access to financial resources to pay for the cost of litigation activities or additional unforeseen costs.
- Illiteracy or low levels of literacy.
- Vulnerability or trauma arising from the matter at issue (e.g. the

matter involves a serious crime such as serious assaults or sexual offences perpetrated against the client).

- Homelessness.
- Drug or alcohol dependency or other addiction issues.

30. The term "vulnerable client" should be interpreted widely. You will need to identify any factors that may make a client vulnerable when considering whether or not to take on their case. Having identified any such factors, you will need to consider what additional measures, if any, are necessary to ensure that the client is supported properly and understands fully any information which you communicate to them, so that you may act in their best interests. This may involve ensuring that documentation provided to your client is translated into another language or into plain English. You should also consider whether you can direct the client to any external resources or agencies for further advice and support.

(C) The basis of the agreement and the client care letter

[3.33]

31. The agreement between barrister and client is contractual. This means that:
    - the barrister is bound by the agreement and may be liable in contract for failure to perform;
    - it should be clear what is to be done under the contract, the charging rate and any other special terms that may be agreed (note your general duties under rC22 in addition to the public access rules);
    - the barrister will be able to sue for fees.

32. There are a number of things a barrister must inform his client about at the outset of the agreement. These are set out in rC125. They include warning a client that you are an independent practitioner and there may be occasions where a clash of professional commitments prevents you from carrying out an instruction.

33. A model client care letter is on the BSB's website. Provided you have promptly written to your client in the terms of the model letter you will have complied with the notification requirements in rC125. Where the client has previously instructed you in respect of the same matter it may well be unnecessary for you to provide a full client care letter in respect of every new instruction received. Barristers must still ensure that the fundamentals of the client care letter are set out in respect of each new instruction i.e. the work that is to be undertaken, the cost and the payment mechanism. Other matters which you are required to inform your client about, such as the barrister's limitations (if any) with respect to litigation, how to complain and the fact the barrister may have to withdraw can be covered by referring the client to the original client care letter.

34. It may also be possible in limited circumstances for you to enter into a retainer or novel fee arrangement with a public access client. However, care should be taken to ensure you continue to observe your general Handbook duties around independence and conflict of interest.

(D) Non-discrimination rules

[3.34]

35. In deciding not to accept an instruction, you should be mindful of rC28 of the Handbook. This states that you must not withhold your services or permit your services to be withheld:

    a. on the ground that that the nature of the case is objectionable to you or to any section of the public;

    b. on the ground that the conduct, opinions or beliefs of the prospective client are unacceptable to you or to any section of the public; or

    c. on any ground relating to the source of any financial support which may properly be given to the prospective client for the proceedings in question.

36. rC12 states that a barrister must not discriminate unlawfully against, victimise or harass any other person on the grounds of race, colour, ethnic or national origin, nationality, citizenship, sex, gender re-assignment, sexual orientation, marital or civil partnership status, disability, age, religion or belief or pregnancy and maternity.

37. The effect of these rules is that, whilst the "cab rank" rule does not apply to public access cases, you must not discriminate in the way you accept, refuse or carry out public access instructions. Potential clients may feel aggrieved if a barrister refuses to take on a case and may allege that they did so for improper reasons. It would be prudent for a barrister refusing a case to make a brief note of the reasons for so doing in case this is questioned in future.

(E) Withdrawal from a case

[3.35]

38. rC25 to rC27 of the Handbook highlight the scenarios where a barrister must or may cease to act and return instructions.

39. In addition to the usual reasons for withdrawal from a case, barristers are required to cease to act in a public access case where they have formed the view (for instance, as a result of receiving further information about the case) that it is in the interests of the client or in the interests of justice for the client to instruct a solicitor or other professional client.

40. If, as a result of being told that you cannot continue to act without a solicitor or professional client being instructed, the client instructs a solicitor or other professional client, then you will be able to continue to act. It is open to you, therefore, to give the client the opportunity to instruct a solicitor or other professional client before you finally withdraw from the case.

41. In a public access case, the issue of withdrawing from a case will only arise once you have accepted the instruction. That will usually be when the client care letter is sent. You will need to take care in deciding whether to withdraw not only because you owe a duty under the Handbook to act in the best interests of your client, but also because you may owe them contractual

duties. Unless your decision to withdraw is justified by your obligations under the Handbook you are likely to place yourself in breach of your contract with the client.

42. It will therefore very rarely be appropriate for you to withdraw where there is simply a difference of opinion between yourself and the client. In particular, the fact that a client legitimately rejects your advice on tactics or a settlement will not of itself justify you in withdrawing from the case; nor does the fact that a client may raise a minor complaint or question about the service provided by you. Where such disagreements arise, however, you would be prudent to make full attendance notes of the discussion and have them agreed by the client.

43. A barrister acting for a client who is a party to proceedings must bear in mind the particular difficulties which the client might encounter if the barrister withdraws. A hearing may be imminent; or the client may experience real difficulty in finding a solicitor willing to take on the case. Where there is doubt, or a difference of opinion as to whether you should withdraw, and withdrawal would or might cause difficulties for the client, it would be prudent for a barrister to contact the Bar Council Public Access enquiries line (0207 611 1472) for guidance.

44. Where you consider that you are required to withdraw and it appears that, by reason of the proximity of a hearing, a client may have difficulty finding another lawyer to take on the case in the time available, you should provide such assistance as is proper to protect the client's position. This can include:

a. applying to the court for an adjournment if it is necessary to withdraw during the course of the hearing;

b. drafting letters for the client to send to the court and the other side seeking an adjournment;

c. providing supporting letters for the client explaining that, for professional reasons, you have had to withdraw and, so far as this is possible without breaching confidentiality or prejudicing the client's position, explaining the reasons;

d. where the matter is urgent or it is otherwise appropriate, contacting solicitors or other suitable intermediaries who may be willing to take on the client's case.

(F) Complaints

[3.36]

45. The Handbook requires barristers to have in-house procedures for dealing with complaints (rC99-rC109). Such procedures can be a useful source of feedback to Chambers and also a way of retaining client goodwill when mistakes occur. Public access work may result in Chambers receiving a substantially greater number of complaints from clients, which may or may not be legitimate. However, all such complaints should be addressed and acted upon within an appropriate timescale.

46. You should have regard to the BSB's guidance on complaints handling. In particular, you must:

a. ensure that the client is told about the procedure in the client care letter;

b. deal with complaints promptly and according to that procedure as they arise;

c. inform the client that, if they are dissatisfied with the way in which the complaint has been handled, they may refer it to the Legal Ombudsman.

Fees

(A) *Notifying the client*

[3.37]

47. If you accept public access instructions you must forthwith notify your client in clear and readily understandable terms of the work you have agreed to perform and the fees which you propose to charge or the basis on which your fee will be calculated. You should therefore complete those parts of the model client care letter which deals with these matters.

48. rC22 and rC88 require barristers to keep adequate records to support fees charged, and to provide such records or details to clients on request. Such records should contain separate items for each piece of paperwork and, where substantial telephone advice is provided, separate items for each piece of such advice. If the client requires further detail and, notably, the exact work done and the cost of it in respect of each item involved this should be provided.

(B) *Payment in advance*

[3.38]

49. rC73 prohibits a barrister from handling client money. The associated guidance (gC106-gC107) clarifies that a fixed fee paid in advance is not client money for the purposes of rC73. If you agree with a client, who can reasonably be expected to understand the implications of such an agreement, that (1) your fee for any work will be charged according to the time spent on it, but (2) you will be paid a fixed fee in advance for it, and (3), when the work has been done, you will pay the client any difference between that fixed fee and the fee which has actually been earned, and (4) you will not hold the difference between the fixed fee and the fee which has been earned on trust for the client, that difference will not be client money. Such fees may be considered as client money if you cannot demonstrate that the agreement was made in advance and on clear terms. You should also consider carefully whether such an arrangement is in the client's interest and that the client fully understands the implications.

(C) *Withholding paperwork until paid*

[3.39]

50. Barristers may withhold paperwork until fees have been received. We recommend, however, that it should be made clear to the client at the time of instruction that this will be the arrangement. It should be expressly stated in the client care letter. Barristers should note that while they are permitted to withhold the work they have done, they may not be permitted to withhold the client's papers.

(D) *Lien*

[3.40]

51. We are not aware of any authority by which barristers gain a general lien on documents belonging to the client until the fees are paid, although there seems to be nothing in the law to invalidate an express agreement made between a barrister and a client permitting the barrister to exercise such a lien. In the absence of a contractually enforceable lien you should return the papers to your client on request, but first ensure that you have complied with your record keeping obligations (see paragraphs 67 to 71 below).

(E) *Disbursements*

[3.41]

52. You may agree with your client that you are entitled to charge disbursements, such as travel and accommodation expenses and photocopying. This can include charging for the work of a clerk, administrative assistant or paralegal. This must be agreed in advance and therefore should be included in the client care letter.

(F) *Over-charging and disputes*

[3.42]

53. It is likely that clients will, on occasion, seek to dispute the amount that is charged by a barrister or to claim that they have been overcharged. The scope for such disputes is obviously greatly reduced if there is clarity about the charging arrangements beforehand.

54. It is obviously appropriate for you to seek to resolve the dispute informally if this is possible. Otherwise two options exist:

   a. the client can refuse to pay and the dispute may have to be resolved by litigation;

   b. the client can complain to the Office of the Legal Ombudsman ("LeO"), if they consider that you have provided inadequate professional services. In appropriate cases LeO has the power to fine you and/or order that fees be repaid. Complaints may also be made to the Bar Standards Board where the alleged conduct may amount to a breach of the Handbook.

(G) *Conditional Fee Agreements (CFA) and Damages-based Agreements*

[3.43]

55. While in principle there is nothing to prevent barristers undertaking public access work on a Conditional Fee Agreement or a Damages-based Agreement, particular care should be taken with such arrangements. You should consider the level of risk and the likelihood of recovering base costs and the success fee in the case of a Conditional Fee Agreement and the likelihood of recovering the percentage of the claimant's damages in the case of a Damages-based Agreement.

56. You should also consider the question of payment. Payment in advance or on completion of a particular piece of work would not be possible since, by definition, no fee is payable until success had been achieved. Generally, any money paid in advance would be considered client money and barristers are not permitted to hold this (see paragraph 49 above for circumstances when payment in advance may be possible). If you require further advice please contact the Bar Council.

Intermediaries

[3.43a]

57. You may find yourself asked to perform legal services by a person or organisation that is an intermediary, for the benefit of a named client. For example, an independent financial adviser may wish to take advice for a client, or arrange to have a document drafted. A son or daughter may want to instruct you on behalf of an elderly parent. A sponsor in this country may wish you to act in an immigration matter for a person who is out of the country. There is no objection in principle to a barrister accepting instructions from such an intermediary, but care must be taken in respect of a number of matters.

58. You must ensure that the intermediary is not acting, or proposing to act, as a "litigator". It is a criminal offence under the Legal Services Act 2007 for an unauthorised person to act as a litigator, and a barrister who facilitated such activity might also be criminally liable.

59. You must ensure that both intermediary and client understand the true nature of the arrangement. To this end, you should send a client care letter to both the intermediary and the client. It is assumed that the intermediary will undertake contractual responsibility for your fees. If the intermediary does not wish to do so, you would be entitled to enquire why you should deal with the intermediary at all, rather than directly with the client. Model letters to both intermediary and client are on the BSB's website at: https://www.barstandardsboard.org.uk/regulatory-requirements/bsb-handbook/code-guidance/.

60. You should bear in mind the possibility that the intermediary may have negotiated a contingent fee arrangement with the client and the potential conflict of interest which could thus arise between the intermediary and the client. Barristers are already familiar with the risks of potential conflicts of

interest between solicitors and clients where conditional fee agreements have been made. However, in the case of unregulated intermediaries you may feel that there is an even greater need to be alert to the risk that the manner in which information is transmitted to you may have been coloured by the intermediary's own commercial interests.

61. If you form the view that there is a conflict of interest between client and intermediary, for example, because the intermediary has been negligent, Core Duty 2, rules such as rC15 and rC17 and related guidance require you to consider whether it would be in the client's interest to instruct another professional, and, if you consider it would be, you must both so advise and take steps to ensure that such advice reaches the client. However, it is not your duty to police the relationship between intermediary and client, which is a private matter to them.

62. Where the intermediary instructs you to perform advocacy services, for example, before a domestic tribunal or in an arbitration, you must take such steps as appear appropriate to ensure that the client does, in fact, wish you to appear for them. In many cases this will involve having a conference with the client. A barrister performing advocacy services should inform the tribunal that they are acting for their client. You have the same obligation to a tribunal to which you send a skeleton argument.

63. You must have regard to the relevant provisions of the Money Laundering Regulations (see paragraphs 72 to 75 below). Where instructed by an intermediary, you must normally follow the identification procedures in respect of the client. The only exception will be where the intermediary is a regulated professional and informs you by letter or certificate that they are a professional within the regulated sector as defined in Proceeds of Crime Act (POCA) and the Money Laundering Regulations and has carried out identification procedures

64. If you are approached by an intermediary you remain under the same obligation to satisfy yourself before accepting the case that it is appropriate to do so without a solicitor or other professional client as you would be under if you were approached by the client direct. If you are familiar with the intermediary and the way in which the intermediary operates then this will be a relevant factor, but will not obviate the need for you, in respect of each prospective case, to satisfy yourself that no solicitor is required.

65. The client care letter to the client should be sent to the client's home or, as appropriate, business address and not to the intermediary's address. The client's address will therefore be one of the pieces of information which you will need before accepting instructions through an intermediary.

66. It is prohibited for you to pay or receive a referral fee to or from an intermediary, or to any other person for introducing a client or providing you with work. Full guidance on referral fees can be found at: https://www.barstandardsboard.org.uk/regulatory-requirements/bsb-handbook/code-guidance/.

Administration and record keeping

[3.43b]

67. When taking on public access work, Chambers need to be aware that the expectations of clients are likely to be very different from those of solicitors. They will not necessarily understand that barristers work on a different basis from solicitors and that it will not always be possible to speak directly to the barrister and that there are limits to what can and cannot be done by barristers. This should be made clear at an early stage and may be something that you would want to discuss with a client at a preliminary meeting. Barristers and clerks may need to adopt a flexible approach to dealing directly with the public and keep under review whether Chambers' administration should be adjusted accordingly.

68. In the absence of a solicitor it will be crucial for you to maintain records about your role in providing advice to the client in case questions or complaints arise afterwards. In particular, if it is not clear from other documentation, you should maintain a record of:

    a. the initial contact with the client;

    b. the work you have been asked to do;

    c. the dates of conferences and notes of advice given;

    d. records of telephone conversations and advice given;

    e. significant changes to instructions; and

    f. hearings attended and advice given.

    These records should be retained for at least seven years.

69. It is likely that clients will provide you with original documents. It is for each barrister to decide, in consultation with the client, whether they wish to retain those documents or work from copies. It is perfectly appropriate to charge for photocopying the documents but you should make it clear in your client care letter what the charge will be. You may also be asked to store the original documents on behalf of the client, but barristers are strongly discouraged from agreeing to do so unless retention by you is required in order to undertake litigation on behalf of the client (if you have been authorised to do so). The following matters should be kept in mind:

    a. the original documents belong to the client and, unless otherwise agreed (for example because a lien has been agreed), must be returned to the client on demand at any stage;

    b. if you agree to store original documents for the client you must keep the documents in a secure place and may be liable in negligence for failing to do so;

    c. it will almost always be impractical for you to store original documents for long periods of time unless your Chambers is prepared to guarantee such a service even after you have left Chambers or ceased to practise. If originals are retained you should specify to the client a date by which they must be collected or will be returned.

70. In any case it is prudent to keep papers following the conclusion of the case because there might be an appeal, a complaint or an action for professional

negligence. If a solicitor is instructed that obligation generally falls on the solicitor. In a public access case the obligation falls on the barrister. You must keep for a period of seven years the originals, copies or a list of all documents you have received or take reasonable steps to ensure that the client will do so.

71. Electronic storage is permissible if appropriate – you may wish to consult the Bar Council for further information on Information Security.

Money laundering and proceeds of crime

[3.43c]

72. The Bar Council has produced detailed briefings on the Money Laundering Regulations 2007 and the Proceeds of Crime Act 2002.

73. The Money Laundering Regulations apply to barristers who are asked to advise at the planning or execution stage in transactions which involve either:

    a. the buying or selling of real property or business entities;

    b. the creation, operation, or management of trusts, companies or similar structures.

74. The requirements upon barristers who conduct relevant business can be summarised as:

    - Customer due diligence e.g. (i) identifying the client or beneficial owner prior to the establishment of the business relationship, or the execution of the transaction, (ii) obtaining information about the business relationship or transaction, (iii) monitoring the business relationship on an ongoing basis.
    - Record keeping procedures – records of all relevant transactions and evidence of client identity must be maintained for five years from the date on which the last transaction was completed.
    - Procedures to forestall money laundering, and training staff – all barristers and sets of Chambers who undertake work within the ambit of the Regulations should have in place and operate general systems and procedures for ensuring compliance with the Regulations. This includes training staff on the law relating to money laundering/terrorist financing and on how to recognise and deal with transactions and other activities which may be related to money laundering/terrorist financing.

75. The POCA makes it an offence to enter into or become concerned in an arrangement which you know or suspect facilitates (by whatever means) the acquisition, retention, use or control of criminal property by or on behalf of another person.

Solicitors and professional clients

[3.43d]

76. Two main issues arise in respect of solicitors and other professional clients in relation to public access work:

a. acceptance of work where there is already a solicitor or professional client advising the client; and

b. the recommendation of solicitors to public access clients.

77. There is no objection to you accepting instructions from a client where a solicitor is currently instructed in the matter, if the solicitor is aware that the client is doing so. There is no obligation on the solicitor to instruct you directly and, in some cases, solicitors having done the necessary preparatory work will be content for the client then to brief you directly. In such circumstances, however, it is important that you should:

a. consider whether there is any reason why the solicitor needs to instruct you directly (for example, because the matter is complex or the client cannot properly undertake the litigation component of the case);

b. be satisfied that the solicitor is aware that the client is instructing you.

If you are satisfied that the client does not require a solicitor's involvement, then you may accept the case.

78. A more difficult question arises where the solicitor does not know that the client is coming to you for advice. In some cases, the client will be seeking advice on the conduct of the solicitor or for a second opinion. Here there is no reason why you should not provide advice. You should not inform the solicitor of this without the client's consent. Where a case is litigious it is advisable for you, if client gives their consent, to liaise with the solicitor as necessary

79. It is possible that clients will wish to seek counsel's advice directly in respect of matters for which a public funding certificate is already in existence and where the certificate does not extend to counsel's advice. Counsel should be alert to guard against any breach of the rules against "topping up". Where the client has indicated that they already have a solicitor, counsel should seek to establish whether or not a certificate is in existence in respect of such work.

80. If you decide that a client should instruct a solicitor or professional client, the client may well ask you to recommend a particular individual. You may properly do this (and, if prudent, may well suggest suitable names) provided that:

a. you have reasonable grounds to believe that the solicitor or professional client is competent to do the work; and

b. you receive no payment for the referral; and

c. the solicitor is free to instruct another barrister.

January 2014

Bar Standards Board

Annex A

The Public Access Scheme – Guidance for Lay Clients

[3.43e]

Introduction

1. The purpose of this Guide is to explain how the public access scheme works and to show how members of the public ("lay clients") can use it to instruct barristers directly.

What is public access?

2. The public access scheme allows members of the public to instruct a barrister directly. In the past it was necessary for clients to use a solicitor or other third party in order to instruct a barrister.

What are the advantages of the public access scheme?

3. The main advantage of the public access scheme is that it could potentially save you money, since you would be paying for a barrister only instead of a barrister and a solicitor. However, although the barrister would be able to deal with many aspects of the case, you may have to assist in some areas, including filing documents with the court, unless the barrister is also authorised to conduct litigation on your behalf. This is explained in more detail below but can be, in some cases, a relatively complex and technical process. In some cases, the barrister may recommend that you instruct a solicitor because of the complexity of the case or because you may need more assistance than the barrister alone can provide.

Is my case suitable for public access?

4. Public access is available for all types of work that barristers can do, except for work that is funded by legal aid. It is worth considering if it would be better to have a solicitor to assist with your case in the first instance. Some cases may not be suitable for public access because of their emotional nature, because they are particularly complex or because the type of work that needs to be done in order to prepare the case would be difficult for you and may not be able to be done by a barrister. If you are not sure whether your case would be suitable for public access, you should contact an appropriate barrister (see below) or their clerk and seek an initial view. If the barrister considers that your case would benefit from the involvement of a solicitor, they will tell you so.

5. You may need to be able to deal with certain administrative tasks in order to help your case along, without the help of another legal professional. For example you may need to be able to gather together the papers and the evidence in support of your case that the barrister will need in order to do the work that you ask them to do. You may also need to file documents at court (that is submit documents such as expert reports, case summaries or witness statements depending on the nature of the case) and correspond with the court and other parties (although the barrister will be able to draft letters and other legal documents on your behalf). If you are not sure if you will be able to assist with the various administrative tasks for whatever reason, it is worth considering if it would be better to have a solicitor assist you with your case.

6. Should your case involve litigation, you should establish whether your barrister is authorised to conduct litigation on your behalf (unlike solicitors, not all barristers are able to conduct litigation). If the barrister cannot do this for you, you will be a "litigant in person" and will be treated by the court and the other side for most purposes as though you were acting without any legal assistance. (Litigation is when a legal case is taken to and through a court or tribunal.) If your case goes to court you will be the person whose name appears in the court's records, and all documents from the other parties and the court will be sent directly to you. However, you can sometimes ask or arrange for the court or tribunal and the other parties to copy documents to a third party other than your barrister. If your barrister has been authorised to conduct litigation then they will be able to undertake these tasks for you.

7. In considering whether your case is suitable for public access, the barrister is likely to take into account the nature and complexity of the case and (if the barrister cannot undertake litigation for you) your ability to deal with those aspects of it which would normally be taken care of by a solicitor. In making a decision the barrister will be guided by the requirements set out in the BSB Handbook. If they decide that your case is not suitable for public access, the rules require them to decline your instructions. If you wish, they may recommend a suitable solicitor for you to instruct.

8. It is also open to a barrister to accept instructions to read the papers and advise whether or not they are able to perform the work which you wish them to do. If your instructions are accepted for these limited purposes, it is important that you are both clear as to whether a charge is to be made. If preliminary work is to be carried out and a charge made for that work, you will be sent a client care letter. Copies of these letters are available on our website.

What if I qualify or may qualify for public funding?

9. If you are eligible for public funding (also known as "legal aid") and wish to take advantage of this funding, a barrister should advise you to approach a solicitor. This is because barristers cannot do legal aid work unless they have been instructed by a solicitor.

10. If you are not sure if you qualify for public funding and you would like to talk to someone in more detail about getting legal aid, you should contact a solicitor who does legal aid work. They will be able to tell you about the legal aid arrangements for a civil case eg when you are in a private dispute with another individual or organisation, and for a criminal case, eg where a

crime may have been committed. It is unlikely that a barrister will be able to carry out the means-test required to establish whether you would qualify for public funding. You can find out more information on the Gov.UK website: https://www.gov.uk/check-legal-aid

11. Whether or not you qualify for public funding, you might like to consider whether you have any insurance policies that might cover your legal fees, or if the fees may be paid by someone else, for example a trade union.

12. You may not wish to investigate whether you qualify for public funding, or if you qualify for legal aid you may prefer to instruct a barrister directly. In this case the barrister should ensure that you fully understand the implications of choosing to instruct them privately and the likely costs which you will incur by not accessing public funds. It is likely that the barrister will ask you to confirm in writing that you fully understand the implications of your decision, for example the client care letter might contain a paragraph indicating that you have made an informed decision not to use legal aid.

Is a barrister obliged to accept public access work?

13. A barrister may choose whether or not to accept a case that is suitable for public access work. However, a barrister may not refuse to accept instructions:

    a. On the grounds of race, colour, ethnic or national origin, nationality, citizenship, sex, gender re-assignment, sexual orientation, marital or civil partnership status, disability, age, religion or belief or pregnancy and maternity;

    b. On the grounds that the nature of the case is objectionable to him or her or to any section of the public; or

    c. On the grounds that your conduct, opinions or beliefs are unacceptable to him or her or to any section of the public.

14. If the barrister decides to accept your instructions, you will be sent a client care letter that, amongst other things, describes the work to be undertaken, sets out the terms and conditions, how much the work will cost and how to complain if something goes wrong.

15. Throughout the case, the barrister remains under an ongoing duty to consider whether a case remains suitable for public access, and they must refuse to continue to act on a public access basis if it is no longer suitable for them to do so.

How do I make use of the public access scheme?

16. To use the scheme, you would have to instruct a barrister yourself. Further details of how to do this are given in this guidance.

The difference between the services offered by a barrister and a solicitor

[3.43f]

17. The historic difference between what a barrister does and what a solicitor does has become less obvious over the last few years. However, barristers

specialise in providing expert legal advice, advocacy in court and the drafting of documents. Solicitors normally give advice to and draft documents for their clients or may instruct a barrister to provide this service. In a public access case you will need to perform these roles yourself.

18. Barristers are not able to provide some of the services that solicitors offer. For example, unless they have been specifically authorised to do so, they will not be able to conduct litigation and they are not allowed to handle client money. Your barrister will advise you if they consider that anything you want done is something which only a solicitor can provide.

19. The following are some examples of **work which a barrister is allowed to do**.

    a. A barrister may appear on your behalf at court.

    b. A barrister may give you legal advice.

    c. A barrister may draft legal documents for you, such as a will or statement of claim.

    d. A barrister may advise you on the formal steps which need to be taken in proceedings before a court or other organisation and draft formal documents for use in those proceedings.

    e. A barrister may draft and send letters for you. A barrister can assist you with drafting letters if your case goes to court but the letters will need to be sent out in your name.

    f. If a witness statement from you is required in proceedings, a barrister may prepare that statement from what you tell them. A barrister may also help to prepare witness statements from another person based on the information which that person has provided.

    g. Where a case requires an expert witness (for example, a surveyor who can provide evidence of a technical or professional nature), a barrister may advise you on the choice of a suitable expert and may draft a letter of instruction which you can then send to the expert as a letter from you on your own notepaper.

    h. Barristers can negotiate on your behalf and can attend employment, police or investigative hearings where appropriate.

20. The following are examples of work that a barrister may do, but only if they have been authorised to conduct litigation.

    a. File proceedings on your behalf with the court or file other applications, or take other formal steps in court or other proceedings. (If the barrister has not been authorised to conduct litigation, you will have to send the documents to the court, although the barrister could help prepare them for you.)

    b. Instruct an expert witness on your behalf.

21. A barrister **is not allowed to handle clients' money** (by comparison, solicitors can hold client money in the firm's trust account).

Does a barrister need special training to take public access work?

[3.43g]

22. Yes. Before a barrister can accept public access work they must satisfy number of conditions. Subject to limited exceptions, before a barrister is permitted to accept public access work they must:

    a. be properly qualified by having more than three years' standing;

    b. have undertaken a "public access" training course approved by the Bar Standards Board (BSB) through which they will demonstrate that they have the necessary knowledge, understanding and skills to conduct such work; and

    c. have notified their regulator (the BSB) that they wish to offer public access services.

Instructing a public access barrister

[3.43h]

How do I find a barrister?

23. It is important to instruct a barrister who specialises in the appropriate area of law for your case. If you do not know who to instruct, there are a number of ways of finding the right barrister. The Bar Council has a directory of public access barristers on its website, at: http://www.barcouncil.org.uk/instructing-a-barrister/public-access/.

24. There are also legal directories which specialise in finding barristers; for example, the Bar Directory (which may be found via the Bar Council's website), Chambers & Partners Guide to the Legal Profession and the Legal 500. In addition, many sets of Chambers have their own web sites which contain information about the different barristers who work there and the type of work they do. A set of Chambers is a practice where a group of independent self-employed barristers share premises and administrative services.

25. Alternatively, if you know of a set of barristers' Chambers which undertake your sort of case, you can telephone them and ask the Senior Clerk or Practice Manager to make a recommendation.

How do I instruct a barrister?

26. Try to clarify in your own mind the nature of your problem and what it is that you want the barrister to do. Telephone the Senior Clerk or Practice Manager of the set of Chambers where the barrister works and tell them that you wish to instruct the barrister directly. They will tell you what to do next.

27. Alternatively, if the barrister works by themselves as a sole practitioner, i e is not a member of a set of Chambers, you should contact the barrister's place of work. You will have to explain that you wish to instruct the barrister

directly and to explain the nature of the work which you wish the barrister to undertake for you. The barrister may want you to send you some further documents or alternatively may decide that the most appropriate option would be to meet and decide on the best way forward.

Proof of your identity

28. In some circumstances, the barrister will be required by law to carry out certain identification procedures. These must be followed as soon as reasonably practicable after you have first made contact with the barrister and it is likely that this will happen after you make the initial contact described above. Whether these procedures apply and, if so, how they should be followed, need to be considered by the barrister when you first make contact.

29. Where the procedure applies, the barrister will require satisfactory evidence of your identity – that is, proof of your name, date of birth and current address. The type of evidence required will depend on the circumstances. For example:

    a. If you are acting as an individual, you may be required to produce in person your current passport or other national identity card or a new form of driving licence (with a photograph) together with a recent utility bill, or bank or building society statement.

    b. If you are acting on behalf of a company, you will need to produce a certified copy of the Certificate of Incorporation, the latest accounts filed at Companies House and evidence that you are authorised to act on behalf of the company.

30. To carry out the procedures properly, the barrister may well have to have a meeting with you. You will be told what to bring to that meeting. The barrister is required to take copies of the documents you bring and to retain those copies for 5 years.

How will I be charged?

31. A barrister usually charges according to their level of experience, the complexity of the case and the length of time involved in dealing with it. It is important that the cost to you, and the stage at which the fee is payable, is agreed at the outset, and that the terms of the agreement are clear to both you and the barrister.

32. There are no formal scales of fees for barristers' work. The amount to be charged for any particular piece of work, and when the fee becomes payable, is a matter for negotiation between you, the barrister and their clerk. All public access barristers are independent self-employed practitioners, competing with each other. If you consider the fee proposed by one barrister to be too high, try another barrister.

33. Where the fee relates to a hearing, the barrister is normally entitled to the fee, regardless of whether or not the hearing goes ahead. If that is to be the case, the barrister should tell you at the outset. You may, if you wish, try to agree a different basis for payment of the fee in such a case.

34. In other cases (whether for a meeting or for a written advice), it may be possible to fix a fee in advance for the work. However, that will not be

possible in every case. Where it is not possible, you should ask for an estimate. You may be able to agree with the barrister that there should be a "ceiling" on the fee charged for a particular piece of work.

35. If you agree a fee in advance of the work being done, then the barrister may require that fee to be paid before carrying out the work. Where a fee is not fixed in advance and the work involves the production of paperwork (for example, the drafting of a contract), the barrister may nevertheless require you to pay for the work after they have completed it and before releasing it to you. If that is to be the case, the barrister should tell you at the outset.

36. Conditional fee agreements (agreements under which a fee becomes payable only in the event of success in a case) are possible. However, it is unlikely that barristers will be willing or able to undertake public access work on a conditional fee basis, save in very rare cases. Again, this is matter of negotiation between you and the barrister.

37. The barrister is required to keep sufficient records to justify the fees that they are charging. You are entitled to ask for details to justify the fee that you are being charged.

Can a barrister stop acting for me after they have accepted my instructions?

38. Yes, but this will only happen in a small number of cases. There will be some rare occasions when the barrister has to stop acting for you. In public access cases, the barrister must stop acting for you if they consider that the case is no longer suitable for public access. The barrister may be able to assist if, as a consequence of them no longer continuing to act for you, you will or may experience difficulties in relation to an imminent hearing.

39. In public access cases, a barrister is also required to cease to act where they have formed the view that it is in your interests or the interests of justice that you instruct a solicitor or other professional person. In such cases:

  a. Your barrister is under a continuing duty to consider whether your case remains a suitable case for public access. If they form the view that it is not, you will be advised of this fact. If you then instruct a solicitor or other professional person able to provide instructions to the barrister, they may continue to act for you. If you do not, your barrister must cease to act for you.

  b. If you are a party to proceedings (ie you have brought a case against another person or a case has been brought against you) in which a hearing is imminent, and you are likely to have difficulty in finding a solicitor in time for the hearing, your barrister should provide you with such assistance as is proper to protect your position. Although your barrister may not continue to work for you on a public access basis, they may be able to assist you by, for example:

    (i) drafting letters for you to send, asking for an adjournment of the hearing;

    (ii) writing a letter to the court in support of that application, explaining that they have had to withdraw and, if appropriate, explaining the reasons for doing so; and

(iii) assisting you to find a solicitor.

Can I instruct a barrister directly when I have already instructed solicitors?

40. Yes, you may instruct a barrister directly even though you have already instructed solicitors. If you do so, the barrister will still have to consider whether they should accept your instructions. However, the fact that you have retained solicitors is not in itself a reason for refusing to accept your instructions; nor may the barrister contact your solicitors without your permission. However, there may be cases, e g where your case involves existing litigation, where a barrister will refuse to accept your instructions unless you give them permission to contact and liaise with your solicitors and you also give your solicitors the necessary permission to provide information to the barrister.

Confidentiality and compulsory disclosure of information

41. Your barrister is under a strict professional duty to keep your affairs confidential. This legal professional privilege protects your communications with your barrister from disclosure. The only exception is that any lawyer, e g a barrister or a solicitor, may be required by law to disclose information to governmental or other regulatory authorities, and to do so without first obtaining your consent to such disclosure or telling you that they have made it.

Complaints

[3.43i]

42. If you have a complaint about your barrister, then in the first instance, you should try the complaints system maintained by your barrister or his or her Chambers. Information on how to do this should have been provided to you in the initial client care letter.

43. If you are not satisfied with the handling or outcome of your complaint by your barrister or his or her Chambers, then you can contact the Legal Ombudsman. The Legal Ombudsman is an independent organisation. It deals with complaints about the service provided by all types of lawyers in England and Wales. The Legal Ombudsman can decide whether or not the service you received from your barrister was satisfactory, and can:

a. award compensation for poor service;

b. consider whether the fees paid, or have been charged, should be reduced; and

c. decide whether you should receive an apology.

44. Any complaint to the Legal Ombudsman should be made within 6 months of receiving the final response to your complaint from your barrister or his/her Chambers (provided the response specifically notifies you of your

right to complain to the Ombudsman and of the six month time limit). A complaint to the Legal Ombudsman must also not be made more than 6 years after the problems arising and not more than 3 years after you become aware of the problem.

45. The Legal Ombudsman will assess your complaint and determine whether there are any concerns about professional misconduct (professional misconduct is when a barrister has not kept to the Code of Conduct for barristers, and, as a result, disciplinary action might need to be taken.). If your complaint relates to potential professional misconduct, the Legal Ombudsman will refer the relevant parts of your complaint to the Bar Standards Board for consideration. If your complaint needs to be referred you do not need to do anything. The Legal Ombudsman will let you know if any aspect of your complaint has been referred and the Bar Standards Board will also contact you to confirm this.

46. The Legal Ombudsman can give you more detailed information on how to make a complaint. You can contact the Legal Ombudsman:

    By phone: 0300 555 0333

    By email: enquiries@legalombudsman.org.uk

    Through their website: www.legalombudsman.org.uk

    By post: PO Box 6806, Wolverhampton, WV1 9WJ

PART III IN PRACTICE

Guidance on prohibition on handling of client money

[3.44]–[3.45]

The prohibition on self-employed barristers handling client money

1. Under the old (8th edition) of the Code of Conduct, self-employed barristers were prohibited from handling client money.

2. This prohibition remains in place under the new Bar Standards Board (BSB) Handbook. It has not been altered or watered down.

3. The prohibition is now in the following terms in Rule C73:

   "Except where you are acting in your capacity as a manager of an authorised (non-BSB) body, you must not receive, control or handle client money apart from what the client pays you for your services."

4. This applies to public access cases just as much as to other cases. It also applies to barristers who obtain authorisation from the BSB to conduct litigation. The sole exception is the receipt of money in payment of fees.

5. Any breach of this prohibition amounts to professional misconduct, and may be subject to enforcement or supervisory action by the BSB.

What is client money?

6. Client money is defined in the Handbook (definition 47) as:

(a) money, securities or other assets beneficially owned by a client; or

(b) money, securities or other assets provided by, or for the benefit of, your client or intended by another party to be transmitted to your client.

So far as self-employed barristers are concerned, it excludes:

(c) a fixed fee paid in advance; and

(d) a payment made in settlement of an accrued debt (i.e. the payment of fees or expenses which are already due to the barrister).

Misconceptions about what this means in practice

7. The prohibition is fairly simple to state, but there may be some misconceptions about its practical application, particularly in relation to payments 'on account' of fees and other payments made in advance.

BSB Guidance

8. The BSB has set out extensive guidance on the prohibition on handling client money in the new Handbook at gC103 to gC112, which repays reading in full, but I hope that it will assist if I draw your attention to some important points in relation to payments on account and other payments in advance.

A practical starting point

9. One practical step to take in deciding whether you can accept a payment from a client might be to ask yourself this question: is it a payment of fees or expenses which are already due to me?

10. If it is, then it is likely to be permissible. If it is not, then it is likely to involve handling client money.

11. That test is too simplistic to cover all situations, but may be a useful starting point. You will find a brief discussion below concerning where the dividing line may lie in cases involving fixed fee amounts payable in advance.

Payments on account

12. A payment on account does not represent fees which are already due: it represents money paid to a barrister, to be held 'on account' until fees fall due in the future.

13 Accordingly, one important effect of the prohibition is that **you cannot accept a payment on account of fees**.

14. The sole exception is where client monies are held by a third party payment service which complies with Rule C74, such as BARCO (see further below).

Payments through chambers or others

15. The prohibition on accepting payments on account applies both to payments made to you **and** to payments made into or held in your chambers' bank account.

16. Monies held by chambers which do not represent fees which are already due to a member of chambers are just as much client monies as monies held by an individual barrister.

17. Accordingly, such monies held by your chambers which relate to you are likely to be held (or are likely to be regarded by the BSB as being held) on your behalf, putting you in breach of the prohibition on handling client money. Similarly, those barristers responsible for administering or controlling your chambers' bank account may also be in breach of the Handbook by permitting or participating in a breach of the prohibition by you.

18. The prohibition also applies to monies paid to or held by a "ProcureCo", and through other arrangements which give you control over monies belonging to a client.

19. As stated in gC103–104:

> "The prohibition in Rule C73 applies to you and to anyone acting on your behalf, including any 'ProcureCo' being a company established as a vehicle to enable the provision of legal services but does not in itself supply or provide those legal services. Rule C73 prohibits you from holding client money or other client assets yourself, or thorough any agent, third party or nominee.
>
> Receiving, controlling or handling client money includes entering into any arrangement which gives you de facto control over the use and/or destination of funds provided by or for the benefit of your client or intended by another party to be transmitted to your client, whether or not those funds are beneficially owned by your client and whether or not held in an account of yours."

20. To put it simply, the prohibition on handling client monies cannot be avoided or side-stepped by using a chambers' bank account (or any other, similar arrangement) to receive or hold monies.

Fixed fees in advance

21. If you agree to be paid a fixed fee for a piece of work, and that the fee will be payable before you start work, then you will be allowed to accept payment of that fee before any work is done. Such a payment is not client money, because it belongs to you as a payment of fees already due as soon as it is received.

Other permitted arrangements

22. There are also two other types of arrangement which are allowed.

23. First, you and your client may agree that you will be paid a fixed minimum amount in advance, with the possibility of an additional fee falling due in defined circumstances (e.g. if the work reasonably takes longer than a defined number of hours).

24. An example might be as follows. Say that you charge an hourly rate of £100, and you anticipate that a piece of work will take ten hours. You thus estimate the resulting fee at £1,000. You and your client might agree that the client will pay you a fixed minimum fee of £1,000 before you do any work, but

that if it reasonably takes you longer than ten hours, then the client will pay for the additional time spent at your hourly rate. The resulting agreement is that you will be paid £1,000 in advance, and will be entitled to keep that full amount even if the work takes you less than ten hours, but you will be entitled to an additional fee if it takes longer.

25. In order to be permissible, the terms of any such agreement will need to be clear, including as to how any additional fee will be calculated, (see Rule C22) and such an arrangement should only be made with a client who can reasonably be expected to understand its effect, and who appears to do so.

26. The second type of arrangement is outlined in the BSB's guidance at gC107:

"If you agree with a client, who can reasonably be expected to understand the implications of such an agreement, that (1) your fee for any work will be charged according to the time spent on it, but (2) you will be paid a fixed fee in advance for it, and (3), when the work has been done, you will pay the client any difference between that fixed fee and the fee which has actually been earned, and (4) you will not hold the difference between the fixed fee and the fee which has been earned on trust for the client, that different will not be client money. Such fees may be considered as client money if you cannot demonstrate that the agreement was made in advance and on clear terms. You should also consider carefully whether such an arrangement is in the client's interest and that the client fully understands the implications."

27. If all of those requirements are strictly complied with, and if the correct legal analysis is that you do not hold money belonging to your client at any point, then there will be no breach of Rule C73. However, as the guidance indicates, it will be far from easy to be confident that this outcome has actually been achieved, and it may be difficult to demonstrate that your client understood the implications of such an arrangement and that it was in your client's interest. You might readily find that you have crossed the line and have handled client money. The Bar Council suggests that the BSB's guidance should be taken as containing a clear warning of the difficulties and risks involved in such an arrangement, and that you should take very great care if you decide to pursue this possibility.

Third party payment services

28. The most straight forward way of achieving a result similar to that of requiring money to be paid on account is likely to be to use a third party payment service which complies with Rule C74, such as BARCO.

29. BARCO is a third party company, owned and operated by the Bar Council, which manages the funds required to facilitate on-going legal services provided by lawyers in England and Wales. The BARCO model allows you to require your clients to pay money to BARCO to cover your fees and expenses, and then to request payment out of that money as and when fees fall due. The model was designed by the Bar Council with the prohibition on handling client money in mind. It fills a gap in public access cases, where there is no professional client who can ask your lay client for monies on account, but its use can also be built into your contracts in other cases as a permissible way of reducing the extent to which the payment of your fees and expenses is dependent upon the actions of your professional clients (particularly in cases in which your professional client is not willing to accept

a primary responsibility for payment). Full details of the BARCO service are available on the Bar Council's website here.

30. Other third party services may also be available, but if you choose to use such a service then you should ensure that both you and it comply with Rule C74 and gC108–111.

31. The availability of such services – and any decision not to use them – might be taken into account by the BSB if you were to breach Rule C73 by entering into an arrangement involving a prohibited payment on account, but that would be a matter for them.

Further information

32. If you need further information or assistance on the prohibition on handling client money, then the Bar Council's ethical enquiries service would be pleased to try to assist you. Full details of the service, including contact details, are available on the Bar Council's website here.

Important Notice

This document has been prepared by the Bar Council to assist barristers on matters of professional conduct and ethics. It is not "guidance" for the purposes of the BSB Handbook I6.4, and neither the BSB nor a disciplinary tribunal nor the Legal Ombudsman is bound by any views or advice expressed in it. It does not comprise – and cannot be relied on as giving – legal advice. It has been prepared in good faith, but neither the Bar Council nor any of the individuals responsible for or involved in its preparation accept any responsibility or liability for anything done in reliance on it. For fuller information as to the status and effect of this document, please refer to the professional practice and ethics section of the Bar Council's website here.

Accepting Instructions in Licensed Access Work

Licensed Access — General and Introductory

[3.46]–[3.49]

To simplify terminology, the names of two schemes "Bardirect" and "Direct Professional Access" have now been changed to the one name – that of "licensed access".

Organisations or individuals that have an identifiable area of expertise or experience can apply to the Bar Standards Board to be licensed to instruct barristers directly. The license holder can instruct any member of the Bar for advice, and in some circumstances representation, on their own behalf or another's behalf in the specialist area.

Licensed Access Guidance – Handbook for Chambers

(INFORMATION PACKS INCLUDING HANDBOOKS AND APPENDICES ARE AVAILABLE FROM THE GENERAL COUNCIL OF THE BAR)

Information for Chambers

[3.50]

Introduction

1.1 This handbook comprises the following sections:

(1) A general introduction which sets out what licensed access is and the nature of the work covered by the scheme.

(2) A check list for barristers considering whether to accept instructions under the licensed access scheme.

(3) Guidance for individual barristers and chambers who are considering whether to accept instructions under the licensed access scheme. The notes cover matters such as the qualifications for acceptance of instructions and the obligations arising upon receipt of instructions and thereafter. Where appropriate, the notes contain references to the relevant rules of the Licensed Access Rules.

1.2 There are also attached to this handbook a number of appendices, as follows:

(1) The information pack given to existing and prospective licensed access clients comprising the following:

(a) an introduction;

(b) guidance for those seeking recognition as licensed access clients;

(c) guidance notes for licensed access clients.

(2) An application form for those seeking recognition as licensed access clients.

(3) The Licensed Access Terms of Work.

(4) The Licensed Access Rules ("the LAR").

(5) The Licensed Access Recognition Regulations ("the LARR").

1.3 To apply for a licence, to amend an existing licence, or to receive further details of the scheme, please visit the Bar Standards Board's website, or contact Joanne Dixon, Manager, ualification Regulations: 020 7611 1444. Members of the Bar or clerks seeking guidance on Licensed Access issues should contact the Ethical Enquiries line on 020 7611 1307, or by email.

Introduction to Licensed Access

[3.51]

What is Licensed Access?

2.1 Licensed access seeks to maximise client access to the legal profession whilst at the same time ensuring that the Bar retains its identity as a referral profession. The legal profession is responsible to the public for the provision of competitive and cost effective legal services of the highest professional standards. In meeting these goals the legal profession must ensure that the interests of the client are prioritised. licensed access has been established to provide those organisations and individuals who possess the necessary skills and knowledge to do so, to have the opportunity to refer to the expertise of a Barrister without the intervention of a solicitor.

2.2 Licensed access recognises that there are significant areas of work in which the traditional two layered legal system in which the Bar insists that only a solicitor can refer work to it may unnecessarily increase the costs which the client is required to bear. Licensed access seeks to highlight the fields of practice in which barristers are positioned to provide specialised advisory and advocacy services on a competitive and cost effective basis without the intervention of a solicitor. It demonstrates the areas of work in which the skills and training of a barrister are compatible with direct access from organisations and individuals whose own training, skills and experience equip them to instruct a barrister directly.

2.3 Building upon the experience of Direct Professional Access (DPA), licensed access will allow direct access to the services of a barrister from a far wider range of organisations and individuals than previously permitted. It will mean that under certain conditions, suitable organisations and individuals (from the business community to the voluntary sector) will have direct access to a Barrister.

2.4 The Bar Council will carefully regulate licensed access to ensure that the organisation or individual is properly equipped to instruct the Bar. Through a Licensing Scheme known as Licensed Access, The Bar Council will identify the particular type and scope of work in respect of which organisations and individuals which it licenses will in future have the opportunity to instruct a Barrister directly. Licensed access will give those organisations the choice of consulting either a solicitor or a barrister in cases where it is unnecessary and not cost effective to instruct both a solicitor and a barrister.

2.5 In short, licensed access is about ensuring that the Bar is a premier provider of competitive and cost effective legal services and that in offering those services to the public it does not impose unnecessary restrictions.

Licensed Access Work

2.6 The Courts and Legal Services Act ("CLSA") recognises a distinction between advocacy services and litigation services. The Bar believes that this is an important distinction in the provision of legal services and one which should be maintained in the interests of the public. The Bar is not equipped to and does not have the facilities to conduct litigation or offer litigation services. The principle of a primarily referral based profession remains central to the profession and practice of a Barrister. Licensed access does not permit barristers to conduct litigation within the definition set out in the CLSA or to perform "excepted work" as defined in the Code of Conduct.

2.7 The licensed access licensing scheme ensures that the referrer has the skills necessary and the facilities available to instruct the Bar direct. Licensed access will not lead to referrals 'off the street'.

Implementation

2.8 Pilot schemes began in the summer of 1999. Client access to the scheme is governed by the LARR a copy of which is at Appendix 5. The role of counsel under the scheme is governed by the Licensed Access Rules ('LAR') which is at Appendix 4. Any barrister wishing to accept instructions under licensed access must be familiar with the terms of both the Regulations and the Rules.

Licensed Access Checklist

[3.52]

The Client

- Is the client an approved organisation permitted to instruct under license access?
- Does the licensed access client have sufficient authority to instruct you on the type of work that it wishes to – i e does the work fall within the authority shown on the licensed access licence forwarded to you at the time of instruction?
- Is the particular type of work actually suitable for instruction under licensed access or will it require the intervention of an intermediary to provide litigation services?

Counsel

- Are you familiar with the terms of the Licensed Access Recognition Regulations and the Licensed Access Rules?
- Are you satisfied that you and your chambers are sufficiently equipped to facilitate the additional administrative requirements necessary to accept licensed access instructions?

Guidance for Barristers and Chambers

[3.53]

Who can accept instructions?

3.1 The LAR covers every barrister in self-employed practice and governs the terms under which they are permitted to accept instructions.

3.2 As set out below, licensed access imposes requirements on Counsel to assess the suitability of instructions under the scheme, obligations to advise clients as to the nature of scheme in each particular case and a duty in respect of the organisation of paperwork etc.

3.3 To be eligible to accept licensed access instructions a barrister must have completed the first six months of pupillage and be either be a tenant in chambers or a working pupil/squatter.

The Obligation Upon Counsel Upon Receipt of Instructions

3.4 Accompanying every instruction the client is obliged to send the barrister a copy of its licensed access licence and identify exactly who is providing instructions (See LAR Rule 4). A barrister can only accept instructions if satisfied that the type of work offered is appropriate for the scheme. Whilst the licensing scheme should result in a clear definition of what work should be forwarded to counsel, it remains the responsibility of a barrister in each individual case to satisfy her/himself that s/he has sufficient facilities to support the case without the need of a solicitor or other similar intermediary (see LAR Rule 5). Similarly, if at any time during the course of a case, a barrister feels that the client's best interests and the interests of justice are best served by the introduction of a solicitor, or other such intermediary, then s/he must advise in writing the client of the need to instruct them forthwith (see LAR Rule 8(a)). If a solicitor (or other duly authorised person) is not so instructed then the barrister is under an obligation to return instructions and cease to act (see LAR Rule 8(b)).

3.5 Upon receipt of instructions a barrister must write to the client stating that the instructions have been accepted (as the case may be) on the standard terms previously agreed in writing with that licensed access client or on the Licensed Access Terms of Work or if s/he has accepted instructions otherwise than on such standard terms a copy of the agreement in writing with the licensed access client setting out the terms upon which s/he has agreed to do the work and the basis upon which s/he is to be paid. If requested so to do a barrister should send a copy of the Licensed Access Terms of Work to the licensed access client. Unless s/he has accepted instructions on the terms of the Licensed Access Terms of Work or on terms which incorporate the following particulars s/he must advise the licensed access client in writing of the effect of paragraph 401 of the Code of Conduct in the circumstances of the instructions, of the fact that the barrister cannot be expected to perform excepted work and that circumstances may arise in which it will be necessary or appropriate, often at short notice and possibly during the case, to retain the services of a solicitor or authorised litigator (see LAR Rule 7).

Administrative Obligations

3.6 A barrister who is instructed by a licensed access client must keep a case record (either on card or computer). Rule 10 sets out what must be included in the record (such as details as to the date of receipt of and acceptance of instructions, time limits, dates of advices and conferences, the fee (when agreed) etc).

3.7 Instructions (including a list of enclosures), advices, drafts of documents, notes of all conferences (including on the telephone) and all advice given must either be retained by the Barrister or the Barrister must take reasonable steps to ensure that the licensed access client will retain these documents for 6 years after the date of the last item of work done. (see LAR Rule 11).

3.8 The barrister is under a duty to ensure that the licence covers the client and the scope and type of work the subject matter of the instructions to the Barrister. A copy of the licensed access Licence must be sent to the barrister with the instructions (see LAR Rule 4). If a barrister believes that a licensed access client has in some significant respect failed to comply with the terms of its licence or with the Terms of Work, then the barrister must report the fact to the Licensed Access Committee (see LAR Rule 9).

Appendices

1. The information pack given to existing and prospective licensed access clients comprising:
   - An introduction;
   - Guidance for those seeking recognition as licensed access clients;
   - Guidance notes for licensed access clients.
2. An application form for those seeking recognition as licensed access clients. (Not printed in this Code) [*This has not been reproduced in this Handbook*].
3. The Licensed Access Terms of Work. [*These are available at the Bar Council website*].
4. The Licensed Access Rules ("the LAR") (Printed in Annex F of this Code). See para **[1.44]** above.
5. The Licensed Access Recognition Rules ("the LARR")

Licensed Access: Information Pack for Client

[3.54]

Introduction

1.1 This handbook, which is provided to existing or potential licensed access clients, comprises the following sections:

(1) Guidance for those seeking recognition under the licensed access scheme. The purpose of this section is to set out, in general terms, the principles which govern the grant of licences to use the licensed access scheme and the nature of such licences.

(2) A check list for licensed access clients who are proposing to instruct a barrister under thE terms of their licence.

(3) Guidance notes for licensed access clients. This section is designed to be of assistance to clients who are proposing to instruct a barrister under the terms of their licence. It covers matters such as the type of cases in which it is appropriate to instruct a barrister, choice of

barrister, the manner in which a barrister should be instructed, the steps following the initial instruction and billing.

1.2 There are also attached to this handbook a number of appendices, as follows:

(1) An application form for those seeking recognition as licensed access clients.

(2) The Licensed Access Terms of Work.

(3) The Licensed Access Rules.

(4) The Licensed Access Recognition Regulations.

1.3 To apply for a licence, to amend an existing licence, or to receive further details of the scheme, please visit the Bar Standards Board's website, or contact Joanne Dixon, Manager, Qualification Regulations: 020 7611 1444. Members of the Bar or clerks seeking guidance on Licensed Access issues should contact the Ethical Enquiries line on 020 7611 1307, or by email.

Guidance for those seeking recognition under the Licensed Access Scheme

[3.55]

2.1 Licensed access recognises that Solicitors are not alone in having the skills and knowledge to benefit from the legal services offered by the Bar. Licensed access provides the opportunity for the widest diversity of organisations and individuals to be licensed to instruct a barrister directly whether in the commercial, profit, non-profit or voluntary sector and irrespective of size or of type of work. These Guidance Notes use the generic term 'organisation' to describe the full range of bodies from large public limited companies to small charities and advice centres.

2.2 A fundamental principle of licensed access is that access under its provisions is licensed. An organisation or individual must be licensed by the Bar Council to use the scheme and the licence will govern who in the organisation may use the scheme and the type and scope of work in respect of which the organisation or individual is licensed to instruct a barrister directly. Within the Bar Council the licensing functions will be carried out by the Access to the Bar Committee (see LARR Regulation 1). The organisation or individual seeking a licence must apply to the Bar Council and for this purpose must complete an Application Form and provide such further information as may be required.

2.3 Whilst there is no limitation to the type of organisation that can seek authorisation the Access to the Bar Committee will ensure that the body is equipped to provide direct instructions to Counsel. The Committee will examine a wide range of criteria in determining whether a proposed organisation or individual should be granted a licence, including for example the type of work which it wishes to refer directly to a barrister, its expertise orexperience, its familiarity with any relevant area of law, its ability to obtain and prepare information and to organise papers and information for the barrister and in a contentious matter for the court, its ability to take charge and have the general conduct of the matter on which it wishes to instruct the barrister directly, the extent to which it has arrangements for holding in separate accounts and maintaining as trust monies any monies received from third parties, the extent to which the affairs and conduct of the person or organisation or its members are subject to professional, disciplinary, regulatory or other organisational rules and have professional indemnity insurance (see LARR Regulation 6).

2.4 The scope and type of work embraced by the licence will depend on the expertise, skills and knowledge of the organisation or individual applying for the licence. For example,whilst some organisations may be licensed simply to use licensed access to obtain written advices on policy matters, others may be permitted to approach counsel for a wide range of services including advocacy (see LARR Regulation 3).

2.5 The terms of a licence specifying the name of the person or organisation, the period for which the licence has been granted, the limitations or conditions on which the licence has been granted are within the complete discretion of the Access to the Bar Committee. Such limitations and conditions may for example define the matters upon which they mayinstruct counsel through licensed access, set out the tribunals or courts in which a barrister may be instructed to exercise a right of audience and/or provide that unless otherwise first agreed in writing all instructions will be deemed to be given and accepted on the terms of the Licensed Access Terms of Work as approved by the Access to the Bar Committee (see LARR Regulation 4(b)). A copy of the Licence must be sent to the Barrister at the time of instruction enabling the barrister to ensure that the licence covers the instructions (see LAR Rule 4(c)).

2.6 The status of an organisation can be considered by the Access to the Bar Committee. Approval can be given to an organisation or an individual, or to all or some of the members of an organisation or to all or some of the employees of an organisation or its members or of the individual (LARR Regulation 3(c)). Approval can be on a provisional or full basis and can be limited in time (LARR Regulation 3(a) (b)).

2.7 The Access to the Bar Committee may from time to time, approve additional persons or organisations, withdraw approval either in whole or in part from any person or organisation who has been licensed, increase reduce or otherwise alter the period for which a licence has been granted, alter or revoke the conditions or limitations which have been imposed under the licence and cancel and demand surrender of any licence which has been issued (see LARR Regulation 5).

2.8 Instructions under licensed access can only be accepted where the client is properly authorised for the type of work sought to be offered (see LARR Regulation 3(e) and LAR Rule 1).

2.9 A barrister is not required to accept work from a licensed access client and should not do so if the barrister considers it in the interests of the lay client or the interests of justice that an intermediary be instructed together with or in place of the barrister. Such intermediary may be a solicitor or other authorised litigator or some other appropriate person or organization (see BDR Rule 5(b)). If a barrister having accepted instructions from a licensed access client considers it in the interests of the lay client or the interests of justice that an intermediary be instructed together with or in place of the barrister the barrister must forthwith advise the licensed access client in writing to instruct such intermediary and unless such intermediary is as soon as reasonably practicable instructed the barrister must cease to act and must return any instructions to the licensed access client (see LAR Rule 8).

Checklist for Licensed Access Clients Proposing to Instruct Barristers

[3.56]

- Is my case an appropriate case for instructing a barrister: see guidance notes in section 3, paragraphs 3.2 to 3.5.
- How do I choose the right barrister for my case: see guidance notes in section 3, paragraphs 3.6 to 3.8.
- How do I go about instructing a barrister: see guidance notes in section 3, paragraphs 3.9 to 3.10.
- How are a barrister's fees calculated and how should they be agreed: see guidance notes in section 3, paragraphs 3.6(4) and 3.10(4).
- What should I send to a barrister: see guidance notes in section 3, paragraphs 3.11 to 3.15.
- What happens after I have instructed a barrister: see guidance notes in section 3, paragraphs 3.16 to 3.20.
- How will I be billed: see guidance notes in section 3, paragraphs 3.21 to 3.22.
- What do I do if I am unhappy about the service which has been provided: see guidance notes in section 3, paragraphs 3.23 to 3.24.

Guidance on Instructing Barristers under the Licensed Access Scheme

[3.57]

Introduction

3.1 These guidance notes are intended for use by licensed access clients who are considering instructing a barrister or barristers direct, whether for the purposes of obtaining their advice or for the purposes of obtaining representation in court under the new arrangements for direct licensed access.

In which cases is it appropriate to instruct a Barrister?

3.2 The overriding consideration when deciding whether it is appropriate to instruct a barrister alone, or whether to instruct a solicitor (whether that solicitor in turn instructs a barrister or not), is whether to do so would be in the best interests of the client. This means that it is essential to have a proper understanding of what a barrister can and cannot do.

3.3 The following is an outline of those things which a barrister is normally expected and entitled to do:

(1) Advisory work (e.g., giving advice on the law generally and/or on the merits of any particular matter, whether contentious or non-contentious, and/or on the drafting of documents such as contracts, standard terms and conditions, correspondence , letters before actions, reports etc.,);

(2) Drafting of claim forms, petitions and other applications;

(3) Drafting of statements of case;

(4) Advice on the factual and expert evidence which will be needed in order to establish the case at the hearing, whether oral or written;

(5) Advice on which witness statements, expert reports and documents must or should be disclosed to the other side;

(6) Assistance in the preparation of affidavits and witness statements for use at a hearing. There is an important distinction between (i) taking a statement from a witness, which involves interviewing the witness in order to elicit his or her evidence, and (ii) assisting in the preparation of a witness statement[1]. The latter task typically includes identifying the matters the statement should cover, reviewing a draft witness statement, advising on questions of admissibility and weight of particular passages of draft statements, and by settling from drafts a final form of witness statement;

(7) Preparation of any documents, such as skeleton arguments, chronologies, etc, used for the purposes of presenting a case in court;

(8) Representation at any court hearing;

(9) Representation at a hearing before a tribunal other than a court, for example a disciplinary tribunal;

(10) Advice on tactics in relation to the litigation generally and its settlement.

3.4 There are some things, on the other hand, which a barrister would not normally be expected or entitled to do. In general barristers do not have the facilities or the office backup to undertake much of the general preparatory work necessary to get a more complex case to trial. In particular, barristers are not permitted to do the following:

(1) the management, administration and general conduct of litigation including written or oral communication between the parties or their advisors;

(2) investigating and collecting evidence for use in court;

(3) the receipt or handling of client money.

3.5 In general, accordingly, unless the licensed access client is equipped and prepared to undertake the type of litigation support function normally undertaken by a solicitor, the typical case in which a barrister might be instructed directly to appear in court will be one:

(1) of lesser factual complexity; and

(2) where there is unlikely to be a need for extensive investigation into

and gathering of evidence, whether oral or documentary. Even in the more complex cases, or cases where extensive investigation is required, it may be appropriate to instruct a barrister direct to advise, or to appear in court on a particular application within the litigation.

Choosing a Barrister

3.6 The following factors are relevant in determining the appropriate barrister.

(1) Whether the case merits more then one barrister. It may be appropriate to instruct two (or more) barristers to work as a team, possibly each from a different field of expertise.

(2) Whether the case merits the use of a Queen's Counsel, or a junior barrister, or both. There is no hard and fast rule as to when it is appropriate to use a Queen's Counsel. In general, it is appropriate where the issues involved in the case are particularly complex, where the result is likely to have significant consequences for the client, and where there is a sufficient amount at stake to warrant the higher cost. Similarly, there is no hard and fast rule as to when it is appropriate to instruct both a junior barrister and a Queen's Counsel. In general, it is appropriate to do so where the criteria for the use of a Queen's Counsel are satisfied and there is likely to be a significant amount of preparatory, drafting or research work which could be carried out by a junior barrister at a significantly lower cost than if the Queen's Counsel were to do so.

(3) The seniority of the barrister. A barrister's seniority is denoted in the various published directories and guides (see below) by reference to the year in which he was called to the bar. A barrister is normally called to the bar during the year between completing his final year of studying for the bar (i.e., taking the exams at the end of the bar vocational course) and completion of his pupillage. In practice this means that a barrister called in, say, 1990 will by October 1999 have been in practice since about October 1991, i.e., 8 years. This is not, however, a hard and fast rule. Some barristers might have followed another career path (for example an academic career) between being called to the bar and entering practice. The various directories of barristers denote the seniority of a Queen's Counsel by the year in which he took silk. Queen's Counsel are appointed in the April of each year. The factors which will dictate the appropriate level of seniority for a particular case are similar to those which dictate whether it is appropriate to employ the services of a Queen's Counsel or a junior barrister (see above).

(4) Expense. Particular regard should be paid to the cost of employing the services of different barristers. In so doing, the following should be taken into consideration:

(a) There are three basic methods by which barristers charge for their services:

(i) an hourly rate so that the fee varies upon the amount of time taken to complete the work;

(ii) a fixed fee agreed in advance for a particular piece of work;

(iii) a "brief" fee, which is a fixed fee to cover preparation for a hearing and the first day in court, and a "refresher" or a daily charge for each subsequent day.

Additionally, some barristers may in certain types of case be allowed and prepared to accept instructions pursuant to a conditional fee agreement, in which the payment or the amount of the fee will depend upon the outcome in the case.

Generally, licensed access clients should be prepared to negotiate with the barrister or his clerk in relation to the method of charging for the barrister's services as well as the overall amount to be charged.

(b) In comparing hourly rates offered in respect of different barristers, it should be borne in mind that a barrister well versed in the relevant field of expertise is likely to spend fewer hours on the matter than one who has a more general experience.

3.7 Each barrister has a professional duty to advise his client whenever he considers either that the client ought to be represented by someone with a different expertise, or by someone at a lower or higher level of seniority. In addition, each barrister owes a duty to consider, and advise, as to whether the case warrants the assistance of (as the case may be) a Queen's Counsel or junior barrister, or alternatively no longer merits the continued use of either the Queen's Counsel or junior barrister. The barrister also has a duty to advise whether the case merits the involvement of a solicitor.

3.8 There are a number of ways in which to identify a suitable barrister for the relevant case.

(1) Recommendation from others;

(2) The Bar Council publishes a Bar Directory that lists all barristers currently practising and gives details of the expertise of barristers in particular chambers. The Directory is available on the Internet at www.BarCouncil.org.uk.

(3) Directories are published by a number of specialist Bar Associations, for example by the Chancery Bar Association and the Commercial Bar Association, which contains lists of barristers (though not all barristers) practising within those fields and details of the expertise of barristers in particular chambers;

(4) There are a number of directories published by private organisations, many of which indicate the views of the editors of the directory of particular barristers operating in particular fields of expertise. These views, being subjective, need to be treated with caution.

(5) Having identified a set or sets of chambers whose members are held out as having expertise in the relevant field, it is worth contacting the chambers to discuss with the clerk the member or members who would be most suitable for your purposes, and to discuss the possible charging structure and charge-out rates of the relevant members.

Instructing a Barrister

3.9 Once the licensed access client has decided upon a barrister to instruct, it is always preferable to contact that barrister's clerk in the first instance in order to ensure that the barrister is available.

3.10 In making enquiries of the barrister's clerk, there are four particular points to check:

(1) Is the barrister available to carry out the specific piece of work in relation to which he or she is to be instructed? Barristers are sole practitioners. This has the advantage that when a barrister is instructed it is the barrister himself or herself who carries out the work. In this respect a barrister differs from a solicitor who will regularly delegate work to an assistant or assistants. It has, however, the disadvantage that any particular barrister will already have commitments to other clients, including commitments to complete paper work by a certain date, or to appear in court on a certain date or dates, so that his or her availability may be limited.

(2) If the barrister is to be instructed in a matter that will be ongoing, is he or she likely to be available for any court dates that are to be arranged in the future? Sometimes court hearings are arranged for the convenience of the parties, so that they can ensure that the barrister of their choice represents them. On other occasions, however, court hearings are arranged without regard to the availability of the parties' barristers. Whilst it will not be possible for the barrister to commit to be free for any lengthy period of time within which hearings might occur, it is sensible when initially instructing a barrister to enquire whether he or she has existing commitments such that it is known, or likely, that they will not be free during the period of time when prospective court hearings are likely to occur. It is sometimes sensible to enquire, at the outset, whether there are other members of chambers of a similar level of experience and with similar expertise who would be able to take over in respect of future court hearings in case the barrister of first choice subsequently became unavailable.

(3) If the barrister is being asked to advise in conference, or to attend a specific court hearing, his or her clerk should be asked at the outset to reserve the date and time in the barrister's diary for that purpose.

(4) Fees. A barrister's fees are normally negotiated with his or her clerk. The way in which barristers charge for their services is referred to in paragraph 3.6(4) above. Negotiations at the outset should include whether a fixed fee should be paid, and if so for how much, whether payment should be on the basis of an hourly rate, in which case an indication of the number of hours which the matter is likely to take should be asked for and given, or whether a brief fee/refresher approach is appropriate, in which case the amounts should be agreed in advance. In addition, in any case where a fixed fee is agreed, you should ensure that there is clear agreement with the barrister's clerk as to the extent of the work to be included in the fee (e.g., whether it is to include advising both in conference and in writing, or only one of these).

Identifying the information and materials to send to the Barrister

3.11 There is no required form or procedure for informing a barrister of the matters in relation to which he is to advise or represent you. The appropriate quantity of material to provide, and the appropriate form in which to provide it, will depend upon the circumstances of each case and, to an extent, the requirements of the particular barrister. Solicitors have developed a particular format and style of expression in instructions to barristers. Whilst there is no reason why licensed access clients should not adopt a similar format and style, there is also no reason why they should. It is the content of the instructions that is important, not the form. In most cases, it is sufficient that the information is provided to the barrister in the form of a letter or a note.

3.12 In an urgent case it is possible to attend a conference with a barrister without any prior written instructions. Similarly, where urgent applications to court are concerned, it is more important that the barrister is provided with the necessary materials to make the application as soon as possible, than that time is spent on drafting written instructions.

3.13 Whenever you are in doubt as to any aspect of the instructions, telephone the barrister direct. A great deal of unnecessary time and expense can be saved by an initial discussion with the barrister as to the materials he will need at the outset to see.

3.14 The following guidelines are to be read in the light of the preceding paragraphs and are intended to be of general assistance only.

3.15 As a general rule, the following is the information and material which a barrister would normally expect to be sent to him upon his initial instruction:

(1) A brief description of the circumstances giving rise to the issue in relation to which he is instructed, including a brief history of the matter and a description of the parties involved.

(2) An outline of the issue or issues in relation to which he is either instructed to appear in court or to advise.

(3) In the case of existing proceedings, copies of any documents already filed with the court, or exchanged between the parties which are relevant to the issue upon which the barrister is instructed;

(4) A clear statement of what it is the barrister is being asked to do. For example:

(a) where advice is sought, state whether the barrister is asked to advise on a specific issue, or to advise more generally on the issues which he thinks arise out of the circumstances identified to him;

(b) where the barrister is requested to draft or settle a document, then state the document or documents which he is required to draft (e.g., a statement of case or application), or settle (e.g., an affidavit or a witness statement);

(c) where the barrister is requested to attend a hearing, identify the hearing and state clearly what result from the hearing the barrister is instructed to try to obtain.

(5) Photocopies of those documents that you think are relevant to the matters upon which his advice is sought. The following should be noted:

(a) It is in relation to this aspect that communication with the barrister is particularly recommended, whether prior to sending any instructions, or having sent instructions with a few "core" documents so as to identify what other documents ought to be sent.

(b) It is important not to send original documents, since these should not be marked and should remain in their original form and should be available for inspection by third parties, whether by reason of disclosure orders which might be made in litigation or otherwise.

(c) Where correspondence or similar documentation is to be sent, it will save time and expense if it is arranged in chronological order.

(d) It is also helpful to include an index of the documents, or of the classes of documents, sent.

(6) A clear statement of the time within which a response is sought from the barrister.

(7) Where there is a time limit on commencing proceedings, or taking a step in existing proceedings, or for any other matter, a clear statement of this in the instructions.

Steps following the initial instructions

3.16 Having received the instructions, the barrister should take an initial look through the papers. There are four potential reasons why at this stage the barrister could decline to continue to act:

(1) It is possible that the barrister will identify a conflict of interest (for example because he is acting or has previously acted for another party in the same case) which was not picked up during your discussions with his or her clerk.

(2) The barrister (in cases other than where the licensed access client is able to undertake litigation support such as that normally undertaken by a solicitor) may decide that, because the case requires taking detailed statements from witnesses, or extensive office back-up that he or she does not have, it is not an appropriate case for direct access and needs the expertise of a solicitor. In those circumstances the barrister is required to take no action until an appropriate intermediary is instructed.

(3) The barrister may decide that on closer inspection of the papers the subject matter falls outside his or her area of expertise, or that the case is more complex than he or she is equipped to deal with. He or she is then entitled to decline the instructions.

(4) The barrister may decide, having accepted the instructions on the basis that they were likely to occupy a certain amount of time, which he or she had available, that the instructions will in fact require considerably more of his or her time, which is not available.

3.17 Alternatively, the barrister may decide that whilst the case is within his or her expertise, it is more suitable for a barrister of different seniority. In that case, the barrister is obliged to advise you of his view, but you may choose whether or not to accept that advice.

3.18 Assuming that the barrister is able to continue to work on the case, the course of conduct thereafter will depend upon the circumstances of the individual case.

3.19 It will often be useful to arrange a face to face meeting with the barrister in order either to discuss the advice that the barrister is to give, or to discuss what work needs to be done in preparing the case for court. Such a meeting may take place either at the barrister's chambers, or at the premises of the licensed access client. It is often easier for the barrister to hold the meeting at his or her chambers, where he or she has ready access to the background material needed in order to advise, unless the volume of material, the need to view equipment or a site or the convenience of the client or witnesses suggests otherwise.

3.20 A face to face meeting is particularly useful in order to discuss and agree upon the division of work as between the barrister and the licensed access client in progressing a case towards a court hearing (bearing in mind those matters which the licensed access client can expect, or should not expect, the barrister to do, as set out earlier in these guidelines).

Billing

3.21 The barrister will send a fee note, either at the end of the case, or after each separate item of work done or, in an ongoing matter, at periodic intervals.

3.22 The licensed access client is contractually liable for the fees of the barrister. Any disputes with the barrister over the fee should be taken up with the barrister's chambers as soon as possible. It will often be the case that any dispute over the fee, or other complaint, can be resolved informally with the barrister's chambers.

3.23 The Bar Council is not usually able to involve itself in disputes over fees, except where there is an allegation of professional misconduct[1]. If the fee dispute cannot be resolved informally, accordingly, there is little alternative but for the matter to go to court.

3.24 If you have any concerns about the services provided by your barrister, you should, in the first instance, refer these to the barrister himself to be resolved through the chambers complaints procedure if possible. If you remain dissatisfied, it is open to you to approach the Bar Council and you should write to the Secretary of the Professional Conduct and Complaints Committee at the Bar Council for further information about this.

Licensed Access Terms of Business

Terms of Work

[3.57a]

1. Application of these terms: These terms apply to all instructions accepted by barristers where the instructions are given by a licensed access client in accordance with the terms of a licence issued by the Bar Standards Board. They apply save to the extent that they have been varied or excluded by written agreement and subject to the following:

   (1) These Terms will apply to instructions only where the instructions have been accepted by the barrister.

   (2) These terms do not apply to legal aid work.

2. The Licence: A copy of the Licence issued to the licensed access client by the Bar Standards Board shall be sent with every set of instructions.

3. Acceptance of Instructions: Notwithstanding that instructions have been delivered to a barrister, he shall not be deemed to have accepted them until he has satisfied himself that the instructions are given in accordance with the licence granted by the Bar Standards Board by a person entitled by that licence to give those instructions and has expressly accepted them orally or in writing.

4. Code of Conduct to prevail: A barrister accepts instructions upon the understanding that in carrying them out he must and will comply with the Code of Conduct and the general law. In this regard

   Paragraph 307 of the Code states:

   307. A barrister must not:

   (a) permit his absolute independence integrity and freedom from external pressures to be compromised;

   (b) do anything (for example accept a present) in such circumstances as may lead to any inference that his independence may be compromised;

   (c) compromise his professional standards in order to please his client the Court or a third party, including any mediator;

   (d) give a commission or present (save for small promotional items) or lend any money for any professional purpose to or (save as a remuneration in accordance with the provisions of this Code) accept any money by way of loan or otherwise from any client or any person entitled to instruct him as an intermediary;

   (e) make any payment (other than a payment for advertising or publicity permitted by this Code or in the case of a self-employed barrister remuneration paid to any clerk or other employee or staff of his chambers) to any person for the purpose of procuring professional instructions;

   provided that nothing in paragraph 307(d) or (e) shall prevent a barrister from paying a reasonable fee or fees required by an alternative dispute resolution body that appoints or recommends persons to provide mediation, arbitration or adjudication services, or from entering into such a reasonable fee-sharing arrangement required by such a body, if the payment or arrangement is of a kind similar to that made by other persons who provide such services through the body;

(f) Deleted from 26th March 2010.

The Licensed Access Rules (which form part of the Code of Conduct) provide:

(a) by rule 5 that a barrister must not accept any instructions from a licensed access client

(i) unless the barrister and his Chambers are able to provide the services required of them by that licensed access client;

(ii) if the barrister considers it in the interests of the lay client or the interests of justice that a solicitor or other authorised litigator or some other appropriate intermediary (as the case may be) be instructed either together with or in place of the barrister;

(b) by rule 8 that if at any stage a barrister who is instructed by a licensed access client considers it in the interests of the lay client or the interests of justice that a solicitor or other authorised litigator or some other appropriate intermediary (as the case may be) be instructed either together with or in place of the barrister:

(i) the barrister the barrister must forthwith advise the licensed access client in writing to instruct a solicitor or other authorised litigator or other appropriate intermediary (as the case may be) ; and

(ii) unless a solicitor or other authorised litigator or other appropriate intermediary (as the case may be) is instructed as soon as reasonably practicable thereafter the barrister must cease to act and must return any instructions.

4A. The work expected of a barrister is defined by his instructions. These only extend to work permitted by the Code of Conduct but which a barrister is not required to undertake (for example conducting correspondence on behalf of the lay client) where that work is the subject of specific instructions and those instructions have been accepted by the barrister in writing.

5. Duty to the lay client: Where instructions are given to a barrister by a licensed access client in relation to a matter concerning a lay client the licensed access client warrants that he has or will as soon as practicable

(1) Send the lay client a copy of the Licensed Access Terms of Work.

(2) Advise the lay client in writing of:

(a) the effect of paragraphs 401 and 401A of the Code of Conduct as it relevantly applies in the circumstances;

(b) the fact that the barrister cannot be expected to perform the functions of a solicitor or other authorised litigator and in particular to fulfil limitation obligations disclosure obligations and other obligations arising out of or related to the conduct of litigation;

(c) the fact that circumstances may require the lay client to retain a solicitor or other authorised litigator at short notice and possibly during the case.

(3) Send to the lay client a copy of any advice received by the licensed access client from the barrister to the effect that:

(a) a solicitor or other authorised litigator or some other appropriate intermediary (as the case may be) is capable of providing any services to the lay client which the barrister himself is unable to provide; or

(b) the barrister considers it in the interests of the lay client or the interests of justice that a solicitor or other authorised litigator or some other appropriate intermediary (as the case may be) be instructed either together with or in place of the barrister; or

(c) the licensed access client should instruct a solicitor or other authorised litigator or other appropriate intermediary (as the case may be).

6. Liability for the fees: The licensed access client is liable for a barrister's fee due in respect of work carried out by the barrister under any instructions. In a case where the matter concerns a lay client, the licensed access client is solely and exclusively liable to the barrister for the fees. In this regard:

(1) The relationship between the barrister and the licensed access client is a contractual one.

(2) Any individual giving or purporting to give the instructions on behalf of any partnership firm, company, individual or other person warrants to the barrister that he is authorised by the latter to do so.

(3) If the licensed access client is a partnership or a firm or unincorporated association, the liability of the partners or members and on death that of their estates for the barrister's fees is joint and several.

(4) Neither the sending by a licensed access client of instructions to a barrister nor the acceptance of those instructions by a barrister nor anything done in connection therewith nor these Terms nor any arrangement or transaction entered into under them shall give rise to any contractual relationship rights duties or consequences whatsoever either (i) between the barrister or the General Council of the Bar and any lay client or (ii) between the General Council of the Bar and the licensed access client.

7. Time for performance of instructions: Unless otherwise expressly stipulated by written agreement:

(1) a barrister will carry out the instructions as soon as he reasonably can in the ordinary course of his work, but

(2) time will not be of the essence.

8. Duty of care: A barrister will exercise reasonable care and skill in carrying out instructions. This is however subject to

   (1) any immunity from suit which the barrister may enjoy under the general law in respect of any work done in the course of carrying out instructions and

   (2) paragraph 11(1) below.

9. Copies of briefs and instructions and records of advice: A barrister shall be entitled on completion of any work to take and retain a copy of such instructions and papers and of any written work.

10. Fees: Other cases. Subject to the Code of Conduct, the following provisions apply:

   (1) Fees and/or charging rates: These shall be as agreed between the barrister and the licensed access client before the barrister commences work under the instructions or, in default of such agreement, shall be a reasonable professional rate for the barrister instructed.

   (2) Submission of fee notes:The barrister shall (a) as soon as reasonably practicable comply with a written request by the licensed access client for a fee note and (b) in any event submit a fee note not later than 3 months after the work to which the fee note relates has been done.

   (3) Time for payment: A barrister's fees in respect of instructions to which these Terms apply are payable and must be paid by the licensed access client 30 days after receipt by the licensed access client of the fee note submitted by him to the licensed access client in respect of such fees.

   (4) Default in payment: In the event that a barrister's fees are not paid in full in accordance with sub-paragraph (3) above, the fees and/or the balance thereof outstanding from time to time will carry simple interest at the stipulated rate from the date they became due until payment in full.

11. Complaints: In the event that the licensed access client or the lay client (if any) has any Complaint about the services provided by a barrister under any instructions

   (1) The fees shall be paid in accordance with paragraph 10(3) above and no Complaint shall afford a valid ground for non-payment of the fees whether on grounds of set-off or otherwise.

   (2) Sub-paragraph (1) above is without prejudice to any rights of the licensed access client and the lay client to institute any proceedings against the barrister and/or a complaint against the barrister under the Complaints Rules in Annexe K to the Code of Conduct.

12. Definitions: In these Terms:

   (1) "Instructions" includes a brief and any other instructions to a barrister.

   (2) "Licensed access Client" means the individual, firm, company or other person instructing or seeking to instruct a barrister, whether on his, their or its own behalf or on behalf of some other person under the terms of a licence issued by the Bar Standards Board.

(3) In a case where the licensed access client is instructing or seeking to instruct a barrister not on his, their or its own behalf but on behalf of some other person, 'lay client' means that other person.

(4) "Written agreement" means an agreement in writing between (a) one or more barristers (including a set of Chambers) and (b) a licensed access client.

(5) "Written work" includes any draft pleading or other similar document, any written opinion or advice, and any other similar document.

(6) "Legal aid work" means instructions which are publicly funded under the Legal Aid Act 1988 or Access to Justice Act 1999 as in force from time to time or any legislation which may replace them, and any work carried out pursuant to such instructions.

(7) "Stipulated rate" means the rate at which interest is payable from time to time on High Court judgment debts.

(8) "Complaint" includes any complaint whatsoever relating to anything done by a barrister pursuant to any instructions or to the time taken or alleged to have been taken by him in carrying them out and whether the same involves issues of competence, quantum or otherwise.

(9) "Code of Conduct" means the Code of Conduct of the Bar of England and Wales as promulgated and amended by the General Council of the Bar from time to time.

(10) In these Terms any reference to the masculine shall be deemed to include the feminine.

Guidance for Clerks Regarding Public Access Rules

[3.58]

The Bar Standards Board has produced guidance specifically for clerks relating to the Public Access Rules, as set out below.

Guidance for clerks regarding Public Access and Licensed Access Rules

[3.59]–[3.61]

Introduction

1. The purpose of this guidance is to explain, in general terms, how the licensed access and public access schemes work and to show how members of the public, also known as lay clients (the "client"), can use the public access scheme to instruct barristers. This document does not deal with obligations under the Proceeds of Crime Act, Money Laundering Regulations or Equality Act 2010. Barristers do not, and cannot, delegate their responsibilities under the Proceeds of Crime Act or the Money Laundering Regulations to their clerks. It will at all times be the responsibility of barristers to ensure compliance with any obligations which may arise.

2. Further guidance for barristers and clients about the public access scheme can be obtained from the Bar Standard Board's (BSB) website at the following link: https://www.barstandardsboard.org.uk/regulatory-requirements/bsb-handbook/code-guidance/.

3. Since 2004 members of the public have been able to go directly to a barrister without having to involve an instructing solicitor or other intermediary. In the past it was necessary for clients to use a solicitor or other recognised third party through whom the barrister would be instructed.

4. Although the barrister's role remains essentially the same, members of the public may instruct a barrister directly through the public access scheme, provided the barrister has a full practising certificate, has undertaken the appropriate training and otherwise complies with their various BSB Code of Conduct obligations.

PART III IN PRACTICE

What is Licensed Access?

5. In 1990 a number of professions were recognised as entitled to instruct barristers without a solicitor: this was at that time called "Direct Professional Access". Accountants, tax specialists and surveyors are the three professions which have made the greatest use of this arrangement. This arrangement has since been extended to members of various other groups and to various individual bodies, which in each case were granted a licence for this purpose: this was then called "BarDIRECT". All these arrangements are now called "Licensed Access".

Initial contact and acceptance of instructions

6. Ascertain whether the client contacting Chambers has a BSB licence to instruct the Bar directly and if so what types of work the licence covers. For practical purposes three categories are so entitled:

   a. Recognised professions (formerly Direct Professional Access): a list is available from the BSB website – See Licensed Access Recognition Regulations https://www.barstandardsboard.org.uk/regulatory-requirements/for-barristers/licensed-access-recognition-regulations/.

   b. Individuals who have been given licences or members of organisations which have group licences (formerly BarDirect): a list is available from the Qualifications Committee of the BSB.

If licensed access

7. If the client is exercising an individual licence, request that a copy be supplied. If the client presents himself as a member of a recognised profession, and if uncertain of client, check in appropriate professional or trade directory.

8. Place the enquiry before the intended barrister to ascertain whether the barrister considers it proper to accept the case on licensed access.

9. If the intended barrister considers it proper to accept the case on licensed access, write to client notifying that the case is accepted, the terms on which it is accepted and the basis upon which he is to be paid (if it is wished to withhold delivery of paperwork until fee paid, set this out expressly in letter).

If public access

10. Check whether the intended barrister:

    a. is properly qualified with a full practising certificate;

    b. has undertaken BSB approved public access training; and

    c. has notified Bar Council that they will accept public access work.

11. Place the enquiry before the intended barrister to ascertain whether the barrister considers it proper to accept the case on public access. This decision will be based on a number of factors including the complexity of the case and the ability of the client to undertake aspects of the case.

12. A barrister may accept public access instructions in any area of practice. However, it should be noted that the restriction on the conduct of litigation will be relevant if they have not been authorised by the BSB to undertake litigation. Barristers should not accept cases where there is an expectation that they will carry out litigation if they are not authorised to do so. It is suggested that in the event of any uncertainty you should contact the Bar Council's Public Access Helpline: 020 7611 1472.

13. Barristers can now also accept public access cases where the client is eligible for legal aid, provided reasonable steps have been taken to ensure the client has made an informed decision to choose public access. It should be noted that barristers are unlikely to be able to conduct a means assessment to establish whether a client will qualify for public funding. Nor are barristers at

present able to apply to the Legal Services Commission for public funding on behalf of a client. Therefore, if a barrister is approached by a person whose circumstances are not such as to make it obvious that he will not be eligible for public funding, the barrister should advise the client that they cannot investigate the possibility of public funding and advise the client to approach a solicitor to investigate this possibility. The barrister should also inform the client that they can visit the www.gov.uk website for further information: https://www.gov.uk/check-legal-aid.

14. Before accepting instructions it is good practice for the barrister to discuss with the client how they will pay and the discussion should cover whether public funding may be available to the client, whether the client has any insurance policies that might cover the fees, and whether the fees may be paid by someone else such as a trade union. It is essential that all clients clearly understand the implications of choosing public access and the likely costs which they will incur by not accessing public funds. If a client is eligible for public funding but has chosen to instruct a barrister directly the client care letter should explain the situation in a clear and understandable fashion. The barrister should obtain written confirmation from the client that they understand that legal aid might be available but the client would prefer to instruct a barrister directly, for example a paragraph to this effect could be inserted into the model client care letter.

15. If the barrister is not willing to accept the case, notify the prospective client as soon as possible. Remind the barrister to keep a record of the reasons for declining the work. If the barrister is uncertain whether it would be proper to accept, and wishes to have a no-fee meeting with the prospective client before deciding, arrange the meeting. Write to the client to ensure that the limited purpose of the meeting is understood.

16. If the barrister is uncertain whether it would be proper to accept and wishes to be paid for having a meeting with the client and/or for reading documents before deciding, ensure that the barrister writes a client care letter to the client in respect of such preliminary work.

17. If and when the barrister decides to accept instructions, ensure that the barrister sends a client care letter. The clerk should assist the barrister to select an appropriate fee option, and to insert suitable figures. The letter forms the basis of the relationship between the barrister and the client, and it will be considered professional misconduct if a properly worded letter is not sent to the client. The model client care letter can be found on the BSB's website at: https://www.barstandardsboard.org.uk/regulatory-requirements/bsb-handbook/code-guidance/.

18. Provided the barrister has promptly written to the client in the terms of the model letter they will have complied with the notification requirements set out in rC124 of the BSB Handbook. Where the client has previously instructed the barrister in respect of the same matter it may well be unnecessary for the barrister to provide a full client care letter in respect of every new instruction received. Barristers must still ensure that the fundamentals of the client care letter are set out in respect of each new instruction i.e. the work that is to be undertaken, the cost and the payment mechanism. Other matters which the barrister is required to inform the client about, such as the barrister's limitations with respect to litigation (if relevant), how to

complain and the fact the barrister may have to withdraw can be covered by referring the client to the original client care letter.

19. Ensure a copy of this letter is filed and stored safely and open a case record on the Chambers computer. Ensure the client countersigns and returns a copy of the client care letter. File the countersigned letter.

20. If the client is acting as an intermediary for the ultimate client, ensure that the barrister not only sends an appropriate client care letter to the intermediary, but also an appropriate letter to the client.

After case accepted (both licensed access and public access)

21. Notify the client when paperwork is done. If the fee has been agreed to be time based, notify the client what the fee has come to. Record such notification on the Chambers computer.

22. If an agreement has been made with the client that the paperwork will not be delivered until the fee is paid, ensure that fee has been received before paperwork is delivered. If the paperwork is delivered by e-mail, consider whether it should also be delivered in hard copy form.

After work done (both licensed access and public access)

23. Maintain the case record on the Chambers computer of all relevant actions and payments, as with a solicitor referral case.

24. Keep in an ordered filing system copies of letters to and from the barrister regarding acceptance of instructions and fees.

25. Remind the barrister to archive necessary papers for at least 7 years for a public access case and 6 years for a licensed access case. This will include:

    a. all drafts and advices prepared by the barrister,

    b. the barrister's notes of all meetings and telephone calls,

    c. either a list of all papers before the barrister, or copies of them,

    d. identification documents if the barrister has considered work to be "relevant business" within the Money Laundering Regulations.

Additional requirements for public access barristers with less than three years' standing

26. The prohibition on barristers with less than three years' standing undertaking public access work has been removed. However, in addition to having access to a qualified person such barristers are also required to:

    a. keep a log of the public access cases they have dealt with and record any issues or problems that have arisen; and

    b. where possible and appropriate, seek feedback from public access clients.

27. A pro forma for logging cases is attached at Annex A of the BSB's guidance for barristers. The purpose of this requirement is to assist the Bar Standards Board in assessing whether the removal of the prohibition has introduced any unacceptable risk in to the process. Therefore the BSB will sample a selection of these logs to gauge the impact of the rule change.

January 2014

Bar Standards Board

Money Laundering and Public and Licensed Access Work

[3.62]–[3.65]

The Bar Council has produced specific guidance in relation to money laundering in respect of public and licensed access work which is produced in full below:

Identification Obligations in Public and Licensed Access Work

The following guidance is the latest version of the guidance but at the time of going to print this is the latest version. In February 2004, the Bar Council published general guidance on the Money Laundering Regulations 2003 ("the 2003 Regulations"). This note develops that guidance in the particular context of public access and licensed access work. This note supplements the general guidance, and does not replace it. Barristers undertaking public and licensed access work should follow all the guidance in the February 2004 Guidance.

When can a Barrister Rely on ID Checks carried out by an Accessor on a Lay Client?

The Bar Council has advised barristers that when instructed by a solicitor they may rely on a letter or certificate from a UK solicitor stating that he has confirmed the lay client's identity in accordance with regulation 4 of the 2003 Regulations. In what, if any, circumstances can a barrister rely on a similar assurance from an accessor who is not a solicitor?

The governing criterion is that the barrister must take reasonable measures. This is likely to involve considering both the accessor and what he has actually done in the particular case.

As a general guide the Bar Council suggests that a barrister would be following a reasonable procedure in relying on an assurance from an accessor who is a member of a professional institution or who is authorised to practise in a field subject to statutory regulation where:

(i) the structure, discipline and training of the profession or regulated group are such that barristers can feel confidence in its members' performance of ID procedures;

(ii) "relevant business" is regularly undertaken by members of the profession or regulated group so that their familiarity with ID procedures is likely to involve practical experience as well as theoretical knowledge.

In the remainder of this note a person fulfilling both those criteria is referred to as a "reliable professional".

The Bar Council considers that amongst "reliable professionals" are likely to be members of the following groups:

Chartered accountants
Certified accountants
Insolvency practitioners
Chartered surveyors
Financial advisers authorised by the Financial Services Authority.

An assurance from a "reliable professional" might reasonably be relied on where:

(a) The "reliable professional" is acting as an intermediary for a client, rather than instructing the barrister on his own behalf; and

(b) the assurance is to the effect that the "reliable professional's" own ID checks have verified the identity of the lay client to the satisfaction of the "reliable professional" for the purpose of the 2003 Regulations.

Broadly speaking, therefore, a barrister may rely on an assurance from an accessor who is under the same duty to carry out ID checks pursuant to the 2003 Regulations as the barrister.

Public Access and Licensed Access Clients who are not Intermediaries

A barrister must normally carry out ID procedures on any client who instructs the barrister on his own behalf in relation to relevant business. This is so even if the client is a member of a professional institute or regulated occupation.

However, in the case of established professions and persons authorised by the Financial Services Authority, the steps necessary to check identity may be quite simple. For instance, if a barrister receives instructions on the printed letterhead of an independent financial adviser, whose name is found in the on-line FSA register at www.fsa.gov.uk/register/, no further check would normally be necessary. Similarly if a barrister receives instructions on the printed letterhead of a chartered surveyor, whose name is found in the RICS directory at http://dir.rics.org/.

In-house assessors

A barrister must normally carry out ID procedures on a lay client if he is instructed for "relevant business" by a professional who is an employee of the lay client – for instance, by an in-house accountant. The Bar Council considers that a barrister cannot rely on an assurance from such professional that he has carried out ID procedures on his employer pursuant to regulation 4: that is because such an employee is not under an obligation under the Regulations to perform ID on his employer.

However, such a professional may quite properly provide to the barrister the materials which identify the employer, or direct the barrister to the simplest ID steps (eg providing the web page of a company's listing on the AIM at the London Stock Exchange web site).

A barrister receiving instructions from a professional or manager by a letter on the printed writing paper of a company would not normally require any further evidence of the individual's authority to act for the company.

The Special Position of Banks and other Regulated Financial Services Firms

There is an exception to the normal requirement for ID procedures in the case of certain firms in the financial services sphere. There is no requirement to carry out ID procedures where the barrister has reasonable grounds for believing that the lay client carries on business in the UK of a type specified in regulation 5(2). The most commonly encountered clients within this exception are likely to be persons who are authorised under the Financial Services and Markets Act 2000 for the following activities:

- accepting deposits;
- dealing in, and arranging deals in, investments;
- managing investments;
- advising on investments.

Long term Insurance by a Person Authorised pursuant to Articles 4 or 51 of the Life Assurance Consolidation Directive.

This exception applies both when such an authorised firm instructs a barrister direct and when the instructions are received from an accessor acting as an intermediary.

Public Corporations

There is no need for a barrister to carry out ID procedures on a publicly funded organisation. Examples of bodies on which no ID procedures are necessary are: a police force, a probation service, the Crown Prosecution Service, a District Council.

Persons already known

There is no need for a barrister to carry out ID procedures on an individual who is already well known to him. Good personal knowledge of an individual may, indeed, be considered to be the best way of verifying an individual's identity.

If a lay client is already well known to a "reliable professional", and the assurance as to ID from the "reliable professional" is based on personal knowledge, a barrister may rely on this in the same way as he would rely on a "reliable professional's" inspection of passport and the like.

Advising on Contracts

Since public and licensed access work will often be non-contentious or pre-litigious work, the question may arise more frequently as to the boundary of "relevant business" in the context of contract advisory and drafting work.

The Bar Council considers that the following are relevant business:

- Drafting a contract with a view to it being executed between known parties for a specific known transaction;
- Advising on the effect of a draft contract proposed to be executed between known parties for a specific known transaction

On the other hand, the Bar Council considers that the following are not "relevant business":

- Advising on the effect of a contract which has already been executed;
- Drafting a set of standard terms for a business;
- Drafting a model form of contract to be published by a institution;
- Record keeping;
- Barristers should keep copies of documents which they inspect for the purpose of ID procedures.

In addition the Regulations contain requirements as to keeping records of transactions by way of "relevant business". But a barrister who complies with the normal public access requirements for record keeping will have done quite sufficient to comply with these Regulations.

Guidance for Chambers on Responding to Potentially Discriminatory Instructions

[3.66]

It is unlawful to instruct a barrister on the basis of his or her gender. The Bar Council has produced guidance clarifying the situation under the Sex Discrimination Act 1975, which follows below.

The Bar Council has received advice from Leading Counsel confirming that it is unlawful to use gender as a basis for selection of counsel. The situation in which the problem often arises is where solicitors make a request to barristers' clerks for a female barrister to prosecute a rape case, or to advise/ represent female clients in immigration and asylum work where there are allegations of sexual abuse. Under the Sex Discrimination Act 1975 it is unlawful:

a) for a solicitor to give instructions to a female barrister on the grounds of her gender, when the effect of doing so is to treat a comparable male barrister less favourably;

b) or a female barrister to accept instructions, knowing that she is being instructed for reasons related to her gender and where a comparable male barrister is treated less favourably in consequence; and

c) for a barrister's clerk or head of chambers/those responsible for the administration of chambers to permit a practice which enables female barristers to gain exposure or undertake a class of work which is denied to male colleagues.

It would be equally unlawful in relation to any of the above for the instructions to be given to a male barrister to the detriment of a female colleague.

Such requests by solicitors would be in breach of their professional obligations under the Solicitors Anti-Discrimination Rules 2004. Members of the Bar would be in breach of the Bar Code of Conduct, which prohibits discrimination. The new Equality and Diversity Code for the Bar provides, at paragraphs 1.36 to 1.47, for non-discriminatory allocation of work within chambers. Paragraph 1.47, repeating similar earlier guidance, provides "any solicitor who insists on a directly discriminatory allocation of work should be reported to his or her professional body. The work should be refused".

Such requests are often justified by the claim that it is what the client/complainant wants. It may be, however, that a solicitor making such a request does not really have instructions to discriminate, nor does the solicitor wish to discriminate. It may be that the solicitor has a client who is very worried and anxious about the hearing and tends to burst into tears if not handled sensitively. It may be that the solicitor has chosen to ask for a female counsel when what they really want is a sensitive counsel. A sensitive counsel may be male or female. Similarly a solicitor may request a male barrister when what they really think they want is an aggressive cross-examiner. They may be under the complete misapprehension that that requires a man. Once the real problem is identified then a proper basis of selection may emerge and the matter can be dealt with amicably and fairly. Chambers who have adopted a positive approach to dealing with these issues have found that rather than creating problems for themselves they have been able to improve their working relations with solicitors and provide a better service to clients. The stages of dealing with this problem are, as they normally are:

(a) Ask why,

(b) Identify the problem,

(c) Share the problem (another person in the clerks room or in chambers may well be able to help to diffuse the position and identify the real problem),

(d) Keep a proper note,

(e) Be polite but firm, clear and fair.

Client Incapacity

[3.67]

The Professional Practice Committee has produced general guidance for Counsel to assist barristers who have doubts about a client's capacity, by reason of mental disorder or by reason of termporary intoxication – to understand advice, give instructions, or follow or take part in proceedings. The Guidance was issued in February 2014.

---

1. Incapacity by reason of lack of mental capacity

[3.68]

1. Counsel should be familiar with the standard texts on the current law and practice relating to:

   (a) The Mental Capacity Act 2005 and the principles set out therein relating to capacity.

   (b) A client lacking capacity for the purpose of managing money and property so that his money and property is under the control of the Court of Protection.

   (c) A client being a "protected party" for the purpose of conducting civil or family proceedings, i.e. lacking capacity (within the meaning of the 2005 Act) to conduct proceedings; see CPR part 21.1 and FPR 2.3. In particular, counsel should be aware of the leading case (as at the date of this guidance) of *Masterman-Lister v Brutton & Co* [2003] EWCA Civ 70, [2003] 1 WLR 1511[2003] which emphasises that:

      (i) There is a presumption of capacity for a person of adult age, but that as a matter of practice the court should investigate the issue where there is any reason to suspect its absence.

      (ii) The test of capacity is issue specific. Accordingly, a client may have capacity to conduct relatively simple litigation, but lack the capacity to conduct more complex litigation.

      (iii) Equally, a client may not lack capacity to pursue or compromise a claim merely because they would be incapable of taking investment decisions in relation to any compensation ultimately received.

   (d) A client being "unfit to plead" for the purpose of criminal proceedings.

2. Once a legal adviser entertains a reasonable doubt about their client's capacity to give proper instructions, it is that adviser's professional duty to satisfy themselves that the client either has or does not have the capacity to give instructions; see *P (a child) (care and placement order proceedings: mental capacity of parent), Re* [2008] EWCA Civ 462, [2009] LGR 213, [2008] 3 FCR 243.

3. As the law and practice presently stand, the Bar Council suggests barristers might adopt the following approach:

4. If Counsel reasonably suspects that the client is or may be a "protected party" (for any relevant purpose) or "unfit to plead", counsel clearly needs to proceed with great care, in particular since:

   4.1 if counsel doubts the client's capacity to give instructions, it follows that counsel cannot be certain that it is proper to act on any instructions which the client may purport to give (although, even where a client definitely lacks the capacity to give instructions, counsel should still seek the client's views and take them into account);

   4.2 additionally, where litigation is being privately funded by the client, the propriety of counsel's instructing solicitor accepting funds from the client may be in doubt; and

   4.3 moreover, revealing counsel's suspicion that the client lacks capacity to the client may well be perceived as offensive, and revealing the suspicion to the court and any other party may well be unauthorised and/or highly prejudicial.

5. Each case will be different, but the following stage by stage approach is suggested.

   5.1 In a case involving an instructing solicitor (or other professional client):

      (i) Counsel should discuss the question of the client's capacity with the instructing solicitor (who is likely to have had more contact with the client than counsel has)

      (ii) If, having done so, counsel still reasonably suspects that the client lacks capacity, then counsel should, if practicable, meet the client, if counsel has not already done so

      (iii) Whether or not counsel meets the client, if counsel's concerns about the client's capacity persist, counsel should ensure that the client is informed of those concerns as tactfully as possible, and that any comments which the client has to make on the issue of capacity are obtained and taken into account.

   5.2 In a matter that does not involve a professional client, counsel should, if practicable, meet the client, and follow the approach in paragraph 1(iii) above. Counsel should also take into account the guidance in the Bar Standards Board's Public Access Guidance for Barristers on identifying and representing vulnerable clients. If, having taken those steps, counsel still reasonably suspects the client lacks capacity, then the appropriate course of action may depend on whether counsel is instructed by a solicitor (or other professional client).

   5.3 In a public access case, counsel is likely to be in the position of being unable to act (if instructions have not been accepted), or of being obliged to cease acting. The practical implications of the client's perceived lack of capacity are likely to be such that counsel will have concluded that the case is not suitable for public access, not least because in all the circumstances, it would in any event be in the interests of the client or in the interests of justice for the client to instruct a solicitor or professional client (BSB Handbook rC123); but even if that is not the case, the Bar Council considers that counsel cannot properly accept instructions from a client, or continue to act for a client, whom counsel reasonably perceives to lack capacity, having taken the steps already identified above. However:

(i) In a case involving withdrawal, counsel should bear in mind paragraphs 38 to 44 and 84 of the Bar Standards Board's Public Access Guidance for Barristers, concerning limitations on withdrawal under rule 608(a) of the Code of Conduct (the equivalent BSB Handbook rules are rC123 and rC25-rC26), cases of potential urgency or prejudice to the client, and referrals to solicitors. Whilst the Bar Council is of the view that counsel cannot continue to act for, or take any further steps on behalf of, a client who is believed not to have the capacity to give instructions (which is not a situation catered for in the BSB guidance), counsel may feel that giving assistance along the lines suggested in paragraph 44 of the Public Access Guidance for Barristers may still be appropriate in cases where the client might otherwise be prejudiced, depending on the circumstances. Counsel will in any event be obliged to explain clearly to the client the reasons for withdrawal (BS Handbook rC27.1.b).

(ii) Even in a case in which counsel is declining to accept instructions, rather than withdrawing, this does not mean that counsel cannot try to assist the client, perhaps by helping to find a solicitor, or by referring the client to a particular solicitor or to CAFCASS Litigation, either of whom may be better placed to assist the client to find a way forward despite the issue of capacity. Counsel may also assist the client to engage a solicitor with a view to counsel and solicitor taking the steps indicated below, if counsel considers that to be in the client's best interests, and if the client agrees. However, counsel should be wary of those situations in which there may be no time for a client to seek alternative advice, or where delay may prejudice the client's position, in which case the client should be told (i) that counsel considers it to be in the client's best interests to inform the court of counsel's suspicions, and (ii) of the relevant procedure(s) identified in paragraph 11 below. Although this does not involve counsel withdrawing from a case, counsel may still be assisted by referring to paragraphs 43 and 84 of the BSB's Public Access Guidance for Barristers as regards situations of urgency and referrals to solicitors.

(iii) In either type of case, counsel is also not prevented from informing the client of the importance of professional assistance, or (where counsel thinks it appropriate) from giving tactful advice about the merits of the client raising the issue of their capacity with a solicitor, or indeed from informing the chosen solicitor of counsel's concerns as to the client's capacity (although counsel should take care not to breach any duty of confidentiality owed to the client when doing so).

5.4 In a case in which counsel is instructed by a solicitor (or other professional client), counsel should advise that evidence about the client's capacity is obtained. Clearly, obtaining the necessary time, funding (particularly if there is doubt about the propriety of relying on private funding from the client), and cooperation from the client, may all be problematic. If an adjournment of a hearing is necessary, counsel will obviously need to be discreet in informing the court and any other party about the reason, but must not be misleading. Circumstances may justify simply saying that counsel and solicitor are in a situation of professional embarrassment which makes it impossible for them to proceed immediately, the nature of which they are not currently at liberty to reveal, and which they need time to resolve.

5.5 Counsel should bear in mind in advising that it may be appropriate for counsel's instructing solicitor to seek advice and/or assistance from the Official Solicitor (or additionally, in family proceedings, CAFCASS Litigation). Evidence about capacity from lay people who know the client well may be useful, although, by its very nature, it may not be independent or disinterested. Evidence from the client's GP may be very helpful, if the client will permit it and the GP knows the client. A report from a suitably qualified Medical Expert, based on an examination of the client, the client's medical records and any of the other evidence obtained, is usually essential. Counsel is entitled to advise the client to cooperate in the obtaining of medical evidence, but is not entitled to insist on the client doing so.

6. If, in the light of such evidence, if any, as can be obtained, counsel still reasonably suspects that the client lacks capacity, counsel should, if practicable, meet the client again, and should, in any event, ensure that any further comments which the client has to make are obtained and taken into account, and should discuss the issue of the client's capacity further with the instructing solicitor.

7. If, having done so, counsel still reasonably suspects that the client lacks capacity, counsel should at this stage advise that the appropriate court be informed of the client's suspected lack of capacity.

8. If this advice is accepted and followed, well and good.

9. If the client rejects this advice but the instructing solicitor nonetheless accepts it, in the Bar Council's view, the court should be informed of the client's suspected lack of capacity (which, in the absence of any special application, will normally mean informing any other party to the proceedings), even if the client purports to forbid this. In the Bar Council's view, this is a situation where counsel's duty to the court overrides the client's purported instructions, even if the client subsequently turns out to have capacity. Disclosure of the client's suspected lack of capacity is necessary for the protection of the client, in case the client lacks capacity, and may be necessary for the protection of counsel and instructing solicitor, since, as pointed out above, if the client lacks capacity to give instructions and/or to authorise private funding, neither counsel nor instructing solicitor can properly act on the basis of the client's instructions and/or any such funding.

10. Once the client's suspected lack of capacity has been disclosed to the court:

 10.1 if the client's capacity to conduct civil or family proceedings is in question, that question can be determined by the civil or family court, and, if the client is a "protected party" for that purpose a "litigation friend" can be appointed to conduct the litigation on the client's behalf. Obviously if the court determines that the client has got capacity to conduct the litigation, then counsel must continue with the case;

 10.2 if the client's capacity to manage any money or property is in question, that question can be determined by the Court of Protection and, if the client is incapable for that purpose, his money and property can be placed under the control of the Court of Protection; or

 10.3 if the client's capacity to defend criminal proceedings is in question, the issue of "fitness to plead" can be determined by the criminal court.

11. If, however, both the lay client and instructing solicitor reject counsel's advice that the client's suspected lack of capacity be disclosed to the court, counsel will probably be in such a situation of professional embarrassment that the only proper course will be to withdraw from the case. In that event, counsel will be obliged to explain clearly to the client the reasons for withdrawal (BSB Handbook rC27.1.b).

12. Equally, in the unlikely event that the court refuses to determine the issue of capacity or fitness to plead, and indicates it intends to continue regardless, counsel may have to withdraw from the case, making clear to the court that they cannot act in the absence of proper instructions. It may also be of assistance at this stage to indicate to the court that counsel wishes to contact the Bar Council's ethics hotline to seek advice on their professional obligations.

2. Incapacity by reason of drink/drugs

(A) Client still capable

[3.69]

13. If a client attends court under the influence of drink or drugs, but counsel reasonably believes that the client is still capable of understanding advice, giving instructions, and following and, if necessary, taking part in the proceedings, counsel's duties are, as always:

 13.1 counsel's overriding duty to the court (BSB Handbook CD1, rC3 and rC4), in particular not to mislead the court; and

 13.2 subject to that, counsel's duty to the client (BSB Handbook CD2 and rC15), which includes to advise the client as to his best interests (which may be to seek an adjournment) but ultimately to follow the client's instructions (which may be to proceed) even if those instructions appear to counsel to be unwise.

(B) Client Incapable

14. If, on the other hand, a client attends court and appears to be so under the influence as to be temporarily incapable of understanding advice, giving the instructions, or following or taking any necessary part in the proceedings:

    14.1 In rare cases, where the particular procedure has previously been explained to the client and his instructions taken at a time when he was capable, and the hearing concerned is a formality which follows its predicted course, it may be appropriate for counsel to allow the hearing to proceed

    14.2 But more often, counsel will need to seek an adjournment, since it would be a breach of counsel's duties to the court and to the client to allow the court to proceed on the assumption that the client is capable when in fact he is not. In practice, this is likely to mean that counsel has to make some disclosure of the client's intoxication (in the unlikely event that it is not already apparent to the court)

3. Contemporaneous notes

[3.70]

15 As ever in difficult situations, counsel is strongly advised at every stage to make and keep a good contemporaneous note, and to ask any representative of his instructing solicitors to do the same.

Important Notice

This document has been prepared by the Bar Council to assist barristers on matters of professional conduct and ethics. **It is not "guidance" for the purposes of the BSB Handbook I6.4, and neither the BSB nor a disciplinary tribunal nor the Legal Ombudsman is bound by any views or advice expressed in it.** It does not comprise – and cannot be relied on as giving – legal advice. It has been prepared in good faith, but neither the Bar Council nor any of the individuals responsible for or involved in its preparation accept any responsibility or liability for anything done in reliance on it. For fuller information as to the status and effect of this document, please refer to the professional practice and ethics section of the Bar Council's website

Common Questions and Answers relating to Acceptance of Instructions

[3.71]–[3.73]

The Bar Council publishes a range of frequently asked ethical questions and answers commonly encountered as part of a barrister's practice (see Part III). Please see para **[3.324]**. There are many others inserted under the relevant subject areas throughout the Handbook.

Section 2: Getting Paid

1. Introduction

[3.74]

The Nature of Barristers' Fees

1. General

Barristers' work is varied and does not just consist of the core skill of advocacy in courts or tribunals but is also made up of the provision of advice (in writing and in conference), drafting pleadings and preparing skeleton arguments. Traditionally, barristers have been remunerated for each separate item of work undertaken, regardless of the length of time that work takes, although that time estimate is a factor in setting the fee in the first place. Increasingly however, barristers in all areas of practice are remunerated in relation to hourly rates, in a similar way to that of solicitors.

2. Brief Fee, plus Refreshers

[3.75]

The traditional format for remuneration is that of the brief fee, covering all work in preparation for the case up to and including the first day of the trial plus, if appropriate, refreshers for appearing at court.

The brief fee is also deemed to cover taking a note of the judgment (where no refresher is payable), any conference with the client after the judgment and, the barrister's time commitment in taking on the case i e that time that he has blocked in his diary for the case to the exclusion of any other booking. These definitions are not enshrined in any professional code point or statutory regulation, although there is case law supporting the interpretation of the constituent parts. This places emphasis on establishing clarity at the point of instruction (possibly couching it in expressly contractual terms) for the avoidance of any doubt should the case not run its expected course. In the absence of such clarity, unforeseen scenarios, such as the case going short, will only be resolved through negotiation between the barrister and the solicitor. Payment for the barrister's time commitment can be one such problematic area. If unexpected listing changes force an adjournment and any substantial period of time elapses, counsel may have to re-read the brief and charge a re-reading fee as a result for example.

The refresher fee is remuneration for counsel's attendance at each day of a hearing after the first day (which is covered by the brief fee), when the court is sitting (it cannot be paid when the court is not). When it is payable, it, rather than the brief fee, covers those other tasks above such as taking a note of the judgment and subsequent conference with the client etc.

Wherever possible, brief fees and refreshers should be agreed in advance (in writing and, for ultimate safety, possibly even contractually). The benefit of such a system has always been that the client knows from the outset the amount payable for all the anticipated work and excessive preparation is discouraged in favour of rewarding the efficient. As well as containing an element related to the estimated time the work will take, the fee will also be based upon the complexity of the case, the seniority of the barrister needed to undertake the work etc. Once agreed, brief fees or refreshers are usually only re-negotiated if unforeseen circumstances occur such as the collapse of a hearing or the case grossly overrunning.

3. Hourly Rates

[3.76]

Barristers, particularly in lengthy civil cases and inquiries, increasingly work on an estimate of hours that the case will take, and will disclose the hourly rates at which they operate for the benefit of clients selecting which counsel to use. Often, there is a notional cap to the maximum number of hours permitted for the work imposed by the client. A client, depending on his "purchasing power", may conduct "beauty parades" of counsel at several chambers before settling on a particular individual. Hours can only, of course, be estimated, as with the brief fee system, have to be reviewed regularly and monitored against how the case is proceeding. The advantages of this type of arrangement, particularly in the lengthier cases, are that the barrister receives regular payment for on-going work (often arranged a specifically agreed staged payments) and the client is better able to budget for the costs.

Staged payments (incurments) of brief fees according to an agreed timetable are also more prevalent in civil cases in recent times. Though a fee is incurred (and a fee note may be raised), it is not paid; the tax point arises at the earlier of the issue of the tax invoice and payment. It is usually issued once payment is received.

Other common forms of fee payment arrangements are dealt with in the subsection 4 (of Part III – Tenancy, Section 2 "How do I get Paid?") "Getting Paid in the most Common Fee Payment Scenarios".

4. Fee Levels and what can be charged

[3.77]–[3.78]

There are no prescribed levels of fees set by the Bar Council in relation to work undertaken by barristers on a private basis. Subject to the various other provisions of the Code of Conduct, a barrister may charge for work undertaken by him on any basis he thinks fit provided that basis is legal and does not involve the payment of a wage or salary (paragraph 405 of the Code of Conduct). However, he must ensure also that he is not in conflict with any other provision of the Code and that he complies with the "Terms of Work on which barristers offer their services to solicitors and the Withdrawal of Credit Scheme 1988", including any withdrawal of credit direction issued by the Chairman of the Bar.

5. Guidance on Producing Fee Notes and Keeping Proper Records

[3.79]

Clients are, however, entitled to know the basis on which fees are charged and counsel should ensure that records of work done are properly kept and fee notes are clear. The Professional Standards and Remuneration Committees of the Bar Council have, in the past, produced guidance in relation to fee notes, which offer good practice guidance in relation to fee notes and records. This guidance was updated in February 2014 and is set out below:

Counsel's Fee Notes and Records

Purpose: To guide barristers on how best to issue and record Counsel's fee notes.

Scope of application: All practising barristers.

Issued by: The Professional Practice Committee.

First issued: February 2014.

Status and effect: Please see the notice at end of this document. This is not "guidance" for the purposes of the BSB Handbook.

1. All clients are entitled to know the basis on which fees are charged, not least so that they can protect their interests in respect of any assessments of costs.

2. You are reminded that rC88 requires you to "ensure that adequate records supporting the fees charged or claimed in a case are kept" and that you "must provide your client with such records or details of the work you have done as may reasonably be required for the purposes of verifying your charges". Accordingly, in order to assist lay and professional clients, Judges, Costs Judges and, in the event of opposed assessments of costs, lay and professional clients justifying your fees to opposing parties, you should keep careful records of the time taken on each individual item of work done, such as:

   (a) Pleadings, indictments, or other procedural documents.

   (b) Witness statements.

   (c) Experts' reports.

   (d) Schedules.

   (e) Written Advices and Opinions.

   (f) Letters.

   (g) Skeleton arguments.

   (h) Written submissions.

   (i) Preparation of Briefs.

   (j) Conferences and telephone conferences and the preparation for such conferences.

3. You are also reminded that paragraph rC88 requires such records to be kept at least until the later of the following: your fees have been paid, any determination or assessment of costs in the case has been completed and the time for lodging an appeal against that assessment or determination has expired without any such appeal being lodged, or any such appeal has been finally determined.

4. The following further steps are also advised as a matter of good practice:

   4.1 When you are instructed orally, including by telephone, you should make a note of the nature of the instructions and of the response given.

4.2 When you ask orally for further information, you should make a note of the nature of the request, and of the answer if the answer is given orally.

4.3 When any particularly novel or complex issue of fact or law arises in the course of the conduct of a case, you should (unless the subject is dealt with in a written advice or opinion) make a note summarising the relevant issue or issues and the research undertaken in like manner as is required by (i) above.

4.4 When a consultation or conference takes place, unless the professional client makes an attendance note which is sent to you for approval or amendment, you should make a note of the topics covered and the general nature of the advice given.

4.5 When you are involved in negotiations, either between Counsel or leading, or assisting or supporting the professional client in the conduct of negotiations, you should make a note of the general nature of the involvement.

4.6 Notes made pursuant to subparagraphs (i) to (v) above should be kept by you unless they are returned to an instructing solicitor.

5. In cases where there is not an instructing solicitor, it may be advisable to keep more detailed records.

6. When a brief fee has not been agreed and is claimed by you in a sum greater than the product of an hourly rate and the number of hours actually worked in preparation of the brief, this should be recorded in a note to be submitted with the fee note. Details in the supplementary note should include, but are not limited to:

(i) The seniority, reputation and relevant expertise of Counsel.

(ii) The complexity of the case.

(iii) The amount of preparation required in advance of the hearing.

(iv) Counsel's commitment to a fixed hearing date, if any.

(v) The expected length of the case and, therefore, the time reserved for it in Counsel's diary.

(vi) The urgency of the matter when Counsel was briefed.

(vii) The amount of work required out of Court and in the preparation of any kind of written submission during the hearing.

(viii) The importance of the case to the parties or any of them, or to the public interest.

(ix) Details of any expenses incurred by Counsel.

7. When a brief fee has been agreed you or your Clerk should keep a written record of the date upon which such agreement was reached, the method by which such agreement was reached and by whom, and of the precise terms of such agreement together with such records as will enable a note containing the details set out at paragraph 6(i)–(ix) above to be produced on request.

8. Clients in cases where you fail to keep proper records to support claimed fees may find the fees reduced. You may then find that a complaint of inadequate

professional service may be upheld, in which circumstance you can be ordered to reduce or waive fees and/or to pay compensation.

9. In any case in which you appear properly in a privately paid case at a hearing without a brief fee having been agreed (for example on an interim application) you should make and keep a record of the time spent at Court before the start of the hearing, and of the length of the hearing.

Important Notice

This document has been prepared by the Bar Council to assist barristers on matters of professional conduct and ethics. **It is not "guidance" for the purposes of the BSB Handbook I6.4, and neither the BSB nor a disciplinary tribunal nor the Legal Ombudsman is bound by any views or advice expressed in it.** It does not comprise – and cannot be relied on as giving – legal advice. It has been prepared in good faith, but neither the Bar Council nor any of the individuals responsible for or involved in its preparation accept any responsibility or liability for anything done in reliance on it.

---

7. Fee Notes and Billing for Work

[3.80]

On the 31 January 2013, Standard Contractual Terms replaced the commonly used terms of engagement for barristers taking instructions from solicitors, (the Terms of Work and the Withdrawal of Credit Scheme). Also on the 31 January, the Bar Code of Conduct was amended so that the Cab Rank Rule applies to instructions offered on the basis of new Standard Contractual Terms or the barrister's own published terms of engagement. This means, instead of the Cab Rank Rule applying to the present Terms of Work, it will apply to these new Contractual Terms or the barrister's own published terms.

Part VIII of this Handbook deals in more detail with the tax and VAT implications of issuing of fee notes. Suffice it to say that except where a barrister ceases practice the tax point is the earlier of the issue of a tax invoice and payment. So as to ensure that VAT is only paid when the fee is paid, barristers should ensure that fee notes which their clerks send out prior to the receipt of any fees do not constitute tax invoices. This can be achieved by ensuring that the fee notes so rendered do not bear a VAT distinct invoice number and contain a box, left blank, for the insertion of the date on which the fee is subsequently received, which will constitute the tax point. Once the fee is paid a tax invoice should be sent to the solicitor bearing a distinct invoice number and having inserted upon it the date on which the fee was received and which is, therefore, the tax point.

8. Billing the Client Direct

[3.81]

However, there are circumstances when a professional client will ask a barrister, or his chambers, to bill a client direct instead. Solicitors will sometimes question to whom the barrister's services (which are standard-rated for VAT) are actually supplied and consequently which party is permitted to reclaim the VAT charge. As seen above, it is customary for barristers to look to solicitors for payment of their fees and they therefore will usually send fee notes/tax invoices to the solicitors firm. In these circumstances, the solicitor may treat the fees as an ordinary business cost, recover the VAT charged and charge VAT on his own invoice to the client. There is, alternatively, a further concessionary treatment in relation to counsel's fees that is not widely known.

In this alternative approach, the solicitor may treat counsel's services as supplied directly to the client and his settlement of counsel's fees as a disbursement. In adopting this treatment, the solicitor would then manually amend counsel's tax invoice by inserting the name and address of the client and putting 'per' before the firm's name and address. Counsel's fee note is then recognised as a valid tax invoice in the hands of the client.

It is therefore important that, when asked to bill differently in this way, counsel bears in mind the customary approach to billing and does nothing that might be seen to undermine the solicitor's liability to pay his fees. It should be noted that in the above concessionary treatment, it is for the solicitor to amend counsel's invoice not for counsel to bi-pass the solicitor altogether. An audit trail for the purposes of liability to pay is therefore maintained.

However, barristers need to also be aware that solicitors' liability to pay counsel's fees as a matter of professional conduct has also been subject to change. See below.

9. The Code of Conduct for Solicitors

[3.82]

On 1 July 2007, the Law Society's Guide to the Professional Conduct of Solicitors was replaced by the Solicitors' Code of Conduct by the Solicitors' Regulation Authority (SRA)[1] (now the SRA Handbook as of October 2011). Among the many changes to the old code, was the removal of the express provision that solicitors were personally liable as a matter of professional conduct for the payment of counsel's fees whether or not they had been placed in funds by the client. There is no measure in the new code that replicates these duties.

There is no doubt that the Bar's position is weakened by this development and the change puts all the greater emphasis on making explicit the terms on which counsel is prepared to accept instructions from the solicitor in the first place. The introduction of new contractual terms of work should assist with this.

1 See http://www.sra.org.uk/solicitors/handbook/welcome.page

Issuing Fee Notes to Lay Clients — Clarification

[3.83]

The Bar Council issued specific further clarification in relation to issuing fee notes to lay clients when in-house solicitors' departments in insurance broking organisations are involved:

The Bar Council has been made aware that some sets of Chambers appear to be attempting to gain a commercial advantage over others by changing the customary way in which fee notes are issued to in-house solicitors' departments in insurance broking organisations, who cannot reclaim VAT.

Some counsel are issuing a fee note/invoice net of VAT to the solicitor and a separate note/invoice for the VAT to the lay client (the insured) who can then recover the VAT. However, counsel should be reminded that Annex G1 of the Code of Conduct states in paragraph 3 of the preamble:

> "By established custom of the profession a barrister looks for payment of his fees to the solicitor who instructs him and not his lay client".

Strictly speaking, the fee should not be regarded as comprising a fee element plus a separate VAT ; rather the fee is a single amount inclusive of VAT (even if described as, say, "£1,000 plus VAT"). This customary treatment is recognised in the concession permitted by HMRC whereby the fee note is issued to the solicitor and he, after obtaining the approval of counsel, may re-address it to the lay client for the latter to pay direct to counsel.

It may be that the insurer in these circumstances has an arrangement with the client whereby the client pays the insurer an amount equal to the VAT on counsel's fee, or even pays the barrister an amount equal to the VAT, because the client can recover it, but counsel should issue a single fee note in the usual way, after which he issues a VAT invoice for the fee to the insurer for the full amount. The insurer can pass this on to the client, so the result is the same as if separate fee notes had been issued.

It is the view of the Remuneration Committee that deviation from the usual practice is both unnecessary and at worst could jeopardise the current concessionary treatment permitted by HMRC. The process has not changed since the original clarification issued by the Committee in 1998.

2. The Terms of Work on which Barristers Offer their Services to Solicitors and the Withdrawal of Credit Scheme

Contractual or non-contractual?

[3.84]

Many barristers have not tended to work on any contractual footing. Instead, the agreement with solicitors has been non-contractual and the fee historically regarded as an *honorarium*. Thus, in the absence of any contractual relationship, barristers have had no basis on which to sue solicitors for unpaid fees. The use of "factoring agents" by chambers is therefore also limited.

Formerly, the "Terms of Work on which barristers offer their services to solicitors and the Withdrawal of Credit Scheme 1988" (originally Annex G1 of the Code of Conduct), which are non-contractual were the default terms: that is to say, that they were deemed to apply to a brief or set of instructions supplied by a solicitor unless there is a mutual agreement between the barrister and the solicitor specifically to amend them, use other terms or agree contractual terms instead.

However, Contractual Terms of Work have been available for use since 2001 (originally Annex G2 of the Code of Conduct). The Contractual Terms, in addition to the normal remedies available for contracts, made provision for interest and for referral to the Bar Council under the Withdrawal of Credit Scheme. The Contractual Terms were not mandatory and barristers could into contracts with solicitors for the provision of services on other terms should they so wish.

The contractual terms were, however, rarely used. Chambers working non-contractually were able to use the Bar Council's Fees Collection Office and Withdrawal of Credit Scheme as a means of recovering unpaid fees from solicitors firms, overdue as defined by the Terms of Work which specify that payment of fees must be within one month of the sending of the fee note unless those fees are challenged in writing within three months.

From 31st January 2013, new Contractual Terms and applicable Code of Conduct changes were introduced. The practical effect of the changes were as follows:

1. The present Terms of Work (both in Annex G1 and G2 of the Bar Code of Conduct) were abolished.
2. The Withdrawal of Credit List was abolished.
3. The Bar Code of Conduct was amended so that the Cab Rank Rule applies to instructions offered on the basis of these new Contractual Terms or the barrister's own published terms of engagement – so that, effectively, instead of the Cab Rank Rule applying to the present Terms of Work, it applies to these new Contractual Terms or the barrister's own published terms.
4. Neither the new Contractual Terms nor the barrister's own published terms became the "new" default terms. Default terms are no longer required because barristers/chambers are obliged to publish their terms under the Provision of Services Regulations 2009.
5. Barristers continued to be free to agree any terms, no terms, or to amend the new Contractual Terms.

6. In place of the Withdrawal of Credit List, a List of Defaulting Solicitors and other Authorised Persons was created. A further change to the Code was that, instead of a barrister being forbidden to take instructions on credit from solicitors named on the Withdrawal of Credit List, the barrister has the right, under the Cab Rank Rule, to refuse instructions on credit but, equally, can decide to accept instructions.
7. The solicitors currently on the Withdrawal of Credit List were transferred to the List of Defaulting Solicitors and other Authorised Persons.
8. For work undertaken on the new Terms (after the implementation date), complaints can be made to the Bar Council for solicitors to be placed on the List of Defaulting Solicitors and other Authorised Persons, if a judgment has been obtained for non-payment of the fees or there is non-payment of a joint tribunal award.

Transitional arrangements

9. When complaints are made after the implementation date of the new Terms, but where the instructions were accepted prior to the implementation date, and thus on the old Terms of Work/Withdrawal of Credit scheme, there will be transitional arrangements to enable those complaints to be made to the Bar Council and for the solicitors to be put on the List of Defaulting Solicitors and other Authorised Persons.
10. Although the new Contractual Terms apply to privately funded cases or where, irrespective of the source of funding, the solicitors are liable to pay barristers, complaints in respect of instructions covered by full publicly funded certificates continue to be made – again, with the solicitors placed on the List of Defaulting Solicitors and other Authorised Persons.
11. The new contractual terms were drafted not just for use in relation to instructions from solicitors, but also all persons/bodies authorised by the SRA to carry out legal services under the Legal Services Act 2007.

PART III
IN PRACTICE

The Bar Council has issued full guidance on the operation of their Fees Collection Service following these changes. Included in the Guidance is information on the List of Defaulting Solicitors and other Authorised Persons, which replaces the Withdrawal of Credit scheme. It is set out below:

Guide to standard conditions of contract for the supply of legal services by barristers to authorised persons 2012

Introduction

[3.84a]

1. For centuries most barristers have accepted instructions from solicitors on a non-contractual basis, where the obligation to pay their fees was binding in

honour only. From 31 January 2013 this has changed. On that date the new Standard Conditions of Contract for the Supply of Legal Services by Barristers to Authorised Persons 2012[1] (the "new Standard Terms") came into force and replaced the previous Terms of Work on Which Barristers Offer their Services to Solicitors and the Withdrawal of Credit Scheme.[2] However, the new Standard Terms do not operate as default terms. It will therefore be essential that barristers expressly agree with solicitors the terms on which they perform any work because there are no longer any terms operating in default of such agreement.

2. These changes are part of bringing into effect the regulatory freedom now enjoyed by barristers to agree a contractual basis for the work they do for solicitors and certain other "Authorised Persons", with the advantages that follow from a contractual relationship.

3. Subject to transitional arrangements,[3] barristers can choose between the following alternatives:

   3.1 Accepting instructions on the new Standard Terms. A detailed explanation of how they operate follows this Introduction.

   3.2 Accepting instructions on "bespoke" terms (contractual or non-contractual) that have been drafted by the barrister or his Chambers or an SBA. Here it will be the responsibility of the individual barrister to ensure that his bespoke terms do not leave him exposed to liabilities that are not covered by the Bar Mutual Indemnity Fund (BMIF). Barristers will be aware that practising without full insurance cover may amount to professional misconduct. Broadly, BMIF will not cover a barrister's contractual liability to the extent that it exceeds his liability at common law in tort. If a barrister is minded to draft or agree a bespoke term which potentially could affect his professional indemnity over, enquiry should be made of BMIF.[4]

   3.3 Accepting instructions on "bespoke" terms that have been drafted by the Authorised Person (e.g. the instructing solicitor – see below for a detailed explanation). Here again it will be the responsibility of the individual barrister to ensure that these bespoke terms do not leave him/her exposed to liabilities that are not covered by BMIF, with the risk of professional misconduct.[5]

   3.4 Accepting instructions on terms that are a negotiated variant of any of the above. Here again it will be the responsibility of the individual barrister to ensure that the negotiated terms do not leave him/her exposed to liabilities that are not covered by BMIF, with the risk of professional misconduct.[6]

4. The new Standard Terms apply only to instructions from Authorised Persons who have been authorised by the Law Society or the Solicitors Regulation Authority[7] (SRA), almost all of whom will be solicitors. "Authorised Persons" is defined more widely in the Legal Services Act 2007 so as to include persons authorised by other approved regulators as well as the Law Society. Barristers are free to adapt the Standard Terms to suit instructions from such persons if they do wish to do so, subject to overall compliance with theBSB Handbook.

5. Barristers who choose to contract on the basis of the new Standard Terms, or the barrister's own standard terms, will need to take effective steps to ensure that such terms form the basis of the contract. Barristers should accordingly consider:

   5.1 Including a sufficiently prominent statement on their website that all instructions are accepted on the basis of the new Standard Terms, or the barrister's own standard terms (as the case may be), and

   5.2 In any communication accepting instructions, stating unequivocally that acceptance is on the new Standard Terms, or the barrister's own terms.

6. The new Standard Terms and the barrister's own standard terms (if any) are subject to the Cab Rank Rule (see below) but if the Authorised Person does not insist on using those terms, counsel and the Authorised Person can agree to amend any of the terms to suit their needs – for example the timing of payment; whether payment is dependent upon the solicitor being placed in funds; the timing and rate of interest and the time limits for challenging fees and referral to the Joint Tribunal.

7. As a consequence of the introduction of the new Standard Terms, the focus of the Cab Rank Rule[8] has shifted so that it now applies to instructions offered to the barrister on either the new Standard Terms or on any terms which the barrister (or his Chambers) publicises as being his standard terms of work. Refusing to accept such instructions will be a breach of the Cab Rank Rule (subject to the usual exceptions e.g. not being available, being professionally embarrassed etc). However, the Cab Rank Rule does not apply to instructions offered on any other basis; barristers are free to choose whether or not to accept such instructions. If instructions are offered on the basis of contractual terms prepared by the Authorised Person, the barrister would be well advised to scrutinise such terms carefully before accepting them and should make sure that the terms on which the instructions are accepted have been properly recorded.

8. In the following notes, clause numbers refer to the clauses of the new Standard Terms[9] unless otherwise stated.

1 As referred to in Rule rC30.9c of the BSB Handbook. The new Standard Terms were approved by the Bar Standards Board and the Legal Services Board ("the Regulators"). See Bar Council's website http://www.barcouncil.org.uk/media/278543/12_7_27_approved_contractual_terms_updated_bsb_handbook.pdf

2 At Annexes G1 and G2 of the old Bar Code of Conduct. See Bar Council website http://www.barcouncil.org.uk/media/278355/annexe_g1_non_contract_tow.pdf and http://www.barcouncil.org.uk/media/278358/annexe_g2_contractual_tow.pdf

3 These provide that where instructions were accepted by the barrister on a non-contractual basis before 31 January 2013 and the work is done after that date, the old Terms of Work, currently found in Annexes G1 and G2 of the old Bar Code of Conduct, will continue to apply.

4 The Bar Mutual Indemnity Fund has indicated that it does not consider the new Standard Terms extend barristers' contractual liabilities beyond those they owe at common law.

5 If bespoke terms of this kind are used, it may not be possible to obtain confirmation of cover from BMIF in advance. In that case, the barrister might indicate that the instructions will only be accepted on those terms subject to a caveat along the following lines: "Notwithstanding [the Authorised Persons'] standard terms of contract, [the barrister's] liability in contract, whether to [the Authorised Persons], the lay client or any third party, shall in no circumstances exceed, whether in the type or extent or quantum of damage, [the barrister's] liability at common law in tort were no such contract to exist". This should ensure that any liability falls within the scope of existing BMIF cover.

6 The comments in the previous footnote are equally valid here and the suggested wording as regards the preservation of BMIF cover could be along the following lines: "In no circumstances shall [the barrister's] liability under this [contract], whether to [the Authorised Persons], the lay client or any

third party, whether in the type or extent or quantum of damage, exceed [the barrister's] liability at common law in tort were no such contract to exist".

7 The Law Society has devolved its authorising power under section 18(1)(a) of the Legal Services Act 2007 to the SRA, so in practice the SRA is responsible for giving authorisation.

8 With the introduction of the new Standard Terms, the Cab Rank Rule in the BSB Handbook (f ormerly the Bar Code of Conduct) is amended.

9 As referred to in Rule rc30.9c of the BSB Handbook – see Bar Council website http://www.barcouncil.org.uk/media/278543/12_7_27_approved_contractual_terms_updated_bsb_handbook.pdf

Chapter 1: what has changed and using the new standard terms

What has changed?

9.1 The new Standard Terms may be used for instructions from all Authorised Persons, which here means all bodies and persons authorised by the Law Society or the SRA under section 18(1)(a) of the Legal Services Act 2007 to carry out reserved legal activities. This includes all practising solicitors but will also include any other bodies that are not solicitors' practices but which the SRA regulates. The SRA at present licences such bodies and persons on behalf of the Law Society, but does not publish a list of those bodies and persons who are authorised.

9.2 The new Standard Terms apply only to cases where the barrister is paid by or through the Authorised Person. Most such cases will be privately funded matters but this does include publicly funded matters where the Authorised Person (usually a solicitor) is paid by the Legal Services Commission and is then liable to pay counsel from those funds.

9.3 The new Standard Terms do not apply where the barrister is paid directly by the Legal Services Commission though the Community Legal Service or the Criminal Defence Service or by the Crown Prosecution Service.

9.4 The new Standard Terms can apply to a Conditional Fee Agreement (CFA) where the CFA specifically incorporates these Terms.

9.5 The new Standard Terms expressly provide that if fees for earlier work on the same case are unpaid for more than 30 days after delivery of the invoice or fee note the barrister is entitled to refrain from doing any further work on the case unless payment for that further work is made in advance, subject to the barrister's obligations to the Court and subject to the other provisions of theBSB Handbook.

9.6 The new Standard Terms expressly provide that barristers can sue for unpaid fees and may claim interest on unpaid fees.

9.7 The new Standard Terms are intended to apply for the whole life of the case. However, they can be adopted (or not adopted) on a per instruction basis; and where they have applied to a case,it can be agreed that they should no longer apply.

10. The old 'Terms of Work' on which barristers offered their services to solicitors and the 'Withdrawal of Credit Scheme'[1] have been abolished. This means that the 'Withdrawal of Credit List' has also been abolished, together with the obligation on barristers to refuse work from solicitors on the List unless payment is received with the brief or special permission has been given by the Chairman of the Bar.

11. The 'Withdrawal of Credit List' is replaced by the new advisory 'List of Defaulting Solicitors and Other Authorised Persons'. Amendments to the Bar's Code of Conduct (now BSB Handbook) provide that a barrister has the option to refuse work offered on credit from solicitors named on the 'List of Defaulting Solicitors and other Authorised Persons 2012'. This option to refuse work applies regardless of whether the fees are to be paid by the instructing solicitors/authorised persons or by the Legal Services Commission or the Criminal Defence Service. Under transitional arrangements, solicitors currently on the 'Withdrawal of Credit List' are automatically transferred to the advisory 'List of Defaulting Solicitors and other Authorised Persons 2012'.

12. Where instructions were received before 31 January 2013 on the basis of the former 'Terms of Work', the transitional arrangements allow complaints about non-payment of fees for that work to be made to the Bar Council, as before, but with the solicitor being placed on the 'List of Defaulting Solicitors and other Authorised Persons 2012' instead of the 'Withdrawal of Credit List'. In relation to instructions accepted on the new Standard Terms, complaints about non-payment of fees can only be made to the Bar Council if a judgment has been obtained or if a joint tribunal award is unpaid.

1 At Annexes G1 and G2 of the old Bar Code of Conduct.

Interaction with Cab Rank Rule and Code of Conduct

13. With effect from 31 January 2013, the Cab Rank Rule in the BSB Handbook (formerly the Bar Code of Conduct) is amended.

14. Barristers are no longer required to accept instructions if the Authorised Person wishes to instruct them on terms other than the new Standard Terms OR the terms of work which the barrister (or his chambers) publicises as being his standard terms of work.

15. On the other hand, it is a breach of the Cab Rank Rule for a barrister to refuse instructions from an SRA "Authorised Person" where he wishes to instruct the barrister on the new Standard Terms or on the terms of work which the barrister (or his chambers) publicises as being his standard terms (unless the instructing "Authorised Person" is on the "List of Defaulting Solicitors and other Authorised Persons 2012").

16. The usual exceptions to the Cab Rank Rule continue to apply e.g. not being available, being otherwise professionally embarrassed etc.

17. Furthermore, it is no longer misconduct for a barrister to accept instructions from a solicitor who has been the subject of a direction to withdraw credit. All such solicitors having a direction to withdraw credit against them on the 31 January 2013 will be transferred to the advisory "List of Defaulting Solicitors and other Authorised Persons 2012".

18. Barristers are reminded that the Provision of Services Regulations 2009 require publication of their normal terms of engagement. Guidance on the Regulations can be found on the Bar Council's website by searching "Provision of Services Regulations 2009" or at the following address: http://www.barcouncil.org.uk/provision-of-service-regulations-2009.

Are the new Terms fixed? Can we deviate from these new Terms?

19. The new Standard Terms have been written to delineate the responsibilities of the parties and to provide a comprehensive but not over-elaborate set of contractual terms. They are standard terms but barristers and SRA Authorised Persons are free to agree variations to them (or to agree entirely different terms) to suit their particular needs.

20. However, particular care must be exercised where barristers undertake work on terms that are different from the new Standard Terms. It is impossible in this guide to summarise all of the areas of difficulty which might arise where alternative terms are canvassed, but we draw attention to the following important points:

    20.1 Barristers will wish to take care to ensure that they do not assume duties or liabilities which are not covered by their professional indemnity insurance cover. In particular, it is essential that the barrister takes into account Clause 3.1(x) of BMIF's Terms of Cover, which excludes cover for "Claims or Disciplinary Proceedings in respect of any liability incurred under any contract, save to the extent that (a) such liability would have been incurred irrespective of the terms of such contract and would otherwise fall within the provisions of these Terms of Cover ..."

    20.2 Examples of clauses which would potentially expose barristers to a greater liability than their BMIF cover, and which would therefore amount to misconduct unless additional insurance cover was obtained, include:

        20.2.1 Clauses seeking to impose liability for the solicitor's loss of profits, for example if the solicitor loses the client because of negligent advice given in a particular case by a barrister.

        20.2.2 Clauses seeking to make the barrister strictly liable for advice given (i.e. liable even in the absence of negligence/failure to take reasonable care).

        20.2.3 Clauses seeking to make the barrister liable for loss suffered by clients of the solicitor other than those on whose behalf he is instructed, for example where the advice is of more general application than the specific case and is used by the solicitor in other contexts as a result.

    20.3 BMIF Guidance on the impact of the contractual terms and insurance cover can be found at http://www.barmutual.co.uk/fileadmin/uploads/barmutual/Guidance%20Note%20to%20Members%20-%20February%202013.pdf.

    20.4 Consideration will have to be given to the suitability and effect of alternative terms in respect of matters such as the payment of fees; the authority of clerks; confidentiality/publicity; conflicts of interest;

copyright; data protection; the retention and storage of documents; devilling/the use of pupils and dispute resolution.

20.5 Barristers should take particular care before agreeing that the "Authorised Person's" liability to pay fees is conditional upon their having received funds from the client. The barrister will wish to ensure that:

20.5.1 the Authorised Person cannot, without the barrister's informed prior consent vary, waive or reduce sums payable to the barrister;

20.5.2 the Authorised Person's commercial interests – for example in relation to promises of future work – cannot prejudice the recovery of the barrister's fees;

20.5.3 the Authorised Person keeps the barrister informed about the solvency of the client;

20.5.4 the Authorised Person provides full and timely information to the barrister about whether fees have been paid on account in full and on time, and

20.5.5 if the Authorised Person refuses to take primary liability for the barrister's fees, the barrister may prefer to be paid by the client directly, so long as arrangements are agreed which are in accordance with the BSB Handbook.[1]

20.6 Heads of Chambers must ensure that no member of chambers or pupil is under any improper commercial pressure to accept onerous or unfairly disadvantageous terms, for example because an Approved Person is a regular client of chambers.

20.7 Chambers will need to implement systems to ensure that:

20.7.1 administrative teams are aware of the risks associated with contracting on alternative terms and so be able to identify the boundaries as to what may be agreed, and

20.7.2 the terms upon which instructions have been accepted are properly recorded and retained.

21. The Law Society issued a Practice Note on the 24 January 2013 to their members, making a number of detailed comments on the terms of the new Contract and suggesting alternative clauses. The Law Society's proposals could give rise to some serious potential difficulties and barristers and clerks are strongly advised to read the Bar Council's guidance on this matter. This guidance can be found on the Bar Council's website, http://www.barcouncil.org.uk/for-the-bar/introduction-tomember-services/fees-collection/guidance-on-law-society'spractice-note/

1 In particular Rules rc73–75 of the BSB Handbook concerning handling of client money etc.

When can you NOT use the new Standard Terms?

21. The new Standard Terms are for use where instructions given by a person authorised by the Law Society or SRA under Section 18(1)(a) of the Legal Services Act 2007 to carry out reserved legal activities, almost all of whom will be solicitors.

22. The new Standard Terms cannot be used:

    22.1 where the lay client is to be party to the contract unless the lay client is the Authorised Person; or

    22.2 for CFAs, unless the CFA specifically provides for the new Standard Terms to apply (clause 2.4.2 of the new Standard Terms); or

    22.3 for publicly funded matters where the barrister is paid direct by the Legal Services Commission as part of the Community Legal Service or as part of the Criminal Defence Service or by the Crown Prosecution Service.[1]

23. However, the barrister and the instructing party are free to adapt the new Standard Terms to meet the above situations if they so agree (or may use different terms), provided that the barrister does not thereby infringe any other provision of the BSB Handbook and subject to the observations made above.

1 However, a barrister may still make complaints to the Bar Council about the solicitors' failure to deal with publicly funded matters covered by full publicly funded certificates under a new complaints scheme.

Chapter 2: informing solicitors and the Authorised Person of the new Terms

Notification of use of the new Standard Terms

24. It has always been commonsense and good practice for chambers to advise their professional clients of the terms on which their members provide services. Barristers are advised to draw attention to the application of the new Standard Terms to particular instructions at the first available opportunity, otherwise the new Standard Terms might not apply. If no alternative terms have been agreed in the meantime, it should be made clear on what terms the instructions are accepted no later than when notification is provided to the solicitor of the acceptance of the instructions.

25. Barristers are again reminded that the Provision of Services Regulations 2009 require publication of their normal terms of engagement. Guidance on the Regulations can be found on the Bar Council's website by searching :_:_entity=#x02BA:_:_Provision of Services Regulations 2009:_:_entity=#x02BA:_:_ or at the following address: http://www.barcouncil.org.uk/provision-of-service-regulations-2009

26. Accordingly, if chambers are expecting that the Standard Terms will be their usual terms of engagement, they should consider their obligation to publish them on, for example, their website, as well as referring to them when confirming the acceptance of instructions.

Chapter 3: responsibilities

Liability to pay

27. Clause 12 of the new Standard Terms provides that payment should be made

within 30 days of the delivery of the barrister's fee note or invoice and that interest can be charged, in accordance with the Late Payment of Commercial Debts (Interest) Act 1998.

28. There is no obligation on the barrister to charge interest if fees are paid late or (where interest might be claimed) to claim it.

29. The former "Terms of Work" provided that the solicitor was liable to pay irrespective of whether the solicitors' practice has been put in funds by the lay client. That provision has not been replicated in the new Terms as it is considered unnecessary.

Is counsel accepting the instructions?

30. The new Standard Terms are intended to apply when the first instructions in a matter are received (and accordingly include obligations relating to the consideration and acceptance of the instructions). The new Standard Terms are also intended to apply to all instructions received thereafter in the same matter.

31. Clause 4 of the new Standard Terms provides that the barrister, having had a reasonable time to review the instructions, must inform the instructing Authorised Person whether or not he accepts the Instructions.

32. Despite having accepted the instructions, if the barrister comes to the conclusion that the requirements of the Money Laundering Regulations have not been satisfied, he may withdraw any acceptance of those instructions without incurring liability (clause 4.4) and it is strongly advised that the client is informed at the earliest opportunity of why the barrister is withdrawing (provided that doing so does not contravene the Regulations).

33. It is obviously important that the communication with the Authorised Person regarding the instructions is clear:

    33.1 Chambers should ensure that an acknowledgement of receipt of papers cannot be taken as acceptance of instructions.

    33.2 Communication of the acceptance or refusal of the instructions must be clear and capable of justification in the event of a subsequent dispute.

34. Clause 4 of the new Standard Terms should be read in conjunction with the BSB Handbook to ensure that any refusal of the instructions is not a breach of the Code.

35. If the solicitors/Authorised Persons are named on the Advisory List of Defaulting Solicitors and other Authorised Persons 2012, the barrister is free to accept or refuse the instructions, as he/she sees fit, without contravening the Cab Rank Rule.

What are the Authorised Person's obligations?

36. Clause 3 spells out the obligations of the Authorised Person regarding the issue and acceptance of instructions. It is the Authorised Person's responsibility:

    36.1 To provide adequate instructions, in sufficient time and ensuring that the relevant documentation and information is included. Requests from the barrister for further information or instructions must be responded to promptly and the Authorised Person must inform the barrister immediately if there is reason to believe that any of the information or documentation is untrue or inaccurate.

36.2 If all or any of the instructions require to be dealt with urgently, then the barrister must be informed of the urgency, and the reason for the urgency, at the time of the delivery of the instructions. In addition, the instructions themselves must be marked "urgent". A barrister is entitled to decline the instructions if he is unable to comply with the urgency required.

What are the barrister's obligations?

37. Clause 4 refers to the Receipt and Acceptance of Instructions (see 'Is Counsel Accepting Instructions?' above). The barrister must review the instructions within a reasonable time of receipt and must advise the Authorised Person whether or not he/she accepts the instructions.

38. Clause 5 details the need for the barrister to keep confidential all information provided to him/her unless he/she is obligated or permitted to disclose it. To the extent that such information is already in the public domain, the barrister may disclose in his/her marketing and similar materials information relating to the case. Where the information is not already in the public domain, the barrister may only refer to it for marketing purposes in a form which preserves the lay client's privilege and confidentiality and (where required) with the lay client's consent.

39. Clause 6 provides that the parties can correspond by means of electronic mail unless otherwise directed. The parties must use reasonable procedures to ensure security.

40. The barrister is the data controller for the purposes of the Data Protection Act and clause 7 makes clear his/her responsibilities as regards data protection.

41. The barrister has a contractual obligation to provide all information reasonably required to enable the lay client and/or the Authorised Person:

41.1 to have an assessment of the costs incurred; and

41.2 to obtain and enforce any order or agreement to pay costs against any third party (Clause 8.4).

42. Clause 8 imposes a contractual obligation upon the barrister to provide the services required by the instructions in a timely manner and using reasonable skill and care. The clause permits the barrister to delegate the provision of any part of those services but specifies that the barrister remains responsible for the work. This provision is to allow devilling or preparation of drafts by pupils; it is not intended to allow other types of delegation of the work required.

43. Clause 10 provides that, so far as such exclusion is not prohibited by law, the barrister is not liable for any loss or damage suffered by any person other than the lay client, nor for any loss or damage caused by inaccurate, incomplete or late instructions.

Intellectual Property Rights

44. Clause 9 makes clear that all copyright and other intellectual property rights

attaching to the barrister's work product belongs to and remains with the barrister. Although the Authorised Person and the Lay Client have the right and licence to use the barrister's work product for the particular case and purpose for which it was prepared, neither are entitled to use copies of the barrister's work product for other purposes without the express written permission of the barrister.

Should the barrister retain instructions and records?

45. The new Standard Terms do not affect the fact that the papers sent by the Authorised Person to the barrister belong to the authorised person, who can therefore ask for the return of those papers at any time.

46. Subject to the provisions in Clause 5 concerning confidential information and publicity, the barrister can retain for the purposes of his records copies of the instructions and written advices. The Bar Council strongly urges barristers to do this, as such information would be required, at the least, to substantiate any claim for his fees should the barrister find himself/herself in the position of having to sue for them and/or substantiate the level of fees claimed.

Chapter 4: fees

47. Clause 11 provides that, subject to the Bar Code of Conduct, a barrister may agree to provide services for a fixed fee or an hourly rate or any such other basis as agreed between himself and the instructing Authorised Person. The new Standard Terms also provide that if fees are agreed at an hourly rate, that rate can be subject to a reasonable periodic review by the barrister.

48. If, when the barrister wishes to carry out such periodic review, the increase in hourly rate and effective date cannot be agreed with the Authorised Person, the barrister is entitled to treat the contract as terminated, subject of course to his obligations to the client under the BSB Handbook.

49. If no fee or hourly rate is agreed, then the barrister is entitled to charge a reasonable fee.

50. Clearly it is very important that any terms agreed as regards fees are clearly documented in case the barrister needs to take enforcement action to recover unpaid fees.

Chapter 5: billing, payment and interest

51. Clause 12 refers to billing, payment and interest and uses the word "invoice". It is important to note that the definition of "invoice" in the new Standard Terms includes a fee note not amounting to a VAT invoice (clause 1.2). Barristers may therefore continue to issue fee notes (followed by the issue of a combined receipt and VAT invoice on receipt of payment), as is the current practice,[1] or they may chose instead to issue VAT Invoices from the outset, but should be aware of the tax consequences of doing so, for example that the barrister's obligation to account for VAT shown on a VAT invoice will arise at the date of invoice, rather than the date of receipt of payment, as is the case with traditional fee notes.[2]

52. Clause 12.2 requires the barrister to deliver the invoice as soon as reasonably practical and in any event not more than three months from the earliest of:

    52.1 a request by the Authorised Person; or

    52.2 notification by the Authorised Person that the case has been settled or otherwise concluded; or

    52.3 termination of the Agreement.

53. Barristers and clerks should be aware that proceedings for detailed assessment of costs must be commenced not more than three months after the date of the relevant judgment, direction, order or award, so that the barrister should endeavour to provide the invoice more quickly than three months to allow sufficient time to prepare the documentation for detailed assessment.

54. Clause 12.3 provides that the invoice must set out an itemised description of the services provided by the barrister and the fees charged, together with details and cost of any disbursements incurred, and VAT (if charged). Although not spelt out in the new Standard Terms, it is obviously important that the invoice contains the Authorised Person's name and address together with the name and reference, if any, of the individual who provided the instructions, the barrister's address, the barrister's VAT registration number (if any), the date of the invoice, the name of the case and the barrister's reference number for it.[3]

55. Clauses 12.4–12.6 provide that the invoice must be paid within 30 days of delivery, without any set off. Failure to pay within that time will entitle the barrister to charge interest in accordance with the Late Payment of Commercial Debts (Interest) Act 1998 and/or sue for payment. In addition, subject to the barrister's obligations to the Court and the other Bar Code of Conduct provisions, the barrister is entitled to refrain from doing any further work on the case unless payment for that further work is made in advance.

1 Clause 12.5 provides that where a barrister has been paid on a fee note, the barrister must provide a VAT invoice following receipt of payment at the request of the Authorised Person, as is the current customary practice of the Bar.

2 This potential disadvantage can be avoided by most barristers by electing for cash accounting for VAT purposes. See paragraphs 321–331 of the Bar Council's Taxation and Retirement Benefits Guidance, seventh edition 2013, at http://www.barcouncil.org.uk/media/171635/taxation_guidance_7th_edition.pdf

3 Where the invoice is also a VAT invoice, it must also comply with the relevant VAT Regulations concerning the contents of a VAT invoice.

Chapter 6: termination of contract

56. Under Clause 13, the Authorised Person can terminate the contract at any time, after giving written notice. The barrister can terminate the contract by written notice if he is entitled to do so under Rules rc25–27 of the BSB Handbookor is otherwise able to withdraw from the case, provided that doing so does not conflict with his obligations under theBSB Handbook. It is obviously sensible for the barrister to explain in writing, at the earliest opportunity, the grounds upon which he has terminated the contract.

Chapter 7: notices and delivery

57. Clause 18 provides that notices or other written communication may be sent electronically (including fax and email).

Chapter 8: challenges to the fees

58. As mentioned above, Clause 12.4 provides that invoices should be paid without any set-off (whether by reason of a complaint made or a dispute between the barrister and the Authorised Person).

59. If there is a dispute, then Clause 19 provides that it can be resolved by any dispute resolution procedure agreed between that the barrister and the Authorised Person. In addition, the Joint Tribunal procedure, which is operated jointly by the Bar Council and the Law Society, without charge, still currently continues for fee disputes between barristers and solicitors. Information on the Joint Tribunal service can be found on the Bar Council's website at http://www.barcouncil.org.uk/jointtribunalservice.

Chapter 9: making a complaint to the Bar Council regarding unpaid fees

60. The scheme for placing solicitors/Authorised Persons on the advisory "List of Defaulting Solicitors and other Authorised Persons 2012" is similar to the old 'Withdrawal of Credit Scheme' except that barristers are not required to refuse instructions from solicitors or Authorised Persons on the advisory "List of Defaulting Solicitors and other Authorised Persons 2012", and instead they may choose whether or not to accept such instructions.

61. Complaints can be made against solicitors and Authorised Persons in the following situations:

    61.1 the barrister has obtained a judgment for fees against the solicitor or Authorised Person;

    61.2 the solicitor has not paid a joint tribunal award;

    61.3 where fees are covered by a full publicly funded certificate but remain unpaid due to the failures of the instructing solicitor. The solicitor may have failed to submit the final claim to the Legal Services Commission or, where there is eventually no claim on the legal aid fund because costs are to be recovered from the other side, the instructing solicitor fails to recover those costs or pass on the monies received to the barrister so that the barrister remains unpaid; and

    61.4 where instructions were received before 31 January 2013 on the basis of the former 'Terms of Work', a complaint about non-payment of fees for that work may be made without having first to obtain a judgment or a joint tribunal award.

62. On receipt of a complaint regarding unpaid fees, the Chairman of the Bar Council will write to the solicitor/Authorised Person in question requiring payment to be made. Normally, the Chairman of the Bar Council will place the solicitor/Authorised Person on the advisory "List of Defaulting Solicitors and other Authorised Persons 2012" if two or more such complaints have been made, unless the Chairman is persuaded that it would be inappropriate to do so.

63. The names of solicitors/Authorised Persons on the Withdrawal of Credit List as at 31 January 2013 will automatically be transferred to the advisory "List of Defaulting Solicitors and other Authorised Persons 2012".

64. The Rules relating to the advisory "List of Defaulting Solicitors and other Authorised Persons 2012" and the Scheme for Complaining to the Bar Council for Publicly Funded matters on the Bar Council's website can be found on the Bar Council's website http://www.barcouncil.org.uk/listofdefaultingsolicitors.

Procedure for making a complaint to the Bar Council – non-payment of a judgment or a joint tribunal award

65. A complaint form must be completed and sent to the Bar Council's Fees Collection Department, together with a copy of the judgment or joint tribunal award, a copy of the fee note and copies ofr any relevant correspondence since the judgment or award.

Non-payment of fees (instructions received before 31 January 2013)

66. The appropriate version[1] of Letter A and then Letter B, as prescribed in Schedule C to the 'Rules Relating to the List of Defaulting Solicitors and other Authorised Persons 2012', must be sent to the solicitor.

67. Letter A[2] must be sent not earlier than one month after the first fee note to which the outstanding fees relate and letter B must be sent not earlier than three months after the first fee note to which the outstanding fees relate.

68. A complaint form must then be completed and sent to the Bar Council's Fees Collection Department, together with a copy of the fee note and copies of all relevant correspondence.

1 One version is for privately funded cases (including those cases which are funded by the Legal Services Commission but where the solicitors pay counsel e.g. for Controlled Legal Representation Cases) and one is for cases which have full publicly funded certificates where counsel should be paid direct by the Legal Services Commission.

2 In privately funded cases only, letter A may include the optional paragraph charging interest on theunpaid fees.

Non payment of fees – cases having full publicly funded certificates

69. "The Scheme for Complaining to the Bar Council for Publicly Funded Matters", which is on the Bar Council's website http://www.barcouncil.org.uk/listofdefaultingsolicitors, applies and relates to matters covered by full publicly funded certificates where the barrister should be paid direct by the Legal Services Commission but remains unpaid due to the failures of the instructing solicitor. The solicitor may have failed to submit the final claim to the Legal Services Commission or, where there is eventually no claim on the legal aid fund because costs are to be recovered from the other side, the instructing solicitor fails to recover those costs or pass on the monies received to the barrister so that the barrister remains unpaid. This provision continues the present scheme operated under the Withdrawal of Credit Scheme though

with the added advantage that the change to the Cab Rank Rule enables a barrister to refuse such publicly funded work if the instructions are from solicitors named on the List of Defaulting Solicitors.

70. Letter A and then Letter B, as prescribed in Schedule to 'The Scheme for Complaining to the Bar Council for Publicly Funded Matters' must be sent to the solicitor.

71. Letter A must be sent not earlier than one month after the first fee note to which the outstanding fees relate and Letter B must be sent not earlier than three months after the first fee note to which the outstanding fees relate and not earlier than two months after Letter A was sent.

72. A complaint form must then be completed and sent to the Bar Council's Fees Collection Department, together with a copy of the fee note and copies of all relevant correspondence.

For queries or further information: contact the Fees Collection Office, General Council of the Bar by telephone: 020 7611 1318, email: fees@barcouncil.org.uk or by post: Fees Collection Office, General Council of the Bar, 289–293 High Holborn, London WC1V 7HZ (DX 240 London Chancery Lane)

Contractual Terms – frequently asked questions

[3.84b]

The new contractual terms of work are set out at annex T of the Code of Conduct and can be found in Part I of this Handbook.

The Bar Council has also produced a 'Frequently Asked Questions' paper to assist in the interpretation and application of the new terms and these are set out here:

Adopting the new Contractual Terms

Q.1 I want to adopt the New Contractual Terms in their entirety, what do I need to do?

A. Under Regulation 8(1) of the Provision of Services Regulations 2009, "providers of services" such as barristers, should make their general terms and conditions of engagement available – and this would normally be on your website. You will therefore need to amend your website. You need not put the whole contract on your website. You can instead simply make reference to the relevant part of the Bar Code of Conduct (Annex T). In addition, you do not have to publish your hourly rates.

You will need to advise your current solicitor clients of the change of your normal terms of engagement. This could also be used as a marketing opportunity. Allow sufficient time for your current solicitor clients to respond to you. Obviously you hope that you will never have to sue for your fees but you need to think in terms of worst case scenario – would you have the evidence in place to prove that your client knew that the instructions were being accepted on these new Contractual Terms?

Your acceptance of instruction letters/emails will need to reflect the fact that the instructions are being accepted on these Contractual Terms.

Any subsequent letters, for example chasing fees, would need to be amended. Your chamber's website or promotional material should be checked to ensure that the old terms are not being quoted.

Internal administrative procedures and policies should be reviewed – for example recording whether a variation or different terms have been agreed, whether there are changes to the billing and reminder cycles.

Work based on instructions accepted prior to the 31 January 2013 would be based on the old Terms/Withdrawal of Credit Scheme, even though the work is actually carried out after that date. Complaints of unpaid fees based on the old Terms of Work can still be made to the Bar Council under the transitional arrangements contained in the Rules relating to the List of Defaulting Solicitors and other Authorised Persons 2012. Check on the Bar Council's website http://www.barcouncil.org.uk/for-the-bar/introduction-to-member-services/fees-collection/ on how to make such complaints after the 30 January 2013.

Q.2 Who and what is an 'Authorised person'? how do I find out if someone is an 'Authorised Person?

A. Unlike the old Terms of Work/Withdrawal of Credit Scheme, these new Terms are for use by all Persons authorised by the SRA to carry out legal activities as defined under section 18(1)(a) of the Legal Services Act 2007. The legal activities are listed in section 12 of that Act as follows:

(a) the exercise of a right of audience;

(b) the conduct of litigation;

(c) reserved instrument activities;

(d) probate activities;

(e) notarial activities;

(f) the administration of oaths.

Schedule 2 of the Legal Services Act 2007 gives the definitions of those legal activities.

The SRA does not publish the names of Authorised Persons but does publish some names of Alternative Business Structures supervised by the SRA. Also, not all solicitors are listed on the Law Society's website. If in doubt about whether your prospective client is able to instruct, contact the SRA on 0870 606 2555 or email contactcentre@SRA.org.uk to check the status of an individual or organisation.

Q.3 I am happy to continue to operate under the Terms of Work on which Barristers offer their Services to Solicitors and the Withdrawal of Credit Scheme in Annex G1 of the Code of Conduct – why has this been annulled?

A. As the Terms of Work were unenforceable, its efficacy was limited. This was exacerbated by the fact that it is no longer a matter of professional conduct for solicitors to pay barristers' fees and the Solicitors Regulation Authority does not deal with complaints of unpaid fees. In addition, the Terms had been criticised for some time as being obsolete and unclear.

Q.4 Can I simply ignore these new terms and carry on as I was before?

A. The Terms of Work/Withdrawal of Credit Scheme will not exist as from the 31 January 2013. It is not therefore possible to carry on as before if you were using those Terms as your normal Terms of engagement.

Q.5 Do I need to have Terms? Do I need to do anything?

A. The Terms of Work/Withdrawal of Credit Scheme were, in the Code of Conduct, the default terms in the absence of alternative Terms having been agreed. With the abolition of those Terms on the 31 January 2013, there are no default terms. If a barrister is unpaid, there is no protection available from the Bar Council as the Withdrawal of Credit Scheme is abolished and the List of Defaulting Solicitors would not apply. The new Contractual Terms are not default terms.

The presumption against barristers and solicitors intending to contract may no longer apply. Therefore you may find that a contract has been agreed in oral negotiations between solicitors and your clerk, or by exchange of emails or a Court may infer terms. A simple contract like that may extend the barrister's liability beyond the cover provided by BMIF. Therefore it is unsafe to do nothing.

Contractual implications

Q.6 BMIF – Insurance – Am I covered ?

A. The new Contractual Terms do not create any liabilities for barristers that do not arise in any event at common law. Neither do they impose any further limitation of liability. BMIF Guidance on the impact of the contractual terms and insurance cover can be found at http://www.barmutual.co.uk/fileadmin/uploads/barmutual/Guidance%20Note%20to%20Members%20-%20February%202013.pdf Further advice can be found in answer to Question 17.

Q.7 Accepting new instructions – can I rely on what is published on my website?

A. There are no default terms in the Bar Code of Conduct on or after the 31 January 2013. Consequently you cannot assume that these new contractual terms or the terms on your website (if different) can be considered automatically as the basis upon which your instructing solicitors or authorised person is instructing you. Although not a professional requirement, it would be unwise not to refer to and to confirm in writing the basis upon which you are accepting instructions. Simply having the terms on your website may not be sufficient notice.

Q.8 What records should I keep of cases not based on the Standard Contractual Terms?

A. You should keep records of the terms upon which the cases were accepted; evidence of the instructions; and evidence of any agreement about fees.

Q.9 Due to the pressure of other commitments I did not respond promptly on receipt of instructions. The solicitor is saying that he took the view that in default of a prompt response, it was OK to assume that the instructions could be considered to have been accepted. I do not like the terms that they are offered on and I wish to refuse them. Can I do this?

A. Whether the delay was such that the solicitor or lay client has good ground to lodge a complaint to the Bar Standards Board is a matter of professional conduct and the decision would be based on the particular facts of the situation – for example, the type and complexity of the instructions, were the instructions marked urgent, how long was the period of delay. Did the acknowledgement of the instructions letter clearly explain that the acknowledgement of receipt is not an acceptance of the instructions? Clause 4.1 of the new Terms provide that a barrister has a reasonable time to review the instructions before informing the Authorised Person whether or not he accepts the instructions.

You are under no obligation to accept the instructions if the solicitor insists on terms other than new Contractual Terms or the barrister's published terms of engagement. However, whether you accepted the solicitor's instructions because of the delay in responding is a legal question and the answer is dependent on the particular circumstances of the situation.

Q.10 An instructing solicitor says that he never received an acknowledgement letter referring to the New Terms (it would appear that one was not sent) and is now refusing to pay in 30 days on the basis that he has not agreed to this or indeed anything. I have referred him to our published terms on the website and he does not accept these. What is my position?

A. You would need to consider whether on the facts you can prove that the contract between you and the solicitor was agreed on the new Contractual Terms. It may assist if the solicitor client received a communication advising of your intention to change your normal terms of engagement from the Terms of Work/Withdrawal of Credit scheme to the new Contractual Terms as suggested in the Q1 above. Ultimately, it is a matter of evidence.

Q.11 The lay client has asked me to enter into a contract in addition to the one that I have with the solicitor. Can I do this?

A. So long as you continue to receive instructions from the solicitor, you can enter into a contract with the lay client – for example for the payment of fees. Barristers should make sure that the terms with the lay client do not conflict, but dovetail, with the contractual terms agreed with the solicitor. You should ensure that the contract does not give rise to liability that is wider than the cover provided by the BMIF.

Q.12 Do I need to agree a new contract for each piece of work?

A. Ultimately, the answer depends on whether you have sufficient evidence should you need to sue for the fees; and whether the solicitor is seeking to rely on different terms. The Bar Council considers that it is probably sufficient if you have advised your existing clients of the change to new terms and that the written acceptance of instructions restates that the new terms are being used. If, however, the solicitor is seeking to rely on different terms, you will have to negotiate directly with the solicitor.

Q.13 I accepted a return from a fellow member of Chambers and I was not aware that a different set of Terms had been agreed with that firm. Am I stuck with those Terms or can I insist on my own standard terms or the new Contractual Terms in Annex T?

A. If you have accepted the return, then you have accepted the terms upon which the instructions were given, including the different set of terms. Once you have accepted the instructions, you are bound by them.

Q.14 The solicitor and I have agreed contractual terms but cannot agree the quantum of the fee nor can we agree when the fees should be paid. How can we resolve this?

A. These matters can only be resolved by negotiation. You may wish to bear in mind that the Code of Conduct, at paragraph 604(b) entitles a barrister to refuse instructions if the instructions are offered at an improper fee. In addition, as the standard Contractual Terms provide for payment within 30 days, the amended Cab Rank Rule entitles the barrister to refuse the instructions if the instructing solicitor or Authorised Person declines to use those Terms or the barrister's own published terms. Consequently the barrister is able to refuse the instructions on the basis that the payment date is not accepted at 30 days (assuming the barrister's own published terms of engagement do not provide a payment date which meets the solicitor's demand). The dispute resolution and joint tribunal procedures are generally suitable for when there are disputes over what has been agreed, rather than what should have been agreed.

Q.15 What is date of delivery?

A. The date of delivery is important for the purposes of being sure when you can start to charge interest or take enforcement action for unpaid barristers' fees. It is the date that the Invoice (which includes a fee note not amounting to a VAT invoice) was received by the solicitor under Clause 12.2 of the Contractual Terms. Dates of deemed receipt are set out in Clause 18.2.

Changing the Contractual Terms

Q.16 The solicitor wants to agree a modest variation to the Standard Terms Contractual Terms. Will an exchange of letters suffice?

A. Yes. Clause 2.2 of the Terms states that the Terms can be varied by the parties, in writing, including by exchange of emails. Be sure to retain the evidence of the change of Terms.

Q.17 The solicitor wants many of the new Contractual Terms changed. Where can I get advice on this?

A. The Bar Council strongly advises that great caution is exercised before entering into a contract which varies from the Standard Contractual Terms. You need to be very sure that the proposed Terms do not conflict with the Bar Code of Conduct. What is more likely to be a danger is that a barrister might be extending his potential liability beyond the limits of his BMIF cover. The new standard Contractual Terms exclude barristers' liability beyond that which exists at common law in the absence of a contract.

Clause 3.1(x) of the Bar Mutual Indemnity Fund's 2013 Terms of Cover excludes "Claims or Disciplinary Proceedings in respect of any liability incurred under any contract, save to the extent that (a) such liability would have been incurred irrespective of the terms of such contract and would otherwise fall within the provisions of these Terms of Cover …".

BMIF Guidance on the impact of the contractual terms and insurance cover can be found at http://www.barmutual.co.uk/fileadmin/uploads/barmutual/Guidance%20Note%20to%20Members%20-%20February%202013.pdf The BMIF guidance seeks to explain the types of contractual term which may, and those which do not, have an impact on the extent to which barristers are insured against claims, and it includes Q&As on this topic. If the guidance note does not address the particular situation, or gives rise to concern over insurance cover, then it may be prudent to check with BMIF directly (the guidance note contains the necessary contact details) before agreeing to alternative terms potentially affecting liability.

It is impossible to list possible variances which would expose barristers to greater liability

than their BMIF cover but possible areas could be where the barrister is made liable for the solicitor's loss of profits, or is made strictly liable for the advice given (i.e. liable even in the absence of negligence or failure to take reasonable care), or where the barrister is held responsible for loss suffered by clients of the solicitor other than those on whose behalf he was instructed (e.g. where the advice is used generally instead of for the specific case for which it was given).

There are other terms you will need to consider: for example, you need to ensure that contract terms do not breach the cab rank rule by purporting to restrict clients from whom you can accept work in the future.

Further, very great caution would have to be exercised before entering into a contract which bound chambers as a whole, because that might give rise to common interests which would prevent members of chambers from acting against each other. Further, you might become liable for each other, which would be outside the scope of BMIF's cover.

The Law Society issued a Practice Note on the 24 January 2013 on the contractual terms and, as a consequence, a number of solicitors are seeking changes to the contractual terms, particularly in respect of Money Laundering, Intellectual Property, liability of barristers and fees. Chambers are strongly advised to read the Bar Council's Guide in respect of this Practice Note before agreeing to these changes. The Guide can be found on the Bar Council's Fees Collection webpage, at http://www.barcouncil.org.uk/for-the-bar/introduction-to-member-services/fees-collection/guidance-on-law-society's-practice-note/

Other amendments being suggested by some solicitors give particular cause for concern. For example, amendments which purport to create an absolute assignment of intellectual property rights in barristers' work leave open the possibility of that work being used inappropriately for other matters.

This issue is also addressed in paragraph 3 of the Bar Council's Guide to the Contractual Terms, which can be found at http://www.barcouncil.org.uk/guidetocontractualterms

Solicitors have also asked that the barrister carry out conflicts checks within chambers, which is wholly inappropriate in the context of individual, self-employed barristers, who could find themselves in breach their duties of confidence to other clients.

As regards liability for and timing of the payment of fees, whilst amendment of those terms would not affect professional indemnity cover, barristers should carefully consider the effects of any proposed amendments, which could in some cases result in giving almost unlimited free credit, or in having to rely on recovery from a third party over whom the barrister has limited control.

Q.18 A solicitor has asked me to enter into a contract that would appear to offend the Code of Conduct. What should I do?

A. Refuse. You are under no obligation to accept the instructions if the solicitor refuses to use the new Contractual Terms or the barrister's published terms of engagement and any breach of the Code of Conduct may lead to disciplinary proceedings.

Q.19 The solicitor is insisting on a 'pay when paid' clause in the contract. In effect, does this remove any liability to pay barristers at all? What incentive is there for a solicitor to chase a client to pay barristers' fees before their own or indeed at all?

A. You are correct that such a clause would leave barristers vulnerable to non-payment in the manner you describe. Obviously whether or not you agree to such a clause is a matter of negotiation. Possibly an option to consider is to have a time limit, so that the solicitor is obligated to pay after a period of time irrespective of being placed in funds. Also think about ensuring that the solicitor will agree to chase your fees properly and will assign to you the right to pursue the client in the event of non payment.

Q.20 One of Chambers biggest clients wants to agree a different set of standard terms with Chambers and not all members are agreeable to the penalty clauses. Their Terms have penalty clauses attached relating to poor service. Can Chambers as an entity sign up to this?

A. Part of the answer lies in the constitution of your chambers. As noted above, agreeing contracts as a chambers may have consequences in terms of being unable to act against each other and/or being liable for each other's defaults. However, it should be pointed out that the new Contractual Terms are between the barrister (not his chambers) and the Authorised Person who is instructing. We strongly advise that barristers do not agree to extending their potential liability beyond the limits of their BMIF cover. The new Contractual Terms do not extend nor restrict the liability of barristers that existed prior to the 31 January 2013. Clause 3.1(x) of the Bar Mutual Indemnity Fund's terms of cover excludes "Claims or Disciplinary Proceedings in respect of any liability incurred under any contract, save to the extent that (a) such liability would have been incurred irrespective of the terms of such contract and would otherwise fall within the provisions of these Terms of Cover …". BMIF Guidance, which includes Q&As on the type of contractual terms which might cause difficulties in this respect can be found at http://www.barmutual.co.uk/fileadmin/uploads/barmutual/Guidance%20 Note%20to%20Members%20-%20February%202013.pdf

Paragraph 604(h) of the Code of Conduct enables a barrister to refuse instructions where the potential liability for professional negligence in respect of the case could exceed the level of professional indemnity insurance which is reasonably available and likely to be available in the market for him.

Q.21 A firm of solicitors wants to enter into a general contract with Chambers. The Terms are different to our Standard Terms but they are generally acceptable. Is this OK?

A. As described above, the new Contractual Terms are between the barrister (not his chambers) and the Authorised Person who is instructing. Barristers are self-employed individuals. Barristers are not employed by the chambers. Besides the question of whether a chambers could agree a general contract which binds the barristers, agreeing contracts as a chambers may have consequences in terms of barristers being unable to act against each other, and/or in being liable for each other's defaults. However chambers can of course come to an arrangement or an understanding as regards terms for particular professional clients, which the chambers' barristers would usually use for accepting instructions.

Q.22 A solicitor has inserted a term into a proposed contract that says that I am liable for consequential loss. Can I agree to this?

A. Barristers are free to agree whatever terms they wish, provided they are legal and do not conflict with the Bar Code of Conduct.

With regard to consequential loss, we would urge great caution before agreeing to this. The new standard contractual terms do not create, extend or reduce any liabilities for barristers that do not arise in any event at common law and consequently do not extend the barrister's potential liability beyond the limits of BMIF cover. Extending the barrister's liability to cover consequential loss may extend the barrister's liability beyond that which is covered by his BMIF insurance. It must be borne in mind that paragraph 604(h) of the Bar Code of Conduct enables a barrister to refuse instructions where the potential liability for professional negligence could exceed the level of professional indemnity insurance which is reasonably available and likely to be available in the market for the barrister to accept. Paragraph 204(c) of the Bar Code of Conduct provides that a barrister may supply legal services to the public only if he is covered by insurance against claims for professional negligence arising out of the supply of his services. If the proposal is regarding the solicitor's consequential loss, then agreement is very likely to be outside the scope of BMIF's cover. If the proposal is about the lay client's consequential loss, then it is likely to be within the scope of BMIF's cover. Further guidance from the Bar Council and BMIF on this matter can be found at http://www.barcouncil.org.uk/for-the-bar/introduction-to-member-services/fees-collection/guidance-on-law-society's-practice-note/ and http://www.barmutual.co.uk/fileadmin/uploads/barmutual/Guidance%20Note%20to%20Members%20-%20February%202013.pdf respectively.

Cab rank rule and withdrawal from a case

Q.23 I started a case under the Chambers Standard Contractual Terms and the solicitor now wants to agree modestly different terms prior to delivering the brief for the final hearing. I have objected to the new terms but the solicitor says that I am instructed on the case and cannot now decline to do the case. Can I refuse to accept the brief?

A. Having agreed terms, neither party (barrister and the instructing Authorised Person) is entitled to demand, unilaterally, that different terms be substituted.

However, the Bar Code of Conduct is paramount and, under paragraph 610(d) of the Code, barristers should not return any instructions or withdraw from a case in such a way or in such circumstances that the client is unable to find other legal assistance in time to prevent prejudice being suffered by the client.

If you are using the Bar Council's new Standard Contractual Terms, then you should note that clause 11.2.1 does allow for the periodic review by the barrister of his fees if the fees had been agreed on a hourly rate basis or if there has been a significant change in his status or seniority.

Q.24 The solicitor has not paid me in a timely way, the final hearing, which will involve a substantial amount of work, is imminent and I doubt the solicitor will pay for that either. The solicitor says that I cannot withdraw at this stage as it would prejudice the client. Can I withdraw?

A. Clause 12.6.3 in the new contractual terms provides that, if fees in a case remain unpaid for 30 days or more, the barrister is able to refrain from doing any further work on the case unless payment for that further work is made in advance, subject to the barrister's obligations to the Court and paragraph 610 of the Bar Code of Conduct. Of particular importance is paragraph 610(d) of the Code which forbids the barrister from returning the instructions or withdrawing in such a way that the client is prejudiced through lack of time to obtain alternative legal assistance.

Fees

Q.25 Using the new Contractual Terms, the solicitor and I agreed the fees and I undertook the work. The solicitor is now disputing the amount of fees that was agreed. What options are available to me?

A. You can seek to resolve the matter by use of any dispute resolution procedure. However, the Joint Tribunal service is still available for use by barristers and solicitors for any fee disputes. The Joint Tribunal service is free and is run jointly by the Bar Council and the Law Society. The Tribunal itself is made up of a member appointed by the Bar Council and a member appointed by the Law Society and usually reaches a decision on the basis of written statements from barrister and solicitor. Information on the Joint Tribunal service can be found on the Bar Council's website at http://www.barcouncil.org.uk/jointtribunalservice

Q.26 The solicitor has not paid my fee – can I report him to the Bar Council for non-payment?

A. Complaints can be made against solicitors and Authorised Persons in the following situations:

1. The barrister has obtained a judgment for fees against the solicitor or Authorised Person

2. The solicitor has not paid a joint tribunal award.

3. Where the instructions were covered by a full publicly funded certificate, but remains unpaid due to the failures of the instructing solicitor. The solicitor may have failed to submit the final claim to the Legal Services Commission or, where there is eventually no claim on the legal aid fund because costs are to be recovered from the other side, the instructing solicitor fails to recover those costs or pass on the monies received to the barrister so that the barrister remains unpaid.

4. Where work was based on instructions accepted before 31 January 2013 on the basis of the former "Terms of Work", a complaint about non-payment of fees for that work may be made without having first to obtain a judgment or a joint tribunal award. On receipt of a complaint regarding unpaid fees, the Chairman of the Bar Council will write to the solicitor in question requiring payment to be made. Normally, the Chairman of the Bar Council will place the solicitor on the advisory "List of Defaulting Solicitors and other Authorised Persons 2012" if two or more such complaints have been made, unless the Chairman is persuaded that it would be inappropriate to do so.

The Rules relating to the advisory "List of Defaulting Solicitors and other Authorised Persons 2012" and the Scheme for Complaining to the Bar Council for Publicly Funded matters on the Bar Council's website can be found on the Bar Council's website http://www.barcouncil.org.uk/listofdefaultingsolicitors and information on making complaints can be found on http://www.barcouncil.org.uk/for-the-bar/introduction-to-member-services/fees-collection/.

Q.27 Who is the contract actually agreed with? And do I sue the firm or the solicitor? Is it a personal liability?

A. The new Contractual Terms are stated to be an agreement between the barrister and the Authorised Person. The Authorised Person is defined as the person approved by the SRA (see Q2 above) and includes all successors and assignees. Although the Authorised Person can be an individual, it is likely to be the "firm" and therefore you would sue the firm. If the firm is a true partnership, then the partners are likely to be joint and severally liable. Save for that, there is no provision in the new Contractual Terms that an individual solicitor is personally liable for the instructions given in the name of the firm.

Q.28 A senior member of Chambers did a small piece of work for one of Chambers biggest clients. The solicitor is declining to pay at this stage saying that the client has cited some minor dissatisfaction with the work of that senior barrister. The senior barrister has said that he will sue for his fees unless he is paid and the firm has said that they will pull all of their work from Chambers if he does. Can Chambers stop him suing the solicitor or could Chambers just cover the fee? Is Chambers obliged to support the senior member of Chambers?

A. The introduction of the contractual terms does not affect the provisions of the Code of Conduct in respect of the position of chambers and the responsibility of the Head of Chambers to ensure that fee notes of all former members, pupils and members irrespective of their standing, are sent expeditiously and pursued efficiently. The Bar Council is not in a position to comment on the procedures or decisions of a chambers unless such procedures or decisions conflict with the Bar Code of Conduct.

Q.29 I have an outstanding fee of £500 for which I wish to sue the solicitor in the small claims court. Where can I find out information about this? What is the maximum amount that I can sue for in the small claims court and does the amount that I sue for include interest?

A. The maximum amount that you can sue for in the small claims court is £5,000. However, creditors can make a claim on line for any amount through the new County Court Money Claims Centre (the CCMCC). The CCMCC centralises the administrative functions and manages the early stages of claims, up to allocation of the case in the relevant court. Information can be found in https://www.gov.uk/make-court-claim-for-money/overview See also the answer to question 33.

Q.30 A firm owes me a substantial amount in fees but it has been taken over and the new firm says that the debt is not their problem. Who do I sue?

A. It is unlikely you would be able to sue the new firm unless (exceptionally) the new firm took over the debts of the old firm. Who or whether you can sue depends very much upon the constitution of the firm who instructed. Was the firm a sole practice or a partnership? If the answer is yes, possibly the individual practitioner or partners can be held liable. However if the "firm" was a limited company or an LLP, you will only be able to sue the old practice – which may or may not have assets.

Q.31 What assistance will the Bar Council give me to sue for my fees?

A. Regrettably the Bar Council does not have the resources to provide practical assistance in enabling barristers to sue for his fees, though of course the Bar Council will happily give advice on these Terms and on the Code of Conduct.

Invoices

Q.32 Invoices – I am using fee notes and wish to continue to do so but one client is insisting that I invoice him. Can I operate both systems concurrently?

A. Yes, but you would have to be very careful with your records as it affects the barrister's tax situation. Essentially, a fee note is not deemed to be an invoice and is not treated as an invoice until the fee note is reissued as a combined receipt and VAT invoice. This practice arises from the Regulation 92 of the VAT (General) Regulations 1995, whereby the barrister's liability for payment of VAT does not arise until the fees are paid. With invoices, the barrister's liability for payment of VAT arises when the invoice is issued, not when the fees are paid. Further information is available on page 48 of the Bar Council's 'Taxation and Retirement Benefits Guidance' http://www.barcouncil.org.uk/media/171635/taxation_and_retirement_benefits_-_6th_edition.pdf

Interest

Q.33 How much interest can I charge? Do I have to charge interest?

A. The new Contractual Terms provide at clause 12.6.1 that interest can be charged in accordance with the Late Payment of Commercial Debts (Interest) Act 1998 and the Terms also provide that the interest can be charged from 30 days after the date of the delivery of the fee note. At present, the rate of interest is governed by the Late Payment of Commercial Debts (Rate ofInterest) (No 3) Order 2002 (SI 2002 no 1675) and provides for interest to be charged at 8% above the Bank of England bank (base) rate. The Bank of England's link to the bank rates is http://www.bankofengland.co.uk/boeapps/iadb/Repo.asp?Travel=NIxIRx

Remember, it is entirely optional as to whether interest is charged. The contractual terms say the barrister is "entitled" to charge interest. This does not mean he "has" to charge interest. In addition, of course, the barrister and instructing person can agree a different rate of interest or agree not to charge interest at all.

The Late Payment of Commercial Debts Regulations 2002 (SI 2002/1674) allows the barrister to charge a fixed sum, in addition to the interest charged under the Commercial Debts (Interest) Act 1998, to compensate for the costs of collecting the debt. The sum is £40 for a debt of less than £1,000, £70 for a debt of £1,000 or more but less than £10,000 and £100 for a debt of £10,000 or more.

Copyright

Q.34 I have prepared an extensive advice and I understand that the solicitor is now using that advice for other clients of his. Can he do this?

A. Clause 9.1 of the standard Contractual Terms clearly require that the barrister's written permission is obtained by the solicitor before he can use that advice for purposes other than those for which it was prepared. The work was carried out by the barrister for a particular case and for a particular purpose and it must not be used for other purposes without the barrister's written consent.

For queries or further information please contact the Fees Collection Office, General Council of the Bar, by telephone 020 7611 1318, email fees@barcouncil.org.uk or by post: Fees Collection Office, General Council of the Bar, 289–293 High Holborn, London WC1V 7HZ (DX 240 London Chancery Lane).

Fees Collection

[3.85]

The Bar Council assists barristers to collect fees owed to them by solicitors in respect of instructions accepted up until the 31 January 2013 on the "Terms of Work on which barristers offer their services to solicitors and the Withdrawal of Credit scheme", or on contractual terms or on instructions covered by full publicly funded certificates.

It also manages the List of Defaulting Solicitors and other Authorised Persons and, jointly with the Law Society, the operation of the Joint Tribunal scheme. If barristers have fees outstanding, they can make complaints in the following circumstances by emailing the relevant linked report form and attaching supporting documents as required.

1. The barrister has obtained a judgment for fees against the instructing Solicitor or Authorised Person.
2. The instructing Solicitor or Authorised Person has not paid a joint tribunal or an arbitration award in respect of a barrister's fees.
3. Where instructions were accepted before 31 January 2013 on the basis of the former "Terms of Work", a complaint about non-payment of fees for that work may be made without having first to obtain a judgment or an award of a joint tribunal or an arbitration (Guidance and application forms for a Private Funding Agreement or a Conditional Fee Agreement).
4. Where fees are covered by a full publicly funded certificate but remain unpaid due to the failures of the instructing solicitor. The solicitor may have failed to submit the final claim to the Legal Services Commission or, where there is eventually no claim on the legal aid fund because costs are to be recovered from the other side, the instructing solicitor fails to recover those costs or pass on the monies received onto the barrister so that the barrister remains unpaid (Application form).

Joint Tribunal Process

The Bar Council also handles the joint tribunal process whereby disputes between barristers and solicitors are resolved regarding the amount of fees charged.

Applications under the Rules relating to the "List of Defaulting Solicitors and Other Authorised Persons 2012" for instructions received before 31 January 2013

[3.86]

Introduction to this guidance

General Introduction

1. For many years the Bar Council has operated the Withdrawal of Credit Scheme[1] which enables barristers to place a solicitors firm on a defaulting list to which no barristers could accept instructions unless full payment was received in advance. Following the introduction of Contractual Terms in 2013 the list became advisory and the prohibition of accepting instructions (without full prior payment) from these firms was lifted. The status of the list is therefore advisory; nonetheless, the Bar Council discourages any barrister to accept instructions from the listed firms. This guidance relates to complaints under the old Withdrawal of Credit Scheme where instructions were received on, or before, 31 January 2013 and how applications to place a solicitor's firm on the list can be made.

Purpose

2. The purpose of this guidance is to outline how applications can be made to place a solicitors firm on the list of defaulting solicitors following the non-payment of barristers' fees. This guidance outlines the process the Bar Council follows when determining an application and how such an application should be made.

3. This guidance has been based on, and should be read in accordance with, the requirements set out in the following documents:

   a. the Withdrawal of Credit Scheme in respect of work undertaken on the old Terms of Work/Withdrawal of Credit scheme (annex G1 and G2 of the Bar Code of Conduct – 6th Edition);

   b. the Rules Relating to the List of Defaulting Solicitors and Other Authorised Persons 2012, and

   c. the Withdrawal of Credit Scheme in respect of work undertaken on the old Terms of Work/Withdrawal of Credit Protocol.

4. Copies of these are available on the Bar Council's website but they are also provided as annexes A, B and C respectively at the end of this guidance.

Roles and responsibilities

5. The success of this scheme depends on both the Bar Council and members of the Bar who use this service working cooperatively and understanding what is expected of each other. To that end the roles and responsibilities of each party should be clear.

6. The Bar Council manage and administer the scheme and:

   a. are accountable for the performance of the service;

   b. are consistent in their decision-making applying discretion only in limited and prescribed areas of the process;

   c. proactively explore opportunities to better serve users of the service;

   d. strive to exceed members' needs and expectations through competence and consistency;

   e. understand that our members deserve a service that is responsive, professional, efficient and timely; and

   f. ensure that the process, including the roles and responsibilities of users of the service, is communicated clearly.

7. The requirements we have of users of the service (applicants) are as follows:

   a. applications should not be sent until both Letter A and Letter B have been sent by the complainant, or by chambers on their behalf;

   b. applications should be sent in good form, first time. Any errors on the application detract attention from other valid claims in the system from progressing;

   c. the Bar Council must be made aware of any changes to the complaint in a timely manner including notifying the Bar Council of receipt of full (or part) payment or where there have been material differences; and

d. users of the service should respond to any request by the Bar Council in a timely manner.

The rules and protocol outlining the process

Introduction

8. On the 31 January 2013, the Terms of Work on which Barristers offer their Services to Solicitors and the Withdrawal of Credit Scheme 1988 were abolished. The "List of Defaulting Solicitors and Other Authorised Persons" replaced the Withdrawal of Credit List.

9. The scheme for placing solicitors/Authorised Persons on the advisory List of Defaulting Solicitors and other Authorised Persons 2012 is similar to the old Withdrawal of Credit Scheme except that barristers are not required to refuse instructions from solicitors or Authorised Persons on the advisory List of Defaulting Solicitors and other Authorised Persons 2012. Instead they may choose whether or not to accept such instructions. The names of solicitors/ Authorised Persons on the Withdrawal of Credit List as at 31 January 2013 were automatically transferred to the advisory List of Defaulting Solicitors and other Authorised Persons 2012.

10. Complaints can be made to the Bar Council against solicitors and Authorised Persons in the following situations:

    a. The barrister has obtained a judgment for fees against the solicitor or Authorised Person.

    b. The solicitor has not paid a joint tribunal or an arbitration award.

    c. Where instructions were received before 31 January 2013 on the basis of the former "Terms of Work", a complaint about non-payment of fees for that work may be made without having first to obtain a judgment or an award of a joint tribunal or arbitration.

    d. Where fees are covered by a full publicly funded certificate but remain unpaid due to the failures of the instructing solicitor. The solicitor may have failed to submit the final claim to the Legal Aid Agency or, where there is eventually no claim on the legal aid fund because costs are to be recovered from the other side, the instructing solicitor fails to recover those costs or pass on the monies received on to the barrister so that the barrister remains unpaid.

11. This guidance relates to applications made under 10.c and 10.d above.

Outline of the process

12. The guiding document that underpins this process is contained in Annex G1 of the sixth edition of the Bar Code of Conduct and sets out a four letter process to which failure to respond, pay or give valid reasons for non-payment leads to the solicitor's firm being placed on the List of Defaulting Solicitors and Other Authorised Persons.

13. Annex G1 divides the responsibility of sending these letters first to the barrister (the first two letters) and the Bar Council (the last two letters) before a listing can be made. The process can be outlined as follows:

(a) Letter "A" (Barrister).

(b) Letter "B" (Barrister).

(c) Application to the Bar Council (Barrister).

(d) Letter "C" (The Bar Council).

(e) Letter "D" (The Bar Council).

(f) Listing (The Bar Council).

14. The first two letters (known as Letter A and Letter B) are prescribed in Annex G1 (though the updated wording in Annex D should be used for those letters). Letter A must be sent one month after the first fee note was submitted and Letter B must be sent after three months has elapsed since the first fee note. Template letters for Letters A and B are available on the Bar Council's website and are reproduced in Annex D.

Letter A

15. The text for Letter A is prescribed (Annex D of this Guidance) and should be substantially reproduced in that form regardless of whether the letter was sent by post or electronically.

16. There is an optional additional paragraph to letter A for instructions to allow for the charging of interest as, under the Terms of Work, interest can be charged one month after the issue of letter A. Please note that the Bar Council does not seek to recover interest through this process.

Letter B

17. The text for Letter B is prescribed (Annex D of this Guidance) and should be substantially reproduced in that form regardless of whether the letter was sent by post or electronically.

18. To ensure that the instructing solicitors or authorised person is fully aware of the outstanding fees a copy of Letter B should be sent to the Senior Partner (or relevant equivalent) of the firm concerned if that is not the same person.

Letter A and B for applications involving Conditional Fee Agreements

19. Where the barrister offered their services under a Conditional Fee Agreement please attach a copy of the Agreement. Different letters A and B need to be used, depending upon whether the Agreement had been terminated and/or payment was dependent upon the completion of the case.

Letter C

20. Following receipt of a valid application the Bar Council will send Letter C seeking to resolve the matter within 14 days the Bar Council. The Bar Council will send letters electronically by default but will revert to the post if that is appropriate.

Letter D

21. A further letter will be sent stating that upon the expiry of a further 14 days the solicitor's firm will be placed on the next published List of Defaulting Solicitors and Other Authorised Persons.

The List of Defaulting Solicitors and Other Authorised Persons

22. The Bar Council will publish an updated list on the Bar Council website.

23. At any time during this process the solicitor's firm can make a full payment and prevent themselves appearing on the List of Defaulting Solicitors. Alternatively, if the fees are disputed the case can be moved to a Joint Tribunal provided jointly by the Bar Council and the Law Society. In the situation where fees are disputed and full payment is unlikely we encourage the use of that process. More details on the Joint Tribunal scheme can be found on the Bar Council's website.[2]

Eligibility

24. Any member of the Bar may use the service, regardless as to whether they have paid the Bar Representation Fee, if they held a valid practising certificate for the year in which they first undertook the work.

25. An application under this process is only valid if:

a. The instructions were accepted on, or before, 31 January 2013

b. Letter A was sent in the correct form and was sent more than one month after the first fee note was submitted

c. Letter B was sent in the correct form and was sent more than three months after the first fee note was submitted and at least 14 days have elapsed after sending letter B

d. Letter B was addressed to the Senior Partner of the solicitor firm as registered with the Solicitors Regulation Authority (SRA) or, if applicable, and individual solicitor unless the solicitor or authorised person responsible for the outstanding fees is also the senior partner or if the solicitor is a sale practitioner.

e. The solicitor firm has changed details

f. The fee note does not relate to criminal legal aid.[3]

g. The date of the first fee note was submitted does not exceed two years from the date the application was made to the Bar Council.

h. The solicitor firm complained of has not been intervened (or has been made bankrupt), and

i. The fee note is submitted within three months after the work has been completed (or sooner if requested by the solicitor).

Validation

26. If the application is invalid in respect of one, or more, reasons relating to 25.a to 25.e then an email will be sent to the applicant informing them of the

error and providing information on how they can correct it. The reason(s) for rejection will be recorded so the prevalence of common errors can be monitored. The application will not progress until all the errors have been rectified. Details on how to ensure that the application is valid is discussed in the next part of this guidance.

27. If the application is rejected under 25.g (fee note exceeds two years from the date the application was received by the Bar Council) or 25.i. (fee note submitted three months after the work has been completed or sooner if the solicitor requests it) it will be rejected unless there is an exceptional reason to disapply the two-year rule. Such exceptional circumstances include:

   a. The fee in question related to a missed instalment of fees relating to instructions of more than two years from the submission of the first fee note but was missed within two years

   b. If the fee note relates to a publicly funded case within two years of the Legal Aid Certificate was discharged or revoked.

   c. If the case relates to a Conditional Fee Agreement or Damages-based Agreement within two years of the case being completed (or terminated), and

   d. Further exceptional reasons may also be accepted at the discretion of the Bar Council.

28. The reason for such an exception to be made must be stated at the time of application and accepting an exception is at the complete discretion of the Bar Council.

29. If the application is invalid due to the fact that the matter relates to criminal legal aid (25.f) the solicitor firm being intervened (25.h) or fee note was submitted three months after the work has been complete (25.i) then the application will be rejected.

Letter "C"

30. Following the determination of a valid application a letter (Letter C) will be sent by email to the solicitor firm. In limited circumstances the letter will be sent in hard copy through the post (if we believe that the email will not reach the required recipient).

31. If the solicitor firm, within three months of the date the fee note was submitted or one month after letter A, disputes the fees then the dispute must be determined by the Joint Tribunal process if the solicitor requests this action. At any stage the application can be moved outside this process and moved to the Joint Tribunal process or be closed as long as both parties agree. We recommend the use of the Joint Tribunal process in cases where the fees are disputed.

32. If the Solicitor firm responds to Letter C and gives a valid or understandable reason why payment remains unpaid, this will be communicated to the applicant to see if the issue can be resolved; either by receiving delayed payment or payment in instalments etc. The principle of OPTP (One Promise To Pay) will be used, and must be agreed to by the applicant, if the Solicitor firm breaks the OPTP then the application will move to the next

stage of the process. If no response is received the next part of the process will commence following the expiry of 14 days from the date Letter C was sent.

Letter "D"

33. Upon expiry of 14 days after Letter C has been sent to which no written representations have been made by the Solicitor's firm, a final Chair's letter (for convenience we refer to it as 'Letter D') will be sent to the Solicitor's firm stating that the Solicitor's firm will go on the next published list of defaulting solicitors.

34. Under the rules in Annex G1, if the Solicitor firm makes full payment but does not provide reasons for the late payment they are still liable to be listed on the List of Defaulting Solicitors and Other Authorised Persons. However, this is discretionary and full payment (in all open applications) will be sufficient grounds to prevent the solicitors firm going on the list.

List of defaulting solicitors

35. Upon the expiry of 14 days of the Letter D being sent and no payment, or reason why there has been non-payment, being received from the solicitor firm, the information relating to the application will be sent to a member of the Bar Council's Fees Collection Panel for approval to include the solicitor's firm in the next iteration of the List of Defaulting Solicitors.

36. Upon approval the solicitors firm will be assigned to go on the next version of the list. If a listing is not recommended, an email will be sent to the applicant detailing the reason why the listing will not occur on this occasion and if any remedial action can be taken to secure a listing in the future.

37. The list of defaulting solicitors will be published on the Bar Council website by 1700 on the first Monday of every month, unless there are no additions or removals on the list. If the Bar Council Offices are closed, it will be published by 1700 on the closest working day to the Monday at the beginning of the relevant month. A hyperlink to the list will also be emailed to all Heads of Chambers within 48 hours of the list being uploaded on the Bar Council website.

Removing solicitors from the list of defaulting solicitors list

38. Any solicitor firm that is on the list may apply after six months to be removed from the list. In practice, such a removal will only occur if all unpaid cases against that solicitor firm have been paid. Any decision to remove an entry on the list requires the positive approval of a member of the Fees Collection Panel.

Payment is received

39. At any stage, the applicant can receive full payment and therefore the application for the solicitor firm to be placed on the list is taken no further with regard to that application. It is the responsibility of applicants to inform

the Bar Council of any payments, part payment or further correspondence relating to an application and this should be done by emailing fees@barcouncil.org.uk

Fee written off

40. At any stage the Barrister can write the debt off. If this happens please inform the Bar Council as soon as possible.

Making an application

Applications to be received by email

41. All applications are to be received by the Bar Council electronically and must be sent either from the barrister's professional email address or, if submitted by a fees clerk, the barrister's professional email address must be copied to the email. Receipt of this email indicates explicit approval for the Bar Council to progress the application and to place a solicitors firm on the list. An email should be sent to fees@barcouncil.org.uk

42. Any application received by post (using the old application forms) after 31 July 2014 will be returned. Any application received by post before this date will be converted to an electronic format and the hard copy will be destroyed confidentially and securely.

43. Any supplementary documentation from barristers or clerks must be received by email after 31 July 2014. Until that time the Bar Council will convert hard copies to electronic PDF format and then destroy confidentially and securely all hard copy documentation. Electronic correspondence from solicitors will be encouraged but will not be mandatory.

Choosing the correct application form

44. The application form is a PDF form that can be completed by the applicant electronically and sent to the Bar Council by email. There are three forms which relate to different areas of work:

    a. Application relating to a private funding agreement.

    b. Application relating to a Conditional Fee Agreement.

    c. Application relating to publicly funded cases (not including criminal legal aid).

45. Copies of the forms are available on the Bar Council website.[4]

Supporting information

46. Documentation is required to support your application. This section provides further information regarding what documentation should be provided relating to the different type of case to which the application relates.

47. All applications require copies of Letter A, Letter B, all fee notes and all other correspondence with the solicitors firm relating to payment. These should be added as attachments to your application.

48. If the application relates to a fee note submitted over two years then please provide in the body of the email an explanation of why the application should be accepted.

49. If the barrister offered their services on Contractual Terms please attach a copy of the agreement to the application of the contractual terms.

50. If the application relates to a Conditional Fee Agreement then the Conditional Fee Agreement should also be attached.

51. If the application relates to a publicly funded matter then the Legal Aid Certificate should be attached. If you do not have a copy of this document please provide us with the certificate number and date of issue.

52. The following table details the supporting documentation required:

	Private funding agreement	**Conditional fee agreement**	**Publically funded agreement**
Application form	✓	✓	✓
Letter A	✓	v	✓
Letter B	✓	✓	✓
All relevant correspondence relating to payment	✓	✓	✓
All Fee Notes	✓	✓	✓
If Contractual Terms were used, a copy of the agreement	✓	✓	
Conditional fee agreement		✓	

The application forms

53. All applications must, after the 31 July 2014 be made by email and using the forms provided on the Bar Council's website. You can make an application through the new process from 2 June 2014. Each electronic form has the following sections that need to be completed:

   a. Counsel details.

   b. Clerks details.

   c. Chamber's details.

   d. Solicitor's details.

   e. Case details.

   f. Correspondence.

54. This section of the guidance details what information is needed in each field of the forms.

Counsel details

55. The following information is required in this section:

a. Name – Please provide the full name of Counsel (including the suffix QC if appropriate) to which this application relates. If different Counsel are involved in the same case a separate application form is needed for each application (but should be sent in the same email).

b. Email – Please provide the professional email address of Counsel (i.e. this should be the chambers address rather than a personal address. In the case of sole practitioners we will accept personal email addresses).

Chamber's details

56. The following information is required in this section:

a. Name – Please provide the full name of the Chambers, or in the case of a sole practitioner please write "Sole Practitioner".

b. Postal address – The full postal address of the Chambers (or Annex) of the barrister, or in the case of a sole practitioner the address as registered with the Bar Council for the purposes of the practising certificate.

c. Telephone Number – Please provide the direct dial telephone number of the person who will be managing the application.

d. DX Number – If you have one please provide the DX number.

Solicitor's details

57. The following information is required in this section:

a. Name – Please provide the full name of the solicitor who instructed the work.

b. Email – If correspondence with the solicitor was undertaken (in part) by email please provide the email address. If all correspondence was carried out by post please leave this blank.

c. Postal address – Please provide the full postal address of the solicitor's firm (including the firm's name) of the barrister, or in the case of a sole practitioner the address as registered with the Bar Council for the purposes of the practising certificate.

Case details

58. The following information is required in this section:

For privately funded cases and Conditional Fee Agreement cases only:

a. Name – Please provide the name of the case to which this application relates.

b. Fees due (incl. VAT) – Please provide the amount of fees due to Counsel under this case including VAT. If more than one Counsel was involved in the case please provide the amount due to the Counsel named in the first section and not the total fees due for the case.

c. Is interest due? – Please indicate if Letter A or Letter B included the paragraph on interest.

For private funding agreements only

d. Were any contractual terms agreed? – Please indicate if there were any contractual terms agreed and if so, on what date.

For Conditional Fee Agreements only

e. Date of agreement – Please provide the date the Conditional Fee Agreement was signed by both parties.

f. Was the case completed – Please indicate whether the case has been completed.

g. Are fees payable on the outcome of the case? – Please indicate either yes or no.

For publicly funded cases only

h. Assisted person's name – Please provide the full name of the person being assisted by legal aid in this case.

i. Certificate number – Please provide the Legal Aid Certificate number.

j. Date of issue – Please provide the date the Legal Aid Certificate was issued.

k. Date of event which gave rise to the right to taxation – this is usually the date the certificate is discharged or revoked.

l. Total of fees claimed (incl. VA 1) – Please provide the amount of fees due to Counsel under this case including VAT. If more than one Counsel was involved in the case please provide the amount due to the Counsel named in the first section and not the total fees due for the case.

m. Payment on Account received (Incl. VAT) – Please provide the total value of any payment(s) received through Payment of Account.

Correspondence

59. The following information is required in this section:

a. Date Letter A was sent – Please provide the date Letter A was sent.

b Date Letter B was sent – Please provide the date Letter B was sent.

c. Date Senior Partner was contacted – Please provide the date the Senior Partner was contracted.

d. Were the fees challenged? – Please indicate if the fees have been challenged at any time by the solicitor.

e. If so, were they challenged in time? – If the fees were challenged within three months of the submission of the first fee note they were challenged in time so please indicate yes otherwise indicate no (or if not relevant leave blank).

Common errors

60. There are a number of common errors where we need to return to the applicant for further information to rectify an error. It is in the interests of everybody to ensure that applications are received in the correct form and valid first time. The following paragraphs detail some of the common errors.

Solicitor who instructed the work moved firms due to the firm ceasing practice or has moved firm

61. If the solicitor who instructed the work moved practice and letter A or B was sent after the cessation of the practice then any letter sent after the date is invalid. The remedy is to res end Letter B, or Letter A and B (if both letters are needed a 14 day interval should bridge the sending of both letters), to the solicitor who instructed the barrister at the firm's new address and be addressed as follows:

    [Solicitor Name],

    previously [Firms address when instructed], c/o [Name of the new firm],

    [Postal Address]

62. Letter B should not be addressed to the Senior Partner as the Senior Partner of the new firm is not liable for the fees.

Solicitor firm changed names

63. If the solicitor firm has changed names then Letter A and B needs to be changed to reflect this. In this circumstance the Bar Council advises that Letter A and Letter B are sent at least 14 days apart, a further 14 days should elapse after the sending of Letter B before an application is made.

Solicitor firm has changed address

64. If the solicitor firm has changed address then Letter A and B needs to be changed to reflect this. In this circumstance the Bar Council advises that Letter A and Letter B are sent at least 14 days apart, a further 14 days should elapse after the sending of Letter B before an application is made to the Bar Council.

Letter A or B not sent at the correct time

65. As a minimum, Letter A must be sent one month after the fee note was submitted and Letter B must follow after three months of the first fee note. One common error is that when the barrister sends a copy of the letter to the Bar Council, the chambers software automatically updates the date of the letter to today's date. Please ensure that true copies or reprints of the letters actually sent are attached to the email. The Bar Council has to accept Letters A and B at face value and we cannot process the application if either letter appears not to have been sent at the correct time interval.

Checklist

66. The following checklist can be used to ensure that the application process can proceed smoothly:

Prior to submitting your application:

- Ensure that the fees remain unpaid.
- Ensure that the case does not relate to criminal legal aid.
- Ensure that Letter A was sent one month after the fee note was submitted and contains the correct wording.
- Ensure that Letter B was sent three months after the fee note was submitted and contains the correct wording.
- Ensure that Letter B is addressed to the Senior Partner.

When completing your application:

- Ensure that you are completing the correct form for the type of case (i.e. privately funded case, Conditional Fee Agreement or publicly funded case).
- Ensure that Letter A is not dated automatically and is a true representation of the date the letter was actually sent.
- Ensure that Letter B is not dated automatically and is a true representation of the date the letter was actually sent.

When submitting your application:

- Ensure that the application form is attached to the email. If the application relates to more than one barrister please provide a separate application for each.
- Ensure that the fee note is not older than two years from the date of application. If it is and the reason is exceptional please provide a brief reason for this in the email.
- Ensure that Letter A is attached to the email Ensure that Letter B is attached to the email Ensure that all fee notes are attached to the email.
- Ensure that all correspondence to the Solicitor relating to the payment of fees are attached to the email.
- Ensure that the email is addressed to fees@barcouncil.org.uk.

A copy of this checklist is provided at Annex E so that it can be printed and used when submitting each application.

Following up an application

67. Applicants will be sent an email detailing when the application has been received and a follow-up email when the application has been validated. If an applicant would like to follow up the progress of any application please email fees@barcouncil.org.uk (if you know the Bar Council reference number please provide the reference in your emai1.)

Making a complaint

68. We endeavour to provide a good professional service. We recognise that there will be times that we fall short of the high standards you rightly expect from us. To make a complaint please complete the following online form (https://adobeformscentra1.com/?f=Lii2bgVYYFhXnKf2UeseOw). We seek to provide a substantive response within two working days.

Further information

69. Email is the preferred method of communication but we understand that applicants, or prospective applicants, might also wish to contact us by telephone. Below are the emails and numbers you should use:

If the matter relates to a prospective or a current application please email fees@barcouncil.org.uk or telephone 020 76111318.

If the matter relates to how the scheme operates in terms of general policy please contact, Christine Power, Fees Collection Supervisor, at cpower@barcouncil.org.uk or telephone 020 7611 1375, or Adrian Vincent, Head of Remuneration and Policy, at avincent@barcouncil.org.uk or telephone 020 76111312.

If you would like more information on the Joint Tribunal Scheme please contact Wendy Dawson, Fees Collection Administrator, at wdowson@barcouncil.org.uk or telephone 020 7611 1376.

Annex A–Annex GI

This annex will be deleted from 31 January 2013 and will be replaced by annex T.

The Terms of work on which Barristers Offer their Services to Solicitors and the Withdrawal of Credit Scheme 1988

(As authorised by the General Council of the Bar on 16 July 1988 and amended by authority of the General Council of the Bar on 10 November 1990, 17 July 1999, and 24 March 2001 and 21 November 2001.)

Whereas:

1. these Terms have been authorised by the General Council of the Bar and are intended to apply (save as hereinafter provided) in any case where a barrister is instructed by a solicitor;
2. any solicitor who sends a brief or instructions to a barrister will be deemed to instruct that barrister on these Terms unless and to the extent that the barrister and the solicitor have agreed in writing in relation to the particular matter or generally (a) that the Contractual Terms on which Barristers Offer their Services to Solicitors 2000 shall apply, or (b) to exclude or vary these Terms;

and whereas:

3. by the established custom of the profession a barrister looks for payment of his fees to the solicitor who instructs him and not to his lay client;
4. except in publicly funded cases a solicitor is personally liable as a matter of professional conduct for the payment of a barrister's proper fees whether or not he has been placed in funds by his lay client;
5. where instructions have been given in the name of a firm all partners at that date incur personal liability and remain liable for the payment of counsel's fees incurred on behalf of the firm by a deceased bankrupt or otherwise defaulting former partner of the firm; and

6. the liability of a sole practitioner and of partners for the liabilities of their co-partners is a continuing one and is not cancelled or superseded by any transfer of the practice or dissolution of the partnership;

General

1. A solicitor may in his capacity as a director partner member employee consultant associate or other agent of a company firm or other body brief or instruct a barrister.

2. In any case where a barrister accepts a brief or instructions from a solicitor in his capacity as a director partner member employee consultant associate or agent of a company firm or other body:

   (1) the solicitor warrants that he is authorised by his company firm or other body to instruct the barrister;

   (2) the obligations of the solicitor under these Terms (including in particular his responsibility for the payment of the barrister's fees) shall be the joint and several obligations of him and that company firm or other body.

Instructions

3. A barrister has the duty or the right in certain circumstances set out in the Bar Code of Conduct to refuse to accept a brief or instructions and these Terms will apply only where the barrister has accepted the brief or instructions.

4. Notwithstanding that a brief or instructions have been delivered to a barrister the barrister shall not be deemed to have accepted that brief or those instructions until he has had a reasonable opportunity:

   (1) to peruse them;

   (2) in the case of a brief to agree a fee with the solicitor.

5. A barrister accepts a brief or instructions upon the understanding:

   (1) that he must and will comply with the Bar Code of Conduct;

   (2) that he will deal with instructions as soon as he reasonably can in the ordinary course of his work;

   (3) that he may return the brief or instructions in accordance with the Bar Code of Conduct, and that, if he does so, he will incur no liability to the solicitor under these terms as a result of so doing.

6.

   (1) Where for any reason time is of the essence the solicitor must at the time when he delivers the brief or instructions but separately from the brief or instructions themselves inform the barrister of that fact and of the particular reason for urgency in order that the barrister may decide whether in those circumstances he can accept the brief or instructions. In addition the brief or instructions must be clearly marked "Urgent".

(2) In the case of publicly funded work, the solicitor must at the time when he delivers the brief or instructions (or if any relevant certificate is not then available to him as soon as reasonably practicable thereafter) supply the barrister with copies of any relevant public funding certificates.

Copies of Briefs and Instructions and Records of Advice

7. A barrister shall be entitled for the purposes of his records (but not otherwise) to retain his brief or instructions or any papers delivered therewith or (if the solicitor requires the return of such brief or instructions and papers) to take and retain a copy of such brief or instructions and papers and of any written advice PROVIDED that nothing shall entitle a barrister to exercise any lien over any brief instructions or papers.

Fees

8. Save in the case of publicly funded work or in the case of a Notified Solicitor a barrister and solicitor may (subject to any rules regarding contingent fees) make such agreement or arrangement between them as to the time or times whether at the time of delivery of the brief or instructions or subsequently thereto or otherwise at which the barrister's fees shall be paid as they may think fit and the barrister's fees shall be paid by the solicitor accordingly PROVIDED that every such agreement or arrangement shall be in writing.

9. Save in the case of publicly funded work or in the case of work the fees for which are to be paid out of a fund but cannot be so paid without an order of the court a barrister may and in the case of fees payable by a Notified Solicitor a barrister (unless and except as otherwise previously authorised in writing by the Chairman) must require his fees to be agreed and paid before he accepts the brief or instructions to which the fees relate.

10.

(1) Fees and/or charging rates shall be (i) as agreed between the barrister and the solicitor before the barrister commences work under the brief or instructions; or, in default of such agreement, (ii) a reasonable professional rate for the barrister instructed

(2) The barrister shall submit an itemised fee note not later than three months after the work to which the fee note relates has been done or at the conclusion of the matter in which the barrister is briefed or instructed whichever is the sooner.

(3) The barrister shall as soon as reasonably practicable comply with a request by the solicitor for a fee note.

(4) Every fee note shall include the solicitor's reference and (where appropriate) the barrister's case reference number, the barrister's relevant account number for the purpose of receiving payment in publicly funded cases and (if known to the barrister) any relevant public funding certificate number and date of issue.

(5) If any fees remain outstanding at the conclusion of a case the solicitor shall as soon as reasonably practicable inform the barrister that the case has concluded.

11. In the case of publicly funded work:

(1) The solicitor and barrister shall respectively take such steps as may be open to each of them to take under the applicable Regulations for the time being in force for the purpose of obtaining payment of the barrister's fees as soon as reasonably practicable.

(2) The solicitor shall as soon as reasonably practicable comply with a request by the barrister for information by (i) notifying the barrister of the date of issue and number and supplying the barrister with copies of any relevant public funding certificates (ii) notifying the barrister of the date of any order for assessment of costs under the relevant certificate or other event giving rise to a right to such assessment (iii) informing the barrister of the steps taken by him pursuant to paragraph 11(1) hereof.

(3) The barrister unless such information and an explanation for non-payment satisfactory to him is thereupon received from the solicitor shall then report the facts to the Chairman.

12. In the case of work the fees for which are to be paid out of a fund but cannot be so paid without an order of the court:

(1) The solicitor shall use his best endeavours to obtain such order or orders as may be requisite to enable payment of the fees to be made as soon as reasonably practicable.

(2) The solicitor shall as soon as reasonably practicable comply with a request by the barrister for information by informing the barrister of the steps taken by him pursuant to paragraph 12(1) hereof.

(3) The barrister unless such information and an explanation for non-payment satisfactory to him is thereupon received from the solicitor shall then report the facts to the Chairman;

(4) Subject to paragraph 12(5) below, the barrister's fees shall be payable one month after the making of the order of the court required for the payment of such fees out of the fund.

(5) In the event of any breach by the solicitor of his obligations under paragraph 12(1) and/or 12(2) above, the fees will be payable forthwith and the amount outstanding from time to time will carry simple interest at the stipulated rate from one month after the date of the letter referred to in paragraph 15(1) hereof until payment.

13.

(1) Subject to any such agreement or arrangement as is referred to in paragraph 8 hereof the barrister's fees if and to the extent that such fees have not been previously paid shall unless challenged by the solicitor as hereinafter provided be paid by the solicitor within one month after the fee note relating thereto has been sent to the solicitor whether or not the solicitor has been placed in funds by his client and whether or not the case is still continuing.

(2) In the event that the barrister's fees are not paid in full in accordance with sub-paragraph (1) above, the fees outstanding from time to time will carry simple interest at the stipulated rate from one month after

the date of the letter referred to in paragraph 15(1) hereof until payment if that letter includes a statement to that effect.

14.

(1) Any challenge by a solicitor to a barrister's fee (whether giving rise to an issue of competence or a dispute on quantum or otherwise) must be made by the solicitor in writing within three months after the first fee note relating to that fee has been sent to him or within one month after such letter relating to that fee as is referred to in paragraph 15(1) hereof has been sent to him whichever is the later.

(2) No challenge to a barrister's fees will be accepted either by the barrister or in the case of a complaint by the barrister to the Bar Council of failure to pay those fees by the Bar Council unless:

(a) the challenge was made in accordance with paragraph 14(1) hereof; and

(b) the solicitor has within 14 days of being requested to do so either by the barrister or by the Bar Council agreed in writing (i) to submit the issue or dispute giving rise to the challenge to the decision of a Tribunal and (ii) to abide by and forthwith give effect to the decision of the Tribunal.

(3) If a dispute is referred to a Tribunal in accordance with paragraph 14(2) above:

(i) The Tribunal shall act as experts and not as arbitrators and its decision shall be conclusive, final and binding for all purposes upon the solicitor and the barrister.

(ii) No payment need be made in respect of the fees (unless the Tribunal orders an interim payment) until the Tribunal has made its decision and communicated it to the parties.

(iii) If the Tribunal determines that any sum is payable in respect of the fees, paragraph 13(2) above shall apply to that sum as if it had become payable when it would have become payable if no challenge had been made, and the Tribunal shall also determine the amount payable in respect of interest thereon under that paragraph.

(4) Unless the solicitor has challenged the barrister's fees and agreed to submit the issue or dispute in accordance with paragraphs 14(1) and (2), the fees will be payable in full, without any set-off whatsoever, in the amount set out in the relevant fee note and at the time specified in paragraph 13(1) above.

15. Save as aforesaid and subject to any such agreement or arrangement as is referred to in paragraph 8 hereof the barrister if and to the extent that his fees have not been previously paid:

(1) may at any time after the expiration of one month after the first fee note relating thereto has been sent send a reminder substantially in the form of the letter annexed hereto and marked "A" or some reasonable adaptation thereof;

(2) unless an explanation for non-payment satisfactory to the barrister has been received shall at the expiration of three months after the first fee

note relating thereto has been sent send a further reminder substantially in the form of the letter annexed hereto and marked "B" or some reasonable adaptation thereof; and

(3) unless an explanation for non-payment satisfactory to the barrister is thereupon received shall then report the facts to the Chairman.

Withdrawal of Credit

16. In any case where a barrister has made a report to the Chairman in accordance with paragraphs 11(3) 12(3) or 15(3) hereof or under the equivalent terms of any contract and in any other case in which he is satisfied that it is appropriate to do so, the Chairman may write a letter in the form of one of the letters annexed hereto and marked "C" or some reasonable adaptation thereof.

17.

(1) This paragraph applies where the following conditions are satisfied namely where:

(a) such a letter as is referred to in paragraph 16 hereof has been sent and no explanation for non-payment satisfactory to the Chairman has been received; and

(b) either (i) any fees referred to in such letter which are in the opinion of the Chairman properly payable remain unpaid or (ii) in the event that all such fees have been paid not more than twelve months have elapsed since payment; and

(c) circumstances have arisen in which the Chairman would otherwise have occasion to send to any person liable for the fees or to any connected person a further letter such as is referred to in paragraph 16 hereof.

(2) In any case in which paragraph 17(1) hereof applies the Chairman shall write to such person or persons (as the case may be) to the effect that unless written representations received by him within 14 days after the date of such letter or within such extended period as he may allow justify an exceptional departure from the following course he will and unless persuaded by such representations not to do so the Chairman whether or not any fees remain unpaid shall:

(a) issue a direction that no barrister may without the written consent of the Chairman (which consent may be sought urgently in exceptional cases) knowingly accept instructions from any person or firm named in such direction or from any person who or firm which is or has at any time since the direction was issued been a connected person unless his fees are to be paid directly by the Legal Services Commission or such instructions are accompanied by payment of an agreed fee for such work or unless he agrees in advance to accept no fee for such work; and

(b) cause the names of the persons or firms named in such direction to be included in a list of persons and firms named in such directions to be circulated by pre-paid firstclass post to all such persons and firms to all the Clerks and Heads of

Chambers in England and Wales to the Master of the Rolls and to the President of the Law Society notifying them of such direction.

18. Notwithstanding anything to the contrary herein if in any case the Chairman is satisfied that it is appropriate to issue a direction such as is referred to in paragraph 17(2)(a) hereof in respect of any person or firm named in such direction and to circulate a list such as is referred to in paragraph 17(2)(b) hereof including the names of the persons or firms named in such direction he may after giving such persons and firms due notice of why he considers it appropriate to take such course and after considering any written representations and after consultation with the Law Society issue a direction in respect of and cause the list to include the names of such persons and firms as may be appropriate.

18.A Upon issuing a direction pursuant to either paragraph 17(2)(a) or paragraph 18 hereof, the Chairman shall report the facts to the OSSand shall request the OSS to commence proceedings before the Solicitors' Disciplinary Tribunal against the persons, the firms, or the partners in the firms named in such direction.

19. The list referred to in paragraphs 17 and 18 hereof shall be circulated monthly unless there have been in the meantime no additions to or deletions from the list.

20. Any Notified Solicitor and any barrister may at any time after the expiration of six months after the name of any person or firm was first included in such a list seek the revocation of any relevant direction and the amendment of the list and the Chairman after considering any written representations and after consultation with the Law Society shall be empowered (but shall not be obliged) to accede to such application upon such terms as he considers appropriate.

Definitions and consequential provisions

21. For the purpose hereof:

(1) "Bar Code of Conduct" shall mean the Code of Conduct of the Bar of England and Wales for the time being in force;

(2) "brief" "instructions" and "lay client" shall have the meanings assigned to them respectively in the Bar Code of Conduct;

(3) "solicitor" shall where the context admits include any solicitor liable for the fees;

(4) "person liable for the fees" shall mean any solicitor liable for the fees and any person company firm or other body responsible by virtue of paragraph 2(2) hereof for the payment of the fees;

(5) Section 5(2), (3) and (4) of the Arbitration Act 1996 apply to the interpretation of all references in these Terms to parties having agreed, or made an agreement, in writing;

(6) "connected person" shall mean any person who from time to time is either

(a) a partner employee consultant or associate of any firm of which any person liable for the fees or any Notified Solicitor is a partner employee consultant or **associate;**

(b) the employer of any person liable for the fees or of any Notified Solicitor;

(c) an employee of any person liable for the fees or of any Notified Solicitor;

(d) a firm of which any person liable for the fees or any Notified Solicitor is a partner employee consultant or associate;

(7) "Notified Solicitor" shall mean any person or firm whose name is for the time being included in the list referred to in paragraphs 17 and 18 hereof and any person who or firm which is or has at any time since the direction was issued been a connected **person;**

(8) "Tribunal" shall mean a Tribunal consisting of a barrister nominated by the Chairman and a solicitor nominated by the President of the Law Society;

(9) "the Chairman" shall mean the Chairman of the Bar Council and shall include any person including in particular the Vice-Chairman of the Bar and the Chairman of the Remuneration and Terms of Work Committee and the Chairman of the Fees Collection Committee to whom the Chairman may have delegated either the whole or any part of his responsibilities hereunder;

(10) "the OSS" shall mean the Office for the Supervision of Solicitors;

(11) "Publicly funded work" shall mean cases funded and paid directly to the barrister by the Legal Services Commission, as part of the Community Legal Service or the Criminal Defence Service;

(12) Where the context admits, references to fees include any interest accrued in respect of them under paragraph 13(2) hereof;

(13) The "stipulated rate" shall mean 2% above the Bank of England base rate from time to time;

(14) Any letter written by the Chairman to any person pursuant to or which would otherwise have been effective for the purposes of either the Withdrawal of Credit Scheme which came into effect on 2 March 1987 or the Withdrawal of Credit Scheme 1988 as originally enacted or in force from time to time shall in relation to such person be deemed to be such a letter as is referred to in paragraph 16 hereof.

22.

(1) Subject to sub-paragraph (2) below, any fee note and any such letter as is referred to in paragraphs 15(1) 15(2) 16 17(2) or 18 hereof may be sent and shall be treated as having been properly and sufficiently sent to each and every person liable for the fees and to each and every connected person (as the case may be) if posted by pre-paid first-class post or sent through any Document Exchange or by facsimile transmission addressed to:

(a) any person liable for the fees; or

(b) if any person liable for the fees is either a partner of or consultant to or associate of or employed by another or others to the person liable for the fees or to his employer or to his senior partner (as the case may be); or

(c) if any such person practises (whether on his own or in partnership with others or otherwise) under a name other than his own, to the firm under whose name he **practises;** and addressed to any place at which such person or his employer or any partner of his **carries on practice.**

(2) Where a firm or a sole proprietor is liable for the fees, if any letter under paragraphs 15(2), 16, 17(2) or 18 hereof is addressed to some person other than the senior partner of the firm or the sole proprietor, a copy must also be sent to the senior partner or sole proprietor at the same time.

23. Any such letter as is referred to in paragraphs 17(2) or 18 hereof shall:

(1) identify any relevant earlier matters of complaint;

(2) state the Chairman's proposed course of action; and

(3) enclose a copy of this document provided that any accidental omission or failure to enclose such a copy may be remedied by the sending of a separate copy as soon as the Chairman is made aware of such omission or failure.

24. Any such direction as is referred to in paragraphs 17 or 18 hereof may contain or be amended so as to add or include any or all of the names and addresses:

(1) of any person liable for the fees;

(2) of any connected person; and

(3) if any such person practises (whether on his own or in partnership with others or otherwise) under a name other than his own, of the firm under whose name he practises.

Status of these Terms

25. Neither the General Council of the Bar in authorising these Terms nor a barrister in offering his services to a solicitor on these Terms has any intention to create legal relations or to enter into any contract or other obligation binding in law.

26. Neither the sending by a solicitor of a brief or instructions to a barrister nor the acceptance by a barrister of a brief or instructions nor anything done in connection therewith nor the arrangements relating thereto (whether mentioned in these Terms or in the Bar Code of Conduct or to be implied) nor these Terms or any agreement or transaction entered into or payment made by or under them shall be attended by or give rise to any contractual relationship rights duties or consequences whatsoever or be legally enforceable by or against or be the subject of litigation with either the barrister or the General Council of the Bar.

Exclusion or variation

27. A solicitor who sends a brief or instructions to a barrister will be deemed to instruct that barrister on these Terms unless and to the extent that the barrister and the solicitor have agreed in writing in relation to the particular matter or generally (a) that the Contractual Terms on which Barristers Offer their Services to Solicitors 2000 shall apply, or (b) to exclude or vary these Terms.

Transitional

28. Unless otherwise agreed in writing:

    (1) Any amendment to these Terms has effect only with regard to briefs and instructions accepted on or after the date the amendment is expressed to take effect; and

    (2) As regards briefs and instructions accepted before that date, these Terms continue to have effect in the form in which they stood before the amendment.

LETTER "A"

(To be sent 1 month after fee note)

Privately funded cases

Dear Sir,

Re:

I refer to the fee note of [name of barrister] in respect of the above case which was sent to you on [date].

My records indicate that this is a privately funded case in which your relationship with [Name of Barrister] is governed by the Terms of Work on which Barristers offer their Services to Solicitors and the Withdrawal of Credit Scheme 1988 (as amended; "the Terms"). Under paragraph 13(1) of the Terms, the fees were due and payable within 1 month of the fee note.

I would be grateful if you could make arrangements for these fees to be paid or let me know when payment may be expected.

[Please note that under paragraph 13(2) of the Terms, any such fees remaining outstanding one month after the date of this letter will carry interest at 2% above the Bank of England base rate from time to time from one month after the date of this letter until payment.]*

Yours faithfully,

Clerk to [name of barrister]

*Words substantially in the form of those shown in square brackets must be included if (but only if) it is wished to charge interest on the fees which are the subject of this letter A.

Publicly funded cases

Dear Sir,

[Relevant Public Funding Certificate Number] [Date of issue]

Re:

I refer to the fee note of [name of barrister] in respect of the above case which was sent to you on [date].

My records indicate that this is a publicly funded case and I would be grateful if you could let me know when payment may be expected.

Yours faithfully,

Clerk to [name of barrister]

LETTER "B"

(To be sent 3 months after fee note)

Privately funded cases

Dear Sir,

Re:

I have referred to [name of barrister] the letter I wrote to you concerning the fees in this matter. To date payment has not been made and no explanation for the non-payment has been forthcoming.

As you know Counsel is required as a matter of professional conduct to report to the Chairman of the General Council of the Bar the fact that these fees have been outstanding for more than three months without satisfactory explanation. Unless, therefore, I hear from you within the next 14 days I regret that Counsel will have no alternative other than to make such a report.

I sincerely trust that this will not be necessary and look forward to hearing from you in early **course.**

Yours faithfully,

Clerk to [name of barrister]

Publicly funded cases

Dear Sir,

[Relevant Public Funding Certificate Number] [Date of issue]

Re:

I have referred to [name of barrister] the letter I wrote to you concerning the fees in this matter. To date payment has not been received.

My records indicate that this is a publicly funded case. I must therefore ask you to notify me of:

(a) the date of issue and number of the relevant public funding certificate(s); (b) the date of any order for assessment of costs under the relevant certificate or other event giving rise to a right to such assessment; and (c) the steps you have taken under the relevant Regulations for the purpose of obtaining payment of [name of barrister]'s fees.

Would you also supply me with copies of the relevant Public Funding Certificate(s).

As you know Counsel is required as a matter of professional conduct to report the matter to the Chairman of the General Council of the Bar unless he receives in response to this letter the information requested above and a satisfactory explanation for the fact that he has not yet been paid. Unless, therefore, I hear from you within the next 14 days I regret that Counsel will have no alternative other than to make such a report.

I sincerely trust that this will not be necessary and look forward to hearing from you in early **course.**

Yours faithfully,

Clerk to [name of barrister]

LETTER "C"

First Chairman's Letter: Private

Private and Confidential Recorded Delivery

The Senior Partner

Dear Sir,

I refer to Counsel's fees particulars of which are set out in the Schedule to this letter. Copies of the relevant fee notes are attached. Letters have been written regarding payment of these fees. Payment has not been received. As a result the matter has been referred to the General Council of the Bar in accordance with Counsel's professional obligations.

I would remind you of your professional obligation to pay Counsel's fees in non publicly funded matters irrespective of whether you have been placed in funds by your client.

Unless you challenged Counsel's fees in writing within 3 months after the first fee note was sent to you, or you are able to provide a satisfactory explanation for non-payment, I would ask you to pay Counsel within 14 days of the date of this letter. In addition, please provide an explanation for the delay in payment, again within 14 days of the date of this letter.

I am also enclosing for your attention a copy of the Terms of Work on which Barristers offer their services to Solicitors and the Withdrawal of Credit Scheme 1988 (as amended). You will appreciate from reading the text of the Scheme that its effect is such that, unless there is a satisfactory explanation for non-payment or you challenged the fees in time, and the Chairman has occasion to write again in respect of other outstanding fees within the period referred to in paragraph 17(1)(b) of the Scheme, then the consequences spelt out in paragraph 17(2) of the Scheme will, save in the most exceptional circumstances, follow. In other words, credit will be withdrawn. Furthermore, the Chairman will report the facts to the Office for the Supervision of Solicitors with a request that it should commence proceedings against you before the Solicitors Disciplinary Tribunal.

If, therefore, you consider that a satisfactory explanation for non-payment exists, it is in your interests to provide it now.

I hope that it will not prove necessary to implement the Scheme in your case and that Counsel's fees will be paid promptly when due. I am, however, concerned that you should be fully informed in advance of the problems which would arise should you fail to pay Counsel's fees on time.

Yours faithfully,

[Name]

CHAIRMAN OF THE BAR encls:

THE SCHEDULE

Name and address of Counsel Fees in the matter of

[Here list name(s) and address(es) of Counsel and name(s) of case(s)]

LETTER "C"

First Chairman's Letter: Publicly funded

Private and Confidential Recorded Delivery

The Senior Partner

Dear Sir,

I refer to Counsel's fees, particulars of which are set out in the Schedule to this letter. Copies of the relevant fee notes are attached. Letters have been written regarding payment of these fees. Payment has not been received. As a result, the matter has been referred to the General Council of the Bar in accordance with Counsel's professional obligations.

Since this complaint relates to a publicly funded matter, I would be grateful if you would supply the following information within 14 days of the date of this letter:

(a) notify me of the date of issue and number and supply me with copies of any relevant publicly funded certificates; (b) notify me of the date of any order for assessment of costs under the relevant certificate or other event giving rise to a right to such assessment; and (c) inform me of what steps you have taken under the relevant Regulations for the purpose of obtaining payment of Counsel's fees.

I am also enclosing for your attention a copy of the Terms of Work on which Barristers offer their services to Solicitors and the Withdrawal of Credit Scheme 1988 (as amended). You will appreciate from reading the text of the Scheme that its effect is such that if (1) no satisfactory explanation for non-payment of the fees referred to in the Schedule to this letter has been provided and (2) the Chairman has occasion to write again in respect of other outstanding fees within the period referred to in paragraph 17(1)(b) of the Scheme, then the consequences spelt out in paragraph 17(2) of the Scheme will, save in the most exceptional circumstances, follow. In other words, credit will be withdrawn. Furthermore, the Chairman will report the facts to the Office for the Supervision of Solicitors with a request that it should commence proceedings against you before the Solicitors Disciplinary Tribunal. If, therefore, you consider that a satisfactory explanation for non-payment exists, it is in your interests to provide it now.

I hope that it will not prove to be necessary to implement the Scheme in your case, and that Counsel's fees will be paid promptly when due. I am, however, concerned that you should be fully informed in advance of the problems which would arise should you fail to pay Counsel's fees on time."

Yours faithfully,

[Name]

CHAIRMAN of THE BAR encls:

THE SCHEDULE

Name and address of Counsel Fees in the matter of

[Here list name(s) and address(es) of Counsel and name(s) of case(s)]

LETTER "C"

First Chairman's Letter: Private and Publicly funded

Private and Confidential Recorded Delivery

The Senior Partner

Dear Sir,

I refer to Counsel's fees, particulars of which are set out in the Schedule to this letter. Copies of the relevant fee notes are attached. Letters have been written regarding payment of these fees. Payment has not been received. As a result, the matter has been referred to the General Council of the Bar in accordance with Counsel's professional obligations.

I would remind you of your professional obligation to pay Counsel's fees in privately funded matters irrespective of whether you have been placed in funds by your client.

Unless you challenged Counsel's fees in writing within 3 months after the first fee note was sent to you, or you are able to provide a satisfactory explanation for non-payment, I would ask you to pay Counsel within 14 days of the date of this letter. In addition, please provide an explanation for the delay in payment, again within 14 days of the date of this letter.

Insofar as this complaint relates to a publicly funded matter, I would be grateful if you would supply the following information within 14 days of the date of this letter:-

(a) notify me of the date of issue and number and supply me with copies of any relevant publicly funding certificates; (b) notify me of the date of any order for assessment of costs under the relevant certificate or other event giving rise to a right to such assessment; and (c) inform me of what steps you have taken under the relevant Regulations for the purpose of obtaining payment of Counsel's fees.

I am also enclosing for your attention a copy of the Terms of Work on which Barristers offer their services to Solicitors and the Withdrawal of Credit Scheme 1988 (as amended). You will appreciate from reading the text of the Scheme that its effect is such that, unless there is a satisfactory explanation for non-payment or you challenged the fees in time, and the Chairman has occasion to write again in respect of other outstanding fees within the period referred to in paragraph 17(1)(b) of the Scheme, then the consequences spelt out in paragraph 17(2) of the Scheme will, save in the most exceptional circumstances, follow. In other words, credit will be withdrawn. Furthermore, the Chairman will report the facts to the Office for the Supervision of Solicitors with a request that it should commence proceedings against you before the Solicitors Disciplinary Tribunal.

If, therefore, you consider that a satisfactory explanation for non-payment exists, it is in your interests to provide it now.

I hope that it will not prove to be necessary to implement the Scheme in your case, and that Counsel's fees will be paid promptly when due. I am, however, concerned that you should be fully informed in advance of the problems which would arise should you fail to pay Counsel's fees on time.

Yours faithfully,

[Name]

CHAIRMAN of THE BAR encls:

THE SCHEDULE

Name and address of Counsel Fees in the matter of

[Here list name(s) and address(es) of Counsel and name(s) of case(s)]

Annex B – Rules Relating to the List of Defaulting Solicitors and Other Authorised Persons

Rules Relating to the List of Defaulting Solicitors and Other Authorised Persons 2012

As approved by the General Council of the Bar on 20 October 2012 and amended by the General Council of the Bar on 2 March 2013.

1. These Rules are intended to be read alongside and to be supplemental to:

   (1) any rules or standing orders for the time being in force concerning the Joint Tribunal procedure for fee disputes;

   (2) instructions accepted under the Terms of Work 1988 where paragraph 2 of these Rules applies; and

   (3) The Scheme for Complaining to the Bar Council for Publicly Funded Matters

2. Where paragraph 15 of the Terms of Work 1988 applies in respect of instructions accepted before 31 January 2013, the reference in that paragraph to Letter "A" and Letter "B" shall be taken to be a reference to the documents marked Letter "A" and Letter "B" contained in Schedule C to these Rules but without prejudice to the validity of any such letters sent before 31 January 2013.

3. In the event that an Authorised Person fails to pay any fees due to a Barrister in respect of legal services determined by a judgment of a court or an arbitration award (which for this purpose includes an award of the Joint Tribunal) to be due and owing to a Barrister within 14 days of the said judgment or award, then the Barrister shall be entitled to report the matter to the Chairman of the General Council of the Bar pursuant to these Rules. For the avoidance of doubt this is without prejudice to the Barrister's rights to enforce the sums determined by the said judgment or award to be due and owing but remaining unpaid by action at law or otherwise.

4. Where a Barrister has made a report to the Chairman in accordance with:

   (1) paragraph 3 of these Rules; or

   (2) paragraph 15(3) of the Terms of Work 1988 as modified by paragraph 2 of these Rules above; or

   (3) the Scheme for Complaining to the Bar Council for Publicly Funded matters, then the Chairman may write to the Authorised Person a letter substantially in the form of Standard Letter 1 contained in Schedule A hereto.

5. Paragraph 6 of these Rules applies where Standard Letter 1 has been sent and either:

   (1) any fees referred to in Standard Letter 1 remain unpaid for more than 14 days after Standard Letter 1 was sent and, in the case of publicly funded matters, there has been no satisfactory explanation provided for the non-payment; or

(2) in the event that all such fees have been paid, not more than twelve months have elapsed since payment and circumstances have arisen in which the Chairman would otherwise have occasion to send to the Authorised Person or to any Connected Person a further Standard Letter 1.

6. Where this paragraph applies, the Chairman shall write a letter to the Authorised Person in substantially the form of Standard Letter 2 contained in Schedule B hereto to the effect that, whether or not any fees remain unpaid, he will:

(1) Include the name of the Authorised Person on the Bar Council's List of Defaulting Solicitors and Other Authorised Persons indicating that they are defaulters, who have in the past failed to pay barristers' fees in accordance with contractual terms on which the barrister was engaged or with the Terms of Work 1988, or that they have been subject to a successful complaint to the Bar Council under the Scheme for Complaining to the Bar Council.

(2) Circulate the Bar Council's List of Defaulting Solicitors and Other Authorised Persons including the name of the Authorised Person to all barristers suggesting that it would be unwise for any barrister to accept instructions from the Authorised Person or from Connected Persons unless they are paid directly by the Legal Services Commission or such Instructions are accompanied by payment of an agreed fee for the services or unless he agrees in advance to accept no fee for the services.

(3) Circulate the Bar Council's List of Defaulting Solicitors and Other Authorised Persons including the Authorised Person's name to the Master of the Rolls, the President of the Law Society and the Solicitors Regulation Authority.

7. If the Chairman is satisfied in any other case that it is appropriate to proceed as provided in paragraph 6 of these Rules, he may do so after giving the Authorised Person (and, if appropriate, any Connected Persons) due notice of why he considers it appropriate to take such course, and after considering any written representations from the Authorised Person, and after consultation with the Law Society.

8. Upon including the Notified Solicitor on the Bar Council's List of Defaulting Solicitors and Other Authorised Persons, the Chairman shall report the fact to the Solicitors' Regulation Authority and shall request the Solicitors' Regulation Authority to commence proceedings before the Solicitors' Disciplinary Tribunal (or any equivalent tribunal for any non-solicitor Authorised Person) against the Notified Authorised Person.

9. The Bar Council's List of Defaulting Solicitors and Other Authorised Persons shall be circulated at least 3 times each year to the persons mentioned in paragraphs 6(2) and (3) of these Rules.

10. Any Notified Authorised Person may at any time after the expiration of six months after his name was first included in the Bar Council's List of Defaulting Solicitors and Other Authorised Persons apply to the Chairman for the removal of their name from that list. The Chairman may, after considering any written representations and after consultation with the Law Society, remove the name of any Notified Authorised Person from the Bar

Council's List of Defaulting Solicitors and Other Authorised Persons unconditionally or upon such terms as he considers appropriate.

11. The Bar Council's List of Defaulting Solicitors and Other Authorised Persons may include, in addition to the name of the Notified Solicitor, the Instructing Solicitor, any other person liable for the fees shown in the Fee Note, and any Connected Person.

Transitional Arrangements:

12. On the date on which the Bar Council's List of Defaulting Solicitors and Other Authorised Persons comes into force, namely 31 January 2013 the names of all the Firms, Solicitors and other persons on the Withdrawal of Credit Scheme 1988 immediately before that date shall be immediately and automatically included on the Bar Council's List of Defaulting Solicitors and Other Authorised Persons. In such cases, paragraph 10 of these Rules will apply as if those Firms, Solicitors and other persons were first included on the Bar Council's List of Defaulting Solicitors and Other Authorised Persons on the date they were included on the Withdrawal of Credit Scheme 1988.

Definitions:

13. The following definitions shall apply to these rules in addition to the definitions contained in the 2012 Terms:

"Authorised Person": a person who is an authorised person for the purposes of s 18(1)(a) of the Legal Services Act 2007 and whose approved regulator under that Act is the Law Society and/or the SRA, and all successors and assignees: (a) of which the barrister's Instructing Solicitor is a director, partner, member, employee, consultant, associate or agent, and (b) on whose behalf, and in such capacity, the Instructing Solicitor instructs the barrister.

"Bar Council's List of Defaulting Solicitors and Other Authorised Persons": the list of Authorised Persons, Firms and persons referred to in these Rules. For the avoidance of doubt, this shall include Authorised Persons who are not solicitors.

"Chairman" shall mean the Chairman of the General Council of the Bar and shall include any person to whom the Chairman may have delegated either the whole or any part of his responsibilities under these Rules.

"Connected Person": shall mean any Authorised Person or Firm or person who from time to time is either a partner, director, associate, member, or employee of, a consultant to, or a person employing, a Notified Solicitor, save that it shall not include an employee of a Notified Solicitor who was not himself the Instructing Solicitor.

"Firm": a company, partnership, firm, limited liability partnership, association, public authority, professional body, sole practitioner or other person or body: (a) of which the barrister's Instructing Solicitor is a director, partner, member, employee, consultant, associate or agent, and (b) on whose behalf, and in such capacity, the Instructing Solicitor instructs the barrister.

"Instructing Solicitor": the person who is responsible for instructing the barrister in his capacity as director, partner, member, employee, consultant, associate or agent of the Authorised Person or Firm as the case may be. For the avoidance of doubt, the term

"Instructing Solicitor" may include any person, whether employed by an Authorised Person or Firm or not, and whether himself qualified as a solicitor or otherwise as an Authorised Person or not, but who instructs or purports to instruct a barrister either on behalf of a solicitor or any other authorised person for the purposes of s 18(1)(a) of the Legal Services Act 2007;

"Notified Authorised Person": any Authorised Person or Firm whose name is for the time being included in the Bar Council's List of Defaulting Solicitors and other Authorised Persons, or any Authorised Person or Firm or person who has, since the said inclusion thereof, been a Connected Person.

"Standard Letter 1": the pro-forma letter whose text is contained in Schedule A hereto.

"Standard Letter 2": the pro-forma letter whose text is contained in Schedule B hereto.

"Terms of Work 1988": the Terms of Work on which Barristers offer their services to Solicitors and the Withdrawal of Credit Scheme 1988 (formerly Annex Gl to the Code of Conduct).

Schedule A: Standard Letter 1

First Chairman's Letter – Privately Funded Cases

To be sent to the Senior Partner, General Manager or equivalent of the Authorised Person:

Dear Sir or Madam,

Bar Council's List of Defaulting Solicitors and other Authorised Persons: The Rules Relating to the List of Defaulting Solicitors and other Authorised Persons ("the Rules")

I refer to the barrister's fees particulars of which are set out in the schedule to this letter. You will be aware that your agreement with the barrister is governed by [the Standard Contractual Terms for the Supply of Legal Services by Barristers to Authorised Persons 2012 ("the 2012 Terms")] or [contractual terms to which the Rules apply] (the "Agreement"). Copies of the Agreement and of the Rules are attached to this letter.

OR

I refer to the barrister's fees particulars of which are set out in the schedule to this letter. You will be aware that these fees were referred, with your agreement, to a Joint Tribunal. Copies of the Joint Tribunal standing orders and the Rules are attached to this letter.

OR

I refer to the barrister's fees particulars of which are set out in the schedule to this letter. You will be aware that your agreement with the barrister is governed by the Terms of Work on which Barristers offer their services to Solicitors and the

Withdrawal of Credit Scheme 1988 ("the Terms of Work 1988"). The Rules also apply to this case. Copies of the Terms of Work 1988 and the Rules are attached to this letter.

Copies of the relevant invoices or fee notes are attached.

{On [insert date] [judgment was entered against you in the Court, case number . in the sum of £ in relation to those fees] or [the Joint Tribunal determined that the sum of £ was due and owing in relation to those fees]. To date [this sum] or [£ of this sum] remains unpaid, with interest accruing thereon daily.} As a result the matter has been referred to the Bar Council under the Rules or [paragraph 15.3 of the Terms of Work 1988, as modified by paragraph 4 of the Rules] or [paragraph 3 of the Rules].

I would ask you to pay these fees at once and in any event within 14 (fourteen) days of the date of this letter. You will appreciate from paragraphs 5 and 6 of the Rules relating to the List of Defaulting Solicitors and Other Authorised Persons that, unless you pay the fees within 14 days of the date of this letter, or if in any event the Chairman has occasion to write again in respect of other outstanding fees within the period referred to in paragraph 5(2) of the Rules, then the consequences spelt out in paragraph 6 of the Rules will follow. In other words, the name of your firm will be included on the Bar Council's List of Defaulting Solicitors and Other Authorised Persons.

Furthermore, the Chairman will report the facts to the Solicitors Regulation Authority with a request that it should commence proceedings against your firm before the Solicitors' Disciplinary Tribunal (or any equivalent tribunal for any non-solicitor Authorised Person).

I hope that it will not prove necessary to include your firm's name on the Bar Council's List of Defaulting Solicitors and Other Authorised Persons, and that you will pay the fees of barristers instructed by your firm promptly when due. I am, however, concerned that you should be fully informed in advance of the problems which would arise should you fail to pay barristers' fees in accordance with your obligations.

Yours faithfully,

First Chairman's Letter – Publicly Funded Cases

To be sent to the Senior Partner, General Manager or equivalent of the Authorised Person:

Dear Sir or Madam,

Bar Council's List of Defaulting Solicitors and other Authorised Persons: The Rules Relating to the List of Defaulting Solicitors and other Authorised Persons ("the Rules")

I refer to Counsel's fees, particulars of which are set out in the Schedule to this letter. Copies of the relevant fee notes are attached.* Letters have been written regarding payment of these fees. Payment has not been received and no satisfactory explanation has been provided for the non-payment. As a result, the matter has been referred to the General Council of the Bar in accordance with the scheme for complaining to the Bar Council for Publicly funded matters ("the Scheme for Complaining")] OR [paragraph 15.3 of the Terms of Work on which Barristers offer their services to Solicitors and the Withdrawal of Credit Scheme 1988 ("the Terms of Work 1988") as modified by paragraph 2 of the Rules.

Since this complaint relates to a publicly funded matter, I would be grateful if you would supply me with the following information within 14 days of the date of this letter:

(a) the date of issue and number of any relevant publicly funded certificates, together with a copy of such certificates;

(b) the date of any order for assessment of costs under the relevant certificate(s) or other event giving rise to a right to such assessment; and

(c) what steps you have taken under the relevant regulations for the purpose of obtaining payment of Counsel's fees.

I am also enclosing for your attention a copy of the Rules and [the Scheme for Complaining] OR [the Terms of Work 1988]. You will appreciate from reading them that their effect is such that if (1) no satisfactory explanation for non-payment of the fees referred to in the Schedule to this letter has been provided and (2) the Chairman has occasion to write again in respect of other outstanding fees within the period referred to in paragraph 5(2) of the Rules, then the consequences spelt out in paragraph 6(1) of the Rules will follow. In other words, the name of your firm will be included on the Bar Council's List of Defaulting Solicitors and Other Authorised Persons. Furthermore, the Chairman will report the facts to the Solicitors Regulation Authority with a request that it should commence proceedings against your firm before the Solicitors' Disciplinary Tribunal (or any equivalent tribunal for any non-solicitor Authorised Person).

I hope that it will not prove necessary to include your firm's name on the Bar Council's List of Defaulting Solicitors and Other Authorised Persons, and that you will pay the fees of barristers instructed by your firm promptly when due. I am, however, concerned that you should be fully informed in advance of the problems which would arise should you fail to pay barristers' fees in accordance with your obligations.

Yours faithfully,

* The fees referred to in this letter must be unpaid more than 14 days after delivery of Letter "B", as set out at the Schedule C to these Rules or the Scheme for Complaining to the Bar Council as the case may be, and the Authorised Person must not have provided a satisfactory explanation for the non-payment.

Schedule B: Standard Letter 2

Second Chairman's Letter – Privately Funded Cases

To be sent to the Senior Partner, General Manager or equivalent of the Authorised Person:

Dear Sir or Madam,

Bar Council's List of Defaulting Solicitors and other Authorised Persons: The Rules Relating to the List of Defaulting Solicitors and Other Authorised Persons ("the Rules")

I refer to the barrister's fees particulars of which are set out in the schedule to this letter. You will be aware that your agreement with the barrister is governed by [the Standard Contractual Terms for the Supply of Legal Services by Barristers to Authorised Persons 2012] or [contractual terms to which the Rules apply] (the "Agreement"). Copies of the Agreement and of the Rules are attached to this letter.

OR

I refer to the barrister's fees particulars of which are set out in the schedule to this letter. You will be aware that these fees were referred, with your agreement, to a Joint Tribunal. Copies of the Joint Tribunal standing orders and the Rules are attached to this letter.

OR

I refer to the barrister's fees particulars of which are set out in the schedule to this letter. You will be aware that your agreement with the barrister is governed by the Terms of Work on which Barristers offer their services to Solicitors and the Withdrawal of Credit Scheme 1988 ("the Terms of Work 1988"). The Rules Relating to the List of Defaulting Solicitors and other Authorised Persons 2012 also apply to this case. Copies of the Terms of Work 1988 and the Rules are attached to this letter.

Copies of the relevant invoices or Fee Notes are attached.

{On [insert date] [judgment was entered against you in case number in the sum of £ in relation to those fees] or [the Joint Tribunal determined that the sum of £ . was due and owing in relation to those fees]. To date [this sum] or [£ of this sum] remains unpaid, with interest accruing thereon daily.} As a result the matter has [again] been referred to the Bar Council under the Rules or [paragraph 15.3 of the Terms of Work 1988, as modified by paragraph 2 of the Rules] or [paragraph 3 of the Rules].

This is the [second] occasion on which it has been necessary to write to you concerning outstanding fees.

I would ask you to pay these fees at once and in any event within 14 (fourteen) days of the date of this letter.

[The schedule to this letter also sets out particulars of previous barristers' fees which have been reported to the Bar Council as being [unpaid by your firm, or its associates, consultants, employers, or employees (as the case may be)] AND/OR [on your firm's instructions and publicly funded but unpaid without a satisfactory explanation for the non-payment].] You will appreciate from reading rules 5 and 6 of the Rules that, since it is now necessary to write to you [again in respect of the outstanding fees referred to in the schedule to this letter] or [within the period referred to in paragraph 5(2) of the Rules], this [new] complaint, if properly made, will have the consequences spelt out in paragraph 6(1) of the Rules. This means that the Chairman will include the name of your firm in the Bar Council's List of

Defaulting Solicitors and Other Authorised Persons, unless (exceptionally) he is persuaded by any representations you may make not to do so.

The consequence of your firm's inclusion in the Bar Council's List of Defaulting Solicitors and other Authorised Persons will be that all barristers will be told that it would be unwise for any barrister to accept instructions from your firm or from Connected Persons unless they are paid directly by the Legal Services Commission or such instructions are accompanied by payment of an agreed fee for such work or unless he agrees in advance to accept no fee for such work.

Furthermore the Chairman will report the fact to the Solicitors Regulation Authority with a request that it should commence proceedings against your firm, its partners, associates, consultants, employers, or employees (as the case may be) before the Solicitors' Disciplinary Tribunal (or any equivalent tribunal for any non-solicitor Authorised Person).

Any representations which your firm may wish to make must be made in writing within the next 14 (fourteen) days. You will be informed of the Chairman's decision in any event and before circulation of any list containing your firm's name.

Yours faithfully,

Second Chairman's Letter – Publicly Funded Cases

To be sent to the Senior Partner, General Manager or equivalent of the Authorised Person:

Dear Sir or Madam,

Bar Council's List of Defaulting Solicitors and other Authorised Persons: The Rules Relating to the List of Defaulting Solicitors and other Authorised Persons ("the Rules")

I refer to the barrister's fees particulars of which are set out in the schedule to this letter. Copies of the relevant Fee Notes are attached. Letters have been written regarding payment of these fees. Payment has not been received and no satisfactory explanation for the non-payment has been provided. As a result the matter has [again] been referred to the Bar Council.

You will be aware that this matter is governed by [the Scheme for Complaining to the Bar Council for Publicly Funded Matters and the Rules relating to the List of Defaulting Solicitors and other Authorised Persons] OR [the Terms of Work on which Barristers offer their services to Solicitors and the Withdrawal of Credit Scheme 1988, as modified by paragraph 2 of the Rules, together with the Rules themselves].

[Since this complaint relates to a publicly funded matter, I would be grateful if you would supply me with the following information within 14 days of the date of this letter:

(a) the date of issue and number of any relevant publicly funded certificates, together with a copy of such certificates;

(b) the date of any order for assessment of costs under the relevant certificate(s) or other event giving rise to a right to such assessment; and

(c) what steps you have taken under the relevant regulations for the purpose of obtaining payment of Counsel's fees.]*

This is the [second] occasion on which it has been necessary to write to you concerning outstanding fees.

[The schedule to this letter also sets out particulars of previous barristers' fees which have been reported to the Bar Council as being [unpaid by your firm, or its associates, consultants, employers, or employees (as the case may be)] AND/OR [on your firm's instructions and publicly funded but unpaid without a satisfactory explanation for the non-payment].] You will appreciate from reading clauses 5 and 6 of the Rules that, since it is now necessary to write to you [again in respect of the outstanding fees referred to in the schedule to this letter] or [within the period referred to in paragraph 5(2) of the Rules], this [new] complaint, if properly made, will have the consequences spelt out in paragraph 6(1) of the Rules. This means that the Chairman will include the name of your firm in the Bar Council's List of Defaulting Solicitors and other Authorised Persons, unless (exceptionally) he is persuaded by any representations you may make not to do so.

The consequence of your firm's inclusion in the Bar Council's List of Defaulting Solicitors and other Authorised Persons will be that all barristers will be told that it would be unwise for any barrister to accept instructions from your firm or from Connected Persons unless they are paid directly by the Legal Services Commission or such instructions are accompanied by payment of an agreed fee for such work or unless he agrees in advance to accept no fee for such work.

Furthermore the Chairman will report the fact to the Solicitors Regulation Authority with a request that it should commence proceedings against your firm, its partners, associates, consultants, employers, or employees (as the case may be) before the Solicitors' Disciplinary Tribunal.

Any representations which your firm may wish to make must be made in writing within the next 14 (fourteen) days. You will be informed of the Chairman's decision in any event and before circulation of any list containing your firm's name.

Yours faithfully

* Delete this section if this is a further complaint about non-payment of fees after Standard Letter 1 has been sent in respect of the same matter.

Schedule C: Letter

LETTER "A" – Privately Funded Cases

Dear Sir, Re:

I refer to the fee note of [name of barrister] in respect of the above case which was sent to you on [date].

My records indicate that this is a privately funded case in which your relationship with [Name of Barrister] is governed by the Terms of Work on which Barristers offer their Services to Solicitors and the Withdrawal of Credit Scheme 1988 (as amended; "the Terms"). The Bar Council's Rules relating to the List of Defaulting Solicitors and other Authorised Persons, pursuant to rule 2 thereof, will now apply to this case.

Under paragraph 13(1) of the Terms, the fees were due and payable within 1 month of the fee note. I would be grateful if you could make arrangements for these fees to be paid or let me know when payment may be expected.

[Please note that under paragraph 13(2) of the Terms, any such fees remaining outstanding one month after the date of this letter will carry interest at 2% above the Bank of England base rate from time to time from one month after the date of this letter until payment.]*

Yours faithfully,

Clerk to [name of barrister]

*Words substantially in the form of those shown in square brackets must be included if (but only if) it is wished to charge interest on the fees which are the subject of this letter A.

LETTER "A" – Publicly funded cases

Dear Sir,

[Relevant Public Funding Certificate Number] [Date of issue]

Re:

I refer to the fee note of [name of barrister] in respect of the above case which was sent to you on [date].

My records indicate that this is a publicly funded case and I would be grateful if you could let me know when payment may be expected.

Yours faithfully,

Clerk to [name of barrister]

LETTER "B" (To be sent not earlier than 3 months after fee note or invoice) – Privately funded cases

Dear Sir,

Re:

I have referred to [name of barrister] the letter I wrote to you concerning the fees in this matter. To date payment has not been made and no explanation for the non-payment has been forthcoming.

As you know the Bar Council's Rules relating to the List of Defaulting Solicitors and other Authorised Persons ("the Rules") now apply to this case. Unless, therefore, I hear from you within the next 14 days with a satisfactory explanation for the non-payment, I regret that Counsel will make a report to the Chairman of the Bar Council, which will be a report for the purposes of rule 4 of the Rules.

I sincerely trust that this will not be necessary and look forward to hearing from you in early **course.**

Yours faithfully,

Clerk to [name of barrister]

LETTER "B" (*To be sent not earlier than 3 months after fee note or invoice*) – *Publicly funded cases*

Dear Sir,

[Relevant Public Funding Certificate Number] [Date of issue]

Re:

I have referred to [name of barrister] the letter I wrote to you concerning the fees in this matter. To date payment has not been received.

My records indicate that this is a publicly funded case. I must therefore ask you to notify me of:

(a) the date of issue and number of the relevant public funding certificate(s);

(b) the date of any order for assessment of costs under the relevant certificate or other event giving rise to a right to such assessment; and

(c) the steps you have taken under the relevant regulations for the purpose of obtaining payment of [name of barrister]'s fees.

Would you also supply me with copies of the relevant Public Funding Certificate(s).

As you know the Bar Council's Rules relating to the List of Defaulting Solicitors and other Authorised Persons ("the Rules") will now apply to this case. Unless, therefore, he receives in response to this letter the information requested above and a satisfactory explanation for the fact that he has not yet been paid within the next 14 days I regret that Counsel will make a report to the Chairman of the Bar Council, which will be a report for the purposes of rule 4 of the Rules.

I sincerely trust that this will not be necessary and look forward to hearing from you in early **course.**

Yours faithfully,

Clerk to [name of barrister]

Annex C – Fees Collection Protocol

Withdrawal of Credit Scheme in respect of work undertaken on the old Terms of Work/Withdrawal of Credit Protocol

Preamble

This Protocol details, at a high-level, the process the Bar Council undertakes when processing applications under the Withdrawal of Credit Scheme in respect of work undertaken on the old Terms of Work / Withdrawal of Credit scheme (annex G1 and G2 of the Bar Code of Conduct – 6th Edition). A separate Protocol applies to the conduct of Joint Tribunals (with the Law Society) and complaints made under the Standard Contractual Terms for the Supply of Legal Services by Barristers to Authorities Persons Rules 2012.

This Protocol supersedes, together with any policy or discretion previously linked to it, the "Revised guide to the operation of the withdrawal of credit scheme" (Third Edition) (December 2001) produced by the Fees Collection Panel.

For the avoidance of doubt, this Protocol outlines the process for the Fees Collection Panel and the Executive[5] *to follow in administering the old Withdrawal of Credit Scheme. Areas where discretion can be applied are clearly outlined and discretion must only be applied in those areas.*

This first Protocol was approved by the Remuneration Committee on 29 April 2014 and comes into effect immediately.

Core values and guiding principles

2. The Bar Council Executive and the Fees Collection Panel who administer the service …
   - (a) are accountable for the performance of the service;
   - (b) are committed to sustainability and acting in an environmentally friendly way;
   - (c) are consistent in their decision-making applying discretion only in limited and prescribed areas of the process;

(d) are accountable to the Remuneration Committee reporting performance information clearly, regularly and transparently;[5]

(e) listen to, and are receptive to, new and diverse ideas from across the organisation;

(f) pro actively explore opportunities to better serve users of the service;

(g) strive to exceed members' needs and expectations through competence, consistency and teamwork;

(h) understand that our members deserve a service that is responsive, professional, efficient and timely;

(i) utilise and embrace modern technology; and

(j) ensure that the process, including the roles and responsibilities of users of the service, is communicated clearly.

Our expectations of users of the service

3. The requirements we have of users of the service are as follows:

(a) Applications for the service should not be sent until both Letter A and Letter B have been sent by the complainant, or by chambers on their behalf.

(b) Applications should be sent in good form, first time. Any errors on the application detract attention from other valid claims in the system from progressing.

(c) The Bar Council must be made aware of any changes to the complaint in a timely manner including notifying the Bar Council of receipt of full payment.

(d) Users of the service should respond to any request by the Bar Council in a timely **manner.**

4. These roles and responsibilities together with tools to assist members in making valid applications right, first time, are communicated in a separate guidance document available on the Bar Council's website.

Overview of the process

5. The high-level overview of the process is as follows:

(a) application received by email;

(b) application validated;

(c) Letter "C" sent;

(d) Letter "D" sent;

(e) determination to list;

(f) listing.

6. The presumption will be that the sending of Letter C will prompt the solicitors to pay barristers what they owe, and that if they fail to do so despite a letter from the Chairman of the Bar, to place the solicitors firm on the list.

Receipt of an application

7. Any member of the Bar may use the service, regardless as to whether they have paid the Bar Representation Fee, if they currently hold (or have held) a valid practising certificate for the year in which they first undertook the work to which the application relates.[6]

8. All applications are to be received by the Bar Council electronically and must be sent either from the barrister's professional email address or, if submitted by a fees clerk, the barrister's professional email address must be copied to the email. Receipt of this email indicates explicit approval for the Bar Council to progress the application and to place a solicitors firm on the list.

9. Any application received by post after 31 July 2014 will be returned. Any application received by post before this date will be manually scanned by the Executive and entered into the Document Management System (DMS); the hard copy will be destroyed confidentially and securely.

10. Any supplementary documentation from barristers or clerks must be received by email after 31 July 2014. Until that time the Executive will convert hard copies to electronic PDF format and then destroy confidentially and securely all hard copy documentation. Electronic correspondence from solicitors will be encouraged but will not be mandatory.

Validation

11. Each application will be assigned and stored in an electronic file on the DMS and will be checked by the Executive for validity. An application is only valid if:

    (a) Letter A was sent in the correct form and was sent more than one month after the first fee note was sent;[7]

    (b) Letter B was sent in the correct form and was sent more than three months after the first fee note;[8]

    (c) Letter B was addressed to the Senior Partner of the solicitor firm as registered with the Solicitors Regulation Authority (SRA) or, if applicable, an individual solicitor;

    (d) The solicitor firm has not changed details;

    (e) The fee note does not relate to criminal legal aid;

    (f) The date of the first fee note does not exceed two years from the date the application was made to the Bar Council;

    (g) The solicitor firm complained of has not been intervened (or has been made bankrupt); and

    (h) The fee note is submitted within three months after the work has been completed (or sooner if requested by the solicitor).[9]

12. If the application is invalid in respect of one, or more, reasons relating to 11.a to 11.e then an email will be sent to the applicant informing them of the error and providing information on how they can correct it. The reason(s) for rejection will be recorded so the prevalence of common errors can be monitored. The application will not progress until all the errors have been rectified.

13. If the application is rejected under 11.f (fee note exceeds two years from the date the application was received by the Bar Council) it will be rejected unless there is an exceptional reason to disapply the two-year rule. Such exceptional circumstances include:

    (a) The fee in question related to a missed instalment of fees relating to instructions of more than two years from date of the first fee note but was missed within two years.

    (b) If the fee note relates to a publicly funded case within two years of the Legal Aid Certificate was discharged or revoked.

    (c) If the case relates to a Conditional Fee Agreement or Damages-based Agreement within two years of the case being completed.

    (d) Further exceptional reasons may also be accepted at the discretion of the Fees Collection Panel. Any discretion under this provision must be recorded and the total number of exceptions should be reported to the Remuneration Committee in the monthly update.

    For the avoidance of doubt, the previous practice known to some as "putting files on hold" has been discontinued as the exceptional circumstances above achieve the same outcome.

14. If the application is invalid due to the solicitor firm being intervened (11.g) or fee note made three months after the work has been complete (11.h) then an email will be sent to the applicant stating that the application has been rejected.

15. If the application is deemed valid then an acknowledgement email will be sent to the applicant and the application will move to the next stage of the process.

    For the avoidance of doubt, the solicitor firm does not need more than one complaint for the application to proceed to any stage of the process

Letter "C"

16. A letter will be sent by email to the solicitor firm if it is the view of the Executive that the solicitor firm is active and appears carrying out business.[10] If it is the view of the Executive that the email address is inactive or unlikely to be received by the intended recipient, then a hard copy letter should be sent.

17. The draft letter will then be kept in a batch of electronic files to be sent to the Chair of the Bar Council (or any person they give authority to sign on their behalf) for negative approval within five working days; at a set day at the Chair's convenience.

18. If no veto is received from the Chair of the Bar within five working days, the Executive will check with the applicant that the payment remains unpaid and the email (or in limited circumstances hard copy letter) will be sent to the solicitor firm.

19. If the Chair does veto the letter then the reasons for a Chair's veto must be recorded and reported to the Remuneration Committee in the monthly update.

Fees disputed

20. If the solicitor firm, within three months of the date of the fee note or one month after letter A, disputes the fees then the dispute must be determined by the Joint Tribunal process if the solicitor requests this action; a separate Protocol details that process. At any stage the application can be moved outside this process and moved to the Joint Tribunal process or be closed as long as both parties agree.

Valid or understandable reasons

21. If the Solicitor firm responds to letter "C" and gives a valid or understandable reason why payment remains unpaid, this will be communicated to the applicant to see if the issue can be resolved; either by receiving delayed payment or payment in instalments etc. The principle of OPTP (One Promise To Pay) will be used, and must be agreed to by the applicant, if the Solicitor firm breaks the OPTP then the application will move to the listing stage.

Letter "D"

22. Upon expiry of 14 days after letter "C" has been sent to which no written representations have been made by the Solicitor's firm, a final Chair's letter ("Letter D"[11]) will be sent to the Solicitor's firm stating that the Solicitor's firm will go on the next list of defaulting solicitors.[12]

Payment made but no explanation for late payment

23. If the Solicitor firm makes full payment but does not provide reasons for the late payment they are still liable to be listed under Annex G1. However, this is discretionary and full payment (in all open applications) will be sufficient grounds to stop the solicitors firm going on the list.

List of defaulting solicitors

24. Upon the expiry of 14 days of the Letter D being sent and no payment, or reason why there has been non-payment, being received from the solicitor firm, the information relating to the application will be sent to a Fees Collection Panel member for positive approval (a reminder will be sent automatically if no response has been received within 10 working days) for inclusion on the next published List of Defaulting Solicitors. At this point the Fees Collection Panel have complete discretion in determining whether the solicitor's firm should go on the List of Defaulting Solicitors but the decision must be recorded centrally and relayed to the applicant.

25. Upon approval the solicitors firm will be assigned to go on the next version of the List of Defaulting Solicitors. If a listing is not recommended, an email will be sent to the applicant detailing the reason why the listing will not occur on this occasion. At this stage, the Fees Collection Panel have full discretion over what actions need to be undertaken on the part of the applicant and solicitors firm; however, the presumption will be that the solicitor firm will go on the next iteration of the list if payment remains unpaid.

26. The list of defaulting solicitors will be published on the Bar Council website by 17:00 on the first Monday of every month; unless there are no additions or removals on the list[13] If the Bar Council Offices are closed, it will be published by 17:00 on the next working day. A hyperlink to the list will also be emailed to all Heads of Chambers within 48 hours of the list being uploaded on the Bar Council website.

27. A satisfaction survey for each applicant that caused a solicitor firm to be put on the list will be sent out by email.

Removing solicitors from the list of defaulting solicitors list

28. Any Solicitor firm that is on the list may apply after six months to be removed from the list.[14] In practice, such a removal will only occur if all unpaid cases against that Solicitor firm have been paid. Any decision to remove an entry on the list requires the positive approval of a member of the Fees Collection Panel.

Payment is received

29. At any stage, the applicant can receive full payment and therefore the application for the solicitor firm to be placed on the list is taken no further with regard to that application. Upon closing the application, a satisfaction survey will be emailed for completion online to the applicant.

General reporting function

30. The Chair of the Fees Collection Panel will attend each Remuneration Committee meeting (or nominate a barrister member of the committee to attend in their place) and report on the performance of the service since the last Remuneration Committee meeting, will report on any extensions to the two year rule, the number and reason's for a Chair's veto, the monthly results from the users feedback survey and highlight any issues with the operation of the Protocol.

31. In terms of the performance of the service, the following information will be sent by email to all Remuneration Committee members and Fees Collection Panel members on a monthly basis:

    (a) Total number of applications received.

    (b) Total number of complaints moved to a Joint Tribunal.

    (c) Number of application rejected outright (in the following categories):

        (i) Fee note relates to criminal legal aid.

        (ii) Solicitor firm has been intervened.

        (iii) Fee note made after three months after the work is completed (or earlier if requested).

        (iv) Fees too old.

    (d) Number of applications rejected for correctable reasons:

        (i) Letter A invalid.

        (ii) Letter B invalid.

(iii) Letter B not sent to senior partner.

(iv) Changes to the solicitor firm after the work was undertaken

(v) Incorrect report form.

(vi) Insufficient evidence to progress the application

(e) Number of Letter Cs sent:

(i) Number of Letter Cs sent by email.

(ii) Number of Letter Cs sent by post.

(f) Number of Letter D's sent:

(i) Number of Letter D's sent by email.

(ii) Number of Letter D's sent by post.

(g) Number of letter Cs vetoed by the Chair Number of Letter D's vetoed by the Chair.

(h) Number of application put on the list of defaulting solicitors.

(i) Number of applications not put list due to FCP determination [LRl].

(j) Number of applications that are closed due to payment.

Annual reporting function

32. Upon completion of each financial year, the Fees Collection Panel will produce a report to the Remuneration Committee that details at least the following information relating to the relevant financial year:

(a) Total cost of running the service for the financial year (including staffing costs, infrastructure costs and postage costs);

(b) Cost per application processed (regardless of outcome);

(c) Total number of barristers that have used the service;

(d) Total number of complaints that have been paid;

(e) Total number of complaints that remain unpaid;

(f) Total number of complaints that move to a Joint Tribunal;

(g) Percentage of applications received in good form at the first attempt;

(h) Percentage of reasons for rejection at the first attempt;

(i) The average time an application takes to place a solicitor firm on the list;

(j) Information at which stage payment is received;

(k) Results of the satisfaction of users based on the satisfaction survey; and

(l) Breakdown of the number of solicitor firms put on the list of defaulting solicitors list each month.

33. The annual report must be presented to the Remuneration Committee within six weeks of the financial year ending.

April 2014

Bar Council

Annex D – Sample Letters A and B

Below are example letters A and B for applicants to use before making an application to the Bar Council.

Letter "A" (for privately funded cases)

Dear Sir,

Re:

I refer to the fee note of [name of barrister] in respect of the above case which was sent to you on [date].

My records indicate that this is a privately funded case in which your relationship with [Name of Barrister] is governed by the Terms of Work on which Barristers offer their Services to Solicitors and the Withdrawal of Credit Scheme 1988 (as amended; "the Terms"). The Bar Council's Rules relating to the List of Defaulting Solicitors and other Authorised Persons, pursuant to rule 2 thereof, will now apply to this case.

Under paragraph 13(1) of the Terms, the fees were due and payable within 1 month of the fee note.

I would be grateful if you could make arrangements for these fees to be paid or let me know when payment may be expected.

[Please note that under paragraph 13(2) of the Terms, any such fees remaining outstanding one month after the date of this letter will carry interest at 2% above the Bank of England base rate from time to time from one month after the date of this letter until payment.]*

Yours faithfully,

Clerk to [name of barrister]

*Words substantially in the form of those shown in square brackets must be included if (but only if) it is wished to charge interest on the fees which are the subject of this letter A.

Letter "A" (for publicly funded cases)

Dear Sir,

[Relevant Public Funding Certificate Number] [Date of issue]

Re: [CASE NUMBER]

I refer to the fee note of [name of barrister] in respect of the above case which was sent to you on [date].

My records indicate that this is a publicly funded case and I would be grateful if you could let me know when payment may be expected.

Yours faithfully,

Clerk to [name of barrister]

Letter "A" (for use in a Conditional Fee Agreement where payment of the fees under the Agreement is to await the outcome of the case)

Dear Sir

Re [CASE NAME]

I refer to the fee note [name of barrister] in respect of the above case which was sent to you on [date].

My records indicate that this is a Conditional Fee Agreement matter in which your relationship with [name of barrister) is governed by the Conditional Fee Agreement and the Terms of Work on which Barristers offer their Services to Solicitors and the Withdrawal of Credit Scheme 1988 (as amended) ("The Terms "). The Bar Council's Rules relating to the List of Defaulting Solicitors and other Authorised Persons, pursuant to Rule 2 thereof, now apply to this case.

Under the terms of the Conditional Fee Agreement, the fees are due and payable within 1 month of the assessment or agreement on the question of costs with the other side, or receipt of costs by the solicitor.

I would be grateful if you could let me know the current position of this case and when payment may be expected.

(Please note that under paragraph 13(2) of The Terms of Work, any such fees remaining outstanding one month after the date of this letter, or one month after the date the fees became due under the Conditional Fee Agreement, whichever is the later, will carry interest at 2% above the Bank of England base rate from time to time until payment.)*

Yours faithfully

Clerk to [name of barrister]

*Words substantially in the form of those shown in round brackets must be included if, but only if, it is wished to charge interest on the fees which are the subject of this letter A.

Letter "B" (Privately funded cases – To be sent not earlier than 3 months after fee note or invoice)

Dear Sir,

Re:

I have referred to [name of barrister] the letter I wrote to you concerning the fees in this matter. To date payment has not been made and no explanation for the non-payment has been forthcoming.

As you know the Bar Council's Rules relating to the List of Defaulting Solicitors and other Authorised Persons ("the Rules") now apply to this case. Unless, therefore, I hear from you within the next 14 days with a satisfactory explanation for the non-payment, I regret that Counsel will make a report to the Chairman of the Bar Council, which will be a report for the purposes of rule 4 of the Rules.

I sincerely trust that this will not be necessary and look forward to hearing from you in early **course.**

Yours faithfully,

Clerk to [name of barrister]

Letter "B" (Publicly funded cases – To be sent not earlier than 3 months after fee note or invoice)

Dear Sir,

[Relevant Public Funding Certificate Number] [Date of issue]

Re:

I have referred to [name of barrister] the letter I wrote to you concerning the fees in this matter. To date payment has not been received.

My records indicate that this is a publicly funded case. I must therefore ask you to notify me of:

(a) the date of issue and number of the relevant public funding certificate(s);

(b) the date of any order for assessment of costs under the relevant certificate or other event giving rise to a right to such assessment; and

(c) the steps you have taken under the relevant regulations for the purpose of obtaining payment of [name of barrister]'s fees.

Would you also supply me with copies of the relevant Public Funding Certificate(s).

As you know the Bar Council's Rules relating to the List of Defaulting Solicitors and other Authorised Persons ("the Rules") will now apply to this case. Unless, therefore, he receives in response to this letter the information requested above and a satisfactory explanation for the fact that he has not yet been paid within the next 14 days I regret that Counsel will make a report to the Chairman of the Bar Council, which will be a report for the purposes of rule 4 of the Rules.

I sincerely trust that this will not be necessary and look forward to hearing from you in early **course.**

Yours faithfully,

Clerk to [name of barrister]

Letter "B" (for use in a Conditional Fee Agreement where the Agreement has been terminated AND counsel requires payment of normal fees without a success fee under Option A)

Dear Sir

Re [CASE NAME]

I have referred to [name of barrister] the letter I wrote to you concerning the fees in this matter.

To date payment has not been made.

As you know, the Bar Council's Rules relating to the List of Defaulting Solicitors and other Authorised Persons ("The Rules") now apply to this case. Unless therefore I hear from you within the next 14 days, I regret that Counsel will have no alternative other than to make such a report.

I sincerely trust that this will not be necessary and look forward to hearing from you in early **course.**

Yours faithfully

Clerk to [name of barrister]

Letter "B" (for use in a Conditional Fee Agreement where payment of the fees under the Agreement is to await the outcome of the case)

Dear Sir

Re [CASE NAME]

I have referred to [name of barrister] the letter I wrote to you concerning the fees in this matter.

To date payment has not been made nor information provided as to the current position of this case and when payment may be expected.

As you know, the Bar Council's Rules relating to the List of Defaulting Solicitors and other Authorised Persons ("The Rules") now apply to this case. Unless therefore I hear from you within the next 14 days, I regret that Counsel will have no alternative other than to make such a report.

I sincerely trust that this will not be necessary and look forward to hearing from you in early **course.**

Yours faithfully

Clerk to [name of barrister]

Annex E – Application Checklist

Prior to submitting your application:

- Ensure that the fees remain unpaid
- Ensure that the case does not relate to criminal legal aid
- Ensure that Letter A was sent one month after the fee note was submitted and contains the correct wording
- Ensure that Letter B was sent three months after the fee note was submitted and contains the correct wording
- Ensure that Letter B is addressed to the Senior Partner

When completing your application:

- Ensure that you are completing the correct form for the type of case (i.e. privately funded case, Conditional Fee Agreement or publicly funded case)
- Ensure that Letter A is not dated automatically and is a true representation of the date the letter was actually sent
- Ensure that Letter B is not dated automatically and is a true representation of the date the letter was actually sent

When submitting your application:

- Ensure that the application form is attached to the email. If the application relates to more than one barrister please provide a separate application for each
- Ensure that the fee note is not older than two years from the date of application. If it is and the reason is exceptional please provide a brief reason for this in the email
- Ensure that Letter A is attached to the email
- Ensure that Letter B is attached to the email
- Ensure that all fee notes are attached to the email
- Ensure that all correspondence to the Solicitor relating to the payment of fees are attached to the email
- Ensure that the email is addressed to fees@barcouncil.org.uk

1 The Withdrawal of Credit Scheme in respect of work undertaken on the old Terms of Work/ Withdrawal of Credit scheme (Annex G1 and G2 of the Bar Code of Conduct – 6th Edition).
2 http://www.barcouncil.org.uk/for-the-bar/fees-collection/joint-tribunal-service/
3 An exception may be made in a Crown Court criminal legal aid defence graduated fee case, where a solicitor advocate is the Instructed Advocate and receives the entire fee for the case from the Legal Aid Agency and then fails to pay a barrister whom the solicitor advocate had instructed to undertake a **hearing or hearings** as a **Substitute** Advocate.
4 www.barcouncil.org.uk.
5 This is the preferred term for members of staff who work for the Bar Council. The members of staff involved in this work are part of the Remuneration Team.
6 Paragraph 15 (3) (Annex G1).
7 Paragraph 15(1) (Annex G1).
8 Paragraph 15 (2) (Annex G1).

9 Paragraph 10(2) and 10(3).
10 Paragraph 16 (Annex G1).
11 NOTE: Letter D is being used for clarity; no description nor prescriptive text is included in .Annex Gl.
12 Paragraph 17(2) (Annex G1).
13 Paragraph 19 (Annex G1).
14 Paragraph 20 (Annex G1).

List of defaulting solicitors and other authorised persons 2012

[3.87]

On the 31 January 2013, the Withdrawal of Credit scheme was replaced by the 'List of Defaulting Solicitors and other Authorised Persons 2012'.

The scheme for placing solicitors on the advisory List of Defaulting Solicitors and other Authorised Persons 2012 is similar to the old Withdrawal of Credit Scheme except that barristers are not required to refuse instructions from solicitors or Authorised Persons on the advisory List of Defaulting Solicitors and other Authorised Persons 2012, and instead they may choose whether or not to accept such instructions.

Complaints can be made against solicitors and Authorised Persons in the following situations:

(1) The barrister has obtained a Judgment for fees against the Authorised Person

(2) The solicitor has not paid a joint tribunal or arbitration award

(3) Where instructions were received before 31 January 2013 on the basis of the former Terms of Work, a complaint about non-payment of fees for that work may be made without having first to obtain a Judgment or a joint tribunal award

(4) Where fees are covered by a full publicly funded certificate but remain unpaid due to the failures of the instructing solicitor. The solicitor may have failed to submit the final claim to the Legal Services Commission or, where there is eventually no claim on the legal aid fund because costs are to be recovered from the other side, the instructing solicitor fails to recover those costs or pass on the monies received onto the barrister so that the barrister remains unpaid.

On receipt of a complaint regarding unpaid fees, the Chairman of the Bar Council will write to the solicitor or authorised person in question requiring payment to be made. Normally, the Chairman of the Bar Council will place the solicitor on the advisory List of Defaulting Solicitors and other Authorised Persons 2012 unless the Chairman is persuaded that it would be inappropriate to do so.

The names of solicitors on the Withdrawal of Credit List as at 31 January 2013 will automatically be transferred to the advisory List of Defaulting Solicitors and other Authorised Persons 2012.

Joint Tribunal Process

[3.88]–[3.90]

The Bar Council offers, in conjunction with the Law Society, a Joint Tribunal service for resolving fee disputes between barristers and solicitors. The service can be invoked by either the barrister or solicitor.

Once both parties have agreed to be bound by the decision of a joint tribunal, the Applicant provides a written Statement of Case with accompanying documents, and the Respondent provides a Statement of Response. Further Statements can be made. A Joint Tribunal then considers all the documentation submitted and makes a decision. A Joint Tribunal may decide to hold an oral hearing, but that is rare.

An award issued by a Joint Tribunal must be settled within 14 days. Any decision of a Joint Tribunal is final and there is no appeal process. Failure to comply with an award is regarded as unbefitting conduct and can lead to disciplinary proceedings.

The Joint Tribunal itself is composed of a barrister, normally a QC, appointed by the Chairman of the Bar Council and a solicitor, often a Council member, appointed by the Law Society.

There is no charge to either the barrister or the solicitor for invoking or participating in the Joint Tribunal process.

To commence a Joint Tribunal, the barrister should send an email to Fees@BarCouncil.org.uk asking for a tribunal, attaching a copy of the fee note in dispute.

The Bar Council will then arrange for the necessary consents to be obtained before the Tribunal process starts and before the barrister has to issue his Statement of Case under the Joint Tribunal Standing Orders.

Joint Tribunal Standing Orders

Standard time scale proposed

[3.91]–[3.112]

1. The purpose of the Joint Tribunal ('the Tribunal') is to resolve disputes between counsel and instructing solicitors relating to a barrister's claim for fees and/or expenses and arising out of a contract between the parties or otherwise. The procedure may be instigated by either party. For the purposes of these Orders, the instigating party is "the Applicant" and the other party "the Respondent".

2. Both parties will be required to agree to be bound by the Tribunal's decision. The Applicant shall, within 28 days of being advised of the Respondent's agreement to be bound, issue a Statement of Case with any supporting documents which must include copies of the agreement, the fee notes in question and relevant correspondence. The Statement and accompanying documents must be sent as follows:

(a) two copies direct to the Law Society;

(b) two copies direct to the General Council of the Bar;

(c) one copy direct to the Respondent.

3. The Respondent shall, within 28 days of receipt of the Applicant's Statement of Case, issue a Statement of Response with any supporting documents which must include a copy of the agreement to be bound by the Tribunal and relevant correspondence. The Statement and accompanying documents must be sent as follows:

(a) two copies direct to the Law Society;

(b) two copies direct to the General Council of the Bar;

(c) one copy direct to the Applicant.

4. All documents which are submitted shall be indexed and paginated consecutively.

5. If either party relies upon the evidence of another person, a statement of such evidence shall be signed and dated by the witness.

6. The Tribunal should be appointed within 44 days of the receipt by the Law Society and the General Council of the Bar of the Statement of Case. The members of the Tribunal shall be supplied with copies of the Statements and accompanying documents sent by the Applicant and Respondent to the Law Society and the General Council of the Bar. Upon receipt of the Statements by the Tribunal, it shall notify the parties of a date for the determination of the dispute which should not be later than 60 days after the supply of the above documents.

7. If, in exceptional circumstances, the Applicant wishes to submit a Statement of Reply, or either party wishes to submit additional material to the Tribunal, they shall submit the Statement or material to the Tribunal, within 14 days of receiving the last Statement or documents from the other party, with a request that is accepted. As in (1) and (2) above, two copies should be sent to the Law Society, two copies to the General Council of the Bar and one copy to the other party in dispute. The Tribunal shall rule upon the admissibility of such documents and its ruling shall be final.

8. The Tribunal is an informal body, fixing its own procedure. It shall rule upon any application by either party in respect of the conduct of its consideration of the matter, and shall notify the parties, the Law Society and the Bar Council, of any consequential directions when giving notice of the date for the determination of the dispute.

9. Any applications by either party in respect of the conduct of the Tribunal's consideration of the matter shall be included within the Statement of Case/Response. The Tribunal shall determine the dispute on the basis of the written submissions of the parties unless in the opinion of the Tribunal an oral hearing is appropriate.

10. If an oral hearing has been requested the Tribunal shall, when fixing the date for the determination of the dispute, inform the parties, the Law Society and the Bar Council, whether or not a hearing is considered to be appropriate, of the date, time and venue for the hearing.

11. The Tribunal's task is to look at all the circumstances in dispute. Where matters touching counsel's conduct or competence are significantly in issue, such matters should be considered through the complaints process of the Bar Standards Board.

12. In exceptional circumstances, the timescales allowed in these Orders may be varied. However, non compliance with these Orders shall entitle the Tribunal to dismiss any case or response and to determine the dispute as the Tribunal thinks fit.

13. Payment of any sum found to be due shall be made within 14 days of the date of notification of any determination by the Tribunal. The Tribunal shall have power to direct payment of undisputed sums forthwith and payment shall be made within 14 days of notification of any interim determination.

14. The Tribunal shall have power in its absolute discretion to award interest upon unpaid fees for such period and at such rate as it deems appropriate in the circumstances.

15. In the event of non-payment within the due time of any determination or interim determination, either the General Council of the Bar or the Law Society may refer the non-payment as a matter as a professional conduct to the Solicitors Regulation Authority or the Bar Standards Board as appropriate.

Further Information

Further information about the complaints procedure for unpaid fees, together with the Joint Tribunal process, can be obtained from the Fees Collection Department: telephone 020 7611 1318, email (fees@barcouncil.org.uk) or by post:

Fees Collection Department
General Council of the Bar
289–293 High Holborn
London
WC1V 7HZ
DX 240 London Chancery Lane

3. Getting Paid in the most Common Fee Payment Scenarios

[3.113]–[3.114]

An outline of how to get paid in the most common scenarios (other than the traditional 'brief fee plus refreshers' arrangement referred to previously[1]) is set out below. Reference is also made to other sources of information and, where appropriate, relevant extracts are included.

1 Section 2, subsection 1 of this Part III, para 2.

Getting Paid: Unassigned Counsel in the Magistrates' Court

[3.115]

The Bar Council has agreed a best practice framework for the instruction of barristers in the Magistrates' Court with the London Criminal Courts Solicitors Association. It is intended to assist in achieving consistent levels of service and fair levels of remuneration for the young bar. It is set out below:

Protocol for the Instruction of Counsel

[3.116]

This protocol shall be referred to as the protocol for instructing counsel in cases covered by Legal Services Commission General Criminal Contract. It will be reviewed on or before 31st December annually.

The object of this protocol is to provide a 'best practice' framework concerning the instruction of counsel to attend Magistrates' Courts on behalf of clients instructed by firms within the Greater London area for work done under the General Criminal Contract. The protocol applies regardless of whether counsel is seconded to a solicitors firm or not.

The London Criminal Courts Solicitors' Association, the Criminal Bar Association and the Young Barristers' Committee of the Bar Council hope that this document will assist in obtaining consistent standards of service and fair levels of remuneration for the young bar.

Counsel shall be the barrister attending a court upon instructions from the solicitor.

A) The solicitor agrees as follows:

1. Those instructions shall be given (except in the case of an emergency) in writing sent by e-mail, fax, DX or post.

2. That instructions shall, whenever appropriate, include at least the following:
   a) Name, address, date of birth and telephone number of the client;
   b) Copies of charges, TICs, advance information (whether case summary or statements) and exhibits;
   c) Bail details or reasons for remand into custody, stage of proceedings, object of the hearing in question and bail instructions;
   d) Unique File Number (UFN) and a copy of the grant of representation order, where available, or instructions to make application for a representation order;
   e) Proof of evidence of client, including antecedents, previous convictions and comment on prosecution case.
3. That payment shall be made in the month following receipt of counsel's fee note and report of result of hearing.
4. Payment to counsel shall be based on the guidance set out in Annex A, attached hereto. The purpose of Annex A is to recommend a minimum basis for payment of counsel's fees that is fair and reasonable.
5. To pay counsel whether or not a representation order exists unless agreed to the contrary.

B) Counsel agrees as follows:

1. On the day of the hearing, or within 24 hours thereof, counsel shall forward a written report on the case to the instructing solicitors.
2. To act as counsel, from the solicitor's approved list of counsel, (save in exceptional circumstances), for the solicitor advising and assisting the client at the relevant hearing.
3. To ensure that the number of cases accepted at any time will not diminish the quality of the service offered to the client of the solicitor.
4. That on the day of the hearing counsel will, by telephone, advise the solicitor of the result of the hearing and any emergency work which is to be carried out.
5. Counsel's chambers will invoice the solicitor collectively, once a month, so that the solicitor may pay the invoice in a single transfer to chambers.
6. If counsel's fees are not paid within 30 days, counsel's clerk will ordinarily require an explanation before a decision is taken to revert to the LSC for payment.

ANNEX A

Minimum fees:

- £50 for first appearances, remands, bail applications, sentences, adjourned trials.
- £75 for half day trials, half day contested committals and where a defendant pleads guilty at trial.
- £150 for full day trials and full day contested committals.

Travel disbursements are to be paid in addition to the above.

[3.117]

In 2008, the Protocol was reissued with an accompanying letter from the then Chairman of the Bar, Tim Dutton QC, commending the adoption and implementation of the Protocol. The substance of the letter is reproduced below:

In 2002, a protocol was agreed with the London Criminal Courts Solicitors Association (LCCSA) as to appropriate levels of remuneration for junior barristers acting as unassigned counsel in the Magistrates' Courts.

The Bar Council has consulted the LCCSA and has updated the protocol. The revised protocol is attached and we request that it is widely circulated.

We stress that the fee levels set in the protocol are minimum levels, and have been set to give a minimum standard in London where remuneration of junior barristers has been particularly poor.

The historical need for chambers to adhere to the protocol has been explained to the profession before and is reiterated here.

The Bar Council remains concerned about the level of fees being paid to junior barristers instructed as unassigned counsel in the Magistrates' Courts. Like the 2002 protocol this new protocol is not compulsory but it is considered that the rates of payment represent fair and appropriate fees for the work likely to be done.

In the past some chambers have been unwilling to offend solicitors who instruct more senior members of chambers regularly and, in some cases, put pressure on junior members to accept very low fees, and certainly not to adhere to the recommended rates of the protocol.

Problems also arise over the, often, excessive delays in obtaining fees from solicitors. Again, the perception has been that chambers are unwilling to press solicitors for the fees.

Both these practices cause considerable hardship to young barristers and are unacceptable and can engage certain specific points of the Code of Conduct which will be treated very seriously. Specifically, under Paragraph 404.2 of the Code of Conduct, Heads of Chambers have a duty to ensure that "the affairs of [their] chambers are conducted in a manner which is fair and equitable for all barristers and pupils". Requiring junior barristers, who are often in no position to refuse, to undertake work as unassigned counsel for rates significantly below the protocol or failure to collect their fees in the times suggested by the protocol, are likely to amount to a breach of the requirement. The Bar Council will view justified complaints of this sort very seriously, and will not hesitate to take appropriate action if necessary by referring a matter to the Bar Standards Board.

The Bar Council recommends that it is good practice for Chambers to adopt the following timetable:

1. put in place systems properly and effectively to submit invoices for work undertaken in the Magistrates' Court within 14 days of the work done;
2. put in place systems to ensure that payment is made within 30 days of the submission of the said invoice;
3. require payment of the invoice within a further 14 days if payment is not made within 30 days of the submission of the invoice;
4. report the matter to the Legal Services Commission if payment is not received within 7 days of (3) above in accordance with Paragraph 2.15(5) of the General Criminal Contract.

If a Chambers fails to have regard to these guidelines and, in particular, if barristers find themselves unable to claim fees as a result of the delay by Chambers, then there may well be a breach of paragraph 404.2 and the barrister or the Bar Council can refer these to the Bar Standards Board. The Bar Standards Board has powers to investigate Chambers and to inspect records. It can also take disciplinary action against Heads of Chambers or others responsible for the administration of Chambers for failure to comply with this paragraph.

I commend the adoption and implementation of the revised Magistrates Courts Protocol to you and urge chambers to ensure that junior members of the Bar are treated fairly and properly if only to maintain the reputation of the entire profession.

Signing an application for legal aid (FORM CRM 14)

[3.118]–[3.120]

Purpose: To draw barristers' attention to the practicalities relating to signing an application for legal aid (Form CRM 14).

Scope of application: All practising, criminal barristers.

Issued by: The Professional Practice Committee.

Reissued: January 2014.

Status and effect: Please see the notice at end of this document. This is not "guidance" for the purposes of the BSB Handbook I6.4.

General approach

1. This provides clarification in relation to the permissibility of you completing and signing, as the legal representative, Part 31 of form CRM 14, "Application for Legal Aid in Criminal Proceedings" (formerly form "CDS 14"), issued by the Legal Aid Authority ("LAA").
2. The Legal Services Commission, the predecessor to the LAA confirmed, in 2006, that barristers could sign form CDS 14 and it was always their intention that they should be able to, as agents of the solicitor. The PPC has considered the replacement form CRM 14 and the guidance notes thereto (available on the Ministry of Justice's website: www.justice.gov.uk). The form

requires the applicant's legal representative to complete and sign Part 31. It does not require you to verify or attest to the accuracy of the information submitted. The PPC considers that it is permissible under the BSB Handbook for barristers to complete and sign Part 31 form CRM 14.

Important Notice

This document has been prepared by the Bar Council to assist barristers on matters of professional conduct and ethics. **It is not "guidance" for the purposes of the BSB Handbook I6.4, and neither the BSB nor a disciplinary tribunal nor the Legal Ombudsman is bound by any views or advice expressed in it.** It does not comprise – and cannot be relied on as giving – legal advice. It has been prepared in good faith, but neither the Bar Council nor any of the individuals responsible for or involved in its preparation accept any responsibility or liability for anything done in reliance on it.

Fees for Counsel in Criminal Cases in the Magistrates' Courts

[3.121]

The following guidance was updated in 2014 and has been produced in relation the practice of solicitors requesting counsel to conduct magistrates' work for NO FEES in return for future Crown Court work:

1. The Bar Council has received enquiries from several sets of chambers in relation to letters and approaches from firms of solicitors on the subject of counsel's fees for work in Magistrates' Courts in criminal cases.
2. The way in which solicitors are remunerated for the conduct of Magistrates' Court hearings in criminal cases was changed. Whereas a separate fee used to be paid for this work, it is now included in the fee paid to the solicitors under the Litigators' Graduated Fee Scheme. Some firms of solicitors have written to sets of chambers claiming that they have no fee from which to pay counsel for attending Magistrates' Courts. This is not correct, as the Legal Services Commission has confirmed. Solicitors are paid for this work.
3. On the basis of this incorrect statement, the solicitors' firms concerned have asked counsel to conduct hearings in the Magistrates' Courts for no fee, in return for which the solicitors' firms state that instructions to conduct the consequent Crown Court trials will, in the absence of unforeseen circumstances, be sent to members of chambers (who may or may not be the counsel who conducted the Magistrates' Court hearing).
4. You will find copies of the following on the Bar Council's website:

   4.1 The Protocol for the instruction of counsel in Magistrates' Court cases. Page 3 of the Protocol sets out recommended minimum rates.

   4.2 A letter from the Chairman of the Bar Council to all heads of chambers in respect of the Protocol. That letter refers to the duty imposed on heads of chambers by the former paragraph 404.2 of the Code of Conduct (the equivalent provision in the BSB Handbook are rC110 and gC141) and points out that requiring junior counsel to conduct cases at rates significantly below the protocol is likely to amount to a breach of this duty.

4.3 Guidance on referral fees. As appears from paragraph 8(8) of the guidance, the view of the Professional Practice Committee of the Bar Council is that the acceptance of an improperly low proportion of the fee paid under a graduated fee scheme can amount to a referral fee.

Payments on Account (and recoupment of) in Publicly Funded Cases

[3.122]–[3.123]

In some publicly funded civil cases barristers claim for a payment on account from the Legal Services Commission. Occasionally a final report or final claim for costs is never submitted by the solicitor.

The Bar Council has worked closely with the LAA and a "Guidance for Counsel" document has been produced, together with revisions to the LSC's standard letter and standard report form. These are set out below.

Members of the Bar will sometimes be contacted by the LAA's Debt Recovery Unit regarding requests for repayment of previous overpayments. In these circumstances The Bar Council recommends that barristers speak to their clerks regarding the regular financial statement/reports that the LAA supply in order to investigate the history of the particular overpayment, and then seek to engage constructively with member of staff at the Debt Recovery Unit who contacted you, in order to resolve the matter. The Unit also has a general email address: DRU@legalservices.gsi.gov.uk .

Example Standard Letter

[3.124]

The Clerk to [Name of Counsel]
Address of Chambers
Address of Chambers
Postcode

Case ref: XX/XX/XXXXX/A/Z/X
Our ref: XX/XX/XXXXXXX
Date

Dear Sir

RE: CLIENT NAME (SOLICITOR: FIRM NAME)

We are currently reviewing certificates on which payments on account have been made but no final bill or report from the solicitor has been received. We have written to the solicitors with conduct of the above case, to ask them either to submit a bill or to justify continuance of the certificate.

My records indicate that counsel (as named above) was instructed in this case and received payments on account in the sum of £xxx.xx on *[insert date]*. As I may be closing this case shortly, I am writing to ask you to complete and return the enclosed form to me, within 21 days, to enable me to deal appropriately with counsel's fee.

If counsel has not been paid for the work carried out via the solicitors, please submit a fee note direct to this office, quoting the reference above. I will arrange for the fee to be assessed and paid (net of any payments on account already received).

If you are not able to submit a fee note, please indicate that on the form. I will treat the payment on account already made as being equivalent to a final claim for fees and close the case without recovering any money from counsel's account.

If you are aware that the costs in this case have been paid by a third party and counsel has not been paid for the work, please complete the form to this effect and I will recoup counsel's payment on account from the instructing solicitors.

I hope this letter is self-explanatory and look forward to receiving your response. If you can scan the attached form and wish to return it to me by e-mail, my address is *name.name@legalservices.gov*.uk. If you wish to contact me by telephone, my number is *[insert telephone number]*.

Yours faithfully

Name

Job Title

Example Report Form

[3.125]

Report On Case (Counsel)

Please return to the Leeds Regional Office

Counsel Account Number:		
Name of Counsel:		
Name of Conducting Solicitor:		
Solicitors reference:		
Certificate Number:		
Name of Assisted Person:		
PLEASE TICK ONE OF THE FOLLOWING:		
It is not my intention to submit a further fee note in this case. Please treat the payments on account made as being a final claim for fees.		

Counsel has not been paid for his/her work by any party and has no reason to believe that an unassisted party has agreed to, or been ordered to, pay the costs or that those costs have been paid to the conducting solicitor. I enclose a fee note for assessment.	
Counsel has not been paid for his/her work by any party; an order for costs has been granted against an unassisted party, or the unassisted party has agreed to pay the costs. It will be for the solicitor to recover those costs. I have completed the additional information box below. I enclose a fee note for assessment.	
Counsel has been paid for his / her work by the conducting solicitors. Costs in the case were awarded against an unassisted party, or the unassisted party agreed to pay costs.	

If you are aware that an order for costs was made against an unassisted party please provide the additional information below:

Name of Court	
Name of Unassisted Party	
Date of Order or Agreement	

Fees received direct from instructing solicitors: Please indicate in the comments box whether counsel was paid in full or paid just the balance due (net of the payment(s) on account made).
If any of the above options are inappropriate please advise as to the position using the comments box below
Comments:
Signed:..Date ....
Contact Name .... Tel No ....
Office Use Only Provider's Account Number .... Caseworker ....

PART III IN PRACTICE

Guidance For Counsel

Payments on Account in Publicly Funded Cases

Payments Under Review

[3.126]–[3.132]

The Legal Aid Agency (LAA) reviews payments on account outstanding on publicly funded cases (and particularly on older, dormant cases), where the conducting solicitor has not yet submitted a final report or final claim for costs. Solicitors are asked to make reports to the LAA, to enable it to determine whether or not the case(s) can be closed.

If as a result of the enquiries made, a solicitor informs the LAA that a case can be closed, the LAA may then write to you as counsel, if you have received a payment or payments on account in the case in question. You will be asked to complete and return a simple form to enable the LAA to determine how your fees should be dealt with.

The LAA's purpose in writing is not to recover the payment(s) on account made to you. Where appropriate it will be open to you to submit a further claim for fees. However, a payment is likely to be recovered if;

(i) it becomes clear that you have been paid in full for your work on the case by a third party (in which case the LAA's payment on account will be an over-payment and will be recoverable), or;

(ii) you fail to respond to the LAA's request for information.

Under the circumstances, should you receive a request to report about a case, it is important to ensure a response is made to the LAA within the 21 days allowed. Failure to make a report may result in a payment being recovered from your account.

A template of the LAA's standard letter and the standard report form being used are annexed to this guidance. The form can be returned by DX, by post, or scanned and returned by e-mail if more convenient. If for any reason you are unable to return the report within the allowed time you should contact the member of the LAA's staff who wrote to you, via the telephone or by e-mail.

Payments on Account in Other Circumstances

There are some circumstances in which the conduct of a solicitor may impact upon counsel's ability to realise his or her fee – if a solicitor fails to include the full amount of counsel's fee in a final claim for example. Situations of this type will be dealt with on a case-by-case basis, taking account of the individual circumstances in each case, but the general approach of the LAA will be to ensure that counsel is not unfairly penalised by the conduct of the solicitor involved. Should a situation of this type arise, counsel should contact the regional office of the LAA that normally deals with claims for fees.

There are also circumstances where counsel can be disadvantaged by events over which they have no control – for example, if a solicitor's firm ceases to trade or is intervened in. Again the LAA will deal with cases of this type individually, taking account of the individual circumstances in each case and the financial interests of all the parties involved. In some circumstances fees may be payable to counsel, in which case a payment can be made. 2

Normally issues relating to payments on account should be resolved with either the author of any correspondence sent by the LAA (if a letter from the LAA has triggered the issue), or through the LAA's regional office that normally pays counsel's fees.

If for any reason it is not possible to resolve matters in this way, counsel may wish to contact Guy Barker, via the addresses below:

By Post:

Guy Barker
Operations Manager
Legal Aid Agency
Harcourt House
21 The Calls
Leeds
LS2 7EH

By DX:

Guy Barker
Legal Aid Agency
DX12068 Leeds

By e-mail:

guy.barker@legalaid.gsi.gov.uk

By telephone:

0113 390 7463

Advice for members of the Bar in relation to payments on account is also available from the Bar Council's Remuneration team.

By e-mail:

Remuneration@BarCouncil.org.uk

By telephone:

020 7611 1323

Getting Paid: Criminal Cases

Criminal Advocates Graduated Fee Scheme (Defence)

[3.133]–[3.135]

Certain proceedings in the Crown Court specified by the Criminal Defence Service ("CDS") at the LSC are paid via a Criminal Advocates Graduated Fees Scheme. Payment under this scheme is calculated using a prescribed formula which takes into account the following elements:

- The basic fee (attributable to the type of offence under which the defendant is tried). This fee is also dependent on the type of case (trial, guilty plea, or cracked trial) and the category of the advocate involved (QC, leading junior, led junior, or junior alone).
- The number of days (or parts of) on which the advocate attends the court beyond the second day.
- Refreshers – the fee payable for daily attendance of the advocate in.
- The number of pages of prosecution evidence.
- The number of prosecution witnesses.

The Background to this system is as follows: In 2006, the Carter Review recommended a revised advocates graduated fee scheme (RAGFS) for the remuneration of advocates in the Crown Court. The RAGFS was set out in The Criminal Defence Service (Funding) Order 2007, SI 2007 No 1174 (the Order), which took effect from 30 April 2007 in respect of representation orders granted on or after 30 April 2007. In April 2010 the government announced a reduction of 13.5% over a three year period in remuneration for criminal graduated fee work. As a consequence, graduated fees were cut by 4.5% in April 2010, 2011 and 2012. In addition, on 3 October 2011, the government harmonised fees for Crown Court cases paid under Class A (homicide and related grave offences) and cases paid under Class J (serious sexual offences) so that they are paid at the same rate. Two other key changes in operation from 3 October 2011 were the introduction of fixed fees for either way cases where an elected Crown Court trial ends in a guilty plea or cracked trial, and treating sentence hearings as standard appearances.

Apportionment of Fees between Advocates

[3.136]

As referred to previously[1] the apportionment of fees between advocates in criminal cases is now therefore the statutory responsibility of the Instructed Advocate rather than the LAA. This raises a number of practical issues in relation to accounting, income tax/VAT, and chambers administration. To assist barristers undertaking this work, the Bar Council has produced a Graduated Fee Payment Protocol (January 2014) offering recommendations to best manage the new system and this is set out below.

1 Part III, Section 2, Subsection 1 Introduction, para 5.

The Graduated Fee Payment Protocol

[3.137]

Introduction

Background

1. In 2006, the Carter Review recommended a revised advocates graduated fee scheme (RAGFS) for the remuneration of advocates in the Crown Court.[1]
2. The RAGFS was set out in The Criminal Defence Service (Funding) Order 2007 SI No 1174 (the Order), which took effect from 30 April 2007 in respect of representation orders granted on or after 30 April 2007.
3. In April 2010 the government announced a reduction of 13.5% over a three year period in remuneration for criminal graduated fee work. As a consequence, graduated fees were cut by 4.5% in April 2010, 2011 and 2012.
4. In addition, on 3 October 2011, the government harmonised fees for Crown Court cases paid under Class A (homicide and related grave offences) and cases paid under Class J (serious sexual offences) so that they are paid at the same rate. Two other key changes in operation from 3 October 2011 were the introduction of fixed fees for either way cases where an elected Crown Court trial ends in a guilty plea or cracked trial, and treating sentence hearings as standard appearances.
5. Since 1 April 2013, the Criminal Legal Aid (Remuneration) Regulations (the Remuneration Regulations) have provided for the payment of graduated fees for Crown Court advocacy.
6. This Fee Payment Protocol (the Protocol) was the subject of consultation by the Bar Council in 2007, and was adapted as a result. It was supported by the Department for Constitutional Affairs, now the Ministry of Justice, and the Protocol meets the requirements of the Remuneration Regulations where necessary.

1 Lord Carter of Cole, Legal Aid: A market-based approach to reform (2006), 76–78. The review is available online at: http://tinyurl.com/7gal2ga

Helpful information

7. The Bar Council publishes a monthly Remuneration Update with information with news, updates and current issues about getting paid as a barrister.

8. The Legal Aid Agency (LAA) also publishes a monthly update, called the Advocates' Bulletin. The Bulletin provides information and advice about ensuring you get paid on time and making sure fee claims are right the first time. You can subscribe to the Advocates' Bulletin on the LAA website

Key definitions and concepts

The instructed advocate and substitute advocate

9. The Order defines the instructed advocate in article 2:

"instructed advocate" means

(a) where a representation order provides for a single advocate, the first barrister or solicitor advocate instructed in the case, who has primary responsibility for the case; or

(b) where a representation order provides for more than one advocate, each of—

(i) the leading instructed advocate; and

(ii) the led instructed advocate.

"leading instructed advocate" means the first leading barrister or solicitor advocate instructed in the case, who has primary responsibility for those aspects of a case undertaken by a leading advocate;

"led instructed advocate" means the first led barrister or solicitor advocate instructed in the case, who has primary responsibility for those aspects of the case undertaken by a led advocate.

10. Any other advocate who carries out paid returned work (as defined below) in relation to the case is referred to in this Protocol as the substitute advocate.

11. This protocol operates most effectively when the instructed advocate and any substitute advocates have a **contractual relationship**. This requires the instructed advocate to contract with any substitute advocates where they are required to undertake any advocacy services. **The instructed advocate is then the contractor and the substitute advocate a subcontractor.** The relationship of contractor and subcontractor does not affect any of the barrister's duties under the BSB Handbook.

12. The instructed advocate's position as contractor and the substitute advocate as subcontractor can be evidenced by the instructed advocate and any substitute advocate agreeing to provide services in accordance with the letter at Annex C.

Withdrawal as instructed advocate

13. It is in the public interest and the criminal justice system that the same advocate should undertake all necessary work on a case and that the advocate of choice should undertake all aspects of the case for the client.

14. There are, however, some limited circumstances where withdrawal as

instructed advocate is inevitable. These circumstances are set out in schedule 1, paragraph 25(10) of the Remuneration Regulations:

(10) An instructed advocate must remain as instructed advocate at all times, except where—

(a) a date for trial is fixed at or before the plea and case management hearing and the instructed advocate is unable to conduct the trial due to the instructed advocate's other pre-existing commitments;

(b) the instructed advocate is dismissed by the assisted person or the litigator; or

(c) the instructed advocate is required to withdraw because of his professional code of conduct.

15. The replacement instructed advocate must then take over all the original instructed advocate's responsibilities. This is established in schedule 1, paragraph 25(11):

(11) Where, in accordance with sub-paragraph (10), an instructed advocate withdraws he must-

(a) immediately inform the court of his withdrawal—

(i) in writing; or

(ii) where the withdrawal takes place at a plea and case management hearing, orally; and

(b) within 7 days of the date of his withdrawal, notify the court in writing of the identity of a replacement instructed advocate, who must fulfil all the functions of an instructed advocate in accordance with the terms of this Order.

16. For the avoidance of doubt, paragraph 25(11) does not impose an obligation on the incumbent instructed advocate to select a replacement instructed advocate, as this would be inconsistent with a client's freedom of choice. The obligation is one of notification and not selection.

Paid returned work and paid retained work

17. Paid returned work is work undertaken by a substitute advocate where the instructed advocate was unable to do the work.

18. Paid retained work is work undertaken by the instructed advocate.

19. Paid returned work covers only the items specified in Annex A below. In particular, there is no separate payment for tape listening, video watching and/or reading unused material. The same applies to retained work.

Total fee

20. The total fee covers all advocacy services provided by the instructed advocate and any substitute advocates. The total fee is paid by the LAA to the instructed advocate. It is then the responsibility of the instructed advocate distribute fees to any substitute advocates

Basic fee and depleted basic fee

21. The basic fee includes payment for:

- First plea and case management hearing (PCMH) or pre-trial review
- First four standard appearances
- First three pre-trial conferences or views
- Reading, listening and watching evidence that is not defined as pages of prosecution evidence.

22. Where a substitute advocate has undertaken work remunerated under the Basic Fee, instructed advocates may have to accept a depleted basic fee to ensure all advocates are adequately paid for their services. This is further explained in paragraph 54–55 and examples of how this works in practice are provided in Annex E below.

Professional obligations to professional and lay client

23. The relationship of contractor and subcontractor does not alter any of the instructed or substitute advocate's professional obligations to their professional or lay client or to the court.

24. It is the duty of all advocates at all times to act in the best interest of their clients, in accordance with the BSB Handbook and the Solicitors Regulation Authority (SRA) Handbook.

Obligations of the instructed advocate

Preparing and submitting fee claims

25. At the end of the case, the instructed advocate must prepare a claim form (in the required format) for all advocacy services and submit it within the required time limit to the LAA for payment (Remuneration Regulations, regulation 4).

26. The claim form itemises the appropriate fee for the case and any items of work that attract discrete payments under the Remuneration Regulations. The total payment will include VAT if the instructed advocate is VAT registered.

Paying substitute advocates

27. The instructed advocate is responsible for arranging payment of fees to any substitute advocates (Remuneration Regulations, schedule 1, paragraph 26(3)). Any payments to substitute advocates will be in accordance with this protocol.

28. Where the instructed advocate is a solicitor, and where work has been undertaken by other advocates on the case (whether barristers or Higher Court Advocates) the solicitor will treat the amounts due to such other advocates from the fee or fees paid by the LAA as client monies and account for them as such.

29. All fees owed to substitute advocates which are received by the instructed advocate, whether a solicitor or barrister, must be paid to substitute advocates within 14 days of receipt.

Redetermination of fees

30. If any advocate is dissatisfied with the determination of fees by the LAA, the instructed advocate may apply for a redetermination. Regulation 28 of the Remuneration Regulations only provides for the instructed advocate to apply for a redetermination.

31. The only exceptions to this are in relation to special preparation and wasted preparation, as regulation 28(1)(a) allows any advocate in proceedings in the Crown Court to seek a redetermination of a decision by the appropriate officer not to allow special or wasted preparation, or to dispute the number of hours allowed in the calculation of the fee.

32. This means that where a substitute advocate is dissatisfied with the appropriate officer's determination of a fee (other than special or wasted preparation), the application for redetermination and any appeal must be brought by the instructed advocate.

33. The instructed advocate is responsible for ensuring that the application for a redetermination is made in accordance with regulation 28.

34. Regulation 29 allows a representative who is dissatisfied with the decision of the appropriate officer to appeal to a Costs Judge.

Obligations of substitute advocates

35. A substitute advocate must invoice the instructed advocate in respect of any paid returned work done for the instructed advocate. This will include VAT where the substitute advocate is VAT registered.

36. Substitute advocates must invoice the instructed advocate promptly, and in good time so as to enable the instructed advocate to submit a correct fee claim to LAA within three months of the conclusion of the case.

37. If the substitute advocate is dissatisfied with the LAA's determination of fees and requires the instructed advocate to apply for a redetermination, the substitute advocate must prepare any written material required by regulation 28 in support of a redetermination. This is because only the substitute advocate will know the precise grounds of dissatisfaction.

Division of fees

Paid returned work contained in the basic fee

38. During the Carter Review, the Bar Council provided the Carter Review Team with a full breakdown of the appropriate fees for the constituent parts of a case (with the exception of the Plea and Case Management Hearing (PCMH) fee). The Carter Review Team agreed that these were the appropriate fees, even though many of them were put into the basic fee rather than being discrete payments as before.

39. Fees (excluding VAT) which should be paid by the instructed advocate to any substitute advocate are included in the tables at Annex A for:

    (a) Table A: Scheme 10 (1 April 2013 –).

(b) Table B: Scheme 9 (1 April 2012 – 31 March 2013).

(c) Table C: Scheme 8 (3 October 2011 – 31 March 2012).

(d) Table D: Scheme 7 (1 April 2011 – 2 October 2011).

(e) Table E: Scheme 5 and 6 (27 April 2010 – 31 March 2011).

(f) Table F: Scheme 4 (30 April 2007 – 26 April 2010).

40. The instructed advocate is obliged to pay any substitute advocate who undertakes any of the work on the case specified in Annex A. Payment for paid returned work is at the rates specified in Annex A, together with any hotel or travel expenses paid by the LAA or other agency in respect of expenses incurred by the substitute advocate.

41. The instructed advocate will retain from the total fee paid for the case the appropriate sums for any work on the case done by them which is specified in Annex A and at the rates shown there, together with any hotel or travel expenses incurred.

Paid returned work covers only the items specified in Annex A. In particular, there is no separate payment for tape listening, video watching and/or reading unused material. The same applies to retained work.

Depleted basic fee

42. If the proportion of the basic fee remaining for the trial, re-trial, cracked trial or guilty plea after following the requirements of Annex A is less than 70 per cent of the basic fee, then the instructed advocate shall reduce the sums payable for all paid returned work and paid retained work (including the trial, included in the starting calculation at 70 per cent of the basic fee) by an equal percentage that will reduce the total to the amount of the basic fee.

43. Examples of how depleted basic fees work in practice are set out in Annex E. The underlying principle is that in determining whether the fees are subject to reduction, both paid returned work and paid retained work must be deducted from the basic fee, otherwise the instructed advocate may be penalised for attending hearings other than the main hearing.

PCMH Fee

44. It is expected that trial advocates will be able to conduct both the PCMH and the trial.

45. Where the PCMH is conducted by an advocate other than the instructed advocate, the PCMH fee will be 15 per cent of the appropriate trial basic fee as shown in Annex B regardless of whether the case ultimately fights or cracks. If the case is disposed of as a guilty plea at the PCMH then the advocate conducting the hearing will receive the appropriate guilty plea fee. This will ensure that the advocate who conducts the PCMH is properly remunerated for the necessary preparation and attendance at court.

Paid returned work where there are two instructed advocates

46. In a case where there are two instructed advocates and a substitute advocate appearing alone undertakes any paid returned work in place of the led junior, the obligation to pay the substitute advocate shall be shared between the instructed advocates in the ratio of two-thirds (leading advocate) to one-third (led advocate).

47. Where a leading advocate (QC or leading junior) is instructed as a trial advocate after the date of instruction of the junior advocate, the leading advocate shall be liable for two-thirds of all of the paid returned work fees, including work undertaken by a substitute advocate appearing alone prior to the date of instruction of the leading advocate.

48. Where a junior advocate (led either by a QC or a leading junior) is instructed after the leading advocate, the junior advocate shall not be liable in respect of any paid returned work undertaken prior to the date of their instruction.

Dispute resolution

49. Chambers must have their own dispute resolution process in relation to the division of RAGFS fees. The Bar Standards Board takes a serious view of any failure by one member of the Bar to honour obligations to another, and barristers must comply at all times with the BSB Handbook.

50. In the first instance, any dispute between barristers should be resolved by the Head of Chambers or Heads of Chambers (where barristers are in different chambers) with the barristers concerned. The Head of Chambers will, with the senior clerk, ensure that a procedure is in place which resolves any dispute quickly and fairly.

51. Where the dispute involves a barrister or barristers less than five years Call, the Head of Chambers will arrange for suitable assistance to be available through the Head of the Chambers Pupillage Committee.

52. Where the dispute involves a barrister and solicitor advocate, the Head of Chambers and the Senior Partner of the firm in question will seek to resolve the dispute quickly and fairly.

53. A written record of the dispute and its resolution should be kept. Where the dispute involves a sole practitioner the parties concerned will seek to resolve the dispute in writing.

54. If a dispute is not resolved under this procedure, the Bar Council should be notified in writing and the matter will be referred to a Dispute Resolution Panel. The Dispute Resolution Panel will resolve disputes between barristers, whether in sole practice or in the same or different chambers.

55. A dispute between a barrister and a solicitor which cannot be resolved informally will be resolved in accordance with the Joint Tribunal Standing Orders for Fee Disputes with Solicitors.

Accounting system

56. The Bar Council considers it essential for chambers to have in place a communal fee accounting system to enable fees for paid returned work to be paid to other advocates.

57. The outline of a model accounting system is set out in Annex D.

Income Tax

58. When the instructed advocate receives the total fee they are only liable to tax on payment for the work they have actually undertaken.

59. The substitute advocate will be liable to tax for their share of the fees at the point when those fees are earned.

VAT

60. The total payment from the LAA to the instructed advocate is inclusive of VAT, if the instructed advocate is VAT registered. The instructed advocate is liable to account to HM Revenue and Customs (HMRC) for the VAT on the value of the whole supply made.

61. If the substitute advocate is VAT registered they will be required to account for VAT on the value of the supplies made to the instructed advocate. The instructed advocate will be liable to pay VAT to the substitute advocate, whether or not the instructed advocate is VAT registered. However, if the instructed advocate is registered for VAT, the VAT may be deducted as input tax (subject to normal VAT rules). For this reason it is strongly advisable for the instructed advocate to be registered for VAT.

62. Appropriate records must be kept for VAT inspection, including copies of VAT invoices issued by the instructed advocate and VAT invoices issued to the instructed advocate by any substitute advocate. The Bar Council recommends that chambers keep these records centrally. An extract of HMRC guidance, and advice received by the Bar Council appears in Annex F. This advice is relevant to both barristers and solicitor advocates who receive fees for Crown Court advocacy.

63. Please note that, whilst the VAT treatment has been discussed with HMRC, the views expressed in this document are based on the Bar Council's understanding of the law as at the date of publication of this protocol. Neither the Bar Council nor HMRC can accept any liability for any reliance placed on this protocol. Barristers, solicitors and their staff should check for changes in the law, and any court or tribunal decisions, and obtain updated official publications. Help can be obtained from HMRC's website at http://www.hmrc.gov.uk/ or by telephoning HMRC VAT Helpline on 0845 010 9000

Annex A: Paid returned and retained work

[3.138]

Key points to note:

When using the tables below, the following points must be taken into account:

- **Conferences:** Fees for conferences are payable to a substitute advocate as Paid Returned Work and deductible by the instructed advocate as Retained

Work at the rates shown in the columns below, but subject to the capping both as to number and length that applies under the current Graduated Fee Scheme.

- **Uplifts for additional cases:** Any uplifts payable under schedule 1, paragraph 27 of the Order are payable to a substitute advocate in respect of Paid Returned Work and are deductible by the instructed advocate for Retained Work.

The figures below are for the following payment schemes:

- Table A: Scheme 10 (representation orders 1 April 2013 –).
- Table B: Scheme 9 (representation orders 1 April 2012 – 31 March 2013).
- Table C: Scheme 8 (representation orders 3 October 2011 – 31 March 2012).
- Table D: Scheme 7 (representation orders 1 April 2011 – 2 October 2011).
- Table E: Scheme 5 and 6 (representation orders 27 April 2010 – 31 March 2011).
- Table F: Scheme 4 (representation orders 30 April 2007 – 26 April 2010).

Table A: Scheme 10 (representation orders 1 April 2013 –)

Category	Comments	Junior	Leading Junior	QC
The trial	The amount paid to the advocate undertaking the trial will be the Total Fee less (a) any sums payable to other advocates for Paid Returned Work apart from the trial, and (b) any sums which the instructed advocate is entitled to deduct for Retained Work.	See adjoining comments column	See adjoining comments column	See adjoining comments column

Category	**Comments**	**Junior**	**Leading Junior**	**QC**
PCMH *Part of Basic Fee*	The amount paid to the advocate undertaking the PCMH will be the amount shown as 15% of the Basic Fee in table B below, or the guilty plea fee less any sums which the instructed advocate is entitled to deduct for Retained Work if the case pleads at the PCMH	See adjoining comments column	See adjoining comments column	See adjoining comments column
Conferences with clients and experts. Views. *Part Basic Fee, part fixed fee under the Order, depending upon the actual or estimated length of the case.*	The first three conferences are included in the Basic Fee. Separate payment is made for fourth and subsequent conferences only in cases lasting or estimated to last 21 days or more.	£39 per hour	£56 per hour	£74 per hour
Standard appearances. *Standard appearances 1–4 part of Basic Fee, 5+ fixed fee under the Order.*	The first 4 standard appearances are included in the Basic Fee. Separate payment is made for fifth and subsequent standard appearance. They are paid as Paid Returned Work at the rates shown in the adjoining columns	£87	£130	£173

Category	Comments	Junior	Leading Junior	QC
Full and Half Day Hearings for PII hearings, bad character hearings, abuse of process, and disclosure hearings. *Fixed fee*		Half Day £130 Full Day £238	Half Day £195 Full Day £346	Half Day £260 Full Day £497
Special and Wasted Preparation. *Fixed fee.*	Wasted preparation to apply only as defined in the Order. This includes research on novel facts.	£39	£56	£74
Ineffective Trial Payment. *Fixed fee.*	A listed trial that does not proceed for any reason.	£130	£195	£281
Sentencing. *Sentence hearing paid as standard appearance. This means there is no separate fee where sentencing hearings are included in the first 4 standard appearances. Deferred sentence hearing paid as fixed fee. Non-effective hearing counts as a standard appearance.*	Sentence Hearings Deferred Sentence Effective Non-effective	£87 £173 £87	£130 £238 £130	£173 £324 £173
Appeals to the Crown Court *Fixed fee*	Against Sentence Effective Non-effective Against Conviction Effective Non-effective	£108 £87 £130 £87	£151 £130 £195 £130	£216 £173 £260 £173

Category	Comments	Junior	Leading Junior	QC
Proceedings for breach of a Crown Court order *Fixed fee under the Order.*	Effective Non-effective	£108 £87	£151 £130	£216 £173
Committal for sentence *Fixed fee*	Effective Non-effective	£130 £87	£195 £130	£260 £173
Noting Brief. *Fixed fee*		£108	-	-

Table B: Scheme 9 (1 April 2012 –)

Category	Comments	Junior	Leading Junior	QC
The trial	The amount paid to the advocate undertaking the trial will be the Total Fee less (a) any sums payable to other advocates for Paid Returned Work apart from the trial, and (b) any sums which the instructed advocate is entitled to deduct for Retained Work.	See adjoining comments column	See adjoining comments column	See adjoining comments column

Category	**Comments**	**Junior**	**Leading Junior**	**QC**
PCMH *Part of Basic Fee*	The amount paid to the advocate undertaking the PCMH will be the amount shown as 15% of the Basic Fee in table B below, or the guilty plea fee less any sums which the instructed advocate is entitled to deduct for Retained Work if the case pleads at the PCMH	See adjoining comments column	See adjoining comments column	See adjoining comments column
Conferences with clients and experts. Views. *Part Basic Fee, part fixed fee under the Order, depending upon the actual or estimated length of the case.*	The first three conferences are included in the Basic Fee. Separate payment is made for fourth and subsequent conferences only in cases lasting or estimated to last 21 days or more.	£39 per hour	£56 per hour	£74 per hour
Standard appearances. *Standard appearances 1–4 part of Basic Fee, 5+ fixed fee under the Order.*	The first 4 standard appearances are included in the Basic Fee. Separate payment is made for fifth and subsequent standard appearance. They are paid as Paid Returned Work at the rates shown in the adjoining columns	£87	£130	£173

PART III
IN PRACTICE

Category	**Comments**	**Junior**	**Leading Junior**	**QC**
Full and Half Day Hearings for PII hearings, bad character hearings, abuse of process, and disclosure hearings. *Fixed fee*		Half Day £130 Full Day £238	Half Day £195 Full Day £346	Half Day £260 Full Day £497
Special and Wasted Preparation. *Fixed fee.*	Wasted preparation to apply only as defined in the Order. This includes research on novel facts.	£39	£56	£74
Ineffective Trial Payment. *Fixed fee.*	A listed trial that does not proceed for any reason.	£130	£195	£281
Sentencing. *Sentence hearing paid as standard appearance. This means there is no separate fee where sentencing hearings are included in the first 4 standard appearances. Deferred sentence hearing paid as fixed fee. Non-effective hearing counts as a standard appearance.*	Sentence Hearings Deferred Sentence Effective Non-effective	£87 £173 £87	£130 £238 £130	£173 £324 £173
Appeals to the Crown Court *Fixed fee*	Against Sentence Effective Non-effective Against Conviction Effective Non-effective	£108 £87 £130 £87	£151 £130 £195 £130	£216 £173 £260 £173

Category	**Comments**	**Junior**	**Leading Junior**	**QC**
Proceedings for breach of a Crown Court order *Fixed fee under the Order.*	Effective Non-effective	£108 £87	£151 £130	£216 £173
Committal for sentence *Fixed fee*	Effective Non-effective	£130 £87	£195 £130	£260 £173
Noting Brief. *Fixed fee*		£108	-	-

Table C: Scheme 8 (3 October 2011 – 31 March 2012)

Category	**Comments**	**Junior**	**Leading Junior**	**QC**
The trial	The amount paid to the advocate undertaking the trial will be the Total Fee less (a) any sums payable to other advocates for Paid Returned Work apart from the trial, and (b) any sums which the instructed advocate is entitled to deduct for Retained Work.	See adjoining comments column	See adjoining comments column	See adjoining comments column

Category	**Comments**	**Junior**	**Leading Junior**	**QC**
PCMH *Part of Basic Fee*	The amount paid to the advocate undertaking the PCMH will be the amount shown as 15% of the Basic Fee in table B below, or the guilty plea fee less any sums which the instructed advocate is entitled to deduct for Retained Work if the case pleads at the PCMH	See adjoining comments column	See adjoining comments column	See adjoining comments column
Conferences with clients and experts. Views. *Part Basic Fee, part fixed fee under the Order, depending upon the actual or estimated length of the case.*	The first three conferences are included in the Basic Fee. Separate payment is made for fourth and subsequent conferences only in cases lasting or estimated to last 21 days or more.	£41 per hour	£59 per hour	£77 per hour
Standard appearances. *Standard appearances 1–4 part of Basic Fee, 5+ fixed fee under the Order.*	The first 4 standard appearances are included in the Basic Fee. Separate payment is made for fifth and subsequent standard appearance. They are paid as Paid Returned Work at the rates shown in the adjoining columns	£91	£137	£182

Category	**Comments**	**Junior**	**Leading Junior**	**QC**
Full and Half Day Hearings for PII hearings, bad character hearings, abuse of process, and disclosure hearings. *Fixed fee under the Order.*		Half Day £137 Full Day £250	Half Day £205 Full Day £364	Half Day £273 Full Day £523
Special and Wasted Preparation. *Fixed fee under the Order.*	Wasted preparation to apply only as defined in the Order. This includes research on novel facts.	£41	£59	£77
Ineffective Trial Payment. *Fixed fee under the Order.*	A listed trial that does not proceed for any reason.	£137	£205	£296
Sentencing. *Sentence hearing paid as standard appearance. This means there is no separate fee where sentencing hearings are included in the first 4 standard appearances. Deferred sentence hearing paid as fixed fee. Non-effective hearing counts as a standard appearance.*	Sentence Hearings Deferred Sentence Effective Non-effective	£91 £182 £91	£137 £250 £137	£182 £348 £182

Category	Comments	Junior	Leading Junior	QC
Appeals to the Crown Court *Fixed fee under the Order.*	Against Sentence Effective Non-effective Against Conviction Effective Non-effective	£114 £91 £137 £91	£159 £137 £205 £137	£228 £182 £273 £182
Proceedings for breach of a Crown Court order *Fixed fee under the Order.*	Effective Non-effective	£114 £91	£159 £137	£228 £182
Committal for sentence *Fixed fee under the Order*	Effective Non-effective	£137 £91	£205 £137	£273 £182
Noting Brief. *Fixed fee under the Order.*		£114	-	-

Table D: Scheme 7 (1 April 2011 – 2 October 2011)

Category	Comments	Junior	Leading Junior	QC
The trial	The amount paid to the advocate undertaking the trial will be the Total Fee less (a) any sums payable to other advocates for Paid Returned Work apart from the trial, and (b) any sums which the instructed advocate is entitled to deduct for Retained Work.	See adjoining comments column	See adjoining comments column	See adjoining comments column

Category	**Comments**	**Junior**	**Leading Junior**	**QC**
PCMH *Part of Basic Fee*	The amount paid to the advocate undertaking the PCMH will be the amount shown as 15% of the Basic Fee in table B below, or the guilty plea fee less any sums which the instructed advocate is entitled to deduct for Retained Work if the case pleads at the PCMH	See adjoining comments column	See adjoining comments column	See adjoining comments column
Conferences with clients and experts. Views. *Part Basic Fee, part fixed fee under the Order, depending upon the actual or estimated length of the case.*	The first three conferences are included in the Basic Fee. Separate payment is made for fourth and subsequent conferences only in cases lasting or estimated to last 21 days or more.	£41 per hour	£59 per hour	£77 per hour
Standard appearances. *Standard appearances 1–4 part of Basic Fee, 5+ fixed fee under the Order.*	The first 4 standard appearances are included in the Basic Fee. Separate payment is made for fifth and subsequent standard appearance. They are paid as Paid Returned Work at the rates shown in the adjoining columns	£91	£137	£182

Category	**Comments**	**Junior**	**Leading Junior**	**QC**
Full and Half Day Hearings for PII hearings, bad character hearings, abuse of process, and disclosure hearings. *Fixed fee under the Order.*		Half Day £137 Full Day £250	Half Day £205 Full Day £364	Half Day £273 Full Day £523
Special and Wasted Preparation. *Fixed fee under the Order.*	Wasted preparation to apply only as defined in the Order. This includes research on novel facts.	£41	£59	£77
Ineffective Trial Payment. *Fixed fee under the Order.*	A listed trial that does not proceed for any reason.	£137	£205	£296
Sentencing. *Fixed fee under the Order if effective. Non-effective hearing counts as a standard appearance.*	Sentence Hearings Effective Non-effective Deferred Sentence Effective Non-effective	£114 £91 £182 £91	£182 £137 £250 £137	£273 £182 £341 £182
Appeals to the Crown Court Fixed fee under the Order.	Against Sentence Effective Non-effective Against Conviction Effective Non-effective	£114 £91 £137 £91	£151 £130 £205 £137	£216 £173 £273 £182
Proceedings for breach of a Crown Court order *Fixed fee under the Order.*	Effective Non-effective	£114 £91	£159 £137	£228 £182

Category	Comments	Junior	Leading Junior	QC
Committal for sentence *Fixed fee under the Order*	Effective Non-effective	£137 £91	£205 £137	£273 £182
Noting Brief. *Fixed fee under the Order.*		£114	-	-

Table E: Scheme 5 and 6 (27 April 2010 – 31 March 2011)

Category	Comments	Junior	Leading Junior	QC
The trial	The amount paid to the advocate undertaking the trial will be the Total Fee less (a) any sums payable to other advocates for Paid Returned Work apart from the trial, and (b) any sums which the instructed advocate is entitled to deduct for Retained Work.	See adjoining comments column	See adjoining comments column	See adjoining comments column

Category	**Comments**	**Junior**	**Leading Junior**	**QC**
PCMH *Part of Basic Fee*	The amount paid to the advocate undertaking the PCMH will be the amount shown as 15% of the Basic Fee in table B below, or the guilty plea fee less any sums which the instructed advocate is entitled to deduct for Retained Work if the case pleads at the PCMH	See adjoining comments column	See adjoining comments column	See adjoining comments column
Conferences with clients and experts. Views. *Part Basic Fee, part fixed fee under the Order, depending upon the actual or estimated length of the case.*	The first three conferences are included in the Basic Fee. Separate payment is made for fourth and subsequent conferences only in cases lasting or estimated to last 21 days or more.	£43 per hour	£62 per hour	£81 per hour
Standard appearances. *Standard appearances 1–4 part of Basic Fee, 5+ fixed fee under the Order.*	The first 4 standard appearances are included in the Basic Fee. Separate payment is made for fifth and subsequent standard appearance. They are paid as Paid Returned Work at the rates shown in the adjoining columns	£96	£143	£191

Category	**Comments**	**Junior**	**Leading Junior**	**QC**
Full and Half Day Hearings for PII hearings, bad character hearings, abuse of process, and disclosure hearings. *Fixed fee under the Order.*		Half Day £143 Full Day £263	Half Day £215 Full Day £382	Half Day £287 Full Day £549
Special and Wasted Preparation. *Fixed fee under the Order.*	Wasted preparation to apply only as defined in the Order. This includes research on novel facts.	£43	£62	£81
Ineffective Trial Payment. *Fixed fee under the Order.*	A listed trial that does not proceed for any reason.	£143	£215	£310
Sentencing. *Fixed fee under the Order if effective. Non-effective hearing counts as a standard appearance.*	Sentence Hearings Effective Non-effective Deferred Sentence Effective Non-effective	£119 £96 £191 £96	£191 £143 £263 £143	£287 £191 £358 £191
Appeals to the Crown Court Fixed fee under the Order.	Against Sentence Effective Non-effective Against Conviction Effective Non-effective	£119 £96 £143 £96	£167 £143 £215 £143	£239 £191 £287 £191
Proceedings for breach of a Crown Court order *Fixed fee under the Order.*	Effective Non-effective	£119 £96	£167 £143	£239 £191

PART III IN PRACTICE

Category	Comments	Junior	Leading Junior	QC
Committal for sentence *Fixed fee under the Order*	Effective Non-effective	£143 £96	£215 £143	£287 £191
Noting Brief. *Fixed fee under the Order.*		£119	-	-

7 As noted above, scheme 5 operated from 27 April 2010 – 6 February 2011. Scheme 6 marked the transfer of RAGFS processing from HM Courts Service to the Legal Services Commission on 7 February 2011. The rates for schemes 5 and 6 are the same.

Table F: Scheme 4 (30 April 2007 – 26 April 2010)

Category	Comments	Junior	Leading Junior	QC
The trial	The amount paid to the advocate undertaking the trial will be the Total Fee less (a) any sums payable to other advocates for Paid Returned Work apart from the trial, and (b) any sums which the instructed advocate is entitled to deduct for Retained Work.	See adjoining comments column	See adjoining comments column	See adjoining comments column

Category	Comments	Junior	Leading Junior	QC
PCMH *Part of Basic Fee*	The amount paid to the advocate undertaking the PCMH will be the amount shown as 15% of the Basic Fee in table B below, or the guilty plea fee less any sums which the instructed advocate is entitled to deduct for Retained Work if the case pleads at the PCMH	See adjoining comments column	See adjoining comments column	See adjoining comments column
Conferences with clients and experts. Views. *Part Basic Fee, part fixed fee under the Order, depending upon the actual or estimated length of the case.*	The first three conferences are included in the Basic Fee. Separate payment is made for fourth and subsequent conferences only in cases lasting or estimated to last 21 days or more.	£45 per hour	£65 per hour	£85 per hour
Standard appearances. *Standard appearances 1–4 part of Basic Fee, 5+ fixed fee under the Order.*	The first 4 standard appearances are included in the Basic Fee. Separate payment is made for fifth and subsequent standard appearance. They are paid as Paid Returned Work at the rates shown in the adjoining columns	£100	£150	£200

Category	Comments	Junior	Leading Junior	QC
Full and Half Day Hearings for abuse of process, admissibility of evidence, disclosure, and withdrawal of plea of guilty. *Fixed fee under the Order.*		Half Day £150 Full Day £275	Half Day £225 Full Day £400	Half Day £300 Full Day £575
Special and Wasted Preparation. *Fixed fee under the Order.*	Wasted preparation to apply only as defined in the Order. This includes research on novel facts.	£45	£65	£85
Ineffective Trial Payment. *Fixed fee under the Order.*	A listed trial that does not proceed for any reason.	£150	£225	£325
Sentencing. *Fixed fee under the Order if effective. Non-effective hearing counts as a standard appearance.*	Sentence Hearings Effective Non-effective Deferred Sentence Effective Non-effective	£125 £100 £200 £100	£200 £150 £275 £150	£300 £200 £375 £200
Appeals to the Crown Court *Fixed fee under the Order. Fixed fee under the Order.*	Against Sentence Effective Non-effective Against Conviction Effective Non-effective	£125 £100 £150 £100	£175 £150 £225 £150	£250 £200 £300 £200
Proceedings for breach of a Crown Court order *Fixed fee under the Order.*	Effective Non-effective	£125 £100	£175 £150	£250 £200
Committal for sentence *Fixed fee under the Order*	Effective Non-effective	£150 £100	£225 £150	£300 £200

Category	Comments	Junior	Leading Junior	QC
Noting Brief. *Fixed fee under the Order.*		£125	–	–

Annex B: PCMH Fees[8]

[3.139]

Table G: Scheme 9 and 10 (1 April 2012 –) PCMH fees in pounds (£)

Class of offence	QC	Leading Junior	Led Junior	Junior alone
A	428.40	321.30	244.80	244.80
B	379.35	284.55	189.75	195.75
C	295.20	221.40	134.70	134.70
D	342.60	257.10	168.75	168.75
E	227.10	170.40	104.10	97.95
F	227.10	170.40	104.10	104.10
G	227.10	170.40	104.10	104.10
H	285.45	214.05	122.40	122.40
I	318.30	238.80	146.85	146.85
J	428.40	321.30	244.80	244.80
K	428.40	321.30	214.20	244.80

60 for further details.

Table H: Scheme 8 (3 October 2011 – 31 March 2012) PCMH fees in pounds (£)

Class of offence	QC	Leading Junior	Led Junior	Junior alone
A	450.75	337.95	257.55	257.55
B	399.15	299.40	199.50	205.95
C	310.50	232.80	141.75	141.75
D	360.45	270.45	177.45	177.45
E	238.95	179.25	109.50	103.05

Class of offence	QC	Leading Junior	Led Junior	Junior alone
F	238.95	179.25	109.50	109.50
G	238.95	179.25	109.50	109.50
H	300.30	225.30	128.70	128.70
I	334.80	251.10	154.50	154.50
J	450.75	337.95	257.55	257.55
K	450.75	337.95	225.30	257.55

Table I: Scheme 7 (1 April 2011 – 2 October 2011) PCMH fees in pounds (£)

Class of offence	QC	Leading Junior	Led Junior	Junior alone
A	605.25	453.90	302.55	347.70
B	399.15	299.40	199.50	205.95
C	310.50	232.80	141.75	141.75
D	360.45	270.45	177.45	177.45
E	238.95	179.25	109.50	103.05
F	238.95	179.25	109.50	109.50
G	300.30	225.30	150.15	193.20
H	300.30	225.30	128.70	128.70
I	334.80	251.10	154.50	154.50
J	450.75	337.95	257.55	257.55
K	450.75	337.95	225.30	257.55

Table J: Scheme 5 and 6 (27 April 2010 – 31 March 2011)[9] PCMH fees in pounds (£)

Class of offence	QC	Leading Junior	Led Junior	Junior alone
A	635.10	476.25	326.55	364.80
B	418.80	314.10	209.40	216.15
C	325.95	244.35	148.65	148.65
D	378.30	283.80	186.30	186.30
E	250.65	188.10	114.90	108.15
F	250.65	188.10	114.90	114.90
G	315.15	236.40	157.65	202.65

Class of offence	QC	Leading Junior	Led Junior	Junior alone
H	315.15	236.40	135.15	135.15
I	351.45	263.55	162.15	162.15
J	472.95	354.75	270.30	270.30
K	472.95	354.75	236.55	270.30

Table K: Scheme 4 (30 April 2007 – 26 April 2010) PCMH fees in pounds (£)

Class of offence	QC	Leading Junior	Led Junior	Junior alone
A	665.10	498.75	332.55	382.05
B	438.60	328.95	219.30	226.35
C	341.25	255.90	155.70	155.70
D	396.15	297.15	195.00	195.00
E	262.50	196.95	120.30	113.25
F	262.50	196.95	120.30	120.30
G	330.00	247.50	165.00	212.25
H	330.00	247.50	141.45	141.45
I	367.95	276.00	169.80	169.80
J	495.30	371.40	283.05	283.05
K	495.30	371.40	247.65	283.05

PART III IN PRACTICE

Annex C: Terms of work in defence criminal legal aid cases

[3.140]

Dear [XXXX],

Thank you for sending me instructions in the case of [XXXX], which I note is or is likely to paid under the Criminal Legal Aid (Remuneration) Regulations 2013 (the Remuneration Regulations).

It is a term of my acceptance of these instructions that applications for payment under the Remuneration Regulations will be made promptly and in accordance with its terms, and no later than 3 months after the conclusion of the case.

I also accept instructions in this case on the basis that the terms and provisions of the Bar Council's Graduated Fee Payment Protocol (the Protocol) apply and will be enforceable in law.

[XXXX] of [XXXX] chambers ***will be/*is** the instructed advocate. The Protocol provides, amongst other things, that in the event that, subject to my professional client's consent, any advocacy work involved in the case is subcontracted to a substitute advocate(s), the fee or fees for work undertaken by any subcontracted advocate(s) will be claimed, accounted for and distributed in accordance with the Protocol.

A copy of the Protocol ***is attached**, or ***has been provided to you by my clerk**, or ***is available on my chambers/the Bar Council website**.

Yours sincerely,

[XXXX]

Annex D: Chambers fee account

The scheme

[3.141]–[3.142]

The advocates' graduated fee scheme involves creating a chambers fee account. All fees are paid in to the account, rather than to an individual barrister. The chambers administrator(s) reconcile the fees received with the work done and make payments (twice monthly) to each barrister. The scheme allows for detailed record keeping and cross-payments to other chambers.

Steps

1. The chambers' constitution needs to have an enabling provision to cover the scheme and each member should sign to show assent. A suitably worded part of the constitution (or side document) will cover pupils' fees. The constitution needs to ensure that cheques made out to members under the graduated fee scheme can be paid into the chambers fee account and distributed in accordance with the terms of the protocol. Arrangements need to be made for pupil's fees to be paid and dealt with under the protocol and distributed through the chambers fee Account. One form of amendment to a fairly standard chambers constitution is as follows:

   Chambers may operate such fees accounts and systems as are reasonable or efficient for the business – and may require members remuneration to be paid into fees accounts and hold such monies for dispersal to members, or other advocates, including pupils.

   Chambers may deduct from any funds received to chambers any monies outstanding to chambers (including expenses, surcharges and contingency funds and any debts that chambers may have incurred for on or behalf of members, or other advocates for whom the fees are held) before release of any net proceeds to members

   Chambers may hold the property of any members or any interest in chambers property, until any sums due and owing to chambers are discharged. Any disputes as to sums owed shall be dealt with by the grievance procedure.

2. Chambers must notify all paymasters of its intention to create a dedicated fees account (the fees account) and supply them with the account details.

3. Each member of chambers must supply their bank account details to the chambers administrator.

4. At the outset, the bank is likely to require one copy of the chambers' constitution which contains details of the fees accounting system. It ought not to require any additional mandate thereafter. The account is both for payments in and out.

5. Payments are made from the fees account to individual barristers twice monthly. These payments are net of payments due to other barristers, chambers contributions and incidentals. On request, the VAT can be held back so that it remains available to be paid at the end of the quarter.

6. The date of cross-payments will appear as the remittance date.

7. Payments to and from other chambers and higher court advocates should be made by direct transfer from one fee account to the other fee account. In order to achieve this, each chambers should open a fee account as described in this document. Details would have to be exchanged with other organisations, thereby allowing payments to be made and received between chambers.

8. Fees accounts should not become overdrawn. Payments out should only be made from cleared funds.

9. If under chambers constitutional arrangements chambers charges or expenses are to be deducted from funds in the fees account, deductions should only be made in respect of the correct amount due from sums held to the credit of individual members of chambers or other advocates.

10. Reference should be made to the VAT advice contained in Annex F. In short, the tax point arises on receipt of money into the chambers fee account and not on payment out to the barrister concerned.

Annex E: Examples of depleted basic fees

[3.143]

The examples below are of a two-day Class E trial conducted by a sole junior. The Basic Fee includes:

- the PCMH
- all conferences and views
- up to four standard appearances (SAF) as defined in Schedule 1, paragraph 1 of the Remuneration Regulations.

The Basic Fee (BF) for the trial is £653

70 per cent of the Basic Fee (BF) is £457

30 per cent of the BF is £195

15 per cent of the BF (the PCMH fee or value) is £97

Example 1

A substitute advocate (SA) conducts one SAF; the instructed advocate (IA) conducts the PCMH and trial.

Advocate	Hearing	Cost	
	30% of BF	£195.00	minus
Instructed advocate	PCMH	£97.00	minus
Substitute advocate	SAF	£87.00	
	Balance	*£11.00*	

*Due to the balance being **greater** than £0.00 the SA's fee is paid out of the instructed advocate's BF.*

Basic Fee Cost Breakdown

Instructed advocate	BF	£653.00	minus
Instructed advocate	PCMH	£97.00	minus
Substitute advocate	SAF	£87.00	
Instructed advocate	**Trial**	**£469.00**	

Example 2

SA conducts two SAFs; the IA conducts the PCMH and trial.

Advocate	Hearing	Cost	
	30% of BF	£195.00	minus
Instructed advocate	PCMH	£97.00	minus
Substitute advocate	SAF	£87.00	minus
Substitute advocate	SAF	£87.00	
	Balance	*-£76.00*	

*Due to the balance being **less** than £0.00 the fees are reduced using the "Depleted Basic Fee" rule*

Depleted Basic Fee Rule

Substitute advocate	SAF	£87.00	
Substitute advocate	SAF	£87.00	
	Substitute Total	£174.00	
Instructed advocate	Trial (@ 70%)	£457.00	
Instructed advocate	PCMH	£97.00	
	Total	£728.00	minus

Depleted Basic Fee Rule

	BF	£653.00
	Excess	*£75.00*
Excess as a proportion of Total		10.30%
Percentage rate payable of each fee		89.70%

Allocation of Amounts		**Fee**	**Paid**
Substitute advocate	SAF	£87.00	£78.00
Substitute advocate	SAF	£87.00	£78.00
Instructed advocate	Trial (@ 70%)	£457.00	£410.00
Instructed advocate	PCMH	£97.00	£87.00
	Total	£728.00	£653.00

Example 3

SA conducts the PCMH and a SAF; the IA conducts the trial.

Advocate	**Hearing**	**Cost**	
	30% of BF	£195.00	minus
Substitute Advocate	PCMH	£97.00	minus
Substitute Advocate	SAF	£87.00	
	Balance	*£11.00*	

Due to the balance being ***greater*** *than £0.00 the SA's fee is paid out of the instructed advocate's BF.*

Fees' Breakdown

Instructed advocate	BF	£653.00	minus
Substitute advocate	PCMH	£97.00	minus
Substitute advocate	SAF	£87.00	
Instructed advocate	**Trial**	**£469.00**	

Example 4

SA conducts three SAFs; the IA conducts the PCMH and trial.

PART III
IN PRACTICE

Advocate	Hearing	Cost	
	30% of BF	£195.00	minus
Instructed advocate	PCMH	£97.00	minus
Substitute advocate	SAF	£87.00	minus
Substitute advocate	SAF	£87.00	minus
Substitute advocate	SAF	£87.00	
	Balance	*-£163.00*	

Due to the balance being **less** *than £0.00 the fees are reduced using the "Depleted Basic Fee" rule*

Depleted Basic Fee Rule

Substitute advocate	SAF	£87.00	
Substitute advocate	SAF	£87.00	
Substitute advocate	SAF	£87.00	
	Substitute Total	£261.00	
Instructed advocate	Trial (@ 70%)	£457.00	
Instructed advocate	PCMH	£87.00	
	Total	£805.00	minus
	BF	£653.00	
	Excess	*£152.00*	
Excess as a proportion of Total		*18.88%*	
Percentage rate payable of each fee		*81.12%*	

Allocation of Amounts		Fee	Paid
Substitute advocate	SAF	£87.00	**£71.00**
Substitute advocate	SAF	£87.00	**£71.00**
Substitute advocate	SAF	£87.00	**£71.00**
Instructed advocate	Trial (@ 70%)	£457.00	**£370.00**
Instructed advocate	PCMH	£97.00	**£78.00**
	Total	£815.00	**£661.00**

Example 5

SA conducts PCMH and three SAFs; IA conducts the trial.

Advocate	**Hearing**	**Cost**	
	30% OF BF	£195.00	minus
Substitute advocate	PCMH	£97.00	minus
Substitute advocate	SAF	£87.00	minus
Substitute advocate	SAF	£87.00	minus
Substitute advocate	SAF	£87.00	
	Balance	*-£163.00*	

*Due to the balance being **less** than £0.00 the fees are reduced using the "Depleted Basic Fee" rule **Depleted Basic Fee Rule***

Depleted Basic Fee Rule

Substitute advocate	PCMH	£97.00	
Substitute advocate	SAF	£87.00	
Substitute advocate	SAF	£87.00	
Substitute advocate	SAF	£87.00	
	Substitute Total	£358.00	
Instructed advocate	Trial (@ 70%)	£457.00	
	Total	£815.00	minus
	BF	£653.00	
	Excess	*£162.00*	
Excess as a proportion of Total		19.88%	
Percentage rate payable of each fee		80.12%	

Allocation of Amounts		Fee	Paid
Substitute advocate	PCMH	£97.00	**£77.00**
Substitute advocate	SAF	£87.00	**£70.00**
Substitute advocate	SAF	£87.00	**£70.00**
Substitute advocate	SAF	£87.00	**£70.00**
Instructed advocate	Trial (@ 70%)	£457.00	**£366.00**
	Total	£815.00	**£653.00**

Example 6

SA conducts the PCMH and four SAFs; IA conducts trial.

PART III
IN PRACTICE

Advocate	Hearing	Cost	
	30% of BF	£195.00	minus
Substitute advocate	PCMH	£97.00	minus
Substitute advocate	SAF	£87.00	minus
Substitute advocate	SAF	£87.00	minus
Substitute advocate	SAF	£87.00	minus
Substitute advocate	SAF	£87.00	
	Balance	*-£250.00*	

Due to the balance being **less** *than £0.00 the fees are reduced using the "Depleted Basic Fee" rule* ***Depleted Basic Fee Rule***

Depleted Basic Fee Rule

Substitute advocate	PCMH	£97.00	
Substitute advocate	SAF	£87.00	
Substitute advocate	SAF	£87.00	
Substitute advocate	SAF	£87.00	
Substitute advocate	SAF	£87.00	
	Substitute Total	£445.00	
Instructed advocate	Trial (@ 70%)	£457.00	
	Total	£902.00	minus
	BF	£653.00	
	Excess	*£249.00*	

Excess as a proportion of Total	27.61%
Percentage rate payable of each fee	72.39%

Allocation of Amounts		Fee	Paid
Substitue advocate	PCMH	£97.00	**£70.00**
Substitute advocate	SAF	£87.00	**£63.00**
Substitute advocate	SAF	£87.00	**£63.00**
Substitute advocate	SAF	£87.00	**£63.00**
Substitute advocate	SAF	£87.00	**£63.00**
Instructed advocate	Trial (@ 70%)	£457.00	**£331.00**
	Total	£902.00	**£653.00**

Example 7

SA conducts the PCMH and five, SAFs; IA conducts the trial

Advocate	Hearing	Cost	
	30% of BF	£195.00	plus
	SAF 5	£87.00	
	Total	**£282.00**	minus
Substitute advocate	PCMH	£97.00	minus
Substitute advocate	SAF 1	£87.00	minus
Substitute advocate	SAF 2	£87.00	minus
Substitute advocate	SAF 3	£87.00	minus
Substitute advocate	SAF 4	£87.00	minus
Substitute advocate	SAF 5	£87.00	
	Balance	*-£268.00*	

Due to the balance being ***less*** *than £0.00 the fees are reduced using the "Depleted Basic Fee" rule*

Depleted Basic Fee Rule

	BF	£653.00	
	SAF 5	£87.00	
	Total	**£740.00**	
Substitute advocate	PCMH	£97.00	
Substitute advocate	SAF 1	£87.00	
Substitute advocate	SAF 2	£87.00	
Substitute advocate	SAF 3	£87.00	
Substitute advocate	SAF 4	£87.00	
Substitute advocate	SAF 5	£87.00	
	Substitute Total	£550.00	
Instructed advocate	Trial (@ 70%)	£457.00	
	Total	£1,007.00	minus
	Total Fee	£740.00	
	Excess	*£267.00*	

Excess as a proportion of Total	25.51%
Percentage rate payable of each fee	73.49%

PART III
IN PRACTICE

Allocation of Amounts		Value	Paid
Substitute advocate	PCMH	£97.00	**£71.00**
Substitute advocate	SAF 1	£87.00	**£64.00**
Substitute advocate	SAF 2	£87.00	**£64.00**
Substitute advocate	SAF 3	£87.00	**£64.00**
Substitute advocate	SAF 4	£87.00	**£64.00**
Substitute advocate	SAF 5	£87.00	**£64.00**
Instructed advocate	Trial (@ 70%)	£457.00	**£336.00**
	Total	£989.00	**£727.00**

Annex F: Extract from HMRC guidance on VAT records

[3.144]

1. HMRC have issued guidance on VAT, Notice 700, which is available to download from the HMRC website. Paragraph 19.2 states:

   You must keep records and accounts of all taxable goods and services which you receive or supply in the course of your business. This includes:

   - standard-rated;
   - reduced-rated; and
   - zero-rated supplies.

   You must also keep records of any exempt supplies that you make.

   In addition, you must keep a summary of the totals of your input tax and output tax for each tax period. This is called a VAT account (see paragraph 19.12).

   All these records must be kept up to date and must be in sufficient detail to allow you to calculate correctly the amount of VAT that you have to pay to, or can claim from, HM Revenue and Customs.

   You do not have to keep these records in any set way. But they must be kept in a way which will enable our officers to check easily the figures that you have used to fill in your VAT return. If your records do not satisfy the requirements set out in this notice, we have the power to direct you to make the necessary changes.

   However you decide to keep your records, you must be able to make them readily available to our officers when they ask to see them.

Advice received on VAT treatment

2. Annex D of the Protocol deals with the chambers fee account into which all fees are paid and distributed by the chambers administrator twice monthly.

3. VAT Regulations 1995 SI 1995/2518, regulation 92 governs the time of supply for supplies of services by barristers and advocates. This regulation

does not relate to any other business activity (to which the normal tax point rules apply as per Notice 700 The VAT Guide) apart from advocacy.

4. Regulation 92 provides:

"Services supplied by a barrister, or in Scotland by an advocate, acting in that capacity, shall be treated as taking place at whichever is the earliest of the following times:

(a) when the fee in respect of those services is received by the barrister or advocate;

(b) when the barrister or advocate issues a tax invoice in respect of them; or

(c) the day when the barrister or advocate ceases to practice as such."

5. The expectation therefore is that for the instructed advocate who issues a "request for payment fee note" to Legal Aid Agency (rather than a tax invoice), the tax point will, as now, continue to be triggered by receipt of the legal aid payment. It is important to note that for chambers operating a fees account, "received" for the purposes of regulation 92 will be the time the payment is received into the fees account, as opposed to the time of the bi-monthly payment to individual barristers.

6. For the substitute advocate, who issues an invoice to the instructed advocate, the time of the substitute advocate's supply to the instructed advocate will be the earlier of receipt of payment or issue of a VAT invoice.

7. Note that regulation 92 only extends to barristers. Solicitors are therefore subject to normal tax point rules.

8. Under the protocol, solicitor instructed advocates must treat the substitute advocate element of any legal aid payments as "client monies and account for them as such". However, the tax point for VAT purposes will be created by the receipt of that payment in the normal way. In other words, the normal practice of disregarding payments into client's accounts will not be appropriate in these circumstances.

Annex G: Email notification to Crown Court centres of the identity of the instructed advocate

Introduction

[3.144a]–[3.151]

1. Schedule 1, paragraph 25(1) of the Criminal Legal Aid (Remuneration) Regulations 2013 (the Remuneration Regulations) requires written notification of the identity of the instructed advocate to the court before the PCMH.

2. If the identity of the instructed advocate is not provided, schedule 1, paragraphs 25(2), 25(3) and 25(4) of the Remuneration Regulations provides that the person who attends the PCMH will be recorded as the instructed advocate. If no barrister or solicitor advocate attends the PCMH then the barrister or solicitor advocate who attends the next hearing will be deemed to be the instructed advocate.

3. Schedule 1, paragraph 25(6) provides that where a representation order is amended after the PCMH an additional advocate must notify the court in writing of their appointment within seven days of the date on which the order is amended. Each instructed advocate must notify the court whether they are the leading instructed advocate or the led instructing advocate.

4. Schedule 1, paragraph 25(7) states that where no notification is given in accordance with paragraph 25(6), the advocate who attends the next hearing will be deemed to be an instructed advocate and the court will record whether they are the leading instructed advocate or the led instructed advocate, as appropriate to the circumstances of the case.

5. This protocol governs written notification and establishes standard delivery arrangements for those wishing to email the notification. The attached list gives the email address for each Crown Court Centre. **These are not secure email addresses**. Those able and wishing to use secure email should add **cjsm.net** to the end of the listed email address for the court.

Protocol

6. Notifications must be sent to the court's 'enquiries' box (shown in the attached address list).

7. Every email notification must have the heading 'Instructed Advocate Notification' and should show the date of the PCMH.

8. The email message must contain the name, telephone number and email address of the sender and should be in plain text or rich text format rather than HTML.

9. It is permissible for notification to be made on behalf of an instructed advocate but the person making the notification must state the capacity in which it is made (e.g. barrister's clerk, another member of the solicitor advocate's firm).

10. To enable the court to identify the correct defendant/case and avoid the need for the notification to be rejected, the email must include:

    - the case number;
    - the full name of the represented defendant;
    - the full name of the instructed advocate;
    - the name and telephone number of the person taking responsibility for the notification;
    - if notification is made on behalf of another, the capacity in which it is made;
    - chambers/firm name and address.

11. The notification is limited to identifying the instructed advocate and any additional information, such as listing information, will not be processed.

12. A separate email notification must be sent for each represented defendant even if the same instructed advocate represents more than one defendant in a multi-handed case.

13. The notification sender must set up the email to give an automatic 'delivery receipt' if they require confirmation of receipt. This will be the only form of acknowledgement.

14. The notification must be received in the correct email box at the correct court before the PCMH or, in the case of an additional instructed advocate, seven days after the date on which the representation order is amended. Otherwise, the advocate who attends the PCMH will be recorded as the instructed advocate. In the case of an additional instructed advocate, where no notification is given within the seven day period, then the advocate who attends the next hearing will be deemed to be an instructed advocate and the court will record whether they are the leading instructed advocate or the led instructed advocate

15. The notifying party is responsible for ensuring that the email transmission is filed within the relevant time limit. An email transmission must be received by the court by 16:00 the day before the PCMH in order to be accepted as being received on that day.

16. The date and time of notification will be the date and time the email is received in the correct email box at the correct court. The time of receipt of a transmission will be recorded electronically on the transmission as it is received. If a transmission is received after 16:00 the day before the PCMH the transmission will be treated as received on the next day the court office is open.

17. The notification sender cannot ask for the email to take effect from a day/time earlier than the day/time it was received in the correct email box at the correct court.

18. An email received by the court before the PMCH will be deemed to be the notification even if not opened until after the PCMH.

19. The email notification will be assumed by the court to be accurate. Any error in notification will be an issue internal to the chambers/solicitor's firm.

20. This protocol is for instructed advocates wishing to use email. Courts can also accept notification by letter.

Crown Court Centre email addresses

Display Name	Email Address
Aylesbury Crown, Enquiries	enquiries@aylesbury.crowncourt.gsi.gov.uk
Basildon Crown Ct, Enquiries	enquiries@basildon.crowncourt.gsi.gov.uk
Birmingham Crown, Enquiries	enquiries@birmingham.crowncourt.gsi.gov.uk
Blackfriars Crown, Enquiries	enquiries@blackfriars.crowncourt.gsi.gov.uk
Bolton Crown, Enquiries	enquiries@bolton.crowncourt.gsi.gov.uk
Bournemouth Crown, Enquiries	enquiries@bournemouth.crowncourt.gsi.gov.uk
Bradford Crown, Enquiries	enquiries@bradford.crowncourt.gsi.gov.uk
Bristol Crown, Enquiries	enquiries@bristol.crowncourt.gsi.gov.uk

Display Name	Email Address
Burnley Crown, Enquiries	enquiries@burnley.crowncourt.gsi.gov.uk
Cambridge Crown, Enquiries	enquiries@cambridge.crowncourt.gsi.gov.uk
Canterbury Crown, Enquiries	enquiries@canterbury.crowncourt.gsi.gov.uk
Cardiff Crown, Enquiries	enquiries@cardiff.crowncourt.gsi.gov.uk
Carlisle Crown Crt, Enquiries	enquiries@carlisle.crowncourt.gsi.gov.uk
Central Criminal Court	enquiries@central.crowncourt.gsi.gov.uk
Chelmsford Crown Court, Enquiries	enquiries@chelmsford.crowncourt.gsi.gov.uk
Chester Crown, Enquiries	enquiries@chester.crowncourt.gsi.gov.uk
Chichester Crown, Enquiries	enquiries@chichester.crowncourt.gsi.gov.uk
Coventry Crown, Enquiries	enquiries@coventry.crowncourt.gsi.gov.uk
Croydon Crown, Enquiries	enquiries@croydon.crowncourt.gsi.gov.uk
Derby Crown, Enquiries	enquiries@derby.crowncourt.gsi.gov.uk
Doncaster Crown, Enquiries	enquiries@doncaster.crowncourt.gsi.gov.uk
Dorchester Crown, Enquiries	enquiries@dorchester.crowncourt.gsi.gov.uk
Durham Crown Court, Enquiries	enquiries@durham.crowncourt.gsi.gov.uk
Exeter Crn, Enquiries	enquiries@exeter.crowncourt.gsi.gov.uk
Gloucester Crn, Enquiries	enquiries@gloucester.crowncourt.gsi.gov.uk
Grimsby Crown, Enquiries	enquiries@grimsby.crowncourt.gsi.gov.uk
Guildford Crown, Enquiries	enquiries@guildford.crowncourt.gsi.gov.uk
Harrow Crown, Enquiries	enquiries@harrow.crowncourt.gsi.gov.uk
Hull Crown, Enquiries	enquiries@kingstonuponhull.crowncourt.gsi.gov.uk
Inner London Crown, Enquiries	enquiries@innerlondon.crowncourt.gsi.gov.uk
Ipswich Crown, Enquiries	enquiries@ipswich.crowncourt.gsi.gov.uk
Isleworth Crown, Enquiries	enquiries@isleworth.crowncourt.gsi.gov.uk
Kingston Crown, Enquiries	enquiries@kingstonuponthames.crowncourt.gsi.gov.uk
Leeds Crn, Enquiries	enquiries@leeds.crowncourt.gsi.gov.uk
Leicester Crown, Enquiries	enquiries@leicester.crowncourt.gsi.gov.uk
Lewes Crown Crt, Enquiries	enquiries@lewes.crowncourt.gsi.gov.uk
Lincoln Crown, Enquiries	enquiries@lincoln.crowncourt.gsi.gov.uk
Liverpool Combined Court, Enquiries	enquiries@liverpool.crowncourt.gsi.gov.uk
Luton Crown, Enquiries	enquiries@luton.crowncourt.gsi.gov.uk
Maidstone Crown, Enquiries	enquiries@maidstone.crowncourt.gsi.gov.uk
Manchester Crown, Enquiries	enquiries@manchester.crowncourt.gsi.gov.uk
Merthyr Tydfil Crown, Enquiries	enquiries@merthyrtydfil.crowncourt.gsi.gov.uk

Display Name	**Email Address**
Middlesex Guildhall Crown, Enquiries	enquiries@middlesexguildhall.crowncourt.gsi.gov.uk
Minshull St Crown, Enquiries	enquiries@manchesterminshullstreet.crowncourt.gsi.gov.uk
Mold Crown, Enquires	enquiries@mold.crowncourt.gsi.gov.uk
Newcastle Crown, Enquiries	enquiries@newcastle.crowncourt.gsi.gov.uk
Newport (Gwent) Crown, Enquiries	enquires@newport-southwales.crowncourt.gsi.gov.uk
Newport (IOW) Crown, Enquiries	enquiries@newportiow.crowncourt.gsi.gov.uk
Northampton Crown, Enquiries	enquiries@northampton.crowncourt.gsi.gov.uk
Norwich Crown, Enquiries	enquiries@norwich.crowncourt.gsi.gov.uk
Nottingham Crown, Enquiries	enquiries@nottingham.crowncourt.gsi.gov.uk
Oxford Crown, Enquiries	enquiries@oxford.crowncourt.gsi.gov.uk
Peterborough Crown, Enquiries	enquiries@peterborough.crowncourt.gsi.gov.uk
Plymouth Crn, Enquiries	enquiries@plymouth.crowncourt.gsi.gov.uk
Portsmouth Crown Crt, Enquiries	enquiries@portsmouth.crowncourt.gsi.gov.uk
Preston Crown, Enquiries	enquiries@preston.crowncourt.gsi.gov.uk
Reading Crown Court, Enquiries	enquiries@reading.crowncourt.gsi.gov.uk
Salisbury Crown, Enquiries	enquiries@salisbury.crowncourt.gsi.gov.uk
Sheffield Crown, Enquiries	enquiries@sheffield.crowncourt.gsi.gov.uk
Shrewsbury Crown, Enquiries	enquiries@shrewsbury.crowncourt.gsi.gov.uk
Snaresbrook Crown Ct, Enquiries	enquiries@snaresbrook.crowncourt.gsi.gov.uk
Southampton Crn, Enquiries	enquiries@southampton.crowncourt.gsi.gov.uk
Southwark Crown, Enquiries	enquiries@southwark.crowncourt.gsi.gov.uk
St Albans Crown, Enquiries	enquiries@stalbans.crowncourt.gsi.gov.uk
Stafford Crown, Enquiries	enquiries@stafford.crowncourt.gsi.gov.uk
Stoke on Trent Crown, Enquiries	enquiries@stoke.crowncourt.gsi.gov.uk
Swansea Crown, Enquiries	enquiries@swansea.crowncourt.gsi.gov.uk
Swindon Crown, Enquiries	enquiries@swindon.crowncourt.gsi.gov.uk
Taunton Crown, Enquiries	enquiries@taunton.crowncourt.gsi.gov.uk
Teesside Crown Crt, Enquiries	enquiries@teesside.crowncourt.gsi.gov.uk
Truro Crown Court, Enquiries	enquiries@truro.crowncourt.gsi.gov.uk
Warwick Crown, Enquiries	enquiries@warwick.crowncourt.gsi.gov.uk

Display Name	Email Address
Winchester Crown, Enquiries	enquiries@winchester.crowncourt.gsi.gov.uk
Wolverhampton Crown Ct, Enquiries	enquiries@wolverhampton.crowncourt.gsi.gov.uk
Wood Green Crown, Enquiries	enquiries@woodgreen.crowncourt.gsi.gov.uk
Woolwich Crn, Enquiries	enquiries@woolwich.crowncourt.gsi.gov.uk
Worcester Crown, Enquiries	enquiries@worcester.crowncourt.gsi.gov.uk
York Crown, Enquiries	enquiries@york.crowncourt.gsi.gov.uk

[3.152]

Since the issue of the Graduated Fee Payment Protocol in 2007, specific issues have arisen in relation to hearings sent for trial in the Crown Court pursuant to s 51 of the Crime and Disorder Act 1998 (related to (i) payment for attendance at such hearings in the Magistrates' Court and (ii) whether a case so sent for trial should be remunerated as a 'standard appearance fee' under the Funding Order) as well as in relation to payment for breach of bail hearings. The Bar Council has therefore issued the following guidance in April 2008 to complement the Fee Payment Protocol:

Revised Advocates Graduated Fee Scheme: Section 51 and Bail Hearings

1. Two issues have arisen in relation to fees payable in respect of hearings where an indictable only offence is sent for trial in the Crown Court, pursuant to section 51 of the Crime and Disorder Act 1998 ("section 51"). A third issue has arisen in relation to remuneration for a hearing in respect of a breach of bail granted by the Crown Court.
2. The first issue concerns payment for attendance at the section 51 hearing in the Magistrates' Court.
3. The second issue is whether the first hearing in the Crown Court in respect of a case sent for trial under section 51 falls to be remunerated as a "standard appearance" under the Funding Order.
4. The third issue is whether a breach of Crown Court bail hearing in the magistrates' court falls to be remunerated out of the Revised Advocates' Graduated Fee Scheme (RAGFS) and if so, at what rate.

Issue 1: the section 51 hearing in the magistrates' court

[3.153]

5. Article 2 of the Funding Order states (so far as is relevant):

"**Interpretation**

2. In this Order—

'advocate' means a barrister, a solicitor advocate or a solicitor who is exercising their automatic rights of audience in the Crown Court;"

6. Article 5 of the Funding Order states (so far as is relevant):

"5.—(1) Claims for fees by an instructed advocate in proceedings in the Crown Court must be made and determined in accordance with the provisions of Schedule 1 to this Order."

7. Article 6 of the Funding Order states (so far as is relevant):

"6.—(1) Claims for fees by litigators in proceedings in the Crown Court must be made and determined in accordance with the provisions of Schedule 2 to this Order."

8. Article 12(1) of the Funding Order (as amended by The Criminal Defence Service (Funding) (Amendment) Order 2007 S.I. 3552 states:

"**Indictable-only offences**

12.—(1) Where a case is sent for trial to the Crown Court under section 51 of the Crime and Disorder Act 1998(**a**) (No committal proceedings for indictable-only offences), the payment in relation to work carried out in the magistrates' court is included within the applicable fee payable under Schedule 1 or Schedule 2."

9. Schedule 1 relates to the Advocates' Graduated Fee Scheme (AGFS) and Schedule 2 relates to the Litigators' Graduated Fee Scheme (LGFS). Article 12 makes it plain that the applicable fee is payable **either** under Schedule 1 **or** under Schedule 2 and therefore not under both.

10. The Bar Council has discussed this issue with the Legal Services Commission (LSC). The reference to Schedule 2 is for the usual circumstances where a solicitor prepares for and attends the section 51 hearing in the magistrates' court. The remuneration is part of the litigators' graduated fee. The LGFS is intended to cover the **whole** of the litigators work in the Magistrates' Court, both preparation and any hearings.

11. It was made clear in the LGFS consultation that the litigators' graduated fee includes the section 51 hearing in the magistrates court:

The Litigator Graduated Fee Scheme: A Response to Consultation, October 2007, http://www.legalservices.gov.uk/docs/cds_main/LGFS-responseto consultation_Oct07.pdf

"Committal Hearings and Sent Cases

4.20. Cases that are transferred under Section 51 contain an element for payment for the transfer within the proposed LGFS. All other committal (and similar) proceedings will continue to be remunerated in the Magistrates' Court."

See also the LSC website the Litigator Graduated Fee Scheme Guidance. Re-Issued 14 March which states: http://www.legalservices.gov.uk/criminal/litigator_graduated_fee_scheme.asp

"5.1.1 Committal for trial payments is separate to the LGFS and remains in the Magistrates' Courts. Payment for section 51 cases that are sent for trial in the Crown Court is included in the LGFS base fees."

Also on the LSC website (same web-link) is the LSC Q&A document of 10 January:

"What about section 51's. Will they be part and parcel of the litigator's fee scheme?

Yes – the LGFS fees include payments for section 51 hearings."

12. The Bar Council understands that the reference in Article 12 to Schedule 1 was intended to cover cases in which the Magistrates' Court grants a Representation Order for an "advocate" to appear in the Magistrates' Court: see Criminal Defence Service (General) (No.2) Regulations 2001, Reg. 12 as amended (*Archbold* 6–163 & supplement).

13. The logical basis for the distinction is that:

If the Magistrates' Court grants a Representation Order for an advocate, then a barrister or solicitor advocate appearing at the section 51 hearing appears qua "advocate". The Representation Order will provide both for an advocate and a solicitor. In these circumstances, the fee for the advocate should properly come from the AGFS and the fee for the solicitor should come from the LGFS.

On the other hand, if the Magistrates' Court has not granted a Representation Order for an advocate, then any barrister or solicitor advocate appearing in the Magistrates' Court does not appear qua "advocate" but as agent for the solicitor/litigator. In the normal course of events, if a solicitor instructs non-assigned counsel to appear in the Magistrates' Court, counsel appears as agent for the solicitor and is entitled to be paid out of the solicitors fees. The same must be true of a non-assigned solicitor advocate. It follows that if the litigator instructs a non-assigned barrister or solicitor advocate to conduct the section 51 hearing in the Magistrates' Court, the barrister /solicitor advocate is instructed as agent of (and in substitution for) the litigator – and the fee should properly come from the LGFS

14. There is no proper basis under the RAGFS scheme for the solicitor conducting the section 51 hearing in the magistrates' court to purport to do so as a Substitute Advocate, as none would be required. The solicitor is able to conduct that hearing as a litigator and is intended to be remunerated under Schedule 2 (LGFS).

Issue 2: the section 51 hearing in the Crown Court

[3.154]

15. Fees under RAGFS are only payable to "advocates" as defined in Article 2 of the Funding Order (see above), namely a barrister or a solicitor with rights of audience for that hearing.

16. A solicitor has a right of audience for a section 51 hearing in the Crown Court.

17. Schedule 1, Part 1 of the Funding Order states (so far as is relevant):

"Advocates Graduated Fee Scheme
PART 1
Definitions and Scope
Interpretation
1.(1) In this Schedule—

"standard appearance" means an appearance by the trial advocate or substitute advocate in any of the following hearings which do not form part of the main hearing—

(a) a plea and case management hearing, except the first plea and case management hearing;

(b) a pre-trial review;

(c) he hearing of a case listed for plea which is adjourned for trial;

(d) any hearing (except a trial, a plea and case management hearing, a pre-trial review or a hearing referred to in paragraph 2(1)(b)) which is listed but cannot proceed because of the failure of the assisted person or a witness to attend, the unavailability of a pre-sentence report or other good reason;

(e) custody time limit applications;

(f) bail and other applications (except where any such applications take place in the course of a hearing referred to in paragraph 2(1)(b)); or

(g) the hearing of the case listed for mention only, including applications relating to the date of the trial (except where an application takes place in the course of a hearing referred to in paragraph 2(1)(b)),

provided that a fee is not payable elsewhere under this Schedule in respect of the hearing;"

Fees for plea and case management hearings and standard appearances

9.—(1) The fee payable in respect of—

(a) an appearance by the trial advocate or substitute advocate at the first plea and case management hearing or pre-trial review; and

(b) up to four standard appearances by the trial advocate or substitute advocate, is included within the basic fee (B) specified in paragraph 5 as appropriate to the offence for which the assisted person is tried and the category of trial advocate.

PART III IN PRACTICE

(2) The fee payable in respect of an appearance by the trial advocate or substitute advocate at a plea and case management hearing or standard appearance not included in sub-paragraph (1) is specified in the Table following paragraph 19 as appropriate to the category of trial advocate or substitute advocate.

(3) The fee payable for preparing and filing the plea and case management questionnaire where no oral hearing takes place is specified in the Table following paragraph 19 as appropriate to the category of trial advocate or substitute advocate.

(4) This paragraph does not apply to a standard appearance which is or forms part of the main hearing in a case or to a hearing for which a fee is payable elsewhere under this Schedule."

18. A section 51 hearing in the Crown Court falls within the definition of a "standard appearance" and falls to be remunerated as such where it is conducted by an "advocate" as defined in Regulation 2.

19. In many cases, a section 51 hearing will be unnecessary in view of the standard directions given in the magistrates' court. Alternatively, such a hearing could take place electronically.

Issue 3: breach of Crown Court bail hearings in the magistrates' court

[3.155]

20. An alleged breach of bail granted by the Crown Court is ordinarily held in the magistrates' court (section 7 of the Bail Act 1976).

21. Under the old Graduated Fee Scheme, this was paid for as a Crown Court matter.

22. Such a hearing does relate to proceedings in the Crown Court and falls to be remunerated under RAGFS.

23. Such a hearing will constitute a Standard Appearance under RAGFS. The Remuneration Committee has been asked to consider whether the fee for such a hearing ought to be at the Crown Court rate (i.e. £100) or at a lesser rate. The LSC has drawn the Bar Council's attention to a Costs Judge's decision that for fees purposes such a hearing should be treated as if it had taken place in the Crown Court. Further, the LSC's Graduated Fee Scheme Guidance document April 2007 states:

"L. Standard and Other Appearance Fee.

L4 The fee is also paid for bail applications, custody time limit applications, mentions and any other applications including applications relating to date of trial subject to the conditions set out in paragraph B7 ante. R v Bailey (X16)

L4A The fee for any bail application or Bench Warrant executed in the Magistrates' Court after the Crown Court is seized of the case is remunerated as if it had been heard in the Crown Court subject to the conditions set out in paragraph B7 ante. See also H11 ante."

24. Accordingly, the fee payable is the Crown Court fee as set out in the Protocol, namely £100.

[3.156]

In January 2009, the Bar Council issued further clarificatory guidance in relation to breach of bail hearings as well as preliminary hearings in the Crown Court:

Confiscation in Graduated Fee Cases: Protocol for Counsel

[3.157]

During 2008, the Bar Council became aware of particular issues in relation to counsel instructed in a criminal matters on behalf of someone who might or might not subsequently become involved in confiscation proceedings if convicted. The following guidance, issued in August of that year, sets out a Protocol aimed at dealing of issues of acceptance of instructions in such situations (also covered in Part III, Section 1) and remuneration for such work:

Introduction to the Protocol

[3.158]

1. This is the Bar Council's Guidance Note and Protocol for counsel who are instructed in a criminal matter on behalf of a person who will or may be involved in confiscation proceedings if convicted.

General Principles

[3.159]

2. A barrister who unconditionally accepts instructions to represent a lay client in criminal proceedings may be expected to conduct all aspects of the case, including any resulting confiscation proceedings. Phrases such as "Brief for Trial" or "Brief for the Defence" are understood by general usage to mean that the barrister is accepting all aspects of the case covered by the Representation Order.

3. A barrister must not accept instructions if he lacks sufficient experience and competence to handle the matter in question. Where a barrister is instructed 'generally' as in paragraph 2 above this experience and competence will apply to all parts of the case, including such confiscation issues as may be reasonably anticipated to arise at the time of accepting the instructions.

4. Where it is anticipated that complex confiscation proceedings will or might follow a conviction in an otherwise straightforward contested trial or plea, instructions should be refused unless:

   a. counsel has sufficient experience and expertise to conduct the anticipated complex confiscation proceedings; or

   b. counsel is instructed only to conduct the trial and sentence hearing (if any) and the areas to be covered by such limited instructions are within counsel's experience and competence.

5. Where junior counsel accepts instructions in a case which is apparently within his expertise and competence, and subsequently become aware that complex confiscations issues will or are likely to arise which are outwith his expertise and competence, he should:

   a. notify his instructing solicitor immediately that he will be professionally embarrassed if he undertakes any confiscation work in the case, and therefore will not undertake such work;

   b. indicate to his instructing solicitor that he can continue to represent the lay client, provided his instructions are limited to the conduct of the trial and sentencing hearing (if any);

   c. offer to withdraw from the case forthwith if required by his solicitor or lay client to do so.

6. For the avoidance of doubt, counsel who is professionally embarrassed and withdraws from undertaking confiscation proceedings because it is anticipated that such proceedings are beyond his expertise or competence, will not thereby offend against the principles set out in *R v Ulcay* [2007] EWCA Crim 2379, [2008] 1 All ER 547, [2008] 1 WLR 1209, CA. Counsel should be aware of both the potential existence and the anticipated complexity of confiscation proceedings long before the relevant confiscation hearings begin.

Remuneration

[3.160]

7. A barrister is entitled to refuse to accept instructions in any publicly funded graduated fee criminal case where he believes that the remuneration which he is likely to receive is inadequate having regard to his experience and expertise. A barrister should, however, be aware that he or she may be asked to justify this objectively, particularly in comparison to other work that has been accepted.

8. A barrister who unconditionally accepts general instructions to represent a lay client in a criminal graduated fee case (see para 2 above), is expected to conduct all aspects of that case, including any resulting confiscation proceedings. This obligation applies even if unexpected and unanticipated complex confiscation proceedings arise after instructions have been accepted provided they are still within the barrister's experience and competence. It is immaterial that the barrister would have refused such instructions had he been aware of the length or complexity of such proceedings.

9. A solicitor is free to instruct counsel of choice to conduct any stage of the proceedings, subject to any limitations imposed by the funding regulations or

Representation Order. This may involve instructing different counsel to undertake or assist in different parts of the same case. A barrister may properly accept instructions to act in this limited manner.

10. A barrister who is offered a criminal graduated fee case may decline to accept instructions to undertake confiscation work relating to that case provided that:

   i. those instructing counsel are aware of the barrister's limitations on what (if any) confiscation work is being accepted by counsel as part of the instructions and the matter is agreed between them in writing; or

   ii. where a barrister discovers after accepting instructions generally that he or she would be professionally embarrassed (due to insufficient experience and competence)

      (a) instructing solicitor is informed of that fact immediately both orally and in writing; and

      (b) the barrister can and is prepared to justify objectively the decision to decline the instructions in respect of confiscation either in respect the fee not being a proper professional fee or the work in question being beyond the barrister's experience and competence.

Explanatory note as regards the limited acceptance oF instructions

[3.161]

The purpose of this Protocol is not to provide barristers in graduated fee criminal cases with a means of refusing to undertake confiscation work. Its purpose is to protect barristers who accept a criminal graduated fee case and subsequently find that the work required to prepare and argue a contested confiscation hearing is wholly disproportionate to that required for the antecedent criminal proceedings.

This Protocol does not attempt to identify the factual circumstances in which a barrister should indicate that instructions will be accepted on a limited basis, nor the conditions on which a barrister might seek to accept instructions.

At one extreme, a barrister who refuses to undertake any confiscation work, even where the anticipated confiscation work is likely to be minimal, is likely not only to fall foul of paragraph 10(ii)(b), but is also unlikely to be offered that brief, or indeed any future work.

At the other extreme, a barrister who is offered a small graduated fee case, in respect of which a substantial confiscation hearing is anticipated, would be wholly justified in accepting the brief on the condition that he is not instructed to undertake the confiscation work.

Within those extremes lie an enormous range of circumstances. Where a barrister seeks to accept a brief on a conditional basis, the nature and terms of the conditions will be determined by the nature and extent of the confiscation hearing anticipated by the barrister and the instructing solicitor when the brief is offered. Conditions suggested by a barrister in a graduated fee case where the trial is estimated to last two days (e.g. not to undertake the confiscation work if the confiscation hearing and/or the preparation is likely to exceed 1 day), which might be regarded as reasonable, would clearly be wholly unreasonable if the trial is estimated to last 5 weeks. Every case must be determined on its own facts.

Where limited instructions subject to conditions are agreed, it is essential that such conditions are reduced to writing.

Explanatory note following an April 2009 House of Lords decision

[3.161a]

On 29 April 2009 the House of Lords confirmed that the prosecution are entitled in confiscation proceedings (i) to prove that the defendant had committed offences other than those to which he had pleaded or in respect of which he had been convicted and (ii) to invite the court to estimate the profit that he must have made from those offences: *R. v. Briggs-Price* [2009] UKHL 19, [2009] AC 1026, [2009] 4 All ER 594. The opinion effectively entitles prosecuting authorities to raise and prove additional offences at confiscation hearings for the purpose of calculating benefit.

The graduated fee scheme does not cater for what amounts to secondary trials. Unless and until provision for the adequate remuneration for such confiscation hearings are put in place, barristers are reminded that they may accept a brief conditionally, and decline to accept instructions to undertake any related confiscation work if, for example, the prosecution subsequently seek to prove that the defendant committed offences other than those for which he was indicted.

Advocacy Payment in Confiscation Cases and Application under Paragraph 11 of Schedule 1 of the Criminal Defence Service (Funding) Order 2007 — Guidance Notes

[3.161b]–[3.161d]

The Criminal Defence Service (Funding) (Amendment No 2) Order 2009 introduced new fees for advocacy in confiscation hearings concluded on or after 21st August 2009 where there are more than 50 pages of evidence. The following letter and guidance was issued by the Bar Council to advise barristers of these changes and how to get paid for such work:

Application under Paragraph 11 of Schedule 1 of the Criminal Defence Service (Funding) Order 2007 — Advocacy Payment in Confiscation Cases

[3.161e]

Guidance Notes

1. The Criminal Defence Service (Funding) (Amendment No. 2) Order 2009 introduced new fees for advocacy in confiscation hearings concluded on or after 21 August 2009 where there are more than 50 pages of evidence.
2. The type of pages that count towards that evidence are set out in the Order and repeated in the form attached that should be used to apply for payment.
3. A form that should be used to claim these fees is attached.
4. Applications for payment in cases with more than 50 pages, and any associated claim for additional half-day or full day advocacy fees for the second and any subsequent days of the confiscation hearing, should be submitted to the National Taxing Team as set out below.
5. Applications sent to the National Taxing Team must be supported by a copy of all the pages that are included in the claim form (at sections A, B and C). Please show clearly, by reference to page number or paragraph number, where any pages claimed under part B are referred to in the statement of information served under section 16 of the Proceeds of Crime Act 2002 (or the other two Acts mentioned). The mention of a witness by name or reference to an exhibit in the statement is not sufficient to mean that the statement of that witness or the exhibit necessarily count towards pages of evidence. The statement must make clear that the witness statement or exhibit itself is specifically relied upon for the purposes of the confiscation hearing and would have been exhibited with the section 16 statement had it not already been served.
6. Claims may include, at part C, pages of a written report of an expert

obtained by the defence with the prior authority of the Commission under CDS Regulations or allowed by the appropriate officer under the Funding Order (in this case that would be allowed by the LSC as part of the LGFS payment). Claims may not include any documents contained in such annexes or exhibits which have already been counted under parts A or B of the claim or which consist of financial records or similar data.

7. Other graduated fees claims for the same case should be submitted to the Crown Court in the usual manner.

8. All other claims for confiscation hearings, where there are less than 50 pages of evidence, should be included in the usual claim for payment and submitted to the Crown Court.

9. The new payments for confiscation are banded according to the number of pages, but advocates should note that page count is used as an approximation of complexity. There is no underlying rate per page that is – used to calculate fees. So, for example, a junior advocate making a claim for a case with 55 pages and a junior advocate making a claim for a case with 240 pages would both receive a fee of £500 (plus VAT if appropriate).

10. Please note that in order to properly assess the overall work on a case where there are 1,001 pages (or more) – all hours worked should be included in Part B. The Determining Officer will allow the number of hours believed to be reasonable in the circumstances of the case, at the appropriate hourly rate. From that allowance the Determining Officer shall subtract the first 25 hours, to reflect the work done on the first 1,000 pages which is paid for at the fixed rate for cases with 750 to 1,000 pages. Advocates may claim the fixed fee for 751 to 1,000 pages of evidence automatically when the total pages of evidence (as defined) are 1,001 or more.

11. Please use part C for claims for additional days and half days of the confiscation hearing. Please note that the first day is included in the fee claimed in Part A.

12. Claims that should be submitted to the National Taxing Team should be sent to:

Birmingham and Cardiff Region; Regional Manager, Phil Sulley
3rd floor, Temple Court , 35 Bull St, Birmingham B4 6LG.
DX 701991 BIRMINGHAM 7
Tel: 0121 681 3262 Fax: 0121 681 3270
Email: Adminntt.bham@justice.gsi.gov.uk

Aylesbury
Basildon
Birmingham
Bristol
Cambridge
Canterbury
Cardiff
Coventry
Croydon
Exeter
Gloucester
Harrow

Ipswich
Leicester
Luton
Maidstone
Merthyr Tydfil
Northampton
Norwich
Nottingham
Oxford
Peterborough
Plymouth
Shrewsbury
St.Albans
Stafford
Stoke
Swansea
Swindon
Taunton
Truro
Warwick
Wolverhampton
Worcester

Doncaster Region; Regional Manager, Roger Pendleton
c/o Crown Court College Road DN1 3HS. DX 703005 DONCASTER 5
Tel: 01302 363 988 Fax: 01302 322441
Email: NTTDONADMIN@hmcourts-service.gsi.gov.uk

Bradford
Derby
Doncaster
Durham
Grimsby
Kingston upon Hull
Leeds
Lincoln
Newcastle
Sheffield
Teesside
York

Manchester and Winchester Region; Regional Manager, Sandra Crossley
3rd Floor, c/o Salford County Court, Prince William House, Salford M5 4RR
DX 702633 Salford 5
Tel: 0161 745 4240 Fax: 0161 745 4268
Email: AdminManchesterNtt@HMCOURTS-SERVICE.GSI.GOV.UK

Blackfriars
Bolton
Bournemouth
Burnley
Caernarfon

Carlisle
CCC (Old Bailey)
Chelmsford
Chester
Chichester
Guildford
Inner London
Isleworth
Kingston
Knutsford
Lewes
Liverpool
Manchester (Crown Square)
Manchester (Minshull St)
Mold
Newport (I.O.W)
Portsmouth
Preston (Barrow and Lancaster)
Reading
Salisbury
Snaresbrook
Southampton
Southwark
Warrington
Weymouth & Dorchester
Winchester
Wood Green
Woolwich

Case No.

Crown Court at ______________________

APPLICATION UNDER PARAGRAPH 11 OF SCHEDULE 1 OF THE CRIMINAL DEFENCE SERVICE (FUNDING) ORDER 2007 – ADVOCACY PAYMENT IN CONFISCATION CASES

NOTE

This application must be forwarded to the appropriate National Taxing Team Office as soon as possible and in any event no later than **THREE** months after the conclusion of the confiscation hearing. This time limit will only be extended by the Determining Officer for good reason.

Name of Defendant(s):	
Date of Conclusion of Confiscation Hearing: (NB Must be on or after 21 August 2009)	/ /
Instructed Advocates Name and Address:	
Advocates Status:	**QC** ☐ **Leading Junior** ☐ **Junior alone** ☐**Led Junior** ☐
Telephone Number:	
VAT Number:	

PART III IN PRACTICE

A – COUNSELS FEES INC VAT

	Specify	No of Pages
A	Total number of pages of the statement of information served under section 16 of the Proceeds of Crime Act 2002* and relied on by the prosecution for the purposes of a confiscation hearing under Part 2 of that Act and any attached annexes and exhibits. (* or any similar statement served under section 2 of the Drug Trafficking Act 1994 or under section 71 of the Criminal Justice Act 1988) **Please supply a copy of all pages above.**	
B	Total number of pages of any other document which— (i) is served as a statement or an exhibit for the purposes of the trial; (ii) is specifically referred to in, but not served with, a statement mentioned at A above; and (iii) the prosecution state that they intend to rely on in the hearing. **Please specify where in the statement at A above these further pages are referred to by page and/or paragraph number.** **Please supply a copy of all pages above.**	
C	Total number of pages of any written report of an expert obtained with the prior authority of the Commission under CDS Regulations or allowed by the appropriate officer under this Order, and any attached annexes and exhibits. This should exclude any documents already served under A or B above or which consist of financial records or similar data. **Please supply a copy of the prior authority and all pages above.**	
	Total Number of Pages (NB if total pages amount to 1,001 or more please claim fee for up to 1,000 pages here, but also complete table B below)	

	Amount Claimed	
	VAT Claimed	
	Total Claimed	
NTT USE ONLY	**Amount Allowed**	
	VAT Allowed	
	Total Allowed	

B – COUNSELS FEES (CASES WITH OVER 1,000 PAGES ONLY)

Date	Work Done (includes all work done)	Hours claimed	Amount Claimed	VAT Claimed	**NTT ONLY** Amount Allowed	**NTT ONLY** VAT Allowed
SUB TOTAL CLAIMED						
LESS 25 HOURS (to account for fee claimed above)						
TOTAL CLAIMED						
NTT USE – TOTAL ALLOWED						

PART III IN PRACTICE

C – Fixed Payments for Additional Days/Half Days

Date(s)	Full or Half Day	Amount Claimed	VAT Claimed	**NTT ONLY** Amount Allowed	**NTT ONLY** VAT Allowed
TOTAL					

I confirm that none of the work/appearances listed above have been claimed as part of the normal Advocates Graduated Fee claim.

Signed by Instructed Advocate:

Date of Application: / /

NTT USE ONLY

Total allowed (Part A)	
Total allowed (Part B)	
Total allowed (Part C)	
Grand Total allowed	

Appendix A

The Criminal Defence Service (Funding) (Amendment No. 2) Order 2009

[3.161f]

Made: 2009

Laid before Parliament: 2009

Coming into force: 21 August 2009

The Lord Chancellor makes this Order in exercise of the powers conferred by section 14(3) of the Access to Justice Act 1999.[1]

He has had regard to the matters specified in section 25(3) of that Act and has consulted the General Council of the Bar and the Law Society in accordance with section 25(2) of that Act.

Citation, commencement, interpretation and application

(1) This Order may be cited as the Criminal Defence Service (Funding) (Amendment No. 2) Order 2009 and comes into force on 21st August 2009.

(2) In this Order "the 2007 Order" means the Criminal Defence Service (Funding) Order 2007.[2]

(3) This Order applies to hearings to which paragraph 11 of Schedule 1 to the 2007 Order applies and which are concluded on or after 21st August 2009.

1 1999 c.22. The reference to the Lord Chancellor was changed to the Secretary of State by S.I. 2003/1887 and changed back by S.I. 2005/3429.

2 S.I. 2007/1174; there is one relevant amending instrument, S.I. 2007/3552.

Amendment to the Criminal Defence Service (Funding) Order 2007

(1) Schedule 1 to the 2007 Order is amended as follows.

(2) In paragraph 11(2), for the words from "for attendance" to the end substitute:

"in respect of such a hearing:

(a) where the number of pages of evidence is fewer than 51, for attendance:

(i) in respect of any day when the hearing begins before and ends after the luncheon adjournment, at the daily rate set out in the first section of the table following this subparagraph; or

(ii) in respect of any day when the hearing begins and ends before the luncheon adjournment, or begins after the luncheon adjournment, at the half-daily rate set out in the first section of that table, as appropriate to the category of trial advocate or substitute advocate;

(b) where the number of pages of evidence is between 51 and 1000:

(i) at the rates for the relevant number of pages set out in the second section of the table following this sub-paragraph; and

(ii) where the hearing lasts for more than one day, for attendance on subsequent days or halfdays at the daily rate or half-daily rate set out in the first section of that table, as appropriate to the category of trial advocate or substitute advocate; or

(c) where the number of pages of evidence exceeds 1000:

(i) at the rates for 751 to 1000 pages set out in the second section of the table following this sub-paragraph;

(ii) with such fee as the appropriate officer considers reasonable for preparation in respect of the pages in excess of 1000, at the hourly rates for preparation set out in the third section of that table; and

PART III
IN PRACTICE

(iii) where the hearing lasts for more than one day, for attendance on subsequent days or halfdays at the daily rate or half-daily rate set out in the first section of that table,

as appropriate to the category of trial advocate or substitute advocate

Fees for confiscation hearings				
	Fee for QC	Fee for leading junior	Fee for junior alone	Fee for led junior
1 Daily and half daily rates				
Half daily rate	£300	£225	£150	£150
Daily rate	£575	£400	£275	£275
2 Pages of evidence				
51–250	£750	£625	£500	£375
251–500	£1,125	£938	£750	£562
501–750	£1,500	£1,250	£1,000	£750
751–1000	£2,250	£1,875	£1,500	£1,125
3 Preparation				
Hourly rates	£85	£65	£45	£45"

(3) After paragraph 11(2) insert:

"(3) In sub-paragraph (2) 'evidence' means:

(a) the statement of information served under section 16 of the Proceeds of Crime Act 2002 and relied on by the prosecution for the purposes of a hearing under Part 2 of that Act, or a similar statement served and so relied on for the purposes of a hearing under section 2 of the Drug Trafficking Act 1994 or under section 71 of the Criminal Justice Act 1988 and, in each case, any attached annexes and exhibits;

(b) any other document which:

(i) is served as a statement or an exhibit for the purposes of the trial;

(ii) is specifically referred to in, but not served with, a statement mentioned in paragraph (a); and

(iii) the prosecution state that they intend to rely on in the hearing; and

(c) any written report of an expert obtained with the prior authority of the Commission under CDS Regulations or allowed by the appropriate officer under this Order, and any attached annexes and exhibits, other than documents contained in such annexes or exhibits which have also been served under paragraph (a) or (b) or which consist of financial records or similar data."

(4) In the table after paragraph 19 omit the entry relating to confiscation hearings.

Signed by authority of the Lord Chancellor.

Name
Parliamentary Under Secretary of State
Ministry of Justice

Date

Explanatory note

(This note is not part of the Order.)

This Order amends the Criminal Defence Service (Funding) Order 2007 which makes provision for the funding and remuneration of services provided as part of the Criminal Defence Service. The Order increases the fees payable to advocates in confiscation proceedings.

Appendix B

[3.161g]

To:

All Heads of Chambers

All Senior Clerks and Practice Managers

4 August 2009

The cases of *Campbell*, *Carlton* and *R v P* have highlighted the difficulty in obtaining Advocates prepared to act in complex confiscation cases under the Advocates Graduated Fees Scheme.

The current payment scheme for defence counsel for confiscation in the CDS Funding Order 2007, pays a daily fixed fee only: there is no remuneration for preparation. In complex confiscation cases this is wholly inadequate.

Following discussions with the Bar Council, the Ministry of Justice has amended the Criminal Defence Service (CDS) Funding Order 2007. Their revised Funding Order will be laid before Parliament and is intended to come into force on 21st August 2009. The final draft of the Order is attached hereto. The formal Order will be available online next week at http://www.opsi.gov.uk/.

The Funding Order will apply to all confiscation hearings which are concluded on or after 21st August 2009. It will, in effect apply to preparatory work currently being undertaken. The effect of the new funding order is to pay increasing levels of enhanced fees in graduated fee cases where the page count in confiscation proceedings exceeds 50 pages. The fees will include the first day of the confiscation hearing. Any subsequent days, or half days will be paid at the current rates. Where the page count exceeds 1,000 pages, the advocate will receive the payment appropriate for 750–1,000 pages, but can apply to the NTT for additional hours properly and reasonably spent in preparation. These will be remunerated at what amount to the current special preparation rates.

Guidelines will be issued to Determining Officers at the NTT in respect of cases in excess of 1,000 pages to the effect that the Determining Officers will calculate the

PART III IN PRACTICE

number of hours reasonably expended, apply the appropriate hourly rate and then deduct from that total the pages of evidence payment less the daily or half daily rate as appropriate.

For example, if 100 hours was reasonably incurred by a Junior in a two day confiscation hearing, the formula would be 100 x £45 = £4,500 less (£1,500 – £275) = £3,275.

Paragraph 5 states that the page count is to be calculated by reference to:

(i) the section 16 (or similar) statement, together with any annexes or exhibits attached thereto;

(ii) documents referred to in that statement which formed part of the trial bundle and are intended to be relied upon by the prosecution for the purpose of the hearing;

(iii) defence expert reports obtained with the prior authority of the LSC and material annexed thereto which is not otherwise relied upon by the prosecution.

Pages from the main bundle relied upon by the prosecution must be clearly identified in the s.16 statement. If these are not clearly identified, then it is recommended that defence counsel write to the prosecution and seek clarification as to precisely what the prosecution are relying on.

All confiscation payments under the revised Funding Order will be channelled through the National Taxing Team (NTT). Page counts will have to be supported by evidence as counsel may be required to produce the pages relied upon to the NTT.

However, it must be stressed that counsel will not qualify for additional hourly payments, even if the page count exceeds 1,000 pages, if they have not kept records of the hours worked and the nature of the work undertaken.

Counsel should be aware that the payment for confiscation proceedings will not be funded through a reduction elsewhere in the legal aid budget, but will come from elsewhere, possibly from monies obtained from confiscation proceedings.

Counsel should also be aware that the *Protocol for Counsel in relation to Confiscation of Graduated Fee Cases* still applies. Whether, and to what extent it may be considered applicable in any given case will depend upon individual assessment of the potential complexity of any confiscation proceedings and the remuneration which may be anticipated for those proceedings.

Andrew Mitchell QC
Treasurer
The General Council of the Bar

Tony Shaw QC
Vice Chairman
Fees and Remuneration Committee

Service Standard on Timely Claim and Payment of Prosecution Fees

[3.162]

The following are Service Standards as to the payment of fees funded by the CPS/Prosecution

---

[3.163]–[3.174]

1. Principle

1.1 The principle upon which this Standard is based is that payment to an advocate for work actually and reasonably undertaken should be achieved without unreasonable delay as soon as is practicable following the conclusion of the case.

1.2 CPS policy is to pay bills in accordance with agreed contractual conditions, or where no such conditions exist, within 30 days of receipt of goods or services or the presentation of a valid invoice, whichever is later.

1.3 CPS instructs advocates, both counsel and solicitor advocates/agents to prepare and present cases for hearing in the criminal courts. Prosecution work funded by CPS falls broadly into 4 categories:

(i) sessional work in the Magistrates' Court for which a whole list fee is payable;

(ii) Crown Court cases for which standard fees are payable;

(iii) cases for which fees are pre-marked;

(iv) cases for which fees are assessed ex posto facto.

1.4 The principle of achieving prompt payment applies equally to each category but different arrangements will apply to meet the different methods by which fees are both claimed and assessed.

1.5 In order that the CPS may achieve prompt payment, the advocate accepts that all claims for payment must be submitted within 3 months of the conclusion of the case, or receipt of a Notification of Fees Form (NOFF), if later. Any claim from the advocate outside that time will be disallowed by the CPS unless good cause for late submission can be demonstrated.

2. Guidance

2.1 Guidance for the payment of fees is contained within the Fee Scheme which confirms that the CPS will use its best endeavours to make payment within 10 working days of the receipt of an agreed invoice. In order to facilitate prompt payment at the conclusion of the proceedings, every effort should be made to ensure that fees are agreed in advance of the hearing. Normal practice is to make one payment per case in respect of all advocates involved in the preparation and the presentation of the case. Where payment is due to more than one advocate it is the responsibility of CPS to indicate clearly on the NOFF to whom individual payment is owing.

2.2 It is the responsibility of the Chambers to apportion the payment on receipt. More than one payment should only be made where:

(i) the advocates employed are from different Chambers;

(ii) one advocate is not registered for VAT;

(iii) where separate advocates each play significant roles in the case (e.g. trial and retrial; leader and junior etc);

(iv) where a staged payment has been agreed.

2.3 For the purposes of fee payment, conclusion of the proceedings means the date that sentence is passed. In addition, to avoid unreasonable delay, payment should also be made:

(i) where sentence is deferred, or final orders such as confiscation are to be delayed for a period of more than 2 months after verdict or plea;

(ii) in cases where a warrant is issued and there is no prospect for the immediate apprehension of the defendant;

(iii) in cases where a retrial is ordered and the case is not to be re-listed immediately.

Sessional Work in the Magistrates' Court

2.4. Fees for sessional work in the Magistrates' Courts by counsel are reviewed periodically and are applied nationally. There are no set fees for solicitors which are locally negotiated.

Standard Fees

2.5 Standard fees apply to about 80% of prosecutions in the Crown Court and subject to the number of appearances, are not normally discretionary. As such, these fees are amenable to speedy assessment and prompt payment.

Pre-marked Fees

2.6 Pre-marked fees can apply to individual cases for hearing in all criminal courts. They are individually assessed both in respect of brief fees and refreshers and the arrangements are such to promote prompt assessment and payment.

Ex Post Facto Fees

2.7 In the larger cases attracting Case Management Plans it may not be possible to agree fees in advance of the hearing, but broad preparation times should regularly be agreed and updated, and where possible an hourly preparation rate agreed to be applied in the assessment.

3. Procedure

Sessional Fees in the Magistrates' Court

3.1 Agent solicitors and barristers are engaged on a personal basis and their commitment should not be transferred to any other person without the prior approval of a Crown Prosecutor. Barrister agents should be included in the circuit lists of advocates approved to prosecute by the Attorney General.

3.2 In respect of each appearance, the advocate should complete a daily court record or attendance certificate and submit an Invoice specifying the name of the advocate, the court sitting(s) together with the times, and the fee claimed.

3.3 The correctly completed invoice should be submitted within 10 working days of the conclusion of the sitting to the CPS Branch that issued the instructions to prosecute. No claim should be submitted more than 3 months from the date of sitting.

3.4 CPS should confirm that the claim is in accordance with the prevailing rates and authorise payment to be made by the Area Finance Office. The CPS Branch should aim to perform this authorisation within 5 working days of receipt of the invoice. The Area Finance Office must aim to pay within 10 working days of the Branch receiving the correctly completed invoice.

Standard Fees in the Crown Court

3.5 At, or shortly before, the conclusion of the case the caseworker at court should ensure that all items, for which separate payment is required, have been recorded on the fee log. The advocate should ensure that similar endorsements have been made on the brief backsheet and, where possible, should check these with the caseworker against the fee log so as to avoid additional claims for work omitted. To facilitate prompt payment, the endorsed brief backsheet must be left with the CPS representative at the court centre. Where this is not possible, the brief should otherwise be returned to the appropriate CPS office within 7 days.

3.6 The advocate will need to have been informed by CPS of the overall fees, witness expenses and CPS costs prior to the conclusion of the case to inform any application for costs against the defendant in the event of a conviction.

3.7 Within 5 working days the caseworker should endorse the amounts to be paid on a NOFF and forward the same to the advocate or his clerk. The advocate should raise an invoice to match the details contained in the NOFF, and quoting the unique NOFF reference number, forward the invoice to the CPS Area Finance Office whose address is shown on the NOFF.

3.8 The advocate, or his clerk, should aim to send the invoice within 5 working days of receipt of the NOFF. If the NOFF is not received within 10 working days of the conclusion of the case, the advocate or his clerk should contact the caseworker at the originating Branch by telephone or letter to ascertain the cause for delay. An invoice should not be issued in advance of receipt of the NOFF as this is contrary to the agreed procedure and will simply add to the delay.

3.9 No invoice should be issued, submitted, more than 3 months after the conclusion of the case and only in exceptional circumstances will invoices submitted after this period be considered. The Area Finance Office must aim to pay within 10 working days of receipt of the correctly completed invoice.

3.10 Where issue is taken with the content of the NOFF, enquiries should be made by telephone or in writing with the CPS caseworker at the originating Branch. Where necessary, and where amendment to the original NOFF is not feasible, the original NOFF should be cancelled by the Branch and a further form issued setting out the agreed amount before a fee note/invoice is forwarded to the Area Finance Office.

3.11 It is important that any invoice from an advocate tallies with the information on the NOFF to enable prompt payment to be made. If it is necessary to amend or cancel the original NOFF it is essential that the Area Finance Office is informed by the Branch in writing so that the records on the Counsel Fee Register can be updated. No invoice should be issued or submitted more than 3 months after the amended NOFF has been received by the advocate or his clerk.

Pre-marked Fees

3.12 As for standard fees, CPS must aim to have assessed and agreed the fees in pre-marked cases at, or immediately before the conclusion of the hearing, again because of the requirement to accurately assess any application for costs against the defendant. In cases where fees are marked £5,000 or more, a Case Management Plan (CMP) should be utilised.

3.13 Records of any adjustments to the pre-marked fees must be retained in the case file. At the conclusion of the case, the advocate should ensure that similar endorsements have been made on the brief backsheet and, where possible, should check these with the case-worker against the fee log so as to avoid additional claims for work omitted. To facilitate prompt payment, the endorsed brief backsheet must be left with the CPS representative at the court centre. Where this is not possible, the brief should otherwise be returned to the appropriate CPS office within 7 days.

3.14 Subject to the delegated authority of the caseworker dealing with the prosecution, there should be no unreasonable delay in completing the NOFF which should be undertaken within 5 working days of conclusion of the hearing.

3.15 This advocate or his clerk should reconcile the NOFF with their records and raise an invoice quoting the NOFF serial number which should be despatched to the Area Finance Office shown on the form within 10 working days of receipt of the NOFF. The copy NOFF should be retained by the advocate or his clerk and endorsed to indicate that an invoice has been submitted.

3.16 The Area Finance Office must aim to pay within 10 working days of receipt of the correctly completed invoice. Any enquiry concerning the content of the NOFF should be directed to the CPS officer from the originating Branch before an invoice is raised.

3.17 The guidelines for notification, claim and payment of pre-marked fees are the same as those for standard fees.

Ex Post Facto Fees

3.18 Case Management Plans should be employed in all cases where agreement has been made to assess fees ex post facto. The advocate or his clerk should aim to submit the agreed action plan and work record with the brief backsheet, fee note/invoice (and note for taxation if applicable) to the reviewing prosecutor/caseworker within 10 working days of the conclusion of the case. No invoice should be issued more than 3 months after the conclusion of the case.

3.19 Within a further 10 working days, the reviewing prosecutor/caseworker should consider the fees claimed against the accompanying documentation and assess a payment that is both fair and reasonable. Details of the fees it is proposed to pay should be passed to the advocate or his clerk by telephone, or in writing if necessary, and efforts made to secure agreement. Records of negotiations should be retained as part of the Case Management Plan.

3.20 Where fees are accepted in accordance with the original claim, a NOFF should be raised by the caseworker/reviewing prosecutor, and sent, accompanied by the fee note/invoice direct to the Area Finance Office to avoid further delay. The Area Finance Office must aim to pay within 10 working days of receipt of the correctly complete invoice. Where agreed fees differ from those originally proposed, a NOFF should be raised in the revised amounts and forwarded to the advocate or his clerk within 5 days thereafter.

3.21 Where agreement cannot be reached, the review and appeal procedures set out in the Fee Scheme should be applied.

Civil Privately Funded

Guidance for Barristers and Clerks relating to Privately Funded Civil Litigation

[3.175]–[3.179]

The Bar Council has produced practical advice about funding civil cases. In recognition of the fact that barristers must survive financially in an increasingly competitive market, it unashamedly focuses on the practical and commercial aspects of civil litigation funding; this includes the methods by which barristers can fairly protect their own business interests whilst at the same time providing excellent service and value for money.

Rather than focusing solely on the means by which counsel's own services may be funded (so-called 'counsel funding'), this guide also addresses funding in general ('case funding'). It addresses the latter only very briefly: it is very much an introductory guide in that regard.

This guidance is not part of the Code of Conduct and (save where clearly indicated) should not be regarded as describing an expected or minimum standard of care. Instead, it is a 'living document' that will be updated as the profession learns how to grapple with the post-Jackson funding regime. It should not be regarded as being a definitive document setting out the duties expected of counsel. It should also be borne in mind that there is no single good practice in relation to funding matters that applies to all types of case. What is good practice in one type of case may not be good practice in another.

The Civil (Private) Panel is able to answer general queries and can be contacted at Remuneration@BarCouncil.org.uk. Please attach any relevant information to the email and provide as much background information as you can.

The guidance is set out in full below.

Introduction

[3.180]–[3.202]

This section introduces the guidance including the flowcharts which are an essential part of the guidance. It also introduces the Bar Council model agreements counsel should use.

The nature of this guide

1. This guidance gives practical advice about funding civil cases. In recognition of the fact that barristers must survive financially in an increasingly competitive market, it unashamedly focuses on the practical and commercial aspects of civil litigation funding; this includes the methods by which barristers can fairly protect their own business interests whilst at the same time providing excellent service and value for money.

2. Rather than focusing solely on the means by which counsel's own services may be funded (so-called '**counsel funding**'), this guide also addresses funding in general ('**case funding**'). It addresses the latter only very briefly: it is very much an introductory guide in that regard.

3. This guidance is not part of the Code of Conduct and (save where clearly indicated) should not be regarded as describing an expected or minimum standard of care. Instead, it is a 'living document' that will be updated as the profession learns how to grapple with the post-Jackson funding regime. It should not be regarded as being a definitive document setting out the duties expected of counsel. It should also be borne in mind that there is no single good practice in relation to funding matters that applies to all types of case. What is good practice in one type of case may not be good practice in another.

4. This Guidance is best read electronically and care should be taken that the most up to date version is accessed. This is to ensure that hyperlinks in the Guidance lead to the correct sources.

5. The Civil (Private) Panel is able to answer general queries and can be contacted at Remuneration@BarCouncil.org.uk. Please attach any relevant information to the email and provide as much background information as you can. For more specific queries you should consult a costs lawyer.[1]

6. The Bar Council has also published a complementary Q&A document to help answer the most common queries.[2]

1 The Association of Costs Lawyers, Directory of Members, http://www.associationofcostslawyers.co.uk/members.

2 Guidance for Barristers and Clerks Relating to Privately Funded Civil Litigation: Q&A.

The flowcharts

7. This guide contains flowcharts (Part 8) that will reward careful scrutiny. If they are to be used (and this is very much recommended), it is important to follow them step-by-step; if this is not done (or if shortcuts are taken) the reader may miss important points or fail to take into account commercially relevant considerations.

Changes in the law in 2013 (the Jackson reforms)

8. In April 2013, success fees became irrecoverable between opposing parties. A number of other changes in the law were also made at that time. These changes will be referred to as "the 2013 Changes". This guide applies to funding arrangements made after those changes.

The model agreements

9. This guidance is intended to be used alongside the suite of templates known collectively as the Bar Council Model Agreements ("the Model Agreements").[3]

10. The Model Agreements should not be confused with the *Standard Conditions of Contract for the Supply of Legal Services by Barristers to Authorised Persons 2012*.[4] Those conditions are standard terms recommended by the Bar Council that may be used where counsel is paid regardless of the outcome of the claim. One of the Model Agreements is based on the *Standard Conditions*, but there is no such thing as the *Standard Conditions of Contract* relating to Conditional Fee Agreements or Damages-based Agreements.

3 The Bar Council Model Agreements, http://www.barcouncil.org.uk/for-the-bar/practice-updates-and-guidance/remuneration-guidance/Guidance-for-Barristers-and-Clerks-Relating-to-Privately-Funded-Civil-Litigation.

4 Standard Conditions of Contract for the Supply of Legal Services by Barristers to Authorised Persons 2012.

Decisions concerning funding

11. Counsel should ensure that their agreements are fair to lay clients and appropriate for the lay clients' needs; no more than a proper fee should be charged in any particular case. This guide does not dwell upon that aspect of the matter because barristers are already well-equipped to ensure that their lay clients' interests come first. Ethically difficult cases may arise from time-to-time. Where this happens, then counsel's first port of call should be the Bar Council's ethical enquires service (020 7611 1307 or ethics@barcouncil.org.uk).

12. The lay client is not the only person to consider, however. Counsel need to consider their position and a balance needs to be struck between their desire to be properly remunerated for the risk that they are taking and the client's right to be charged no more than a proper and fair fee. Barristers tend not to be very good at taking risk and their own financial interests into account, so in order to make this task easier, this guide identifies three commercial considerations that may assist in this regard.

The three commercial considerations

This section introduces the three considerations (suitability, viability and transparency) that should underpin counsel's commercial decision making.

The three principles

13. While there is no obligation to do so, it is recommended that whenever counsel makes a commercial decision about funding, the following three factors are taken into account:

(a) **Suitability:** Where appropriate, counsel should ensure that the proposed method of funding is suitable for the category of case in question. This means ensuring that the correct type of agreement – such as a Damages-based Agreements, a CFA Lite, etc – has been chosen and that where necessary, it has been properly adapted for use in the case in question.

(b) **Viability:** The type of agreement may be suitable (see above), but the case itself may not be up to scratch. Counsel should ensure that the case is viable in terms of potential profit and good cash flow.

(c) **Transparency:** The type of agreement may be suitable and the case may be commercially viable, but the proposed written agreement may not accurately reflect what has been agreed or counsel's expectations. Counsel must ensure that the agreement is transparent (which, in this context, means that it is accurate, complete, and comprehensive).

14. The last of these points may lead to counsel changing the way in which they interact with those who instruct them. Counsel may need to have discussions about how and when they are going to get paid. In particular, thought should be given to what would happen in the following hypothetical circumstances:

(a) if the lay client fails to put the professional client in funds for counsel's fees;

(b) if the recovery of costs from the opponent is markedly less than the amount claimed; and

(c) if counsel's fees are assessed downwards by the court (between opposing parties).

15. The ideal is to create a written agreement that is clear, complete and comprehensive so that no subsequent discussions will need to take place. Put otherwise, it should negate the need for any discussions at the end of the claim about how much counsel is going to get paid. This ideal may not be achievable in some instances, but the vast majority of other businesses manage to achieve that ideal – it is not an impossible goal to reach.

16. In summary, where appropriate, counsel should choose the most suitable type of agreement. Once this has been done, then it will be necessary to consider whether the case is commercially viable. If it is viable, then the parties to the agreement should communicate with each other and ensure the proposed agreement is transparent (i.e., it is comprehensive and that it reflects what counsel will actually be paid).

The responsibilities of counsel

17. As set out in the introduction to this guide, there are two broad issues that counsel may need to comment upon when considering the suitability of any given method of funding: the the method by which counsel's own fees are to be funded (**counsel funding**) and the method by which the claim in general is to be funded (**case funding**). Each is considered in turn, but counsel would need to get involved with the latter only rarely; this is because, in general, the professional client would be responsible for giving the requisite advice. Circumstances in which counsel might wish to advise on **case funding** would include:

(a) where they have been instructed to advise on that issue and are competent to do so;

(b) where there is no instructing solicitor (or other professional client); and

(c) where it becomes clear that the professional client's advice was obviously wrong or substantially incomplete.

18. Even in these situations, it is questionable whether counsel has a duty to advise (other, of course, than (a)). In most cases there is no general duty to give advice about **case funding**, though in certain types of case it may be desirable to address that issue. This may be so where the proposed funding arrangement has the potential to erode the lay client's damages (as may happen with a Damages-based agreement). Counsel should be careful, however, not to undermine their professional clients, who, as a rule, will already have advised the lay client about **case funding** (often because they are under a professional duty to do so). Counsel should be careful not to meddle by giving advice that is neither required nor desired.

19. The issue of **counsel funding** is very different, however, in that counsel will always owe a duty to themselves to ensure that they are going to be properly and fairly remunerated for their work. Counsel (or, in reality, counsel's clerks) will need to address their minds to that issue. This may be a very brief exercise. If, for example, the case is offered on a CFA Lite basis (see Part Four), then there would be little point in considering other methods of funding. The only question would be whether the case was sufficiently viable to be commercially worthwhile. At the other end of the spectrum, if instructions are received from a commercial organisation on a private client basis (i.e. the level of the barrister's fee is not dependent on the outcome or success of the case), no one is going to be assisted by counsel questioning that arrangement.

20. **Counsel funding** is usually about what is suitable for counsel, but the position of the lay client may be a relevant factor in certain types of case. From time-to-time that may become an issue upon which counsel should give advice. Any advice should be on the basis of what counsel has been told. Other than the circumstances where there is no professional client, it would almost never be the case that counsel would be expected to initiate or supervise a search for alternative means of funding. If counsel believes that the lay client's best interests would be served by a method of funding that is different to that which has been proposed, it would usually be appropriate to explain why. Similarly, if counsel is not prepared to accept any of the methods of funding that are appropriate for the case in hand, then it would usually be helpful to explain that that is the case and to point the professional client in the right direction (such as to another barrister).

Where there is a professional client

21. Where counsel gives advice about **counsel funding**, that advice would normally be given to the professional client. Counsel would not be expected to check the advice that the professional client had given to the lay client (unless, of course, there was a specific reason why counsel should do that). Where advice needs to be given, however, and where it is complex or likely to be controversial, it would usually be befitting to give that advice in writing this often saves time and reduces the risk of misunderstanding.

Where there is no professional client

22. Where written advice is given in a form that is intended to be considered directly by the lay client, it would be helpful to ensure that it is written in language that the lay client is likely to understand. Where there is no professional client (or where the professional client is not a lawyer or is not the type of lawyer who is under a professional duty to give advice about funding), then it may – depending on the facts – become appropriate to give full advice about both **case funding** and **counsel funding**. Further guidance is provided in Annex 1.

Case funding

This section deals with case funding whether directly with a lay client or a professional client.

Determining the most suitable type of funding for the case in general

23. The following applies to the commonest type of case, namely, where instructions have been received from a solicitor[5] (or equivalent[6]). If no such professional client exists or if **case funding** has become germane for other reasons, then the guidance given in Annex 1 (i.e. full advice about **case funding**) may become relevant, particularly where:

    (a) the instructions come directly from a lay client;

    (b) counsel has been instructed to consider the issue of **case funding**;

    (c) it has become clear that the advice given to the lay client is based on a mistake or is otherwise wrong;[7]

    (d) the professional client is not a lawyer; or

    (e) the professional client is that type of lawyer who does not owe a professional duty to give advice about funding (such as a costs lawyer).

    For most counsel these situations will arise only rarely. What is set out below is what should be done in those cases that do not fall within any of those categories (i.e., the vast majority of cases).

24. There are three topics that merit some discussion:

    (a) how to find out what the options are (so called "funding enquiries");

    (b) how to choose the best of those options (i.e., the best way of funding the claim); and

    (c) how to consider the effect of the proposed method of funding on the lay client.

PART III IN PRACTICE

5 The reason that solicitors fall into a separate category is because they are under a professional duty to enter into funding arrangements that are suitable for their lay clients' needs and that take account of the clients' best interests (see SRA Code of Conduct 2011, O(1.6)); moreover, they are under a duty to ensure that lay clients have the best possible information about the likely overall costs of the matter (see SRA Code of Conduct 2011, O(1.13)).

6 Most other professional clients do not have a professional duty to give advice about funding.

7 Where a mistake has been made, it would usually be appropriate to draw it to the professional client's attention. For the avoidance of doubt, this does *not* mean that barristers must double-check the professional client's advice in every case. The circumstances in which a barrister would have an affirmative duty to advise would very rarely arise.

Funding enquiries: discovering the options

25. Where there is no professional client then the guidance in Annex 1 will become appropriate instead of the guidance below.

26. Funding enquiries are enquiries made for the purposes of deciding how the case is to be funded and what the options are; they are intended to find out whether the lay client has legal expenses insurance, trades union legal assistance, etc. In the vast majority of cases they will be of little interest to counsel other than as a background fact. If, however, counsel suspects that the lay client has been misadvised, then it would usually be appropriate to ask what the funding enquires revealed.

27. As a matter of professional courtesy, any corrective or additional advice would normally be given first to the professional client rather than directly to the lay client. It would usually be sensible to record that advice in a written note. It may, however, be necessary to give the advice directly to the lay client if, for example, there is a conflict of interest.[8] In this regard, it is worth bearing in mind that counsel's primary duty is to the lay client.[9]

8 Where this is so, then it would be sensible to discuss the matter with the Bar Council's ethical helpline on 020 7611 1307 or ethics@barcouncil.org.uk.

9 See paragraph 303 of the Code of Conduct of the General Council of the Bar of England and Wales.

Selecting the most appropriate method of funding

28. In the vast majority of cases counsel will not have to consider this issue at all. That said, it is useful to be able to recognise mistakes. It has to be emphasised, however, that in the vast majority of cases counsel is not under a duty to check the advice given to the lay client.

29. A selection of common mistakes are as follows:

(a) **Rejecting BTE funding or trades union funding because the professional client is "off-panel":** A frequent occurrence is that a lay client has been advised not to use BTE insurance (or trades union funding, as the case may be) because the professional client is not a member of the funder's panel. Where this is the only reason for rejecting that form of funding, advice of that nature is nearly always incorrect. This is for two reasons:

(i) firstly, if the funder is a BTE insurer and if the claim has already been issued, then the insurer is obliged to allow the insured (i.e., the lay client) to choose their lawyer; it is only in pre-issue that the client does not have a choice, and

(ii) secondly, even where the lay client does not have a choice, it is rarely in the lay client's interests to eschew an entirely suitable form of funding solely for the purposes of instructing a particular firm of solicitors.

(b) **Rejecting BTE funding because the limit of indemnity is too low**: If the limit of cover is too low for the purpose of funding the whole of the case, there is usually no reason why it cannot be used for funding part of the claim; it would rarely be necessary to reject that form of funding altogether.

(c) **Accepting public funding without considering alternatives**: Public funding is very far from being perfect and it would be wrong to use it merely because it is available. This is particularly so where the statutory charge is likely to "bite" (i.e., where the client is likely to have to pay part of their damages as being a contribution towards the costs); in those circumstances, other forms of funding may well be better in the long run.

The effect of the method of funding of the lay client

30. Unlike the two considerations set out above, this is an issue that will often arise, especially in claims in which the costs are likely to be large in comparison to the damages. It will also be particularly relevant in cases that are funded by litigation funding agreements. Indeed, the issue will arise whenever the lay client is asked to bear the difference between the fees charged by the lawyers and the costs recovered from the opponent (e.g. most types of Conditional Fee Agreement).

31. It may be appropriate to consider the effect of the method of funding on both the management of the litigation and on the overall benefit that the client is likely to get from the claim. Any such advice would form part of counsel's advice about the claim generally. It is often a good idea to calculate the "net benefit" – the figure that is likely to be allowed once costs, fees and expenses have all be paid – for a number of different outcomes.

Counsel funding

This part deals with counsel funding and determining the most suitable way forward for funding counsel.

32. The issue here is what barristers should do about how their own fees are to be funded. This is an issue that is usually focuses on counsel rather than the lay client. When reading what is set out below, it should be borne in mind that most of what is said is directed at counsel's interests rather than the lay client's interests; nothing in what is set out below is intended to create any duties towards the lay client.

33. The three criteria in Part 2 form the basis of the discussion; they were:

(a) suitability;

(b) viability; and

(c) transparency.

34. Again, it is important to recognise that whilst it is possible to apply those factors to the interests of the lay client, that is not their primary function. Their primary function is to assist counsel in their deliberations about their own commercial interests. Each is considered in turn.

Determining the most suitable type of funding for counsel's own fees

35. The issue here is what barristers should do when they are deliberating how their own services are to be funded. Counsel is under no obligation to enter into a Conditional Fee Agreement or a Damages-based Agreement, and as such, the starting point is the type or types of agreement counsel is willing to accept. Factors counsel may wish to take into account include:

(a) the level of fee;

(b) the amount that the client can fairly be asked to pay and is willing to pay; and

(c) the risks involved.

36. This question will arise only infrequently because instructions are usually proffered on a take-it-or-leave-it basis or on a privately-funded basis.[10] In the first of those circumstances (take-it-or-leave-it), the question is not whether the proposed agreement is suitable but whether the case is viable: this is addressed in the next section. In the second (private fee agreement), issues may arise as to the terms of the agreement; some of those issues – can be surprisingly problematic. Where, on the other hand, instructions are offered on the "Standard Conditions of Contract for the Supply of Legal Services by Barristers to Authorised Persons 2012", counsel would have no option but to accept those instructions under the cab-rank rule.

37. Cases will arise, however, in which counsel would be expected to express a view as to the best method by which their own services could be funded. These would include:

(a) where counsel is tendering for bulk instructions;

(b) where counsel is competing with other barristers for instructions;

(c) where counsel is instructed to give that advice;

(d) where counsel's fees are likely to be unusually large in comparison to the damages; and

(e) where the lay client asks for such advice.

38. To put it candidly, counsel may be expected to bid for instructions on the basis that they provide better value than their competitors; those barristers who are familiar with the ways in which their services can be funded will be at a distinct advantage. This will be particularly so if they are so familiar with the topic that they can suggest novel and ingenious methods of funding. The commonly encountered methods of funding are set out below along with their pros and cons, and "risk ratings".[11]

10 For the avoidance of doubt, where instructions are received on a private fee basis, there is no obligation upon counsel to consider whether the lay client would be better off with a conditional fee agreement.

11 The risk rating is an indication of the risk to counsel; the greater number of stars, the less suitable the fee arrangement is likely to be in riskier cases.

The methods of funding that are available

Traditional private fee agreement

Counsel will be paid their full fees regardless of the outcome of the claim. Expenses may or may not be payable in addition.

Pros and cons: This type of agreement is simple and easy to understand (namely, the client must pay for the supply of legal services notwithstanding the fact that the claim may ultimately fail).

Risk rating: Nil to ★ (depending on probity and solvency of the professional or lay client).

Traditional Conditional Fee Agreement ("no win, no fee") with no quantum risk

If the claim is successful, counsel will be paid their full fee (with or without a success fee) but if it is unsuccessful, no fees at all are payable. Expenses may or may not be payable if the case is lost. If the client wins but fails to beat a Part 36 offer, fees are still payable even for work done after the offer was made.

Pros and cons: The client must bear the risk of fees being incurred but not recovered in the litigation. Counsel bears all other risks (including the risk that the case is lost). It is suitable for cases that have reasonable prospects of success.

Risk rating: ★★★

Ordinary Conditional Fee Agreement with quantum risk

As above, save that if the client wins but fails to beat a Part 36 offer, fees will not be payable for work done after the expiry of the 'relevant period' which is generally 21 days after the offer was made but the offer may specify a longer period.

Pros and cons: As above, but counsel bears the additional risk posed by Part 36 offers. If liability has already been admitted or if an offer has already been made, this may be a very important factor.

Risk rating: ★★★★

CFA Lite ("no-cost-to-you" or "eat what you kill")

The main characteristic of a CFA Lite is that in ordinary circumstances the client will be liable only for those costs which are recovered in the litigation. Escape provisions may exist to take account of the possibility that the lay client may behave unreasonably or dishonestly.

Pros and cons: This type of agreement is simple to understand, namely, counsel bears all of the risks in the case and, unless the lay client acts dishonestly or unreasonably, the client bears no part of the risk of having to pay counsel's fees. After the 2013 Changes counsel will not be compensated for bearing those risks (i.e., no success fee will be payable).

Risk rating: *****

CFA Max ("success-fee-only agreement")

This is a type of agreement that would be worth considering after the 2013 Changes. In so far as base fees are concerned it is a CFA Lite, but in addition to the monies that are recovered from the other side, a success fee is payable. That success fee is based on the amount of base costs recovered (i.e. an agreed percentage increase will apply to whatever is recovered from the other side). Escape provisions may exist to take account of the possibility that the lay client may behave unreasonably or dishonestly.

Pros and cons: Counsel bears considerable risks but, unlike under CFA Lite made after the 2013 Changes, counsel will be compensated by way of a success fee.

Risk rating: ****

Discounted Conditional Fee Agreement ("no win, low fee")

This is otherwise known as a 'partial Conditional Fee Agreement' or a 'guaranteed fee agreement'. Counsel's fees are payable in full in the event of success (with or without a success fee in addition), but a discounted fee will apply if the case is lost. Escape provisions may exist to take account of the possibility that the lay client may behave unreasonably or dishonestly.

Pros and cons: Counsel has the comfort of knowing that they will be paid something regardless of the outcome of the litigation. The client must bear the risk of fees being incurred in the event of a win, but not recovered in the litigation.

Risk rating: * to ** (depending on level of discount).

Discounted CFA Lite

The oxymoronic phrase 'discounted CFA Lite' is used to describe a type of agreement in which a discounted fee is payable regardless of whether the case is won or lost, but any fees in addition to that guaranteed minimum will ordinarily be limited to those costs recovered in the litigation. Where the agreement has been made after the 2013 Changes, this would preclude the payment of a success fee. Escape provisions may exist to take account of the possibility that the lay client may behave unreasonably or dishonestly.

Pros and cons: Counsel has the comfort of knowing that they will be paid something regardless of the outcome of the litigation and the client has the comfort of knowing that ordinarily they will not have to pay any more than the discounted fees. If it provides for a success fee, it is suitable only if success fees are recoverable in principle; this will not be the case if the agreement is made after the 2013 Changes.

Risk rating: ★★ to ★★★ (depending on level of discount).

Discounted CFA Max

This is a type of agreement in which a discounted fee is payable regardless of whether the case is won or lost, but any base fees in addition to that guaranteed minimum will ordinarily be limited to those costs recovered in the litigation. A success fee is then payable in addition, that fee being calculated as an agreed percentage of the recovered base costs. Escape provisions may exist to take account of the possibility that the lay client may behave unreasonably or dishonestly.

Pros and cons: Counsel has the comfort of knowing that they will be paid something regardless of the outcome of the litigation and the client has the comfort of knowing that ordinarily they will not be required to pay more than discounted fees or a success fee (whichever is appropriate).

Risk rating: ★★ to ★★★ (depending on level of discount).

Damages-based Agreement (or contingency fee agreement)

A Damages-based Agreement is an agreement where the amount of counsel's fee is linked to the amount of damages or debt recovered (or, in non-contentious matters, to the price received, the premium, etc).

Pros and cons: The main benefit of a Damages-based Agreement is that the client will pay costs which are proportionate to the benefit received. The main disadvantage is that the costs actually paid may bear no relation to the work undertaken. Another disadvantage is that Damages-based Agreements are fairly heavily regulated.

Risk rating: ★★ to ★★★★ (depending on the facts).

Before the event insurance

Many lay clients will have before the event insurance (otherwise known as legal expenses insurance). It is a type of insurance that will protect the client for having to pay their own lawyers' fees or those of the other side. It will usually result in counsel being paid on a private fee basis (often at a lower hourly rate than would normally be appropriate), but some insurers will require counsel to work on a conditional fee basis.

If counsel is asked to accept a lower rate than they would normally be paid, it would usually be worth asking the insurer to work on a discounted CFA Lite basis such that the lower fee is payable regardless of the outcome of the claim, but if the case is won, then counsel keeps whatever is recovered from the other side.

Pros and cons: Unless they asked to work on a conditional fee basis (which is rare) counsel has the comfort of knowing that they will be paid something regardless of the outcome of the litigation. Most polices are limited to either £50,000 or £100,000.

Risk rating: Nil to ★ (unless funded on a conditional fee basis and/or if the limit of cover is exceeded).

Litigation funding (otherwise known as third-party funding)

A litigation funding agreement is an agreement where a commercial organisation (often a hedge fund) will purchase a share in the litigation (often 30 to 40 percent of the damages) in return for providing funding. This form of funding would almost never be made solely for the purposes of funding counsel, but it is commonly used to fund counsel's fees (often on a discounted Conditional Fee Agreement basis) as part of a larger funding package. Before the 2013 Changes it was a type of financial product that was almost always combined with after the event insurance; it is not known what will happen after the 2013 Changes.

Pros and cons: From counsel's point of view, litigation funding may either be irrelevant (i.e., it will not be used to fund counsel's fees) or it will provide a degree of relatively risk-free funding (be that under a private fee agreement or a discounted Conditional Fee Agreement). From the point of view of the lay client, it will spread the risk of litigation but at the cost that the client will recover less if they win: it is, therefore, best used in cases that cannot be funded solely on a conditional-fee-agreement basis.

Risk rating: Nil to ★ (unless funded on a conditional fee basis).

Civil legal aid

Civil legal aid is available for certain types of civil action, in the following categories: actions against the police, clinical negligence, community care, consumer and general contract, debt, education, employment, family, housing, immigration and asylum, mental health, public law and welfare benefits.

Whether or not cases within these categories are covered by civil legal aid is mandated by the Legal Aid, Sentencing and Punishment of Offenders Act 2012 (LASPO). Individual eligibility for legal aid is determined by a means test and an interest of justice test. Applications for civil legal aid funding are submitted by providers who hold contracts with the Legal Aid Authority to provide publicly funded legal work.

The Bar Council has produced guidance on the scope of civil legal aid following LASPO.[12]

12 See Changes to civil legal aid: Practical guidance for the Bar.

How to choose the best form of counsel funding

39. This guide contains two sources on this topic: the first is the set of flowcharts in Part 8, and the second is the commentary above of the different methods of funding. The flowcharts are self-explanatory. The text gives general guidance and deals with each form of funding in turn, but it will not provide much assistance with the decision-making process; this is better addressed by faithfully following the flowcharts.

40. Neither the flowcharts nor the text cover every contingency. If the case is particularly difficult or if the answer cannot be found in the flowcharts, then it would be best to discuss the matter with a costs lawyer or other specialist.

Which flowchart to use

41. The decision as to which type of agreement to select will depend on many factors; there are several flowcharts and sub-flowcharts that may be relevant. The decision-making process will depend on counsel's instructions:

(a) **Instructions on a private-client basis or as a disbursement***:* Where instructions are received to act on a private-client basis or as a disbursement (i.e., where counsel will get paid in full regardless of the outcome of the matter), then it would rarely, if ever, be necessary for counsel to spend much time considering the issue of funding.[13] Consideration may need to be given to the terms of the agreement, and in particular, consideration may need to be given to how payment is going to be enforced.

(b) **Instructions to act on a basis to be agreed or to tender for work**: If counsel is asked to tender for work the significant thought ought to be given to the issue of funding. This may, in some cases, merely be a matter of offering the best hourly rate or the most competitive fixed price, but in other cases it will mean offering the most appropriate form of retainer for the purposes of satisfying the lay client's (or, on occasion, the professional client's) commercial requirements. In this regard, all three of the considerations set out above will be relevant. The starting point will be *Flowchart A: Main Chart*.

(c) **Instructions to act under a Conditional Fee Agreement where the type of agreement is not specified**: Where counsel is asked to act under a Conditional Fee Agreement, then the first step will be to find out what the client actually means. If the reality is that the client is prepared to pay only those monies that are recovered from the other side, then there is no point in considering anything other than a CFA Lite. Very often, however, the client will have only a rough idea of what is required, and in those circumstances, counsel may wish to offer some guidance (assuming this has not already been given by the professional client).

There are two routes. The first would be to consult *Flowchart A: Main Chart* (but to disregard those questions and options that do not relate to the Conditional Fee Agreements), and the second route – and, in most cases, the preferred route – would be to use the *Flowchart B: Selecting the type of Conditional Fee Agreements to use*. If, however, counsel's fees are likely to be substantial, it may be best to apply the numeric analyses detailed in *Flowchart C: Traditional CFA sub-flowchart* and Flowchart *D: Discounted CFA Sub-flowchart*; this would mean that the first route would be appropriate:

(a) **Instructions to act under a specific type of Conditional Fee Agreement**: Where instructions are to act under a specific type of Conditional Fee Agreement (such as a traditional Conditional Fee Agreement, a CFA Lite, a discounted Conditional Fee Agreement, etc), then the first task will be to ensure transparency by asking the clients to confirm that they actually intend to pay those monies that may fall due but which are not recovered from the other side; it may be that the reality is that the offer of a putative traditional Conditional Fee Agreement is, in reality, an offer to enter into a CFA Lite (or

CFA Max). Assuming this not to be the case, then the only issue that will arise in most cases will be whether the case is viable (i.e., whether to accept the case on the offered terms); this can be addressed by one of the following:

(i) *full method:* follow one or the two routes described under the previous heading (Instructions to act under a Conditional Fee Agreement where the type of arrangement is not specified) and disregarding those parts of the flowcharts that do not apply; or

(ii) *shortcut:* carry out the calculations in *Flowchart E: CFA Lite sub-flowchart* and deciding whether the likely reward justifies the work involved.

(b) **Instructions to act under a Damages-based Agreement**: This will largely be a matter of considering whether the proposed agreement is likely to be sufficiently profitable to justify the work involved (i.e. whether the case is viable). In this regard, *Flowchart G: DBA sub-flowchart* might be of assistance. It may be that counsel is not willing to supply legal services on the basis that has been suggested; if so, then in most cases it would usually be good client care both to explain why and to say whether counsel would be prepared to act on some other basis. In this regard, it may be necessary for counsel to work through the *Flowchart A: Main Chart* for the purposes of determining the basis or bases upon which services could be offered.

13 Any such advice would form part of counsel's advice about the claim generally. It is often a good idea to calculate the "net benefit" – the figure that is likely to be allowed once costs, fees and expenses have all been paid – for a number of different outcomes but that would be far from mandatory.

Factors relevant to the choice of counsel funding

42. The following very general comments are intended to supplement (but not replace) *Flowchart A: Main Chart* (i.e. the central flowchart that is used when selecting the basis upon which counsel would be prepared to supply legal services):

(a) **The type of case:** Certain types of fee agreement are not lawful in certain types of cases. Conditional Fee Agreements may not be used to fund family or criminal matters[14] and Damages-based Agreements are lawful only in certain circumstances.

(b) **The wishes of the client:** The wishes of the client are a highly relevant factor. Usually the client will want the type of agreement that is the best in terms of containing costs, but this would not always be the case. Some clients (especially businesses) will want to 'incentivise' their lawyers, and this may mean that they specifically want to pay more than is strictl\y necessary. This is done in the hope that they will get a better result.

(c) **Legal expenses insurance and other forms of funding:** Some clients will have legal expenses insurance (otherwise known as 'before the event' or 'BTE' insurance). Others may have trades union legal aid or legal aid as a perk of membership of a professional body.

(d) **Commercial realities:** If the commercial reality is that the case is *de facto* offered on a CFA Lite or CFA Max basis, then this needs to be identified at an early stage; this is so that counsel can get the benefit of that knowledge either by declining the work or by claiming an appropriately high success fee.

(e) **The level of risk generally:** If a case is laden with risk, it would be best to avoid any form of Conditional Fee Agreement or damages based agreement entirely. In general, if a client wishes to pursue a case that is risky, it is only fair that the client bears that risk; this would tend to indicate a private fee agreement. Alternatively, thought should be given to a discounted Conditional Fee Agreement with a relatively high discounted fee (such as 75 or 80 percent of normal fees). A CFA Lite and a CFA Max should be avoided entirely.

(f) **The nature of the risk:** In general, there are three types of risk:

(i) **Liability risk:** the risk of losing.

(ii) **Quantum risk:** the risk of not beating Part 36 offer or admissible offer, and

(iii) **Recovery risk:** the risk of not getting paid in full because the costs are reduced on assessment or the court awards only part of the full costs.

It is usually best to match the risk to the type of agreement. CFA Lites and discounted CFA Lites expose counsel to all three types of risk. Ordinary Conditional Fee Agreements with quantum risk provide for liability risk and quantum risk. The other types tend to provide only for liability risk.

(g) **Specific risks:** Counsel is not obliged to accept each and every risk that the case presents, and it may be that counsel wants to avoid a particular aspect of the risk by writing it out of the agreement. If, for example, counsel are prepared to accept the risk of losing but not the risk of failing to beat a Part 36 offer, they may choose an ordinary agreement without a quantum risk. This may be done even though the quantum risk is considerable.

(h) **Whether it will be practicable to determine if the case has been 'won':** If it is likely to be difficult to decide whether the case has been 'won'[15] then it might not be appropriate to enter into a Conditional Fee Agreement at all; usually, however, the definition of 'win' can be adapted to suit the case.

(i) **Whether a success fee is likely to be recoverable from the other side:** Save for limited exceptions,[16] no success fee is recoverable under a Conditional Fee Agreement made after 1 April 2013. This means that, in an appropriate case, the lay clients will have to decide which risk they want to bear and which risk they want counsel to bear: the greater the risks borne by counsel, the higher the success fee. Where the success fee is not recoverable, the clients must pay that success fee themselves. A compromise may have to be reached where counsel bears some of the risk (say, the liability risk), but the client bears the other risks.

(j) **Whether a success fee is payable by the client:** If the reality is that no success fee is going to be paid to counsel at all, then – in the interests of transparency – that fact needs to be identified at an early stage. If counsel has other work that is more profitable, it would be commercially sensible to reject the claim entirely. Alternatively, counsel may agree to bear only part of the risk (i.e. a discounted conditional fee agreement).

(k) **The amount counsel is prepared to risk:** In addition to the level of risk, another factor to be borne in mind is the effect that losing would have on counsel's finances; it would make no sense at all to accept a risk (even a very low risk) that might lead to bankruptcy if it eventuated. Thus, if the case is a very large case in terms of counsel's fees, then caution should be exercised; on the whole, only agreements with lower risk ratings should be used.

(l) **Cash flow:** Some types of agreement (such as private fee agreements) will lend themselves to prompt payment and interim payments; others (such as CFA Lites) will mean that payment is likely to be made only at the very end of the case. Some types (such as discounted Conditional Fee Agreements) are in-between in terms of cash flow.

(m) **The difference between the damages, debt or value of the matter and costs:** Where the ratio of damages, debt or value of the matter is very high when compared with the costs, then it may be to counsel's advantage to enter into a Damages-based Agreement (assuming this to be lawful). Where the ratio is very low, however, in personal injury cases, thought should be given to the restriction imposed in such cases.[17]

14 Proceedings under section 82 of the Environmental Protection Act 1990, may be conducted under a conditional fee agreement provided that no success is charged.
15 Such as where liability is not in dispute and no clear offers have been made.
16 Mesothelioma proceedings (see section 48 of the Legal Aid, Punishment of Offenders and Sentencing Act 2012 and CPR rule 48.2) and insolvency-related proceedings (see CPR rule 48.2).
17 See article 5 of the Conditional Fee Agreement Order 2013.

Factors relevant to specific types of funding

43. The following paragraphs expand upon some of the factors that might be relevant to the following specific types of funding:

(a) alternative means of funding (such as BTE insurance, trades union funding, etc);

(b) private fee agreements and funding as a disbursement (including via litigation funding);

(c) Conditional Fee Agreements (or all types); and

(d) Damages-based Agreements.

Alternative means of funding

44. "Alternative means of funding" is a catchall phrase that includes before the event (BTE) insurance, trades union funding, civil legal aid, etc.; in a nutshell, it means any form of funding where someone other than the client has an obligation to fund the claim or part thereof. Its relevance is that where it exists and where it is suitable, it may be better to make use of it rather than to ask the lay client to bear the cost. This would be particularly true if the arrangements that would otherwise be proposed required the lay client to pay fees that would, in principle, be irrecoverable (such as a success fee or a damages-based fee).

45. Save where it is obvious from the facts that he has a duty to do so, counsel is not obliged to make enquiries of the lay client as to the existence of alternative means of funding.

46. It is possible to make an offer to supply legal services conditional on the professional client confirming that the lay client does not have alternative means of funding. There are many circumstances in which such a conditional proposal would not be necessary. These include:

    (a) where counsel already knows that the funding enquiries have been carried out and that the lay client does not have suitable alternative means of funding;

    (b) where, on the facts of the case in question, there is a good reason why alternative means of funding should not be used for counsel funding; and

    (c) where, through previous experience, counsel knows that the professional client has put in place a funding regime that is suitable overall notwithstanding the terms on which counsel is to be funded.

Where legal expenses insurance already exists

47. A fairly common situation is where a client has legal expenses insurance but the instructing solicitors still wish to act (or for counsel to act) under a Conditional Fee Agreement. Counsel should be aware that more often than not this is because professional clients are concerned about not being on the insurers' panel of solicitors. In those circumstances it may be helpful to advise the professional client about the matters referred to in paragraph 28. Once the professional client knows the true position they may not feel that a Conditional Fee Agreement is necessary.

48. Where counsel has explained the correct law to the professional client and where the professional client still wishes to instruct counsel under a Conditional Fee Agreement (or, for that matter, a damages based agreement), then counsel will have to decide whether to accept the case on those terms. Counsel may do this only if the proposed method of funding is fair to the lay client. The pros and cons need to be weighed. They are likely to be:

Advantages of using a Conditional Fee Agreement	Disadvantages of rejecting BTE insurance
Free choice of lawyer even before the claim is issued (NB the free choice of lawyer under BTE exists only after the claim is issued).	No access to the insurer's panel of counsel (if there is one).
No restriction on the hourly rate charged by counsel (which may be a decisive factor in whether counsel accepts the instructions).	No funder willing to pay the lawyer in the event that there is a shortfall in the recovery of costs.
Possibility that the use of the counsel (i.e., the particular barrister in question) will result in better recovery of damages.	No cover for costs orders made against the lay client (although in personal injury cases this is a fairly low risk because of one-way costs shifting).

49. The issue usually boils down to a question of whether the use of the particular barrister in question is likely to result in sufficiently higher damages to justify the success fee and to justify the risk of the lay client having to pay legal costs.

Private fee agreements and funding as a disbursement

50. In most instances in which counsel are instructed under a private fee agreement, this is on the specific instructions of the lay client (or other person paying counsel's fees). Where this is so, then it would be rare for any issues concerning funding to arise. It would generally be prudent (from counsel's point of view) to ensure that neither the lay client nor the professional client expect an adjustment to the fees if the case goes badly; if the reality is that such an adjustment would be required, the it would be best to look at discounted Conditional Fee Agreements (or something similar).

51. It may be that the impetus that counsel be paid under a private fee agreement comes from counsel or from the professional client rather than from the lay client. This may happen in the following circumstances:

(a) **Where counsel is not prepared to act on any other basis**: It may be that counsel has rejected a Conditional Fee Agreement (perhaps because the case is too risky), and that the only basis on which they are prepared to provide legal services is under a private fee agreement. This is counsel's prerogative and there is no duty to give reasons or to give advice about how counsel's fees may be funded. That said, many counsel would seek to be helpful and would comment on those two matters, where appropriate.

(b) Where the professional client is not prepared to allow counsel to act on any other basis: This may happen in a number of circumstances. These include the following:

(i) where the professional client wishes to act under a Conditional Fee Agreement that is limited by damages but wishes to fund counsel as a disbursement for the purposes of avoiding the need to share the success fee with counsel;

(ii) where the professional client wishes to act under a Damages-based Agreement but wishes to fund counsel as a disbursement for the purposes of avoiding the need to share the damages-based fee with counsel;

(iii) where the professional client intends to or has already arranged litigation funding for the purposes of funding counsel's fees; and

(iv) where the professional client has some other form of funding in mind or has already arranged that other form of funding.

Where one or more of these situations exists, counsel will often be unaware of that fact; this is because counsel's instructions will usually be ordinary instructions to which the cab-rank rule will apply. This is not usually a problem, however, as it would be very rare that counsel would be able to – or wish to – object to receiving instructions on any of these bases.

(c) **Where litigation funding is being considered:** It may be that counsel is not prepared to stake the fruits of their labours on the case being successful. Where this is so, one option that may be worth bearing in mind is litigation funding. In order to attract the interests of a funder the merits of the case have to be good (i.e., the prospects of success need to be at least 60 percent or, for many funders, 70 percent) and the case has to be large (i.e., theoretically cases as small as £500,000 can be funded, but in practice, the case must be worth at least £2m-£3m). One way of managing the situation is to invite instructions to draft a full advice once a funder has indicated that it is interested in the case.

In large cases there is often a degree of negotiation as to whether that advice should be funded by the funder, by the lay client, by the professional client, or by counsel (i.e., through a conditional fee agreement relating just to the advice). If counsel agrees to act under such a conditional fee agreement, care must be taken to ensure that (a) the ambit of the conditional fee agreement is clearly and accurately set out therein, and (b) a private fee agreement (preferably in writing) can be evidenced for any subsequent work. If the Advice is to be funded by the funder or the professional client but not by the lay client, then the advice of a costs lawyer should be obtained as to how that arrangement can be made to comply with the indemnity principle; any such enquiry should be accompanied by a copy of the retainer (or proposed retainer) between the lay client and the professional client and (if it exists) the most recent draft of the litigation funding agreement.

Enforcement provisions

52. There are only limited ways in which counsel can enforce payment of his fees, and now that the Withdrawal of Credit Scheme 1988 no longer exists, it is essential that the agreement contains a contractual provision relating to enforcement. Any request to act on the basis of a "gentleman's agreement" or on the basis of there being no contractual rights at all ought to be rejected out of hand.

53. The following contractual methods of enforcement are available. There is not a great deal that can be done about the second of these problems other than by asking for payment in advance. As to the first, this should not be a problem if it has been possible to make an agreement that deals with every

eventuality (including the possibility of the lay client not putting the professional client in funds for counsel's fees); in reality, however, many professional clients will be reluctant to do this. It may be worth explaining why a solicitor should be liable for counsel's fees. Those reasons include (but are not limited to) the following:

(a) **Unqualified enforcement against the professional clients**: This is the usual (i.e. traditional) method of enforcing a contractual right to payment. The two largest problems with it are:

   (i) that it is unpopular with professional clients and some may refuse to offer instructions on that basis; and

   (ii) that if the professional clients become insolvent, counsel's fees may be reduced accordingly.

   As to the first, this should not be a problem if it has been possible to make an agreement that deals with every eventuality (including the possibility of the lay client not putting the professional client in funds for counsel's fees); in reality, however, this is difficult to do. The rationale for fixing the professional client (and in particular, solicitors) includes (but is not limited to) the following:

   (i) *consumer protection*: There is no method of assessing counsel's fees as against counsel; as such, consumer protection is best achieved by the solicitors standing between the lay client and counsel (this being because counsel's fees can be assessed as against the solicitor (i.e. A solicitor and client assessment);

   (ii) *no handling of client monies*: Barristers, unlike solicitors, are not permitted to handle client money; as such, it is not possible to take fees from monies already held. In certain circumstances BARCO may be able to provide assistance;[18]

   (iii) *no effective lien*: Solicitors often (or usually) hold items belonging to the client which are of sufficient value to be able to claim effective lien (such as money, the case papers, documents, etc); barristers rarely hold such items and if they were to claim lien, it would almost always be ineffective;

   (iv) *no statutory right to security for costs*: Solicitors have a statutory right to seek security for costs;[19] barristers do not have that right;

   (v) *no statutory right to charging orders*: Solicitors have a statutory right to seek a charging order in the event of non-payment of fees;[20] barristers do not have that right;

   (vi) *design of system*: The system of the Bar is based on the premise that counsel is able to rely on professional clients for the purposes of enforcing fees as against the lay client; if this were not the case, then barristers would have to carry similar overheads to those carried by solicitors, and this would increase fees; and

   (vii) *preservation of market forces*: The market will become distorted if the person carrying out the negotiations has no genuine interest in the amount charged by counsel.

(b) **Qualified enforcement against the professional clients**: This is becoming a much-requested form of contract. It is based on the premise that the professional client will go so far in trying to enforce the debt against the lay client, but if that fails, the debt is assigned to counsel; this is not recommended for the following reasons:

(i) *no right to render "final bill"*: the right that would be assigned would be the same right as the solicitor had, and in view of that, if a final bill has not been rendered, it would need to be rendered in a way that is compliant with the relevant provisions in the Solicitors Act 1974; barristers are not able to do that;

(ii) *no ability to attend solicitor and client assessment*: likewise, the client's right to a solicitor and client assessment is in no way diminished by the assignment, and it is highly doubtful whether counsel can attend a solicitor and client assessment in place of the assignor-solicitors;

(iii) *no statutory safeguards*: The points made above about "no statutory right to charging orders" and "no statutory right to security for costs" are just as relevant in this context as they were in the context above; this is particularly so when one takes into account the fact that it will only be difficult lay clients – i.e., where those rights may be most relevant – whose debts will be assigned;

(iv) *no effective redress for male fides behaviour*: It is not unknown for solicitors to seek to prefer their own financial well-being over that of counsel whom they instruct; if this happened to an improper degree (such as the solicitors taking counsel's fees from the client but then not paying them to counsel, or solicitors claiming for the same work as that done by counsel) it would be very difficult for counsel to seek redress;

(v) *enforcement against the lay clients*: The points made immediately above are repeated (although those points do not apply where counsel is instructed directly by a lay client);

(vi) *enforcement against the funders (if any)*: The Third Parties (Rights against Insurers) Act 1930 does not apply to enable a lawyer to recover costs directly from insurers upon the bankruptcy.[21] This situation was going to be remedied by the Third Parties (Rights against Insurers) Act 2010, but the relevant sections have not been bought into force. In any event, it would be very difficult indeed to bring a claim against an insurer under those Acts. It is possible that a claim could be brought against a funder (be it a liability insurer or another type of funder) under the Contracts (Rights of Third Parties) Act 1999, but this would be possible only if the retainer between the insurer and the professional client contained a provision that gave counsel a right to payment; this is rarely the case.

PART III
IN PRACTICE

18 See BARCO website.
19 See section 65 of the Solicitors Act 1974.

20 See section 73 of the Solicitors Act 1974.
21 *Tarbuck v Avon Insurance plc* [2001] 2 All ER 503 at 509.

Conditional Fee Agreements

Counsel may have to decide whether to enter into a Conditional Fee Agreement, and if so, what type of agreement to make. This section deals with the decision process that spans all three 'principles' (i.e., the Suitability Principle, the Viability Principle, and the Transparency Principle).

Whether to enter into a Conditional Fee Agreement

54. The "cab rank rule" does not apply to Conditional Fee Agreements; as such, counsel should decide whether to accept instructions offered on the basis of such factors as the merits of the case, the needs of the client and the chances of making a profit. In addition to the issue of whether there are alternative means of funding (where this is relevant: see paragraphs 44 to 49), counsel's decision will depend on factors that will include the following:
    (a) the category of case;
    (b) commercial considerations; and
    (c) ethical considerations.

55. Each of those considerations is considered in turn, but first, attention is drawn to the decision-making process as set out in the flowcharts. There are two routes by which counsel may wish approach the flowcharts. The first would be to consult Flowchart A: Main Chart and the associated sub-flowcharts and, where appropriate, to disregard those questions and options that do not relate to the Conditional Fee Agreements, and the second route, and if other forms of retainer have been ruled out, the generally preferred route, would be to consult Flowchart B: Selecting the type of Conditional Fee Agreement to use. The latter is easier to use and is less demanding in terms of numeric analysis.

Category of case

56. Criminal proceedings and family proceedings[22] may not be the subject of a Conditional Fee Agreement.

57. Another factor that may be worth considering is whether a success fee would be recoverable from the opposing parties; this would be so only if the proceedings are mesothelioma proceedings (see section 48 of the Legal Aid, Punishment of Offenders and Sentencing Act 2012 and CPR rule 48.2) or insolvency-related proceedings (see CPR rule 48.2).

22 There is an exception for proceedings under section 82 of the Environmental Protection Act 1990; that type of case may be funded by way of a conditional fee agreement that does not provide for a success fee.

Commercial considerations: Conditional Fee Agreements

58. There are three factors that might be relevant to the issue of whether a Conditional Fee Agreement is commercially viable; the first is the level of risk, the second is likely recovery of base costs, and the third is the likely recovery of the success fee.

Risk

59. A risk assessment should be carried out in all cases (see Administrative matters); that assessment should take into account the risk of losing (this being "the liability risk"), and – where appropriate – the risk of failing to beat Part 36 offers ("the quantum risk" or "risk on quantum") and the risk of recovering only a part of the base costs ("the recovery risk"). If the success fee (or other commercial benefits) do not justify the risk, then it would normally be prudent to reject the case. That said, it may be worth considering the options set out in paragraphs 39 and 40. This is because riskier cases can be made commercially viable by tailoring the agreement to those risks. Thus, if (for example) the risk is too great to bear the whole of the liability risk, then it may be worth looking at discounted Conditional Fee Agreements.

Base costs

60. A view needs to be taken at an early stage as to whether (in reality) counsel is going to be paid base costs in full. In this regard, it will be necessary directly to ask the instructing solicitor what is going to happen if only part of counsel's fee is recovered from the opponent. If the answer is that counsel will not be paid the shortfall (or if the answer is vague or inconclusive), then this is a factor to be taken into account (either when setting the success fee, or when deciding whether to accept the case).

Success fee

61. Thought needs to be given to whether the client is going to be asked to pay a success fee and if so, how much.

62. Success fees may or may not be fixed by law. If they are not fixed, then the table attached to the Model Agreements will help set the appropriate amount. The maximum that can be charged is 100 percent. An additional limit applies to personal injury work, where at first instance the success fee will be limited to 25 percent of the damages (excluding damages for future pecuniary loss and net of CRU) or, on appeal, to 100 percent of those damages.[23] In many (if not most) cases, this will be the limiting factor rather than the aforesaid 100 percent cap.

63. It is worth pausing here to say that some personal injury solicitors are seeking to avoid the effect of that cap by entering into discounted Conditional Fee Agreements that do not provide for a success fee but which provide for payment of a much higher rate of base costs in the event of a win. The Bar Council neither endorses nor condemns such an approach, but it is worth

pointing out that if the court were to find that such an agreement was a sham and that in reality it was a Conditional Fee Agreement that provided for a success fee that exceeded the aforesaid cap, then it is possible that counsel would not get paid anything at all.

64. Once these factors have been addressed, then a view needs to be taken as to the 'present value' of the proposed arrangement (i.e., the present value to counsel; this would include monies recovered from the client but not recovered from the other side). The 'present value' is the overall amount that is likely to be recovered in the event of a win is adjusted for risk (i.e., a 40% chance of getting £1,000 is a present value of £400). Once the present value has been estimated, then this needs to be compared with the sums that would be earned doing other work. The relevant arithmetic can be fairly complex, but the formulas are set out in the sub-flowcharts governed by Flowchart A: Main Chart.

23 See The Conditional Fee Agreements Order 2013.

Ethical considerations relating to Conditional Fee Agreements

65. It would not be appropriate to enter into an agreement where there was an unacceptable conflict of interests between counsel and the lay client. This will be exceptionally rare, however, and counsel should be careful not to get tied up in knots by focussing on unlikely, extreme or unreal hypothetical circumstances. In this regard it should be remembered that all Conditional Fee Agreements will, to some extent, give rise to a conflict of interests. That conflict will become unacceptable if, for example, it interfered with counsel's freedom to comply with the Code of Conduct or if it was obviously in the lay client's best interest to fund the matter in some other way. Detailed guidance is not given here because if a barrister is concerned about his or her ethical position, he or she should seek guidance on the matter from the Bar Council. If counsel wishes to do this, the following information or documentation should be to hand: a copy of the agreement between the lay client and the professional client or a brief description as to the nature of that agreement; a copy of the proposed agreement with counsel or a brief description as to the nature of that agreement; some indication as to the benefit that the lay client will obtain if the case is successful; some indication as to the lay client's *realistic* options if counsel were to decline to act under the proposed Conditional Fee Agreement; and some indication as to the likely merits of the claim and the nature of the main areas of risk.

Damages-based Agreements (or contingency fee agreements)

This section deals with Damages-based Agreements which have been widened in the Legal Aid, Sentencing and Punishment of Offenders Act 2012 to cover all areas of civil litigation which can be otherwise funded by a Conditional Fee Agreement.

Regulatory requirements

66. Damages-based Agreements must specify the following:[24]

(a) the claim or proceedings or parts of them to which the agreement relates;

(b) the circumstances in which the representative's payment, expenses and costs, or part of them, are payable; and

(c) the reason for setting the amount of the payment at the level agreed.[25]

67. A Damages-based Agreement must not require an amount to be paid by the client other than:[26]

"(a) the payment,[27] net of:

(i) any costs (including fixed costs under Part 45 of the Civil Procedure Rules 1998); and

(ii) where relevant, any sum in respect of disbursements incurred by the representative in respect of counsel's fees, that have been paid or are payable by another party to the proceedings by agreement or order; and

(b) any expenses incurred by the representative, net of any amount which has been paid or is payable by another party to the proceedings by agreement or order."

68. Persons who are considering entering into a Damages-based Agreement should be aware that some commentators are of the opinion that it is not possible to comply with these requirements in such a way as to be able to enforce the entirety of the fee. This is because the provisions in regulation 4 of the Damages-based Agreements Regulations 2013 mean that the only way that costs can be recovered from an opponent is by setting aside the indemnity principle. Surprisingly, they say, that has not been done (this being despite the fact that the CPR has set it aside for other purposes). As such, the lay client will not be able to obtain a costs order, so – they say – they would have a reasonably good case for refusing to pay those monies to the lawyers who created that problem. It remains to be seen whether that view is correct.

24 See regulation 3 of the Damages-Based Agreements Regulations 2013.
25 In an employment matter, this must "include having regard to, where appropriate, whether the claim or proceedings is one of several similar claims or proceedings".
26 See regulation 4 of the Damages-Based Agreements Regulations 2013.
27 "[P]ayment" means that part of the sum recovered in respect of the claim or damages awarded that the client agrees to pay the representative, and excludes expenses but includes, in respect of any claim or proceedings to which these regulations apply other than an employment matter, any disbursements incurred by the representative in respect of counsel's fees: see regulation 1(2) of the Damages-Based Agreements Regulations 2013.

Whether to enter into a Damages-based Agreement

69. The "cab rank rule" does not apply to Damages-based Agreements; as such, counsel should decide whether to accept instructions offered on the basis of such factors as the merits of the case, the needs of the client, and the chances of making a profit. That decision will depend on factors that will include the following:

(a) the category of case;

(b) whether there are alternative means of funding (which in this context will mean alternatives such as Conditional Fee Agreements and litigation funding) commercial considerations; and

(c) ethical considerations.

70. Each of those considerations is considered in turn, but first, the reader should look at the decision-making process as set out in Flowchart A: Main Chart and Flowchart F: DBA Sub-Flowchart.

Category of case

71. There are three types of work that need to be considered:

(a) **True non-contentious work**: Whilst there is a small risk that Damages-based Agreements are unlawful at common law, the Bar Council believes that there can be no objection in principle to a DBA-like agreement (i.e. a traditional contingency agreement) in those cases that do not involve disputes between parties.[28] This is often called "true non-contentious work". Thus, if counsel were to advise on the sale of a company's assets or on a tax-saving measure, there would be no objection in principle to counsel being paid on a percentage of that company's assets or fraction of the tax saved. Certainly, there is no rule or policy that would specifically prevent barristers from entering into such agreements.

It is not clear whether the legislation covering Damages-based Agreements is intended to extend to true non-contentious work.[29] It would appear that the provision that disapplies the regulation of Damages-based Agreements in non-contentious work applies only to solicitors.[30] The most cautious route counsel can take is to comply with the relevant legislation. The Model Agreements can easily be modified for that purpose.

(b) **Disputatious non-contentious work**: Work becomes contentious if proceedings are issued in a court (or a tribunal that has the same status as a court); this will not be the case if proceedings have not yet been issued or if proceedings are issued in other tribunals, such as an employment tribunal.[31] This means that non-contentious work may be carried out in a dispute that a layman would describe as being contentious. That type of work is disputatious non-contentious work (otherwise known as "litigated non-contentious work"). Section 58AA of the Courts and Legal Services Act 1990 will apply.[32] As such, the Model Agreements ought to be used. A Damages-based Agreement must not relate to work which is of such a type that it cannot be the subject of an enforceable Conditional Fee Agreement.[33]

(c) **Contentious work**: This means business that is litigation in court (or in a tribunal that has the same status as a court). By and large, the comments made immediately above apply.

28 The Bar Council's view as to the legality of damages-based agreement in non-contentious work (see below) has changed since the last time it issued guidance on this topic; any previous guidance the Bar Council may have given is revoked.

29 This is because there are competing arguments. On the one hand, sub-section 58AA(3) of the Courts and Legal Services Act 1990 appears to define damages-based agreement by reference to advocacy

services and litigation, yet sub-section 58AA(9) of that Act and the draft delegated legislation made under that Act appears to contain a provision that disapplies that legislation in non-contentious work, but only for solicitors.

30 See sub-paragraph 1(4) if the Damages-Based Agreements Regulations 2013.

31 See section 87 of the Solicitors Act 1974 and *In Simpkin Marshall Ltd* Re [1959] Ch 229, [1958] 3 All ER 611.

32 See section 58AA(7A) of the Courts and Legal Services Act 1990.

33 See sub-section 58AA(4)(aa) of the Courts and Legal Services Act 1990.

Alternative means of funding and Damages-based Agreements

72. Given the special features of Damages-based Agreements, it would often be necessary to consider litigation funding (but, assuming the market conditions have not substantially changed since the time of writing, only in cases where the sums involved are in the millions or at least high six figures) and the various flavours of Conditional Fee Agreement.

Commercial considerations: Damages-based Agreements

73. There are three factors that are likely to be relevant to the issue of whether a damages fee agreement is commercially viable; the first is the level of risk in terms of whether a payment will be made, the second is the way in which that risk is distributed, and the third is the amount that is likely to be recovered.

74. A good way to decide whether a Damages-based Agreement is likely to create a profit is to work out the "present value" of the proposed agreement; this would involve estimating the monies that are likely to be recovered and adjusting them for risk. In a simple case this may be as simple as multiplying the likely size of the damages-based fee (in money terms) and then multiplying this by the percentage chance that the case will be won. This should then be compared the present values of other types of agreement (or other types of work). The starting point is Flowchart A: Main Chart but this will then lead to Flowchart F: DBA Sub-Flowchart. Where it is not possible to estimate the amount of likely damages, then (in very large cases) it may be necessary to take advice from an actuary.

75. When calculating the "present value", it should not be forgotten that there are limits on the amounts that may be recovered. The relevant limits will be as follows:

(a) in a personal injury matter, the damages-based fee must not exceed 25 percent of the damages (excluding damages for future pecuniary loss);

(b) in an employment matter, the damages-based fee must not exceed 35 percent of the monies recovered; and

(c) In any other matter, the damages-based fee must not exceed 50 percent of the monies recovered.

76. All of these figures are inclusive of VAT. Those limits apply only at first instance. It is not clear what the interplay is where both counsel and the professional client are acting under Damages-based Agreement; it could well

be the case that the aforesaid limits apply to the aggregate of their damages-based fees rather than to each individually.

Ethical considerations: Damages-based Agreements

77. As with Conditional Fee Agreements, it would not be appropriate to enter into a Damages-based Agreement where there was an unacceptable conflict of interests between counsel and the lay client. In this regard, the following factors should be taken into account:

    (a) **The views of the lay client:** Some lay clients want to "incentivise" counsel, and they may prefer to pay more in order to get a better result; if a client wishes to do this and if he or she fully understands the alternatives, then this is not in any way objectionable.

    (b) **The alternatives available to the lay client**: Very often, the alternatives available to the lay client would be more unattractive than a Damages-based Agreement; in particular, for a commercial client the alternative would often be a litigation funding agreement. It should be borne in mind that if the lay client cannot instruct counsel in the way that he or she wants, he or she may be forced to instruct someone other than counsel or a less suitable barrister; thus, it may be in the client's best interests to accept an invitation to work under a Damages-based Agreement if this is the only means by which they can receive expert legal advice.

    (c) **Access to justice**: Sometimes (such as where the chances of success are remote but the damages are very large) a Damages-based Agreement is the only method by which a lay client can secure the services of legal advisors without having to fund the proceedings privately; where this is the case, then it would usually be wrong to reject the case on the basis that it was not in the lay client's best interests to enter into a Damages-based Agreement.

78. Finally, it should be borne in mind that where there are concerns about the amount that the lay client may have to pay, this can be addressed by limiting that amount in the agreement.

Miscellaneous matters

The section deals with the model agreements and some other matters.

How to complete the model agreements

79. The following guidance refers to the standard Model Agreements. Variants of the Model Agreements exist for use where the lay client is a defendant and where the agreement is intended to be a collective Conditional Fee Agreement. The latter should only be completed with the assistance of a specialist and therefore no guidance is given in this guidance.

80. The Model Agreements[34] are intended to be completed part-by-part:

    (a) **Part One**: The administrative details should be entered. The details of the claim and the opponent should be sufficient to allow the case to be identified; they should not be so specific as to narrow the ambit of the agreement. Thus, "the claim for damages arising out of the road traffic accident in February 2011" is better than "the Part 7 claim for damages for injury to the left arm arising out of the road traffic accident on 24 February 2011 at 2.32 pm". The Agreement Date is merely a date for identifying the Conditional Fee Agreement; it does not matter whether it is the date the agreement was signed or whether it is the date it was printed.

(b) **Part Two:** Thought should be given to whether the agreement is or is not retrospective.

(c) **Part Three:** The type of agreement should be selected.

(d) **Part Four:** The default success fee is the relevant fixed success fee (if there is one) or a sliding scale. The agreement will still work if no risk assessment is entered, but this is poor practice. A risk assessment should be entered and a success fee recorded accordingly.

There are, in essence, two approaches to a success fee that is not fixed:

(i) *Single stage success fee:* This is the traditional method. The risk as estimated as a single figure (which should include an allowance for quantum risk and recovery risk). That figure is then turned into a success fee by using the ready reckoner at the end of this guidance. This will, in a personal injuries case, need to be limited to the appropriate percentage of damages.

(ii) *Staged success fee:* This is the preferred method. The success fee rises as the case goes on. The final stage is nearly always 100%. The starting stage will depend on the level of risk generally, but – obviously – the first stage should not be higher than the amount that would have been sought if a single stage success fee had been claimed. The stages can be based on any identifiable step or steps in the proceedings: thus, the first stage could be, for example, up to 14 days before trial or service of the Directions Questionnaire. Again, in a personal injuries case, then be limited to the appropriate percentage of damages (see page 155).

(e) **Part Five:** Counsel's normal fees should be recorded.

(f) **Part Six:** A record should be made of what counsel will charge if only a part of their fees are recovered. It is good practice to discuss this with the solicitor in advance of the agreement being made.

(g) **Part Seven:** Definition of "win": The standard definition will usually work, but it may not be optimal for the case in hand. In a case involving non-financial matters, this definition should be examined very carefully indeed.

(h) **Part Eight:** The agreement should be signed.

(i) **Part Nine:** Some versions have a Part Nine which sets out certain advice that needs to be given to the lay client; the correct advice needs to be selected.

81. Some of the variants of the Model Agreements (such as the Private Fee Agreement) do not have all of the above Parts; the number is the same as in other agreements, however, so Part Two might be followed by Part Five with no intervening Parts Three and Four.

82. There are two types of agreement that merit special attention: Damages-based Agreements and Conditional Fee Agreements which are the first to be made with the lay client in the claim in question.

34 See The Model Agreements, http://www.barcouncil.org.uk/for-the-bar/practice-updates-and-guidance/remuneration-guidance/Guidance-for-Barristers-and-Clerks-Relating-to-Privately-Funded-Civil-Litigation.

Damages-based Model Agreement

83. The following applies to the Damages-based Agreement Model Agreement:

(a) It contains a section that deals with the damages-based fee rather than the success fee. Again, however, the numbering is broadly the same as the other variants.

(b) It is particularly important that the following details are entered correctly (because otherwise it may be found to be unenforceable):[35]

(i) the reason for setting the amount of the payment at the level agreed, including having regard to, where appropriate, whether the claim or proceedings is one of several similar claims or proceedings;

(ii) the claim or proceedings or parts of them to which the agreement relates;

(iii) the circumstances in which the representative's payment, expenses and costs, or part of them, are payable; and

(iv) an explanation as to the point at which expenses become payable; and a reasonable estimate of the amount that is likely to be spent upon expenses, inclusive of VAT.

(c) It will rarely be the case that the first of these points will require counsel to set out any form of mathematical calculation; this is because no calculation exists that would allow one to calculate "the" fee. Whilst there is no authority on the point, it is likely that a narrative explanation would be appropriate where each factor is identified and then taken into account in the round; if so, the following forensic sieve would be as good as any (it being loosely based on the "seven pillars of wisdom"[36]):

(i) *Risk:* The risk that the claim will not be successful or that only a relatively small amount is recovered (this may need to be set out in some detail).

(ii) *Value:* The amount or value of any money or property involved.

(iii) *Counsel's skill and position in the market:* The skill, effort and specialised knowledge that counsel would have to bring to bear on the matter and what other counsel with the same skills and knowledge would be likely to charge (i.e., the state of the legal services market and counsel's position).

(iv) *Importance:* The importance of the matter to all the parties.

(v) *Time and conduct:* The time spent on the case; the anticipated conduct of all the parties may be relevant, especially where the other side's conduct is likely to generate extra work;

(vi) *Complexity:* The particular complexity of the matter or the difficulty or novelty of the questions raised; and

(vii) *Other circumstances:* Where relevant, the place where and the circumstances in which the work or any part of it will be done.

(d) In addition, whilst not a regulatory requirement, the client should be given such further explanation, advice or other information about any of those matters as the client may request.

(e) In a personal injuries case, an explanation must be given as to how the damages-based fee will be calculated; whilst there is no authority on this point, counsel would be well advised to deal with the interplay (if any) with the fees sought by their professional client.

(f) In a claim for personal injuries, there must be an explanation as to how the payment will be calculated; if the Model Agreements are used, then this should not be a problem.

(g) In an employment matter, the client must be told about the following (in writing):

(i) the circumstances in which the client may seek a review of costs and expenses of the representative and the procedure for doing so;

(ii) the dispute resolution service provided by the Advisory, Conciliation and Arbitration Service (ACAS) in regard to actual and potential claims; and

(iii) whether other methods of pursuing the claim or financing the proceedings, including (i) advice under the Community Legal Service, (i) legal expenses insurance, (iii) pro bono representation, or (iv) trade union representation, are available, and, if so, how they apply to the client and the claim or proceedings in question.

(h) The regulations relating to Damages-based Agreements differ from those that relate to Conditional Fee Agreements in that there is no provision that releases additional legal representatives from the obligation to provide the type of advice set out above.

35 See regulation 3 of the Damages-Based Agreements Regulations 2013.
36 See CPR rule 44.5(3).

Administrative matters

84. The Model Agreements work best with Word 2007 or later; with earlier versions, the drop-down lists may not work.

Points for chambers and for groups of barristers

85. The following miscellaneous matters may apply to chambers or other groups of barristers (such as departments and specialist groups within chambers):

(a) **Equality and diversity (maternity leave, paternity leave, disability, illness, etc)**: The Model Agreements contain a provision that permits counsel to suspend the agreement and to ask a counsel of similar standing to carry out the work in the event of counsel being unable to provide legal services because of maternity leave, paternity leave, disability, etc. Chambers should make sure that that there is a proper system for supporting counsel who transfer cases in this way. That system should be sufficiently reliable for counsel to be able to accept cases without having to be concerned about whether cover is available. Chambers should specifically consider:

(i) whether the case should be covered by another member of chambers until the chosen Counsel is expected to be available again;

(ii) whether the case should be transferred to another to handle until its conclusion; or

(iii) whether the issue could best be dealt with by chosen Counsel retaining overall control but another member of chambers assisting.

(c) **Screeners**: Some chambers operate a screening policy where cases are screened before they are allocated. Where this is done, a record must be kept of the name of the person or persons who have carried out the screening. They must not act for the opponent in any case that they have screened. Issues of client confidentiality may arise, and as such, it is best to obtain the client's consent to the case being screened.

When withdrawal is permitted

86. Counsel may withdraw from the case in any of the circumstances set out in the agreement (regardless of its type), but only if satisfied that they are permitted to withdraw pursuant to Part VI of the Code of Conduct.

87. The Code of Conduct takes priority over the agreement. Thus, if counsel is required to withdraw for professional reasons, they must do so regardless of whether the agreement is silent on the point.

How to repair 'broken' agreements

88. It will often be the case that counsel will find that their agreement (be it a Conditional Fee Agreement, Damages-based Agreement or other type of agreement) is defective. If this happens after conclusion of the claim or matter, then there is not a lot that counsel can do to save the situation. In those circumstances, counsel will have to make the best of it. If, on the other hand, counsel discovers the error before the conclusion of the claim or matter, then steps can be taken to secure their position. Those steps include the following:

(a) asking the client to enter into a new (retrospective) agreement;

(b) asking the client to agree to the existing agreement being remedied;

(c) formulate an argument that will persuade the court to interpret the agreement in a way that is favourable to counsel; and

(d) rely on the fact that it is rare for counsel's fees to be challenged on the grounds of a defective retainer.

The flowcharts and sub-flowcharts

This part contains the decision flowcharts mentioned in the guidance.

89. The flowcharts are as follows:

(a) Main Chart.

(b) Selecting the type of CFA to use.

(c) Traditional CFA Sub-Flowchart.

(d) Discounted CFA Sub-Flowchart.

(e) CFA Lite Sub-Flowchart.

(f) DBA Sub-Flowchart, and

(g) Quantum risk Sub-Flowchart.

90. All the flowcharts are available in a separate document.[37]

NOTE: Red Flags in the flowcharts warn of a particular danger and red diamonds indicate troublesome issues.

37 See Guidance for Barristers and Clerks Relating to Privately Funded Civil Litigation: The Flowcharts.

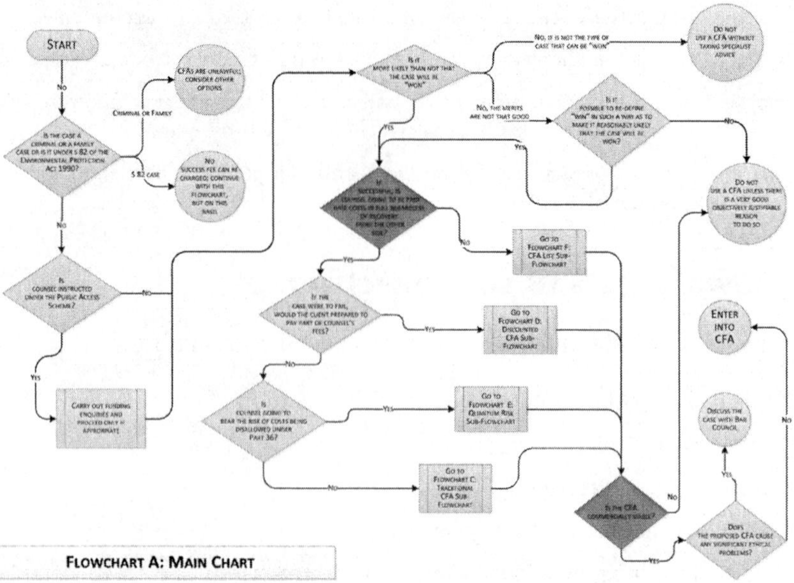

Flowchart A: Main Chart

Flowchart B: selecting the type of conditional fee agreement to use

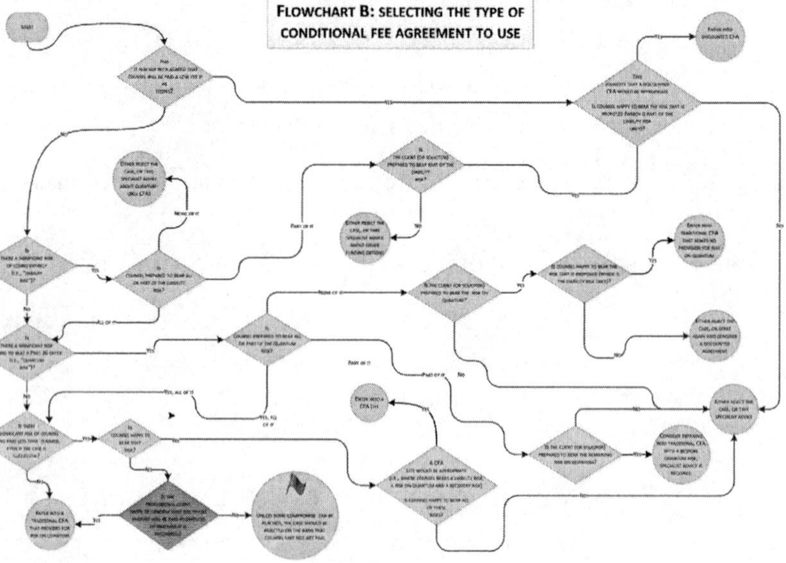

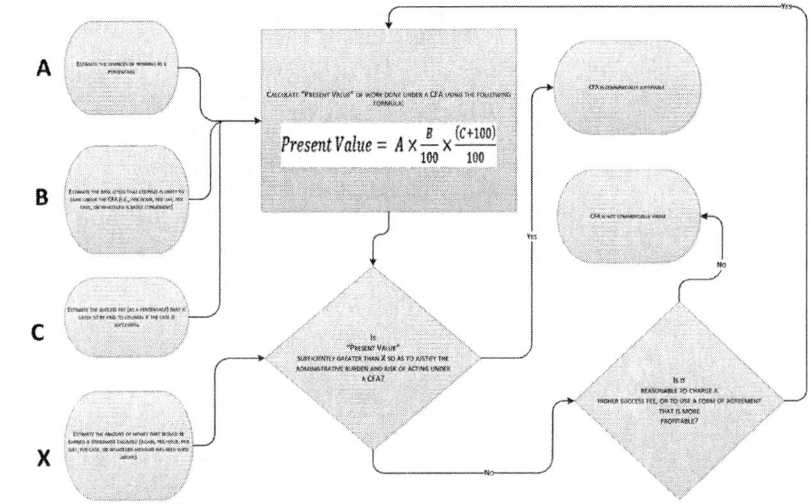

FLOWCHART C: TRADITIONAL CFA SUB-FLOWCHART

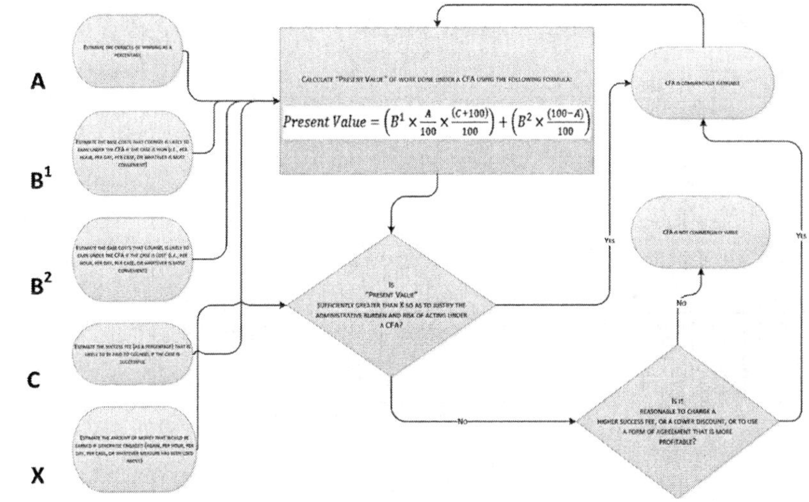

FLOWCHART D: DISCOUNTED CFA SUB-FLOWCHART

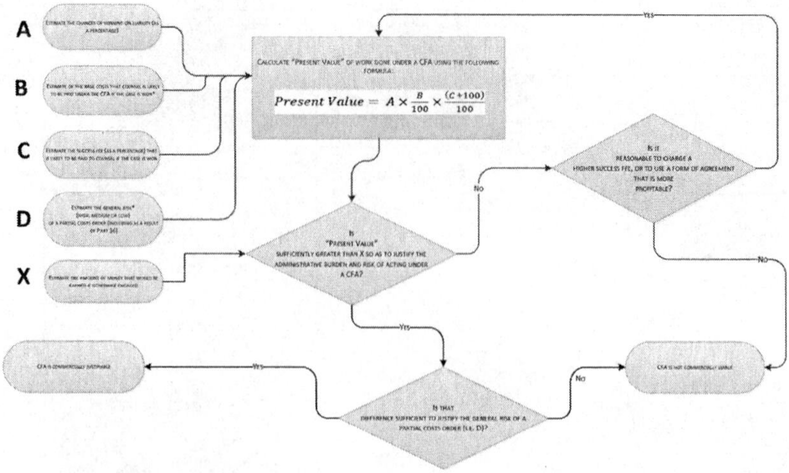

FLOWCHART E: CFA LITE SUB-FLOWCHART

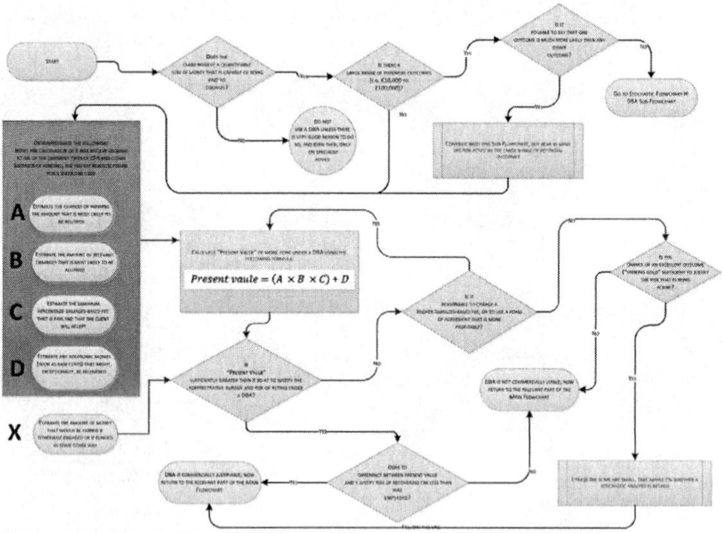

FLOWCHART F: DBA SUB-FLOWCHART

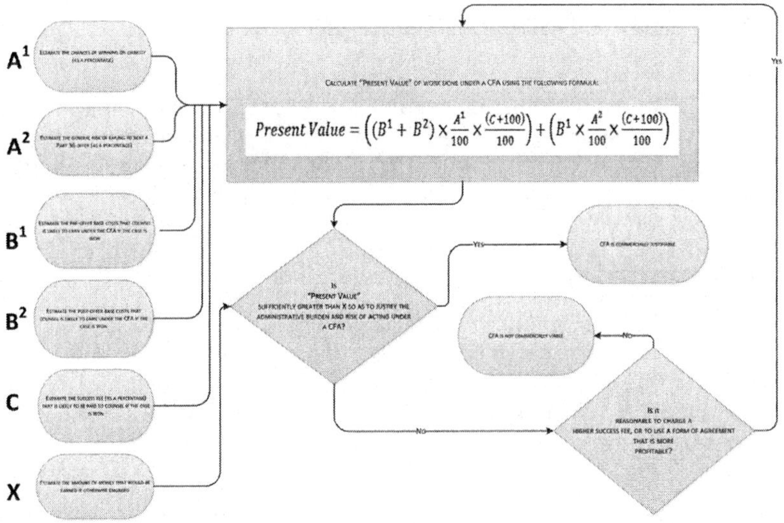

Flowchart G: Quantum Risk Sub-Flowchart

Annex 1: Full advice on funding

1. Where counsel is primarily responsible for giving advice about funding directly, then it will usually be the case that **counsel funding** and **case funding** will be very similar. The following issues might need to be addressed.

Funding enquiries

2. The starting point would be to make funding enquiries (which are those enquiries that are made of or on behalf of the lay client for the purposes of deciding how the case is to be funded). They are intended to find out whether the lay client is able to use any of the following:

   (a) before the event (BTE) insurance (also known as "legal expenses insurance");

   (b) legal assistance funded by a trades union or other similar body; and

   (c) civil legal aid.

3. Where counsel has not been instructed by a solicitor (or by another lawyer who is under a comparable duty to carry out funding enquiries), then it may be appropriate directly to ask the lay client whether any of these forms of funding exist. If they do exist, it would usually be appropriate to ask the lay client to produce the relevant documents for inspection, if the client agrees, by counsel. It is worth considering whether a charge should be made for this service and in any event how much time is required as part of the engagement of counsel (or considering whether to engage counsel). Any time spent on this topic needs to be factored in, especially if there is an urgency to the case.

4. In general terms, the following enquiries ought to be borne in mind:

   (a) If it exists, the lay client may be asked to produce any legal expenses policy (also known as a "before the event policy").

   (b) In view of the fact that legal expenses policies are usually incorporated into other contracts of insurance, it may be appropriate to ask to see those other policies; home contents insurance, buildings insurance and motor insurance often contain legal expense insurance.

   (c) If a legal expenses policy does exist, then it would be appropriate to form a view as to whether it is suitable for the matter in hand. Factors that may be relevant include:

      (i) the limit of insurance as compared to the likely cost of the claim (on both sides, where that is relevant);

      (ii) the stage reached in the litigation (this being relevant because the right to choose a lawyer generally applies only after proceedings have been issued);

      (iii) whether it is in the lay client's best interests to use a "panel" firm and whether the lay client reasonably objects to doing that;

(iv) the limit on the hourly rate for "off panel" firms (if any) and whether this would realistically be sufficient to purchase the relevant legal services; and

(v) whether the insurance is for both sides' costs or only for an opponent's costs.

(d) If the legal expenses insurance is not suitable, then it may be worth making enquires of the insurer as to whether it is prepared to fund the matter notwithstanding the strict terms of the policy:

(i) It may also be appropriate to ask whether the lay client is or was previously a member of any trades union or professional (not regulatory) body; if so, it may be helpful to make enquiries as to whether that body or union provides suitable funding.

(ii) The task of examining the policies is, in general, not a job for the lay client to do themselves. In particular, if comparison with the duties owed by solicitors is any guide, it would not be appropriate routinely to ask the lay client whether they have insurance that could be used for covering the claim in question. The better approach would be to ask them to produce all of the potentially relevant policies themselves. It is normally fairly easy to determine whether a policy contains legal expenses insurance as it is regulatory requirement to set it out in a separate section. Nonetheless, if counsel feels that considering the terms of the policy is something that requires advice from someone specialised in such matters, they should inform the client who should have the choice whether to seek separate specific advice on the scope of any insurance cover. Any such advice will have to be the subject-matter of separate instructions from the client.

The lay client should to be told of all the potentially available funding options, including those that may be available if the lay client were to instruct someone else. If counsel reasonably believes that a funding option is, in practice, not going to be available, then there is no need to mention it. The lay client must be given clear and focussed advice and should not be overburdened with irrelevant information.

(e) If counsel believes that the lay client's best interests would be served by a method of funding that is different to that which their client proposed and if counsel is prepared to accept that method of funding, then it should be offered; if counsel is not prepared to accept that method of funding, then they should explain that that is the case and that other lawyers may be willing to provide legal services on terms that are more favourable to the lay client. If counsel reasonably believes that that option is, in reality, not going to be available, then there is no need to mention it.

(f) Having identified all the funding options (including those that might be offered by other lawyers), counsel should explain the differences between them, including their most important pros and cons. Counsel should, in addition, make a recommendation as to which method of funding is best; if counsel is not prepared to act under those terms, then they should explain why. Counsel is under no duty to offer only the best method of funding but is under a duty to give best advice about funding.

(g) Counsel should explain the terms of the proposed agreement and (in general terms) its effect; the amount of information should meet the lay client's reasonable needs and should be proportionate to the matter in hand.

(h) Counsel should consider whether the lay client is at risk of being ordered to pay the other side's costs; if there is a significant risk of this, then counsel should consider how that risk could be minimised (such as by making tactical offers) or managed (such as by purchasing after the event insurance). If the lay client is at risk of paying costs in certain circumstances (such as if they behave unreasonably), then counsel should state what those circumstances are.

(i) Counsel should then provide their best estimate of the total costs of the matter (or, if appropriate, part of the matter) both in terms of their own fees, the lay client's own costs generally and the other side's costs generally. Counsel should then explain what is likely to happen in the event of the lay client winning, losing and (if appropriate) winning only part of the matter. The lay client should be told what their net liability or benefit is, this being the total that the client will actually pay or receive once all counterclaims, costs orders, fees, disbursements, etc, have been taken into account. That figure (which may be qualified in appropriate circumstances) should be given for: (1) the worst case scenario assuming that there is no dishonesty or unreasonable conduct, and (2) the most likely outcome. Unless it is inappropriate to do so, counsel should provide their best estimate of the chances of success.

(j) Counsel should express a view in clear and reasoned terms as to whether the likely benefit to the lay client of continuing with the matter justifies the costs. If the costs are likely to be disproportionate, counsel should state that fact and should explain what the effect of such a finding is likely to be.

Conditional Fee Arrangements — Guidance for barristers appearing before a fee paid judge who is a current member of their Chambers

[3.203]–[3.204]

The Standards Committee of the Bar Standards Board has produced guidance specifically addressing the scenario in which barristers appear before a judge who is a current member of their chambers in terms of potential conflicts of interest etc:

If a barrister acting on the basis of a conditional fee arrangement appears in a case to be heard by a fee paid judge who is a current member of his or her chambers there is a risk of the need to recuse on the grounds of bias. Depending on arrangements within chambers for sharing expenses the judge may be said to have a financial interest in the outcome of the case.

Barristers and heads of chambers should therefore ensure that clerking arrangements, including a system to carry out appropriate monitoring of diaries, are in place which will enable the court to be notified in advance before a case is listed where there is a risk that a barrister acting on the basis of a conditional fee may be be listed at that court at a time when another member of chambers is sitting at that court as a fee-paid judge. In such circumstances, the court should be given as much notice as possible.

A barrister instructed on the basis of a conditional fee who becomes aware that his or her case has in fact been listed before a fee paid judge who is a member of his or her chambers should take steps to alert the court as soon as practicable, and to inform the lay client what has occurred. If the matter is nonetheless listed before that fee paid judge the barrister should ensure that it is drawn to the attention of the fee paid judge and his or her opponent, preferably in advance of the hearing,—that: (a) the fee paid judge is a member of his or her chambers; and (b) the barrister concerned is acting on the basis of a conditional fee arrangement.

It then remains a matter for the court to decide whether it is appropriate for the case to proceed before that judge and if so, on what basis. In terms of best practice to be followed by judges in any cases in which bias is or might be alleged, barristers are referred to the guidelines suggested by the Court of Appeal in *Jones v DAS Legal Expenses Insurance Co Ltd* [2003] EWCA Civ 1071, para 35, [2004] IRLR 218, para 35, 147 Sol Jo LB 932, para 35.

It is recommended that any communication referred to above should be in writing or confirmed in writing as far as practicable. For the avoidance of doubt, apart from indicating that he or she is acting under a conditional fee agreement as indicated above, nothing in this guidance implies that a barrister should provide any additional information about the details of the conditional fee arrangements in place in excess of such disclosure as is required by the Civil Procedure Rules and relevant Practice Directions.

Guidance to Barristers Undertaking Civil Legal Aid Work

[3.205]

In March 2013, the Bar Council produced the following guidance specifically for barristers undertaking civil legal aid work after 1 April 2013 in all categories of civil cases other than family cases.

The Guidance is intended to help explain how civil legal aid work has been changed by the legal aid reforms introduced by the Legal Aid, Sentencing and Punishment of Offenders Act 2012 (LASPO) and the secondary legislation made under it.

The Guidance cannot, and does not, seek to cover all dimensions of the changes which have taken place. It focuses only on one specific issue – the remaining scope of civil legal aid – with the intention of helping a barrister determine whether a case can be brought within one of the new prescribed categories where civil legal aid remains available or within the new exceptional funding criteria.

The Guidance provides an overview of the scope of civil legal aid now available in each of the following categories of law:

- actions against the police;
- clinical negligence;
- community care;
- debt;
- education;
- employment;
- housing;
- immigration and asylum;
- inquests;
- mental health;
- personal injury;
- public law and judicial review; and
- welfare benefits.

The Guidance has been prepared by a team of practising barristers and clerks who comprise the Bar Council's Civil (Public) Panel. It will be regularly revised and updated and the Bar Council welcomes any comments or suggestions to inform future revisions of the Guidance. Any comments should be sent to Remuneration@BarCouncil.org.uk

This Guidance does not address alternative methods of funding civil cases whether by private payment, conditional fee agreements, damages-based agreements or otherwise. Barristers seeking guidance on those funding methods should consult the Bar Council's Guidance for Barristers and Clerks Relating to Privately Funded Civil Litigation.

Overview

Summary

1. This Guidance is directed to barristers undertaking civil legal aid work after 1 April 2013 in all categories of civil cases other than family cases.

2. The Guidance is intended to help explain how civil legal aid work has been changed by the legal aid reforms introduced by the Legal Aid, Sentencing and Punishment of Offenders Act 2012 (LASPO) and the secondary legislation made under it. This material has been prepared by a team of practising barristers and clerks who comprise the Bar Council's Civil (Public) Panel. It will be regularly revised and updated. The Bar Council welcomes any comments or suggestions to inform future revisions of the Guidance.

3. This Guidance cannot, and does not, seek to cover all dimensions of the changes which have taken place. It focuses only on one specific issue – the remaining scope of civil legal aid – with the intention of helping a barrister determine whether a case can be brought within one of the new prescribed categories where civil legal aid remains available or within the new exceptional funding criteria. This Guidance provides an overview of the scope of civil legal aid now available in each of the following categories of law:

- actions against the police;
- clinical negligence;
- community care;
- debt;
- education;
- employment;
- housing;
- immigration and asylum;
- inquests;
- mental health;
- personal injury;
- public law and judicial review; and
- welfare benefits.

4. Readers interested in pursuing other dimensions of the legal aid reforms are directed to guidance available from the following sources:

- *The Lord Chancellor's Guidance on Civil Legal Aid* (February 2013) Ministry of Justice;
- *Legal Aid Reforms: Frequently Asked Questions* (July 2012) Ministry of Justice;
- *Out of scope, out of mind: Who really loses from legal aid reform* (March 2012) Citizens Advice Bureau Service; and
- *Legal Aid Handbook 2013/2014* (April 2013) Legal Action Group.

5. This Guidance does not address alternative methods of funding civil cases whether by private payment, conditional fee agreements, damages-based agreements or otherwise. Barristers seeking guidance on those funding methods should consult the Bar Council's *Guidance for Barristers and Clerks Relating to Privately Funded Civil Litigation.*

6. This Guidance is best read electronically and care should be taken that the most up to date version is accessed. This is to ensure that hyperlinks in the Guidance lead to the correct sources.

Keeping up to date

7. The Bar Council and the Legal Aid Agency (LAA) have agreed that there should be regular opportunities for the exchange of information between the

Bar and legal aid officials about the operation of the legal aid reforms, including the matters covered in this Guidance. Individual barristers can get involved in this process by:

- attending the meetings held in London and on Circuit where barristers can meet and discuss issues directly with legal aid officials. These are known as Bar Reference Group meetings
- raising issues of concern about the general administration of civil legal aid for the Bar Council to canvass at its regular liaison meetings with senior legal aid officials.[5]

8. Regular updates on aspects of the material covered in this Guidance are available free of charge from three sources to which all civil legal aid practitioners should consider subscribing:
   - Remuneration Update (issued by the Bar Council).
   - Advocates' Bulletin (issued by the Legal Aid Agency).
   - Latest News and Updates (issued by the Legal Aid Agency).
9. The LAA have also published online training modules covering the impact of the legal aid reforms.
10. Barristers regularly undertaking civil legal aid casework may benefit from membership of the Legal Aid Practitioners Group (LAPG).

Legal Aid, Sentencing and Punishment of Offenders Act 2012

The headline changes

11. In April 2013 civil legal aid underwent its biggest shake-up in a generation. The driving force for change was the Government policy to reduce public spending.
12. The changes were first outlined in a consultation paper issued in 2010. There were some 5,000 representations received in the consultation process but the Government's response to the consultation, published in 2011, advised that it would press forward with the reforms largely as originally proposed. LASPO was the subsequent legislative vehicle for the central reforms. It completed the Parliamentary process and received Royal Assent on 1 May 2012. Since then the detail of the changes has been supplied in a series of statutory instruments.
13. The 'headline' changes include:
   - **Abolition of the Legal Services Commission**. The LSC was abolished on 1 April 2013. Decision-making on legal aid is now the role of a Director of Legal Aid Casework and administration of applications, claims and payments is now handled by the Legal Aid Agency (LAA) based within the Ministry of Justice. All policy responsibility is taken directly by the Lord Chancellor and other ministers in the Ministry of Justice.
   - **Reduced scope of civil legal aid**. Before 1 April 2013 the assumption was that civil legal aid was available to help on almost all

aspects of English law, with narrowly prescribed exceptions. Since 1 April 2013 the situation has been completely reversed – civil legal aid is now only available for prescribed topics and types of legal work, subject to a narrow override for exceptional funding in other cases.

- **Reduced access to civil legal aid through means-testing**. There has long been an element of means-testing to determine who qualifies for legal aid. From 1 April 2013 the means-test has been tightened so that fewer individuals qualify for legal aid.
- **Tightened merits testing**. Before 1 April 2013, LSC officials decided legal aid applications by applying criteria in the Funding Code and Guidance. Since 1 April 2013 the basis on which civil legal aid will be made available has been circumscribed by statutory instrument (see Civil Legal Aid (Merits Criteria) Regulations 2013 SI No. 104 and its subsequent amending regulations). From 27 January 2014 the criteria have been further tightened in that it is no longer possible to obtain legal aid for a case with only "borderline" merits (see Civil Legal Aid (Merits Criteria) (Amendment) Regulations 2014 SI No. 131).
- **Shift away from face-to-face access**. Government is increasingly keen that publicly-funded legal services should be accessed otherwise than through the traditional 'high street solicitor' route. From 1 April 2013 there is a greater emphasis on call-centre provision under which legal advice is sought and provided by telephone, email and online from the service called Civil Legal Advice (CLA). Those call-handlers giving advice are not usually solicitors but the intention is that their work be supervised by solicitors. For some subject areas it will only be possible to access legal aid by first passing through a 'gateway' of telephone advice services. The announcement of the successful bidders to provide the telephone advice services from 1 April 2013 was made in November 2012.
- **Reduced remuneration for undertaking legal aid work**. The cuts in rates of pay for solicitors, barristers and experts handling civil legal aid work were implemented early in the process of legal aid reform and apply to all work done in legal aid cases where legal aid applications were made after 3 October 2011. The rates of payment in effect from 3 October 2011 were implemented by The Community Legal Service (Funding) (Amendment No.2) Order 2011 SI No. 2066, Schedules 1 and 2. Rates of pay were, in effect, cut by 10 percent. From 1 April 2013, the rates of payment to solicitors, barristers and experts in civil legal aid cases have been prescribed by new regulations (see Civil Legal Aid (Remuneration) Regulations 2013 SI No. 422). A second round of even more significant cuts in rates of pay for junior barristers undertaking civil legal aid work came into effect for new cases on 2 December 2013 (see Civil Legal Aid (Remuneration) (Amendment) Regulations 2013 SI No. 2877).
- **Changes in the supplier-base**. Most front line suppliers of civil legal aid services were given notice ending their contracts with the LSC from 31 March 2013. Following a tendering-exercise, new contracts with the LAA were issued with effect from 1 April 2013. Other suppliers continue to work under the terms of the 2010

contract, which was subject to variation in order to bring it into line with LASPO and to provide as much consistency with the 2013 contract as possible. The amended contract documents are available on the Ministry of Justice website. Some previous suppliers have left the market. Many new providers have contracts to supply services in subject areas in respect of which they have not previously practised. Because some subject areas were exposed to over-bidding, the number of cases offered to successful bidders may have been so limited as to make contracts non-viable. But, as before, there are legal aid 'deserts' in which no local provider of specialist legal services is available to take on particular types of legal aid cases. The Bar Council understands that no contracts have been issued to barrister-led bidders.

- **Changes to civil legal aid procedures**. The rules about how legal aid applications are made, processed and determined and the various forms in which civil legal aid can be provided are detailed in a new statutory instrument (see Civil Legal Aid (Procedure) Regulations 2012 SI No. 3098). They are no longer the subject of procedural guides produced by the legal aid authorities.
- **Changes in the Civil Procedure Rules**. The availability of civil legal aid has also been affected by the changes introduced to the management of civil cases by amendments to the Civil Procedure Rules which came into effect on 1 April 2013.[1] Most obviously, the doubling of the upper limit of the small claims track from £5,000 to £10,000 has meant that civil legal aid effectively ceased to be available in respect of the taking or defending of most claims for sums between £5,000 and £10,000.
- **Changes to forms and in technology**. All the forms used to apply for legal aid or be paid for the provision of civil legal aid services were changed on 1 April 2013.[2] All claims submitted on the old forms after that date will be rejected. Later in 2013 the LAA will implement a new online computer system through which it will deal with applications for civil legal aid, with most other civil legal aid transactions, and with claims for payment presented by barristers and solicitors. All barristers doing civil legal aid work will need to register for participation in the new computerised system when it is rolled-out nationally. That roll-out had been intended to begin in January 2014 but it has been delayed following a pilot involving providers and chambers in the North East of England.
- **Changes to costs protection**. As with the old legal aid arrangements, the new scheme provides some measure of costs protection for circumstances in which a legally aided client loses their case. The details are given in a new set of regulations.[3] These also set out the circumstances in which the Lord Chancellor can be ordered to meet the costs of the successful party.
- **Supplementary Legal Aid Scheme**. It had been envisaged that a new Supplementary Legal Aid Scheme might be introduced alongside the mainstream legal aid reforms. That proposal has not been taken forward, at least for the time being.

- **Arrangements for payment of barristers**. Under the new civil legal aid scheme there is no contract between the LAA and any barrister for the payment by the LAA of a barrister's fees. Nor does counsel have any statutory entitlement to be paid for his or her services by the LAA. The scheme for payment of barristers in civil legal aid cases is intended to "work" by the LAA requiring its contracted suppliers to themselves pay professionals whom they engage in legal aid cases, including barristers and experts, and by the LAA agreeing, under those contracts, that in some cases it will pay barristers directly. It is therefore for each barrister to make their own agreement with a legal aid supplier, such as a solicitor, as to the terms on which they will accept a brief or instructions to undertake civil legal aid work. The old default Terms of Work between barristers and solicitors ceased to apply on 31 January 2013 and as a result any liability on the solicitor to pay (or arrange for the LAA to pay) in a civil legal aid case will only be enforceable if the barrister enters into a contract with the supplier.[4] The Bar Council's Fee Collection Service remains available to assist counsel if a solicitor will not pay (or will not arrange for a barrister to be paid by the LAA) in a civil legal aid case.[5]
- **Very High Cost Civil Cases**. As with the pre-reform arrangements, civil legal aid cases likely to incur costs of over £25,000 for the assisted client will be treated as "high cost" cases and subject to special measures.[6] In each such case, the solicitor will enter into an individual contract with the LAA specifically designed to manage high cost cases. Since 1 April 2013 the form of the contract has changed but not its essential structure which requires prior LAA approval of each "stage" of the case and imposes a reduced (risk rate) payment from the LAA if the case does not result in full costs recovery at *inter partes* rates. For counsel, the risk rates are at the same rates which have been frozen since 2000.[7] A barrister instructed by a solicitor holding a high cost contract does not become a party to the contract and has no statutory or contractual right to payment from the LAA. Although the LAA issued guidance on 1 April 2013 for barristers instructed in high cost cases,[8] the guidance was not drafted jointly with, or approved by, the Bar Council. An updated revision of the guidance was issued in December 2013.

PART III IN PRACTICE

1 Civil Procedure (Amendment) Rules 2013 SI No. 262.
2 The forms are available on the Ministry of Justice website.
3 Civil Legal Aid (Costs) Regulations 2013 SI No. 611.
4 Contractual terms that can be used for civil (non-family) legal aid work are available on the Bar Council website.
5 Further information on the Fees Collection Service is available on the Bar Council website.
6 Further information about civil VHCCs is available on the Ministry of Justice webpage for civil high cost cases.
7 £50 per hour for a junior, £90 per hour for a QC.
8 The guidance is available on the Ministry of Justice website.

How the Act works

14. This part of this Guidance offers an outline of how LASPO "works" and how barristers can identify what is within, and what is now outside, the scope of civil legal aid.

15. "Civil legal aid" is once again the term covering non-crime legal aid services. It is defined as constituting the "civil legal services" required to be made available under sections 9 or 10 of LASPO or under paragraph 3 of Schedule 3 of the Act.[9]

16. Civil legal aid services are services providing advice and assistance both as to the application of the law and legal proceedings. The term also covers providing advice and assistance to prevent or resolve legal disputes and for enforcing decisions in legal proceedings or other decisions resolving legal disputes.[10]

17. Sections 9 and 10 of LASPO deal respectively with first "General cases" and then "Exceptional cases".

9 LASPO, s 1(2)(a).
10 LASPO, s 8.

General cases

18. General cases are now those cases in which the subject is brought within the scope of the civil legal aid scheme because it is listed in Part 1 of Schedule 1 of LASPO and the Director of Legal Aid Casework (through LAA officials) has determined that the individual qualifies for civil legal aid services. Exceptional cases are those limited number of cases where civil legal aid remains available notwithstanding that they would not otherwise qualify as general cases.

19. The starting point in most cases will be to determine whether or not the case is of a type which falls within scope (i.e. is specified in Schedule 1 Part 1). The Schedule works by identifying a particular subject, describing which services within that subject are covered, and then applying a series of definitions, conditions and exclusions. The amount of cross-referencing within the Schedule produces a snakes-and-ladders type exercise to determine whether a particular sub-class of case is in or out of scope. The function of the detailed chapters in this Guidance is to break the back of that exercise so that barristers can more readily discern what is in or out of scope.

20. The fundamental concept is that if a case does not fall within the parameters of Schedule 1, Part 1, and cannot be treated as an exceptional case, it is out of scope. The net effect is that the following matters are now outside the scope of civil legal aid:[11]

- asylum support (except where accommodation is claimed);
- consumer and general contract;
- Criminal Injuries Compensation Authority cases;
- debt, except where there is an immediate risk to the home;
- employment cases;

- education cases, except for cases of Special Educational Needs;
- housing matters, except those where the home is at immediate risk (excluding those who are "squatting"), homelessness assistance, housing disrepair cases that pose a serious risk to life or health and anti-social behaviour cases in the County Court;
- immigration cases (non-detention);
- appeals to the Upper Tribunal from the General Regulatory Chamber of the First- tier Tribunal;
- cash forfeiture actions under the Proceeds of Crime Act 2002;
- legal advice in relation to a change of name;
- actions relating to contentious probate or land law;
- court actions concerning personal data;
- actions under section 14 of the Trusts of Land and Appointment of Trustees Act 1996;
- legal advice on will-making for those over 70; disabled people; the parent of a disabled person; the parent of a minor who is living with the client, but not with the other parent, and the client wishes to appoint a guardian for the minor in a will;
- private family law (other than cases where criteria are met regarding domestic violence or child abuse);
- tort and other general claims; and
- welfare benefits, except for appeals on a point of law in the Upper Tribunal (but not advocacy in the Upper Tribunal), and onward appeals to the Court of Appeal and Supreme Court.

21. The Lord Chancellor has power to alter, amend and add to Schedule 1 Part 1 and has already exercised that power.[12] This means that the Schedule must always be read in an updated or revised form in the light of the exercise of those powers.

22. Even if a case is within scope, the qualifying criteria for civil legal aid remain governed by tests of means and merits.[13] The means test is established by section 21, as again detailed in regulations. The merits test is framed by the general criteria in section 11 of LASPO which have subsequently been fleshed out in detailed regulations.[14]

23. The way in which the merits criteria are drawn means that it is not sufficient for a case to be within the scope of Schedule 1 Part 1. It must also meet the criteria set out in the regulations for the funding of such a case.[15] Again, the detail is in the respective subject-related chapters of this Guidance.

11 A summary of these areas is found in *Reform of Legal Aid in England and Wales: the Government Response* (2011). Do note that that response was published prior to the Parliamentary passage of LASPO and some changes were made to scope, such as the minor provision for some welfare benefits work to remain in scope.

12 See, for example, Civil Legal Aid (Preliminary Proceedings) Regulations 2013 SI No. 265. See also The Legal Aid, Sentencing and Punishment of Offenders 2012 (Amendment of Schedule 1) Order 2013 SI No. 748.

13 See LASPO, s 11.

14 Civil Legal Aid (Merits Criteria) Regulations 2013 SI No. 104.

15 Including amending regulations such as Civil Legal Aid (Merits Criteria) (Amendment) Regulations 2013 SI No. 772.

Exceptional cases

24. As indicated above, failure to bring a case within the parameters of Schedule 1 Part 1 is not necessarily fatal to legal aid entitlement. Two classes of exceptional case are provided for under section 10.

25. The first and more limited class applies to inquests and that class is dealt with in the Inquests chapter of this Guidance.

26. The second and broader class is set out in section 10(2)–10(3) of LASPO in these terms:

"(2) This subsection is satisfied where the Director—

(a) has made an exceptional case determination in relation to the individual and the services, and

(b) has determined that the individual qualifies for the services in accordance with this Part,

(and has not withdrawn either determination).

(3) For the purposes of subsection (2), an exceptional case determination is a determination—

(a) that it is necessary to make the services available to the individual under this Part because failure to do so would be a breach of—

(i) the individual's Convention rights (within the meaning of the Human Rights Act 1998), or

(ii) any rights of the individual to the provision of legal services that are enforceable EU rights, or

(b) that it is appropriate to do so, in the particular circumstances of the case, having regard to any risk that failure to do so would be such a breach."

27. How particular cases in specific subject areas can satisfy that test – and be brought back into scope – is considered in the subject-specific chapters of this Guidance. The Lord Chancellor has issued specific guidance to LAA officials on the operation of this category of 'non-inquest' exceptional funding.[16] Although it had been expected that significant numbers of applications would be successfully made for exceptional funding, only a small number of applications have been made of which only a tiny number has been successful. The first official figures on applications and awards of exceptional funding will be made available by the Ministry of Justice in March 2014.

28. Although every effort has been made to describe the provisions of LASPO accurately in this Guidance there can be no substitute for the legislation itself. This Guidance can usefully be read with:

- The Act itself.
- The Explanatory Memorandum.

Provider contracts

29. Providers are entitled to carry out work where they have a contract schedule authorisation for specified Categories of Law. The 2013 and amended 2010 Civil Contract definitions of categories of law do not purport to state what is in scope or what cases are eligible for exceptional funding. They do, however, define what cases providers can carry out under their contract. Any work that is in scope but is not within a Contract category is known as Miscellaneous Work and can be carried out by any Civil Contract holder.[17]

16 Lord Chancellor's Exceptional Funding Guidance (Non-Inquests).
17 Further information is available in the Standard Civil Contract 2013, Category Definitions and Standard Civil Contract 2010, Amended Category Definitions.

Regulations and official guidance

30. As the numerous references in the text and footnotes to this Guidance indicate, there are many regulations and orders published in exercise of the powers to make delegated legislation given in LASPO. Where possible this guidance provides hyperlinks to them.

31. The Lord Chancellor has published various pieces of official guidance, including:[18]

- *The Lord Chancellor's Guidance on Civil Legal Aid* (February 2013) Ministry of Justice;
- *The Lord Chancellor's Guidance on Exceptional Funding (Non-Inquests)* (February 2013) Ministry of Justice; and
- *The Lord Chancellor's Guidance on Exceptional Funding (Inquests)* (February 2013) Ministry of Justice.

32. This official guidance was written by civil servants in the Ministry of Justice. Its content was not the subject of any prior consultation with the Bar or with any other external body. It cannot substitute for the wording of the Act or the Regulations and the legal accuracy of the guidance that it gives cannot necessarily be assured. By way of illustration only, the *Guidance on Exceptional Funding* (*Non-Inquests*) states that whether or not there is a McKenzie friend (MF) who could be granted permission to speak on behalf of a party to proceedings is something a caseworker should consider when determining how capable an applicant for exceptional funding is of presenting their case effectively.[19] Compare and contrast this with the Master of the Rolls Practice Guidance 2010 on the role of MFs:[20]

"Courts should be slow to grant any application from a litigant for a right of audience or a right to conduct litigation to any lay person, including a MF."

33. Those interested in identifying the precise intended consequences of particular aspects of the new regime will find the detail set out in a host of impact assessments and equality impact assessments,[21] including assessments dealing specifically with the changes to scope.[22]

18 Civil legal aid funding guidance is available on the Ministry of Justice website
19 See Lord Chancellor's Exceptional Funding Guidance (Non-Inquests), page 9
20 Practice Guidance – McKenzie Friends (Civil and Family Courts), paragraph 19

21 The impact assessments and equality impact assessments are available on the archived Ministry of Justice website.

22 See the Impact Assessment specifically dealing with changes to scope and the Equality Impact Assessment.

Actions against the police

Category definition and scope

LASPO Schedule 1, Part 1

34. The LASPO categories of most relevance to Actions Against the Police (AAP) are those set out in Schedule 1, Part 1, paragraphs 21 and 22. Paragraphs 3 and 39 will also assist in some cases.

35. Paragraph 21 covers cases involving "abuse by a public authority of its position or powers". However, Schedule 1, Part 1, paragraph 21(4) goes on to provide that

> "For the purposes of this paragraph, an act or omission by a public authority does not constitute an abuse of its position or powers unless the act or omission –
>
> (a) is deliberate or dishonest, and
>
> (b) results in harm to a person or property that was reasonably foreseeable."

36. Paragraph 22 covers claims in tort or claims for damages (other than claims in tort) in respect of a "significant breach of Convention rights" by a public authority.[23]

37. Paragraphs 21(5) and 22(4) provide that for the purposes of paragraphs 21 and 22 "public authority" has the same meaning as in the Human Rights Act 1998, section 6:

> "(3)[…] 'public authority' includes—
>
> (a) a court or tribunal, and
>
> (b) any person certain of whose functions are functions of a public nature, but does not include either House of Parliament or a person exercising functions in connection with proceedings in Parliament
>
> […]
>
> (5) relation to a particular act, a person is not a public authority by virtue only of subsection (3)(b) if the nature of the act is private."

38. Paragraph 3 brings within scope cases involving the physical or mental abuse of children or vulnerable adults, and paragraph 39 covers assistance to the victims of certain sexual offences.

23 Further information on the meaning of "significant breach" is provided by the Lord Chancellor's Guidance Under Section 4 of Legal Aid, Sentencing and Punishment of Offenders Act 2012, paragraphs 11.1–11.3

Regulations

39. Chapter 3 of the Civil Legal Aid (Merits Criteria) Regulations 2013 sets out specific merits criteria provisions for claims against public authorities.[24]

40. Regulation 57 provides that where a claim is made for **investigative representation** in relation to a matter described in paragraphs 21 and 22, the "minimum damages" criteria set out in regulations 40(1)(c),[25] and (2),[26] only apply to the extent that the case:[27]

    (a) is part of a multi-party action; and

    (b) does not relate to:

        (i) the abuse of a child or a vulnerable adult; or

        (ii) a contravention of the Equality Act 2010 or of a previous discrimination enactment.

41. Following amendment by the Civil Legal Aid (Merits Criteria) Amendment Regulations 2014,[28] which came into force on 27 January 2014. Regulation 58 now provides that where a claim is made for **full representation** in relation to such cases the applicable criteria are those set out in regulation 39,[29] regulation 43 and Regulation 58(2).

42. Regulation 43 and 58(2) between them provide that funding will be granted if the proportionality test is met[30] and the prospects of success are either very good, good or moderate.[31] Funding will no longer be granted for cases with borderline prospects of success.

43. Regulation 59 sets out the criteria for **full representation** in relation to multi-party claims against public authorities: multi-party action damages criterion.

44. Under Regulation 20 of the Civil Legal Aid (Procedure) Regulations 2012,[32] discrimination cases that fall within the AAP contract category are exempt from the "gateway" provisions.

45. The Lord Chancellor's Guidance,[33] at parts 4–5 and 7, provides further guidance on the merits and costs benefit tests. These parts of the guidance should be examined closely by AAP practitioners given the different merits and costs benefit tests that apply to claims under paragraphs 21 and 22.

PART III IN PRACTICE

24 Civil Legal Aid (Merits Criteria) Regulations 2013 SI No. 104.
25 Which provides that "if the individual's claim is primarily a claim for damages or other sum of money in which the likely damages do not exceed £5,000, the case must be of significant wider public interest".
26 Which provides that "[f]or the purposes of paragraph (1)(c), if the claim forms part of a multi-party action only the lead claim within that action is capable of being a case of significant wider public interest".
27 Civil Legal Aid (Merits Criteria) Regulations 2013 SI No. 104, regulation 57(2).
28 Civil Legal Aid (Merits Criteria) Amendment Regulations 2014 SI No. 131.
29 Standard criteria for determinations for legal representation.
30 Civil Legal Aid (Merits Criteria) Regulations 2013 SI No. 104, regulation 58(2).
31 Civil Legal Aid (Merits Criteria) Regulations 2013 SI No. 104, regulation 43.
32 SI No. 3098.
33 Lord Chancellor's Guidance Under Section 4 of Legal Aid, Sentencing and Punishment of Offenders Act 2012.

Standard Civil Contract 2010 (as amended)

46. The Standard Civil Contract 2010 (between the then Legal Services Commission and contracted legal aid providers) previously included, within its "Actions Against the Police, etc" category, reference to claims arising out of the deliberate/dishonest torts such as assault, wrongful arrest and malicious prosecution but also claims arising from "... other abuse of authority or neglect of duty against anybody or person, public or private, with power to detain, imprison or prosecute".

47. The amended category definitions that apply from 1 April 2013[34] make clear that funding is now only available for cases within Schedule 1, Part 1, paragraphs 3, 21, 22 and 39 of LASPO.

48. The amended category definition refers to claims only being within scope if they relate to claims against public or private authorities with "... the power to prosecute, detain, or imprison". This limitation on the definition of public authority is not to be found in LASPO (which would prevail over the guidance) but this category would nevertheless appear to embrace the main types of authorities against which claims of this nature are brought (namely the police, prisons, immigration authorities and private bodies carrying out these functions).

49. The amended category definition also provides that claims for damages for clinical negligence (including claims funded via exceptional funding) are included only if the clinical negligence forms part of a claim which includes another cause of action against a body or person with power to detain or imprison.

50. The amended contract category definition also makes clear that exceptional funding under section 10 of LASPO can be made available for applications to the Home Office under the Criminal Justice Act 1988, section 133 or the *ex gratia* scheme for compensation for wrongful conviction and claims under the Criminal Injuries Compensation Authority Scheme, including any applications to the First-Tier Tribunal arising out of such a matter. It also makes clear that claims for damages in respect of alleged professional negligence in the conduct of a matter included in the category are covered.

34 Standard Civil Contract 2010, Amended Category Definitions, paragraphs 31–33.

Types of cases covered in practice

51. It is likely that most AAP cases will fall to be considered under LASPO Schedule 1, Part 1, paragraphs 21 and 22.

52. The reference in paragraphs 21(5) and 22(4) to the Human Rights Act 1998 definition of a public authority makes clear that where a private body is carrying out public functions it will be regarded as a public authority for these purposes. This is welcome given the increasing privatisation of public functions. It means that, for example, actions against those running private prisons or court escort services will continue to be within scope.

53. The main limitation on the scope of paragraph 21 claims is the provision in paragraph 21(4) confining claims under this category to those which arise

from "deliberate or dishonest" acts or omissions of public authorities and which result in "reasonably foreseeable harm to a person or property".

54. It is likely that the first limb of this definition will cause most difficulty, because it is hard to envisage many deliberate or dishonest acts by public authorities that do not also result in reasonably foreseeable harm to a person or property.

55. However, the limitation of claims to those arising from deliberate or dishonest acts means that the following sorts of cases are now likely to fall out of scope:

- claims of loss of liberty arising from the negligence of the police and/or immigration authorities;
- claims in respect of arrests pursuant to defective warrants; and
- cases where, due to negligence of the detaining authorities, a prisoner has been in a position to assault another prisoner due to negligence by the supervising officers.

56. The LAA has refused at least one funding application on the basis that an arrest alleged to have been carried out without the required reasonable suspicion did not involve a 'deliberate or dishonest act'. This is based on a questionable interpretation of paragraph 21(4)(a), and in particular the term 'deliberate'. It does not appear to be the position generally taken by the LAA.

57. The main limitation on the scope of paragraph 22 is the requirement that a claim only falls within it if it involves a "significant" breach of Convention rights by a public authority. Guidance on the meaning of "significant breach" is provided by the *Lord Chancellor's Guidance on Civil Legal Aid*, at paragraphs 11.1–11.3 (which replaces the previous Funding Code guidance on the meaning and effect of "Significant Human Rights Issue").[35] The new Guidance indicates that:

- this category is "intended to focus legal aid on the most serious cases";
- the word "significant" should be given its natural meaning; and
- factors which might be relevant in considering whether there has been a significant breach of a Convention right by a public authority include whether the breach was deliberate, and whether the individual has suffered a significant disadvantage taking account of both his or her subjective perceptions and what is objectively at stake in a particular case.

58. It is unsurprising that the Guidance seeks to focus funding for human rights cases on the most serious claims. In the police context, this provision is perhaps most likely to be of use in civil claims involving breaches of the rights set out in Articles 2, 3, 5, 8, 9, 10 and 14 of the European Convention on Human Rights (ECHR). In particular, it appears likely that any loss of liberty in contravention of Article 5 would amount to a "significant breach".

59. There has been widespread publicity recently over the issue of sexual offences committed by police officers and the victims of those offences may be assisted by LASPO Schedule 1, Part 1, paragraphs 3 and 39 (although many of those cases would also fall under paragraphs 21 and/or 22).

60. As indicated above, the amended contract category definition makes clear that exceptional funding under section 10 of LASPO can be made available for applications to the Home Office under the Criminal Justice Act 1988, section 133 or the *ex gratia* scheme for compensation for wrongful conviction and claims under the Criminal Injuries Compensation Authority Scheme. However, claims for exceptional funding in these cases and any other AAP claims which fall outside the general AAP funding provisions (such as those relating to negligence by the police or other authorities which do not on their facts fall within LASPO paragraphs 3, 21, 22 or 39) will need to meet the criteria for exceptional funding.

61. The *Lord Chancellor's Guidance on Exceptional Funding (Non-Inquests)* makes clear that the overarching question to be considered in determining such applications is whether the withholding of legal aid would make the assertion of the claim practically impossible or lead to an obvious unfairness in proceedings. Claims for compensation for miscarriages of justice are notoriously difficult, and such cases should have reasonable prospects of obtaining exceptional funding, as should complex claims relating to negligence by the police or other authorities. Particularly complicated Criminal Injuries Compensation Authority claims may well also meet the exceptional funding threshold.

62. The provisions of regulation 57 disapplying the "minimum damages" criteria to certain cases are welcome and should mean that even discrimination claims against public authorities that are worth less than £5,000 are brought within scope.[36]

35 Lord Chancellor's Guidance Under Section 4 of Legal Aid, Sentencing and Punishment of Offenders Act 2012.

36 See Civil Legal Aid (Merits Criteria) Regulations 2013 SI No. 104, regulation 57.

Clinical negligence

Category definition and scope

LASPO Schedule 1, Part 1

63. Clinical negligence is defined for the purposes of LASPO by paragraph 23(5) of Part 1 of Schedule 1 as "breach of a duty of care or trespass to the person committed in the course of the provision of clinical or medical services (including dental or nursing services)".

64. LASPO removed all claims for damages for clinical negligence from the scope of civil legal aid, with one exception: clinical negligence during pregnancy, child birth, or the postnatal period (eight weeks), which causes a child to suffer severe disability due to a neurological injury.

65. The conditions which must be met are set out in LASPO Schedule 1, Part 1, paragraph 23. They are that:

- clinical negligence caused "a neurological injury" to the individual (V)[37] and, as a result of the neurological injury, V is "severely disabled";[38]

- the clinical negligence occurred:
  - "while V was in his or her mother's womb"; or
  - "during or after V's birth"; and:
    - (i) if V was born before the beginning of the 37th week of pregnancy, the period of eight weeks beginning with the first day of what would have been that week; or
    - (ii) if V was born during or after the 37th week of pregnancy, the period of eight weeks beginning with the day of V's birth.[39]

66. Paragraph 23(5) provides that "disabled" means "physical or mentally disabled" and defines "birth" as "the moment when an individual first has a life separate from his or her mother" and references to an individual being born are interpreted accordingly.

67. The services under the certificate of public funding must be provided to V, or where V has died, to his or her "personal representatives", defined as being:[40]

"(a) a person responsible for administering the individual's estate under the law of England and Wales, Scotland or Northern Ireland, or

(b) a person who, under the law of another country or territory, has functions equivalent to those of administering the individual's estate."

68. Other clinical negligence claims can still secure civil legal aid if the LAA makes an "exceptional case determination" under section 10(2) of LASPO.

69. Section 10(2) applies where it is "necessary to make the services available to the individual under this Part because failure to do so would be a breach of ... the individual's Convention rights (within the meaning of the Human Rights Act 1998)", or where "... it is appropriate to do so, in the particular circumstances of the case, having regard to any risk that failure to do so would be such a breach".[41]

PART III
IN PRACTICE

37 The individual is defined as "V" throughout LASPO Schedule 1, Part 1, paragraph 23.
38 LASPO, Schedule 1, Part 1, paragraph 23(1).
39 LASPO, Schedule 1, Part 1, paragraph 23(2).
40 LASPO, Schedule 1, Part 1, paragraph 23(5).
41 LASPO, s 10(3).

Regulations

70. The same merits and financial eligibility criteria apply to clinical negligence claims which fall within the scope of civil legal aid as apply to a general case under paragraph 23 of Part 1 of Schedule 1 of LASPO and to those where an exceptional funding application is made under section 10(2) of LASPO.

71. There is no longer a specific category for clinical negligence claims in the relevant merits criteria. Instead, clinical negligence claims are subject to the general merits criteria before legal representation (investigative or full representation) can be granted or continue.[42]

72. Essentially, for **investigative representation** to be granted:

- the prospects of success must be "unclear" and substantial investigative work required before the prospects can be determined to be "poor", "moderate", "good" or "very good"; and
- there must be reasonable grounds for believing that once the investigative work is performed, the criteria for full representation will be met.

73. To qualify for **full representation** both the "cost benefit" criteria in regulation 42 and the "merits" criteria in regulation 43 must be met.

74. In terms of "merits", the prospects of success must not be "poor" or "borderline" but must be at least "moderate" (50 percent or more, but less than 60 per cent) or greater.

75. The "cost benefit" criteria, which relate to likely damages versus likely costs, are in the form of a sliding scale, depending upon whether the merits of the claim are moderate, good or very good.[43] In short, likely damages must exceed likely costs by the following ratios:

- moderate prospects of success – 4:1;
- good prospects of success – 2:1; and
- very good prospects of success – 1:1.

76. The definitions of "likely damages" and "likely costs" in regulations 9 and 10 respectively bear careful examination. "Likely damages" means the amount of damages that the individual is likely to receive if "substantially successful" at trial or other final hearing. "Likely costs" means the total costs to final settlement or judgment calculated on legal aid rather than *inter partes* rates. The prospects of the claim settling before trial are explicitly to be taken into account in assessing "likely damages". Because there may be legitimate debate over when an individual case may compromise, the application of the "cost benefit" criteria may not be straightforward.

77. Because of the costs involved in claims involving serious disabilities caused by neurological injury, it is almost certain that every clinical negligence claim which falls within the scope of LASPO will be treated as "Special Case Work" within the meaning of Part 6 of the Civil Legal Aid (Procedure) Regulations 2012.[44] A fully costed case plan is likely to be required,[45] which will include details of the tasks to be undertaken by counsel.

42 Civil Legal Aid (Merits Criteria) Regulations 2013 SI No. 104, regulations 40–43, as amended.
43 Civil Legal Aid (Merits Criteria) Regulations 2013 SI No. 104, as amended. The definitions of likely damages and likely costs are set out in regulations 9 and 10 respectively.
44 SI No. 3098.
45 Civil Legal Aid (Procedure) Regulations 2012 SI No. 3098, regulation 55.

Standard Civil Contract 2010 (as amended)

78. The amended category definition of the Standard Civil Contract 2010 (between the then Legal Services Commission[46] and contracted legal aid providers) refers to the provisions of LASPO Schedule 1, Part 1, paragraph 23.[47] The Contract also refers to grants of exceptional funding including:[48]

"all proceedings in relation to a claim for damages or a complaint to a relevant professional body in respect of an alleged breach of duty of care or trespass to the person committed in the course of the provision of clinical or medical services (including dental or nursing services); or a claim for damages in respect of alleged professional negligence in the conduct of such a claim."

46 Now the Legal Aid Agency (LAA).
47 See Standard Civil Contract 2010, Amended Category Definitions, paras 24–25.
48 See Standard Civil Contract 2010, Amended Category Definitions, para 25.

Types of cases covered in practice

Claims within scope

79. **Identity of the negligent healthcare professionals**. Paragraph 23 of Part 1 of Schedule 1 does not limit the healthcare professionals whose negligence could give rise to a claim. So long as the other criteria are met, clinical negligence claims could be brought as a result of negligence not only of doctors, nurses, or dentists, but midwives, physiotherapists, healthcare visitors or any other healthcare professional.

80. **Neurological injury not confined to the brain**. The definition of neurological injury is not confined to injury of the brain. It could encompass injury to other parts of the nervous system, although such a case may not qualify under the criteria which relate to the severity of the injury or the timing of the negligence. The definition in paragraph 23 is probably wide enough to cover claimants suffering from severe Erbs' palsy caused during delivery.

81. **Requirement for there to be negligence in the course of treatment of a patient**. For a prospective claim to fall within the scope of civil legal aid under paragraph 23, the neurological injury must be caused by clinical negligence. This will exclude claims where the occurrence of the injury is incidental to the claimant's presence in a hospital or other location where healthcare services are provided. For instance, a serious neurological injury caused by a slip or trip on the premises will not fall within this category. The qualifying injury must be caused by a negligent act or omission in the treatment of a patient.

82. **Common scenarios**. There are countless scenarios in which healthcare professionals can injure, or fail to prevent injury to, a child in utero or in the first eight weeks of life so as to cause a serious neurological injury. The most common of these is likely to be obstetric negligence where mismanagement of a mother's labour leads to deprivation of oxygen for the foetus, resulting in hypoxic ischaemic brain injury. Alternatively, negligence by paediatricians or neonatologists where a newborn infant is not resuscitated adequately in the immediate aftermath of birth, or where serious illness is not recognised on attendance to hospital. Another common species of claim will relate to General Practitioners who fail to refer to hospital infants who are suffering serious illness, such as meningitis or septicaemia.

83. **Exclusion of claims based on pre-conception negligence**. Claims where the clinical negligence occurs before conception will not be eligible

for legal aid under this paragraph. For example, in cases where drugs administered to the mother before conception cause malformation of the brain, or other serious neurological abnormality, the child would not be eligible for legal aid.

84. **Latent injury**. The drafting of paragraph 23 makes it clear that it is the time of the negligence not the injury which is relevant. Consequently, even if the injury did not declare itself until much later – as may be the case with neurological injury causing only cognitive disabilities – the claim would still fall within scope so long as the first act of negligence occurred within the qualifying timeframe.

85. **Treatment of third parties**. Paragraph 23 is sufficiently wide to encompass clinical negligence in the treatment of a patient other than the child (V). For example, the following situation would potentially remain within the scope of civil legal aid: administration of a drug to treat a medical condition in V's mother during her pregnancy, the direct effects of which cause a serious neurological injury to V in utero, preventing V's mother's ability to deliver V without such an injury.

86. **Legal aid available for all parts of the proceedings**. Subject to the criteria in paragraph 23 of Part 1 of Schedule 1 of LASPO, civil legal aid will be available for advocacy services in all courts in which clinical negligence claims are heard, from the County Court to the Supreme Court.[49]

49 See LASPO, Schedule 1, Part 3 (Advocacy: exclusion and exceptions).

Exceptional funding

87. Exceptional case determinations are made by the LAA applying the guidance in the *Lord Chancellor's Exceptional Funding Guidance* (*Non-Inquests*). The guidance recognises that the overarching question to be asked is "will withholding of legal aid make assertion of the claim practically impossible or lead to an obvious unfairness in the proceedings?"[50] Guidance which is specific to clinical negligence cases is found at paragraphs 46 and 47. The following factors may be particularly relevant:

- in relation to the importance of the matter at stake, whether the applicant is a disabled person who is seeking to recover damages which would in whole or in part cover adjustments, adaptations, equipment, or care;
- in relation to the complexity of the case, how complex the case is bearing in mind the complexity and volume of any medical expert evidence and any medico-legal arguments in the case; and
- in relation to the ability of the applicant to present their own case, how able he/she is to do so bearing in mind any disabilities, medical problems, or caring responsibilities they have for others.

88. If alternative funding is available, a claim will not qualify for civil legal aid under the exceptional funding scheme. Because the same means criteria apply to legal aid under the exceptional funding scheme as to general cases, the claimants who potentially would qualify are unlikely to have the means to litigate using their own private funding. In the main, the scheme will only

benefit those claimants of qualifying means who do not have any form of before-the-event (BTE) insurance and are unable to secure a conditional fee agreement (CFA).

89. All clinical negligence claims require medical expert evidence on breach of duty, causation and quantum. Because of their complexity, lay people are usually ill-equipped to present these claims effectively. The type of clinical negligence claim that is most likely to succeed in an application for exceptional funding is a claim of moderate to high value where the claimant has failed to find a solicitor to accept it as a CFA because its merits appear to be moderate rather than good.

50 See Lord Chancellor's Exceptional Funding Guidance (Non-Inquests), page 3

Community care

Category definition and scope

LASPO Schedule 1, Part 1

90. Community Care was one of the areas of civil legal aid least affected by the April 2013 changes. Under LASPO Schedule 1, Part 1, paragraph 6(3), funding available for "community care" includes services which a relevant person (namely a local authority Primary Care Trust or Local Health Board) may provide or arrange to be provided under the following provisions:

"(a) Part 3 of the National Assistance Act 1948(local authority support for children and families);

(b) section 47 of the 1948 Act (removal to suitable premises of persons in need of care and attention);

(c) section 48 of the 1948 Act (temporary protection for property of persons admitted to hospital);

(d) section 45 of the Health Services and Public Health Act 1968 (arrangements for promoting welfare of old people);

(e) section 117 of the Mental Health Act 1983 (after-care);

(f) section 17 of the Children Act 1989 ("the 1989 Act") (provision of services for children in need);

(g) section 20 of the 1989 Act (provision of accommodation for children);

(h) sections 22A, 22B, 22C and 23 of the 1989 Act (accommodation and maintenance for children in care and looked after children);

sections 23B and 23C of the 1989 Act (local authority functions in respect of relevant children);

(j) sections 24, 24A and 24B of the 1989 Act (provision of services for persons qualifying for advice and assistance);

(k) section 2 of the Carers and Disabled Children Act 2000 (services for carers);

section 254 of, and Schedule 20 to, the National Health Service Act 2006 (functions of local social service authorities); and

(m) section 192 of, and Schedule 15 to, the National Health Service (Wales) Act 2006 (functions of local social service authorities)."

Standard Civil Contract 2010 (as amended)

91. The amended category definition of the Standard Civil Contract 2010 (between the then Legal Services Commission and contracted legal aid providers) states that civil legal aid for community care "includes legal services provided in relation to community care assessments, service provision decisions, and issues around the delivery of services". It does not include, however, "any matter falling within the Welfare Benefits Category or Clinical Negligence Category and proceedings before the First-Tier Tribunal (Mental Health)".[51]

92. The category definition also specifies that Community Care work covers advocacy in proceedings to the extent set out at paragraph 4 of Part 3 of Schedule 1 to LASPO, regarding a person's capacity, their best interests (welfare and/or medical treatment) and deprivation of liberty issues.

93. LASPO Schedule 1, Part 3, paragraph 4 provides that civil legal aid covers:

"Advocacy in proceedings in the Court of Protection to the extent that they concern:

(a) a person's right to life;

(b) a person's liberty or physical safety,

(c) a person's medical treatment (within the meaning of the Mental Health Act 1983);

(d) a person's capacity to marry, to enter into a civil partnership or to enter into sexual relations; or

(e) a person's right to family life."

94. If there is a grant of exceptional funding, the Community Care category will also cover advocacy for matters arising under the Mental Capacity Act 2005 which are not listed at paragraph 4 of Part 3 of Schedule 1 in LASPO.[52]

51 See Standard Civil Contract 2010, Amended Category Definitions, paragraphs 28–30.
52 See Standard Civil Contract 2010, Amended Category Definitions, paragraph 30.

Types of cases covered in practice

95. In practice, the overwhelming majority of Community Care cases will be applications for judicial review arising out of alleged breach of statutory duty by the local authority or Primary Care Trust in any of the above examples. The most common types of case will tend to be those in which accommodation is sought under the National Assistance Act 1948 or Children Act 1989.

96. For further information about the circumstances in which funding for judicial review is available, please see the chapter of this Guidance on Public Law and Judicial Review.

Debt

Category definition and scope

LASPO Schedule 1, Part 1

97. LASPO Schedule 1, Part 1, has effectively removed debt work from the scope of legal aid. A residual category of housing-related debt is within scope and, under paragraph 33, can cover civil legal services relating to:

- court orders for sale of an individual's home;
- court orders for the possession of an individual's home following failure to make mortgage payments (which could include a "secured loan"[53]); and
- bankruptcy orders under Part 9 of the Insolvency Act 1986 where the estate includes the individual's home and where the petition for bankruptcy was not presented by the individual.

Standard Civil Contract 2013

98. No contracts to provide freestanding debt work have been available since 1 April 2013. The Standard Civil Contract 2013 reiterates the provisions of LASPO Schedule 1, Part 1 to define what work is covered by the new Housing and Debt contracts.[54]

99. Legal help is available for work that is in scope. However, because Debt is a subject area covered by the 'Gateway' arrangements, such help must be sought first through the Civil LegalAdvice online and telephone service.55 That is not to say that a defendant to a Debt-related claimcannot ever get full legal representation. The LAA has clarified that "providers can use their delegated functions in Debt where proceedings have been issued (as opposed to threatened) togrant legal representation where the relevant scope, means and merits criteria are met. ... Where advice under Controlled Work would be more appropriate clients must be signposted to CLA at the earliest opportunity (unless they are an exempted person). Any delay would be contrary to s.2.49 of the 2013 Standard Civil Contract Specification and s.7.2 of the 2013 Standard Civil Contract Standard Terms relating to acting in the best interests of potential clients and contract sanctions could be applied"56

100. In response to a specific question, the LAA has also clarified that an order for sale made under the Proceeds of Crime Act 2002 could fall under the scope of the Debt category. However, it added that confiscation or restraint orders made under the same Act would not be in scope of the Debt category. Certain work under the Proceeds of Crime Act, including restraint orders, will fall under miscellaneous work. 57

101. The category definition of Debt clarifies that possession of an individual's home arising out of any matter other than failure to make mortgage payments, falls within the Housing category. To undertake such Housing work, a provider must hold a Housing contract as the categories of work are exclusive.

102. To the extent that any relevant grant of exceptional funding is made in the Debt category, the grant can include legal help and all proceedings[58]

(a) For the payment of monies due or the enforcement of orders in such proceedings (excluding any matter which falls within the Housing category); and

(b) arising out of personal insolvency, including bankruptcy, administration, Debt Relief representation or IVA proceedings, but excluding representation in proceedings against parties in default of a fine or other order in criminal proceedings in the magistrates' court who are at risk of imprisonment.

53 See Legal Aid Agency, Frequently Asked Questions – Civil Legal Aid Reforms, FAQ 92.
54 Standard Civil Contract 2013, Category Definitions.
55 Further information is available on the Ministry of Justice website.
56 See Legal Aid Agency, Frequently Asked Questions – Civil Legal Aid Reforms, FAQ 91.
57 See Legal Aid Agency, Frequently Asked Questions – Civil Legal Aid Reforms, FAQ No 76.
58 Standard Civil Contract 2013, Category Definitions, paragraph 19.

Types of cases covered in practice

103. The thrust of the April 2013 legal aid reforms was to exclude most debt cases from scope, leaving only a small residual category where enforcement of the debt puts a home in jeopardy (usually where a lender seeks to enforce a secure loan).

104. The *Lord Chancellor's Guidance on Exceptional Funding (Non-Inquests)* does canvass the possibility that some other debt cases might be brought back into scope,[59] but only where legal aid is essential to avoid obvious unfairness in proceedings where the party is faced with enforcement action in respect of a debt.

105. The LAA has answered two specific questions from providers about the availability of legal aid under the Debt category in relation to bankruptcy proceedings:[60]

> 89. What happens where a creditor pays the charges for bankruptcy proceedings? Would this be classed as voluntary or involuntary bankruptcy as client could agree to it but creditor pays the actual charge?
>
> The Act specifies that cases where the petition for a bankruptcy order against a client is made by a person other than the client would be in scope. However, providers should also be mindful of the Civil Legal Aid (Merits Criteria) Regulations 2013 which provide that legal help may only be provided where there is sufficient benefit to the client to justify work being carried out. For example, a case where a petition made by a creditor is undefended or otherwise agreed with the debtor would be unlikely to meet the merits criteria or to justify the provision of specialist legal advice.
>
> 90. Bankruptcy matters where the petition for bankruptcy was issued by a creditor are in scope. Can advice be given to clients who are not being made bankrupt themselves but co-own a property with the person who is being made bankrupt e.g. a spouse or partner?
>
> Advice in relation to a bankruptcy order against the individual is within scope; BUT a co-owner would not qualify. Such a co-owner may qualify if an order for sale of the property was sought or if they were made homeless and were making an application for re-housing.

59 See Lord Chancellor's Exceptional Funding Guidance (Non-Inquests), paragraphs 48–50.
60 See Legal Aid Agency, Frequently Asked Questions – Civil Legal Aid Reforms, FAQ 89 and 90.

Education

Category definition and scope

LASPO Schedule 1, Part 1

106. LASPO Schedule 1, Part 1, Paragraph 2 defines civil legal services for "Special Educational Needs" as:

"(1) Civil legal services provided in relation to:

(a) matters arising under Part 4 of the Education Act 1996 (special educational needs);

(b) assessments relating to learning difficulties under sections 139A and 140 of the Learning and Skills Act 2000."

107. It is worth noting that this definition will have to be amended once the Children and Families Bill 2014 comes into force. This will probably be in September 2014. Part 3 of the Bill extends special educational needs provision to young people up to the age of 25, and accordingly will repeal Part 4 of the Education Act 1996 and ss. 139A and 140 of the Learning and Skills Act 2000. Unlike the version of the SEN Code of Practice in place from 2001, the new draft 0–25 SEN Code of Practice refers at page 171 to circumstances in which legal aid will be available.

108. Education cases also fall within the:

(a) judicial review civil legal services definition in Schedule 1, Part 1, paragraph 19; and

(b) Equality Act 2010 civil legal service definition in Schedule 1, Part 1, paragraph 43.

Standard Civil Contract 2013

109. The Standard Civil Contract 2013 category of Education (Special Educational Needs) is defined as:[61]

"1. Legal Help and all proceedings in relation to:

(a) matters arising under Part 4 of the Education Act 1996 (Special Educational Needs) (under paragraph 2(1)(a) of Part 1 of Schedule 1 to the Act as set out above);

(b) assessments relating to learning difficulties under sections 139A and 140 of the Learning and Skills Act 2000 (under paragraph 2(1)(b) of Part 1 of Schedule 1 to the Act); and

(c) any other matter within the scope of Part 1 of Schedule 1 to the Act where the primary problem or issue relates to the provision of, or failure to provide, education or funding for education.

2. For the avoidance of doubt, the following are included in the category:

   (a) Legal Help and all proceedings in relation to a contravention of Part 6 of the Equality Act 2010 (Education); and

   (b) Legal Help and all proceedings in relation to a contravention of a previous discrimination enactment as far as the matter concerns the provision or funding of education.

3. Proceedings in relation to judicial review of an enactment, decision, act or omission as far as this concerns the provision or funding of education. To the extent that exceptional funding is granted (in accordance with section 10 of the Act) this category includes Legal Help and proceedings in relation to any matter where the primary problem or issue relates to the provision of or failure to provide education or funding for education."

110. This is a significant departure from the previous Education category under the Standard Civil Contract 2010, where Education was defined as:

"1. Legal Help in relation to matters where the primary problem or issue relates to the provision of or failure to provide education or funding for education, including special educational needs. This would include such issues or problems relating to admissions, exclusions or Disability Discrimination Act claims.

2. Any proceedings before a court concerning the above issues. This excludes claims for damages falling within the Personal Injury, though claims for damages arising out of a failure to provide adequate education or assessment for education are included."

61 Standard Civil Contract 2013, Category Definitions.

Types of cases covered in practice

111. Legal help is available in cases before the First Tier Tribunal:

   (a) appeals against the contents of a Statement of Special Educational Needs ("a Statement") under the Education Act 1996 (EA), section 326 and other related Local Authority decisions, i.e. refusal to assess, refusal to issue a Statement, and

   (b) Equality Act 2010 claims for disability discrimination in the First Tier Tribunal, i.e. claims that a school discriminated against a pupil by excluding him/her or claims based on failures to make reasonable adjustments.

112. Legal representation is available for appeals to the Upper Tribunal from the First-Tier Tribunal or Special Educational Needs Tribunal for Wales (SENTW) on a challenge to special needs decisions, which include:

   (a) A reasons appeal in relation to waking day curriculum issues and links to social care.

   (b) An appeal on section 316 EA 1996 regarding integrated education.

   (c) An appeal on education otherwise and home education under section 319 EA 1996.

(d) An appeal to the Upper Tribunal on post-16 provision, and

(e) An appeal on practice and procedure in the First-Tier Tribunal.

113. However, Schedule 1, Part 3 of LASPO makes it clear that Special Educational Needs civil legal services do not include advocacy at the First-Tier stage. Save in complex cases or on points of law, cases at this stage are normally dealt with by solicitors.

114. Advocacy is funded in proceedings in the Upper Tribunal under the Tribunals, Courts and Enforcement Act 2007[62] from decisions made by the First-Tier Tribunal or the Special Educational Needs Tribunal for Wales (SENTW) in proceedings under the following:[63]

(a) Part 4 (special educational needs) of the Education Act 1996 ("EA 1996"); or

(b) The Equality Act 2010 ("the Equality Act").

115. Appeals to the Upper Tribunal from the First-Tier Tribunal or SENTW on a discrimination claim under the Equality Act 2010 (legal representation and advocacy funding is available) are included. Examples of this include:

- the application of the Equality Act 2010 Disability Regulations on excluded conditions;
- a school's failure to make reasonable adjustments; and
- direct discrimination.

116. Some Equality Act education cases will be brought outside the First-Tier Tribunal, suchas claims by University students. These will be brought in the county court and both legalrepresentation and advocacy are covered for these claims.[64]

117. If an SEN or an Equality Act case is appealed from the Upper Tribunal to the Court ofAppeal and then to the Supreme Court, there is cover for legal representation and advocacy.[65]

118. There is cover for legal representation and advocacy in judicial reviews.[66] Examples of education-related judicial reviews include challenges to:

- a Local Authority's decision not to provide transport for an eligible child pursuant to section 508B EA 1996. Legal representation and funding for advocacy is available;
- a Local Authority's failure to comply with section 324 EA 1996 and make the provision specified in a Statement;
- a Local Authority's failure to implement the First-Tier Tribunal's decision;
- decisions regarding religious education to include human rights issues;
- a Local Authority's failure to comply with section 19 EA 1996 and provide lawful and adequate out of school provision for those out of school for medical, exclusion, or other reasons; and
- decisions regarding post-19 continued education in complex cases including where there are links to social care. Here the issues will plainly overlap with work covered by Community Care.

PART III IN PRACTICE

Education cases that are no longer covered by civil legal aid include:

- bullying and other educational negligence cases;[67]
- schools exclusions and admissions cases, save:
  - — where there is an Equality Act 2010 claim to the First-Tier Tribunal (in which case legal help but not advocacy will be available), or
  - — an appeal to the Upper Tribunal, or
  - — where a judicial review arises following an ultimate determination in those cases, and
- breach of contract in education cases.

62 See section 11 – appeals on a point of law.
63 LASPO, Schedule 1, Part 3, paragraph 17.
64 Schedule 1, Part 3, paragraph 5.
65 Schedule 1, Part 3, paragraphs 1 and 2.
66 See LASPO, Schedule 1, Part 3, paragraph 3 which provides for funding for advocacy in proceedings in the High Court. See further the relevant chapter of this Guidance on Public Law and Judicial Review.
67 LASPO, Schedule 1, Part 2, paragraph 2 excludes civil legal services provided in relation to a claim in tort in respect of negligence.

Employment

Category definition and scope

120. LASPO defines employment law as "an enactment or rule of law relating to employment, including in particular an enactment or rule of law conferring powers or imposing duties on employers, conferring rights on employees or otherwise regulating the relations between employers and employees".[68]

121. Since April 2013, there has been no civil legal aid available for employment law cases except for cases which involve a contravention of the Equality Act 2010 or the legislation which preceded it ("discrimination claims") or cases in connection with the exploitation of an individual who is a victim of trafficking in human beings ("trafficking claims").[69]

68 LASPO Schedule 1, Part 1, paragraph 32(8)
69 LASPO Schedule 1, Part 1, paragraphs 32 and 43; Part 3, paragraph 20. The Government has also proposed to extend the current RTA Portal Scheme to cover Employers' Liability claims up to £25,000. Further information is available on the Ministry of Justice website.

Types of cases covered in practice

122. Prior to April 2013, the most common type of advocacy funded under legal aid was bringing or defending appeals to the Employment Appeal Tribunal, Court of Appeal or Supreme Court. Since April 2013, advocacy for these types of cases has continued to attract legal aid where the underlying claim is a discrimination claim.[70] Advocacy in trafficking appeals before the Court of

Appeal or the Supreme Court is also eligible for legal aid.[71] Schedule 1, Part 3 of LASPO excludes advocacy in the Employment Tribunal.

123. Prior to April 2013, legal help (i.e. legal aid amounting to assistance short of advocacy) was available in employment cases. While legal help would not cover advocacy, it was possible for barristers to be compensated via "disbursements" for drafting in particular cases, for example settling particulars of claim or schedules of loss. Since April 2013, legal help has only remained available for discrimination claims[72] and trafficking claims.[73]

124. Employment practitioners may be able to make use of exceptional funding, which is available where failing to provide legal aid "would result in a breach of the individual's rights to legal aid under the Human Rights Act 1998 or European Union law".[74]

125. The *Lord Chancellor's Guidance on Civil Legal Aid* provides that an application for exceptional funding in the Employment Tribunal in a discrimination claim will be assessed under the "general merits" criteria for legal representation.[75] This is explained in the Civil Legal Aid (Merits Criteria) Regulations 2013 as follows:[76]

(a) if the prospects of success of the case are very good, the Director must be satisfied that the likely damages exceed likely costs;

(b) if the prospects of success of the case are good, the Director must be satisfied that the likely damages exceed likely costs by a ratio of two to one; or

(c) if the prospects of success of the case are moderate, the Director must be satisfied that the likely damages exceed likely costs by a ratio of four to one.

126. The *Lord Chancellor's Exceptional Funding Guidance (Non-Inquests)* provides that such funding may be made available in claims relating to a private contract of employment. The Guidance invites caseworkers to consider "whether the withholding of legal aid would make the assertion of the claim practically impossible or lead to an obvious unfairness in proceedings"[77]

127. In *Steel and Morris v The United Kingdom*,[78] the European Court of Human Rights (ECtHR) found significant unfairness where the claimant was a large multinational and the case was an exceptionally lengthy non-employment (libel) hearing and the defendants were refused legal aid. Generally, the lengthiest and most complex Employment Tribunal cases are direct discrimination, harassment or equal pay claims, which, depending on the circumstances, may require exceptional funding for advocacy in the Employment Tribunal. At appeal stage they are eligible for funding under the provision for funding of discrimination claims.

128. It is possible to imagine cases raising the claimant's capacity to represent themselves (for example, a claim brought by a disabled person for "ordinary" unfair dismissal, where the facts of the dismissal were unusually complex) or cases of particular legal difficulty (for example, raising statutory interpretation under human rights or European law) which might come within this test.

129. Significantly, the Exceptional Funding Guidance envisages that exceptional funding might be appropriate not merely in Employment Tribunal proceedings and appeals from the Tribunal but also potentially in professional

..sciplinary proceedings where the proceedings will have a substantial effect on the applicant's civil right to practice his or her profession.[79]

70 LASPO, Schedule 1, Part 3, paragraphs 1, 2 and 20.
71 LASPO, Schedule 1 Part 3, paragraphs 1 and 2.
72 LASPO, Schedule 1 Part 1, paragraph 43.
73 LASPO, Schedule 1, Part 1, paragraph 32.
74 LASPO, s 10(2)–10(3) sets out the statutory requirements.
75 Lord Chancellor's Guidance Under Section 4 of Legal Aid, Sentencing and Punishment of Offenders Act 2012, paragraph 7.10.
76 SI No. 104, regulation 42(2).
77 See *Lord Chancellor's Exceptional Funding Guidance* (Non-Inquests), paragraphs 53–54.
78 [2005] ECHR 103; 18 BHRC 545.
79 See *Lord Chancellor's Exceptional Funding Guidance* (Non-Inquests), paragraphs 53–54.

Housing

Category definition and scope

LASPO Schedule 1, Part 1

130. Schedule 1, Part 1, paragraphs 33–36 of LASPO describe housing law matters as including:

- loss of home;
- homelessness;
- risk to health or safety in rented home;
- anti-social behaviour;
- protection from harassment;
- immigration: accommodation for asylum seekers etc.;
- judicial review (but only arising out of matters that are already covered in this category); and
- exceptional funding cases.

Regulations

131. The Civil Legal Aid (Merits Criteria) Regulations 2013 implements specific merits criteria that have to be met for certain types of housing work in addition to the general merits test.[80] These Regulations have been amended with effect from 27 January 2014 to remove borderline cases from scope.[81] The prospects of success criterion for full representation provided by Regulation 43 have been amended. The provision for borderline cases of significant wider public interest or overwhelming importance to the individual have now been removed. Regulation 43, as amended, has been incorporated into the Regulations dealing with criteria for full representation in specific areas. This includes public law claims,[82] claims against public authorities,[83] and possession claims.[84] These changes do not affect applications made before the commencement date.

132 The specific merits criteria for housing cases include:

- **For full representation in relation to a claim for a court order for possession of an individual's home.** The Director must be satisfied the individual has a defence; the prospects of success are very good, good, moderate or borderline; and the proportionality test is met.[85]
- **For full representation in relation to other housing matters to which specific merits criteria apply (this covers eviction, risk to health or safety in a rented home and harassment, by a landlord or other person, that interferes with the individual's enjoyment of their home).** The Director must be satisfied that the proportionality test is met; the landlord or other person responsible for the matter complained of has been notified of the complaint (an exception is where this is impracticable) and been given a reasonable opportunity to resolve the matter.[86]
- **For investigative representation in unlawful eviction cases.** Where the claim is primarily for damages and the damages do not exceed £1,000 the case must be of significant wider public interest.[87] Where the claim is part of a multi-party action only the lead claim in the action is capable of being of significant wider interest.[88]

80 See Civil Legal Aid (Merits Criteria) Regulations 2013 SI No. 104, regulations 61–63.
81 See Civil Legal Aid (Merits Criteria) (Amendment) Regulations 2014 SI No. 131, regulation 2.
82 Regulation 56.
83 Regulation 58.
84 Regulation 61.
85 Civil Legal Aid (Merits Criteria) Regulations 2013 SI No. 104, regulation 61.
86 Civil Legal Aid (Merits Criteria) Regulations 2013 SI No. 104, regulation 62.
87 Civil Legal Aid (Merits Criteria) Regulations 2013 SI No. 104, regulation 63(2).
88 Civil Legal Aid (Merits Criteria) Regulations 2013 SI No. 104, regulation 63(3).

Standard Civil Contract 2013

133. Housing is now a stand-alone category of legal aid.[89] Mortgage repossession cases fall within the Debt contract and are not covered by the Housing contract.

134. The Standard Civil Contract 2013 covers legal help and proceedings in housing law areas specified under LASPO. Where exceptional funding is granted, the contract category definition makes it clear that housing work also includes:[90]

> "any matters which concern the possession, status, terms of occupation, repair, improvement, eviction from, quiet enjoyment of, or payment of rent or other charges for premises (including vehicles and sites they occupy) which are occupied as a residence, including the rights of leaseholders under the terms of their lease or under any statutory provision (including enfranchisement). Cases including allocation, transfers and the provision of sites for occupation are also included."

89 Housing and debt were previously joined in the Standard Civil Contract 2010.
90 Standard Civil Contract 2013, Category Definitions.

# of cases covered in practice

135. Advocacy for housing work that remains in scope is covered for proceedings in all courts from the County Court to the Supreme Court

Loss of home

136. Loss of home includes possession and eviction proceedings in respect of an individual's home.[91] Home can include house, caravan, houseboat or other vehicle that is an individual's only or main residence.[92] This includes applications under the Trusts of Land and Appointment of Trustees Act 1996 by the trustee of a bankrupt's estate and proceedings in relation to bankruptcy or a statutory demand where the individual's estate includes their home. Cases of unlawful eviction and planning eviction are also covered. Cases under the Matrimonial Causes Act 1973 and under the Civil Partnership Act 2004 are excluded.

137. Instances of loss of home include claims in tort for assault, battery and false imprisonment, as well as trespass to goods and land. Damage to property and breach of statutory duty are covered where they relate to counterclaims in proceedings for court orders for possession or sale, or where there has been an unlawful eviction.[93]

91 LASPO, Schedule 1, Part 1, paragraph 33.
92 LASPO, Schedule 1, Part 1, paragraph 33(9).
93 LASPO, Schedule 1, Part 1, paragraph 33(6).

Homelessness

138. Legal services for homeless persons or persons threatened with homelessness extend to work under Part 6 (allocation) and 7 (homelessness) of the Housing Act 1996.[94] The terms "homeless" and "threatened with homelessness" have the same meaning as section 175 of the Housing Act 1996.

94 LASPO, Schedule 1, Part 1, paragraph 34.

Risk to health or safety in a rented home

139. Civil legal aid will be available for housing disrepair claims brought to reduce or remove a risk to the health or safety of an individual or family member as a result of deficiency in a home that is rented or leased.[95] The deficiency can be caused by the construction of the building or absence of maintenance and repair. Harm includes temporary harm and health includes mental health.[96]

140. The *Lord Chancellor's Guidance on Civil Legal Aid* sets out those matters to which the Director must have regard when determining whether legal aid should be made available to an individual in regard to housing disrepair.[97] The Civil Legal Aid (Merits) Regulations 2013 provide specific merits criteria for legal representation in disrepair cases.

141. Where there is a credible allegation of disrepair, within the LASPO definition, civil legal services are available from an early stage to fund expert reports. In appropriate cases this will mean not only a report on the state of the property and causation but also medical reports. Joint experts should be instructed in keeping with the Pre-Action Protocol save where an urgent injunction is needed. If after reports are obtained the Director is not satisfied that the case is one of serious risk then funding will cease.

142. The Lord Chancellor's Guidance also sets out factors that the Director may take into account.[98] It is made clear that the Director must take into account all relevant factors and the examples given are not an exhaustive list. Some factors may make the issue clear cut such as where there are gas leaks or dangerous electrical installations. In less clear cut cases there are a number of factors that need to be taken into account. These will include whether there has already been harm to the applicant or a member of the family. Consideration should be given to whether the applicant or those in the applicant's family are members of a high risk or vulnerable group. It will also be relevant if the local authority has identified hazards under the Housing Health and Safety Rating System.

95 LASPO Schedule 1, Part 1, paragraph 35.
96 LASPO Schedule 1, Part 1, paragraph 35.
97 See *Lord Chancellor's Guidance Under Section 4 of Legal Aid, Sentencing and Punishment of Offenders Act 2012*, Part 12.
98 See *Lord Chancellor's Guidance Under Section 4 of Legal Aid, Sentencing and Punishment of Offenders Act 2012*, paragraphs 12.9–12.11.

Anti-social behaviour and protection from harassment

143. Legal aid is available to individuals where an order has been sought or made in the County Court under the *Crime and Disorder Act 1998* and under the *Housing Act 1996* for anti-social behaviour.[99]

144. Civil legal aid is also available for work in relation to injunctions under section 3 or section 3A of the Protection from Harassment Act 1997 and the variation or discharge of restraining orders under section 5 or section 5A of the same Act.[100]

99 LASPO, Schedule 1, Part 1, paragraph 36.
100 LASPO, Schedule 1, Part 1, paragraph 37.

Immigration: accommodation for asylum seekers etc.

145. Individuals can seek legal aid for claims in respect of the Secretary of State's powers to provide accommodation for asylum seekers under the Immigration and Asylum Act 1999 and to provide support for destitute asylum seekers under the Nationality, Immigration and Asylum Act 2002.[101]

146. Civil legal services are only available for proceedings challenging these specific powers. Any claims for any injury or damage suffered as a consequence of the Secretary of State failing to exercise these powers or an improper exercise of the powers are excluded.[102]

101 LASPO, Schedule 1, Part 1, paragraph 31.
102 LASPO, Schedule 1, Part 2.

Judicial review and public law

147. Challenges by way of judicial review or counterclaim to acts, omissions or decisions of public bodies will be covered by the category in which the main challenge proceeds. Judicial review challenges of housing matters within the housing contract are included in that contract. This includes, in the housing context, challenges under the Human Rights Act 1998.[103]

148. To qualify for legal services for judicial review, an individual must show the judicial review has a potential to produce a benefit for themselves or their family or the environment. This cuts out challenges brought for the benefit of the public but without benefit to the individual seeking the judicial review.

[103] LASPO Schedule 1, Part 1, paragraph 19.

Immigration and asylum

Category definition and scope

LASPO Schedule 1, Part 1

149. LASPO constitutes a significant change in legal aid funding for immigration and asylum work. Most non-asylum immigration work is out of scope, including children's cases. Legal aid is only available in the following circumstances:

- asylum cases;[104]
- immigration cases involving applications for leave to enter or remain made by a victim of trafficking and applications for indefinite leave to remain under the domestic violence rule;[105]
- cases relating to immigration detention, including bail applications and matters/conditions relating to temporary admission and release on restrictions;[106]
- habeus corpus;[107]
- asylum support where accommodation is sought under sections 4 and 95 of the Immigration and Asylum Act 1999;[108] and
- proceedings before the Special Immigration Appeals Commission.[109]

150. All other immigration applications are out of scope. Significantly, this includes applications on the basis of Article 8 of the European Convention on Human Rights (ECHR),[110] or otherwise on grounds of long residence.

[104] LASPO, Schedule 1, Part 1, paragraph 30(1).
[105] LASPO, Schedule 1, Part 1, paragraph 28, 32(1).
[106] LASPO, Schedule 1, Part 1, paragraph 25–27.
[107] LASPO, Schedule 1, Part 1, paragraph 20.
[108] LASPO, Schedule 1, Part 1, paragraph 31.

[109] LASPO, Schedule 1, Part 1, paragraph 24.
[110] Right to respect for private and family life.

Regulations

151. The Civil Legal Aid (Merits Criteria) Regulations 2013 provide specific merits tests that must be passed to qualify for **full representation** in immigration cases.[111] An individual will qualify for full representation in any area of immigration work covered by LASPO if:

- the reasonable private paying individual test is met (if the case is not of significant wider public interest) or if the case is of significant wider public interest; or
- the proportionality test is met and the prospects of success are very good, good or moderate.

[111] See Civil Legal Aid (Merits Criteria) Regulations 2013 SI No. 104, regulation 60.

Types of cases covered in practice

Asylum cases

152. Asylum cases are covered where they involve rights to enter and remain in the United Kingdom arising from:

- the Refugee Convention;
- Articles 2 and 3 of the ECHR;
- the Temporary Protection Directive;[112] and
- the Qualification Directive.[113]

153. Asylum support cases are covered where accommodation is sought under sections 4 and 95 of the Immigration and Asylum Act 1999. However, as previously, legal aid will not be available for representation before the First-tier Tribunal (Asylum Support).

[112] Council Directive 2001/55/EC of 20 July 2001.
[113] Council Directive 2004/83/EC of 29 April 2004.

Immigration cases

154. Immigration cases are only covered where they:

- involve applications for leave to enter or remain made by a victim of trafficking, where there has been a conclusive determination under the Trafficking Convention, or there are reasonable grounds to believe that the person is a victim of trafficking and there has not yet been a conclusive determination that they are not;[114]

PART III
IN PRACTICE

- involve applications for indefinite leave to remain under the domestic violence rule. This only includes people with leave under the immigration rules as partners/spouses who have suffered domestic violence, not children or other family members who have suffered domestic violence;[115]
- involve applications and for EU residence permits on the grounds of a retained right of residence arising from domestic violence under regulation 10(5) of the Immigration (European Economic Area) Regulations 2006;[116]
- relate to immigration detention. This includes bail applications and matters/conditions relating to temporary admission and release on restrictions. There is no legal aid for the detainee's substantive immigration application.[117]

[114] LASPO, Schedule 1, Part 1, paragraph 32(1).
[115] LASPO, Schedule 1, Part 1, paragraph 28.
[116] LASPO, Schedule 1, Part 1, paragraph 29.
[117] LASPO, Schedule 1, Part 1, paragraph 25–27.

Judicial review

155. Judicial review remains in scope,[118] but in immigration cases it is restricted by specific exclusions preventing the provision of civil legal services where judicial review is sought:

- in relation to an issue in respect of which an appeal or judicial review of the same or substantially the same issue was resolved adversely to the applicant/appellant, less than one year previously;[119] and
- for removal directions given not more than one year after a decision was made to remove the individual or any appeal against such a decision was determined.[120]

156. These specific exclusions do not apply to judicial review of a negative decision in relation to an asylum application where there is no right of appeal to the First-tier Tribunal against the decision,[121] or to judicial review of a certificate under section 94 or 96 of the Nationality, Immigration and Asylum Act 2002 (NIAA 2002).[122]

157. Surprisingly, "asylum application" is defined by reference to the EU Procedures Directive, which limits the meaning of 'asylum application' to claims under the Refugee Convention.[123]

[118] LASPO, Schedule 1, Part 1, paragraph 19. See further the relevant chapter of this Guidance on Public Law and Judicial Review.
[119] LASPO, Schedule 1, Part 1, paragraph 19(5).
[120] LASPO, Schedule 1, Part 1, paragraph 19(6).
[121] This will mainly be refusals of further representations under paragraph 353 of the Immigration Rules.
[122] See LASPO, Schedule 1, Part 1, paragraph 19(7).
[123] This excludes claims based on Article 2 or 3 ECHR, or humanitarian protection claims under the Qualification Directive.

Exceptional cases

158. Section 10 of LASPO allows for "exceptional case determinations" to provide funding for cases which do not fall within Part 1 of Schedule 1 where it is necessary to provide civil legal services to avoid a breach of an individual's Convention rights or enforceable EU rights, and it is appropriate to do so, having regard to the risk that a failure to provide civil legal services would be such a breach.

159. The government's view has been that immigration cases will not qualify for this funding, on the basis of established European case law that the right to a fair trial under Article 6(1) of the ECHR does not cover immigration cases.[124] The Lord Chancellor's Guidance states as follows:[125]

> "59. Proceedings relating to the immigration status of immigrants and decisions relating to the entry, stay and deportation of immigrants do not involve the determination of civil rights and obligations.
>
> 60. The Lord Chancellor does not consider that there is anything in the current case law that would put the State under a legal obligation to provide legal aid in immigration proceedings in order to meet the procedural requirements of Article 8 ECHR."

160. The Ministry of Justice had estimated that in the first year of LASPO there would be 5000–7000 applications for exceptional funding. This estimate had taken into consideration the areas that had been taken out of scope of legal aid and the expected number of litigants who would be unable to represent themselves. The Public Law Project revealed the underuse of exceptional funding, reporting that the LAA received only 223 applications for exceptional funding from April–June 2013, with 83 of these applications being rejected for being incomplete or in relation to areas of law that are covered by legal aid the usual way. It was further reported that only two grants of exceptional funding have been made in non-inquest matters: one in a family law case where the applicant had very serious mental health problems and the other in a particularly complex immigration case. To further highlight the difficulty in obtaining funding, the immigration case was only granted funding when judicial review proceedings were threatened after the initial funding application was refused.

161. Not satisfied with the restrictions on access to legal aid achieved by LAPSO, the government issued a further consultation paper on 9 April 2013, Transforming legal aid: delivering a more credible and efficient system. The more pertinent proposals advanced in this paper were:

(a) introduction of a residence test whereby a person would have to be lawfully resident in the UK at the date of application for legal aid and have had been so for twelve months previously;

(b) synchronization of payments to barristers to that paid to Solicitors;

(c) removal of borderline cases for qualification in legal aid; and

(d) payment for Judicial Review claims to be made only on permission being obtained from the Administrative Court to bring the claim.

162. The residence test has not yet been brought into force. The intention was for it to come into force on 31 March 2014. However, the Public Law Project

obtained permission to challenge the lawfulness of the test and the Ministry of Justice has indicated that it will not now seek to bring it into force until May 2014.126 In the event that the test is enforced it will have disproportionate impact on immigration cases for obvious reasons as the matter at issue in immigration proceedings is usually the status of the claimant, it being argued that they should be granted residence rights in the UK which they do not have.

124 *Maaouia v France* (Application 39652/98) (2000) 33 EHRR 1037, 9 BHRC 205, ECtHR.
125 *Lord Chancellor's Exceptional Funding Guidance* (Non-Inquests), paragraphs 59–60.
126 A substantive hearing of the issue is expected the first week of April 2014: CO/17247/2013.

Inquests

Category definition and scope

LASPO Schedule 1, Part 1

163. Inquests are covered by LASPO, Schedule 1, Part 1, section 41(1), where the inquest involves "a member of the individual's family".

164. However under the Civil Legal Aid (Merits Criteria) Regulations 2013,[127] regulation 30, legal help is the only form of civil legal services which is appropriate in relation to any matter described in paragraph 41.

165. Under the Civil Legal Aid (Merits Criteria) Regulations 2013, regulation 19, advocacy for inquests is deemed "other legal services" and therefore falls to be considered for exceptional"funding.

166. Section 10 of LASPO provides that exceptional funding will be granted where the criteria in either section 10(2) or section 10(4) are met.

167. Section 10(2) applies where it is "necessary to make the services available to the individual under this Part because failure to do so would be a breach of ... the individual's Convention rights (within the meaning of the Human Rights Act 1998)", or where "... it is appropriate to do so, in the particular circumstances of the case, having regard to any risk that failure to do so would be such a breach".[128]

168. Section 10(4) applies where a "wider public interest determination" has been made. This is a "determination that, in the particular circumstances of the case, the provision of advocacy under this Part for the individual for the purposes of the inquest is likely to produce significant benefits for a class of person, other than the individual and the members of the individual's family".

169. Under section 41(2) and section 10(6) for these purposes an individual is a member of another individual's family if:

- they are relatives (whether of the full blood or half blood or by marriage or civil partnership);
- they are cohabitants (as defined in Part 4 of the Family Law Act 1996); or

- one has parental responsibility for the other.

170. Under the Civil Legal Aid (Merits Criteria) Regulations 2013,[129] regulation 48, when considering an application for exceptional inquest funding, the Director of Legal Aid Casework must apply the merits criterion in regulation 45. Regulation 45 provides that an individual may qualify for other legal services, i.e. inquest advocacy, only if the Director is satisfied that it would be reasonable in all the circumstances of the case for the individual to be provided with such other legal services.

171. The LAA's current position is that preparation for inquests cannot be claimed as exceptional funding meaning funding for such work will not be available where, for example, families do not qualify under the means test for legal help. The LAA's *Inquests – Exceptional Cases Funding – Provider Pack* states that there is no longer any provision to add the costs of preparatory work to any certificate for "other legal services" for advocacy at an inquest.[130]

172. In order for an exceptional inquest case to be funded the client must in general satisfy the financial eligibility limits as set out in the Civil Legal Aid (Financial Resources and Payment for Services) Regulations 2013.[131] This is subject to possible waiver of the eligibility criteria asset out in the *Lord Chancellor's Exceptional Funding Guidance (Inquests)*,[132] which is discussed below.

173. The Civil Legal Aid (Procedure) Regulations 2012,[133] regulations 66–69, set out the procedure for applying for exceptional funding.

174. The LAA's *Inquests – Exceptional Cases Funding – Provider Pack* sets out guidance on the procedure for applying for inquest exceptional funding, as well as guidance on, inter alia, funding expert reports, remuneration (including increased remuneration for counsel in exceptional circumstances) and the statutory charge.[134]

127 SI No. 104.
128 LASPO, s 10(3).
129 SI No. 104.
130 Inquests – Exceptional Cases Funding – Provider Pack, page 4.
131 SI No. 480. See also Inquests – Exceptional Cases Funding – Provider Pack page 3.
132 *Lord Chancellor's Exceptional Funding Guidance (Inquests)*, paragraphs 37–38.
133 SI No. 3098.
134 See *Inquests – Exceptional Cases Funding – Provider Pack* pages 5–11.

Standard Civil Contract 2010 (as amended)

175. The amended category definitions to apply from April 2013 state at paragraphs 17 and 18 that legal help or exceptional funding in relation to an inquest will fall into the category which relates to the underlying subject matter of the inquest. For example, legal help for an inquest where the client died in prison will be funded in the Actions Against the Police etc Category. Where an inquest does not fall within one of the categories, it will be included in the Miscellaneous Category.[135]

135 Standard Civil Contract 2010, Amended Category Definitions.

Types of cases covered in practice

176. Caseworkers (on behalf of the Director of Legal Aid Casework) must have regard to the *Lord Chancellor's Exceptional Funding Guidance (Inquests)* in determining whether civil legal services in relation to an inquest are to be made available under section 10 of LASPO.[136]

177. The Guidance sets out some of the factors that caseworkers should take into account in deciding exceptional funding applications in relation to inquests. It is not intended to be an exhaustive account of those factors, nor to replace the need for consideration of representations in individual cases and new case law that arises. The Guidance stresses that applications should be considered on a case by case basis.[137]

178. The Guidance reiterates that there are two grounds on which exceptional funding can be made available for inquests: (i) where the failure to provide such assistance would lead to a family member's rights under Article 2 ECHR[138] being breached; and (ii) if an inquest raises wider public interest issues within the LASPO definition.[139]

179. In respect of the Article 2 ground, caseworkers need to be satisfied that: (i) there is an arguable breach of the State's substantive obligation under Article 2; and (ii) funded representation is required to discharge the procedural obligation under Article 2 to investigate that arguable breach.[140]

180. As to (i), the Guidance provides that:

- it is likely that there will be an arguable breach of the substantive obligation where State agents have killed the individual: for example, a police shooting. It is also likely that an arguable breach of the substantive obligation will occur where the individual has died in State custody other than from natural causes: for example, killings or suicides in prison;[141]

- it is unlikely that there will be an arguable breach of the substantive obligation where there is no State involvement in the death, for example, the fatal shooting of one private individual by another private individual (where the authorities had no forewarning or other knowledge prior to the death). Another example is a death (in State detention) through natural causes;[142]

- There is more likely to be an arguable breach of the substantive obligation for deaths that occur where the deceased has been under the compulsory detention of the State. "Compulsory detention" refers to deaths that occur (i) in police or prison custody, (ii) during the course of police arrest, search, pursuit or shooting, or (iii) during the compulsory detention of the deceased under the Mental Health Act 1983;[143]

- It is unlikely that there will be an arguable breach of the substantive obligation where there is no State involvement in the death, for example, the fatal shooting of one private individual by another private individual (where the authorities had no forewarning or other knowledge prior to the death). Another example is a death (in State detention through natural causes;[144]

- There may be an arguable breach of the substantive obligation where it is alleged that theState has played some role in the death, including a failure to take reasonable steps to prevent the death;[145] and
- in the context of allegations against hospital authorities, there will not be a breach of the substantive obligation where a case involves only allegations of ordinary medical negligence as opposed to where the allegations of negligence are of a systemic nature.[146]

181. As to whether funded representation is required to discharge the procedural obligationunder Article 2 to investigate that arguable breach, the Guidance states that all the individualfacts and circumstances of the case must be taken into account by caseworkers, including:[147]

- the nature and seriousness of the allegations against State agents (with particular regard being given to allegations based on evidence of gross negligence or systemic failures, for example, closely related multiple and avoidable deaths from the same cause within the same institution; criminal conduct; and attempts to conceal information or otherwise interfere with an investigation into the circumstances surrounding the death);
- the previous investigations into the death and whether the family has been involved in such investigations; and
- the particular circumstances of the family (such as whether the applicant is suffering from severe mental health problems, potentially arising from the circumstances of the death, or has a learning disability).

182. In respect of the "wider public interest" ground, the Guidance provides that:

- a "wider public interest determination" is a determination that, in the particular circumstances of the case, the provision of advocacy for the individual for the purposes of the inquest is likely to produce significant benefits for a class of person, other than the applicant and members of the applicant's family;[148]
- in the context of an inquest, the most likely wider public benefits are the identification of dangerous practices, systematic failings or other findings that identify significant risks to the life, health or safety of other persons;[149]
- whether the wider public interest is "significant" will depend on a number of factors: what the benefits are; whether the benefits are more or less tangible; whether they will definitely flow to other persons or whether this is just a possibility; and the numbers of people who will benefit (it will be unusual for significant wider public interest to apply to something that benefits fewer than around 100 people, for example);[150]
- it is not sufficient that there is significant wider public interest in the inquest itself. There must be significant wider public interest in the client being represented at the inquest for the case to qualify for a wider public interest determination. This means that an applicant must be able to demonstrate that representation is necessary to obtain any benefits that may arise, not just that the inquest itself may provide benefits;[151] and

- in deciding whether to make a wider public interest determination, caseworkers should consider the nature of any allegations of systemic failings, and whether there are likely to be improvements to systems as a result of the inquest.[152]

183. The Guidance also makes provision for the waiver of the financial eligibility limits relating to inquests if, in all the circumstances, it would not be reasonable to expect the family to bear the full costs of legal assistance at the inquest. Whether this is reasonable will depend in particular on the history of the case and the nature of the allegations to be raised against State agents, the applicant's assessed disposable income and capital, other financial resources of the family, and the estimated costs of providing representation.[153] Provision is also made for the waiver of contributions in whole or part, which again is determined on the basis of the applicant's disposable income and disposable capital in the usual way ignoring upper eligibility limits.[154] The LAA's *Inquests – Exceptional Cases Funding – Provider Pack* also addresses the waiver of financial contributions.[155]

[136] Lord Chancellor's Exceptional Funding Guidance (Inquests), paragraph 1.
[137] Lord Chancellor's Exceptional Funding Guidance (Inquests), paragraph 2.
[138] The investigative obligation derived from the right to life.
[139] Lord Chancellor's Exceptional Funding Guidance (Inquests), paragraph 5.
[140] Lord Chancellor's Exceptional Funding Guidance (Inquests), paragraphs 6–7.
[141] Lord Chancellor's Exceptional Funding Guidance (Inquests), paragraph 12.
[142] Lord Chancellor's Exceptional Funding Guidance (Inquests), paragraph 25.
[143] Lord Chancellor's Exceptional Funding Guidance (Inquests), paragraph 26.
[144] Lord Chancellor's Exceptional Funding Guidance (Inquests), paragraph 13.
[145] Lord Chancellor's Exceptional Funding Guidance (Inquests), paragraph 14.
[146] Lord Chancellor's Exceptional Funding Guidance (Inquests), paragraph 15.
[147] Lord Chancellor's Exceptional Funding Guidance (Inquests), paragraphs 20–24.
[148] Lord Chancellor's Exceptional Funding Guidance (Inquests), paragraph 28.
[149] Lord Chancellor's Exceptional Funding Guidance (Inquests), paragraph 29.
[150] Lord Chancellor's Exceptional Funding Guidance (Inquests), paragraph 30.
[151] Lord Chancellor's Exceptional Funding Guidance (Inquests), paragraph 31.
[152] Lord Chancellor's Exceptional Funding Guidance (Inquests), paragraphs 32–36.
[153] Lord Chancellor's Exceptional Funding Guidance (Inquests) paragraph 37.
[154] Lord Chancellor's Exceptional Funding Guidance (Inquests), paragraph 38.
[155] inquests – Exceptional Cases Funding – Provider Pack pages 7–8.

Mental health

Category definition and scope

LASPO Schedule 1, Part 1

184. LASPO Schedule 1, Part 1, paragraph 5(1), defines mental health work as covering three areas of work where matters arise under:

- the Mental Health Act 1983;
- paragraph 5(2) of the Schedule to the Repatriation of Prisoners Act 1984; and
- the Mental Capacity Act 2005.

185. There are, however, specific exclusions and the following matters are not covered:[156]

- the creation of lasting powers of attorney under the Mental Capacity Act 2005, and
- the making of advance decisions under the Mental Capacity Act 2005.

186. These exclusions, though, do not exclude services provided in relation to determinations and declarations by a court under the Mental Capacity Act 2005 as to the validity, meaning, effect or applicability of a lasting power of attorney that has been created, or an advance decision that has been made.[157]

187. In relation to Court of Protection Proceedings, (which fall under the Mental Capacity Act 2005), advocacy work is only available to the extent that the relevant proceedings concern:[158]

- a person's right to life;
- a person's liberty or physical safety;
- a person's medical treatment (within the meaning of the Mental Health Act 1983);
- a person's capacity to marry, to enter into a civil partnership or to enter into sexual relations; and
- a person's right to family life.

[156] LASPO, Schedule 1, Part 1, paragraph 5(3).
[157] LASPO, Schedule 1, Part 1, paragraph 5(4).
[158] LASPO, Schedule 1, Part 3, paragraph 4.

Regulations

188. Civil Legal Aid (Merits Criteria) Regulations 2013[159] provide further information about the type of legal aid that can be provided for Mental Health work.

189. Regulation 21 states that **investigative representation** will not be awarded for Mental Health work where it relates to proceedings before the First-tier Tribunal or the Mental Health Review Tribunal for Wales.

190. Regulations 51 and 52 stipulate criteria that must be taken into account when considering determinations for **full representation** in relation to mental health proceedings and mental capacity proceedings.

Standard Civil Contract 2010 (as amended)

191. Mental Health work is covered by the Standard Civil Contract 2010 (as amended). The amended category definition notes that the Mental Health category covers legal help and proceedings under LASPO Schedule 1, Part 1, paragraph 5.

192. The definition also clarifies that where there is a grant of exceptional funding, the Mental Health category also includes advocacy for matters arising under the Mental Capacity Act 2005 in addition to those listed in LASPO.[160]

159 SI No. 104.
160 See LASPO, Schedule 1, Part 3, paragraph 4.

Types of cases covered in practice

193. In practice, funding will be available for medical treatment cases, cases concerning a right to life and cases concerning capacity to marry, enter into a civil partnership or sexual relations.

194. Cases involving liberty will continue to be covered and so will those concerning a person's right to family life. This will mean that there will be funding in cases where there is a deprivation of liberty, and in cases where an incapacitated adult is being removed from their family or where contact with their family is restricted.

Personal injury

Category definition and scope

LASPO Schedule 1, Part 1

195. There is no separate category for, or definition of, claims involving personal injury in LASPO. Claims for damages arising out of personal injury or death can arise in numerous contexts and as a result of a number of different legal wrongs.

196. Regardless of their basis, the default position is that claims for damages arising out of personal injury or death are excluded from the scope of civil legal aid by paragraphs 1–3 and 8 of Part 2 of Schedule 1 of LASPO.[161]

197. There are a limited number of exceptions to this general position. Part 1 of Schedule 1 sets out a number of categories of claim which remain within the scope of civil legal aid which can involve a claim for damages for personal injury. Those categories are summarised in the paragraphs that follow, but require careful reading.

198. The category of abuse of a child or vulnerable adult relates to claims arising out of the abuse of an individual that took place at a time when they were a child or vulnerable adult.[162] Clinical negligence claims are excluded from this category.

199. Civil legal aid is available in relation to abuse by a public authority of its position or powers.[163] Again, clinical negligence claims are excluded from this category.

200. Civil legal aid is also available in relation to a claim in tort in respect of an act or omission by public authority that "involves" a "significant breach of Convention Rights" by the authority.[164] Clinical negligence claims are once again expressly excluded from this category of work.[165]

201. Civil legal aid is available for specific clinical negligence claims where an infant is left severely disabled.[166] This category is considered in fuller detail in the chapter of this Guidance on Clinical Negligence.

202. A claim for damages by a victim of conduct amounting to a sexual offence under a provision of the Sexual Offences Act 2003 or section 1 of the Protection of Children Act 1978, or their personal representative, will fall within the scope of civil legal aid, regardless of whether there have been criminal proceedings in relation to their conduct, or the outcome of any such proceedings.[167]

203. Even if it does not fall within any of the general cases listed above, a claim for damages for personal injury can still secure civil legal aid if the LAA makes an "exceptional case determination" under section 10(2) of LASPO.

204. Section 10(2) applies where it is "necessary to make the services available to the individual under this Part because failure to do so would be a breach of… the individual's Convention rights (within the meaning of the Human Rights Act 1998)", or where "… it is appropriate to do so, in the particular circumstances of the case, having regard to any risk that failure to do so would be such a breach".[168]

[161] See the Ministry of Justice website for further information about changes to civil litigation affecting personal injury claims.
[162] LASPO, Schedule 1, Part 1, paragraph 3.
[163] LASPO, Schedule 1, Part 1, paragraph 21.
[164] LASPO, Schedule 1, Part 1, paragraph 22. Further information about the meaning of "significant breach" is provided by the *Lord Chancellor's Guidance Under Section 4 of Legal Aid, Sentencing and Punishment of Offenders Act 2012*, paragraphs 11.1–11.3.
[165] LASPO, Schedule 1, Part 1, paragraph 22(3).
[166] LASPO, Schedule 1, Part 1, paragraph 23.
[167] LASPO, Schedule 1, Part 1, paragraph 39.
[168] LASPO, s 10(3).

Regulations

205. If a claim is eligible for civil legal aid under any of these categories, legal aid is available for advocacy services in all courts in which such claims are heard, from the County Court through to the Supreme Court.[169]

206. Claims under any of these categories which fall within the scope of civil legal aid, or obtain it via an exceptional case determination, still need to satisfy relevant financial eligibility and means criteria before civil legal services will be available for legal representation (either investigative or full representation). The merits criteria are contained in the Civil Legal Aid (Merits Criteria) Regulations 2013.[170]

207. For claims involving the abuse of a child or vulnerable adult[171] or sexual offences[172] the 'merits' criteria and 'cost benefit' criteria apply.[173] Essentially, for **investigative representation**, this requires the prospects of success to be unclear and substantial investigative work to be required before the prospects can be determined, but there to be reasonable grounds for believing that once the investigative work is performed, the criteria for full representation will be met, and that (unless the claim is of wider public interest) the likely damages will exceed £5,000.

208. To qualify for **full representation** both the "cost benefit" criteria in regulation 42 and the 'merits' criteria in regulation 43 must be met. The prospects of success must be at least moderate (50 per cent or more) to satisfy the merits criteria. The cost benefit criteria, which relate to likely damages

versus likely costs, are in the form of a sliding scale, depending upon whether the merits of the claim are moderate, good or very good. The definitions of likely damages and likely costs are set out in regulations 9 and 10 respectively. In short, likely damages must exceed likely costs by the following ratios:

- moderate prospects of success – 4:1;
- good prospects of success – 2:1; and
- very good prospects of success – 1:1.

209. In the case of the abuse of position or powers,[174] or the breach of Convention Rights,[175] by a public authority, the criteria in the Civil Legal Aid (Merits Criteria) Regulations 2013 are less exacting.[176]

210. The minimum £5,000 limit on the likely damages, which would otherwise preclude a case being eligible for **investigative representation**, does not operate where the claim is part of a multi-party action or there was abuse of a child or vulnerable adult.

211. For **full representation**, the "merits" criteria is in effect modified so that the prospects of success must be at least "moderate" .

212. The "cost benefit" criterion does not apply. Instead, the "proportionality test" in regulation 8 must be satisfied. The proportionality test is met if the likely benefits of the proceedings to the individual and others justify the likely costs, having regard to the prospects of success and all the other circumstances of the case.

[169] LASPO, Schedule 1, Part 3.
[170] SI No. 104.
[171] LASPO, Schedule 1, Part 1, paragraph 3.
[172] LASPO, Schedule 1, Part 1, paragraph 39.
[173] See Part 4, and in particular regulations 39–43, of Civil Legal Aid (Merits Criteria) Regulations 2013 SI No. 104.
[174] LASPO, Schedule 1, Part 1, paragraph 21.
[175] LASPO, Schedule 1, Part 1, paragraph 22.
[176] See Part 6, and in particular regulations 57–58, of *Civil Legal Aid (Merits Criteria) Regulations 2013* SI No. 104.

Types of cases covered in practice

Abuse of child or vulnerable adult and Sexual Offences

213. Claims involving abuse of children or vulnerable adults arise in a variety of guises, usually as trespass to the person where the abuse may take the form of violence, a sexual assault, or rape. There is a clear overlap with the category of sexual offences. The defendants to such claims may be family members, schools, religious orders, care homes, local authorities, prisons, the police, or similar bodies. Claims can also lie in negligence for neglect, or for failing to detect, prevent, or act upon the abuse. Claimants in such cases are entitled to damages for personal injuries arising out of the physical and psychiatric effects of their experiences.

Abuse of position or powers by a public authority

214. Deliberate or dishonest abuse of position or powers by a public authority so as to cause personal injury to a claimant might arise in a number of contexts. One may be in the use of police or other regulatory powers, where a dishonest or deliberate detention could include the use of force which causes the claimant to suffer physical and/or psychiatric injury. Another area where personal injury can occur in the exercise of statutory powers by a public authority is in the context of the detention and restraint of psychiatric patients. However, it is very unlikely that such claims will fall within this category because of the breadth of the definition of clinical negligence in paragraph 21(5) of Part 1 of Schedule 1, which should exclude such claims from this category.

Breach of Convention rights by public authority

215. A claim in tort against a public authority which involved a "significant breach"[177] of one of the Convention Rights will most frequently occur where the operational obligation in Article 2 of the European Convention on Human Rights[178] is engaged because of the presence of a real and immediate risk of suicide or death on the part of an individual, yet negligence allows the death to occur. In such circumstances, damages for personal injury would be included in the claim on behalf of the estate under the Law Reform (Miscellaneous Provisions) Act 1934. A relative may suffer a psychiatric injury ("nervous shock") as a result of witnessing the immediate aftermath of the death.

216. Paragraph 22 of Part 1 of Schedule 1 of LASPO does not restrict civil legal aid services to the direct victim of the significant breach of the Convention Rights. It is therefore likely that a nervous shock claim could be brought as a result of witnessing the aftermath of a significant breach of Article 2.

217. Although this factual matrix is most likely to occur in the context of mental health patients informally or compulsorily admitted to a hospital for assessment and treatment, such claims are likely to be excluded because they fall within the definition of clinical negligence which is excluded from this category by paragraph 22(3) of Part 1 of Schedule 1. The same exclusion does not apply to other public authorities, such as the police or the prison service. Claims in tort involving serious breaches of Articles 3,[179] and Article 8,[180] which encompasses bodily integrity could also give rise to an eligible claim under this category.

218. By necessity, whether a claim involves a "significant breach" of Convention Rights will be highly fact-sensitive.[181]

177 Further information on the meaning of "significant breach" is provided by the *Lord Chancellor's Guidance Under Section 4 of Legal Aid, Sentencing and Punishment of Offenders Act 2012*, paragraphs 11. 1–11.3.

178 Right to life.

179 Prohibition of torture.

180 Right to respect for private and family life.

181 Further information on the meaning of "significant breach" is provided by the *Lord Chancellor's Guidance Under Section 4 of Legal Aid, Sentencing and Punishment of Offenders Act 2012*, paragraphs 11. 1–11.3.

Public law and judicial review

Category definition and scope

LASPO Schedule 1, Part 1

219. Under LASPO Schedule 1, Part 1, legal aid is available for "civil legal services provided in relation to judicial review of an enactment, decision, act or omission".[182] Legal aid is also available for habeas corpus proceedings.[183]

220. Paragraph 18 of Part 2 of Schedule 1[184] excludes judicial review from services for which legal aid is available except as provided under Schedule 1. This is to ensure that judicial review can only be funded via paragraph 19 of Part 1 of Schedule 1 and not under other paragraphs.[185] The effect is that the limitations contained in that paragraph apply to all judicial review claims, whatever their subject matter.

[182] LASPO, Schedule 1, Part 1, paragraph 19.
[183] LASPO, Schedule 1, Part 1, paragraph 20.
[184] Inserted by the Legal Aid Sentencing and Punishment of Offenders Act 2012 (Amendment of Schedule 1) Order SI No. 748.
[185] See the explanatory memorandum to the Legal Aid Sentencing and Punishment of Offenders Act 2012 (Amendment of Schedule 1) Order SI No. 748.

Regulations

221. **Full representation** will only be granted where the requirements of Civil Legal Aid (Merits Criteria) Regulations 2013 are met, i.e.:[186]

- there has been a letter before claim and reasonable time to respond (except where this is impracticable);
- the proportionality test is met, meaning "the likely benefits of the proceedings to the individual and others justify the likely costs having regard to the prospects of success and all the other circumstances of the case";[187] and
- the prospects of success are 50 per cent or above.

222. For cases where the application for legal aid was made before 27 January 2014 legal aid may also be granted where the merits are borderline and the case is either of significant wider public interest, of overwhelming importance to the individual or "the substance of the case relates to a breach of Convention Rights". A case is of significant wider public interest for these purposes:[188]

if the Director is satisfied that the case is an appropriate case to realise real benefits to the public at large, other than those which normally flow from cases of the type in question; and benefits for an identifiable class of individuals, other than the individual to whom civil legal services may be provided or members of that individual's family.

223. The borderline category was removed with effect from 27 January 2014 by the Civil Legal Aid (Merits Criteria) (Amendment) Regulations 2014.[189] Transitional provisions in Regulation 6 have the effect that the category still exists for cases in which the application is made after 27 January 2014 where civil legal services have already been provided pursuant to an earlier application and the new application "relates to the same case". There are other conditions and reference must be made to the Regulations but the effect will be, for example, that the borderline test will continue to apply to applications for legal aid for an appeal in respect of cases where the initial application was made earlier than 27 January 2014.

224. Note that if the application is for **investigative representation** then the proposed defendant must still be notified of the potential claim before legal aid is granted. This need not be a full pre-action protocol letter and is expected to be most relevant in cases of failure to act (such as failure to carry out an assessment) where mere notice of the claim may prompt action.[190]

[186] SI No. 104, Regulation 60.
[187] Civil Legal Aid (Merits Criteria) Regulations 2013 SI No. 104, regulation 8.
[188] Civil Legal Aid (Merits Criteria) Regulations 2013 SI No, 104, regulation 6.
[189] SI No. 131.
[190] See Lord Chancellor's Guidance Under Section 4 of Legal Aid, Sentencing and Punishment of Offenders Act 2012, paragraphs 7.38–7.39.

Standard Civil Contract 2010 (as amended) and Standard Civil Contract 2013

225. Public law contracts have not been terminated and continue on the 2010 terms (as amended). The public law category covers:[191]

"34 Legal Help and related proceedings concerning:

a. The human rights of the client or a dependant of the client other than matters which fall within the definition of another category.

b. Public law challenges to the acts, omissions or decision of public bodies, including challenges by way of judicial review or habeas corpus.

35. To the extent that any relevant grant of exceptional funding is made (in accordance with section 10 of the Act) this category also include Legal Help and all proceedings concerning data protection and freedom of information issues."

226. This is narrower than the original category definition in the 2010 contract which covered civil liberties more generally, proceedings under section 222 of the Local Government Act 1972 and freedom of information.

227. The 2010 (as amended) and 2013 contracts both refer to the relationship between this and other categories in the following terms:[192]

19."Public law challenges to the acts, omissions or decision of public bodies (including under the Human Rights Act 1998), in particular challenges by way of judicial review ...and habeas corpus are covered by the Category in which the principal matter or proceedings appear or by the Category which relates to the underlying substance of the case (as referenced by the widest Category Definition incorporating excluded work). They are also covered by the Public Law Category.

20 If arising in respect of matters or proceedings within the Crime Category, these cases will also fall within the Crime Category.

21 Note that the fact that a Defendant is a Public Authority does not bring a case within the Public Law Category. For a case to constitute a public law challenge it must be determined according to judicial review principles (limited to paragraph 19 Part 1 of Schedule 1 to the Act). Claims for damages against Public Authorities, other than Human Rights Act claims, do not usually fall within Public Law but may come within Actions Against the Police etc. Claims under the Human Rights Act may well come within both Public Law and Actions Against the Police etc."

228. As pointed out in the *Bhatia Best* case,[193] this is subject to the definition in paragraph 19(10) of schedule 1 to LASPO so, in order to fall within the terms of a public law contract a matter must be both within this definition and within that paragraph.

229. Paragraph 2.28 of the Standard Civil Contract 2013 specification provides that:[194]

All Categories of Work are exclusive under this Contract. You must have Schedule Authorisation in a Category to undertake work in that Category unless it is Miscellaneous Work.

230. The effect is that:

(a) If a judicial review claim arises out of a matter that is in scope in some other category then the solicitor bringing the claim must either have a contract in that category or a public law contract. So, the holder of a community care contract can bring a judicial review claim to challenge an assessment under section 21 of the National Assistance Act 1948 and a housing contract holder can bring a claim for judicial review to challenge a refusal to accept a homelessness claim.

(b) If a judicial review claim arises out of a matter that is not within one of the other contract categories then the solicitor must have a public law contract to bring the claim. The important point to note is that the contract categories do not necessarily overlap with the ordinary meaning of the category heading. So, for example, housing does not include non-homeless allocation decisions. A judicial review claim in such a case would have to be brought under a public law contract and not a housing contract.[195]

(c) Where a provider does not hold a contract permitting them to undertake work of a particular kind then it may still be possible to enter into an individual contract through the LAA Special Cases Unit. It will be necessary to satisfy the criteria in Regulation 31(5) of the Civil Legal Aid (Procedure) Regulations 2012,[196] namely:

31(5) The effective administration of justice test is satisfied if the Director decides that it is necessary for a provider to provide the services which are the subject of the application under an individual case contract having considered—

(a) the provider's knowledge of the particular proceedings or dispute and expertise in providing the civil legal services which are the subject of the application;

(b) the nature and likely length of the particular proceedings or dispute;

(c) the complexity of the issues; and

(d) the circumstances of the individual making the application.

In the *Bhatia Best* case[197] these criteria seems to have been satisfied because the firm in question had particular expertise in dealing with cases arising from the decision of the ECJ in *Ruiz Zambrano v Office National de l'Emploi* (ONEm): C-34/09 [2012] QB 265, [2011] ECR I-1177.[198]

231. Solicitors cannot exercise delegated powers to grant representation in a judicial review case except in homelessness cases and some community care matters.[199] The LAA has given guidance as to emergency applications and states that it "will" process them within 48 hours. Email applications can be made where work has to be undertaken in less than 48 hours.[200]

Payment for work at the permission stage

232. The Civil Legal Aid (Remuneration) (Amendment) (No. 3) Regulations 2014,[201] amend the Civil Legal Aid (Remuneration) Regulations by inserting a new Regulation 5A to prevent payment for "civil legal services consisting of making" an application for judicial review unless permission is granted. This is subject to an exception in Regulation 5A(1)(b) to the following effect:

(b) the court neither refuses nor gives permission and the Lord Chancellor considers that it is reasonable to pay remuneration in the circumstances of the case, taking into account, in particular—

(i) the reason why the provider did not obtain a costs order or costs agreement in favour of the legally aided person;

(ii) the extent to which, and the reason why, the legally aided person obtained the outcome sought in the proceedings; and

(iii) the strength of the application for permission at the time it was filed, based on the law and on the facts which the provider knew or ought to have known at that time.

233. There is some doubt about what exactly is excluded from payment under this provision. An application for judicial review is defined "as an application for judicial review made, or treated as made, in accordance with (i) Part 54 of the Civil Procedure Rules 1998 or (ii) Part 4 of197 the Tribunal Rules".[202] However, paragraph 119 of the consultation paper which preceded these changes stated:[203] Legal aid would continue to be paid in the same way as now for the earlier stages of a case, to investigate the prospects and strength of a claim (including advice from Counsel on the merits of the claim) and to engage in pre-action correspondence aimed at avoiding proceedings under the Pre-Action Protocol for Judicial Review. In addition, payment for work carried out on an application for interim relief in accordance with Part 25 of the Civil Procedure Rules would not be at risk, regardless of whether the provider is ultimately paid in relation to the substantive judicial review claim.

PART III IN PRACTICE

234. No express exclusion for interim relief has been made in the Regulations but it is plain from this history that such applications are not intended to be caught by the prohibition on payment. This can only be because the amended Regulations adopt a narrow meaning of "making an application" for judicial review to cover only those parts of the application that necessarily fall under the Civil Procedure Rules (CPR) Part 54. Other steps (including an application for an injunction) do not fall within that phrase even though they would ordinarily be treated as the costs of those proceedings (for example on a costs order from the opponent). If this is right then it may well be that other ancillary steps not within CPR Part 54 are also excluded from the narrow definition and could also attract payment even if permission is refused. For example, an application for disclosure is not within CPR Part 54 but is made under CPR Part 31. Conversely, the new Regulation 5A makes clear that the prohibition payment relates to the whole of the making of the application and not just the permission stage. So there can be no payment for a rolled up hearing unless the court grants permission.

191 Standard Civil Contract 2010, Amended Category Definitions.

192 See Standard Civil Contract 2013, Category Definitions and Standard Civil Contract 2010, Amended Category Definitions.

193 [2014] EWHC 746 (QB).

194 Standard Civil Contract 2013. All contract documents are available on the Ministry of Justice website.

195 See the Legal Aid Agency's Frequently Asked Questions for the civil legal aid reforms, paragraph 77.

196 SI No. 3098.

197 [2014] EWHC 746 (QB).

198 2011] ECR I-1177.

199 2010 Specification, paragraph 5.3(b).

200 See Applications for emergency funding in Judicial Review cases: Processes and Procedures from 1 April 2013.

201 SI No. 607.

202 Civil Legal Aid (Remuneration) (Amendment) (No. 3) Regulations 2014, SI No. 607, Regulation 5A(3)(c).

203 Ministry of Justice, "Judicial Review – Proposals for Further Reform" (2013).

Types of cases covered in practice

Courts and Tribunals covered

235. LASPO Schedule 1, Part 1, paragraph 19(10) defines judicial review as including "any procedure" in which a court or body in Schedule 3 "is required by an enactment to make a decision applying the principles that are applied by the court on an application for judicial review".

236. Various statutes make such provision but the main effect seems to be to include judicial review in the Upper Tribunal under section 15 of the Tribunals Courts and Enforcement Act 2007. It is doubtful whether collateral challenges before other statutory Tribunals are covered by legal aid.[204]

237. Where a statute allows for an appeal on a point of law (for example homelessness appeals)[205] then that normally includes the same grounds as are available on a judicial review but that does not seem to be what is intended here. Otherwise funding would now be available for all appeals on a point of law. In relation to homelessness appeals, this has now been confirmed by *Bhatia Best Limited v Lord Chancellor* [2014] EWHC 746 (QB), [2014] 3 All

ER 573.[206] Silber J held that an appeal on a point of law under s.204 of the Housing Act 1996 did not fall within paragraph 19. The effect was that the Claimant could not bring such appeals under their public law contract but would have to hold a housing contract to do so (subject to the possibility of entering individual case contracts). An odd consequence of this case is that homelessness appeals in respect of interim accommodation pending appeal under s. 204A will still be within the judicial review category because s. 204A(4) does require that the court apply "the principles that are applied by the court on an application for judicial review".

238. Paragraphs 1, 18 and 19 of Schedule 3 include legal aid for advocacy services in the Upper Tribunal exercising its judicial review powers.

239. Proceedings will cease to qualify as judicial review if the court orders that they should continue as if brought by ordinary action.[207] The claim will then have to qualify for funding under a different category.

Personal benefit mandatory

240. LASPO provides that a judicial review claim must "have the potential to produce a benefit for the individual, a member of the individual's family, or the environment".[208] Benefit is not defined but this is intended to exclude a pure "public interest" challenge.

241. If proceedings become academic for the individual after legally aided services have been provided then the exclusion does not apply. So, for example, if the individual claimant in a community care claim receives the relief they are seeking then legal aid can continue to allow the claim to proceed for the purpose of pursuing costs or on wider public interest grounds.

[204] For example, a challenge to the validity of Housing Benefit Regulations in the First Tier Tribunal.
[205] However, homelessness cases are treated as public law cases for the purposes of the application of the Civil Legal Aid (Merits Criteria) Regulations 2013 SI No. 104.
[206] [2014] EWHC 746 (QB).
[207] See Civil Procedure Rules Part 54.20.
[208] LASPO Schedule 1, Part 1, paragraph 19(3).

Alternative proceedings

242. Under the Civil Legal Aid (Merits Criteria) Regulations 2013, the case must meet the standard criteria under regulation 39. In particular:

"the individual has exhausted all reasonable alternatives to bringing proceedings including any complaints system, ombudsman scheme or other form of alternative dispute resolution."

243. In addition, the claim must meet the criteria in regulation 53, meaning the claim must appear to be susceptible to challenge and that:[209]

"there are no alternative proceedings before a court or tribunal which are available to challenge the act, omission or other matter, except where the Director considers that such proceedings would not be effective in providing the remedy that the individual requires."

244. This applies only to alternatives before a court or tribunal, but where such a remedy exists then it must be used first unless it would be ineffective. For example, the alternative procedure might not be mandatory if the case is urgent and the tribunal cannot grant interim relief.[210]

[209] Regulation 53(b) as substituted by the Civil Legal Aid (Merits Criteria) Amendment Regulations 2013 SI No. 772.
[210] See further Lord Chancellor's Guidance Under Section 4 of Legal Aid, Sentencing and Punishment of Offenders Act 2012, paragraph 7.37.

Subject-based limitations

245. As a general rule legal aid for judicial review is not limited to particular subject areas, although contract holders who do not hold public law contracts (see above) will be limited in the kinds of case they can take on. This means that judicial review claims can still be brought in respect of issues that would otherwise be excluded. For example:

- It is still possible to include a claim for damages for most non-defamation torts in a judicial review application where that arises out of the claim. This will include a restitutionary claim provided that it is not based on trust law. The circumstances in which such claims can be made are governed by section 31(4) of the Senior Courts Act 1981.
- It is still possible to bring a judicial review for claims in relation to welfare benefits, including those excluded from legal aid generally by paragraph 15 of Part 2 of Schedule 1. However, in most cases a judicial review claim will not be possible because there will be an alternative remedy.

246. There are, however, various exclusions. Some general exclusions in LASPO, Schedule 1, Part 2 apply to judicial review claims:

- defamation and malicious falsehood;[211]
- in relation to conveyancing;[212]
- in relation to the making of wills;[213]
- in relation to matters of trust law;[214]
- company or partnership law;[215]
- civil legal services provided to an individual in relation to matters arising out of or in connection with the establishment, carrying on, termination or transfer of their business;[216] and
- changing an individual's name.[217]

247. If the subject matter of the claim falls within any of the above then it will not qualify for legal aid including for judicial review, although in principle the Director could make an exceptional case determination under section 10 of LASPO.[218]

248. In relation to immigration claims, LASPO Schedule 1, Part 1, paragraph 19(5) creates a general rule that legal aid is not available for judicial review in respect of an immigration issue where substantially the same "issue" has been determined against the claimant within the preceding year on an application for judicial review or an appeal to a court of tribunal. Paragraph 19(6) provides that legal aid is not available to challenge removal directions given not more than a year after the making of the relevant decision to remove or the conclusion of any appeal against that decision.

249. The one year rule does not apply to asylum applications where there is no right of appeal,[219] to certificates under the Nationality Immigration and Asylum Act 2002 sections 94 and 96,[220] or of removal directions in prescribed circumstances.[221] At the time of writing no such circumstances had been prescribed.

Forthcoming changes

250. At the time of writing the MOJ intends to introduce changes by secondary legislation that will restrict legal aid so that it is not available where the client has not been lawfully resident in the UK for more than 12 months. This will apply to all cases and not only judicial review but is likely to have a particularly significant impact on judicial review claims. Permission has been granted to judicially review this proposal. Regulations have now been delayed pending a decision on that claim.

[211] LASPO, Schedule 1, Part 2, paragraph 7.
[212] LASPO, Schedule 1, Part 2, paragraph 9.
[213] LASPO, Schedule 1, Part 2, paragraph 10.
[214] LASPO, Schedule 1, Part 2, paragraph 11.
[215] LASPO, Schedule 1, Part 2, paragraph 13.
[216] LASPO, Schedule 1, Part 2, paragraph 14.
[217] LASPO, Schedule 1, Part 2, paragraph 17.
[218] The Lord Chancellor's Guidance expressly gives a judicial review claim arising out of a business as an example of a case where a determination might be made. An example might be where statutory powers have been used to close down a business that is the claimant's sole source of income and where a challenge requires extensive expert evidence. See *Lord Chancellor's Guidance Under Section 4 of Legal Aid, Sentencing and Punishment of Offenders Act 2012*, paragraph 7.10.
[219] LASPO, Schedule 1, Part 2, paragraph 19(7).
[220] LASPO, Schedule 1, Part 2, paragraph 19(7).
[221] LASPO, Schedule 1, Part 2, paragraph 19(8).

Welfare benefits

Category definition and scope

LASPO Schedule 1, Part 1

251. Paragraph 15 of Part 2 of Schedule 1 of LASPO excludes civil legal services in relation to a benefit, allowance, payment, credit or pension under any enactment relating to social security as well as tax credits, pension credit and vaccine damage payments.

252. The exception to this is under paragraph 8 of Schedule 1, Part 1 which allows for civil legal services to be provided on a point of law in the Upper Tribunal, the Court of Appeal or Supreme Court in relation to a benefit, allowance, credit or pension under enactments relating to social security, tax credits and pension credits.

253. A further important exception is that of judicial review in respect of welfare benefits, which continue to remain in scope under paragraph 19(2)(a) of Schedule 1, Part 1, under the category of Public Law. There may be circumstances where the judicial review of a welfare benefits issue overlaps

with another category, such as Housing. Consideration will then need to be given as to which category the work falls under, Public Law or Housing. This will depend on what is the "overall substance or predominant issue" in the case "when taken as a whole".[222]

254. Finally, there is an exception for cases which involve a contravention of the Equality Act 2010,[223] which includes disability discrimination, especially a failure to make reasonable adjustments.

Regulations

255. The effect of regulation 2 of the Civil Legal Aid (Preliminary Proceedings) Regulations 2013,[224] is that requests to the First Tier Tribunal for permission to appeal a decision of a First-tier Tribunal to the Upper Tribunal are not eligible for legal aid.[225] This means work undertaken in respect of an appeal to the Upper Tribunal only comes within scope once a First-tier Tribunal Judge has issued a determination on an application for permission (either granting or refusing permission to appeal).[226]

[222] Standard Civil Contract 2013, Category Definitions paragraph 8.

[223] LASPO Schedule 1, Part 1, paragraph 43(1) and (2)(a).

[224] SI No. 265.

[225] Requests are a requirement under Rule 38 of The Tribunal Procedure (First-tier Tribunal) (Social Entitlement Chamber) Rules 2008 SI No. 2685.

[226] Rule 39 of The Tribunal Procedure (First-tier Tribunal) (Social Entitlement Chamber) Rules 2008 SI No. 2685.

Standard Civil Contract 2013

256. Welfare benefits no longer form part of the Standard Civil Contract. However, the Law Centres Network has been awarded a civil contract which allows them to undertake free-standing work on welfare benefits. A Standard Civil Contract (Welfare Benefits) was awarded to the Law Centres Network from 1 November 2013 for the procurement areas in London & the South East of England, and Midlands & East of England.[227] A further contract was awarded to the Network from 1 February 2014 for the procurement areas in the North and the South West & Wales.[228] The contract permits work to be undertaken under the following categories for Welfare Benefits:[229]

(a) Legal Help in relation to appeals on a point of law in the Upper Tribunal, Court of Appeal and Supreme Court for all welfare benefits (including housing benefit, war pensions, state pensions and other similar benefits under a social security enactment, the Vaccine Damage Payments Act 1979 or Part 4 of the Child Maintenance and Other Payments Act 2008).

(b) Legal Help in relation to appeal on a point of law relating to a council tax reduction scheme from the Valuation Tribunal England and the Valuation Tribunal Wales to the High Court, Court of Appeal and Supreme Court.

(c) Legal representation for appeals to the Court of Appeal and the Supreme Court on a point of law in relation to all welfare benefits (including housing benefit, war pensions, state pensions and other similar benefits under a social security enactment, the Vaccine

Damage Payments Act 1979 and Part 4 of the Child Maintenance and Other Payments Act 2008) and appeals on a point of law relating to a [council tax reduction scheme] to the Court of Appeal and Supreme Court.

257. Advocacy is not funded at the Upper Tribunal unless the Tribunal is exercising its judicial review functions under section 15 of the Tribunals, Courts and Enforcement Act 2007 or it is an exceptional case under section 10 of LASPO and Part 8 of the Civil Legal Aid (Procedure) Regulations 2012.[230]

258. To the extent that any relevant grant of exceptional funding is made in the Welfare Benefits category, it includes:[231]

(a) Legal Help in relation to all welfare benefits (including [council tax reduction scheme appeals], housing benefit, war pensions, state pensions and vaccine damage payments or similar payments), and in relation to proceedings before any welfare benefit review or appeal body;

(b) any subsequent or related proceedings before a court.

259. An exceptional case is one where the failure to provide legal aid would be a breach of the individual's convention rights or the rights of the individual to the provision of legal services that are enforceable EU rights.

260. Appeals on the right to reside requirement and other determinations concerned with free movement may raise issues of enforceable EU rights. Further, where the decision concerns an assertable right to welfare benefit (i.e. one that does not involve the exercise of a discretion), a claim for exceptional funding could be made under Article 6 of the European Convention on Human Rights.

261. The Lord Chancellor's Exceptional Funding Guidance (Non-Inquests) makes clear that in determining whether Article 6 would be breached, what has to be shown is that the failure to fund means that bringing the case would be "practically impossible or lead to an obvious unfairness in proceedings".[232] The factors that may be particularly relevant include:

(a) The legal complexity of the matter, i.e. is there a cross over with EU/immigration law?

(b) the importance of the issue at stake , and

(c) the inability of the claimant to argue their case, for example, because of vulnerability or disability.

Types of cases covered in practice

262. The stated purpose of the April 2013 legal aid reforms, now enshrined in LASPO, is to exclude welfare benefits from the scope of civil legal aid (with the exception of judicial review). This means that only a small residual category remains, namely appeals before in the Upper Tribunal, the Court of Appeal or Supreme Court.

263. This means that only the following types of cases are covered in practice:

(a) Legally aided advice and assistance for advice on whether or not to submit an application for permission to appeal to the Upper Tribunal (following a refusal of permission by the First-tier Tribunal);

(b) Legally aided advice and assistance for an application to the Upper Tribunal for permission to appeal to the Upper Tribunal;

(c) Legally aided advice and assistance for substantive appeals on a point of law at the Upper Tribunal;

(d) Legally aided advice and assistance for advice on whether or not to submit an application for permission to appeal to the Court of Appeal or Supreme Court;

(e) Legally aided advice, assistance and representation for an application to the Court of Appeal or Supreme Court for permission to appeal, and for a substantive appeal;

(f) Legally aided advice and assistance for advice on whether or not to appeal to the High Court relating to a council tax reduction scheme;[233]

(g) Legally aided advice and assistance for substantive appeals to the High Court on a point of law, relating to a council tax reduction scheme;[234]

(h) Legally aided advice and assistance for advice on whether or not to submit an application for permission to appeal to the Court of Appeal or Supreme Court, relating to a council tax reduction scheme;

(i) Legally aided advice, assistance and representation for an application to the Court of Appeal or Supreme Court for permission to appeal, and for a substantive appeal, relating to a council tax reduction scheme;

(j) Legally aided advice and assistance for advice on whether or not to apply for judicial review relating to welfare benefit in the Administrative Court; and

(k) Legally aided advice, assistance and representation for an application for judicial review relating to welfare benefits in the Administrative Court.

227 Further information is available on the Ministry of Justice website.
228 Further information is available on the Ministry of Justice website.
229 Standard Civil Contract 2013, Category Definitions paragraphs 33–35
230 SI No. 3098.
231 Standard Civil Contract 2013, Category Definitions, paragraph 36.
232 Lord Chancellor's Exceptional Funding Guidance (Non-Inquests), paragraphs 63.
233 The Legal Aid, Sentencing and Punishment of Offenders Act 2012 (Amendment of Schedule 1) Order 2013 SI No. 748.
234 The Legal Aid, Sentencing and Punishment of Offenders Act 2012 (Amendment of Schedule 1) Order 2013. SI No. 748.

Assessment of Fees and Costs

The Detailed Assessment Process

[3.206]

Detailed Assessment is one of two forms of assessment that the court may carry out when it comes to assessing costs on an inter partes basis. Summary Assessment is the other form of assessment and that is discussed below.

The procedure for detailed assessment is set out in CPR 47.6–CPR 47.10 and the Costs Practice Direction Sections 31–42. The procedure is commenced by the receiving party serving on the paying party a Notice of Commencement in accordance with one of the precedents annexed to the Costs Practice Direction. Service has to be effected within 3 months of the order or other authority for the assessment. A failure to commence within that period enables the paying party to apply to the court requiring the proceedings to be commenced. Failure to commence thereafter may lead to a disallowance of costs altogether. It is the responsibility of the solicitor to carry in the assessment proceedings (on the instructions of the lay client) and so invariably counsel will not be involved at all in the assessment process. However, it is important that counsel, through his clerk, keeps up to date on the progress of any assessment proceedings.

Whilst it is the solicitor who will seek to ensure that all of counsel's fees are properly accounted for in the claim for costs the solicitor may be assisted by counsel in providing breakdowns or written explanations for fees incurred. This is particularly so where specific challenge is made by the paying party to counsel's fees.

If the paying party wishes to dispute the bill then they must serve points of dispute (Precedent G) within 21 days of service of the Notice of Commencement. It is at this stage that counsel will often be contacted by the instructing solicitor to report as to the challenges that are being made to counsel's fees. It is then that counsel may consider it helpful to provide breakdown's and explanations for the disputed fees to assist the solicitor, or his costs draftsman, at the assessment hearing. A failure to provide breakdowns (itemising hours spent and briefly describing the work done) can have a detrimental effect on the ultimate recovery of the disputed fees.

It is not usually necessary for counsel to attend the detailed assessment proceedings himself. The bill is supported at the hearing usually by the instructing solicitor and/or costs draftsman. In exceptional cases the court may require counsel or his clerk to attend to explain particular challenged items. The significance of the detailed assessment as part of the overall litigation process has led to specialist barristers being instructed to represent parties at detailed assessments. It is not at all unusual for specialist costs counsel to be instructed to appear at the detailed assessment hearing.

In a non-legal aid case which goes to assessment, as a general rule the client must pay the barrister's fees in full for work done prior to any assessment, thus enabling receipted (paid) fee notes to form part of the bill being assessed. The solicitor should have agreed the fees with counsel's clerk and got the agreement of the client prior to the work being carried out. The inter partes assessment should have no impact on the level of fees between the barrister and the client although many will look again at their fees if there are drastic reductions.

The general position as described above applies equally to detailed assessments undertaken a legal aid case where there is a paying party. However, in a legal aid only assessment (such as where legal aid costs are being assessed following a discharge of a legal aid certificate or pursuant to an order for the legal aid assessment of costs where the client has lost) there will be no paying party and so there will no points of dispute served. However, counsel's fees will still need to be justified in the same way to the costs judge assessing the costs.

Further information in relation to counsel's position vis-à-vis the detailed assessment process can be found in the Civil Legal Aid (General) Regulations 1989[1] and the Civil Procedure Rules[2].

1 Civil Legal Aid (General) Regulations 1989, SI 1989/339.
2 CPR 47 and CPD PD 43–48.

The Summary Assessment Process

[3.207]

Most barristers will be much more familiar with the summary assessment process than they are with the detailed assessment process simply because they themselves will have participated in summary assessments. The relevant rules are to be found in CPR 44.6 and Section 9 of the Cost Practice Direction. A statement of costs itemising the costs incurred (sometimes estimating) will be presented to the court for the court to summarily assess the costs claim. Counsel appearing at the assessment will necessarily be in a good position to justify his own fees if a challenge is made.

The existence of a conditional fee agreement or other funding arrangement is not by itself a sufficient reason for not carrying out a summary assessment. The basic costs can be summarily assessed with the additional liabilities (success fee) being assessed at the end of the case in the event of a successful outcome. In some cases the trigger for a success fee may have been met at the time the summary assessment takes place in which case the court will assess the success fee at the summary assessment.

In connection with conditional fee agreements entered into before 1 November 2005 it remains open to a legal representative to apply to the court for an order that he be permitted to recover from his client an agreed success fee which has been disallowed inter partes. See former CPR 44.16 and Section 20 of the Costs Practice Direction. There are some important provisions under this section which counsel should be aware of. They are set out below:

Section 20.4 (of the former costs rules pre 1 April 2013)

(1) Where detailed assessment proceedings have been commenced, and the paying party serves points of dispute (as to which see Section 34 of this Practice Direction), which show that he is seeking a reduction in any percentage increase charged by counsel on his fees, the solicitor acting for the receiving party must within 3 days of service deliver to counsel a copy of the relevant points of dispute and the bill of costs or the relevant parts of the bill.

(2) Counsel must within 10 days thereafter inform the solicitor in writing whether or not he will accept the reduction sought or some other reduction. Counsel may state any points he wishes to have made in a reply to the points of dispute, and the solicitor must serve them on the paying party as or as part of a reply.

(3) Counsel who fails to inform the solicitor within the time limits set out above will be taken to accept the reduction unless the court otherwise orders.

Section 20.5 (of the former costs rules pre 1 April 2013)

Where the paying party serves points of dispute seeking a reduction in any percentage increase charged by a legal representative acting for the receiving party, and that legal representative intends, if necessary, to apply for an order that any amount of the percentage disallowed as against the paying party shall continue to be payable by his client, the solicitor acting for the receiving party must, within 14 days of service of the points of dispute, give to his client a clear written explanation of the nature of the relevant point of dispute and the effect it will have if it is upheld in whole or in part by the court, and of the client's right to attend any subsequent hearings at court when the matter is raised.

Section 20.6 (of the former costs rules pre 1 April 2013)

Where the solicitor acting for a receiving party files a request for a detailed assessment hearing it must if appropriate, be accompanied by a certificate signed by him stating:

(1) that the amount of the percentage increase in respect of counsel's fees or solicitor's charges is disputed;

(2) whether an application will be made for an order that any amount of that increase which is disallowed should continue to be payable by his client;

(3) that he has given his client an explanation in accordance with paragraph 20.5; and,

(4) whether his client wishes to attend court when the amount of any relevant percentage increase may be decided.

Section 20.7 (of the former costs rules pre 1 April 2013)

(1) The solicitor acting for the receiving party must within 7 days of receiving from the court notice of the date of the assessment hearing, notify his client, and if appropriate, counsel in writing of the date, time and place of the hearing.

(2) Counsel may attend or be represented at the detailed assessment hearing and may make oral or written submissions.

Section 20.8 (of the former costs rules pre 1 April 2013)

(1) At the detailed assessment hearing, the court will deal with the assessment of the costs payable by one party to another, including the amount of the percentage increase, and give a certificate accordingly.

The Role of the Costs Draftsman/Costs Lawyer

[3.208]

As discussed above, most solicitors will instruct a costs draftsman to prepare the bill of costs. The costs draftsman will then usually be instructed to attend any detailed assessment to support the bill of costs. They will invariably prepared points of reply to any points of dispute challenging the bill (they will prepare points of dispute when challenging a bill). Costs draftsman are specialists in their chosen area; many now have specific rights of audience and the right to conduct costs litigation. More information about costs draftsman can be found on the Association of Costs Lawyers ("ACL") web site: http://www.associationofcostslawyers.co.uk. You will find information here about the work of the ACL, its bye-laws and code of conduct, membership details and links to other relevant web sites.

Other Types of Fee Arrangements and Scenarios Affecting Charging

Commitment Fees

[3.209]

A barrister has to ensure that he does not accept money other than by way of remuneration or his independence could be seen to be compromised, in accordance with the provisions of the Code of Conduct (see paragraph 307 of the Code). However, commitment fees can be charged; such a fee is very similar to a brief fee, in that it is payable further in advance of the date of the arbitration (or other attendance) but is only a proportion of the fee which will be earned for the attendance. Traditionally, a barrister will accept a reservation for a case and will take the risk that the case settles before the brief for the case is actually delivered. In such circumstances the space booked in the diary will be empty, and there is a risk that the barrister will be unemployed for all or part of that time, and a risk that, in the meantime, he has been forced to refuse work which might have been remunerative during that period. On the other hand, if the brief is delivered and the case settles thereafter, the barrister would normally be entitled to retain the brief fee, and may have the added benefit of obtaining other work during the newly void period in the diary.

The reason for the traditional approach of not demanding commitment fees is justified by the understanding in England and Wales, as between solicitors and barristers, that the barrister may not be able to attend on the dates booked because of supervening events, for instance involvement in a case which remains part heard. In such circumstances the case has to be returned to alternative counsel. There is therefore a *quid pro quo* for the solicitor's (and client's) right to settle the case and cancel the barrister.

Abated Brief Fees

[3.210]

An 'abated brief fee' is a reduced brief fee payable when a case is compromised. It is the belief of the Bar Council's Remuneration Committee, that it is possible to charge such an abated brief fee if the brief has been delivered but more difficult to do so if the brief has never been delivered. Instead of charging an abated brief fee, it is the practice of some chambers to construct a 'structured brief fee' which allows for circumstances and payment in scenarios when the case is compromised.

Re-reading Fees

[3.211]

Adjournments are a common problem faced by advocates. They are often caused by listing problems well beyond the control of counsel. Although the brief fee is expected to cover all preparation for the trial, it is not unreasonable for counsel to charge a re-reading fee if a substantial amount of time has elapsed since the case was adjourned and he has to re-read the brief as a result.

Becoming a QC – the Effect on Charging Rates

[3.212]

It is generally understood that once a barrister has been briefed for a particular piece of work as a junior and at junior's rates then he must complete that work at the rate agreed. This obviously applies only to the actual work that he has been asked to do. Thus, if he is asked to do an initial advice only, this does not commit him to doing the whole case as a junior and if subsequent instructions come in, then it is open to him to charge at a silk's level. It is equally open to the solicitor not to instruct the barrister.

There is a grey area where there is a clear implication that a barrister will have taken on a piece of litigation as a junior and were expected to see it through. If fees have, in effect, been agreed to cover the whole of the work (either a full fee or an hourly rate) then he must abide by them. If they simply covered a single piece of work, then he need not be so bound. There appear to no formal authorities on this point, however; the basic principle is that once fees have been agreed for work then a barrister is in a relatively weak position if he or she tries to re-negotiate.

There are particular rules in the LSC Manual relating to legal aid which state that when a junior who has been instructed takes silk, the regional office will, on an application for authority for him or her to continue as a leader, take the following into account:

(a) Queen's Counsel is permitted, and should normally be willing at any time before the first anniversary of being appointed as Queen's Counsel, to do any ordinary work of a junior in any proceedings he or she was instructed to settle before appointment;

(b) he or she may, at his or her discretion, continue to act as a junior for an unlimited time, inter alia, in a civil suit in which he or she was instructed before being appointed as Queen's Counsel and appeared as a junior at the trial or on an appeal before the first anniversary of the appointment;

(c) except as above, he or she should refuse to act as a junior after the first anniversary of being appointed as Queen's Counsel unless, in his or her opinion, such a refusal would cause harm to the client. In that event he or she may, at his or her discretion, continue to act until the second anniversary of the appointment;

(d) in the event of Queen's Counsel not electing or being able to continue as a junior, it is open to a solicitor to instruct a fresh junior.

Payment of Arbitrators' Fees via the creation of a Limited Company

[3.213]

Under the definitions of the Code of Conduct, sitting as an arbitrator does not constitute offering 'legal services'. The provisions of the Code that might therefore otherwise prevent independent self-employed members of the Bar from doing so, do not therefore prevent barristers from setting up a limited company to administer arbitration services.

Payment of Pupils

[3.214]–[3.223k]

If a pupil does any work for a barrister, then that barrister must pay that pupil for that work because it has been of value to him and therefore warrants payment[1]. Pupils in turn need to make themselves aware of the various obligations and tax liabilities pertaining to their earnings and any awards they received[2].

1 Paragraph 805 of the Code of Conduct.
2 See Part VIII Taxation and Accounts, Part 2.

Section 3: Guidance in Practice

Guidance in Practice

1. Good Practice and advice relating to the Code

[3.223l]

Introduction

This chapter brings together guidance issued by the Bar Council in respect of a number of significant issues that commonly arise for the barrister in practice on a day-to-day basis.

We begin the chapter by considering the guidance that has general application to all areas of practice. Of general application is BARCO.

BARCO

BARCO, the Bar's own escrow service, was officially launched to the profession in April 2013 and since then has grown from strength to strength and is now being used by practitioners across a wide range of disciplines. It is helping the Bar to win work and secure their fees in advance without being in breach of the BSB's prohibition on handling client money, therefore eliminating the risk of unpaid fees. It also assists in allowing practitioners to undertake the type of work they previously couldn't do, such as litigation and class actions.

BARCO is a third party company, owned and operated by the Bar Council. It is regulated by the Financial Conduct Authority and is fully insured. The escrow service is an arrangement made under contractual provisions between transacting parties, whereby an independent trusted third party, in this case BARCO, receives and disburses money for the transacting parties, with the timing of such disbursements dependent on the fulfilment of contractually-agreed conditions by the transacting parties.

The service may be used to receive funds from clients, which are required in relation to legal fees, alternative dispute resolution costs, disbursements and settlements.

For further information please contact the BARCO team on 020 7611 4680 or email contact.us@barco.org.uk

Part A: Application of the BSB Handbook

[3.223m]

The purpose of the following guidance is to draw barristers' attention to issues relating to the application of the BSB Handbook to barristers acting outside England or Wales.

General approach

1. Concern has been expressed to the Bar Council that some barristers may not be aware that the BSB Handbook applies to your conduct in court and before tribunals (including arbitrators) wherever those courts and tribunals may be sitting, and whatever law they may be applying.

2. The BSB Handbook rC2 states that if you are practising or otherwise providing legal services (as defined in the BSB Handbook), then Sections 2.B, 2.C and 2.D of the BSB Handbook will apply. This is so whether you are practising or providing legal services in England and Wales or elsewhere.

3. The BSB Handbook rC2 also makes clear that CD5 and CD9 apply at all times, as does rC2, rC9 and rC64 to rC70 and the associated guidance. They will thus apply wherever you may be.

4. In addition, rC13 requires you, in connection with any "*foreign work*", to comply with any applicable rule of conduct prescribed by the law or by any national or local Bar of (a) the place where the work is or is to be performed, and (b) the place where any proceedings or matters to which the work relates are taking place or contemplated, unless such rule is inconsistent with any requirement of the Core Duties.

5. The BSB Handbook defines "*foreign work*" as legal services of whatsoever nature relating to (a) court or other legal proceedings taking place or contemplated to take place outside England and Wales; or (b) if no court or other legal proceedings are taking place or contemplated, any matter or contemplated matter not subject to the law of England and Wales.

6. gC35 explains that it is your responsibility to inform yourself as to any applicable rules of conduct. This is likely in practice to require you to contact the relevant national or local Bar(s). You may also wish to take note of the International Bar Association's International Principles for the Conduct of the Legal Profession.

7. rC14 also stipulates that if you solicit work in any jurisdiction outside England and Wales, then you must not do so in a manner which would be prohibited if you were a member of the local Bar.

8. D6 of the BSB Handbook also lays down further rules applicable when you are engaged in cross border activities (as defined in the BSB Handbook) within a CCBE State other than the UK. These rules are derived from the Code of Conduct for European Lawyers, adopted by the Council of Bars and Law Societies of Europe ("CCBE"). CCBE States are those states whose legal profession is a full, associate or observer member of the CCBE. The Guidance at gC35 makes clear that the rules under D6 are in addition to rC13 and rC14.

Important Notice

This document has been prepared by the Bar Council to assist barristers on matters of professional conduct and ethics. It is not "guidance" for the purposes of the BSB Handbook I6.4, and neither the BSB nor a disciplinary tribunal nor the Legal Ombudsman is bound by any views or advice expressed in it. It does not comprise – and cannot be relied on as giving – legal advice. It has been prepared in good faith, but neither the Bar Council nor any of the individuals responsible for or involved in its preparation accept any responsibility or liability for anything done in reliance on it. For fuller information as to the status and effect of this document, please refer to the professional practice and ethics section of the Bar Council's website

Guidelines for Barristers on commenting to the Media on Cases

[3.224]

Introduction

1. Prior to the introduction of the BSB Handbook, the old Code of Conduct was updated in April 2013 to remove the prohibition on media comment.

2. The Bar Standards Board believes that, consistent with the rights of freedom of expression that are enjoyed by all, the starting point is that barristers are free to make comments to or in the media (this includes both conventional media – speaking to newspapers or broadcasters – and new media – social media, blogs and websites). However, because of the special position they occupy, certain rules will continue to limit the circumstances in which it will be appropriate for barristers to comment on cases in which they have been instructed and what they can properly say.

3. The purpose of this guidance is to clarify the remaining ethical obligations in relation to media comment and to suggest some of the issues that the barrister should bear in mind whilst exercising professional judgment about whether and how to comment. This will require an assessment of many factors, including the nature and type of proceedings, the stage they have reached, the need to ensure that media comment does not prejudice the administration of justice and the nature of the comment that is proposed to be made. More generally, barristers need to consider carefully whether commenting on individual cases in which they have acted would be appropriate and whether the proposed comment would require any individual client's consent. Ill-judged comments on an individual case may cause unintended harm to the interests of the client. The rule change does not, of course, oblige the barrister to make comments. Indeed, many barristers will decline to do so on the basis that they lack experience in speaking to the press and/or commenting in other media.

Ethical obligations

4. The ethical obligations that apply in relation to your professional practice generally continue to apply in relation to media comment. In particular, barristers should be aware of the following:

   a. **Client's best interests**: Core Duty 2 and Rules C15.1-.2 of the BSB Handbook require a barrister to promote fearlessly and by all proper and lawful means the lay client's best interests and to do so without regard to his or her own interests.

b. **Independence**: Core Duties 3 and 4 provide that you must not permit your absolute independence, integrity and freedom from external pressures to be compromised.

c. **Trust and confidence**: Core Duty 5 provides that you must not behave in a way which is likely to diminish the trust and confidence which the public places in you or the profession.

d. **Confidentiality**: Core Duty 6 and Rule C15.5 require you to preserve the confidentiality of your lay client's affairs and you must not undermine this unless permitted to do so by law or with the express consent of the lay client.

Legal issues

5. Media comment which causes a substantial risk of serious prejudice of current or pending proceedings may lead to proceedings for contempt of court.

6. Barristers should also be aware of the risk of personal liability for claims in defamation or malicious falsehood against the barrister, or even against the client (if the barrister is speaking on the client's behalf). Barristers' professional indemnity insurance does not usually cover liability for such claims.

Insurance and Limitation of Liability

Insurance & Limitation of Liability

Barristers occasionally need to seek clarification about the way in which they are able to limit their liability in negligence. The Bar Council has produced guidance in relation to this point and this is set out below. This guidance was issued in November 2011 and reviewed in January 2012 by the Standards Committee:

Insurance and Limitation of Liability Guidance

[3.225]

1. Advice is sometimes sought from members of the Bar dealing with substantial claims about the extent to which they can limit their liability in negligence.

2. This is a complex question and one that involves not simply the Bar's Code of Conduct, but also the substantive law.

3. The following guidance was reviewed by the Standards Committee in January 2014.

The Code of Conduct and the Law

4. Barristers are subject to the general law. There are circumstances at law in which barristers may limit or exclude their liability. However, the question of when and how they may do so, and how such exclusions or limitations can be made effective, raises complex legal issues upon which the BSB cannot advise. In particular, barristers considering excluding or limiting liability should consider carefully the ramifications of the Unfair Contract Terms Act 1977 and other legislation and case law.

5. There is nothing in the Code of Conduct to prevent barristers limiting their liability in ways which are permitted at law. If a barrister is found by the court to have limited liability in a way which is in breach of the Unfair Contract Terms Act, that might amount to professional misconduct.

6. rC30.3 provides an exemption from the "cab rank" rule if "the potential liability for professional negligence in respect of the particular matter could exceed the level of professional indemnity insurance which is reasonably available and likely to be available in the market for you to accept".

Generally

7. All barristers in independent practice should regularly review the amount of their professional indemnity insurance cover, taking into account the type of work which they undertake and the likely liability for negligence. They should be aware that claims can arise many years after the work was

undertaken and that they would be prudent to maintain adequate insurance cover for that time since cover operates on a "claims made" basis and as such it is the policy and the limits in force at the time a claim is made that are relevant, not the policy and limits in force when the work was undertaken. They should also bear in mind the need to arrange run-off cover if they cease practice. If in doubt, it would be prudent to seek advice from the BMIF.

Issued: November 2011

Reviewed: January 2014

Standards Committee

Entertainment of Solicitors and Others by the Bar

[3.226]

The increase in the extent of entertainment of clients by the Bar, particularly of solicitors, necessitated the introduction of the following guidance by the Standards Committee in June 2007. It was reviewed in September 2008. It continues to appear on the Bar Standards Board website under "Old Code Guidance" with the all encompassing reminder that "From 6 January 2014 the Bar should refer to the new Handbook for rules and guidance on their conduct as barristers."

Guidance on Referral and Marketing Arrangements for Barristers

The Bar Standard Board Guidance

[3.227]

In January 2014 the Bar Standards Board issued the following guidance to barristers as to referral and marketing arrangements in practice.

Guidance on referral and marketing arrangements for barristers permitted by the BSB

Referral fees

The BSB will consider a number of features when determining whether a payment to a third party making a referral, acting as an introducer or providing administrative and marketing services constitutes a prohibited referral fee. A payment for these purposes includes not only a financial payment but also any benefits in kind such as the provision of services or facilities for no cost or at a reduced rate.

Features which will indicate that the payment is a prohibited referral fee:

1. The payment is made in circumstances which amount to bribery under the Bribery Act 2010.
2. The payment is made in connection with personal injury work and is prohibited by the Legal Aid, Sentencing and Punishment of Offenders Act 2012.

Features which are likely to indicate that the payment is a prohibited referral fee:

1. The payment is made to a professional person acting for the lay client who has a duty to act in the best interests of that client when making a referral.
2. The payment to an introducer is linked to specific referrals.
3. The payment to an introducer for services provided by the barrister is not a set fee but is linked to the number of referrals.
4. In a publicly funded case, the fee paid to an instructed barrister is less than the Legal Aid Agency fee for those advocacy services.
5. The payment is a condition of receiving a referral.
6. A payment for marketing or related services is higher than market rates.

Features which may suggest that the payment is not a referral fee:

1. The payment is made to an employee or agent of the barrister making the payment, e.g. a clerk or an outsourced clerking service, in return for the services they provide to the barrister and not for onward payment to any person who refers work to the barrister.
2. The payment is made to a marketing or advertising agency and the amount does not depend on whether any instructions are received or on the value of any instructions received.
3. The payment is made to an introducer who is not an authorised person or other professional person for the purpose of being included in a list of providers of legal services and the amount is not dependent on the number of referrals received from that introducer.

In considering whether to take enforcement action in cases where payments have been made which may amount to referral fees, the BSB will take a purposive approach and will consider the underlying nature and purpose of the arrangements and whether or not they were in the best interests of clients, either by helping them to access legal services not otherwise readily accessible by them or by providing some benefit to them which is directly attributable to the payment made. For example, where a professional person is under a duty to act in their client's best interests when making a referral, receipt of any payment from barristers seeking to be instructed by that professional person's client creates a risk to their independence and integrity in discharging that duty to the client, without any concomitant benefit to the client in improving their access to justice. Where, on the other hand, the payment is made by the barrister to a third party whose business is to make information about choices of barrister more readily accessible by clients so that they can make an informed choice of barrister, that is in principle capable of promoting access to justice by clients.

Where on the face of it a payment appears to be related to referrals (for example where the payment varies according to whether work is received) the barrister will need to demonstrate that the payment is genuinely made in return for a service other than in return for the decision by the person who instructs the barrister to instruct that barrister. Where a payment has been made other than to an agent or employee of the barrister (such as a clerk), the BSB will also consider whether the client has been informed of the fee and had an opportunity to challenge it.

The following are examples of cases in which a payment is not likely to be a prohibited referral fee

Example 1 (outsourced clerking arrangements)

A barrister or Chambers arranges to outsource its administrative and clerking arrangements. The barrister or Chambers pay fixed fees on a contractual basis to a company providing these arrangements, which may also include marketing and advertising services. The outsourcing company acts as a barrister's agent and liaises with solicitors and other professional clients, including over billing and fees. The role of the outsourcing company, in respect of referrals of work, is to market the services of the barristers who retain them to those who are looking to instruct them, in the same way that in-house clerks would do. By competing with others to secure the work from referrers they contribute to a competitive, efficient and informed market place. The outsourcing company does not purport to make recommendations that are independent of the barristers who retain it and does not assume a duty to advise the client in the client's best interest as to selection of a barrister, so as to owe any duty to the client that would conflict with the duty they owe to those whom they represent. Rather, the outsourcing company represents the barristers. It is the barrister who has a duty to the client not to take on work that is outside his competence or which he does not have time to carry out.

Example 2 (marketing services)

Members of a Chambers appoint a marketing or advertising business to promote their services. Clients who contact chambers in answer to the advert are asked to identify this at the point of instruction in order to measure the effectiveness of the advertising campaign. Members pay a fee for these services which is reviewed quarterly based on the number of instructions identified as being referable to the marketing campaign or adverts. The marketing techniques used do not mislead clients into believing they are receiving independent advice as to their choice of barrister and are clearly identifiable as advertising. The members are able to demonstrate that the payment was genuinely made for the purpose of receiving the marketing services. (See general guidance above.)

Example 3 (barrister owned referral company)

Members of a Chambers establish, own and manage a limited company in order to advertise and market their services more effectively. The company provides no legal services itself but operates a website or 'shop front' which advertises to potential clients how to instruct barristers on a direct access basis. It is comparable in nature to other limited companies owned by barristers in Chambers which provide administrative and accommodation services to them. Members of the public get in touch by telephone, email or by visiting in person. Clients who are introduced in this way then instruct individual barristers in Chambers via the clerks in the traditional way, paying fees directly to them. Members of Chambers pay regular fixed fees to the company which reflect the costs of the advertising services provided and are not linked to individual referrals. The company acts as agent for Members of Chambers, not as agent for potential clients. The role of the company is analogous to that in example 1 and the analysis is therefore the same.

Example 4 (third party introducer)

A company sets up a service which introduces direct access clients to barristers. The introducer operates a commercial website and a call centre for consumers to phone and outline their legal problems. The introducer provides no legal advice or services itself and is not an authorised body under the LSA 2007. It trades on its offer to put consumers in touch with individual self-employed barristers who have the relevant expertise to meet their needs and who are able to be instructed on a direct access basis. The introducer introduces potential clients to barristers who are on a national panel, pre-selected by the introducer. The introducer undertakes the costs of advertising, operating the website and call centre, setting up the panels and vetting potential clients and recoups these costs from its fees. Barristers on the panel may also be charged a one off or annual fixed fee to the agency but this does not vary depending on the number of referrals received.

Example 5 (third party introducer)

The facts are as in example 4 but the introducer's fee does vary with the number of referrals received. However, the barrister is able to demonstrate (see general guidance above) that the introducer makes its own independent judgment as to which barrister best meets the client's needs for the given case and advises the client accordingly, and that the percentage the introducer receives is the same regardless of which of the barristers on its panel is instructed, rather than it auctioning cases to the highest bidder. The fact that payment varies with success in attracting instructions is then a fair commercial reflection of the value of the service provided to the barrister in vetting the barrister and maintaining the barrister on the panel and does not adversely affect the client's interests. (Note, however, that quite independently of whether or not the arrangements involve any referral fee, barristers need to ensure they do not enter into any terms with an introducer that would interfere with their ability act independently and in their client's best interests.)

Example 6 (membership subscriptions)

Barristers pay individual membership subscriptions to a body which maintains a panel of accredited barristers from which it proposes barristers to those who contact the body requiring those with particular expertise (for example an alternative dispute resolution (ADR) body, which appoints or recommends persons to provide mediation, arbitration or adjudication services from a list of barristers who pay to maintain their membership of the ADR body). The membership subscriptions paid by barristers are on an annual or regular, fixed basis and are not per referral made or otherwise linked to the number of referrals.

Example 7 (membership subscription)

If the facts are as in example 6 but, instead, fees were paid to the ADR body as a percentage of the fees received for acting, it would be necessary to consider whether the situation was truly analogous to example 1 or example 5, in which case it would not be a referral fee.

By way of contrast, an arrangement such as that in examples 6 or 7 is likely to be a referral fee where the facts are such that clients are likely to be under a mistaken impression that the introducer or ADR body was acting independently in selecting the barrister, when in reality their recommendation was procured by the highest bid, for example, because the percentage to be paid is not fixed in advance or the same for all.

Bar Standards Board

6 January 2014

The Referral Fee Prohibition

The Referral Fee Prohibition

[3.227a]

In October 2012 the Professional Practice Committee issued guidance drawing attention to issues relating to the payment for professional instructions. The guidance was reviewed in January 2014.

Status and effect: Please see the notice at end of this document. This is not "guidance" for the purposes of the BSB Handbook I6.4.

General approach

1. There has been a proliferation in recent years of the payment of, or requests for payment of, referral fees in connection with the provision of legal services. In the Final Report of his Costs Review,[1] Jackson L.J. recommended that they should be prohibited in relation to personal injury cases. This recommendation has been adopted by the Ministry of Justice and may be extended to other areas of work.
2. You are reminded that the payment by a barrister of a referral fee for the purpose of procuring professional instructions is forbidden under the BSB Handbook. The Professional Practice Committee of the Bar Council ("the PPC") endorses this approach, for the reasons set out in the Annex below.
3. You are also reminded that the payment of a referral fee whether or not it is disclosed to the lay client is potentially both a civil wrong and a criminal offence, whether or not it is also prohibited in connection with personal injury work by the Legal Aid, Sentencing and Punishment of Offenders Act 2012.

4. The BSB Handbook rC10 prohibits both the payment and receipt of referral fees. The term "referral fee" is defined in the BSB Handbook (definition (187)) as follows:

"any payment or other consideration made in return for the referral of professional instructions by an intermediary."

5. The definition goes on to clarify that a payment is not a referral fee if it is a payment either (1) for the provision of a particular service or (2) for some other reason, other than for the provision or referral of professional instructions.

6. Definition (114) defines "intermediary" for this purpose as any person by whom a self-employed barrister or authorised body is instructed on behalf of a client; and in the context of referral fees, "intermediary" includes a professional client (as defined in definition (162)).

7. It would thus be a breach of the BSB Handbook for you:

a. to make or receive <u>any</u> payment or other consideration;

b. to or from <u>any</u> intermediary (as defined);

c. <u>in return for</u> the referral of professional instructions.

8. At the BSB Handbook gC29 to gC31 is also relevant. This provides as follows:

"gC29 Making or receiving payments in order to procure or reward the referral to you by an intermediary of professional instructions is inconsistent with your obligations under CD2 and/or CD3 and/or CD4 and may also breach CD5.

gC30 Moreover:

1 where public funding is in place, the Legal Aid Agency's Unified Contract Standard Terms explicitly prohibit contract-holders from making or receiving any payment (or any other benefit) for the referral or introduction of a client, whether or not the lay client knows of, and consents to, the payment,

2 whether in a private or publicly funded case, a referral fee to which the client has not consented may constitute a bribe and therefore a criminal offence under the Bribery Act 2010,

3 referral fees are prohibited where they relate to a claim or potential claim for damages for personal injury or death or arise out of circumstances involving personal injury or death ...: section 56 Legal Aid, Sentencing and Punishment of Offenders Act 2012.

gC31 Rule rC10 does not prohibit proper expenses that are not a reward for referring work, such as genuine and reasonable payments for:

1 clerking and administrative services (including where these are out-sourced),

2 membership subscriptions to ADR bodies that appoint or recommend a person to provide mediation, arbitration or adjudication services, or

3 advertising and publicity, which are payable whether or not any work is referred. On the other hand, payments which purport to represent fees payable for the out-sourcing of clerking or administrative or other

services but which in fact are expressly or implicitly linked to, or conditional on, or vary in amount with, the receipt of instructions, are referral fees and are prohibited."

9. The BSB Handbook rC8 and rC9, and gC18–gC21 and gC25, also explain how Core Duties 3, 4 and 5 may be engaged:

a. rC8 provides as follows:

"You must not do anything which could reasonably be seen by the public to undermine your honesty, integrity (CD3) and independence (CD4)."

b. rC9 provides as follows:

"Your duty to act with honesty and integrity under CD3 includes the following requirements: .7 you must only propose, or accept, fee arrangements which are legal."

c. The guidance provides as follows:

"Examples of how you may be seen as compromising your independence

gC18 The following may reasonably be seen as compromising your independence in breach of rC8 (whether or not the circumstances are such that rC10 is also breached): .1 offering, promising or giving: .a any commission or referral fee (of whatever size) – note that these are in any case prohibited by rC10 and associated guidance, or .b a gift (apart from items of modest value), to any client, professional client or other intermediary, or .2 lending money to any such client, professional client or other intermediary, or .3 accepting any money (whether as a loan or otherwise) from any client, professional client or other intermediary, unless it is a payment for your professional services or re-imbursement of expenses or of disbursements made on behalf of the client.

gC19 If you are offered a gift by a current, prospective or former client, professional client or other intermediary, you should consider carefully whether the circumstances and size of the gift would reasonably lead others to think that your independence had been compromised. If this would be the case, you should refuse to accept the gift.

gC20 The giving or receiving of entertainment at a disproportionate level may also give rise to a similar issue and so should not be offered or accept if it would lead others reasonably to think that your independence had been compromised.

gC21 Guidance gC18 to gC20 above is likely to be more relevant where you are a self-employed barrister … If you are a BSB authorised individual who is an employee or manager of an authorised (non-BSB) body or you are an employed barrister (non-authorised body) and your approved regulator or employer (as appropriate) permits the payments to which Rule rC10 applies, you may make or receive such payments only in your capacity as such and as permitted by the rules of your aprpoved regulator or employed (as appropraite). For further information on referral fees, see the guidance at gC32)."

Other possible breaches of CD3 and/or CD5:

gC25 A breach of Rule rC9 may also constitute a breach of CD3 and/or CD5. Other conduct which is likely to be treated as a breach of CD3 and/or CD5 includes (but is not limited to): .1 … breaches of Rule rC8, .2 breaches of Rule rC10.

10. See also the BSB's "Guidance on referral and marketing arrangements for barristers permitted by the BSB".[2]

11. The PPC also takes the following views:

The position of clerks and other staff:

a. In the light of CD10, oC24, and rC89 and rC90, you will be responsible for the conduct of your staff, and must take steps to ensure that members of your staff are not paying commissions or giving other consideration on their own account in respect of professional instructions for members of chambers.

Publicly funded cases:

b. Where public funding is in place, the Legal Services Commission's Unified Contract Standard Terms explicitly prohibit contract-holders from making or receiving any payment (or any other benefit) for the referral or introduction of a client, whether or not the lay client knows of, and consents to, the payment.[3]

c. In relation to criminal cases specifically, the PPC takes the view that the payment or acceptance of a referral fee is also contrary to the Criminal Defence Service (Funding) Order 2007.[4]

d. The PPC takes the view that the acceptance of an improperly low proportion of the fee paid under the Advocates Graduated Fee Scheme where the solicitor is the "instructed advocate" in a case amounts to the payment of a referral fee by a barrister, and is thus prohibited.[5]

e. Such a payment would also be a breach of the Legal Services Commission's Unified Contract Standard Terms.[6]

Civil and Criminal Law:

f. Where the lay client does not know of and consent to the payment of the referral fee:

   i. it constitutes a bribe, and is recoverable by the lay client from the solicitor or other intermediary or the advocate, and

   ii. the offer, promise or giving or the request, agreement to receive or acceptance of a referral fee may amount to a criminal offence under the Bribery Act 2010,

   and this applies to both private and publicly funded cases.

g. Even where the barrister believed that the solicitor or other intermediary would tell or had told the lay client of the fee, you will be treated in civil law as a party to the solicitor's or other intermediary's breach of duty if the solicitor or other intermediary had not told the client and not obtained his consent to make the payment.

Provision of the services of junior barristers at discounted fee rates

12. As already explained, disguised commission payments are prohibited as much as apparent commission payments.

13. In this context, the PPC takes the view that the provision of junior barristers for a fee clearly below the market rate, or below that prescribed by regulation or subject to an applicable protocol, is capable of amounting to a disguised commission payment.

14. This may be for one or more of the reasons already outlined earlier in this ethical assistance document.

15. In addition, however, the PPC takes the view that the provision of junior barristers at discounted fees of this sort (or even for no fee at all) in return for securing instructions for other members of chambers, particularly more senior members, is also prohibited. Not only does this involve a disguised referral fee, but it also involves a serious abuse of the most vulnerable in the profession.

Advice

16. If you are uncertain whether a particular arrangement is consistent with the BSB Handbook are encouraged to seek advice:

    a. by writing to Ethical Enquiries Service, The Bar Council, 289–293 High Holborn, London WC1V 7HZ;

    b. by email; or

    c. by calling the Ethical Enquiries Line on 020 7611 1307.

Important notice

This document has been prepared by the Bar Council to assist barristers on matters of professional conduct and ethics. **It is not "guidance" for the purposes of the Bar Standards Board Handbook I6.4, and neither the Bar Standards Board nor a disciplinary tribunal nor the Legal Ombudsman is bound by any views or advice expressed in it.** It does not comprise – and cannot be relied on as giving – legal advice. It has been prepared in good faith, but neither the Bar Council nor any of the individuals responsible for or involved in its preparation accept any responsibility or liability for anything done in reliance on it. For fuller information as to the status and effect of this document, please refer to the professional practice and ethics section of the Bar Council's website here.

Annex: explanatory note

1. The PPC is firmly of the view that referral fees in the legal market, and in the provision of advocacy services in particular, operate against the public interest.

2. The PPC views referral fees as:

    (1) threatening the quality of the service the lay client receives, since:

(a) willingness and ability to pay a referral fee may have more influence upon the choice of advocate than the ability of the advocate in question; and

(b) advocates are no longer forced to rely upon the quality of their advocacy to attract work.

(2) limiting client choice, by reducing the pool of advocates from which the solicitor will make a selection, and

(a) compromising the independence of the advocate.

3. The PPC agrees with the views expressed by Jackson L.J. in *Civil Litigation Costs Review: Final Report by Lord Justice Jackson* (21 December 2009):

(1) Jackson L.J. highlighted the negative effects of non-advocacy referral fees upon personal injury cases and came to the conclusion that they should be prohibited. He found that referral fees in personal injury cases "... add to the costs of litigation, without adding any real value to it."

(2) Jackson L.J. found that referral fees there were of no benefit to the lay client: "... the effect of referral fees can only be to drive up legal costs (since the referee must recoup its outlay) and/or to depress quality of service."

(3) The fact that referral fees are paid as a matter of routine was found to be one of the factors that contribute to the high costs of personal injuries litigation. The lifting of the ban on referral fees in 2004 by solicitors had not proved to be of benefit either to claimants or to the providers of legal services: "The only winners are the recipients of referral fees."

4. The very high standards which the Bar sets and maintains are given regulatory force in Core Duties 2, 3, 4 and 5, and by the specific obligations on barristers in rC15:

"1 you must promote fearlessly and by all proper and lawful means the client's best interests;

2 you must do so without regard to your own interests or to any consequences to you;

3 you must do so without regard to the consequences to any other person (whether to your professional client, employer or any other person)".

5. Members of the Bar also compete in an open market with other members of the profession who practise in the same field and are of similar experience. The strength of a barrister's reputation for providing a high-quality service for his client is the main reason why a barrister attracts instructions. This need to compete creates the climate at the Bar which has consistently produced the highest standards in both advocacy and legal representation throughout the profession.

6. The payment of referral fees undermines those standards and the public's confidence that the profession is maintaining them. It risks corrupting the Bar's integrity, the service provided to lay clients (who are often from the most vulnerable sectors in society) and the professional relationship between the solicitor and the advocate.

7. The payment of referral fees within the legal market is also having a damaging effect upon the viability of practice for younger members of the Bar, particularly where representation is publicly funded. In the long run this can only damage the whole of the Bar.

8. Since the Access to Justice Act 1999, there has been a steady increase in the number of solicitors practising advocacy, whether as solicitor advocates or "higher court advocates" ("HCAs"), particularly in family and in criminal law. The payment of referral fees between solicitors' firms and freelance HCAs is now commonplace, particularly in criminal practice, where cross-referrals between solicitors happen regularly.

9. Economic pressure upon publicly funded solicitors' practices, and particularly criminal practices, will continue to intensify as a result of the further reduction of police station fixed fees in some areas and the proposed introduction of Best Value Tendering.

10. These pressures will increase the drive towards the request for referral fees. Thus solicitors will be incentivised to brief advocates based on economic criteria rather than on which advocate would provide the best representation for the lay client. The Bar Council is aware of the increasing pressure being put upon members of the Bar by certain solicitors to enter into referral fee agreements.

11. The payment between solicitors of referral fees and the consequent increased use of solicitor advocates has diverted work away from young practitioners at the family and criminal Bars. As a result, young barristers are losing valuable experience at an important stage in their career, are suffering financial hardship and, in crime, are finding difficulty in establishing a crown court practice. This has affected not only those barristers who are currently at the Bar, but is likely to discourage the brightest and best applicants from coming to the Bar.

12. Pupils typically begin their career at the Bar many thousands of pounds in debt. An effect of referral fees is ultimately likely to be to dissuade those from less privileged backgrounds from a career at the Bar. The junior Bar will not only see the quality of its new members diminish, but also its diversity. In time, this will impact upon the quality and diversity of the senior Bar and the judiciary.

13. Accordingly, for the reasons set out above, the PPC takes the view that referral fees have a negative rather than a positive impact for the client, and operate against the public interest. They threaten to compromise the integrity of those who receive them. At best they limit the client's choice of advocate: at worst, they can result in the lay client receiving a substandard service.

1 *Civil Litigation Costs Review: Final Report* by Lord Justice Jackson (21 December 2009).

2 At paras 20.1, 20.2 and 20.3.

3 At paras 11, 21(3) and 21(4).

4 The practice has developed among some solicitors of using the "one-case one-fee" rules in para 21, Pt. 5, Sch 1 to the Criminal Defence Service (Funding) Order (2007) to the solicitors' own financial advantage. Under those rules, all fees in the case are paid by the Legal Aid Agency to the "Instructed Advocate" for him to distribute to other advocates who also appear to represent the defendant. The "Instructed Advocate" is supposed to be the advocate with primary responsibility for the case (see the definition of "instructed advocate" in para 1(1), Sch. 1 to the Order). But some solicitors with higher court rights of audience seek to take improper advantage of the deeming provision (in para 20(2) of Sch. 1 of the Order) which deems the advocate who attends the PCMH to be the instructed advocate. They appear at the PCMH in order to be deemed to be the instructed advocate and thereby

to gain control over the distribution of the advocacy fee for the case, but with no intention of conducting the trial. Instead, they exploit their position as fund-holder to retain as much of the fee as possible, seeking to negotiate down the payments made to any advocate (typically counsel) from outside their firm who appears at the trial.

5 The PPC considers this an abuse of the system and one that will, usually, involve a breach of para 20(10), Sch 1 of the Order and section IV.41.8 of the Consolidated Criminal Practice Direction (2007).In such a scenario, neither the client nor the LAA as the paymaster benefits from the payment of a lower fee for advocacy in this way; the only effect is to inflate the solicitor's profit margin. This cannot be in the public interest.

6 There is a divergence of view between the PPC and the Legal Aid Agency as to this situation in cases where the Instructed Advocate is an in-house advocate: "Fees Sharing/Referral Fees, Important guidance for holders of LSC Crime Contracts" (November 2009).

Holding Out – Barristers without Practising Certificates

Barristers without Practising Certificates

[3.227b]

The Bar Standards Board issued the following guidance to barristers practising without holding a practising certificate in order to supplement the general rule that any barrister who does not hold a practising certificate must not hold himself out as a Barrister in connection with the supply of legal services.

Introduction

This note gives guidance to barristers without practising certificates on the exceptions to the general rule which bans them from holding themselves out as barristers when providing legal services.

The general rule

Any barrister who does not hold a practising certificate must not hold him or herself out as a barrister in connection with the supply of legal services.

Exceptions to the general rule

The general rule is subject to limited exceptions for certain categories of barristers without practising certificates who are allowed to hold themselves out as barristers when providing legal services provided that they comply with specified requirements.

The following categories of barristers without practising certificates may rely on the exceptions:

- Those who were called to the Bar before 31 July 2000, and who have notified the Bar Council by 31 March 2012 that they are holding themselves out as a barrister in connection with the supply of legal services, and who provide an annual notification thereafter (see paragraph 206.1 of the Code, as amended on 1 January 2012).

- Those barristers who are also qualified and authorised to practise by another Approved Regulator (for example as a solicitor holding a practising certificate from the SRA) (see paragraph 808.4 of the Code).
- Those who supply legal services only outside England and Wales (see paragraph 206.2 of the Code).

You must meet the following requirements in order to comply with the exceptions:

(i) unless you are authorised by another approved regulator, you must have first notified the Bar Council, that you are supplying legal services on or before 31 March 2012, and thereafter, provide full details of your employer and/or of the premises from which you intend to supply legal services in March of each succeeding year;* and

(ii) unless you are providing legal services only to your employer or you are authorised by another approved regulator, you (or where relevant your employer) must be insured against claims for professional negligence up to at least £250,000; and

(iii) you must provide a written to any potential client, employer or third party a "health warning", explaining your status, any relevant limitations on the legal services you may undertake, the fact that you are not fully regulated by the Bar Standards Board and the absence of any compensatory powers for any inadequate professional service you may provide.

Further detail of the provisions

I do not have a practising certificate and do not practise as a barrister. May I call myself "barrister (non-practising)" when providing legal services?

No. The transitional provisions allowing certain barristers to supply legal services as a "barrister (non-practising)" ended on 31 July 2005. All barristers without practising certificates must either comply with the current provisions, or stop using any title containing the word "barrister".

Who are the other Approved Regulators?

Under the Legal Services Act 2007, only Approved Regulators can authorise the supply of reserved legal activities, such as the exercise of rights of audience, or the conduct of litigation. The following Approved Regulators can currently authorise the conduct of litigation and/or exercise of rights of audience: the Law Society, the Institute of Legal Executives, the Chartered Institute of Patent Agents and the Institute of Trade Mark Attorneys. If you are practising as a person authorised by one of these Approved Regulators, you may hold yourself out as a barrister in addition to your other qualification, provided that you comply with the "health warning" requirement in para 808.4 of the Code. For example, this applies to you if you hold a practising certificate as a solicitor, which will authorise you to conduct litigation, or if you have rights of audience as a Higher Courts Advocate. (NB There is no requirement for this category to notify the Bar Council or to obtain insurance unless that is required by another Approved Regulator).

I am qualified and practise as a lawyer in another country, but also use the title "barrister". Do I need to comply with the rules?

The rules do not affect rule 4(e) of the International Practice Rules, which allows barristers qualified and practising as lawyers in jurisdictions other than England and Wales to hold themselves out as barristers, provided that:

(i) they are undertaking international work substantially performed outside England and Wales; and

(ii) they do not give advice on English law; and

(iii) they do not supply legal services in connection with any proceedings or contemplated proceedings in England and Wales (other than as an expert witness on foreign law).

If you meet these requirements, you may use the title "barrister" alongside the title under which you primarily practise, without needing to comply with the other requirements. If not (e.g. if you are only qualified as a lawyer in England and Wales or if you give advice on English law), you must comply with the Code provisions in order to hold yourself out as a barrister.

What notification do I need to give to the Bar Council of my intention to supply legal services under the exceptions?

Barristers without practising certificates who wish to hold themselves out as barristers in connection with the supply of legal services, under rule 206 must have notified the Bar Council that they are practising in this way before 31 March 2012. You will then need to provide an annual notification with updated details in March of each succeeding year. You will be able to provide your notification online through Barrister Connect. Details of how to set up an account will have been sent to all barristers in February 2012.

How do I arrange insurance?

You should consult a broker specialising in professional indemnity insurance. We understand that the following insurance companies provide such insurance, but there are likely to be many others that do so also:

(i) Lonmar global risks Ltd *www.onmar.com*. Contact Robin Wilson 020 7204 3625.

(ii) TLO Ltd www.tloinsurance.co.uk. Contact Vernon Taylor v**ernon.taylor@ tloinsurance.co.uk** 020 7839 0472.

(iii) S-Tech Insurance Services Ltd, **www.s-tech.co.uk**. Contact Martin Taylor 01223 445408.

What must be included in the "health warning"?

The warning must cover all of the following:

(i) your status and the fact that you do not hold a practising certificate under the Bar's Code of Conduct; and

(ii) the limitations on the legal services you may undertake; and

(iii) that you are not fully regulated by the Bar Standards Board; and

(iv) that no-one has power to order you to pay compensation for any inadequate professional service you may provide.

A suggested health warning is attached to these guidelines. However, it is not compulsory to use the suggested warning, so long as you include all the compulsory elements.

To whom must I supply the health warning, and when?

If you are already employed to supply legal services, you must give the warning to your employer before you start holding yourself out as a barrister under the current rules. For any future employment, you should give the warning before you start employment.

Whether you are employed or self-employed, you must give the warning to anyone to whom you propose to supply legal services, before you make any agreement to supply such services.

During the course of supplying legal services, you must give the warning to any third party, as soon as you first deal with them.

What title may I use?

If you fall within one of the exceptions and so long as you have complied with all of the relevant requirements, you may use the title "barrister".

Can I use the title "barrister" on my business card?

If you use it in connection with the supply of legal services, you should only provide the card to clients or third parties in connection with those services if you fall within one of the exceptions and you have given them the "health warning".

What are the limitations on what I can do?

Essentially, you must not undertake work that you could only do if you were an authorised person under the Legal Services Act 2007. You are not an authorised person because you do not hold a practising certificate. Certain types of work are reserved to authorised persons under the Legal Services Act 2007 and it is an offence to provide these services without authorisation. In essence this includes:

- exercising rights of audience in those courts where such rights are restricted (the magistrates' courts, the county courts, the Crown Court, the High Court, the Court of Appeal and the Supreme Court);
- exercising a right to conduct litigation on behalf of someone else (including issuing proceedings, or taking other formal steps in the action);
- providing such conveyancing and probate services as are reserved legal activities under the Legal Services Act 2007;

- the administration of oaths;
- providing immigration advice or representation unless you are registered with the Office of the Immigration Services Commissioner.

You can undertake legal services which are not reserved legal activities under the Legal Services Act 2007, subject to the requirements described above as to the "health warning" you must give if you hold yourself out as a barrister.

Does this mean that I cannot appear as an advocate?

No. You have exactly the same rights as any other member of the public and there is nothing to prevent you appearing on behalf of a client in tribunals where rights of audience are not restricted or, with the permission of the court, in one of the higher courts. You must not, however, claim to have a right of audience as of right as a barrister and, if seeking leave, should not mislead the court as to your status.

Does the work I do constitute "legal services"?

The Code of Conduct (paragraph 1001) defines "legal services" as follows:

> "'legal services' includes legal advice representation and drafting or settling any statement of case witness statement affidavit or other legal document but does not include:
>
> (a) sitting as a judge or arbitrator or acting as a mediator;
>
> (b) lecturing in or teaching law or writing or editing law books articles or reports;
>
> (c) examining newspapers, periodicals, books, scripts and other publications for libel, breach of copyright, contempt of court and the like;
>
> (d) communicating to or in the press or other media;
>
> (e) exercising the powers of a commissioner for oaths;
>
> (f) giving advice on legal matters free to a friend or relative or acting as unpaid or honorary legal adviser to any charitable benevolent or philanthropic institution;
>
> (g) in relation to a barrister who is a non-executive director of a company or a trustee or governor of a charitable benevolent or philanthropic institution or a trustee of any private trust, giving to the other directors trustees or governors the benefit of his learning and experience on matters of general legal principle applicable to the affairs of the company institution or trust."

If all the work that you do falls outside the definition of "legal services", you may hold yourself out as a barrister without complying with the "health warning" provisions described above.

What rules of professional conduct apply to me?

The Code of Conduct still covers you and the Bar Standards Board can consider complaints against you. While it is true that many of the rules apply only to practising barristers (notably paras. 302–307 and Parts IV–VII), you should note that you are still covered by paragraph 301 of the Code and that there are a number of circumstances (for example, acting where there is a conflict of interest, misleading a court or failing to act in good faith) which would be very likely to put you in breach of that paragraph. While neither the Bar Standards Board not the Legal Ombudsman has the power to take action against a barrister without a practising certificate for inadequate professional service, it is possible that seriously poor service to a client or succession of clients might justify an action for misconduct under this paragraph.

Who Should I Contact With Questions?

Please contact the Bar Standards Board, 289–293 High Holborn, London WC1V 7HZ; Tel 020 7611 1444. Questions about the extent to which barristers without practising certificates are subject to the Code of Conduct and complaints procedures should be directed as follows:

Authorisation to conduct litigation – guidance for applicants

Authorisation to conduct litigation

[3.227c]

Do I need to be authorised to conduct litigation?

1. The new BSB Handbook allows both self-employed and employed barristers to be authorised to conduct litigation. Employed barristers who are already authorised to conduct litigation will retain their authorisation, provided that they remain in employed practice. Other barristers will be able to apply for authorisation from 22 January 2014.
2. Authorisation to conduct litigation is an additional authorisation which can be added to your rights to practise and to your practising certificate. It is optional and you will need to decide whether you need it for your practice or employment.

What is the conduct of litigation?

3. The conduct of litigation is a 'reserved legal activity' in the terms of the Legal Services Act 2007. This means that it can only be undertaken legally by a person who is authorised to undertake that activity. The Bar Standards Board (as a relevant "approved regulator") is entitled to authorise barristers to conduct litigation.
4. It is important to distinguish the conduct of litigation from the exercise of rights of audience, and other reserved legal activities. A barrister's entitlement to exercise rights of audience does not entitle him or her to conduct litigation.
5. The Bar Standards Board does not itself define what is meant by conducting litigation as this is a matter of law. However, the following is intended to provide some guidance on interpretation and to illustrate the types of litigation activities.

6. The conduct of litigation has a statutory definition in Schedule 2 of the Legal Services Act:

   "4 (1) The 'conduct of litigation' means –

   (a) the issuing of proceedings before any court in England and Wales,

   (b) the commencement, prosecution and defence of such proceedings, and

   (c) the performance of any ancillary functions in relation to such proceedings (such as entering appearances to actions)."

7. The last subheading 'ancillary functions' has been defined further, in relation to civil litigation, by *Agassi v Robinson (Inspector of Taxes) (Bar Council intervening)* [2005] EWCA Civ 1507, [2006] 1 All ER 900, [2006] 1 WLR 2126. The definition of ancillary functions is construed narrowly and is limited to the formal steps required in the conduct of litigation.

8. The remaining restrictions on activities associated with the conduct of litigation for barristers who are not authorised to conduct litigation include:

   - issuing any claim or process or application notice;
   - signing off on a list of disclosure;
   - instructing expert witnesses on behalf of a lay client;
   - accepting liability for the payment of expert witnesses; and
   - any other "formal steps" in the litigation of a sort that are currently required to be taken either by the client personally or by the solicitor on the record.

   If you want to be able to carry out any of these activities for your clients, then you need to seek a litigation extension to your practising certificate.

9. *O'Connor v Bar Standards Board* [2012] All ER (D) 108 (Aug) (which addressed the scope of the meaning of the conduct of litigation, citing *Agassi*) established that signing a declaration of truth did not amount to conducting litigation, and has further underlined that litigation is narrowly defined.

Criminal litigation

10. If you are authorised to conduct litigation, this authorisation extends to both civil and criminal litigation. You will, however, need to ensure that you meet the Core Duty to act within your competence in undertaking any litigation activity (see below).

11. The conduct of criminal litigation is more limited in scope than the conduct of civil litigation because of the role of the prosecuting authorities. For example, prosecution disclosure is undertaken by the police and is overseen by the CPS (who are already authorised to conduct litigation by virtue of provisions in the Prosecution of Offences Act 1985) and there are limited duties to disclose for the defence beyond drafting defence statements (a task which is already undertaken by barristers).

12. Other formal steps involved in criminal litigation may also be more limited because the prosecution process is shorter than the equivalent civil procedure and is largely the responsibility of the prosecution. Nevertheless there may be some processes for which you would need authorisation.

13. Barristers may already undertake many of the drafting tasks, such as completing Criminal Procedure Rules forms (for example the Plea and Case Management Form at the Crown Court, notices and grounds of appeal to the appellate courts). Such drafting does not constitute the conduct of litigation.

Am I eligible to obtain authorisation to conduct litigation?

14. In order to be eligible to apply for authorisation to conduct litigation, you will need to hold a current practising certificate. This can be a self-employed, employed or dual capacity practising certificate.

15. There is an additional requirement which applies if you are a less experienced barrister. If you are:

- a self-employed barrister under three years' standing; or
- an employed barrister under three years' standing who supplies legal services to the public via an authorised body; or
- an employed barrister under one year's standing who supplies legal services only to your employer;

you will need to confirm that you have a 'qualified person' in your place of practice, who is readily available to provide guidance to you when conducting litigation.

16. A qualified person who can supervise you in the conduct of litigation is:

- an individual who has been entitled to practise and has practised as a barrister (other than as a pupil who has not completed pupillage in accordance with the Bar Training Regulations), or as a person authorised by another approved regulator (such as a solicitor) (which need not have been as a person authorised by the same approved regulator);
  - for at least six years in the previous eight years;
  - for the previous two years has made such practice his main occupation;
  - is entitled to conduct litigation before every court in relation to all proceedings;
  - is not acting as a qualified person in relation to more than two other people;
  - and has not been designated by the BSB as unsuitable to be a qualified person.

17. Alternatively, if you are barrister exercising a right to conduct litigation in a Member State other than the United Kingdom pursuant to the Establishment Directive or in Scotland or Northern Ireland pursuant to the European Communities (Lawyer's Practice) Regulations 2000, a qualified person has been designated by the BSB as having qualifications and experience in that state or country which are equivalent to the qualifications and experience (see Rule rS22.3 for further details).

18. You must ensure you have appropriate insurance in place (see below).

How do I apply?

19. In order to apply for an extension to your practising certificate authorising you to conduct litigation, you will need to complete an application form. The form consists of a self-assessment questionnaire, which you should download from the following link: https://www.barristerconnect.org.uk/login/

20. You will also need to pay the application fee, covering the administrative costs of the application to the BSB.

21. The information you provide in the form will be assessed by authorisation staff at the BSB, who will also have access to further records about you and your practice. In reviewing your application, authorisation staff will assess whether you meet the criteria for authorisation.

22. The authorisation criteria are:

   - That you have appropriate systems in your place of practice to enable you to conduct litigation (Rule S47.3).
   - That you have the requisite skills and knowledge of litigation procedure to enable you to provide a competent service to clients (Rule S47.4).
   - That you have adequate insurance (Rule C76).

23. In order to satisfy itself that you meet these mandatory criteria, the BSB will need to consider a number of factors. These include:

   - The training in and experience of litigation you have previously undertaken.
   - The policies and procedures that you have in your place of practice.
   - Insurance.

Knowledge and training in litigation

24. It is your responsibility to ensure that you have the appropriate level of knowledge and training in litigation. You should demonstrate on your application form that you have such knowledge and that it is up-to-date. If you intend only to provide either civil or criminal litigation, you need to supply evidence only in relation to the relevant kind of litigation.

25. The outcome we wish to achieve is that:

   "Barristers authorised to do litigation have adequate knowledge of civil and/or criminal litigation procedures to enable them to conduct litigation competently."

   You can demonstrate that you are in a position to meet this outcome by confirming or providing relevant information about the following. For your knowledge to be adequate, it must be up-to-date. When any relevant training was undertaken some time ago, you will need to show how you meet the requirement for your knowledge to be up-to-date. This might be through more recent raining or practical experience.

Completion of the BPTC or equivalent

26. You should confirm whether you completed the BPTC or an equivalent qualification within the last three years. The BPTC includes component modules on civil and criminal litigation procedure which we ordinarily judge to be sufficient training, in conjunction with pupillage, in knowledge of litigation procedure.

Additional training

27. Where you completed the BPTC or equivalent qualification over three years ago, it is important to demonstrate that you have taken any necessary further training to ensure that your knowledge is up-to-date.

28. You should provide details of any additional training in litigation that you have completed within the last three years.

29. We would ordinarily expect you to have undertaken the public access training course, or to have renewed your public access training. Further details are available on the public access section of the BSB website.

30. The BSB does not accredit litigation courses and it is up to you to demonstrate that the training you have undertaken is appropriate.

31. There are courses on litigation available from postgraduate law colleges and universities, such as City University, the University of Law (College of Law) and Kaplan Law School. We may publish further information about these in the litigation section of the BSB website otherwise you should contact training providers directly for further details.

32. You should also detail here whether you have undertaken any other form of relevant learning within the last three years and provide an explanation of any activities you might have undertaken. For example, this might include additional CPD, self-directed learning, or other relevant work experience.

Prior experience of litigation

33. You should provide details of any prior experience of litigation.

Prior experience of conducting litigation

34. If you have previously been authorised to conduct litigation, and have conducted litigation within the last three years, by virtue of authorisation by another approved regulator, for example as a practising solicitor, or by virtue of a statutory right to do so, you should set out the details of this. You should include the dates and time period of your authorisation and confirmation that your practice has included litigation within the last three years.

Other experience of litigation

35. You may have other prior experience of litigation, through your involvement in preparing cases for courts or tribunals or helping to manage trials, even if you have not previously conducted litigation. For example, you may have provided advice on aspects of litigation procedure, such as providing advice

on the use of evidence or instructing expert witnesses. You may also have undertaken the drafting of documents concerned with litigation, such as particulars of claim, or provided advice on the drafting of such documents.

36. You should describe your prior experience of litigation in this context. It is your responsibility to assess whether this experience has provided you with sufficient knowledge and skills to enable you to conduct litigation. Some of the areas of litigation procedure which you may wish to consider include:

- Pre-action.
- Issue and acknowledgement of proceedings.
- Statements of case.
- Interim remedies.
- Judgment without trial.
- Track allocation and case management.
- Disclosure.
- Part 36 offers to settle.
- Preparations for trial and evidence.
- Costs.
- Enforcement of judgments.

37. We do not expect you to list all aspects of litigation procedure where you have experience, but you should provide an overview of the sort of work you have undertaken and should be able to clearly demonstrate how this experience is relevant to the litigation work you expect to take on once you are authorised. Ordinarily, we would expect this to have been a significant component of your practice. You should detail the number of years of practice in which you gained this experience.

38. You should be prepared to provide specific examples if asked to do so.

Administration and management of litigation

39. You must ensure that there are appropriate administrative and management procedures in your place of practice and all persons involved in the conduct of litigation are familiar with them.

40. If your place of practice already has an individual barrister who is authorised to conduct litigation and you will be adopting the same procedures, you should state this clearly and you do not need to complete this section of the application. You should, however, confirm that you are familiar with the relevant procedures.

41. You are expected to take responsibility for ensuring that appropriate procedures are in place in your practice. It is important that you can satisfy yourself that you are personally familiar with these procedures and know how they operate. You should also ensure that anyone else who has a role in the litigation for which you are responsible has been trained in such procedures.

42. A series of outcomes relating to administration and management of your practice are listed in the checklist section of the questionnaire. Under each

outcome there is a list of procedures and policies which we believe should normally form the minimum arrangements your practice should have in place.

43. You should tick off each item, confirming that your practice has relevant policies and procedures in place. Alternatively, you should add an explanation of how you believe each issue is otherwise addressed.

44. Where possible, you should add a document reference, which could be the name or number of the policy or procedure. We may ask you to provide further evidence, such as a copy of a policy and this will assist that process.

45. The outcomes we expect you to achieve are:

- Clients understand the service they will receive and how fees will be charged.
- Clients receive a timely and consistent service.
- Clients receive a service when they need it.
- All litigation cases are managed effectively.
- All matters relating to litigation cases are recorded fully and accurately.
- Support staff are adequately trained and supervised.

The core duties

All the core duties and relevant conduct rules will apply to the conduct of litigation as to the conduct of the rest of your practice. Core duties which are particularly relevant are:

You must provide a competent standard of work and service to each client [CD7]

46. Once you become authorised to conduct litigation, you will remain subject to Core Duty 7 in the Code of Conduct to provide a competent standard of work and service to each client. This obligation applies to conducting litigation as it does to any other type of legal service you provide. You must ensure that you do not take on instructions, or seek to undertake tasks, if you are not competent to do so.

47. As with all public access work, you must also consider whether it would be in the client's interests to instruct a solicitor or other authorised person, for example because the litigation in question would benefit from more experience or resources than you have.

You must take reasonable steps to manage your practice, or carry out your role within your practice, competently and in such a way as to achieve compliance with your legal and regulatory obligations [CD10]

48. You must also comply with Core Duty 10 and take reasonable steps to manage any aspects of your practice concerned with the conduct of

litigation. You must also carry out your role as an individual who is authorised to conduct litigation within your practice competently and in such a way as to achieve compliance with any relevant legal and regulatory objectives.

49. For the purposes of this application, you will need to satisfy the BSB that you have made a thorough assessment of your skills and competencies relating to your ability to conduct litigation on behalf of each client, and to do so to a competent standard.

Intended areas of practice

50. If you are granted a litigation extension to your practising certificate you will be authorised to conduct litigation in all areas of practice. For the purposes of future supervision and monitoring by the BSB, you should indicate on your application form the areas of practice in which you intend to conduct litigation. This will help allow us to assess the risks of barristers conducting litigation across different practice areas.

Review of applications and sampling

51. The BSB will review all applications and may seek further information or ask to talk to you on the phone in order to discuss any aspects of your application, for example the nature of your prior experience of litigation. The BSB will also undertake random sampling of a proportion of applications for more in-depth investigation. If selected for this sample, this is likely to mean that BSB authorisation staff will contact you for further information relating to your application, such as documentary evidence of any courses you have stated that you have undertaken, or copies of policies and procedures in your place of practice. This will allow us to evaluate your application more fully.

Supervision

52. The BSB's Supervision strategy includes a focus on the conduct of litigation, because this is a new area of practice for many barristers and we wish to ensure that we identify and mitigate any risks appropriately.

53. Once you are authorised to conduct litigation, you may be subject to further supervision and the information you provide at authorisation stage may be reviewed. Further details of the BSB's supervision arrangements are available on our website.

Boundaries of the Barrister's Litigation Services

Boundaries of Litigation Services

[3.228]

The Bar Council has issued guidance related to the extent to which barristers are permitted to issue documents in the High Court on behalf of solicitors, and this is set out below:

Introduction

In October 2003, the Professional Conduct and Complaints Committee ("PCC") and the Professional Standards Committee ("PSC") considered the position under the Code of Conduct of Chambers issuing proceedings in court on behalf of solicitor clients. Both the PSC and PCC formed the view that this kind of conduct would be likely to breach the Code of Conduct. In particular, it would be contrary to paragraph 401(b), as it would amount to the barrister, on behalf of whom the clerk was acting, conducting litigation and/or undertaking the administration and general conduct of a lay client's affairs. It was likely that a barrister who allows their clerk to undertake this work would also find that BMIF would not cover them in the event of any failure to issue the petition.

In November 2003, a letter was sent to all Heads of Chambers notifying them of the stance of the PCC and PSC and advising that barristers should not permit their clerks to issue proceedings for solicitors in this way. As a result of this letter, the Bar Council has received a certain amount of correspondence seeking further clarification. In the light of this, it was decided that further guidance should be issued.

This guidance[1] addresses the main areas where there appears to be some confusion over the position of the barrister and his clerk in issuing proceedings and in other related situations. The guidance is set out below:

1 Issued by the Professional Standards Department, May 2004, and reviewed in September 2008.

Lodging Bundles for Hearings

It is proper for clerks to lodge bundles for hearings, provided that they are doing so on behalf of barristers. Barristers often draft the case summary, chronology etc; these are either contained within a separate bundle or are placed at the front of the main bundle. There is nothing wrong with clerks lodging either sort of bundle.

Covering applications to Fix Trial Dates on behalf of Solicitors

It is our understanding that clerks regularly fix trial dates to ensure that the date fixed is convenient for counsel instructed. They do so on behalf of barristers and as a result is permissible under the Code of Conduct.

Issuing applications for hearings, which will involve receiving a cheque from the solicitor to pay the fee on the application

Issuing applications is the work of the solicitor and it would be unacceptable for a barrister or his clerk to do it. A barrister who carries out, or permits his clerk to carry out, such work would be in breach paragraph 401(b) of the Code of Conduct. Moreover, issuing proceedings amounts to the conduct of litigation for the purposes of the Courts and Legal Services Act 1990, self-employed barristers do not have the right to do so and would be likely to commit an offence if they did.

It is arguable that a barrister, in receiving the cheque to pay the court fee for issuing the proceedings, would be in breach of paragraph 307 of the Code of Conduct, as barristers are not permitted to hold client money or security. There is no protection for the client if the barrister loses the cheque or is negligent and they would not be covered by the BMIF for this work.

If the lay client is present, it may be appropriate for a barrister to provide some general assistance to them in issuing the proceedings themselves but only if they have been instructed by a solicitor to do so. Again, the barrister should not hold the cheque or issue the proceedings on behalf of the client.

It follows that issuing claim forms is equally unacceptable.

Making Representations to the Masters in relation to Hearing Dates

We understand that this is done regularly on an informal basis. If the Masters are prepared to hear the clerks on such applications, it is permissible, provided that they are doing so on behalf of a barrister.

Sealing Court Orders

Clerks regularly deal with the sealing of court orders. The Code of Conduct does not prohibit such work.

Conclusion

The above examples are not exhaustive but address the main issues of what is and what is not permitted by the Code of Conduct and/or statute. The Bar Council would be grateful if this guidance could be made available to all clerks and members of chambers.

Searches as Independent Counsel

Searches as Independent Counsel

[3.229]

The instruction of independent counsel by investigating agencies has become increasingly common in the context of search and seizure warrants obtained from the criminal courts by a variety of UK law enforcement agencies, such as the Police, Serious Organised Crime Agency, Serious Fraud Office and the Financial Services Authority to name just a few. Independent counsel may be asked by the investigating authority to give an opinion as to whether a particular document contains material that may be subject to legal professional privilege. On 17th May 2010 the Professional Practice Committee issued the following guidance to barristers attending searches as independent counsel. The guidance was reviewed in January 2014.

Independent Counsel

Status and effect: Please see the notice at end of this document. This is not "guidance" for the purposes of the BSB Handbook I6.4.

Introduction

1. Warrants to permit the search of premises are frequently obtained from the courts by UK law enforcement agencies. The search of such premises will be conducted with a view to seizing relevant material.

2. The power to seize property during such a search does not (save for the statutory 'seize and sift' exception) extend to material that is subject to legal professional privilege, (hereafter "privilege").

3. Law enforcement agencies therefore routinely instruct counsel to advise them in relation to material where privilege may exist or has been claimed. As counsel play no role in the conduct of the investigation or any subsequent prosecution they are referred to as "Independent Counsel". This title has become almost universally applied despite it not being entirely accurate: counsel is instructed by and acting for the investigating body.

4. The use of independent counsel has become commonplace, particularly in relation to the seizure of mixed material and the search of solicitors' premises.

5. You may be instructed to assist an investigating agency either at the time of the execution of a warrant or at a later date, such as where material has been seized for later sifting or if it has been obtained as a result of a Production Order.

6. This process has been considered by the courts – see e.g. *R (on the application of Rawlinson and Hunter Trustees) v. Central Criminal Court* [2012] EWHC 2254 (Admin), [2013] 1 WLR 1634, the Director of the Serious Fraud Office [2012] EWHC 2254 (Admin) – but the full nature of, and legal

basis for, the role of independent counsel has not, to the Bar Council's knowledge, been subject to detailed consideration. As a result, this guidance can only be based on the Bar Council's current understanding and appreciation of the issues involved.

Counsel's role

7. Independent counsel's role is to assist the investigating authority in maintaining the proper protections of privilege. Accordingly where it is believed that material the investigators wish to seize, or mixed material that has been seized, might contain privileged information, or where a claim of privilege is made, the opinion of independent counsel may be sought. If you are instructed, you will be asked to consider the material and give an opinion as to whether or not its contents are privileged.

8. Independent counsel should not normally expect to be required to advise upon wider issues in relation to the search, for example whether the seizure of any item would comply with the terms of the warrant.

9. The decision whether to inspect material over which a claim of privilege has been made, or which counsel has advised is privileged or contains privileged information (or, indeed, what to do with such material), is for the investigating agency; counsel can only provide his opinion.

10. You must consider carefully whether given your expertise, experience and the scope of the information provided to you, you are competent to provide, and capable of providing, such an opinion.

11. Your opinion is wholly dependent upon the material provided to you, and if you feel that you have been provided with insufficient information to be able to advise properly you must decline to so do and inform the law enforcement agency accordingly.

Counsel's instructions

12. Prior to acting independent counsel should obtain clear written instructions from the investigating authority. Those instructions should contain sufficient information to permit you to make an informed assessment of the content of any material provided to you for consideration. Your ability to provide an opinion is dependent upon the amount and quality of information that you have been provided with.

13. Your instructions should set out clearly that you are being instructed to act solely in the role of independent counsel as explained in this guidance, i.e. to provide your opinion in relation to whether material shown or given to you for review is subject to privilege.

14. The statutes that grant a power of search and seizure do not have a uniform approach to the issue of privilege. Your instructions should set out in clear terms the test that the law enforcement agency is asking you to apply in relation to the existence of privilege, and should identify the statutory provisions under which the search will be, or has been, carried out. You should ensure that you are familiar with those provisions, particularly the limitations on the power of search and seizure as regards privileged material, before reviewing any material.

15. As the role of independent counsel is to ensure that privilege is not encroached upon, you should ensure that you are instructed on the basis that you would not be permitted to divulge to the investigators or those who instruct you any information seen by you or disclosed to you in the course of your duties that is subject to the privilege of someone other than the investigating agency.

16. Equally, both in providing your opinion and in the course of communications with the investigators or your instructing solicitors, as independent counsel you must be careful not to disclose the content of any privileged material seen by you.

17. You should ensure that your instructions address the issue of communications made to you on behalf of someone asserting privilege, including:

    (a) Whether you may or may not receive communications from such persons,

    (b) If you are permitted to receive such communications, whether they are confidential as between that person and you or are to be communicated to those who instruct you, and

    (c) Your obligations to explain to persons making representations to you the basis on which you are receiving those representations and whether they are confidential or not.

18. Where it is proposed that independent counsel should enter the premises being searched this should be expressly stated in your instructions and confirmation should be provided that the warrant authorises such entry.

19. Where there is any potential safety issue for those conducting the search, the investigating authority's risk assessment must include consideration of the role of independent counsel and confirmation of this should be in your instructions.

20. Where entry upon premises is required your instructions should also contain an indemnity for you against any damages arising out of the lawfulness of the warrant or the conduct of the search.

Some practical issues

21. Where you are present at the execution of a warrant you will be asked to examine material that the investigators wish to seize either because the investigators believe that it may contain privileged information or because a claim to privilege has been raised.

22. There is no bar to independent counsel being informed by the person making a claim to privilege their reasons for making such a claim. You will be required to make a determination as to the existence of privilege as a result of all the information provided to you. If the person claiming privilege does not accept your opinion, you can expect that the disputed items will be 'blue bagged' for later determination, whether by agreement or by the appropriate court under section 59 of the CJPOA (although this is a matter for those instructing you, and not for you).

23. Where you as independent counsel are present at the execution of the warrant you will be required to give an oral opinion to those conducting the search. You should keep a careful written record of all documents provided to

or seen by you and the opinion that you have provided in relation to the same. You should reduce that opinion into writing and provide it to his instructing solicitors as soon as practicable thereafter.

24. Independent counsel may also be asked to examine material, for example 'mixed material', on a date after a search has taken place. Again you should keep a careful written record of all documents provided to or seen by you and the opinion that you has provided in relation to them; recording that opinion in writing and providing it to his instructing solicitors as soon as practicable thereafter.

25. Independent counsel remains at risk of being called as a witness in the event that the seizure of material becomes contentious, but instructions to act as independent counsel during or after a search do not offend rC21.10 of the BSB Handbook (which, in conjunction with gC73, includes the prohibition upon accepting instructions in a matter where you are likely to be called as a witness).

R v Cox & Railton, the "fraud/crime exception"

26. Independent counsel may well be asked by the law enforcement agency to advise as to whether, in his opinion, the principle in *R v Cox & Railton* (1884) 14 QBD 153, 49 JP 374 applies to material in relation to which a claim of LPP has been made. Even where you are not expressly instructed in relation to this issue the point may arise. Accordingly you must be familiar with the relevant principle and have it in mind when carrying out his instructions and providing your opinion. If you do not have the information necessary in order to be able to advise on this, then you should say so, and if the necessary information is not provided to you or if insufficient information is available, then you should either refuse to give such advice or should qualify your advice (as appropriate).

Checklist for Counsel

27. Have you ensured that:

(a) You are competent to advise on the doctrine and case law on privilege as it applies to search warrants and seized material (BSB Handbook rC21.8)?

(b) If you are asked to attend at premises, the warrant specifically authorise you to enter the premises? If not, has written permission for you to enter been obtained from the owner or occupier of the premises?

28. Are you in receipt of written instructions?

29. Do your instructions:

(a) Make clear that you are being instructed only to act as 'independent counsel', i.e. to provide his opinion in relation to whether material that is shown to you or given to you for review is subject to privilege?

(b) Set out what test the law enforcement agency is asking you to apply in relation to a claim of privilege, and identify the statutory provisions under which the search is being conducted?

(c) Address the issue of communications made to you by a person making a claim of privilege, including:

  (i) whether you may or may not receive communications from such a person or their representative;

  (ii) if you are permitted to receive such communications, whether they are confidential or are to be communicated to those who instruct you; and

  (iii) your obligation to explain to the person making such representations the basis on which they will be received, and whether they may be communicated to those who instruct you or not?

(d) Make clear that you must not divulge to the investigators or those who instruct you any information seen by him that is subject to the privilege of someone other than the investigating agency?

(e) Where you are to enter premises being searched, demonstrate that the investigating authority's risk assessment included consideration of independent counsel's attendance?

(f) Contain an indemnity for you against any damages arising out of the lawfulness of the warrant or the conduct of the search?

30. If you are unsure of the status of the material inspected or unable to provide the advice sought of you, you are entitled to ask for further information from those who instruct you.

31. You should bear in mind that you may be asked to provide evidence in relation to your role as independent counsel.

32. If you have concerns as to the content of you instructions or how you are being asked to conduct you duties then you should consult the Bar Council's Ethical Enquiries Service on: 020 7611 1307 or by email: Ethics@BarCouncil.org.uk

Important notice

This document has been prepared by the Bar Council to assist barristers on matters of professional conduct and ethics. **It is not "guidance" for the purposes of the BSB Handbook I6.4, and neither the BSB nor a disciplinary tribunal nor the Legal Ombudsman is bound by any views or advice expressed in it.** It does not comprise – and cannot be relied on as giving – legal advice. It has been prepared in good faith, but neither the Bar Council nor any of the individuals responsible for or involved in its preparation accept any responsibility or liability for anything done in reliance on it. For fuller information as to the status and effect of this document, please refer to the professional practice and ethics section of the Bar Council's website.

Confidentiality

Confidentiality

[3.229a]

Concern has been expressed that the profession is not taking its responsibilities to protect confidential client data and confidential financial data of members of Chambers sufficiently seriously. As a consequence the Standards Committee has issued the following guidance:

Maintaining Confidentiality

Concern has been expressed that the profession is not taking its responsibilities to protect confidential client data and confidential financial data of members of Chambers sufficiently seriously. Examples have been given that client papers and Chambers' data are not being disposed of securely and are simply being discarded in waste paper baskets within Chambers.

The Standards Committee of the Bar Standards Board would like to remind barristers that all client communications are privileged and that such communications, client information and Chambers confidential data (financial or otherwise) must be stored, handled and disposed of securely.

Attention in particular is drawn to paragraph 702 of the Bar's Code of Conduct which requires barristers to preserve the confidentiality of the client's affairs. Any barrister who does not adhere to this rule by, for example, allowing other people to see confidential material, losing portable devices on which unprotected information is stored, or not disposing of client papers securely could face disciplinary action by the Bar Standards Board.

Barristers are data controllers under the Data Protection Act and must comply with the requirements of the Act in handling data to which that Act applies.

Barristers are responsible for the conduct of those who undertake work on their behalf and are advised to ensure that clerks and other Chambers' staff are aware of the need to handle and dispose of confidential material securely. Heads of Chambers are responsible for ensuring that Chambers have appropriate systems for looking after confidential information.

In making arrangements to look after the information entrusted to them, barristers should seek to reduce the risk of casual or deliberate unauthorised access to it. Consideration needs to be given to information kept in electronic form as well as on paper. The arrangements should cover:

- The handling and storage of confidential information. Papers should not be left where others can read them, and computers should be placed so that they cannot be overlooked, especially when working in public places. When not being used, papers should be stored in a way which minimises the risk of unauthorised access. Computers should be password protected.

- Suitable arrangements should be made for distributing papers and sending faxes and emails.
- Particular care should be taken when using removable devices such as laptops, removable discs, CDs, USB memory sticks and PDAs. Such devices should be used to store only information needed for immediate business purposes, not for permanent storage. Information on them should be at least password protected and preferably encrypted. Great care should be taken in looking after the devices themselves to ensure that they are not lost or stolen.
- When no longer required, all confidential material must be disposed of securely, for example by returning it to the client or professional client, shredding paper, permanently erasing information no longer required and securely disposing of any electronic devices which hold confidential information.

Additional safeguards will need to be put in place for particularly sensitive information, or for cases in which Counsel from the same Chambers are appearing on opposing sides (see separate guidance).

Confidentiality – previous instructing solicitors sued

[3.229b]

The following guidance has been issued by the Professional Conduct and Complaints Committee to cover concerns about confidentiality arising from approaches to counsel by former clients who are suing the solicitor who instructed counsel in the particular matter. The guidance was reviewed in January 2014.

Duty of Confidentiality when previous Instructing Solicitors are sued

Status and effect: Please see the notice at end of this document. This is not "guidance" for the purposes of the BSB Handbook I6.4.

General approach

1. The instructing solicitor is sued by his former lay client; s/he approaches you who were instructed on the client's behalf to request that you provide the solicitor with a witness statement of your recollections for use in the solicitors defence. What is your duty?
2. Your primary duty as between your lay client and professional client is owed to the lay client (BSB Handbook, rC15(3)). Counsel has a positive obligation to preserve the confidentiality of his client's affairs (BSB Handbook, CD6, rC15(5)).

3. A client who sues his solicitor impliedly waives privilege and confidence in relation to his dealing with that solicitor (see *Lillicrap v Nalder (a firm)* [1993] 1 All ER 724, [1993] 1 WLR 94 and other decisions including *Nederlandse Reassurantie Groep Holding NV v Bacon & Woodrow (a firm)* [1995] 1 All ER 976, [1995] 2 Lloyd's Rep 77, *Kershaw v Whelan* [1996] 2 All ER 404, [1996] 1 WLR 358 and *Hayes v Dowding* [1996] PNLR 578. The client is precluded from *both* asserting a breach of duty, *and* enforcing the professional confidence where such enforcement would deprive the solicitor of his defence to the allegation of breach of duty. The implied waiver may extend to privileged communications between the client and a third party.

4. There can be no doubt that where you are sued, there is a corresponding implied waiver in relation to you. It has further been suggested that, in a case where the solicitor only is sued, there is automatically an implied waiver in relation to duties of counsel instructed by that solicitor. The PPC considers that whether there is such an implied waiver, is a matter of law and may well be dependent on the particular facts of an individual case. In making your own decision as to whether his former client's conduct amounts to an implied waiver takes the risk that the court, the PPC or a Disciplinary Tribunal might not agree with him. Similar considerations may arise with regard to the question whether information has lost any character of confidentiality through being placed in the public domain.

5. There is no objection to you informing the solicitor (if it is the case) that you are willing to provide a witness statement subject to the written consent of the former lay client being obtained. Such consent can be given by the client's new solicitor on his behalf.

6. Problems of professional conduct and complaint are liable to arise where such consent is requested and refused. It is not your duty to arbitrate, on this question of implied waiver, between the interests and arguments of his instructing solicitor and those of his/her former lay client. If consent is refused, or simply not provided, you would be wise to decline to provide a statement until provided with a suitable order of Court.

Important notice

This document has been prepared by the Bar Council to assist barristers on matters of professional conduct and ethics. **It is not "guidance" for the purposes of the BSB Handbook I6.4, and neither the BSB nor a disciplinary tribunal nor the Legal Ombudsman is bound by any views or advice expressed in it.** It does not comprise – and cannot be relied on as giving – legal advice. It has been prepared in good faith, but neither the Bar Council nor any of the individuals responsible for or involved in its preparation accept any responsibility or liability for anything done in reliance on it. For fuller information as to the status and effect of this document, please refer to the professional practice and ethics section of the Bar Council's website.

Jury Service

Jury Service

[3.230]

Since the enactment of the Criminal Justice Act 2003, barristers are no longer exempt from jury service. Consequently, guidance was issued offering some clarification in relation to this relatively new situation. The guidance has been updated for 2014, and this follows below:

Status and effect: Please see the notice at end of this document. This is not "guidance" for the purposes of the BSB Handbook I6.4.

General approach

1. Criminal Justice Act 2003 s21 came into force on 5 April 2004. The effect is that members of the Bar are no longer entitled to be excused from jury service as of right.

2. *Guidance for summoning officers when considering deferral and excusal applications* at paragraphs 5 to 20 govern excusal and deferral. The more likely course is deferral, and it is only in the most "extreme circumstances" that a person will be excused completely.

3. A common problem is likely to be where you are summoned to attend as a juror where you practise and/or sit as a Recorder. It would be inappropriate for a juror to have any special knowledge of any person involved in a trial: that applies not just to defendants or witnesses, but also to members of the judiciary, and to the legal representatives involved in a trial. Personal knowledge of the jury bailiff or other court staff will not be considered a reason to be excused from service.

4. If a member of the Bar receives a summons to attend the court at which you regularly practise and/or sits as a Recorder, you should apply to the summoning officer not to serve at that particular court. If deferral would not solve the problem, the summoning officer should consider whether jury service could be undertaken at a different court. It is to be borne in mind that no juror is expected to travel more than one and a half hours from home in order to serve on a jury.

5. As with any other potential juror, valid professional or business reasons may justify deferral or excusal. However as the Guidance makes clear, such applications will be "looked at closely and granted only if there would be unusual hardship". If you have a fixture which was arranged prior to receipt of a jury summons, and where it would be contrary to the interests of the client to return the brief, then application for deferral should be made. Such an application should contain sufficient information to enable the summoning officer to make an informed decision.

6. If selected to serve on a jury, it is axiomatic that you do so as part of your duty as a private citizen. It is neither necessary nor appropriate to conceal

your profession from other jurors, but nor is it necessary to volunteer such information immediately. You should expect to be treated as equal members of the jury, and should insist that you are not accorded any special status.

7. The most important thing for you to note is that you are sitting on the jury as part of the tribunal of fact, and not in your capacity as a barrister.

8. Where a jury is required to leave court during the trial, you should not offer any explanation as to the reason, and should not give any explanation beyond what the Judge has told the jury, even if asked.

9. You should not express any advice or opinion as to the law, or as to any direction of law given by the Judge, at any time. You may, like any other jury member, send a note to the Judge asking any relevant question of fact or law. However, also like every other member of the jury, you must accept that it is for the Judge, not the jury, to decide issues of law. You must, therefore, accept the Judge's directions as to any issue of the law, even if you consider it to be incorrect.

Important notice

This document has been prepared by the Bar Council to assist barristers on matters of professional conduct and ethics. **It is not "guidance" for the purposes of the BSB Handbook I6.4, and neither the BSB nor a disciplinary tribunal nor the Legal Ombudsman is bound by any views or advice expressed in it.** It does not comprise – and cannot be relied on as giving – legal advice. It has been prepared in good faith, but neither the Bar Council nor any of the individuals responsible for or involved in its preparation accept any responsibility or liability for anything done in reliance on it. For fuller information as to the status and effect of this document, please refer to the professional practice and ethics section of the Bar Council's website.

Reporting Professional Misconduct: Guidance

Reporting Professional Misconduct

[3.231]–[3.232]

This guidance was issued by the General Management Committee of the General Council of the Bar in October 2005. The guidance was last reviewed in February 2009. It addresses the circumstances in which a barrister will be expected to report the conduct of another barrister to the Bar Council.

The guidance is reproduced below:

Introduction

1. It is essential within a system of self-regulation, such as that operated at the Bar, that barristers recognise the important role that they play in ensuring

that the profession conducts itself in the public interest and in a manner that is not discreditable, disreputable or dishonest.

2. The Bar Standards Board (BSB) is reliant on its members and members of the public to contact them if they are concerned about a barrister's conduct, ability to practise competently or if they are aware that a barrister has been convicted of a serious criminal offence.

Conduct that should be reported

3. The categories of conduct that we believe barristers should report can be separated into two discrete areas:

- What is in the public interest to be reported.
- What is in the best interests of the reputation of the profession to be reported.

4. In both of these categories the misconduct, incapacity or offence to be reported must be serious and of the sort which, if proved, would suggest to the public that the individual ought not to continue to be permitted to practise as a barrister offering advice to the public and might justify a sentence of disbarment or suspension from practise from a Disciplinary Tribunal. Barristers are not expected to report every minor offence or breach of the Code.

The "public interest" category

5. This category can be further sub-divided into the following areas:

Unfit to practise

6. This is defined in Annex O of the Code as meaning that:

"(a) the barrister is suffering from serious incapacity due to his mental or physical condition (including any addiction); and

(b) as a result the barrister's fitness to practise is seriously impaired."

7. The BSB accepts that barristers are not usually medically trained, but in our view this is not necessary when deciding whether in their opinion a barrister is fit to practise. The crucial question is whether, by reason of incapacity, the ability to appear in court, advise clients or to make judgements in the client's interests is impaired. Such an assessment is something that any barrister could reasonably be expected to undertake. If the answer to the question is yes, for the protection of the public, the barrister ought to be reported to the BSB:

Gross incompetence

8. We would expect a report to be made under this category only in relation to an act, or series of acts, which seriously calls into question whether a barrister is competent to practise or offer legal services to the public of the standard expected by the profession. It is not necessary to report all acts of negligence or poor service, however the cumulative effect of a number of such acts might be sufficient to suggest that a barrister is not competent. The

assessment of conduct within this category is very much subjective in nature, barristers who are unsure whether to make a report can contact the BSB to discuss the issues on a confidential and anonymous basis.

The "reputation of the profession" category

9. This category can be sub-divided into the following areas:

Indictable offence

10. Paragraph 905(b) of the Code of Conduct requires barristers to report to the Bar Council if they have been charged with an indictable criminal offence of if they have been convicted of any relevant criminal offence.

11. We would only expect a report to be made if a member of the Bar believes on reasonable grounds that another barrister has been convicted of a serious criminal offence but had not reported it to the BSB. If you are uncertain whether a barrister has reported his/her conviction you should contact the BSB who will have a record of the convictions reported to it.

Disreputable conduct

12. This applies to conduct in the course of a barrister's practice whether in self employed or employed practice The following are examples of the kind of conduct that we believe should be brought to the attention of the BSB:-

Disreputable conduct within Chambers/place of work

13. Conduct which constitutes an indictable offence, eg.:

(a) theft from another member of Chambers or staff or pupil, or any visitor to Chambers;

(b) assault on another member of Chambers or staff or pupil, or any visitor to Chambers.

14. Dishonest or deceitful conduct towards other members of Chambers or staff or pupils, eg:

(a) seking to gain access without consent to papers or confidential information relating to a case in which a member of Chambers is instructed on the other side;

(b) seeking to gain access without consent to information confidential to another member of Chambers or pupil in relation to his practice or his personal affairs (except in appropriate circumstances by a pupil supervisor in relation to a pupil).

15. In all such cases arising in self-employed practice, the person who would usually be expected to report the matter to the BSB is the Head of Chambers or the person or Committee within Chambers which has responsibility for the proper administration of Chambers or for investigating the matter in the first instance. However, if a barrister with knowledge of the conduct in question is aware that the Head of Chambers or other responsible person has

failed to report the matter to the BSB, the barrister with such knowledge should bring the matter to the attention of the BSB.

16. For those cases arising in employed practice, barristers may wish to discuss the matter with their Head of Department or line manager before deciding who should make the report.

Disreputable conduct in relation to court proceedings

17. The BSB recognises that barristers cannot reasonably be expected to police the conduct of their opponents in the course of adversarial litigation. However, the profession has a duty to ensure that cases are presented fairly and honourably, so that justice can properly be done. In most cases, the Court will be able to make use of its own powers to control its procedures and to ensure that cases are properly presented. Misconduct in the face of the Court will usually be apparent to the Judge, and in such cases, it is expected that the Judge hearing the matter will bring the misconduct in question to the attention of the BSB. However, there are some instances in which misconduct by a barrister may not come to the attention of the Court. In addition, there are other instances in which the misconduct in question so fundamentally undermines the proper and fair administration of justice that members of the profession are expected to ensure that it is brought to the attention of the BSB. The following are examples of such misconduct:

    (a) Dishonest or disreputable conduct, such as:

        (i) seeking to gain access without consent to instructions or other confidential information relating to the opposing party's case;

        (ii) encouraging a witness to give evidence with is untruthful;

        (iii) misleading or allowing the Court or opponent to be misled.

    (b) Being drunk or under the influence of drugs at Court.

Racial or sexual discrimination/harassment

18. This is an extremely sensitive area and one in which victims can be reluctant to come forward themselves. We do not advocate that a report that a colleague has committed an act of racial or sexual discrimination or harassment should be made without first discussing the matter with the victim , who may have strong views that a report should not be made, however we would stress that conduct that falls within this category is wholly unacceptable and should be reported wherever possible. The BSB will of course offer support and assistance to the victim if a report is made.

19. It may well be the case that Chambers will be considering the matter through their own procedures and in those circumstances we would not expect a report to be made to the BSB unless it is deemed necessary following Chambers' investigation of the allegation.

Issues to take into consideration before making a report

20. Before making any report to the BSB, members of the Bar should give careful consideration to the following:

Evidence

21. What evidence or information is there of the barrister's conduct conviction or fitness to practise which causes a report to be made. A belief based on gossip or hearsay would not be sufficient. For the Bar Council to take the report forward they will need prima facie evidence either in the form of documents or witness statements.

22. If there is in any doubt before making a report as to whether it is justified, it is open to barristers to make additional investigations and to contact the barrister concerned for an explanation.

Privilege/confidentiality

23. Barristers should not breach their own duties of privilege or confidentiality in reporting misconduct without the client's consent. They must take into account the law of privilege and before reporting members of the bar on the other side of a case for what may appear to be dishonesty or gross incompetence should ensure that they have prima facie evidence to support it. Consideration should also be given to the comments made by the House of Lords in the case of *Medcalf v Mardell* [2002] UKHL 27, [2003] 1 AC 120, [2002] 3 All ER 721 about the dangers of making assumptions on apparently damning facts without first having heard the full story.

24. When deciding whether a report should be made, it may be useful to look at the provisions of the Code of Conduct to see whether the conduct causing the report seems to fall within any particular rule. This is not, of course, an exact science but it might be helpful in determining whether a report is appropriate or necessary.

25. Reports of serious misconduct, or allegations of unfitness to practise, that are made out of malice, or without supporting evidence, may be considered by the Complaints Committee actually themselves to amount to professional misconduct. Barristers should, therefore, if they are in any doubt, contact the Complaints Team at the BSB to discuss the possible report on a confidential and anonymous basis.

What action the BSB will take if a report is made

26. The action taken by the BSB will depend on the nature of the allegation and the evidence contained in the report. In all cases, the matter will be referred either to the Complaints Commissioner or to the Chairman of the Complaints Committee for instructions. As guidance, the following action is likely to be taken:

27. Where a report advises that a barrister has been convicted of a serious criminal offence the BSB is likely to institute proceedings under the Interim Suspension Rules (see Annex N to the Code of Conduct) and will also consider disciplinary action.

28. If the evidence suggests that the barrister is unfit to practise, the BSB is likely to institute proceedings under the Fitness to Practise Rules (see Annex O of the Code of Conduct). It is important to note, however, that these proceedings do not amount to disciplinary proceedings and are intended to provide support for a barrister to deal with his or her problems so that disciplinary proceedings are avoided. The main aim of the Fitness to Practise Rules is to protect the public but it is also a means of protecting the profession as it removes from individual barristers and their chambers the burden of deciding whether they are fit to practise and places it upon the BSB.

29. In other cases the BSB is likely to raise a complaint against the barrister concerned or to seek their comments prior to raising any complaint.

30. If a complaint is raised, the BSB may require the assistance of the barrister making the report in supplying witness statements and/or attending at any Tribunal proceedings that may follow.

Reporting the matter to the Bar Standards Board

31. Should a barrister wish to make a report to the BSB they should write to the Complaints Section, 289–293 High Holborn, London, WC1V 7HZ, enclosing any evidence that they have in support of their report. Barristers should therefore, if they are in any doubt, contact the Complaints Team at the BSB to discuss the possible report on a confidential and anonymous basis.

Conclusion

32. The Bar functions on a system based on trust and confidence between colleagues and the Bar Council and the BSB would not wish to suggest anything that might put this in jeopardy. There is however a need to ensure that the profession continues to operate at the high standard it has historically maintained. The role that self-regulation plays in achieving this is essential and, in order for the BSB to effectively police the profession, assistance from members of the Bar is encouraged. Our net does not extend wide enough to be able to uncover every instance of serious misconduct, incompetence or unfitness to practise. Barristers have a responsibility to uphold the reputation of the profession and we would urge them strongly therefore to bring to our attention anything that might call this into question.

Guidance on Acting as a Commissioner for Oaths

Guidance on Acting as Commissoner for Oaths

[3.232a]

The following guidance was last reviewed in January 2014.

General approach

1. If you were Called to the Bar before 1 January 2010 you were advised that you were entitled to administer an oath and that this did not depend on whether you had a right of audience or a practising certificate. However, that position has changed. The Legal Services Act 2007 (sections 12–13, and Schedule 5) provides that the administration of oaths is now a reserved legal activity. Such activities may only be carried out by authorised persons.
2. Although as a barrister you are deemed to be authorised by the Bar Council to carry out the reserved legal activities specified in paragraph 4(2) of Schedule 5 of the 2007 Act (which includes, in sub-paragraph 4(2)(d), the administration of oaths) , paragraph 4(4) of Schedule 5 of the 2007 Act states that a person is not so authorised unless they have "in force a certificate issued by the General Council of the Bar authorising the person to practise as a barrister".
3. Section 14 of the 2007 Act effectively makes it a criminal offence for you to undertake reserved legal activities without a current practising certificate.
4. These provisions came into force on 1 January 2010 (SI 2009/3250). Barristers without a practising certificate are therefore unable to administer an oath.
5. Barristers who are not sure whether they are entitled to a practising certificate should consult the BSB Handbook rS67.

PART III
IN PRACTICE

Important notice

This document has been prepared by the Bar Council to assist barristers on matters of professional conduct and ethics. **It is not "guidance" for the purposes of the BSB Handbook I6.4, and neither the BSB nor a disciplinary tribunal nor the Legal Ombudsman is bound by any views or advice expressed in it.** It does not comprise – and cannot be relied on as giving – legal advice. It has been prepared in good faith, but neither the Bar Council nor any of the individuals responsible for or involved in its preparation accept any responsibility or liability for anything done in reliance on it. For fuller information as to the status and effect of this document, please refer to the professional practice and ethics section of the Bar Council's website.

Guidance on Witness Preparation

Guidance on Witness Preparation

[3.233]

Following a significant case which highlighted the issue of witness coaching, the Bar Council issued the following advice:

This guidance has been prepared by the Professional Standards Committee of the Bar Council to provide assistance to barristers on the difficult issues that arise in respect of witness coaching in the light of the recent decision of the Court of Appeal in *R v Momodou* [2005] EWCA Crim 177, [2005] 2 All ER 571, [2005] 1 WLR 3442. This guidance applies simply to the issues surrounding witness preparation and should be read in conjunction with the relevant provisions of the Code of Conduct (notably paragraph 705) and the Written Standards for the Conduct of Professional Work (notably Section 6 on Witnesses). The guidance is not intended to affect the barrister's ability to discuss the merits of the case with his lay client.

Barristers play a significant role in the preparation and presentation of witness evidence. They have a duty to ensure that the evidence in support of their client's case is presented to best effect. It is also the responsibility of a barrister to ensure that those facing unfamiliar court procedures are put at ease as much as possible, especially when the witness is nervous, vulnerable or apparently the victim of criminal or similar conduct: see the Bar Council's Written Standards for the Conduct of Professional Work (para 6.1.4). Barristers are being asked to prepare witnesses or potential witnesses for the experience of giving oral evidence in criminal and civil proceedings. The purpose of this guidance is to clarify what is and what is not permissible by way of witness preparation, in whatever form it is conducted.

The rules which define and regulate the barrister's functions in relation to the preparation of evidence and contact with witnesses are set out in paragraphs 704–708 of the Code of Conduct. The fundamental prohibition regarding the preparation of witness evidence is expressed in paragraph 705(a) of the Code: a barrister must not rehearse, practise or coach a witness in relation to his/her evidence. However, the line between (a) the legitimate preparation of a witness and his/her evidence for a current or forthcoming trial or hearing and (b) impermissible rehearsing or coaching of a witness, may not always be understood.

Criminal Cases

[3.234]

The Court of Appeal has recently considered this question in connection with witness training courses in the criminal case of *R v Momodou* [2005] EWCA Crim 177: see paras. 61–65 of the Judgment. The Court of Appeal emphasised that witness coaching is not permitted. However, the Court drew a distinction between witness coaching (which is prohibited) and arrangements to familiarise witnesses with the layout of the court, the likely sequence of events when the witness is giving evidence, and a balanced appraisal of the different responsibilities of the various participants ("witness familiarisation"). Such arrangements prevent witnesses from being disadvantaged by ignorance of the process or taken by surprise at the way in which it which it works, and so assist witnesses to give of their best at the trial or hearing in question without any risk that their evidence may become anything other than the witnesses' own uncontaminated evidence. As such, witness familiarisation arrangements are not only permissible; they are to be welcomed.

Although the Court of Appeal did not expressly address the point in *Momodou*, it is also appropriate, as part of a witness familiarisation process, for barristers to advise witnesses as to the basic requirements for giving evidence, e g the need to listen to and answer the question put, to speak clearly and slowly in order to ensure that the Court hears what the witness is saying, and to avoid irrelevant comments. This is consistent with a barrister's duty to the Court to ensure that the client's case is presented clearly and without undue waste of the Court's time.

The Court of Appeal in *Momodou* further stated that it is permissible to provide guidance to expert witnesses and witnesses who are to give evidence of a technical nature (eg. crime-scene officers and officers with responsibility for the operation of observation or detection equipment) on giving comprehensive and comprehensible evidence of a specialist kind to a jury, and resisting the pressure to go further in evidence than matters covered by the witnesses' specific expertise. Again, this would not diminish the authenticity or credibility of the evidence which is given by such witnesses at trial.

In relation to witness familiarisation or expert training programmes offered by outside agencies, the Court of Appeal provided the following broad guidance:

General requirements:

The witness familiarisation or expert training programme should normally be supervised or conducted by a solicitor or barrister with experience of the criminal justice process, and preferably and if possible by an organisation accredited for the purpose by the Bar Council and Law Society.

None of those involved should have any personal knowledge of the matters in issue in the trial or hearing in question.

Records should be maintained of all those present and the identity of those responsible for the programme, whenever it takes place.

The programme should be retained, together with all the written material (or appropriate copies) used during the sessions.

None of the material should bear any similarity whatever to the issues in the criminal proceedings to be attended by the witnesses, and nothing in it should play on or trigger the witness's recollection of events.

If discussion of the instant criminal proceedings begins, it must be stopped, and advice must be given as to precisely why it is impermissible, with a warning against the danger of evidence contamination and the risk that the course of justice may be perverted. Note should be made if and when any such warning is given.

Prosecution witnesses:

The CPS should be informed in advance of any proposal for a witness familiarisation course for prosecution witnesses.

The proposals for the intended familiarisation course should be reduced into writing, rather than left to informal conversations.

If appropriate after obtaining police input, the CPS should be invited to comment in advance on the proposals.

If relevant information comes to the police, the police should inform the CPS.

If, having examined them, the CPS suggests that the course may be breaching the permitted limits, it should be amended.

Defence witnesses:

Counsel's advice should be sought in advance, with written information about the nature and extent of the familiarisation course for defence witnesses.

The proposals for the intended familiarisation course should be reduced into writing.

Counsel has a duty to ensure that the trial Judge and the CPS are informed of any familiarisation process organised by the defence using outside agencies.

Two points arise from the Court of Appeal's guidance in relation to courses offered by outside agencies:

- First, the advice referred to in paragraph 7(3)(a) should be sought from defence counsel or independent counsel with no involvement in the proposed witness familiarisation course. Such advice should be provided in writing.
- Second, in view of the Court of Appeal's warning that none of the course materials should bear any similarity to the issues in the relevant criminal proceedings, it would be good practice for both the party subscribing to the familiarisation course and the participants to provide signed written confirmation that the course materials do not have similarities with any current or forthcoming case in which the participants are or may be involved as witnesses.

As part of a familiarisation process, barristers may be asked to take witnesses through a mock examination-in-chief, cross-examination or re-examination. The following points must be borne in mind when advising on, preparing or conducting any such exercise:

- Subject to sub-paragraphs (2)–(4) below, a mock examination-in-chief, cross-examination or re-examination may be permissible if, and only if, its purpose is simply to give a witness greater familiarity with and confidence in the process of giving oral evidence.

- If, however, there is any risk that it might enable a witness to add a specious quality to his or her evidence, a barrister should refuse to approve or take part in it.
- A barrister who is asked to approve or participate in a mock examination-in-chief, cross-examination or re-examination should take all necessary steps to satisfy himself or herself that the exercise is not based on facts which are the same as or similar to those of any current or impending trial, hearing or proceedings at which a participant is or is likely to be a witness. If it appears that such an exercise may not satisfy these requirements, the barrister should not approve or take part in it.
- In conducting any such mock exercises, barristers are reminded that they must not rehearse, practise or coach a witness in relation to his/her evidence: see para.705(a) of the Code. Where there is any reason to suspect that a mock examination-in-chief, cross-examination or re-examination would or might involve a breach of the Code, a barrister should not approve or take part in it.

Civil Cases

[3.235]

Civil proceedings differ from criminal proceedings in the form of witness evidence and the process of its preparation. The Civil Procedure Rules provide that witness evidence is to be adduced by way of witness statements and expert reports exchanged before trial, which are to stand as the evidence-in-chief of the witness in question unless the court orders otherwise: CPR Part 32.4(2) and 32.5.

The principles set out in *Momodou* apply in criminal proceedings. However, there is currently no authority on these matters in relation to civil proceedings. Until such authority emerges, it would be prudent to proceed on the basis that the general principles set out in *Momodou* also apply to civil proceedings. Thus while witness coaching is prohibited, a process of witness familiarisation is permissible in order to prevent witnesses from being disadvantaged by ignorance of the process or taken by surprise at the way it which it works.

[*Further guidance on preparing witness statements in civil proceedings can be found at paragraph* **[3.237]**].

Witness Familiarisation

The following guidance should be observed in relation to any witness familiarisation process for the purpose of civil proceedings:

- Any witness familiarisation process should normally be supervised or conducted by a solicitor or barrister.
- In any discussions with witnesses regarding the process of giving evidence, great care must be taken not to do or say anything which could be interpreted as suggesting what the witness should say, or how he or she should express himself or herself in the witness box – that would be coaching.

If a witness familiarisation course is conducted by an outside agency:

- It should, if possible, be an organisation accredited for the purpose by the Bar Council and Law Society.
- Records should be maintained of all those present and the identity of those responsible for the programme, whenever it takes place.
- The programme should be retained, together with all the written material (or appropriate copies) used during the sessions.
- None of the material used should bear any similarity whatever to the issues in the current or forthcoming civil proceedings in which the participants are or are likely to be witnesses.
- If discussion of the civil proceedings in question begins, it should be stopped.
- Barristers should only approve or take part in a mock examination-in-chief, cross-examination or re-examination of witnesses who are to give oral evidence in the proceedings in question if, and only if:
  (i) its purpose is simply to give a witness greater familiarity with and confidence in the process of giving oral evidence; and
  (ii) there is no risk that it might enable a witness to add a specious quality to his or her evidence; and
  (iii) the barrister who is asked to approve or participate in a mock examination-in-chief, cross-examination or re-examination has taken all necessary steps to satisfy himself or herself that the exercise is not based on facts which are the same as or similar to those of any current or impending trial, hearing or proceedings at which a participant is or is likely to be a witness; and
  (iv) in conducting any such mock exercises, the barrister does not rehearse, practise or coach a witness in relation to his/her evidence: see para 705(a) of the Code. Where there is any reason to suspect that a mock examination-in-chief, cross-examination or re-examination would or might involve a breach of the Code, a barrister should not approve or take part in it.

Witness Statements

Barristers in civil proceedings are typically involved in settling witness statements. However, the courts have emphasised that a witness statement must, so far as possible, be in the witness's own words: see eg *Aquarius Financial Enterprises Inc. v Certain Underwriters at Lloyd's* [2001] 2 Ll Rep 542 at 547; Chancery Guide, Appendix 4, para 1; Commercial Court Guide para H1.1(i) and H1.2 and Technology and Construction Court Guide para 6.10. When settling witness statements, great care must be taken to avoid any suggestion:

- that the evidence in the witness statement has been manufactured by the legal representatives; or
- that the witness had been influenced to alter the evidence which he or she would otherwise have given.

Furthermore, the evidence in a witness statement must not be partial; it must contain the truth, the whole truth and nothing but the truth in respect of the matters on which the witness proposes to give evidence: see Chancery Guide, Appendix 4, para 6 and Queen's Bench Guide, para 7.10.4(1). A barrister may be under an obligation to check, where practicable, the truth of facts stated in a witness statement if he or she is put on enquiry as to their truth: see Chancery Guide, Appendix 4, para 6. Moreover, if a party discovers that a witness statement which has been served is incorrect, it must inform the other parties immediately: see Chancery Guide, Appendix 4, para 6 and Queen's Bench Guide, para 7.10.4(6). Barristers therefore have a duty to ensure that such notice is given if they become aware that a witness statement contains material which is incorrect.

Experts

It is standard practice in civil cases for barristers to be involved in discussions with experts and to consider drafts of the expert's report prior to service of the report on the other side. In this connection, barristers have a proper and important role in advising experts as to:

- the issues which they should address in their report;
- the form of the report and any matters which are required by the rules of court to be included in it; and
- any opinions and comments which should not be included as a matter of law (eg. because they are irrelevant or usurp the function of the court or go beyond the expert's experience and expertise).

Beyond this, however, the courts have repeatedly emphasised that expert reports should be, and should be seen to be, the independent product of the expert in question: see *The Ikarian Reefer* [1993] 2 Ll Rep 68 at 81; Practice Direction – Experts and Assessors, para 1.2; Commercial Court Guide, Appendix 11, para 1. Therefore, a barrister should not seek to draft any part of an expert's report. His or her involvement may, however, include discussing or annotating on a draft report observations and questions for the expert to consider in any revisions to the draft.

A barrister may, however, familiarise experts with the process of giving oral evidence, including:

- explaining the layout of the Court and the procedure of the trial, and
- providing guidance on giving comprehensive and comprehensible specialist evidence to the Court, and resisting the pressure to go further in evidence than matters covered by his or her specific expertise.

See paragraph 6 above. However, great care must be taken not to do or say anything which could be interpreted as manufacturing or in any way influencing the content of the evidence that the expert is to give in the witness box.

Further Guidance related to Witness Preparation

[3.236]

As well as the guidance above, the Bar Council has also issued other guidance in relation to dealing with witnesses and preparing witness statements in civil proceedings, set out below (last reviewed September 2008:

Preparing Witness Statements for use in Civil Proceedings

[3.237]

Introduction

1 The purpose of this guidance which has the approval of the Professional Standards Committee of the General Council of the Bar, is to offer guidance to members of the Bar instructed to prepare or settle a witness statement and as to dealings with witnesses. Guidance already exists for practice in some Courts, notably Appendix 4 to the Chancery Guide, Part H1 of the Commercial Court Guide and CPR Part 32 and 32PD paragraphs 17 to 25, to which attention is drawn. The intention is that this paper should be consistent with that guidance.

2 This guidance is not applicable to criminal proceedings. Attention is drawn to the Guidance Note "Written Standards for the Conduct of Professional Work" in Section 3 of the Code of Conduct

Witness statements

3 The cardinal principle that needs to be kept in mind when drafting or settling a witness statement is that, when the maker enters the witness box, he or she will swear or affirm that the evidence to be given will be the truth, the whole truth and nothing but the truth. In most civil trials almost the first question in chief (and not infrequently the last) will be to ask the witness to confirm, to the best of his belief, the accuracy of the witness statement. It is therefore critical that the statement is one that accurately reflects, to the best of Counsel's ability, the witness's evidence.

4 Witnesses often misunderstand the function of those drafting and settling witness statements. The function of Counsel is to understand the relevant evidence that a witness can give and to assist the witness to express that evidence in the witness's own words. It is important it is made clear to the witness (by reminder to the professional client or the witness, if seen by Counsel) that the statement once approved is the witness's statement. Ultimately it is the witness's responsibility to ensure that the evidence he gives is truthful. It is good practice to remind witnesses expressly of this from

time to time, especially where Counsel is assisting the witness to formulate in his own words a particular aspect of the evidence or putting forward a particular piece of drafting for the witness' consideration (which is expressly permitted by the proviso to Rule 704 of the Code of Conduct).

5 It is not Counsel's duty to vet the accuracy of a witness's evidence . We all may doubt the veracity of our clients and witnesses occasionally. Counsel is, of course, entitled and it may often be appropriate to draw to the witness's attention to other evidence which appears to conflict with what the witness is saying and is entitled to indicate that a Court may find a particular piece of evidence difficult to accept. But if the witness maintains the evidence, it should be recorded in the witness statement. If it is decided to call the witness, it will be for the Court to judge the correctness of the witness's evidence.

6 It follows that the statement:

(i) Must accurately reflect the witness's evidence. Rule 704 of the Code of Conduct states:

"A barrister must not devise facts which will assist in advancing the lay client's case and must not draft any … witness statement [or] affidavit … containing:

…

(d) in the case of a witness statement or affidavit any statement of fact other than the evidence which in substance according to his instructions the barrister reasonably believes the witness would give if the evidence contained in the witness statement or affidavit were being given in oral examination;

provided that nothing in this paragraph shall prevent a barrister drafting a document containing specific factual statements or contentions included by the barrister subject to confirmation of their accuracy by the lay client or witness."

(ii) Must not contain any statement which Counsel knows the witness does not believe to be true. Nor should the witness be placed under any pressure to provide other than a truthful account of his evidence.

(iii) Must contain all the evidence which a witness could reasonably be expected to give in answer to those questions which would be asked of him in examination in chief. The witness statement should not be drafted or edited so that it no longer fairly reflects the answers which the witness would be expected to give in response to oral examination-in-chief in accordance with the witness's oath or affirmation. Although it is not the function of a witness statement to answer such questions as might be put in cross-examination, great care should be exercised when excluding any material which is thought to be unhelpful to the party calling the witness and no material should be excluded which might render the statement anything other than the truth, the whole truth and nothing but the truth. While it is permissible to confine the scope of examination-in-chief to part only of the evidence which a witness could give, that is always subject to Counsel's overriding duty to assist the Court in the administration of justice and not to deceive or knowingly or recklessly to mislead the Court (Rule 302 of the Code of Conduct). Consequently, it would be improper to exclude material whose omission would render untrue or misleading anything which remains in the statement. It would also be improper to include fact A while excluding fact B, if evidence-in-chief containing fact A but excluding fact B could not have been given consistently with the witness's promise to tell the truth, the whole truth and nothing but the truth. Whether it is wise and in the client's interest in any given case to exclude unfavourable material which can properly be excluded is a matter of judgment.

Save for formal matters and uncontroversial facts, should be expressed if practicable in the witness's own words. This is especially important when the statement is dealing with the critical factual issues in the case–e.g. the accident or the disputed conversation. Thus the statement should reflect the witness's own description of events. It should not be drafted or edited so as to massage or obscure the witness' real evidence.

Must be confined to admissible evidence that the witness can give, including permissible hearsay. Inadmissible hearsay, comment and argument should be excluded.

Should be succinct and exclude irrelevant material. Unnecessary elaboration is to be avoided. It is not the function of witness statements to serve as a commentary on the documents in the trial bundles. Nor are they intended to serve as another form of written argument.

7. Sometimes it becomes apparent, after a witness statement has been served, that the witness's recollection has altered. This may happen if the witness sees or hears how another witness puts the facts in a witness statement served by another party. Where Counsel learns that the witness has materially changed his evidence –

(i) He should consider with, and if necessary advise, his professional or BarDirect client whether, in the circumstances, a correction to the original statement needs to be made in order to avoid another party being unfairly misled.

(ii) Where a correction to the original statement is appropriate, this should be done by recording the changed evidence in an additional witness statement and serving it on the other parties (and if appropriate filing it at court). If this is impracticable, e.g. because it occurs very shortly before the hearing, the other parties should be informed of the change immediately and the statement should be corrected at an early stage in court.

(iii) The underlying principle is that it is improper for a litigant to mislead the court or another party to the litigation

(iv) If a lay or BarDirect client refuses to accept Counsel's advice that disclosure of a correction should be made, Counsel's duty is to withdraw from further acting for the client.

Formalities

8 A witness statement:

(i) Should be expressed in the first person;

(ii) Should state the full name of the witness and the witness's place of residence or, if the statement is made in a professional, business or other occupational capacity, the address at which he works, the position he holds and the name of the firm or employer;

(iii) Should state the witness's occupation or if he has none his description;

(iv) Should state if the witness is a party to the proceedings or is an employee of such a party;

(v) Should usually be in chronological sequence divided into consecutively numbered paragraphs each of which should, so far as possible, be confined to a distinct portion of the evidence;

(vi) Must indicate which of the statements in it are made from the witness's own knowledge and which are matters of information and belief, indicating the source for any matters of information and belief;

(vii) Must include a statement by the witness that he believes that the facts stated in it are true;

(viii) Must be signed by the witness or, if the witness cannot read or sign it, must contain a certificate made by an authorised person as to the witness's approval of the statement as being accurate;

(ix) Must have any alterations initialled by the witness or by the authorised person;

(x) Should give in the margin the reference to any document or documents mentioned;

(xi) Must be dated.

There are further formal requirements in CPR PD 32 paras 17–19, relating to intitulement, exhibits, pagination, production and presentation, to which attention is directed.

Dealings with Witnesses

Counsel seeing witnesses

9 The old rules preventing Counsel from seeing a witness, other than the client, have been progressively relaxed over recent years. The current position in civil proceedings can be summarised as follows:

(i) There is no longer any rule which prevents a barrister from having contact with any witness. Indeed, in taking witness statements and generally, it is the responsibility of a barrister, especially when the witness is nervous, vulnerable or apparently the victim of criminal or similar conduct, to ensure that those facing unfamiliar court procedures are put as much at ease as possible.

(ii) Although there is no longer any rule which prevents a barrister from having contact with witnesses, a barrister should exercise his discretion and consider very carefully whether and to what extent such contact is appropriate, bearing in mind in particular that it is not the barrister's function (but that of his professional client) to investigate and collect evidence.

(iii) The guiding principle must be the obligation of Counsel to promote and protect his lay client's best interests so far as that is consistent with the law and with Counsel's overriding duty to the Court (Code of Conduct paragraphs 302, 303). Often it will be in the client's best interests that Counsel should meet witnesses whose evidence will be of critical importance in the case, so as to be able to form a view as to the credibility of their evidence and to advise the lay client properly;

(iv) A barrister should be alert to the risks that any discussion of the substance of a case with a witness may lead to suspicions of coaching, and thus tend to diminish the value of the witness's evidence in the eyes of the court, or may place a barrister in a position of professional embarrassment, for example, if he thereby becomes himself a witness in the case. These dangers are most likely to occur if such discussion takes place:

(a) before the barrister has been supplied with a proof of the witness's evidence; or

(b) in the absence of the barrister's professional client or his representative.

(v) Rule 705 of the Code of Conduct provides that a barrister must not rehearse practise or coach a witness in relation to his evidence. This does not prevent Counsel giving general advice to a witness about giving evidence e.g. speak up, speak slowly, answer the question, keep answers as short as possible, ask if a question is not understood, say if you cannot remember and do not guess or speculate. Nor is there any objection to testing a witness's recollection robustly to ascertain the quality of his evidence or to discussing the issues that may arise in cross-examination. By contrast, mock cross-examinations or rehearsals of particular lines of questioning that Counsel proposes to follow are not permitted. What should be borne in mind is that there is a distinction, when interviewing a witness, between questioning him closely in order to enable him to present his evidence fully and accurately or in order to test the reliability of his evidence (which is permissible) and questioning him with a view to encouraging the witness to alter, massage or obscure his real recollection (which is not). The distinction was neatly drawn by Judge Francis Finch in *In Re Eldridge* in 1880, where he said:

> "While a discreet and prudent attorney may very properly ascertain from witnesses in advance of the trial what they in fact do know and the extent and limitations of their memory, as guide for his own examinations, he has no right legal or moral, to go further. His duty is to extract the facts from the witness, not to pour them into him; to learn what the witness does know, not to teach him what he ought to know."

At the risk of stating the obvious, this is a difficult area calling for the exercise of careful judgment.

(vi) A barrister should also be alert to the fact that, even in the absence of any wish or intention to do so, authority figures do subconsciously influence lay witnesses. Discussion of the substance of the case may unwittingly contaminate the witness's evidence.

(vii) There is particular danger where such discussions:

(a) take place in the presence of more than one witness of fact; or

(b) involve the disclosure to one witness of fact of the factual evidence of another witness.

These practices have been strongly deprecated by the courts as tending inevitably to encourage the rehearsal or coaching of witnesses and to increase the risk of fabrication or contamination of evidence: *R v Arif* (1993) Times, 17 June, CA; *Smith New Court Securities Ltd v Scrimgeour Vickers (Asset Management) Ltd (Roberts, third party)* [1994] 4 All ER 225, [1994] 1 WLR 1271.

(viii) That is not to suggest that it is always inappropriate to disclose one witness's evidence to another. If conflicting witness statements have been obtained from different witnesses or served by the other side, it may be appropriate or necessary for a witness to be further questioned about, or have his attention drawn to, discrepancies between statements. Discretion is, however, required, especially where the evidence of independent witnesses is involved.

(ix) Whilst there is no rule that any longer prevents a barrister from taking a witness statement in civil cases, there is a distinction between the settling of a witness statement and taking a witness statement. Save in exceptional circumstances, it is not appropriate for a barrister who has taken witness statements, as opposed to settling witness statements prepared by others, to act as Counsel in that case because it risks undermining the independence of the barrister as an advocate. Exceptional circumstances would include:

(a) The witness is a minor one;

(b) Counsel has no choice but to take the proof and this is the only practical course in the interests of justice – this would apply, for instance, where a witness appears unexpectedly at Court and there is no one else competent to take the statement;

(c) Counsel is a junior member of a team of Counsel and will not be examining the witness.

The Cab Rank rule does not require a barrister to agree to undertake the task of taking witness statements.

(x) A barrister should be prepared to exchange common courtesies with the other side's witnesses. However, a barrister should only discuss the substance of the case or any evidence with the other side's witnesses in rare and exceptional circumstances and then only with the prior knowledge of his opponent.

Court Dress

Court Dress

[3.238]

On 31 July 2008 the then Chairman of the Bar issued the following directive to members of the Bar as to Court Dress. The full text of the Chairman's letter is set out below.

SBA Chairs
Circuit Leaders
Heads of Chambers

Dear Colleague

COURT DRESS: GUIDANCE FROM CHAIRMAN OF THE BAR COUNCIL

1. The Lord Chief Justice has issued a Practice Direction dated 31 July indicating when the Judiciary will, from 1 October 2008 wear their new robes in civil cases. It will be for each Head of Division, if there is considered to be good reason, thereafter to issue a further direction as to the practice of the judiciary in that Division.

2. The Bar Council, following two surveys of the profession and in the light of consultations with the Specialist Bar Associations, at its meeting on 12 July 2008 indicated its strong preference in favour of the position that presently prevails both as to (a) the dress that should be worn and (b) the occasions upon which it is worn. It is felt that the present situation reflects sensible working practices which have evolved in each Division and reflect the nature of the work and the preferences of both the Judges and the Bar. It is important that such practices should be consistent throughout the courts of England and Wales.

3. The Guidance below is intended to reflect present practice in civil cases though certain changes have been made in respect of the Chancery Division to remove the distinction between different types of appeal. The position in the criminal courts is provided for below for the sake of completeness.

4. In the Court of Appeal, in the House of Lords and in the Privy Council Counsel will wear court dress.

5. Subject to paragraph 10 below in the High Court Counsel will wear the following:

   — In the Commercial and Admiralty Court business suits on all occasions;

   — In the Technology Court business suits on all occasions;

   — In the Chancery Division court dress for all trials and appeals and business suits on all other occasions;

   — In the Family Division Counsel will wear business suits save for contested divorce/nullity petitions when court dress will be worn;

— In the Administrative Court court dress on all occasions;

— In the Queen's Bench Division on occasions not covered by the above court dress for trials and business suits on all other occasions.

6. In the County Court Counsel will wear business suits for applications (including all interim and final hearings in children and ancillary financial relief cases) and court dress for trials (including contested divorce/nullity petitions).

7. Before Masters, Registrars and District Judges Counsel will wear business suits (save in the Chancery Division where in hearings before Masters, Registrars and District Judges where the hearing takes place in the Judges room Counsel will wear business suits and where the hearing takes place in court Counsel will wear court dress).

8. In the Magistrates Court Counsel will wear business suits.

9. In the Crown Court Counsel will wear court dress (save for bail applications which are held in Chambers).

10. In any case where the liberty of the subject is in issue (save in the Magistrates Court and during Crown Court bail applications which are held in Chambers) Counsel will wear court dress.

11. In this guidance "business suits" means dark coloured formal non-court dress as appropriate; "court dress" means wigs, gowns, wing collars and bands or collarettes; "trials" include, for the avoidance of doubt, any final hearing of a Part 7 Claim, Part 8 Claim or a petition.

Timothy Dutton QC
Chairman of the Bar Council of England and Wales
31 July 2008

[3.238a]

On 2 June 2009 the then Chairman of the Bar issued the following further directive to members of the Bar as to Court Dress. The full text of the Chairman's letter is set out below:

SBA Chairs
Circuit Leaders
Heads of Chambers

Dear Colleague

Court Dress: Revised Guidance from the Chairman of the Bar Council

1. On 31 July 2008 Timothy Dutton QC, then Chairman of the Bar, wrote to the profession about the Lord Chief Justice's Practice Direction of the same day indicating the occasions when, as from 1 October 2008, the Judiciary would be wearing their new robes in civil cases. As he said, it is for the Head of each Division to issue directions as to the practice of the Judiciary in that Division.

2. The Bar Council carried out two surveys of the profession and consulted with the Specialist Bar Associations prior to indicating at its meeting on 12 July 2008 its strong preference for the maintenance of the prevailing position as to what should be worn and when. The position reflected the working practices in each Division and Court, the nature of the work concerned and the preference of Bar and Bench.

3. It is obviously important that the practice should be consistent throughout the courts of England and Wales. The Revised Guidance now given is intended to reflect the present practice in civil cases, but changes have been made to remove the distinction between different types of appeal in the Chancery Division and to clarify the position in the County Court. For the sake of completeness, the present Guidance re-states the existing position in the criminal courts.

4. The Court of Appeal, the House of Lords and the Privy Council:

   As before, Counsel will wear court dress.

5. The High Court:

   As before, subject to the qualification in paragraph 10, Counsel will wear the following:

   - Commercial Court and Admiralty Court: business suits on all occasions.
   - Technology Court: business suits on all occasions.
   - Chancery Division: court dress for all trials and appeals, and business suits on all other occasions.
   - Family Division: business suits, save for contested divorce and nullity petitions when court dress will be worn.
   - Administrative Court: court dress on all occasions.
   - Queen's Bench Division: court dress for trials save on the occasions mentioned above; business suits on all other occasions.

6. The County Court:

   For hearings before Circuit Judges, Deputy Circuit Judges and Recorders, Counsel will wear business suits for applications (including all interim and final hearings in children and ancillary financial relief cases). They will wear court dress for trials (included contested divorce and nullity petitions).

   In appeals in the County Court, Counsel will wear business suits for appeals from applications, and court dress for appeals from trials and appeals under sections 204 and 204A Housing Act 1996.

7. Masters, Registrars and District Judges:

   Counsel will wear business suits, save that court dress will be worn:

   (1) in the Chancery Division where the hearing takes place in court (and not in the Judge's Room), and

   (2) on winding-up hearings heard by District Judges in the County Court.

8. Magistrates' Courts:

As before, Counsel will wear business suits.

9. Crown Court:

As before, Counsel will wear court dress, save on bail applications heard in chambers.

10. Cases involving the liberty of the subject:

As before, Counsel will wear court dress in any case where the liberty of the subject is in issue, save in:

(1) the Magistrates' Court, and

(2) the Crown Court when a bail application is heard in chambers.

11. In this Guidance:

"business suits" means dark-coloured, formal non-court dress as appropriate,

"court dress" means wigs, gowns, wing collars and bands or collarettes,

"trials" include, for the avoidance of doubt, any final hearing of a CPR Part 7 claim, a Part 8 claim or a Petition.

DESMOND BROWNE QC
Chairman of the Bar Council of England and Wales
2 June 2009

Guidance on Non-Disclosure by a Barrister to his Own Client

[3.238b]

In February 2011, the Professional Practice Committee issued the following guidance as to the disclosure of information to the barrister's own client and in particular practitioners are likely to find the guidance as "counsel" to "counsel" discussions of interest. The guidance was reviewed in February 2014.

Status and effect: Please see the notice at end of this document. This is not "guidance" for the purposes of the BSB Handbook I6.4.

1. As a general rule, your Core Duty to act in the best interests of your lay client (BSB Handbook, CD2) requires you to disclose to the lay client any documents or information relevant to the instructions in your possession of which the lay client may be unaware.

Agreement by counsel not to disclose information or documents to the lay client

2. However, in an increasing number of situations, barristers are invited to receive information or documents on the basis that they will not communicate that information or those documents to their lay client. In these circumstances:

    (a) you should not agree to receive information or documents on this basis unless your lay client consents to you doing so; and

    (b) you should advise your lay client as to the consequences of consenting or not consenting to such a course of action.

3. In advising your client, you will need to consider the practical implications of receiving information on this basis. These include:

    (a) an inability to take the lay client's instructions on the material;

    (b) a difficulty in giving full advice if you has been given information that you cannot pass on to the lay client;

    (c) a difficulty in deciding how to conduct the case in the lay client's best interests;

    (d) the need to exercise great caution to guard against the risk of inadvertent disclosure of the material;

    (e) the possibility of damage to the relationship between you and your lay client; and

    (f) the possibility that you may find yourself to be professionally embarrassed.

4. These issues are discussed in the judgment of the Criminal Division of the Court of Appeal in *R v B & G* [2004] EWCA Crim 1368, [2004] 1 WLR 2932, [2004] 2 Cr App Rep 630.

5. The appropriate advice to give in any individual case will depend on the circumstances of the case. For example:

(a) In civil cases concerning trade secrets it is common for barristers and solicitors to agree (with their lay client's consent) not to disclose certain information to anyone (including representatives of their lay client) other than the members of a small "confidentiality club" (although even then the club usually includes one nominated representative of the lay client).

(b) In criminal cases, it will very rarely, if ever, be in the defendant's best interests to consent to their barrister receiving information on the basis that that information or those documents will not be communicated to the defendant.

The supposed rule of "counsel to counsel" confidentiality

6. There is a common misconception that discussions between barristers are automatically subject to a "counsel-to-counsel" obligation of confidentiality, such that you are prohibited from disclosing to your lay client information conveyed to you by an opposing barrister (save with the consent of that opposing barrister).

7. However, neither the law nor the BSB Handbook recognises any such rule of automatic "counsel-to-counsel" confidentiality. Accordingly, unless it is expressly agreed between the barristers concerned that information conveyed by one barrister to another is not to be disclosed to the receiving barrister's lay client, such disclosure is permitted.

8. A request by one barrister to another to speak on a "counsel-to-counsel" basis is an invitation to which the guidance set out in paragraphs 2 to 5 above applies.

9. Where it becomes apparent to you that your opponent is proceeding on the mistaken basis that their discussion is subject to "counsel-to-counsel" confidentiality, you should explain that this is not the case. Otherwise, you risk a finding either that you have consented to receive information on the "counsel-to-counsel" basis or that you have misled or taken unfair advantage of your opponent.

Documents disclosed to counsel by mistake

10. It sometimes happens that confidential documents are sent to an opposing barrister by mistake.

11. If you realise that you have received such documents by mistake you should not read them (or not read them any further) and should return them.

12. You should also note that where you become aware of confidential or privileged information or documents of another person which relate to the matter on which you are instructed, you may become professionally embarrassed as a result of such knowledge. Consequently rC26.6 provides that in such circumstances you may cease to act on the matter and return you instructions.

13. The BSB Handbook at gC86 provides that, when considering whether or not you are required to return your instructions in accordance with rC26.6, you should have regard to relevant case law including: *English and American Insurance Co Ltd v Herbert Smith & Co* [1988] FSR 232, [1987] NLJ Rep 148

and *Ablitt v Mills & Reeve (a firm)* (1995) Times, 25 October. It is suggested that reference should also be made to *Al-Fayed v Commissioner of Police and the Metropolis* [2001] EWCA 780 and to *R v B & G* [2004] EWCA Crim 1368.

14. The above case law establishes that where you read a confidential document disclosed to you by mistake, then you may come under a duty of confidence (enforceable by order of the court) to your opponent or to another person not to use that document or the information contained in it for any purposes or to disclose the same to any other person including your lay client. If the information contained in the document is relevant to the matter upon which you are instructed, then you may decide that you are professionally embarrassed by reason of that duty of confidence in that you are no longer able to act in the best interests of your lay client (CD2) and/or to maintain your independence (CD4). In these circumstances, you should cease to act and return your instructions.

15. The BSB Handbook at gC83 provides that in deciding whether to cease to act and to return existing instructions in accordance with rC26, you should, where possible and subject to the your overriding duty to the court, ensure that the client is not adversely affected because there is not enough time to engage other adequate legal assistance.

16. If the lay client does not consent to you ceasing to act, then you must clearly explain to the lay client or to the professional client the reason for doing so (rC27.1).

17. In the context of the inadvertent disclosure of a privileged document in civil litigation, CPR Rule 31.20 provides that where a party inadvertently allows a privileged document to be inspected, the party who has inspected the document may use it or its contents only with the permission of the court. If such permission is refused, the court may also restrain by injunction the further use or disclosure of the document in question (see Al-Fayed v Commissioner of Police and the Metropolis [2001] EWCA 780). As regards confidential material inadvertently disclosed in the course of criminal proceedings, the Crown Court also has jurisdiction to grant an injunction restraining further use or disclosure of the material in question (see *R v B & G* [2004] EWCA Crim 1368).

Important notice

This document has been prepared by the Bar Council to assist barristers on matters of professional conduct and ethics. **It is not "guidance" for the purposes of the BSB Handbook I6.4, and neither the BSB nor a disciplinary tribunal nor the Legal Ombudsman is bound by any views or advice expressed in it.** It does not comprise – and cannot be relied on as giving – legal advice. It has been prepared in good faith, but neither the Bar Council nor any of the individuals responsible for or involved in its preparation accept any responsibility or liability for anything done in reliance on it. For fuller information as to the status and effect of this document, please refer to the professional practice and ethics section of the Bar Council's website

Written standards for the conduct of professional work

Written standards for the conduct of professional work

[3.238c]

From 6 January 2014 the Bar should refer to a new Handbook for rules and guidance on their conduct as barristers.

---

1 Introduction

1.1 These Standards are intended as a guide to the way in which a barrister should carry out his work. They consist in part of matters which are dealt with expressly in the Code of Conduct and in part of statements of good practice. They must therefore be read in conjunction with the Code of Conduct, and are to be taken into account in determining whether or not a barrister has committed a disciplinary offence. They apply to employed barristers as well as to barristers in independent practice, except where this would be inappropriate. In addition to these General Standards, there are Standards which apply specifically to the conduct of criminal cases.

2 General

2.1 The work which is within the ordinary scope of a barrister's practice consists of advocacy, drafting pleadings and other legal documents and advising on questions of law. A barrister acts only on the instructions of a professional client, and does not carry out any work by way of the management, administration or general conduct of a lay client's affairs, nor the management, administration or general conduct of litigation nor the receipt or handling of clients' money.

2.2 It is a fundamental principle which applies to all work undertaken by a barrister that a barrister is under a duty to act for any client (whether legally aided or not) in cases within his field of practice. The rules which embody this principle and the exceptions to it are set out in paragraphs 303, 601, 602, 603, 604 and 605 of the Code of Conduct.

3 Acceptance of work

3.1 As soon as practicable after receipt of any brief or instructions a barrister should satisfy himself that there is no reason why he ought to decline to accept it.

3.2 A barrister is not considered to have accepted a brief or instructions unless he has had an opportunity to consider it and has expressly accepted it.

3.3 A barrister should always be alert to the possibility of a conflict of interests. If the conflict is between the interests of his lay client and his professional client, the conflict must be resolved in favour of the lay client. Where there is a conflict between the lay client and the Legal Aid Fund, the conflict must be resolved in favour of the lay client, subject only to compliance with the provisions of the Legal Aid Regulations.

3.4 If after a barrister has accepted a brief or instructions on behalf of more than one lay client, there is or appears to be a conflict or a significant risk of a conflict between the interests of any one or more of such clients, he must not continue to act for any client unless all such clients give their consent to his so acting.

3.5 Even if there is no conflict of interest, when a barrister has accepted a brief or instructions for any party in any proceedings, he should not accept a brief or instructions in respect of an appeal or further stage of the proceedings for any other party without obtaining the prior consent of the original client.

3.6 A barrister must not accept any brief or instructions if the matter is one in which he has reason to believe that he is likely to be a witness. If, however, having accepted a brief or instructions, it later appears that he is likely to be a witness in the case on a material question of fact, he may retire or withdraw only if he can do so without jeopardising his client's interests.

3.7 A barrister should not appear as a barrister:

(a) in any matter in which he is a party or has a significant pecuniary interest;

(b) either for or against any local authority, firm or organisation of which he is a member or in which he has directly or indirectly a significant pecuniary interest;

(c) either for or against any company of which he is a director, secretary or officer or in which he has directly or indirectly a significant pecuniary interest.

3.8 Apart from cases in which there is a conflict of interests, a barrister must not accept any brief or instructions if to do so would cause him to be otherwise professionally embarrassed: paragraph 603 of the Code of Conduct sets out the general principles applicable to such situations.

4 Withdrawal from a case and return of brief or instructions

4.1 When a barrister has accepted a brief for the defence of a person charged with a serious criminal offence, he should so far as reasonably practicable ensure that the risk of a conflicting professional engagement does not arise.

4.2 The circumstances in which a barrister must withdraw from a case or return his brief or instructions are set out in paragraph 608 of the Code of Conduct; the circumstances in which he is permitted to do so are set out in paragraph 609 the circumstances in which he must not do so are set out in paragraph 610.

5 Conduct of work

5.1 A barrister must at all times promote and protect fearlessly and by all proper and lawful means his lay client's best interests.

5.2 A barrister must assist the Court in the administration of justice and, as part of this obligation and the obligation to use only proper and lawful means to promote and protect the interests of his client, must not deceive or knowingly or recklessly mislead the Court.

5.3 A barrister is at all times individually and personally responsible for his own conduct and for his professional work both in Court and out of Court.

5.4 A barrister must in all his professional activities act promptly, conscientiously, diligently and with reasonable competence and must take all reasonable and practicable steps to ensure that professional engagements are fulfilled. He must not undertake any task which:

(a) he knows or ought to know he is not competent to handle;

(b) he does not have adequate time and opportunity to prepare for or perform; or

(c) he cannot discharge within a reasonable time having regard to the pressure of other work.

5.5 A barrister must at all times be courteous to the Court and to all those with whom he has professional dealings.

5.6 In relation to instructions to advise or draft documents, a barrister should ensure that the advice or document is provided within such time as has been agreed with the professional client, or otherwise within a reasonable time after receipt of the relevant instructions. If it becomes apparent to the barrister that he will not be able to do the work within that time, he must inform his professional client forthwith.

5.7 Generally, a barrister should ensure that advice which he gives is practical, appropriate to the needs and circumstances of the particular client, and clearly and comprehensibly expressed.

5.8 A barrister must exercise his own personal judgment upon the substance and purpose of any advice he gives or any document he drafts. He must not devise facts which will assist in advancing his lay client's case and must not draft any originating process, pleading, affidavit, witness statement or notice of appeal containing:

(a) any statement of fact or contention (as the case may be) which is not supported by his lay client or by his brief or instructions;

(b) any contention which he does not consider to be properly arguable;

(c) any allegation of fraud unless he has clear instructions to make such an allegation and has before him reasonably credible material which as it stands establishes a prima facia case of fraud; or

(d) in the case of an affidavit or witness statement, any statement of fact other than the evidence which in substance according to his instructions, the barrister reasonably believes the witness would give if the evidence contained in the affidavit or witness statement were being given viva voce.

5.9 A barrister should be available on reasonable notice for a conference prior to the day of hearing of any case in which he is briefed; and if no such conference takes place then the barrister should be available for a conference on the day of the hearing. The venue of a conference is a matter for agreement between the barrister and his professional clients.

5.10 A barrister when conducting proceedings at Court:

(a) is personally responsible for the conduct and presentation of his case and must exercise personal judgment upon the substance and purpose of statements made and questions asked;

(b) must not, unless asked to so by the Court or when appearing before a tribunal where it his duty to do so, assert a personal opinion of the facts or the law;

(c) must ensure that the Court is informed of all relevant decisions and legislative provisions of which he is aware, whether the effect is favourable or unfavourable towards the contention for which he argues, and must bring any procedural irregularity to the attention of the Court during the hearing and not reserve such matter to be raised on appeal;

(d) must not adduce evidence obtained otherwise than from or through his professional client or devise facts which will assist in advancing his lay client's case;

(e) must not make statements or ask questions which are merely scandalous or intended or calculated only to vilify, insult or annoy either a witness or some other person;

(f) must if possible avoid the naming in open Court of third parties whose character would thereby be impugned;

(g) must not by assertion in a speech impugn a witness whom he has had an opportunity to cross-examine unless in cross-examination he has given the witness an opportunity to answer the allegation;

(h) must not suggest that a victim, witness or other person is guilty of crime, fraud or misconduct or make any defamatory aspersion on the conduct of any other person or attribute to another person the crime or conduct of which his lay client is accused unless such allegations go to a matter in issue (including the credibility of the witness) which is material to his lay client's case, and which appear to him to be supported by reasonable grounds.

5.11 A barrister must take all reasonable and practicable steps to avoid unnecessary expense or waste of the Court's time. He should, when asked, inform the Court of the probable length of his case; and he should also inform the Court of any developments which affect information already provided.

5.12 In Court a barrister's personal appearance should be decorous, and his dress, when robes are worn, should be compatible with them.

6 Witnesses

6.1.1 The rules which define and regulate the barrister's functions in relation to the preparation of evidence and contact with witnesses are set out in paragraphs 704, 705, 706, 707 and 708 of the Code of Conduct.

6.1.2 There is no longer any rule which prevents a barrister from having contact with any witness.

6.1.3 In particular, there is no longer any rule in any case (including contested cases in the Crown Court) which prevents a barrister from having contact with a witness whom he may expect to call and examine in chief, with a view to introducing himself to the witness, explaining the court's procedure (and in particular the procedure for giving evidence), and answering any questions on procedure which the witness may have.

6.1.4 It is a responsibility of a barrister, especially when the witness is nervous, vulnerable or apparently the victim of criminal or similar conduct, to ensure that those facing unfamiliar court procedures are put as much at ease as possible.

6.1.5 Unless otherwise directed by the Court or with the consent of the representative for the opposing side or of the Court, a barrister should not communicate directly or indirectly about the case with any witness, whether or not the witness is his lay client, once that witness has begun to give evidence until it has been concluded.

6.2 Discussing the evidence with witnesses

6.2.1 Different considerations apply in relation to contact with witnesses for the purpose of interviewing them or discussing with them (either individually or together) the substance of their evidence or the evidence of other witnesses.

6.2.2 Although there is no longer any rule which prevents a barrister from having contact with witnesses for such purposes a barrister should exercise his discretion and consider very carefully whether and to what extent such contact is appropriate, bearing in mind in particular that it is not the barrister's function (but that of his professional client) to investigate and collect evidence.

6.2.3 The guiding principle must be the obligation of counsel to promote and protect his lay client's best interests so far as that is consistent with the law and with counsel's overriding duty to the court (Code of Conduct paragraphs 302, 303).

6.2.4 A barrister should be alert to the risks that any discussion of the substance of a case with a witness may lead to suspicions of coaching, and thus tend to diminish the value of the witness's evidence in the eyes of the court, or may place the barrister in a position of professional embarrassment, for example if he thereby becomes himself a witness in the case. These dangers are most likely to occur if such discussion takes place:

(a) before the barrister has been supplied with a proof of the witness's evidence; or

(b) in the absence of the barrister's professional client or his representative.

A barrister should also be alert to the fact that, even in the absence of any wish or intention to do so, authority figures do subconsciously influence lay witnesses. Discussion of the substance of the case may unwittingly contaminate the witness's evidence.

6.2.5 There is particular danger where such discussions:

(a) take place in the presence of more than one witness of fact; or

(b) involve the disclosure to one witness of fact of the factual evidence of another witness.

These practices have been strongly deprecated by the courts as tending inevitably to encourage the rehearsal or coaching of witnesses and to increase the risk of fabrication or contamination of evidence: *R v Arif* (1993) Times, 17 June, CA; *Smith New Court Securities Ltd v Scrimgeour Vickers (Asset Management) Ltd (Roberts, third party)* [1994] 4 All ER 225, [1994] 1 WLR 1271.

That is not to suggest that it is always inappropriate to disclose one witness' evidence to another. If the witness is one to be called by the other party, it is almost inevitable that a witness' attention must be drawn to discrepancies between the two statements. Discretion is, however, required, especially where the evidence of independent witnesses is involved.

6.2.6 Whilst there is no rule that any longer prevents a barrister from taking a witness statement in civil cases (for cases in the Crown Court see below), there is a distinction between the settling of a witness statement and taking a witness statement. It is not appropriate for a barrister who has taken witness statements, as opposed to settling witness statements prepared by others, to act as counsel unless he is a junior member of the team of Counsel and will not be examining the witness or there are exceptional circumstances, because it risks undermining the independence of the barrister as an advocate. Exceptional circumstances would include:

(a) the witness is a minor one;

(b) Counsel has no choice but to take a proof and this is the only practical course in the interests of justice – this would apply, for instance, where a witness appears unexpectedly at Court and there is no one else competent to take the statement.

The Cab-rank Rule does not require a barrister to agree to undertake the task of taking witness statements.

6.2.7 There is no rule which prevents a barrister from exchanging common courtesies with the other side's witnesses. However, a barrister should not discuss the substance of the case or any evidence with the other side's witnesses except in rare and exceptional circumstances and then only with the prior knowledge of his opponent.

6.3 Criminal cases in the Crown Court

6.3.1 Contested criminal cases in the Crown Court present peculiar difficulties and may expose both barristers and witnesses to special pressures. As a general principle, therefore, with the exception of the lay client, character and expert witnesses, subject to 6.3.2, it is wholly inappropriate for a barrister in such a case to interview any potential witness. Interviewing includes discussing with any such witness the substance of his evidence or the evidence of other such witnesses.

6.3.2 Prosecution counsel may, if instructed to do so, interview potential witnesses for the purposes of, and in, accordance with the practice set out in the Code for Pre-Trial Witness Interviews.

6.3.3 There may be extraordinary circumstances in which a departure from the general principles set out in paragraphs 6.3.1 and 6.3.2 is unavoidable. An example of such circumstances is afforded by the decision in *R v Fergus* (1993) 98 Cr App 313, 158 JP 49, CA.

6.3.4 Where any barrister has interviewed any potential witness or any such witness has been interviewed by another barrister, that fact shall be disclosed to all other parties in the case before the witness is called. A written record must also be made of the substance of the interview and the reason for it.

7 Documents

7.1 A barrister should not obtain or seek to obtain a document, or knowledge of the contents of a document, belonging to another party other than by means of the normal and proper channels for obtaining such documents or such knowledge.

7.2 If a barrister comes into possession of a document belonging to another party by some means other than the normal and proper channels (for example, if the document has come into his possession in consequence of a mistake or inadvertence by another person or if the document appears to belong to another party, or to be a copy of such a document, and to be privileged from discovery or otherwise to be one which ought not to be in the possession of his professional or lay client) he should:

(a) where appropriate make enquiries of his professional client in order to ascertain the circumstances in which the document was obtained by his professional or lay client; and

(b) unless satisfied that the document has been properly obtained in the ordinary course of events at once return the document unread to the person entitled to possession of it.

7.3

7.3.1 If having come into possession of such a document the barrister reads it before he realises that he ought not to, and would be embarrassed in the discharge of his duties by his knowledge of the contents of the document, then provided he can do so without prejudice to his lay client he must return his brief or instructions and explain to his professional client why he has done so.

7.3.2 If, however, to return his brief or instructions would prejudice his lay client (for example, by reason of the proximity of the trial) he should not return his brief or instructions and should, unless the Court otherwise orders, make such use of the document as will be in his client's interests. He should inform his opponent of his knowledge of the document and of the circumstances, so far as known to him, in which the document was obtained and of his intention to use it. In the event of objection to the use of such document it is for the Court to determine what use, if any, may be made of it.

7.4 If during the course of a case a barrister becomes aware of the existence of a document which should have been but has not been disclosed on discovery he should advise his professional client to disclose it forthwith; and if it is not then disclosed, he must withdraw from the case.

8 Administration of practice

8.1 A barrister must ensure that his practice is properly and efficiently administered in accordance with the provisions of paragraph 304 of the Code of Conduct.

8.2 A barrister should ensure that he is able to provide his professional client with full and proper details of and appropriate justification for fees which have been incurred, and a proper assessment of any work to be done, so that both the lay client and the professional client are able to determine the level of any financial commitment which has been incurred or may be incurred.

Standards applicable in criminal cases

9 Introduction

9.1 These standards are to be read together with the General Standards and the Code of Conduct. They are intended as a guide to those matters which specifically relate to practice in the criminal Courts. They are not an alternative to the General Standards, which apply to all work carried out by a barrister. Particular reference is made to those paragraphs in the General Standards relating to the general conduct of a case (5.8), conduct in Court (5.10), discussion with witnesses (6.1, 6.2) and the use of documents belonging to other parties (7.1, 7.2, 7.3), which are not repeated in these standards.

10 Responsibilities of prosecuting counsel

10A The Standards and principles contained in this paragraph apply as appropriate to all practising barristers, whether in independent practice or employed and whether appearing as counsel in any given case or exercising any other professional capacity in connection with it.

10.1 Prosecuting counsel should not attempt to obtain a conviction by all means at his command. He should not regard himself as appearing for a party. He should lay before the Court fairly and impartially the whole of the facts which comprise the case for the prosecution and should assist the Court on all matters of law applicable to the case.

10.2 Prosecuting counsel should bear in mind at all times whilst he is instructed:

(i) that he is responsible for the presentation and general conduct of the case;

(ii) that he should use his best endeavours to ensure that all evidence or material that ought properly to be made available is either presented by the prosecution or disclosed to the defence.

10.3 Prosecuting counsel should, when instructions are delivered to him, read them expeditiously and, where instructed to do so, advise or confer on all aspects of the case well before its commencement.

10.4 In relation to cases tried in the Crown Court, prosecuting counsel:

(a) should ensure, if he is instructed to settle an indictment, that he does so promptly and within due time, and should bear in mind the desirability of not overloading an indictment with either too many defendants or too many counts, in order to present the prosecution case as simply and as concisely as possible;

(b) should ask, if the indictment is being settled by some other person, to see a copy of the indictment and should then check it;

(c) should decide whether any additional evidence is required and, if it is, should advise in writing and set out precisely what additional evidence is required with a view to serving it on the defence as soon as possible;

(d) should consider whether all witness statements in the possession of the prosecution have been properly served on the defendant in accordance with the Attorney-General's Guidelines;

(e) should eliminate all unnecessary material in the case so as to ensure an efficient and fair trial, and in particular should consider the need for particular witnesses and exhibits and draft appropriate admissions for service on the defence;

(f) should in all Class 1 and Class 2 cases and in other cases of complexity draft a case summary for transmission to the Court.

10.5 Paragraphs 6 to 6.3.4 of the Written Standards for the Conduct of Professional Work refer.

10.6 Prosecuting counsel should at all times have regard to the report of Mr Justice Farquharson's Committee on the role of Prosecuting Counsel which is set out in Archbold. In particular, he should have regard to the following recommendations of the Farquharson Committee:

(a) Where counsel has taken a decision on a matter of policy with which his professional client has not agreed, it would be appropriate for him to submit to the Attorney-General a written report of all the circumstances, including his reasons for disagreeing with those who instructed him;

(b) When counsel has had an opportunity to prepare his brief and to confer with those instructing him, but at the last moment before trial unexpectedly advises that the case should not proceed or that pleas to lesser offences should be accepted, and his professional client does not accept such advice, counsel should apply for an adjournment if instructed to do so;

(c) Subject to the above, it is for prosecuting counsel to decide whether to offer no evidence on a particular count or on the indictment as a whole and whether to accept pleas to a lesser count or counts.

10.7 It is the duty of prosecuting counsel to assist the Court at the conclusion of the summing-up by drawing attention to any apparent errors or omissions of fact or law.

10.8 In relation to sentence, prosecuting counsel:

(a) should not attempt by advocacy to influence the Court with regard to sentence: if, however, a defendant is unrepresented it is proper to inform the Court of any mitigating circumstances about which counsel is instructed;

(b) should be in a position to assist the Court if requested as to any statutory provisions relevant to the offence or the offender and as to any relevant guidelines as to sentence laid down by the Court of Appeal;

(c) should bring any such matters as are referred to in (b) above to the attention of the Court if in the opinion of prosecuting counsel the Court has erred;

(d) should bring to the attention of the Court any appropriate compensation, forfeiture and restitution matters which may arise on conviction, for example pursuant to sections 35–42 of the Powers of Criminal Courts Act 1973 and the Drug Trafficking Offences Act 1986;

(e) should draw the attention of the defence to any assertion of material fact made in mitigation which the prosecution believes to be untrue: if the defence persist in that assertion, prosecuting counsel should invite the Court to consider requiring the issue to be determined by the calling of evidence in accordance with the decision of the Court of Appeal in *R v Newton* (1982) 77 Cr App Rep 13, 4 Cr App Rep (S) 388, CA.

11 Responsibilities of defence counsel

11.1 When defending a client on a criminal charge, a barrister must endeavour to protect his client from conviction except by a competent tribunal and upon legally admissible evidence sufficient to support a conviction for the offence charged.

11.2 A barrister acting for the defence:

(a) should satisfy himself, if he is briefed to represent more than one defendant, that no conflict of interest is likely to arise;

(b) should arrange a conference and if necessary a series of conferences with his professional and lay clients;

(c) should consider whether any enquiries or further enquiries are necessary and, if so, should advise in writing as soon as possible;

(d) should consider whether any witnesses for the defence are required and, if so, which;

(e) should consider whether a Notice of Alibi is required and, if so, should draft an appropriate notice;

(f) should consider whether it would be appropriate to call expert evidence for the defence and, if so, have regard to the rules of the Crown Court in relation to notifying the prosecution of the contents of the evidence to be given;

(g) should ensure that he has sufficient instructions for the purpose of deciding which prosecution witnesses should be cross-examined, and should then ensure that no other witnesses remain fully bound at the request of the defendant and request his professional client to inform the Crown Prosecution Service of those who can be conditionally bound;

(h) should consider whether any admissions can be made with a view to saving time and expense at trial, with the aim of admitting as much evidence as can properly be admitted in accordance with the barrister's duty to his client;

(i) should consider what admissions can properly be requested from the prosecution;

(j) should decide what exhibits, if any, which have not been or cannot be copied he wishes to examine, and should ensure that appropriate arrangements are made to examine them as promptly as possible so that there is no undue delay in the trial.

(k) should as to anything which he is instructed to submit in mitigation which casts aspersions on the conduct or character of a victim or witness in the case, notify the prosecution in advance so as to give prosecuting Counsel sufficient opportunity to consider his position under paragraph 10.8(e).

11.3 A barrister acting for a defendant should advise his lay client generally about his plea. In doing so he may, if necessary, express his advice in strong terms. He must, however, make it clear that the client has complete freedom of choice and that the responsibility for the plea is the client's.

11.4 A barrister acting for a defendant should advise his client as to whether or not to give evidence in his own defence but the decision must be taken by the client himself.

11.5

11.5.1 Where a defendant tells his counsel that he did not commit the offence with which he is charged but nevertheless insists on pleading guilty to it for reasons of his own, counsel should:

(a) advise the defendant that, if he is not guilty, he should plead not guilty but that the decision is one for the defendant; counsel must continue to represent him but only after he has advised what the consequences will be and that what can be submitted in mitigation can only be on the basis that the client is guilty.

(b) explore with the defendant why he wishes to plead guilty to a charge which he says he did not commit and whether any steps could be taken which would enable him to enter a plea of not guilty in accordance with his profession of innocence.

11.5.2 If the client maintains his wish to plead guilty, he should be further advised:

(a) what the consequences will be, in particular in gaining or adding to a criminal record and that it is unlikely that a conviction based on such a plea would be overturned on appeal;

(b) that what can be submitted on his behalf in mitigation can only be on the basis that he is guilty and will otherwise be strictly limited so that, for instance, counsel will not be able to assert that the defendant has shown remorse through his guilty plea.

11.5.3 If, following all of the above advice, the defendant persists in his decision to plead guilty:

(a) counsel may continue to represent him if he is satisfied that it is proper to do so;

(b) before a plea of guilty is entered counsel or a representative of his professional client who is present should record in writing the reasons for the plea;

(c) the defendant should be invited to endorse a declaration that he has given unequivocal instructions of his own free will that he intends to plead guilty even though he maintains that he did not commit the offence(s) and that he understands the advice given by counsel and in particular the restrictions placed on counsel in mitigating and the consequences to himself; the defendant should also be advised that he is under no obligation to sign; and

(d) if no such declaration is signed, counsel should make a contemporaneous note of his advice.

12 Confessions of guilt

12.1 In considering the duty of counsel retained to defend a person charged with an offence who confesses to his counsel that he did commit the offence charged, it is essential to bear the following points clearly in mind:

(a) that every punishable crime is a breach of common or statute law committed by a person of sound mind and understanding;

(b) that the issue in a criminal trial is always whether the defendant is guilty of the offence charged, never whether he is innocent;

(c) that the burden of proof rests on the prosecution.

12.2 It follows that the mere fact that a person charged with a crime has confessed to his counsel that he did commit the offence charged is no bar to that barrister appearing or continuing to appear in his defence, nor indeed does such a confession release the barrister from his imperative duty to do all that he honourably can for his client.

12.3 Such a confession, however, imposes very strict limitations on the conduct of the defence, a barrister must not assert as true that which he knows to be false. He must not connive at, much less attempt to substantiate, a fraud.

12.4 While, therefore, it would be right to take any objections to the competency of the Court, to the form of the indictment, to the admissibility of any evidence or to the evidence admitted, it would be wrong to suggest that some other person had committed the offence charged, or to call any evidence which the barrister must know to be false having regard to the confession, such, for instance, as evidence in support of an alibi. In other words, a barrister must not (whether by calling the defendant or otherwise) set up an affirmative case inconsistent with the confession made to him.

12.5 A more difficult question is within what limits may counsel attack the evidence for the prosecution either by cross-examination or in his speech to the tribunal charged with the decision of the facts. No clearer rule can be laid down than this, that he is entitled to test the evidence given by each individual witness and to argue that the evidence taken as a whole is insufficient to amount to proof that the defendant is guilty of the offence charged. Further than this he ought not to go.

12.6 The foregoing is based on the assumption that the defendant has made a clear confession that he did commit the offence charged, and does not profess to deal with the very difficult questions which may present themselves to a barrister when a series of inconsistent statements are made to him by the defendant before or during the proceedings; nor does it deal with the questions which may arise where statements are made by the defendant which point almost irresistibly to the conclusion that the defendant is guilty but do not amount to a clear confession. Statements of this kind may inhibit the defence, but questions arising on them can only be answered after careful consideration of the actual circumstances of the particular case.

13 General

13.1 Both prosecuting and defence counsel:

(a) should ensure that the listing officer receives in good time their best estimate of the likely length of the trial (including whether or not there is to be a plea of guilty) and should ensure that the listing officer is given early notice of any change of such estimate or possible adjournment;

(b) should take all reasonable and practicable steps to ensure that the case is properly prepared and ready for trial by the time that it is first listed;

(c) should ensure that arrangements have been made in adequate time for witnesses to attend Court as and when required and should plan, so far as possible, for sufficient witnesses to be available to occupy the full Court day;

(d) should, if a witness (for example a doctor) can only attend Court at a certain time during the trial without great inconvenience to himself, try to arrange for that witness to be accommodated by raising the matter with the trial Judge and with his opponent;

(e) should take all necessary steps to comply with the Practice Direction (Crime: Tape Recording of Police Interviews) [1989] 1 WLR 631.

13.2 If properly remunerated (paragraph 502 of the Code), the barrister originally briefed in a case should attend all plea and directions hearings. If this is not possible, he must take all reasonable steps to ensure that the barrister who does appear is conversant with the case and is prepared to make informed decisions affecting the trial.

14 Video recordings

14.1 When a barrister instructed and acting for the prosecution or the defence of an accused has in his possession a copy of a video recording of a child witness which has been identified as having been prepared to be admitted in evidence at a criminal trial in accordance with Section 54 of the Criminal Justice Act 1991, he must have regard to the following duties and obligations:

(a) Upon receipt of the recording, a written record of the date and time and from whom the recording was received must be made and a receipt must be given.

(b) The recording and its contents must be used only for the proper preparation of the prosecution or defence case or of an appeal against conviction and/or sentence, as the case may be, and the barrister must not make or permit any disclosure of the recording or its contents to any person except when, in his opinion, it is in the interests of his proper preparation of that case.

(c) The barrister must not make or permit any other person to make a copy of the recording, nor release the recording to the accused, and must ensure that:

  (i) when not in transit or in use, the recording is always kept in a locked or secure place; and:

  (ii) when in transit, the recording is kept safe and secure at all times and is not left unattended, especially in vehicles or otherwise.

(d) Proper preparation of the case may involve viewing the recording in the presence of the accused. If this is the case, viewing should be done:

  (i) if the accused is in custody, only in the prison or other custodial institution where he is being held, in the presence of the barrister and/or his instructing solicitor;

  (ii) if the accused is on bail, at the solicitor's office or in counsel's chambers or elsewhere in the presence of the barrister and/or his instructing solicitor.

(e) The recording must be returned to the solicitor as soon as practicable after the conclusion of the barrister's role in the case. A written record of the date and time despatched and to whom the recording was delivered for despatch must be made.

15 Attendance of counsel at Court

15.1 Prosecuting counsel should be present throughout the trial, including the summing-up and the return of the jury. He may not absent himself without leave of the Court; but, if two or more barristers appear for the prosecution, the attendance of one is sufficient.

15.2

15.2.1 Defence counsel should ensure that the defendant is never left unrepresented at any stage of his trial.

15.2.2 Where a defendant is represented by one barrister, that barrister should normally be present throughout the trial and should only absent himself in exceptional circumstances which he could not reasonably be expected to foresee and provided that:

(a) he has obtained the consent of the professional client (or his representative) and the lay client; and

(b) a competent deputy takes his place.

15.2.3 Where a defendant is represented by two barristers, neither may absent himself except for good reason and then only when the consent of the professional client (or his representative) and of the lay client has been obtained, or when the case is legally aided and the barrister thinks it necessary to do so in order to avoid unnecessary public expense.

15.2.4 These rules are subject to modification in respect of lengthy trials involving numerous defendants. In such trials, where after the conclusion of the opening speech by the prosecution defending counsel is satisfied that during a specific part of the trial there is no serious possibility that events will occur which will relate to his client, he may with the consent of the professional client (or his representative) and of the lay client absent himself for that part of the trial. He should also inform the judge. In this event it is his duty:

(a) to arrange for other defending counsel to guard the interests of his client;

(b) to keep himself informed throughout of the progress of the trial and in particular of any development which could affect his client; and

(c) not to accept any other commitment which would render it impracticable for him to make himself available at reasonable notice if the interests of his client so require.

15.3.1 If during the course of a criminal trial and prior to final sentence the defendant voluntarily absconds and the barrister's professional client, in accordance with the ruling of the Law Society, withdraws from the case, then the barrister too should withdraw. If the trial judge requests the barrister to remain to assist the Court, the barrister has an absolute discretion whether to do so or not. If he does remain, he should act on the basis that his instructions are withdrawn and he will not be entitled to use any material contained in his brief save for such part as has already been established in evidence before the Court. He should request the trial judge to instruct the jury that this is the basis on which he is prepared to assist the Court.

15.3.2 If for any reason the barrister's professional client does not withdraw from the case, the barrister retains an absolute discretion whether to continue to act. If he does continue, he should conduct the case as if his client were still present in Court but had decided not to give evidence and on the basis of any instruction he has received. He will be free to use any material contained in his brief and may cross-examine witnesses called for the prosecution and call witnesses for the defence.

16 Appeals

16.1

16.1.1 Attention is drawn to the Guide to Commencing Proceedings in the Court of Appeal Criminal Division ("the Guide") . The current edition is dated October 2008 and can be found at http://www.hmcourts-service.gov.uk/docs/proc_guide.pdf

16.1.2 In particular when advising a defendant following conviction or sentence Defence Counsel is encouraged to follow the procedures set out at paragraphs A1–1 of the Guide.

16.2 Defence Counsel who represents the Defendant at the sentencing hearing at which the facts are opened and a plea in mitigation is advanced and where the sentence is being passed at that hearing, should see the defendant immediately following sentence. He should then proceed as follows:

(a) If he is satisfied that there are no reasonable grounds of appeal he should so advise orally and certify in writing. Counsel is encouraged to certify using the form set out in Appendix 1 to the Guide. No further advice is necessary unless it is reasonable for a written advice to be given because the client reasonably requires it or because it is necessary e.g. in the light of the circumstances of the conviction, any particular difficulties at trial, the length and nature of the sentence passed, the effect thereof on the defendant or the lack of impact which oral advice given immediately after the trial may have on the particular defendant's mind.

(b) If he is satisfied that there are more reasonable grounds of appeal or if his view is a provisional one or if he requires more time to consider the prospects of a successful appeal he should so advise orally and certify in writing. Counsel is encouraged to certify using the form set out in Appendix 1 to the Guide. Counsel should then furnish written advice to the professional client as soon as he can and in any event within 14 days.

(c) If sentence is not passed at the sentencing hearing but is adjourned to another hearing then if the Counsel who represents the defendant on the day on which sentence is passed ("Counsel B"), was not the Defence Counsel ("Counsel A") who had conduct of the sentencing hearing at which the facts were opened and a plea in mitigation made.

(d) Counsel B should, if satisfied that he/she is adequately briefed as to the opening and the plea in mitigation presented on the Defendant's behalf, express his/her view orally as to the prospects of appeal but state that his/her view is subject to written confirmation from Counsel A.

(e) If Counsel B is not satisfied that he/she is adequately briefed as to the opening and the plea in mitigation presented on the Defendant's behalf, then he/she should explain this clearly to the Defendant and indicate how and by when they will receive advice on appeal from Counsel A;

(f) In either case, Counsel A is then responsible for certifying in writing that there are no reasonable grounds of appeal, or for:

 (i) considering whether it is nevertheless reasonable to provide a written advice and for providing that advice in accordance with paragraph 16.2(a); or

 (ii) acting in accordance with paragraph 16.2(b).

16.3 Counsel should not settle grounds of appeal unless he considers that such grounds are properly arguable, and in that event he should provide a reasoned written opinion in support of such grounds.

16.4 In certain cases counsel may not be able to perfect grounds of appeal without a transcript or other further information. In this event the grounds of appeal should be accompanied by a note to the Registrar setting out the matters on which assistance is required. Once such transcript or other information is available, counsel should ensure that the grounds of appeal are perfected by the inclusion of all necessary references.

16.5 Grounds of Appeal must be settled with sufficient particularity to enable the Registrar and subsequently the Court to identify clearly the matters relied upon.

16.6 If at any stage counsel is of the view that the appeal should be abandoned, he should at once set out his reasons in writing and send them to his professional client.

Guidance on practice in authorised bodies (such as LDPs and ABSs) permitted by amendments to Code of Conduct

Amendments to Code of Conduct

[3.238d]

1. On 26 March 2010, the prohibition in the Bar's Code of Conduct on barristers (other than employed barristers) supplying legal services to the public through or on behalf of any other person ceased to have effect. Part 5 of the Legal Services Act 2007 (LSA 2007) came into effect on 6 October 2011and barristers are now permitted to supply legal services to the public in three different ways: as a self-employed barrister (as previously), as a manager or employee of an *authorised body*, subject to the rules of the approved regulator of that body, or as an employed barrister (to the same extent as previously permitted under rule 502). The significant recent change is that barristers are now permitted to practise as managers or employees of Alternative Business Structures (ABSs), which are bodies licensed by a licensing authority under Part V of the LSA 2007.

2. An Authorised Body is defined in part X of the code as follows:

   (a) ***authorised body*** means a body that has been authorised by an approved regulator to practise as a *licensed body* or a *recognised body.*

   (b) ***licensed body*** means a body licensed by a licensing authority, other than the Bar Standards Board, under Part 5 of the *LSA*.

   (c) ***recognised body*** *means a partnership, LLP, company or sole principal authorised to provide reserved legal services by an Approved Regulator other than the Bar Standards Board other than a licensable body as defined in s.72 of the Act of 2007 but does not include a body which is deemed to be authorised by reason of s.18(3) of the Act of 2007.*

3. "Recognised bodies" are entities of all kinds, or sole principals, authorised to provide reserved legal activities by an approved regulator other than the Bar Standards Board (BSB) i.e. a law firm regulated by the Solicitors Regulation Authority (SRA) is a recognised body. A "manager" for these purposes is a partner of a firm, a director of a limited company or a member of a limited liability partnership which is a recognised body, as the case may be.

4. Recognised bodies include what are generally known as Legal Disciplinary Practices (LDPs). These are a creature of the LSA 2007. They can have different kinds of qualified lawyer and non-lawyers as managers and employees (or just lawyers). At present, no more than 25% of the managers (or shareholding) in an SRA-regulated LDP can be non-lawyers, and only non-lawyers who are managers can own a shareholding. At present, only the SRA can regulate LDPs that are authorised to conduct litigation and exercise rights of audience, though the Council for Licensed Conveyancers (CLC) also has power to regulate Legal Disciplinary Practices (LDPs). At present, recognised bodies can only supply legal services (restricted or not) to the public, not other services such as accountancy or valuation services.

5. The Legal Services Board has now enabled the licensing of bodies under Part V of the LSA 2007 that can be externally owned and supply other

services as well as legal services. These are generally known as ABSs. Some LDPs (those that include non-lawyer managers) will have to become ABSs once a transitional period has expired after the start of the licensable body regime.

6. Barristers are permitted to become managers of SRA-regulated LDPs, alongside solicitors, other qualified lawyers and non-lawyers. A barrister can also be a manager of a CLC-regulated LDP but as such cannot conduct litigation or exercise rights of audience. Most barristers who become managers and employees of recognised bodies are therefore likely to be in SRA-regulated firms. Barristers are now also permitted to become managers of ABSs regulated by either the SRA or the CLC.

7. Barristers practising in SRA regulated entities will be subject to the whole of the SRA's Code of Conduct, save to the extent that this is expressed to apply only to solicitors or trainee solicitors. Barristers practising in SRA-regulated entities will therefore be amenable to the jurisdiction of the SRA and the Solicitors Disciplinary Tribunal in the event of breaches of the SRA rules of conduct. The practicalities of managing disciplinary procedures, when individuals are subject to the regimes of more than one Approved Regulator, has been addressed through the development of a Framework Memorandum of Understanding between the relevant Approved Regulators.

8. Barristers practising in SRA-regulated entities will remain subject to certain parts of the Bar's Code of Conduct. These are the provisions that are regarded as necessary or fundamental to all practising barristers. The provisions of the Code that apply to barristers so practising are identified in rule 105C.1 of the Code. The cab-rank rule does not apply to barristers who are managers or employees of authorised bodies, as it does not apply to employed barristers generally. Barristers practising in authorised bodies are strongly advised to ensure that they are aware of the provisions of the Bar's Code that will remain applicable to them. It is a disciplinary offence under the Bar's Code for a barrister to be convicted of a disciplinary offence by another approved regulator, such as the SRA. A barrister so convicted therefore is liable to further disciplinary action by the BSB (rule 901.8) so far as necessary in the public interest and proportionate.

9. The opportunity for barristers to become managers of authorised bodies means that barristers may be exposed, for the first time, to business practices that are unfamiliar to them. In particular, the SRA rules make all managers of authorised bodies responsible for (and entitled to deal with) client monies. This is something that barristers have not previously been entitled to do. In order to qualify, a solicitor has to pass examination papers in accounting for client monies. Any barrister managers of authorised bodies are strongly urged not to personally deal with client monies until they have received adequate training and have acquired a sufficient understanding of the Solicitors' Accounts Rules. Similarly those with managerial responsibility for handling clients' money should ensure that they are familiar with the relevant Rules. Entitlement to handle client monies is, however, a matter for the SRA as regulator of the entity and subject to that for the regulated entity, and not for the BSB as the professional regulator of the individual barrister.

10. Both the SRA Code (O 1.4) and the Bar's Code (paras 606.1, 701(b)) contain rules that require a barrister not to act beyond his professional

competence. Any barrister acting as manager of an authorised body should ensure that he/she does not infringe this rule.

11. The amendments to the Code give barristers who are managers of authorised bodies the right to conduct litigation (employed barristers already have this right), subject to complying with the Employed Barristers (Conduct of Litigation) Rules (Annex I of the Code) and the Approved Regulator's rules. Rule 1(b) of the former requires a period of practice under the supervision of a qualified person who has been entitled to conduct litigation for the previous 2 years, unless the BSB grants an exemption on the grounds of relevant experience.

12. Rules 407, 505 and 507 (which came into effect on 26 March 2010) replace rule 307(f) on client money. For self-employed barristers and all employed barristers, the existing prohibition on receiving and handling client money is maintained, but the prohibition does not apply to managers of authorised bodies. They will therefore be able to be responsible for client money, subject to the rules of the Approved Regulator for the entity of which they are a manager. Such rules may include requirements as to training and they will, in any case, be subject to the Code requirements not to undertake any task which they are not competent to handle.

Dual practice

13. Under the amendments made to the Code, a barrister may now practise in more than one of the ways identified in paragraph 1 above at the same time. That is to say, a barrister may practise in the self-employed model from chambers but work part time as an employed barrister for the Government, or for a law firm regulated by the SRA; or may practice part time in the employment of the Serious Fraud Office and part time as a manager of an LDP or ABS. A common example is expected to be that of young barristers who wish to practise self-employed in publicly-funded criminal or family work, but who may need to be employed part-time in complementary work for a law firm or a Government body.

14. Although such dual practice may be complementary and beneficial, both to the barrister and in the public interest, there are also increased risks of conflicts of interests and duty and added risks that the confidentiality of a client's affairs may be compromised. This is particularly an issue in a case where a barrister conducts a self-employed practice at the same time as working for an employer or authorised body, or where the barrister works for more than one employer or authorised body. The barrister will not be free to disclose to his employer or the body details (or the existence) of clients from his/her self-employed practice or another employer's or body's practice. That means that conflicts of interest and of duty for the barrister will be harder to identify and manage in advance of their arising, in ways that barristers in self-employed practice are used to dealing with and barristers hitherto employed by firms of solicitors may not have had to deal with. On the other hand, in many cases of dual practice, the likelihood of a conflict of this kind will be extremely small, e.g. because the kind or level of work done in self-employed practice is different from the work done for an employer. Barristers considering dual practice should review carefully the risks of conflicts and in relation to maintaining confidentiality of clients' affairs, and should ensure that by one means or another such risks are avoided or dealt with in advance of their arising wherever possible.

15. In order to manage these risks and prevent avoidable conflicts from occurring, rules 207 and 208 of the Code impose restrictions and requirements for barristers who wish to practice in more than one capacity:

(1) *Notification.* The fact of practice in more than one capacity must be notified to the Board in writing and in advance (rule 207(b)(i)). Note that this is an additional requirement going beyond the requirements of rule 202(d) to notify the Board of the identity and contact details of any employer or authorised body. If the Board requires further information about the capacities in which the barrister is supplying legal services, the barrister must then supply such information as the Board requires.

(2) *Protocol.* The barrister must agree in advance with each of his employers or with each authorised body a written protocol, under which the barrister and the employer or body agree how, consistently with maintaining the confidentiality of clients' affairs, conflicts will be avoided or will be resolved if they exist. The Board would regard it as quite wrong for a self-employed barrister to refuse to act further for a pre-existing client on the basis that his employer or authorised body has subsequently been instructed by someone whose interests conflict or potentially conflict with the interests of the first client. It would equally be wrong, save in extreme circumstances of greater prejudice to a client being caused by refusing to act, for the barrister and the employer or body to continue to act for persons whose interests conflict.

Accordingly, before acting in two or more capacities, a barrister will need to ensure, by the terms of some written protocol agreed with his employer or authorised body, that such conflicts can be avoided or can be resolved if they arise without causing prejudice to either or any clients concerned. Clearly, this is likely to involve the barrister either himself being involved in decisions that his employer or body takes relating to conflicts of interest, or at least in reviewing client lists so that any apparent conflict of interest may be resolved in accordance with the terms of the protocol agreed. The Board does not intend to draft a standard protocol for these purposes, since no one agreement can possibly suit the greatly variable circumstances that may arise. It is the responsibility of the barrister considering practising in more than one capacity to address these issues and reach a satisfactory, written agreement with his employer or body in a way that preserves client confidentiality and avoids or resolves conflicts of interest and duty without prejudicing the interests of clients.

A copy of any such protocol must be provided to the Board on request.

(3) *Working in only one capacity at the same time on the same matter* (rule 208 (d)). Potential regulatory issues arise where the barrister works on the same matter in more than one capacity. Firstly, the potential for client confusion is self-evident. Secondly, in many circumstances it is unlikely to be in the best interests of the client.

The Bar Standards Board considered prohibiting a barrister from acting in more than one capacity in the same matter, but in the event has decided that such a prohibition would not be proportionate. There will be some circumstances where it may be appropriate for a barrister to act in more than one capacity at different stages of the case. For example, the barrister may work on the case whilst employed by the solicitors' firm, but subsequently the firm may wish to instruct him as a self-employed barrister as advocate at trial. A barrister licensed to carry out public access work may give preliminary advice as a self-employed barrister and subsequently (subject to his doing so being in the client's best interests) may refer the matter to the law firm which employs him when the matter becomes litigious, so that the client can have the benefit of the firm's resources in the litigation, with the barrister conducting the litigation in his or her capacity as an employee or manager of the firm (or working under the supervision of the person doing so). Such an arrangement has the advantage, from the client's perspective, that the client does not pay the firm's overheads when the barrister is carrying out work that can be done on a self-employed basis but does so only when the barrister's role involves work of a sort that can and should properly be done in their capacity as a manager/employee of the firm.

The risk of client confusion means that it is essential that the barrister makes it clear to the client in writing the capacity in which he is working on the case at each stage. This is necessary so that the client knows when the firm is and is not responsible for the barrister's work and which code of conduct and regulatory regime applies to the barrister's work at any given time.

Whilst in appropriate circumstances a barrister may thus work on the matter in different capacities at different stages of the matter, Rule 208(d) prohibits the barrister from working on the case in different capacities at the same time. "At the same time" is to be distinguished from different stages of the case. Thus a barrister who works in chambers on Monday and Friday and works as an employee of a solicitor's firm on Tuesday, Wednesday and Thursday could not work on the same matter in different capacities on different days of the week.

The barrister must at all times have regard to the best interests of the client (and solicitors have a like duty). There are always particular concerns as to whether the client's best interests are served where one-off arrangements are made in relation to a specific case and this issue is of particular importance here. Thus it would be unlikely to be in the best interests of the client for the barrister to enter into a one-off arrangement where a matter on which the barrister has already acted in a self-employed capacity is transferred to the firm which then employs the barrister to do work which could perfectly well have been done by the barrister on a self-employed basis, without the client having to pay the firm's overheads. On the face of it, such an arrangement has no purpose other than to charge the client a higher fee for the barrister's work. In contrast, arrangements which are not one-off may well have other legitimate purposes (such as enabling the barrister to develop a given specialism by securing a flow of work of that type through the firm or ensuring that the barrister can draw directly on relevant resources and personnel available within the firm). It is likely to be prudent to cover such issues in the protocol agreed between barrister and law firm. It should at all times be borne in mind that both the barrister and the solicitors involved have a duty to act in the client's best interests. The purpose of allowing barristers to practise in a dual capacity is that this flexibility can promote diversity in the profession and benefit clients: for example, enabling barristers to develop not to enable law firms to charge clients more for work than they would otherwise.

16. Where acting in a dual capacity, there is nothing to prevent a barrister from referring a client to a firm of which he is an employee or manager, provided of course that the barrister is acting in what he reasonably considers to be the best interests of the client and in doing so, that full disclosure of his interest is made, and that no referral fee is paid to him by the firm or any intermediary for the referral (rule 209(b). Similarly, the firm might properly refer the client to the barrister subject again to the barrister ensuring that full disclosure has been made and no referral fee paid. Such referrals should, however, be approached with a degree of caution, as the possibility exists for the referring party to be unduly influenced by his own interests, and for complaints to be made at a later time unless the referral was scrupulously fair and transparent (rule 208 (e)).

17. In order to ensure that the client is making a properly informed choice as to what is in his best interests, the barrister is therefore required to disclose to the client in writing, before making or accepting the referral, as the case may be, the nature and extent of his interest in the firm, and to advise the client of his right to instruct another barrister or retain another firm of his choice to act for or represent him. The referral should only proceed if the barrister is satisfied that the client fully understands and is able to make his choice freely.

18. The barrister is also required to keep a record of all cases in which he made or received a referral to or from his employer or recognised body (rule 208(b)). The records should be kept for a minimum of 6 years from each referral.

Ownership of LDPs

Note: The BSB is currently reviewing the necessity of rule 209 with a view to potentially relaxing the rule in favor of existing provisions in the Code. Amendments to rule 209 will be subject to consultation in early 2012, but for the time being this guidance remains valid.

19. Unlike lay people, who can only own shares in a LDP if they are managers of it, there is no restriction in the Act on any qualified lawyer owning shares in an LDP. There is currently no restriction in the Code on barristers owning shares in law firms or LDPs.

20. It is to be expected that barristers who are managers or employees of LDPs may wish to have an ownership interest in the LDP that they manage or that employs them, and such a course is unobjectionable. However, where barristers seek to take an ownership interest in an LDP where they are not involved in the management, entirely different considerations and regulatory risks arise.

21. The Board has taken the view that a complete ban on such interests, which will normally be for investment purposes, would be disproportionate as it would catch situations where there is no regulatory risk. Accordingly, the amended rules permit ownership but subject to some conditions and safeguards in the public interest. These conditions and safeguards do not

apply where the barrister is a manager or employee of the LDP, though the dual practice rules (above) will apply if the barrister is also practising in another capacity at the same time.

22. Before taking such ownership interests, barristers must consider carefully the risks and restrictions which arise in consequence of such ownership interests. Those risks are more acute than may appear on the surface, and will, in very many cases, make it impractical for a practising barrister to acquire such an ownership interest unless there is no prospect of having any professional dealings with the LDP concerned in circumstances in which a conflict of interest and duty could arise.

23. Where a barrister has an ownership interest in a LDP, it will be inappropriate for the barrister to act where the LDP is itself an opposing party to litigation. Where the financial interest is non-trivial it will be inappropriate for the barrister to act where the LDP acts for an opposing party, as the barrister will have a financial interest on both sides of the litigation. This may require the barrister to cease to act where the opposing party's lawyers change in the course of the litigation and the LDP in which the barrister has an interest is instructed. Although it will be permissible for the barrister to obtain the informed consent of the client to acting in such circumstances, it is essential that the client is fully aware of the issues involved, and in particular when the client is not a sophisticated user of legal services, there may be real risks of misunderstanding.

24. There is no objection in principle to the LDP in which the barrister has an interest instructing the barrister. However such instruction gives rise to potential issues of lack of independence and as to whether the LDP is necessarily acting in the best interests of the client.

25. Whilst ownership by barristers of interests in LDPs gives rise to the same kinds of issues and concerns as dual practice (see para 11 above), the issues here are significantly more acute. Barristers' involvement is likely to be less obvious to clients. It is essential that such interests are disclosed to clients, where material, and disclosed to the Board so that the impact of them can be monitored as part of the Board's general jurisdiction to ensure that barristers practise is a way that protects and promotes clients' and the public interest above their own private interests.

26. Barristers are advised to consider carefully the implications of owning an interest in an LDP, either directly or indirectly, in circumstances in which they are not employees or managers of that LDP. As explained below, in some cases ownership would require the barrister to take steps to manage or avoid conflicts that might arise. The responsibility to avoid causing prejudice to his client is, in these circumstances, that of the barrister.

27. In order to manage the risks and avoid conflicts of interest and duty from occurring, rules 209 of the Code imposes restrictions and requirements for barristers who wish to own interests in LDPs:

    (1) *Notification.* The fact of an ownership interest must be notified to the Board in writing. The interest must be notified as soon as practicable after the interest is acquired or the barrister ceases to be an employee or manager of the LDP in question, as the case may be. At present, the rules do not require the extent or nature of the ownership interest to be disclosed to the Board. The Board intends to keep that matter

under review and the rules may change in future. If the extent or nature of the interest is material to any client of the barrister, however, that does not mean that the extent or nature need not be disclosed to the client, as explained below.

(2) *Conflict of interest and duty.* If a barrister has a more than trivial ownership interest in an LDP, then, as explained above, there is scope for a conflict or potential conflict to arise between a barrister and his client, where the LDP is acting for another party or for a person with a conflicting interest. It is the responsibility of the barrister to ensure that conflicts are avoided. Save in exceptional circumstances, a barrister must not act or continue to act where there is a conflict or possible conflict between his interests and those of his client or his duty to his client.

Becoming a Sole Practitioner – Creating a new set of Chambers

Becoming a Sole Practitioner

[3.238e]

The Bar Standards Board Handbook provides that you may practise on your own provided that you have practised for a total of three years with a qualified person following the completion of your pupillage (BSB Handbook rS20). The following guidance provides further guidance.

Setting up your own practice

Sole practitioners

1. The Bar Standards Board Handbook provides that you may practise on your own provided that you have practised for a total of three years with a qualified person following the completion of your pupillage (BSB Handbook rS20).

2. Please note that:
   - a "qualified person" is defined at rS22;
   - periods of "squatting" or third-six pupillages count towards the three years;
   - periods spent in employment as an employed barrister with full rights of audience;
   - after 31st July 2000 also count towards the three years;
   - the period of three years need not be continuous: breaks may have been taken provided that the total time spent in practice amounts to three years;
   - if you are practising in a dual capacity you must work with a qualified person in both capacities. You may not therefore set up as a sole practitioner even if you have worked with a qualified person in your employed capacity.

3. In certain circumstances, the Bar Standards Board may waive the requirement to have practised for three years post-pupillage. Please contact the Qualifications Department of the Bar Standards Board (020 7611 1444) for more information.

4. Assuming you meet the basic qualification, you do not need special permission from the Bar Standards Board in order to establish your own chambers. You should, however:
   - update your records through BarristerConnect or inform the Records department (020 7242 0934) immediately of the address from which

you will practise and the telephone number. This is of considerable importance and is your responsibility. It is not sufficient to rely on your former chambers to do so

- inform the Bar Mutual Indemnity Fund (0207 621 0405) of your new status – they are unlikely to require an additional premium.

5. Finally, you should note the requirements in the BSB Handbook to administer your practice efficiently and to have an effective complaints procedure. (see rC88–98).

6. You may wish to notify the Circuit on which you are practising and your Inn of Court.

Things to consider

7. Before deciding to practise alone, you should think carefully, not merely about how to comply with the Handbook but also about how you will deal practically with the different regime involved.

8. The advantages of sole practice can include:
   - reduction in the costs of running a practice;
   - control of your administration and marketing;
   - a freer lifestyle in running your practice;
   - saving time and money by travelling less.

9. Disadvantages can include:
   - increased administrative burdens which are ongoing and not just limited to the initial setting up
   - lack of support to expand your practice and isolation from others, limiting exchange of views
   - difficulties with work that has to be returned
   - receiving fewer returns.

10. You should weigh these issues up and should think about:
    - whether solicitors will continue to brief you if you are on your own;
    - how you will inform/market yourself to solicitors;
    - how you will deal with returned work;
    - what administrative support you need in place;
    - whether as a self-employed barrister you will undertake public access work and/or apply for an extension to your practising certificate to conduct litigation.

11. The Sole Practitioners Group may be able to provide advice on these points.

Questions and answers for sole practitioners

Do I need to have a clerk?

No. The requirement is simply that you administer your practice efficiently. You need to assess whether you will be able to undertake the necessary administration yourself or whether you need somebody else to assist. If your practice is largely paper-based, then you can probably manage without any assistance. Most sole practitioners manage without a clerk.

Can I conduct litigation?

You may apply for a litigation extension to your practising certificate from the Bar Standards Board. This way you can run a case from cradle to grave if you are granted extension and comply with requirements, if you wish, laid down by the Bar Standards Board.https://www.barstandardsboard.org.uk/regulatory-requirements/for-barristers/authorisation-to-conduct-litigation/

Where can I hold conferences?

Conferences can be held wherever is convenient. There is nothing to stop them taking place in solicitors' offices, or your own office.

How can I market myself to solicitors?

In any way which is consistent with the advertising rules – you can contact solicitors directly, provide details of your skills, experience and fees. You should be careful about direct comparisons with other professionals (gC57).

Questions and Answers about creating a new set of Chambers

Can I outsource work?

Yes.

The BSB Handbook at rC86 states that:

> "you must ensure that such outsourcing is subject to contractual arrangements which ensure that such third party:
>
> (a) is subject to confidentiality obligations similar to the confidentiality obligations placed on you in accordance with this Handbook
>
> (b) complies with any other obligations set out in this Code of Conduct which may be relevant to or affected by such outsourcing
>
> (c) processes any personal data in accordance with your instructions and, for the avoidance of doubt, as though it were a data controller under the Data Protection Act, and
>
> (d) is required to allow the Bar Standards Board or its agent to obtain information from, inspect the records (including electronic records) of, or enter the premises of such third party in relation to the outsourced activities or functions."

What do I do if someone makes a complaint against me?

You must comply with the Complaints Rules at D1.1 rC99–109.

What Equality and Diversity obligations do I have?

The BSB Handbook at rC110–112 set out extensive equality and diversity obligations for Chambers and self-employed barristers.

Do I need to register for the Quality Assurance Scheme for Advocates (QASA)?

All criminal barristers must register for QASA within the following timescales:

Circuits	Start	Close
Midland and Western	30 September 13	30 May 14
South Eastern	31 May 14	3 October 14
Northern, North Eastern and Wales and Chester	4 October 14	31 December 14

Please see the BSB website FAQs for more information: https://www.barstandardsboard.org.uk/media/1566645/qasa_faqs_-_policy_v4_.pdf

Do I need to let the BSB have access to my premises?

Yes. The BSB Handbook at rC70 states that:

> "You must permit the Bar Council, or the Bar Standards Board, or any person appointed by them, reasonable access, on request, to inspect:
>
> (1) any premises from which you provide, or are believed to provide, legal services, and
>
> (2) any documents or records relating to those premises and your practice, or BSB authorised body.
>
> and the Bar Council, Bar Standards Board, or any person appointed by them, shall be entitled to take copies of such documents or records as may be required by them for the purposes of their functions."

What is meant by "Chambers is administered competently and efficiently"?

Essentially, you need to have the office systems which will ensure that, amongst other things:

- briefs and instructions are logged in on arrival;
- you have adequate facilities to ensure that work is completed in good time and do not take on more work than you can manage;

- you have suitable diary facilities to identify clashes of dates of hearings, conferences and other appointments at the earliest possible stage and to remind you of those appointments;
- you keep adequate records of your work;
- fee notes are sent out in good time and adequate records of fees are kept;
- you have effective arrangements for handling complaints and inform clients about them;
- you are able to identify and take notice of all relevant guidance and rule changes issued by the Bar Standards Board.

There is no single right way of achieving this. Due to the diverse nature of sole practitioners' practice no specific software package can be recommended. You would be wise to consider the requirements of quality accreditation, so if you apply your system is already in place. The longer the system has been in place the more impressive it will be to the person who assesses your application.

Can I handle client money?

No. Self-employed barristers cannot handle client money see the BSB Handbook at rC73–75. You may be interested in using BARCO, the Bar Council escrow service: http://www.barcouncil.org.uk/for-the-bar/barco/

Can I accept or pay referral fees?

No. Referral fees are strictly prohibited by rC10.

Can I negotiate my own fees?

Yes.

Can I practise from my own home?

Yes.

Do I have to have my name outside the place where I practise?

No.

What equipment and support will I need?

This will depend on the nature of your practice. It is likely that you will need a computer with access to the internet.

For information about IT security best practice please see: http://www.barcouncil.org.uk/for-the-bar/professional-practice-and-ethics/it-panel-articles/

Sources of advice

If there are matters that are not covered here or if there are issues on which you need further advice or guidance, the following places may be able to assist:

- The Bar Council, Ethical Enquiries Service – 020 7611 1307
- BMIF– 020 7621 0405
- Bar Sole Practitioners' Group – Contact Numbers:
- East Anglia
  Lorraine Webb – 01245 248341
- London
  Wendy Datta – 07785 564775
  Philip Proghoulis – 020 8788 1238
- Midlands
  Karen Boyes – 01234 720952
- North
  Fauz Khan – 07973 133594
- Southern England
  Doug Cracknell – 01959 522325
- West Country
  Elizabeth Hailstone – 01179 624138

Important notice

This document has been prepared by the Bar Council to assist barristers on matters of professional conduct and ethics. **It is not "guidance" for the purposes of the BSB Handbook I6.4, and neither the BSB nor a disciplinary tribunal nor the Legal Ombudsman is bound by any views or advice expressed in it.** It does not comprise – and cannot be relied on as giving – legal advice. It has been prepared in good faith, but neither the Bar Council nor any of the individuals responsible for or involved in its preparation accept any responsibility or liability for anything done in reliance on it. For fuller information as to the status and effect of this document, please refer to the professional practice and ethics section of the Bar Council's website.

The Provision of Services Regulations 2009

The Provision of Services Regulations 2009

[3.238f]

The purpose of this guidance is to draw barristers' attention to issues relating the application for the Provision of Services Regulations 2009 which came into force in December 2009. They impose obligations on barristers as to the information to be made available or made by services providers to the receivers of those services.

---

1. The Provision of Services Regulations 2009[1] ("the Regulations") came into force on 28 December 2009. They give effect, in English law, to the EU Services Directive[2] ("the Directive").

2. Although the Directive is a milestone in the creation of a single European market for the provision of services, the market for legal services had already been liberalised by earlier European legislation (including Directives 77/249/EEC, 98/5/EC and 2005/36/EC). The Services Directive takes effect subject to this earlier legislation, and therefore has had little impact on the way in which lawyers can provide their services generally within Europe.

3. However the Directive and the Regulations have imposed additional obligations and requirements on ***all*** service providers (including barristers), principally in terms of the information to be given or made available by service providers to the receivers of their services. The purpose of this letter is to draw your attention to the relevant terms of the Regulations, and to provide advice as to the way in which the requirements may best be met.

1 SI 2999/2009: available at http://www.legislation.gov.uk/uksi/2009/2999/pdfs/uksi_20092999_en.pdf; with an explanatory memorandum at http://www.legislation.gov.uk/uksi/2009/2999/pdfs/uksiem_20092999_en.pdf.

2 2006/123/EC; available at http://eur-lex.europa.eu/LexUriServ/site/en/oj/2006/l_376/l_37620061227en00360068.pdf

The Regulations

4. The critical Regulations are Regulations 7–12. In summary, they impose the following requirements:

5. Every service provider must *"make available"* to all recipients of their service:

   (a) "contact details" including at least the following:

      (i) a postal address, fax number or email address;

      (ii) a telephone number; and

      (iii) where applicable, an official address,

   to which the recipients of services can send a complaint or make a request for information about the service.

(Regulation 7)

(b) The following information:

(i) The provider's name,

(ii) The provider's legal status and form,

(iii) The "geographic address" at which the provider is established, and details by which the provider can be contacted rapidly and communicated with directly,

(iv) Where the provider is registered in a public register, the name of the register and the provider's registration number (or other means of identification in the register),

(v) Where the activity is subject to an "authorisation scheme"[1] in the UK, the particulars of the relevant competent authority,

(vi) Where the activity is subject to a scheme equivalent to an "authorisation scheme" in another EEA State, the particulars of the relevant authority involved or the "Point of Single Contact" in that state,

(vii) Where the activity is subject to VAT, the provider's VAT number,

(viii) Where the provider is carrying on a regulated profession, the professional body with which the provider is registered, their professional title and the EEA state that granted it,

(ix) The general terms and conditions (if any) used by the provider,

(x) The existence of any contractual terms concerning the competent court or law applicable to its contracts,

(xi) The existence of any "after sales guarantee" (not imposed by law) given by the provider,

(xii) The price of the service (where pre-determined by the provider for a given type of service),

(xiii) The main features of the service, if not apparent from the context, and

(xiv) Where the provider is subject to a requirement to hold professional indemnity insurance, information about the insurance; and in particular:

(1) the contact details of the insurer, and

(2) the territorial coverage of the insurance.

1 It is not entirely clear what is meant by an "authorisation scheme" or how it relates to membership of a regulated profession. However, in the present context, the obligations imposed on service providers subject to an authorisation scheme do not appear different in substance from those imposed on members of a regulated profession.

(Regulation 8(1))

6. For the purposes of Regulation 8(1), information is "made available" if:

(a) It is supplied to the recipient on the provider's own initiative;

(b) It is easily accessible to the recipient at the "place where the service is provided" or where the contract for the service is "concluded";

(c) It is easily accessible to the recipient electronically by means of an address supplied by the provider; or

(d) It appears in any information supplied in the recipient by the provider in which the provider gives a detailed description of the service.[1]

(Regulation 8(2))

7. In addition, the following information must be provided on request:

(a) Where the price of the service is not pre-determined by the provider for a given type of service, the price of the service in question, or the method of calculating it so that it can be checked by the recipient, or a "sufficiently detailed estimate";

(b) Where the provider is carrying on a regulated profession, a reference to the rules applicable in their State of establishment and how to access them;

(c) Information on other activities undertaken by the provider which are "directly linked" to the service in question and on the measures taken to avoid conflicts of interest;[2] and

(d) Any codes of conduct to which the provider is subject and the address at which the codes may be consulted electronically, specifying the language available.

(Regulation 9(1))

8. Where the service provider is subject to a code of conduct or is a member of trade association or professional body which provides for a non-judicial dispute resolution procedure, the service provider must:

(a) inform a recipient of the service of that fact; and

(b) mention it in any document providing a detailed description of the service specifying how detailed information about the procedure may be accessed.

(Regulation 10)

9. Where information must be made available or supplied that must be done:

(a) in a clear and unambiguous manner; and

(b) in good time before the conclusion of the contract, or, where there is no written contract, before the service is provided.

(Regulation 11)

10. There is also a specific obligation with regard to complaints. The service provider must:

(a) respond to complaints "as quickly as possible"; and

(b) make "best efforts" to find a satisfactory solution to complaints.

The latter duty does not apply to vexatious complaints.

1 This sub-paragraph of Regulation 8(2) contemplates the provision by the service provider of a detailed written statement of the service to be provided, which in the usual case a barrister is unlikely to do.

2 The meaning of this provision is obscure, but appears to contemplate that a service provider may be involved in other activities which might, unless safeguards are taken, provide an incentive in conflict with the interests of the recipient of the service (e.g. a financial adviser who also acts as an insurance intermediary). A barrister is unlikely to find themselves in that position.

(Regulation 12)[1]

Suggestions to the profession – General

11. The first issue that self-employed barristers and their Chambers will need to address is how to that ensure that information which needs to be "made available" before a contract is concluded or service provided (i.e. within the timescale required by Regulation 11) can best be made available to clients.

12. For most Chambers this will most conveniently be done through the Chambers website. It is however likely that, for most Chambers, rather more information will have to appear on the website than is presently the case. Thus, in addition to details of the Chambers postal address, telephone number, and fax number, it will probably be convenient for websites to include the following:

(a) Each barrister's:

(i) Professional title(s) (barrister, QC, avocat, Rechtanswalt);

(ii) VAT number (see further below); and

(iii) Registered name on the BSB Register.

(b) Statements, either in relation to each barrister, or in relation to all members generally, of:

(i) their legal status (i.e. that they are sole practitioners);

(ii) that they are barristers registered with the Bar Standards Board of England and Wales,

(Those professing foreign qualifications will in addition have to identify their foreign professional titles, the State granting that title and the regulating body in that State.)

(iii) the general terms and conditions on which services are provided;

(iv) any choice of jurisdiction and/or choice of law that the barristers' contracts will create;

(v) that the barristers have professional liability insurance provided by the Bar Mutual Indemnity Fund Limited; contact details for the Bar Mutual; and a statement of the territorial coverage of the Bar Mutual insurance cover held;

(vi) the website address of the Bar Mutual is http://www.barmutual.co.uk/. The postal address of the Bar Mutual Management Company is 90 Fenchurch Street, London EC3M 4ST. Territorial coverage is world-wide, subject to the terms of cover of the Bar Mutual, which may be accessed at http://www.barmutual.co.uk/fileadmin/uploads/barmutual/Bar_Mutual_Terms_of_Cover_01.pdf.;

(vii) those members of Chambers professing foreign qualifications and practising under their foreign professional titles will have to provide equivalent information about any insurance coverage they may be required to have under applicable laws or codes of conduct as foreign lawyers.; and

(viii) that any complaint about a barrister should, in the first instance be, made to the barrister in question or to their Chambers (the Chambers website should specify how/ to whom complaints should be made) – but that if a satisfactory solution to the complaint is not obtained from these sources, that the members are subject to a non-judicial dispute resolution procedure, which may be accessed through the Legal Ombudsman's website at http://www.legalombudsman.org.uk.[2]

1 Cf. BSB Handbook rC99 – rC105.
2 Cf Regulation 10.

13. The provision of individual email addresses and VAT numbers are matters of sensitivity to some barristers.

(a) So far as concerns email addresses, the obligation to make available "details by which the provider can be contacted rapidly and communicated with directly" would plainly be met by giving details of each individual barrister's email address. But this could attract unwanted "spam"; and there is no reason why a central Chambers'/ clerks' email address should not be given on the website, so long as there is in place an efficient system for forwarding emails received at that address to the barrister concerned (or a system by which the clerks make available to a client the barrister's personal email address promptly after instructions are received).

14. It will be for each set of Chambers to decide how they wish to meet the requirement outlined above.

15. It will also be a matter for individual Chambers whether they will wish to provide on their websites the information which they will be required to provide on request (under Regulation 9). Chambers may wish to consider having available on their websites some of this information: e.g.

(a) Indicative hourly rates, and a statement that the members are, as barristers/ QCs, governed by the BSB Handbook; available in

English at the relevant page of the Bar Standards Board's website at https://www.barstandardsboard.org.uk/regulatory-requirements/the-code-of-conduct/handbook/.)

(b) (NB Those professing foreign qualifications will, on request, have to identify their foreign professional codes of conduct, and how/ where those codes may be accessed (e.g. the relevant website address(es)); and the languages in which they are available.)

16. It does not appear practical to include in advance on the website any information about "other activities undertaken by the provider which are directly linked to the service in question and on the measures taken to avoid conflicts of interest", since – in the unlikely event that a barrister does undertake other activities directly linked to his or her provision of advocacy services – any relevant information is likely to be case-specific.

17. Those Chambers and sole practitioners who do not have a website will need to consider how they are to meet the informational requirements of the Regulations. Plainly, it will be necessary to have available a written "Information Sheet" detailing the matters outlined above. Since it may be unpredictable or unclear in a particular case where a barrister's service is provided or where the contract for that service is concluded, it may not be sufficient simply to have that Information Sheet available in Chambers, or at the sole practitioner's practising address. The safest course will be to supply a copy of the Information Sheet spontaneously i.e. "on the provider's own initiative" at first meeting or telephone contact with every professional and lay client (in accordance with Regulation 8(2)(a)); for which purpose a barrister will need to keep copies of the Information Sheet to hand at conferences before court or out of Chambers (as well as in Chambers).

Insurance

18. The requirement to provide information about insurance coverage raises particular sensitivities.

(a) Regulation 8(1)(n) requires that "where the provider is subject to a requirement to hold any professional liability insurance or guarantee" information about the insurance or guarantee must be made available "and in particular (i) the contact details of the insurer or guarantor, and (ii) the territorial coverage of the insurance or guarantee."

(b) The view of the Professional Practice Committee is that this requires the provision of information only about such insurance as is professionally compulsory i.e. the minimum cover which barristers must have as members of the Bar Mutual Indemnity Fund (currently £500,000). There is no requirement to provide information about any additional insurance or additional level of cover that a barrister may have taken out (whether with the Bar Mutual or with other insurers); and indeed there is no requirement to specify the level of cover which is professionally required; though this will be apparent from the Terms of Cover which appear on the Bar Mutual Website.

(c) Those terms of cover provide that territorial coverage is world-wide; albeit that:

(i) the costs of defending a claim brought before a court or tribunal in the United States or Canada are (unlike the costs of defending other claims) included within the limit of indemnity; and

(ii) the award of punitive, exemplary or multiple damages by a court or tribunal in the United States or Canada is excluded from coverage.

The Professional Practice Committee considers that if there is any conceivable possibility that a member of Chambers might be exposed to a claim which could be brought before a court or tribunal in the United States or Canada, recipients of Chambers services should be made aware of the terms of cover by specific reference to the relevant page of the Bar Mutual's website i.e. http://www.barmutual.co.uk/fileadmin/uploads/barmutual/Bar_Mutual_Terms_of_Cover_01.pdf.

(d) Those members of Chambers professing foreign qualifications and practising under their foreign professional titles will have to provide equivalent information about any insurance cover they may be required to have by virtue of their practice as foreign lawyers.

Important notice

This document has been prepared by the Bar Council to assist barristers on matters of professional conduct and ethics. **It is not "guidance" for the purposes of the BSB Handbook I6.4, and neither the BSB nor a disciplinary tribunal nor the Legal Ombudsman is bound by any views or advice expressed in it.** It does not comprise – and cannot be relied on as giving – legal advice. It has been prepared in good faith, but neither the Bar Council nor any of the individuals responsible for or involved in its preparation accept any responsibility or liability for anything done in reliance on it. For fuller information as to the status and effect of this document, please refer to the professional practice and ethics section of the Bar Council's website.

Client Incapacity

[3.238g]

The purpose of this guidance is to draw barristers' attention to issues relating client incapacity. This is a complex area and the guidance helps to distil the essential guidance. It was last updated in February 2014.

Incapacity by reason of lack of mental capacity

1. Counsel should be familiar with the standard texts on the current law and practice relating to:

   1.1 the Mental Capacity Act 2005 and the principles set out therein relating to capacity;

   1.2 a client lacking capacity for the purpose of managing money and property so that his money and property is under the control of the Court of Protection;

   1.3 a client being a "protected party" for the purpose of conducting civil or family proceedings, i.e. lacking capacity (within the meaning of the 2005 Act) to conduct proceedings; see CPR part 21.1 and FPR 2.3. In particular, counsel should be aware of the leading case (as at the date of this guidance) *of Masterman-Lister v Brutton & Co* [2003] EWCA Civ 70, [2003] 1 WLR 1511 which emphasises that:

      1.3.1 there is a presumption of capacity for a person of adult age, but that as a matter of practice the court should investigate the issue where there is any reason to suspect its absence;

      1.3.2 the test of capacity is issue specific. Accordingly, a client may have capacity to conduct relatively simple litigation, but lack the capacity to conduct more complex litigation;

      1.3.3 equally, a client may not lack capacity to pursue or compromise a claim merely because they would be incapable of taking investment decisions in relation to any compensation ultimately received.

   1.4 a client being "unfit to plead" for the purpose of criminal proceedings.

2. Once a legal adviser entertains a reasonable doubt about their client's capacity to give proper instructions, it is that adviser's professional duty to satisfy themselves that the client either has or does not have the capacity to give instructions; see *P (a child) (care and placement order proceedings: mental capacity of parent), Re* [2008] EWCA Civ 462, [2009] LGR 213, [2008] 3 FCR 243.

3. As the law and practice presently stand, the Bar Council suggests barristers might adopt the following approach.

4. If Counsel reasonably suspects that the client is or may be a "protected party" (for any relevant purpose) or "unfit to plead", counsel clearly needs to proceed with great care, in particular since:

4.1 if counsel doubts the client's capacity to give instructions, it follows that counsel cannot be certain that it is proper to act on any instructions which the client may purport to give (although, even where a client definitely lacks the capacity to give instructions, counsel should still seek the client's views and take them into account);

4.2 additionally, where litigation is being privately funded by the client, the propriety of counsel's instructing solicitor accepting funds from the client may be in doubt; and

4.3 moreover, revealing counsel's suspicion that the client lacks capacity to the client may well be perceived as offensive, and revealing the suspicion to the court and any other party may well be unauthorised and/or highly prejudicial.

5. Each case will be different, but the following stage by stage approach is suggested:

5.1 In a case involving an instructing solicitor (or other professional client):

5.1.1 Counsel should discuss the question of the client's capacity with the instructing solicitor (who is likely to have had more contact with the client than counsel has)

5.1.2 if, having done so, counsel still reasonably suspects that the client lacks capacity, then counsel should, if practicable, meet the client, if counsel has not already done so

5.1.3 whether or not counsel meets the client, if counsel's concerns about the client's capacity persist, counsel should ensure that the client is informed of those concerns as tactfully as possible, and that any comments which the client has to make on the issue of capacity are obtained and taken into account.

5.2 In a matter that does not involve a professional client, counsel should, if practicable, meet the client, and follow the approach in paragraph 5.1.3 above. Counsel should also take into account the guidance in the Bar Standards Board's Public Access Guidance for Barristers on identifying and representing vulnerable clients. If, having taken those steps, counsel still reasonably suspects the client lacks capacity, then the appropriate course of action may depend on whether counsel is instructed by a solicitor (or other professional client).

5.3 In a public access case, counsel is likely to be in the position of being unable to act (if instructions have not been accepted), or of being obliged to cease acting. The practical implications of the client's perceived lack of capacity are likely to be such that counsel will have concluded that the case is not suitable for public access, not least because in all the circumstances, it would in any event be in the interests of the client or in the interests of justice for the client to instruct a solicitor or professional client (BSB Handbook rC123); but even if that is not the case, the Bar Council considers that counsel cannot properly accept instructions from a client, or continue to act for a client, whom counsel reasonably perceives to lack capacity, having taken the steps already identified above. However:

5.3.1 In a case involving withdrawal, counsel should bear in mind paragraphs 38 to 44 and 84 of the Bar Standards Board's Public Access Guidance for Barristers, concerning limitations on withdrawal under rule 608(a) of the Code of Conduct (the equivalent BSB Handbook rules are rC123 and rC25-rC26), cases of potential urgency or prejudice to the client, and referrals to solicitors. Whilst the Bar Council is of the view that counsel cannot continue to act for, or take any further steps on behalf of, a client who is believed not to have the capacity to give instructions (which is not a situation catered for in the BSB guidance), counsel may feel that giving assistance along the lines suggested in paragraph 44 of the Public Access Guidance for Barristers may still be appropriate in cases where the client might otherwise be prejudiced, depending on the circumstances. Counsel will in any event be obliged to explain clearly to the client the reasons for withdrawal (BS Handbook rC27.1.b).

5.3.2 Even in a case in which counsel is declining to accept instructions, rather than withdrawing, this does not mean that counsel cannot try to assist the client, perhaps by helping to find a solicitor, or by referring the client to a particular solicitor or to CAFCASS Litigation, either of whom may be better placed to assist the client to find a way forward despite the issue of capacity. Counsel may also assist the client to engage a solicitor with a view to counsel and solicitor taking the steps indicated below, if counsel considers that to be in the client's best interests, and if the client agrees. However, counsel should be wary of those situations in which there may be no time for a client to seek alternative advice, or where delay may prejudice the client's position, in which case the client should be told (i) that counsel considers it to be in the client's best interests to inform the court of counsel's suspicions, and (ii) of the relevant procedure(s) identified in paragraph 11 below. Although this does not involve counsel withdrawing from a case, counsel may still be assisted by referring to paragraphs 43 and 84 of the BSB's Public Access Guidance for Barristers as regards situations of urgency and referrals to solicitors.

5.3.3 In either type of case, counsel is also not prevented from informing the client of the importance of professional assistance, or (where counsel thinks it appropriate) from giving tactful advice about the merits of the client raising the issue of their capacity with a solicitor, or indeed from informing the chosen solicitor of counsel's concerns as to the client's capacity (although counsel should take care not to breach any duty of confidentiality owed to the client when doing so).

5.4 In a case in which counsel is instructed by a solicitor (or other professional client), counsel should advise that evidence about the client's capacity is obtained. Clearly, obtaining the necessary time, funding (particularly if there is doubt about the propriety of relying on private funding from the client), and cooperation from the client, may all be problematic. If an adjournment of a hearing is necessary, counsel will obviously need to be discreet in informing the court and any other party about the reason, but must not be misleading. Circumstances may justify simply saying that counsel and solicitor are in a situation of professional embarrassment which makes it impossible for them to proceed immediately, the nature of which they are not currently at liberty to reveal, and which they need time to resolve.

5.5 Counsel should bear in mind in advising that it may be appropriate for counsel's instructing solicitor to seek advice and/or assistance from the Official Solicitor (or additionally, in family proceedings, CAFCASS Litigation). Evidence about capacity from lay people who know the client well may be useful, although, by its very nature, it may not be independent or disinterested. Evidence from the client's GP may be very helpful, if the client will permit it and the GP knows the client. A report from a suitably qualified Medical Expert, based on an examination of the client, the client's medical records and any of the other evidence obtained, is usually essential. Counsel is entitled to advise the client to cooperate in the obtaining of medical evidence, but is not entitled to insist on the client doing so.

6. If, in the light of such evidence, if any, as can be obtained, counsel still reasonably suspects that the client lacks capacity, counsel should, if practicable, meet the client again, and should, in any event, ensure that any further comments which the client has to make are obtained and taken into account, and should discuss the issue of the client's capacity further with the instructing solicitor.

7. If, having done so, counsel still reasonably suspects that the client lacks capacity, counsel should at this stage advise that the appropriate court be informed of the client's suspected lack of capacity.

8. If this advice is accepted and followed, well and good.

9. If the client rejects this advice but the instructing solicitor nonetheless accepts it, in the Bar Council's view, the court should be informed of the client's suspected lack of capacity (which, in the absence of any special application, will normally mean informing any other party to the proceedings), even if the client purports to forbid this. In the Bar Council's view, this is a situation where counsel's duty to the court overrides the client's purported instructions, even if the client subsequently turns out to have capacity. Disclosure of the client's suspected lack of capacity is necessary for the protection of the client, in case the client lacks capacity, and may be necessary for the protection of counsel and instructing solicitor, since, as pointed out above, if the client lacks capacity to give instructions and/or to authorise private funding, neither counsel nor instructing solicitor can properly act on the basis of the client's instructions and/or any such funding.

10. Once the client's suspected lack of capacity has been disclosed to the court:

10.1 If the client's capacity to conduct civil or family proceedings is in question, that question can be determined by the civil or family court, and, if the client is a "protected party" for that purpose a "litigation friend" can be appointed to conduct the litigation on the client's behalf. Obviously if the court determines that the client has got capacity to conduct the litigation, then counsel must continue with the case

10.2 If the client's capacity to manage any money or property is in question, that question can be determined by the Court of Protection and, if the client is incapable for that purpose, his money and property can be placed under the control of the Court of Protection; or

10.3 If the client's capacity to defend criminal proceedings is in question, the issue of "fitness to plead" can be determined by the criminal court.

11. If, however, both the lay client and instructing solicitor reject counsel's advice that the client's suspected lack of capacity be disclosed to the court, counsel will probably be in such a situation of professional embarrassment that the only proper course will be to withdraw from the case. In that event, counsel will be obliged to explain clearly to the client the reasons for withdrawal (BSB Handbook rC27.1.b).

12. Equally, in the unlikely event that the court refuses to determine the issue of capacity or fitness to plead, and indicates it intends to continue regardless, counsel may have to withdraw from the case, making clear to the court that they cannot act in the absence of proper instructions. It may also be of assistance at this stage to indicate to the court that counsel wishes to contact the Bar Council's ethics hotline to seek advice on their professional obligations.

Incapacity by reason of drink/drugs

(A) Client still capable

13. If a client attends court under the influence of drink or drugs, but counsel reasonably believes that the client is still capable of understanding advice, giving instructions, and following and, if necessary, taking part in the proceedings, counsel's duties are, as always:

13.1 Counsel's overriding duty to the court (BSB Handbook CD1, rC3 and rC4), in particular not to mislead the court; and

13.2 Subject to that, counsel's duty to the client (BSB Handbook CD2 and rC15), which includes to advise the client as to his best interests (which may be to seek an adjournment) but ultimately to follow the client's instructions (which may be to proceed) even if those instructions appear to counsel to be unwise.

(B) Client Incapable

14. If, on the other hand, a client attends court and appears to be so under the influence as to be temporarily incapable of understanding advice, giving the instructions, or following or taking any necessary part in the proceedings:

14.1 In rare cases, where the particular procedure has previously been explained to the client and his instructions taken at a time when he was capable, and the hearing concerned is a formality which follows its predicted course, it may be appropriate for counsel to allow the hearing to proceed.

14.2 But more often, counsel will need to seek an adjournment, since it would be a breach of counsel's duties to the court and to the client to allow the court to proceed on the assumption that the client is capable when in fact he is not. In practice, this is likely to mean that counsel has to make some disclosure of the client's intoxication (in the unlikely event that it is not already apparent to the court).

14.3 Contemporaneous Notes

14.4 As ever in difficult situations, counsel is strongly advised at every stage to make and keep a good contemporaneous note, and to ask any representative of his instructing solicitors to do the same.

Important notice

This document has been prepared by the Bar Council to assist barristers on matters of professional conduct and ethics. **It is not "guidance" for the purposes of the BSB Handbook I6.4, and neither the BSB nor a disciplinary tribunal nor the Legal Ombudsman is bound by any views or advice expressed in it.** It does not comprise – and cannot be relied on as giving – legal advice. It has been prepared in good faith, but neither the Bar Council nor any of the individuals responsible for or involved in its preparation accept any responsibility or liability for anything done in reliance on it. For fuller information as to the status and effect of this document, please refer to the professional practice and ethics section of the Bar Council's website.

Investigating or collecting evidence and taking witness statements

Investigating or collecting evidence

[3.238h]

1. There is no longer a rule which prohibits a self-employed barrister from investigating or collecting evidence generally or therefore from taking statements from potential witnesses (which is treated for these purposes as investigating or collecting evidence). By taking witness statements is meant interviewing the potential witness with a view to preparing a statement or taking a proof of evidence. A barrister has always been entitled to settle a witness statement taken by another person, and this is not investigating or collecting evidence. However, rule 401(b)(iii) provides that a self-employed barrister must not in the course of his practice conduct a case in court if the barrister has previously investigated or collected evidence for that case unless the barrister reasonably believes that the investigation and collection of that evidence is unlikely to be challenged.

2. It follows that if the nature of the evidence or the circumstances in which it was investigated or collected are such that there is likely to be an issue about that in court, where the barrister might be needed to give evidence, the barrister can properly be involved in the preparations for a case but cannot accept a brief to conduct the case in court, even as the junior member of a team of barristers. Only if the barrister reasonably believes that the investigation and collection of that evidence (as distinct from the evidence itself) is unlikely to be challenged can the barrister properly conduct the case in court. Nothing in the rule is intended to apply to the case where a barrister properly accepts a brief and then, as part of his conduct of the case at court, has urgently to take a statement from his client or a potential witness (see rule 707 of the Code). The rule applies where a barrister has investigated or collected evidence before arriving at court at the start of the case.

3. In this regard, barristers should note that rule 401(b)(iii) is in one respect more restrictive in its effect than the previous Written Standards (which are being revised to reflect the new rules) relating to witnesses, which enabled barristers to take witness statements and then act as the junior barrister in the case. The Written Standards stated that it was not appropriate for a witness statement taker "to act as counsel unless he is a junior member of the team of Counsel and will not be examining the witness". The Bar Standards Board considers that it is a key function of a junior member of a team of Counsel that s/he should be in a position to conduct the case in court if and when required, and that it is unacceptable to have briefed as junior counsel in a case someone who may not be in a position to take on the full advocacy role in that case by reason of professional embarrassment should it become necessary. The risks to the client's interests and to the due administration of justice generally are too great to allow a barrister to conduct a case in court, even as a junior in a team of barristers, if there is a real risk that the circumstances of the taking of the evidence that barrister has collected will be challenged in the case. If a junior member of the team is called upon to conduct the case and the circumstances of his investigation and collection of evidence is an issue in the case,, the barrister might have to stand down, damaging the

client's interests (the client having then been deprived of each member of his/her chosen team) and the due administration of justice (through the inconvenience and delay in the conduct of the case).

4. When investigating or collecting evidence, barristers should bear carefully in mind the dangers of unconsciously affecting or contaminating the evidence that a witness is able to give. These are discussed in detail in the Written Standards at paragraphs 6.2.1–6.2.7. Barristers should also be aware of the risks of professional embarrassment as a result of becoming involved in investigating or collecting evidence, and take these risks into account when deciding:

   (a) whether to undertake such work in the first place; and

   (b) if they have done, whether or not they can properly accept a brief at a subsequent trial.

5. The rules place the onus squarely on the barrister who has investigated or collected evidence prior to accepting a brief to consider and reach a reasonable conclusion whether or not his/her involvement is likely to be challenged.

6. In assessing whether to accept a brief in these circumstances, the barrister should be mindful of the dangers of professional embarrassment where s/he has been involved in the collection or investigation of evidence. The barrister's duty is to reach a reasonable decision on the risk of embarrassment before accepting a brief. The brief can only properly be accepted if it is reasonable for the barrister to conclude that the circumstances of his investigation or collection of evidence are unlikely to be challenged. If the barrister's decision is not a reasonable one, and the trial is subsequently adjourned as a result of his professional embarrassment, the barrister risks being exposed to an order for wasted costs as well as prosecution for a breach of the Code.

7. Even where a brief is properly accepted, the question of whether the barrister is professionally embarrassed is a matter that s/he must keep under review during the case in light of any later developments.

8. Investigation or collection of evidence (save for taking proofs of evidence or preparing witness statements urgently as part of the barrister's conduct of the case at court) is not subject to the cab-rank rule: see rule 604(i). If barristers wish to concentrate on advice and advocacy services and do not wish to undertake other types of activity (especially ones which may reduce their opportunity to undertake an advocacy role), that should be their choice and it is in the public interest that they cannot be forced to accept such work.

Conduct of correspondence

9. The extent to which self-employed barristers are permitted to conduct correspondence is addressed in rule 401A of the Code. These provisions are separate from the provisions under the Public Access Rules and apply generally. Conducting correspondence under rule 401A does not extend to the conduct of litigation, as explained by the Court of Appeal in *Agassi v Robinson (Inspector of Taxes) (Bar Council intervening)* [2005] EWCA Civ 1507, [2006] 1 All ER 900, [2006] 1 WLR 2126. Barristers should be mindful of the inherent risks (including of negligence claims) involved in the conduct of correspondence on behalf of lay clients.

10. It will not always be in the best interests of the client for barristers to conduct correspondence. It may be better for the barrister to draft a letter for the solicitor or other professional client to send. There is a danger of confusion where some letters are written by a barrister and some by a solicitor.

11. If the barrister is instructed to write a letter, addressees of letters written by the barrister must be made aware to whom any response should be addressed (and, for example, that it is unnecessary to reply to both the barrister and any solicitor or other professional who is also instructed). The barrister must keep the client and any professional client apprised promptly of any response, and seek further instructions at that juncture.

12. Barristers who become involved in the conduct of correspondence on behalf of lay clients will need to institute appropriate systems to deal promptly with responses and to keep records of the correspondence. Such systems should make provision to cover periods when the barrister is on holiday, or conducting a trial elsewhere, or otherwise unavailable to receive letters.

13. Barristers should consider whether it would be appropriate for them to undertake training in the conduct of inter-partes correspondence before agreeing to enter into any such correspondence.

14. It is also important for barristers embarking on the conduct of correspondence to ensure that, so far as possible, their actions do not create any threat to either their actual or their perceived independence, or any risk of subsequent professional embarrassment. For example, they should not appear personally to endorse statements by clients or witnesses, since that might appear to conflict with arguments or evidence which they subsequently present to the Court.

15. The conduct of correspondence with other parties (save where reasonably necessary as part of the barrister's conduct of the case at court) is not subject to the cab-rank rule: see rule 604(i).

Sharing premises

16. Rule 403.2 permits self-employed barristers to share office facilities and other premises with any person provided that certain conditions are met.

17. The rule relaxes a previous prohibition on the sharing of office facilities and premises with persons other than those specified in rule 403.1. The relaxation is intended to:

    (a) allow barristers to make use of any surplus space and to reduce administrative costs; and

    (b) enable a wider range of services to be provided from the same premises, and provide opportunities for reducing costs.

18. The five conditions in rule 403.2 have been imposed to address and manage risks thought to be engendered by the relaxation of the rule.

19. The first two conditions (that there must be complete separation between the provision of services by the barrister and the services provided by any other person with whom the barrister shares the premises or facilities, and that nothing be done that might reasonably create the impression that there is any sharing of work, income or profits of the businesses) are imposed to prevent informal business sharing arrangements that are not transparently regulated as

such in the public interest, to address the concern that the sharing of facilities might create confusion for the public, and to mitigate the risk of a perception developing that barristers lack independence. These rules are intended to ensure that chambers and individual barristers do not allow clients to be misled into thinking that the barristers have some responsibility for, or endorse, the services provided by others (or vice versa). Barristers must operate independently and must be seen to be operating independently.

20. Thus, whilst barristers might share premises (including conference or meeting rooms), neither the signage at the premises, nor the headed paper used by any of the businesses sharing those premises, nor the marketing or promotional material (including headed paper and website pages) must convey the impression of conducting business in concert or coordination with those with whom the premises are shared.

21. Further, whilst businesses might jointly employ a telephonist, they must have separate telephone numbers, and the greeting deployed by the telephonist must be specific to the business to which any given call is made.

22. The requirement that the barrister has effective arrangements in place to protect the confidentiality of the clients' affairs is regarded as of particular importance where sharing of premises or other facilities is occurring. Those intending to share office space should give careful consideration to the need for separate telephone and computer systems, coded door locks and lockable storage cupboards, and to the identity of those supplied with keys.

23. The prohibition of any general referral arrangement or understanding between the barrister and the person/people with whom they are sharing is intended to ensure that any referrals that do take place must be made at arm's length and in the best interests of the client on a case by case basis. The prohibition is intended to address the concern that barristers might refer work (or might unfairly be perceived as referring work) to others with whom they are sharing for reasons of convenience or financial advantage, rather than because the referral is in the client's best interest. Correspondingly, the sharer might refer clients to the barrister with whom they are sharing for the same reasons. The prohibition of a general referral arrangement or understanding is intended to ensure that referrals are only made on an individual basis, when it is in the client's best interest. A 'general referral arrangement or understanding' means an arrangement or understanding that, as and when the barrister has cause to refer work or certain categories of work to someone in the profession(s) of the person(s) with whom the barrister shares office facilities and other premises, or vice versa, s/he will refer that work (or some of that work) to those with whom s/he shares facilities. What the Code requires is that, on each occasion that it becomes necessary to refer work, careful consideration must be given to the needs of the individual client in question. The barrister must in each case assess the suitability of the person to whom the referral will be made.

24. Rule 403.4 imposes a record keeping requirement which is intended to ensure that the Bar Standards Board is able to monitor the referrals which are made, to ensure that the prohibition is being observed and that it is effective to control the regulatory risks to which sharing gives rise. Records should be kept for at least 6 years. Barristers availing themselves of the opportunity to share office facilities or other premises who make referrals to those with whom they share should note that they may be required to demonstrate the

basis on which any particular referral was made, and that the records maintained should, therefore, include the reasons for the decision to refer a client to the sharer

25. Before a barrister can embark upon a sharing arrangement permitted by rule 403.2, prior notification in writing of the sharing must have been give to the Bar Standards Board. No approval from the Bar Standards Board is required, but the fact that premises and office facilities are being shared will be taken into account by the Bar Standards Board in ascertaining appropriate monitoring programmes to ensure that those sharing facilities abide by the terms of the rule.

Attendance at police stations

26. The previous rules prevented barristers from attending on clients at police stations. That absolute bar has now been removed. Rule 401(b)(iv) provides that a self-employed barrister must not (except as permitted by the Public Access Rules) attend at a police station without the presence of a solicitor to advise a suspect or interviewee as to the handling and conduct of police interviews unless the barrister has complied with such training requirements as may be imposed by the Bar Standards Board in respect of such work. Advising at police stations is specialist work; any barrister who performs such work must complete any relevant training imposed by the Bar Standards Board.

27. Barristers undertaking publicly funded police station work under a criminal contract must comply with the training requirements specified by the Legal Services Commission. Barristers undertaking privately funded police station work must complete the Police Station Qualification ("PSQ") and (if they do not hold higher rights of audience) the Magistrates Court Qualification. If a barrister who wishes to undertake privately funded police station work considers they hold relevant previous experience that would exempt them from completing the PSQ, they should contact the Professional Practice Team at the Bar Standards Board with full details of their previous experience.

28. Rule 401(b)(vi) provides that a self-employed barrister must not (except as permitted by the Public Access Rules) conduct in court any criminal proceedings in which the barrister has attended at a police station for any defendant in connection with those proceedings or any associated proceedings unless the barrister reasonably believes that nothing said, done, heard or seen by the barrister at the police station might require him/her to give evidence in those proceedings.

29. A particular difficulty facing a barrister who attends at a police station to advise suspects and interviewees or to take part in identification procedures is that the barrister may have to advise the client whether or not to answer police questions or to volunteer a statement, or may see or hear something that is material to the evidence that will be presented in court. The client's decision whether or not to answer questions, and if so which, is very likely to be a significant matter in any subsequent court hearing. So might compliance with PACE Codes of interviews or identification procedures that the barrister sees or hears. If these are significant evidential matters at trial, the barrister in question may find him or herself in serious professional difficulties if acting as advocate in the case.

30. Advising a suspect at the police station or attending on his behalf at an interview or identification procedure always gives rise to the risk that you may become a witness at the trial or at a Newton hearing or pre-trial admissibility hearing. The fact of advising a suspect or being present in those circumstances does not of itself prevent you from appearing as an advocate for that defendant in all circumstances. If the defendant you have advised is going to enter a guilty plea which you know to be acceptable to the Crown, or has given a full comment interview which remains as his account, then the degree of risk may be relatively low. But if the defendant declined, on your advice or not, to answer all or any questions in interview (whether or not there was a prepared statement) then the risk of becoming a witness will, inevitably, be too great to allow you to deal with the case at trial or at a Newton hearing or pre-trial admissibility hearing. This guidance applies equally whether you were to appear as an advocate alone or being led or leading (see paragraph 3 above).

31. Given the possibility that you may be required to give evidence of events at the police station, you should keep detailed, contemporaneous notes of those events.

32. For the reasons already discussed in relation to collecting evidence (as to which, see paragraph 8 above), attending at police stations is not subject to the cab rank rule: see rule 604(i).

Bar Standards Board

March 2010

Last reviewed: January 2011

Clash of hearing dates (listings)

[3.238i]

Introduction

1. This guidance provides further explanation of the application of the BSB Handbook in the event that you have a clash of hearing dates (listings).

2. Rule c18 in the BSB Handbook states that your duty to provide a competent standard of work and service to each client (CD7) includes a duty to inform your professional client, or your client if instructed directly by a lay client, as far as reasonably possible in sufficient time to enable appropriate steps to be taken to protect the client's interests, if:

   (a) it becomes apparent to you that you will not be able to carry out the instructions within the time requested, or within a reasonable time after receipt of instructions; or

   (b) there is an appreciable risk that you may not be able to undertake the instructions.

3. Rule c26 states that you may cease to act on a matter on which you are instructed and return your *instructions* if you are a *self-employed barrister* and despite all reasonable efforts to prevent it, a hearing becomes fixed for a date on which you have already entered in your professional diary that you will not be available. This may include a prior arranged hearing relating to another case.

Preventing clashes

4. You should make all reasonable efforts to prevent a clash of dates. This involves communicating effectively with the Court and managing and diarising your cases effectively.

What to do if there is a clash

5. In some instances it may be impossible to prevent a clash of hearing dates. Where there is a clash, you must exercise your professional judgement in deciding which hearing is most important to attend.

6. In addition particular types of hearings may have to take precedence as a matter of law or procedure. You should take direction from the Court and have regard to any relevant case management rules.

7. Where an order of precedence is not clear, you should consider your duty to act in the best interests of each of your clients and, in particular, which of you clients is likely to be most prejudiced by alternative representation being arranged at short notice. You should take particular care to consider the needs of vulnerable clients and the impact of your decision on access to justice.

8. You should consider all the relevant circumstances relating to each case including the following issues:

   (a) the length of time that you have been instructed on each case;

(b) the complexity and difficulty of each case;

(c) the amount of work you have already done on the case;

(d) relevant access to justice considerations and the likely impact on your client.

What to do in respect of the missed hearing

9. You should at all times take reasonable steps to keep all parties concerned informed of any clash of hearing dates. In particular you should ensure that your clients are informed of any clash as soon as possible.

10. You should take all reasonable steps to assist clients to find alternative representation where you are unable to attend a hearing date.

Part B: Good Practice Guidance for Barristers practising Criminal Law

Criminal Law — Good Practice Guidance

[3.239]

For barristers working as prosecution advocates, the CPS has issued guidelines (the "Farquharson Guidelines") on their role and responsibilities, set out below.

Farquharson Guidelines

[3.240]

The Crown Prosecution Service ("CPS") introduced the Farquharson Guidelines on the role and responsibilities of the Prosecution Advocate with effect from 15 February 2002. The Guidelines build on, and develop, the principles established by the Farquharson Committee in 1986 and are intended to provide practical guidance for all prosecutors:

Foreword

The Prosecution Advocate plays an important public role and as such may be considered a cornerstone of an open and fair criminal justice system. The principles so well articulated by Farquharson LJ and his committee as to the role of the prosecution advocate have served us well since they were published in 1986. However, the time has come for new guidance which, whilst building on the established principles, reflects the changes that have occurred in the criminal courts, at the Bar and within The Crown Prosecution Service over recent years. I welcome and commend the new Guidelines which, whilst not legally binding unless expressly approved by the Court of Appeal, nonetheless provide important practical guidance for practitioners involved in the prosecution process.

LORD CHIEF JUSTICE OF ENGLAND AND WALES

Introduction

The work undertaken in 1986 by the committee chaired by Farquharson LJ has, for over 15 years, provided valuable guidance as to role of the prosecution advocate and their relationship with The Crown Prosecution Service ("CPS"). However, the ever-evolving criminal justice system, changes at the Bar and developments in The CPS brought about by the implementation of Sir Iain Glidewell's Review, mean that the environment in which we all operate has radically changed since the original report was published. Whilst the principles established by Farquharson LJ's committee have been enormously helpful and will continue to apply, the time has come for new guidance that reflects the changes and emphasises the new relationship that is developing between CPS Areas and the local Bar. The new Guidelines have therefore been developed to take account of the changes and are the result of the Bar and CPS working in partnership and in consultation with the judiciary, Bar Council and Law Society. We commend the Guidelines as providing valuable guidance and a framework within which the Bar and The CPS can work effectively together.

ATTORNEY GENERAL

DIRECTOR OF PUBLIC PROSECUTIONS

The Role and Responsibilities of the Prosecution Advocate

1. Pre-Trial Preparation

[3.241]

Farquharson

(a) It is the duty of Prosecution Counsel to read the Instructions delivered to him expeditiously and to advise or confer with those instructing him on all aspects of the case well before its commencement.

1.1 The Crown Prosecution Service (CPS) will deliver instructions at a stage in the proceedings that allows sufficient time for the prosecution advocate adequately to consider, prepare and advise on the evidence before the court hearing or draft/agree the indictment.

1.2 Where a CPS Higher Court Advocate represents the prosecution at a Plea and Directions Hearing ("PDH"), The CPS will deliver instructions to the trial advocate no later than 10 working days after the date of the PDH.

1.3 The CPS will deliver instructions which:

- i. address the issues in the case including any strategic decisions that have been or may need to be made;
- ii. identify relevant case law;
- iii. explain the basis and rationale of any decision made in relation to the disclosure of unused material;
- iv. where practical, provide specific guidance or indicate
- v. where a case is an appeal either to the Crown Court from the magistrates' court or is before the Court of Appeal, Divisional Court or House of Lords, address the issues raised in the Notice of Appeal, Case Stated, Application for Judicial Review or Petition.

Action on receipt of instructions

1.4 On receipt of instructions the prosecution advocate will consider the papers and advise The CPS, ordinarily in writing, or orally in cases of urgency where:

- i. the prosecution advocate forms a different view to that expressed by The CPS (or where applicable a previous prosecution advocate) on acceptability of plea;

ii. the indictment as preferred requires amendment;

iii. additional evidence is required;

iv. there is an evidential deficiency (which cannot be addressed by the obtaining of further evidence) and, applying the Code for Crown Prosecutors, there is no longer a realistic prospect of conviction; or the prosecution advocate believes that it is not in the public interest to continue the prosecution;

v. in order to expedite and simplify proceedings certain formal admissions should be made;

vi. the prosecution advocate, having reviewed previous disclosure decisions, disagrees with a decision that has been made; or is not satisfied that he or she is in possession of all relevant documentation; or considers that he or she has not been fully instructed regarding disclosure matters;

vii. a case conference is required (particularly where there is a sensitive issue e.g. informant/PII/disclosure etc); parameters on acceptable plea(s); and

viii. the presentation of the case to the court requires special preparation of material for the jury or presentational aids.

1.5 The prosecution advocate will endeavour to respond within five working days of receiving instructions, or within such period as may be specified or agreed where the case is substantial or the issues complex.

1.6 Where the prosecution advocate is to advise on a specific aspect of the case other than 1.4(i–viii), the advocate should contact The CPS and agree a realistic timescale within which advice is to be provided.

1.7 The prosecution advocate will inform The CPS without delay where the advocate is unlikely to be available to undertake the prosecution or advise within the relevant timescale.

1.8 When returning a brief, the advocate originally instructed must ensure that the case is in good order and should discuss outstanding issues or potential difficulties with the advocate receiving the brief. Where the newly instructed advocate disagrees with a decision or opinion reached by the original advocate, The CPS should be informed so that the matter can be discussed.

Case summaries

1.9 When a draft case summary is prepared by The CPS, the prosecution advocate will consider the summary and either agree the contents or advise The CPS of any proposed amendment.

1.10 In cases where the prosecution advocate is instructed to settle the case summary or schedules, the document(s) will be prepared and submitted to The CPS without delay.

Case Management Plan

1.11 On receipt of a Case Management Plan the prosecution advocate, having considered the papers, will contact the Crown Prosecutor within seven days, or such period as may be specified or agreed where the case is substantial or the issues complex, to discuss and agree the plan. The plan will be maintained and regularly reviewed to reflect the progress of the case.

Keeping the prosecution advocate informed

1.12 The CPS will inform the prosecution advocate of developments in the case without delay and, where a decision is required which may materially affect the conduct and presentation of the case, will consult with the prosecution advocate prior to that decision.

1.13 Where The CPS is advised by the defence of a plea(s) of guilty or there are developments which suggest that offering no evidence on an indictment or count therein is an appropriate course, the matter should always be discussed with the prosecution advocate without delay unless to do so would be wholly impracticable.

Victims and witnesses

1.14 When a decision whether or not to prosecute is based on the public interest, The CPS will always consider the consequences of that decision for the victim and will take into account any views expressed by the victim or the victim's family.

1.15 The prosecution advocate will follow agreed procedures and guidance on the care and treatment of victims and witnesses, particularly those who may be vulnerable or have special needs.

Appeals

1.16 Where the prosecution advocate forms a different view to that expressed by The CPS on the conduct/approach to the appeal, the advocate should advise The CPS within FIVE working days of receiving instructions or such period as may be specified or agreed where the case is substantial or the issues complex.

PDH and other preliminary hearings

1.17 The principles and procedures applying to trials as set out in the following paragraphs will be equally applicable where the prosecution advocate is conducting a PDH or other preliminary hearing.

2. Withdrawal of Instructions

[3.242]

Farquharson

(b) A solicitor who has briefed Counsel to prosecute may withdraw his instructions before the commencement of the trial up to the point when it becomes impracticable to do so, if he disagrees with the advice given by Counsel or for any other proper professional reason.

2.1 The CPS will consult and take all reasonable steps to resolve any issue or disagreement and will only consider withdrawing instructions from a prosecution advocate as a last resort.

2.2 If the prosecution advocate disagrees with any part of his or her instructions, the advocate should contact the responsible Crown Prosecutor to discuss the matter. Until the disagreement has been resolved the matter will remain confidential and must not be discussed by the prosecution advocate with any other party to the proceedings.

"Proper Professional Reason"

2.3 The prosecution advocate will keep The CPS informed of any personal concerns, reservations or ethical issues that the advocate considers have the potential to lead to possible conflict with his or her instructions.

2.4 Where The CPS identifies the potential for professional embarrassment or has concerns about the prosecution advocate's ability or experience to present the case effectively to the court, The CPS reserves the right to withdraw instructions.

Timing

2.5 It is often difficult to define when, in the course of a prosecution, it becomes impracticable to withdraw instructions as circumstances will vary according to the case. The nature of the case, its complexity, witness availability and the view of the court will often be factors that will influence the decision.

2.6 In the majority of prosecutions it will not be practicable to withdraw instructions once the judge has called the case before the court as a preliminary step to the swearing of the jury.

2.7 If instructions are withdrawn, the prosecution advocate will be informed in writing and reasons will be given.

2.8 Instructions may only be withdrawn by or with the consent of the Chief Crown Prosecutor, Assistant Chief Crown Prosecutor, Head of a CPS Trials Unit or, in appropriate cases, Head of a CPS Criminal Justice Unit.

2.9 In relation to cases prosecuted by The CPS Casework Directorate, the decision may only be taken by the Director Casework or Head of Division.

3. Presentation and Conduct

[3.243]

Farquharson

(c) While he remains instructed it is for Counsel to take all necessary decisions in the presentation and general conduct of the prosecution.

3.1 The statement at 3(c) applies when the prosecution advocate is conducting the trial, PDH or any other preliminary hearing, but is subject to the principles and procedures relating to matters of policy set out in section 4 below.

Disclosure of material

3.2 Until the conclusion of the trial the prosecution advocate and CPS have a continuing duty to keep under review decisions regarding disclosure. The prosecution advocate should in every case specifically consider whether he or she can satisfactorily discharge the duty of continuing review on the basis of the material supplied already, or whether it is necessary to inspect further material or to reconsider material already inspected.

3.3 Disclosure of material must always follow the established law and procedure. Unless consultation is impracticable or cannot be achieved without a delay to the hearing, it is desirable that The CPS and, where appropriate, the disclosure officer are consulted over disclosure decisions.

4. Policy Decisions

[3.244]

Farquharson

(d) Where matters of policy[1] fall to be decided after the point indicated in (b) above (including offering no evidence on the indictment or on a particular count, or on the acceptance of pleas to lesser counts), it is the duty of Counsel to consult his Instructing Solicitor/Crown Prosecutor whose views at this stage are of crucial importance.

(e) In the rare case where Counsel and his Instructing Solicitor are unable to agree on a matter of policy, it is, subject to (g) below, for Prosecution Counsel to make the necessary decisions.

Policy issues arising at trial

4.1 The prosecution advocate should alert The CPS at the first opportunity if a matter of policy is likely to arise.

4.2 The prosecution advocate must not give an indication or undertaking which binds the prosecution without first discussing the issue with The CPS.

1 "policy" decisions should be understood as referring to non-evidential decisions on: the acceptance of pleas of guilty to lesser counts or groups of counts or available alternatives: offering no evidence on particular counts; consideration of a re-trial; whether to lodge an appeal; certification of a point of law; and the withdrawal of the prosecution as a whole.

CPS representation at Crown Court

4.3 Whenever possible, an experienced Crown Prosecutor will be available at the Crown Court to discuss and agree any issue involving the conduct or progress of the case.

4.4 When it is not possible to provide a Crown Prosecutor at court, an experienced caseworker will attend and facilitate communication between the prosecution advocate and the Crown Prosecutor having responsibility for the case.

4.5 In exceptional circumstances where it is not possible to contact a Crown Prosecutor, the prosecution advocate should ask the court to adjourn the hearing for a realistic period in order to consult with The CPS. Where an adjournment is refused, the prosecution advocate may make the decision but should record his or her reasons in writing.

Referral to senior CPS representative

4.6 Where an issue remains unresolved following consultation with a Crown Prosecutor; or where the case/issue under consideration is substantial, sensitive or complex; or the prosecution advocate disagrees with the advice of the Crown Prosecutor, the matter may be referred to the Chief Crown Prosecutor, the Director Casework or to a senior Crown Prosecutor with delegated authority to act on their behalf.

4.7 In order to ensure consultation takes place at the highest level appropriate to the circumstances and nature of the case, the court should be asked to adjourn if necessary. When an adjournment is sought, the facts leading to the application should be placed before the court only in so far as they are relevant to that application.

4.8 Where a Chief Crown Prosecutor has been directly involved in the decision making process and the issue remains unresolved, the matter may be referred to the Director of Public Prosecutions.

Farquharson

(f) Where Counsel has taken a decision on a matter of policy with which his Instructing Solicitor has not agreed, then it would be appropriate for the Attorney General to require Counsel to submit to him a written report of all the circumstances, including his reasons for disagreeing with those who instruct him.

4.9 It will only be in exceptional circumstances that the Attorney General will require a written report. The prosecution advocate will first discuss the decision with the Chief Crown Prosecutor or the Director, Casework. Where, by agreement, the issue remains one that either party considers should be drawn to the attention of the Director of Public Prosecutions the prosecution advocate will, on request, provide a written report for submission to the Director of Public Prosecutions. If he considers it appropriate to do so, the Director of Public Prosecutions may refer the matter to the Attorney General.

4.10 Where there has been a disagreement on a matter of policy, provided that The CPS is satisfied that the prosecution advocate followed the principles set out in this document, the professional codes of conduct and was not Wednesbury unreasonable, The CPS will not apply sanctions in respect of any future work solely as a result of the decision in a particular case.

5. Change of Advice

[3.245]

Farquharson

(g) When Counsel has had the opportunity to prepare his brief and to confer with those instructing him, but at the last moment before trial unexpectedly advises that the case should not proceed or that pleas to lesser offences should be accepted, and his Instructing Solicitor does not accept such advice, Counsel should apply for an adjournment if instructed so to do.

5.1 The CPS and the prosecution advocate should agree a period of adjournment that would allow a newly instructed advocate to prepare for trial. The period should be realistic and acknowledge that in such circumstances a case conference will usually be required.

5.2 The facts leading to the application for the adjournment should be placed before the court only in so far as they are relevant to that application.

6. Prosecution Advocate's Role in Decision Making at Trial

[3.246]

Farquharson

(h) Subject to the above, it is for Prosecution Counsel to decide whether to offer no evidence on a particular count or on the indictment as a whole and whether to accept pleas to a lesser count or counts.

6.1 The prosecution advocate may ask the defence advocate whether a plea will be forthcoming but at this initial stage should not suggest or indicate a plea that might be considered acceptable to the prosecution before a plea is offered.

6.2 Where the defence advocate subsequently offers details of a plea, the prosecution advocate may discuss the matter with a view to establishing an acceptable plea that reflects the defendant's criminality and provides the court with sufficient powers to sentence appropriately.

Responsibility of prosecution advocate to consult

6.3 Where the prosecution advocate forms the view that the appropriate course is to accept a plea before proceedings commence or continue, or to offer no evidence on the indictment or any part of it, the prosecution advocate should:

i. whenever practicable, speak with the victim or victim's family attending court to explain the position;

ii. ensure that the interests of the victim or any views expressed by the victim or victim's family are taken into account as part of the decision making process; and

iii. keep the victim or victim's family attending court informed and explain decisions as they are made.

6.4 Where appropriate, the prosecution advocate may seek an adjournment of the court hearing in order to facilitate discussion with the victim or victim's family.

6.5 The prosecution advocate should always comply with paragraph 6.3 and, where practicable, discuss the matter with The CPS before informing the defence advocate or the court that a plea is acceptable.

6.6 Where the defendant indicates an acceptable plea, unless the issue is simple, the defence should reduce the basis of the plea writing. The prosecution advocate should show The CPS any written record relating to the plea and agree with The CPS the basis on which the case will be opened to the court.

6.7 It is the responsibility of the prosecution advocate to ensure that the defence advocate is aware of the basis on which the plea is accepted by the prosecution and the way in which the prosecution case will be opened to the court.

6.8 It will not be necessary for the prosecution advocate to consult The CPS where the plea or course of action accords with the written instructions received from The CPS, although paragraph 6.3 may still apply.

Prosecution advocate's role in sentencing

6.9 The prosecution advocate should always draw the court's attention to any matters, including aggravating or mitigating features, that might affect sentence. Additionally, the advocate should be in a position to assist the court, if requested, with any statutory provisions or sentencing guidelines and should always draw attention to potential sentencing errors.

6.10 Where a discussion on plea and sentence takes place, the prosecution advocate must adhere to the Attorney General's Guidelines on The Acceptance of Pleas published on 7 December 2000.

7. Seeking Judicial Approval

[3.247]

Farquharson

(i) If Prosecution Counsel invites the Judge to approve the course he is proposing to take, then he must abide by the Judge's decision.

7.1 A discussion with the judge about the acceptability of a plea or conduct of the case should be held in the presence of the defendant unless exceptional circumstances[1] apply.

7.2 In exceptional circumstances, where the prosecution advocate considers it appropriate to communicate with the judge or seek the judge's view in chambers, The CPS should be consulted before such a step is taken.

7.3 Where discussions take place in chambers it is the responsibility of the prosecution advocate to remind the judge, if necessary, that an independent record must always be kept.

7.4 The prosecution advocate should also make a full note of such an event, recording all decisions and comments. This note should be made available to The CPS.

1 For the purposes of these guidelines, "exceptional circumstances" would include the following:

i. Where there is material or information which should not be made public, e.g. a police text, or for some other compelling reason such as a defendant or witness suffering, unknown to them, from a serious or terminal illness; or

ii. There are sensitivities surrounding a prosecution decision or proposed action which need to be explained in chambers with a view to obtaining judicial approval. Such approval may be given in open court where it is necessary to explain a prosecution decision or action in order to maintain public confidence in the criminal justice system.

Farquharson

(j) If Prosecution Counsel does not invite the Judge's approval of his decision it is open to the Judge to express his dissent with the course proposed and invite Counsel to reconsider the matter with those instructing him, but having done so, the final decision remains with Counsel.

7.5 Where a judge expresses a view based on the evidence or public interest, The CPS will carry out a further review of the case.

7.6 The prosecution advocate will inform The CPS in a case where the judge has expressed a dissenting view and will agree the action to be taken. Where there is no CPS representative at court, the prosecution advocate will provide a note of the judge's comments.

7.7 The prosecution advocate will ensure that the judge is aware of all factors that have a bearing on the prosecution decision to adopt a particular course. Where there is a difference of opinion between the prosecution advocate and The CPS the judge will be informed as to the nature of the disagreement.

Farquharson

(k) In an extreme case where the Judge is of the opinion that the course proposed by Counsel would lead to serious injustice, he may decline to proceed with the case until Counsel has consulted with either the Director or the Attorney General as may be appropriate.

7.8 As a preliminary step, the prosecution advocate will discuss the judge's observations with the Chief Crown Prosecutor in an attempt to resolve the issue. Where the issue remains unresolved the Director of Public Prosecutions will be consulted. In exceptional circumstances the Director of Public Prosecutions may consult the Attorney General.

These Guidelines are subject to the Code of Conduct of the Bar of England and Wales (barrister advocates) and The Law Society's The Guide to the Professional Conduct of Solicitors (solicitor advocates). Whilst reference is made in the guidelines to The CPS and levels of authority within the Service, the guidelines may be adopted as best practice, with consequential amendments to levels of authority, by other prosecuting authorities.

Refusing work on the basis of fees

[3.247a]

Guidance has been issued by the Professional Practice Committee to draw barristers' attention to issues relaing to refusal of work by members of the criminal Bar on grounds relating to fees. The guidance was received in January 2014 and is set out below.

General approach

1. If you are a self-employed barrister, then the "Cab-rank" rule (BSB Handbook rC29) obliges you to accept instructions if they are appropriate taking into account your experience, seniority and field of practice, subject to the exceptions in the BSB Handbook rC30.

2. Accordingly, unless one of the exceptions in the BSB Handbook rC30 applies, you must accept instructions if the BSB Handbook rC29 requires you to do so.

3. Similarly, the BSB Handbook rC28 requires you not to withhold services or permit your services to be withheld (e.g. by your clerk) on various grounds relating to the nature of the case, the client or the source of financial support. As regards the last of those grounds, the BSB Handbook rC28.3 prohibits you from doing this on any ground relating to the source of any financial support which may properly be given to the prospective client for the proceedings in question, and the BSB Handbook gC88 makes clear that this includes a refusal on the ground that support may be given to the prospective client as part of the Community Legal Service or Criminal Defence Service.

4. One of the exceptions to the Cab Rank rule is where you have not been offered a proper fee for the required services (BSB Handbook rC30.8), although this exception does not apply if you have not made or responded to any fee proposal within a reasonable time after receiving the instructions. A prompt decision is necessary.

5. The BSB Handbook gC90 provides that, in determining whether or not a fee is proper for the purposes of the BSB Handbook rC30.2, regard shall be had to the following:

   (a) the complexity, length and difficulty of the case;

   (b) your ability, experience and seniority; and

   (c) the expenses which you will incur.

6. With effect from 6th January 2014, the BSB Handbook no longer deems any fee to be, or not to be, a proper fee.

7. In deciding in any particular case whether a fee is 'proper', you must consider two questions:

   (a) whether you in good faith regards the fee as proper; and

(b) if in good faith you do not regard the fee as proper, whether you are acting reasonably and justifiably in reaching that decision.

8. Whether a fee is proper will vary from case to case.

9. If you are considering refusing instructions in a type of case for which the fees payable have actually been reduced since you last accepted a case of that type, then you are unlikely to be vulnerable without more to an allegation that you are in breach of the BSB Handbook in declining affected work after that date. But you will need to consider whether the reduced fees are proper fees.

10. On the other hand, if you are considering refusing instructions in a type of case for which the fees payable have not been reduced since you last accepted a case of that type, then it will obviously be less easy to demonstrate that an unreduced fee is not a proper fee. The tests set out above must be applied carefully in each case before you make a decision to refuse such work in any particular case.

Return of instructions/brief that you have already accepted where fees are later reduced

11. Where you have already accepted a brief or instructions, and the fee rates payable to you are reduced subsequently, then you will need to consider BSB Handbook rC26 to rC28. These lay down when you can, and when you cannot, return instructions which have already been accepted. More widely, in deciding what approach to take, you will need to focus on the BSB Handbook CD1 (duty to the court in the administration of justice), CD3 (to act with honesty and integrity) and CD5 (not behaving in a way which is likely to diminish the trust and confidence which the public places in you or in the profession).

12. If what has happened is that the basis on which you are to be paid has been changed fundamentally since you accepted the instructions, then the BSB Handbook gC87 will be of particular relevance. This provides as follows:

"If a fundamental change is made to the basis of your remuneration, you should treat such a change as though your original instructions have been withdrawn by the client and replaced by an offer of new instructions on different terms."

13. The BSB Handbook gC87.1–87.3 goes on to explain that you must then judge the offer of new instructions afresh in accordance with the BSB Handbook. Thus, if the fee is not a proper fee for the purposes of the BSB Handbook rC30.8 (as explained above), then you may decline to accept the brief, subject to the qualification identified in paragraphs 15 to 18 below.

14. The BSB Handbook gC87.4 also states that in declining to accept the 'new' instructions in those circumstances, you will not be regarded as returning the instructions, as withdrawing from the case, or as ceasing to act, for the purposes of the BSB Handbook rC25 and rC26 (the rules ordinarily governing such matters). It explains that this is because the previous instructions have been withdrawn by the client.

Qualifications on the current BSB guidance

15. Although paragraphs 11 to 14 above reflect the existing guidance in the BSB Handbook, they now need to be qualified.

16. In its policy statement published on 25 November 2013 in relation to Very High Cost Cases in crime, the Bar Standards Board said this, with reference to the guidance on which those paragraphs are based:

> "... the BSB is minded to review this guidance, in order to ensure that the public interest is adequately protected in circumstances where the person whom the barrister represents is not himself responsible for adversely altering the basis of the barrister's engagement and where exercising any right to withdraw would be disproportionate in view of the degree of prejudice to that person and/or to the administration of justice.
>
> In particular, it will be clear from the discussion of the BSB's approach to VHCCs, above, that a critical element is the fact that transitional arrangements are in place which protect the interests of consumers and the administration of justice. In relation to other types of legally aided cases, where no such transitional arrangements have been proposed, there will be a risk to consumers and the administration of justice if barristers were to treat themselves as free to withdraw from an ongoing case regardless of how serious and disruptive the consequences may be for the client and for others involved in the trial, for example, withdrawing mid-trial. The BSB believes that it may be in the public interest to require barristers in these situations to consider a number of factors and assess the proportionality of ceasing to act, in order to protect the interests of consumers and the wider regulatory objectives. The BSB is therefore urgently considering revised guidance on the rules relating to withdrawal of instructions, clarifying the relationship of those rules to the rules defining a barrister's obligations to the client and the court. In the meantime, barristers are reminded that they must reconcile any right to withdraw, because of a change in terms effected by the Ministry of Justice, with their professional obligations towards the individual whom they represent, who is not responsible for that change. The BSB will consult fully in the New Year on the updated guidance. That consultation will not take place until after the launch of the new Handbook on 6 January."

17. The Bar Council will respond to any such consultation; but in the meantime, you should take account of this statement by the BSB, particularly the passage we have underlined, in considering what the Core Duties require of you, and in reaching any decision to return instructions in a situation to which the statement applies.

18. If and when any revised guidance is published by the BSB, then that will supersede the current guidance, and paragraphs 12 to 14 above may no longer be accurate.

The position of pupils and pupil supervisors

19. In the context of the above guidance, you are reminded that:

    (a) A barrister who is a pupil supervisor with a pupil must not allow any decisions with regard to the acceptance of new instructions to affect or disrupt the pupillage training which the pupil supervisor is obliged to give.

(b) Whatever decisions may be taken, the pupil supervisor remains under an obligation to ensure that the pupil receives the required training so that the pupil can in turn apply themselves diligently to the pupillage and properly complete the checklist and of course the pupillage.

(c) Similarly, all members of Chambers will be obliged to ensure that, if any pupil supervisor in chambers makes a decision to refuse work, arrangements are in place which allow pupils to be properly trained. This flows from the obligation on all members of Chambers to take reasonable steps to ensure that proper arrangements are made in their Chambers for dealing with pupils and pupillage (BSB Handbook rC89.4). The steps required by each member of Chambers will depend on the circumstances, including the internal arrangements within Chambers (BSB Handbook rC90). You should also note that one of the outcomes provided for under the Code is that all pupils must be treated fairly (oC29).

(d) Pupils have a legitimate right to proper training irrespective of any such decisions which a pupil supervisor may take, and that right should be fully recognised and respected, regardless of any steps which may be taken over the acceptance or refusal of work.

20. The respective duties of pupils and pupil supervisors are set out in the BSB Handbook rQ38 and rQ54 respectively.

Important notice

This document has been prepared by the Bar Council to assist barristers on matters of professional conduct and ethics. **It is not "guidance" for the purposes of the BSB Handbook I6.4, and neither the BSB nor a disciplinary tribunal nor the Legal Ombudsman is bound by any views or advice expressed in it.** It does not comprise – and cannot be relied on as giving – legal advice. It has been prepared in good faith, but neither the Bar Council nor any of the individuals responsible for or involved in its preparation accept any responsibility or liability for anything done in reliance on it. For fuller information as to the status and effect of this document, please refer to the professional practice and ethics section of the Bar Council's website.

Public Interest Immunity ("PII") Hearings and Disclosure

[3.248]

Specific issues arise for counsel conducting Professional Interest and Immunity (PII) Hearings and disclosure. Guidance developed by the Standards Committee, following consultation with the Criminal Bar Association and the Circuits, is set out below. The guidance was reissued in January 2014.

General approach

1. The Bar Council has issued ethical assistance on the appropriate conduct for barristers acting in cases where they are invited to consider material on the basis that they undertake not to disclose it to their defendant client. The Bar Council consulted the Criminal Bar Association and the Circuits on this point.
2. It is noted first that neither the law nor the BSB Handbook recognised any concept of "counsel to counsel" confidentiality and that when told something on this basis which would be to his client's advantage, you should inform your client and use it.
3. The BSB Handbook CD2, CD3, CD7 are the relevant references when approached on this basis. Failure to disclose material to a client could cause serious difficulties including an inability to take the lay client's instructions on the material, almost impossible difficulties in deciding how to conduct the defence in the client's best interests and generally a risk that disparity could develop in the practice of disclosure between counsel.
4. These disadvantages appeared to override any very rare advantages that might result of such a practice. You should not agree to proceed on this basis and support the direction in the Attorney General's guidelines that the practice of counsel to counsel disclosure should cease: it is inconsistent with the requirement of transparency in the prosecution process.

Important notice

This document has been prepared by the Bar Council to assist barristers on matters of professional conduct and ethics. **It is not "guidance" for the purposes of the BSB Handbook I6.4, and neither the BSB nor a disciplinary tribunal nor the Legal Ombudsman is bound by any views or advice expressed in it.** It does not comprise – and cannot be relied on as giving – legal advice. It has been prepared in good faith, but neither the Bar Council nor any of the individuals responsible for or involved in its preparation accept any responsibility or liability for anything done in reliance on it. For fuller information as to the status and effect of this document, please refer to the professional practice and ethics section of the Bar Council's website.

Guidance on the Money Laundering Regulations

Guidance on the Money Laundering Regulations 2007

[3.249]–[3.261]

At the time of going to print the Bar Council guidance on Money Laundering is currently being revised. The Bar Council recommends practitioners refer to the guidance published by the Chancery Bar Association, prepared for the Chancery Bar Association by Paul Marshall, No5 Chambers.

The link is http://www.chba.org.uk/for-members/library/professional-guidance.

Amended Guidance on the Proceeds of Crime Act

Proceeds of Crime

[3.262]

Following a notable Court of Appeal case (*Bowman v Fels*) affecting the circumstances for disclosure, in 2005 the Bar Council issued guidance in relation to the Proceeds of Crime Act 2002. In January 2008, this guidance was updated and is set out below:

This guidance supersedes all previous guidance on the Proceeds of Crime Act 2002. Guidance on the Money Laundering Regulations 2007 has already been published and should be read by all whose practice may bring them within the regulated sector. None of the guidance is a substitute for the relevant legislation:–

Proceeds of Crime Act 2002, as amended. Most recently schedule 9 of the Proceeds of Crime Act 2002 has been amended by the Proceeds of Crime Act 2002 (Business in the Regulated Sector and supervisory Authorities) Order 2007 which came into force on 15th December 2007 and by the Terrorism Act 2000 and the Proceeds of Crime Act 2002 (Amendment) regulations 2007 which came into force on 26th December 2007.

The Money Laundering Regulations 2007 which came into force on 15th December 2007.

See also the decision of the Court of Appeal in *Bowman v Fels* [2005] EWCA Civ 226, [2005] 4 All ER 609, [2005] 1 WLR 3083.

You may also wish to read the relevant EU directives.

The website of the Serious and Organised Crime Agency is useful www.soca.gov.uk

PART III
IN PRACTICE

Introduction

[3.263]

1. Money Laundering is now a familiar concept. It is the process whereby assets which are the proceeds of crime and the true ownership of those proceeds are changed or disguised so that they appear to come from a legitimate source.

Part 7 of POCA

[3.264]

2. Part 7 of POCA may affect members of the Bar. The main offences are set out in sections 328 and 330. The old section 333 (Tipping Off offence) has been repealed and replaced by sections 333A to 333D. These new sections

apply **only** to the regulated sector but are broader in scope than the old section 333 (see below under Regulated Sector). Section 342 remains in force.

Section 328

[3.265]

3. By section 328(1) a person commits an offence if he enters into or becomes concerned in an arrangement which he knows or suspects facilitates (by whatever means) the acquisition, retention, use or control of criminal property by or on behalf of another person.

4. Criminal Property is defined at section 340(3). It is a wide definition. Property is criminal property if

(a) it constitutes a person's benefit from criminal conduct or represents such benefit (in whole or part and whether directly or indirectly), and

(b) the alleged offender knows or suspects that it constitutes or represents such a benefit.

For example property that represents the benefit of the non payment of tax constitutes criminal property for the purposes of the Act.

5. Section 328(2) provides defences. By Section 328(2)(a) a person does not commit an offence if he makes an authorised disclosure under section 338 and (if the disclosure is made before he does the act mentioned in subsection (1) he has the appropriate consent.

Disclosure is considered at paragraphs below.

6. There is no definition of what constitutes becoming "concerned in an arrangement" for the purposes of section 328. The decision in *Bowman v Fels* is extremely helpful in this regard. The Court of Appeal held that;

(i) Section 328 does not extend to the involvement of a barrister in the ordinary conduct of litigation or its consensual resolution; and

(ii) even if it did the section would be subject to a full saving for common law legal professional privilege (LPP) notwithstanding the absence of any express statutory saving for LPP in that section.

7. In the light of the decision in *Bowman v Fels* [2005] EWCA Civ 226, [2005] 4 All ER 609, [2005] 1 WLR 3083 a barrister will only fall within the ambit of section 328 if he is not involved in the ordinary conduct of litigation (see paragraph 83) but in the extraordinary conduct of litigation. Although the Court of Appeal nowhere sets out what it has in mind by the extraordinary conduct of litigation, the Bar Council submissions had put forward an example of bogus or sham litigation, where the barrister instructed came to suspect that there was no genuine dispute between the parties, but a dispute concocted as a cover for the transfer of ill gotten gains; and this seems to be reflected in other passages of the judgment (see for example paragraph 101). Clearly such cases will be extremely rare. When they do arise barristers must consider carefully whether an authorised disclosure should be made, so as to avoid committing a section 328 offence.

Disclosure and consent

[3.266]

8. Section 328(2) provides that a person does not commit an offence if he makes an authorised disclosure under section 338 and (if the disclosure is made before he does the act mentioned in subsection (1)) he has the appropriate consent. Thus where a member of the Bar is instructed to advise or appear in court in circumstances where he might commit a section 328 offence (for example because he suspects the litigation is a sham or because he is being asked to provide advice which he foresees may be used for money laundering purposes) he must consider whether he should make a disclosure before continuing to act.

9. Where the barrister considers that he should make a disclosure in order to continue to act without committing a criminal offence (and his solicitor has not already done so) then (subject to his assessment of the impact of sections 333 (as amended) and 342 he should inform his solicitor and his client that he must make a disclosure to a constable, customs officer or SOCA (in practice, usually SOCA) and seek consent before continuing to act. He should also inform his solicitor and his client that in order for them to proceed without committing a criminal offence they too should seek consent from SOCA. The solicitor (who is subject to the same regulation as the barrister) will almost certainly support the barrister in making disclosure, and advising the client of the wisdom of doing so. Thereafter events will take one of three courses:–

   a) The client objects to this course of action, in which case he will no doubt withdraw his instructions. If he does so there is no difficulty and there is no need for the barrister to make a disclosure under section 328 (although a duty may still arise under section 330, subject to the LPP defence, see below).

   b) If the client objects to the report and does not withdraw instructions, the barrister should withdraw from the case to avoid committing the offence. Having withdrawn, there is no duty upon the barrister under section 328 to make a disclosure (although a duty may still arise under section 330, subject to the LPP defence).

   c) If the client agrees to the proposed course of action, the barrister makes disclosure to SOCA and seeks consent. The barrister should consider (and advise his client in this regard) whether he should make a disclosure jointly with his solicitor and/or his client. If the client makes a report, he also has the protection of the defence. In practical terms it may well be the case that the disclosure is made jointly by barrister, solicitor and client.

10. A disclosure report must be made in writing. The report can be downloaded from www.soca.gov.uk. Consent may be express or deemed. SOCA has 7 working days (the notice period) within which to notify the person making the disclosure of its consent/refusal, starting with the first working day after the person makes disclosure. If no notice is received from SOCA during the notice period a person is deemed to have appropriate consent. If a notice of refusal is served on the person making disclosure there is then a moratorium

period (31 days starting with the day on which the person receives notice of refusal). At the expiry of that period the person is deemed to have consent.

Regulated Sector

[3.267]

11. The definition has been amended and is set out in the new schedule 9. It is consistent with the definition within the Money Laundering Regulations 2007.

Subparagraphs 1(m) and (n) are most likely to be relevant to some barristers;

"1. A business is in the regulated sector to the extent that it consists of ...

...

m) the provision of advice about the tax affairs of other persons by ... a sole practitioner ... who by way of business provides advice about the tax affairs of other persons

n) the participation in financial or real property transactions concerning

i) the buying and selling of real property ... or business entities

v) the creation operation or management of trusts, companies or similar structures

by ... a sole practitioner who by way of business provides legal or notarial services to other persons".

12. As set out above it is implicit in the Court of Appeal's reasoning in *Bowman v Fels* [2005] EWCA Civ 226, [2005] 4 All ER 609, [2005] 1 WLR 3083 that a barrister involved in the ordinary conduct of litigation or its consensual resolution does not fall within the regulated sector (see in particular paragraphs 58–62 and paragraph 99). A barrister will fall within the regulated sector if he is undertaking non contentious advisory or transactional work of the type set out in paragraph 1 above. A barrister within the regulated sector must comply with sections 330 and 333A and with the Money Laundering Regulations 2007.

13.

"**1. Section 330**

By section 330 a person in the regulated sector commits an offence if four conditions are satisfied.

a) That he

i) knows or suspects, or

ii) has reasonable grounds for knowing or suspecting, that another person is engaged in money laundering.

b) that the information or other matter

i) on which his/her knowledge or suspicion is based, or

ii) which gives reasonable grounds for such knowledge or suspicion came to him in the course of a business in the regulated sector

c) that he

i) can identify the other person engaged in money laundering or the whereabouts of any of the laundered property, or

ii) he believes, or it is reasonable to expect him/her to believe, that the information or other matter mentioned above will or may assist in identifying that other person or the whereabouts of any of the laundered property

d) that he does not make the required disclosure to the appropriate recipients as soon as is practicable after the information or other matter came to him"

14. **Section 330 and Legal Professional Privilege**

There is, however, an express statutory saving for legal professional privilege ("LPP"); Section 330 (6) provides that a person does not commit an offence under the section if he is a professional legal adviser and the information came to him in privileged circumstances. Section 330 (10) defines LPP for these purposes. Nearly all information that will be provided to a barrister in the context of non-contentious advisory work will be privileged, and, if the information is privileged, no disclosure to SOCA should be made.

15. NB Section 330 (11) makes it clear that LPP does not extend to information which is communicated with the intention of furthering a criminal purpose. Under the criminal law, one intends something if one can foresee its natural consequences. It is not clear whose intention is relevant for the purposes of this section. At common law, the client's fraudulent intention is sufficient to throw aside the cloak of LPP even if the legal adviser is unaware of it: see *R v Cox and Railton*)1884) 14 QBD 153, 49 JP 374. However, in *Bowman v Fels* the Court of Appeal expressed some sympathy for the view that unless a barrister is actually aware of his client's intention to further a criminal purpose, the information would be protected from disclosure and no offence would be committed: see paragraphs 93 and 94. Given the serious penal consequence of the statute for barristers if they do not make a relevant disclosure, the Bar Council believes the views tentatively expressed by the Court of Appeal in those passages are correct.

16. **Section 333A (Tipping Off)**

This offence no longer applies outside the regulated sector. It is markedly different from its predecessor and the relevant provisions are set out in full below.

By Section 333A: regulated sector

(1) A person commits an offence if–

(a) the person discloses any matter within subsection (2);

(b) the disclosure is likely to prejudice any investigation that might be conducted following the disclosure referred to in that subsection; and

(c) the information on which the disclosure is based came to the person in the course of a business in the regulated sector

(2) the matters are that the person or another person has made a disclosure under this Part–

(a) to a constable,

(b) to an officer of Revenue and Customs,

(c) to a nominated officer, or

(d) to a member of staff of the Serious Organised Crime Agency authorised for the purposes of this Part by the Director General of that Agency, of information that came to that person in the course of a business in the regulated sector.

(3) A person commits an offence if –

(a) the person discloses that an investigation into allegations that an offence under this Part has been committed is being contemplated or is being carried out;

(b) the disclosure is likely to prejudice that investigation; and

(c) the information on which the disclosure is based came to the person in the course of a business in the regulated sector.

17. There are a number of exceptions. Most relevant to the Bar are likely to be those set out at Section 333D which provides:

(1) A person does not commit an offence under section 333A if the disclosure is –

(a) to the authority that is the supervisory authority for that person by virtue of the Money Laundering Regulations 2007 [here, the General Council of the Bar]; or

(b) for the purpose of–

(i) the detection, investigation or prosecution of a criminal offence (whether in the UK or elsewhere),

(ii) an investigation under this Act, or

(iii) the enforcement of any order of a court under this Act.

(2) A professional legal adviser … does not commit an offence under section 333A if the disclosure –

(a) is to the adviser's client, and

(b) is made for the purpose of dissuading the client from engaging in conduct amounting to an offence.

(3) A person does not commit an offence under section 333A (1) if the person does not know or suspect that the disclosure is likely to have the effect mentioned in section 333A(1)(b).

(4) A person does not commit an offence under section 333A(3) if the person does not know or suspect that the disclosure is likely to have the effect mentioned in section 333A(3) (b).

18. The mischief at which the section is aimed is clear; to prevent those about whom disclosures have been made from acting so as to frustrate the investigation. It is not aimed at preventing all disclosure. The wording of section 333A would allow a barrister in the regulated sector to tell his own client of a disclosure made about (eg) another party – provided that to do so was not likely to prejudice any subsequent investigation.

As to disclosures to a client about whom a disclosure has been made a barrister in the regulated sector must not inform his client of a disclosure or investigation unless he does so in order to dissuade him from engaging in conduct amounting to an offence (subsection 333D (2)). It is not apparent how this will work in practice.

Section 342 of POCA sets out the offences of prejudicing an investigation which are unchanged.

Duty to Disclose Previous Convictions (Aug 2001)

Disclosure of Previous Convictions

[3.268]

The Professional Conduct and Complaints Committee has issued guidance applicable to all barristers in relation to their obligations to disclose previous convictions of the defendant and how they must not become party to any deception of the court:

Counsel has an overriding duty to the Court to ensure in the public interest that the proper and efficient administration of justice is achieved; he must assist the Court in the administration of justice and must not deceive or knowingly or recklessly mislead the Court. For example, where the Court and prosecution are misled as to the existence of previous convictions as a result of the conduct of the defendant, in providing false information as to his identity, counsel would be associating himself with the deception if he continued to act in the knowledge of that fact and the client declined to indicate his true identity to the Court.

The PSC has been asked for further guidance about counsel's professional duty to reveal the existence of convictions of which the Court and prosecution are unaware in circumstances other than those described above. The PSC gave the following guidance in August 2001:

The Professional Standards Committee has concluded that counsel is not under a duty to reveal previous convictions to the prosecution or the court, but nor should counsel withdraw if his client refuses to reveal the convictions. In circumstances where counsel is aware of previous convictions, regardless of the nature of the case or potential sentence, counsel should give the defendant clear advice as to all the options. He should:

- Inform the defendant that the information as to the previous conviction will remain confidential unless the client specifically waives privilege;
- Inform the defendant that whilst the information remains confidential, he will be restricted in what he can say in mitigation;
- Advise the defendant that nothing can be said as to the defendant's record which expressly or impliedly adopts the position as outlined by the prosecution and in particular, that nothing can be said as to:
  - (a) the absence of convictions of the type or gravity of the undisclosed conviction;
  - (b) a period of time as being free from convictions if the undisclosed conviction occurred during that period;
  - (c) the absence of a particular sentence or disposal in the defendant's antecedents if such sentence or disposal was in fact imposed in respect of the undisclosed conviction; or
  - (d) an apparently good character of the defendant.

- Specifically advise the defendant as to the nature of the sentencing exercise if the court became aware of the undisclosed conviction, whether by virtue of the defendant's voluntary disclosure or by some other means.
- Specifically advise the defendant as to the consequences of a mandatory life sentence under section 2 of the 1997 Act, and the process of fixing a specified period under section 28 of that Act;
- Further advise him as to the release provisions and the licence provisions;
- Specifically consider and advise the defendant in relation to the issue of "exceptional circumstances";
- Advise the defendant as to the possibility of the prosecution subsequently discovering the undisclosed conviction;
- Advise of the real possibility that failure of counsel to refer to the defendant's antecedents would not go unnoticed by experienced prosecution counsel or judge. This could lead to an adjournment, to the matter being relisted for alteration of the sentence, or to a reference by the Attorney General under section 36 of the Criminal Justice Act 1998.
- Advise that so long as the conviction remains undiscovered, the mandatory sentencing provisions will not operate, but that if any of the above events occur, sentencing will take place in accordance with those revisions.

The defendant should be told that the choice as to what course to adopt is his, but that if he decides to reveal the qualifying conviction, he would be entitled to expect significant credit from the court in fixing the specified period.

If counsel is in any doubt as to the action he needs to take, he should contact the PCCC for advice.

Preparation for PCMH Hearings

[3.269]

Adequate preparation is vital for any advocate and the Bar Council has issued guidance specifically for criminal practitioners conducting Plea and Case Management Hearings ("PCMH"s), set out below:

This guidance was prepared by the Professional Practice Committee of the Bar Council in October 2006 and was sent to all Circuits for dissemination.

1. It is unacceptable for Counsel to be under prepared for the PCMH so as to be of little or no assistance to the Court. This view is of course dependent upon full and proper primary disclosure having been completed, and Counsel having sufficient instructions from their instructing solicitor including in the case of defence work a proof and comments on the prosecution statements.
2. If Counsel conducting the PCMH is not Trial Counsel then he/she must have fully read the Brief and have liaised with Trial Counsel to ensure that all

appropriate measures and directions are taken at the PCMH. It is good practice for Counsel in those circumstances to have liaised over the work required at the PCMH.

3. The Defence Case Statement must be completed at the earliest possible time after completion of Primary Disclosure and the taking of a signed proof. Counsel should remember that the late service of this document could subsequently prejudice a defendant.

Guidance on Preparation of Defence Case Statements

Preparation of Defence Case Statements

The Preparation Of Defence Case Statements Pursuant To The Criminal Procedure And Investigations Act 1996

[3.270]

Guidance on the duties of Counsel (as approved by the Standards Committee in March 2011) was issued in respect of the drafting/settling of Defence Case Statements under the 1996 Act. The guidance is reproduced below.

Guidance On The Duties Of Counsel

[3.271]

1. It is becoming increasingly common for solicitors to instruct counsel to draft or settle Defence Statements, required under section 5 of the Criminal Procedure and Investigations Act 1996. Often these instructions are given to counsel with no or little previous involvement in the case shortly before the expiry of the time limit.

2. The relevant legislation is set out at paras 12–52 et seq. of the 2011 edition of Archbold. In summary, however:

   (i) the time limit for compliance is short – 14 days from service of prosecution material or a statement that there is none. The permitted grounds for an extension of time are limited[1];

   (ii) the contents of the Defence Statement are obviously of great importance to the defendant. An inaccurate or inadequate statement of the defence could have serious repercussions for the defendant, if the trial judge permits "appropriate" comment;

   (iii) whilst it will be the natural instinct of most defence counsel to keep the Defence Statement short, a short and anodyne statement may be insufficient to trigger any obligation on the prosecution to give further disclosure under section 7A of prosecution material.

3. Normally it will be more appropriate for instructing solicitors to draft the Defence Statement, since typically counsel will have had little involvement at this stage.

However, there is nothing unprofessional about counsel drafting or settling a Defence Statement, although it must be appreciated that there is no provision in the current regulations for graduated fees allowing for counsel to be paid a separate fee for his work. A barrister has no obligation to accept work for which he will not be paid. The absence of a fee will justify refusal of the instructions of counsel who are not to be retained for the trial and are simply asked to do no more than draft or settle the Defence Statement. Where counsel is retained for the trial, Rule 604(b) of the Code of Conduct deems instructions in a legally aided matter to be at a proper professional fee. Where counsel accepts the trial brief, his fee will include all necessary preparation, including (if so instructed) drafting or settling the Defence Statement.

Many members of the Bar will nevertheless feel that, in the interests of their lay client and or of good relations with instructing solicitors, they cannot refuse work, even where they would otherwise be entitled to do so. Those who do so need to recognise the crucial importance of:

(i) obtaining all prosecution statements and documentary exhibits;

(ii) getting instructions from the lay client, from a properly signed proof and preferably a conference. Those instructions need to explain the general nature of the defence, to indicate the matters on which issue is taken with the prosecution and to give an explanation of the reason for taking issue. They must also give details of any alibi defence, sufficient to give the information required by Section 6A(2) of the 1996 Act;

(iii) getting statements from other material witnesses;

(iv) ensuring that the client realises the importance of the Defence Statement and the potential adverse consequences of an inaccurate or inadequate statement;

(v) getting proper informed approval for the draft from the client. This is particularly important, given the risks of professional embarrassment if the client seeks to disown the statement during the course of the trial, perhaps when the trial is not going well or when under severe pressure in cross-examination. Counsel ought to insist on getting written acknowledgement from the lay client that:

    (a) he understands the importance of the accuracy and adequacy of the Defence Statement for his case;

    (b) he has had the opportunity of considering the contents of the statement carefully and approves it.

    This may often mean having a conference with the lay client to explain the Defence Statement and to get informed approval, although in straightforward cases where counsel has confidence in the instructing solicitor, this could be left to the solicitor. Where the latter course is taken, a short written advice (which can be in a standard form) as to the importance of obtaining the written acknowledgement before service of the statement should accompany the draft Defence Statement. A careful record should be kept of work done and advice given.

(vi) If there is inadequate time, counsel should ask the instructing solicitor to apply for an extension of time. This needs to be considered at a very early stage, since the application must be made before the expiry of the time limit.

4. It follows that counsel ought not to accept any instructions to draft or settle a Defence Statement unless given the opportunity and adequate time to gain proper familiarity with the case and to comply with the fundamental requirements set out above. In short, there is no halfway house. If instructions are accepted, then the professional obligations on counsel are considerable.

1 See the Defence Disclosure Time Limit Regulations 1997 made pursuant to the Act: Archbold paras 12–94.

Defence Statements and Skeleton Arguments

[3.272]

As well as adequate preparation, counsel also needs to ensure that they do not draft a defence statement without adequate instructions, see below:

This guidance was prepared by the Professional Practice Committee of the Bar Council and was reviewed in January 2014.

General approach

1. You cannot, and should not, draft a defence statement without adequate instructions, which amounts to either a signed proof of evidence or having advised the client in conference. These statements are of increasing importance and defendants are frequently cross-examined, to their detriment, on such documents. You should be formally instructed to draft them. If you fail to comply, there are already sanctions within the BSB Handbook.

2. Skeleton arguments are not actually required in every case. If submissions are to be made on legal or evidential points, then they should, when necessary, be drafted in a concise and efficient form. Again existing provisions of BSB Handbook seem to cover this area.

3. It may be wise to remind you of the duty to draft a skeleton to assist the court, when necessary. This is of particular importance when the court is being asked to deal with applications in respect of bad character or hearsay

pursuant to the Criminal Justice Act 2003. There are, of course, considerations of remuneration in respect of this and the drafting of defence statements in graduated fee cases.

4. It must be remembered that unnecessary or over long written submissions may add to the length of a trial.
5. You are reminded of the benefits that will accrue to defendants by the early indication of a plea of guilty.
6. It would be professional misconduct to delay a plea of guilty until a late stage if that is motivated by a desire to obtain a higher fee (such a course also amounts to a failure in the duty owed to the lay client since he will usually receive a lesser discount for his plea if it is entered at a later stage in the proceedings).
7. It is important to draft Defence Statements and Skeleton Arguments in good time.

Important notice

This document has been prepared by the Bar Council to assist barristers on matters of professional conduct and ethics. **It is not "guidance" for the purposes of the BSB Handbook I6.4, and neither the BSB nor a disciplinary tribunal nor the Legal Ombudsman is bound by any views or advice expressed in it.** It does not comprise – and cannot be relied on as giving – legal advice. It has been prepared in good faith, but neither the Bar Council nor any of the individuals responsible for or involved in its preparation accept any responsibility or liability for anything done in reliance on it. For fuller information as to the status and effect of this document, please refer to the professional practice and ethics section of the Bar Council's website.

Special Measures Guidance from the Professional Practice Committee (Part 29, Criminal Procedure Rules)

[3.273]

Specific guidance has been issued by the Professional Practice Committee in relation to special measures applications under the Criminal Procedure Rules:

Part 29 of the Criminal Procedure Rules sets out the timetable in respect of special measures applications. The requirements in CPR 29.1(4)(c) in particular pre-suppose that the court should be in a position to deal with an application at the pleas and case management hearing, and that by the date of the PCMH all parties will have already received notice and copies of any evidence on which the applicant seeks to rely.

Counsel should upon receipt of the brief check to see if a special measures application is likely in respect of any of the witnesses and ensure that the Crown Prosecution Service or their instructing solicitors have taken the necessary steps in time.

It should be noted that the purpose of the Youth Justice and Criminal Evidence Act 1999 is to allow such steps as would maximise the quality of an eligible witness's evidence. Any opposition to an application should concentrate on that. The Act already requires the trial judge to give an appropriate direction to the jury to mitigate any possible prejudice to the defendant.

CPR 29.2 sets out the procedure for applying for an extension of time. CPR 29.3 allows for an application to be made orally at the trial. Where appropriate, every step should be taken to avoid a late application.

In the case of an application under section 29 of the Act for the use of an Intermediary, counsel should be aware that there has from time to time been a late recognition of the communication needs of the witness. The fact that an Intermediary was not used in interview is therefore not in itself evidence that one is not needed at trial. The grounds for opposing a late application are the same as for one made on time, that is, the needs of the witness, and counsel should seriously consider the extent to which the client they represent would be prejudiced if the witness were assisted by an Intermediary. Above all, counsel should only raise such grounds in opposition as are properly arguable and not pursue a hidden agenda simply to deprive the witness of the opportunity of giving evidence effectively.

Counsel faced with making a late application in respect of their own witness should therefore not disregard the possibility of making an application at trial. If a report is available from the Intermediary, then they should take heed of its findings. It should be recognised that the Intermediary is exercising an expertise when assessing the witness's needs. Counsel does not normally possess any such expertise and they should not take it upon themselves to decide what the communications needs are of any of their potentially vulnerable witnesses, and, in particular, children. They should not make themselves personally responsible for the quality of their own witness's evidence or abandon their responsibility to the witness simply to avoid an adjournment or because a late application may be unpopular with the court.

When an Intermediary is used at trial, it is essential, before the witness's evidence begins, for counsel, the Intermediary and the judge to hold a hearing to discuss the recommendations in the Intermediary's report and to set down the ground rules for the examination of the witness.

Procedure in the Court of Appeal Criminal Division

[3.274]

Guidance reminding counsel of the procedure in the Criminal Court of Appeal in relation to advice on appeal is set out below:

A Reminder

The Registrar of Criminal Appeals asked the Bar Council to publicise the following points:

1. If a positive advice on appeal is given then it should always be incorporated into the same document as the grounds of appeal, thus generating a single document rather than the two that often appear at the moment. This enables an assessment of the strength of the appeal to be made more easily.
2. An adverse advice should never be lodged with the Registrar so that if there is a new, personal appeal, there will be nothing adverse in the file and the application can be considered entirely on its merits.

We understand that a large number of cases arrive in the Criminal Appeal Office where it seems clear that counsel are unaware of this message. It is important that this should be remembered in future.

Court Appointed Legal Representatives

Court Appointed Legal Representatives

[3.275]

The Criminal Bar Association, at the request of the General Management Committee of the Bar Council produced the following guidance in relation to court appointed legal representatives:

Commentary

[3.276]

1. The Criminal Bar Association was asked by the General Management Committee of the Bar Council to draft brief guidance to assist with the issues which arise when the court appoints legal representatives to act on behalf of defendants and to consider whether a list of suitable counsel and solicitors should be drawn up from which the courts can make such appointments. The text that follows is the guidance issued by the Criminal Bar Association[1]. There have been previous reports written on this subject[2] and, although in practice, the appointment of counsel by the court is not likely to occur often, as a matter of common sense, when it does occur, it is likely to involve a defendant who is either not cooperating or who is "playing the system" and such guidance will have to be interpreted liberally if the interests of the defendant are to be preserved and justice is seen to be done.

This guidance sets out in full the background and statutory basis for these issues in order to explain why the guidance has been drafted in the terms that it has. References to "we" in this section is of course a reference to the Criminal Bar Association.

1 November 2003.
2 Peter Rook QC 27th January, 2001 and Nicholas Price QC March 2002.

2. The Background

2.1 The legislation which has provided for this procedure was passed as a result of two widely publicised cases in which a defendant acting in person cross-examined the complainant on an allegation of rape[3]. The Lord Chief Justice gave guidance (in the then absence of statutory reform) in the case of *R v Brown (Milton)* [1998] 2 Cr App R 364 to assist trial judges confronted with such a problem:

> "It will often be desirable, before any question is asked by the defendant in cross-examination, for the trial judge to discuss the course of the proceedings with the defendant in the absence of the jury. The judge can then elicit the general nature of the defence and identify the specific points in the complainant's evidence with which the defendant takes issue and any points he wishes to put to her. If the defendant proposes to

call witnesses in his own defence, the substance of their evidence can be elicited so that the complainant's observations on it may, so far as it is relevant, be invited."

There was further guidance set out as to the steps to be taken to restrict repetition or the intimidation or humiliation of the witness by way of the defendant's dress, bearing, manner or questions

3 *R v Brown (Milton)* [1998] 2 Cr App Rep 364, [1998] NLJR 694, CA and *R v Edwards (Ralston)* (1996) Times, 23 August.

2.2 Statutory restrictions on cross-examination of the complainant by a defendant in person charged with a sexual offence[4] were imposed by Section 34 of the Youth Justice and Criminal Evidence Act 1999 ("the Act") and this provision is now in force in respect of proceedings commencing on or after 4th September, 2000. This prohibition covers any other offence (of whatever nature) with which that person is charged in the proceedings[5].

4 Defined in s 62 Youth Justice and Criminal Evidence Act 1999.
5 Section 34(b) Youth Justice and Criminal Evidence Act 1999

2.3 Section 34A of the Criminal Justice Act, 1988 prohibited cross-examination in person of child witnesses in certain cases and Section 35 of the Act extended this to include the alleged victims of kidnapping, false imprisonment and abduction. This prohibition also extends to cross-examination in respect of other offences with which a defendant is charged in the proceedings[6].

6 Section 35(b) Youth Justice and Criminal Evidence Act 1999.

2.4 There is a further power under Sections 36 and 37 of the Act to prohibit a defendant in person from cross-examining witnesses not covered by Sections 34 & 35 if the court is satisfied, first, that the quality of the witness's evidence is likely to be diminished if the defendant is allowed to proceed and improved if he is prohibited from doing so and secondly, that it would not be contrary to the interests of justice to give such a direction. These provisions came into force on the 24th July 2002.

2.5 Section 38 of the Act makes provision for the appointment of a qualified legal representative for the purposes of cross-examination of a witness where an accused in person has been prevented from so doing by virtue of Section 34, 35 or 36.

3. Section 38.

3.1 Section 38 allows the accused to have the opportunity of appointing his own legal representative to conduct the cross-examination on his behalf. If he does not, Section 38(4) of the Act specifies that where the court has decided that it is necessary in the interests of justice for the witness to be cross-examined by a court appointed legal representative, the court must appoint a qualified legal representative[7] (chosen by the court) to cross-examine the witness in the interests of the accused. A person so appointed shall not be responsible to the accused[8]. Any reference to cross-examination includes (in a case where a direction under Section 36 has been given after the accused has begun cross-examining the witness) a reference to further cross-examination[9]. Even after the appointment by the court under Section 38(4) of such a legal representative, the accused may arrange for that legal representative to be appointed to act for him and it is then as though he had done so at the outset under Section 38(2)(a) of the Act[10].

7 Defined in s 38(8)(b) as a legal representative who has a right of audience (within the meaning of the Courts and Legal Services Act 1990) in relation to the proceedings before the court.
8 Section 38(5) Youth Justice and Criminal Evidence Act 1999.
9 Section 38(8)(b) Youth Justice and Criminal Evidence Act 1999.
10 Crown Court Rules 1982 r 24D.

The legal representative is then no longer the representative of the Court.

[3.277]

3.2 We have set out the statutory framework in some detail because the provisions themselves make it clear that there are the two underlying principles behind the appointment of such a legal representative, namely, that such an appointment is in the interests of justice and that the legal representative is appointed to represent the interests of the accused although not responsible to him. They may sound obvious principles but the tensions which are likely to flow from such a situation make any court appointed legal representative liable to face a number of extremely difficult decisions and it will be a testing task for the judge to ensure that the balance between the interests of justice and the interests of the accused is maintained. One of the obvious problems which we try to deal with in the guidance is the effect of disclosure material. This may well contain material which could properly be used in cross-examination where it was relevant but in the absence of specific issues identified by the defendant to the Court, it will be extremely difficult for its relevance to be assessed.

4. Code of Conduct

Paragraph 401(a) of the Code of Conduct has been amended to allow for a barrister in independent practice to be appointed by the court but it seems to us very likely that there will have to be other amendments made since the role of court appointed counsel who is expressly not responsible to the defendant is quite different from the role of counsel appointed to represent the defendant. An example is under Paragraph 708(a) which deals with conduct in court and which requires that a barrister is personally responsible for the conduct and presentation of his case and must exercise personal judgement upon the substance and purpose of statements made and questions asked. This is likely to be very difficult since the questions asked are likely to be constrained by the judge who will ultimately be responsible for parameters of appropriate cross-examination.

It will also be very important that any court-appointed counsel is as clear as possible as to the purpose and the parameters of any questions to be asked since it is not difficult to foresee a situation where questions asked without instructions may receive answers which either make matters worse for the defendant or open up previously unexplored areas which the Crown may use to their advantage. This may be unavoidable but if both the judge and counsel are fully aware of the nature of the questions to be asked, the danger will be lessened and, if it occurs, counsel will not be at fault. A simple instruction from the court to "test the evidence" will not be sufficient and the judge will have to be as specific as possible and counsel equally careful as to the questions asked to avoid unnecessarily exposing themselves to complaint from the defendant of unfairness.

5. List of Suitably Qualified Legal Representatives

5.1 As previously set out, "qualified legal representative" is defined in Section 38(8)(b) as a "legal representative who has a right of audience (within the meaning of the Courts and Legal Services Act,1990) in relation to the proceedings before the Court".

It is, in our view, essential that only legal representatives with the appropriate number of years experience (we suggest seven) in predominantly criminal law with previous experience of cross-examining complainants in sexual cases and children be considered for what is going to be a difficult task. Whilst these cases may not be restricted to allegations of sexual abuse, they are more likely to be generated by them. The Code of Conduct provisions would in any event apply to the Bar which would prevent counsel from accepting any instructions if to do so would cause him to be professionally embarrassed which includes having insufficient experience or competence to handle the matter[11].

11 Paragraph 603(a).

5.2 The task of appointing counsel is likely to be done on a practical level by the associate in consultation with the judge and perhaps the List Office. Who is appointed will depend on the stage at which the appointment is made. If it is early in the proceedings, there should be ample time to appoint an appropriate representative. In the absence of a list, this is likely to be from counsel who regularly appear in that court or who are well known. It seems to us there should at least be the opportunity for counsel to have their name on the list. It may be the appropriate course would be for all Chambers to be asked to provide a list of counsel with the appropriate experience who would like to be included on the list. Remuneration would have to be appropriate[12] because it will be necessary for counsel to familiarise themselves with all the material including unused which in these unusual circumstances should also be made available to the judge.

12 Section 40 Youth Justice and Criminal Evidence Act 1999 makes provision for payment out of central funds.

5.3 Although an appointment of a legal representative will normally terminate at the conclusion of the cross-examination[13], there is provision for the court to determine otherwise and we consider that it may well be necessary for counsel to remain for the duration of the trial in case evidence is given by the defendant or another witness which needs to be put to the complainant who will then have to be recalled and re-cross-examined. This situation may arise where the defence is not known and the issues have not been fully identified because the defendant is being uncooperative and may have given a no comment interview. The cross-examination will have been based on the papers and, whilst obvious issues will have been covered, it may well be that the questions asked do not, in fact, cover the defendant's case as given from the witness box. To avoid the whole scenario becoming a sham, the defendant's case will have to be put to the complainant. It follows from this that counsel appointed by the court will have to be available for the whole trial as opposed to simply cross-examination. There is also the possibility that the judge may intervene during the trial to make a direction under Section 36 preventing the defendant from cross-examining other witnesses.

13 Crown Court Rules 1982 r 24C-(2).

5.4 Such a list will need maintaining as well as setting up. Although there are a number of sources which could probably provide the relevant information, for example, the individual Bar Messes, the CBA, the circuit, none of these include solicitor advocates and although there may not presently be many with the necessary experience, the Law Society will need to be involved in this process to maintain equal opportunity for all those with suitable qualifications.

5.5 Once such a list is set up, it will be for the court to select the appropriate advocate and the cab-rank principle should apply to all approached, subject to an advocate feeling they are insufficiently experienced.

6. Duties of Court Appointed Legal Representative

6.1 It is expressly set out that the legal representative is not responsible to the defendant[14]. It follows that there will not be any meetings with the defendant nor any instructions taken directly from him unless he chooses to "adopt" the court appointed representative as his own (see para 3.1).

14 Section 38(5) Youth Justice and Criminal Evidence Act 1999.

6.2 Rules of court may make provision in particular for securing that the legal representative will be provided with "evidence or other material relating to the proceedings"[15] and this can include disclosure of material in connection with criminal proceedings under Part 1 of the Criminal Procedure and Investigations Act, 1996[16]. It will be the duty of the legal representative to read all such material and watch any videos of disclosure interviews.

15 Section 38(6)(b) Youth Justice and Criminal Evidence Act 1999.
16 Section 38(7)(a) Youth Justice and Criminal Evidence Act 1999.

6.3 If the appointment is made at a relatively early stage in the proceedings, presence at preparatory hearings may seem sensible if there is to be a ruling on the admissibility of evidence or any similar ruling prior to the swearing of the jury and it may well be useful to attend simply to clarify the issues. It should be borne in mind, however, that the role of the legal representative is clearly intended to be limited to cross-examining witnesses whom the defendant is prohibited from cross-examining and although it may be thought that such a representative could be useful to the court in other areas, that does not seem to be intended by the legislation. Ultimately, it will be matter for the judge to decide and, no doubt if there is a point which can be properly taken on admissibility of a witness's evidence which is not dependent on the defendant's instructions, the legal representative will make the appropriate submissions, either of his own volition or at the invitation of the judge and these are areas which may well be identifiable at an early stage in the proceedings.

6.4 If it is possible, the legal representative should be present during the opening of the case to the jury and it is after this that there should be a hearing in the absence of the jury but in the presence of the defendant and both prosecuting counsel and the legal representative at which the judge will have to take steps to establish the issues in the case. Concern has been expressed that the defendant may refuse to tell the judge anything in the presence of prosecuting counsel and there is always the possibility that the defendant may inadvertently say something to the judge which could provide material in cross-examination. The problem is that prosecuting counsel has an ongoing duty of disclosure and they have to know what the defence is in order to comply with their duty. If the defendant makes it clear that he will not say anything if prosecuting counsel remains present, the Judge must decide what to do and this may well include explaining to the defendant the duty of the Crown and how limited the judge's powers are on disclosure without input from the Crown. Subject to that, if the Judge feels that the interests of justice are best served by a hearing in the absence of the Crown, then, no doubt, that is what he will do.

There are a number of possible scenarios:–

(i) The defendant has given a full interview to the police setting out his defence. In this case, the defendant can simply be asked whether he will confirm the defence set out in the interview. If he does so, then it seems to us that the legal representative is justified in putting a positive case to the witness although no doubt in a moderate way. This will assist the jury to assess the credibility of the witness. If the defendant will not confirm that this is his defence, the witness should nonetheless be cross-examined on that basis but not as a positive case and any other relevant points need to be identified before cross-examination.

(ii) There is a defence statement setting out a defence. The same question can be asked but as the defendant will have presumably sacked whoever was responsible for that statement, care will need to be taken in putting that forward even if the defendant confirms that is his defence. There are often significant differences between an interview and a defence statement and all that will be required will be to give the witness the opportunity of dealing with any points made in either. It is important, however, that the cross-examination is not conducted in a way which invites scepticism because of how it is put as opposed to the actual content of the questions being put because the legal representative has been appointed to represent the interests of the defendant.

(iii) There is a no comment interview and no defence statement. Although the defendant can be asked by the judge if he will outline the points on which he takes issue in the case, it is not hard to foresee the scenario where a defendant is being completely uncooperative, no doubt wishing to make a point to the jury (which some may think has some force) that he has not been able to defend himself properly because he has been unable to cross-examine the main witness against him. In those circumstances, the legal representative is likely to be constrained by the issues which the judge directs are relevant as far as can be ascertained from the papers although no doubt the submissions of the legal representative will be sought. Once those issues have been identified, they should be explained to the defendant and he should again be asked whether he is now willing to indicate his defence. It should be noted that it is for the court to decide in the first place whether it is necessary in the interests of justice for the witness to be cross-examined by a legal representative appointed to represent the interests of the defendant and it is only if the court does so decide that a legal representative has to be appointed. Strictly speaking, if there is no sensible basis upon which a witness can be cross-examined, it may not be in the interests of justice for this to be done and it is open to the judge to refuse to appoint a legal representative to do so. This would be a brave decision to take and one which would seem likely to strike the average juror as unfair. The more likely scenario and the more sensible one would be for the legal representative to be invited to test the evidence as if a certain line of defence was being put forward but not putting any positive case to the witness.

(iv) Where the defendant refuses to be represented because of a psychiatric condition such as mental illness or a personality disorder. It is obvious in these very unfortunate cases that every effort should be made to persuade the defendant to be represented but that if they will not, then all proper and available lines of defence should be put to the witness and all proper legal arguments mounted.

6.5 Once the relevant areas of cross-examination have been identified, the legal representative must consider any proper legal arguments relevant to the cross-examination. This would include questions relating to the sexual history of the witness for which leave must be given or whether a particular line of cross-examination may lead to an application to adduce the defendant's previous convictions in the event of him giving evidence. We do not consider it is the duty of the legal representative to raise other legal arguments which are not relevant to cross-examination. It may be that such representatives would wish to ensure that either the court or the prosecution was made aware of such points to avoid a miscarriage of justice but it would not appear to be within the limited confines of their duty which is to cross-examine. There will no doubt be a strong temptation for the legal representative to be treated as amicus in the trial generally. We do not consider that to be appropriate unless the judge specifically requests that that role be adopted as it will be extremely difficult for the legal representative then to be confident that he or she is fully aware of the parameters of their role in the case. It would also be confusing for the jury who may well think that the defendant has actually got full representation even though he didn't want it.

6.6 There will be circumstances where the legal representative considers that it is in the interests of the defendant that they remain until the end of the evidence. If so, application should be made to the judge for leave to remain.

6.7 It may also be sensible for the defendant to be reminded at the end of the cross-examination that they can "adopt" the legal representative. If that is done, there will need to be the opportunity for the defendant to give instructions and, if necessary, further cross-examination but care will have to be taken to prevent a defendant manipulating or appearing to manipulate the court process and also to prevent a witness being cross-examined more than is necessary.

7. It is our view that many of these decisions can only be taken on an individual case basis and will depend upon the sensible handling of the defendant by the judge. The legal representative will need to be alive to the limitations of their role and not to be beguiled into acting as the defendant's representative generally. There is a requirement in Section 40 of the Act that the judge gives such warning to the jury as he considers necessary to prevent prejudicial inferences being drawn either from the fact that the defendant is not cross-examining or (where this occurs) the fact that a court appointed representative has cross-examined on his behalf. It remains to be seen whether the difficult balance between maintaining the interests of justice whilst making sure that justice is being seen to be done can be achieved in practice.

Guidance for Court Appointed Legal Representatives

[3.278]–[3.279]

1. A court appointed legal representative will not meet privately with the defendant nor take instructions directly from the defendant.
2. All matters relevant to the cross-examination to be conducted by the legal representative will ordinarily be dealt with in open court in the presence of the prosecution and the defendant but in the absence of the jury.
3. The legal representative will be provided with the evidence in the case comprising all prosecution statements and exhibits and have access to unused material. It will be the duty of the legal representative to familiarise him/herself with the evidence and be in a position to assist the judge as to the likely material issues as disclosed on the papers.
4. Before the start of the trial, the judge will identify as far as possible the likely issues in the case. This will involve the prosecution and the legal representative and where possible, the defendant.
5. Where the defendant has given a full account in interview and has confirmed to the judge that this account is to be maintained at trial identifying, if appropriate, any material differences etc, the legal representative should prepare cross-examination on the basis of that defence. It is a matter for the legal representative's judgement in each case as to whether that is put forward as a positive defence in cross-examination or simply used as a basis for testing the evidence.
6. Where there is only a defence statement which the defendant has not confirmed as his defence, the legal representative should not put this forward as a positive defence. It should only be used as a basis from which to test the evidence of the witness.
7. Where there is only a defence statement but the judge has elicited from the defendant that this accurately represents his defence, the legal representative should prepare cross-examination on the basis of that defence but should not

generally put it as a positive defence unless there is good reason so to do, for example, if the defendant indicates that the defence to a rape allegation is to be one of consent.

8. Where the defendant has made no comment in interview and there is no defence statement but the judge has elicited from the defendant what his defence is to be, the legal representative should prepare cross-examination on the basis of that defence but should not generally put it as a positive defence unless there is good reason so to do, for example, if the defendant indicates that the defence to a rape allegation is to be one of consent.

9. Where the defendant has made no comment in interview and there is no defence statement and declines to indicate what his defence is to be, the legal representative should prepare cross-examination in accordance with the directions of the judge after discussion with both prosecution and the legal representative as to the material issues in the case. This should not be put forward as a positive case. The only proper basis is to test the evidence of the witness on the specific areas identified by the judge.

10. Where the defendant has given an account in interview and/or his defence statement but has indicated that his defence is different and will not indicate in what way it differs, the same approach as in para 9 above should be followed.

11. Although the appointment by the court of a legal representative implies that the court considers that cross-examination of the relevant witness will be in the interests of the defendant, it is a matter for the legal representative to judge whether, in the event, it is in the interests of the defendant for there to be cross-examination as, for example, where the witness has not come up to proof on a material point.

12. It will be the duty of the legal representative to raise any points of law relevant to the conduct of the cross-examination prior to the cross-examination such as whether there are relevant and admissible questions on the witness's sexual history or whether a particular line of cross-examination is likely to result in the defendant's "shield" being lost in the event of him giving evidence.

13. Whilst in the normal course of events, the appointment of the legal representative terminates at the conclusion of the cross-examination of the particular witness, the legal representative should consider whether there is a need for the appointment to remain until a later stage in the trial if, for example, it may be necessary for the witness to be recalled for further cross-examination and if there is, to make the appropriate application to the judge.

Barristers making payments to secure criminal work

[3.280]–[3.282]

The following is some further guidance forbidding the making of payments to secure work.

Reports have been received of solicitors requiring payments to be made to them by barristers in return for work to be referred to the barristers in criminal cases. Barristers are reminded that the making of payments in order to secure instructions is **forbidden** by paragraph 307 (e) of the Bar Code of Conduct, which states:

> 307. A barrister must not:
>
> ...
>
> (e) make any payment (other than a payment for advertising or publicity permitted by this Code or in the case of a self-employed barrister remuneration paid to any clerk or other employee or staff of his chambers) to any person for the purpose of procuring professional instructions;

Further, the profession is reminded that a payment agreed by a clerk, on behalf of a barrister for the purpose of procuring professional instructions, would similarly put the barrister in breach of paragraph 307 (e).

If you have concerns as to your position under the Code, it is recommended that you telephone the Bar Council's ethics line. The number is 020 7611 1307.

Criticism of Former Counsel in Criminal Cases

Criticism of Former Counsel

[3.283]

The following guidance has been approved by the Lord Chief Justice and the Bar Council in respect of the sometimes sensitive issue of having to formally criticise a former barrister in a case in support of the client's grounds of appeal. The guidance was reissued in January 2014.

1. Allegations against former counsel may receive substantial publicity whether accepted or rejected by the court. You should not settle or sign grounds of appeal unless you are satisfied that they are reasonable, have some real prospect of success and are such that you are prepared to argue before the court (Guide to Commencing Proceedings in the Court of Appeal Criminal Division Para A2–6). When such allegations are properly made, however, in accordance with the BSB Handbook rC15.1, if you are newly instructed counsel must promote fearlessly and by all proper and lawful means your lay client's best interests without regard to others, including fellow members of the legal profession.

2. When you are newly instructed counsel and satisfied that such allegations are made, and a waiver of privilege is necessary, you should advise the lay client fully about the consequences of waiver and should obtain a waiver of privilege in writing signed by the lay client relating to communications with, instruction to and advice given by former counsel. The allegations should be

set out in the Grounds of Application for Leave to Appeal. Both waiver and grounds should be lodged without delay; the grounds may be perfected if necessary in due course.

3. On receipt of the waiver and grounds, the Registrar of Criminal Appeals will send both to former counsel with an invitation on behalf of the Court to respond to the allegations made. Having obtained the signed waiver, the 'waiver of privilege' procedure above should not be instigated by newly instructed counsel.

4. If former counsel wishes to respond and considers the time for doing so insufficient, s/he should ask the Registrar for further time. The court will be anxious to have full information and to give former counsel adequate time to respond.

5. The response should be sent to the Registrar. On receipt, s/he will send it to you as newly instructed counsel who may reply to it. The grounds and the responses will go before the single judge.

6. The Registrar may have received grounds of appeal direct from the applicant, and obtained a waiver of privilege before fresh counsel is assigned. In those circumstances, when assigning counsel, the Registrar will provide copies of the waiver, the grounds of appeal and any response from former counsel.

7. This ethical assistance covers the formal procedures to be followed. It is perfectly proper for you as newly instructed counsel to speak to former counsel as a matter of courtesy before grounds are lodged to inform him/her of the position.

Important notice

This document has been prepared by the Bar Council to assist barristers on matters of professional conduct and ethics. **It is not "guidance" for the purposes of the BSB Handbook I6.4, and neither the BSB nor a disciplinary tribunal nor the Legal Ombudsman is bound by any views or advice expressed in it.** It does not comprise – and cannot be relied on as giving – legal advice. It has been prepared in good faith, but neither the Bar Council nor any of the individuals responsible for or involved in its preparation accept any responsibility or liability for anything done in reliance on it. For fuller information as to the status and effect of this document, please refer to the professional practice and ethics section of the Bar Council's website.

Part C: Good Practice Guidance for Barristers practising Family Law

Family Law – Good Practice Guidance

[3.284]

The Professional Practice Committee has provided advice for family counsel in relation to material disclosed to them in confidence which might undermine the case of the client or adversely affect the welfare of a child in the case:

Professional Practice Committee Guidance on Unhelpful Material Disclosed to Counsel in Family Proceedings

[3.285]

1. The Professional Practice Committee of the Bar Council regularly receives enquiries from barristers undertaking family law cases about the nature and extent of professional obligations when the question of whether or not to disclose unfavourable material to their client's case arises. The unfavourable material may be provided in the form of instructions given at conference; or may be contained within documents generated for the purposes of family proceedings in which counsel is instructed e.g. witness proofs. In many cases where queries arise, the client seeks to withhold information which is likely to be relevant to the court in determining the child's welfare; and may even be detrimental to the child if the same is withheld. Alternatively, queries may relate to a client's expressed intentions towards other family members.

2. Family law practitioners should be familiar with the Code of Conduct of the Bar of England and Wales; a barrister's duty to the client; a barrister's duty to the court; duties of disclosure generally; the principles of privilege, particularly legal professional privilege and privilege against self-incrimination, and relevant case law.[1] Essential principles only are distilled below from paragraph 5 onwards.

3. It has become clear to those responding to ethical enquiries that if, at the outset, Counsel explain to clients their professional obligations in the context of family proceedings, difficulties which may emerge surrounding disclosure of information can be avoided.

4. Counsel should advise the client at the earliest opportunity:

   (i) Counsel's role is to represent the client and to present the client's case to the best of his or her ability;

   (ii) Counsel has a duty of "full and frank" disclosure in respect of relevant material that is disclosed by the client and which impacts upon the welfare of the child;

   (iii) Counsel is not in a position to conduct a trial or proceedings whilst withholding or concealing relevant information from the parties and the Court;

(iv) The duty of confidentiality to the client owed by Counsel and contained in paragraph 702 of the Code of Conduct may be overridden as permitted by law. In particular, any information which reveals a serious risk to the welfare of a child, or serious harm to a third party, may have to be disclosed even if Counsel's instructions are discontinued.

Professional obligations

5. Paragraph 302 of the Code of Conduct of the Bar of England and Wales states:

"A barrister has an overriding duty to the court to act with independence in the interests of justice: he must assist the court in the administration of justice and must not deceive or knowingly or recklessly mislead the court."

Clearly, therefore, counsel must not make representations to the parties or the court which are not accurate in the face of unfavourable material which has been provided by a client, and barristers must not mislead the court.

6. According to paragraph 303(a) of the Code, a barrister:

"must promote and protect fearlessly and by all proper and lawful means the lay client's best interests and do so without regard to his own interests or to any consequences to himself or to any other person ..."

7. In relation to disclosure and in particular the failure to make proper disclosure to the court or to another party, paragraphs 608(d) and (e) of the Code provide:

"A barrister must cease to act and if he is a self-employed barrister must return any instructions:

...

(d) if the client refuses to authorise him to make some disclosure to the Court which his duty to the Court requires him to make;

(e) if having become aware during the course of a case of the existence of a document which should have been but has not been disclosed on discovery the client fails forthwith to disclose it;"

8. In relation to the duty of confidentiality owed by Counsel to the client, paragraph 702 of the Code provides:

"Whether or not the relation of counsel and client continues a barrister must preserve the confidentiality of the lay client's affairs and must not without the prior consent of the lay client or as permitted by law lend or reveal the contents of the papers in any instructions to or communicate to any third person ... information which has been entrusted to him in confidence or use such information to the lay client's detriment or to his own or another client's advantage."

9. In the Practice Direction (Family Proceedings: Case Management) [1995] 1 WLR 332 Sir Stephen Brown P set out the principle of disclosure in family proceedings as follows:

"It is a duty owed to the court both by the parties and by legal representatives to give full and frank disclosure in ancillary relief applications and also in respect of children".

The duty is owed both by the parties and by the legal representatives of the parties. However the Practice Direction does not, of itself, deal with the principle of legal professional privilege, or the status of a client's instructions. Furthermore, this Practice Direction does not mean that counsel has a duty to disclose that is distinct from that of the client, save in the exceptional circumstances considered at paragraphs 25 -28 below.

10. The express duty of full and frank disclosure outlined in this Practice Direction, together with a number of decisions to the same effect by various Family Division Judges at first instance (see, in particular, judgment of Wall J in *Re DH (a minor) (child abuse)* [1994] 1 FLR 679, at 703–704),[2] has led to a culture in family proceedings whereby upon advice and with the client's consent, unfavourable material affecting the welfare of the child is often disclosed to the other parties, and ultimately the court, and any privilege arising in respect of such material is waived. This may be because clients are advised:

(i) that whilst the advocate has a duty to present the client's case to the best of his or her ability, the advocate has a higher duty to the court to disclose relevant material to the court even if that disclosure is not in the interests of the client (per Wall J in *Re DH (a minor) (child abuse)* at 704/C);

(ii) that full disclosure of relevant material will result in a fair and proper assessment of the child's welfare and will assist the court in arriving at the best possible outcome for the child (usually their child);

(iii) that full and frank disclosure is more likely to result in parents and/or carers needs being properly identified, which in turn will impact positively upon the child if they are considered able to care for the child;

(iv) that if relevant information were to be withheld (such as a new relationship with an unsuitable partner), then almost invariably it would emerge during cross-examination or further investigation within the proceedings, and the client might then be heavily criticised and his or her case damaged because of his or her failure to be honest and open with the court at the earliest possible stage;

(v) that in acting for a client counsel cannot mislead the court in any way. Thus where unfavourable information is withheld on the grounds of privilege against self-incrimination, counsel may be obliged to withdraw at a later stage if the client continues to withhold that unfavourable material in oral evidence (where no such privilege can be claimed)[3] and in so doing directly or indirectly misleads the court.

11. Subject to questions of privilege which are considered below, where a client does not accept the merits of disclosing unhelpful material to the other parties and the court, and does not consent to disclosure as advised, counsel should withdraw from the case and return his or her instructions. Counsel should not continue to act for a client knowing that there exists information which ought to have been disclosed in accordance with the duty of full and

PART III
IN PRACTICE

frank disclosure but which, in breach of that duty, has not been disclosed because the client has refused to permit its disclosure.

12. Counsel may also have to make difficult decisions in respect of what can and/or should be disclosed to the other parties and the court notwithstanding counsel's withdrawal. Such decisions require an evaluation of counsel's duty to the client (see below); and whether and how that duty may conflict with professional duties to the court and the duty for full and frank disclosure.

Legal professional privilege

13. Legal professional privilege may be classified under two sub-headings: legal advice privilege and litigation privilege. Legal advice privilege covers communications between a client and his legal adviser and is available whether or not proceedings are in existence or contemplated. Litigation privilege embraces a wider class of communications, such as those between the legal adviser and potential witnesses. These communications are privileged only where proceedings are in existence or contemplated.

Litigation privilege

14. In *Re L (minors)(police investigation: privilege), Re* [1997] AC 16, [1996] 2 All ER 78, HL the House of Lords decided that litigation privilege does not apply in care proceedings. Lord Jauncey of Tullichettle, with whom the majority agreed, was of the view that care proceedings are non-adversarial in nature. Litigation privilege has no place, therefore, in relation to reports based on the papers disclosed in the proceedings and obtained from a third party within them. Accordingly all such reports must routinely be disclosed and served within proceedings; as should communications from any party with court appointed experts.

15. However if the report in question was not prepared for the purposes of the care proceedings but for the purposes of criminal proceedings, legal professional privilege may still arise. In *S County Council v B* [2000] 2 FLR 161, Charles J. held (at 174/C-E) that the father could claim legal professional privilege in care proceedings in respect of his communications with medical experts who had been instructed solely for the purposes of criminal proceedings. Further the privilege is absolute (see p173/B-D) and the duty of full and frank disclosure which arises in care proceedings does not override that privilege (see p183/E-185/H).

Communications between clients and their advisers (legal advice privilege)

16. In *Re L* above, Lord Jauncey stated that his decision in relation to litigation privilege "... does not of course affect privilege arising between solicitor and client". In *S County Council v B* (above), Charles J decided (at 179/E-F) that *Re L* preserved legal professional privilege in respect of communications between solicitor and client, and draft statements and discussions as to the relevant facts between solicitor and client for the purposes of proceedings under the Children Act 1989. See also Wall J. in *A Chief Constable v A County Council* [2002] EWHC 2198 (Fam), paragraph 96. Currently, therefore, legal

professional privilege applies to communications with the client in family proceedings (see also Lord Nicholls, in *Re L* on this point).

17. Legal professional privilege rests upon the principle that a client must be free to consult his legal advisers without fear of his communications being revealed. In this way, the interests of the administration of justice are maintained. Privilege is absolute, and remains even where he who asserts the privilege no longer has any recognisable interest in upholding that privilege (*R v Derby Magistrates Court ex p B* [1996] AC 487, [1995] 4 All ER 526, HL.

18. *R v Cox and Railton* (1884) 14 QBD 153, 49 JP 374 provides a well recognised exception to legal professional privilege: namely, where the disclosure or communication amounts to a crime or is intended to further a criminal purpose. Within the judgment of Stephen J who gave the judgment of the court in *Cox v Railton* the following passage appears:

> "The reason on which the rule [of legal professional privilege] is said to rest cannot include the case of communications, criminal in themselves, or intended to further any criminal purpose, for the protection of such communications cannot possibly be otherwise than injurious to the interests of justice, and to those of the administration of justice. Nor do such communications fall within the terms of the rule".

19. The limits of what is protected by legal professional privilege should also be noted. Where the client knows of relevant information which ought to be disclosed in accordance with the duty of full and frank disclosure (such as a new relationship with an unsuitable partner), that information does not become entitled to legal professional privileged simply by the act of telling it to Counsel. The client remains under a duty to disclose the information in accordance with the duty of full and frank disclosure notwithstanding the communication of the information to Counsel.

20. On the other hand, the same reasoning would not necessarily apply to information which is likely to lead to a danger of self-incrimination by the client. Such information, if entitled to privilege against self-incrimination before it was told to Counsel, would continue to be entitled to that privilege after being told to Counsel.

21. It is for counsel to decide, as a matter of law, whether legal professional privilege arises in respect of any unfavourable information which is disclosed to Counsel during the course of dealings with the client. Broadly speaking, and subject to the comments in paragraphs 16–18 above, LPP may arise in respect of discussions between counsel and client; and documents generated as a result of legal advice or instructions (such as witness proofs), whether in contemplation of a case or in the course of it.

Privilege against self-incrimination

22. Privilege against self-incrimination may arise in respect of the disclosure of information which is likely to lead to a danger of self-incrimination by the client or his/her spouse or civil partner (see *Rank Film Distributors Ltd v Video Information Centre (a firm)* [1982] AC 380, 416C, 419F).

23. Privilege against self-incrimination may permit the withholding of information and non-co-operation with the court's investigation which would otherwise be required in accordance with the duty of full and frank

disclosure which arises in care proceedings. However the privilege does not excuse the client from giving evidence on any matter or entitle the client to refuse to answer any question put to him in the course of his giving evidence (Children Act 1989, s.98(1)). As Wall J. said in *A Chief Constable v A County Council* [2002] EWHC 2198 (Fam), paragraph 96:

"A lawyer whose client admits child abuse in a conversation covered by legal professional privilege is placed in a very difficult position. Lawyers have a professional duty not to mislead the court, and plainly cannot conduct the parent's case in a manner which is inconsistent with any admission made to them. However, lawyers cannot, without the consent of their clients, breach or waive the privilege. Thus although lawyers may advise their clients to be open and honest with the court, they are also entitled, without breaching professional standards, to advise parents in care proceedings that, subject to section 98(1) of the Children Act 1989, they are not bound to co-operate with the court's investigation. They should, however, in my judgment, advise their clients that anything they say to an expert witness in the context of the latter's investigations, is protected by section 98(2) of the 1989 Act."

24. Likewise where a child who is in care has been abducted and a recovery order has been made requiring a person with information as to the child's whereabouts to disclose it, the privilege against incrimination does not excuse compliance with the requirement (Children Act 1989, s.50(11). Similarly, under the Family Law Act 1986, s 33(2) or where a Location Order is made in the High Court, in a private law context, the privilege against incrimination does not excuse non disclosure.

The duty of confidentiality

25. The duty of confidentiality owed to the client by Counsel is contained in paragraph 702 of the Code of Conduct which is set out at paragraph 6 above.

26. As stated in paragraph 702, client confidentiality may be overridden where "permitted by law". This exception would apply where the law specifically requires or authorises the disclosure of the information in question notwithstanding the duty of confidentiality. The exception may also apply where disclosure is in the public interest and, in proceedings for breach of confidence, it is referred to as "the defence of just cause and excuse". A balancing exercise is required in the application of the public interest exception. Each case will turn on its own facts.

27. In considering whether to disclose any information covered by client confidentiality without the clients' consent, Counsel should bear in mind the importance which the law attaches to the right of every person to obtain legal advice in confidence. Further if any disclosure is to be made without the client's consent, it should not be any wider than is reasonably necessary in the circumstances, e.g. disclosure to the relevant authorities but no more.

28. Counsel should also keep in mind that *In Re D* (*Minors*) (*Conciliation: Disclosure of Information*) Re [1993] Fam 231, [1993] 2 All ER 693, CA, the Court of Appeal refused to allow any exception to the privilege which attaches to statements made by one or other of the parties in the course of conciliation "save in the very unusual case where a statement is made clearly indicating that the maker has in the past caused or is likely in the future to cause serious harm to the well being of a child". (see p 241/A-B).

Guiding principles

29. The Code of Conduct of the Bar of England and Wales sets out duties which all barristers must obey. It is professional misconduct to breach the rules and can result in a barrister being charged with misconduct upon receipt of a complaint by his professional body. Barristers should be aware of the content of the Code; and of the relevant law in the context of potentially conflicting duties between the interests of the client and duties to the court in family proceedings.

30. Counsel should advise the client of the duty of full and frank disclosure in family proceedings and of Counsel's higher duty to the Court at the outset of any meeting with the client. If a client wishes to withhold relevant information in respect of the welfare of the child, the client should be advised of the importance of disclosing relevant information. In most cases, the information is likely to emerge in any event, in cross-examination or in further investigation within the context of the proceedings. It is usually less damaging to a client's case to be honest and open with the court at the outset; and it is always better in assessing the child's welfare that parties are honest. If privilege arises in respect of such information, the client should be advised of his or her right to claim privilege subject to the matters set out at paragraph 21 above.

31. If no privilege arises in respect of the unfavourable information but the client rejects Counsel's advice and seeks to withhold that information, counsel should withdraw from the case and return his or her instructions. Counsel should not continue to act for a client knowing that there exists information which ought to have been disclosed in accordance with the duty of full and frank disclosure but which, in breach of that duty, has not been disclosed because the client has refused to permit its disclosure.

32. If LPP does apply, the privilege is absolute and information cannot be disclosed without the permission of the client. Likewise, the duty of confidentiality cannot be breached, other than as permitted by law. Counsel may contact the Ethical Enquiries Line (020 7611 1307 or email ethics@barcouncil.org.uk), where those dealing with such queries are not permitted to advise on the law, but can discuss the judgment to be exercised.

Professional Practice Committee
Bar Council
Dec 2012

1 For duties to the court and disclosure see: *Ali (Saif) v Sydney Mitchell & Co (a firm)* [1980] AC 198, [1978] 3 All ER 1033, HL; *Re R (minors)(police investigation: privilege), Re* [1997] AC 16, [1996] 2 All ER 78, HL [1994] Fam 167; [1993] 2 FLR 826; [1993] 4 ALL ER 702; *Oxfordshire County Council v M* [1994] Fam 151; [1994] 2 All ER 269, CA [1994] 1 FLR 175; *DH (a minor) (child abuse)*, Re [1994] 2 FCR 3, [1994] 1 FLR 679; *Oxfordshire County Council v P* [1995] Fam 161; [1995] 2 ALL ER 225; *Vernon v Bosley (No 2)* [1999] QB 18, [1997] 1 ALL ER 614; *Arthur J S Hall v Simons* [2002] 1 AC 615, [2000] 3 ALL ER 673, HL. For Legal Professional Privilege see: *R v Derby Magistrates' Court ex p B* [1996] AC 487, [1995] 4 All ER 526, HL; [1996] 1 FLR 513; *R v Cox and Railton* [1884] 14 QBD 153; *L (a minor) (Police Investigation: Privilege), Re* [1997] AC 16, [1996] 2 All ER 78; *S County Council v B* [2000] 3 WLR 53, [2000] 1 FCR 536. For privilege against self-incrimination see: *Rank Film Distributors Ltd v Video Information Centre (a firm)* [1982] AC 380, 416C, 419F; *A Chief Constable v A County Council* [2002] EWHC 2198 (Fam).

2 See also Thorpe J. in *Essex County Council v R* [1994] Fam 167n, [1994] 2 WLR 407n; Ward J. in *Oxfordshire County Council v P* [1995] Fam 161, 166; Charles J. in *S County Council v B* [2000] 2 FLR 161, 183/A-B.

3 Children Act 1989, s 98(1).

Representation of Children in Care Proceedings

Advice from the Bar Council

[3.286]

The following is some brief guidance issued by the Bar Council in respect of representation of children in cases where no Guardian has been appointed.

It has come to the attention of the Bar Council that counsel are at times appearing in court on behalf of children even before a Guardian has been appointed. Frequently, the child's solicitor is not at court. Counsel finding themselves in that situation are reminded that they may not make submissions on the child's behalf and hold no more than a watching or noting brief in such circumstances. More generally, counsel are reminded that their active participation in such proceedings depends upon their having clear instructions which will be given by the Guardian through a solicitor.

Illegally Obtained Evidence in Civil and Family Proceedings

Illegally Obtained Evidence

[3.287]

The Bar Council has issued the following guidance for counsel who are given advice which has been obtained illegally. The guidance was reissued in January 2014.

General approach

1. It is increasingly common for counsel to have to advise in cases where evidence has, or may have been, obtained illegally.

2. Whilst it will be for you to decide, in each particular case, whether or not the evidence falls into the category of illegally obtained evidence, this ethical assistance is designed to assist in any situation in which it appears that the evidence has, indeed, been so obtained.

3. It should go without saying that it would be serious professional misconduct for counsel to advise or otherwise participate in the obtaining of information illegally. In this respect attention is drawn to the BSB Handbook CD1, CD3 and CD5:

"CD1 – You must observe your duty to the court in the administration of justice."

"CD3 – Your must act with honesty and integrity"

"CD5 – You must not behave in a way which is likely to diminish the trust and confidence which the public places in you or in the profession."

4. Clearly advising or participating in any criminal act would be in breach of this provision. Depending on the precise factual circumstances, it may be that advising or otherwise participating in some non-criminal but otherwise unlawful action – such as breach of confidence – could also be in breach of this provision.

5. Furthermore, you may find yourself in professional difficulties simply by having sight of improperly obtained documents. In this respect attention is drawn to gC11 and gC13:

"gC11 – If there is a risk that the court will be misled unless you disclose confidential information which you have learned in the course of your instructions, you should ask the client for permission to disclose it to the court. If your client refuses to allow you to make the disclosure you must cease to act, and return your instructions: see Rules C25 to C27 below. In these circumstances you must not reveal the information to the court."

"gC13 – Similarly, if you become aware that your client has a document which should be disclosed but has not been disclosed, you cannot continue to act unless your client agrees to the disclosure of the document. In these circumstances you must not reveal the existence or contents of the document to the court".

And rC25 and rC26:

"rC25 – Where you have accepted instructions to act but one or more of the circumstances set out in Rules C21.1 to C21.10 above then arises, you must cease to act and return your instructions promptly. In addition, you must cease to act and return your instructions if:

2 the client refuses to authorise you to make some disclosure to the court which your duty to the court requires you to make, or

3 the client refuses to authorise you to make some disclosure to the court which your duty to the court requires you to make ..."

"rC26 – You may case to act on a matter on which you are instructed and return any instructions if:

6 you become aware of confidential or privileged information or documents on which you are instructed ..."

Claims to privilege in illegally obtained evidence

6. In *Dubai Aluminium Co Ltd v Al Alawi* [1999] 1 All ER 703, [1999] 1 All ER (Comm) 1, Rix J ruled that legal professional privilege did not apply in relation to any relevant documents unlawfully obtained. It follows that all such data obtained, the source of the data and the letters of instruction to the person who obtained them, will have to be disclosed to the other side in any case in which data has already been so obtained. This will be the case whether or not so doing will assist the client or prejudice him and his

sources, by revealing unlawful activity. However, see Neuberger MR's comments in *Imerman v Tchenguiz* [2010] EWCA Civ 908 [2011] 2 WLR 592 at paragraph 42 as to the possibility of claiming privilege from self-incrimination to avoid explaining how documents have been acquired, but not the fact that such documents have been acquired. See also *Hildebrand v Hildebrand* [1992] 1 FLR 244, [1992] Fam Law 235, as considered in *Imerman* for when such documents must be disclosed.

Imerman, breach of confidentiality and computers:

7. The case of *Imerman* (*supra*) has highlighted three particular issues that counsel should be award of in this area:

   (i) breach of confidence;

   (ii) the Computer Misuse Act 1990; and

   (iii) the Data Protection Act 1988.

8. *Imerman* has underlined the fact that documents obtained in breach of confidence, at least when they are not yet disclosable, must be returned to the owner, although this ought to be subject to any available defences as a matter of law or equity. If they must be returned, then it appears almost inevitable that they would fall within the issues covered by the BSB Handbook set out above.

9. It may or may not be professionally embarrassing to continue to act in such a situation. Whether this is so will depend on the circumstances.

10. *Imerman* also gives a helpful example of where copying data from a computer for the purpose of helping in legal proceedings at least raised the possibility of criminal offences having occurred under the two statutes.

11. The Computer Misuse Act 1990 s.1 provides that it is an offence for a person to cause "a computer to perform any function with intent to secure access to any program or data held in any computer", where "the access ... is unauthorised" and "he knows at the time ... that that is the case". Securing access includes taking copies of any data or moving any data to "any storage medium" or using such data. And an act is "unauthorised, if the person doing [it] ... is not [and does not have the authority of] a person who has responsibility for the computer and is entitled to determine whether the act may be done".

12. The Data Protection Act 1988 s.55(1)(a) states that "a person must not knowingly or recklessly" and "without the consent of the data controller obtain or disclose personal data". Section 55(2) exempts from the ambit of section 55(1) cases where (a) the obtaining or disclosing was "necessary for the purpose of preventing or detecting a crime" or "required ... by any rule of law", (c) the person reasonably believed that he had the consent of the data controller, or (d) the action was "justified as being in the public interest". Section 55(3) provides that a person who breaches section 55(1) "is guilty of an offence". In this respect clients often seek to argue that their case was 'justified as being in the public interest'. In such cases it may be useful to refer to Neuberger MR's comments at paragraph 103 of Imerman on one such attempt.

Conclusion

13. The following principles therefore apply:

(a) You must never advise that evidence be obtained illegally.

(b) If evidence has already been so obtained, you must advise the client of both (a) the client's disclosure obligations and (b) where applicable, counsel's own disclosure obligations, including the ramifications of the decision in *Dubai Aluminium*.

(c) If the client is in breach of the consequent disclosure obligations, you will almost invariably have to return the case.

Important notice

This document has been prepared by the Bar Council to assist barristers on matters of professional conduct and ethics. **It is not "guidance" for the purposes of the BSB Handbook I6.4, and neither the BSB nor a disciplinary tribunal nor the Legal Ombudsman is bound by any views or advice expressed in it.** It does not comprise – and cannot be relied on as giving – legal advice. It has been prepared in good faith, but neither the Bar Council nor any of the individuals responsible for or involved in its preparation accept any responsibility or liability for anything done in reliance on it. For fuller information as to the status and effect of this document, please refer to the professional practice and ethics section of the Bar Council's website

President of Family Division's Guidance on McKenzie Friends

Guidance on McKenzie Friends

[3.287a]

Practitioners should be aware that the President of the Family Division has recently issued guidance on the advantages to the Court of Mackenzie friends and, in particular, how useful they are to the Court when dealing with litigants in person. The guidance is set out below.

President's Guidance

1. This Guidance applies to civil and family proceedings in the Court of Appeal (Civil Division), the High Court of Justice, the County Courts and the Family Proceedings Court in the Magistrates' Courts.[1] It is issued as guidance (not as a Practice Direction) by the Master of the Rolls, as Head of Civil Justice, and the President of the Family Division, as Head of Family Justice. It is intended to remind courts and litigants of the principles set out in the authorities and supersedes the guidance contained in *Practice Note (Family Courts: McKenzie Friends) (No 2)* [2008] 1 WLR 2757, which is now withdrawn.[2] It is issued in light of the increase in litigants-in-person (litigants) in all levels of the civil and family courts.

The Right to Reasonable Assistance

2. Litigants have the right to have reasonable assistance from a layperson, sometimes called a McKenzie Friend (MF). Litigants assisted by MFs remain litigants-in-person. MFs have no independent right to provide assistance. They have no right to act as advocates or to carry out the conduct of litigation.

What McKenzie Friends may do

3. MFs may:

   (i) provide moral support for litigants;

   (ii) take notes;

   (iii) help with case papers;

   (iv) quietly give advice on any aspect of the conduct of the case.

What McKenzie Friends may not do

4. MFs may not:

   (i) act as the litigants' agent in relation to the proceedings;

   (ii) manage litigants' cases outside court, for example by signing court documents; or

   (iii) address the court, make oral submissions or examine witnesses.

Exercising the Right to Reasonable Assistance

5. While litigants ordinarily have a right to receive reasonable assistance from MFs the court retains the power to refuse to permit such assistance. The court may do so where it is satisfied that, in that case, the interests of justice and fairness do not require the litigant to receive such assistance.

6. A litigant who wishes to exercise this right should inform the judge as soon as possible indicating who the MF will be. The proposed MF should produce a short curriculum vitae or other statement setting out relevant experience, confirming that he or she has no interest in the case and understands the MF's role and the duty of confidentiality.

7. If the court considers that there might be grounds for circumscribing the right to receive such assistance, or a party objects to the presence of, or assistance given by a MF, it is not for the litigant to justify the exercise of the right. It is for the court or the objecting party to provide sufficient reasons why the litigant should not receive such assistance.

8. When considering whether to circumscribe the right to assistance or refuse a MF permission to attend the right to a fair trial is engaged. The matter should be considered carefully. The litigant should be given a reasonable opportunity to argue the point. The proposed MF should not be excluded from that hearing and should normally be allowed to help the litigant.

9. Where proceedings are in closed court, i.e. the hearing is in chambers, is in private, or the proceedings relate to a child, the litigant is required to justify

the MF's presence in court. The presumption in favour of permitting a MF to attend such hearings, and thereby enable litigants to exercise the right to assistance, is a strong one.

10. The court may refuse to allow a litigant to exercise the right to receive assistance at the start of a hearing. The court can also circumscribe the right during the course of a hearing. It may be refused at the start of a hearing or later circumscribed where the court forms the view that a MF may give, has given, or is giving, assistance which impedes the efficient administration of justice. However, the court should also consider whether a firm and unequivocal warning to the litigant and/or MF might suffice in the first instance.

11. A decision by the court not to curtail assistance from a MF should be regarded as final, save on the ground of subsequent misconduct by the MF or on the ground that the MF's continuing presence will impede the efficient administration of justice. In such event the court should give a short judgment setting out the reasons why it has curtailed the right to assistance. Litigants may appeal such decisions. MFs have no standing to do so.

12. The following factors should not be taken to justify the court refusing to permit a litigant receiving such assistance:

    (i) the case or application is simple or straightforward, or is, for instance, a directions or case management hearing;

    (ii) the litigant appears capable of conducting the case without assistance;

    (iii) the litigant is unrepresented through choice;

    (iv) the other party is not represented;

    (v) the proposed MF belongs to an organisation that promotes a particular cause;

    (vi) the proceedings are confidential and the court papers contain sensitive information relating to a family's affairs

13. A litigant may be denied the assistance of a MF because its provision might undermine or has undermined the efficient administration of justice. Examples of circumstances where this might arise are:

    (i) the assistance is being provided for an improper purpose;

    (ii) the assistance is unreasonable in nature or degree;

    (iii) the MF is subject to a civil proceedings order or a civil restraint order;

    (iv) the MF is using the litigant as a puppet;

    (v) the MF is directly or indirectly conducting the litigation;

    (vi) the court is not satisfied that the MF fully understands the duty of confidentiality.

14. Where a litigant is receiving assistance from a MF in care proceedings, the court should consider the MF's attendance at any advocates' meetings directed by the court, and, with regard to cases commenced after 1.4.08, consider directions in accordance with paragraph 13.2 of the Practice Direction Guide to Case Management in Public Law Proceedings.

15. Litigants are permitted to communicate any information, including filed evidence, relating to the proceedings to MFs for the purpose of obtaining advice or assistance in relation to the proceedings.

16. Legal representatives should ensure that documents are served on litigants in good time to enable them to seek assistance regarding their content from MFs in advance of any hearing or advocates' meeting.

17. The High Court can, under its inherent jurisdiction, impose a civil restraint order on MFs who repeatedly act in ways that undermine the efficient administration of justice.

Rights of audience and rights to conduct litigation

18. MFs do not have a right of audience or a right to conduct litigation. It is a criminal offence to exercise rights of audience or to conduct litigation unless properly qualified and authorised to do so by an appropriate regulatory body or, in the case of an otherwise unqualified or unauthorised individual (i.e., a lay individual including a MF), the court grants such rights on a case-by-case basis.[3]

19. Courts should be slow to grant any application from a litigant for a right of audience or a right to conduct litigation to any lay person, including a MF. This is because a person exercising such rights must ordinarily be properly trained, be under professional discipline (including an obligation to insure against liability for negligence) and be subject to an overriding duty to the court. These requirements are necessary for the protection of all parties to litigation and are essential to the proper administration of justice.

20. Any application for a right of audience or a right to conduct litigation to be granted to any lay person should therefore be considered very carefully. The court should only be prepared to grant such rights where there is good reason to do so taking into account all the circumstances of the case, which are likely to vary greatly. Such grants should not be extended to lay persons automatically or without due consideration. They should not be granted for mere convenience.

21. Examples of the type of special circumstances which have been held to justify the grant of a right of audience to a lay person, including a MF, are:

    (i) that person is a close relative of the litigant;

    (ii) health problems preclude the litigant from addressing the court, or conducting litigation, and the litigant cannot afford to pay for a qualified legal representative;

    (iii) the litigant is relatively inarticulate and prompting by that person may unnecessarily prolong the proceedings.

22. It is for the litigant to persuade the court that the circumstances of the case are such that it is in the interests of justice for the court to grant a lay person a right of audience or a right to conduct litigation.

23. The grant of a right of audience or a right to conduct litigation to lay persons who hold themselves out as professional advocates or professional MFs or who seek to exercise such rights on a regular basis, whether for reward or not, will however only be granted in exceptional circumstances. To do otherwise would tend to subvert the will of Parliament.

24. If a litigant wants a lay person to be granted a right of audience, an application must be made at the start of the hearing. If a right to conduct litigation is sought such an application must be made at the earliest possible time and must be made, in any event, before the lay person does anything which amounts to the conduct of litigation. It is for litigants to persuade the court, on a case-by-case basis, that the grant of such rights is justified.

25. Rights of audience and the right to conduct litigation are separate rights. The grant of one right to a lay person does not mean that a grant of the other right has been made. If both rights are sought their grant must be applied for individually and justified separately.

26. Having granted either a right of audience or a right to conduct litigation, the court has the power to remove either right. The grant of such rights in one set of proceedings cannot be relied on as a precedent supporting their grant in future proceedings.

Remuneration

27. Litigants can enter into lawful agreements to pay fees to MFs for the provision of reasonable assistance in court or out of court by, for instance, carrying out clerical or mechanical activities, such as photocopying documents, preparing bundles, delivering documents to opposing parties or the court, or the provision of legal advice in connection with court proceedings. Such fees cannot be lawfully recovered from the opposing party.

28. Fees said to be incurred by MFs for carrying out the conduct of litigation, where the court has not granted such a right, cannot lawfully be recovered from either the litigant for whom they carry out such work or the opposing party.

29. Fees said to be incurred by MFs for carrying out the conduct of litigation after the court has granted such a right are in principle recoverable from the litigant for whom the work is carried out. Such fees cannot be lawfully recovered from the opposing party.

30. Fees said to be incurred by MFs for exercising a right of audience following the grant of such a right by the court are in principle recoverable from the litigant on whose behalf the right is exercised. Such fees are also recoverable, in principle, from the opposing party as a recoverable disbursement: CPR 48. 6(2) and 48(6)(3)(ii).

Personal Support Unit & Citizen's Advice Bureaux

31. Litigants should also be aware of the services provided by local Personal Support Units and Citizens' Advice Bureaux. The PSU at the Royal Courts of Justice in London can be contacted on 020 7947 7701, by email or at the enquiry desk. The CAB at the Royal Courts of Justice in London can be contacted on 020 7947 6564 or at the enquiry desk.

Lord Neuberger of Abbotsbury, Master of the Rolls
Sir Nicholas Wall, President of the Family Division
12 July 2010

1 References to the judge or court should be read where proceedings are taking place under the Family Proceedings Courts (Matrimonial Proceedings etc) Rules 1991, as a reference to a justices' clerk or

assistant justices' clerk who is specifically authorised by a justices' clerk to exercise the functions of the court at the relevant hearing. Where they are taking place under the Family Proceedings Courts (Childrens Act 1989) Rules 1991 they should be read consistently with the provisions of those Rules, specifically rule 16A(5A).

2 *R v Leicester City Justices, ex p Barrow* [1991] 2 QB 260, [1991] 2 All ER 437, *Chauhan v Chauhan* [1997] 2 FCR 206, CA, *R v Bow County Court, ex p Pelling* [1999] 4 All ER 751, [1999] 1 WLR 1807, CA, *A-G v Purvis* [2003] EWHC 3190 (Admin), *Clarkson v Gilbert* [2000] 3 FCR 10, [2000] CP Rep 58, CA, *Uhbi (t/a United Building & Plumbing Contractors) v Kajla* [2002] EWCA Civ 628, [2002] All ER (D) 265 (Apr), *O (children), Re* [2005] EWCA Civ 759, [2006] Fam 1, [2005] 3 WLR 1191, *Westland Helicopters Ltd v Sheikh Salah Al-Hejailan (No 2)* 2004] EWHC 1688 (Comm), [2004] 2 Lloyd's Rep 535, [2006] 4 Costs LR 549. *Agassi v Robinson (Inspector of Taxes) (Bar Council intervening)* [2005] EWCA Civ 1507, [2006] 1 All ER 900, [2006] 1 WLR 2126, *N (a Child) (McKenzie friends: rights of audience)* [2008] EWHC 2042 (Fam), [2008] 1 WLR 2743, [2008] 3 FCR 642.

3 Legal Services Act 2007 ss 12–19 and Schedule 3.

Part D: Good Practice Guidance for Barristers practising Civil Law

Retainers and Novel Fee Arrangements

Retainers and Other Fee Arrangements — Guidance Note

[3.288]

The Professional Practice Committee is sometimes asked to consider the propriety of "retainers" or other novel fee arrangements, particularly in relation to problems of conflict of interest in appearing against the party paying the retainer.

The guidance that follows was issued by the PPC in October 2012.

Introduction

This guidance from the PPC concerns fee arrangements, with particular reference to "retainers" of various types. It does not cover the prohibition on referral fees (and other commission-type payments): the PPC has given separate guidance on that topic.

There is no generally-accepted definition of "retainer" (for example, in the Bar Council's standard-form Contractual Terms and CFA, it appears to be used simply to mean a barrister's agreement with a solicitor to provide legal services). To avoid issues of terminology, we have set out below various types of arrangement that are sometimes called "retainers", and may give rise to problems in practice, together with our views about such arrangements.

At the end, there is a checklist which is intended to assist barristers to analyse whether or not it is permissible for them to enter into a particular fee arrangement.

Retainer-type arrangements

Rule 405 of the Code of Conduct provides that (subject to rule 307) a self-employed barrister may charge for any work undertaken by him on any basis or by any method he thinks fit provided that such basis or method is permitted by law and does not involve the payment of a wage or salary. Thus, any particular arrangement may be prohibited because it is unlawful, or because it involves the payment of a wage or salary. This may not, however, be the only relevant rule to be considered in relation to a retainer-type arrangement.

Payments giving the client a "call option" on the barrister's services and barring him from appearing against that client.

This is the traditional type of retainer which was abolished in the 1980s. In our view:

(a) A "general retainer" (whose effect is that the barrister is debarred from acting against that client in any matter, whether or not he has received instructions to act for him in a particular case) will not usually be permissible. This is because, in the absence of a true conflict, it is an affront to the cab rank rule, and to the free availability of legal services.

(b) A "special retainer" (debarring the barrister from accepting a brief from any other party in a particular case) is likely to be subject to the same objections, at least up to the time when instructions are received.

Payments in the nature of "booking" fees

Whether it is permissible to charge a "booking" fee depends on what is meant by a booking fee in any particular case.

Where it is proposed to charge or incur fees before work has been undertaken, the question whether the arrangement is permissible will depend on whether the fee can be said to be incurred on account of work undertaken or to be undertaken.

For example, where a barrister agrees to keep himself free in order to undertake a particular piece of work, it will be acceptable to charge a non-refundable fee so long as that fee is genuinely a payment in respect of the work it is anticipated will be carried out. The fact that the barrister is in the event not required to carry out the work does not affect the fee being paid for work to be undertaken. Such an arrangement is no different in principle from a brief fee which is incurred in whole or part before the papers are delivered and is treated as non-refundable if the case settles. Similarly, it is permissible to charge and receive a fee if the fee is in respect of the barrister making him/herself available for a defined period of time: e.g. for blocking out a defined period of time in his/her diary for a case.

However, there are cases where barristers have sought to charge merely for "agreeing to act" in respect of a particular matter (but not for undertaking any further obligation). Such a fee is not a fee for work undertaken or to be undertaken, and is potentially objectionable for the reason given in section 1 above.

A condition, attached to a standard brief or instructions, purporting to debar the barrister from acting against that client in the future

Some major clients are said to seek to impose this as a pre-condition of receiving instructions from them. We believe that the problem most commonly occurs in relation to insurance companies, national newspapers, large accountancy firms, and some US clients. We have also been made aware that those who are members of certain government panels at times feel under (or are placed under) pressure not to accept instructions to act against the governmental body on whose panel they serve.

In our view, it is professionally improper for counsel to agree, expressly or implicitly, to such a condition. In effect, it is an attempt to "contract out" of the Cab-rank rule, which positively obliges counsel to accept instructions against an existing or former client unless a specific conflict, generally relating to confidential information, would result. Counsel must be free to test the proposed new instructions against the existing ones on a case-by-case basis; or else major clients could quickly "scoop the pool" and monopolise competent representation in their field.

A condition attached to a particular brief or instructions, precluding counsel from carrying out other work during that case

There appears to be no objection in principle to this, provided (1) the object is genuinely to ensure that the barrister has sufficient time to deal with the work, (2) the condition, and its extent, are objectively justifiable, and (3) it does not prejudice other, pre-existing clients.

An arrangement whereby counsel is not paid on the traditional "piecework" basis, per case, day or hour, but rather is "retained", in return for periodic payments, to deal generally with whatever legal matters may arise

It is not unusual, particularly at the junior end of the common law bar, for such flat-fee arrangements to be proposed by solicitors, clients or claims handlers who wish to cap their counsels' bills.

In principle, the Code permits any lawful fee arrangements except a "wage or salary" (rule 405(b)).

In practice, there is a real risk that such fee arrangements may be linked with doubtful work practices that prejudice the young barristers' professional independence and lead them into danger of breaching other Code rules.

We have set out below a checklist intended to assist barristers to identify and resolve such problems.

There is also a danger that such an arrangement will amount to or involve a disguised referral fee or commission, which is prohibited under the Code (as explained in the separate guidance which has been given on this topic).

Guidance on Commissions and Payment by Barristers for Work

Civil Law – Commissions Practice Guidance

[3.289]–[3.291]

Following the outcome of the Claims Direct Personal Injury programme, the Professional Standards Committee issued the following guidance to the Bar to clarify the permissibility of barristers offering payment in return for work:

This guidance is issued following recent communications from the Professional Standards Committee (PSC) concerning schemes under the aegis of the Claims Direct Personal Injury programme. The Committee's view was that these schemes appeared to involve members of the Bar paying outside consultants in order to obtain work and could not fairly be construed as arrangements under which barristers pay for preparation and administrative work which is necessary to enable them to give good professional advice. The Professional Standards Committee established a Working Group to consider the issues raised by such schemes and generally.

We understand that the original scheme which gave rise to our concerns is no longer applicable. So far, no similar schemes have been proposed and we therefore do not think it necessary or appropriate to look at the issue in respect of hypothetical cases. If further schemes are suggested we will look at those and see whether this advice needs amendment.

We think, however, that it would be helpful to the Bar to state what the rules currently are and how we believe they affect particular sets of circumstances that have arisen. In particular, we bear in mind the following principles:

- barristers should be instructed for their expertise and suitability for the task, not because they have paid either the client or any third party to receive instructions;
- fee notes should be transparent and not have the effect of misleading a court or any party as to what they contain.

The Rules

We draw the Bar's attention particularly to the following passage of the Code of Conduct:

"Paragraph 307

A barrister must not:

(a) permit his absolute independence integrity and freedom from external pressures to be compromised;

(b) do anything (for example accept a present) in such circumstances as may lead to any inference that his independence may be compromised;

(c) compromise his professional standards in order to please his client the Court or a third party, including any mediator;

(d) give a commission or present or lend any money for any professional purpose to or (save as a remuneration in accordance with the provisions of this Code) accept any money by way of loan or otherwise from any client or any person entitled to instruct him as an intermediary;

(e) make any payment (other than a payment for advertising or publicity permitted by this Code or in the case of a barrister in independent practice remuneration paid to any clerk or other employee or staff of his chambers) to any person for the purpose of procuring professional instructions;..."

Sub-paragraphs (d) and (e) are of particular relevance to this issue. In addition, attention should also be drawn to paragraphs 205 (prohibition on supplying services to the public through or on behalf of anyone other than solicitors, the LSC or a Law Centre).

We now give advice on the following issues.

Payments for work

In our view:

- schemes which require barristers to pay for services provided outside chambers in order to accept work are likely to contravene paragraph 307(e) and to involve a hidden commission contrary to 307(d);
- 307(e) in our view precludes payments to clerks of other chambers in return for forwarding work;
- an "introduction" fee of a set amount per case or a percentage-based "administration charge" or "advertising fee" where the amount is linked to the work actually received is also likely to breach paragraph 307; and
- if the "advertising" or "publicity" fee paid by a barrister is periodic e.g. annual or monthly (for as long as the service continues to be supplied) and: (a) can be shown to be payable whether any referrals result or not, (b) does not vary with the number of referrals, and (c) is priced in a way that seems to be a fair commercial reflection of the services that are actually being supplied, then the payment is unlikely to be interpreted as a referral fee, even if paid afterwards rather than before.

Agreements with lay clients providing "bulk" work

We are aware that a number of protocols exist with lay clients who instruct the Bar regularly (particularly insurers) whereby barristers agree to undertake work at particular rates or to discount fees if payment is made promptly. In principle, the Bar Council has no objection to such arrangements but care needs to be taken to ensure that:

- the agreement does not amount to a contract with the lay client (and if it is in writing this should be clear) – otherwise it would breach paragraph 401;

PART III
IN PRACTICE

- where the agreement includes a reduction for early settlement of fees, this should be made clear on the fee note;
- 307(a) and (b) in our view have the effect of prohibiting barristers from agreeing to schemes whereby different fees are routinely paid according to the nature of the advice given (eg: a lower fee for negative advice).

Responsibility for Members of Chambers

Barristers are reminded that they are responsible for the conduct of their staff and should ensure that members of their staff are not paying commission on their own account in respect of work received by Chambers.

Other Guidance Concerning the Claims Direct Scheme

We have received a number of additional queries arising out of the particular arrangements proposed under the scheme from Brown Associates and the Bar Council's advice. It should be made clear that:

- barristers retain responsibility for the contents of their fee notes and should not: (i) permit blank fee notes to be sent out to be completed by third parties; (ii) be party to arrangements where fee notes are altered by third parties.
- fee notes should record the fee that the barrister is actually being paid for professional services. There is obviously no need to refer to ordinary professional expenses, such as clerks' fees, chambers rent and administration, travel costs and the like. A special payment to be made to a third party for preparation or administrative work of the kind that would normally be undertaken by instructing solicitors would, however, be regarded as an extraordinary expense. Such payments should be recorded on the fee note so that the document is transparent and so could be challenged by the party ultimately responsible for paying the fee.
- there are doubts about whether the instructions that counsel received under this scheme and the timescales in which the work was required to be done were necessarily sufficient. Barristers must take care to ensure that they are satisfied that the advice they give is competent and sufficiently full, and even where counsel is invited to use a standard form, that they have seen and had time to consider all the relevant documents in a case before completing any work.
- there is nothing inherently wrong in undertaking work which has been generated by Claims Direct or any similar organisation but, in doing so, barristers must ensure that any arrangements pursuant to which the work is done by them comply with the Code. If the terms do not comply then the barrister should seek to re-negotiate the terms with the instructing solicitor (who, of course, remains liable for the fee). If that is unsuccessful then the barrister is professionally embarrassed under paragraph 603(c) of the Code.

Generally

If barristers are uncertain about whether particular schemes fall within the Code, they are urged to seek advice in writing from the Professional Standards Department of the Bar Council. It is essential that when writing barristers should provide comprehensive information about the schemes including any relevant materials which the barristers have concerning the schemes. That Department will attempt to provide advice as quickly as possible, but it may well be that advice may need to be sought from the relevant Committees and this may take some weeks. If Chambers are negotiating such schemes, they should raise them with the Bar Council as early as possible. This can be done on a confidential basis.

In particular, Chambers should not rely on statements from others that approval has been gained or is being sought for particular schemes. The PCC is unlikely to look favourably on requests for waivers to enable Chambers to complete work on terms which are in breach of the Code and which were entered into without having consulted the Bar Council and may, indeed, take disciplinary action against Chambers which do so.

Conflict with the rules of other Approved Regulators (s 52 of the LSA 2007)

The BSB has become aware that some barristers may be attempting to circumvent the prohibition on the payment of referral fees by obtaining a dual practising certificate and entering into arrangements with SRA regulated entities.

Barristers in this position may take the view that no issues of professional misconduct arise because (a) the 2010 changes to the Code of Conduct allow "dual capacity", (b) the SRA's Handbook specifically permits referral payments, and (c) where the SRA's rules conflict with those of the BSB, the SRA's rules (as the entity regulator) are to be preferred in accordance with section 52 of the LSA 2007 ("the Act").

The BSB will apply a purposive interpretation to the prohibition on referral fees, and will consider taking enforcement action against any barrister who enters into arrangements whose object is to circumvent the prohibition. The BSB considers that on a correct application of section 52, that section does not have the effect of overriding the BSB's prohibition on referral fees.

Section 52 of the Act provides that:

"52 Regulatory conflict with approved regulators

(1) This section has no associated Explanatory Notes(1)The regulatory arrangements of an approved regulator must make such provision as is reasonably practicable to prevent regulatory conflicts.

(2) For the purposes of this section and section 53, a regulatory conflict is a conflict between:

(a) a requirement of the approved regulator's regulatory arrangements; and

(b) a requirement of the regulatory arrangements of another approved regulator.

(3) Subsection (4) applies where a body is authorised by an approved regulator ('the entity regulator') to carry on an activity which is a reserved legal activity.

(4) If a conflict arises between:

(a) a requirement of the regulatory arrangements of the entity regulator, in relation to the body authorised by the entity regulator or an employee or manager of the body ('an entity requirement'); and

(b) a requirement of the regulatory arrangements of another approved regulator in relation to an employee or manager of the body who is authorised by it to carry on a reserved legal activity ('an individual requirement'), the entity requirement prevails over the individual requirement.

(5) The BSB's view is that in section 52 the meaning of the word 'requirement' is limited to mandatory regulatory requirements. It does not extend to permissive arrangements.

(6) Therefore "regulatory conflict" for the purposes of ss 52 and 54 occurs only where a mandatory provision in the regulatory arrangements of one approved regulator is incompatible with a mandatory provision in the regulatory arrangements of another approved regulator. Itdoes notoccur where:

(a) a mandatory provision in the regulatory arrangements of one approved regulator is more restrictive than an equivalent provision in the regulatory arrangements of another approved regulator; or

(b) a permissive provision in the regulatory arrangements of an approved regulator would otherwise allow a person to act in a way which is prohibited by a mandatory provision in the regulatory arrangements of another approved regulator, because the former provision is not a 'requirement' and thus outside the sub-class of regulatory arrangements identified in ss 52(2) and 54(2).

(7) In the BSB's view the qualified permission to pay referral fees contained in the SRA's regulatory arrangements does not amount to a 'requirement of the SRA's regulatory arrangements'. Therefore, no regulatory conflict within the meaning of s.52 arises and that section does not have the effect of overriding the BSB's prohibition.

(8) Whether or not enforcement action is taken against barristers is a fact sensitive issue and will depend on whether the arrangements have as their object evading the prohibition. Examples of behavior that will make prosecution more likely include:

(a) A set of Chambers creates an LLP formed of all members of Chambers and one solicitor, from which the members of Chambers receive a profit share (or even a salary as mployees) on terms which effectively amount to a pass-through of fees attributable to the work actually done by each barrister. Here the entity is merely a front for members of Chambers designed to evade the requirements of the Code of Conduct and they should be regarded as one and the same, such that payment of referral fees by the entity amounts to a breach of the Code by the barristers involved.

(b) A self-employed barrister, who has obtained a dual practising certificate, enters into a case-by-case contract for service with a SRA regulated entity on the understanding that they will undertake the advocacy component of the case for 80% (or similar) of the prescribed legal aid fee.

(c) An LLP is established and regulated by the SRA. It is comprised inter alia of a number of barristers who seek to be instructed to provide advocacy services. The barristers are either members of the LLP, or are employed by it, as the case may be. In accordance with the SRA's rules on referral fees, the LLP agrees to accept instructions for 80% (or similar) of the advocacy fee. The advocacy is then undertaken by the barristers, acting as either members or employees of the LLP (pursuant to paragraph 207 of the Code), in return for 100% of the 80% of the fee paid to the LLP. The commercial purpose and effect of the arrangements is to enable the individuals to pay a referral fee and receive a pass-through of the balance of the fee attributable to their individual work. "

Guidance on Pleading Fraud

Guidance on Pleading Fraud

[3.292]

This short guidance note was issued by the PSC in March 2003 and last reviewed in September 2008..

In the case of *Medcalf v Mardell* [2002] UKHL 27, [2003] 1 AC 120, [2002] 3 All ER 721, the House of Lords considered paragraph 704(c) of the Code of Conduct and a barrister's duties in considering whether or not to draft a document including an allegation of fraud.

Paragraph 704 (c) states that a barrister should not draft a document containing any allegation of fraud "unless he has clear instructions to make such an allegation and has before him reasonably credible material which as it stands establishes a prima facie case of fraud". In this case, the Court of Appeal had taken the view that a barrister in making such an allegation should have before him "evidence which can be put before the court to make good the allegation".

The House of Lords rejected this interpretation. Lord Bingham of Cornhill, with whom the other law lords agreed, said that:

> "... the requirement is not that counsel should necessarily have before him evidence in admissible form but that he should have material of such a character as to lead responsible counsel to conclude that serious allegations should properly be based upon it".

The Professional Standards Committee ("PSC") takes the view that there is no litmus test for determining whether it is proper to allege fraud. As Lord Bingham made clear: "Counsel is bound to exercise an objective professional judgment whether it is in all circumstances proper to lend his name to the allegation". That decision will depend on the individual facts of each case.

It should be noted that although paragraph 704 refers specifically to fraud, the same principle would apply to any other allegation of serious misconduct.

1 Subject to approval by the DCA.

Bar Equality and Diversity Rules of the BSB Handbook

[3.293]–[3.318]

The Bar Standards Board has produced a BSB Handbook Equality Rules Supporting Information guidance booklet. This can be accessed via the BSB website. This information pack is designed to be a tool for the administration of chambers, to enable chambers to meet their legal and regulatory duties, and to follow best practice in equality and diversity.

Guidance for Chambers on Equality Act Changes

Guidance for Chambers on Equality Act changes

[3.318a]–[3.319]

The Bar Council Equality and Diversity Committee issued the following guidance in December 2010 as to the effect of the Equality Act 2010.

Introduction

The Equality Act 2010 ("the Act") replaces the numerous Acts and Regulations which previously dealt with race, sex, disability, religion or belief, sexual orientation, age, pregnancy and maternity, marriage and civil partnership and gender reassignment discrimination. The Act consolidates the previous legislation, retaining many of the same legal principles and concepts, but organising them in a more coherent and accessible manner. However, there are also some significant changes made to the law (see below).

As with the old discrimination legislation, Chambers are affected in a number of ways. Firstly, as employers, they are subject to the non-discrimination provisions as regards their treatment of chambers' employees (see Part 5 Chapter 1 of the Act). Secondly, barristers and clerks are bound by provisions relating to the Bar in section 47 of the Act (prohibiting discrimination against pupils, tenants and would-be pupils or tenants). Thirdly, as service providers, chambers are covered by Part 3 of the Act in relation to service recipients.

Date From Which the Equality Act 2010 Applies

1. The majority of the provisions of the Equality Act 2010 came into force on 1 October 2010. A number of the remaining provisions will be brought into force in April 2011.
2. Where an act which is unlawful under previous discrimination legislation continues after 1 October 2010, it is also unlawful under the Equality Act.
3. The Equality Act, however, will not apply to acts which occur wholly before 1 October 2010.
4. Further, the victimisation provisions in section 27 are to be read as applying equally to victimisation as a result of bringing proceedings under the previous legislation as to proceedings brought under the Equality Act.
5. The transitional provisions also state that the existing guidance on disability remains in force until new guidance comes into force.

The Following Sections of the Equality Act 2010 have not yet been Brought into Force

1. The socio-economic inequality duty on public authorities (section 1) (the new coalition Government has said that it has no intention of bringing this into force).
2. Dual discrimination i.e. claims combining two protected characteristics (section 14).
3. The requirement on private sector employers to publish gender pay gap information (section 78).
4. Positive action in recruitment and promotion (section 159) (this is due to come into force in April 2011).
5. Compulsory retirement at 65 will be phased out from April 2011. Protection from age discrimination in the provision of services will come into force in 2012.
6. The single public sector equality duty (sections 149–157) due to come into force in April 2011.

Protected Characteristics

The 2010 Act brings together all the grounds previously protected by anti-discrimination legislation, describing them as "protected characteristics". Those characteristics are:

1. Age
2. Disability
3. Gender reassignment
4. Marriage and civil partnership
5. Pregnancy and maternity
6. Race
7. Religion or belief
8. Sex
9. Sexual orientation

Key Changes Made by the Equality Act 2010

1. **Discrimination "arising from" disability**: this is a new form of unlawful discrimination which is intended to address problems that had occurred with "reason related" discrimination under the old law. The Equality Act 2010 states that if a chambers treats an employee or a barrister treats a pupil or tenant "unfavourably because of something arising in consequence of disability" and the chambers or barrister cannot show that the treatment is a "proportionate means of achieving a legitimate aim", it will be unlawful.
2. **Duty to make reasonable adjustments**: the duty which existed previously under the Disability Discrimination Act 1995 is now extended to

require chambers to take such steps as are reasonable to provide auxiliary aids or services to a disabled employee who would otherwise be put at a substantial disadvantage in relation to a non disabled employee. The same applies to barristers vis-a-vis disabled pupils and tenants.

3. **Harassment**: the Act extends the definition of harassment to harassment related to an employee's, tenant's or pupil's race, colour or nationality. Thus unlawful harassment can now relate to any of the protected characteristics set out above, save for pregnancy, maternity, marriage and civil partnership.

Another key change to the old law relates to an employer's responsibility for harassment of its employees by a third party. A chambers will now be liable where a third party (which would include a barrister or a solicitor) harasses an employee in the course of that employee's employment and the chambers is found not to have taken such steps as would have been reasonably practicable to prevent the third party from doing so. This requires the chambers to have known about harassment of that employee by a third party on at least three occasions. Note that the chambers would still be responsible even if the harassment they were aware of had come from a different barrister or solicitor (or other third party) on each of those three occasions.

Individual barristers and clerks are not subject to these rules on third parties and will only be held personally liable for unlawful harassment of a pupil or tenant (or would-be pupil or tenant) by their own conduct.

4. **Enquiries about disability and health prior to appointment**: The Equality Act 2010 prohibits pre-selection questions of a candidate (whether orally or in writing) about their health save as set out below. These rules apply to the appointment process for an employee or the process for offering a pupillage or tenancy. Questions *can* be asked where the question is necessary for the purpose of:

(a) establishing whether the applicant will be able to undergo an assessment in order to determine whether the chambers will be under a duty to make reasonable adjustments;

(b) establishing whether the applicant will be able to carry out a function that is intrinsic to the work involved in the job being applied for (for example, will a post room clerk be able to carry a reasonable weight of parcels to the post office);

(c) monitoring the diversity of those applying to chambers;

(d) the chambers taking positive action for the benefit of disabled applicants; or

(e) if chambers specifically requires someone with a particular disability, establishing whether the applicant has it. A chambers can only rely on this provision if it is an occupational requirement to employ someone with that disability.

Only the Equality and Human Rights Commission can bring proceedings against a chambers for a breach of this provision of the Equality Act 2010. However, the Act stresses that whilst merely asking about an applicant's health will not breach the other rules regarding disability discrimination (e.g. direct or indirect discrimination), how a chambers reacts to and uses information about an applicant's health might do so.

5. **Associative discrimination**: The Act clarifies that in relation to direct discrimination and harassment, an individual can claim they have been less favourably treated not just because of *their* race, sex, disability etc, but also "because of" race, sex disability etc in a more general sense. The most likely scenario this will cover is where it is claimed the less favourable treatment arises because the individual in question is associated with someone of a particular race, sex, disability etc.

6. **Perception discrimination**: This is where someone claims that they have been discriminated against because of a mistaken perception that they are of a particular religion, sexual orientation, age etc. Under the old law, this concept was not obviously covered in relation to sex, gender reassignment, disability, colour and nationality. The Equality Act 2010 has addressed that inconsistency and claims can now be brought on these bases.

7. **Contractual gagging clauses**: that seek to prevent disclosure of terms or conditions relating to pay and bonus are unenforceable against employees seeking or making a "relevant pay disclosure". The context of the discussion in which the relevant pay disclosure takes place must be discrimination, for example, a conversation where the employee seeks to discover whether there is a connection between how much people are paid and one or more of the protected characteristics, and in the course of that conversation, reveals pay data.

Further Changes Made by the Equality Act 2010

1. **Victimisation**: there is no longer a need to ask whether a person has been treated less favourably than someone who did not commit the protected act. Rather than comparing the treatment of the claimant with someone else's treatment, the question is simply whether the claimant was treated to their detriment because of a protected act.

2. **Sharing the same protected characteristic**: The fact that a person accused of discrimination shares the protected characteristic with the claimant is irrelevant. For example, a black junior clerk can bring a claim of race discrimination against a black senior clerk.

3. **Indirect discrimination**: the law on indirect discrimination now applies to disability and gender reassignment as well as all the other areas previously covered.

4. **Pregnancy and maternity discrimination**: breast feeding. The new Act states that it will be unlawful discrimination to treat a woman less favourably because she is breast-feeding within 26 weeks of her giving birth.

5. **Positive action**: The Act extends existing positive action provisions so a chambers or a barrister or clerk will be able to single out persons with a particular protected characteristic and take any action which is a proportionate means of achieving the aim of enabling or encouraging them to overcome a disadvantage connected to the protected characteristic. A chambers or barrister or clerk can also take action to meet any needs the employees, pupils or tenants have as a result of disadvantage connected to the protected characteristic or to encourage them to participate in an activity where participation by people with the protected characteristic is disproportionately low.

From April 2011, when faced with two or more candidates of equal merit in recruitment and selection exercises only, the Act will permit more favourable treatment of (i.e. selection of) someone because of a particular protected characteristic if people with that particular characteristic are underrepresented in the chambers. In practice it is rare for any two candidates to be of equal merit, and until this aspect of the law is clarified, chambers, barristers and clerks should be cautious in exercising positive action of this kind.

Further Practical Steps for Chambers to Consider

1. Chambers should update their Equal Opportunities Policies to reflect the changes made by the Equality Act 2010.
2. Pupillage/job/ tenancy application procedures should also be up dated to reflect the changes.
3. Chambers should consider sending their Equality Officers, Heads of Chambers, Heads of Pupillage Committees, clerks and members in other relevant positions on a course providing a basic grounding in equality and diversity issues relevant to the provision of legal services, practice management and the administration of chambers. Ideally all members should be encouraged to attend such training.

Bar Council Equality and Diversity Committee, December 2010. (PBhalla@barcouncil.org.uk)]

The Bar Council Gender Equality Scheme

Bar Council Gender Equality Scheme

[3.319a]

The Bar Council, as a body with public functions, is committed to fulfilling its statutory duties to eliminate discrimination and to promote race, gender and disability equality. The following sets out the text of the Bar Council's Gender Equality Scheme:

The Bar Council Gender Equality Scheme

1. Introduction

Plan

1.1 The Bar Council, as a body with public functions, is committed to fulfilling its statutory duties to eliminate discrimination and to promote race, gender and disability equality. This is a long term commitment and, over many years, the Bar Council has developed policies, a regulatory framework and issued guidance to help meet all its obligations under the equalities legislation. We have single equality schemes to promote race, gender and disability equality and will give consideration to merging these into a single Diversity Equality Scheme for the Bar.

1.2 This Gender Equality Scheme sets out our commitment to our general duty to have due regard to the need to:

- Eliminate unlawful discrimination and harassment on the grounds of gender; and
- Promote equality of opportunity between women and men.

1.3 The Gender Equality scheme applies to all Bar Council (including the BSB) functions but public functions will be given priority.

2. Consultation

2.1 The Bar Council is committed to consulting all its stakeholders, on the operation of its Gender Scheme and action plan, on the review of progress and development of future action plans. The Scheme has been considered by members of the Bar Council's Equality and Diversity Committee and the Association of Women Barristers.

We welcome views from all individuals and groups and ask that they be submitted to the Equality and Diversity Advisers at the Bar Council:

Address:289–293 High Holborn
London, WC1V 7HZ

Email: EqualOpps@BarCouncil.org.uk

3. Objectives and Goals of the Gender Equality Scheme

3.1 The Bar Council aims to promote equality and diversity both within the profession, so that those with the right abilities are able to succeed as barristers, and in the services it provides, irrespective of sex or gender re-assignment.

3.2 Our objectives are:

(a) To promote gender equality and eliminate and prevent any discriminatory difference in treatment on the grounds of sex or of gender identity across all Bar Council functions, including the regulation and representation of barristers and in the services the Bar Council provides to the public and its membership.

(b) To promote gender equality and eliminate or prevent any discriminatory difference in treatment on the grounds of sex or of gender identity in relation to the participation of men, women and trans people in the policy and decision making activities of the Bar's regulatory or representational arms.

(c) To ensure that there are no unjustified earnings or remuneration differentials, including scholarships, bursaries and pupillage awards, which have a disproportionate negative impact on male, female or trans barristers or bar students.

(d) To promote policies, which encourage fair and open access to quality work at the Bar and the retention of barristers with child care responsibilities so that there is an increase in the gender diversity of the pool of barristers ready for judicial, silk or other senior appointment.

(e) To promote gender equality and eliminate or prevent any discriminatory difference in treatment on the grounds of sex or of gender identity in the recruitment, employment, training, promotion of staff and in the range of pay, benefits, other emoluments and opportunities offered to staff.

3.3 Our goal is to make visible and faster progress towards gender equality and indicators of our progress will include the following outcomes:

- Language used in the Bar Council and BSB publications and documents is inclusive and gender neutral.
- Meetings are arranged at times that enable those with caring responsibilities to attend.
- Women feel effectively engaged in decision and policy making and become involved in Bar Council and BSB committees and activities in greater numbers than before.
- Women and men are employed at all levels of the secretariat and in all areas of work.

- Sexual harassment of staff, barristers (including pupils) and others is dealt with promptly and systematically according to agreed procedures and any tolerance of harassment drops within the Bar as a whole.
- The reported level of disadvantage experienced by pregnant barristers and those returning to practice from maternity leave reduce significantly and is eliminated and more women barristers are retained in practice.
- To the extent that there is any gap between men and women's pay for work of equal value in the secretariat's staff, it narrows and is eventually eliminated.
- Those with caring responsibilities, both in the secretariat's staff and at the employed and self-employed Bar are receiving greater support from the Bar Council (and via the Bar Council through chambers) including flexible and part-time working opportunities at all levels of work.
- Barristers and secretariat staff are aware of their equality duties, understand how the duties affect their work and have the skills to improve the duties in their work.
- Equality issues and their budgetary and other implications are considered at the beginning of policy-making.

4. The Gender Context

Gender Profile of barristers

4.1 The practising Bar at the end of 2008 consisted of 12,136 self-employed barristers practising from chambers, and 3.046 employed barristers who practised across a spectrum of legal careers including the government legal service, commerce, industry, solicitors' firms and the voluntary sector.

4.2 The first woman barrister was called to the Bar in 1922 but women did not enter practice in significant numbers until the seventies and eighties. Women were 3% of self-employed barristers in 1955, 7% in 1975, 13% in 1985, 22% in 1995 and 31% in 2008. Women's representation is stronger in employed practice where they were 38% of employed practitioners in 1995 rising to 42% in 2002 and 46% in 2008. Men and women graduate from the Bar Vocational Course in roughly equal numbers. Between 2001–2006 the female proportion of pupil barristers varied from 47% to 52%.

4.3 Female self-employed barrister representation on the six Bar Circuits at the end of 2008 ranged from 30% on the Western circuit to 33% on the Wales and Chester Circuit. Female representation on the Bar Council reached a low of 12.6% in 2000 and a high of 33% in 2003. There has been one female Chair of the Bar Council in 1998; two female Circuit Leaders over the last decade and the first and second Chairs of the Bar Standards Board are women.

Queens Counsel

4.4 The percentage of women appointed as Queens Counsel has risen from 4% in 1990 to 10% in the 2008 silk round. By comparison 20% of self-employed barristers over 15 years of call are female.

Judiciary

4.5 In April 2008 women were 10% of High Court Judges (further appointments were made later in the year), 13% of Circuit Judges, 15% of Recorders, 22% of District Judges and 23% of District Judges (Magistrates Court).

4.6 Gender monitoring data on barristers is published annually on the Bar Council website (http://www.barcouncil.org.uk/about/statistics/)

5. *Key Gender Issues*

5.1 Retention of Female Practitioners

5.1.1 A Bar Council study of barristers ceasing self-employed practice found that the proportion of women who began a tenancy between the years 1988–98, and who ceased to practice between the 6th and 10th year of call was up to twice that of men. For both men and women the significant departure years were between the second year of call and the sixth. The Bar Council has instituted an annual exit survey to identify the reasons why barristers leave practice or change their practising status. Over half of barristers responding to the Exit Survey, who were in self-employed practice, cited level of income or the uncertainty over future income as a factor in their decision to leave chambers. Female practitioners were more likely to have had a practice reliant on publicly funded work than male respondents. A high proportion of female respondents considered that having children had adversely affected their careers at the Bar and respondents referred to particular difficulties where practice requirements necessitated frequent appearances in court.

5.1.2 The Bar Council has issued maternity leave guidelines to chambers and clerks and practice managers are advised to assist returners to build up their practices and to enable flexible working. Workaholism and presenteeism culture does exist at the Bar, as in many other professions and our guidance on flexible working and career breaks is aimed at providing alternatives to this culture. We have introduced an annual one day course to assist returners to re-enter practice. The exit survey will continue so that we can ensure our policies and strategies are accurately targeted at retaining barristers in practice.

5.2 Access to Quality Work and Progression

5.2.1 Opportunities for barristers to develop a successful practice in their chosen area of work can be affected by the recruitment process into pupillage and tenancy, career development support and the range and quality of work they receive in the early stages of their careers. The Code of Conduct requires that chambers are conducted in a fair and equitable manner and the Equality

Code sets out guidance on fair recruitment, career development and fair allocation of work between members and pupils in chambers. Data from the annual Exit Survey suggest that women, disproportionately compared to men, work in crime, family and publicly funded areas of work where earnings are typically lower than in private commercial, chancery and civil work. The Bar's pupillage survey indicates that female pupils on average receive lower pupillage awards than male pupils.

5.2.2 Experience gained on government advocacy panels provides a stepping-stone to judicial and other senior appointments and we welcomed measures to increase the transparency and objectivity of the recruitment process for these panels as well as for silk and judicial appointment. In 2007 we jointly launched with the CPS an Equality and Diversity Expectations Statement which sets out the CPS's diversity expectations of chambers it uses and negotiated a new and fairer grading system for the allocation of CPS prosecution work in London. Together with the CPS we will be monitoring the implementation of the Statement and the grading scheme and will provide barristers guidance on implementation and meeting monitoring reviews. In 2008 the Attorney General launched an equivalent statement for chambers whose members are appointed to Civil Prosecution Panels. We will work with the AG's staff to encourage implementation of this statement and offer guidance to barristers on meeting its requirements. We hold regular information events in London and the circuits jointly with the Treasury Solicitors to widen access to their panel appointments.

5.2.3 We will continue to support initiatives to increase the gender diversity of applicants for judicial and silk appointment, review monitoring data following competitions and consult on strategies to improve diversity that lie within the Bar's sphere of responsibility or influence.

5.3 Mentoring

5.3.1 Lack of role models and career development support, particularly in small sets of chambers, are seen as restraints on the career progress of women barristers. Groups such as the Association of Women Barristers and a specialist bar association offer some mentoring assistance to their members. The Equality and Diversity Committee will promote mentoring schemes for the profession as an aid to both quality assurance and increasing the diversity of applicants for senior appointments.

6. Structure and Role of the Bar Council and Bar Standards Board

6.1 The Bar Council is the governing body for all barristers in England and Wales. It provides representation and services for the Bar and guidance on becoming a barrister and professional practice. One of its priorities is widening access to and retaining the diversity of the profession.

6.2 The representative side of the Bar Council undertakes its work through a structure of committees reporting to the Council. The Central Services Division of the Bar Council supports the work of the Bar Council and its regulatory arm.

6.3 The Bar Council created the Bar Standards Board as an independent regulatory arm in January 2006. It sets the education and training requirements for entry to the profession and the continuing training requirements and standards for practice at the Bar. It enforces the Professional Rules of Conduct, monitors the service provided by barristers and handles complaints against barristers and students taking disciplinary or other action where appropriate. One of its eight principles is to promote equality and diversity throughout the Bar and within the organisation. It conducts its work through a structure of committees and sub committees reporting to the Board.

7. Equality and Diversity Framework

7.1 The BC Equality and Diversity Committee was established at the beginning of 2007 from the merged Bar Committees on Race, (formed in the mid eighties) and on gender and disability (both formed in 1992). It is located in the central services division. Its membership includes representatives of BME, women and disabled barrister groups, discrimination practitioners and others with an interest in equality and diversity. The Sub-Group on Disability drives forward work on increasing disability access to and throughout the profession. The BSB set up an Equality and Diversity Committee at the end of 2009 which includes lay and barrister members. The Board has approved 3 strategic equality and diversity objectives for its work: to promote equality and diverse entry into the profession; to promote equality and diversity throughout the profession; and to ensure that the BSB conducts its regulatory activities fairly and in accordance with its duty to promote equality and eliminate discrimination. It has developed a timetabled action plan to meet these objectives, which sets out a number of specific activities to promote equality.

7.2 The BC and BSB have their own lead Equality and Diversity Advisers who work with the BC and BSB Equality and Diversity Committees. A small support team based in the central services division supports equality and diversity work on the regulatory and representational sides

7.3 The Code of Conduct for the Bar of England and Wales prohibits discrimination on the grounds of race, sex, disability, sexual orientation, religion or belief and age. The Bar Council adopted an Equality Code for the Bar in 1995 and this was updated in 2004. It offers practical guidance to chambers on complying with equality duties and can be downloaded from the Bar Standards Board website –

(http://www.barstandardsboard.room.net/standardsandguidance/codeofconduct/).

7.4 The Code of Conduct requires barristers working together in chambers to have a written equal opportunity policy and appoint an Equal Opportunity Officer from among chambers' members before taking pupils.

7.5 Impact Assessment

The Bar Council is committed to assessing the impact of its current and future policies on gender equality in respect of the profession, the services it provides and the employment of its staff. In this way we aim to ensure that equality and diversity considerations are built into the core business thinking and processes of the Bar Council.

7.6 Monitoring Review

The Bar Council and Bar Standards Board collect diversity data and monitor entrants to the profession and their progress, staff recruitment and progression, the complaints service and the impact of policy decisions on diverse groups. Data on the profession and staff has been collected and reported on for many years. We wish to track the progress of different groups of barristers more effectively and are putting in place a new comprehensive data collection system. A full range of diversity information will be collected from students as they enter the Bar vocational Course. Until this system is fully developed information will be collected through the annual chambers' returns and supplemented by snapshot surveys. The Bar Council will report on the implementation and operation of its gender equality scheme every year and review the scheme every three years.

7.7 Diversity Training

The Bar Council offers a programme of courses throughout the year for chambers on meeting their equality and diversity obligations under the Equality Code and diversity training qualifies for continuing education hours. The Bar Standards Board require all barristers entering the profession to be sufficiently trained in equality and diversity issues so that their practices promote equality of opportunity and are free from discrimination. The effectiveness of all training for members of the profession will be kept under review.

7.8 Procurement

In procurement of goods, services or staff the Bar Council will extend its equality requirements within the contract arrangements to its contractors. We will build relevant gender equality considerations into the procurement process to ensure that all our functions meet the requirements of the gender duty, irrespective of who is carrying them out.

7.9 Where ever possible, we will use public bodies' equality schemes to ensure equal access to their advocacy work. We will use opportunities to raise awareness at the Bar of the business case for diversity and of supplier diversity requirements from both public bodies and private sector corporations.

7.10 The Bar Council will continue to negotiate with the Government to fulfil their obligations to undertake gender impact assessments on the proposed Carter reforms to the funding of legal aid.

7.11 Sex Discrimination

The Equality and Diversity Code summaries the law on direct and indirect discrimination. The Code of Conduct prohibits direct and indirect sex discrimination.

7.12 Sexual Harassment

The Equality and Diversity Code advises chambers on adopting procedures to prevent and discourage harassment and discrimination and to provide formal and informal mechanisms for raising complaints by members, pupils, staff and service users. Evidence from pupillage surveys indicates that the incidence of harassment has declined in the last 4–5 years. We will continue to review progress.

7.13 Multiple Discrimination

We will address evidence of multiple discrimination experienced by men, women or transsexual people who may be disadvantaged because of their racial group, religion or belief, sexual orientation, marital or civil partnership status, whether or not they have a disability and whether or not they have undergone gender re-assignment.

8. *Circuits and Specialist Bar Associations*

8.1 The Circuits and Specialist Bar Associations will be encouraged to participate in all initiatives to promote gender diversity so that there membership benefits from these.

9. *The Complaints Service*

9.1 The Bar Standards Board runs the service for complaints against barristers. An independent Complaints Commissioner reviews every complaint received. The Commissioner's Strategic Review of the Complaints Process recommended more effective communication with consumers and service users to make the system more accountable and transparent and to increase its accessibility. Data is collected on the gender of complainants and barristers complained against and on the outcome of cases. This is monitored annually and progress kept under review.

10. *Staff of the Bar Council*

10.1 The Bar Council employs the staff of the regulatory and representational arms. Its equality policy commits it to fair and open recruitment and fair treatment within the work place. Gender data is collected on applicants, appointees and staff in post and analyses are published on the website every year. At the end of 2008 there were 99 members of staff in post and 70% of the staff was female. Except at most senior levels (chief executive and directors) at which level one woman has been appointed, women outnumber men at manager level by 2 to 1 and at administration level by over 3 to 1. In 2006 men were 48% of applicants for posts and 25% of those appointed. The reasons for the lack of success of male applicants will be examined and an evaluation of work and pay is planned for 2009–10. The staff induction programme includes equality and diversity briefing. A programme of equality and diversity training has commenced for staff and committee members with reference to their job functions and the requirement to assess the impact of their policy decisions on diverse groups.

Positive Action Guidance – Under-representation

Positive Action Guidance – Under-representation

[3.319b]

The following guidance sets out the positive action measures that should be taken by chambers where under-representation is established.

"Positive action" is the term used for permitted measures under the Sex Discrimination and Race Relations Acts to remedy the under-representation of men, women or members of different racial groups in the work force. These measures relate to special encouragement and in some cases training to assist under-represented groups to compete for work. Following any positive action programme, participants must compete for any position or work on equal terms with all other applicants and any appointments must be on merit. Positive discrimination in favour of men, women or particular racial groups at the point of selection is unlawful.

Under-representation arises where there is ongoing and enduring under representation of women, members of ethnic minorities or disabled people as barristers compared to their representation in the wider applicant pool or in the population at large. In the case of pupils the relevant comparison might be with the proportion of the group among BVC graduates excluding overseas students. Approximately fifty percent of BVC graduates are female and twenty-five percent are home BME students.

Where under-representation is established, chambers should consider taking the following positive action measures:

- Using messages in recruitment advertisements or literature that particularly encourage under-represented groups to apply to chambers.
- Publicising mini-pupillage and pupillage opportunities to under-represented groups by using media that targets these groups and by messages that particularly welcome applications from these groups.
- Visiting universities or BVC providers known to have a strong representation among the students of the under-represented groups and encouraging applications from them.
- Including in careers visits members of the under-represented groups from your Specialist Bar Association who are established in practice as role models.

Separately to positive action disability legislation requires barristers to make "reasonable" adjustments to the recruitment process and working environment to remove barriers for disabled people. For example this may include changes to the physical environment, the types of duties undertaken or provision of accessible IT equipment. Making clear chambers' willingness to make reasonable adjustments and providing information on chambers' level of accessibility will encourage disabled applicants. Guidance and financial help for reasonable adjustments is available through the government's Access to Work scheme.

Collecting and examining equalities monitoring information will help determine the need for and type of positive action or other measures appropriate to the particular set of chambers. Data should be analysed after each major recruitment exercise and at least annually. Each stage of the selection process should be analysed from application, to shortlisting and, finally, appointment. At each stage the proportion of disabled, male and female applicants, and applicants from different ethnic groups should be checked. Equalities data on mini pupils should also be collected and examined. Further guidance on analysing monitoring data is included in the Equality and Diversity Code, Annexe E.

The under-representation of particular groups among applicants or mini pupils should lead to the re-examination of advertising methods, re-targeting of adverts and careers visits with content that encourages interest in chambers from the under-represented groups. If equalities data show that the under-represented groups are represented among applicants and mini pupils, chambers should identify the reasons why the groups fail to make it through the selection process and seek to adjust any chambers processes that appear to be excluding applicants for reasons unrelated to merit. If under-represented groups are obtaining mini-pupillages and pupillages, chambers should identify the reasons why the groups fail to stay in chambers on completion of pupillage.

Work allocated to chambers' pupils and pupils' training experience and opportunities should be examined to ensure chambers' practices do not unfairly or unintentionally disadvantage particular groups. For example, do opportunities to socialise and develop working relationships within chambers favour some groups more than others? Positive action requires the creation of measures that encourage all groups within chambers and create new opportunities for those that have been disadvantaged or excluded. Equality and diversity training for chambers' clerks, staff and members will help to create a more open and welcoming working environment that will encourage the under-represented groups to stay in chambers.

Crown Prosecution Service Equality And Diversity Expectations Statement For The Bar

Crown Prosecution Service — Equality and Diversity

[3.320]

THE CPS has issued its own Equality and Diversity Expectations statement for the Bar. The full text of the statement is set out below.

Contents

1. Context

1.1 The CPS secures a range of external legal services each year. The service spends approximately £130 million of a total annual budget of £580 million on external legal services.

1.2 The CPS has a long standing commitment to and increasing positive reputation in respect of equality and diversity across all of its activities. As a public body the CPS also has positive duties to promote disability equality, gender equality and race equality across its activities including where relevant when it secures external services. The Bar Council itself has a general duty to promote disability, gender and race equality. Both CPS and the Bar council also have obligations to ensure equality in employment and training in respect of sexuality and religion or belief. Similar obligations are also forthcoming in respect of age.

1.3 Given the firm commitment to furthering equality and diversity and our legal obligations, the CPS has decided to put in place a clear statement of equality and diversity expectations with the Bar.

1.4 In setting out these expectations the CPS recognises that our objectives and duties in relation to equality and diversity do not overrule other laws or regulations on public procurement.

Guidance on implementation

1.5 This Equality and Diversity Expectations Statement reflects the requirements of both the Bar Council's Code of Conduct and the Equality and Diversity Code for the Bar. The latter provides guidance on the implementation of good equality and diversity practice in Chambers and will assist Chambers in implementation of this Statement. Throughout this Statement, there is clear cross referencing where CPS expectations reflect the Bar Council's Code of Conduct and the Equality and Diversity Code for the Bar. There also is guidance in the form of frequently asked questions for Chambers.

2. Purpose

2.1 The purpose of this expectation statement is to:

provide for the Bar a clear concise statement of expectations on equality and diversity when seeking to work and when working for CPS;

ensure that the CPS can continue to meet its legal obligations to promote equality when it secures external legal services from the Bar.

3. Equality and Diversity Expectations

The following are the elements of a framework to address equality and diversity which the CPS expects to see in place and actively implemented in Bar Chambers from which it secures legal services.

3.1 Equality and Diversity Policy Statement and Actions

The CPS expects Chambers through which it secures legal services to have a written policy statement of its commitments to equality and diversity have a timetabled action plan or set of actions in a wider Chambers Business Plan to implement this policy implement the policy and action plan report to its JASC and as required by CPS on achievements in implementing the Plan have a designated equal opportunity officer or equality and diversity officer (also required by the Bar Council's Code of Conduct para 404.2(d)).

This policy statement should address recruitment of pupils and members; retention and career development; training; equal access to work and opportunities within chambers; reasonable adjustment to promote disability equality, maternity and parental leave and flexible working, and handling of complaints of discrimination and harassment; the outcomes the Chambers is seeking to achieve and roles and responsibilities in relation to the policy. These expectations are consistent with existing Bar Council Codes, in particular the Bar Council's Code of Conduct para 404.2(d) requires that Chambers have a written equal opportunity policy which will set out Chambers' policies in relation to each of the action areas in the Equality and Diversity Code.

3.2 Equalities Monitoring

The CPS expects chambers through which it secures legal services to:

monitor all applicants for pupillage and membership by disability, ethnicity and gender and likewise to monitor all appointees;

monitor all staff, pupils and members in chambers;

make publicly available the results of this monitoring to the JASC and to CPS as required.

These expectations are consistent with para 1.16 of the Bar Council's Equality and Diversity Code.

3.3 Addressing Under Representation in Chambers

The CPS expects chambers through which it secures legal services to

analyse recruitment monitoring data at least annually;

take corrective action where there is significant under representation of any particular group compared to their representation in the potential applicant pool;

take corrective action where there are significant differences between those applying and those appointed to pupillage and as members;

take steps, including the setting of measurable objectives where necessary in terms of gender, ethnic and disability representation to help secure a more representative Chambers (including staff, members and pupils);

focus recruitment efforts on addressing under representation;

evaluate its monitoring results against relevant benchmarks including Bar Council vocational course graduate data and pupillage data and begin to build up data on disabled practitioners and BVC students. (Guidance on relevant benchmarks is given in para 1.17 of the Bar Council's Equality and Diversity Code);

report progress in addressing under representation.

These expectations are consistent with paragraph 1.16 of the Bar Council's Equality and Diversity Code. Further guidance for Chambers on monitoring and tackling under-representation is available in Annex E of the Bar Council's Equality and Diversity Code.

3.4 Positive Action

In some circumstances it will be appropriate for Chambers to take positive action to address significant under representation of particular groups. Positive action refers to measures that Chambers may lawfully take under equalities the sex discrimination and race relations legislation to meet special needs or to train or encourage people from a specific group that is under represented in particular work. Following the positive action programme, participants must then compete for any established posts on equal terms with all other applicants and all appointments must be on merit. This may be for example where there is ongoing and enduring under representation of women, or members of ethnic minorities or disabled people as barristers compared to their representatives on in the wider applicant pool. In such circumstances the CPS expects Chambers through which it secures legal services to:

actively consider and put in place positive action programmes where the evidence warrants such programmes;

explain the reasoning and benefits of positive action to all staff, members, pupils and potential applicants;

evaluate the impact of any positive action programme and cease the programme once the results have been achieved.

(Para 2.25 of the Bar Council's Equality and Diversity Code sets out a definition of lawful positive action and distinguishes this from positive discrimination.)

There is no prohibition in the disability discrimination legislation against positive measures in favour of disabled people. It anticipates that such measures, including reasonable adjustments (see para. 3.8), will be taken. Chambers are expected to:

encourage disabled people to apply to chambers;

review their recruitment and marketing literature to include appropriate references to disability access;

identify chambers' level of accessibility to disabled people;

offer mini-pupillages to appropriately qualified disabled students;

take other appropriate outreach steps.

These expectations are consistent with para 1.107 of the Bar Council's Equality and Diversity Code which sets out the position in relation to disability legislation.

3.5 Training on Equality and Diversity

The CPS expects Chambers through which it secures legal services to:

ensure all members, staff and pupils receive basic training on equality and diversity which covers both legal obligations and good practice;

ensure equality and diversity training covers all equality strands including age, disability, faith, ethnicity, gender and sexuality;

Integrate equality and diversity issues into other training provided for chambers staff, members and pupils;

keep training under review and in line with current developments.

(Para 1.8 of the Bar Council's Equality and Diversity Code recommends a least one member of the selection committee is trained in fair selection methods.)

3.6 Familiarisation with and Commitment to Key CPS Policies

The CPS expects Chambers through which it secures legal services to ensure that its members are:

familiar with and competent in the application of CPS policies when prosecuting on behalf of CPS;

demonstrate a detailed familiarity with and commitment to the consistent implementation of CPS hate crime policies in the areas of domestic violence, homophobic crime and racist and religious crime;

able to meet the needs of a diverse client base.

3.7 Equal Access to and Fair Allocation of Work Within Chambers

The CPS instructs members of Chambers on the basis of appropriate skills and experience. This means that CPS may instruct specialist prosecutors to prosecute particular crimes. Such instruction is on the basis of specialist skills and experience and merit, not on personal attribute. CPS recognises that Chambers Clerks play a crucial role in this process and expects that when work is allocated or returned to Clerks they will follow the same fair allocation procedure based on skills, experience and merit.

The CPS expects Chambers through which it secures legal services to:

ensure equal access to the range of work available;

ensure a fair allocation of work within Chambers;

monitor pupils and junior tenant access to work by disability, ethnicity and gender;

monitor the allocation to barristers of all returns and unnamed work coming into Chambers by disability, ethnicity and gender;

address any significant differences in work access and work allocation;

reallocate any work on the basis of skills and experience ensuring no discrimination in work reallocation;

provide appropriate guidance for Clerks on the fair allocation of work including allocation of returns.

(Para 1.46 of the Bar Council's Equality and Diversity Code refers to Chambers duties to brief their clerks in fair allocation of work and in monitoring work allocation. Paras 1.36 to 1.52 of the Bar Council's Equality and Diversity Code also refers to fair access to and fair allocation of work. Also para 404.2(b) of the Bar Council's Code of Conduct requires Heads of Chambers to ensure that the affairs of their Chambers are conducted in a manner which is fair and equitable for barristers and pupils.)

3.8 Reasonable Adjustments to Promote Disability Equality

There is a recognition that disability equality issues are both less well developed in this sector and require specific practical responses.

In this context the CPS expects Chambers through which it secures legal services to:

> take steps to raise the awareness of members and staff of their obligations under the disabilities legislation;
>
> advertise their commitment to providing reasonable adjustments in relation to the recruitment of members, staff and pupils and the provision of legal services;
>
> respond appropriately to requests for reasonable adjustments.

(These expectations are consistent with paras 1.2 and 1.3 of the Bar Council's Equality and Diversity Code. Also relevant is Annex D to the Bar Council's Equality and Diversity Code guidance on reasonable adjustments in pupillage and tenancy recruitments.)

3.9 Maternity, Paternity, Parental Leave and Flexible Working

The CPS expects Chambers through which it secures legal services to:

> have a written policy on maternity, paternity and paternal leave which contains particulars of:
>
> (a) the extent of period of leave offered free of rent and Chambers expenses;
>
> (b) the member's right to return to Chambers after a specified period of leave.
>
> Have a written policy permitting members of Chambers to take career breaks or work flexibly.

3.10 Handling of Complaints

The CPS expects Chambers from which it procures legal services to: -

> have a complaints policy including harassment which sets out standards for acceptable and unacceptable behaviour and procedures for dealing with complaints of such behaviour;
>
> have a procedure for resolving complaints informally and promptly;
>
> have a formal procedure for investigating and resolving complaints which become formalised;
>
> have a clear policy statement which treats breaches of equality and diversity policies and procedures as a disciplinary issue;

(This reflects Annexes E and F of the Bar Council's Equality and Diversity Code on harassment and on complaints and grievances.)

3.11 Reviewing and Reporting Achievements against the Expectations Statement

The CPS requires reporting by Chambers of progress against the Statement. The CPS will support this reporting by Chambers with its own review activity. The CPS operates a tiered progress reporting system to check progress in the implementation of this Statement. This tiered reporting system involves different frequencies of reporting based on the size of Chambers. The tiered reporting system involves:

> annual reporting for larger sets of Chambers (i e sets with 45 or more members and undertaking or seeking to undertake CPS work);
>
> biannual reporting for medium sets of Chambers (i e sets comprising 20 to 45 members and undertaking or seeking to undertake CPS work); and
>
> three yearly reporting for smaller sets of Chambers (i e sets comprising under 20 members and undertaking or seeking to undertake CPS work).

The progress reports will be produced in accordance with a standard CPS reporting format. The progress report will be expected to be a clear, concise and verifiable statement of the position and progress at a given point in the reporting cycle. The reports will be submitted to the Joint Advocate Selection Committee (JASC) for their circuit. The reports should be copied to the local CCP as well as to the Chair of the JASC and to the CPS Equality and Diversity Unit in CPS HQ. (This builds on existing practices where JASCs have been receiving analyses of ethnic and gender data from Chambers).

The JASC will review each Chambers report and decide whether it meets CPS expectations, or contains realistic plans to meet them. If the JASC view is that Chambers should do more to comply with CPS expectations, Chambers will be given the opportunity to improve their systems and processes. Ultimately, if Chambers cannot demonstrate that it meets CPS expectations, or has reasonable timetabled and realistic plans to meet them, the CPS must decide whether it wishes to continue to send work to that Chambers.

Before any decision is taken the Head of Chambers will be invited to discuss findings with the JASC Chair and Circuit Leader. The Head of Chambers will be given an opportunity to make representations or submit a reasonable timetabled plan to meet CPS expectations. Care will be taken to ensure that individual members of Chambers do not lose the opportunity to undertake CPS work because their Chambers fails to meet CPS expectations, without being given a reasonable period of time to make necessary improvements.

New applicants to the CPS lists will be asked to confirm that their Chambers has policies in place which meet CPS expectations, perhaps by reference to the last Chambers annual report to the JASC or that their Chambers have a timetabled and realistic plan to meet the CPS expectations.

In addition to the basic review and reporting arrangements set out above, the CPS Equality and Diversity Unit will through its team of regional Projects and Performance Advisors undertake a series of annual randomly selected but pre-announced monitoring visits and reviews of Chambers performance against this Expectations Statement. This will complement and support the assessment under-taken via the JASCs system set out above.

Sources of Additional Information

1. The Bar Council, Code of Conduct
2. The Bar Council, Equality and Diversity Code for the Bar (Nov 2004)
3. Commission for Racial Equality, Guide on Race Equality and the Procurement of Public Services 2002–03.
4. Race Relations Act 1976
5. Disability Discrimination Act 1995
6. Sex Discrimination Act 1975

CPS: Equality and Diversity Expectations Statement: Template for First Progress Reports

[3.321]

The Crown Prosecution Service has issued its own Equality and Diversity Expectation statements. Templates have been issued in respect of each stage of implementation of the policy by sets of chambers. The templates are all set out below. The templates are followed by a series of FAQ's relating to the Equality and Diversity Expectations Statement.

Please note: This template will be required to be completed by large sets (45+) within one year of the Expectations Statement coming into effect; by medium sets (20 to 45) within two years of the Expectations Statement coming into effect; and by smaller sets (under 20) within three years of the Expectations Statement coming into effect. There is also a separate template for second and subsequent progress reports. As a guide, progress reports should be four sides of A4 in length.

1. Introductory Paragraph

This should be a brief description of the Chambers, its size, numbers of members, pupils, staff.

2. Equality and Diversity policy or policies

This should be a summary paragraph on the steps to be taken to produce an equality and diversity policy or policies. It should indicate what the policy or policies cover against the areas identified in the Expectations Statement including maternity, paternity, parental leave and flexible working and reasonable adjustments to improve access. It should indicate where the JASC and CPS can obtain copies.

3. Equality and Diversity actions to implement the policy or policies

This should be a summary paragraph on the actions taken, being taken or planned to implement the equality and diversity policy or policies. It should indicate what the main actions cover against the areas identified in the Expectations Statement. It should indicate where the JASC and CPS can obtain copies of the action taken or planned.

4. Equalities monitoring and under-representation

This should include a summary paragraph which includes a demographic breakdown of members, staff and pupils by ethnicity, gender and disability. It should summarise any actions taken or planned to address any under-representation identified in the demographic breakdown. It should summarise any positive action taken or planned including in relation to disabled people. It should also include any objectives set to help secure a more representative Chambers. It should indicate where the JASC and CPS can obtain more detailed information if required including on applicants, interviewees and appointees.

5. Training

This should include a summary paragraph on any equality and diversity training undertaken or being planned including topics to be covered and who is to be trained (ie members, pupils and/or staff). This should also summarise any action taken or planned to ensure familiarisation with CPS key policies. It should indicate where the JASC and CPS can obtain more detailed information on equalities training and training plans if required.

6. Ensuring equal access to and fair allocation of work

This should include a summary paragraph on how the Chambers ensure or plans to ensure equal access to and fair allocation of work. It should summarise the work to ensure equal access and fair allocation against the areas identified in the Expectations Statement. It should indicate where the JASC and CPS can obtain more detailed information on Chambers' activity to ensure equal access and fair allocation of work if required.

7. Handling complaints

This should be a summary paragraph on the Chamber's policy and arrangements for handling of complaints including harassment complaints. It should indicate where the JASC and CPS can obtain further detail if required.

Please note: No documents should be attached to this progress report. Any additional information which is required will be requested.

CPS: Equality and Diversity Expectations Statement: Template for Second and Subsequent Reports

[3.322]

1. Equality and Diversity policy and actions

This should be a summary of the key actions taken to implement the equality and diversity policy. It should summarise the results and outcomes of the key actions taken. It should provide a clear overview of the main actions to progress equality and diversity in the reporting period. It should indicate where the JASC or CPS can obtain further information if required.

2. Equalities monitoring and under-representation

This should be a summary of progress made in the reporting period to secure a representative chambers in terms of pupils, members and staff by disability, ethnicity and gender. It should basically report progress against starting positions in terms of gender, ethnicity and disability composition, and against any objectives set for the reporting period. It could be structured somewhat as follows:

Chambers Category	Gender Profile					
	Start	Now	Start	Now	Start	Now
Pupils						
Members						
Staff						

Chambers may wish to break down these categories further by age or length of call.

It should summarise any further action to be taken to make further progress in securing a representative workforce. It should also summarise the progress from any positive action undertaken in the reporting period. As above for further information.

3. Training

This should be a paragraph which summarises the numbers of members, staff and pupils trained and the topics on which they were trained and dates when training took place. It should also summarise the steps that have been taken to ensure familiarisation with CPS key policies. It should also summarise any further actions to be taken. As above for further information.

4. Equal access to and fair allocation of work

This should include a paragraph which summarises the outcomes of monitoring by ethnicity, disability and gender of work allocation and any reallocations. It should include a summary of any actions taken to address the outcomes of this monitoring. It should also summarise any further actions to be taken. As above for further information.

5. Handling complaints

This should include a paragraph which summarise the numbers of complaints of discrimination and/or harassment received in the reporting period; the numbers upheld and any improvement actions taken or planned. As above for further information.

CPS: Equality and Diversity Expectations Statement: FAQs

[3.323]

1. What is Positive Action?

Positive Action is the term used for measures taken under the provisions of the Race Relations and Sex Discrimination Acts where one sex or racial or ethnic group is under-represented in particular areas of work. Positive Action through encouragement, training and development of potential is an important part of any equal opportunity programme. It should be taken only in the context of such a programme and where the conditions of under-representation are established through the regular review of ethnic and gender monitoring data.

Positive Action measures enable recruiters to encourage applications from suitable ethnic minority candidates or women so that they can be considered equally with other candidates. Under some circumstances it may be appropriate to offer training of ethnic minorities and women to assist them to compete for work where they are under-represented.

2. Does the requirement to take Positive Action conflict with the requirement for open competition in pupillage and tenancy recruitment?

No, Positive Action are special measures taken before selection. It is unlawful to discriminate in favour of women or people from ethnic minority backgrounds in the arrangements made for shortlisting or selecting candidates for appointment. Positive Action does not permit the selecting of ethnic minority or female candidates irrespective of merit for the purposes of increasing diversity among shortlisted or appointed candidates. Recruitment to chambers should follow open advertisement and be based on objective selection criteria related to the work to be done.

3. What form of Positive Action will be appropriate to chambers?

Women and members of ethnic minority groups are well represented among graduates of the Bar Vocational Course and, if the applicants to your chambers are not from diverse backgrounds, you may wish to consider the following Positive Action measures:

- Review marketing materials to ensure that the messages they give to prospective candidates are welcoming and inclusive and make reference to chambers commitment to its equality and diversity policy.
- Particularly encourage members of under-represented groups to apply to chambers.
- At recruitment fairs, provide information about chambers' equality and diversity policies and opportunities within chambers.

Career development support provided by chambers to pupils and junior tenants will influence their opportunities to obtain senior appointments or positions as experienced practitioners. Chambers could ensure regular feedback sessions for working pupils and practice development meetings for junior tenants (see recommendation para. 1.48 in the Equality and Diversity Code for the Bar). Chambers could set up mentoring schemes whereby a junior tenant may be a pupil's mentor and a junior tenant may be linked to a more senior member of chambers who can offer advice and guidance regarding practice development in a mentoring role. This would be relevant also to barristers returning to practice following a career break.

4. How frequently should we review equality and diversity recruitment monitoring data?

Data should be checked after each major recruitment exercise or at least, annually. The data should be obtained from an ethnic origin, gender and disability monitoring form attached to the application form (see Annexe E of the Equality and Diversity Code for the Bar). If an application form is not used all candidates responding to an advertisement, or seeking a position, should be sent a monitoring form at the outset of the process. Statistical summaries should be produced which identify applicants by ethnicity, gender and disability for each of the following stages of the process:

- Applications.
- Shortlisting.
- Interviews.
- Appointments.

Differential success rates at any stage should be investigated to ensure that there is no direct or indirect discrimination in the treatment of candidates. Under-representation at the application stage may indicate the need for Positive Action measures.

5. What are the relevant benchmarks against which to compare data in pupillage and tenancy recruitment monitoring reviews?

Relevant benchmark data to compare applicants for pupillage are provided in the breakdown of BVC Graduate Data published on the Equality and Diversity website (attached). Benchmark data to compare applicants for starter tenancies are provided by the Bar Council's pupillage breakdown published on the Equality and Diversity website. For staff recruited nationally, the Census provides an ethnic minority benchmark of between 7–8%. The equivalent figure in the Greater London travel-to-work area is between 15–25%.

6. Our chambers is small and recruits staff and tenants infrequently and only has one pupil per year. It is hard to achieve diversity in chambers with such a low level of recruitment.

In these circumstances patterns of representation will take years to become apparent. It may not be possible to discern much from one year's figures but they should indicate whether chambers is attracting a diverse group of applicants. If not, the Positive Action measures referred to above should be considered. It is recommended that data on previous years' analyses be compiled so any trends can be identified over time and, if necessary, addressed.

7. Is it necessary to conduct diversity monitoring of work allocation when established tenants in chambers receive very little unnamed work?

It is recommended that unallocated work and all returns are monitored by ethnicity and gender in chambers. There should be regular reviews of work undertaken by pupils and junior tenants to ensure that they have the opportunity to develop their practices in a fair and equal manner and that stereotypical assumptions about suitable areas of work for particular groups are not influencing patterns of instruction and allocation to them. Guidance is offered in Action Area B of the Equality and Diversity Code. If briefing practices are identified that disadvantage a particular group (e.g. allocating sex and child abuse cases predominantly to female practitioners) these should be addressed in the clerk's room and ultimately by the Head of Chambers and the CPS.

8. Meridian Software does not offer an ethnicity, gender or disability field and to monitor either recruitment or work allocation without this facility is too onerous for chambers.

Meridian is redeveloping its software and has agreed, at the request of the Bar Council, to provide ethnic, gender and disability monitoring fields in its new software. Other software providers are being approached by the Bar Council to provide similar facilities.

9. What is the position of barristers wishing to take CPS work if their chambers do not comply with the CPS' Equality and Diversity Expectation Statement?

It is hoped that there will be few barristers in this position given the new requirements in the Code of Conduct that chambers appoint an Equal Opportunity Officer and have a written equality policy consistent with the action areas in the Equality and Diversity Code. Where a chambers fails to provide an annual report to the Joint-Advocacy Selection Committee (JASC), or the JASC takes the view that the chambers are not complying with the statement, the chambers will be given the opportunity to meet the standard required. Guidance will be available from the Equality and Diversity Advisers at the Bar Council and from the CPS' Equality and Diversity team. Ultimately, if the chambers decides not to comply with the statement or it fails to comply, the CPS will decide whether or not it should withdraw work from those chambers. It is intended that chambers will be given every opportunity to comply and that no hasty decisions will be made. Should the CPS decide to withdraw work the head of chambers will be invited to discuss this decision with the JASC chair and circuit leader. The Expectations Statement states that care will be taken to ensure that individual members of chambers do not lose the opportunity to undertake CPS work because their chambers fails to comply without being given a reasonable period of time to make necessary improvements.

10. If I work from chambers on a flexible basis will this impact on the quality of work the CPS sends me?

There should be no barrier to combining a successful career at the Bar with childcare or other domestic responsibilities. Annexe L in the Equality and Diversity Code provides a range of examples of flexible working arrangements within chambers. These arrangements may vary according to area of practice but invariably it is possible, with the support of clerks, to make a flexible arrangement work satisfactorily. For example a court-based practice may not permit working a two or three-day week but it may be possible to take a break between trials. The Equality and Diversity Code advises chambers to ensure that rental arrangements do not inadvertently restrict opportunities for flexible working. It is the policy of the CPS to support flexible working patterns as far as possible within the confines of the criminal justice system.

11. Can the Bar Council ensure there is consistency between the various equality and diversity standards as set out in the Equality and Diversity Code, BarMark, Practice Management Guidelines and Quality Mark and the CPS Expectation Statement?

The Practice Management Guidelines are currently under review. Amendments will be made to ensure consistency with the Equality and Diversity Code and, in due course, we expect this to influence the BarMark and Quality Mark standards. The CPS Expectation Statement is derived from the Equality and Diversity Code and the attached document links each of the statement's recommendations with the Code recommendations.

12. What can chambers do to ensure that disabled applicants are not put at any disadvantage in the recruitment process?

Under the Disability Discrimination Act all chambers are under an existing duty to have completed adjustments (including alterations to the building and reviews of processes and procedures) to make chambers and the services it offers accessible to disabled persons. The work already completed will make adjustments for the recruitment process much simpler.

It is convenient to consider, firstly, reasonable adjustment for the recruitment process. Any advertising of vacancies should not put disabled persons who may wish to apply at a disadvantage, and the whole process should be accessible. The Disability Discrimination Act places a positive duty on barristers in chambers to make reasonable adjustments to accommodate a disabled person. At this stage the objective is to ensure that the disabled applicant has the same opportunity of success as an applicant without a disability. The applicant should always be consulted about the adjustment as he or she is an expert. All tenants and staff dealing with applications should be fully briefed on this duty.

In determining what is reasonable the following should be taken into account:

- The effectiveness of the adjustment in overcoming the disability.

- How practicable is the adjustment.
- The cost of the adjustment. The resources of chambers are relevant but the availability of assistance from other sources should be considered.

The following are examples of some 'reasonable adjustments':

- Applicants submitted in alternative formats to the standard written application form such as an on cassette tape or electronically.
- Accessible venue provided for the interview.

The work previously undertaken may help so that, for example, an interview could use the procedure used for a conference in chambers for a client with the same or similar disability.

Chambers should brief its members and staff that any request for an adjustment will be fully considered and agreed to if reasonable. There should be a procedure to consider each such request. This could be delegated to, or involve, the chambers Equal Opportunity Officer and another senior member. In some cases chambers may find it helpful to consult a disability charity, which works in the relevant disability field, or some other expert. The objective is to ensure that a disabled applicant can take part in the normal recruitment and interview process, and the procedure to consider adjustments should not be complex or cumbersome.

Once a disabled applicant has been successful further or different adjustments may be required. The individual should be able to obtain funding for some assistance and equipment through the Access to Work Scheme, administered through local offices of JobCentre Plus. Their general aim is to pay, or subsidize, the disability costs leaving the business costs to the individual or chambers, so that the disabled person can work more effectively.

Chambers may need to make some further adjustments. The chambers' Equal Opportunity Officer in conjunction with another senior member could consider these, as for recruitment. While broadly the same factors apply as for recruitment, what is not reasonable for an interview may be reasonable for a successful applicant. By considering these adjustments with the disabled person chambers may be able to improve facilities for disabled clients, to whom chambers also owes a similar duty to make reasonable adjustments.

Attorney General's Civil and Criminal Panel Counsel

[3.323a]

Equality and Diversity Expectations Statement

Reporting format for first progress reports required by 1 October 2009

Please note: This template will be required to be completed by all sets by 1 October 2009

There is a separate template for second and subsequent progress reports. As a guide, progress reports should be about four sides of A4 in length.

References to numbers in brackets below are references to the paragraphs so numbered in the Attorney General's Equality and Diversity Expectations Statement for Civil and Criminal Panel Counsel and their Chambers ("the Expectations Statement"). Such paragraphs are the basis of the requirements set out below. A copy of the statement can be found on the Treasury Solicitor's website.

The Attorney General's statement builds on the CPS Equality and Diversity Expectations Statement for the Bar, launched in March 2007. It imposes only requirements that are parallel, not additional, to the CPS statement.

1. Introductory paragraph

This should be a brief description of the Chambers, its size, numbers of members, pupils, staff.

2. Equality and diversity policy or policies

This should be a summary paragraph on the steps taken or to be taken to produce an equality and diversity policy or policies. It should indicate what the policy or policies cover against the areas identified in the Expectations Statement including maternity, paternity, parental leave and flexible working and reasonable adjustments to improve access. It should indicate where the AGO and TSol can obtain copies. (*Paras 3.1 and 3.8*)

3. Equality and diversity actions to implement the policy or policies

This should be a summary paragraph on the actions taken, being taken or planned to implement the equality and diversity policy or policies. It should indicate what the main actions cover against the areas identified in the Expectations Statement. It should indicate where the AGO and TSol can obtain copies of the action taken or planned. (*Para 3.1*)

4. Equalities monitoring and under-representation

This should include a summary paragraph which includes a demographic breakdown of members, staff and pupils by ethnicity, gender and disability. It should summarise any actions taken or planned to address any under-representation identified in the demographic breakdown. It should summarise any positive action taken or planned including in relation to disabled people. It should also include any objectives set to help secure a more representative Chambers. It should indicate where the AGO and TSol can obtain more detailed information if required including on applicants, interviewees and appointees. (*Paras 3.2, 3.3, 3.4 and 3.7*)

5. Training

This should include a summary paragraph on any equality and diversity training undertaken or being planned including topics to be covered and who is to be trained (i e members, pupils and/or staff). It should indicate where the AGO and TSol can obtain more detailed information on equalities training and training plans if required. (*Para 3.5*)

6. Ensuring equal access to and fair allocation of work

This should include a summary paragraph on Chambers' monitoring of access to and allocation of work, any conclusions drawn and action taken. It should indicate where the AGO and TSol can obtain more detailed information on Chambers' activity in this area if required. (*Para 3.6*)

7. Handling complaints

This should be a summary paragraph on the Chamber's policy and arrangements for handling of complaints including harassment complaints. It should indicate where the AGO and TSol can obtain further detail if required. (*Para 3.9*)

Attorney General's Equality and Diversity Expectations Statement for Civil and Criminal Panel Counsel and their Chambers

Reporting format for second and subsequent progress reports 2010 and beyond.

This template should completed by large sets (45+) every year commencing in 2010 (by 1 October); by medium sets (20 to 45) every two years commencing in 2011 (by 1 October); and by smaller sets (under 20) every three years commencing in 2012 (by 1 October).

1. Equality and diversity policy and actions

This should be a summary of the key actions taken to implement the equality and diversity policy. It should summarise the results and outcomes of the key actions taken. It should provide a clear overview of the main actions to progress equality and diversity in the reporting period. It should indicate where the AGO or TSol can obtain further information if required.

2. Equalities monitoring and under-representation

This should be a summary of progress made in the reporting period to maintain or secure a representative chambers in terms of pupils, members and staff by disability, ethnicity and gender. It should report progress against starting positions in terms of gender, ethnicity and disability composition, and against any objectives set for the reporting period. It could be structured as follows:

Chambers Category	Gender Profile					
	Start	Now	Start	Now	Start	Now
Pupils						
Members						
Staff						

It should summarise any further action to be taken to make further progress as regards maintaining or securing a representative workforce. It should also summarise the progress from any positive action undertaken in the reporting period.

3. Training

This should be a paragraph which summarises the numbers of members, staff and pupils trained and the topics on which they were trained and dates when training took place. It should also summarise any further actions to be taken. As above for further information.

4. Equal access to and fair allocation of work

This should include a summary paragraph on Chambers' monitoring of access to and allocation of work, any conclusions drawn and action taken. It should indication where the AGO and Tsol can obtain more detailed information on Chambers' activity in this area if required.

5. Handling complaints

This should include a paragraph which summarise the numbers of complaints of discrimination and/or harassment received in the reporting period; the numbers upheld and any improvement actions taken or planned.

Attorney General: Equality and Diversity Expectations Statement: FAQs

Frequently Asked Questions relating to the Attorney General's Equality and Diversity Expectations Statement for Civil and Criminal Panel Counsel and their Chambers

1. What is Positive Action?

Positive Action is the term used for measures taken under the provisions of the Race Relations and Sex Discrimination Acts where one sex or racial or ethnic group is under-represented in particular areas of work. Positive Action through encouragement, training and development of potential is an important part of any equal opportunity programme. It should be taken only in the context of such a programme and where the conditions of under-representation are established through the regular review of ethnic and gender monitoring data.

Positive Action measures enable recruiters to encourage applications from suitable ethnic minority candidates or women so that they can be considered equally with other candidates. Under some circumstances it may be appropriate to offer training of ethnic minorities and women to assist them to compete for work where they are under-represented.

2. Does the requirement to take Positive Action conflict with the requirement for open competition in pupillage and tenancy recruitment?

No, Positive Action are special measures taken before selection. It is unlawful to discriminate in favour of women or people from ethnic minority backgrounds in the arrangements made for shortlisting or selecting candidates for appointment. Positive Action does not permit the selecting of ethnic minority or female candidates irrespective of merit for the purposes of increasing diversity among shortlisted or appointed candidates. Recruitment to chambers should follow open advertisement and be based on objective selection criteria related to the work to be done.

3. What form of Positive Action will be appropriate to chambers?

Women and members of ethnic minority groups are well represented among graduates of the Bar Vocational Course and, if the applicants to your chambers are not from diverse backgrounds, you may wish to consider the following Positive Action measures:

- review marketing materials to ensure that the messages they give to prospective candidates are welcoming and inclusive and make reference to chambers commitment to its equality and diversity policy;
- particularly encourage members of under-represented groups to apply to chambers;
- at recruitment fairs, provide information about chambers' equality and diversity policies and opportunities within chambers.

Career development support provided by chambers to pupils and junior tenants will influence their opportunities to obtain senior appointments or positions as experienced practitioners. Chambers could ensure regular feedback sessions for working pupils and practice development meetings for junior tenants (see recommendation para. 1.48 in the Equality and Diversity Code for the Bar). Chambers could set up mentoring schemes whereby a junior tenant may be a pupil's mentor and a junior tenant may be linked to a more senior member of chambers who can offer advice and guidance regarding practice development in a mentoring role. This would be relevant also to barristers returning to practice following a career break.

4. How frequently should we review equality and diversity recruitment monitoring data?

Data should be checked after each major recruitment exercise or at least, annually. The data should be obtained from an ethnic origin, gender and disability monitoring form attached to the application form (see Annexe E of the Equality and Diversity Code for the Bar). If an application form is not used all candidates responding to an advertisement, or seeking a position, should be sent a monitoring form at the outset of the process. Statistical summaries should be produced which identify applicants by ethnicity, gender and disability for each of the following stages of the process:

- Applications
- Shortlisting
- Interviews
- Appointments

Differential success rates at any stage should be investigated to ensure that there is no direct or indirect discrimination in the treatment of candidates. Under-representation at the application stage may indicate the need for Positive Action measures.

5. Our chambers is small and recruits staff and tenants infrequently and only has one pupil per year. It is hard to achieve diversity in chambers with such a low level of recruitment.

In these circumstances patterns of representation will take years to become apparent. It may not be possible to discern much from one year's figures but they should indicate whether chambers is attracting a diverse group of applicants. If not, the Positive Action measures referred to above should be considered. It is recommended that data on previous years analyses be compiled so any trends can be identified over time and, if necessary, addressed.

6. Is it necessary to conduct diversity monitoring of work allocation when established tenants in chambers receive very little unnamed work?

Even though there is much less unallocated work on the AG's panels than on the CPS panel it is nevertheless still necessary to monitor pupils and junior tenants access to work by disability, ethnicity and gender and, in so far as there is any unallocated work, to monitor that in the same way. There should be regular reviews of work undertaken by pupils and junior tenants to ensure that they have the opportunity to develop their practices in a fair and equal manner and that stereotypical assumptions about suitable areas of work for particular groups are not influencing patterns of instruction and allocation to them. Guidance is offered in Action Area B of the Equality and Diversity Code.

7. What is the position of barristers wishing to undertake Government work if their chambers do not comply with the AG's Equality and Diversity Expectation Statement?

It is hoped that there will be few barristers in this position given the new requirements in the Code of Conduct that chambers appoint an Equal Opportunity Officer and have a written equality policy consistent with the action areas in the Equality and Diversity Code. Where a chambers fails to provide the reports requested or do not otherwise comply with the statement, the chambers will be given the opportunity to meet the standard required. Guidance will be available from the Equality and Diversity Advisers at the Bar Council and from the Treasury Solicitor's Department. Ultimately, if the chambers decides not to comply with the statement or it fails to comply, the Attorney General will have to decide whether instructions can continue to be given to members of those chambers. It is intended that chambers will be given every opportunity to comply and that no hasty decisions will be made. The aim is to encourage chambers to make the necessary improvements rather than to deprive members of those chambers of the opportunity to undertake Government work.

8. What can chambers do to ensure that disabled applicants are not put at any disadvantage in the recruitment process?

Under the Disability Discrimination Act all chambers are under an existing duty to have completed adjustments (including alterations to the building and reviews of processes and procedures) to make chambers and the services it offers accessible to disabled persons. The work already completed will make adjustments for the recruitment process much simpler.

It is convenient to consider, firstly, reasonable adjustment for the recruitment process. Any advertising of vacancies should not put disabled persons who may wish to apply at a disadvantage, and the whole process should be accessible. The Disability Discrimination Act places a positive duty on barristers in chambers to make reasonable adjustments to accommodate a disabled person. At this stage the objective is to ensure that the disabled applicant has the same opportunity of success as an applicant without a disability. The applicant should always be consulted about the adjustment as he or she is an expert. All tenants and staff dealing with applications should be fully briefed on this duty.

In determining what is reasonable the following should be taken into account:

- the effectiveness of the adjustment in overcoming the disability;
- how practicable is the adjustment;
- the cost of the adjustment. The resources of chambers are relevant but the availability of assistance from other sources should be considered.

The following are examples of some 'reasonable adjustments':

- applicants submitted in alternative formats to the standardwritten application form such as an on cassette tape or electronically;
- accessible venue provided for the interview

The work previously undertaken may help so that, for example, an interview could use the procedure used for a conference in chambers for a client with the same or similar disability.

Chambers should brief its members and staff that any request for an adjustment will be fully considered and agreed to if reasonable. There should be a procedure to consider each such request. This could be delegated to, or involve, the chambers Equal Opportunity Officer and another senior member. In some cases chambers may find it helpful to consult a disability charity, which works in the relevant disability field, or some other expert. The objective is to ensure that a disabled applicant can take part in the normal recruitment and interview process, and the procedure to consider adjustments should not be complex or cumbersome.

Once a disabled applicant has been successful further or different adjustments may be required. The individual should be able to obtain funding for some assistance and equipment through the Access to Work Scheme, administered through local offices of JobCentrePlus. Their general aim is to pay, or subsidise, the disability costs leaving the business costs to the individual or chambers, so that the disabled person can work more effectively.

Chambers may need to make some further adjustments. The chambers' Equal Opportunity Officer in conjunction with another senior member could consider these, as for recruitment. While broadly the same factors apply as for recruitment, what is not reasonable for an interview may be reasonable for a successful applicant. By considering these adjustments with the disabled person chambers may be able to improve facilities for disabled clients, to whom chambers also owes a similar duty to make reasonable adjustments.

9. Where can I find out more about the Attorney General's Civil and Criminal Panels?

There is more information on both the Attorney General's website and the Treasury Solicitor's website.

Equality Rules of the BSB Handbook

[3.323b]

Frequently Asked Questions

1. How might chambers approach the monitoring of unassigned work?

   Chambers should consider keeping a database of work allocation. Monitoring data will need to be kept in a form that allows Equality and Diversity Officers to identify individuals for work allocation purposes and identify any patterns or discrepancies. Fair allocation means that a barrister's knowledge and level of expertise is taken into account, and that work is allocated for justifiable reasons. It does not mean blindly equal allocation of work. Devilled work should also go through the clerks' room to ensure that it too is being allocated fairly.

2. Do chambers have to publish monitoring information on unassigned work?

   No, requirement rC110(3)(f) covers the monitoring and review of allocation of unassigned work only.

3. Are sole practitioners covered by the E&D rules for the self-employed Bar?

   No, only the core duty not to discriminate at rC12 applies to sole practitioners. The requirements at rC110 do not apply to sole practitioners.

4. If all members of chambers answer 'prefer not to say' to every question on the diversity monitoring questionnaire, does this data still have to be published?

   Yes. The requirement is to undertake the data collection and publication exercise, irrespective of the results.

5. How has the new core duty changed from what was previously in the Code of Conduct at 305.1?

   The fundamental principle now applies to a barrister in the course of his of her professional practice as opposed to applying generally in relation to any other person. The principle clearly prohibits unlawful discrimination as opposed to discrimination generally. The principle has also been updated to include the protected characteristics set out in the Equality Act 2010.

6. Where can I get fair recruitment training?

   Fair recruitment training may be undertaken through:

   (a) Private study of the Bar Council's Fair Recruitment Guide (which can be downloaded for free from www.barcouncil.org.uk/media/165213/recruitment_guidev22_18sept_merged_readonly.pdf).

   (b) Classroom sessions.

   (c) Online courses.

   Details on appropriate online or classroom courses may be obtained by contacting the Bar Council Equality and Diversity Helpline 0207 611 1321.

7. What does the BSB consider "recent" in terms of the training requirement?

Recent for the purposes of rules rC110 (3)(b) & (c) is training undertaken in the last 5 years before the selection panel sitting.

8. What is a "flat rate"?

A flat rate system is one where charges are made on a pre-defined sum as opposed to on a percentage rate of earnings.

9. What if someone in chambers does not want to provide their diversity data?

Provision of equality data is entirely voluntary, if an individual does not feel comfortable providing the data they do not have to provide it.

10. Who should draft the equality policy and action plan?

The rules do not require a particular person to draft the policy and action plan but it is suggested, in the BSB Supporting Information, that chambers' EDO ensures they are developed. All members of chambers workforce should contribute to the development of both documents.

11. My chambers does not have a website – how do we publish our diversity data?

The rules provide that where a chambers does not have a website, it is sufficient for chambers to ensure that diversity data is available to the public on request.

12. What is remedial action?

Remedial action is defined in the Supporting Information as "*Any action aimed at removing or reducing the disadvantage experienced by particular groups*". For example monitoring reveals that chambers has an underrepresentation of female members. An example of remedial action might be for female members to attend pupillage recruitment events as role models and to provide information.

13. How often does diversity data need to be reviewed?

In respect of data on pupils, it is suggested that data be reviewed annually. As regards data on tenants data should be reviewed every 3 years.

14. If we pay rent as a percentage of receipts – will chambers be required to waive that rental payment for 6 months?

No, the requirement relates to chambers operating a flat rate rental structure only.

15. If I undertake work to keep my hand in during my time on rent free paternity leave will I have to pay rent on anything I earn?

No, but you will need to negotiate with chambers how much and what type of work they will allow you to do during this time. Informal working arrangements to keep your hand in during parental leave do not affect a member's entitlement to a six month rent free period provided that the head of Chambers is kept informed of the arrangements and is satisfied that the level of work being undertaken does not constitute a return to practice.

16. If someone attends a pupillage interview in a wheelchair are we allowed to ask them how they intend to get to Court given that many Courts are inaccessible?

Questions about the health of an applicant may not be asked before pupillage is offered. However a question about the disability of a pupil may be asked in interview if the question is asked with the aim of establishing whether s/he will be able to carry out a function intrinsic to the role (e.g. getting to court, if regular court appearances are intrinsic to the role).

17. Should chambers EDOs ensure that if a disability is declared in monitoring information, that may require a reasonable adjustment, they proactively ask the disabled applicant about the need for an adjustment?

There is a legal requirement to avoid health related questions prior to a selection decision. Information packs/websites should encourage applicants to contact chambers in advance for a reasonable adjustment where needed. The checking of monitoring data for reasonable adjustment requests is not a correct use of monitoring data and may not be feasible for pupillage portal users when monitoring data is analysed and passed to chambers. It should be made clear to applicants that their response to the disability monitoring question will be used for monitoring purposes only.

18. How do you make a listed building accessible?

Easy Access to Historic Buildings booklet from English Heritage: http://www.english-heritage.org.uk/content/publications/publicationsNew/guidelines-standards/easy-access-to-historic-buildings/eheasyaccess2004.pdf.

This booklet is from 2004, but is comprehensive. In summary, if disability access provisions are treated as additions which respect existing historic architecture, rather than alterations, and skilfully integrated, they need have no more effect on historic buildings than sympathetically designed modern services, health & safety and fire precautions. Crucially, all buildings are different and it is best to speak to the local planning authority before knocking down any walls!

The Bar Council has produced a document containing guidance about making chambers accessible which can be found here: http://www.barcouncil.org.uk/media/43938/disability_access_making_chambers_accessible.pdf.

19. Why is there no sample flexible working or equal opportunity policy in the Supporting Information whilst there is a sample reasonable adjustments and anti-harassment policy?

The Supporting Information does not contain model E&D or FW policies as such policies will need to be tailored to the specific needs of each chambers, addressing the particular equality issues facing that chambers and setting out the aims and objectives of chambers in relation to equality. An E&D policy should cover all the areas set out in Section 3 of the Supporting Information on the rules. As regards reasonable adjustments and anti-harassment measures in chambers, appropriate provisions are likely to be broadly similar across most chambers and for this reason sample policies have been drafted for chambers to adapt. These may be found at section 13 of the Supporting Information.

20. Can chambers' Equality and Diversity Officer (EDO) be the same person as the Diversity Data Officer (DDO)?

Yes, and in many chambers it is likely that these two positions will be held by the same person.

21. Does headcount diversity data collected on all members of the chambers' workforce need to be analysed in the same way as the race, disability and gender data collected on numbers of barristers/applications/unassigned work?

There is no requirement for headcount diversity data (other than race, gender and disability data) to be analysed or for chambers to take remedial action, but chambers are encouraged to do this as a matter of best practice.

22. Is "fair and appropriate" training by way of accredited training courses? Or will any courses which meet the requirements be acceptable?

Courses will be deemed acceptable by the BSB as long as they cover the following areas: fair and effective selection and unconscious bias, selection criteria, short-listing and interviewing skills, assessment and making a selection decision; monitoring and evaluation. Remember you can satisfy the training rules by privately studying the Bar Council's Fair Recruitment Guide which can be downloaded for free from www.barcouncil.org.uk/media/165213/recruitment_guidev22_18sept_merged_readonly.pdf.

23. Where pupillage or tenancy recruitment decisions are taken by chambers as a whole (or by a chambers' meeting) would all members who participate have to be trained as set out in the training rule for panel members?

Where pupillage or tenancy recruitment decisions are taken by chambers as a whole then effectively the panel comprises every member of chambers and therefore every member of chambers should be trained as the rules require. However panels made up of every member of chambers (unless the set is very small) are discouraged as such panels are less likely to reach a full consensus on the appropriate candidate in a reasonable timeframe.

24. Does the BSB hold a list of approved providers for the fair recruitment training courses?

The BSB does not hold lists of approved providers for fair recruitment training courses however details of courses currently on offer from the Bar Council and some other providers can be obtained by contacting the Bar Council Equality Helpline on 0207 611 132. The training rules can also be satisfied by privately studying the Bar Council's Fair Recruitment Guide which can be downloaded for free from www.barcouncil.org.uk/media/165213/recruitment_guidev22_18sept_merged_readonly.pdf.

25. Do the requirements include gathering information on gender reassignment?

Following advice from trans equality organisations and data protection specialists the BSB has decided against requirement data collection in this area. The rules therefore do not require the collection or publication of data on gender reassignment. The BSB plans to conduct qualitative research into the experiences of trans barristers in the future separately to the data collection exercise.

26. Can a DDO be a member of staff?

Yes. The DDO role is a largely administrative one, requiring the holder to undertake tasks such as gathering data, ensuring monitoring forms are disseminated and ensuring relevant data is published. However if the DDO/EDO are one and the same person, that person should be a barrister.

27. Can an EDO be a member of staff?

The equality and diversity officer (EDO) should be a barrister, ideally a senior member of chambers as the role includes the provision of advice on equality issues to those in chambers.

28. How do you determine socio economic status?

The questionnaire on p.25 of the Supporting Information contains the relevant questions to ask members of your workforce to determine socio-economic status. The questions cover whether or not the individual was the first member of their family to attend university and whether or not they attended private school.

29. What is expected of a Sole Practitioner?

Sole practitioners are only covered by the core duty. The rules at rC110 do not apply.

30. What is "unassigned work"?

Unassigned work" is work that comes into chambers that is not assigned to a named person. Unassigned work may come into chambers by post, email, or may come in the form of a phone call from an instructing solicitor (or in public access cases, directly from a client). Any matter coming into chambers, by any means, that does not have a named individual assigned to it, is unassigned work.

31. How do we monitor unassigned work where the collection of diversity information is anonymous?

There are two types of monitoring required by the rules. The first is that which relates to recruitment and unassigned work allocation. Data must be collected on race, gender and disability, the data must be analysed and remedial action must be taken to tackle any disparities. Such monitoring should not be anonymous as it is necessary to link individuals with unassigned work coming into chambers and with recruitment exercises.

The second type of monitoring required by the rules is workforce headcount monitoring. This may be done anonymously but that would require a further monitoring exercise as distinct from that set out in the above paragraph. It may also be carried out non-anonymously but publication must be anonymous unless full consent is obtained from the workforce. This monitoring must be undertaken using the monitoring form at p.25 of the Supporting Information to which a section for the individual's name can be added if monitoring is not going to be anonymous. Other changes may not be made to this form as it is the form used by all branches of the legal profession (including solicitors/paralegals/legal execs) in order that profession wide comparisons can be made.

32. Does the monitoring of unassigned work allocation extend to QC choice of junior?

Monitoring of unassigned work includes but is not limited to work allocated to: pupils, barristers of fewer than four years' standing and barristers returning from parental leave. These groups must be covered by such monitoring but the rule does not exclude unassigned work monitoring of others in chambers such as QCs. Although not expressly set out in the rule "unassigned work" is likely to extend to QC choice of junior and therefore should be covered.

33. Do we need to inform anyone at the BSB/Bar Council about the name of our DDO?

Yes, you should email the Bar Standards Board equality team at equality@barstandardsboard.org.uk to notify us of the name of your DDO.

2. Ethical Advice in respect of all areas of Practice

Ethical Advice

Frequently Asked Questions

[3.324]

This Section sets out some of the questions put to the Bar Council's Professional Practice Committee concerning the BSB Handbook and related professional matters, and our responses to those questions.

If members of the Bar have particular questions about professional conduct matters that they would like to see addressed on this web page they should write to James Woolf at the Bar Council.

---

1. Acting as a Commissioner for Oaths or Notary Public – Q&As

Q1.1. Can I act as a Commissioner for Oaths?

A. Yes all practising barristers can act as a Commissioner for Oaths.

As of 1 January 2010, the right to administer an Oath has been limited to members of the Bar with a practising certificate. Part 2 of Schedule 5 of the Legal Services Act 2007, which came into force on this date, limits the right to administer oaths to 'authorised persons'. The 2007 Act defines 'authorised persons' as individuals who have 'in force a certificate issued by the General Council of the Bar authorising the person to practise as a barrister.' The practical effect of this is that since 1 January 2010 if you do not hold a current practising certificate you are prohibited from acting as a Commissioner for Oaths.

The Professional Practice Committee and Ethical Enquiries Service is unable to state which activities fall within the terms of reference for a Commissioner for Oaths as this is an area that goes beyond the BSB Handbook.

2. Work at Legal Advice Centres – Q&As

Q2.1. Does the BSB Handbook include any guidance on acting in a Legal Advice Centres?

A. The BSB Handbook B9 rS41–42 covers this in detail.

3. Personal Issues and Relationships – Q&As

Q3.1. I have a dispute with a builder over work that he has carried out on my home. Is it appropriate for me to write to him on Chambers' notepaper setting out what I believe to be my legal rights?

A. You should not attempt to gain an advantage or put any pressure on other people by virtue of your position as a barrister (BSB Handbook gC26.) It would be inappropriate for you to use your status as an implied threat to those with whom they are in dispute. Using chambers' notepaper in correspondence about a personal dispute, or when conducting personal business, could well constitute an implied threat and leave you open to a justified complaint of professional misconduct. Thought should also be given as to whether the use of an email address identifying chambers in the context of such a dispute might also contain an implied threat.

Q3.2. An opposing solicitor has indicated a wish to start a sexual relationship with me. Are there any problems with me starting such a relationship?

A. It would be unwise to start such a relationship during a case in which you are both involved. Perception is important, as well as reality, and clients (or, in a case which attracts publicity, the press and wider public) might perceive a danger of breach of confidence or of a conflict of interest or that you may not act in the best interests of your client. The BSB Handbook rC3 prohibits you from doing anything which could reasonably be seen by the public to undermine your honesty, integrity and independence.

The existence of any pre-existing relationship ought usually to be disclosed to clients in cases in which you are both instructed. If, for some reason, one of you is, or both of you are, unwilling for this disclosure to be made, you should consider carefully whether it is proper for you to act. If appropriate, you may wish to discuss the particular circumstances with the Ethical Enquiries Service.

4. Lay client relations and communications – Q&As

Q4.1. My client wishes to record a conference. Can I refuse this request?

A. You have no obligation to permit a recording to be made and are entitled to refuse. But before doing so you should consider, and if appropriate discuss with the client, preferably in the presence of your instructing professional, why the request is made and is whether it is the right thing to do. It may, e.g. inhibit discussion. On the other hand, there may be many reasons for it: the client may have some relevant physical or mental condition; they may be nervous and not confident of their ability to understand or to remember; they may not be confident of their ability to take adequate notes; or they may wish to discuss the details of the conference with someone else afterwards. If, but only if, you conclude that the request suggests that the client lacks confidence in you, it may be appropriate for you to suggest that the client consider instructing somebody else.

5. Pupils undertaking Work – Q&As

Q5.1. I am a pupil in my first six months and have been asked to take a noting brief. Am I allowed to do so?

A. Yes, provided that your pupil supervisor or Head of Chambers has given his permission, you can accept a noting brief during your non-practising six. Please see rS11. You may also charge for this work. You are only able to supply legal services and exercise a right of audience once you have completed, or been exempted from, the non-practising six months of pupillage and have the permission of your pupil supervisor or Head of Chambers.

Q 5.2. A solicitor who is a friend of mine sits on the board of a small company. He would like to use chambers for pro bono advice on contracts and other arrangements. We are a criminal set without much experience in this area. He thought that some of our pupils might be competent to do this.

A. The Handbook prohibits you from undertaking work which is outside of your competence. If you are a Pupil chambers, you should not undertake work which cannot be adequately supervised by your Pupil Supervisor (by whose insurance you are covered); and whose obligations under rQ54.1 extend to adequate supervision of pupils. You should not be given permission to do this if you are in your non-practising six months (BSB Handbook rS19). The fact that the work may be done pro-bono does not change this: you are under the same duty to act competently.

6. Writing for Legal Journals – Q&As

Q6.1. I am writing an article to be published in a legal journal. Am I able to describe myself as a barrister?

A. Yes. Whether or not you hold a practising certificate as a barrister, writing or editing law books articles or reports is specifically excluded from the definition of 'legal services' in Part 6 of the BSB Handbook, definition 122. You do not therefore need to be instructed by a professional client to write the article, and can refer to yourself as a barrister. The same principle applies for lecturing in or teaching law and examining publications for libel, breach of copyright and the like. Any member of the Bar can undertake these activities and hold out as a barrister.

7. Communications with other barristers and advocates – Q&As

Q7.1. In the course of a conversation with opposing counsel, I discovered information to which I would not normally have been privy which could affect the way I conduct my lay client's case. What should I do?

A. There is no such thing as 'counsel to counsel' confidentiality. If you learn something, which will affect you lay client's case, and which it is in his/her best interests to know, you should tell him/her and adjust the way in which you handle the case accordingly.

There is a common, but mistaken, belief, that communications between counsel are automatically subject to 'counsel to counsel' confidentiality, with the result that you cannot tell your client anything which opposing counsel told you unless you have opposing counsel's permission. Communications between counsel are no different from any other communication between the lawyers for opposing parties.

It sometimes happens that opposing counsel offers to speak to you on a 'counsel to counsel" basis, or otherwise indicates that they want you to agree not to tell your client what they are about to tell you. You should tell your opponent that you will not agree to do this without first getting your lay client's permission. If they wish to tell you without you seeking that permission, it will be at the risk that you will disclose the material. You will have to advise your client whether it is in their best interest for you to be given information which you cannot communicate to them. You will need to consider the practical implications of receiving information on this basis, which may lead to your becoming professionally embarrassed. (See *R v. B. & G.* [2004] EWCA Crim 1368, [2004] 1 WLR 2932, [2004] 2 Cr App Rep 630 for an example of a case in which counsel considered that they were unable to continue once they became aware of relevant information which the Judge ordered them not to communicate to their clients.)

Q7.2. I acted for the wife in a family matter. During counsel to counsel discussions, I told opposing counsel that I had advised against a particular application being made. My instructing solicitors have now received a letter from the husband's solicitors making a claim for wasted costs in respect of the application on the basis that it was against my advice. It is clear that opposing counsel has revealed matters which I discussed with him in confidence. Is there anything I can do about it?

A. There is no such thing as 'counsel to counsel' confidentiality. You have disclosed, without instructions to allow you to do so, material which was subject to your client's legal professional privilege. Your opponent's duty is to use the information if it is in his own client's best interests. The circumstances may support an argument that you made a careless disclosure, which could not reasonably be regarded as amounting to an informed waiver by the client of her own legal professional privilege. In those circumstances, an argument may be advanced that privilege has not been waived and that the material about your advice is not admissible on the husband's application against your instructing solicitors. Even if you are asked to do so, you should not act for the solicitors on this application without inviting them to consider whether that argument might be better advanced by other counsel. You should also consider whether the possibility of a complaint being made against you makes it inappropriate for you to act in that application.

8. Chambers Administration and Internal Issues – Q&As

Q8.1. One of the clerks in chambers is having an affair with a member of chambers. Does this cause any professional conduct problems?

A. While it is unlikely that the individual member is committing any misconduct, this can have serious ramifications for the remainder of chambers, particularly if the clerk concerned is involved in the allocation of work. If you are a self-employed barristers in chambers you have a duty to ensure that chambers are administered fairly and properly. This must include ensuring that work is distributed fairly and that no member is seen or perceived to be obtaining more favourable treatment than others (BSB Handbook rC110). It is easy to see how such a perception could arise. If serious concerns arise within chambers about this, then it may be appropriate that one or other should leave but, in any case, the other members of chambers will need to ensure that there is sufficient monitoring of the allocation of work to ensure that any perceptions are unfounded.

Q8.2. In order to monitor distribution of work and to ensure that members are informed about chambers' financial position and prospects, we propose to circulate details of members' receipts to all members of chambers. Are we able to do so?

A. There is nothing in the BSB Handbook to prevent you from doing so, provided that members of chambers consent.

9. Client Confidentiality and Threats of Violence – Q&As

Q9.1. I am instructed in a residence and contact case to represent the father. In conference, the father has told me that if he does not get custody of the child he will make sure that no one else will. I am very concerned by what he might do to the child. However, he has told me that I must not mention what he said to anyone else. Am I able to breach client confidentiality and report the matter to the proper authorities?

A. You should first satisfy yourself that the threat is genuine. The BSB Handbook rC15.5 allows a barrister to breach his duty of confidentiality 'as permitted by law'; broadly, the law permits you to do so where there is a danger of harm to a third party. In such circumstances a barrister should report the threat to the police or other agency (such as the local authority social services department) able to take appropriate protective measures. This subject is also covered in more detail in the following ethical assistance document: Disclosure of Unhelpful Material Disclosed to Counsel in Family Proceedings. If you are in any doubt you should contact the Ethical Enquiries Service: 020 7611 1310.

10. Employed Barristers – Q&As

Q10.1. I am an employed barrister working for a firm of solicitors. I have been invited to become a partner. Am I able to do so?

A. Yes, you are now able to become a partner in a firm of solicitors. The prohibition on barristers supplying legal services to the public through, or on behalf of any other person, (including a partnership company or other corporate body) has been removed. The BSB Handbook rS16 allows legal services to be supplied to the public by:

(1) a self-employed barrister, subject to the limitations imposed by Section 3.B3;

(2) as a BSB authorised body, subject to the limitations imposed by Section 3.B4;

(3) as a manager of a BSB authorised body or as an employed barrister (BSB authorised body), subject to the limitations imposed by Section 3.B5;

(4) A manager of an authorised (non-BSB) body or as an employed barrister (authorised non-BSB body), subject to the limitations imposed by Section 3.B6;

(5) an employed barrister (non-authorised body), subject to the limitations imposed by Section 3.B7; or

(6) a registered European lawyer in any of the above capacities, in which case the equivalent limitations that would have applied if you were practising as a barrister shall apply to your practice as a registered European lawyer.

The precise provisions, which apply to barristers practising as managers or employees of Authorised Bodies is set out in the BSB Handbook rS35–37.

11. Non-Legal Roles – Q&As

Q11.1. I have been asked to be a non-executive director of a company. Is this permitted?

A. For the purposes of the BSB Handbook, acting as a non-executive director does not fall within the definition of providing a legal service, (if the company is not in itself an authorised (non-BSB) body). You can therefore be a non-executive director. The BSB Handbook definition 122(f) also exempts from the definition of legal services, giving to the other directors the benefit of his learning and experience on matters of general legal principle applicable to the affairs of the company.

If you have a material interest in an organisation which is proposing to refer a matter to you, you must tell the client about your interest before you accept instructions, and must have clear agreement with the organisation how relevant issues, such as conflicts, will be resolved. You also have a duty to keep records must be kept in accordance with BSB Handbook rC82.

Q 11.2. May I be a director of a company?

A. Yes. If the company provides legal services, specific requirements apply dependent on the nature of the corporate structure, and your role within it. If you hold other directorships in corporate entities, which do not provide legal services, then you must not do anything which could reasonably be seen by the public to undermine your honesty, integrity) and independence (BSB Handbook CD3–5) as a BSB regulated person.

12. Clashes of Cases – Q&As

Q12.1. I have a clash of cases on the same day. Which one should I choose?

A. It is ultimately your responsibility to decide which case is the most important for you to attend. As a general guide:

(1) criminal cases take precedence over civil;

(2) a part-heard case takes precedence over a new matter; and

(3) a case for which a fixed date has been obtained takes precedence over a "floater".

If none of the above apply, you should take into consideration the amount of work that you have done on the case, the length of time that you have been instructed on each case, each case's complexity and difficulty and, perhaps most importantly, which lay client will be most prejudiced by someone else taking the case over at short notice.

You should also bear in mind the following points: you should notify the professional client or client, as far as reasonably possible, in sufficient time to enable appropriate steps to be taken to protect the client's interests, if there is an appreciable risk that that you might not be able to conduct a case: see the BSB Handbook rC18. BSB Handbook rC17 provides that the duty to act in the best interests of each client includes a duty to consider whether the client's best interests are served by different legal representation, and if so, to advise the client to that effect: see guidance on this rule at gC49.

Q12.2. Can I be instructed as leading counsel for two clients in separate cases where there is a danger of a clash of cases? Both clients have consented to me representing them and being absent for part of the case. I have advised both clients that if the first client withdraws this consent I would have to return the second case altogether.

A. A Disciplinary Tribunal has ruled on a complaint raising similar issues under the former Code of Conduct. The Tribunal took the view that counsel should have considered their duty to the clients, to maintaining confidence in the legal profession, and to the administration of justice generally.

Such a scenario has the potential to engage your Core Duties to: observe your duty to the court in the administration of justice (CD1); act in the best interests of each client (CD2); and not behave in a way which is likely to diminish the trust and confidence of the public (CD5). BSB Handbook rC21 provides that you must not accept instructions to act: if due to any existing or previous instructions you are not able to fulfil your obligation to act in the best interests of the prospective client; or you do not have enough time to deal with the particular matter, unless the circumstances are such that it would still be in the client's best interests to accept. BSB Handbook rC17 provides that the duty to act in the best interests of each client includes a duty to consider whether the client's best interests would be better served by different legal representatives, and if so, to advise the client to that effect: see guidance on this rule at gC49. CD7 provides a competent standard of work and service to each client is also potentially relevant. BSB Handbook rC18 provides that this includes a duty to inform the professional client, or client, as far as reasonably possible in sufficient time to enable appropriate steps to be taken to protect the client's interests, if there is an appreciable risk that you may not be able to undertake the instructions.

Accepting both sets of instructions will not be appropriate in many cases. For example, if the first client withdraws their consent late in the day, the complexity of the second case could mean that alternative counsel would require a lengthy period of time to be instructed and master the brief, and the second trial may need to be adjourned. In a criminal case this could result in considerable cost to the public purse, depending on the availability of the other counsel in the case, of trial Judge, and of witnesses, as well as the additional time the defendant would need to spend in custody. In these situations, the best interests of clients and the administration of justice will not be well-served.

However, there may be situations, where consent has been given by both of the clients and professional clients, where it would be reasonable to accept both cases. For example, if the first case is likely to settle promptly and the second is reasonably straightforward; in these circumstances, if the first case does not settle it would not prejudice the client in the second case by them having alternative counsel as they would have adequate time to prepare.

You should consider your position carefully if you find yourself in a similar situation. If you have any doubt they should contact the Ethical Enquiries Service.

13. Media Comment in Current Cases – Q&As

Q13.1. I have been approached to appear on a television/radio discussion programme to put forward the legal position on a particular area of the law. Can I do this?

A. There is nothing in the Handbook that prohibits you from discussing the legal standpoint on a given issue in general terms. However, you should avoid being drawn into giving advice on a specific person's case without being properly instructed as this might place you in breach of the BSB Handbook rS24.

The former prohibition on practising barristers expressing a personal opinion in the media, in relation to any future or current proceedings in which they are briefed, has been removed. If you are a practising barrister you must nonetheless, ensure that any comment that you make does not undermine, and is not reasonably seen as undermining, their independence. Furthermore, any such comment must not bring the profession nor any other barrister into disrepute.

14. Conflicts – Q&As

Q14.1. A solicitor for a defendant has spoken briefly to me about his client's case. The prosecution subsequently sought to brief me and sent me the papers. I have not had the opportunity to read the papers. Now the defence solicitor is seeking to brief me. Which set of instructions should I take?

A. This will depend upon the nature of the discussion with the defence solicitor, the information provided at that time and, in particular, whether you learned anything about the defence case which would give you an undue advantage in presenting the prosecution case. If you have such knowledge then you ought to return the prosecution brief unread. There would be nothing then to prevent you accepting the defence brief in those circumstances. If you has no such knowledge then, the prosecution brief having arrived first, you should take that.

15. Sole Practitioners and Establishing New Sets of Chambers – Q&As

Q15.1. Yesterday, my client instructed me that he wished to plead guilty to an offence. We went carefully through all the defences available to him and he signed instructions saying he wished to plead guilty. He did so. Today he has written to the Judge indicating that he wishes to change his plea because he was under pressure from others to plead guilty. Am I in difficulties?

A. Probably. Your duty is to ensure that the court is not knowingly or recklessly misled (BSB Handbook CD1, oC1 and rC3.1). In this situation, it would be appropriate to ask the client (a) why this was not raised with you originally, and (b) why he chose to write to the judge about it. It may be that he can provide an explanation for the sudden change which satisfies you that you will be able to represent him. If he does not provide a satisfactory explanation, then you should withdraw.

If the explanation is satisfactory, then it would be sensible to explore why he thought it right to approach the judge rather than deal with this through his legal advisers. The action suggests a lack of confidence in you which, of itself, might be reason either for you to withdraw or for him to seek to instruct new counsel.

16. Acting for Yourself and for Friends – Q&As

Q16.1. I am in litigation and wish to represent myself. May I do so?

A. You have the same right as every other citizen to act as a litigant in person. What you may not do is appear as a barrister in your own case e.g. by wearing robes and appearing in counsel's row.

Q16.2. A friend has asked me for some legal advice. Am I able to help?

A. You are allowed to give pro-bono legal advice to friends and relations without instructions from a solicitor, even if you have not completed the public access training. You should bear in mind that this is limited to advice and does not cover representation. If you wish to go further, you would need to be instructed by a solicitor or undertake the required public access training. In particular, you should not correspond with the other side on your friend's behalf (although you could draft letters for him to sign).

You should consider the BSB Handbook CD4 and whether your connection with the client is so close that you might find it difficult to maintain your professional independence. Clearly, the more serious the matter, the more likely it is that you will find it difficult to advise as independently as someone not connected with the client.

Q16.3. A friend has asked me to appear at an Employment Tribunal hearing on her behalf. May I do so without instructions from a professional client? I will not be charging a fee and do not want my friend to go to the trouble and expense of instructing a solicitor. If this is not possible may I assist as a McKenzie friend?

A. The BSB Handbook permits you to offer advice free to a friend or relative and, as this is not deemed to be a legal service, you do not need instructions from a professional client in order to give such advice. Of course, were you to provide advice on an aspect of the law with which you were unfamiliar, you might run the risk of a complaint being made against you under BSB Handbook CD5 (You must not behave in a way which is likely to diminish the trust and confidence which the public places in you or in the profession). On the other hand, representation is a legal service even if you undertake the work on a pro-bono basis. If you wish to appear on behalf of a friend or relative you must get instructions from a solicitor or, alternatively, accept instructions directly from the client if comply with the Public Access Rules (BSB Handbook D2).

The BSB Handbook does not prevent you from appearing as a McKenzie Friend but you should be careful not to go further than the traditional role.

17. Issuing Proceedings – Q&As

Q17.1. Our clerks have been asked by solicitors to issue proceedings in the High Court. All the papers have been prepared by the solicitor and they will provide the fee. It is simply more convenient for us to provide this service. Can we do so?

A. No. Unless you have applied for, and been granted, a litigation extension you cannot conduct litigation. You cannot handle client money save through a third party payment service approved by the BSB, such as BARCO, unless you are acting in your capacity as a manager of an authorised (non-BSB) body.

You can apply for an extension to your practising certificate from 22 January 2014.

18. Gifts and Presents – Q&As

Q18.1. My chambers would like to give a gift of a food hamper to one of our regular instructing solicitors. Is this permissible?

A. Under CD3 and CD5 you must maintain your independence, and act with honesty and integrity. The BSB Handbook rC3 stipulates that the offering, promising or giving of a gift (apart from items of modest value) to any client, professional client or other intermediary may reasonably be seen to compromise your independence (see gC18).

The giving or receiving of entertainment at a disproportionate level may also give rise to a similar issue, and therefore, should not be offered or accepted if it would lead others reasonably to think that your independence had been compromised (gC20).

It is considered to be acceptable for you to take a solicitor or intermediary out for dinner at the conclusion of a case. The same would apply for chambers offering proportionate hospitality to a firm of solicitors or other intermediary.

Q18.2. A grateful client is offering me a present. Can I accept it?

A. It will depend on the nature of the present and whether you are continuing to represent the client. The Conduct Committee has ruled that if your involvement in a case has ended and that there is unlikely to be any appeal, you may accept a gift from a lay client, provided that the gift is relatively modest and the circumstances and size of the gift are unlikely to bring your independence into question. See BSB Handbook gC19 in this context. Money, gift vouchers and so forth, should generally be avoided. Furthermore, any gift received should not be of excessive value or disproportionate to the work done by you. If you feel that accepting a particular gift will cause you embarrassment, it should be returned with a suitable note of thanks either to the client direct or through the instructing solicitor. If in doubt about individual gifts, you should seek advice from the Ethical Enquiries Service.

19. Appearing as both advocate and witness – Q&As

Q19.1. I am instructed in a contested childcare case on behalf of the mother. At a hearing outside court, the father attacked my client's ex-husband. I was present. The judge heard about this and has ordered a contempt hearing against the father. He has ordered that I supply a witness statement. Can I continue with the original case?

A. Possibly. This will depend upon, whether there is a dispute about your evidence in the contempt matter, and/or whether you consider evidence in respect of the attack is relevant and should be heard within the childcare case. The contempt action and the childcare case are different proceedings. In principle, you could act as advocate in one and witness in the other. However, if there is some serious allegation about your impartiality, or you seek to cross-examine using evidence which you are able to give yourself, you are likely to be professionally embarrassed and unable to continue with the original case.

20. Liens over Papers – Q&As

Q20.1. My lay client and his instructing solicitor have fallen out and my lay client is now instructing another firm. He has not paid his previous solicitors. I still possess a number of papers in the case forwarded to me by the first solicitors. The second solicitors wish to instruct me. Am I able to make use of the papers?

A. You should ask the first solicitors whether they wish to claim a lien over the papers. If they do not, you may use the papers. If they do wish to claim a lien, you should return the papers to them (not to the new solicitors) without copying them or using them. There is nothing to prevent you from keeping and using your own notes at any stage. You do not need to send your own notes, or copies of them, to the first solicitors.

Part IV
Foreign Work

1. Foreign Work and the BSB Handbook

[4.1]

There have been significant changes in the new Handbook regarding what was previously termed "international work". "International work" has been changed and replaced by three new definitions of "foreign work", "foreign clients" and "foreign lawyers." The rationale is that the new definitions allow the Handbook to be applied to foreign work in a more consistent and logical way than was achieved by the previous Code. Public Access rules now apply to foreign work when instructions are received directly from a lay foreign client or a lay client in England and Wales in relation to foreign work.

The new Handbook no longer separates the rules relating to foreign work in an annex. Instead the rules are incorporated into the main body of the Handbook.

The changes in more detail

[4.2]–[4.3]

Under the Old Code of Conduct, there was a set of rules called the International Practice Rules ("IPRs") at Annex A to the Code. In essence, the IPRs, by reason of their definition of "International Work", disapplied the Cab Rank Rule for:

(a) some but not all English proceedings (depending on the residence of the lay client and where, geographically, the instructions came from; and

(b) some but not all foreign proceedings (depending on where the work was actually carried out).

The other significant relaxation under the old IPRs was the disapplication of the old rule 401(a) for International Work, thereby permitting the Bar to accept instructions directly from lay clients.

In addition, the old IPRs relaxed and modified the Code in relation to International work substantially performed outside England and Wales. The old IPRs made distinctions based on:

(a) where the "substantially performed" his instructions;

(b) the residence of his lay client; and

(c) the location from which his instructions emanated.

The new Handbook replaces the old concept of "international work" with fresh definitions of "foreign client", "foreign work" and "foreign lawyer" (see the definitions in Part VI of the Handbook).

Foreign client

A foreign client is, as "a lay client who has his centre of main interests outside England and Wales, or who reasonably appears as having that characteristic."

The foreign client definition is tied to the concept of "Centre of Main Interests" which is borrowed from European and UN law and is best domestically in the law of cross-border insolvency. This is an international and objective test, independent of the type of legal entity concerned, which has been considered and refined in the ECT and the English Courts (e.g. see Re *Stanford International Bank Ltd* Re [2010] EWCA Civ 137), [2011] Ch 33, [2010] 3 WLR 941.

Foreign work

Foreign work is defined in the handbook as legal services of whatsoever nature relating to:

(a) court of other legal proceedings taking place or contemplated to take place outside England and Wales; or

(b) if no court or other legal proceedings are taking place or contemplated, any matter or contemplated matter not subject to the law of England and Wales.

As before, albeit with potentially different limits, foreign work is not subject to the cab rank rule – see the Handbook rC30.5.

As with all other work, a barrister undertaking foreign work remains under a duty to ensure that the client is well-served by the composition of the legal team, and to advise if they take the view that the client would be better served with different legal representation – see the Handbook rC17 and gC49.

Broadly, as before, a barrister undertaking foreign work is obliged to comply with the applicable rules of the relevant jurisdiction, subject always to the overriding Core Duties – see the Handbook rC13. Furthermore, soliciting work outside England and Wales must not be carried out in a manner which would be prohibited if done by a member of the local Bar – see the Handbook rC14.

Unless the barrister has undertaken Public Access training, they are not permitted to accept instructions for foreign work directly from a lay foreign client. Please note, the BSB allowed barristers who undertake foreign work a period of grace in which to complete Public Access training until 30 June 2014. From 1 July 2014, barristers must have undertaken the training in order to accept foreign work directly from a lay client.

Foreign Lawyer

Foreign Lawyer is defined substantially but not precisely as per the Courts and Legal Services Act 1990 as a person who is a member, and entitled to practise as such, of a legal profession regulated within a jurisdiction outside England and Wales and who is not an authorised person for the purposes of the Legal Services Act 2007 (as amended).

Instructions from a Foreign Lawyer, whether to carry out domestic or foreign work, need not be accepted under the cab rank rule, unless the foreign lawyer is from Europe – see Handbook rC30.6.

As before, any barrister may take instructions from a foreign lawyer without the need for an English solicitor as the definition of professional client in Part VI includes a foreign lawyer. Accordingly, as before, there is no need under the Handbook for a barrister to have a public access qualification before being able to accept instructions from a foreign lawyer. However, there has been a significant relaxation in that a barrister can now take instructions from a foreign lawyer to provide advocacy services, which used to be prohibited.

The new rules change the old position in this respect: under the old Code of Conduct, no intermediary was needed for international work – that was effected by disapplying para 401(a) of the Code in relation to International Work. But in relation to foreign work, a barrister cannot now take instructions directly from a lay client because the equivalent provision in the Scope of Practice Rules section in the new Handbook (rS24) does not have any carve out for foreign work.

For example, in 2013 a barrister might have chosen to (but was not obliged to) accept instructions directly from a foreign client to advise on an English law matter or appear in an English arbitration: that would have been International Work then and there was no requirement under the old Code to have an English solicitor involved in such matters because they did not entail advocacy services in an English court. A common example of this used to be a London construction arbitration in which the barrister was instructed by an in-house surveyor at the client. Under the new Handbook, such work cannot be accepted by a barrister who is not authorised to undertake public access work (rS24.3.a.iii).

The same is true of direct instructions from a lay client to advise or work on a foreign law matter, or appear in a foreign arbitration or an overseas Court. Under the old Code, with limited exceptions, such instructions could have been accepted by any barrister as the work was likely to have been International Work. However, under the new Handbook, only barristers licensed to undertake public access work could accept them under rS24.3.a.iii.

Other differences in form and practice

Unlike the Code of Conduct, the Handbook does not contain annexes. Much of the substance of the previous Code's Annex A, the International Rules, has been incorporated into the body of the Handbook. Subject to the points set out above, there are few radical changes to the limits and rules of international practice per se.

One other significant change to the rules is that a barrister can now accept instructions directly from a foreign lawyer to provide advocacy services to appear in Court in England or Wales without an English solicitor intermediary. However, unless the barrister has the requisite conduct of litigation extension, a suitable solicitor may still be needed.

The above change is a result of the fact that under the old Code of Conduct a barrister could take instructions from "a professional client" which included a foreign lawyer "in a matter which does not involve the barrister supplying advocacy services". Advocacy services are defined in the Courts and Legal Services Act 1990 (s 119) as "any services which it would be reasonable to expect a person who is exercising, or contemplating exercising, a right of audience in relation to any proceedings, to provide", and so would include writing a skeleton argument of preparing for court. The net effect of this was that a barrister could not take instructions to prepare arguments to deploy in an English Court on the instructions of a foreign lawyer.

However, in the Handbook, there is no such restriction in the definition of "professional client", so the barrister can provide advocacy services on the instructions of a foreign lawyer, albeit neither of them can conduct the ensuing litigation unless as stated above the barrister has the requisite extension to their practising certificate. In practice, the barrister will also be best placed to identify and recommend a suitable solicitor which is a further reason why the rule change could be advantageous to the profession.

Other changes have the effect of permitting a barrister to refuse to accept instructions in some rare situations which the previous rules treated somewhat anomalously as being governed by the Cab Rank Rule. The following are provided as examples:

(a) A foreign matter in which the barrister is instructed by a lawyer (foreign or English) on behalf of an English lay client, and where the work is then carried out in England. Under the old rules, this would not have been International Work, but under Handbook is within the definition of "foreign work". The effect is that this situation is no longer caught by the Cab Rank Rule:

(b) A foreign matter in which the barrister is instructed by an English solicitor on behalf of a foreign client where the work is carried out in England. This is likely to be rare but could conceivably happen, for example a Russian company retaining a City law firm which instructs a barrister in London to advise on a specialised point of law in a contract governed by the law of Hong Kong, whose law on the point is similar to English law. Under the old Code of Conduct, this would not have been International work but it is foreign work as defined under the new code. The effect once again is that it would no longer be governed by the Cab Rank Rule.

The old International Practice Rules relaxed the rules on overseas associations between barristers and other lawyers, restrictions on the type of work which barristers could do abroad, their insurance requirements and the ways in which barristers charged for their services. Many of the restrictions have been dismantled by the BSB as part of its wider plan to free up the profession from historic barriers to work. Accordingly, the new Code does not need to refer expressly to the relaxation of former restrictions. For that reason, there are only limited equivalent provisions in the new Code to what was previously set out in the IPR Rules 4(a) to (c).

However, there is in the Scope of the Practice Rules section of the Handbook, rS26, a relaxation on the management administration and general conduct of a client's affairs where the work is foreign work carried out at an office outside England and Wales which a barrister established or joined primarily for the purpose of carrying out that particular foreign work or foreign work in general.

The old rules on dual qualified barristers and barristers working outside England and Wales are not significantly changed in the Handbook.

Under the old rules an unregistered barrister practising as a foreign lawyer who neither advised on English law nor supplied legal services in respect of English proceedings was not treated as a practising barrister. The position is preserved under rS13.

The former rules set out who would be qualified to supervise a barrister of less than 3 years' standing who works from an office in the EU outside England and Wales. This is reproduced at rS22.b.

How the Handbook applies to European and Foreign Lawyers

[4.4]–[4.5]

In much the same way as the previous Code, the Handbook stipulates how a registered European lawyer must comply with the Code. However, rather than a dedicated annex, the rules regarding European Lawyers have been split up and moved to different parts of the Handbook. The parts that cover Registered European Lawyers can be found at rC142–rC143. The rules governing registration of European Lawyers are at rS78–rS81. Registered European Lawyers enjoy largely the same practice rights as the host profession with which they are registered. Foreign Lawyers working in Chambers are no longer dealt with by way of a separate annex. Instead, they are dealt with more briefly at rC89.7.

2. International Relations and Bar Council

[4.6]

The International Relations Secretariat is the principal point of contact for enquiries relating to the international relations of the Bar Council with jurisdictions in other countries including the work of the International Relations Committee.

The International Relations Secretariat performs three functions. Firstly, it promotes the international business interests of the Bar, through a variety of high-level business developments visits (both incoming and outgoing), publications and training for commercial officers of HMG. Secondly, it informs the Bar Council and the BSB on international regulatory developments and seeks to influence these as appropriate. Thirdly, it undertakes legal co-operation projects which seek to strengthen legal professions abroad and the rule of law generally.

In relation to the business development function, the Bar Council has significantly extended its services to members in recent years. In addition to the many business networking activities offered, it has produced the following three publications aimed at explaining to international clients the advantages of using the Bar:

- "Services of the International Criminal and Regulatory Bar;
- "Barristers in the International Legal Market"; and
- "Barristers in International Arbitration".

These publications are all available from the Bar Council website at http://www.barcouncil.org.uk/instructing-a-barrister/information-for-international-clients/or in hardcopy from the International Team. It makes good sense for chambers to have a supply of these brochures available for international clients or refer them to the weblink.

Barristers interested in developing their international careers now also have the opportunity to join one of three regional interest groups, which will provide them with information on business development opportunities. Interest Groups have so far been set up for the Middle East, India and China. Depending on resources new groups will be created in future. Members interested in joining any of these should contact the Secretary to the International Team.

In promoting the Bar abroad, the Bar Council works closely with UK Trade & Investment, which undertakes a number of business development activities in which chambers and individual barristers can take part in. Further information can be found at https://www.uktradeinvest.gov.uk/. The Bar Council is also a member of CityUK (www.thecityuk.com) and takes part in their promotional work to strengthen England & Wales as an international legal centre.

In addition to its three international policy functions, the International Relations Secretariat can provide the contact details of the competent regulators for barristers seeking rights of audience in jurisdictions outside England and Wales.

Barristers and lawyers who have qualified in other jurisdictions and who wish to practise in England and Wales should contact the Secretary to the Joint Regulations Committee at the Bar Standards Board.

News and information on all areas of international relations work are published regularly in *BarNews* (within *Counsel Magazine*) and on the Bar Council website.

The Bar Council's Brussels Office

[4.7]

The Bar Council monitors developments at the EU institutions and works for the interests of the Bar through a dedicated office in Brussels.

The Brussels Office works closely with the Bar Council's European Committee, and other Bar bodies where appropriate, in order to develop positions on, and provide expert input into, the EU legislative and policy-making processes that may have a bearing on the practice of barristers, whether in the regulatory, procedural or substantive law sense.

Current issues with which the Office is concerned include the review of the Brussels I regulation and several related PIL developments; an important proposal on Wills and Succession; key milestones on European Contract law and the CFR; the proposal for a Consumer Rights Directive; the possible introduction of system(s) of collective redress at EU level; progress towards a European Patent system; and developments in the field of e-justice, including the encouragement of the use of ID cards and e-signatures by lawyers.

In pursuit of the Bar's objectives at EU level, from time to time the Brussels Office arranges for evidence to be provided by the Bar to the European Parliament and to the UK Parliament on matters of EU law and policy, thus helping to communicate the Bar's experience and expertise in legislative and policy development.

Regular summary reports from the Brussels Office are published in the Bar News supplement of *Counsel*, as well as in a regular newsletter produced by the office called 'Brussels News'. Further information is also posted on the Bar Council's website. Barristers or chambers interested in receiving the office newsletter 'Brussels News' electronically, should contact the Brussels Office at the e-mail address below.

The Bar Council's Brussels office is conveniently located close to the European Commission and the European Parliament in central Brussels. It provides modern office facilities which are available for members of the Bar visiting Brussels. The Director of the Office will be pleased to provide further details on request.

The Brussels office contact details are:

Ave des Nerviens 85
B-1040 Brussels
Belgium

Tel: 00 322 230 4810
Fax: 00 322 230 4596
Email: evanna.fruithof@barcouncil.be

Barristers Appearing before Courts and other Tribunals outside England and Wales

[4.7a]

Purpose: To draw barristers' attention to issues appearing outside England or Wales.

Scope of application: All practising barristers.

Issued by: The Professional Practice Committee.

Originally issued: 2012.

Last reviewed: January 2014.

Status and effect: Please see the notice at end of this document. This is not "guidance" for the purposes of the BSB Handbook I6.4.

1. Concern has been expressed to the Bar Council that some barristers may not be aware that the BSB Handbook applies to your conduct in court and before tribunals (including arbitrators) wherever those courts and tribunals may be sitting, and whatever law they may be applying.

2. The BSB Handbook rC2 states that if you are practising or otherwise providing legal services (as defined in the BSB Handbook), then Sections 2.B, 2.C and 2.D of the BSB Handbook will apply. This is so whether you are practising or providing legal services in England and Wales or elsewhere.

3. The BSB Handbook rC2 also makes clear that CD5 and CD9 apply at all times, as does rC2, rC9 and rC64 to rC70 and the associated guidance. They will thus apply wherever you may be.

4. In addition, rC13 requires you, in connection with any "foreign work", to comply with any applicable rule of conduct prescribed by the law or by any national or local Bar of: (a) the place where the work is or is to be performed, and (b) the place where any proceedings or matters to which the work relates are taking place or contemplated, unless such rule is inconsistent with any requirement of the Core Duties.

5. The BSB Handbook defines "foreign work" as legal services of whatsoever nature relating to (a) court or other legal proceedings taking place or contemplated to take place outside England and Wales; or (b) if no court or other legal proceedings are taking place or contemplated, any matter or contemplated matter not subject to the law of England and Wales.

6. gC35 explains that it is your responsibility to inform yourself as to any applicable rules of conduct. This is likely in practice to require you to contact the relevant national or local Bar(s). You may also wish to take note of the International Bar Association's International Principles for the Conduct of the Legal Profession.

7. rC14 also stipulates that if you solicit work in any jurisdiction outside England and Wales, then you must not do so in a manner which would be prohibited if you were a member of the local Bar.

8. D6 of the BSB Handbook also lays down further rules applicable when you are engaged in cross border activities (as defined in the BSB Handbook) within a CCBE State other than the UK. These rules are derived from the Code of Conduct for European Lawyers, adopted by the Council of Bars and Law Societies of Europe ("CCBE"). CCBE States are those states whose legal profession is a full, associate or observer member of the CCBE. The Guidance at gC35 makes clear that the rules under D6 are in addition to rC13 and rC14.

Important notice

This document has been prepared by the Bar Council to assist barristers on matters of professional conduct and ethics. It is not "guidance" for the purposes of the BSB Handbook I6.4, and neither the BSB nor a disciplinary tribunal nor the Legal Ombudsman is bound by any views or advice expressed in it. It does not comprise – and cannot be relied on as giving – legal advice. It has been prepared in good faith, but neither the Bar Council nor any of the individuals responsible for or involved in its preparation accept any responsibility or liability for anything done in reliance on it. For fuller information as to the status and effect of this document, please refer to the professional practice and ethics section of the Bar Council's website here.

3. Bar Associations Abroad

[4.8]

The Bar Council has close links with Bar Associations in other jurisdictions and is an active member of the Council of European Bars and Law Societies ("CCBE")[1], the International Bar Association ("IBA")[2], the Commonwealth Lawyers Association ("CLA")[3] and the International Criminal Bar ("ICB")[4]. There are also links to the websites of these and other international organisations in the 'Links' section of the Bar Council website. Below are details of a selection of those organisations.

1 http://www.ccbe.eu/
2 http://www.ibanet.org/
3 http://www.commonwealthlawyers.com/
4 http://www.bpi-icb.com/index.php?lang=en

The CCBE

[4.9]

The CCBE is the representative body for the bars and law societies in the European Union and the European Economic Area (covering some 700,000 lawyers).

Head Office
Rue Joseph II, 40 / 8

B-1000 BRUSSELS

Tel: +32 (0)2 234 65 10
Fax: +32 (0)2 234 65 11/12
Email: ccbe@ccbe.org

The CCBE only admits organisational members (individual lawyers may not become members) which have to organise themselves in national delegations. The Bar Council therefore is a member of the UK Delegation to the CCBE, which consists of the six bars and law societies of the UK.

The CCBE has agreed a Code of Conduct which applies only to cross-border delivery of legal services and which is binding in all Member States, since all regulatory bars and law societies in the EU, including the Bar Council of England & Wales have incorporated the CCBE Code into their domestic Code of Conduct.

The CCBE produces material for advocates appearing in the European Court of Justice. The guidance below, 'Practical Guidance for Advocates before the Court of Justice in Preliminary Reference Cases', is set out in full:

This practical guidance is addressed principally to those appearing for the first time in the Court of Justice of the EU. They have been drafted by the Permanent Delegation to the Court of Justice of the Council of Bars and Law Societies of Europe (CCBE) in order to enhance the efficiency of the preliminary reference procedure. These tips are designed to complement the Court's own guidance set out on the Court's website under the heading "Procedure" and in particular in the Notes for the Guidance of Counsel.

Written Pleadings in Preliminary Reference Cases

General

- Keep pleadings as short as reasonably possible.

- Do not repeat material which is already in the judgment or order of the referring court (the Court has this in translation already).
- If your client has the same interest as other parties pleading before the Court (including Member States), discuss in advance who is going to focus on which points.
- Before starting, consider writing out your opponent's main points in order to focus your own arguments.
- It is vital to note that extensions of the deadline of two months and 10 days cannot be granted.
- Bear in mind that an oral hearing may not be granted and therefore the written pleading may be the sole opportunity to influence the result of the case.

Drafting style

- Keep the style simple so that it translates easily – punchy uncomplicated sentences are best.
- Consider asking a non-native speaker to read your text to check for likely ease of translation.
- Avoid use of national legal jargon which may be difficult to translate easily.
- As far as possible, try to be concise.

Structure

- Consider starting with a brief summary to focus the mind of the Court on the key issues.
- Avoid long introductions and do not rehearse the questions of the referring court or the order for reference at great length throughout the document.
- Restrict any statement of facts to what is strictly necessary for the resolution of the questions of EU law before the Court, bearing in mind that judgments are usually brief on the facts of the case.
- Be aware that the Court will rely on the statement of facts and law as contained in the referring court's judgment unless clearly challenged by one of the parties.
- In general, it is advisable to address each question from the national court in the order in which it is asked: however should you suggest that the questions be reformulated or answered in a different order, do so clearly.
- Conclude your written pleadings with proposed answers to the questions which the Court can use in the operative part of the judgment.

Content

- Written pleadings generally have more impact on the Court than oral pleadings.
- Focus on the good points.
- Remember that there is only one round of written pleadings with any reply points being exclusively for the oral hearing if there is one.
- So far as possible, anticipate the issues likely to arise at the oral hearing.
- A concise statement of the national legal framework can be important and should be prepared in a style that is easily comprehensible to lawyers from other legal traditions and which could be slotted into the judgment.

- Where the procedural context is relevant (e.g. Brussels Regulation cases) and is not apparent from the order for reference, describe it precisely.
- If not clear from the order for reference, summarise the facts underlying the decision to refer.
- Note that Annexes are not translated into the Court's working language (French) and that Judges will not even see them unless they request to do so.
- Avoid repetition.
- Suggest rephrasing the questions referred only where you consider it absolutely necessary.

Oral pleadings

Generally

- Respond promptly to the Registry's letter enquiring about an oral hearing, giving reasons why one is necessary.
- Once allotted a time for the main pleading (normally 15 mins in three judge chamber and 20 mins in five judge chamber) this time limit will be strictly adhered to unless an extension is granted in advance on written application to the Registry.
- Contact the Registry by e-mail or telephone to ask which parties are attending the oral hearing (and to obtain their advocates' contact details if needed).
- Confer, if possible, with parties with the same interest to agree which party is to focus on which argument.
- If the Court requests the parties to deal with particular issues, consider whether it is necessary to focus exclusively on these issues.
- If possible, send a summary of your pleading (e.g. 3–4 pages with highlights/bullet points) – including references to any judgments from which you intend to quote – to the interpreters in advance at the following e-mail: interpret@curia.europa.eu . In any event, bring a paper copy with you for the interpreters at the hearing or, if you lend your notes for photocopying, paginate them first.
- If you intend to refer in your presentation to case-law that has not previously been cited in the written pleadings, bring copies to the hearing.
- Do not forget to bring the robes you normally wear when appearing before the referring Court.

What to expect

- Find your Courtroom and the Salon des Avocats allocated to it where you can deposit any luggage you may have and put on your Court robes.
- After arrival at the Courtroom, one of the interpreters is likely to ask for a copy of any speaking notes you have for your presentation – so bring a spare copy (otherwise, they will ask to photocopy your notes).
- Immediately before the hearing commences, the Registrar or his representative will invite the advocates who are pleading to meet the Judges – a frequently asked question is whether you are going to need all of the time that has been allotted. On occasion the President of the formation will ask the advocates to address certain issues or to deal with a specific question.

- The order of pleadings is the main pleadings, followed by questions from the Bench and an opportunity to reply to any of the issues raised in the course of the hearing.
- The order of main pleadings is set by the President but usually consists of the parties before the referring court, the originating Member State of reference and then other Member States in alphabetical order and finally the European Institutions (usually the European Commission).
- Questions may or may not arise – you must be prepared to answer questions both on the facts and on the law (in particular on the applicable national law).
- Ensure that associates who may be able to assist with questions are seated in such position as to be able to assist the speaker in responding to questions.
- Replies must be kept short and should be limited to points that arise from the oral pleadings of the other parties and, where appropriate, questions from the Bench not addressed to you. They are not an opportunity to restate your main case and can be dispensed with unless you have something to say.

The pleading itself

- Focus on the members of the court – and in particular the reporting judge, the President of Chamber and the Advocate General (indicated on a sheet of paper attached to the lectern).
- Speak into the microphone (otherwise the interpreters cannot hear you!).
- Reading out a written speech runs the risk that you speak too quickly, fail to keep the attention of the Court and to lack flexibility to deal with the points made by others.
- Remember the interpreters, and speak slowly.
- Cut your speaking points down in length, rather than trying to speak very fast in order to get through the material in the time available.
- Avoid literary flourishes, jokes and idiomatic speech – they translate poorly.

Content

- Open with a brief statement of what you say the case is about.
- Do not repeat your written arguments in detail – seek to convey the fundamental reason why the Court should adopt your position, and if needed respond to points made by others in their written observations.
- Focus on the two or three most important points whilst showing that you are ready to deal with all other points.
- The Court's task is to provide an interpretation of EU law that can be applied in all Member States – the focus must therefore be on the law and not on the facts of the particular case.
- Avoid repetition of points made by others – if appropriate, simply adopt the previous speaker's points.
- Comply promptly with requests from the Bench, including a request to stop speaking.

Practical issues

Advance preparations

- The Court is on the Kirchberg Plateau in Luxembourg. See map at: http://curia.europa.eu/jcms/jcms/Jo2_7021/.
- The entrance to the Court for advocates is in the Rue du Fort Niedergruenewald.
- There are several hotels within five minutes walk of the Court, which may also permit a reconnaissance visit the afternoon before.
- Kirchberg is close to Luxembourg Airport – direct buses from the airport stop outside the Philharmonie, which is three minutes walk from the Court entrance.
- From the town centre, buses will likewise take you to the Philharmonie, see www.vdl.lu.
- Luxembourg City's roads – including the motorway to and from the airport – suffer bad congestion at peak times, so plan your arrival accordingly.

Arriving at the Court

- Arrive in good time for the hearing and in any event no less than 45 minutes beforehand – security checks can be time consuming.
- Bring passport for security checks, identify yourself as an "Avocat" (e.g. using CCBE card available from all national Bars) & refer to the security official at the head of the counter reserved to lawyers and parties in cases (do not wait in the queue for visits!).
- Ask for which courtroom (*salle d'audience*) your case is scheduled and where it is.
- Outside security, turn left into broad corridor (*la Galerie*) and after 30m, turn right up wide stairs past Rodin sculpture.
- At top of the stairs you are in the *Salle des Pas Perdus*. On the left is the *la Grande Salle d'audience.* The last office in the corridor immediately to the right hand side is the advocates' robing room/Salon des Avocats.
- Lockers are available for personal items and three computers are available with printers of which one has a connection to the internet.
- Do not count on being able to make photocopies at the Court.
- There is an alternative robing room on level 6 – coming out of the lift, it is on the right across the hall.

Arriving in the Court room

- Cases before the *Grande Chambre* will be in the *Grande Salle d'Audience.*
- Otherwise the court room is likely to be on one of the floors above the *Salle des Pas Perdus* (though there are also two court rooms at the bottom of Tower A).
- Although seats for litigants and their advocates are not specifically allocated, Institutions tend to sit on the left but Member States and parties can choose – those with similar interests would normally sit on the same side of the courtroom.
- Normally, advocates will sit at the desks in front of the Bench, while their clients/advisors sit on the front row of the seating immediately behind these desks.

- Do not attempt to sit on the "sideways" facing desks: these are for *référendaires* who assist the judges and the Court Clerk (*huissier*).
- With multiple parties, it will be necessary to use sequentially the podium and the microphone from which to speak.
- Check out your interpretation earphone and verify that it is on the correct channel – for channel numbers, check the number on the window of the booth.
- The lectern can be adjusted to your height if necessary.
- Power points are provided for laptops – switch off mobile phones.
- There will often be a comfort break after approximately two hours if a hearing is less than 3/4 complete. If necessary, there will be a lunch break at 13.00, with the resumption of the hearing at 14.30 – plan your day accordingly.

The IBA

[4.10]

The International Bar Association (IBA) is one of the largest organisations of international legal practitioners, Bar Associations and Law Societies with a membership of some 30,000 individual lawyers and 195 national bodies. It is structured into two divisions (the Legal Practice Division and the Public and Professional Interest Division).

The principal aims and objectives of the IBA are:

- To promote an exchange of information between legal associations worldwide;
- To support the independence of the judiciary and the right of lawyers to practise their profession without interference;
- Support of human rights for lawyers worldwide through its Human Rights Institute.

The IBA works towards these objectives through three main areas of activity:

- Services for individual lawyer members through its Divisions, Committees and Constituents;
- Support for activities of Bar Associations and in particular, developing bars;
- Support of human rights for lawyers worldwide.

The IBA Annual Conference has in recent years become the main global platform for international practitioners to meet, network and carry out law reform initiatives. The meeting attracts between 2000 and 3000 delegates, who nearly all have international practices (including around 300–500 solicitors from leading commercial firms) and is well worth attending for barristers wishing to develop their international practice. The International Relations Secretariat organises business development activities at the Conference and can give further advice.

The CLA

[4.11]

The Commonwealth Lawyers Association (CLA) is the most significant organisation bringing together the key jurisdictions practising the common law (with the exception of the USA). Apart from activities to promote the rule of law it has an important function in promoting the practice of the common law around the globe and to that organises very useful biannual Commonwealth Law Conferences. These bring together well over 1000 common law practitioners. The Bar Council considers the CLA as useful as the IBA for the purposes of business networking and organises its business development activities for the profession at the Conference. More details can be obtained from the International Team at the Bar Council.

The ICB

[4.12]

The International Criminal Bar (ICB) acts as the representative body of counsel appearing before the International Criminal Court regarding issues that affect their practice. It is a worldwide organisation whose members are drawn from many national and regional Bars.

Head Office
Neuhuyskade 94
Box Office 30851
2500 GW The Hague
The Netherlands

Tel: 0031 (70) 3268070
Fax: 0031 (70) 3353531
Email: info@bpi-icb.com

The Faculty of Advocates – the Scottish Bar

[4.13]

The Faculty of Advocates is a body of independent lawyers who have been admitted to practise as advocates before the Courts of Scotland[1]. As well as being the professional body in Scotland which oversees the training requirements needed to practise at the Scottish Bar, it is also via the 'stable listings' of advocate members that Scottish advocates may be instructed.

The Faculty of Advocates
Parliament House
EDINBURGH
EH1 1RF

Tel: 0131 226 5071

1 http://www.advocates.org.uk/

The Bar Council of Northern Ireland[1]

[4.14]

The Bar Council of Northern Ireland is responsible for regulating barristers in Northern Ireland, including in relation to professional conduct, remuneration, organisation and conditions of work, and its relationships with other professions and the Law Society.

PART IV FOREIGN WORK

The Bar Library
91 Chichester Street
Belfast
BT1 3JQ
DX 002 NR BELFAST

Practising in Northern Ireland

[4.15]

Members of the Bar of England and Wales of the Council's are required to be called to the Bar of Northern Ireland and hold a practising certificate in order to be able to practise in Northern Ireland. Both the Inn of Court and Bar Council of Northern Ireland have a requirement that the documentation in respect of Call applications and the issuing of practising certificates be provided at least eight weeks before a case starts.

***The Bar Council of Ireland*[1]**

[4.16]

Bar Council Administration Office,
Four Courts,
Dublin 7

Tel: +353 1 817 5000
Fax: +353 1 817 5150
Email: barcouncil@lawlibrary.ie

1 http://www.lawlibrary.ie/viewdoc.asp?DocID=4

Part V
Sole Practitioners

The Bar Council produces guidance specifically for sole practitioners and those setting up their own chambers and this is set out below:

Introduction

[5.1]

Purpose: To guide barristers setting up their own Chambers or as a sole practitioner.

Scope of application: Self-employed practising barristers.

Issued by: The Professional Practice Committee.

First issued: February 2014.

Status and effect: Please see the notice at end of this document. This is not "guidance" for the purposes of the BSB Handbook I6.4.

Sole practitioners

[5.2]

The Bar Standards Board Handbook provides that you may practise on your own provided that you have practised for a total of three years with a qualified person following the completion of your pupillage(BSB Handbook rS20).

Please note that:

- a "qualified person" is defined at rS22;
- periods of "squatting" or third-six pupillages count towards the three years;
- periods spent in employment as an employed barrister with full rights of audience after 31 July 2000 also count towards the three years;
- the period of three years need not be continuous: breaks may have been taken provided that the total time spent in practice amounts to three years;
- if you are practising in a dual capacity you must work with a qualified person in both capacities. You may not therefore set up as a sole practitioner even if you have worked with a qualified person in your employed capacity.

In certain circumstances, the Bar Standards Board may waive the requirement to have practised for three years post-pupillage. Please contact the Qualifications Department of the Bar Standards Board (020 7611 1444) for more information.

Assuming you meet the basic qualification, you do not need special permission from the Bar Standards Board in order to establish your own chambers. You should, however:

- update your records through BarristerConnect or inform the Records department (020 7242 0934) immediately of the address from which you will practise and the telephone number. This is of considerable importance and is your responsibility. It is not sufficient to rely on your former chambers to do so
- inform the Bar Mutual Indemnity Fund (0207 621 0405) of your new status – they are unlikely to require an additional premium.

Finally, you should note the requirements in the BSB Handbook to administer your practice efficiently and to have an effective complaints procedure. (see rC88–98).

You may wish to notify the Circuit on which you are practising and your Inn of Court.

Things to consider

[5.3]

Before deciding to practise alone, you should think carefully, not merely about how to comply with the Handbook but also about how you will deal practically with the different regime involved.

The advantages of sole practice can include:

- reduction in the costs of running a practice;
- control of your administration and marketing;
- a freer lifestyle in running your practice;
- saving time and money by travelling less.

Disadvantages can include:

- increased administrative burdens which are ongoing and not just limited to the initial setting up;
- lack of support to expand your practice and isolation from others, limiting exchange of views;
- difficulties with work that has to be returned;
- receiving fewer returns.

You should weigh these issues up and should think about:

- whether solicitors will continue to brief you if you are on your own;
- how you will inform/market yourself to solicitors;
- how you will deal with returned work;
- what administrative support you need in place;

- whether as a self-employed barrister you will undertake public access work and/or apply for an extension to your practising certificate to conduct litigation.

The Sole Practitioners Group may be able to provide advice on these points.

Questions and answers for sole practitioners

[5.4]

Do I need to have a clerk?

No. The requirement is simply that you administer your practice efficiently. You need to assess whether you will be able to undertake the necessary administration yourself or whether you need somebody else to assist. If your practice is largely paper-based, then you can probably manage without any assistance. Most sole practitioners manage without a clerk.

Can I conduct litigation?

You may apply for a litigation extension to your practising certificate from the Bar Standards Board. This way you can run a case from cradle to grave if you are granted extension and comply with requirements, if you wish, laid down by the Bar Standards Board.https://www.barstandardsboard.org.uk/regulatory-requirements/for-barristers/authorisation-to-conduct-litigation/

Where can I hold conferences?

Conferences can be held wherever is convenient. There is nothing to stop them taking place in solicitors' offices, or your own office.

How can I market myself to solicitors?

In any way which is consistent with the advertising rules – you can contact solicitors directly, provide details of your skills, experience and fees. You should be careful about direct comparisons with other professionals (gC57).

Questions and answers about creating a new set of Chambers

[5.5]

Can I outsource work?

Yes.

The BSB Handbook at rC86 states that "you must ensure that such outsourcing is subject to contractual arrangements which ensure that such third party:

a. is subject to confidentiality obligations similar to the confidentiality obligations placed on you in accordance with this Handbook;

b. complies with any other obligations set out in this Code of Conduct which may be relevant to or affected by such outsourcing;

c. processes any personal data in accordance with your instructions and, for the avoidance of doubt, as though it were a data controller under the Data Protection Act; and

d. is required to allow the Bar Standards Board or its agent to obtain information from, inspect the records (including electronic records) of, or enter the premises of such third party in relation to the outsourced activities or functions."

What do I do if someone makes a complaint against me?

You must comply with the Complaints Rules at D1.1 rC99–109.

What Equality and Diversity obligations do I have?

The BSB Handbook at rC110–112 set out extensive equality and diversity obligations for Chambers and self-employed barristers.

Do I need to register for the Quality Assurance Scheme for Advocates (QASA)?

All criminal barristers must register for QASA within the following timescales:

Circuits	Start	Close
Midland and Western	30 September 13	30 May 14
South Eastern	31 May 14	3 October 14
Northern, North Eastern and Wales and Chester	4 October 14	31 December 14

Please see the BSB website FAQs for more information: https://www.barstandardsboard.org.uk/media/1566645/qasa_faqs_-_policy_v4_.pdf

Do I need to let the BSB have access to my premises?

Yes. The BSB Handbook at rC70 states that:

> "You must permit the Bar Council, or the Bar Standards Board, or any person appointed by them, reasonable access, on request, to inspect:

1 any premises from which you provide, or are believed to provide, legal services, and

2 any documents or records relating to those premises and your practice, or BSB authorised body.

and the Bar Council, Bar Standards Board, or any person appointed by them, shall be entitled to take copies of such documents or records as may be required by them for the purposes of their functions."

What is meant by "Chambers is administered competently and efficiently"?

Essentially, you need to have the office systems which will ensure that, amongst other things:

- briefs and instructions are logged in on arrival;
- you have adequate facilities to ensure that work is completed in good time and do not take on more work than you can manage;
- you have suitable diary facilities to identify clashes of dates of hearings, conferences and other appointments at the earliest possible stage and to remind you of those appointments;
- you keep adequate records of your work;
- fee notes are sent out in good time and adequate records of fees are kept;
- you have effective arrangements for handling complaints and inform clients about them;
- you are able to identify and take notice of all relevant guidance and rule changes issued by the Bar Standards Board.

There is no single right way of achieving this. Due to the diverse nature of sole practitioners' practice no specific software package can be recommended. You would be wise to consider the requirements of quality accreditation, so if you apply your system is already in place. The longer the system has been in place the more impressive it will be to the person who assesses your application.

Can I handle client money?

No. Self-employed barristers cannot handle client money see the BSB Handbook at rC73–75. You may be interested in using BARCO, the Bar Council escrow service: http://www.barcouncil.org.uk/for-the-bar/barco/

Can I accept or pay referral fees?

No. Referral fees are strictly prohibited by rC10.

Can I negotiate my own fees?

Yes.

Can I practise from my own home?

Yes.

Do I have to have my name outside the place where I practise?

No.

What equipment and support will I need?

This will depend on the nature of your practice. It is likely that you will need a computer with access to the internet.

For information about IT security best practice please see: http://www.barcouncil.org.uk/for-the-bar/professional-practice-and-ethics/it-panel-articles/

Sources of Advice

[5.6]

If there are matters that are not covered here or if there are issues on which you need further advice or guidance, the following places may be able to assist:

- The Bar Council, Ethical Enquiries Service – 020 7611 1307.
- BMIF– 020 7621 0405.

Bar Sole Practitioners' Group

Contact Numbers

[5.7]

East Anglia

Lorraine Webb
Tel: 01245 248341

London

Wendy Datta
Tel: 07785 564775

Philip Proghoulis
Tel: 020 8788 1238

Midlands

Karen Boyes
01234 720952

North

Fauz Khan
Tel: 07973 133594

Southern England

Doug Cracknell
Tel: 01959 522325

West Country

Elizabeth Hailstone
Tel: 01179 624138

Important Notice

[5.8]

This document has been prepared by the Bar Council to assist barristers on matters of professional conduct and ethics. It is not "guidance" for the purposes of the BSB Handbook I6.4, and neither the BSB nor a disciplinary tribunal nor the Legal Ombudsman is bound by any views or advice expressed in it. It does not comprise – and cannot be relied on as giving – legal advice. It has been prepared in good faith, but neither the Bar Council nor any of the individuals responsible for or involved in its preparation accept any responsibility or liability for anything done in reliance on it. For fuller information as to the status and effect of this document, please refer to the professional practice and ethics section of the Bar Council's website here.

Part VI
Regulation and the Bar Standards Board

[6.1]

The Bar Standards Board ("BSB") was established by the Bar Council in January 2006 to regulate barristers called to the Bar in England and Wales in the public interest.

The Bar Council is the "Approved Regulator" of barristers, as specified by the Legal Services Act 2007 but it has delegated its regulatory functions to the Bar Standards Board. "Internal Governance Rules" have been put in place to ensure the principle of the BSB's regulatory independence is safeguarded and its composition, function, duties, and powers are governed by its own Constitution. It is responsible for:

- Setting the education and training requirements for becoming a barrister;
- Setting continuing training requirements to ensure that barristers' skills are maintained throughout their careers;
- Setting standards of conduct for barristers;
- Monitoring the service provided by barristers to assure quality;
- Handling complaints against barristers and taking disciplinary or other action where appropriate.

Its mission is to be recognised as promoting and safeguarding the high standards of practice and safeguard clients and the public interest.

The BSB's vision is that, by the end of 2016 it will have become a more modern and efficient regulator operating to externally agreed high standards, fulfilling our mission and upholding and promoting the regulatory objectives and professional principles.

In achieving this vision, the BSB remains focused upon the "Regulatory Objectives" set out in the Legal Services Act 2007:

The regulatory objectives:

- Protecting and promoting the public interest;
- Supporting the constitutional principle of the rule of law;
- Improving access to justice;
- Protecting and promoting the interests of consumers;
- Promoting competition in the provision of services;
- Encouraging an independent, strong, diverse and effective legal profession;

- Increasing public understanding of citizens' legal rights and duties; and
- Promoting and maintaining adherence to the professional principles.

The Board

[6.2]–[6.3]

The Board comprises 16 people, a combination of barristers and lay people including the Chair Baroness Ruth Deech. None of the members are members of the Bar Council or any of its representational committees. All members are appointed to work in the public interest. The current Vice Chair is Patricia Robertson QC. It has had a lay majority since 2012. The most recent version of the full Standing Orders for the BSB may be found at :https://www.barstandardsboard.org.uk/media/1550246/standing_orders_-_amended_june_2014.pdf. Its work and functions are undertaken by its eight regulatory committees:

1. Professional Conduct Committee

[6.4]

The Professional Conduct Committee has the full delegated authority to take decisions on complaints. It has the power to refer complaints to disciplinary action, decide to take no further action or to dismiss a case due to lack of evidence.

Terms of Reference

[6.5]

(1) to carry out the functions and exercise the powers under Part 5 of the BSB Handbook;

(2) to respond to and, where appropriate, defend appeals against and other challenges to actions and decisions of the Committee and of disciplinary tribunals and panels constituted under the rules referred to at (1) above;

(3) to make recommendations to other committees or to the Board about matters of professional conduct, including changes to rules referred to at (1) above when the Committee considers it appropriate to do so;

(4) to liaise, where appropriate, with other BSB Committees, the Bar Tribunals and Adjudication Service, the Legal Ombudsman and any other bodies relevant to the work of the Committee in exercising its functions;

(5) to undertake such other tasks as the Board may require; and

(6) to report to the Board on its work as and when required.

The membership of the Professional Conduct Committee shall be:

(7) a chair and 4 vice chairs. There must be 2 lay and 2 barrister vice chairs. The chair can be either a lay or barrister member;

(8) a minimum of 10 lay members and a maximum of 24 lay members; and

(9) subject to a minimum of 10, a number of barristers to enable the Committee in the judgment of the Chair to carry out its business expeditiously.

2. Qualifications Committee

[6.6]

The Qualifications Committee deals with applications for waivers or exemptions from the Bar Training Regulations and from a small number of paragraphs of the Code of Conduct, as well as applications for licensed access.

The Committee is split into six panels as follows, the membership of which is taken entirely from the Committee:

- Transferring Qualified Lawyers Panel;
- Pupillage Panel;
- Continuing Professional Development Panel;
- Practising Rules Panel;
- Pupillage Funding & Advertising Panel;
- Exemptions Panel.

Terms of Reference

[6.7]

(1) to consider and determine:

(a) applications for exemption from any requirement of the Bar Training Rules (Section 4B of the Handbook); and

(b) any request for review made under 4B10, 3C6 or 3E11 of the Handbook.

(2) to consider and determine all applications for authorisation under the following (including dispensations from and waivers):

(a) waivers from the requirement to work with a "qualified person" (rS20 and rS21);

(b) authorisation to conduct litigation (rS49);

(c) waivers from the requirement to undertake Public Access work (rC120);

(d) waivers or extensions of time in relation to the Continuing Professional Development Regulations (section 4C);

(e) waivers from the pupillage funding and advertising requirements (rC113);

(f) authorisation of Approved Training Organisations (rQ39);

(g) approval for licensed access; and

(h) any other rule or regulation as may be delegated to it by the Board.

(3) to discharge the functions of the Bar Council and the Inns in respect of the recognition of European lawyers conferred upon them pursuant to the European Communities (Recognition of Professional Qualifications) Regulations 2007 and the European Communities (Lawyers' Practice) Regulations (2000);

(4) to exercise the powers of the Board to designate Legal Advice Centres;

(5) to supervise and, where necessary, decide questions concerning the issue of practising certificates and the registration of pupil supervisors;

(6) to liaise, where appropriate, with other BSB Committees, representative committees of the Bar Council, the Inns' Council and any other body on any matters of concern or common interest;

(7) to undertake such other tasks as the Board may require; and

(8) to report to the Board on its work as and when required.

The membership of the Qualifications Committee shall be:

(1) a chair and three vice-chairs, of whom two must be lay persons and two must be practising barristers;

(2) at least 3 lay persons; and

(3) at least 6 practising barristers.

3. Supervision Committee

[6.8]

The Supervision Committee has replaced the Quality Assurance Committee to lead on providing assurance to the Board on the supervision of barristers, chambers and entities.

Terms of Reference

[6.9]

(1) To provide assurance to the Board on the supervision of barristers, chambers and entities.

(2) To review and challenge proposals brought by the executive relating to the supervision of barristers, chambers and entities, including:

- a. the application of the risk assessment framework to supervision activity;
- b. the application of the supervision strategy;
- c. authorisation of entities;
- d. future priorities for supervision.

(3) To have strategic oversight of, and to provide guidance and advice on the operational delivery of the supervision of barristers, chambers and entities, including:

- a. the monitoring of chambers and entities;
- b. the monitoring of individuals;
- c. thematic reviews;
- d. the authorisation of entities.

(4) To receive from the executive:

- a. Reports on general supervision activity;
- b. Data analysis reports on identified themes and trends arising from all supervision activity;
- c. Reports on the authorisation of entities.

and to reach agreement with the executive on recommendations to the Board resulting from these reports.

(5) To provide an independent perspective on proposals by the executive for thematic reviews.

(6) To undertake such other tasks as the Board may from time to time require; and

(7) To report to the Board on its work as and when required. Membership:

(8) A chair who must also be a Board member.

(9) One vice chair, who will be a lay member if the chair is a barrister and vice versa.

(10) One other practising barrister (excluding chair and vice chairs).

(11) Three other lay members (excluding chair and vice chairs).

Quorum

(12) No business may be transacted at any meeting of the Supervision Committee unless one third of the members are present of whom one must be a chair or vice chair.

Meetings

(13) Meetings to be held six times a year. If the need arises, the Chair or Vice Chair may convene additional meetings, which may take place by telephone if appropriate.

Chambers monitoring

[6.10]

Information on the scheme

The Chambers Monitoring 2012 round was launched in June and closed in August 2012.

This follows the success of the 2010 round of monitoring, which provided the BSB with crucial information on the levels of compliance with administrative and other code requirements, as well as identifying rules which chambers were finding more difficult to implement.

Chambers Monitoring is an important part of the BSB's Supervision Strategy. The BSB intends to develop its Supervision Strategy around this model but with a greater focus on regulatory risk. A consultation with proposals on this will be launched in March 2013 and will close after a period of 3 months.

The results of the Chambers Monitoring 2012 round are available in a PDF document from the BSB at chambersmonitoring@barstandardsboard.org.uk.

The Chambers Monitoring 2012 Process

On 11th June 2012, all Chambers, including sole practitioners, were sent a questionnaire. This questionnaire covered compliance with two areas: chambers complaints handling requirements and the Money Laundering Regulations 2007.

There was also a section on future compliance issues. At this stage, these questions were for data gathering purposes only although they may inform future compliance requirements.

The questionnaire aimed to establish whether and how chambers are complying with their regulatory and legal requirements. Once the questionnaires were completed online, they were sent to the BSB for analysis. Once this process was complete, chambers were assigned a risk rating. A risk rating determines the level of follow up action that is required and the level of regulatory supervision needed.

[The BSB has published Frequently Asked Questions in relation to this new initiative:]

Chambers Monitoring – Frequently asked questions

[6.10a]

1. Why is the BSB monitoring Chambers?

Monitoring compliance with the Code of Conduct is a vital part of the BSB's supervision strategy. Chambers monitoring enables the BSB to systematically gather information from all chambers in order to inform regulatory policy and future supervisory activity. Importantly for chambers, it will either provide them with the re-assurance that they are compliant with their regulatory requirements or help them to identify areas of non-compliance which need to be addressed.

2. Is the completion of the monitoring questionnaire compulsory?

Yes, all Chambers are required to complete the questionnaire and are obliged to do so under 905(a)(i) of the Code of Conduct. Failure to complete and return the questionnaire could result in disciplinary action being taken by the BSB. The action is likely to be taken against the Head of Chambers, as they have overall responsibility for the management and administration of Chambers.

3. I am a sole practitioner, do I still have to complete the monitoring questionnaire?

Yes, all Chambers including sole practitioners are required to complete the questionnaire.

4. Chambers does not have access to the internet, is a hard copy of the questionnaire available?

Chambers who have no recorded email address, will automatically be sent a hard copy of the questionnaire. If Chambers do not receive a hard copy but are unable to submit the questionnaire online, Chambers can request one by email chambersmonitoring@barstandardsboard.org.uk

5. What happens if Chambers are unable to submit the questionnaire by the deadline?

All Chambers have 3 weeks to complete the questionnaire, if Chambers experience difficulty in completing the questionnaire by the deadline date, please contact the BSB on 020 7611 1444 or email chambersmonitoring@barstandardsboard.org.uk

6. What is the Chambers Monitoring timetable for 2012?

The questionnaire will be sent to all chambers in June. We aim to notify all chambers within one month of the submission of the questionnaire of the outcome and whether any follow up action is required. For more detailed dates please see the main Chambers Monitoring page.

7. What will happen once Chambers has submitted the questionnaire?

Once the completed questionnaire has been submitted, the information provided will be analysed, as part of the risk assessment process, in order to determine Chambers compliance in each of the areas.

8. Will those Chambers who are considered not to be in compliance with the Code of Conduct be subject to disciplinary action?

The results of the questionnaire will be analysed and where non-compliance is identified the BSB will contact Chambers to discuss how it can be addressed and to agree appropriate follow up action. If the recommended remedial action is not taken or there are serious concerns about the compliance of a particular set of Chambers, the BSB may visit Chambers and take further action. Disciplinary action will be a last resort and only after attempts to work with Chambers to help them to comply have failed.

9. Chambers does not take pupils or undertake work that brings them within the Money Laundering Regulations 2007, do we have to complete the questions in relation to these areas?

Chambers will not be required to answer these questions, if they do not apply.

10. Is there any guidance to assist Chambers to complete the questionnaire and to understand what the compliance requirements are? Can Chambers have a copy of the questionnaire submitted to the BSB?

There will be guidance available on the BSB website. When chambers are emailed the questionnaire, a link to this guidance will be included. This guidance will explain the process and how to access the questionnaire. It will also link each question to the relevant section of the Code of Conduct and other reference documents. Chambers can obtain a copy by contacting chambersmonitoring@barstandardsboard.org.uk.

11. Who can I speak to at the BSB, if I need advice about any of the areas covered in the questionnaire?

Initially, if you have difficulty in completing the questionnaire, or have further queries in relation to Chambers Monitoring, please contact Jennifer Hart on 020 7611 1444. If your query is in relation to a specific area, Jennifer will direct you to the relevant members of staff who will be able to assist you.

12. Some of Chamber's answers are the same as the 2010 round, do I need to complete the questionnaire?

Yes. The questionnaire still needs to be completed. The questionnaire will also include new questions and cover different areas.

13. I'm having difficulty accessing the questionnaire online, who do I contact?

If you have difficulty in completing or accessing the questionnaire online please contact Jennifer Hart on 020 7611 1444 or email chambersmonitoring@barstandardsboard.org.uk

14. If I require any reasonable adjustments due to a disability who do I contact?

If you have difficulty in completing, accessing or understanding the questionnaire due to a disability please contact Jennifer Hart to arrange an alternative format or method of completion on 020 7611 1444 or emailchambersmonitoring@barstandardsboard.org.uk.

Guidance in relation to completing the chambers monitoring questionnaire may be found at http://www.barstandardsboard.org.uk/regulatory-requirements/for-chambers-and-education-providers/chambers/ .

Quality Assurance Scheme for Advocates (QASA)

[6.10b]

The Quality Assurance Committee also maintains the BSB's oversight of the Quality Assurance Scheme for Advocates (QASA).

QASA will be launched in January 2013. As the launch date approaches, we will provide updates and further information about what barristers need to do to prepare for the Scheme launch.

What is QASA?

QASA is a joint scheme being developed by the BSB, the Solicitors Regulation Authority and ILEX Professional Standards. The Scheme will regulate the quality of all advocates appearing in the criminal courts in England and Wales, whether they are barristers, solicitors, or legal executives. The Scheme will apply to all advocates, whether they are self-employed or employed, and whether they are acting for the prosecution or defence.

The Scheme will systematically assess and assure the quality of criminal advocacy in the courts in England and Wales and will ensure that the performance of all advocates is measured against the same set of standards, regardless of an advocate's previous education and training.

Latest news on QASA

Implementation of the Quality Assurance Scheme for Advocates (QASA) has been delayed by a judicial review of the scheme and subsequent litigation. Judgment was initially handed down on 20 January leading to a review of the QASA timetable. At the time of going to press, the Claimants were granted leave to appeal the original decision, on all grounds. The appeal hearing will be expedited and we understand that a date is likely to be set for mid-July 2014.

In the meantime, the Court of Appeal has ordered the following aspects of the Scheme to be stayed until the outcome of the appeal is known:

- the compulsory registration of advocates who would register at level two – as a trial advocate – or above; and
- the judicial evaluation of advocates in trials.

The Order allows the compulsory registration and accreditation of those who would register at level one, or at level two as a non-trial advocate, to proceed if the frontline regulators wish to do so. The regulators may proceed with background work to be ready for the Scheme in due course, and compulsory assessment – via assessment centres – of advocates who have or would have registered at level two as a non-trial advocate can continue, if the regulators wish.

Any advocates who have already registered under the Scheme will remain registered until further notice.

The voluntary registration of advocates who would register at level two as a trial advocate, level three, or level four can also continue.

The Bar Standards Board (BSB) has already decided to suspend phased geographical registration in the Scheme and, whilst we will continue to work with the Joint Advocacy Group to be ready for implementation, we will not be requiring barristers who may have sought to be assessed as non-trial advocates at an assessment centre to do so until further notice.

Finally, the Court also made a new Protective Costs Order (PCO). This applies reciprocally to the Legal Services Board and theBSB, and the Claimants, and is capped at £65,000. The Claimants have been granted time-limited leave to apply to vary the terms of the PCO, until 16.00pm on 23 May 2014.

Barristers have to register in the principal Circuit in which they practise. Full details of the Scheme requirements will be included in the Scheme Handbook and can be found on the scheme website at http://www.qasa.org.uk/. The BSB has also published "Frequently Asked Questions" in relation to the Scheme:

General – Why does there need to be a Scheme?

The criminal justice system is dependent upon good quality advocacy to deliver fair results.

Lord Carter made it clear in his report in 2006 that market forces alone can no longer be relied upon to eliminate under-performing advocates. Developments in the structure of advocacy services, a widening of the potential training routes and economic pressure are contributing to increased inconsistency in the quality of advocacy.

Criminal advocacy is the practice area which presents the greatest risk; both in terms of perceived incidence of underperformance and the consequences of this for defendants, witnesses and public confidence in the Criminal Justice System.

The public interest and consumer protection require a proactive approach to assuring advocacy competence in the criminal courts. Under the Legal Services Act 2007, the regulators are responsible for setting and maintaining standards within their respective professions.

Where is the evidence?

Criminal advocacy is a high risk area for the regulators for the following reasons:

- It attracts a mix of solicitors, barristers and legal executives who will have taken different routes for training and will be subject to different regulatory requirements.
- It frequently involves vulnerable individuals who may be unable to exercise informed choice as to who represents them.
- Changes to legal aid funding and associated financial pressures are putting pressure on quality.
- There have been changes to the structures for delivery of advocacy services.
- Lord Carter noted in his report of 2006 that market forces can no longer be relied upon to eliminate underperforming advocates.

The judiciary has increasingly expressed concern to the regulators that the risks present in criminal advocacy are in fact materialising in the shape of underperformance. There have been a number of high profile judicial pronouncements on poor quality advocacy and these have been echoed by judges during a series of visits by members of the Joint Advocacy Group to Crown Courts in England and Wales. As a result of these concerns the scheme has the full support of the Lord Chief Justice and the Council of Circuit Judges.

In 2012 the BSB commissioned a Perceptions Study which sought to gauge the level of concern amongst barristers about underperformance in criminal advocacy. Over half of the barristers who took part in the survey (629) stated that they frequently encountered advocates acting beyond their competence. Over three quarters believed that advocacy standards had worsened over the last five years and a similar proportion believed that standards would continue to decline in the coming years in the absence of measures to address it. The decline in standards was attributed by many respondents to public funding pressures as well as differing standards between the Bar and other advocates.

Criminal advocacy is a high risk area that requires an appropriate regulatory response. This response needs to establish a common set of standards that apply to all criminal advocates, regardless of who regulates them. No single group can be the subject of regulation; all criminal advocates must be subject to the same high standards.

What is the Joint Advocacy Group?

The Joint Advocacy Group (JAG) comprises the three main regulators of advocacy; the Bar Standards Board, Solicitors Regulation Authority and ILEX Professional Standards.

The Scheme is being developed through the JAG so that all advocates will be assessed against the same standards regardless of who regulates them and what route they took to qualification.

Is the Scheme compulsory?

Yes. Any advocate (barrister, solicitor advocate, CPS prosecutor etc.) wishing to undertake criminal advocacy will be required to register within the Scheme and be fully accredited. It will be a breach of the regulators' rules to conduct criminal advocacy and not be QASA accredited.

Who does the scheme apply to?

The scheme will apply to those undertaking traditional criminal hearings. This will include cases prosecuted by the CPS following a police investigation as well as fraud cases.

Non-traditional criminal cases that are not compatible with the assessment framework are outside of the scope of the scheme. An example is planning prosecutions, where specialised and complex proceedings could be heard within the Magistrates Court. Barristers whose practices are focussed on planning will not appear in the Crown Court with sufficient regularity to become accredited under the scheme. Applying the scheme to planning prosecutions would prevent planning specialists from undertaking planning prosecutions, which is not a desirable outcome in the public or client's interest, so those types of cases will be outside the scope of QASA.

The scheme will also allow some flexibility for specialist practitioners to appear in traditional criminal cases if they are instructed as a result of their specialism. For example, a health and safety specialist might be instructed on a health and safety breach that has resulted in manslaughter charges prosecuted by the CPS. The QASA Handbook will contain further guidance on when specialists might be able to appear in the criminal courts without QASA accreditation.

When will the scheme come into effect?

QASA was approved in July 2013. Following a judicial review of QASA in January 2014, the BSB has decided to suspend phased geographical QASA registration. All barristers who wish to undertake criminal advocacy remain required to register by 31 December 2014.

As phase one continues, we will provide updates and further information about what barristers need to do to prepare for the Scheme launch.

The Scheme will be implemented for all advocates on a phased basis by geographic area based on Circuit. It is likely that two or more Circuits may be grouped together into "Circuit areas" for the implementation phases. The Scheme went "live" in the first Circuit area on 30 September 2013. Advocates practising in each Circuit area may enter the Scheme from this time. The current timetable of key dates is below:

August 2013: Scheme Handbook published.

All barristers who wish to undertake criminal advocacy remain required to register by 31 December 2014. Registration period in the first area – Midlands and Western Circuits.

All barristers who wish to undertake criminal advocacy remain required to register by 31 December 2014. Registration period in the second area -- South Eastern Circuit.

All barristers who wish to undertake criminal advocacy remain required to register by 31 December 2014. Registration period in the third area – North East, Northern and Wales and Chester Circuits.Once they have registered, barristers will have 24 months from that date in which to obtain two pieces of judicial evaluation which confirm their competence at the level at which they registered.

The BSB will monitor those who appear in circuits that have become operational. Barristers who are appearing within a live circuit who have not registered for QASA should be prepared to justify their decision to register under another circuit.

Will the scheme have any benefits for barristers?

The scheme should have the following benefits for barristers:

- It will create a level playing field across the legal professions.
- Competent advocates will not need to compete for work with those who are not competent at their level.
- The scheme should ensure that all advocates in a case are competent for that level of case, which should encourage the proper administration of justice.

What will happen if I refuse to register under the Scheme?

It will be a breach of each regulator's rules to conduct criminal advocacy and not be QASA accredited.

The BSB will pursue enforcement action against barristers who do not register under the scheme but continue to undertake criminal advocacy. This could ultimately result in suspension or disbarment.

Level 2 accreditation

Why is there a separate route to accreditation for advocates who don't do full trials?

Research undertaken by the Solicitors Regulation Authority into the patterns of practice of solicitor advocates with Higher Rights of Audience suggests that a significant percentage of these advocates do not undertake full trials. The practice of these advocates is focussed on advocacy in PCMHs, guilty pleas and bail applications.

The BSB is also aware of similar patterns of practice amongst some barristers, including those with childcare responsibilities.

As a result, a substantial number of advocates would not be able to meet the requirements of a scheme if the only method of entry was through judicial evaluation in full trials. Such an advocate would be removed from practice not on the basis of competence but as a result of their chosen pattern of practice.

JAG has considered the responses to the fourth consultation concerning this issue, including a significant number of responses from the Bar expressing concern. However, the intention of the Scheme is not to require advocates to alter their current patterns of practice in order to fit within a new assessment framework. The Scheme is designed to ensure that those advocates undertaking criminal advocacy are competent to do so and that this has been confirmed by reliable and rigorous assessment. Therefore the Scheme will provide a means to be accredited, at level 2, via an assessment centre. Advocates who are assessed via this route will not be accredited to undertake trials.

The Scheme will put in place quality assurance mechanisms, where currently there are none, to assure the competence of all criminal advocates. The review of the Scheme will seek to review coverage of advocacy standards via the different assessment methods as well as whether the Scheme adequately assures the competence of all criminal advocates. This will provide the basis for a decision on whether this assessment route is providing adequate quality assurance.

Silks

Why do QCs need to be included within the scheme?

QASA is a regulatory scheme and as such must apply to all advocates. It is important for the credibility of the Scheme that all barristers undertaking criminal advocacy have been subject to the same independent assessment. It is therefore not appropriate for any category of advocate to be excluded from the Scheme.

The Scheme does provide for a modified entry route for recently appointed silks to recognize the fact that they have been assessed recently through the QC application process.

In addition, the regulators will commence discussions with QCA to see whether there is any scope for a continuing quality assurance role that they could play in the re-accreditation of silks which could be recognised under QASA.

Why is there not a level 5 for QCs?

It would be inappropriate for a regulatory scheme that is designed to ensure a minimum level of competence to include within it a level reserved for those who have been assessed against higher standards by an external, non-regulatory body.

The regulators must provide a route of assessment that they have control over for all levels within the scheme. Moreover, as a competency based scheme, all advocates who are able to demonstrate that they meet a required level of competence must be permitted to be accredited at that level. Therefore if a level 5 were to be introduced, this could not be reserved for QCs. Instead, the scheme provides for a level 4 QC, which denotes that an advocate is accredited by their regulator at level 4 and has also been awarded the rank of QC by QCA for excellence in practice.

Determining the level of a case

How will the level of a case be determined?

The instructing party and the advocate will initially be responsible for establishing the level of the case, based on guidance produced by JAG.

There will be a degree of judicial oversight of this process as when a judge is asked to evaluate an advocate they can refer a matter to the regulators if they believe that the level of the case has been set too low. Judges will also be able to make monitoring referrals if the advocate before them has not reached the level of competence required for the case; this will also identify instances in which the grading system has been abused.

At this time any further involvement in the setting of the level of the case was seen, by the judiciary, as being too burdensome and likely to interfere with the criminal justice process. This will be kept under review.

Judicial assessment

Is the Scheme supported by the judiciary?

The Scheme has the support of the Lord Chief Justice and other senior members of the judiciary. At a meeting on 18 May 2012, the Council of Circuit Judges gave their continued support for the Scheme and judicial participation within it.

Why use judges to assess the competence of advocates?

The judiciary are uniquely placed to observe and evaluate the advocates appearing in their courts. The judiciary are in effect the ultimate consumers of all advocates and are in an unparalleled position to provide evaluations across the full range of advocates and in the full range of cases in the Crown Courts.

Will enough judges participate?

Judges in the Midlands and Western circuits have been trained. There was a high level of engagement with the training and 95 per cent of eligible judges undertook training. This level of participation should ensure that sufficient assessors are available.

Will a single evaluation ever be determinative?

No. Regulators will take a decision on an advocate's competence in the light of a body of evidence before it. This will include a number of judicial evaluations and/or assessment reports by an assessment organisation.

Will I be required to tell my client that I am being assessed?

There will be no requirement to inform a client that you are being assessed. Assessment should not impact upon your performance; the judiciary will be trained in how to undertake objective assessments of performance against the QASA standards.

Availability of trials

I do not undertake many criminal trials within a normal year. Will I still be able to enter the scheme?

In order to be accredited under the scheme you will need to be assessed in a minimum of two criminal trials over a period of 24 months. The BSB appreciates that those with mixed practices as well as those who are involved in particularly long running trials might not be able to meet this criterion. However, if you anticipate undertaking any criminal advocacy you should register under the scheme. Extensions will be available for those who can prove that they have not completed two eligible trials within 24 months.

Legal Aid

Is there a link between QASA and Legal Services Commission contracting?

QASA has been developed by the three advocacy regulators, through the JAG, as a regulatory scheme to ensure minimum standards of advocacy.

The Legal Services Commission has been consulted during development of the scheme, as have all other key stakeholders.

The BSB is not aware of any plans to link QASA to LSC contracting. It is a matter for the Bar Council, as the representative body, to negotiate with the LSC in relation to any proposals relating to contracting.

Impact of scheme

Will the scheme make a difference?

The scheme will provide an assessment framework to ensure that all criminal advocates are competent to undertake advocacy at their appropriate level. It will also provide a means of identifying those who are acting beyond their competence. It should therefore provide assurance to consumers that they will receive the required level of competence from their advocate. It should also ensure that only advocates who are competent at the appropriate level should be conducting cases.

The impact of the scheme will be monitored and JAG has committed to a review of the scheme after two years of operation. This will provide an opportunity to assess the success of the scheme as well as identifying any areas that require improvement.

Cost

How much does it cost to be accredited?

There will be charges applied when barristers apply for registration, progression or re-accreditation under the scheme. The fees for each application will be as follows:

Registration

- No charge for registration at Level 1.
- £80 for registration at Level 2.
- £100 for registration at Level 3.
- £120 for registration at Level 4.

Progression

- £125 for applications to progress from Level 1 to Level 2.
- £325 for applications to progress from Level 2 to Level 3.
- £375 for applications to progress from Level 3 to Level 4.

Re-accreditation

It is anticipated that costs for re-accreditation (required if you remain at the same level for 5 years) will be between £100–200.

On the basis of these fees, the average annual cost over the course of a barrister's career should be in the region of £35 to £55, dependent upon the length of career and the rate of progression.

Where can I read the full details of the Scheme?

The Scheme rules and a handbook containing guidance on the scheme are available from the Key QASA Materials section of the BSB website.

4. Standards Committee

[6.11]

The Standards Committee is responsible for recommending rule changes to the Bar Standards Board in respect of the BSB Handbook. Further, the Committee issues guidance in relation to the Handbook and has a significant role in developing policy in respect of professional standards and training.

Terms of Reference

[6.12]

(1) to formulate policy for approval by the Bar Standards Board on all matters relating to the setting of standards for:

  (a) standards of professional practice and conduct of students; and

  (b) administration of practice by BSB regulated persons.

(2) to keep under review and propose changes as necessary to:

  (a) the Handbook; and

  (b) the rules relating to the ways in which barristers conduct their practices and to the conduct of students;

(3) to issue guidance on the interpretation of rules and regulations;

(4) to grant waivers from requirements of the Handbook where appropriate, except those which are the responsibility of the Qualifications Committee;

(5) to liaise and consult with the representative committees, the Inns' Council and the judges as appropriate in exercising its functions;

(6) to undertake such other tasks as the BSB may from time to time require; and

(7) to report to the Board on its work as and when required.

The membership of the Standards Committee shall be:

(1) A chair and 3 vice-chairs of whom 2 must be lay members and 2 must be practising barristers.

(2) Between 3 and 5 lay members, provided that the total number of lay members shall not be less than half the number of barristers appointed to the Committee.

(3) Not fewer than 6 and not more than 12 barristers.

5. Education & Training Committee

[6.13]

The Education & Training Committee oversees all regulatory activity relating to education and training for the Bar. This includes setting the standards of education and training that people must pass before being able to practise as barristers, together with the further training requirements that barristers must comply with throughout their careers.

Terms of Reference

[6.14]

(1) to formulate policy for approval by the BSB on all matters relating to the setting of standards for:

(a) entry to the Bar;

(b) education and training for barristers, including CPD;

(2) in conjunction with the Qualifications Committee, to keep under review and propose changes to the Bar Training Regulations and any regulations replacing them in respect of entry and training;

(3) to supervise the development of effective processes and procedures for monitoring standards in relation to:

(a) entry to the profession;

(b) provision and the quality of education and training for the profession including the validation and revalidation of courses of training and of organisations offering training, advocacy training and CPD;

(4) to issue guidance on the interpretation of rules and regulations;

(5) to liaise, where appropriate, with the Inns' Council, the Solicitors Regulation Authority, the Law Society or any other body on the monitoring of standards of courses or provision; to liaise, where appropriate, with other organisations on matters related to education and training for the profession;

(6) to liaise and consult with the other BSB committees, the Inns' Council and the judges as appropriate in exercising its functions;

(7) to take responsibility for the consideration and approval of Public Access Training Courses. The Education and Training Committee may seek advice from any other BSB committees when considering applications, if deemed appropriate.

(8) to undertake such other tasks as the BSB may from time to time require; and

(9) to report to the Board on its work as and when required.

The membership of the Education and Training Committee shall be:

(1) A chair and 3 vice-chairs of whom 2 must be lay members and 2 must be practising barristers.

(2) Between 3 and 5 lay members, provided that the total number of lay members shall not be less than half the number of barristers appointed to the Committee.

(3) Not fewer than 6 and not more than 12 practising barristers.

(4) At least 2 members who are senior legal academics with experience of vocational training (in addition to the lay members above).

6. Equality and Diversity Committee

[6.14a]

The Bar Standards Board has its own Equality and Diversity Committee chaired by a lay member – Rolande Anderson. The Committee is responsible for:

- scrutinising Equality and Diversity Impact Assessments to ensure that the BSB's functions have given due consideration to eliminating discrimination and promoting equality;
- identifying and reporting regularly to the Board on areas of risk in relation to equality and diversity issues and compliance with relevant legislation;
- championing equality and diversity issues with the Board, its committees and within the BSB generally.

The Board and the Equality and Diversity Committee are supported by an Equality and Diversity Adviser.

Terms of Reference

The terms of reference for the BSB Equality and Diversity Committee are:

(1) to promote equality and diversity in the profession so that profession is open to all on merit and reflects the diversity of society;

(2) to ensure that the BSB acts in accordance with its statutory duties to eliminate unlawful discrimination, advance equality of opportunity and foster good relations between persons who share a protected characteristic and persons who do not share it, and in particular to:

  (a) make strategic recommendations for equality policy development and implementation and, where necessary, submit proposals for policy changes or initiatives to the Board or relevant committee;

  (b) monitor, revise and update the BSB's Equality and Diversity Strategy and Action Plan;

  (c) scrutinise equality assessments to ensure that the BSB's functions have given due consideration to eliminating discrimination and promoting equality; and

  (d) identify and report regularly to the Board on areas of risk in relation to equality and diversity issues and compliance with relevant equalities legislation;

(3) to champion equality and diversity issues with the Board, its committees and within the BSB generally;

(4) to provide appropriate expert advice and guidance to the Board and its committees on equality issues where requested;

(5) to liaise and consult with the other regulatory committees, the Inns' Council and the judges as appropriate in exercising its functions;

(6) to undertake such other tasks as the BSB may from time to time require; and

(7) to report to the Board on its work as and when required.

The membership of the Equality and Diversity Committee shall be:

(1) a chair;

(2) a vice-chair;

(3) up to 5 lay members; and

(4) up to 5 practising barristers.

7. Governance, Risk & Audit Committee

[6.14b]

The Governance, Risk & Audit Committee is responsible for ensuring The Board's corporate governance standards and internal controls are maintained. The Committee keeps under review and advises the Board on all matters relating to the risk management framework and the BSB's internal audit function.

Terms of reference

Terms of Reference of the Governance, Risk and Audit Committee are:

(1) to advise the Board on the effectiveness of the corporate governance structures, and to monitor and recommend to the Board action in respect of the effectiveness of the strategic arrangements for governance, risk management and audit. This includes agreeing a programme of Board member training and development to satisfy corporate governance guidelines;

(2) to monitor and recommend to the Board action in respect of the Board's management of risks, including arrangements for business continuity and disaster recovery;

(3) to agree action in respect of the effectiveness of the Board's financial management and control systems, and internal business processes, including accounting policies, anti-fraud and whistle-blowing arrangements;

(4) to develop the BSB's internal audit function including the appointment of the Board's Internal Auditors. To agree the annual audit plan and include any audit reviews that the Board wishes to see conducted. To monitor and recommend to the Board the results of the Board's internal audit arrangements and the effectiveness of the response to issues identified by audit activity; and

(5) to review relevant assessment reports and assurance reports provided by third parties (including the Independent Observer) to secure an understanding improvements that could be made and best practice revealed by such reports. To provide necessary assurances to the Board, that in turn provides assurances to the Bar Council's Audit Committee.

Membership

(1) A lay chair who must also be a Board member.

(2) A lay or barrister vice chair.

(3) Three other members who must not be Board members.

8. Planning, Resources and Performance Committee

[6.14c]

The Planning, Resources and Performance Committee is responsible for work relating to development of strategic direction and plans for the BSB. It advises the Board on developments to the planning, resource setting and performance monitoring processes. It also considers whether financial and operational resources are properly and effectively allocated and efficiently managed across the BSB.

The Terms of Reference of the Planning, Resources and Performance Committee are:

(1) to consider and support the Board and the executive in formulating the overall strategy for the BSB, with particular emphasis on horizon scanning, vision, mission statement, priorities, activities and outcomes. To scrutinise the BSB's three-year strategic plan and annual business plan before the Board's signoff is sought. Agree actions to ensure that the BSB's associated strategies (Communications, IT, HR and research) are aligned to the corporate strategy;

(2) to oversee operational and programme delivery (without duplicating the detailed oversight provided by any other committee or programme/project governance structure) as well as financial performance against the objectives and targets set out in the Business Plan. To support the Board and executive with finalising the BSB's Annual Report publications;

(3) to consider the annual budget and revenue, in the context of the strategic and business plans, to question whether proposed funding is adequate and properly and effectively allocated across the business, and agree certain levels of virement between programmes (as anticipated in the Finance Manual with levels set by the Committee from time to time);

(4) to consider how the BSB presents financial information to best effect and with appropriate transparency and comprehensiveness. To consider the reliability of forecasting and how the pursuit and achievement of efficiency savings are reported;

(5) to review and agree actions on the effectiveness of service level agreements within the organisation;

(6) to consider how the BSB undertakes planning activity to best effect and in a timely and consistent manner, as well as to review the robustness of programme and project plans. To support the Board and the executive with the planning and monitoring of the implementation of the Regulatory Standards Framework; and

(7) to agree how the BSB monitors, measures and reports performance to best effect, with appropriate transparency and in a timely and consistent manner. To consider the quarterly performance reports prior to submission to the Board.

Membership

The membership of the Planning Resources and Performance Committee shall be:

(1) A chair and vice chair who are members of the Board. Subject to temporary exceptions which may be agreed by the Board, one will be a lay member and one a practising barrister;

(2) two lay members; and

(3) one barrister member (who may be practising or non-practising).

Section 2: Complaints against Barristers

The Complaints Process

[6.15]

Set out below are extracts from the Professional Conduct Committee Information and Guidance pack 2014 explaining the complaints process. The full pack may be downloaded at http://www.barstandardsboard.org.uk/about-bar-standards-board/how-we-do-it/our-committees/professional-conduct-commitee/committee-information-and-guidance-pack/:

Aims and objectives of the complaints system

4.1 The Bar Standards Board Business Plan for 2013/14 sets out five strategic aims, one of which, Strategic Aim 4, is to become more evidence and risk based in the regulatory approach. This aim is further underpinned by a specific objective to implement a framework for regulatory standards, which depends on identifying risk and using evidence on which to base all regulatory decisions The Bar Standards Board has stated that the following are its main **aims** when it investigates complaints and, where appropriate, takes action against barristers who have breached the BSB Handbook:

- act in the public interest;
- protect the public and other consumers of legal services;
- maintain the high standards of the Bar;
- promote confidence in the complaints and disciplinary process, and,
- make sure that complaints about conduct are dealt with fairly, consistently and with reasonable speed.

The following are its stated **objectives** in relation to complaints:

- deal with complaints made against barristers promptly, thoroughly and fairly;
- ensure appropriate action is taken against barristers who breach the BSB Handbook; and,
- be open, fair, transparent and accessible.

4.2 The BSB is also under a statutory obligation under section 28 of the Legal Services Act 2007, when discharging its regulatory functions to act in a way which is compatible with the regulatory objectives as section out in section 1 of the Act, which are:

a. protecting and promoting the public interest;

b. supporting the constitutional principle of the rule of law;

c. improving access to justice;

d. protecting and promoting the interests of consumers;

e. promoting competition in the provision of services;

f. encouraging an independent, strong, diverse and effective legal profession;

g. increasing public understanding of the citizen's legal rights and duties; and

h. promoting and maintaining adherence to the professional principles.

4.3 The "professional principles" referred to at paragraph 4.2 (h) above are also set in section 1 of the LSA and are;

a. that authorised persons[1] should act with independence and integrity;

b. that authorised persons should maintain proper standards of work;

c. that authorised persons should act in the best interests of their clients;

d. that persons who exercise before any court a right of audience, or conduct litigation in relation to proceedings in any court, by virtue of being authorised persons should comply with their duty to the court to act with independence in the interests of justice; and

e. that the affairs of clients should be kept confidential.

1 The term "authorised person" covers only practising barristers but the BSB's regulatory remit is wider and also covers unregistered barristers.

4.4 Not all of the Regulatory Objectives and professional principles apply directly to the enforcement system but it is the potential risk to those that are applicable that is now central to taking decisions on enforcement action. Committee members should therefore have the regulatory objectives at the forefront of their minds when considering what action to take in an individual case.

Rules and Regulations covering the complaints and disciplinary system

4.5 Part 5 of the Handbook (Enforcement Regulations) sets out the Regulations applicable to all aspects of the enforcement system (see Section 3 – paragraphs 3.32–3.33). The Complaints Regulations and the Disciplinary Tribunals Regulations are those that are most directly applicable to the work of the Committee. The rest of this section provides an overview of the processes set out in, and designed to support, the Complaints Regulations (the Regulations): i.e. initial consideration of complaints, formal investigation, imposition of administrative sanctions and referral to disciplinary action. The disciplinary processes are, on the whole, governed by the Disciplinary Tribunal Regulations and are covered in Section 5 of this pack.

4.6 Professional Conduct Committee powers: the Regulations vest all decision making powers in the Committee as a whole. However, it would be impossible to operate the enforcement system effectively if all decisions had to be taken by the full Committee. Therefore, a scheme of authorisations by the Committee under Regulation 3 of the Complaints Regulations has been put in place to allow staff and certain members of the Committee to take decisions on complaints outside full Committee meetings.

Regulatory responsibility for dealing with complaints – client/non-client complaints

4.7 The BSB's remit, and by definition that of the Committee, is limited by the terms of the LSA 2007 to considering complaints about conduct only. Complaints about the service provided to clients by barristers fall exclusively within the remit of the Legal Ombudsman (LeO) and the BSB is prohibited from considering or awarding redress to clients of barristers.

4.8 As a result, the emphasis of the enforcement system is on ensuring that the regulatory objectives are met and in particular that standards at the Bar are maintained in the public interest. The needs and views of complainants still remain an important focus but decisions on complaints must be based on the risk to the regulatory objectives and the proportionality of any action, and not on resolving the complaint to the complainant's satisfaction.

4.9 In light of LeO's remit, the BSB has had to make a distinction between "client" complaints and "non-client" complaints. While the BSB is able to deal with conduct complaints from both clients and non-clients, the initial processes for handling complaints from the two sources are slightly different. In relation to client complaints, these must be channelled first through LeO, regardless of their subject matter: any issues of professional conduct will only be formally referred to the BSB once LeO has had an opportunity to consider whether the complaint includes issues of service. (See Section 6 for further information on the process for handling conduct referrals from LeO and the interface with LeO).

The Professional Conduct Committee's role in the complaints process

4.10 The Complaints Regulations vest all decision making powers in the Committee. Therefore the Committee's functions and powers now extend to cover those previously exercised by the Complaints Commissioner.[2] However, it would be impossible to operate the complaints system effectively if all decisions had to be taken by the full Committee. Therefore, a scheme of authorisations under rE3 of the Rules allows the PCC to authorise any person group or body to fulfil any function or exercise any power give to them under Section 5 of the Handbook. In practice, this has been put in place to allow staff in the Assessment Team and certain members of the Committee to take decisions on complaints outside full Committee.

4.11 The Assessment Team is responsible for: responding to general enquiries about making complaints; referrals from and to the Legal Ombudsman; and preliminary assessment of complaints (external) or information received (internal complaints) to decide whether a matter should be referred to formal investigation. The work of the Team is high volume, with an intended fast turnaround time, which allows complainants to know as quickly as possible whether their complaint is going to be pursued by the BSB. The aim is to conclude the preliminary assessment within eight weeks of receipt of an external complaint.

2 The role of the Complaints Commissioner was to provide an independent and lay "sifting" mechanism, identifying those complaints where there is sufficient evidence to warrant referral to the Committee for consideration of further action, and dismissing all others. This role was removed as of January 2011 and replaced with staff and Committee decision making.

Types of conduct complaint

4.12 Complaints about the conduct of barrister are divided into two types:

a. external complaints; and

b. internal complaints.

4.13 External complaints are those made by anyone other the BSB, which can include, but are not limited to clients, members of the public, solicitors and judges.

4.14 Internal complaints are those raised by the BSB of its own motion under Regulation 10. They are raised as a result of information received other than via an external complainant and by definition do not involve a third party complainant. Internal complaints are only raised where there is evidence of a breach of the old Code/Handbook that warrants investigation.

4.15 The power to raise internal complaints can also be used where it is not appropriate for a complainant to be directly involved or the person does not wish to continue with the complaint. In such circumstances, the BSB can "adopt" the complaint by raising it as an internal matter. This happens most often in relation to complaints made by judges.

4.16 Except at the preliminary assessment stage (see below), the processes for dealing with both internal and external complaints are the same.

Types of breaches of the Code

4.17 The Committee has the power to take enforcement action in relation to any breach of the Handbook. Given the terms of the new definition of professional misconduct in the Handbook, breaches occurring after 6 January 2014 fall into categories:

(i) those which can be appropriately addressed by the Committee by way of no further action or administrative sanctions (i.e. non-disciplinary action) and thereby Re-issued November 2013 The Enforcement Process and Administrative Sanctions are not serious enough to amount to professional misconduct. The standard of proof in relation to such breaches is the balance of probabilities; and,

(ii) those which are serious and would not be appropriate for disposal by means of administrative sanctions and need to be addressed by disciplinary action for professional misconduct (i.e. a referral to the Determination by Consent procedure or a Disciplinary Tribunal). The standard of proof applied in relation to professional misconduct is beyond reasonable doubt.

4.18 The nature of the breach only becomes directly relevant at the post-investigation stage of the process when a decision needs to be taken as to what type of enforcement action, if any, is appropriate. However, it should be noted that the imposition of an administrative sanction is not a disciplinary disposal and details of the decision and the sanction imposed will not be made publically available: this includes communication to the Queen's Counsel Appointment Body and the Judicial Appointments Commission. On the other hand, while no further action decisions are also not formally classed as disciplinary disposals and are not made publically available, they are disclosed in relation to applications for silk or judicial appointment.

Initial assessment and investigation of complaints and decision whether or not to refer for further action

4.19 Where a complaint is received from an external source, the BSB makes an initial assessment of it. If it decides, following that initial assessment, that the complaint should be referred for formal investigation then a case officer is appointed to undertake that investigation. Barristers and complainants are informed who their case officer is so they can correspond with them. Internal complaints are treated in much the same way save for the fact that there is no complainant involved and the initial assessment is made before deciding whether to raise the complaint. All investigations are carried out by staff. Committee members have no role in conducting investigations but may advise staff from time to time about enquiries that should be made.

4.20 DECIDING TO TAKE FURTHER ACTION: Once the investigation is finished and all relevant evidence has been compiled, the BSB will consider whether there is enough evidence to prove that the barrister has breached the Code of Conduct. If it does do not have enough evidence, it will normally dismiss the complaint, but it may decide to give the barrister formal advice about their behaviour. If the BSB considers that it has enough evidence to prove that the barrister has breached the Code of Conduct, it will consider whether to refer the case for disciplinary action. The decision to refer the case for disciplinary action will be taken by the Professional Conduct Committee or, in a limited set of circumstances, by senior staff within the Professional Conduct Department.

4.21 Decisions to refer complaints for disciplinary action are not taken lightly. The BSB only takes action where it considers there is a reasonable prospect of proving misconduct in front of an independent Tribunal and the regulatory objectives set out in the Legal Services Act 2007 would be best served by taking such action. It knows that disciplinary action against barristers, or indeed any other professional expected to abide by a Code of Conduct, may have a detrimental impact on their career. However, that possibility cannot be a factor in deciding whether to take action or not. The BSB appreciates the inevitable stress experienced by barristers who are subject to the complaints and disciplinary system. It tries to deal with complaints as efficiently and promptly as it can in order to minimise stress for complainants and barristers. To seek to minimise stress, and because barristers are innocent until proven guilty, the BSB does not give out details of complaints, or even confirm that they exist, until a Tribunal hearing is scheduled.

Risk assessment

4.22 The BSB's remit, and by definition that of the Committee, is limited by the terms of the LSA 2007 to considering complaints about conduct only. Complaints about the service provided to clients by barristers fall exclusively within the remit of the Legal Ombudsman (LeO) and the BSB is prohibited from considering or awarding redress to clients of barristers.

4.23 As a result, the emphasis of the enforcement system is on ensuring that the regulatory objectives are met and in particular that standards at the Bar are maintained in the public interest. The needs and views of complainants still remain an important focus but decisions on complaints must be based on the risk to the regulatory objectives and the proportionality of any action, and not on resolving the complaint to the complainant's satisfaction.

4.24 In light of LeO's remit, the BSB has had to make a distinction between "client" complaints and "non-client" complaints. While the BSB is able to deal with conduct complaints from both clients and non-clients, the initial processes for handling complaints from the two sources are slightly different. In relation to client complaints, these must be channelled first through LeO, regardless of their subject matter: any issues of professional conduct will only be formally referred to the BSB once LeO has had an opportunity to consider whether the complaint includes issues of service. (See Section 6 for further information on the process for handling conduct referrals from LeO and the interface with LeO).

The complaints processes

4.25 An overview of the processes for dealing with complaints is set out below.

4.26 The same processes are applied to both internal and external complaints although the preliminary assessment (see paragraph 4.27 below) is not necessary in relation to internal complaints as such complaints are only raised where there is sufficient evidence to justify a formal investigation. As previously stated at paragraph 4.11, the preliminary assessment stage is also different for client complaints referred by LeO (see Section 6). However, the process for conducting investigations applies to all complaints whether internal/external or client/non-client.

4.27 **Preliminary assessment:** While substantial changes to the details of the processes have been made, the fundamental structure of the enforcement system (previously referred to as the "complaints and disciplinary system") remains the same and the overall process still consists of the following main stages:

a. Preliminary assessment to determine whether a potential breach of the old Code/Handbook has occurred and whether an investigation is warranted or another disposal is appropriate;

b. Investigation;

c. Review of the outcome of an investigation to determine whether there is evidence of a breach of the old Code/Handbook and, if so, what action is appropriate;

d. Final decision on whether and what action should be taken; and,

e. Implementation of any enforcement action.

4.28 If the complaint reveals a potential breach of the Code and further consideration is justified, then it will normally be referred immediately to formal investigation unless a referral to chambers is considered appropriate.

4.29 **Dismissal of complaints following preliminary assessment:** where the preliminary assessment indicates insufficient evidence of breach of the Handbook, the complaint will be dismissed. In most cases, the decision to dismiss will be taken by the ATM or one of the Assessment Officers who will send the dismissal letters. However, some complaints cannot be dismissed by staff and must be referred to the Committee for a final decision.

4.30 **Referral to chambers:** these disposals will only be appropriate in very few cases, where the final risk level is "low" and it is considered that the matter can be effectively resolved at chambers level or by another body or person.

4.31 **Referral to the Supervision Team**: such a referral is unlikely to be appropriate in many cases, but generally will only be made where the final risk category is either "low" or "medium". The decision as to whether to refer a matter for supervision will be based on affirmative answers to specific questions within the risk assessment relating mainly to issues regarding the barrister's practice and compliance with the practising requirements, which would indicate that there could be wider issues that would warrant supervisory intervention to mitigate the risk of further and on going non-compliance.

4.32 **Investigation:** Medium/high risk complaints will be referred to investigation subject to consideration of other forms of disposal such as referral to chambers/another body or referral of the barrister to the Supervision Team for supervisory action.

4.33 **Conduct of investigations:**The purpose of formal investigation is to gather evidence to establish whether the potential breach of the old Code/Handbook can be proved either on the balance of probabilities (to support a decision to impose administrative sanctions) or beyond a reasonable doubt (to support a referral to disciplinary action for professional misconduct).

4.34 Investigations are carried out by Case Officers in the Investigations and Hearings Team and allocation depends on the category in which the complaint is placed. The Case Officer will compile a summary of the aspects of the complaint to be investigated and, where a complainant is involved, forward the summary to the complainant for comments on its accuracy. This summary will then be used as the basis for the investigation.

4.35 After the summary has been confirmed, the Case Officer will write to the barrister and other relevant witnesses involved, including, where appropriate, any instructing solicitors. Complainants will normally be sent a copy of the barrister's response to the complaint and, where the complainant's comments are required, copies, or a summary of any responses received from others involved in the investigation.

4.36 As with the preliminary assessment, advice on an interim decision can be sought from any member of the Committee.

Conclusion of investigation

4.37 At the conclusion of the investigation, the Case Officer will carry out a post investigation assessment to determine what action should be taken. This involves reviewing the evidence to determine whether it is sufficient to prove a breach of the old Code/Handbook. If there is sufficient evidence of a breach, the Case Officer will then review the risk assessment and, if necessary, amend the answers to any of the risk questions in light of the information received during the investigation. As at the preliminary assessment stage, the risk level arising from the number of affirmative answers can be overridden, if there is a justified reason for doing so: the reasons will be recorded on the assessment form.

4.38 Overriding the risk level at the post-investigation stage: the decision on whether to override a risk level is based on the evidence and all the circumstances and facts of the case. However, specific individual factors relating to medium risk complaints are likely to result in the risk level being adjusted to high. Such factors relate to whether the imposition of an administrative sanction is proportionate and sufficient in the public interest (see rE50.2). They include but are not limited to:

(i) The barrister having a previous disciplinary history in relation to conduct which is similar or the same;

(ii) The barrister having previously been subject to an administrative sanction which is similar of the same;

(iii) The conduct has wider implications for the administration of justice or public confidence in the regulatory system;

(iv) Information about the breach should be in the public domain in order to protect the public; and,

(v) The Sentencing Guidance indicates that a suspension or disbarment might be imposed by a Disciplinary Tribunal in relation to the conduct.

4.39 **Outcome of the post-investigation assessment:** The options for disposal available to staff following a post investigation review are:

a. Staff dismissal of the complaint on the basis of insufficient evidence of breach of the Handbook;

b. A recommendation to the Experienced Members of the Committee to dismiss but with formal advice given to the barrister (see paragraphs 4. 81–4.84);

c. Staff decision to impose an administrative sanction (see paragraphs 4. 66–4.76) where there is clear evidence, on the balance of probabilities, that a breach has occurred which is not sufficiently serious to warrant disciplinary action for professional misconduct;

d. Staff referral direct to disciplinary action (Disciplinary Tribunal or, the Determination by Consent procedure); and,

e. Referral to the Professional Conduct Committee for a final decision.

4.40 The appropriate option will depend on the circumstances of the complaint, including the outcome of the risk assessment and the categorisation of the complaint. However, breaches with a low or medium risk level will be subject to a presumption that the imposition of an administrative fine would be appropriate. Breaches falling into the high risk category will be subject to the presumption that administrative sanctions are not appropriate and the matter is sufficiently serious to warrant disciplinary action for professional misconduct.

Authorisations and categorisation of complaints to be investigated

4.41 Authorisations: the processes described above can only operate effectively if staff and certain members of the Committee are authorised to take decisions outside full meetings. Regulation rE3 of the Complaints Regulations allows the Committee or the Chair of the Committee to authorise any person, group or body to fulfil any function or exercise any power given to the Committee under the Regulations. Therefore the Committee has put in place a range of authorisations that allow staff, Experienced Members and Officer Holder(s) to take decision outside meetings and thereby support the processes outlined in this section of the pack. Full details of the authorisations can found in Annex 4 under "P09 – Complaints Regulations – Authorisation of functions/powers".

4.42 It should be emphasised that merely because an authorisation has been given to a member of staff or members of the Committee, this does not mean that the relevant decision must be taken by those authorised to do so. All decisions, at any stage of the complaints or disciplinary processes, can be referred to the full Committee for the decision to be taken

4.43 Categorisation of complaints: the investigation and post-investigation process described above requires that staff have the ability to take decisions on complaints following an investigation. However, staff do not have the ability to take decisions on all complaints and the extent of their authority depends on the category of the complaint. A summary of the categories and associated decisions staff can take is set out below but full details can be found in "PG11 – Categorisation of complaints and staff authority to take decisions" (see Annex 4).

4.44 It should be noted that staff do not have the authority to take decision on complaints, regardless of their category, that:

a. have attracted, or are likely to attract, media attention;

b. may have wider implications for the public interest, the Bar or any section of the Bar or the BSB; and/or

c. have been referred to the BSB by another "approved regulator" as defined by the Legal Services Act 2007.

All such complaints must be referred to the full Committee, or in certain circumstances Office Holders, for decisions to be taken.

4.45 There are three categories into which complaints are put at the investigation stage:

a. Category 1: this category covers internal complaints relating to breaches of the practising requirements, convictions for dishonesty or deception and failures to comply with orders of Disciplinary Tribunals or sanctions imposed under the Determination by Consent (DBC) procedure. Staff have the power to dismiss such complaints (except those related to criminal offences which must be referred to disciplinary action), withdraw them, impose administrative sanctions and refer the complaints direct to a Disciplinary Tribunal or the DBC procedure. Category 1 complaints can be allocated to any Case Officer.

b. Category 2: this category is defined by reference to the other categories and covers all external complaints that do not fall into Category 3 and all internal complaints that do not fall into Category 1 or Category 3. Staff are able to dismiss complaints in Category 2, but only where it is clear that no breach of the old Code/Handbook is disclosed or the evidence is so weak that it would not support any type of enforcement action. Staff also have the authority to impose administrative sanctions where there is clear evidence of a breach, based on the balance of probabilities and such action is clearly proportionate and sufficient based on the risk level. All other complaints must be referred to the Committee for a decision. Staff cannot refer Category 2 complaints direct to disciplinary action. Category 2 complaints can be allocated to any Case Officer.

c. Category 3: this category includes both external and internal complaints that: are complex either factually or legally; have or may attract media attention; or involve wider implications for the public interest, the profession or the BSB. All complaints in this category must be referred to the Committee to take the decision whether to dismiss, impose administrative sanctions or refer to disciplinary action. Category 3 cases can only be allocated to a legally qualified Case Officer to investigate.

4.46 The category in which a complaint is placed is not related to the risk level for that complaint. For example, a complaint arising from a criminal conviction for dishonesty would inevitably be high risk but would fall within category 1 as referral of the complaint to disciplinary action is not subject to individual judgement, but is prescribed by the Regulations.

Administrative sanctions

4.47 The decision as to whether an administrative sanction is an appropriate disposal in an individual case will be taken as part of the post-investigation assessment stage either by staff or the Committee. Where it is considered that an administrative sanction is appropriate, a decision will be need to be taken either by the staff or the Committee as to what type and level of sanction should be imposed. The following paragraphs set out the approach and procedure for making such decisions.

4.48 The Handbook defines administrative sanctions (at Part 6, definition 5) as "an administrative warning, fixed penalty fine or other administrative fine up to the prescribed maximum, or any combination of the above in accordance with the [Complaints Regulations]". The maximum penalty for individual barristers is £1,000.

4.49 The Regulations do not prescribe the level of administrative sanction that should be imposed in any particular case, but Regulation 51 stipulates that "in determining the level of [sanction] the PCC must have due regard to the enforcement strategy and may have due regard to such other matters as the Bar Standards Board may consider relevant from time to time".

4.50 Warnings: these are generally imposed where some or all of the following factors are present:

- the barrister has no previous disciplinary findings or record of administrative sanctions for similar behaviour in the past two years;
- the breach has been remedied or the barrister has taken all reasonable steps to mitigate the impact of the conduct;
- there have been no adverse consequences for any persons;
- there has been no adverse impact on the public confidence in the administration of justice or the profession;
- there are exceptional circumstances that make the imposition of a financial penalty inappropriate.

4.51 Fixed penalty fines (FPF): these are generally imposed in relation to referrals from other sections of the BSB/Bar Council (see paragraphs 4.49–4.51 above) where the barrister has not previously been subject to an administrative fine for the same or similar conduct. Examples of types of breaches that could attract a FPF include but are not limited to:

- failures to complete the authorisation to practise process;
- failures to complete chambers monitoring or supervisory risk assessments; failures by chambers to publish equality and diversity information; and,
- failures to register for QASA.

4.52 The level of the FPF has been set at £400. However, this is subject to a 50% reduction for early payment if payment is made within 14 days of the fine being imposed.

4.53 Discretionary Fines: these are based on the individual circumstances and nature of a complaint and the risk factors involved. The starting point is £400 and the amount will be adjusted according to the mitigating and aggravating circumstances of the breach.

4.54 The financial circumstances of the barrister need to be taken into account when deciding on the level of discretionary fine. In order to facilitate this, barristers will be informed when the investigation is commenced that, if at the end of the investigation a decision is taken to impose an administrative sanction, if they want their financial circumstances to be taken into account they should submit evidence in relation to this with their response to the complaint.

4.55 Multiple Breaches: Where a complaint involves more than one breach, all of which are suitable for disposal by administrative sanctions separate sanctions for each breach should not be imposed but a global sanction imposed covering all the breaches based on the most serious breach. This in line with the approach taken at the preliminary and post-investigation stages where a "complaint" is risk assessed as whole rather than individually by its constituent aspects. The fact that a complaint involves multiple breaches will be an aggravating factor. Note: this does not prevent different aspects of a complaint being subject to different disposals at the post investigation assessment stage.

4.56 Staff authority to take decisions on administrative sanctions: Staff have the authority to take decisions on the imposition of all types of administrative sanctions including, in theory, up to the maximum of £1,000. However, this authority is restricted by the category of the complaint as set out in paragraphs 4.62–4.65, above. Therefore in practice, given the nature of the authorities, staff will only be taking decisions in relation to clear cut cases and where the level of sanction is either a warning or fine in the mid-range of the maximum.

4.57 Appeals: barristers subject to the imposition of administrative sanctions have a right to appeal the decision to an independent panel, appointed by the Bar Tribunal and Adjudication Service. The appeal process is governed by the provisions set in out the Complaints Regulations, rE84–E89. Barristers have 28 days in which to submit an appeal and appeals can be heard on the papers or, at the request of the barrister, at an oral hearing in front of the panel which consists of three persons: a Queen's Counsel as chair, a lay member and a barrister member.

Committee decisions

4.58 As stated at paragraph 4.13 above, all decision making powers in relation to complaints are vested in the Professional Conduct Committee. While staff are authorised to take some decisions, there is no requirement that they must take those decisions and complaints can be referred to the full Committee at any stage of the process. However, as outlined in the preceding paragraphs, the Committee, or individuals on it, will generally be responsible for the following decisions:

a. deciding in relevant cases whether complaints referred by the Legal Ombudsman should be investigated immediately or await the outcome of the Legal Ombudsman's consideration (see Section 6 of this Pack);

b. dDismissing all Category 3 complaints and also Category 2 complaints where the evidence presents some level of ambiguity and the need for dismissal is not self-evident;

c. imposing administrative sanctions in Category 3 complaints and in Category 2 complaints where the evidence presented some level of ambiguity and/or is it not easily apparent what level of sanction would be proportionate;

d. referring relevant complaints in Categories 2 and 3 to disciplinary action;

e. referring complaints that potentially satisfy the disqualification condition to a Disciplinary Tribunal or the Determination by Consent procedure: and

f. generally considering any complaints where the decision on what action to take following an investigation is not clear, or the PCD consider the matter is best decided by the Committee.

4.59 Where a complaint is referred to the Committee, the options available for the disposal of the complaint are, in the main, the same as those available to staff both at the preliminary and post-investigation stages, but with some slight variance. As is reflected by the terms of the Complaints Regulations, the Committee can:

a. dismiss the complaint, provided that the majority of the lay members present at a meeting consent to the dismissal;

b. dismiss the complaint but advise the barrister as to his/her future conduct in writing or direct the barrister to attend on the Chair or a Vice Chair for such advice (the latter is only available to the Committee);

c. decide that no further action should be taken on the complaint (only available to the Committee (but see Section 9, paragraph 9.58);

d. refer a complaint at the preliminary assessment stage for supervisory action by the Supervision Team;

e. impose an administrative sanction;

f. where administrative sanctions are not appropriate due to the seriousness of the conduct or its surrounding circumstances, there is a realistic prospect of a finding of professional misconduct being made and the regulatory objectives would be best be served by doing so, refer the complaint to the Determination by Consent procedure or a Disciplinary Tribunal on charges of professional misconduct;

g. refer a complaint that potentially satisfies the disqualification condition to a Disciplinary Tribunal (only available to the Committee).

4.60 Process for Committee decisions: Where a complaint is referred to the Committee for a decision, the file will normally be allocated to a member of the Committee, lay or barrister, who acts as a "Case Examiner" for the case. The Case Examiner is expected to compile a written report for the Committee, including recommendations for the disposal of the complaint based on the options listed at paragraph 4.59 above and, where applicable, draft relevant letters for the complainant and/or the barrister.

4.61. The written report by the Case Examiner should be compiled in accordance with a standard template. Sections 8, 9 and 10 of this pack provide further information on the processes related to Case Examiner reports and the preparation of letters.

Decisions by experienced members

4.62 There are some decisions that are not appropriate for staff to take but are also not of a nature that would require a full Committee decision. Therefore "Experienced Members" of the Committee are authorised to take a number of decisions outside meetings. An "Experienced Member" is defined as "a member of the Committee who has served at least two years or is an Office Holder of the Committee". The term "Experienced Members" refers to one lay member and one barrister member of the Committee, acting collectively to take decisions.

4.63 The decisions EMs can take are:

a. whether complaints referred to the BSB by the Legal Ombudsman (LeO) should be investigated immediately or await the outcome of the LeO consideration (see Section 6);

b. whether a complaint should be investigated where staff cannot decide;

c. to dismiss complaints with advice; and,

d. to refer barristers to the Fitness to Practise or Interim Suspension procedures (see Section 7).

4.64 The EMs will be expected to make a joint decision on the complaint. Where they cannot agree or decide on what action to take, the complaint can be referred to the full Committee with the approval of an Office Holder. If referral to the Committee is necessary, then generally one of the EMs should act as Case Examiner and write a report for the Committee but if this is not possible the complaint should be referred back to the relevant Officer for an alternative Case Examiner to be appointed.

4.65 Any complaints referred to Experienced Members (EMs) will be accompanied by a note prepared by the relevant Officer setting out the background to the case, the issues involved, and the reasons why the complaint has been referred for a decision. Experienced members will be expected to make a joint decision and communicate that decision to the relevant Officer. Section 9 provides further information on the role and responsibilities of Experienced Members.

"Intelligence reports" to the supervision team

4.66 In order to ensure that the BSB is generally taking a holistic approach to assessing risks arising from the behaviour of the regulatory community, and thereby updating and developing its risk framework, it is important that relevant information is shared between BSB departments/teams. Information on enforcement action is crucial to this and such information, in summary/anonymised form, will be available to other sections. Information in relation to complaints, which have been dismissed and did not result in an internal complaint being raised or is received by the PCD/PCC by any other avenue, could also be relevant to the BSB's wider assessment of risk, particularly the work of the Supervision Team. Therefore a system for submitting "intelligence reports" from the PCD to the Supervision Team has been put in place.

4.67 Staff in the PCD will be responsible for submitting such reports, but the Committee (or individual members dealing with cases) can ask for a report to be submitted. As a guide, the following types of information might warrant the submission of an "intelligence report":

- indications of systematic problems with the administration of a chambers;
- indications that a chambers may have a widespread problem in relation to the conduct of its members in a specific area;
- indications that a chambers is condoning, or facilitating, breaches of the Handbook;
- information about potential issues of discrimination or harassment, particularly in relation to pupils, within a chambers.

4.68 The submission of an "intelligence report" does not amount to a formal "referral" and it will be for the Supervision Team to decide what use is made of the information (for example, it could inform whether attention needs to be paid to a particular chambers or whether a "thematic" review in a certain area of regulatory activity is warranted).

Checks and balances on staff decision making

4.69 It is not possible to assess at this stage the volume of complaints that will be subject to staff decisions under the new processes. However, the fact that staff are authorised to take decisions does not mean that they have to take such decisions. In the first six months or so of the application of the risk based approach, it is likely that some decisions staff are authorised to take will be referred to the Committee. Further, in relation to the imposition of administrative actions, up until the end of 2014, all final decisions will be taken by the Investigations and Hearings Manager or the Head of Professional Conduct, However, the principle that decisions should be taken at the lowest level appropriate to the case is one that the Legal Services Board is keen that approved regulators abide by and implement.

4.70 Several forms of checks and balances are in place to monitor staff decisions. These include:

a. Regular reports to the Committee – a summary report of all staff decisions to dismiss complaints and impose administrative sanctions is included in the papers for each Committee meeting.

b. Quality Review Sub Committee of the PCC – a standing sub-committee of the Committee reviews a percentage of staff decisions on a quarterly basis to consider whether they were taken in line with the procedures and whether, on their merits, the decisions were reasonable (see Section 9 and "PG18 – Review of Staff Decisions by the Quality Review Sub Committee" for full details).

c. Independent Observer (IO) – the IO has a remit to look at the way in which the agreed processes are being applied and whether the aims and objectives of the system are being met. The IO does not have a role in looking at the merits of individual outcomes of complaints but can take these into account when making recommendations for improvements in the operation of the wider system (see Section 13, paragraphs 13.10–13.12 for more information).

Overview of Complaints Handling Process

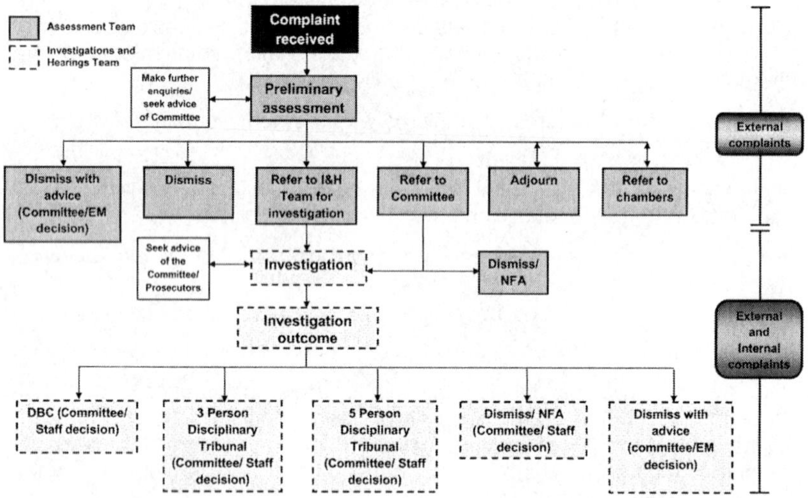

Concerns about a barrister

[6.16]

The BSB explains the process for making complaints about barristers' services in the following terms:

- If the barrister is acting for you and you are not satisfied with their service you should contact the Legal Ombudsman.

- If the barrister is *not* acting for you and you want to complain about their behaviour, sometimes referred to as professional misconduct, you should contact the BSB.

Examples of professional misconduct include:

- misleading the court;
- failing to keep information confidential;
- acting dishonestly or in a way that damages the profession's reputation;
- discriminating against you because or your race, sex, disability, religion or belief, sexual orientation, gender reassignment, age or marital/ civil partnership status.

In order to make your complaint you will need to download and complete our Complaint form, which you will find in the 'Resources' box on the relevant page of the BSB website (http://www.barstandardsboard.org.uk/complaints-and-professional-conduct/concerns-about-a-barrister/). The form has guidance attached to help you complete the form.

The BSB publishes general FAQs about the complaints and disciplinary processes (set out below) as well separate ones for complaints about a barrister that has acted for you and complaints about one that has not (available on the website):

1. I am disabled and need assistance in making a complaint, how can you help me?

If you are disabled and require assistance in making a complaint, it is important that you let us know as soon as possible. We will make all reasonable adjustments to the complaints process to ensure that you are not disadvantaged in making your complaint. We can, for example, provide our literature in different formats such as Braille, large print or on audio tape or compact disc. We can also give you additional time to respond to our enquiries.

We normally expect complaints to be submitted to us on our standard complaints form. However, if your impairment makes it difficult for you to complain to us in writing, we can take the details of your complaint over the telephone or arrange for you to be interviewed. It may, however, be that a friend or relative, your solicitor, local Citizen's Advice Bureau, Law Centre or other organisation can assist you in making your complaint and communicating with us generally.

If you have access requirements, or would like advice on the complaints process, please contact our Information Line on 020 7611 1445.

2. Are there any complaints which you will not normally investigate?

We can only consider complaints about the professional conduct of barristers as defined by the terms of the Bar's Code of Conduct. Therefore there are some types of complaints that we would not normally consider:

Professional Negligence: We are unable to investigate complaints of professional negligence. Professional negligence is a legal concept which may ultimately have to be adjudicated on by the courts. If you think that your barrister may have been negligent then it may be that the Legal Ombudsman can assist. Alternatively you may need to consider obtaining legal advice as to whether you have grounds for a claim of professional negligence that should be pursued in the courts.

Professional Judgment: We cannot deal with complaints about a barrister's legal judgment on the law or facts of a case or the barrister's professional judgement about how a case should be presented to a court. This would require us to put our legal judgement above the barrister's and we are not qualified, or able, to "second guess" a barrister's professional opinion.

Private life: We do not usually deal with complaints about barristers" behaviour when they are acting outside their professional role, unless that behaviour has resulted in a criminal conviction or finding of a court or Tribunal. If you consider that a barrister has committed a criminal offence, you should report the matter to the police. Also, we will not normally investigate a complaint of misconduct which relates to a barrister's private or non-professional life where there is a clear legal remedy available to you which you have not yet pursued. It is only in exceptional circumstances that we will deal with complaints about something a barrister has done in his or her private life.

Debts: We do not usually deal with complaints against barristers who are in debt to members of the public. We have no power to enforce the payment of debts and you may be able to take legal action through the courts to recover the debt. However, if a barrister has not complied with a court order, we may be able to consider the matter but we will need to know what steps you have taken to enforce any judgment obtained against the barrister. Although we may be able to take disciplinary action for failure to comply with a court order, we have no powers to make the barrister pay you or comply with the order.

Disputes within chambers: Our complaints system is not designed to resolve disputes between barristers in chambers or between former members and their previous chambers. This includes disputes concerning money allegedly owed to/by clerks or chambers. Our primary function is to protect members of the public affected by professional misconduct by barristers. The aims and objectives of our disciplinary process are, among other things, to investigate complaints and take action against barristers who have breached the Code of Conduct in order to:

- act in the public interest;
- protect the public and other consumers of legal services;
- promote access to, and the proper administration of, justice; and
- maintain high standards of behaviour and performance for the Bar.

The Bar Council has established an arbitration and mediation service to resolve disputes arising between individual members of chambers or between a member or members of chambers and a senior clerk. Details of the arbitration and mediation service can be found on the Bar Council's website.

We will consider complaints made by barristers and chambers' employees where it is alleged that they have been discriminated against in connection with any of the protected characteristics referred to in the Equality Act 2010 (i.e. age; disability; gender reassignment; marriage and civil partnership; pregnancy and maternity; race; religion and belief; sex; and sexual orientation). We will also consider complaints made by an employee or a barrister in a set of chambers, where the allegation is that the barrister has acted dishonestly. It may, however, be that the allegation should be referred to the police.

Judges, recorders (part time judges) or Tribunal Chairs: we cannot deal with complaints about barristers who are acting in a judicial role. If you wish to complain about the conduct of a barrister acting in a judicial capacity then you will need to complain to the Office for Judicial Complaints.

3. Can you grant me compensation?

No. We have no powers to order compensation. This power is only available to the Legal Ombudsman and only in relation to poor service provided by barristers to their clients. The Legal Ombudsman has the ability to order compensation as well as order that the barrister reduce or return their fees.

4. Can you help me with my court case?

No. We cannot help you with your court case. Amongst other issues related to court proceedings, we are unable to:

- get involved in your court case;
- stop a barrister from acting for the other side in a case;
- prevent a barrister presenting evidence to a court or acting in a way you disagree with; or
- order that you should have another trial.

These are matters for the courts and you should speak to your legal representative if you want this kind of action.

5. If I complain about my opponent's barrister, can you require the barrister to disclose to me confidential or privileged information?

No. If you are complaining about a barrister who does not act for you, then the barrister will have a duty of confidentiality to their client. That duty continues even after the barrister has stopped being instructed by that client. Without the client's consent the barrister is not allowed to disclose what instructions they received from the client or what legal advice was given to the client.

6. What can you do about my complaint?

Our role is to decide whether or not there has been a breach of the Code of Conduct and whether disciplinary action is necessary and justified. If disciplinary action is considered appropriate, we will refer the case to an independent Disciplinary Tribunal for a final decision on what action, if any, should be taken against the barrister. **Find out more about the disciplinary process**

Initial assessment: when we first receive your complaint, we will make an initial assessment about whether it shows sufficient evidence of a possible breach of the Code of Conduct to take the complaint further. We may ask you to provide more information in order to decide this.

Following the initial assessment, we may decide that there has been no breach of the Code or that the information you have provided is not enough to show there has been a possible breach of the Code. Also, in some cases, we may decide that your complaint has been submitted too late (i.e.12 months after the events) and there is no justification for taking the complaint further. If we decide not to take any further action as a result of the initial assessment, we will write to you explaining the reasons for the decision. We may also decide that the barrister should be referred to the Supervision Team for supervisory action to be taken.

Formal investigation: if we think there may have been a possible breach of the Code, we will carry out a formal investigation of the complaint. This will involve asking the barrister for comments and contacting any relevant witnesses or others involved in the complaint.

Once we have gathered all the information, we will then decide whether the evidence indicates that there has been a breach of the Code which warrants taking disciplinary action. If, after investigating the complaint, we do not consider the complaint to reveal sufficient evidence to take disciplinary action, or that such action is not justified, we will not take any further action in relation to your complaint. We will write to you letting you know our decision and giving you reasons for it.

Referral to disciplinary action: if we think that there is sufficient evidence to show that the barrister has breached the Code of Conduct, we will then decide whether it is appropriate to refer the case, or parts of it, to an independent

Disciplinary Tribunal for a hearing to decide what action should be taken. The decision about whether to refer a case to a Tribunal will normally be made by our Complaints Committee.

7. Why have you adjourned your investigation of my complaint?

If your complaint is adjourned, it is put on "hold" to wait for the outcome of issues related to the complaint which need to be resolved before we can continue with our consideration of a complaint. We consider the following factors when deciding whether a complaint should be adjourned:

- Are there any ongoing proceedings which relate to similar allegations?; and/or
- Is there is a risk that our investigation of the complaint would interfere with, prejudice or undermine ongoing proceedings or their outcome?

8. What is the Professional Conduct Committee and what powers does it have?

The Professional Conduct Committee is one of our regulatory Committees which has been given full delegated authority to take decisions on complaints. It is made up of barristers and lay members (non barristers) and meets once every two weeks to consider relevant complaints. The Committee has the power to: refer complaints to disciplinary action; decide to take no further action; or to dismiss a case due to lack of evidence.

The test the Committee applies when deciding whether to refer a case to disciplinary action is whether there is "a realistic prospect of success" at the Tribunal of proving the barrister is guilty of professional misconduct. This may mean that, although there is some evidence of a breach of the Code, it is not enough to refer a case to a Tribunal. If this happens, the Committee will not take any further action in relation to your complaint but you will be informed in writing of the reasons for the decision.

9. Can I appeal decisions taken in relation to my complaint?

No. There is no right of appeal against decisions taken either by staff or the Committee in relation your complaint. We are, however, able to reconsider decisions, but only where you have new evidence relevant to the decision or where you can show any other good reason for a review. Please note that neither the Chair nor the Director of the BSB have any powers to overturn decisions taken by staff or the Committee in relation to individual complaints.

10. Does the BSB arrange the Disciplinary Tribunal?

No. Disciplinary tribunals are arranged by an independent organisation called the Bar Tribunals and Adjudication Service (BTAS). It appoints the members of disciplinary tribunals and arranges the hearings. We have no influence over the members chosen to hear disciplinary cases.

11. What happens at a Disciplinary Tribunal?

In general, only Disciplinary Tribunals can make the final decision about whether a barrister has breached the Code of Conduct. Therefore, after preparing the disciplinary case (which can take several months), there will be a Tribunal hearing where we will present the evidence to support the "charges" of professional misconduct. The barrister can admit the charges but if the barrister denies them, they will be given an opportunity to present any evidence in defence.

The Tribunal will then make a decision as to whether the barrister has breached the Code of Conduct. They must be satisfied to the criminal standard of proof (i.e. "beyond reasonable doubt") that the barrister has breached the Code of Conduct.

If they decide that the barrister has breached the Code of Conduct, the Tribunal will then need to decide what sentence should be imposed.

12. What powers does a Disciplinary Tribunal have?

If a Disciplinary Tribunal makes a finding of professional misconduct, it can:

- give the barrister advice or a reprimand;
- order the barrister to pay a fine to the BSB;
- suspend the barrister from practise;
- disbar (strike off) the barrister.

A Disciplinary Tribunal will only consider suspending or disbarring a barrister in the most serious cases. Further information about the potential sentences Tribunals may impose for common types of breaches of the Code of Conduct can be found in the "Sentencing Guidance" (link to Sentencing Guidance).

13. I am a complainant, what rights do I have in relation to a Disciplinary Tribunal?

Your complaint, or parts of your complaint, may result in disciplinary proceedings but the proceedings are taken by us as the regulator of the profession and are not taken on your behalf. Therefore, all decisions about what charges to bring against the barrister, and what evidence to present to the Tribunal, are taken by us and you do not have a right to object to the charges or the evidence. You will, however, be given an opportunity to comment on the charges and the evidence before the hearing.

You may also be asked to be a witness at the Tribunal, and if this happens we will give you further information and will pay your reasonable expenses to attend the hearing. .The Tribunal will decide whether the barrister has breached the Code of Conduct and, if so, what sentence to impose. It may be that you are not entirely satisfied with the Tribunal's decisions, however, you do not have a right to appeal the decision or the sentence imposed.

14. I am a barrister who is the subject of a complaint, what can I do if I don't agree with the decision that has been made about the complaint made against me?

Decisions made by the Professional Conduct Committee

Decisions made by the Professional Conduct Committee are not subject to formal appeal and are regarded as final. However, the Complaints Regulations allow for decisions on complaints to be reviewed if any new evidence comes to light or for any other good reason. New evidence is evidence not previously provided to the BSB that may indicate that your behaviour does not amount to a potential breach of the Handbook.

Examples of any other good reasons include, but are not limited to:

- errors by staff e.g. existing evidence/aspects of a complaint were not taken into account or overlooked;
- errors by the Committee; e.g. a Case Examiner failed to mention a fundamental and material fact in a Committee report (you can request a copy of the Committee Report by contacting the Case Officer with the day-to-day conduct of your case);
- legal provisions or case law that were not taken into account when taking the original decision; and/or,

- serious illness or incapacity (in relation to either the complainant or barrister) that calls into question the efficacy or reasonableness of continuing with disciplinary proceedings.

Administrative sanctions

If you have had an administrative sanction of any type imposed on you by the BSB, you have a right to appeal against the decision to an independent panel appointed by the Bar Tribunal and Adjudication Service.

The appeal process is set out in BSB Handbook under the Complaints Regulations: rE84–89. An appeal is a review of the original decision and not a reconsideration of the complaint. Appeals are normally carried out on the papers although you can request an oral hearing. A notice of appeal must be lodged within 28 days of the sanction being imposed i.e. within 28 days of the date of the letter informing you of the sanction. As at May 2014, the fee for lodging an appeal is £100.

If you submit an appeal, it will initially be reviewed by a more senior decision maker. If there is clear merit in your appeal e.g. because there was a fundamental flaw in the process or the regulations were wrongly applied, the administrative sanction may be withdrawn and the complaint against you dismissed but it is unlikely that such circumstances will arise. If the decision maker decides there is no obvious reason to overturn the original decision, the administrative sanction will remain in place and the appeal will proceed.

More information on administrative sanctions can be found in the leaflet 'Administrative Sanctions: imposing warnings and fines' and further information on the appeals process can be found here.

Decisions made by a Disciplinary Tribunal

All defendant barristers have the right to appeal to the High Court findings made by a Disciplinary Tribunal and/or the sentence imposed. Complainants do not have a right of appeal. We will tell the complainant (if there is a complainant) of your intention to appeal and inform them of any progress. If the charges have been dismissed or the BSB thinks that the sentence is too lenient the BSB has the right to appeal but only if the Chair of the Bar Standards Board or the Chair of the Professional Conduct Committee agrees. This happens rarely.

Further information on the appeals process can be found here (for tribunal decisions made on or after 7 January 2014) and here (for tribunal decisions made on or before 6 January 2014).

15. What if I have concerns about the service provided by staff?

The BSB has a procedure in place for addressing complaints about the service provided by staff. This procedure is separate to the procedure for making complaints about the conduct of a barrister and is only applicable to concerns about how BSB staff have behaved.

Complaints may be made about any aspect of the service we have provided, for example:

- mistakes or lack of care in dealing with the complaint;
- providing misleading information or wrongly signposting you to other services;
- unreasonable delay in responding or taking action;
- unprofessional behaviour or attitude by staff;

- discrimination (in the way staff have treated you);
- lack of integrity.

Further details about what you can do if you are dissatisfied with the way the BSB handles complaints can be found on the BSB website.

Please note, if your complaint is about a decision we have made about the conduct of a barrister, we will not normally treat it as a complaint about our service. Instead, if appropriate, we will treat your complaint as a request to review the decision made about the barrister's conduct.

For further information on what you can do if you do not agree with the decision taken on your complaint, please click here if you are a complainant, or refer to question 14, above, if you are a barrister subject to a complaint.

16. Further information

If you have any questions about how to make a complaint, require further advice on the complaints process or need adjustments to be made if you are disabled, then please contact the our Information Line on 020 7611 1445 or write to:

Assessment Team
Bar Standards Board
289–293 High Holborn
London WC1V 7HZ

Or send an e-mail to:
contactus@barstandardsboard.org.uk

Facing a complaint?

[6.17]

The BSB also provides advice for barristers who might be facing a complaint. This can be found on the BSB website at http://www.barstandardsboard.org.uk/complaints-and-professional-conduct/facing-a-complaint/ and includes further leaflets that may be downloaded.

If you are a barrister facing a complaint, you may find it helpful to read our guidance.

Assistance for barristers facing a complaint

BMIF: The Bar Mutual Indemnity Fund (BMIF) can provide advice and representation while we are investigating a complaint, and in relation to any disciplinary action that may follow. You can phone the BMIF on 020 7621 0405.

BCAS: The Bar Council operates the Barrister's Complaints Advisory Service (BCAS). This is a list of barristers who have volunteered to provide free advice and/or representation to barristers subject to a complaint or disciplinary action.

Sentencing guidance

[6.18]

The BSB produces guidance in relation to sentencing by disciplinary tribunal.

The Sentencing Guidance was developed by the Council of the Inns of Court (COIC) and the Bar Standards Board in 2009. It is designed to promote consistency in the imposition of proportionate sanctions and to assist those who have to pass sentence under the disciplinary processes for breaches of the Code of Conduct of the Bar of England and Wales (namely the Professional Conduct Committee of the BSB and members of the Bar Tribunals and Adjudication Services Disciplinary Tribunals).

Please note: From 1 April 2011, as a consequence of the Legal Services Act 2007, the BSB's regulatory arrangements were changed and no longer include powers of "redress". In practice, this means that a Disciplinary Tribunal can no longer order a defendant to forgo or refund fees, or order an apology. Additionally, the jurisdiction to deal with outstanding issues of inadequate professional service has been transferred from the BSB to the Legal Ombudsman.

The Guidance was amended by the Bar Tribunals and Adjudication Service in April 2013 to reflect these changes. The amended guidance does however refer to the old Code of Conduct and not the new BSB Handbook.

Sentencing Guidance: Breaches of the Code of Conduct of the Bar of England and Wales

This document is intended to provide guidance and is not intended to inhibit decision makers from using their own discretion when considering an appropriate sanction in individual cases.

Version 2

April 20013

Introduction from the President of the Council of the Inns of Court

I am pleased to present the second edition of the Sentencing Guidance endorsed by the Council of the Inns of Court. It seeks to correct minor inaccuracies in the first edition and to remove sections which no longer fall within the jurisdiction of the Bar Standards Board's regulatory powers. There will be a full review of the guidance in due course.

The function of the guidance is unchanged; it is designed to assist those whose responsibility it is to impose the appropriate sanction under the disciplinary processes for breaches of the Code of Conduct of the Bar of England and Wales. The aim of this guidance is to promote consistency and transparency. It will inform the profession and the public about the principles on which sanctions will be applied and identify the probable range of sentence for the misconduct under consideration.

Professional sanctions are imposed to protect the public from further harm and to maintain the standards imposed by the Code of Conduct in the interests both of the public and the profession. As Lord Bingham observed in *Bolton v Law Society* [1994] 2 All ER 486, [1994] 1 WLR 512, CA:

> "Lawyers practising in this country … should discharge their professional duties with integrity, probity and complete trustworthiness … A profession's most valuable asset is its collective reputation and the confidence which that inspires. … the reputation of the profession is more important than the fortunes of any individual member. Membership of a profession brings many benefits, but that is a part of the price."

Part I of the guidance provides general information about the range of sanctions available and the circumstances in which they may be imposed. Part II of the guidance sets out the "starting points" for sentencing in relation to the most common breaches of the Code. The examples given do not represent all potential breaches of the Code. Decision makers should use their judgement and discretion to meet the requirements of the case.

The contents of this document are intended as guidance. It is not prescriptive. Decision makers are free to depart from the guidance but if they do they should explain their reasons with clarity.

Lord Justice Pitchford
President of the Council of the Inns of Court
April 2013

Part I – General guidance

Section 1 – Introduction

1.1. This guidance has been developed by the Bar Standards Board ("BSB") and The Bar Tribunals and Adjudication Service ("BTAS") for use by the Professional Conduct Committee of the BSB and members of BTAS's Disciplinary Tribunals ("decision makers") when considering what sanctions should be imposed where a barrister has been found to be in breach of the Code of Conduct of the Bar Council of England and Wales ("the Code").

1.2. The guidance is publicly available and allows defendant barristers, complainants and other interested parties to gauge, in advance, the potential sanction that might be imposed in a particular case. For more information about the complaints process, please see the Complaints and Professional Conduct section on the BSB's website (www.barstandardsboard.org.uk).

1.3. The guidance provides decision makers with a basis for considering what sanctions are appropriate in any given case and is intended to promote proportionality, consistency and transparency in sentencing. **However, it must be stressed that it is not intended to interfere with decision makers' powers to impose whatever sanctions are appropriate in the circumstances of individual cases. Decision makers must exercise their own judgement when deciding on the sanctions to impose and must also ensure that any sentence is appropriate and fair, based on the individual facts of the case.** Written reasons should be given for all sanctions imposed including any aggravating or mitigating factors. **Care should be taken to include in the written reasons the basis for departing a significant extent from this guidance.**

Equality and diversity statement

1.4 Effective regulation requires procedures to be fair and free from unlawful discrimination. One of the BSB's priorities is to ensure that it conducts its regulatory activities fairly and in accordance with its duty under the Equality Act 2010 to pay due regard to the need to: eliminate discrimination, advance equality of opportunity and foster good relations between different groups.

1.5. The BSB monitors the outcomes of the exercise of its regulatory powers and is committed to analysing the results and taking action, where appropriate, to reduce/remove inequality.

1.6. The Bar Tribunals and Adjudication Service is equally committed to eliminating discrimination and encouraging diversity. BTAS will monitor and publish equality and diversity data in line with any similar requirement placed upon the BSB by the Legal Services Board. Similarly, BTAS will monitor and publish equality and diversity data to describe our disciplinary panel members, clerks and ICC lay members. BTAS oppose all forms of unlawful and unfair discrimination.

Section 2 – aims and objectives of the Bar's complaints and disciplinary system

2.1 The BSB came into existence on 1 January 2006 following a decision to separate the regulation of the Bar from the representative functions of the Bar Council. The Bar Council has delegated to the BSB all of its regulatory functions including investigation of complaints and the subsequent prosecution of barristers for breaches of the Code. However, the final decision as to whether a barrister has breached the Code is a matter for independent panels appointed by the Bar Tribunals and Adjudication Service (BTAS). In limited circumstances, the Professional Conduct Committee of the BSB can impose sanctions with the agreement of the barrister.

2.2 The operation of the Bar's complaints and disciplinary system is governed by the BSB's high level strategic objectives as well as the specific aims and objectives of the complaints and disciplinary system. Therefore, all decisions regarding the action to be taken in relation to individual complaints are taken by the BSB in the context of the objectives and aims set out below.

2.3 The BSB's strategic objectives applicable to the complaints and disciplinary system are:

- to establish systems to identify areas of risk to consumers; to take action to remedy poor performance by barristers; and where things go wrong, to provide an efficient and fair complaints and disciplinary system;
- to be recognised as a respected, independent regulator according to best regulatory principles with the confidence of the Legal Services Board, consumers, the Bar and other stakeholders.

2.4 In taking these higher level strategic objectives forward, the BSB is committed to ensuring that the Bar's complaints and disciplinary system operates according to the following aims:

- to act in the public interest;
- to protect the public and consumers of legal services;
- to promote access to, and the proper administration of, justice;
- to maintain high standards of behaviour and performance for the Bar;
- to provide appropriate and fair systems for the barrister who is subject to regulatory action;
- to ensure complaints are dealt with fairly, expeditiously and consistently; and
- to promote public and professional confidence in the complaints and disciplinary process.

2.5 BTAS is committed to the statement of purpose set out in the Browne report[1] to:

- provide a hearings service that is efficient, effective, timely, professional and transparent and one that uses up to date practises and approaches;
- facilitate high quality decision-making in the public interest; and
- be independent, providing clear separation of the adjudicatory function from the BSB, as the prosecuting body for the Bar.

2.6 Most decisions regarding the sanctions to impose in relation to breaches of the Code are taken by the independent panels appointed by BTAS who are not directly subject to the aims and objectives of the BSB. Nevertheless, BTAS fully supports the BSB's aims and objectives and, urges disciplinary panel members to adopt them when dealing with disciplinary cases.

1 In late 2011, COIC commissioned a Review Group, chaired by Desmond Browne QC, to examine its disciplinary procedures. The Review Group published their report ("the Browne Report") to COIC on 18 July 2012; the full report is available at: http://www.graysinn.info/index.php/disciplinary-tribunals-review-coic. The statement of purpose can be found at annex 15, paragraph 2 in the summary of recommendations.

Section 3 – Purpose and principles of sentencing

3.1 The purposes of applying sanctions for breaches of the Code are:

a) To protect the public and consumers of legal services;

b) To maintain high standards of behaviour and performance at the Bar;

c) To promote public and professional confidence in the complaints and disciplinary process.

3.2 The primary purpose of imposing sanctions is to protect the public. This is of paramount importance and should be the fundamental guiding factor when considering what sanctions to impose. However, in fulfilling the other purposes it is also important to avoid recurrence of the behaviour by the individual as well as provide an example to other barristers in order to maintain public confidence in the profession. Decision makers must take all of these factors into account when determining the appropriate sanction to be imposed in an individual case. Decision makers should also bear in mind that sanctions are not intended to be punitive in nature but nevertheless may have that effect.

3.3 **Deterrence and upholding standards**: in some cases, the sanction imposed may be necessary to act as a deterrent to other members of the profession. Therefore, when considering a sentence, it may be necessary not only to deter the individual barrister from repeating the behaviour, but also to send a signal to the profession and the public that the particular behaviour will not be tolerated. A deterrent sentence would be most applicable where there is evidence that the behaviour in question seems to be prevalent in relation to numbers of barristers within the profession.

Proportionality

3.4 In deciding what sanctions (if any) to impose, the decision maker should ensure that the sanctions are proportionate, weighing the interests of the public with those of the practitioner. Proportionality is not a static concept and will vary according to the nature of the breach and the background of the individual barrister. For example, a first time breach of the Continuing Professional Development requirements would rarely, if ever, warrant a suspension or disbarment but a similar breach, having been committed many times without remorse or any attempt to remedy the situation, might warrant consideration of suspension or disbarment. Repeated breaches of relatively minor provisions of the Code may indicate a significant lack of organisation, integrity, or insight on the part of the barrister which could represent a risk to the public and undermine confidence in the profession.

3.5 In order to ensure that any sanction imposed is proportionate to the seriousness of the breach of the Code, decision makers should consider all the circumstances of the case including the following:

- the seriousness of the breach;
- whether the breach may have an impact on the general reputation of the Bar;
- whether the breach was intentional;
- whether the breach has lasting consequences;
- any aggravating or mitigating factors relevant to the conduct in question (see Annex 1);
- the personal circumstances of the individual barrister;
- the previous professional history of the barrister, in particular whether the barrister is of previous good professional standing; and
- to a limited and cautious extent, any character references or testimonials provided by the barrister (see paragraphs 7.1–7.2 below).

Section 4 – Types of breaches of the Code and powers to address breaches

Introduction

4.1 The behaviour of barristers both in their professional lives and, to a limited extent their personal lives, is governed by the Code. There are three ways in which the Code can be breached and any subsequent action by the BSB will be dependent on the nature of the breach.

4.2 The two main ways to breach the Code are:

(i) **Professional Misconduct:** According to paragraph 901.7 of the Code, failure to comply with any provision of the Code, except for those covered by paragraph 901.1 (see paragraph 4.2.ii below) is classed as "professional misconduct" for which disciplinary action can be taken.

(ii) **Paragraph 901.1:** The Code can also be breached by a barrister failing to comply with the paragraphs of the Code listed in paragraph 901.1. Failure to comply with these paragraphs does not automatically amount to professional misconduct and will initially only result in a "non-disciplinary" warning or fine being imposed by the Professional Conduct Committee. However, repeated or serious breaches of the relevant paragraphs will amount to professional misconduct. The main provisions to which paragraph 901.1 applies are failures to comply with practising requirements such as completing Continuing Professional Development ('CPD'), paying practising certificate fees and obtaining professional indemnity insurance; however, it also includes the obligations on Heads of Chambers, inappropriate media comment, rudeness and various other breaches.

Powers to address breaches of the Code

4.3 The way in which a breach of the Code will be addressed is determined by the type of breach as set out in 4.2 above. Currently, only breaches of the Code which amount to **professional misconduct** are registered on a barrister's disciplinary record and thereby are available to the public. Findings of IPS are not at present disclosed to the public but will be disclosed to the relevant authorities in the event that the barrister applies for judicial office or Queen's Counsel status. Paragraphs 4.4–4.6 and Section 5 provide details of which "bodies" have the power to impose sanctions for the various breaches of the Code.

4.4 **Administrative warnings and fines**: the Complaints Committee and Disciplinary Tribunals have the power to impose administrative warnings and fines under paragraph 901.1 of the Code. The Complaints Committee has given delegated authority to the staff of the BSB to impose warnings and fines in relation to breaches of the practising requirements (completion of CPD, payment of practising certificate fees and insurance subscriptions) and therefore these breaches can be dealt with by administrative action without the intervention of the Committee. Under paragraph 901.6 of the Code, if a barrister is given two separate administrative warnings or fines, then any further failure to comply with the relevant provisions of the Code will constitute professional misconduct.

4.5 **Professional misconduct**: the Complaints Committee has the power to determine cases of professional misconduct but only with the agreement of the barrister ("Determination by Consent"). The Complaints Committee has no power to impose a direct suspension from practice. In order for the Committee to impose a formal finding and sanction, the barrister must agree to the procedure and accept the final outcome. Otherwise, only Disciplinary Tribunals have the power to make findings of professional misconduct. A three person Disciplinary Tribunal can impose any sanction up to three months' suspension and a five person Disciplinary Tribunal can impose the full range of sanctions including disbarment (see Section 5).

Section 5 – Available sanctions

5.1 This section of the guidance sets out the various sanctions available in relation to the types of breaches outlined in Section 4. The available sanctions are based on the nature and seriousness of the breach of the Code and vary according to the type of breach. There is nothing to prevent a sentence including more than one sanction and in many cases a combination of sanctions will be appropriate (e.g. a fine, a suspension and an apology). A general overview of how to approach each sanction is provided in Section 6. Section 7 includes other important information to consider.

5.2 Administrative warnings and fines

The sanctions available under paragraph 901.1 of the Code are:

- A warning to remedy the breach identified; and
- A fine of £300[2] for any failure to remedy the breach within a specified period.

5.3 Professional misconduct

The sanctions available for professional misconduct are:

- Disbarment (only available to a five-person Disciplinary Tribunal);
- Suspension from practice (a three-person panel can only impose a suspension of up to three months; there is no limit on the period of suspension a five-person panel can impose);
- Prohibition (temporary or permanent) from accepting public access instructions;
- Exclusion from providing representation funded by the Legal Aid Agency;
- A fine of up to £15,000 (f or acts or omissions that took place on or after 31 March 2009) or up to £5,000 (f or acts or omissions that took place prior to 31 March 2009);
- Additional CPD requirements, including in specific areas of law;

- Reprimand;
- Advice as to future conduct.

5.4 Costs

Disciplinary Tribunals have the power to award costs both for and against the BSB. A Costs Order is not a sanction and therefore not covered in this guidance.

2 Subject to change from time to time by the BSB.

Section 6 – General approach to individual sanctions

6.1 This section gives guidance on the approach to take in relation to the application of individual sanctions. Decision makers should always take into account that a combination of sanctions may be appropriate in relation to a single breach of the Code. Also, it is important that the terms of any sanction are clear and therefore guidance is provided in Annex 2 as to the suggested wording to be used on findings and sentence sheets.

Disbarment (Disciplinary Tribunal only)

6.2 The sanction of disbarment is only available to five-person Disciplinary Tribunals. Disbarment is the most serious sanction that can be imposed and should be reserved for cases where the need to protect the public or the need to protect the reputation of the profession is such that the barrister should be removed from the profession. It is not possible to provide a definitive list of the circumstances in which disbarment will be appropriate as it will depend on the facts of the case and the individual background of the barrister. However, as Sir Thomas Bingham M.R. stated in *Bolton v The Law Society* [1994] 2 All ER 486: "*To maintain [the] reputation and sustain public confidence in the profession, it is often necessary that those guilty of serious lapses are not only expelled but denied readmission … the reputation of the profession is more important than the fortunes of any individual barrister.*" Therefore, disbarment may be appropriate where some or all of the following factors apply:

a) serious and/or persistent departures from professional standards or practising requirements;

b) serious harm has been caused to either the administration of justice, the reputation of the Bar or the individual complainant and there is a continuing risk to the public or the reputation of the profession if the barrister is permitted to continue in practice;

c) the barrister has committed a serious criminal offence involving dishonesty, violence or sexual offences;

d) the barrister has acted dishonestly regardless of whether it was in connection with a criminal offence (see 6.3 below)

e) the barrister has shown a persistent lack of insight into the seriousness of his/her actions or the consequences for his/her practice, the administration of justice or the reputation of the Bar.

6.3 **Dishonesty:** any dishonesty on the part of a member of the Bar, in whatever circumstances it may occur, is a matter of great seriousness. It damages the reputation of the profession as a whole, quite apart from its effect on the reputation of the individual barrister. Dishonesty is incompatible with membership of the Bar given the duties placed on barristers to safeguard the interests of their clients and their overriding duty to the law, justice and the courts.

Public interest requires, and the general public expects, that members of the Bar are completely honest and are of the highest integrity. Therefore, in cases where a barrister has proved to be dishonest, even where no criminal offence has been committed, disbarment will almost always have to be considered (see section 7 – Acts of dishonesty). For guidance on dealing with situations where the barrister has been, or may have been, dishonest during the course of proceedings, see paragraph 7.5.

Suspension from practice (Disciplinary Tribunal only)

6.4 This sanction is only available to Disciplinary Tribunals. Suspension from practice is a serious matter and should be reserved for cases where the barrister represents a risk to a public which requires that he/she be unable to practise for a period of time and/or the behaviour is so serious as to undermine public confidence in the profession and therefore a signal needs to be sent to the barrister, the profession and the public that the behaviour in question is unacceptable. Relevant factors to take into account include, but are not limited to:

a) risk to the public;

b) there has been a serious departure from the professional standards expected of a barrister;

c) abuse of position or abuse of trust;

d) the barrister has shown a lack of insight into and understanding of his/her actions and their consequences;

e) the barrister has shown a lack of integrity that is not so serious as to warrant disbarment; and

f) the behaviour is likely to be repeated or has been repeated since the initial incident.

6.5 **Period of suspension:** it is usual to impose a suspension for a specified period of time. The Disciplinary Tribunal Regulations do not stipulate an upper limit to the period of suspension a five person panel can impose. However, very long periods of suspension are tantamount to disbarment and therefore where a suspension of more than three years is considered appropriate, the Disciplinary Tribunal should give serious consideration to disbarring the barrister unless the circumstances are exceptional. The Visitors to the Inns of Court stated in the case of *Durand* (1961) that *"three years … must … be the maximum sentence of suspension which in practice can properly be given"*. Any period of suspension will inevitably have a serious negative impact on the barrister's level of knowledge and up to date experience. Therefore, the longer the period of suspension the more difficult it will be for the barrister to return to practice as an effective advocate. If exceptionally a period of suspension longer than three years is considered appropriate, it should be combined with conditions regarding retraining such as to ensure that before the barrister returns to practice appropriate refresher training has been undertaken.

6.6 **Suspension subject to conditions**: while a specific period of suspension is the norm it is also acceptable to make the period of suspension dependent on the occurrence of a specified event or completion of a specified activity. For example, a barrister could be suspended pending completion of a specified training course or other similar activity. In these circumstances, the suspension would cease when acceptable evidence is provided to the BSB of the relevant activity being completed. The Tribunal should ensure that the terms of any order of suspension from practice are clear particularly where conditions on the suspension are imposed. Barristers should be in no doubt about what actions they need to take to bring a suspension to an end and what evidence they need to present to allow the suspension to be lifted.

Prohibition from accepting public access instructions (Disciplinary Tribunal or adjudication Panel)

6.7 This sanction is only available to Disciplinary Tribunals. It is generally applicable in cases where the barrister was acting under formal Public Access instructions; however, there may be circumstances where a barrister's treatment of a client, even when instructed by a solicitor, indicates that the barrister should not be allowed to accept Public Access instructions. It is a requirement that any barrister providing this type of access must have completed a Public Access training course and must also provide the client, in advance, with prescribed information about the terms and extent of the work that can be carried out. Clients who instruct barristers by this means are exposed to greater risk than those who use a solicitor and therefore panels need to look carefully at whether the barrister's behaviour represents a risk to the public which requires some level of restriction on his/her ability to continue accepting Public Access instructions.

6.8 In general, such a sanction would be appropriate where the barrister's behaviour directly relates to, or arises from, the circumstances of the public access instructions. For example, the barrister has either failed completely, or in part, to comply with the prescribed terms for Public Access or has in some way exploited the Public Access relationship to the detriment of the client. In particular, panels should take into account the manner in which the barrister has handled the issue of fees including both the way in which the fee level has been set and the arrangements for payment. A time-limited prohibition would be appropriate where the barrister's behaviour indicates a level of risk that could be addressed via a period of contemplation and a review of his/her practices which would mitigate the potential risk to clients (this may apply to situations where the barrister has failed during the proceedings to recognise the seriousness of the effect of his or her conduct). A permanent prohibition would be appropriate where there is evidence that the barrister has intentionally exploited the relationship, has persistently provided a poor service to clients, has charged unreasonable rates, or has taken on instructions with no chance of success.

Fines (Disciplinary Tribunal or Complaints Committee)

6.9 The imposition of a fine is a sanction that can easily be combined with other sanctions and decision makers should always consider whether this would be appropriate. The maximum limit of a fine is £15,000 but fines at the upper end of the scale should be reserved for serious breaches of the Code where the barrister does not represent an ongoing risk to the public but appears to have profited substantially from the breach. Fines, on the whole, are a "deterrent" sanction and their main purpose is to mark the severity of the breach and prevent its reoccurrence.

6.10 **The means of the barrister:** when considering whether to impose a fine, the financial means of the barrister should not be the determining factor. If a fine is considered appropriate in the light of the seriousness of the breach, then it should be imposed regardless of the barrister's means. Therefore, the decision maker should first decide if a fine is the appropriate sanction, then consider the appropriate level of fine based on the breach, and finally look at adjusting the fine level in order to take into account a barrister's financial situation. A fine should not be increased merely because a barrister can afford it but it is reasonable to reduce the level of fine to take into account the barrister's financial circumstances or increase it where there is evidence that indicates that the barrister has profited from the breach.

6.11 **Time to pay and instalments:** When a decision maker orders that a fine should be paid, the sum will technically become due for payment immediately after the appeal period has expired or, in the case of Determination by Consent, when the finding is accepted by the barrister. It is, however, good practice for decision makers to specify when the fine is due in their decision (see paragraph A2.8 for wording of the sentence).

6.12 Decision makers should bear in mind that it is open to a barrister to negotiate a payment plan with the BSB following a Tribunal. In most cases, the issue of payment by instalments is better left to the BSB to negotiate with the barrister after the hearing as the BSB will be able to make more detailed enquiries regarding the barrister's financial situation and will have time to negotiate a mutually acceptable plan. Where decision makers consider that it is appropriate to order an instalment plan they should take into account the cost to the BSB of administering the plan. It is helpful to limit any instalment plan to a maximum period of eight months because small instalments over a lengthy period of time can be expensive to administer and involve costs to the profession far in excess of the original fine. Additionally, lengthy instalment plans can lead to substantial delay in it becoming apparent that action needs to be taken for non-compliance.

Additional CPD requirements (*Disciplinary Tribunal, Adjudication Panel or Complaints Committee*)

6.13 The purpose of ordering that a barrister complete additional Continuing Professional Development (CPD) hours is to ensure that barristers are sufficiently trained and knowledgeable in areas where the breach of the Code may demonstrate that they are lacking in the required expertise. It is a rehabilitative sanction and can often be appropriately combined with other sanctions. Decision makers should avoid making a general order to complete further hours but instead specify the area or subject matter in which additional training is required. Further, the order should stipulate a specific date by which the hours should be completed and the completion reported to the BSB. Additional CPD hours should not be imposed solely as a punishment but should serve a useful purpose that will help to prevent the breach of the Code being repeated in the future.

6.14 Where a barrister has failed to complete the required number of CPD hours for a particular year or years, then it is important that the decision maker orders that the outstanding hours be completed within a specified period. It may also be appropriate to order that failure to complete the outstanding hours within the specified period will result in an automatic suspension from practice for a specified period.

Reprimands (*Disciplinary Tribunal or Complaints Committee*)

6.15 A reprimand is appropriate in cases where the breach of the Code is minor and there is no continuing risk to the public but the decision maker wishes to indicate formally that the behaviour is unacceptable and should not occur again. A reprimand is a "backwards looking" sanction and represents censure of previous behaviour. It is therefore appropriate where the behaviour is unlikely to be repeated in the future. The sanction should include an order as to how the reprimand should be made. In most cases, it will be made at the Tribunal and probably form part of the general sentencing decision. However, Tribunals may consider that it is appropriate to order that the reprimand be made in the form of a written document. Reprimands can be given by the decision maker at the hearing or in the report, or by ordering the barrister to attend on a nominated person to be reprimanded. Relevant positive factors that would indicate whether a reprimand is appropriate include, but are not limited to, the following:

a) no evidence of loss to the complainant

b) appreciation and understanding on behalf of the barrister of the failings;

c) the behaviour was isolated and not intentional;

d) genuine expressions of regret/remorse; and

e) previous good history.

Advice as to future conduct (Disciplinary Tribunal or Complaints Committee)

6.16 Advice as to future conduct will be appropriate in cases where the breach is minor and has not had any lasting consequences for the complainant but the decision maker considers it would be helpful if the barrister is given some guidance as to how to behave in the future. Advice is a "forward looking" sanction which should be used where it is thought that the barrister needs to change his/her behaviour. Advice as to future conduct would be particularly appropriate where a barrister appears to have a lack of appreciation or understanding of the nature of the breach and the reasons why disciplinary action was considered necessary. The advice can be given by the decision maker at the hearing or in the report, or by ordering the barrister to attend on a nominated person to be given advice. Such sanctions are particularly appropriate where the barrister is inexperienced in the profession and could benefit from guidance rather than censure.

No further action (Disciplinary Tribunal, Adjudication Panel, or Complaints Committee)

6.17 The option to take no further action in cases where a breach of the Code has been proved is open to all decision makers. It is only appropriate where the barrister's behaviour presents no risk to the public and there are no ongoing or lasting effects in relation to the behaviour. Taking no further action would be appropriate in cases where the barrister has fully acknowledged the breach; the effects of bringing disciplinary act ion have already had a significant impact on the barrister's reputation or practice and where no purpose would be served by ordering other sanctions.

Section 7 – Other important issues to consider

Character evidence

7.1 Barristers are entitled, as part of their mitigation, to put forward character references/witnesses to support their submissions. However, while such evidence can be relevant to the sanctions imposed, it should be treated with caution and panels should be wary of becoming distracted from the main issues by an abundance of character evidence. The fact that a barrister was previously of "good character" and has a good reputation, can only go so far in mitigating his/her behaviour and the more serious the breach of the Code, the less weight should be attached to character evidence. The emphasis should be on the nature of the breach of the Code and the circumstances in which the breach occurred.

7.2 If the character evidence indicates that the person providing it knows the barrister well and has a clear basis for assessing that the behaviour in question was a genuine anomaly/one-off then some weight should be given to it. However, if the character evidence indicates that the person supplying it can only have limited direct knowledge of the barrister, then it should be treated with caution and it may be that little or no weight can be given to it. The general approach should be that character evidence is treated with caution and should not unduly affect the sanctions imposed: a person of good character and impeccable reputation can still commit breaches of the Code that are serious and warrant the same sanctions as any other barrister.

Fitness to practise

7.3 In the Bar's complaints and disciplinary system, the term "fitness to practise" is only used when considering whether a barrister is suffering from a physical or mental condition (including addiction) that may affect the barrister's ability to practise. The Fitness to Practise Rules are contained at Annex O to the Code of Conduct. Fitness to Practise proceedings are not disciplinary in nature and are run entirely separately from any disciplinary proceedings. The primary purpose is to ensure the protection of the public by considering whether a barrister is medically fit to practise and if not, imposing any necessary restrictions.

7.4 Some complaints may give rise to concern about a barrister's fitness to practise as a result of material submitted as part of the barrister's defence and/or mitigation or as a result of their behaviour during the proceedings. This will often include information relating to, or indicating, an ongoing or recurring addiction or mental health problem. If a decision maker has information before it that gives rise to concern about a barrister's fitness to practise, it should:

a. Proceed with making a decision on the case before it based on all the facts and evidence;

b. State in the decision sheet (along with the decision on the case) that there is concern about the barrister's fitness to practise and give reasons for such concern (including reference to relevant documents); and

c. Formally refer their concerns to the Complaints Commissioner of the BSB, who will consider the evidence and, if necessary, invoke the relevant procedure under the Fitness to Practise Rules.

Dishonesty during the course of disciplinary proceedings

7.5 Where the barrister is not facing a specific charge alleging dishonest conduct, but the panel nonetheless decides that he/she has engaged in dishonest behaviour during the course of the disciplinary proceedings, the panel may refer the matter to the Complaints Committee of the BSB to consider raising a fresh complaint. The panel should ensure that it fully particularises any concerns it has so that the Complaints Committee can properly consider whether or not it wishes to take further action and raise a fresh complaint. The panel must sentence the barrister only in relation to the charges currently before it; however, it should ensure that it details the circumstances and basis of any concerns of dishonest behaviour by the barrister as this will be relied upon in any future disciplinary proceedings.

Multiple charges

7.6 When dealing with multiple charges, it is tempting to impose one sentence for the most serious charge and then impose no separate sanction for the more minor charges. However, this can cause problems if the barrister decides to appeal the decision because, if a decision is taken on appeal to overturn the finding or sentence on the most serious charge but not any of the other charges, it can be difficult to establish what sanction should apply to those charges that remain or determine how seriously the original Tribunal viewed each of the remaining charges. To avoid this situation, it is helpful to impose a separate sentence for each charge.

Concurrent and consecutive suspensions

7.7 Where there are multiple proved charges that warrant a period of suspension on each charge, the decision maker will have to decide whether the suspensions on each charge should run concurrently or consecutively: imposing a concurrent sentence means that the suspensions will run alongside each other, whereas imposing a consecutive sentence means that the suspensions will run after each other. Decision makers should be cautious about imposing consecutive suspensions unless they are sure that the totality of the consecutive suspensions is warranted based on the cumulative seriousness of the charges.

Deferred sentences

7.8 The Complaints Committee and Disciplinary Tribunals have the power to defer sentences. This means that a sanction can be imposed but be subject to deferred implementation based on whether a further breach of the Code occurs within a stipulated period. The stipulated period should be between six months and two years. Further breaches of the Code within the stipulated period will leave the barrister open to activation of the original deferred sentence as well as sanctions for the new breach.

7.9 A deferred sentence can only be imposed where the sanction is a fine or a suspension. Therefore, it is appropriate in circumstances where the behaviour is relatively serious (and therefore warrants a fine or suspension), the behaviour is unlikely to be repeated and there is no immediate need to protect the public, but the barrister needs to be encouraged to change the way in which he/she behaves. Lengthy periods of suspended sanctions should be reserved for cases where the barrister may need to have a control mechanism in place to temper his/her behaviour.

Suspension of practising certificate pending appeal

7.10 The Disciplinary Tribunal Regulations give Disciplinary Tribunals the power to order that the BSB suspend a barrister's practising certificate pending the outcome of an appeal where the sanction imposed is one of more than one year's suspension or disbarment. This power is different from imposing a sanction of suspension or disbarment in that suspension of a practising certificate only affects the barrister's ability to provide legal services as a barrister. Only the Inns of Court have the ability to suspend barristers formally or disbar them and in doing so also remove other privileges attached to call to the Bar including membership and use of the Inn's facilities

7.11 The need for a provision that allows the BSB to suspend the right to have a practising certificate arises because sanctions imposed by Tribunals will not be implemented until after the outcome of any appeal is known. Clearly where a Tribunal considers that the barrister represents an immediate risk to the public which warrants a lengthy suspension or disbarment, it would be wrong to allow the barrister to continue practising merely because an appeal has been submitted. The Regulations stipulate that a Tribunal should order that the barrister's practising certificate be suspended pending appeal unless there is good reason not do so.

Reporting the barrister's unsuitability as a pupil supervisor

7.12 In any case where a barrister is a pupil supervisor and the breach of the Code indicates that the barrister may no longer be suitable to continue in that role, the decision maker should order that a report be made to the barrister's Inn so that consideration can be given to removing the barrister from the list of pupil supervisors. Decision makers do not have the power to order that a barrister's status as a pupil supervisor be removed: this is a matter solely for the Inns of Court but it is important that a report is made to the relevant Inn where the circumstances warrant it.

Part II – Guidance on common breaches of the Code

1. This section provides guidance in relation to the starting points for sanctions in respect of the most common breaches of the Code. Sections A to J provide information related to charges of professional misconduct and Section K relates to Inadequate Professional Service. The guidance is not intended to represent a tariff for the breaches and decision makers must decide each case on its own facts. The suggested sanctions do not necessarily represent the "going rate" and the guidance merely indicates where a decision maker might start before considering all the relevant factors.

2. It is important that consistency and proportionality in sentencing are maintained and therefore where a decision maker imposes a lesser or higher sanction than suggested by this guidance, it is important that full reasons are given as to why the sanction is considered appropriate. This will not only give the barrister and the complainant a clear indication of the reasons for a lenient or harsh sentence but will provide justification for the decision should the case go to appeal. It is particularly important for decision makers to give full written reasons for the sentencing should they impose a deferred sanction, as the decision to activate the sanction will be taken by a different body and that body will require detailed reasons in order to make a fair decision.

3. In assessing the appropriate sanction for a breach of the Code, decision makers must consider any aggravating or mitigating factors that may cause the sanction to be increased or decreased. Details of aggravating and mitigating factors applicable to all breaches are set out in Appendix 1. In addition to this, the individual tables relating to common breaches provide examples of aggravating and mitigating factors applicable to each breach. The factors listed are examples and the lists are not intended to be exhaustive.

4. It must be made clear that the guidance in relation to the common breaches is not intended to detract from decision maker's complete discretion to impose any sanction which is appropriate to an individual case: the final decision is a matter for decision maker's alone.

5. In relation to fines and suspensions, rather than including specific amounts, the following table shows three bands for fines and suspensions which are referred to in the rest of Part II. The ranges represent the following:

Fines	**Suspensions**
Low level = up to £1,000	Short = up to 3 months
Medium level = over £1,000 and up to £3,000	Medium = over 3 months and up to 6 months
High level = over £3,000 and up to £15,000	Long = over 6 months and up to three years

Section A – Criminal Convictions

A.1 Conviction for drink driving and related offences

<table>
<tr><th colspan="2">Description</th></tr>
<tr><td colspan="2">A criminal conviction for drink driving is normally charged under paragraph 301(a)(iii) (conduct which brings the legal profession into disrepute); however, depending on the nature of the circumstances, it may also be charged under paragraph 301(a)(i) (engaging in conduct discreditable to a barrister). It may also be accompanied by a separate charge for any other related convictions, such as dangerous driving.
It may also be accompanied by a separate charge for any other related convictions, such as dangerous driving.

The sanction that is imposed should relate to the breach of the Code of Conduct for a barrister having been convicted of a criminal offence. It is not intended to be a second form of punishment, or "double jeopardy", for the actual criminal offence.

Range of sanctions: The starting point for a first time conviction for drink driving should normally be a reprimand and a low level fine. Where a conviction results in a custodial sentence, the general starting point should be disbarment unless there are clear mitigating factors that indicate that such a sanction is not warranted.

Listed below are common circumstances in which breaches might occur set out according to severity.</td></tr>
<tr><th>Common circumstances</th><th>Sanction starting point</th></tr>
<tr><td>a. A first time conviction for drink driving only
b. A conviction for drink driving that involves an element of dangerous driving
c. A conviction for drink driving that is accompanied by further related convictions (e.g. leaving the scene, driving whilst disqualified)</td><td>a. A reprimand and a low level fine
b. A medium level fine and/or a short suspension
c. A short to medium suspension</td></tr>
<tr><th>Aggravating factors</th><th>Mitigating factors</th></tr>
<tr><td>• Injury to persons
• High alcohol level
• Lack of cooperation with the police</td><td>• Compelling emergency situation</td></tr>
<tr><td colspan="2">The aggravating and mitigating factors listed above should be considered in addition to the factors listed at Annex 1.</td></tr>
</table>

A.2 Conviction for assault and violent acts

Description	
A criminal conviction for violence is normally charged under paragraph 301(a)(iii) (conduct which brings the legal profession into disrepute); however, depending on the nature of the circumstances, it may also be charged under paragraph 301(a)(i) (engaging in conduct discreditable to a barrister). The guidance below is also applicable to charges relating to domestic violence, which should not be treated any less seriously than other forms of violence. The sanction that is imposed should relate to the breach of the Code of Conduct for a barrister having been convicted of a criminal offence. It is not intended to be a second form of punishment, or "double jeopardy", for the actual criminal offence. **Range of sanctions:** The starting point for a conviction of minor assault should normally be a reprimand and a medium level fine, which may increase to a short suspension. Where a conviction results in a custodial sentence, the general starting point should be disbarment unless there are clear mitigating factors that indicate that such a sanction is not warranted. Listed below are common circumstances in which breaches might occur set out according to severity.	
Common circumstances	**Sanction starting point**
a. A conviction for low level assault	a. Reprimand and medium level fine to a short suspension
b. A conviction for an act of violence causing injury	b. A medium level suspension
c. A conviction for an act of serious violence	c. Disbarment (or in exceptional circumstances, a long suspension)
Aggravating factors	**Mitigating factors**
• Previous criminal convictions • Lack of cooperation with the police • Use of a weapon • Victim was particularly vulnerable • Intent to cause harm • Discriminatory motivation • Serious injury to the victim	• Isolated incident in difficult and unusual circumstances • Element of self protection or protection of others/property
The aggravating and mitigating factors listed above should be considered in addition to the factors listed at Annex 1.	

A.3 Conviction for drug possession or supply

Description	
A criminal conviction for drug possession or supply is normally charged under paragraph 301(a)(iii) (conduct which brings the legal profession into disrepute); however, depending on the nature of the circumstances, it may be charged under paragraph 301(a)(i) (engaging in conduct discreditable to a barrister). The sanction that is imposed should represent the offence under the Code of Conduct for a barrister having been convicted of a criminal offence. It is not intended to be a second form of punishment, or "double jeopardy", for the actual criminal offence. **Range of sanctions:** The starting point for a conviction of drug possession (normally tried in the Magistrates' Court) should be a reprimand and a medium level fine. A period of suspension or disbarment would be appropriate where there is has been intentional supply for profit. Where a conviction results in a custodial sentence, the general starting point should be disbarment unless there are clear mitigating factors that indicate that such a sanction is not warranted. Listed below are common circumstances in which breaches might occur set out according to severity.	
Common circumstances	**Sanction starting point**
a. A conviction for drug possession (any class) b. A conviction for supply or intent to supply (any class)	a. A reprimand and a medium level fine b. Disbarment
Aggravating factors	**Mitigating factors**
• Previous criminal convictions • Lack of cooperation with the police • Medium/large scale operation	• No intention to gain financially
The aggravating and mitigating factors listed above should be considered in addition to the factors listed at Annex 1.	

A.4 Failure to report a criminal charge or conviction promptly

Description
Barristers are required to report nearly all criminal convictions and also the fact that charges have been preferred in relation to a range of criminal offences. Failure to report a criminal charge or conviction is charged under paragraph 905(b) of the Code. Failure to report a criminal conviction will usually be accompanied by a disciplinary charge relating to the specific conviction. Although there may be multiple charges, a separate sanction should be imposed for each.

Range of sanctions: The starting point for failure to report a criminal charge or conviction promptly should be a low level fine. Given the nature of the offence, the range of appropriate sanctions is limited and it is unlikely that more than a medium level fine will be appropriate. However, the sanctions for the criminal conviction itself are likely to more severe (see A.1 – A.3).

Listed below are common circumstances in which breaches might occur set out according to severity.

Common circumstances	Sanction starting point
a. Failure to report promptly being charged with a relevant criminal offence	a. A low level fine
b. Failure to report promptly a relevant criminal conviction	b. A low to medium level fine
Aggravating factors	**Mitigating factors**
• Substantial delay in reporting the conviction • Attempts to conceal conviction and/or relevant facts or details relating to the conviction	• genuine and understandable ignorance of the duty to report

The aggravating and mitigating factors listed above should be considered in addition to the factors listed at Annex 1.

Section B – Acts of dishonesty

Description

Please see paragraphs 6.3 above regarding the general approach to be taken towards dishonesty within the profession.

There are a number of different types of breaches of the Code that involve dishonesty and different charges that may be brought in relation to each. In general such breaches will be charged under paragraph 301(a)(i) of the Code because they involve either direct allegations of dishonesty or allegations of otherwise bringing the Bar into disrepute.

Dishonesty can amount to criminal dishonesty (even though no criminal charges may have been brought – see also criminal convictions) or personal or professional dishonesty that not does not amount to a crime.

Some examples of dishonest behaviour that form the basis for charges of processional misconduct include:

- Making a false declaration on Call
- Inflating marks or experience on an application form
- Falsification of documents
- Certain types of criminal convictions, such as theft, perjury, or fraud
- Deliberate misuse of client money
- Dishonesty in connection with disciplinary proceedings (see paragraph 7.5)

Range of sanctions: Dishonesty is not compatible with practice in a profession which requires exceptional levels of integrity. The general starting point should be disbarment unless there are clear mitigating factors that indicate that such a sanction is not warranted. Therefore no common circumstances are listed below but instead the emphasis should be on the potential mitigating factors that might reduce the sanction from disbarment.	
Common circumstances	**Starting Point**
	a Disbarment
Aggravating factors	**Mitigating factors**
	• Clear evidence that behaviour was out of character and the consequences were not intended (to be treated with caution- see 7.1 & 7.2 of this guidance) • Behaviour limited to personal life and no evidence of dishonesty in professional life (to be treated with caution- see 7.1 & 7.2 of this guidance)
The aggravating and mitigating factors listed above should be considered in addition to the factors listed at Annex 1.	

Section C – Conduct during proceedings and in court

C.1 Making submissions that are not properly arguable or making allegations of fraud not supported by evidence

Description	
Barristers have a duty to ensure they do not make submissions, or draft documents, that are not properly arguable or supported by evidence. In particular, allegations of fraud should be supported by evidence regardless of the client's instructions. These types of breaches are normally charged under paragraph 704 or 708 of the Code. **Range of sanctions:** As the circumstances surrounding these breaches can vary widely, the appropriate sanction may range from giving advice to disbarment. One key factor to take into account in determining the level of sanction is whether the breach was committed intentionally. Protection of the public is particularly relevant in relation to allegations of fraud, as such allegations are usually made against an individual and therefore may impact on the credibility and reputation of that person. Listed below are common circumstances in which breaches might occur set out according to severity.	
Common circumstances	**Sanction starting point**
a. Recklessly making unsupported submissions	a. Reprimand and/or advice as to future conduct

b. Recklessly making allegations of fraud c. Making intentional unsupported submissions or allegations of fraud	b. Medium level fine to short suspension c. Medium suspension to disbarment
Aggravating factors	**Mitigating factors**
• Personal or professional advantage gained (financial or otherwise) • Negative impact on the complainant, client or other party • Dishonest motive	• Immediate apology • Remedial action taken at an early point
NB – Acting on a client's instructions should not be considered as a mitigating factor, as this runs contrary to a barrister's overriding duty to the Court.	
The aggravating and mitigating factors listed above should be considered in addition to the factors listed at Annex 1.	

C.2 Misleading the Court

Description	
Barristers are under a duty not to mislead the Court and doing so is usually considered to be a serious breach of the Code. The breach is normally charged under paragraph 302 of the Code of Conduct. **Range of sanctions:** As the circumstances surrounding this offence can vary widely, the appropriate sanction may range from giving advice to disbarment. One key element that could warrant more serious sanctions for this breach is whether or not the breach was committed intentionally. Listed below are common circumstances in which breaches might occur set out according to severity.	
Common circumstances	**Sanction starting point**
a. Recklessly misleading the Court b. Knowingly misleading the Court	a. Reprimand and/or advice as to future conduct b. A short suspension to disbarment
Aggravating factors	**Mitigating factors**
• Personal or professional advantage gained (financial or otherwise) • Negative impact on the complainant, client or other party • Actions of the barrister adversely affected the course of the proceedings.	• Immediate apology • Remedial action taken at an early point
NB – Acting on a client's instructions should not be considered as a mitigating factor as this runs contrary to a barrister's overriding duty to the Court.	

The aggravating and mitigating factors listed above should be considered in addition to the factors listed at Annex 1.

Section D – Acceptance and return of instructions

D.1 Acting without a professional client

Description	
A barrister may only supply legal services to a client if he/she is instructed by a professional client (normally a solicitor) or the barrister is acting under Licensed or Public Access. The rules prohibiting acting directly for a client are designed to protect the public and accepting instructions without a professional client can put the public at risk. Breaches are normally charged under paragraph 401(a) of the Code. **Range of sanctions:** The starting point should normally be a reprimand and/or a medium level fine. The main factors in determining the sanction will be the risk posed to the client, whether the breach involved a level of exploitation of the client and/or whether the behaviour was motivated by financial gain. Listed below are common circumstances in which breaches might occur set out according to severity.	
Circumstances	**Starting point**
a. Acting without a professional client (not financially motivated)	a. Reprimand and/or advice as to future conduct
b. Acting without a professional client (financially motivated)	b. Medium level fine to a short suspension
c. Acting without a professional client over a prolonged period of time	c. Short to medium suspension
Aggravating factors	**Mitigating factors**
• Negative impact on the client • Particularly vulnerable client	• Limited level of legal services provided • Remedial action taken at an early point
The aggravating and mitigating factors listed above should be considered in addition to the factors listed at Annex 1.	

D.2 Breach of cab-rank rule

Description
A barrister must not withhold services on the basis of the nature of the case, the client's opinions or beliefs or on the basis of the source of the financial support. These requirements are known collectively as the "cab-rank rule". Breaches of these obligations are normally charged under paragraphs 601 and 602 of the Code.

Range of sanctions: The starting point should normally be a reprimand and/or a medium level fine.

Listed below are common circumstances in which breaches might occur set out according to severity.

Circumstances	Starting point
a. Breach of cab-rank rule (financial motive) b. Breach of cab-rank rule (discriminatory motive)	a. Reprimand and medium level fine b. Reprimand and short suspension
Aggravating factors	**Mitigating factors**
• Actions of the barrister adversely affected the course of the proceedings	• Immediate apology

The aggravating and mitigating factors listed above should be considered in addition to the factors listed at Annex 1.

D.3 Accepting instructions when professionally embarrassed

Description

There are a range of circumstances in which a barrister may be professionally embarrassed. These include (but are not limited to) accepting instructions when the barrister is likely to be a witness or his/her connection to the case will make it difficult to maintain independence, when there is a potential conflict of interest and when there is a significant risk of confidential information being communicated. Breaches are normally charged under paragraph 603 of the Code of Conduct.

Range of sanctions: The sanctions should normally be a reprimand and/or a medium to high level fine. More serious sanctions should be imposed where the breach has had a significant impact on the client or the progress of the proceedings.

Listed below are common circumstances in which breaches might occur set out according to severity.

Circumstances	Starting point
a. Accepting instructions when professionally embarrassed (inadvertently) b. Accepting instructions when professionally embarrassed (intentionally)	a. Reprimand and/or advice as to future conduct and refund/forego fees to client b. Reprimand, medium to high level fine and refund/forego fees to client
Aggravating factors	**Mitigating factors**
• Actions of the barrister adversely affected the course of the proceedings • Financial motivation	• Immediate apology • Remedial action taken at an early point

The aggravating and mitigating factors listed above should be considered in addition to the factors listed at Annex 1.

D.4 Late withdrawal

Description	
A late withdrawal from a case is normally charged under paragraph 610(d) of the Code. **Range of sanctions:** The starting point should normally be a reprimand and/or a medium to high level fine. Listed below are common circumstances in which breaches might occur set out according to severity.	
Circumstances	**Starting point**
a. Late withdrawal (not financially motivated)	a. Reprimand and/or advice as to future conduct and refund/forego fees to client
b. Late withdrawal (financially motivated)	b. Reprimand, medium to high level fine and refund/forego fees to client
Aggravating factors	**Mitigating factors**
• Actions of the barrister adversely affected the course of the proceedings • Lateness/complexity of case prevents client from finding suitable alternative representation	• Immediate apology • Positive steps taken to find/assist an alternative barrister.
The aggravating and mitigating factors listed above should be considered in addition to the factors listed at Annex 1.	

Section E – Management of professional practice/obligations

E.1 Holding out

Description
"Holding out" is the short hand term to describe a barrister who is not entitled to practise presenting him/herself to others in a way that would lead people to believe that he/she is entitled to practise and offer legal services as a barrister. The breach is normally charged under paragraph 202 of the Code on the basis that the barrister will not have complied with the stipulated requirements for practise. Holding out can occur in a variety of circumstances. At one end will be cases where a barrister has provided a misleading description of his/her status on a business card or letter head. At the other end will be cases where the barrister has deliberately stated that he is entitled to practise and has provided legal services for financial gain when he/she is not entitled to do so.

Range of sanctions: This breach is one that could be subject to an administrative warning or fine: therefore any cases which reach a Tribunal will have been considered by the Complaints Committee as unsuitable for such a disposal. The starting point should be a reprimand or advice as to future conduct with fines being more appropriate where the behaviour is deliberate/financially motivated.

Listed below are common circumstances in which breaches might occur set out according to severity.

Common circumstances	Starting Point
a. Using misleading description of status on a business card/letter head	a. Reprimand/advice as to future conduct
b. Inappropriate use of title as a marketing device	b. Reprimand/advice as to future conduct and low level fine
c. Providing legal services for financial gain in circumstances where the client is misled into believing the barrister is entitled to practise.	c. Medium level fine to suspension dependent on the extent of the financial gain (disbarment could be considered where there is a clear risk to the public and the barrister may be likely to persist in the behaviour)

Aggravating factors	Mitigating factors
• Failure to pay administrative fine on time or at all • Providing legal services in return for payment • Persistent pattern of behaviour • Motivation is financial gain • Using status of barrister to threaten or exploit • Failure to take remedial action when asked to do so by the BSB	• No direct impact on members of the public • Breach was inadvertent and unintentional

The aggravating and mitigating factors listed above should be considered in addition to the factors listed at Annex 1.

E.2 Breach of practising requirements

Description

The requirements a barrister must meet to practise as a self-employed barrister are set out in Part II of the Code, Practising Requirements. The requirements include completion of Continuing Professional Development (CPD), payment of practising fees and obtaining insurance cover.

In 2005, a system of administrative warnings and fines was introduced which allows a warning or fine to be imposed by the Complaints Committee for breaches of the practising requirements. Such actions do not result in a disciplinary finding and do not form part of the barrister's disciplinary record.

Therefore any breaches of the practising requirements which reach a Tribunal are likely to have previously been subject to the warnings and fines system or will have been considered by the Committee as unsuitable for such a disposal (usually because the barrister has repeatedly breached the requirements in the past). Therefore panels should bear in mind that the cases that come before them will often be persistent or recalcitrant defaulters who will have received repeated warnings as to the potential consequences of their continued default.

An exception will be cases where a barrister has failed to obtain a practising certificate via the Bar Council's authorisation to practise procedure. The PCC considers that it would normally be inappropriate to deal with such failures by means of an administrative warning or fine given that the Legal Services Act 2007, section 14 has made it a criminal offence for a barrister to carry out a reserved legal activity, such as exercising a right of audience, unless they are authorised to do so.
Often panels will be faced with a charge sheet which includes up to three charges for: failing to pay the administrative fine, failing to meet the relevant requirement and failure to respond.

Panels should treat any of the above failures seriously given that the barrister will have had a number of previous opportunities to rectify his/her non-compliance and considerable resources will have been expended in trying to make the barrister meet his/her obligations. Each breach should be sentenced separately.

Range of sanctions: the starting point for each charge should be a low level fine towards the top end. Therefore in cases where three charges are included on the charge sheet, the total fine could amount to £3,000. The starting point for persistent offenders should be a short conditional suspension – the condition being the barrister should meet the practising requirement by a specified date. Immediate suspensions should be considered where the barrister has previously been subject to a conditional suspension of a similar offence.

Listed below are common circumstances in which breaches might occur set out according to severity.

Common circumstances	**Starting Point**
a. Failing to meet practising requirements in due time (compliance achieved late)	a. Low level fine with starting point of £600
b. Failing to meet practising requirements (compliance still outstanding)	b. Low to medium level fine with starting point of £900 and an order to comply with outstanding requirements by a specified date
c. Failure to pay an administrative fine	c. Low to medium level fine with starting point of £900
d. Repeated failures to meet practising requirements (but no previous disciplinary history of this)	d. Short suspension (usually conditional)

e. Previous disciplinary history of failing to meet practising requirements (including previous suspension)	e. Medium to long suspension conditional on requirements being met
Aggravating factors	**Mitigating factors**
• Previous disciplinary findings for failing to meet practising requirements • Failure to attend a Disciplinary Tribunal without explanation	• Attempts to comply and/or • previous responses to BSB enquiries • Attempts to prevent recurrence Financial hardship causing inability to pay
The aggravating and mitigating factors listed above should be considered in addition to the factors listed at Annex 1.	

E.3 Poor administration of practice/chambers

Description	
All self-employed barristers have an obligation to ensure that their practices are efficiently and properly administered and they can be held personally responsible for any failures to do so. However, Heads of Chambers also have a general responsibility for ensuring the efficient and proper administration of chambers. Breaches of these obligations are charged under paragraph 403 and 404 respectively. **Range of sanctions**: In most cases advice as to future conduct will normally be appropriate. Fines in the low to medium range would be appropriate where there is financial gain or the problems are systemic within a practice/chambers. Fines for Heads of Chambers would not normally be appropriate given the collective nature of chambers but could be appropriate for sole practitioners. Listed below are common circumstances in which breaches might occur set out according to severity.	
Common circumstances	**Starting Point**
a. Failure to return papers/keep proper records of cases/fees	a. Advice as to future conduct
b. Systemic failures to manage a wide-range of areas of practice/chambers in order to save money or increase income	b. Reprimand and a low to medium fine (dependent on potential financial gain)
Aggravating factors	**Mitigating factors**
• Financial gain • Persistent or wide ranging failures in administration • Adverse impact on other members of chambers	• One off/limited duration due to break down in technical support or staff mistakes • Problems in staffing outside the control of an individual barrister • Remedial action taken at an early point
The aggravating and mitigating factors listed above should be considered in addition to the factors listed at Annex 1.	

E.4 Breach of pupillage advertising/funding requirements

Description	
All pupillages must be advertised in order to allow for open selection and equality of opportunity. It is also a requirement that pupillages are funded at a minimum prescribed level or more. Breaches are charged under paragraph 402.2(c) of the Code. Breaches of the advertising requirements may be unintentional and stem from lack of knowledge of the requirements. However, failures to provide funding are more serious as they are likely to be motivated by financial gain and in most cases will involve some level of exploitation of the pupil. Deliberate evasion/circumvention of both requirements should be taken seriously. **Range of sanctions:** Where the breach is unintentional, a reprimand or advice as to future conduct would be appropriate. Intentional breaches of the funding requirements should attract a relatively heavy fine, particularly where the arrangements involved a level of exploitation of the pupil. Listed below are common circumstances in which breaches might occur set out according to severity.	
Common circumstances	**Starting Point**
a. Failure to advertise but no pupillages were offered in contravention of the rules	a. Reprimand/advice as to future conduct
b. Deliberate failure to advertise where pupils have been taken on in contravention of the rules	b. Reprimand and low level fine
c. Deliberate failure to provide funding motivated by financial gain	c. Medium to high level fine dependent on the level of potential or actual financial gain
d. Intentional failure to comply with recruitment requirements as well as failure to provide funding requirements	d. Short suspension
Aggravating factors	**Mitigating factors**
• Financial gain • Exploitation of a pupil • Breach resulted in the pupillage not being registered • Persistent breaches involving numbers of pupils • Lack of response to warnings from Pupillage and Training Committee of the BSB	• Unintentional • One off where previous pupillages had been properly handled • Remedial action taken at an early point
The aggravating and mitigating factors listed above should be considered in addition to the factors listed at Annex 1.	

E.5 Failure to report bankruptcy and provide regular updates to the BSB

Description	
Barristers are required to report the fact of their bankruptcy and thereafter the BSB monitors progress of the administration of the bankruptcy to check that the barrister is complying with all relevant enquiries. The barrister is always asked to provide regular updates to the BSB. If a bankruptcy is reported, and updates provided, no further action will be taken and the barrister is free to continue practising. Charges are normally brought under 905(c) and (d) of the Code. **Range of sanctions:** While there will be a range of circumstances relating to the failure to report the bankruptcy, even with aggravating circumstances, a reprimand is still likely to be the appropriate sanction but the terms of the reprimand need to be considered carefully. A fine will be inappropriate in most circumstances given the barrister's financial position unless the bankruptcy came to light after discharge. Listed below are common circumstances in which breaches might occur set out according to severity.	
Common circumstances	**Starting Point**
a. Failure to report the bankruptcy	a. Reprimand
b. Failure to respond to BSB enquires for updates	b. Reprimand
c. Substantial delay in reporting the bankruptcy	c. Reprimand and low level fine
Aggravating factors	**Mitigating factors**
• Persistent non-compliance with bankruptcy requirements	
The aggravating and mitigating factors listed above should be considered in addition to the factors listed at Annex 1.	

E.6 Failure to respond

Description
Barristers are required, under paragraph 905(d) of the Code, to respond promptly to enquiries from the BSB regarding complaints or potential breaches of the Code. This means that a charge for failure to respond could result from a delay in responding as well as a total absence of response. Failure to respond is most often accompanied by other charges for breaches of the Code. However, in some circumstances, a late response from the barrister results in the main issues of complaint being dismissed but a charge for failing to respond is still brought because of the inconvenience/delay caused either to the BSB or the complainant and/or because of the barrister's attitude towards the authority of the BSB.

Range of sanctions: In most cases the starting point should be a low level fine increasing according to the circumstances, the barrister's attitude and the level of delay/inconvenience caused. A short suspension might be appropriate where the behaviour has been repeated in relation to a number of separate complaints. Listed below are common circumstances in which breaches might occur set out according to severity.	
Common circumstances	**Starting Point**
a. Delays in responding but with some level of engagement with the BSB	a. Low level fine
b. Failure to respond at any point to BSB enquiries	b. Low level fine (upper end)
c. Deliberate decision not to engage with the BSB showing a disregard for the authority of the regulator	c. Medium level fine
Aggravating factors	**Mitigating factors**
• Lack of explanation for the failure to respond • Distress and inconvenience to the complainant • Substantial delay in being able to deal with the complaint • Persistent failures to respond	
The aggravating and mitigating factors listed above should be considered in addition to the factors listed at Annex 1.	

Section F – Failure to comply with a Direction, Order or Judgment

F.1 Failure to comply with an Order of a BTAS Tribunal, the Complaints Committee

Description
The BSB does not have powers of enforcement. Where a barrister fails to comply with an Order of a previous Tribunal or disciplinary panel (including financial penalties) the only option available is to bring further disciplinary proceedings for failure to comply. Breaches are charged under paragraph 905(f) of the Code. **Range of sanctions:** The appropriate sanction will depend on the nature of the original sentence, whether compliance of whole or part of the order remains outstanding and the reasons why the breach occurred. It is therefore difficult to set an overall starting point. A financial penalty may not be appropriate where previous financial orders remain outstanding. In most cases, where order(s) remain outstanding, and no serious attempts have been made to comply, a conditional short suspension could be appropriate (i.e. the suspension does not become operative unless the barrister fails to comply with conditions set by the Tribunal).

Where compliance has been achieved by the date of the Tribunal, the starting point should be a low level fine combined with a reprimand/advice as to future conduct.

Listed below are common circumstances in which breaches might occur set out according to severity.

Common circumstances	Starting Point
a. Failure to comply in due time or with only part of an order	a. Low level fine and reprimand/advice as to future conduct
b. Failure to comply with any part of the orders of the Tribunal/panel	b. Conditional short suspension
c. Deliberate decision not to engage with the BSB showing a disregard for the authority of the regulator	c. Medium suspension

Aggravating factors	Mitigating factors
• Similar previous findings • No attempt to comply with the order	• Genuine attempts to comply • Late compliance

The aggravating and mitigating factors listed above should be considered in addition to the factors listed at Annex 1.

F.2 Breach of Court Direction or failure to comply with a Court Order

Description

Breach of a Court direction or order usually occurs in the course of a barrister representing a client. However it is possible that such a breach may occur in the course of a case that a barrister is involved with on a personal level. Charges are usually brought under paragraph 301(a)(ii) of the Code for diminishing public confidence in the profession or bringing the Bar into disrepute.

Given a barrister's responsibilities to the Court and for upholding the integrity of the profession, such behaviour should be considered more seriously than if committed by a lay person. Disrespect for the authority of a Court should be considered as a serious matter.

Range of sanctions: In most cases the starting point should be a reprimand and/or a fine. The level of fine will be dependent on the circumstances of the breach and the barrister's attitude. In cases where the breach might amount to a criminal offence (usually this occurs in relation to personal matters where a barrister, for example, breaches a restraining order), a medium level fine or a suspension would be appropriate. Suspensions should be reserved for cases where the impact on the complainant is significant.

Listed below are common circumstances in which breaches might occur set out according to severity.

Common circumstances	Starting Point
a. Inadvertent breach of a direction/order that did not have implications for the future course of the proceedings	a. Reprimand
b. Inadvertent breach of a direction/order that resulted in a change to the course/outcome of the proceedings	b. Reprimand and low level fine
c. Deliberate breach of an order/direction in order to gain advantage	c. Medium fine and/or medium suspension
Aggravating factors	**Mitigating factors**
• Deliberate disobedience based on gaining advantage for the barrister or his/her client • Continued breach in face of warnings from the Court • Evidence of previous failures to obey Court Orders/Directions • Significant impact on the complainant or case	• Unintentional • Confusion as to the nature of the order • Immediate apology • Remedial action taken at an early point
The aggravating and mitigating factors listed above should be considered in addition to the factors listed at Annex 1.	

F.3 Failure to comply with a Court judgment

Description

Usually a failure to comply with a Court judgment will occur as result of an event in the barrister's personal life although it is possible that it will result from representing a client. Charges are usually brought under paragraph 301(a)(ii) of the Code for diminishing public confidence in the profession or bringing the Bar into disrepute.

It is a serious matter for a barrister to fail to comply with a Court judgment because it shows a level of contempt for the legal process which is not compatible with the standards expected of professionals with a responsibility to the Court. Therefore, a barrister's non-compliance with a Court judgment should be considered to be more serious than that of "lay person". However, the nature of the judgment will be relevant as will be the point at which the non -compliance has reached.

Range of sanctions: The starting point should be a fine with the level increasing according to the circumstances. A deliberate breach of a judgment resulting in significant implications for the complainant/proceedings may warrant a short suspension.

Listed below are common circumstances in which breaches might occur set out according to severity.

Common circumstances	Starting Point
a. Breach of judgement related solely to personal financial obligations b. Deliberate disregard for the authority of the court combined with a significant impact on the complainant/case	a. Low level fine as well as reprimand and/or advice as to future conduct b. Medium level fine and/or medium suspension
Aggravating factors	**Mitigating factors**
• Deliberate attempt to evade financial obligations	• Late compliance with the judgment • Genuine attempts to meet the judgment
The aggravating and mitigating factors listed above should be considered in addition to the factors listed at Annex 1.	

Section G – Financial Issues

G.1 Overcharging

Description	
Overcharging will normally be charged under paragraph 301(a)(iii) of the Code (diminishing public confidence in the Bar and/or bringing the Bar into disrepute). It is a serious breach in that it will inevitably involve a victim whether that it is the public purse, a company or an individual. **Range of sanctions:** Normally a starting point of medium level fine would be appropriate but the level of fine will be highly fact specific and should reflect the extent and circumstances of the overcharging. In all cases, unless the overcharged fees have already been repaid, an order to repay or forego fees should be made. Where the overcharging consists of knowingly charging for work/hours not completed, decision makers should carefully consider whether the behaviour includes an element of dishonesty and may warrant disbarment (see paragraph 6.3 on dishonesty). Listed below are common circumstances in which breaches might occur set out according to severity.	
Common circumstances	**Starting Point**
a. Overcharging of a privately paying or commercial client	a. Medium level fine, repay/forego fees and an order to apologise
b. Overcharging of a client who is publicly funded	b. High level fine or short suspension, repay/forego fees and an order to apologise
c. Knowingly charging for work/hours not completed.	c. Medium suspension to disbarment

Aggravating factors	Mitigating factors
• Significant amount of overcharging • Particularly vulnerable client • Pattern of repeated behaviour • Public Access client	• Overcharged fee repaid voluntarily • Genuine mistake
The aggravating and mitigating factors listed above should be considered in addition to the factors listed at Annex 1.	

Section H – Discourtesy

Description	
Discourtesy, in most cases, will be directed towards a Judge or Magistrate but can also involve conduct towards a lay client or other individual involved in the proceedings. Charges are normally brought under paragraph 701(a) of the Code. When considering discourtesy it will be important to consider the circumstances of the act and whether or not it was an isolated incident as opposed to repeated acts of discourtesy in the face of repeated warnings from the Judge or Magistrate. **Range of sanctions:** In most cases the starting point should be a reprimand and an apology accompanied by a low level fine. Listed below are common circumstances in which breaches might occur set out according to severity.	
Common circumstances	**Starting Point**
a. An isolated incident within proceedings	a. Reprimand and an apology, possibly accompanied by a low level fine
b. Repeated pattern of discourtesy against a background of repeated warnings or interventions from the Judge/Magistrate	b. Reprimand and an apology accompanied by a medium level fine
c. A high level of the discourtesy that had a significant impact on the victim	c. Reprimand and an apology accompanied by a medium to high level fine
Aggravating factors	**Mitigating factors**
• Lack of remorse • Failure to acknowledge impact of behaviour • Adverse impact on the course of the proceedings • Bullying behaviour	• An isolated incident in difficult or unusual circumstances • Immediate apology
The aggravating and mitigating factors listed above should be considered in addition to the factors listed at Annex 1.	

Section I – Harassment, discrimination and behaviour towards others

I.1 Discrimination and harassment

Description	
Discrimination will normally be charged under paragraph 305.1 of the Code of Conduct and relates to behaviour both in the course of profession work as well as in a barrister's personal life which amounts to discrimination based on race, colour, ethnic or national origin, nationality, citizenship, sex, sexual orientation, marital status, disability, age, religion or belief. **Harassment** will normally be charged under paragraph 301(a)(i) of the Code (conduct discreditable to a barrister). This type of breach is **not** intended to cover the situation where a barrister has been convicted of a criminal offence for harassment in his/her personal capacity. This section relates to behaviour in the course of a barrister's professional work that amounts to any form of harassment or bullying. **Range of sanctions:** The starting point for a finding of either discrimination or harassment should be a medium level fine, although a suspension or disbarment would be appropriate in circumstances where the behaviour is of a serious nature and/or continues over an extended period of time. Listed below are common circumstances in which breaches might occur set out according to severity.	
Common circumstances	**Starting Point**
a. An isolated incident which had a limited impact on the complainant	a. A medium level fine
b. The behaviour took place over an extended period of time and/or the barrister was in a position of power or acting in a supervisory role	b. A high level fine and a short suspension
c. Physical or particularly strong verbal actions towards a vulnerable individual or group	c. A medium suspension to disbarment
Aggravating factors	**Mitigating factors**
• A significant negative impact on the victim • Failure to accept responsibility for actions • The vulnerability of the victim in the circumstances	• Immediate apology
The aggravating and mitigating factors listed above should be considered in addition to the factors listed at Annex 1.	

I.2 Conduct towards witnesses and other advocates

Description	
Section 3 of the Code of Conduct consists of guidance called "Written Standards For The Conduct of Professional Work". While failure to follow this guidance does not in itself amount to a breach of the Code, it may lead to a breach of other provisions of the Code, particularly paragraph 301(a)(ii) (actions prejudicial to the administration of justice). Further, paragraph 701(d) of the Code states that a barrister must have regard to the Written Standards. Common examples are inappropriate contact with witnesses and improper conduct towards opposing advocates. An important element to take into account is whether or not the offence was committed intentionally or inadvertently thorough ignorance of the appropriate guidance. Any findings made in this regard should be noted in the written reasons of the decision maker. A charge involving inappropriate contact with witness should normally be deemed to be more serious than behaviour towards opposing advocates as witnesses are likely to be more vulnerable and less able to protect themselves. **Range of sanctions:** The starting point should be a low level fine for cases of inadvertent behaviour rising to disbarment for more serious sanctions for intentional acts which may be likely to pervert the course of justice. In all cases, consideration should be given to whether it is appropriate to require the barrister to undertake the Professional Ethics Test (see paragraph 6.19 for more details), or be ordered to apologise to the complainant. Listed below are common circumstances in which breaches might occur set out according to severity.	
Common circumstances	**Starting Point**
a. Inadvertent contact with a witness or an act towards another advocate in ignorance of the rules or accepted etiquette	a. A low level fine and advice as to future conduct
b. An intentional act towards a witness or other individual that had (or was likely to have) an adverse effect on the proceedings	b. A medium level fine and medium suspension
c. An intention to act towards a witness or other individual that was likely to pervert the course of justice	c. Disbarment
Aggravating factors	**Mitigating factors**
• The behaviour took place over an extended period of time	• An isolated incident • Immediate apology
The aggravating and mitigating factors listed above should be considered in addition to the factors listed at Annex 1.	

I.3 Using status to influence

Description	
The circumstances in which a barrister may attempt to use his/her status to influence usually arise in relation to the barrister's personal life. A typical breach under this heading might arise where a barrister sends correspondence on a personal matter on chambers' letterhead holding him or herself out as a barrister in an attempt to influence or pressurise someone to accede to a course of action. The breach is usually charged under paragraph 301(a)(iii) of the Code (conduct likely to diminish public confidence or otherwise bring the legal profession into disrepute). **Range of sanctions:** In most cases the starting point should be an apology accompanied by a low level fine. However, if the pressure is severe and amounts to "bullying", then a higher level fine would be appropriate. Listed below are common circumstances in which breaches might occur set out according to severity.	
Common Circumstances	**Starting Point**
a. A single incident of using status to influence when he or she ought to have realised that it was inappropriate	a. A low level fine and an apology
b. Repeated incidents where the barrister is attempting to exploit his/her status as a means of exerting pressure or there is a financial motivation involved	b. A medium level fine and an apology
Aggravating factors	**Mitigating factors**
• Victim is particularly vulnerable • Behaviour over an extended period of time • Motivation is financial gain	• An isolated incident • Immediate apology
The aggravating and mitigating factors listed above should be considered in addition to the factors listed at Annex 1.	

I.4 Inappropriate media comment

Description
Inappropriate media comment is normally charged under paragraph 709.1 of the Code of Conduct and relates to a barrister giving a personal opinion on any current or anticipated proceedings in which he is instructed or expects to appear. Given the potential for self-publicity and commercial advantage this confers, a financial penalty is usually the starting point. Other relevant factors will be the sensitivity of the information imparted to the media, the likelihood of further proceedings being affected by the comments and whether the comment was made in an attempt to place unfair pressure on an opposing party.

Range of sanctions: In most cases the starting point should be an apology accompanied by a medium level fine. Listed below are common circumstances in which breaches might occur set out according to severity.	
Common circumstances	**Starting Point**
a. A relatively uncontroversial comment made where it was unlikely that there would be any further proceedings	a. A medium level fine and an apology
b. Controversial comments when further proceedings were likely and may have been adversely affected by the barristers' comments	b. A high level fine to a short suspension and an apology
Aggravating factors	**Mitigating factors**
• Lack of remorse • The comments were intended to self- publicise • The comments were intended to place unfair pressure on an opposing party • Particularly sensitive information disclosed • Failure to take responsibility for actions • Personal or professional advantage gained (financial or otherwise)	• Remedial action taken at an early point • Immediate apology
The aggravating and mitigating factors listed above should be considered in addition to the factors listed at Annex 1.	

Section J – Incompetence and delay

J.1 Incompetence

Description
Incompetence or delay amounting to discreditable conduct will usually be charged under paragraph 301(a)(iii) of the Code of Conduct (conduct likely to diminish public confidence in the legal profession or otherwise bring the legal profession into disrepute). The level of incompetence and seniority of the particular barrister concerned will be important factors in deciding what sanction is appropriate. It will also be important to consider whether the incompetence has had a direct impact on the client's case. **Range of sanctions:** In most cases the starting point should be an apology however this may be accompanied by a fine for more serious cases.

Listed below are common circumstances in which breaches might occur set out according to severity.	
Common circumstances	**Starting Point**
a. An isolated act on the part of an inexperienced barrister which did not adversely affect the client's case	a. An apology and low level fine
b. Significant or repeated acts of incompetence which had an adverse effect on the proceedings	b. An apology and a medium level fine to a short suspension
Aggravating factors	**Mitigating factors**
• Failure to take responsibility for actions	• Immediate apology • Remedial action taken at an early point
The aggravating and mitigating factors listed above should be considered in addition to the factors listed at Annex 1.	

J.2 Delay

Description	
Delay will usually be charged under 701(b)(iii) of the Code of Conduct. The length of the particular delay will be relevant and persistent instances of ignoring related communications from the client. The workload of the barrister is not a relevant factor to take into account as barristers are required by the Code to refuse instructions if they do not have adequate time or opportunity to prepare that which is required. It will also be important to consider whether or not the delay had a direct impact on the client's case. **Range of sanctions:** In most cases the starting point should be a low level fine. Listed below are common circumstances in which breaches might occur set out according to severity.	
Common circumstances	**Starting Point**
a. A delay with limited impact on the proceedings	a. An apology and/or a low level fine
b. A significant delay in the face of repeated communications seeking a response	b. An apology and a medium level fine

Aggravating factors	Mitigating factors
• Lack of remorse • Previous convictions for similar breaches • Adverse effect on the course of the proceedings • Distress or worry caused to client	• Immediate apology • Remedial action taken at an early point
The aggravating and mitigating factors listed above should be considered in addition to the factors listed at Annex 1.	

Annex 1 – Aggravating and mitigating factors

Aggravating factors

The following factors, if present, may determine whether a higher sanction for a breach should be imposed. The factors listed are only examples and are not exhaustive:

- Premeditation
- Motive of financial gain
- Corruption/gross deception
- Coercion
- Involvement of others
- Persistent conduct or conduct over a lengthy period of time
- Undermining of the profession in the eyes of the public
- Attempts to hide the misconduct or wrongly lay blame elsewhere
- Effect on the complainant or particular vulnerability of the complainant
- Actions accompanied by discriminatory behaviour or motivation (does not require intent)
- Breach of trust
- Position of responsibility within the profession
- Previous disciplinary findings for similar breaches
- Previous disciplinary findings for any types of breaches, particularly where the breaches show an unwillingness to comply with the Code
- Lack of remorse for having committed the offences
- Failure to respond promptly to communications from the BSB, or inappropriate behaviour that frustrates the administration of the complaint
- Failure to attend a Tribunal without explanation
- Indication of an element of dishonesty (see paragraph 6.3 on a finding of dishonesty and paragraph 7.5 on dishonesty during proceedings)

Mitigating factors

The following factors, if present, may determine whether a lower sanction for a breach should be imposed. The factors listed are only examples and are not exhaustive:

- Guilty plea
- Genuine remorse (as expressed in e.g. a willingness to apologise to the complainant and/or compromise over matters such as fees)
- Limited experience within the profession
- The breach was unintentional
- Single incident (not applicable if behaviour involves discrimination)
- Heat of the moment (not applicable if behaviour involves discrimination)
- Co-operation with the investigation
- Voluntary steps have been taken to remedy or rectify the breach
- Evidence of attempts to prevent reoccurrence
- Previous good character (not applicable if behaviour involves discrimination)
- Evidence of financial hardship (only applicable when it has had a direct impact on the commission of the offence)
- Advice was sought and obtained from the Bar Council's professional ethics helpline
- Unusual personal circumstances that provide a reasonable explanation for the behaviour. In particular, bereavement, relationship breakdown and divorce (matters such as pressure of work and bankruptcy should be treated with caution as these factors may indicate a greater risk to the public in the barrister's ongoing practice)
- Good references (only of limited applicability and very much dependent on the nature of the offence and the role and identity of the referee)

Annex 2 – Wording of sentences and Findings and Sentence sheet

Wording of sentences

A2.1 Prescriptive requirements for the wording of sanctions are no longer included in the Disciplinary Tribunal Regulations but it is still important that panels include on the findings and sentence sheet clear details of the sanction(s) imposed. Therefore set out below is guidance on the wording that should be used when imposing each of the individual sanctions, including any sanction imposed under the Determination by Consent procedure. It is based on the previous wording of the Disciplinary Tribunal Regulations and may appear very formal but it provides a sound basis for ensuring that any sanctions imposed are not subject to confusion. It is mandatory to use one of the statements contained in paragraph A2.2 below where a defendant is absent from a Tribunal hearing.

Absence of the barrister charged

A2.2 Where the barrister charged has not been present throughout the proceedings, the sentence must include one of the following two statements:

(i) If the relevant procedure under Regulation 14(1) has been complied with, that the finding and sentence were made in the absence of the barrister in accordance with Regulation 14(1).

(ii) If the procedure under Regulation 14(2) has been complied with, that the finding and the sentence were made in the absence of the barrister and that he has the right to apply to the Directions Judge for an order that there should be a new hearing before a fresh Disciplinary Tribunal.

Disbarment

A2.3 "That [X] be disbarred and expelled from the Honourable Society of [X} [and *any other Inn of which he is a member*] ..."

Removal from the Register of European Lawyers

A2.4 "That [X] be removed from the register of European lawyers maintained by the Bar Council."

Suspension from practice

A2.5 "That [X] be suspended for [X] weeks/months/year."

"That [X] be suspended until he has complied with [state the practising requirement with which the barrister should comply]."

"That [X] be suspended from accepting or carrying out any [state the area of practice that the suspension shall apply to] for [X] weeks/months/years."

"That [X] be suspended from accepting or carrying out any [state the area of practice that the suspension shall apply to] until he has complied with [state the practising requirement with which the barrister should comply]."

Suspension from the Register of European Lawyers

A2.6 "That [X] be suspended from the register of European lawyers maintained by the Bar Council for [X period]."

"That [X] be suspended from the register of European lawyers maintained by the Bar Council until he has complied with [state the practising requirement with which the barrister should comply]."

"That [X] be suspended from the register of European lawyers maintained by the Bar Council with regards to accepting or carrying out any [state the area of practice that the suspension shall apply to] for [X] weeks/months/years."

"That [X] be suspended from the register of European lawyers maintained by the Bar Council with regards to accepting or carrying out any [state the area of practice that the suspension shall apply to] until he has complied with [state the practising requirement with which the barrister should comply]".

Prohibition on accepting or carrying out public access instructions

A2.7 "That [X] be prohibited from accepting or carrying out any public access instructions."

"That [X] be prohibited from accepting or carrying out any public access instructions for [X] weeks/months/years."

"That [X] be prohibited from accepting or carrying out any public access instructions until he has complied with [state the practising requirement with which the barrister should comply]."

Payment of fine

A2.8 "That [X] pay a fine of £[ ] to the Bar Standards Board, within [X] weeks/months of the expiry of any appeal period."

"That [X] pay a fine of £[ ] to the Bar Standards Board, to be paid in monthly instalments of £[ ] to commence within [X] weeks/months of the expiry of any appeal period."

Continuing Professional Development

A2.11 "That [X] shall by [date] complete a minimum of [X] hours of continuing professional development (in addition to the mandatory requirements set out in the Continuing Professional Development Regulations at Annex C to the Code of Conduct) [in the subject of …] and provide satisfactory proof of compliance with this Order to the Complaints Committee of the Bar Standards Board."

Reprimand

A2.13 "That [X] has been reprimanded by the Tribunal."

"That [X] is ordered to attend on [X- the nominated person] to be reprimanded."

Advice as to future conduct

A2.15 "That [X] has been advised by the Tribunal as to his future conduct in regard to …."

"That [X] is hereby ordered to attend on [X – the nominated person] to be given advice as to his future conduct in regard to …".

Order for reduction of Legal Aid fees

A2.16 "That the fees otherwise payable to [X] by the Legal Services Commission in connection with the legal services provided by him are reduced in the following sum £[ ] according to the attached list. (*a list of the reductions should be provided*) "

Order for cancellation of Legal Aid fees

A2.17 "That the fees otherwise payable to [X] by the Legal Services Commission in connection with services provided by him should be cancelled in accordance with the attached list. (*a list of the cancelled services should be provided*) "

Exclusion from Legal Aid work

A2.18"That [X] be excluded from providing representation funded by the Legal Services Commission (as explained in Section 42(4)(b) of the Administration of Justice Act 1985 as substituted by Section 33 of the Legal Aid Act 1988 and amended by Schedule 4 to the Access to Justice Act 1999) until [X date] or for a period of [X time]beginning on [X date].

Determination by Consent ("DBC")

[6.19]

The BSB also manages an alternative means of dealing with complaints which might otherwise be referred to a Disciplinary Tribunal known as the "Determination By Consent" process. The flowing guidance is published in relation to that process:

What is Determination by Consent "DBC"?

The DBC procedure is an alternative means of dealing with complaints which would otherwise be referred to a Disciplinary Tribunal. Involvement in the process is entirely voluntary and requires your express written consent at different points in the procedure to continue. Under DBC, if you agree, the case against you will be dealt with on the papers and the Professional Conduct Committee ("the Committee") of the Bar Standards Board ("BSB") will decide whether you are in breach of your professional obligations as set out in the Handbook (or for conduct that happened before 6 January 2014, the Code of Conduct 8th edition) and, if so, what sentence to impose. You will then be given the opportunity to accept or reject the Committee's finding and sentence.

DBC avoids the case being referred to a full disciplinary tribunal hearing and will hopefully, with your co-operation, conclude the disciplinary process more quickly.

What rules govern DBC?

The rules that govern the DBC procedure can be found in the BSB Handbook, Part 5 (the Enforcement Regulations) section A5.

What makes a case suitable for DBC?

There are five criteria that must be met for a complaint to be deemed suitable for DBC:

- there is a realistic prospect of a finding of professional misconduct being made;
- there are no substantial disputes of fact;
- the circumstances do not warrant the complaint being dismissed or no further action being taken;
- it is in the public interest to resolve the complaint using DBC; and
- if the alleged professional misconduct is admitted or proved, it would not warrant a period of suspension, a disqualification order, or disbarment (bearing in mind your previous disciplinary history, if any).

How is a case referred to DBC?

There are two ways that a complaint can be referred to the DBC procedure:

(1) a member of staff (authorised by the Committee) can deem the case suitable for DBC; or

(2) the full Committee can consider the complaint and decide that that it is suitable for DBC.

What are the stages of the DBC procedure?

A flow chart of the stages listed below can be found at the end of this explanatory note.

Stage 1 – If the complaint against you is deemed suitable for DBC, the first step is for the BSB to write to you to seek your confirmation as to whether you agree in principle to the DBC procedure. **In order for the DBC procedure to continue, you must respond in writing within 14 days to say whether you agree in principle to continuing with DBC.** If you do not agree, or do not respond within 14 days, the complaint will not be referred for DBC and will either be put before the Committee for a decision as to how to proceed or will automatically be referred to a three-person Disciplinary Tribunal. If you respond and agree to DBC, the case will move to Stage 2.

Stage 2 – A Case Officer in the Investigation and Hearings Team will prepare a draft DBC report on the case. The draft report will include the following sections:

A. Background;

B. Charge(s);

C. Summary of Facts ("SoF"); and

D. Previous disciplinary findings.

The BSB aims to serve the draft report on you within 21 days of receiving your written agreement to DBC (see Stage 1). You will be asked to respond within 21 days to say whether or not you agree the SoF and admit the charge(s).

If you admit the charge(s), you will be invited to provide any mitigation (with relevant supporting documents). If you would like the Committee to take into account your financial circumstances as part of your mitigation you should provide supporting information and documents.

If you accept the facts but deny that the facts amount to professional misconduct (and therefore deny the charge(s)), you will be invited to provide a written explanation (with any supporting documents) as to why the facts do not amount to professional misconduct.

The SoF can be amended by agreement – if you wish to request amendments to the SoF, you should contact the Officer responsible for your case. If the SoF is agreed, the case will move to Stage 3.

If you do not respond by the deadline, or respond and indicate a significant dispute as to the facts, the case will automatically proceed to a three-person disciplinary tribunal unless issues are raised that require further consideration. For DBC to proceed, the barrister must continue to consent to the procedure, the SoF must be agreed, and the Committee must continue to consider that the procedure is suitable for the particular case.

Stage 3 – Presentation of report to the Committee

After you have agreed the SoF and responded to the charge(s), we will add the following sections (where appropriate) to the draft report:

E. Your plea in respect of the charge(s);

F. If the charge(s) are denied, a summary of your reasons as to why the facts do not amount to professional misconduct and a recommendation to the Committee as to whether or not the charge(s) should be found proved, along with draft reasons; and/or

G. If the charges are admitted, a summary of your mitigation and a recommended sentence based on the circumstances of the case and the Sentencing Guidance.

The draft report will not be sent to you at this stage but it will be presented to the Committee, which can decide to:

- dismiss some or all of the charges of professional misconduct;
- find some or all of the charges of professional misconduct proved;
- if you have admitted the charge(s) of professional misconduct, impose a sentence for each charge; or
- refer the complaint to a disciplinary tribunal if DBC is no longer appropriate.

The final DBC report will only be sent to you after it has been approved by the Committee.

Charge(s) admitted: if you have admitted the charges, the Committee will approve the contents of the report and decide the sentence for each charge.

Charge(s) denied: If you deny the charge(s), the case will be considered by the Committee twice. On the first occasion, the Committee decides whether or not the charge(s) of professional misconduct against you are proved. If the Committee finds the charges proved, we will send you the DBC report, which will explain the Committee's findings and reasons and we will ask you whether you accept the Committee's findings. If you accept the findings, you will be invited to provide any mitigation including supporting documents) that you wish the Committee to take into account when making the decision on sentence.

The report will be updated to include a summary of your mitigation (if any) and a recommended sentence. It will be presented to the Committee for a second time to decide the sentence in respect of the charge(s).

When the Committee has decided on sentence we will send you the final DBC report, which will explain the sentence the Committee imposed and we will ask you whether you accept the sentence. If you respond and accept the sentence, the case will move to Stage 4.

If you do not confirm in writing within 14 days that you accept the Committee's findings and/or sentence, or you reject the Committee's decision, the case will automatically be referred to a three-person disciplinary tribunal unless issues are raised which require further consideration by the Committee.

What sanctions can the Committee impose?

The Committee will consider our enforcement strategy and take into account the Bar Tribunals and Adjudication Services' ("BTAS") Sentencing Guidance. The sentencing guidance is published on the BTAS website (http://www.tbtas.org.uk) and we encourage you to look at it. Under DBC, the Committee is able to impose the following sanctions:

- order you to pay a fine;
- reprimand you (or order you to attend on a nominated person to be reprimanded);
- give you advice (or an order to attend on a nominated person to be given advice); and/or

- order you to complete CPD of such nature and duration as the PCC directs and provide satisfactory proof of compliance.

The Committee cannot suspend or disbar you or make a costs order against you – these powers are reserved for disciplinary tribunals. **Stage 4** – If you accept the Committee's finding and sentence, a disciplinary finding will be formally recorded against you as of the date when we receive your written acceptance. Details of the charge(s), the finding and sentence will be posted on the BSB's website and publication will be to the same extent as a finding and sentence by a disciplinary tribunal.

Can I appeal the Committee decision?

You cannot appeal against a finding made by the DBC procedure because your express consent is required for a finding to be made and a sanction imposed. You can end the DBC procedure at any time up until your acceptance of the finding and sentence if you would prefer that the case is dealt with by a disciplinary tribunal. The Committee may also terminate the DBC procedure at any time if it no longer considers the criteria are satisfied or for any other good reason.

Compliance

If the sentence includes a requirement for you to take action, for example to pay a fine or complete CPD, the case will move into the compliance stage. We will tell you what you need to do to comply with the sentence and the deadline for doing so. After you have complied with the sentence, we will close our file and mark the case as complete. Failure to comply with the sentence by the deadline is likely to be treated as professional misconduct and the Committee may refer the matter to a disciplinary tribunal.

What if I wish to proceed with DBC but cannot respond during the required time?

Reasonable extensions to the time limits can be given if there is good reason to do so such as a work or family commitment, or the need to seek advice. You should contact the Officer who has conduct of your case as soon as possible to discuss any extensions of time.

Who should I contact if I have any questions about DBC?

If you wish to discuss any aspect of the DBC procedure, please c
Officer who has conduct of the complaint against you by telephoni
main switchboard on 020 7611 1444 and quoting the reference n
at the top of the letters sent to you by the BSB.

Bar Standards Board
Updated March 2014
Originally published August 2009

DBC procedure flow-chart

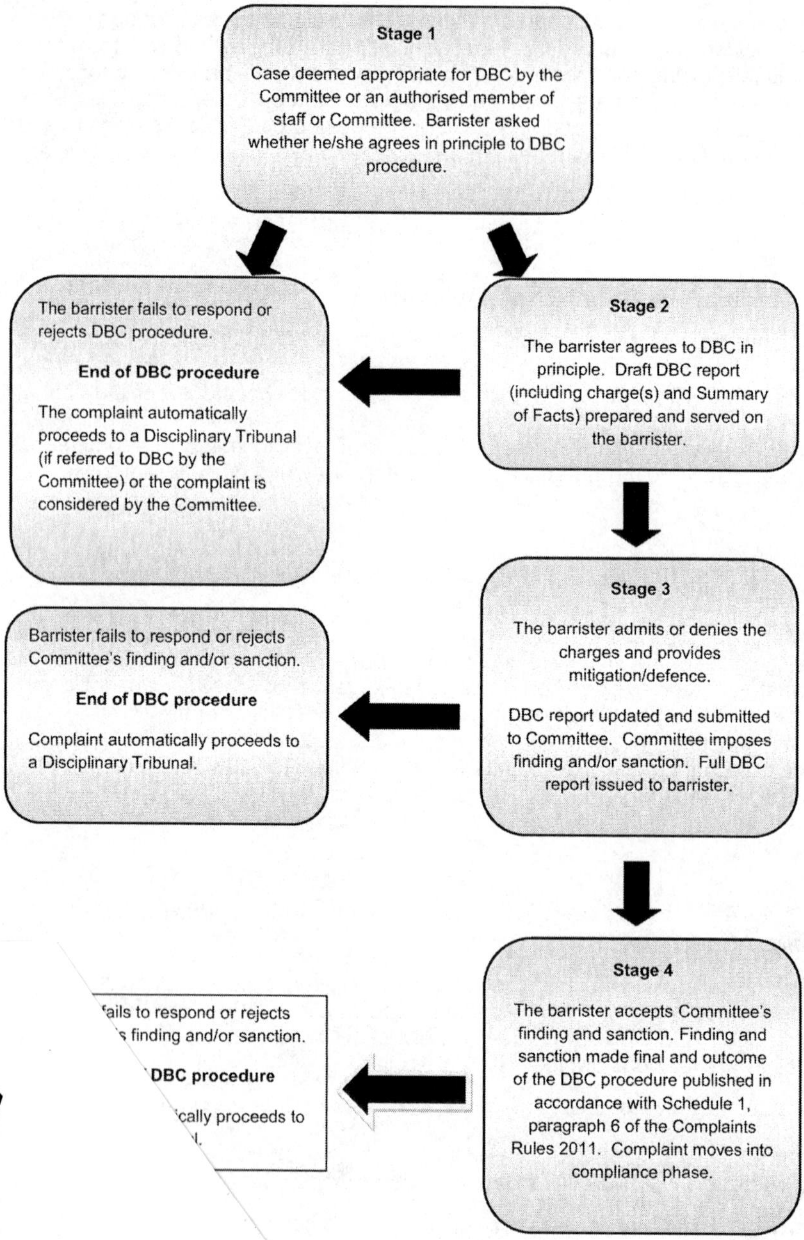
Stage 1
Case deemed appropriate for DBC by the Committee or an authorised member of staff or Committee. Barrister asked whether he/she agrees in principle to DBC procedure.
The barrister fails to respond or rejects DBC procedure.
End of DBC procedure
The complaint automatically proceeds to a Disciplinary Tribunal (if referred to DBC by the Committee) or the complaint is considered by the Committee.
Stage 2
The barrister agrees to DBC in principle. Draft DBC report (including charge(s) and Summary of Facts) prepared and served on the barrister.
Barrister fails to respond or rejects Committee's finding and/or sanction.
End of DBC procedure
Complaint automatically proceeds to a Disciplinary Tribunal.
Stage 3
The barrister admits or denies the charges and provides mitigation/defence.
DBC report updated and submitted to Committee. Committee imposes finding and/or sanction. Full DBC report issued to barrister.
finding and/or sanction.
DBC procedure
Stage 4
The barrister accepts Committee's finding and sanction. Finding and sanction made final and outcome of the DBC procedure published in accordance with Schedule 1, paragraph 6 of the Complaints Rules 2011. Complaint moves into compliance phase.

Disciplinary tribunals and findings

[6.20]

Following the investigation of a complaint, the BSB may decide to formally refer it to a disciplinary tribunal for consideration.

Disciplinary tribunals are arranged by an independent organisation called the Bar Tribunals and Adjudication Service ("BTAS"). It appoints the members of disciplinary tribunals and arranges the hearings.

Tribunal panels are made up of barristers, people who are not from the legal profession (lay people), and sometimes judges. All panels will include at least one lay person.

There are two types of Disciplinary Tribunal: three-person panels and five-person panels. The BSB decides which type of panel is most suitable to hear a case, depending on the seriousness of the potential breach of the Code of Conduct. Both types of panel follow the same process, but the sentencing powers are slightly different.

Publication of Disciplinary Findings

[6.21]–[6.36]

The BSB website provides details of all publishable findings and sentences imposed by Disciplinary Tribunals since 2002.

Details of findings and sentences, including the identity of the barrister concerned, are published in accordance with the BSB's Publications Policy. In summary, all findings will be removed from the website after 2 years, unless the finding of the Disciplinary Tribunal involves a suspension or disbarment. In these cases, the finding will be posted on the website indefinitely.

However, a barrister's full disciplinary record can be obtained by contacting the Professional Conduct Department directly on 0207 611 1444.

You can use the website to search by name of barrister (last name), month and/or year, sentence (whether disbarred, suspended or other sentence), type of hearing (whether visitors hearing (appeal) or disciplinary tribunal), and type of offence (keyword search).

Each set of findings is accorded a status on the following basis:

- **Open to Appeal** – The case is within the period that a barrister can appeal the finding but no appeal has been submitted;
- **Appeal Pending – Sentence Stayed/Appeal Pending** – The barrister h submitted an appeal, which is yet to be heard. Unless the Disciplinary Tr has ordered that the sentence should take effect immediately (Appe ing), the sentence will not be implemented until after the outco appeal is known (Appeal Pending – Sentence Stayed).
- **Final** – The finding has been pronounced either after the a s and expired or following the result of an appeal.

New findings are posted within seven days of a decision, alt **24 hours** for the finding to appear on the website followin information about individual cases can be obtained Hearings Team on **020 7611 1444**.

Information about forthcoming hearings that BTAS will publish

Information regarding the public disciplinary hearings will be made available by the following methods:

- the BTAS website; and
- telephone or written enquiries to BTAS.

The information about hearing dates will be available, on the date that, or shortly after that BTAS issues a Convening Order for a Disciplinary Tribunal on behalf of the President of the Council of the Inns of Court (COIC).

In most cases, details of forthcoming hearings will be available between two to three weeks prior to the date of the hearing. These time periods can vary and information may be available at an earlier point or only very shortly before the hearing date.

The details available to the public about a forthcoming hearing will be:

- name of the defendant barrister;
- the barrister's Inn and date of call;
- the type of hearing;
- the names of the panellists and their current Register of Interests information;
- the paragraphs of the Bar Standards Board's Handbook under which the charges are laid;
- in the case of Appeals, the paragraphs of the Handbook under which the proved charges were laid and whether the Appeal is against conviction or sentence; and
- the venue and time of the hearing.

Information about forthcoming hearings that BTAS will not publish

Details of preliminary hearings that are held in private will not be made available to the public.

Details of hearings under the Fitness to Practise Regulations that are held in private will not be made available to the public.

…s of hearings under the Interim Suspension and Disqualification Regulations … held in private will not be made available to the public.

… hearings under the Inns' Conduct Committee Rules will not routinely be …le to the public as the proceedings do not relate to members of the Bar …eed to provide the public with information about a hearing which might …ual member of the Bar's ability to practice does not arise.

… BTAS website

In circu… posting on … website details of all relevant forthcoming hearings and the hearing but w… in accordance with above.

resumed hearing. will be amended on … hearing is adjourned or goes part heard following a …ntry will be amended to indicate the change to the … website pending a new, confirmed date for the … for the hearing has been confirmed, the posting

In circumstances where a … amended and the name of … panel is no longer able to sit, the entry will be … ute panel member provided as soon as possible.

If a Directions Judge or disciplinary panel order that a hearing shall take place in private, the fact of the hearing will still be posted on the website and all relevant information will be listed. However, the posting will make clear that the hearing has been ordered to take place in private and therefore members of the public are not able to attend.

Information about hearing dates will be removed from the website as soon as possible after the conclusion of the full hearing and at the latest within seven days.

Other means of providing information

Telephone and written enquiries requesting information about forthcoming hearings can be made to BTAS. Anyone making a telephone or written enquiry about forthcoming hearings is entitled to be given the relevant information listed.

The Hearings before the Visitors Rules

The Hearings before the Visitors Rules, which were housed at Annex M of the previous Code of Conduct have expired and therefore have ceased to have effect in respect of appeals against relevant decisions made on or after 7 January 2014. However, the rules continue to have effect in respect of appeals against relevant decisions made before 7 January 2014 and where notice required under rule rE233.1 (notice of intention to appeal) is served before 18 April 2014, until the disposal of the appeal.

The relevant provisions concerning the above can be found at Part 5 Section C of the BSB Handbook.

Fitness to Practise proceedings – guidance

[6.37]

Fitness to Practise proceedings are governed by the Fitness to Practise Rules which are at Annex O of the Bar's Code of Conduct.

These proceedings are confined to determining whether a barrister's fitness to practise is impaired as a result of his or her health and, if so, whether any restrictions on practice should be imposed.

Guidance on the fitness to practice procedure has also been produced for the benefit of barristers, their representatives and members of any Medical or Review Panel established under the Fitness to Practise Rules.

The guidance is not exhaustive and will be reviewed from time to time in light of experience and any relevant case law.

Introduction

1. The purpose of this guidance is to provide an overview of the procedures for determining whether an Individual's[1] fitness to practise is impaired by reason of his or her health, and to provide guidance on the application of the Fitness to Practise Regulations which are included in Part 5: Section E of the Bar

Standards Board BSB) Handbook 2014. The guidance has been prepared in liaison with the Council of the Inns of Court (COIC) and is issued jointly by the BSB and COIC.

2. This guidance is primarily for members of Medical and Review Panels. It will also be of assistance to barristers and their representatives, complainants and members of the public. This guidance is primarily for members of the BSB's Professional Conduct Committee (PCC) and Professional Conduct Department (PCD) and the COIC Fitness to Practise Panels and Appeal Panels ("Panels") administered by Bar Tribunal and Adjudication Service (BTAS), however, it will also be of assistance to the Individual and his or her representatives, complainants and members of the public.

3. This guidance is not exhaustive and will be reviewed from time to time in the light of experience and any relevant case law.

1 Please note: "Individual", for the purpose of these Regulations, means any BSB authorised individual, as defined under Part 6 of the Handbook.

Public protection and proportionality

4. Fitness to Practise and Appeal Panels are responsible for determining whether or not an Individual is unfit to practise, and, if so, what restrictions should be imposed on his or her right to practise. The Fitness to Practise Regulations should be read in conjunction with the BSB Handbook of the Bar of England and Wales, in particular the Complaints Regulations and the Disciplinary Tribunal Regulations.

5. In every case, a Panel must consider all the available evidence and must act to protect the public. Protection of the public, which is key, will require consideration of whether the Individual puts clients, or any other member of the public, at physical risk, or whether his or her judgment is impaired to such an extent that he or she is unable to adequately protect the client's interests.

6. Action may also be required in the public interest or in the interests of the Individual, where he or she puts himself or herself at risk, either professionally or personally, for example as a result of a lack of insight into his or her condition or capabilities.

7. Panels must at all times have regard to the requirements of natural justice and the principles of proportionality, and must deal with cases before them fairly, justly and efficiently. This involves:

   a. dealing with a case in ways which are proportionate to the complexity of the issues and the resources of the parties;

   b. seeking flexibility in proceedings wherever possible;

   c. ensuring that all parties have been given an opportunity to participate fully in the proceedings;

   d. using the Panel members' knowledge and experience effectively; and,

   e. avoiding delay, as far as possible.

The Equality Duty and duty to make reasonable adjustments

8. Panels need to be aware of their obligations under equality legislation. The following characteristics are protected under the Equality Act 2010:

   a. Age.

   b. Disability.

   c. Gender re-assignment.

   d. Pregnancy and maternity.

   e. Race.

   f. Religion or belief.

   g. Sex.

   h. Sexual orientation.

   i. Marriage and civil partnership.

9. Issues relating to the protected characteristics of age, disability and pregnancy and maternity are more likely than other protected characteristics to arise in fitness to practise proceedings (for the purposes of the Equality Act the protected period for pregnancy and maternity is the period of pregnancy and six months after the baby is born).

10. A person is disabled if they have a physical or mental impairment, and that impairment has a substantial and long-term adverse effect on his or her ability to carry out normal day-to-day activities (Equality Act 2010, section 6).

11. Panels must, in the exercise of their functions as defined under section 149 of the Equality Act 2010:

    a. have due regard to eliminate unlawful discrimination, harassment and victimisation and other conduct prohibited by the Act;

    b. seek to advance equality of opportunity between people who share a protected characteristic and those who do not; and,

    c. foster good relations between people who share a protected characteristic and those who do not.

12. Panels also have an obligation under the Equality Act 2010 to make reasonable adjustments for disabled persons. The duty to make reasonable adjustments is anticipatory and is defined under the Equality Act s.20 as the duty to take reasonable steps to avoid substantial disadvantage to disabled people in relation to:

    a. Provisions, criteria or practices.

    b. Physical features eg premises where tribunals are held.

    c. Provision of auxiliary aids eg induction loops.

13. Where an Individual coming before a Panel has a disability, the Panel must consider whether the Individual is fit to practise, on the assumption that reasonable adjustments will be made. This is because Individuals' chambers

and courts (except in relation to the exercise of their judicial function) have a duty to make reasonable adjustments to meet the requirements of disabled Individuals.

14. It should be borne in mind that even where reasonable adjustments have been made, an impairment may affect the ability of an Individual to undertake certain aspects of a role. However, the focus must be on his/her fitness to practise. For example, if an Individual is unable to travel long distances because of his/her impairment this may restrict him/her to practising in a smaller geographical area, but this is not in itself an issue relating to fitness to practise.

Initial consideration and referral of cases to a Fitness to Practise Panel

15. A case does not need to be referred to a Fitness to Practise Panel merely because an Individual is unwell, even if the illness is serious. However, an Individual's fitness to practise is brought into question if it appears that he/she has an incapacity due to a medical condition (including an addiction to drugs or alcohol), and as a result, the Individual's fitness to practise is impaired to such an extent that restrictions on practise are necessary (refer to paragraph 39 below for further discussion of the meaning of "unfit to practise"). For example, an Individual who has an incapacity but does not appear to be following appropriate medical advice about modifying his or her practice as necessary in order to minimise risk to the public may be "unfit to practise".

16. Information raising a question regarding an Individual's fitness to practise may be received from a variety of sources, for example, from a judge, other barristers, through another complaint, as a result of a self-referral from the Individual or from the findings of the Disciplinary Tribunal. The fitness to practise issues may also come to the PCC attention where it is considering a complaint of professional conduct.

17. The PCC must refer a case to a Fitness to Practise Panel if it considers that an Individual may be unfit to practise. The PCC may also refer a matter to a Fitness to Practise Panel where another Disciplinary Panel or Tribunal considering the matter considers an Individual may be unfit to practise, or where an Individual requests that the matter be referred (Regulation 18).

18. The complaint or information must raise genuine concerns as to the Individual's fitness to practise for the PCC to refer it to the Fitness to Practise Panel. It must not be frivolous, vexatious, or without merit. In considering whether to refer a case, the PCC will apply the "realistic prospect" test, and will consider whether there is a realistic prospect of establishing that the Individual's fitness to practise is impaired by reason of incapacity due to his or her physical or mental condition, to a degree justifying restrictions on practise.

19. No decision to refer shall be taken unless the Individual has had a reasonable opportunity to comment upon the matter (see Regulation 9). In practice, unless the Individual has already had an opportunity to comment on the information, upon receipt of any written information or complaint, the Chair of the PCC shall notify the Individual of that information and invite him or her to submit written representations to the PCC, normally within

14 days. This period will vary depending on the nature of the case, the level of risk to the public, or the need to make reasonable adjustment (which may involve allowing the Individual more time to respond). Any such representations made by the Individual will be taken into consideration by the PCC when deciding whether to refer the matter to a Fitness to Practise Panel. The PCC has a duty to act quickly to protect members of the public and the wider public interest and it is important for cases presenting the most risk to be referred to a Preliminary Hearing in short order after information suggesting that interim restrictions on an Individual's practice are required. It will therefore not always be possible to gather all the evidence that might potentially be available before referring the matter to a Preliminary Hearing, particularly in the most serious cases.

20. In addition, in reaching a decision regarding referral, the PCC should have regard to:

a. the standard of proof which will apply before the Panel when considering facts in dispute (i.e. the civil standard of proof);

b. the weight of the evidence (and any finding of fact); and,

c. the Bar Standard Board's duty to act in the public interest, which includes the protection of the public and maintaining public confidence in the profession.

21. If in doubt, the PCC should lean in favour of allowing the case to proceed to a Fitness to Practise Panel, and should be slower to halt a case concerning an Individual who continues to practise than one who does not.

Preliminary hearing of a Medical Panel

22. Once a matter is referred to a Fitness to Practise Panel, a preliminary hearing will be held.

23. At the preliminary hearing the Fitness to Practise Panel will consider:

a. whether to give directions for a full hearing of the Panel (see paragraphs 24 to 29 below);

b. whether the Individual should be suspended or prohibited from accepting or carrying out any public access instructions pending the conclusion of the matter; and,

c. any undertakings as to the Individual's conduct or behaviour pending the conclusion of the full hearing.

Directions for the full hearing

24. At a preliminary hearing the Fitness to Practise Panel may direct that the Individual undergo an examination by a Medical Examiner nominated by the Panel (Regulation 12(a)). On nominating the Examiner, the Panel will take into account the available information about the Individual's condition and have regard to any reasonable objections to the nominated Medical Examiner raised by the Individual.

25. The examination will involve an assessment of the Individual's physical and/or mental condition by a Medical Examiner who is a registered medical

practitioner appointed by the Panel. The Medical Examiner will then prepare a report which shall be disclosed to the Panel and the Individual in accordance with Regulation 13(b).

26. The Individual may also be asked to authorise disclosure of his or her relevant medical records to such Medical Examiner for the purpose of the examination and producing the report. Such disclosure will only be required to the extent that is reasonably necessary to enable the Medical Examiner to perform the examination to the appropriate standard and to report to the Fitness to Practise Panel on any relevant matters.

27. While the Fitness to Practise Panel cannot compel an Individual to submit to an examination or agree to disclosure of his or her medical records, it shall be entitled to take any refusal to supply relevant medical records into consideration when deciding if the Individual is unfit to practise.

28. The Fitness to Practise Panel may also direct the PCC to carry out such other investigations as the Panel considers appropriate to the matters for consideration at the full hearing. The nature of any further investigations required will depend on the circumstances of the case, but may include obtaining documentary evidence and taking statements from witnesses.

Interim restrictions

29. When considering whether to direct an interim suspension or disqualification, the Panel should bear in mind that its primary duty is to protect members of the public and the wider public interest, and not to assume responsibility for, or give priority to, the treatment or rehabilitation of the Individual.

30. If the Panel is satisfied that:

    a. in all the circumstances, there may be impairment of an Individual's fitness to practise which poses a real risk to members of the public (as discussed at paragraph 5), or is otherwise in the public interest or the interests of the Individual; and,

    b. after balancing this against the impact on the Individual, the Panel considers that an interim order is a proportionate response; the appropriate order should be made.

31. In reaching a decision whether to direct an interim order, the Panel should consider the following issues:

    a. the seriousness of the risk to members of the public if the Individual continues to practise pending conclusion of the full hearing. In assessing this risk the Panel should consider the seriousness of the allegations, and the weight of the information, including information about the likelihood of a further incident(s) occurring during the relevant period. For this purpose the Panel should pay no regard to the complexity of the legal work generally undertaken by the Individual;

    b. whether public confidence in the profession is likely to be seriously damaged if the Individual continues to practise during the relevant period;

c. whether it is in the Individual's interests to practise unrestricted. For example, the Individual may clearly lack insight as to the impact of his or her health condition or ability to practise;

d. whether the public can be sufficiently protected by accepting any undertakings as to their practise, and the Individual's willingness to make such undertakings (discussed below).

32. The period of any interim suspension or disqualification must be specified. Except in exceptional circumstances, the period shall not exceed 3 months (Regulation 16). In considering the period for which an interim suspension or disqualification should be imposed, the Panel should bear in mind the time that is likely to be needed before the matter is resolved (for example, the time needed to complete any investigation into allegations regarding the Individual's fitness to practise, including obtaining assessments of the Individual's health and for the case to be listed for a full hearing of the Fitness to Practise Panel). For a period of interim suspension or disqualification to exceed 3 months, there must be "exceptional circumstances". To be "exceptional", the circumstances must be out of the ordinary course, unusual, special, or uncommon. To be exceptional a circumstance need not be unique or unprecedented or even very rare, but it cannot be one that is regularly, routinely, or normally encountered (Lord Bingham CJ in *R v Kelly* (*Edward*) [2000] QB 198 at page 208). The Panel will need to decide what is exceptional on a case by case basis. When the Panel decides to direct an interim restriction, it must give reasons for that decision, including reasons for the period of time for which it is directed, particularly where the period exceeds 3 months. The reasons do not need to be long or detailed but must be clear and explain how the decisions were reached, including identifying the reasons for which the order is considered necessary.

Reviewing interim restrictions

33. The Panel, Chair of the PCC, the PCC (or PCD, acting under authority from the PCC), or the Individual may direct that a review of the interim restriction is held, before the period expires (Regulation 18(a)).

34. The Individual may also request a review in the event of a significant change in circumstances or other good reason (see paragraph 67 below in relation to the meaning of "significant change in circumstances"). A review shall be by way of rehearing of the case by the Fitness to Practise Panel in accordance with Regulation 27.

35. When reviewing an interim order or undertakings, the Panel must fully consider all the circumstances relating to the case, including any new information and may exercise any of the powers of the Fitness to Practise Panel under Regulation 28 confirm, extend, vary or replace the previous direction. In doing so, the Panel should apply the same test and take account of the same factors as set out in paragraph 31 above.

Full hearing of the Fitness to Practise Panel

36. At the end of the investigation period, once any relevant medical reports have been received, the PCC will prepare a summary of the case. Once this has been prepared, the Individual shall be notified of the arrangements for a full hearing of the Fitness to Practise Panel.

37. At the conclusion of a full hearing of the Fitness to Practise Panel it shall determine whether the Individual is unfit to practise, and if so, what restrictions to impose.

Determining whether the barrister is unfit to practise

38. Under definition 218 of Part 6 of the BSB Handbook, an Individual is "unfit to practise" where he or she:

    a. is incapacitated due to his physical or mental condition (including any addiction); and,

    b. as a result, the Individual's fitness to practise is impaired; and,

    c. his or her suspension or disqualification, or the imposition of conditions is necessary for the protection of the public.

39. "Incapacity" means that the Individual is unable to function or incapable of functioning as normal. The incapacity must have a material effect on his or her ability to function on a day-to-day basis. The incapacity must impair the Individual's fitness to practise, in that, his or her ability to practise must be damaged or harmed by reason of his or her incapacity. Finally, it must be necessary to restrict the Individual's ability to practise either in the public interest or in the Individual's own interests.

40. The Panel must first determine whether any facts in dispute are proved, and shall apply the civil standard of proof. This is the balance of probabilities; in other words, the Panel must be satisfied that it is more likely than not that an event occurred. It is then for the Panel to decide, exercising its judgment, whether, on the basis of the facts proved, the Individual is unfit to practise.

41. The following evidence may be taken into account when considering if an Individual is unfit to practise:

    a. any evidence of actual self-harm or a risk of self-harm;

    b. any evidence of actual harm, or a risk of harm to clients, colleagues or to the public;

    c. the Individual's current physical or mental condition;

    d. whether the Individual's condition is episodic, recurrent, or in remission, if it is likely to recur, and whether it is capable of causing impairment if it recurs;

    e. whether the Individual's condition has been sustained over a long period;

    f. whether there has been a failure by the Individual to seek relevant help, treatment or support for the condition;

    g. whether there has been a failure by the Individual to comply with reasonable undertakings which were intended to assist him or her to work effectively within the constraints of his or her condition;

    h. whether there has been a failure by the Individual to comply with a drug regime, treatment regime or medical supervision relating to the condition;

i. whether there has been a failure by the Individual to comply with instructions from a health professional about relevant testing, investigations and medical assessment relating to the condition;

j. whether circumstances have prevented the individual from seeking treatment, or the receipt of treatment is not relevant or available;

k. the Individual's insight in relation to the condition and the impact on his or her ability to practise;

l. any previous findings that the Individual was unfit to practise or otherwise impaired by reason of his or her health by any other regulatory body. However, in such cases the Panel should bear in mind that the findings may have been made at a time when equality legislation such as the Equality Act 2010 or Disability Discrimination Act 2010 did not exist; or,

m. any refusal to comply with reasonable requests in relation to a medical examination or the disclosure of relevant medical records.

42. If the Individual's fitness to practise is not impaired by any incapacity, or if restricting practise is not necessary for the protection of the public or in the Individual's own interests, the Panel must conclude that an Individual is not unfit to practise, and no action needs to be taken.

43. The Panel must give reasons for its determination as to whether the Individual is unfit to practise. Where facts are disputed, the Panel must also give reasons as to why an Individual's evidence was not preferred. Such reasons need not be detailed and need only refer to, for example, the Individual's demeanour, attitude or approach to specific questions (*Southall v General Medical Council* [2009] EWHC 1155 (Admin), [2009] 3 FCR 223, [2009] 2 FLR 1246). However, the demeanour of an individual may be directly related to a disability or impairment and Panels should ensure they take this into account when assessing the evidence.

Restrictions

44. If the Fitness to Practise Panel is satisfied that the Individual is unfit to practise, the Panel will then consider what directions to make in relation to the Individual's practice. The directions available to the Panel are set out at Regulation 22.

45. In deciding what restriction to impose, the Panel should weigh the interests of the public against the interests of the Individual, and should have regard to any mitigating factors, which may include, but are not limited to:

a. evidence of the Individual's insight and understanding of his or her condition, and his or her attempts to address it, which may include seeking and undergoing relevant treatment for his or her condition (where relevant and available), and expressions of regret and apology;

b. evidence of the Individual's overall adherence to important principles of good practice. Mitigation could relate to the circumstances leading up to the incidents as well as the character and previous medical history of the Individual; and/or,

c. matters of personal and professional mitigation, such as testimonials, or evidence of personal hardship and work related stress. However, features such as these should be considered and balanced carefully against the central aim of restrictions, that being the protection of the public and the maintenance of standards and public confidence in the profession.

46. When assessing whether an Individual has insight, the Panel will need to take into account whether he or she has demonstrated insight consistently throughout the hearing, eg the Individual has not given any untruthful evidence to the Panel or falsified documents. But the Panel should be aware that there may be differences in the way that insight is expressed, for example, whether or how an apology or expression of regret is framed and delivered and the process of communication, and that this may be affected by the Individual's circumstances, for example, his or her ill health.

47. The Panel should also have regard to any aggravating factors, such as any previous findings and restrictions imposed by a Fitness to Practise Panel at a full hearing or by any other regulator. The Panel must not, however, give undue weight to any decision to impose an interim suspension or disqualification pending full hearing, as the Panel, when considering whether to direct an interim restriction at a preliminary hearing applies a lower test. That decision will also have been reached without making a finding on the facts or on the Individual's fitness to practise.

48. Whatever restriction is directed, the Panel must explain its reasons for doing so. This will help show that all relevant issues have been addressed and why a particular course of action has been taken. The explanation should include:

    a. the factual basis of the decision;

    b. the legal power or authority being relied upon; and,

    c. conclusions on the main submissions made by the parties or representatives.

49. Reasons must be given in sufficient detail so that interested parties may understand why a determination has been made and should include reference to the mitigating and aggravating factors that influenced its decision. The determination should include an explanation as to why a particular period of restriction was considered necessary, and, in the interest of proportionality, must also demonstrate that the less serious conditions and restrictions were considered, and the reasons as to why the Panel did not consider they were appropriate.

Conditions on practise

50. The Fitness to Practise Panel may make the Individual's right to continue to practise (or right to resume practise after any period of suspension n or disqualification) subject to such conditions as it thinks fit. The purpose of conditions is to enable the Individual to deal with his or her health issues while continuing to practise in a way that protects the public.

51. Before imposing conditions the Panel should satisfy itself that:

    (a) the Individual's medical condition can be appropriately managed through conditions;

    (b) the Individual has genuine insight into his or her health problem(s);

    (c) the Individual will abide by conditions relating to his or her medical condition(s), treatment and supervision, and that circumstances do not prevent the Individual from doing so;

(d) the public will be protected and will not be put at risk either directly or indirectly; and,

(e) it is possible to formulate appropriate and practical conditions to impose on registration.

52. Where conditions are imposed they should be:

a. clear, so that an Individual knows what is expected of him or her, and a Panel at any future review hearing is able to ascertain the original concerns and the exact proposals for their correction;

b. relevant;

c. addressed to the Individual (not to third parties);

d. necessary in order to protect the public or in the interests of the Individual;

e. proportionate to the impairment;

f. formulated so that the conditions are not in effect a suspension; and,

g. written in such a way that compliance can be easily verified, for example by providing for reports prepared by treating medical practitioners to be provided to the PCC or a Panel considering the matter on review (see below).

53. It is open to a Panel to impose conditions as it sees fit in the circumstances of any particular case, whilst taking account of the general principles outlined above. However, appropriate conditions may include conditions relating to relevant medical treatment, as well as conditions relating to an Individual's day-to-day practise. For example, appropriate conditions may include:

a. a requirement to place him or herself under the care of a medical practitioner/health care practitioner specialising in the Individual's condition, attend upon them as required and follow their advice as to treatment of his or her condition;

b. allowing the PCC to exchange information with the medical practitioner/health care practitioner responsible for the Individual's care about his or her health and any relevant treatment he or she is receiving, such information to be disclosed to the Fitness to Practise Panel when reviewing the case;

c. a requirement to attend upon one or more Medical Examiners for regular examination, whose reports will be made available to the Chair of the PCC and/or any Fitness to Practise Panel when reviewing the case;

d. a requirement to place him or herself under the care of a professional supervisor as nominated by the Panel, to attend upon them as required and to follow their advice and recommendations as to day-to-day practise;

e. allowing the PCC to exchange information with the Individual's Supervisor on his or her progress under supervision and compliance with these conditions, such information being disclosed to the Fitness to Practise Panel when reviewing the case; and,

f. where an Individual is unfit to practise by reason of a substance addiction, appropriate conditions may include limiting consumption of that substance in accordance with relevant medical advice obtained.

54. Where an Individual is subject to undertakings or conditions following a hearing, these will be monitored and reviewed by the PCC. If evidence suggests that these have been breached or that the Individual's fitness to practise has otherwise deteriorated, then the Individual will generally be referred for a review hearing under Regulation 26 in order that appropriate action may be taken. Where the breach raises a question of professional misconduct, the matter will be referred to the PCC to consider a referral to the Disciplinary Tribunal.

Suspension (applicable to "BSB authorised individuals" only)

55. If a Fitness to Practise Panel determines that a period of suspension is necessary for public protection, it may direct a suspension, either for a period of up to six months or indefinitely.

56. Suspension will be appropriate where the Panel is satisfied that no conditions can be formulated to protect the public or the barrister's interests.

57. The Fitness to Practise Panel does not have the power to disbar a barrister only by reason that he or she is unfit to practise. However, it can impose an indefinite period of suspension (Regulation 22(a)).

58. Indefinite suspension should only be directed where the Fitness to Practise Panel considers that this is the only means of protecting the public and the wider public interest, which includes maintaining public trust and confidence in the profession.

59. Indefinite suspension may be appropriate where:

a. the authorised individual demonstrates a persistent lack of insight into the seriousness of his or her condition and its impact on his or her fitness to practise;

b. as a result of the authorised individual's incapacity, he or she has displayed a reckless and continuing disregard for the protection of the public;

c. the authorised individual is incapacitated to the extent that his or her behaviour is fundamentally incompatible with the behaviour reasonably expected of a barrister.

60. The Panel is required in the interests of proportionality to balance the need to take action to protect the public, with the interests of the member, including any personal misfortune that a period of suspension would result in for the authorised individual or his or her family. However, the Panel must remember that its primary function is to protect the public.

61. A Panel must provide reasons for the period of suspension chosen, including the factors that led them to conclude that the particular period of suspension was appropriate.

Undertakings

62. In lieu of making a direction to impose a period of restriction or to make his or her practise subject to conditions, a Panel may accept undertakings from an Individual. Those undertakings may relate to any conditions on practise, or any period of suspension or disqualification, and must be such as a Panel would have imposed.

63. Undertakings will only be appropriate where a Panel is satisfied that an Individual will comply with them, for example, because the Individual has shown genuine insight into his or her condition. The Panel may wish to see evidence that the Individual has taken responsibility for his or her own actions and/or otherwise taken steps to mitigate his or her actions.

64. Panellists should ensure that any undertakings are appropriate, proportionate, are sufficient to protect clients and the public, and are an effective way of addressing the concerns about the Individual. The guidance above in relation to conditions similarly applies where undertakings impose conditions on the right to practise.

65. Where a Panel accepts undertakings, the PCC will monitor the Individual's progress and consider any new information received in relation to him or her, including any representations from the Individual to suggest that the undertakings are no longer appropriate.

66. Where there has been a breach of an undertaking, or where further concerns about the Individual's fitness to practise arise (including new information indicating a deterioration in the Individual's health), the matter may be referred for a review hearing at the discretion of the Chair of the PCC. Where the breach raises a question of professional misconduct, the matter will be referred to the PCC to consider a referral to the Disciplinary Tribunal.

Review hearings

67. Where restrictions are directed by the Fitness to Practise Panel under Regulation 15 or 22 or undertaken under Regulation 23, they shall be reviewed at the discretion of the Chair of the PCC, either on his own motion or at the request of the PCD, acting under authority from the PCC, or the individual in the event of a significant change in circumstances, or other good reason (Regulation 26).

68. There may be a "significant change in circumstances or other good reason" where, for example, new and relevant evidence has come to light which could not reasonably have been known before the restrictions were imposed, or where circumstances have changed. Any change in circumstances must be significant having in mind the issues in the case, that is, be capable of leading the Panel on review to revoke or vary the order. Whether there is a significant change in circumstances or other good reason warranting a review hearing will be a question of judgment for the Chair of the PCC, who shall decide whether to convene a Fitness to Practise Panel to review the case.

69. On review, the Fitness to Practise Panel must determine whether the Individual remains unfit to practise, and if so, whether the restriction imposed should be extended or varied.

70. It is important that no Individual should be allowed to resume unrestricted practise following a period of conditional registration or restriction unless the Panel considers that he or she is fit to resume practise and that the public will not be placed at risk by resumption of practise or by the imposition of conditions on practice.

71. The Panel will take into account any evidence produced in relation to the Individual's conduct or behaviour following the imposition of a restriction, including any evidence arising from any conditions made under Regulation 22(b), as well as evidence from any medical examinations undertaken in accordance with Regulation 13.

72. Where a review hearing cannot be concluded before the expiry of the period of conditional registration or restrictions, the Panel may extend that period for a further short period to allow for re-listing of the review hearing as soon as practicable, with the objective of preserving the status quo pending the outcome of the review hearing (Regulation 29).

73. If a Panel finds that the Individual failed to comply with any term of suspension or disqualification or any conditions imposed [or undertaken], it may refer the matter to the PCC to consider whether a charge of professional misconduct should be brought before a Disciplinary Tribunal.

Appealing the Fitness to Practise Panel's decision

74. The Individual has a right to appeal against any decision made under the Regulations (except a previous decision made by an Appeal Panel), including a decision to refer a case to the Fitness to Practise Panel. Any appeals are heard by way of rehearing before an Appeal Panel, and the burden will be on the appellant to establish that the original decision was wrong in fact or in law.

75. Upon determination of any hearing of the Appeal Panel, the Panel may decide to:

   a. allow the appeal;

   b. confirm the decision that is the subject of the appeal;

   c. exercise any of the powers of a Fitness to Practise Panel.

76. The guidance above in relation to procedure and decision-making similarly applies to hearings before an Appeal Panel.

The role of the Medical Examiner as compared to the role of the Panel's Medical Member

77. A Medical Examiner is a registered medical practitioner, nominated by the Panel to conduct a medical examination of the Individual. The Medical Examiner is responsible for reporting his or her findings to the Panel, and may be required to give evidence of those findings before the Panel and/or provide expert advice or opinion on the case. The Individual or his or her representative shall be entitled to cross-examine the Medical Examiner. In contrast, the role of the Medical Member on the Panel is to provide general experience and context as part of the panel's overall ability to determine the

issues in relation to the barrister's fitness to practise. It is not their role to provide expert or medical evidence in relation to proceedings.

Attendance at hearings

78. The attendance of the Individual at any hearing of the Fitness to Practise Panel and Appeal Panel is required (Regulation 37(b)).

79. However, if the Individual does not attend, the Panel may proceed in his or her absence if it is satisfied that:

 a. it is appropriate to do so; and,

 b. all reasonable efforts have been made to serve the Individual with notice of the hearing, by post to the Individual's address or, where agreed, by email; and

 c. no acceptable explanation for the Individual's absence has been provided. Examples of what is acceptable may include ill health supported by relevant medical evidence, child/dependent care arrangements falling through unexpectedly, death/bereavement or serious accident involving family members.

80. If the Panel is not satisfied the above conditions have been met, it shall adjourn.

81. In considering whether proceeding in the absence of the Individual is appropriate, the Panel should take into account the following factors, where applicable:

 a. the nature and circumstances of the Individual's behaviour in absenting himself or herself from the hearing, and in particular whether the behaviour was voluntary and deliberate and so plainly waived the right to be present;

 b. whether an adjournment might result in the Individual attending voluntarily;

 c. the likely length of such an adjournment;

 d. whether the Individual, though absent, is, or wishes to be represented or has, by his or her conduct, indicated that he/she does not wish to be represented;

 e. whether the Individual's representative was able to receive instructions from him or her and the extent to which they could present his or her defence;

 f. the extent of the disadvantage to the Individual in not being able to present his or her account of events, having regard to the nature of the evidence against him or her;

 g. the risk of the hearing reaching an improper conclusion about the absence of the Individual;

 h. the general public interest and the particular interest of any witnesses that a hearing should be held within a reasonable time; and,

 i. the effect of the delay on the memories of witnesses.

Listing and vacating hearing dates

82. Fitness to Practise Panels and Appeal Panels are convened by the President of the Council of the Inns of Court. The President maintains a COIC panellist pool, which includes members eligible to sit on a Panel and consider fitness to practise issues; the pool includes practising barristers and lay members. In order to be eligible to sit on a Fitness to Practise Panel, a barrister must be at least 7 years Call, and to be a Chair, must be Queen's Counsel. To be eligible to sit on an Appeal Panel, a barrister member must be Queen's Counsel who is entitled to sit as a Recorder or Deputy High Court Judge, or have been Queen's Counsel for at least 7 years. In accordance with Schedule 1, Paragraph 3 of the Regulations, the President will have in place separate arrangements for the appointment Medical Members, as these members will not form part of the COIC panellist pool.

83. Before a hearing is listed, the Individual will be notified of the proposed time and date, and one alternative. The Individual will have an opportunity to accept one of the dates proposed, or to make representations proposing two further alternative dates.

84. Where the notice of hearing has been served, a hearing scheduled before a Fitness to Practise or Appeal Panel may be postponed by the Chair of the Panel under Regulation 44. Where a hearing before a Fitness to Practise or Appeal Panel has commenced, the Panel may, at any time, adjourn a hearing in accordance with Regulation 45.

85. In deciding whether to postpone or adjourn a hearing, the decision-maker must take into account all material circumstances, including:

    a. the public interest in the expeditious disposal of the case;

    b. the potential inconvenience caused to a party or any witnesses to be called by that party;

    c. the conduct of the party seeking the postponement or adjournment; and,

    d. the effect of any delay on the fairness of proceedings.

86. Where the Individual applies for a postponement or adjournment on grounds of ill health:

    a. the Individual must adduce appropriate medical certification in support of that application; and,

    b. the decision-maker may, if not satisfied by the medical certification produced, require the person to submit to be examined by a registered medical practitioner approved by the President.

Administrative matters

87. Where a Panel is convened, it will be assisted by a secretary who will be responsible for providing administrative support to the Panel, but who will carry out this role independently of the Bar Standards Board. A representative of the Professional Conduct Committee of the Bar Standards Board will be responsible for matters relevant to the preparation of the papers for presentation before a Panel hearing, including obtaining any reports or undertaking such other investigations as directed by Panel.

88. Panel hearings shall be recorded electronically, and the records shall be retained in accordance with the Professional Conduct Department's Data Retention Policy or, if any charges of professional misconduct are brought against the Individual arising from the case, until those proceedings have been finally disposed of or any appeal in relation to those proceedings has been exhausted.

Chambers Complaints Processes – First Tier Complaints Handling

[6.38]–[6.74]

The BSB also provides guidance for chambers in relation to the management of their own complaints processes.

1. This guidance supplements Section D1.1 of the Code of Conduct. It covers three areas:

    (a) the scope of chambers complaints handling;

    (b) the obligation to notify clients of their right to complain;

    (c) guidance to chambers in developing chambers complaint procedures.

2. References to "client" in this guidance are to the lay client.

A. Scope of chambers complaints handling

Complaints are expressions of dissatisfaction by clients. This guidance draws a distinction between complaints that relate to service, professional negligence and misconduct. A single complaint may have elements of all three and the obligations on chambers are different for each aspect.

Service complaints

The requirements set out in Section D1.1 of the Code of Conduct relate to the handling of service complaints which are within the jurisdiction of the Legal Ombudsman.

Chapter 2 of the Legal Ombudsman's scheme rules set out the types of complaint that are within its jurisdiction. These are complaints that relate to an act or omission by an authorised person in relation to services provided to the complainant (directly or indirectly).

In addition, the Legal Ombudsman's website sets out a list of the categories of complaint which it investigates. These include the following categories (some of which may also include aspects of negligence or misconduct):

- Costs information deficient
- Costs excessive
- Delay
- Unreasonably refused a service to a complainant
- Persistently or unreasonably offered a service that the complainant does not want
- Failure to advise
- Failure to comply with agreed remedy
- Failure to follow instructions
- Failure to investigate complaint internally
- Failure to keep complainant informed of progress
- Failure to keep papers safe
- Failure to progress complainant's case
- Failure to release files or papers
- Failure to reply

Misconduct and professional negligence

Chambers may not be best placed to seek to resolve or provide redress for complaints which relate to misconduct or professional negligence and there is no positive obligation to investigate matters of misconduct.

However, it is likely that in many cases a complaint which raises issues relating to professional misconduct or professional negligence will also amount to an accusation of the provision of poor service or will include a service element. Where this is the case, the service issues should be dealt with in accordance with Section D1.1 of the Code of Conduct. It is not acceptable for chambers not to investigate elements of a complaint which relate to service because the complaint also amounts to, or includes elements which relate to, misconduct or could potentially give rise to a negligence claim.

Complainants should be informed in writing if any aspects of their complaint are deemed to be outside of chambers' complaints handling procedures. This should include information on how to complain to the Legal Ombudsman.

Bar Mutual Indemnity Fund

Where a complaint raises an allegation of negligence it may be appropriate to inform BMIF and to consult them before any proposals for resolution are made to the client.

Non-client complaints

The Legal Ombudsman will only deal with complaints from consumers of lawyers' services. This means that only complaints from the barrister's clients fall within the Ombudsman's jurisdiction. This does not mean that non-client complaints should not be investigated by Chambers. Some non-client complaints, such as discourtesy, may be capable of resolution by Chambers. However, the BSB recognises that Chambers' ability to resolve many kinds of non-client complaints is limited and that they are more suited to consideration under the disciplinary processes of the Bar Standards Board. Accordingly, if Chambers feel that the issues raised by non-clients cannot be satisfactorily resolved through the Chambers complaints process they should refer the complainant to the Bar Standards Board.

B. *Notifying the client of the right to complain*

The New Regime

3. From 6 October 2010, Barristers must notify clients in writing at the time of engagement or if not practicable at the next appropriate opportunity:

   (a) Of their right to make a complaint, how and to whom this can be done, including their right to complain to the Legal Ombudsman at the conclusion of the complaints process, the timeframe for doing so and the full details of how to contact the Legal Ombudsman;

   (b) That the lay client may complain directly to Chambers without going through solicitors.

4. At the conclusion of the complaints process, complainants must be informed in writing of their right to complain to the Legal Ombudsman, who from 6 October 2010 has taken on responsibility for dealing with all service complaints against legal professionals, the timeframe for doing so and the full details of how to contact them.

Complaints to chambers

5. The Legal Services Board (LSB) have specified a requirement to which the BSB is obliged to give effect under s 112(2) of the Legal Services Act 2007. The requirement relates to "first-tier" complaints which, and so far as self-employed barristers are concerned, relate to the procedure whereby a client makes a complaint to Chambers in the first instance.

6. The LSB seeks to ensure consumers have confidence that:

   (a) complaint handling procedures provide effective safeguards for them;

   (b) complaints will be dealt with comprehensively and swiftly, with appropriate redress where necessary.

7. Chambers complaint handling processes must be convenient and easy to use (in particular for those that are vulnerable or have disabilities). They should make provision for complaints to be made by any reasonable means. The way in which complaints are dealt with must be transparent and clear in relation to process, well publicised and free. The process itself should be prompt and fair, with decisions based on a sufficient investigation of the circumstances. Where appropriate, there should be an offer of a suitable remedy.

8. Most consumers will be able to make a complaint to the Legal Ombudsman about the services they received after they have exhausted Chambers complaints processes. Sufficient information must be provided to all clients to

identify whether they do have a right to take their complaint to the Legal Ombudsman and to contact the Legal Ombudsman direct to clarify whether they can.

9. Please note that the Legal Ombudsman, the independent complaints body for service complaints about lawyers, has time limits in which a complaint must be raised with them. The time limits are:

    a. Six years from the date of the act/omission.

b. Three years from the date that the complainant should reasonably have known there were grounds for complaint (if the act/omission took place before the 6 October 2010 or was more than six years ago).

    c. Within six months of the complaint receiving a final response from their lawyer, if that response complies with the requirements in rule 4.4 of the Scheme Rules (which requires the response to include prominently an explanation that the Legal Ombudsman was available if the complainant remained dissatisfied and the provision of full contact details for the Ombudsman and a warning that the complaint must be referred to them within six months. The Ombudsman can extend the time limit in exceptional circumstances. Chambers must therefore have regard to that timeframe when deciding whether they are able to investigate your complaint. Chambers will not therefore usually deal with complaints that fall outside of the Legal Ombudsman's time limits.

10. Clients who have, or may have, a right to complain to the legal Ombudsman, must at the conclusion of the complaint process be informed of their right to complain to the Legal Ombudsman, the timeframe for doing so and full details of how to contact the Legal Ombudsman.

11. Where a barrister accepts instructions from a new client, or instructions on a new matter from an existing client, the client must be notified of the right to make a complaint, how and to whom this can be done. It is essential that systems be set up by Chambers to ensure that these requirements are properly complied with. This will be straightforward for public access clients, but because self-employed barristers will usually be instructed by a solicitor or other professional client on behalf of the client, new procedures will need to be put in place for notifying other clients.

Compliance with requirements to notify clients

12. The LSB has specified a requirement that the BSB must require all individuals and entities they regulate to notify all clients in writing at the time of engagement, or existing clients at the next appropriate opportunity, of their right to make a complaint, how and to whom this can be done (including their right to complain to the Legal Ombudsman at the conclusion of the complaint process, the timeframe for doing so and full details of how to contact the Legal Ombudsman).

13. The Bar Standards Board is required to enforce the LSB requirement and compliance by Chambers. The BSB will monitor Chambers to ensure that the requirement is being complied with.

14. Significant concerns have been expressed by barristers in a variety of fields of practice that a requirement to notify clients directly of their right to

complain would be difficult or impossible to comply with. The BSB are fully aware of these concerns and have discussed them with the LSB. The guidance below is set out to assist barristers and Chambers in setting up systems to effect compliance with the requirement of the LSB in a way that is neither disproportionate nor onerous.

15. Where the barrister is aware of the contact details for the client, the obligation can be satisfied by a letter or e-mail sent directly to the client (which may be sent by someone else on his behalf) providing the required information.

16. If the information has not been provided beforehand in writing, it may be provided on the first occasion that the barrister meets the client at court, or in conference.

17. Subject to the points made below, it is not acceptable for barristers simply to make the information available to solicitors. Nor is it sufficient that the information is available on Chambers' website. There is a positive obligation on the barrister to provide it to the client.

18. An unequivocal agreement by the professional client to pass on chambers' complaint information to the client, either in a particular case, or in relation to each case in which a member of chambers is instructed by that professional client, will serve to discharge the obligation to provide the client with the information. However, there must be a positive agreement on the part of the professional client: silence is not sufficient. Where Chambers receive high volume instructions from a particular professional client it will not be necessary to obtain written confirmation in relation to each instruction. In those circumstances, positive written confirmation should be obtained at regular and reasonable intervals from the professional client that complaints information continues to be passed on to lay clients.

Client information sheets

19. Some barristers may be unhappy at the prospect that the first thing they do when they meet the client is to advise the client how to make a complaint. A "client information sheet" is one way in which the information may be communicated to the client. The information sheet giving details about the barrister as well as information on how to complain could be given to the client by the barrister. An example of a client information sheet is annexed. Whilst the information sheet carries the necessary information, it also carries helpful information for the client about the barrister and should not give rise to any negative impression. The client information sheet may be sent or handed out to the client; it may also be provided by the clerk or receptionist when the client arrives for a conference.

Compliance

20. Whilst these requirements came into force on 6 October 2010, since 2008 Annex S of the Code of Conduct has required barristers or a member of staff when first instructed to notify clients of their Chambers Complaints Procedure. The principal difference was that the requirement in force since 2008 permitted compliance by requesting in writing the solicitor or intermediary to pass the information on to the client. These requirements since 2008 have not given rise to concerns on the part of the profession.

21. It is recognised that there will be circumstances in which, in individual cases, it is impractical to comply strictly with the requirements. What is important is that Chambers set up systems, and establish procedures, to effect compliance with these requirements consistent with this guidance. The precise solutions will differ according to different fields of practice. If this has been done responsibly, then the BSB will in their monitoring visits regard sympathetically particular and specific problems and difficulties which occur or are likely to occur in individual cases.

Cases where the procedure cannot be followed

22. Where the barrister has the contact details of the client, or when the barrister meets the client in the course of the matter, compliance should not in general present a problem.

23. However, there will be areas of practice, and particular cases, where it is not possible or practical for the barrister to satisfy the notification requirement in this way. For example, the barrister may not have the contact details of the client, cannot readily obtain them, and does not anticipate meeting the client in the course of being instructed or at least not for some time.

24. Some common sense is required in setting up procedures so as to fulfil the notification requirements. For example, where a barrister acts for government departments or public bodies it should be possible to agree a standing arrangement with treasury solicitors or other inhouse lawyers whereby details of the complaints system is provided to the professional client to be passed on to the client body. Most barristers will be able to think of examples within their own field of practice where procedures can be responsibly adopted so as to fulfil the notification requirement.

25. In some cases there will be no realistic alternative to compliance by providing the requisite information to the solicitor or other professional client with instructions to provide that information to the client on behalf of the barrister, even when the solicitor has not expressly agreed to do so. But this course should only be adopted when other better means of compliance are not practical.

C. Chambers complaints procedure: guidance

26. This guidance is provided to Chambers to assist them to develop a complaints procedure which is compliant with the mandatory requirements set out at Section D1.1 of the Code of Conduct. Chambers are not obliged to follow the guidance absolutely. If Chambers decide not to adopt the model procedure provided at Appendix 1 below, they should have regard to this guidance when devising their own complaints handling arrangements.

27. All barristers must be familiar with the requirements of Section D1.1 of the Code of Conduct.

28. Those barristers who are responsible for dealing with complaints should ensure that they and any staff who deal with complaints are adequately trained. The Bar Standards Board will audit and monitor Chambers complaints handling, including the sufficiency of training.

29. This annex sets out the contents of an effective procedure. Model complaints procedures are at Appendix 1 (multi member sets of Chambers) and Appendix 2 (sole practitioners). Chambers will need to insert names/positions etc into the sections in square brackets. Chambers must ensure that their website and brochure carries information about the Chambers' Complaints Procedure.

30. Chambers are not obliged to adopt the model complaints procedures provided below. The model procedures set out good practice arrangements for handling complaints but the BSB is aware that there are alternative methods that may be just as effective. Chambers have discretion to either devise their own procedure or to amend the model procedure to best fit their own administrative arrangements or the particular circumstances of a complaint. The only requirements are that Chambers adopts a complaints procedure that includes the mandatory requirements laid down in the complaints protocol set out at Section D1.1 of the Code of Conduct.

31. Possible alternatives to the arrangements in the model procedure have been provided where appropriate. These alternatives are not exhaustive but are used to highlight that other procedures may be more suitable for Chambers depending on their size, practice type or administrative set up.

Chambers complaints procedure: first stage

32. Where a client is dissatisfied with some aspect of the service provided by a barrister or by Chambers he should be invited to telephone an individual nominated under the Chambers Complaints Procedure to deal with complaints. For example, the Chambers Director, Practice Manager or Head of Chambers. In order to ensure consistency of approach, this individual should be the first point of contact for all complaints. The client should also be told that if he prefers he may make the complaint in writing and the Chambers Complaint Procedure should be sent to him unless it has already been provided.

33. Where a complaint is made by telephone, a note of the complaint should be made. It should record:

- the name and address of the complainant;
- the date of the complaint;
- against whom the complaint is made;
- the detail of the complaint; and
- what the complainant believes should be done about the complaint.

34. In many cases the complaint will be resolved over the telephone during the first call. When that occurs the individual nominated to deal with complaints should record the outcome on the note of complaint. The client should be asked whether he is content with the outcome and informed of the Legal Ombudsman's complaints procedure. If he is, that fact will be recorded. The complaints procedure should suggest that the client may wish to make his own note. If the client is not content he should be invited to put the complaint in writing so that it may be investigated formally. At that stage he should be sent a copy of the Chambers' Complaints Procedure unless it has already been provided: The client should also be informed of the Legal Ombudsman's complaints procedure.

Chambers complaint procedure: second stage

35. It is recommended that Chambers set up a complaints panel made up of experienced practitioners from different practice areas and a senior member of staff. A head of panel should be appointed. There should be a nominated deputy. All complaints (other than those resolved at stage one) should be put before the head of the panel or, in his absence, the deputy. The role of the panel is to appoint from its members an independent person to investigate a complaint and to ensure that all complaints are handled consistently and in accordance with the Chambers complaints procedure.

36. It may not be appropriate or possible for a small set of Chambers to convene a complaints panel. Chambers are encouraged to set up a complaints panel where possible or otherwise nominate an individual or individuals to investigate the complaint.

37. Sole practitioners may not feel able to investigate independently a complaint raised against them and should therefore offer mediation or arbitration if a complaint remains unresolved. A suggested approach to mediation/arbitration is set out in the model procedure for sole practitioners at Appendix 2 below.

38. A complaint received in writing should, where possible, be acknowledged within two days of receipt and, in any event, promptly. Within 14 days of that acknowledgment the head of the panel (where one has been set up) (or his deputy) should appoint a member of the panel to investigate the complaint. Where the complaint is against a member of staff the person appointed normally will be the senior staff member. Where the complaint is against the senior staff member the head of the panel should appoint another member of the panel to investigate. Where the complaint is against the head of the panel, the Head of Chambers should investigate or, in his discretion, appoint a member of the panel to investigate. Where the Head of Chambers is the head of the panel, the deputy head of the panel should be the appointed person. No barrister should investigate a complaint of which he is the subject. Where no panel has been established, Chambers should ensure that the individual or individuals nominated to investigate the complaint is impartial.

39. The appointed person/nominated individual should write to the client as soon as he is appointed. He should inform him that he is to investigate the complaint and that he will report back to the client within 14 days. If it becomes plain that a response cannot be sent within 14 days a realistic time frame should be set and the client informed accordingly.

40. The appointed person/nominated individual should investigate the complaint. He should speak to the barrister/member of staff complained against, and any other people he identifies as having something to contribute. He should review all relevant documents. If necessary he should revert to the client for further information and clarification.

41. The appointed person/nominated individual should prepare a report to the client (with a copy to the barrister/member of staff complained against). The report should set out all the matters referred to at paragraph 33 above, the nature and scope of the investigations carried out in respect of each complaint, his conclusions and the basis for his conclusions. The report should be drafted using clear and concise language. Where a complaint is

found to be justified, the report should provide proposals for resolution (e.g. reduction in fees, apology, compensation).

42. The report should be sent to the client within 14 days of the appointed person's appointment (or such longer period as has been communicated to the client in advance – see paragraph 39). A copy of the report should be provided to the barrister/member of staff complained against.

Charging for complaints

45. Chambers should not charge clients for dealing with their complaint. To do so brings the Bar into disrepute and could amount to professional misconduct.

Confidentiality

46. All conversations and documents shall be confidential and disclosed only to the extent necessary. They may be disclosed only to the client, the person complained about, the Head of Chambers, the head of the complaints panel or relevant senior member of the panel, the nominated individual, the management committee (for carrying out the task at paragraph 41) and any other individual with whom enquiries need to be made for the purpose of the investigation.

Record keeping

47. Where the procedure ends after the first stage the person responsible for recording the outcome on the note of complaint should ensure that the note of complaint is placed on the Chambers complaints file.

48. Where the procedure ends after the second stage the head of the panel/ nominated individual should ensure that the following documents are placed on the Chambers complaints file:

- Note/letter of complaint; (see paragraph 33);
- Appointed person's/nominated individual's report; (see paragraph 41).

Review, monitoring and audit

52. The Chambers complaints file should be inspected regularly by the management committee. Papers should be anonymised where necessary. The person responsible for the administration of the system should report at least annually to such appropriate committee of Chambers on the number of complaints received and the subject area of the complaints. In such a report all the details should be anonymised, but should be reviewed for trends and possible training issues.

53. The Bar Standards Board will audit and monitor Chambers complaints handling, including, where appropriate, the sufficiency of training. All barristers must comply promptly with requests for information from the committees of the Bar Standards Board dealing with monitoring and auditing.

Appendix I

The model procedures for Chambers and for Sole Practitioners are based on the suggested arrangements for handling complaints set out in the above guidance. Chambers or sole practitioners may decide to adopt the model procedure but are free to develop their own procedure or set of rules for dealing with complaints. Chambers' must ensure that any procedure they develop is compliant with the mandatory requirements, Section D1.1 of the Code of Conduct.

Model Chambers complaints procedure for multi member sets

1. Our aim is to give you a good service at all times. However if you have a complaint you are invited to let us know as soon as possible. It is not necessary to involve solicitors in order to make your complaint but you are free to do so should you wish.

2. Please note that the Legal Ombudsman, the independent complaints body for service complaints about lawyers, has time limits in which a complaint must be raised with them. The time limits are:

   a. six years from the date of the act/omission;

   b. three years from the date that the complainant should reasonably have known there were grounds for complaint (if the act/omission took place before the 6 October 2010 or was more than six years ago);

   c. within six months of the complaint receiving a final response from their lawyer, if that response complies with the requirements in rule 4.4 of the Scheme Rules (which requires the response to include prominently an explanation that the Legal Ombudsman was available if the complainant remained dissatisfied and the provision of full contact details for the Ombudsman and a warning that the complaint must be referred to them within six months.

3. The Ombudsman can extend the time limit in exceptional circumstances. Chambers must therefore have regard to that timeframe when deciding whether they are able to investigate your complaint. Chambers will not therefore usually deal with complaints that fall outside of the Legal Ombudsman's time limits.

4. The Ombudsman will also only deal with complaints from consumers. This means that only complaints from the barrister's client are within their jurisdiction. Non-clients who are not satisfied with the outcome of the Chambers' investigation should contact the Bar Standards Board rather than the Legal Ombudsman.

5. It should be noted that it may not always be possible to investigate a complaint brought by a non-client. This is because the ability of Chambers to satisfactorily investigate and resolve such matters is limited and complaints of this nature are often better suited to the disciplinary processes maintained by the Bar Standards Board. Therefore, Chambers will make an initial assessment of the complaint and if they feel that the issues raised cannot be satisfactorily resolved through the Chambers complaints process they will refer you to the Bar Standards Board.

Complaints made by telephone

6. You may wish to make a complaint in writing and, if so, please follow the procedure in paragraph 7 below. However, if you would rather speak on the telephone about your complaint then please telephone the individual nominated under the Chambers Complaints Procedure to deal with complaints – NAME or (if the complaint is about a member of staff) the [senior member of staff-NAME]. If the complaint is about the [senior member of staff] telephone [the Head of Chambers – NAME or other member of Chambers appointed by head]. The person you contact will make a note of the details of your complaint and what you would like done about it. He will discuss your concerns with you and aim to resolve them. If the matter is resolved he will record the outcome, check that you are satisfied with the outcome and record that you are satisfied. You may also wish to record the outcome of the telephone discussion in writing.

7. If your complaint is not resolved on the telephone you will be invited to write to us about it so it can be investigated formally.

Complaints made in writing

8. Please give the following details:

- your name and address;
- which member(s) of Chambers you are complaining about;
- the detail of the complaint; and
- what you would like done about it.

9. Please address your letter to [name of preferred recipient and Chambers' address]. We will, where possible, acknowledge receipt of your complaint within two days and provide you with details of how your complaint will be dealt with.

10. Our Chambers has a panel headed by [name] and made up of experienced members of Chambers and a senior member of staff, which considers any written complaint. Within 14 days of your letter being received the head of the panel or his deputy in his absence will appoint a member of the panel to investigate it. If your complaint is against the head of the panel, the next most senior member of the panel will investigate it. In any case, the person appointed will be someone other than the person you are complaining about.

11. The person appointed to investigate will write to you as soon as possible to let you know he has been appointed and that he will reply to your complaint within 14 days. If he finds later that he is not going to be able to reply within 14 days he will set a new date for his reply and inform you. His reply will set out:

- the nature and scope of his investigation;
- his conclusion on each complaint and the basis for his conclusion; and
- if he finds that you are justified in your complaint, his proposals for resolving the complaint.

Confidentiality

12. All conversations and documents relating to the complaint will be treated as confidential and will be disclosed only to the extent that is necessary. Disclosure will be to the head of Chambers, members of our management committee and to anyone involved in the complaint and its investigation. Such people will include the barrister member or staff who you have complained about, the head or relevant senior member of the panel and the person who investigates the complaint. The Bar Standards Board is entitled to inspect the documents and seek information about the complaint when discharging its auditing and monitoring functions.

Our policy

13. As part of our commitment to client care we make a written record of any complaint and retain all documents and correspondence generated by the complaint for a period of six years. Our management committee inspects an anonymised record regularly with a view to improving services.

Complaints to the Legal Ombudsman

14. If you are unhappy with the outcome of our investigation and you fall within their jurisdiction you may take up your complaint with the Legal Ombudsman, the independent complaints body for complaints about lawyers, at the conclusion of our consideration of your complaint. The Ombudsman is not able to consider your complaint until it has first been investigated by Chambers. Please note that the Legal Ombudsman has a twelve-month time limit from the date of the act or omission about which you are complaining within which to make your complaint. You can write to them at:

    Legal Ombudsman
    PO Box 6806,
    Wolverhampton
    WV1 9WJ

    Telephone number: 0300 555 0333

    Email: enquiries@legalombudsman.org.uk

15. If you are not the barrister's client and are unhappy with the outcome of our investigation then please contact the Bar Standards Board at:

    Bar Standards Board
    Professional Conduct Department
    289–293 High Holborn
    London
    WC1V 7JZ

    Telephone number: 0207 6111 444

    Website : www.barstandardsboard.org.uk

Appendix 2

Model complaints procedure – sole practitioners

1. My aim is to give all my clients a good service at all times. However if you have a complaint please let me know as soon as possible, by telephone or in writing. I will treat your complaint as confidential although I may discuss it with other barristers or officials from the Bar Standards Board for their advice. I will not reveal your name to others unless I am setting up mediation or arbitration. I will deal with your complaint promptly.

2. Please note that the Legal Ombudsman, the independent complaints body for service complaints about lawyers, has time limits in which a complaint must be raised with them. The time limits are:

a. Six years from the date of the act/omission.

b. Three years from the date that the complainant should reasonably have known there were grounds for complaint (if the act/omission took place before the 6 October 2010 or was more than six years ago).

c. Within six months of the complaint receiving a final response from their lawyer, if that response complies with the requirements in rule 4.4 of the Scheme Rules (which requires the response to include prominently an explanation that the Legal Ombudsman was available if the complainant remained dissatisfied and the provision of full contact details for the Ombudsman and a warning that the complaint must be referred to them within six months.

3. The Ombudsman can extend the time limit in exceptional circumstances. Chambers must therefore have regard to that timeframe when deciding whether they are able to investigate your complaint. Chambers will not therefore usually deal with complaints that fall outside of the Legal Ombudsman's time limits.

4. The Ombudsman will also only deal with complaints from consumers. This means that only complaints from the barrister's client are within their jurisdiction. Non-clients who are not satisfied with the outcome of the investigation should contact the Bar Standards Board rather than the Legal Ombudsman.

5. It should be noted that it may not always be possible to investigate a complaint brought by a non-client. This is because my ability to satisfactorily investigate and resolve such matters is limited and complaints of this nature are often better suited to the disciplinary processes maintained by the Bar Standards Board. Therefore, I will make an initial assessment of the complaint and if I feel that the issues raised cannot be satisfactorily resolved through my complaints process I will refer you to the Bar Standards Board.

Complaints made by telephone

6. If you wish to make a complaint by telephone, I will make a note of the details of your complaint and what you would like done about it. I will endeavour to resolve matters with you on the telephone. If after discussion you are satisfied with the outcome I will make a note of the outcome and the fact that you are satisfied. If you are not satisfied you may wish to make a written complaint.

Complaints made in writing

7. If you wish to make a written complaint please give me the following details:

- your name, telephone number and address;
- the detail of your complaint; and
- what you would like done about it.

Procedure for dealing with your complaint

8. There are a number of ways in which your complaint may be dealt with:

(a) discussion over the telephone;

(b) dealt with by correspondence;

(c) discussion at a meeting between us;

(d) the appointment of a mediator who will try to facilitate the resolution of your complaint;

(e) the appointment of an arbitrator whose decision we both agree shall be binding.

9. If we decide to appoint an arbitrator we both would need to agree how the arbitrator should approach his/her task and the limit of the compensation that can be awarded. The Bar Sole Practitioners Group (BSPG) or local Circuit will be approached and a barrister will be appointed to arbitrate. We will decide together whether it will be the BSPG or the local Circuit who should be approached. However neither of us may veto the person chosen. It is expected that the BSPG and the Circuit will chose someone who has considerable experience in the area that is the subject matter of the dispute.

10. Upon receipt of a written complaint I will:

(a) Reply in writing, normally within 48 hours, to acknowledge the complaint and inform you how I shall be dealing with it.

(b) Reply within 14 days responding in full to your complaint. I will offer you the opportunity to meet with you if that is appropriate. If I find later that I am not going to be able to reply within 14 days I will set a new date for my reply and inform you. My reply will set out:

- the nature and scope of my investigation;
- my conclusion on each complaint and the basis for my conclusion; and
- if I find that you are justified in your complaint, my proposals for resolving the complaint.

11. If you indicate that you are not happy with my written response you may ask for mediation or arbitration or, if you fall within their jurisdiction, you may make a formal complaint to the Legal Ombudsman, the independent complaints handling body for complaints about lawyers. Please note that the Legal Ombudsman has a twelve-month time limit from the date of the act or omission about which you are complaining within which to make your complaint.

They can be contacted at:

Legal Ombudsman
PO Box 6806,
Wolverhampton
WV1 9WJ

Telephone number: 0300 555 0333

Email: enquiries@legalombudsman.org.uk

12. If you are not my client and are unhappy with the outcome of our investigation then please contact the Bar Standards Board at:

    Bar Standards Board
    Professional Conduct Department
    289–293 High Holborn
    London
    WC1V 7JZ

    Telephone number: 0207 6111 444

    Website: www.barstandardsboard.org.uk

13. I will maintain confidentiality at all times and discuss your complaint only to the extent that is necessary for its resolution and to comply with requests for information from the Bar Standards Board discharging its auditing and monitoring functions.

14. I will retain all correspondence and other documents generated in the course of your complaint for a period of six years and I will review complaints at least once a year to ensure that I maintain good standards of service.

Appendix 3

Example client information leaflet

Barrister XXXXX

Client Information Leaflet

About XXXX

I am a barrister at xxxx Chambers in xxxx

Include a statement about yourself and your experience eg

I specialise in xxxxxx

How I will work for you

My work for you may involve giving advice, writing legal documents, or representing you in a court, tribunal or meeting.

As your barrister, I will work closely with your solicitor. But my duty is to you. I will do whatever I legally can to protect and advance your interests. However, my overriding duty is to the court so I cannot knowingly or recklessly mislead the court.

I will keep what you tell me confidential if that is what you want. But I cannot tell a court (or anyone else) anything that I know is not true.

I will do whatever I can to help you through the legal process. Please tell me or your solicitor about any concerns you have. And do ask all the questions you want to ask.

Feedback and complaints

I value all feedback. Please do let me know, at any time, what you think.

If anything is wrong, I would always want to know and to put it right. Please tell me, or your solicitor, straight away.

You can also contact the Legal Ombudsman (Tel: 0300 555 0333), enquiries@legalombudsman.org.uk

More information

You can find out more about me and my chambers on Chambers website at xxxx

Section 3: The Legal Services Act and the Future of Regulation

Legal Services Act 2007

[6.75]

The Legal Services Act 2007 reforms the way in which legal services are regulated in England and Wales. The Act creates a new regulatory structure for legal services, which allows different types of lawyer and non-lawyer to form businesses together. It also permits non-lawyers to be involved in the management or ownership of businesses that provide legal services.

Under the Act the LSA has a duty to promote the following regulatory objectives:

- Protecting and promoting public interest;
- Supporting the constitutional principles of the rule of law;
- Improving access to justice;
- Protecting and promoting the interests of consumers;
- Promoting competition in the provision of services;
- Encouraging an independent, strong, diverse and effective legal profession;
- Increasing public understanding of the citizen's legal rights and duties;
- Promoting and maintaining adherence to the professional principles.

The main effects of the Legal Services Act

Legal Services Board

[6.76]–[6.81]

The Legal Services Act creates a new regulatory organisation called the Legal Services Board (LSB). This will supervise the work of the various approved regulators, which are permitted by law to regulate the supply of legal services. The LSB became fully constituted on 1st January 2009. Further information about the developing work of the LSB and the Office for Legal Complaints, below, can be found on the LSB's website at http://www.legalservicesboard.org.uk. The approved regulators are:

1. The Law Society
2. The Bar Council
3. The Master of the Faculties
4. The Council for Licensed Conveyancers
5. The Institute of Legal Executives
6. The Chartered Institute of Patent Agents
7. The Institute of Trade Mark Attorneys
8. The Association of Law Costs Draftsmen

Office for Legal Complaints

The creation of the Office for Legal Complaints (OLC). The OLC is a single, independent body, which deals with complaints made by consumers about the provision of legal services. The Legal Ombudsman was established by the OLC under the Legal Services Act 2007 and began accepting complaints on 6 October 2010.

New Business Structures

It permits business structures for firms providing legal services. To begin with, the Act permitted the formation of "Legal Disciplinary Practices" (LDPs), which are firms providing legal services that involve different kinds of lawyers, and can include up to 25 per cent non-lawyers. These came into effect on 31 March 2009 and are regulated by the SRA and the CLC. Following this, the Act permitted Alternative Business Structures (ABSs), which allow external ownership of legal businesses, and multidisciplinary practices which provide a mixture of legal and other services. The CLC started regulating ABSs in October 2011 and the SRA expected to start regulating ABSs in January 2012

Self-Employed Practice

[6.82]

Other changes relate to the structure of self-employed practice and consider barristers sharing premises and office facilities, investigation and collecting evidence and taking witness statements, attendance at police stations and conduct of correspondence. The implementation of these changes has resulted in amendments to Parts IV and VI of the Code. Following the Board meeting the proposed changes were submitted to the Legal Services Board (LSB) for consideration and approval. The amendments took effect on 31st March 2010.

Accompanying the Code changes, the BSB has produced the following guidance (please note that at the time of going to press, the guidance had not been updated to take account of the BSB Handbook which became operational in January 2014):

Guidance on Self-Employed Practice

[6.83]

Investigating or collecting evidence and taking witness statements

1. There is no longer a rule which prohibits a self-employed barrister from investigating or collecting evidence generally or therefore from taking statements from potential witnesses (which is treated for these purposes as investigating or collecting evidence). By taking witness statements is meant interviewing the potential witness with a view to preparing a statement or taking a proof of evidence. A barrister has always been entitled to settle a witness statement taken by another person, and this is not investigating or collecting evidence. However, rule 401(b)(iii) provides that a self-employed barrister must not in the course of his practice conduct a case in court if the barrister has previously investigated or collected evidence for that case unless the barrister reasonably believes that the investigation and collection of that evidence is unlikely to be challenged.

2. It follows that if the nature of the evidence or the circumstances in which it was investigated or collected are such that there is likely to be an issue about that in court, where the barrister might be needed to give evidence, the barrister can properly be involved in the preparations for a case but cannot accept a brief to conduct the case in court, even as the junior member of a team of barristers. Only if the barrister reasonably believes that the investigation and collection of that evidence (as distinct from the evidence itself) is unlikely to be challenged can the barrister properly conduct the case in court. Nothing in the rule is intended to apply to the case where a barrister properly accepts a brief and then, as part of his conduct of the case at court, has urgently to take a statement from his client or a potential witness (see rule 707 of the Code). The rule applies where a barrister has investigated or collected evidence before arriving at court at the start of the case.

3. In this regard, barristers should note that rule 401(b)(iii) is in one respect more restrictive in its effect than the previous Written Standards (which are being revised to reflect the new rules) relating to witnesses, which enabled barristers to take witness statements and then act as the junior barrister in the case. The Written Standards stated that it was not appropriate for a witness statement taker "to act as counsel unless he is a junior member of the team of Counsel and will not be examining the witness". The Bar Standards Board considers that it is a key function of a junior member of a team of Counsel that s/he should be in a position to conduct the case in court if and when required, and that it is unacceptable to have briefed as junior counsel in a case someone who may not be in a position to take on the full advocacy role in that case by reason of professional embarrassment should it become necessary. The risks to the client's interests and to the due administration of justice generally are too great to allow a barrister to conduct a case in court, even as a junior in a team of barristers, if there is a real risk that the circumstances of the taking of the evidence that barrister has collected will be challenged in the case. If a junior member of the team is called upon to conduct the case and the circumstances of his investigation and collection of evidence is an issue in the case,, the barrister might have to stand down, damaging the client's interests (the client having then been deprived of each member of his/her chosen team) and the due administration of justice (through the inconvenience and delay in the conduct of the case).

4. When investigating or collecting evidence, barristers should bear carefully in mind the dangers of unconsciously affecting or contaminating the evidence that a witness is able to give. These are discussed in detail in the Written Standards at paragraphs 6.2.1–6.2.7 (available at the time of publication on the BSB website at https://www.barstandardsboard.org.uk/regulatory-requirements/the-old-code-of-conduct/written-standards-for-the-conduct-of-professional-work/). Barristers should also be aware of the risks of professional embarrassment as a result of becoming involved in investigating or collecting evidence, and take these risks into account when deciding:-

   a. whether to undertake such work in the first place; and

   b. if they have done, whether or not they can properly accept a brief at a subsequent trial.

5. The rules place the onus squarely on the barrister who has investigated or collected evidence prior to accepting a brief to consider and reach a reasonable conclusion whether or not his/her involvement is likely to be challenged.

6. In assessing whether to accept a brief in these circumstances, the barrister should be mindful of the dangers of professional embarrassment where s/he has been involved in the collection or investigation of evidence. The barrister's duty is to reach a reasonable decision on the risk of embarrassment before accepting a brief. The brief can only properly be accepted if it is reasonable for the barrister to conclude that the circumstances of his investigation or collection of evidence are unlikely to be challenged. If the barrister's decision is not a reasonable one, and the trial is subsequently adjourned as a result of his professional embarrassment, the barrister risks being exposed to an order for wasted costs as well as prosecution for a breach of the Code.

7. Even where a brief is properly accepted, the question of whether the barrister is professionally embarrassed is a matter that s/he must keep under review during the case in light of any later developments.

8. Investigation or collection of evidence (save for taking proofs of evidence or preparing witness statements urgently as part of the barrister's conduct of the case at court) is not subject to the cab-rank rule: see rule 604(i). If barristers wish to concentrate on advice and advocacy services and do not wish to undertake other types of activity (especially ones which may reduce their opportunity to undertake an advocacy role), that should be their choice and it is in the public interest that they cannot be forced to accept such work.

Conduct of correspondence

[6.84]

9. The extent to which self-employed barristers are permitted to conduct correspondence is addressed in rule 401A of the Code. These provisions are separate from the provisions under the Public Access Rules and apply generally. Conducting correspondence under rule 401A does not extend to the conduct of litigation, as explained by the Court of Appeal in *Agassi v Robinson (Inspector of Taxes) (Bar Council intervening)* [2005] EWCA Civ 1507, [2006] 1 All ER 900, [2006] 1 WLR 2126. Barristers should be mindful of the inherent risks (including of negligence claims) involved in the conduct of correspondence on behalf of lay clients.

10. It will not always be in the best interests of the client for barristers to conduct correspondence. It may be better for the barrister to draft a letter for the solicitor or other professional client to send. There is a danger of confusion where some letters are written by a barrister and some by a solicitor.

11. If the barrister is instructed to write a letter, addressees of letters written by the barrister must be made aware to whom any response should be addressed (and, for example, that it is unnecessary to reply to both the barrister and any solicitor or other professional who is also instructed). The barrister must keep the client and any professional client apprised promptly of any response, and seek further instructions at that juncture.

12. Barristers who become involved in the conduct of correspondence on behalf of lay clients will need to institute appropriate systems to deal promptly with responses and to keep records of the correspondence. Such systems should make provision to cover periods when the barrister is on holiday, or conducting a trial elsewhere, or otherwise unavailable to receive letters.

13. Barristers should consider whether it would be appropriate for them to undertake training in the conduct of inter-partes correspondence before agreeing to enter into any such correspondence.

14. It is also important for barristers embarking on the conduct of correspondence to ensure that, so far as possible, their actions do not create any threat to either their actual or their perceived independence, or any risk of subsequent professional embarrassment. For example, they should not appear personally to endorse statements by clients or witnesses, since that might appear to conflict with arguments or evidence which they subsequently present to the Court.

15. The conduct of correspondence with other parties (save where reasonably necessary as part of the barrister's conduct of the case at court) is not subject to the cab-rank rule: see rule 604(i).

Sharing premises and associations with others

[6.85]

16. Previous rules preventing self-employed barristers from sharing premises and forming associations with non-barristers have been removed, allowing barristers to pool together risks and resources (subject to not misleading clients, notifying the BSB and keeping appropriate records).

17. The rules governing associations with others are provided at rC79-rC85 of the Handbook. Where you are in an association on more than a one-off basis, you must notify the Bar Standards Board that you are in an association, and provide such details of that association as are required by the Bar Standards Board. If you have a material commercial interest in an organisation to which you plan to refer a client, you must tell the client in writing about your interest in that organisation before you refer the client; and keep a record of your referrals to any such organisation for review by the Bar Standards Board on request. Similar rules apply when you have a material commercial interest in an organisation which is proposing to refer a matter to you.

Attendance at police stations

[6.86]

18. The following guidance is available on the BSB website (please note that at the time of going to press, the guidance had not been updated to take account of the BSB Handbook which became operational in January 2014).

19. The previous rules prevented barristers from attending on clients at police stations. That absolute bar has now been removed. Rule 401(b)(iv) provides that a self-employed barrister must not (except as permitted by the Public Access Rules) attend at a police station without the presence of a solicitor to advise a suspect or interviewee as to the handling and conduct of police interviews unless the barrister has complied with such training requirements as may be imposed by the Bar Standards Board in respect of such work. Advising at police stations is specialist work; any barrister who performs such work must complete any relevant training imposed by the Bar Standards Board.

20. Barristers undertaking publicly funded police station work under a criminal contract must comply with the training requirements specified by the Legal Services Commission. Barristers undertaking privately funded police station work must complete the Police Station Qualification ("PSQ") and (if they do not hold higher rights of audience) the Magistrates Court Qualification. If a barrister who wishes to undertake privately funded police station work considers they hold relevant previous experience that would exempt them from completing the PSQ, they should contact the Professional Practice Team at the Bar Standards Board with full details of their previous experience.

21. Rule 401(b)(vi) provides that a self-employed barrister must not (except as permitted by the Public Access Rules) conduct in court any criminal proceedings in which the barrister has attended at a police station for any defendant in connection with those proceedings or any associated proceedings unless the barrister reasonably believes that nothing said, done, heard or seen by the barrister at the police station might require him/her to give evidence in those proceedings.

22. A particular difficulty facing a barrister who attends at a police station to advise suspects and interviewees or to take part in identification procedures is that the barrister may have to advise the client whether or not to answer police questions or to volunteer a statement, or may see or hear something that is material to the evidence that will be presented in court. The client's decision whether or not to answer questions, and if so which, is very likely to be a significant matter in any subsequent court hearing. So might compliance with PACE Codes of interviews or identification procedures that the barrister sees or hears. If these are significant evidential matters at trial, the barrister in question may find him or herself in serious professional difficulties if acting as advocate in the case.

23. Advising a suspect at the police station or attending on his behalf at an interview or identification procedure always gives rise to the risk that you may become a witness at the trial or at a Newton hearing or pre-trial admissibility hearing. The fact of advising a suspect or being present in those circumstances does not of itself prevent you from appearing as an advocate for that defendant in all circumstances. If the defendant you have advised is going to enter a guilty plea which you know to be acceptable to the Crown, or has given a full comment interview which remains as his account, then the degree of risk may be relatively low. But if the defendant declined, on your advice or not, to answer all or any questions in interview (whether or not there was a prepared statement) then the risk of becoming a witness will, inevitably, be too great to allow you to deal with the case at trial or at a Newton hearing or pre-trial admissibility hearing. This guidance applies equally whether you were to appear as an advocate alone or being led or leading (see paragraph 3 above).

24. Given the possibility that you may be required to give evidence of events at the police station, you should keep detailed, contemporaneous notes of those events.

25. For the reasons already discussed in relation to collecting evidence (as to which, see paragraph 8 above), attending at police stations is not subject to the cab rank rule: see rule 604(i).

Part VII
Taxation and Retirement Benefits

The General Council of the Bar of England and Wales Taxation and Retirement Benefits Handbook

[7.1]

In July 2014 the Bar Council published the 8th Edition of its Taxation and Retirement Benefits Handbook which is set out in its entirety below.

Part I

[7.2]

Income tax

[7.3]

Introduction

1. This part is concerned with the taxation of self employed barristers' income. It covers how that income is quantified for tax purposes and what deductions are allowed.

Income tax for barristers

2. The income of a self employed barrister is professional income and is therefore taxed on the basis of accounting periods (or periods of account).

3. For income tax purposes income is divided into different categories: trading, professional, employment and investment income. Different tax rates and rules may apply in establishing the income to be returned. Furthermore, different deductions may be allowed before the income is taxed and the set-off of losses and allowances may be different. Also, the impact of National Insurance Contributions (NIC) will depend upon the type of income.

4. Income tax is charged on the income for a particular year of assessment (or "tax year"). For individuals the year of assessment runs from 6 April one year to 5 April the next. For some types of income (e.g. interest and dividends),

the income for a given year of assessment is simply the income received in that year. For professional income, however, the income for a year of assessment is generally the income for the accounting period ending in that year and the accounting period is generally a year ending with the date in respect of which the taxpayer draws up the accounts. For example, a barrister drawing up accounts to 31 March each year would pay tax on their professional income for the accounting period ending 31 March 2014 in the tax year ending 5th April 2014 (referred to as tax year 2013/2014) and would therefore be required to include that income in their return to be filed by 31 January 2015. A barrister drawing up accounts to 30 April each year would pay tax on their professional income for the accounting period ending 30 April 2014 in the tax year 2014/2015 (which runs from 6 April 2014 to 5 April 2015) and include this income in their return filed by 31 January 2016.

5. Returns of income and capital gains tax can be made in paper form (non-electronic return) or online (electronic return). Returns must be made by the filing date. A non-electronic return must be made on or before 31 October following the tax year to which it relates. An electronic return must be made on or before 31 January following the tax year to which it relates.

6. The electronic tax return is called a self assessment return and must include a calculation of the liability to tax on the income and capital gains included in the return. Her Majesty's Revenue and Customs (HMRC) will calculate the liability, where the return is made within the time limits.

7. Tax due under self-assessment is paid as follows:

   (a) on 31 January during the tax year and on 31 July after the end of the tax year, the taxpayer must make a payment on account. Each payment is generally half the tax due for the previous year; and

   (b) on 31 January after the end of the tax year, the taxpayer must make a balancing payment or, where the payments on account exceed the liability, claim a repayment.

8. There is further detail on self-assessment in Part Seven of this guidance.

9. Thus, a barrister will need to pay:

   (a) first instalment of tax for **current** tax year ending on 5 April 2015 (year 2014/2015) on 31 January 2015;

   (b) balancing payment of tax for **previous** year of assessment (tax year 2013/2014) on 31 January 2015; and

   (c) second instalment of tax for the current tax year ending on 5 April 2015 (tax year 2014/2015) on 31 July 2015.

10. The sequence of events for payment of income tax for the tax year 2014/2015 is:

Date	Event
6 April 2014	Tax year 2014/2015 begins
31 July 2014	2nd instalment payment for tax for 2013/2014
31 October 2014	2013/2014 filing date for paper returns
31 January 2015	Filing date for electronic tax returns for tax year 2013/2014
31 January 2015	1st instalment payment for tax year 2014/2015
31 January 2015	Balancing payment (or credit) for tax underpaid (overpaid) by instalments for 2013/14
5 April 2015	Tax year 2014/2015 ends
6 April 2015	Tax year 2015/2016 commences
31 July 2015	2nd instalment payment for tax year 2014/2015
31 October 2015	Filing date for non-paper tax returns for tax year 2014/2015
31 January 2016	Filing date for electronic returns for tax year 2014/2015
31 January 2016	1st instalment payment for tax year 2015/16
31 January 2016	Balancing payment (or credit) for tax underpaid (overpaid) by instalments for 2014/15

11. If no return is issued, a taxpayer in receipt of taxable income must notify HMRC by 5 October after the year of assessment. Therefore, a taxpayer in receipt of taxable income in the year ended 5 April 2014 who does not receive a return from HMRC must notify them by 5 October 2014.

12. Returning to the examples given above, it can be seen that with an accounting period ending early in the year of assessment there is a greater deferral of payment of the related tax liability on those earnings compared with an accounting period ending later in the year. Consider a fee earned in March 2014. The barrister drawing up accounts to 31 March would pay tax on that fee in tax year 2013/2014 whereas the barrister drawing up accounts to 30 April would pay tax on that fee in tax year 2014/2015 (i.e. a year later). Broadly, taxpayers are free to choose when their accounting periods end. There are other factors to consider that may influence this decision (which are outside the scope of this guidance). These are important decision and it might be sensible to seek advice from members of chambers who have recently had to consider these questions themselves or an accountant knowledgeable in the tax and accounting of practising at the Bar. There are anti-avoidance provisions to prevent tax advantage being obtained by repeatedly changing accounting dates. Special rules apply to calculate how profits are taxed in the first years of practice.

13. A barrister's profits may be computed in one of three ways, as follows:

(a) The earnings basis in accordance with Generally Accepted Accounting Principles (GAAP). In essence, barristers are taxed on the billable value of their work, whether or not paid (and even whether or not billed) and expenditure is relieved when incurred, whether or not settled, by the end of the accounting period.

(b) The simplified cash basis. The Finance Act 2013 introduced a new basis of cash accounting available to most unincorporated businesses, which includes barristers. It applies from the tax year 2013/14 onwards and has its own special set of rules which are discussed in paragraph 37 and 38. For the remainder of this guidance this basis of accounting is referred to as the "new cash basis".

(c) The cash basis. This basis was withdrawn in Finance Act 2013 with retrospective effect from 6 April 2013, but can continue to be taken advantage by those barristers who used this basis of accounting for the tax year 2012/13 (e.g. accounts for the year ending 31 March 2013) until the seven years has lapsed. Essentially this was a special basis available to barristers only during the first seven years of practice, whereby their self-employed income is taxed when received and expenditure is relieved when paid. For the remainder of this guidance this basis of accounting is referred to as the "old cash basis".

14. As well as fees received (if on the old or new cash basis) earned income would include any other profits which the barrister derives from their profession; for example, income as royalties or commissions for books and articles and fees for acting as an arbitrator. Salaries for teaching law and from part-time judicial appointments are employment income and included in the return, though Pay As You Earn (PAYE) income tax will normally have been deducted from such payments. Certain other types of income, such as that from investments, are taxed in the year of assessment in which the income arises. For example, if a barrister's accounts are drawn up to 30 June each year and in addition they hold some shares and receive bank interest, the tax return for the fiscal year 2014/2015 would include:

(a) taxable profits from the Bar from 1 July 2013 to 30 June 2014;

(b) fees for sitting as a Recorder between 6 April 2014 and 5 April 2015; and

(c) share dividends and bank interest received between 6 April 2014 and 5 April 2015.

15. Except for tax withheld at source, the tax on all this income will be payable at the same time in accordance with the self assessment regime.

Expenses

16. For expenditure to be deducted from income, it must be:

(a) of a revenue nature and

(b) incurred wholly and exclusively for the purposes of the profession.

17. There are also some specific statutory restrictions, for example a deduction for entertaining defined as hospitality of any kind is prohibited.

Capital or revenue expenditure

18. The category into which expenditure falls will depend on the precise facts of the expenditure in question. As a general rule, an expense which is incurred repeatedly would tend to be regarded as revenue; whereas an expense incurred as a one off would tend to be capital. For example, lease payments for the rental of equipment would be regarded as revenue expenses but the purchase of the equipment outright would be treated as capital.

19. Generally, the following will be regarded as revenue expenses:

- Stationery
- Repairs
- Professional fees
- Telephone charges (line rental and call charges)
- Off street parking
- Hotels
- Travel
- Library and periodical subscriptions
- Devilling fees
- Robing room fees
- Chambers' rent
- Professional indemnity insurance premiums
- Bank charges
- Bar Council subscriptions
- Circuit subscriptions
- Specialist Bar Association subscriptions
- Other professional association subscriptions
- Staff costs
- Equipment rental (e.g. computer leasing)
- Law report subscriptions
- Silk application and award fees
- Software licence where the useful economic life of the software is less than two years, and
- Website expenditure.

20. The following will be capital, if purchased and not rented:

- Furniture
- Sets of law reports
- Computers, peripheral equipment and initial purchase of software
- Wigs and gowns, and
- Cars.

21. Her Majesty's Revenue and Customs have issued a Capital v Revenue Toolkit which gives guidance on the application of the distinction.

Wholly and exclusively

22. Not all revenue expenditure is deductible. The main test is that the expense be incurred "wholly and exclusively" for the purposes of the profession. It is specifically provided that if an expense is incurred for a dual purpose, that expense may be apportioned between any identifiable part or any identifiable proportion incurred wholly and exclusively for the purposes of the trade, and the part of proportion of the expense incurred for a non-business purpose If the barrister works at home, they can claim a proportion of domestic expenses as the costs of maintaining an office at home. This is usually undertaken by reference to the floor area of study compared with the floor area of whole dwelling. Likewise, if a barrister uses his or her car partly for business, a proportion of the running costs may be claimed as a business expense and this is usually calculated by reference to the business mileage as a percentage of total mileage.

23. In many cases it should be clear whether a cost is incurred for professional or personal reasons. Difficulties arise where the barrister has a dual purpose in incurring the expense, and it does not lend itself to apportionment between business and non-business use. In that case the expense is non-deductible in its entirety. The situations in which this rule applies include:

(a) **Subsistence**: Subsistence when in chambers is not deductable (although the costs of modest expenditure on subsistence away from chambers and home should be allowable, along with costs of accommodation, travel etc.).

(b) **The cost of court clothing**: Following the decision of the House of Lords in *Mallalieu v Drummond*,[1] the cost of court clothing, including dark suits and court shirts, is not allowed as a deduction, since the barrister is said to be wearing these clothes partly for the personal reasons of modesty and warmth. This analysis should not extend to collars, bands and studs, or laundry costs of the same (as indicated above, the costs of wigs and gowns are capital so cannot be deducted in any event), and

(c) **Dining expenses:** HMRC takes the view that the social element of dining is inseparable from the professional.

1 See *Mallalieu v Drummond (Inspector of Taxes)* [1983] 2 AC 861, [1983] 2 All ER 1095.

Travel and motor expenses

24. The cost of travel between a barrister's home and chambers (and associated costs such as that of a parking space) is generally not allowable. In rare cases, the barrister may be able to demonstrate that their work base is the home rather than chambers so that all travel expenditure from home for professional purposes would be allowable. The costs of travelling from home or chambers direct to Court and between Courts are generally allowable deductions in practice.

25. The treatment of motor expenses generally follows that of travelling as above with the same restriction on deduction for travel between home and chambers.

26. As it is often difficult to determine the percentage of total motoring costs that relate to business, taxpayers are encouraged to keep a log of business mileage and establish the appropriate percentage. In certain circumstances reasonable estimates might be accepted.

27. As an alternative, barristers may wish to keep a log of their business mileage and claim at the statutorily fixed rate of 45p per mile for up to 10,000 business miles each year and 25p per mile in excess of that. From the tax year 2013/14, these rates have statutory authority to be used when preparing self-employed accounts. The use of these rates precludes a separate claim for tax relief (in the form of capital allowances) on the cost of the car itself.

Use of Home as office/study

28. For use of home as an office/study, barristers can opt to claim a statutorily fixed rate deduction from the tax year 2013/14 onwards, in substitution of the actual (apportioned) expenditure The deduction is calculated by reference to the number of hours worked at home in a month as follows:

Number of hours worked	Applicable amount
25 or more	£10
51 or more	£18
101 or more	£26

The total fixed deduction for a year is the sum of the monthly amounts. This calculation assumes, of course, detailed record-keeping of hours worked at home.

Capital allowances

29. Allowances are given for capital expenditure incurred wholly and exclusively for the purposes of the profession. These are "capital allowances" and are discussed further in Part Four. Essentially, a proportion of the capital expenditure, known as the Annual Investment Allowance (AIA) or Writing Down Allowance (WDA) is allowed as a deduction from income each year as if it were a revenue expense.

30. Under the new cash basis with the exception of cars, capital expenditure (which would otherwise be eligible for capital allowances) is immediately deductible against income when paid.

Calculation of profits

31. The tax rules on the calculation of barristers' profits for income tax purposes are largely set out in the Income Tax (Trading and Other Income) Act 2005 (ITTOIA).

32. Barristers in self employed practice who are UK resident in a tax year are carrying on a profession and are charged to income tax on the "full amount of the profits of the tax year."[2]

33. Two question arise:

(a) what are the profits of the tax year?, and

(b) what is the full amount of the profits?

34. The tax year runs from 6 April to the following 5 April. The profits of the tax year are the profits for the accounting period which ends in the tax year. As noted above, a barrister can choose which accounting period to use.

Accounting period	**Tax year**
6 April 2013 to 5 April 2014	2013/2014
1 May 2013 to 30 April 2014	2014/2015
1 January 2014 to 31 December 2014	2014/2015

35. It follows that the barrister commencing professional practice must decide what accounting period to use. Those already in practice may wish to change their accounting date at some future point in time for tax planning or for other reasons. But anti-avoidance rules may apply which prevent a change more than once every five years unless the change brings the accounting year end close to the end of the tax year.

2 See s 5(8) of the Income Tax (Trading and Other Income) Act 2005.

Commencement of practice

36. Commencement of practice at the Bar starts from the beginning of the second six months of pupillage. This is discussed further in Part Two.

The new cash basis

37. From the tax year 2013/14 onwards, barristers have the option of using the new cash basis of accounting. Unlike the old cash basis, there is no seven year time limit but there are entry and exit thresholds based on the level of receipts. It is recommended that a barrister applying this basis of accounting read the HMRC guidance to confirm their eligibility to use it.

38. The principal features of the new cash basis are:

(a) It can be joined where receipts for the accounting year of assessment do not exceed the VAT registration threshold (currently £81,000 or the pro-rated equivalent where the accounting period is less than a year).

(b) Receipts are all "professional receipts" together with those from asset disposals to the extent that tax relief was claimed on such business capital expenditure previously.

(c) Entry into the new cash basis requires an election being made in the first tax return for which it applies. Tax returns from 2013/14 onwards include a box to tick for this purpose.

(d) Where receipts for an accounting period exceed twice the amount of the VAT threshold (£162,000 for 2014/15 or the pro-rated equivalent where the accounting period is less than a year), it is mandatory to leave the new cash basis for the earnings basis when preparing the next set of accounts, unless receipts in the subsequent accounting period fall back below the entry threshold.

(e) If a barrister is VAT registered, it may be dealt with either by excluding it altogether or by including it on a VAT-inclusive gross receipts and payments basis. If the latter is chosen, VAT payments to HM Revenue & Customs will be treated as an expense when paid and VAT repayments as a taxable receipt. If VAT is accounted for in this way, then the gross receipts plus VAT repayments count towards the entry and exit limits.

(f) Interest charges on business borrowings are restricted to a £500 deduction.

(g) The general treatment for capital expenditure with the exception of cars is that the expenditure is deductible when paid where it would otherwise qualify for capital allowances.

(h) Expenditure on cars can be calculated by reference to existing capital allowances and expenditure on actual running costs rules or alternatively, the fixed mileage rates can be used as discussed at paragraph 22 above.

(i) Losses can only be carried forward for relief against future profits as a barrister. Special rules apply on retirement (see Part Four).

(j) The new cash basis may only be exited early if there is a change in commercial circumstances and by making a formal election to that effect. There must be an objective change of circumstances relating to the profession which makes an earnings basis more appropriate. Two of the examples given by HMRC are where more than £500 in interest deductions are being incurred and losses are suffered which the taxpayer wishes to relieve against other sources of income.

(k) Leaving the new cash basis for the earnings basis may give rise to 'adjustment income', a special form of relief to ameliorate the effect of the change. This is dealt with in paragraphs 54 and 55 below.

(l) There are also relieving provisions when a business changes from an earnings basis to a cash basis to avoid double counting. This is dealt with in paragraphs 56 and 57 below.

Earnings basis

39. The profits for a tax year are the profits earned in that year. Once use of the old or cash basis has to be discontinued, "full profits" means the profits calculated in accordance with GAAP.[3]

40. Accounting practice requires the following:

(a) profits are the profits earned for the year, not cash received in the year;

(b) a net increase in debtors (closing debtors – opening debtors) constitutes income, which must be included in profits. A net decrease will conversely be a reduction in income and hence will reduce profits;

(c) deductible expenses are expenses incurred in the year, not expenses paid in the year; and

(d) capital expenditure (e.g. purchase of computer or furniture) is non-deductible.

41. As regards the format of accounts, "profits" will consist of:

Fees received in year	x	
Devilling fees	x	
Debtors at year end (billed)		x
Complete and incomplete work at year end (unbilled)		x
Less:		
Opening debtors (billed)		x
Opening complete and incomplete work (unbilled)		(x)
Gross profit		x

42. For completed work at year end, a barrister has to bring in the fee that is reasonably expected to be received (whether or not billed). For incomplete work, the barrister must make a reasonable assessment of the amount earned so far.[4]

3 See s 25(1) of the Income Tax (Trading and Other Income) Act 2005.

4 See the Bar Council Guidance Computation of Profits for Income Tax Purposes: application of UITF 40 to Barristers' earnings.

Particular situations

Conditional Fee Agreements and Damages-based Agreements

43. In the case of agreements where payment is contingent on outcome, no right to consideration arises until the contingency occurs (i.e. the case is won). In those circumstances, no amount can be brought into account until the result of the case is known.

Pay at end

44. Where there is no fixed fee, but payment is to be made when work is completed, an estimate of the fee earned up to the accounting date should be made.

Fixed fees

45. In the case of fixed fees it should be possible to quantify "work in progress" at year end but the simpler course is to complete the piece of work and transfer "work in progress" to debtors.

Legal Aid

46. In legal aid cases "work in progress" should be recognised as it is done, not as payments on account are received. Allowance should also be made for the fact that some amounts may have to be repaid.

Fee sharing protocol

47. Under the Revised Advocacy Graduated Fee Scheme (RAGFS), fees are paid into a chambers fee sharing account.[5] The whole graduated fee is regarded as the income of the first barrister instructed. Where a fee is split between the instructed advocate and a substituted advocate, the amount paid into the fee sharing account will be allocated between the two. The first instructed should then treat the substituted barrister as a sub-contractor. For example, if the fee is £200, the first instructed advocate will treat the full amount as their income. If the fee is split £80 as to the first instructed advocate, and £120 to the substituted advocate, the income of the first instructed advocate remains £200. However, they will bring in as an expense the payment of £120 plus Value Added Tax (VAT) to the substituted advocate.

48. It should be noted that in practice most chambers operate a computerised system for recording these fees. The payment to the substituted barrister is usually entered on to the system as a reduction in the fee income of the first instructed barrister.

5 See the separate Bar Council guidance entitled *Graduated Fee Payment Protocol*.

Bad debts

49. Where an amount included in debtors at the year end is unlikely be paid or paid in full, the difference between the amount included in debtors and the amount received or likely to be received is a bad debt. Tax relief is granted for bad debts because they are deductible from income.

50. There are two methods of recognising bad debts:

(a) direct write-off method, or

(b) allowance method.

51. Under the direct write-off method the bad debt is recognised in the year in which it becomes uncollectable.

Example

Geoff has an accounting period ending on 31 March issued a fee note to a solicitor for £5,000 in the year to 31 March 2013. The fee had not been received at year end so it was included in closing debtors of £40,000, and he paid tax on the amount in question.

In the year to 31 March 2014 he agrees to reduce the fee to £2,500 because the solicitor has not been able to collect the money from the lay client. At 31 March 2014 his debtors (ignoring this case) are £50,000. Two accounting entries are made to account for this:

Closing debtors are reduced by £2,500, so

(Closing debtors – opening debtors) = (50,000 – 2,500) – 40,000 = 7,500

This prevents the carrying forward of fictional income.

Deductible expenses for the year 31 March 2014 are increased by £2,500.

This makes good the over-payment of tax for the year to 31 March 2013.

The loss is only expensed a year after the income had been recognised. Geoff could have avoided the time lag if it had been possible to recognise the bad debt when drawing up his accounts for the year to 31 March 2013.

52. To avoid the time lag, and in situations where bad debts are a recurrent feature of a practice, the allowance method should be used. At the year end an estimate of uncollectable amounts is made, and the corresponding adjustments to closing debtors and expenses are made in the accounts for that year.

53. If an amount which has been written off as a bad debt is subsequently recovered, it is simply included in the fees received for the accounting period in which it is received. This reverses the bad debt and restores the original income and taxation position.

Change from old cash basis to earnings basis

54. By the end of their seventh year of practice, barristers on the old cash basis must (if they have not made the change earlier) ascertain their debtors and "work in progress" at the last year end accounting date falling in the seventh year[6]. This amount will constitute "adjustment income". Their accounts for year eight of practice will need to bring in closing debtors and "work in progress" at full value, with opening amounts as at the end of year seven deductible. The opening debtors and "work in progress" are separately brought into charge to tax as adjustment income.

55. Adjustment income is income for tax and pension purposes, but not for NIC purposes. The tax charge on adjustment income arising on cessation of the cash basis can be spread over ten years. Instalments for the first nine years are the lower of one-tenth of the catch-up charge or 10% of the barrister's pre-capital allowance profits. In the tenth year, the balance is brought into account. A barrister can elect to accelerate taxation of the catch-up charge.

Example

Sheila commences pupillage in Planet Chambers on 1 October 2008. On 30 September 2009, on completion of her second six months pupillage, she becomes a tenant. She adopts a 31 March accounting date, with her first accounting period commencing on 1 April 2009.

For her first seven year of practice (tax years 2009/2010 – 2016/2017) she uses a cash basis.

On 31 March 2017 the value of her debtors and "work in progress" is £50,000.

She prepares her accounts for 2017/2018 (eighth year of practice) on an accounts basis, bringing in at the year end the full value of her debtors and "work in progress", and with opening balances of £50,000.

In the years 2017/2018 – 2027/2028 she is charged to tax on £5,000 of "adjustment income", unless her pre-capital allowance profits fall below £50,000. In 2017/2018 her profits are £40,000. Thereafter they exceed £50,000. In 2022/2023 (13th year of practice) she elects to accelerate taxation of the entire balance of the catch up charge. It then becomes taxable:

2017/2018	£4,000
2018/2019–2021/2022 (5,000 x 4)	£20,000
2022/2023 (balance)	£26,000
Adjustment income	£50,000

6 If a barrister commences in practice on 1 April 2010, with a 30 April accounting date, the last year end ending in the seventh year would be 30 April 2016. The adjustment income would be calculated as at close of business on this date.

Change from earnings basis to new cash basis

56. Where a barrister moves from the earnings basis to the new cash basis, the closing debtors and work in progress (as computed under the earnings basis) are treated as deductions in the first accounts prepared under the new cash basis. This is necessary to avoid double counting of income and expenses, initially under the earnings basis and again later as a receipt or payment under the new cash basis.

57. Except for cars, any residual unrelieved capital allowances pools may be deducted as an expense in the first year under the new cash basis provided that the expenditure has been fully paid for. Otherwise, a restriction applies with the unpaid portion deducted as an expense when paid

Example

Alexander is currently 6 years' call and his receipts are currently under the threshold. In order to move to the new cash basis when the first seven years has elapsed he needs to elect to be taxed under the new cash basis in his return. Alexander will then be able to take advantage of the cash basis until his receipts exceed the threshold.

Juliette is currently 8 years call and is on the earnings basis with a catch-up charge. Like Alexander she can switch to the new cash basis provided that her receipts are below the entry level. However, she should bear in mind that to the extent that her profits in the year prior to the change include debtors and WIP that have been taxed as earnings, the related receipts coming through in subsequent periods are not taxed again an appropriate adjustment should be made to prevent duplication. If she is within the period to which she is assessed on the catch-up, that is generally the ten years following her first seven years, that will continue until it has all been assessed. It is important to remember that even though Juliette has elected to transfer to the new cash basis from an earnings basis whilst in the catch up charge period, the annual catch up charge will still need to be declared until extinguished.

Change from new cash basis to earnings basis

58. On leaving the new cash basis, a barrister may elect for the opening debtors and the work in progress for the subsequent accounting period to be treated as 'adjustment income', the basis of calculation following that discussed at paragraphs 54 and 55. The 'adjustment income' is brought into charge in equal instalments over six years beginning with the first of the years in which the whole of the adjustment would otherwise be chargeable to tax.

Example

Lisa commences pupillage in Planet Chambers on 1 April 2013 and elects to join the new cash basis, her receipts for the year ending 31 March 2014 being £75,000. In the next year ending 31 March 2015, her receipts are £170,000 and she has to leave the new cash basis. At that date her debtors and WIP are £75,000. She elects for the £75,000 to be treated as 'adjustment income'. In the following year ending 31 March 2016, her receipts are again £170,000 and her closing debtors and work in progress are £80,000. Lisa's assessable income would be as follows:

Tax year 2013/14: new cash basis year ending 31 March 2014 £75,000.

Tax year 2014/15: new cash basis year ending 31 March 2015 £170,000.

Tax year 2015/16: earnings basis for year ending 31 March 2016 [£170,000 of receipts plus net movement in debtors/wip £5,000, (closing £80,000 less opening £75,000); £175,000, plus adjustment income 1/6 x £75,000= £12,500;

Total assessable income £187,500.

Tax years 2016/17 to 2020/21: profit on Earnings basis plus Adjustment income to be recognised of £12,500 a year for the five remaining years.

The barrister can make an election to accelerate the charge if desired.

Change from old cash basis to new cash basis

59. It is expected that normally the cross over should not result in any adjustment. In the event of any unrelieved residual pool of capital expenditure eligible for capital allowances (except for cars), this may be deducted as an expense in the first year under the new cash basis provided the expenditure has been fully paid for.

Business records

60. All records necessary to deliver a full and complete tax return must be preserved for five years and nine months following the end of the year of assessment to which the records relate. Where an enquiry is started into a

return, the records must be kept until the enquiry is completed. Copies (including electronic records) are generally acceptable.

Part 2

Advice to pupils and barristers starting practice

[7.4]

Introduction

61. This section deals with two questions that barristers and pupils face when they start practice:

    (a) how should any pupillage award should be treated, and

    (b) what accounting period should be chosen for their professional profits?

62. These are important decisions and it might be sensible to seek advice from members of chambers who have recently had to consider these questions themselves, or an accountant knowledgeable in the tax and accounting of practising at the Bar.

Pupillage awards

63. In the past, Her Majesty's Revenue and Customs (HMRC) accepted that all pupillage awards (whether from the Inns or from the pupil's chambers) have been exempt from income tax in the pupil's hands as "scholarships."

64. Her Majesty's Revenue and Customs still accepts this as far as awards from the Inns are concerned; nothing in this discussion affects such awards, which are still tax-free. However, since the Bar began formally to encourage the payment of pupillage awards, HMRC has argued that the treatment of chambers' pupillage awards as "scholarships" can no longer be maintained, and that they fall to be taxed as income.

65. Exactly how they should be taxed is, as a matter of strict law, debatable. A case can be made for saying that they are receipts of the pupil's new profession (at least once the pupil has done six months' pupillage and is thus able to accept briefs) and are chargeable as normal professional earnings under Part two of Income Tax (Trading and Other Income) Act 2005 (ITTOIA). Alternatively it can be argued that they are income chargeable under the general sweep-up provisions.[7]

7 See Part 5, Chapter 8 of the Income Tax (Trading and Other Income) Act 2005.

66. The Bar Council has agreed with HMRC that each pupil may choose in which of the two ways they should be taxed. The options are as follows:

    Option 1: The pupillage award in respect of the pupil's first six months will continue to be tax-free, but the award in respect of the second (or subsequent) six months will be included as normal professional earnings in the year of receipt;

Option 2: Both the "first six" and the "second six" awards will be taxable in the fiscal year of receipt under the general sweep-up provisions.

Matters to be considered in making your decision

67. In cases where the award is modest Option 2 may be preferred. Although the first six award will be charged to tax there may well be little or no tax payable if the barrister has no other income and hence the award is covered, or substantially so, by the tax free personal allowance.

68. In cases of substantial awards the decision is more difficult. Option 1 will result in the first six award being tax free but there is a potential for the second six award to be taxed, in part, on two separate occasions should the accounting period end early in the tax year. In these circumstances Option 2 is likely to result in less tax being paid but with the liability arising sooner.

69. One other important factor is the liability to Class 4 National Insurance c (NICs). Under Option 1 the pupillage award would be chargeable, but under Option 2 it is exempt. The NIC is currently 9% on profits between £7,956 and £41,865 and 2% on profits above £41,865 so this is an important consideration.

70. It should be noted that under Option 1 no expenses (e.g. travelling) incurred in the first six months would be deductible. Under Option 2 HMRC accept that they would be deductible, subject to the normal tax rules.

Third and subsequent six awards

71. The Bar Council's view is that any awards received in third six months pupillage or any subsequent period, will be treated in the same way as second six awards. That is, if Option 1 is chosen the third six award will form part of fee income and if Option 2 is chosen it will be treated as a separate source of income.

72. It should be noted that HMRC regard the first 12 months pupillage as a period of training and hence there is no liability to Class 2 NICs. Even in the case of third six, or subsequent periods of pupillage, if it can be demonstrated that no substantial fee earning work is carried out, then there is no requirement to make contributions.

Draw down

73. In cases where a pupillage award is available for "draw down" before the commencement of the pupillage it is considered that any amounts taken prior to the date of commencement are treated as a loan and not as income until pupillage starts subject, of course, to the terms of the agreement. Most chambers' pupillage agreements provide for any "draw down" to be repaid over the 12 months of pupillage once the student commences pupillage. Thus by taking a "draw down" tax is not avoided on the amount of the "draw down" as the awards made in respect of the first and second six months 12 months pupillage have to be considered before the deduction of the repayment of the "draw down"

Awards dependent on fees earned or received

74. A further agreement has been reached with HMRC concerning the tax treatment of "first six" and "second six" pupillage awards in cases where the awards are related to the amounts either earned or received during pupillage.

75. Her Majesty's Revenue and Customs has agreed that a pupillage award which is expressed to be "of an amount equal to the difference between £x and the gross amount received during the period of the award" or alternatively "of an amount equal to the difference between £x and the gross amount earned during the period of the award" will be eligible for the agreed tax treatment described above.

76. It will be apparent that the amount of the award (whether calculated by reference to receipts or to earnings) will be known by the end of the pupillage in question. Insofar as the amount actually advanced by chambers during the pupillage exceeds the award, the excess (repayable out of future receipts) will be regarded as a loan and will be ignored for tax purposes.

General notes

77. The agreement is quite clear that it is the amounts of the pupillage award in respect of the first and second six months that have the choice of treatment. Once the choice has been made the manner in which the awards are charged to tax then depends on the dates of payment. Generally a pupillage award should be assumed to accrue evenly over the 12 months unless the Pupillage award agreement states otherwise. For example if a £30,000 award is assumed to accrue evenly and the first six is treated as tax free £15,000 will be exempt from tax. The £15,000 in respect of the second six will then be taxed in the tax year or years in which it is received. If however the agreement states that £20,000 is in respect of the first six and £10,000 is in respect of the second then £20,000 will be exempt and £10,000 will be taxed in the tax year or years in which it is received.

78. The arrangements outlined above apply to all genuine pupillage awards irrespective of amount and exact date of payment. Payments made by chambers in return for services provided by pupils are not covered by the arrangements but will be taxable in the normal and appropriate manner.

79. In *Edmunds v Lawson*[8] the Court of Appeal held that pupillage is a contract between chambers and pupil for education and training and is not a contract of employment, thus the national minimum wage does not apply and there should be no need to operate Pay As You Earn (PAYE) or employers National Insurance.

8 See *Edmunds v Lawson* [2000] QB 501, [2000] 2 WLR 1091, CA.

80. Her Majesty's Revenue and Customs accept that a barrister's contribution to pupillage awards made by their chambers is deductible in computing that barrister's taxable profits, whether or not chambers has adopted Trade Protection Association (TPA) status. Additionally the deduction will not be affected by the tax treatment of the award in the hands of the recipient, as discussed above.

81. The European Working Time Directive[9] applies to pupils at the Employed Bar. It has not been established that it applies to the self employed Bar but it may be taken as a guide to good practice, at least in relation to holidays.[10]

9 See European Working Time Directive 2003/88/EC.

10 See the Bar Standard Board's Pupillage Handbook (http://www.barstandardsboard.org.uk/media/23648/pupillage_handbook_august_2011_final.pdf).

82. The Department of Work and Pensions (DWP) regarded the whole of the first 12 months of any period of pupillage as a period of training and not of gainful occupation, even though work may be done for a fee under the guidance of the pupil master after the first six months pupillage has been completed. In the decision *Edmonds v Lawson*[11] in the Court of Appeal the Judge commented on the remuneration a pupil receives as follows:

"[It] cannot be conclusive that pupils are not now generally paid. This is true even of funded pupils since, as we understand, chambers grants are treated as professional earnings for tax purposes only in part. But the fact that the generality of barrister pupils have been unpaid, not just in the distant past but also in modern times, is in our view of significance in determining whether a relationship of or equivalent to apprenticeship exists. For although trade apprentices have always received reduced wages, reflecting both the value of the practical training they receive and their reduced productivity, they have always in modern times received some wages and in earlier times board and lodging ... The freedom of a pupil who has obtained a provisional practising certificate to practise during the second six months of pupillage, not for the benefit of the chambers or the pupil master but for their own sole benefit and reward, would be highly anomalous if this were anything approaching an orthodox employment or apprentice relationship. While a small point in itself it is in our view another pointer against such a relationship."

83. If a period of pupillage extends beyond 12 months, the DWP had regard to the frequency of paid briefs in deciding whether the extended pupillage constitutes training or gainful occupation. If training is minimal and paid briefs are accepted regularly the DWP regarded the barrister as a self employed earner.

84. A barrister who has completed their pupillage but cannot find a full tenancy in chambers may become a "squatter" in chambers. The DWP regard a squatter as a self employed earner.

11 *Edmonds v Lawson* [2000] QB 501, [2000] 2 WLR 1091.

Part 3

Starting practice

[7.5]

Introduction

85. Barristers who have been in practice and prepared accounts ending before 6 April 2013 rather than prepare accounts on the usual earnings basis are entitled to prepare their accounts on a cash basis for the first seven years of assessment.[12] However this legislation was abolished retrospectively from 6 April 2013 and was replaced with a general cash basis election available to most unincorporated businesses. Barristers preparing accounts on the cash basis under the old legislation (i.e. the old cash basis) are able to continue to take advantage of those provisions and thus can remain in this regime for seven years.

86. The new cash basis for Small Businesses was introduced by the Finance Act 2013 and may be adopted by any business subject to certain conditions. To be eligible the business must not be a limited company or a limited liability partnership and the fee income must not be greater than the VAT registration threshold which is £81,000 for 202014/15. There are a number of other circumstances where a person is ineligible to elect for this new cash basis, but these are unlikely to apply to the majority of individuals. Once adopted an individual must leave the cash basis when fee income exceeds twice the VAT threshold (£162,000 for 2014/15). As this guide may be used by both barristers under the old legislation as well as under the new the two will be distinguished by being described as the old cash basis and the new cash basis.

87. Under both the old and the new cash bases only expenses actually paid for are allowable as a tax deduction. The one exception concerns pre-commencement expenditure. Under the old cash basis a barrister commencing practice is allowed to claim capital allowances in respect of all expenditure incurred for the purpose of their profession before commencement. In most cases the significance of this will be to allow claims in respect of books bought at university and Bar school (if used in practice) and items such as a wig and gown bought during the first six months of pupillage.

88. Under the new cash basis there are some items of expenditure that have special rules:

    (a) Capital expenditure – provided the expenditure would ordinarily qualify for capital allowances deductions expenditure on capital items will be deductible as an expense when paid. The only exception being expenditure on motor cars which must be dealt with in accordance with the capital allowances regime. Thus pre-commencement expenditure is deductible in the first set of accounts prepared for a barrister commencing in practice.

(B) Interest paid on loans – if interest is paid on any loan that would ordinarily be deductible this is limited to a maximum deduction of £500.

12 See section 160 of the Income Tax (Trading and Other Income) Act 2005.

Commencement of practice

89. A number of points should be noted relating to the commencement of practice:

(a) ordinarily, practice will commence on, but not before, completion of the first six months of pupillage;

(b) there may be circumstances, however, which justify claiming that practice commences later. For example, if a particular barrister does not hold themselves out as being available for work until after completion of 12 months of pupillage, commencement only after that time may be justified. However, if a barrister has a break between first and second six month pupillages, commencement only at the beginning of the second may be justified; and

(c) establishing an early date for the start of practice was at one time important because expenditure incurred prior to commencement was not eligible for tax relief. Expenditure incurred in the seven years prior to the commencement of practice is now eligible.

The early years

90. There are particular rules specifying which accounts form the basis of assessment for a particular fiscal year. Generally the period of account which ends in a particular fiscal year forms the basis of assessment for that year. This means that if accounts are made up to a date early in a year of assessment there is a greater gap between the time money is brought into account and the time tax is due. Moreover the maximum amount of time will be available to prepare accounts and calculate the tax liability under the self assessment provisions. As a general rule, the greatest cash flow benefit will be achieved if the first set of accounts is drawn up to a date early in the year of assessment following that in which practice commenced. Subsequent sets of accounts will use the same date. 30 April may be regarded as a convenient terminal date.

91. The law is found in Chapter 15 of Income Tax (Trading and Other Income) Act 2005 (ITTOIA). The effect is as follows:

92. **First year:** The basis period for the first tax year of practice:

(a) begins with the date on which one commences in practice; and

(b) ends on the following 5 April.

93. **Second year:** The basis period for the second tax year of practice is:

(a) the twelve month period of account ending in the tax year following the year of commencement, or

(b) if there is no twelve month period of account ending in the tax year following of commencement more complicated rules, apportioning the profits of one or more accounting periods, are brought to bear.

Example

Lisa commenced on 20 April 2013 and prepared her first accounts to 30 April 2014, showing a profit of £20,000. Accounts are subsequently prepared to 30 April each year. She would be taxed as follows:

- for 2013/2014, the proportion is 350 days (from 20/4/13 to 5/4/14) divided by 375 days (from 20/4/13 to 30/4/14), so the assessable profits are £18,667;
- for 2014/2015, the proportion is 365 days (from 1/5/13 to 30/4/14) divided by 375 days, so the profits are £19,467, and
- for 2015/2016, she will be taxed on her accounts for the year ended 30 April 2015; for 2016/17, the profit to 30 April 2016 et seq.

Example

Daniel's first period of account covered three fiscal years so the profits would be divided between those years in the same way. So if Daniel commenced on 31 March 2013 and made up his first accounts to 30 April 2014, again showing a profit of £20,000, his taxable profits in the years concerned would be:

- for 2012/2013, the proportion is six days (from 31/3/2013 to 5/4/2013) divided by 395 days (from 31/3/2013 to 30/4/2014), so assessable profits are £304;
- for 2013/2014, the proportion is 365 days (from 6/4/2013 to 5/4/2014) divided by 395 days, so profits are £18,481; and
- for 2014/2015, the proportion is again 365 days (this time from 1/5/2013 to 30/4/2014), so profits are £18,481.

Example

Mark commenced on 6 April 2013 and prepared his first accounts to 5 April 2014, showing a profit of £20,000. Accounts are subsequently prepared to 5 April each year. He would be taxed as follows:

- For 2013/2014, the profit to 5 April 2014.
- For 2014/2015, the profit to 5 April 2015, et seq.

Example

Elizabeth commenced on 1 May 2013 and prepared her first accounts to 31 December 2013 showing a profit of £12,000. Accounts are prepared to 31 December in following years, those to 31 December 2014 showed a profit of £20,000. She would be taxed as follows:

- for 2013/2014, the proportion is the full first period, 245 days, (from 1/5/13 to 31/12/13) plus 95 days (from 1/1/14 to 5/4/14). So assessable profits are £12,000 + £5,205 (£20,000 x 95/365). A total of £17,205;
- for 2014/2015, the year ended 31 December 2014 £20,000; and
- for 2015/2016, the profit to 31 December 2015, et seq.

94. As can be seen, the first set of accounts a barrister draws up may affect the liability to income tax for one or two (or even three) years of assessment. The principle underlying the current rules, however, is that the profits of a practice will be assessed only once over the life of that practice. Where the same profits, or part of the same profits, form the basis for more than one year of assessment, the overlap profits are determined and these may be set off on either a change in accounting date which involves a period of account of more than 12 months or the cessation of practice.

95. The earlier the date in the fiscal year to which accounts are made up, the greater the deferral and the greater the overlap period are. For example, comparing two barristers who earn approximately the same amounts after commencement:

Example

Richard starts practice on 1 May 2013. He makes up his first set of accounts to 5 April 2014 and they show a profit of £8,500. He makes up his second set of accounts to 5 April 2015 and they show a profit of £15,000. He would be taxed as follows:

- 2013/2014 £8,500.
- 2014/2015 £15,000.
- 2015/2016 Profits to 5 April 2016 (likely to be more than £15,000).
- No overlap profits occur so no overlap relief will be available for future use.

Example

Jessica also starts to practise on 1 May 2013. She makes up her first set of accounts to 30 April 2014 and they show a profit of £9,000. She makes up her second set of accounts to 30 April 2015 and they show a profit of £15,600. She would be taxed as follows:

- 2013/2014 £8,383 (340 / 365 of £9,000).
- 2014/2015 £9,000.
- 2015/2016 £15,600.

Jessica's overlap profits are those for the period 1 May 2013 to 5 April 2014, that is, £8,383.

Clearly Jessica, by sole virtue of her accounting date, is paying less tax than Richard in the early years.

96. In different circumstances, different accounting periods may be appropriate. Before drawing up your first set of accounts all considerations relevant to your particular circumstances should be addressed. This is a most important decision and it may well be sensible to seek advice from members of chambers who have recently had to consider these questions themselves, or an accountant knowledgeable in the accounting and tax issues of practising at the Bar.

Timetable

97. Under the self assessment, tax for each year of assessment is paid by way of two instalments on account; 31 January in the year of assessment and 31 July after the end of the year of assessment. The payment on account is generally 50% of the previous year's liability, unless there is reason to believe that the following year's liability will be smaller. Any additional tax is due on 31 January following, once the actual liability has been ascertained. In respect of the year of commencement, however, no payments on account will have been made, so all the tax for the year will be due on 31 January following the end of the fiscal year in which practice commenced. At that time, the first payment on account for the following year will also be due. In total, an amount of 150% of the tax due in respect of the profits for the first year of assessment must be paid.

Notification dates

98. For a barrister starting pupillage in September 2013, commencing in practice on 10 April 2014, and with no other income, the important dates are as follows.

99. If choosing to tax the entire pupillage award as miscellaneous income:

(a) notify HMRC immediately on commencement of practice, if HMRC have not been notified by 5 October 2014 a penalty may be levied;

(b) file first return by 31 October 2014 (if filing a paper return); and

(c) pay tax by 31 January 2015 (and file return if filing by internet).

100. If choosing the first six award tax-free route:

(a) notify HMRC immediately on commencement of practice, if HMRC have not been notified by 5 October 2015 a penalty may be levied;

(b) file first return by 31 October 2015 (if filing a paper return); and

(c) pay tax by 31 January 2016 (and file return if filing by internet).

This example assumes there are no other sources of income or gains that have their own return filing requirements.

National Insurance contributions

101. All self employed individuals must register with HMRC in order to make National Insurance Contribution (NIC). There are two classes of contributions relevant to the self employed: Class 2 and 4.

Class 2 contributions

102. These contributions are a flat rate of £2.75 per week. The contributions are normally paid by direct debit to HMRC.

103. A penalty is charged if there is a failure to notify liability to Class 2 NICs before 31 January following the end of the fiscal year in which the Class 2 contributions should have been paid.

Class 4 contributions

104. These contributions are calculated on the profits chargeable to income tax for a given fiscal year at 9% of profits between £7,956 and £41,865 and then 2% on profits over £41,865. The contributions are paid with the income tax for the year as set out above.

Notification

105. By completing a form CWF1 and sending this to HMRC this will ensure that both the notification requirements for Income Tax and NIC have been complied with. This form should therefore be submitted well before the dates set out above.

Part 4

Capital Allowances and chambers expenditure

[7.6]

Introduction

106. If you buy an asset (e.g. a computer, a table) for use in your practice you cannot deduct the cost of that asset from your profits, unless you are applying the new cash basis of accounting applicable from the tax year 2013/14 onwards. Instead you may be able to claim a capital allowance for that expenditure. The relevant statutory provisions are contained in Capital Allowances Act 1990 supplemented and amended by later Finance Acts. Her Majesty's Revenue and Customs (HMRC) guidance can be found on their website.

107. For those on the new cash basis (see Part 1) expenditure on assets used for business purposes is generally an allowable deduction when paid, as though it were a revenue expense. However, to be so allowable the asset must be such that it would be eligible for capital allowances under the earnings basis. This general rule does not necessarily apply to cars (see below).

Expenditure and allowances

108. Expenditure incurred on "plant and machinery" used for business purposes is eligible for capital allowances. To qualify, the expenditure must be of a capital

nature and the barrister must own or be capable of becoming the owner of the asset (e.g. hire purchase) as a result of incurring the expenditure.

109. There are three allowances relevant to barristers: the Annual Investment Allowance (AIA), the First Year Allowance (FYA) and the WDA. Broadly, the AIA provides for 100% relief against income on qualifying expenditure in the year of purchase, subject to monetary limits. The FYA provides for a 100% relief in the year of spend on certain categories of new plant and machinery. Writing Down Allowances are annual allowances which are claimed on the balance of capital expenditure on qualifying plant and machinery ineligible for either the AIA or the FYA or otherwise where these allowances are not claimed.

Annual Investment Allowance

110. The AIA provides 100% relief for the first £500,000 of qualifying expenditure each year incurred from 6 April 2014 to 31 December 2015. Subject to future Finance Acts, the limit will reduce to £25,000 from 1 January 2016. The limit was £250,000 from 1 January 2013 to 5 April 2014. Cars are excluded from the AIA.

111. The AIA is claimed for the accounting period in which the expenditure is incurred. The AIA is proportionally increased or reduced where the accounting period is more or less than a year. It is time-apportioned where the accounting period overlaps a change in the maximum allowed. The AIA cannot be claimed in the final period of account ending with the death or retirement of a barrister.

112. Where an accounting period straddles a change in the limit the rules for calculating the maximum AIA are complicated.[13] It may be of relevance to Chambers registered as a TPA or as a chambers service company.

113. In general, the AIA will provide a 100% allowance for qualifying expenditure incurred by a barrister leaving the WDA available to relieve any balance of expenditure incurred before the AIA was introduced.

13 For detailed guidance please refer to HMRC (http://www.hmrc.gov.uk/manuals/camanual/ca23085.htm).

First Year Allowance

114. Expenditure on certain types of asset and at certain periods is eligible for enhanced allowances known as FYA.

115. A 100% FYA is available on designated energy-saving and/or environmentally beneficial plant and machinery and there is no cap on the level of expenditure. A 100% FYA is also available on certain low-emission cars. The Department of Energy and Climate Change provides a list of specific products.

116. For expenditure incurred in the fiscal year 2009/10 barristers would receive a FYA of 40% on any balance of qualifying expenditure in excess of the AIA (but excluding cars). There was no FYA for 2008/09 and for 2006/07 and 2007/08 the rate was 50%.

Writing Down Allowance

117. A WDA is currently available on the reducing balance basis at 18% (rounded up to the nearest pound) of the balance of any expenditure not covered by the AIA and any balance of expenditure brought forward from previous years. It is not available on expenditure for the year of acquisition where FYA is claimed. Prior to 6 April 2012 the WDA rate was 20%.

118. The WDA is claimed for an accounting period. It is proportionally increased or reduced where the accounting period is more or less than a year. It is time-apportioned where the accounting period overlaps a change in the rate of allowance (e.g. for the year ended 30 June 2012 the WDA rate is 19.53% following the change in rates from 20% to 18% on 6 April 2012.)

119. Where the written down value of a plant and machinery pool is not more than £1,000 a WDA equal to the entire value of the pool can be claimed.

Example

Josephine buys a desk for her room in chambers for £1,600, in July 2013 having previously incurred £3,000 on computer equipment in May 2009 and makes up her accounts annually to 30 June. They will qualify for the following capital allowances which she may set off against her profits for the corresponding years:

		Allowances
Accounts to 30 June 2009		
Cost	3,000	
FYA @ 40%	(1,200)	1,200
Accounts to 30 June 2010		
Balance brought forward	1,800	
WDA @ 20%	(360)	360
Accounts to 30 June 2011		
Balance brought forward	1,440	
WDA @ 20%	(288)	288
Accounts to 30 June 2012		
Balance brought forward	1,152	
WDA @19.53%[14]	(225)	225
Accounts to 30 June 2013		
Balance brought forward	927	
Write off pool (<£1,000)	(927)	927
Accounts to 30 June 2014		
Balance brought forward	0	
Cost	£1,600	
AIA @ 100%	(1,600)	1,600

120. In general, all qualifying expenditure, is aggregated, known as "pooled" for capital allowance purposes with the consequence that it is unnecessary to make separate calculations for each item of plant and machinery. After

deducting the allowances the resulting balance is known as the "main pool." Expenditure on various types of assets is excluded from the main pool including assets used partly for business purposes, integral features and certain cars.

14 Average rate following reduction in WDA from 20% to 18% on 6 April 2012.

Private use

121. Relevant expenditure incurred on an asset used partly for business use must be included in a separate single pool. Allowances are calculated in the normal way and then the amount claimed for tax purposes is restricted for private use on a just and reasonable basis.

Integral features and special rate

122. Expenditure on integral features for which a WDA is given is included in a special pool. The rate of WDA is currently 8% (10% prior to 6 April 2012). Integral features include electrical (including lighting systems), cold water, heating and ventilation systems and lifts. As the WDA applies after deduction of the 100% AIA this special pool will not normally apply to individual barristers, given that the AIA is now £500,000 (to 31 December 2015) but it may apply to expenditure by chambers.

123. Where the cost of repair on an integral feature which is more than 50% of the cost of replacing the entire integral feature it is required to be treated as a capital replacement (again generally likely to be relevant for chambers only).

124. Expenditure on equipment at a private residence which is used wholly or partly for business purposes may also qualify for capital allowances.

125. Until a profession or trade ceases, balancing allowances or charges may not occur and individual items of plant can continue to attract WDAs at an ever-decreasing rate long after the item has been sold or scrapped. However where expenditure is on assets with a short life, particularly computer equipment, they can form their own separate pool of expenditure and be written off over a shorter period of up to eight years (four years for expenditure prior to 6 April 2011). The ability to claim AIA and write off pools with less than £1,000 means that this facility is more appropriate to chambers' expenditure than to barristers.

Leasing

126. Relevant expenditure incurred using hire purchase or using leasing where the leasing agreement provides that the barrister shall or may become the owner, is eligible for capital allowances purposes.

127. Where the agreement does not provide for ownership to pass to the lessee, but the asset is "capitalised" in the accounts in accordance with accounting standards, the lessee can claim the finance interest and depreciation charged in the accounts on that asset as a deduction for tax purposes.[15] This is not relevant to barristers applying the old and new cash basis who claim relief for expenditure on a paid basis.

128. Otherwise, where assets are rented rather than purchased, the rental payments may be deducted in full for tax purposes since they are regarded as revenue payments (with the exception of motor vehicle leasing). Accordingly, the respective merits of purchasing or leasing assets should therefore be considered in the light of the differing tax treatments.

15 See HMRC Statement of Practice 3/91.

Motor vehicle leasing

129. For leases of cars commencing before April 2009 with an original cost of more than £12,000, there is a formula applied to establish the proportion that may be deducted which would then itself be reduced for any personal element.

130. For leases commencing from April 2013 generally there is a disallowance of 15% of the hire cost where the car in question has carbon dioxide emissions of more than 130g per kilometre. For leases which commenced during the period from 6 April 2009 to 5 April 2013 the 15% disallowance applies where the emissions figure is more than 130g.

Motor cars

131. The rules changed in April 2009. Expenditure incurred before then continues to be subject to the old rules until April 2014. Any balance of capital allowances is transferred to the main pool at the start of the first accounting period commencing after 5 April 2014 unless there is private use (see 135 below).

Expenditure before April 2009

132. For barristers using their vehicles for professional purposes, WDAs of 18% are available.

133. A car costing in excess of £12,000 is required to be kept in its own pool and the annual WDA is restricted to £3,000, proportionally adjusted for accounting periods more or less than 12 months.

Expenditure from April 2009

134. Generally allowances are based on carbon dioxide emissions and changes were made from 6 April 2013. Electric cars and those with carbon dioxide emissions up to 95g per kilometre qualify for a 100% allowance. For emissions between 95g and 130g the 18% main rate of WDA applies. For emissions in excess of 130g the expenditure is allocated to the 8% special pool (along with for example integral features as discussed above) or in its own 8% pool where private use is relevant. For expenditure prior to 6 April 2013 the respective emissions thresholds are 110g and 160g.

135. In almost every case, there will be a degree of non-business use of a vehicle so that the corresponding proportion of the allowance is disallowed. This is regardless of when the car was acquired and each car used privately needs to be kept in a single asset pool.

136. As mentioned in the section on motoring expenses, HMRC look to taxpayers to keep records of business and private mileage in order to justify the proportion claimed as business use. They will often ask for such records as part of self assessment enquiries.

137. On the sale of a motor vehicle that has been used for business purposes, the sale proceeds are compared with the written down value and, subject to adjustment for non-business use, the resulting excess or deficit is charged or allowed in the profit computation of the barrister for the year of the disposal. These are referred to as balancing charges and balancing allowances, respectively and are calculated independently from other capital allowances.

138. For barristers on the new cash basis, capital expenditure on cars can be calculated using the capital allowances rules. Alternatively the mileage rate (see Part 1) can be used to cover both capital and running costs in which case there will be no claim for capital allowances.

Pre-commencement expenditure and/or change of use

139. A barrister commencing in practice is allowed to claim capital allowances in respect of expenditure incurred prior to commencement. The expenditure is treated as if it had been incurred on the first day of practice. In most cases, the significance of this rule is that claims are allowed in respect of earlier purchases of books and computer equipment and items such as a wig and gown.

140. A barrister may introduce into the practice an asset originally acquired for a non-business purpose (e.g. a car) where the qualifying expenditure is taken as the lower of cost or market value at the date it is brought into use.

Discontinuation of practice

141. On ceasing to practice, the disposal proceeds of assets sold together with the market values of assets retained are compared with the tax pool of unallowed expenditure. In the same manner as that described above for motor vehicles, this will result in balancing allowances if the unallowed expenditure is greater than the disposal proceeds or in balancing charges if the disposal proceeds are greater than the unallowed expenditure.

Leaving and entering the new cash basis

142. Where a barrister who joins the new cash basis from the earnings basis, or indeed the old cash basis, has any balances in the capital allowances tax pools (except in relation to cars), this may be claimed as an allowable deduction in the first accounts under the new cash basis provided it has been fully paid for. Where the asset is used partly for private purposes, the deduction should be restricted accordingly.

143. On leaving the new cash basis to enter the earnings basis, any unrelieved qualifying expenditure, e.g. such as under a hire purchase scheme, can be allocated to a new capital allowances pool in the subsequent accounting period.

Capital Allowances and Computation of Profits

144. There are a number of situations in which the accounts computation of profits departs from the computation of profits for tax purposes. Commercial accounts must provide for loss of value (value consumed) each year in relation to capital assets employed in the business. Depreciation is a mechanism for writing off the cost of fixed assets over their predicted useful economic life. Depreciation records a reduction in the value of fixed assets arising from their use in the business. Fixed assets for these purposes would include computers and furniture. In the commercial accounts these will be depreciated each year, and depreciation will appear as expenditure in HMRC accounts. For tax purposes, depreciation is non-deductible and has to be added back to profits. Instead, traders can claim capital allowances, which can then be deducted from profits for tax purposes.

Example

Nick has an accounting period ending on 30 April. On 1 May 2013 the tax Written Down Value (WDV) of his existing computer was £1,533. On 1 March 2014 he buys a laptop for use in his practice for £1,000. His commercial accounts show profits of £60,000, after deducting depreciation of £280.

His capital allowances are (for accounting period ended 30 April 2014):

Item		Capital allowances	Values c/f
Opening value (computer)	1,533		
WDA @ 18%	(276)	276	
Closing value			1,257
Additions (laptop)	1,000		
AIA @ 100%	(1,000)	1,000	
Closing value			0
Total		1,276	1,257

His accounts for tax purposes will show:

Profits per accounts	£60,000
Add back deprecation	£280
Total	£60,280
Less: capital allowances	(£1,276)
Taxable profits	£59,004

Part 5

Chambers expenses, TPAs and service companies

[7.7]

Introduction

145. This part deals with the tax treatment of chambers' contributions and the alternative structures for chambers which deal with some of the issues arising.

Chambers expenditure

146. Whilst it may seem obvious that contributions to chambers expenses should be tax deductible in the accounts of the individual barrister, the matter is not as straightforward.

147. At its simplest, chambers is no more than a group of individuals who have banded together to share common business expenses. Chambers is not a separate legal entity and therefore the tax treatment of members' contributions will depend on when and how those monies are applied by chambers. That is to say, it is not what the members pay into chambers that determines the tax deduction in their accounts, but rather how chambers uses those contributions or indeed if they do not (thus giving rise to a surplus).

148. Where some chambers expenditure does not qualify for a tax deduction, or is of a capital nature, then the members need to make adjustments in their own accounts to reflect this.

149. Chambers must advise each member of their share of non-deductible revenue or capital expenditure. This information must include the date on which the cost was incurred in order that the barrister is able to make the appropriate adjustments.

150. Chambers must also advise each member of their share of chambers capital expenditure qualifying for capital allowances. Again, this information must include the date on which the cost was incurred. Further, where chambers have surplus funds as a result of members' contributions exceeding chambers' expenditure, this also has to be reflected in the members' accounts. Members' contributions have to have been expended by chambers in order to be tax deductible, and chambers must advise each member of their share of unexpended chambers contributions

151. The apportionment of these adjustments can be administratively complex where members have different accounting year ends, and where some members prepare their accounts on the cash basis, whereas others use the earnings basis. Chambers records need to be kept in a manner that permits them to identify the tax adjustments so that the information can be provided to the members.

152. Barristers need this information if they are to complete their self assessment tax returns correctly. It is open to Her Majesty's Revenue and Customs (HMRC) to enquire into a barrister's tax return to ensure that the correct tax treatment has been applied. If on enquiry it is found that chambers have

not provided this information to a member, there is a likelihood that this could trigger enquiries into the tax returns of all the members of that set.

153. Simply setting up a service company does not circumvent the tax difficulties. Members' contributions to these service companies are treated as mutual income, and the "mutual trading" rules apply. Consequently, the service company is transparent for tax purposes, and the tax deductibility of members' contributions to such companies depends on the end use of those contributions, in exactly the same manner as if the company did not exist.

154. Chambers organise themselves in widely differing ways, and the function of what is written here is to alert barristers to the problem, rather than to provide solutions for every situation. The apportionment of expenses is dealt with differently in different sets of chambers. Whatever system is used, however, it is important that it aims to charge for a year only the amount actually expended by chambers in the year, and that any deficit or surplus is made up, or returned to members, as soon as possible after the end of the chambers' accounting period.

Treatment of chambers as a Trade Protection Association

155. The situation is much simplified if chambers adopt the arrangements applicable to Trade Protection Associations (TPAs). The Bar Council has agreed with HMRC that most sets of chambers may be treated as a TPA for tax purposes; this agreement does not affect the substantive question of whether sets of chambers actually are TPAs.

156. The main practical effect of the TPA arrangement is that any tax adjustments are made in chambers' tax computation rather than in those of individual members

157. Chambers wishing to adopt this basis need to proceed as follows:

(a) write to HMRC stating that chambers wishes to adopt TPA status. This letter is best sent to Central London Area, Euston Tower, 286 Euston Road, London, NW1 3UH. This office is familiar with the procedures; and

(b) The letter should be accompanied with:

(i) a copy of the chambers constitution;

(ii) a full list of members annotated with their 10 digit Unique Taxpayer References (UTRs). Changes in the make-up of chambers members need to be notified within a reasonable period of each change (e.g. six months), and

(iii) state the date from which the arrangement is to take effect.

158. Her Majesty's Revenue and Customs will then write to say that the TPA arrangement has been approved in principle, sending three copies of a document setting out the terms of the agreement. All three copies require signature (by the Head of Chambers and Chambers' Treasurer) and will need to be returned to HMRC. One copy will be signed on behalf of HMRC and returned to chambers.

159. The arrangement must effectively start with a neutral opening statement of affairs and the following matters need to be addressed by way of an adjustment in the tax computation of the first accounting period:

(a) Any surplus brought forward into the accounts of the first year should be treated as fully taxable in that year, regardless of its component parts and, regardless of the accounts basis adopted by the barristers involved. Likewise any deficit brought forward should be treated as an allowable expense in that first year

(b) A review should also be made into the central "pot" of the chambers' expenses for the three years prior to it entering into a TPA in order to identify inadmissible expenditure such as entertainment etc. Any such amount identified should be brought into account as income in that first year, and

(c) Any amounts identified under a and/or b above which have already been notified by chambers to the individual barristers, and taken into account by them on their tax returns, can be ignored.

The tax consequences for chambers

160. As a TPA, chambers will be required to prepare accounts in accordance with Generally Accepted Accountancy Practice. Profits arising from members' contributions would be computed using the rules for income from a trade. Losses, caused by a deficiency of members' contributions, would be computed using the same principles as used to calculate profits, and may be relieved against profits of the previous six years or profits of future years.

161. Where chambers make a return of contributions it may be deducted in arriving at the profit for tax purposes.

162. The charge to tax would be at the applicable corporation tax rate (currently less than marginal income tax rates) and normally payable nine months and one day after the end of the accounting period.

The tax consequences for the barrister

163. An individual barrister's chambers contributions to the TPA are wholly deductible in their own accounts whether on a cash or earnings basis. There is therefore no requirement for the barrister to obtain details of how and when their contributions have been applied by chambers.

164. It follows that any return of contributions to the barrister by chambers is taxable. In practice this is achieved by reducing (in the year of receipt for those on a cash basis, in the year in which they arose for those on an earnings basis) the quantum of otherwise tax deductible contributions in the relevant accounts.

The VAT consequences for chambers

165. It is considered that a set of chambers that is actually a TPA (as opposed to one which has simply adopted TPA status for income tax purposes) has in fact the obligation to register for VAT with the following consequences:

(a) VAT will be charged on all "supplies", which will, of course, include contributions levied on members of chambers;

(b) VAT incurred on expenditure will be recoverable subject to the normal rules; and

(c) Completion of a VAT return in the name of chambers, rather than chambers VAT being included on the VAT return of the head of chambers.

The VAT consequences for the barrister (if chambers is registered)

166. The barrister registered for VAT will be able to recover the VAT charged on their contributions by chambers, unless they have adopted the Flat Rate Scheme (FRS). There will be a cash flow disadvantage in that individual members of chambers would have to pay VAT to chambers on their contributions and then reclaim the VAT as "input tax" in their quarterly returns.

167. Those barristers not registered for VAT will not be able to recover VAT charged.

Service companies

168. Simply setting up a service company does not circumvent the tax difficulties associated with a set of chambers which has not adopted TPA status.[16] Contributions to these service companies are treated as mutual income, and the "mutual trading" rules apply. Consequently, the service company is transparent for tax purposes, and the tax deductibility of members' contributions to such companies depends on the end use of those contributions, in exactly the same manner as if the company did not exist. It is, however, open to service companies to apply for TPA status in the same way as chambers generally. The same procedures would need to be followed as described above.

169. Some chambers have formed service companies to assist in the general administration of chambers. Such companies may have commercial advantages (e.g. in providing continuity of employment as regards staff). Fiscal considerations applicable to such companies are complex and are not covered in this guidance. It is considered that there is no fiscal advantage in adopting service companies and there are quite likely to be fiscal disadvantages (especially as regards the ownership and leasing of plant and machinery). Any set of chambers proposing to form a service company to own chambers' assets should seek particular tax advice of its own. No particular problems arise if a company is used merely to employ staff and pay expenses etc. (without owning assets). This is attractive to some Heads of Chambers who do not wish to their name to appear as the employer as would normally be the case under Pay As You Earn (PAYE) legislation. However the cost and the statutory administrative requirements of forming and operating such a company should be taken into account.

170. Annual costs would vary with the size and turnover etc. of chambers and whether or not chambers' accounts are already audited, but it is estimated that the minimum additional cost of having such a company is £3,000 and it could be much more.

16 Typically, a service company is set up as a non-profit making company limited by guarantee. The members of chambers are usually members of the company and hence members.

ProcureCo

171. A ProcureCo is in effect a vehicle by which contracts maybe be entered into by a set of chambers or a consortium of chambers and other professional advisers. The intention being to secure work for the Bar and to compete with other legal service providers. In its current form the ProcureCo acts as an agent for a panel of professionals and is not intended to make a profit. The Bar Council guidance recommends the use of a company limited by guarantee. As the ProcureCo is non-profit making and passes all income direct to the panel members there should be no corporation tax consequences. However if the ProcureCo incurs expenditure and charges the panel members for providing its services there could be a corporation tax issue if any of the expenses are not tax deductible.

172. The ProcureCo will also need to consider the Value Added Tax (VAT) position. It is believed that it will be necessary for the ProcureCo to register for VAT. Even though it is acting as an agent for the panel members it will need to charge VAT on the fees payable by the client and will then be charged VAT on the fees when passing the fees onto the panel member that undertook the work.

173. The ProcureCo will be obliged to prepare accounts and file corporation tax returns in exactly the same way as any other corporate body.

Specialist Bar Associations

174. There are numerous specialist Bar associations that barristers become members of and to which they pay regular subscriptions. The subscriptions paid will normally be tax deductible in the accounts of the paying barrister. However, as with a set of chambers if the association uses the subscriptions for settling expenditure that would not be tax deductible if paid by the barrister then strictly a proportion of the subscription would not be tax deductible in the barrister's accounts. A similar problem arises if the association makes a profit out of the subscriptions and retains that surplus.

175. In addition if the association puts on events that are open to non-members for a fee and makes a profit from the event there is a corporation tax liability on that part of the profit that relates to non-members.

176. These difficulties can be dealt with in a simplified manner if the association registers with HMRC as a TPA. The Bar Association will have to pay corporation tax on all profits but the subscriptions of the members will be fully tax deductible without any concerns over the use to which those subscriptions have been put.

Part 6

VAT and the Bar

[7.8]

Introduction

177. Value Added Tax (VAT) a tax levied on the supply of goods and services by a person registrable for VAT. In general, VAT will apply to barrister's fees.

178. The relevant statutory provisions are contained in the Value Added Tax Act 1994 (VATA) supplemented and amended by later Finance Acts and Statutory Instruments. HMRC have issued a notice[17] which is of general application.

179. This *Notice* may be considered valuable as a background to the information provided here, which is designed to be of specific use to barristers in explaining how the tax applies to barristers, and how barristers and their clerks should deal with the necessary documentation.

17 Notice No. 700, The VAT Guide.

What must be paid

180. In principle VAT is a tax to which barristers are chargeable on the services they render in the exercise of their profession. In general, the services provided are either taxable supplies or outside the scope supplies. Taxable supplies are subject to VAT at the rate of 20% currently. Outside the scope supplies attract no UK VAT charge. Accordingly, once registered a barrister must account for VAT on all taxable supplies made in the course or furtherance of their profession. Taxable supplies extend, for example, to a sale by the barrister of any of their chambers furniture and, unless a separate employment is involved, to fees for lecturing and writing articles. He must charge VAT on such supplies and account for it to HMRC. Furthermore, the accounting for VAT will include any other business activity he undertakes in their own individual capacity that may be entirely unrelated to their work as a barrister. Registration, and the requirement to register, applies to the individual person in respect of all business supplies he makes, not just those made in the course of their professional chambers work.

181. In general VAT is not payable by barristers until fees for their services are actually received. The actual receipt of fees by barristers will almost invariably include VAT and the moment of such receipt is called the tax point. This moment will fall in a tax period, each of such periods being of three calendar months, for which a VAT return is required to be made to HMRC.

182. The standard rate of VAT has been 20% since 4th January 2011. Typically, this means that barristers will levy 20% to their base fee charged for professional work as the receipt is regarded as including VAT. This 20% is called output tax. Subject to the deductions mentioned below, it must be accounted for and paid by barristers to HMRC within the one month period next after the end of the tax period in which the particular fee is received.

183. Thus a barrister who charges £1,000 for a piece of work must account for an additional £200 representing output tax. If they receive that total sum of £1,200 on 1 November and the next VAT period ends on 30 November, they must pay the £200 VAT element to HMRC before 31 December, together with all other VAT received between 1 September and 30 November, but subject to the deduction for all input tax in the course of their profession during that period.

184. Arrangements can be made for payment by direct transfer to HMRC via electronic means of payment for which an allowance of an additional seven days is granted. If filing is done online, such electronic payments are mandatory. Payments must be in HMRCs bank account in principle on or before the seventh calendar day from the standard due date, but the seven day allowance is restricted if the seventh day falls on a weekend or bank holiday in which case payment must be received by the last working day beforehand.

185. "Input tax" is the name given to VAT charged by a supplier on goods or services used by the barrister in the course or furtherance of their profession (i.e. VAT which has been paid by the barrister).

186. Consideration for goods and services is deemed inclusive of VAT (e.g. if a barrister agrees to a fee of £600 for lecturing, £100 is VAT unless the agreement makes it clear that the fee is exclusive of VAT). This is an essential principle to bear in mind when agreeing a fee for any services provided. The barrister must guard against the risk that they have to account to HMRC for VAT out of a fee which they had assumed was exclusive of VAT.

187. Devilling fees paid to a barrister who is registered for VAT are liable to VAT which should therefore be added to the fees and included in the recipient's quarterly return. The payer takes credit for the VAT as deductible input tax in their quarterly return, and is entitled to be given a tax invoice for it. The result is neutral in the sense that the VAT cost to the barrister and the devil is nil, but it is important that barristers and their devils should know the strict legal position.

188. If a barrister, in carrying on their practice, uses certain services supplied from outside the UK, then they are deemed to have supplied those services in the UK. Accordingly, they will have to account for VAT on the value of the supply received from abroad, but unless the circumstances are unusual, they will also be entitled to a corresponding input tax credit, so there is no net effect. This process is called "the Reverse Charge." It is a mystifying mechanism at first sight, but it may help to understand it by reference to the apparent policy reason for its existence, which is to prevent distortion of competition by removing any VAT advantage in a UK business outsourcing services it needs from the UK to non-UK suppliers.

Part-time Judicial appointments and other offices

189. As indicated above, once a barrister is registered, VAT will apply to all supplies made in the course or furtherance of their profession. Section 94(4) of VATA provides that:

> "Where a person, in the course or furtherance of a trade, profession or vocation, accepts any office, services supplied by him as the holder of that office are treated as supplied in the course or furtherance of the trade, profession or vocation."

190. As a matter of law, therefore, it might well be that remuneration of a barrister holding a part-time judicial appointment could be subject to VAT. Any appointment to an office needs to be considered from this aspect. As stated below, not all appointments are regarded as being taken in the course or furtherance of the profession.

191. Her Majesty's Revenue and Customs treat certain such appointments as outside the scope of the Section. The HMRC Customs and Excise Manual states:

"Judicial appointments

Full time, salaried judicial appointments, although technically public offices, are not caught by section 94(4) since the services are regarded as supplied in the course of employment.

Part-time judicial appointees who carry out the same functions and have the same powers as their full time colleagues are not treated as making supplies in the course or furtherance of business"

192. Examples of part-time judicial appointments outside the scope of the tax given by HMRC are:

- Deputy High Court Judge
- Recorder
- Deputy Circuit Judge/Assistant Recorder
- Deputy Metropolitan Magistrate
- Deputy Provincial Stipendiary Magistrate
- Deputy County Court and District Registrar
- Deputy Master/Registrar of the Supreme Court of High Court
- Deputy Assistant Chancery Registrar
- Coroner
- Deputy and Assistant Coroner
- Dean of the Court of Arches
- Auditor of the Province of York (Church of England)
- Assistant Local Government Boundary Commissioner
- Temporary Supreme Court Judge (Scotland), or
- Temporary Sheriff Principal (Scotland).

193. It is considered that in practice this treatment may extend to part-time chairmen and members of the Tax Tribunal and other Tribunals. In view of the absence of an express statement to that effect, however, in HMRC manuals any barrister in this position should take specific advice, and, as appropriate, obtain a ruling from HMRC.

194. Section 94(4) of VATA only applies in terms to "offices." Accordingly, it is important to note that where a barrister is employed to carry out some particular function and is taxed under PAYE as employment income rather than as professional income) VAT will not be chargeable, as section 94(4) would not as such apply. For example, a barrister may be retained to give a

series of lectures either on a self employed basis as part of their profession or in a separate employment capacity. Only in the first case would they have to account for VAT.

VAT paid on receipts

195. VAT on supplies made by members of the Bar is chargeable at the earliest of the following times:[18]

(a) when the fee is received;

(b) when the barrister issues a VAT invoice; or

(c) the day when the barrister ceases to practice.

196. Accordingly, if a practising barrister wishes to postpone the tax point to the time of payment, they should ensure that their Fee Note is not a VAT invoice,[19] as otherwise the VAT element will then arise and become due for payment one month from the end of the quarter involved, even though the fees are still outstanding. This possibility of postponement also applies to part payments when a VAT invoice should only be issued for the amount received, but not the amount outstanding (for which a further fee note could be issued at the same time as the invoice).

197. The position on retirement or death is set out in paragraphs 243 to 250. Subject to that, if the procedure set out in paragraph 253 is adopted, the tax point will always be the day when the fee is received.

198. VAT is not due on any interest charged on fees paid late.

18 See VAT (General) Regulations 1995, SI 1995/2518, reg 92.
19 See reg 92.

Fee-sharing protocol

199. Following the introduction of a Revised Advocates Graduated Fees Scheme making payments for publicly funded criminal work, the Bar Council has produced a Fee Payment Protocol containing recommended, practical ways of managing the allocation of payments under the new arrangements. This specifically addresses the new basis of remuneration in criminal legal aid cases whereby payment is made on a per case rather than a per advocate basis.

Fees payable to the Instructed Advocate

200. The total fee for the case will be paid to the Instructed Advocate together with VAT (if they are VAT registered). Where it is necessary for a Substitute Advocate to undertake any advocacy services that will be as subcontractor.

201. The Instructed Advocate will be liable to account to HMRC for the VAT on the value of the whole supply made. The Substitute Advocate (if VAT registered) will be required to invoice the Instructed Advocate and account for VAT on the value of the supplies made to the Instructed Advocate. The Instructed Advocate may, however, reclaim (on their VAT return) the VAT which was made accountable to them by a Substitute Advocate, on these supplies as input tax, subject to normal VAT rules.

202. Appropriate records must be kept for VAT inspection, including copies of VAT invoices issued by the Instructed Advocate and VAT invoices issued to the Instructed Advocate by any Substitute Advocate. The Bar Council recommends that chambers keep these records centrally.

Registration threshold

203. This is dealt with in more detail in the sections below. In essence a barrister is liable to be registered if the value of their annual supplies (from practice and any other business supplies) exceeds £81,000 or there are reasonable grounds to believe that it will exceed such a figure within the next thirty days taken from any point of time. The figure of £81,000 is applicable from 1 April 2014 and is usually increased at Budget Day each year. Persons whose annual turnover does not reach these figures may apply for voluntary registration.

Deductible sums – Input Tax

204. Before paying over to HMRC the VAT element in their receipts, the barrister is entitled to deduct any VAT added to the cost of the goods or services for which they have paid and has received a tax invoice in the course of their practice during the same tax period. They may, for instance, have bought stationery for £100 in that period, carrying an additional VAT element of £20 and incurred hotel bills of £200 carrying an additional VAT element of £40. They are entitled to set off against their VAT liability for that tax period the sum of £60 which they have paid out as VAT charged by others. This sum of £60 is called input tax and is deductible against their output tax. For income tax purposes £300 of the above mentioned expenses may be treated as deductible expenditure against their income tax liability, but the £60 is not so deductible since it reduces their VAT liability and is wholly recovered. A different option is available under the 2013 cash basis where receipts and expenses may include VAT – see paragraph 38e.

205. Where a barrister does not claim input tax on supplies against the output tax on their supplies, for example because they are below the registration limit and not voluntarily registered, the total cost of their purchases, including the VAT element, may be deducted for income tax purposes. In practice the principle of deducting for income tax what is not recovered for VAT purposes may extend more widely, (e.g. if input tax relief is denied because of lack of an appropriate VAT invoice) but as this course would only give the barrister relief in respect of the input tax at their highest rate of income tax, it is always preferable to recover the VAT element in full and they should endeavour to retain all VAT invoices in respect of their inputs and recover the input tax against the output tax.

The expenses which attract and do not attract VAT

206. Input tax incurred can only be reclaimed where it is incurred for business purposes and must not be specifically disallowed by statute (e.g. entertaining and private motor cars). Furthermore some expenditure is exempt, zero-rated, or outside the scope of VAT, that is does not involve incurring VAT in the first place. A barrister cannot recover any input tax on expenditure in these latter three categories, as none will have been paid.

Standard rate expenditure attracting the tax

207. Examples of expenses falling into the various categories are shown below

- Computer costs
- Stationery
- Repairs and renewals
- Accountancy charges
- Telephone, including mobile charges
- Off street parking
- Hotel bills
- Subsistence when away from chambers
- Car repairs and servicing
- Car, Petrol and oil
- Subscriptions to law libraries, as distinct from purchase of law books
- Taxi fares (if the driver is registered for VAT)
- Devilling charges (if the devil is registered)
- Robes, wigs, collars, bands, two dark suits and six tunic shirts for appearance in Court.
- Robing room fees for locker use
- Chambers' contributions – where a VAT invoice is issued
- Capital expenditure (e.g. furniture, equipment but not books or sets of cases), and
- Domestic fuel and power (e.g. electricity and gas) attracts VAT at a lower rate, currently 5%.

208. In all of these instances it is assumed that the supplier is registered. If they are not registered they cannot add VAT to their fees so there is nothing to reclaim. The barrister should always obtain a VAT invoice in respect of any of these supplies, otherwise the VAT may not be deductible.

209. As indicated above a barrister can deduct for VAT purposes the input tax on the cost of a dark suit and similar items of clothing purchased specifically for Court wear: *Alexander v Customs and Excise Commissioners* [20] HMRC are prepared to accept limited claims where the dark clothing would not have been purchased but for Court requirements. The effect of this decision is confined to VAT. The VAT rules are less stringent than the "wholly and exclusively" test for income tax, discussed elsewhere in this guidance. Consequently this input tax may be deducted even though the barrister is not entitled to deduct the actual cost of such clothes for income tax purposes.

210. Examples of expenditure which is exempt from the tax include:

(a) insurance premiums;

(b) bank charges;

(c) rent of chambers and other accommodation for professional purposes (unless your landlord has exercised their option to charge VAT at the standard rate); and

(d) Bar Council, Circuit, Specialist Bar Association and other professional Association subscriptions.

20 See *Alexander v Customs and Excise Commissioners* [1976] VATTR 107.

211. Examples of zero rated expenditure include:

(a) books and other publications;

(b) newspapers/magazines; and

(c) travel by public transport.

212. Examples of expenditure outside the scope of the tax altogether include:

(a) wages and National Insurance of the barrister's employees;

(b) Council Tax;

(c) payments for services or goods from non-registered persons; and

(d) parking fines.

VAT and chambers expenditure

213. VAT registered barristers are entitled to deduct from their VAT payments all input tax in relation to the VAT elements of their chambers expenses. Thus, for example, the cost of a new computer paid for by chambers as a whole will carry a VAT element which can be deducted by the registered barristers in those chambers in whatever proportion is appropriate.

214. Different chambers adopt different systems for charging and apportioning chambers expenditure. There are three general systems known to exist in practice and HMRC are prepared to accept the application of any of these systems. The three systems are set out below.

215. There is no requirement that sets adopting the Trade Protection Association (TPA) arrangement for income tax must be registered separately for VAT purposes. The TPA arrangement is simply a contract between a set of chambers and HMRC and does not in itself affect the VAT position. Many sets adopting the TPA arrangements have applied to be registered for VAT but this is not necessary and whether it is advisable will depend on the circumstances of the set and its members.

216. Other sets have arranged for the incorporation of a service company. It is usual for the service company to register for VAT in its own right so that the following provisions will not apply.

Method 1 – supplies by the Head of Chambers or other nominated member

217. The nominated member, to whom the invoice has been addressed, treats the full amount of VAT as input tax. Output tax is accounted for on the shares charged to all the other members of chambers.

218. Those members who are VAT registered are entitled to deduct the VAT charged to them as their input tax.

219. As a concession by HMRC, tax invoices need not be issued by the nominated member. However, to help HMRC to ensure that no more than the total VAT stated on the invoice is deducted, it will be necessary for each member's records to be cross-referenced to:

(a) output tax charged by the nominated member;

(b) the input tax deducted by other members; and

(c) the original tax invoice.

220. The records of all members of chambers must be available during a VAT control visit by HMRC to any one of them.

Method 2 – proportional attribution of input tax

221. The nominated member, to whom the invoice has been addressed, does not charge output tax on the members' contributions. The input tax on the supply is apportioned so that VAT registered members may deduct it on the basis of their own contributions.

222. Records must be kept of the apportionment of input tax between the members of chambers. Each member's records should cross-reference the input tax deducted to the tax invoice.

223. The records of all members of chambers must be available during a VAT control visit by HMRC to any one of them.

Method 3 – the combination method

224. The nominated member, to whom the invoice has been addressed, deducts the whole amount of input tax but also pays an equal amount into the common fund. This method may only be used when all members of chambers are registered for VAT.

225. Special accounting rules apply to those barristers or advocates who are on the flat-rate scheme and whose chambers use Method 3.

226. Sets of chambers are entirely free to adopt whichever of the above methods best satisfies their needs. Once a particular system has been adopted it is recommended that the system be maintained. The concern of HMRC is of tax claims by all the members of chambers exceeding the actual input tax suffered on supplies to chambers. Consequently adequate records of the manner of attribution etc. should be maintained so that the position can readily be checked by HMRC.

227. Alternatively, the chambers itself may be registered for VAT as described below.

Chambers registered for VAT

228. If a set of chambers or a chambers service company is registered for VAT it will have to account for VAT on the supplies it makes to members of chambers and will receive credit for input tax paid on the supplies it receives. Whether the chambers have to levy VAT on all supplies to members will

depend on the precise circumstances. For example, if the set makes separate supplies of accommodation (paid for by rent) and general administrative services (paid for by a percentage contribution), the percentage element will attract VAT but the rental element will be liable for VAT if and only if the set has "waived the exemption" to VAT (or "opted to tax") in respect of its premises. The set should issue invoices to members who will then, if themselves registered for VAT, be able to reclaim the VAT element.

229. This system may be administratively simpler than those outlined above but results in a cost for those members who are not themselves registered and could lead to the earlier payment of VAT by members. Care should be taken in choosing the chambers VAT quarters relative to those of members. Before registering for VAT, a set of chambers should seek appropriate professional advice.

VAT and personal expenditure

230. VAT registered barristers may also deduct the VAT element in their business expenditure paid personally against their output tax.

Example

Fiona is a London based barrister who does a two day case in Birmingham. Her expenses may look like this:

Item	Expenses	VAT
Taxi to Euston	15.00	3.00
Taxi to hotel	12.00	0.00[21]
Hotel bill	100.00	20.00
Lunches	20.00	4.00
Train fares	115.00	0.00
Taxi Euston to chambers	5.00	3.00
	£277.00	£30.00

The sum of £30.00 can be deducted in the relevant quarterly return against output tax, whether or not the fees for that case were paid in the same period. The sum of £277 should qualify for deduction against income tax as ordinary professional expenses, but the sum of £30.00 does not, on the basis that it has been claimed in the VAT return as input tax.

21 Taxi driver is not VAT registered.

Obligatory registration

231. A barrister is required to be registered:

(a) after the end of any month, if the value of their taxable supplies (whether as a barrister or otherwise) in the period of one year then ending has exceeded £81,000, or

(b) at any time if there are reasonable grounds for believing that the value of their taxable supplies within the next thirty days will exceed £81,000.[22]

232. If the fees of a barrister (inclusive of the monetary amount of any other taxable supplies they may make from other activities) who is not registered exceed the figure of £81,000 for any year they are still not obliged to be registered if Her Majesty's Revenue and Customs (HMRC) can be satisfied that the value of their total taxable supplies in the following year will not exceed £79,000.

233. The figures of £81,000 and £79,000 referred to above are applicable from 1 April 2014 and may be increased by subsequent Treasury Orders.

22 See VAT Act 1994, Sch 1, para 1, as amended.

Voluntary registration

234. Even though a barrister may not be obliged to register under the tests set out above they may apply to be registered voluntarily. This is a personal decision for the barrister concerned. Reasons why a barrister with a tenancy might wish to register voluntarily include:

(a) a barrister who registers can claim recovery of their input tax against their VAT liability. Otherwise this is not recoverable and the barrister will only be able to obtain relief against their income tax liability;

(b) their clerk can commence a system of accounting which can be permanently adhered to without alteration and which is identical to that of the other members of their chambers;

(c) they do not disclose to their clients that their gross earnings are comparatively low; or

(d) their chambers can only use the third method of dealing with VAT on chambers expenditure described above if *all* members of chambers are registered.

235. It might be thought that barristers in the early stages of their career would be at a disadvantage in voluntarily registering for VAT as they would be obliged to account for VAT when other, unregistered barristers in a similar position are not charging VAT. However this is not invariably so and depends upon the source of work undertaken. In particular instructing solicitors can generally claim back as their own input tax the VAT so charged, and the VAT the solicitors themselves must charge may be to commercial or business clients who can recover the VAT themselves.

236. There will, however, be a relative disadvantage where fees are borne by clients who cannot reclaim the VAT element themselves, that is where private client work predominates.

What follows registration

237. The form by which the barrister applies for registration is VAT 1. Shortly after a barrister's application has been accepted and they are registered they will receive from HMRC a certificate of registration (VAT 4), stating their

registration number. This number must be used in all subsequent communications with HMRC and must appear on all VAT invoices of registered barristers which are tax invoices. The barrister will also be told the effective date of their registration, that is to say the date from which their obligation to pay output tax and their entitlement to deduct input tax will start. A registered barrister is also under an obligation to notify HMRC of any change of professional address and of their retirement.

238. The quarterly return period will also be advised. The barrister can apply for this to be altered to a more conventional date (e.g. to coincide with their annual accounting date).

Deregistration

239. A barrister ceases to be liable to be registered at any time, if they can satisfy HMRC that the value of their taxable supplies in the period of one year then beginning will not exceed £79,000 (this figure is applicable from 1 April 2014 but can be changed by Treasury Order).

240. The current Form for deregistration is VAT 7.

Retirement or death

241. The provisions for deregistration set out above apply where the barrister continues to carry on their practice but the value of their supplies has fallen. Ordinarily it would not be recommended that they should seek to deregister in such circumstances.

242. Where a barrister retires which includes discontinuance for any other reason (e.g. to take up full-time employment) they should notify HMRC of the fact within thirty days. HMRC will then cancel their registration.

243. When a barrister dies whilst in practice, their clerk should inform HMRC as soon as possible of the death. The personal representatives of a deceased barrister should likewise inform HMRC within 10 days of the grant of probate or letters of administration whether they wish to elect for the deferment procedure.

244. References should be made to Part Seven of this guidance regarding discontinuance generally. Technically,[23] the output VAT on all of the barrister's work completed prior to the date of retirement or death becomes payable. However, HMRC are prepared to allow payment of the VAT as and when the fees are received provided the barrister or their personal representatives makes a specific election (referred to as "deferment") shortly after the cessation of practice. It is considered that such an election will almost invariably be advisable. It has been agreed with HMRC that, when they receive an application for deregistration by or on behalf of a retired or deceased barrister, they will send in reply a copy of their leaflet explaining the special arrangement for post-cessation receipts of barristers and the appropriate form for election to defer payment of VAT until the fees are received. That form must be completed and returned to the HMRC if VAT is not to be paid at once on all outstanding fees.

245. Where deferment of the liability has been accepted by HMRC in these circumstances, a form will be sent to the barrister or their representative, on which is to be listed:

(a) all the outstanding fees subject to the standard rate of VAT;

(b) the name of the relevant case;

(c) the professional client; and

(d) the date of the first fee note.

246. Subsequently HMRC will send each quarter a form which will be used to show:

(a) any fees which have been received in the period;

(b) any fees for which a VAT invoice has been issued in the period; or

(c) any fees, previously shown as free of VAT, which are now subject to the standard rate.

247. After the first year, the barrister may choose to submit the form on a six monthly basis, until such time as all the fees have been collected. At this stage the declaration on it "declaration of final payment" may be completed. This finalises the matter. In the event there are fees outstanding which the barrister or personal representative determines cannot be collected, the reason should be stated in the declaration of final payment.[24]

248. On deregistration the barrister is deemed to have supplied (at market value) all goods then owned which had been acquired for the purposes of their profession and on which they had claimed an input tax deduction, and account for output tax thereon. This usually applies to capital items. Subsequent actual sales of the goods will not attract VAT.

249. Any input tax incurred after registration has been cancelled may be repaid by HMRC on submission of a separate claim. The claim must normally be made within six months of deregistration, but in any case within three years of the date on which the input tax arises.

23 See VAT (General) Regulations 1995, reg 92.

24 Her Majesty's Revenue and Customs have published a special leaflet for barristers on this subject, Leaflet 700/44/07, which can be obtained from any VAT Office.

The need to maintain records

250. Every taxable barrister must keep records of all services they supplied and the goods and services they received in the course of their profession in sufficient detail, for a minimum of six years:[25]

(a) to allow them to calculate correctly the amount of VAT they have to pay HMRC

(b) to allow them to calculate the amount of money they can offset against their VAT liability

(c) to complete the necessary VAT returns, and

(d) to provide documentation to allow HMRC to check the completeness and accuracy of these returns.

251. In particular they must retain VAT invoices in respect of supplies so as to enable them to recover the VAT thereon as input tax.

25 See para 2.4 *Notice 700/21/07* "Keeping VAT records".

Tax invoices

252. Except where a barrister ceases practice, the tax point is the earlier of the issue of a tax invoice and payment. So as to ensure that the VAT only becomes due when the fee is paid, barristers may wish to ensure that fee notes which their clerks issue prior to the receipt of any fees do not constitute tax invoices. This can be achieved by ensuring that the fee notes so rendered do not bear a distinct VAT invoice number and contain a box, left blank, for the insertion of the date on which the fee is subsequently received, which will constitute the tax point. Once the fee is paid a tax invoice should be sent to the solicitor, or other instructing professional, bearing a distinct invoice number and having inserted upon it the date on which the fee was received and which is, therefore, the tax point.

253. A VAT invoice should contain the following information

(a) a unique, sequential tax invoice number;

(b) the date of the tax point (generally payment);

(c) the barrister's name, address, and VAT registration number;

(d) the professional instructor's name and address;

(e) details of the work done;

(f) the nature of the services charged for (which will always be professional services);

(g) the amount of the fees charged for each item;

(h) the total fees (i.e. the taxable amount); and

(i) the rate and amount of VAT charged.

254. Fee notes rendered prior to payment do not need to be formal VAT invoices and, therefore, should not contain these requirements where the barrister has chosen to defer the tax point until payment.

Local authority payments

255. It has been common practice for barristers' clerks to issue a fee note, and only when payment has been received, to issue that invoice which enables the recipient of the service to reclaim VAT. An increasing number Chambers has found that this practice has become unacceptable to an increasing number of local authorities, who are now seeking to change their payment practices, so they will only pay on receipt of a formal VAT invoice.

256. Where this occurs, the advantage of the traditional procedure under which the barrister only pays VAT on receipt of the actual payment for their services is set aside, since the local authority assert that they do not accept the traditional fee note as a valid request for payment but instead insist a VAT invoice. This means barristers not only may have to wait payment, but they may well need to find the VAT element out of their own resources whilst so doing.

257. Subject to certain restrictions and conditions, a facility is generally available to businesses, provided that currently VAT chargeable turnover is expected to

be less than £1.35m (excluding VAT and capital items). Using cash accounting a business does not need to pay VAT until their own customers have paid it, thus if barristers used it, it would overcome the problem now being raised by local authorities.

258. Using standard VAT accounting, VAT is paid on any VAT invoices issued, even if no payment has been received; and VAT can be reclaimed on input VAT on any invoices received, even if payment has not yet been made to the supplier.

Changes in rates of VAT

259. In the case of barristers' fees the rate of tax payable will often be the rate in force at the time at which the fees are received by the barrister. However, if the rate of VAT goes up, the position may be different. It may be that barristers' fees paid after the change are subject to liability at the old rate if the fees relate to services rendered before the change of rate.[26] Whenever there is a rate change there is also usually anti-forestalling legislation which also needs to be considered.

260. There was a change to the VAT rate from 17.5% to 20% on 4th January 2011. Detailed guidance on this change as it affects barristers was issued at the time. It should also be taken into account that those on the flat-rate scheme are affected differently than those not on the scheme. The principles involved are likely to apply to future VAT rate changes. VAT on fees outstanding at registration.

26 See VAT Act 1994, s 88 (2), and VAT (General) Regulations 1995/2518, regs 92 and 95.

261. Most barristers do not become registered for VAT before they receive their first sets of instructions, and therefore they will probably have undertaken a number of items of work before their registration takes effect. This will apply to many pupils in the second six months of their pupillage.

262. If a fee note is issued in respect of such work before the barrister is registered the fee note will not show any VAT as an addition to the fee. If the fee is paid before the barrister is registered there is no difficulty, but a problem arises if payment is received after the barrister has become registered, for work carried out beforehand.

263. It would obviously be inconvenient for barristers if VAT had to be accounted for after registration for work performed before registration, and the Bar Council regards the legal position as not entirely clear. HMRCs view is that VAT should be levied on all fees received after the date of registration.[27]

264. However, they accept that the point is not wholly free from doubt and, since only small sums of VAT are involved which in practice would probably either be deductible as input tax by the instructing solicitor or would fall on legal aid funds, they are prepared to accept that VAT need not be accounted for on fees received by barristers in such circumstances.

265. Therefore, when a barrister becomes registered it is unnecessary for their clerk to send out new VAT inclusive fee notes in substitution for those still outstanding at the time. However, HMRC are concerned that solicitors should not misunderstand the position and deduct tax which barristers have

not accounted for. The arrangement is therefore subject to the condition that fee notes issued in such circumstances should specify the date the work was performed and have stamped or written on them, the following words:

Note: This is not a VATable invoice. No VAT is included in this fee.

266. Since this is a practice of HMRC, the current text from the relevant Customs and Excise Manual[28] is reproduced in full:

"5.1 Fees outstanding at registration

In nearly all cases most barristers will have fees outstanding due to them at registration for work undertaken prior to VAT registration. If a receipted fee note is sent out before VAT registration, no VAT should be shown for the work undertaken.

However, from the VAT registration date fees will be paid for work undertaken prior to registration. ***A newly registered barrister is not required to account for VAT on fees that were outstanding at the time of registration.*** (*Our emphasis*)

In these cases barristers or their administrative clerks should ensure that no VAT is shown on the receipted fee note and it is quite clear that the recipient should not claim any input tax in relation to the fee. The actual tax invoice should show the actual date the work was performed, and to avoid any misunderstandings the phrase "This is not a VATable invoice" should be clearly printed on the receipted fee note issued.

If part of the work is undertaken prior to registration and part after but a request for payment [occurs after registration] sent out and payment is made, VAT should be charged on the total cost of the service provided, ***unless the actual dates and work performed are shown on the fee note.*** (*Our emphasis*)"

267. Where registration and requests for payments take place prior to the issue of receipted fee notes, even though some of the relevant work may have been performed prior to registration, the view of HMRC is that VAT must be accounted for. This creates no practical inconvenience for the barrister, and the council recommends that in such cases the fee note should add VAT to the basic amount of the fee in the usual way.

27 See reg 92 of the VAT (General) Regulations 1995.
28 See HMRCs V1–37 – Control Notes – Section 5 Accounting information.

VAT and insured clients

268. The usual practice in issuing fee notes applies to work undertaken for insurance companies. This remains the case even if the insurance company acts through an in house solicitor. A barrister cannot properly issue a fee note/invoice net of VAT to the insurance company and a separate note/invoice for the VAT to the lay client (the insured) in the hope that the lay client can recover the VAT even though the insurer (who cannot normally recover VAT) has paid the fee.

269. It is understood that the special procedure which has been agreed between HMRC and the Bar Council whereby it is possible to treat the supply of counsel's services as having been made directly to a solicitor's overseas client does not apply in the case of insurance companies and their customers. Counsel should issue a single fee note in the usual way, after which they should issue a VAT invoice for the fee to the insurer for the full amount.

Special concessionary procedure in relation to legal services with foreign element

270. *De Voil* states the general rule at V6.135:

"[The] Commissioners advise that a barrister is regarded as making supplies of legal services to the instructing solicitor (or other person entitled to instruct him). Accordingly it will be the place where the solicitor has their business rather than the location of the solicitor's client that will determine where any legal services are supplied."

271. Nevertheless a special concessionary procedure was agreed between HMRC, the Law Society and the Bar Council. This was when VAT was first introduced and the procedure was published in the 4th April 1973 edition of Law Society Gazette. *The Law Society's VAT Guide* also refers to it. It should be noted that the concession only applies to solicitors, despite the fact that other professionals are now authorised to instruct Counsel.

272. Under this procedure it is possible for the instructing solicitor to treat the supply of counsel's services as having been made directly to the ultimate client. This entails the solicitor re-addressing counsel's fee note by adding the client's name and address and the word "per" before the solicitor's. Once receipted, the fee note should be passed by the solicitor to their client thus enabling them to treat the VAT as input tax, if they are a taxable person and the supply of counsel's services was obtained for the purposes of their business.

273. If, because of the nature of counsel's services and the identity and location of the solicitor's client, the supply of those services is not subject to UK VAT, for example legal advice to a business abroad, the solicitor is entitled to certify the fee note accordingly and ask their client to pay the VAT exclusive amount only. Alternatively they may ask counsel's clerk to cancel the original fee note and submit a new one; this will have no adverse VAT implications in that counsel's fee note only becomes a tax invoice when receipted. In either case, the fee note will have to be addressed to the ultimate client.

274. It is important to note that it is the UK solicitor who decides whether to adopt the concessionary treatment. It is not the barrister; if the solicitor does not elect for the concessionary treatment, VAT remains chargeable under the general rule.

275. De Voil[29] comments that "unfortunately this concession is not widely known and can often lead to problems with local VAT offices." In this context we add text which can be found currently in the Customs and Excise Manual.[30] It reads:[31]

"Barristers and advocates

Invoices from barristers and advocates (known as Counsel) are usually addressed to the firm which instructed them, rather than the ultimate client. Most practices will recover the VAT on Counsel's fees and account for output tax when they are charged on to the client. However, under an agreement between the Department and the Law Society, they may opt to treat Counsel fees as disbursements, in which case the firm will manually write the client's name and 'per' above their own name on the Counsel fee note. The original Counsel fee note must be forwarded to the client."

276. As stated previously this concession does not apply to insurance companies and their clients.

29 See De Voil at V6.360.
30 See De Voil at V1.37.
31 See 3.41 under the heading Solicitor's Control Note.

VAT and work for foreign clients

277. In view of the special concession referred to above which UK based instructing solicitors may elect to use to treat Counsel's legal services as generally supplied to the ultimate client and there are rules which apply that treat legal advice as outside the scope of UK VAT when supplied to a person who belongs abroad. They may also be directly applicable to barristers should instructions be accepted from outside the UK instead of from a UK solicitor.

Client "belonging" overseas

278. When the client "belongs" overseas, the supply is either outside the scope, as being deemed to have been made outside the UK, or standard-rated.

279. The supply will be outside the scope, firstly, if the client "belongs" in a country outside the EU (other than the Isle of Man). Under this heading it is not relevant whether the supplies are for private or business purposes. It is sufficient that the client is outside the EU.

280. Alternatively, outside the scope treatment will apply if the client "belongs" in an EU country other than the UK and receives the barrister's services otherwise than wholly in a private capacity. For this purpose the barrister should be provided with the client's VAT registration number or other satisfactory evidence that they are in business. HMRC[32] state that:

"[To] satisfy yourself that this section applies you should obtain commercial evidence showing that your customer belongs outside the UK and does not receive your supply for a wholly private purpose. For some supplies of services it will be clear that the supply would not be purchased by anyone for a wholly private purpose. VAT registration numbers are the best evidence that the supply is not received for a wholly private purpose and should be requested. If your customer is unable to provide a VAT number, you can accept alternative evidence. This includes certificates from fiscal authorities, business letterheads, or other commercial documents indicating the nature of the customer's activities."

32 See HMRCs *Notice 741A* at 2.7.

"Belonging"

281. The country in which a person "belongs" can be a complex matter and advice should be taken in any case which is not straightforward because the client appears to be based in several countries or has branches or places of business in the UK.

282. If the case in question is legally aided, you should also consider the Legal Aid Agency's guidance on this issue.[33]

33 See Section 4 of the Legal Aid Agency's *Costs Assessment Guidance* for civil work completed under the 2013 contract, and the 2010 contract.

Exclusion of land services

283. Legal services related to UK land are always supplied in the UK and chargeable to VAT. Conversely legal services related to land outside the UK in another EU country are always supplied in the relevant EU country. In this context the private/business distinction is not relevant.

284. Her Majesty's Revenue and Customs state that legal services such as conveyancing or dealing with applications for planning permission are covered by this rule; whereas services with no direct land element, such as the legal administration of a deceased person's estate which happens to include property, are not so covered and remain general legal services.

Car expenses

"Business use" and "private use"

285. Please see Part One for information on what constitutes business and private use.

Fuel

286. Provided a barrister uses their car at least partly for "business" purposes, they have an option of claiming all the VAT they pay on all fuel purchases as input tax, subject to obtaining and retaining supporting invoices in the usual way.

287. However, assuming that they use the car at least partly for private use, which will almost invariably be the case, they must account for "output tax" at a flat rate according to a scale which depends upon the car's CO_2 emissions. The scale charge is the same whatever the private mileage in the VAT quarter.

288. The only alternatives to adopting the scale charge are; for input tax to be apportioned on a mileage basis between business and non-business/private use, and thus the use of detailed time-consuming logs of every journey; or, alternatively, for no input tax to be claimed at all on road fuel.

289. The quarterly scale charge applicable from May 2014 increases in steps from £26 for 120 g/km (or less) to £91.33 for over 225 g/km. These charges usually change annually on 1 May and when there is a change in the VAT rate.

290. Assuming the scale charge is adopted, the barrister should include the amount of VAT due under the appropriate scale in Box 1 of their VAT Return.

291. Barristers should consider carefully whether they travel sufficient "business" miles to justify claiming VAT on petrol. It may be advisable to opt out of

accounting for VAT using the scale charges by not reclaiming input tax on any fuel bought, whether they use it for business or private motoring.

Leasing or hiring a vehicle

292. When a barrister leases or hires a vehicle at least partly for "business use", they may reclaim 50% of the VAT incurred on the rental.

Repairs and maintenance

293. Provided that the barrister uses their car at least partly for "business use", they may treat *all* the VAT paid on repairs and maintenance as input tax. This applies even if the car is used partly for private purposes. If a car is hired with a contract that incorporates servicing and repairs, the leasing company may be able to apportion the VAT to show that which is attributable to the leasing charges (VAT deduction restricted to 50%) and that attributable to servicing etc. (VAT fully deductible).

Purchase of a car

294. A barrister cannot reclaim *any* VAT on the purchase or importation of a car, unless it is used wholly for business use. Even one journey for private use will result in disallowance of all of the tax.

295. "Purchase" means not only outright purchase but also any purchase made under a hire-purchase, lease-purchase or other agreement whereby property in the car eventually passes to the purchaser.

VAT returns

The barrister's personal records

296. For the purposes of recording their personal expenses, which are relevant to both VAT and income tax, a barrister may find it convenient to keep a VAT and expenses book in which can be entered all of their professional expenses. HMRC are entitled to demand to see receipts (tax invoices) for any items on which it is claimed that input tax is deductible. Such documents should be retained for six years after the end of each accounting period.

The quarterly return

297. Once registered a barrister will have to account quarterly for VAT. From April 2012 virtually all VAT businesses have to file VAT Returns online and pay electronically.

Information required

298. For the purpose of VAT accounting, the barrister will need to be given by their clerk the following information in relation to the relevant accounting period:

(a) the amount of their gross receipts excluding VAT;

(b) the amount of VAT charged;

(c) the share of their deductible input tax from chambers, if any;

(d) the total of their "taxable" professional expenses (excluding VAT) incurred during that period through chambers (i.e. those taxed for VAT at the standard rate and those which are zero rated); and

(e) the total value of all services supplied to, and purchases from, EU Member States.

299. They must also obtain from their own records:

(a) their deductible VAT from business expenses paid personally, and

(b) the total of their personal "taxable" (as in (d) above) professional expenses which they have personally incurred during that period.

300. They should also provide their clerk with details of the amount of any VAT paid in previous accounting periods which, for any reason, they have failed to pay and/or has overpaid so that the clerk may use the appropriate error correction procedures, depending on the net amount involved in the error.

301. In general where the net value of errors found on previous returns is below £10,000, it is possible to adjust the current VAT Return. For larger errors a special error correction notification procedure using a special form VAT 652 must be followed. In general there is a four year time limit for such adjustments or notifications and special advice should be taken in relation to errors discovered for out-of-time periods. Specific advice should be taken where it is proposed not to use VAT 652 to make a correction, as the penalty position is dependent upon it.

What each clerk must record

302. All registered barristers must account for VAT in relation to all professional services with which their clerks are likely to be concerned. Consequently they must levy 20% on the fee amount in respect of all work except that which is outside the scope of VAT. VAT registration applies to all business activities so the records must contain details of other goods and services provided and VAT unless the goods and services are zero-rated, exempt or outside the scope of VAT. Sufficient and suitable records must be kept by all clerks so as to enable them:

(a) to record how much VAT output tax has been received by each of their principals;

(b) to record how much input tax has been paid out by chambers generally on behalf of those principals;

(c) to record chambers' taxable expenses whether zero-rated or not;

(d) to inform those principals at suitable intervals of those amounts;

(e) to divulge and demonstrate these records to Inspectors from HMRC if required;

(f) to retain these records for a period of six years from each accounting period or for such less period as HMRC may allow; and

(g) to keep a VAT summary showing how much VAT those principals have paid.

Foreign currencies and the Euro

303. Invoices showing values computed in foreign currencies (including the Euro) must be converted into sterling at the rates available from HMRC. VAT payments may be made in Euros with conversion costs being absorbed by HMRC.

Special accounting schemes

304. There are three special accounting schemes designed to assist "small" businesses as defined; the Annual Accounting Scheme (AAS), Flat Rate Scheme (FRS) and Cash Accounting Scheme (CAS).

Annual accounting scheme

305. The first special scheme is an annual accounting scheme for small businesses (defined as those with an annual turnover of less than £1,350,000). Under this scheme a barrister is entitled to submit a single annual VAT return. Provided accounting records are properly maintained, kept up-to-date and not left until the year end, the scheme provides some simplification and, of course, removes the need for quarterly VAT returns. However, there is a different more onerous payment regime, in that regular instalments on account are required.

Flat rate scheme: turnover of less than £150,000

306. Businesses with a VAT-exclusive turnover of less than £150,000 can apply to be registered under the "flat-rate" scheme. A flat-rate scheme means (a) charging output tax as normal; (b) accounting for output tax at a reduced rate; (c) not recovering input tax. The purpose of the scheme is to reduce the administrative burden imposed when operating VAT. The scheme is optional and is open to businesses whose annual taxable turnover (not including VAT) does not exceed £150,000 or whose total turnover including the value of exempt income (e.g. rents and non taxable income) does not exceed £191,500. Turnover for these purposes does not include the proceeds from the sale of capital assets. The turnover test applies to anticipated turnover in the following 12 months. This can be calculated in any reasonable way but would normally be based on the previous 12 months turnover. Businesses not already VAT registered may do so at the same time as applying to use the scheme. There is no penalty for exceeding the turnover limits but if the VAT inclusive turnover exceeds £230,000 the business must leave the scheme.

307. Under the scheme a set percentage is applied to the turnover of the business as a one off calculation instead of having to identify and record the VAT on each sale and purchase. There is no input tax deduction for purchases except capital assets valued over £2,000, inclusive of VAT.

308. The flat-rate which is applicable to barristers is 14.5% from 4 January 2011.

309. As the flat-rate is applied to the total of the fee plus VAT the saving in tax is therefore not 5.5% (as it might appear) but 2.6% of the net fee. This is shown as follows:

Fee	Fee plus VAT	VAT	Flat rate output tax
£1,000	£1,200	£200	£174

310. Thus the VAT saving in output tax accounted to HMRC is £200-£174 = £26, or 2.6% of the fee.

311. It should be noted that there is a 1% discount on flat-rate for the first year of VAT registration.

312. Barristers whose chambers use any of the methods of accounting for common expenses may use the scheme. However, those chambers using "the combination method" must follow special rules if they have any members using the flat-rate scheme. Furthermore, chambers must ensure that input tax claims are apportioned and only relate to those barristers who are not on the flat-rate scheme by additional record-keeping. This presents an administrative burden on chambers and results in the VAT related to those barristers on the flat-rate scheme not being recovered.

Example

Maureen in LegalEagle chambers has annual fees of £60,000 and VATable expenses of £1,000 plus VAT. Her fee charges are £60,000 plus £12,000 of output VAT; her recoverable input tax is £200; she accounts to HMRC for (£12,000 – £200) = £11,800.

Sebastian joins the flat-rate scheme, the applicable flat-rate being 14.5%. As before their fee charges are £72,000. He pays over to HMRC £72,000 x 14.5% = £10,440.

The net result is:

	Normal	Net- Normal	Flat-Rate	Net – Flat-rate
Fees	60,000		60,000	
VAT	12,000		12,000	
Expenses	(1,000)		(1,200)	
Pay HMRC	(11,800)		(10,440)	
		59,200		60,360

The saving arises because Sebastian is allowed to keep part of the output tax, and this exceeds the amount of input tax which he could otherwise reclaim. On the other hand, an example could be produced just as easily demonstrating that the barrister loses by adopting the scheme due to the VAT on expenditure exceeding the reduction in tax due on income. This would be particularly relevant to the leading advocate under a fee-sharing protocol where VAT is charged on the invoice from the "sub-contracted" barrister.

Records and invoicing/income tax

313. A record of the flat-rate calculation showing the flat-rate turnover for the accounting period, the flat-rate percentage used and the tax calculated as due must be kept with the VAT account.

314. Invoices for clients will still need to be shown at the standard rate of 20%.

315. For income tax purposes barristers using the scheme should prepare accounts using earnings inclusive of VAT (gross receipts, again inclusive of VAT, if on cash basis) less flat-rate VAT applying the relevant percentage. Expenses will include the irrecoverable input VAT.

Pros and cons of the flat-rate scheme

316. The scheme offers a simplified expedient procedure for dealing with VAT. Those interested in taking up the scheme should identify whether it is suitable for them and whether or not an advantage accrues.

317. Method 3 (the combination method) accounting does mean that there is an additional burden on their chambers where members use the flat-rate scheme.

318. The flat-rate scheme can be used in conjunction with the annual accounting scheme requiring a single annual return. This could save time and money.

319. It is important to note that the flat-rate applies to all the supplies the barrister makes, including the value of exempt supplies, such as rental income from buy-to-let property. As exempt and zero-rated supplies are included in the flat rate turnover, it is possible depending on circumstances to pay more VAT by being on the scheme.

Cash accounting

320. Using cash accounting, VAT is accounted for to HMRC each quarter on the basis of payments received and made (rather than by reference to the tax point of supplies made and received). In other words, a business does not need to pay VAT until its own clients have paid it and conversely, VAT on expenses cannot be reclaimed until settled.

321. This scheme is generally available to businesses, provided that the annual taxable turnover is expected to be less than £1.35 million (excluding VAT and capital items). After joining a barrister can remain in the scheme until the annual taxable turnover exceeds £1.6m. "Outside the scope" supplies are disregarded for the purposes of the threshold tests.

322. The scheme tends not to be used by barristers as they will normally only have to account for VAT on receipt of the fee under the special rules for barristers.

323. Using cash accounting, VAT is paid on sales and customers pay; VAT is recoverable purchases only when suppliers have been paid. This may be helpful for cash flow, especially if recipients of the particular barristers' services are slow payers. Indeed, if the recipient never pays, VAT will not be due on that bad debt so long as the cash accounting scheme continues to be used.

324. On the other hand the following disadvantages should be noted:

(a) the VAT cannot be reclaimed purchases until they have been paid for. Where most purchases involve credit this may be disadvantageous, and

(b) similarly when the circumstances are regular payments are being made, under cash accounting they will normally fall later.

325. In start-up circumstances where then maybe substantial outlays incurred. On leaving the cash accounting scheme, account will have to be made for all outstanding VAT dude including any bad debts.

326. Cash accounting cannot be used:

(a) by anyone in default on their VAT obligations;

(b) in relation to purchases or sales involving leasing, hiring, conditional or credit sales;

(c) in relation to acquisitions imports from other EU states;

(d) in relation to invoices issued in advance services rendered; or

(e) in relation to the users of the flat rate scheme.

327. There is no need to complete application form or advise HMRC to start using cash accounting. It is possible to start at the beginning of any VAT period for barristers already registered for VAT; and, in other cases, from the day the VAT registration commences.

328. It should be noted that those already registered to take care that they do not accountant VAT twice on any sales or purchasing. It is necessary to identify and separate any transactions in existing records where account has been rendered for them using the standard procedures.

Joining and leaving the cash accounting scheme

329. The scheme can be left at the end of any VAT accounting quarter. It does not need to be notified to HMRC. As discussed above, the scheme ceases to be available where the taxable turnover is over £1.6 million.

330. Broadly, on leaving the cash accounting scheme, account has to be made for all outstanding VAT due, save for a deferment option of up to 6 months on uncollected amounts subject to conditions.

Penalties for late VAT returns

331. If a taxable person is in default in sending in their VAT return and/or making payment of the VAT shown as due for the period, HMRC will serve a surcharge liability notice. The notice is a warning that a penalty will be imposed if they default again within a period ending one year after the last day of the accounting period for which the tax was due. This period is known as the "notice period." The penalty for the first default following the issue of a surcharge liability notice is 2%. In addition, to the penalty, the notice period is extended to the anniversary of the last day of the prescribed accounting period for which the return was late or tax was not paid.

332. Further default will result in increased penalties and further extensions of the notice period. The rate of penalties is:

Default	
First	Warning notice
Second	2% of tax due
Third	5% of tax due
Fourth	10% of tax due
Fifth and subsequent defaults	15% of tax due

333. If on a default no tax is due, there is no penalty but the notice period will be extended.

334. A prescribed percentage penalty can be avoided by showing that there is a "reasonable excuse", but reliance on a third party (e.g. a clerk) or insufficiency of funds will not usually constitute a reasonable excuse.[34]

34 See s 71 (1) of VATA 1994.

Part 7

Discontinuance of Practice at the Bar – The Tax Position

[7.9]

Introduction

335. On discontinuance of practice, either on retirement (including taking a full-time judicial appointment, but not taking silk) or on death, a number of major issues need to be considered. The most important are

(a) the tax liability arising from the final period in practice, where a number of adjustments need to be made

(b) the tax position in respect of post-cessation adjustments, both receipts and payments, and

(c) other matters:

(i) VAT, or

(ii) Professional indemnity insurance.

Tax position on final accounts

336. It is assumed the barrister will always keep to the same accounting date. They can of course change their accounting date any time they wish, but if they do so extra complications, not dealt with here, are likely to arise.

337. When you cease practice, the profits assessable in the final tax year (whether calculated under a cash basis or earnings basis) of your practice will be those arising in the period beginning immediately after the end of the basis period

for the preceding year and ending on the date of cessation.[35] This period may be more than twelve months. Where overlap relief has arisen on commencement this is available to offset against the profits assessable in the final period.

338. The following illustration may be of interest:

"Matthew ceases to practice on 30 June 2013. He has always prepared accounts to 31 March each year and they show a profit of £115,000 for the year to 31 March 2013 and his profits for the final three months are £45,000.

2012/2013	£115,000
2013/2014	£45,000

Felicity ceases to practice on 30 June 2013. She has always prepared accounts to 30 April each year and they show a profit of £115,000 for the year to 30 April 2013 and her profits for the final two months are £23,000."

2013/2014	£
Profits for 14 month period of cessation	138,000
Less: overlap relief	8,383
	£129,617

339. As can be seen from the examples above there can be large differences in the amount of profit being assessed to tax in the final year. Matthew above is required to pay tax on a final year profit of £45,000 whereas Felicity is required to pay tax on a final profit of £129,617. The reason for the large difference is clearly because Matthew is required to pay tax on three months' profits whereas Felicity is required to pay on 14 months (less a small amount of overlap relief). Felicity has, however, had the advantage throughout her career of paying tax in arrears on what was generally speaking a rising income. Matthew, however, was paying tax very much on an actual basis. Whilst some of Felicity's profit was doubly assessed to tax in the second year of practice, hence giving rise to some overlap relief, such relief is likely to be small when compared to the final year profits. This is simply because profits would have been small in the first years of practice and much larger in the final years. Those worse affected on cessation will be those with an accounting period ending shortly after 5 April (i.e. 30 April), whilst those least affected, will be those with an accounting period ending on 5 April or close to (i.e. 31 March).

340. It is therefore especially important that someone with an accounting period ending shortly after 5 April is aware of the position and makes due provision by maintaining an adequate tax reserve.

341. It should also be recognised that this aggregation of profits can lead to part of the profits falling into a higher tax bracket compared to the position for just 12 months' profits. Barristers wishing to avoid assessability on more than 12 months profits (less overlap relief) on retirement should arrange (where possible) to retire on a date after 5 April.

Example

Stephen prepares accounts to 30 April each year and retires on 10 April 2014. Assessments will be:

2013/2014 – 12 months to 30 April 2013.

2014/2015 – period 1 May 2013 to 10 April 2014.

By contrast, if retirement had occurred on 5 April 2014, all the profits would have been assessable in 2013/2014.

35 See s 202 of the Income Tax (Trading and Other Income) Act 2005.

Maintenance of a tax reserve

342. It is not easy to establish a tax reserve. Early in a barrister's career other demands on their cash resources often make it impracticable to set money aside for future tax payments. Similarly, a barrister in mid-career who does not have a tax reserve is hard-pressed to create one, since much of the current year's profits goes to pay the current tax bills.

343. Nevertheless, many barristers do maintain tax reserves, and they are plainly in a much better position to sustain the tax costs of a cessation after periods of rising profits. Their tax reserves will cover any extra tax arising and, even after payment of that, some of the reserves may not be needed to pay tax liabilities and will provide welcome uncommitted cash resources.

344. All barristers are recommended to do whatever they can to establish out of current receipts reserves to meet future tax liabilities. Following the cessation of a barrister's practice, tax payments will continue to become due for a period extending as long as 21 months. These may form a considerable burden if adequate provision has not been made to build up tax reserves out of current receipts.

Terminal loss relief

345. Relief may be claimed to set a loss incurred in the final 12 months of practice against the practice income of the tax year of cessation and the three previous tax years. The terminal loss may include any available overlap relief.

Adjustments on final accounts on earnings basis

346. If the earnings basis applies a number of adjustments need to be made in the final accounts:

(a) a more critical assessment of the value of outstanding fees is advisable;

(b) any future liability for the payment of chambers rent after cessation should be brought into account; and

(c) any future liability for the payment of clerks' fees after cessation should be brought into account.

347. For those assets still held on which capital allowances have been claimed on discontinuance, the "disposal value" of any assets still held, on which capital allowances have been claimed, is brought into account. If the written-down value in the pool exceeds the disposal value, a balancing allowance is given equal to the difference. If disposal value exceeds written-down value, there is a balancing charge on the excess. "Disposal value" means sale price or, if there is no sale, market value, but disposal value cannot exceed original cost.

Outstanding fees at cessation

348. For those preparing final accounts on the earnings basis the most important item, which is a matter of judgement in individual cases, is the assessment of the value of outstanding fees (billed and unbilled but not received by the time final accounts prepared). It is almost certain that the amount ultimately received will be greater or lesser than the figure included in the final accounts. Any difference, either greater or lesser, needs to be accounted for in future tax returns. These adjustments are dealt with as follows:

(a) where the figure received in total is greater, the surplus must be declared in the tax return covering the year in which the surplus arose. It is possible that such a declaration may need to be made in more than just one return. For example: a barrister retired on 30 June 2013 with outstanding fees owed of £87,000. It was considered that some fees may not be paid at all, and that a reduced sum might be paid on others, especially those subject to Legal Aid taxation. After due consideration the barrister decided that a fair and prudent assessment of what he might ultimately obtain was £65,000. By 5 April 2014 he had received £58,000. During the year to 5 April 2015 he received a further £11,000. On the tax return to 5 April 2015 he would have to declare, as miscellaneous income, the "windfall" profit of £4,000 (£58,000 plus £11,000 less £65,000). If any further monies are received in future years those would also have to be returned on a future tax return(s). Alternatively, surplus receipts received in a tax year beginning no later than six years after the date of cessation may, on election, be treated as received at the date of cessation. This may be of benefit if the tax rate applying to the barrister in the year of receipt is greater than that in the year of cessation. Effect is given to the election by an adjustment to the tax return of receipt, and

(b) where the figure received in total is lesser, relief can be claimed for the shortfall. Using the example under (a) if by, say, 5 April 2015 the £58,000 received to 5 April 2014 is known to be all that will be received, then the barrister has paid tax on £7,000 more profit than actually made. On the tax return to 5 April 2015 they can make a claim for relief for this sum against their other income for 2013/2014.

Practical issues to be considered regarding outstanding fees

349. Whilst there is no time limit for declaring any "windfall" profit, a claim for relief in respect of any shortfall must be made within seven years of the profession ceasing. This seems unfair, and so the advice must be that on assessing the amount that is likely to be received for fees owing at cessation, a particularly prudent approach should be adopted.

350. It is quite possible that relief for any shortfall will be at a lesser tax rate than was originally paid on the figure; dependent on the retired barrister's tax rate in the year the claim is made. Provided the figure is known by 31 January, 21 months after the tax year of cessation, it may be advisable to make an amendment to the tax return covering the year of cessation. In this way there is no danger of receiving relief at a lesser tax rate (i.e. where cessation happened on 30 June 2013 an amendment to the tax return for the year of cessation, 2013/2014, can be made by 31 January 2016).

351. Relief against post cessation receipts is allowed for expenses, such as clerk's fees, falling due to be paid as outstanding fees are received, to the extent that they exceed the amount provided for in the final accounts

New cash basis

352. If the new cash basis applies, the value of any Work in Progress[36] at the time of the cessation is brought into account as a deemed receipt in calculating the profit. It is difficult to envisage any significant work in progress for a typical retiring barrister, as inevitably it will have been "billed". Nonetheless, it is required to be considered and brought into account where relevant. By contrast fees received after cessation are taxed as post cessation receipts except to the extent that they are already included in closing work in progress.

353. Relief against post cessation receipts is allowed for expenses, such as clerk's fees, falling due to be paid as outstanding fees are received, to the extent that they exceed the amount provided for in the final accounts

Old cash basis

354. For those on the old cash basis a post cessation receipt is taxable as miscellaneous income.

355. Relief against post cessation receipts is allowed for expenses, such as clerk's fees, falling due to be paid as outstanding fees are received, to the extent that they exceed the amount provided for in the final accounts.

Catch up charge

356. Part One explained the change from the old cash basis to the earnings basis results in adjustment income which can be spread and taxed over 10 years. If a barrister retires within the 10 years, he or she can continue to take advantage of the spreading provisions. Hence, post cessation, the adjustment income continues to be charged each tax year over the remaining years of the spreading period, until the tenth year, when the balance of the adjustment income is taxable. The figure needs to be declared on the tax return as miscellaneous income.

357. Similarly, for those changing from the new cash basis to the earnings basis, any "adjustment income" on changing is spread over six years. If a barrister retires within these 6 years, he or she can continue to take advantage of the spreading provisions.

VAT

358. A barrister is normally accountable for Value Added Tax (VAT) on their fees when the fees are paid. On discontinuance, the strict position is that they are accountable for VAT on all outstanding fees. However, by concession, HMRC allow retired members of the Bar to defer payment of VAT on outstanding fees until the fees are paid. The relevant VAT rate will be that in force at the date of cessation. This concession must be applied for and form 811 completed. [37]

359. Retirement involves de-registration, and on de-registration, a barrister is treated as making a supply of any assets that they still own and for which they have taken a credit for input tax (e.g. carpets, furniture, computers). The supply is treated as made for a price equal to the second hand value of the assets. Books are zero-rated so this rule has no application to law reports, nor does it apply to antiques bought from a dealer operating the special scheme for dealers under which they apportion VAT on their margin but no input tax is allowed to the purchaser.

36 Work in progress on cessation means: services performed in the ordinary course of the profession the performance of which is wholly or partly completed at the time of cessation, and for which it would be reasonable to expect that a charge would be made if there were no cessation and, in the case of partly completed services, their performance were fully completed, see section 183 ITTOIA 2005.

37 See HMRCs leaflet 700/44 which details the procedures to be followed.

Professional indemnity insurance considerations

360. The Bar Mutual Indemnity Fund (BMIF) provides, free of charge, cessation cover of £500,000 for six years from the date of retirement. One should consult the BMIF in good time before cessation and consider carefully whether additional cover may be needed.

361. Generally, a premium paid for excess run-off cover should be deductible against the final profits.

362. Her Majesty's Revenue and Customs expresses the view that …:

"… premiums paid after cessation can be relieved against post cessation receipts; and that they would not seek to disallow premiums paid whilst in practice where the cover extends to claims lodged after cessation." [38]

38 HMRC, October 1995, Revenue Tax Bulletin.

Part 8

Self assessment

[7.10]

Introduction

363. Under self assessment a barrister must calculate their own tax liability and ensure the tax is paid on time. Even when an accountant is engaged to deal with these matters, responsibility for self assessment remains with the barrister.

364. The barrister will receive a tax return designed to disclose their income and capital gains and enable them to calculate their tax liability. This tax is due on set dates each year. Interest and penalties are charged where returns or payments are late.

365. The return consists of core pages that are common to every taxpayer. For barristers, this is supplemented by the six self-employment pages in which they disclose their professional profits and expenses.

366. If their annual turnover, (i.e. receipts/earnings before deductions) is less than the Value Added Tax (VAT) registration threshold (currently £81,000), the only details they need provide are the turnover and expenses.

367. If the turnover is above this figure, the form requires the recasting of the barrister's accounts information in a standard layout which is used by Her Majesty's Revenue and Customs (HMRC) for their risk assessment procedures.

368. Her Majesty's Revenue and Customs publish a number of help sheets and explanatory pages which together should be reviewed before the return is filled in.

369. In order to reduce the possibility of HMRC opening an enquiry into a return, it is worth ensuring that:

(a) in each year's return expenses are put under the same head, for example, professional subscriptions should not be switched between such categories as "general administrative expenses" one year and "other expenses" the next; and

(b) if accounts are prepared so that the proportions of expenditure representing private use are excluded, those figures can be used on the return without the gross equivalent but it is advisable that a note be added on the return explaining that this has been done.

370. In order to assess the tax liability there are two alternative procedures from which the barrister is able to choose:

(a) submission of the paper return manually by 31 October following the end of the tax year (or two months after the issue of the return if later). In this case HMRC will calculate the tax position; or

(b) submission of the return electronically by 31 January following the end of the tax year (or within three months of the date of issue of the return if later). This is known as the filing date. In this case the taxpayer must assess their own tax liability and the amount of tax due must be shown on the return.

371. If the self assessment return is not filed on time there is an automatic penalty of £100. If the return is still not submitted after a further 90 days HMRC can impose a daily penalty of £10 for each day that the failure continues. If the failure continues after six months from the filing date there is a liability to a penalty equal to the greater of £300 and 5% of any tax liability which would have been shown in the return in question. There is a right of appeal if the taxpayer has a reasonable excuse for late submission but this only covers circumstances beyond the taxpayer's control, such as unforeseen illness. Furthermore, there are provisions for further tax geared penalties if the failure continues for 12 months from the filing date.

372. After the return is filed, HMRC have nine months from the date the return is filed to correct any obvious errors or mistakes on the return. The taxpayer has a similar right, but has 12 months from the filing date as long as HMRC have not started an enquiry. The filing date being 31 January following the tax year to which the return relates.

373. HMRC will select returns for enquiry each year and can issue a notice to this effect up to 12 months after the date the return was filed or, if the return is filed late, by the quarter-day following the first anniversary of the date of delivery or amendment to the return. A notice is sent to the taxpayer, and if they are represented, to their agent.

Payment of tax

374. For this purpose, tax includes Class 4 NICs.

375. Income tax will generally be due in two equal instalments on 31 January during the tax year and 31 July after the end of the tax year. The amount of each of these instalments is half the liability of the previous year excluding capital gains tax. The balancing tax together with tax on capital gains is payable on 31 January after the end of the tax year.

376. Provisions exist for claiming reduced instalment payments if the taxpayer anticipates the liability for that year will be less than the liability for the previous year. However, interest is charged on any underpayment by reference to the instalments that would otherwise have been payable.

377. Where the payments on account exceed the liability for the year, the excess may be refunded or set off against future tax instalments.

378. Interest is charged on the late payment of tax. Such interest is not tax deductible. Furthermore, a 5% late payment penalty arises in respect of the balancing tax and any capital gains tax unpaid after 30 days. There is a further 5% penalty on tax still unpaid after six months and yet another 5% penalty if the tax is unpaid after 12 months.

Example

For an established barrister

Tax year 2013/2014

31 January 2014	First instalment
31 July 2014	Second instalment
31 January 2015	Balance of tax due, or refund of excess of instalment payments over the liability, if not made earlier

Income tax overlap relief

379. It is a basic principle of self assessment that over the lifetime of the profession, all of the profits will be charged to tax; none of the profits will fall out of charge and if any profits are charged to tax more than once, appropriate relief is given.

380. In the early years of a barrister commencing in practice, it is possible for profits to be assessed more than once and so overlap relief is created as discussed in Part Two of this guidance.

381. There is, however, a further form of overlap which was established on the commencement of self assessment referred to as "transitional overlap relief." This is defined as the amount of profits, before capital allowances which were taxed in the 1997/98 tax year but which arose prior to 6 April 1997. Where applicable, the transitional overlap would have already been established and should appear at box 70 on the full Self Employment supplementary pages to the self assessment tax return.

382. Overlap relief (of both types) is frozen and is carried forward and deducted from profits in the final year of the profession.

383. Overlap relief can be used earlier by extending a barrister's accounting period to a date closer to the end of the tax year. A proportion of the overlap relief representing a period in excess of one year would then be available as a deduction. It is worth bearing this in mind as a barrister approaches retirement and finds that their earnings are reducing. If they have traditionally paid tax at higher rates they should also consider changing their accounting date if it might otherwise mean that the relief would only be available at the lower rate. On the basis that the relief is not index-linked, barristers may also consider changing their accounting date to make use of the relief while its inherent value is greater.

Part 9

Retirement provision for barristers

[7.11]

Introduction

384. As self employed persons, barristers in independent practice face the particular responsibility of making their own retirement provision. What follows deals with pensions, which are the main vehicle for retirement planning because of their favourable tax treatment. However, there are restrictions on the amount one can invest in pensions and higher earners should consider supplementing their pensions with other forms of savings.

385. On 1 July 1988, Personal Pension Plans (PPPs) replaced Retirement Annuity Contracts (RACs). This means that no new RAC contracts can be effected after 1 July 1988, but existing RAC contracts may continue and in most cases it is possible to increase the premiums without effecting a new policy. From 6 April 2006 both types of policy are subject to the new rules governing registered pension schemes.

Pension contributions

Net relevant earnings

386. Pension contributions are calculated by reference to Net Relevant Earnings (NRE). These are earnings arising from self-employment, either alone or in partnership, less allowable expenses. In brief this is the profit figure less capital allowances plus, where applicable, the "catch-up" charge. It also includes sitting earnings as this is not from a pensionable employment.

Lifetime allowance

387. From 6 April 2006 the total value of all an individual's tax privileged pensions must fall below a new limit, known as the Standard Lifetime Allowance (SLA), and any excess over the SLA will be subject to a tax charge. The SLA was set at £1.8m for the tax year 2011/2012 but reduced to £1.5m in the tax year 2012/2013, with subsequent years' allowances being no lower than that for the preceding year.

388. In some circumstances an individual's lifetime allowance will actually be higher than the standard lifetime allowance, as they may benefit from one of the following "protections":

(a) Primary Protection – protection is given to the value of pre "A" day (5 April 2006) pension rights and benefits in excess of £1.5m. The pre A-day value will be indexed in parallel with the indexation of the statutory lifetime allowance up to the date that benefits are taken. It is possible to accrue "Relevant Benefit Accrual" post A-Day. To be able to elect for Primary Protection, an individual's A-day value must have exceeded £1.5mm, or

(b) Enhanced Protection – this was available to individuals who ceased all "Relevant Benefit Accrual" after 5 April 2006. There is no requirement for the "A" day value of their benefits to have been greater than £1.5m.

389. In both of these cases you must have registered with Her Majesty's Revenue and Customs (HMRC) by 5 April 2009.

390. Fixed Protection – if you did do not have either primary or enhanced protection, then until 5 April 2012, "Fixed Protection" could have been can be applied for. This was limited to £1.8m and required cessation of all accrual of benefits by 6 April 2012. This was available to those with pension savings above £1.5m or those who believed their value would rise to above this level without further contributions being paid.

Contribution Limits pre 6 April 2006

391. Prior to 6 April 2001, the maximum aggregate contributions which a barrister could pay into an approved pension contract depended on their age at the beginning of the year of assessment in which contribution was to be relieved.

392. From 6 April 2001, maximum contributions continued to be determined by percentages of NRE and the earnings cap, but the "earnings" employed in

the calculation did not have to be current year earnings. Instead, barristers could nominate any of the previous five tax years as their "basis year" (a basis year could have been before 2000/01). The percentage, however, was always related to current age. Eligibility to contribute was also extended: contributions of up to £3,600 pa gross could be made without the need for any NRE to justify the contribution.

Contribution Limits post 5 April 2006 until 5 April 2011

393. Individuals could contribute up to the higher of £3,600 gross and 100% of relevant UK earnings. However, there was a single limit on the tax-advantaged contributions that could be paid each year into pension schemes by an individual. This limit was known as the "annual allowance." The annual allowance for the tax year 2006/07 was set at £215,000, increasing by £10,000 each tax year to £255,000 in the tax year 2010/2011. If contributions exceeded the annual allowance then the individual was taxed on the excess, via the annual allowance charge.

Contribution Limits post 5 April 2011 and Carry Forward of Unused Annual Allowance

394. The annual allowance of £255,000 was reduced to £50,000 on 6 April 2011 and has been reduced further to £40,000 from 6 April 2014. Where an individual's pension savings exceed the Annual Allowance for a tax year, a tax charge may apply.

395. However, it is now possible for a barrister to "carry forward" any unused allowance from the three previous tax years, provided the individual has been a member of a registered pension scheme in each of those years – this includes where a barrister may have established a pension arrangement a number of years before with a single contribution and made no further pension savings in the intervening years.

396. The annual allowance for the tax years 2008/09 to 2013/14 inclusive, for the purposes of carry forward, is limited to £50,000.

Payment of premiums

397. Up to 6 April 2006, self employed barristers paid PPP premiums net of basic rate tax and had to claim higher rate tax relief via their tax returns. Retirement Annuity Policies (RAP) were paid gross and all tax relief was claimed back through their tax returns.

398. From a legislative perspective post 6 April 2006 all premiums to registered pension schemes, including those to retirement annuity policies, can be paid net of basic rate tax, currently 20%. However, retirement annuity providers have to change their policy terms to allow this to happen, but few providers have actually done this, so the contributions system will stay as it was pre 6 April 2006 for the majority of providers.

399. The premiums can be paid by means of regular contributions or by a series of single contributions. The latter method is advantageous since it provides flexibility both in terms of the amount to be paid and also as to the choice of pension provider.

Combining a Personal Pension Plan with life assurance

400. Pension Term Assurance (PTA) is standard term life insurance but with premiums that attract tax relief so the net cost could be cheaper. However, in respect of PTA policies linked to Personal Pension Plans, tax relief will no longer be available for contributions made on or after 6 April 2007 in respect of PTA policies, unless the insurer received the policy application before 14 December 2006 and the policy was taken out before 6 April 2007.

401. Tax relief on premiums for policies that continue to qualify will be stopped if the policy is varied to increase the sum assured or extend the term, unless the variation is as a result of the exercise of an option within the policy.

Death benefits before retirement (vesting)

402. Individuals aged under 75 – in the event of death before retirement, Retirement Annuity Contracts (RACs) can provide for no return of contributions, for the return of contributions, or for the accumulated fund to be paid. PPPs normally provide for the accumulated fund to be paid on the individual's death. Any lump sum benefit will normally be paid free of tax, provided it is paid within two years.

403. From 6 April 2006 the above position remains but any lump sum payable above the Standard Lifetime Allowance will be subject to the Lifetime Allowance Charge (LAC). The lump sum could include the return of pension funds or contributions and any pension life assurance benefits.

404. For those aged 75 or over who have not taken any benefits, there will be a tax charge of 55%. Dependant's pensions may also be paid but these will not count towards the Standard Lifetime Allowance (SLA).

405. It will generally be advisable for barristers to have their pensions written in trust (f or members of their families) for Inheritance Tax (IHT) purposes, but advice must be sought depending on the individual's circumstances.

Waiver of premium

406. Waiver of premium is an additional form of protection whereby pension premiums continue to be paid in the event of permanent or prolonged ill health. Even where Permanent Health Insurance cover has been affected, the proceeds are not treated as earned income and thus are not NRE for premium purposes.

407. The benefit will usually be payable after three, six or 12 months of incapacity and will continue up to the selected retirement age.

408. It is no longer possible to add waiver of premium benefit to an existing pension contract or include it in a new pension contract, unless a contractual right to do so existed on 5 April 2006. If this is considered important to your planning, consideration of a separate protection policy may be required.

Stakeholder rules

409. Under current legislation stakeholder pensions must offer certain features, including penalty free transfers, no initial charge and a cap of 1.5% for ten years and 1% thereafter in respect of annual management charges. Whilst

these are also a feature of personal pensions they are not subject to the same legislative requirements and the providers could increase the charges or impose exit penalties in respect of their personal pension contracts at any time.

Benefits at retirement

Retirement age

410. Subject to the terms of the policy, the benefits from a PPP can be taken at any time from the age of 55, irrespective of whether or not the barrister has actually retired.

411. With a RAC the retirement age prior to 6 April 2006 was between 60 and 75, although it is normally possible to transfer to a PPP in order to take advantage of the lower retirement age.

412. Post 6 April 2006 legislation allows benefits from RACs to be taken at the same time as PPPs. However, this will once again rely on the individual company changing its policy terms, and not all companies will have done this.

413. From 6 April 2010 it has not normally been possible for individuals under age 55 to commence pension income benefits. Between 6 April 2006 and 6 April 2010 it was possible for those over the age of 50 to begin any pension benefits.

414. In addition, from 6 April 2011 the requirement to take a tax free lump sum and/or commence income drawdown or buy an annuity by age 75 has ended.

Tax-free lump sum

415. Under a PPP, up to 25% of the pension fund can be taken as a tax-free lump sum on the chosen retirement date.

416. Under a Retirement Annuity Policy (RAP) prior to 6 April 2006 the tax free lump sum could not exceed three times the pension remaining after commutation. It was possible to transfer into a PPP if this produced a higher tax-free lump sum.

417. From 6 April 2006 the maximum tax-free lump sum available from both PPP and RACs will be 25% of the capital value of the pension up to the statutory Lifetime Allowance. This tax-free lump sum is otherwise known as the Pension Commencement Lump Sum (PCLS).

418. An individual may have accrued occupational scheme benefits prior to joining the Bar, in this instance they may have the right to take more than 25% of the value of the pension accrued as a tax-free sum and these rights will be automatically retained within that pension scheme. If benefits are individually transferred away from the scheme the 25% limit will apply and the protection of lump sum rights is lost.

Annuities

419. The pension fund can be used to purchase an annuity which is in effect the pension. Most pension providers offer an open market option that enables the barrister to transfer pension funds to whichever insurance company is offering the best annuity rates at the time.

420. It can then be decided which of the various types of pension/annuity is best suited to the individual's requirements.

421. As a result of falling interest rates and increasing longevity, there has been a sharp decrease in annuity rates in recent years. The Finance Act 1995 introduced income withdrawal which is an alternative method of taking retirement benefits.

Drawdown pension (previously known as unsecured pension/income withdrawal/income drawdown)

422. This provision was originally designed to allow an individual to draw income from their pension fund without purchasing an annuity. The income that can be paid from a drawdown arrangement is defined by reference to a standard table of annuity rates published by the Government Actuaries Department, which is amended from time-to-time to reflect changes in long-term interest rates.

423. From 6 April 2011 two versions of drawdown pension became available, namely "capped drawdown" and "flexible drawdown."

424. Drawdown Pension is likely to be most effective for barristers who have a fund of at least £100,000 and who are prepared to accept some investment risk in retirement. The advantage is that it allows flexibility in the timing of the purchase of the annuity to avoid having to secure an annuity when rates may be very low, allowing the barrister to retain control over their pension funds for as long as possible.

Capped drawdown

425. The minimum and maximum amounts that can be taken under a drawdown arrangement were revised. Between 6 April 2006 and 5 April 2011, for barristers under age 75, the minimum amount was £0 per annum and the maximum was 120% of the highest annual annuity that could otherwise be purchased, based on the rates set by the government actuary. From 6 April 2011, subject to some transitional rules, the maximum reverts to 100% from 120%, but the limit applies at all ages, and not just ages below 75.

426. Between 6 April 2006 and 5 April 2011, the maximum had to be reviewed every five years or earlier if any further funds under the arrangement are used for drawdown, or an annuity is purchased or the funds are subject to a pensions share following a divorce. From 6 April 2011, subject to some transitional rules, the normal review period reverts to three years for those under 75, but reviews are required every single year for those over age 75.

427. Upon death, a dependant's annuity or drawdown may commence, or the value of the unused pension funds may be paid as a one-off lump sum, subject to a tax charge. Until 6 April 2011, lump sums were taxed at 35%, but from this date the tax charge has risen to 55%.

428. Between 6 April 2006 and 5 April 2011, once age 75 was reached an annuity had to be purchased or drawdown could continue subject to revised limits. After age 75, drawdown was known as Alternatively Secured Pension (ASP). From 6 April 2011, ASP ceased to exist because normal drawdown rules were extended to cover all ages.

Flexible drawdown

429. Under flexible drawdown, there is no limit on the amount that can be drawn from the available pension fund. It is therefore possible to take the entire fund as a one-off income payment, subject to income tax under PAYE.

430. To avoid the risk of people taking all of their pension funds and spending them, and then falling on to the State for income benefits, flexible drawdown is only available to those who meet a Minimum Income Requirement (MIR). The MIR is initially £20,000 per annum.

431. Relevant income that can be included in MIR is:

(a) payments of a lifetime annuity from a registered pension scheme;

(b) in certain circumstances, payments of a "scheme pension" from a registered pension scheme;

(c) payments under an overseas pension scheme which, if the scheme were a registered pension scheme, would fall within one of the above categories; and

(d) payments of social security pension (also referred to as state pension).

Phased annuity purchase

432. The phased retirement option allows you to make tax-efficient use of your pension income. It also allows you to build up the value of your uncrystallised pension fund which can then be drawn upon at a time that suits you.

433. Your pension fund can be crystallised (benefits commenced in payment) on a gradual basis. Each time you crystallise part of your pension fund, you can choose to receive a PCLS of up to 25% of the value crystallised with the remainder of the fund being used to purchase an annuity. The pension bought will be guaranteed to be paid to you for life (as a normal conventional lifetime annuity).

434. The uncrystallised element of your pension fund will continue to be invested in a tax-efficient environment.

435. You can decide when you wish to crystallise pension funds. On each occasion you crystallise benefits you will benefit from a further PCLS (if selected) and increase your pension income through the purchase of another annuity. This will continue until your entire pension fund has been used up.

436. Some pension providers offer a combination of Phased Retirement and Drawdown Pension. This is a flexible arrangement that enables barristers to maximise IHT efficiency and to adapt their income according to their requirements.

Choosing a pension

437. Pensions are usually arranged through insurance companies that offer a choice between With-Profits Funds, Unit-Linked Funds and Self-Invested Funds.

With profits

438. Historically this has been a popular type of pension. It provides a fund and/or pension benefits on retirement that derive from bonuses paid at intervals in accordance with the level of contributions payable.

439. Bonuses are of two types:

(a) **Reversionary bonus**: usually declared annually, which once added forms a permanent part of the emerging policy benefits, and

(b) **Terminal bonus:** added only when the pension becomes payable. Reversionary bonuses generally have regard to the long-term investment performance of the fund, and past bonus declarations are only an indication of future levels.

440. Terminal bonuses have regard to the surplus earned in the fund over the life of the policy and (sometimes) to market conditions at retirement and should not be relied upon when projecting future fund values.

441. However, in recent times with-profit funds have had a large amount of negative press due to the introduction of Market Value Reductions (MVRs), and this has led people to question the opacity in setting bonus rates and the over-complexity of the product in general.

442. In addition, the failure of the Equitable Life to have the money to meet the guarantees it had made, led to considerable negative publicity and damaged the reputation of with-profit policies.

Unit-linked

443. Units in one or more selected funds are purchased as each premium is paid, usually at the offer price. The unit value is based on the market value of the underlying fund. The value of the policy on retirement is the bid value of the units but there is rarely a minimum guaranteed value. Unit-linked policies give access to a range of funds which can be selected according to one's attitude to risk.

444. Some policies offer an option under which the pension continues to be linked to the units after retirement, which may provide the possibility of the pension keeping pace with inflation, but with a corresponding risk.

Self Invested Personal Pension Schemes

445. Self Invested Personal Pension Schemes (SIPPs) were introduced on 11 October 1989 to give members a wider degree of investment choice, including the ability to determine what assets should be held and when they should be bought or sold. The rules offer access to a wide range of assets that may be held in a SIPP, but barristers may be most interested in the option to invest directly into the stockmarket.

446. In addition, a large number of barristers have used SIPPs as a mechanism for purchasing their own chambers premises in a tax-efficient manner. Not only will the rental income paid by tenants and members be added to the SIPP without any deduction for income tax, any appreciation in the value of the chambers building will also be free from capital gains tax.

The importance of making a pension provision

447. All being well, practitioners will be in retirement for over twenty years and they will need to accumulate a substantial amount of money in order to provide for a good standard of living.

448. However, when taking advice on a choice of pensions bear in mind the following: Pension providers and advisers often prepare illustrations of projected benefits on retirement without taking into account the effects of inflation on the value of the benefits. As a result, the annuity values quoted will appear far greater than they will be in real terms. The impact of inflation is particularly important when looking at long term contracts.

449. It is difficult to estimate the real values of projected returns from pensions, nevertheless it is reasonable to assume that the accumulated pension fund will equal the real value of the premiums put into it. However, if the barrister elects to commute part of the fund or takes a reduced annuity during their life in order to provide a continuing annuity for their spouse, the purchasing power of the annuity will obviously be smaller.

450. It is very important to review pension contributions on an ongoing basis, taking into account personal circumstances and ideally make substantial pension contributions each year, if possible. It is also extremely important to increase the contributions at least in line with inflation. To determine what appears to be a reasonable contribution in one year and then simply to continue paying the same amount each year will inevitably lead to an inadequate pension.

Part 10

Making a will

[7.12]

Introduction

451. It is generally sensible to make a will and review it regularly. This should not only ensure that the estate passes to the right beneficiaries but also make administration of the deceased's affairs much simpler. This applies not only to barristers, of course, but also to their husbands, wives, civil partners, parents and adult children.

452. Without a will it is entirely possible that the operation of the rules of intestate succession will make things even worse for surviving relatives than they need have been. Intestacy can cause many problems. It will often throw up a greater tax burden than need have arisen; it may create difficulties between a widow, widower or partner and the other beneficiaries; it may force a sale of the family home.

453. Although it is perfectly possible to produce a valid and effective home-made will, in all but the simplest cases it will be sensible to take advice from a solicitor (or other relevantly qualified professional) with whom all relevant matters can be discussed in detail, including all possibilities and the various fiscal considerations. This might include, for example, details of all life insurances or pension policies to ensure that these can be found promptly after death. A full and accessible statement (again regularly reviewed) of all assets and liabilities together with details of the locations of these, and the will itself, will assist enormously. It is also helpful to keep a list of internet account details and passwords.

454. Detailed advice on inheritance tax planning is outside the scope of this guidance but the following general points should be noted.

455. First, as the law now stands, any property left to a spouse or civil partner in trust for life or absolutely will be free of inheritance tax at that stage (except where the deceased is domiciled in the UK and the spouse or civil partner is not). There is also an exemption for gifts to charities.

456. Secondly, there is a "nil rate band" (£325,000 from 6 April 2009) meaning that gifts of property to this value do not attract IHT even if the relevant gift is not exempt. Taking these two points together, a person can leave £325,000 to children, for example, and the balance to a spouse or civil partner without there being any liability to Inheritance Tax (IHT). Until 9 October 2007, it was important to make use of this nil rate band. A straightforward way to do this was to leave an amount equal to the nil-rate band on discretionary trusts for family as a whole, so that it can be used to benefit children or widow(er)/ surviving civil partner as required (with the residue left to the spouse/civil partner). Otherwise, if the whole estate were left to the spouse/civil partner, and was therefore exempt, the benefit of that nil rate band would be lost.

457. On 9 October 2007, however, the "transferable nil rate band" was introduced. This means that if a nil rate band is unused on the first death, the estate of the survivor benefits from an enhanced nil rate band. If the nil rate band was wholly unused on the first death, the nil rate band on the second death is doubled; if partly used, the increase is proportionate. This reduces the importance of the nil rate band discretionary trust, where property is otherwise to be left to the surviving spouse or civil partner (although there are still some situations in which it may be appropriate).

Redirection of the estate

458. It is possible for a person's estate to be redirected within two years of death in such a way that inheritance tax is charged on the basis of the new disposition. In other words, the redirection is read back to death for inheritance tax purposes. This can be done either by the original beneficiaries (by "deed of variation") or, if the will is drafted to allow this, by the executors.

459. The second option can be very attractive to those who are not sure what they want done because they do not know what the circumstances will be when they die. But one or two things must be borne in mind before opting to create such a discretion. First of all, it places a burden on the executors; they must be clear as to what is expected of them, and they must be trusted to get things right. The provisions of such a proposed will must therefore be discussed with them first and their selection must be done with care, possibly

consisting of one member of the family and one or two independent professionals who know the family circumstances. Secondly, if it is thought likely that the executors in the end will be asked to give everything to the widow(er)/civil partner, this sort of arrangement may not be all that satisfactory, because inheritance tax will have to be paid on the grant of probate without regard to the possibility that they will ultimately take, and this can involve a considerable difficulty in terms of cash flow.

Outstanding fees

460. It is worth noting Her Majesty's Revenue and Customs (HMRCs) acceptance that fees outstanding at death are not liable to inheritance tax. This practice is set out in the Inheritance Tax Manual:[39]

"Outstanding barrister's fees or the fees due to a member of the Faculty of Advocates in Scotland do not form part of an estate. This is because they are deemed to be honoraria and, as such, are not recoverable by legal process. This applies even if the client has paid the fees into the hands of the instructing solicitor, Wells v Wells [1914] P157."

461. It may therefore be sensible to consider leaving outstanding fees to children/ grandchildren (or a family trust).

39 See the inheritance tax manual at 10121 (April 2010).

Bar Council

July 2014

Part VIII
Becoming a QC

QC Appointments

[8.1]

The process for the award of Queen's Counsel is the responsibility of Queen's Counsel Appointments, an independent secretariat and organisation[1], conceived and agreed between the Bar Council and the Law Society and approved by the then Lord Chancellor and Secretary of State for Constitutional Affairs (Lord Falconer) in 2004.

The application process is designed to be in the public interest, through a fair and transparent method of identifying excellence in advocacy rigorously and objectively while promoting fairness, excellence and diversity. It is self-financing with a fee charged on application and a further fee charged on appointment.

Applicants are assessed against the Competency Framework. Each standard must be demonstrated to the level of excellence and where applicable, must be demonstrated in cases of substance, complexity, or particular difficulty or sensitivity.

These arrangements have been in place since 2005 and now run on an annual basis. The list of successful applicants and other information relating to that competition can be found on the QC Appointments website, www.qcapplications.org.

Set out below is Guidance for Applicants for the most recent competition. Please note, the most recent competition and while this process is run on an annual basis QC Appointments guidance is subject to change and review and final confirmation of the application processes and requirements should be sought from the QCA website at: http://www.qcapplications.org.uk or by contacting them by telephone on 020 7831 0020.

1 http://www.qcapplications.org.uk

The Guidance for Applicants for the most recent competition is reproduced below:

General Information

[8.2]

Introduction: Queen's Counsel

1. The award of Queen's Counsel is made for excellence in advocacy in the higher courts. All applicants must hold rights of audience in the higher courts and a current practising certificate. Applicants are judged against a Competency Framework (at Appendix A). To recommend appointment, the Queen's

Counsel Selection Panel is looking for strong and consistent evidence of excellence in the demonstration of each of the competencies and across all the competencies in cases of substance, complexity, or particular difficulty or sensitivity.

2. The advocacy may be written or oral but must relate to developing and advancing a client's case to secure the best outcome for the client in a dispute. That outcome may, for example, be secured through arbitration, court determination or a settlement agreement. There are no age requirements for applications; however, it is unlikely that you will have acquired the necessary skills and expertise for appointment without extensive experience in legal practice.

Selection Process

3. The summary of the Process (i.e. the way the competition will be conducted) has been agreed by the Law Society and the Bar Council and approved by the (then) Lord Chancellor. This is available on our website at **www.qcapplications.org.uk**

4. The competition is overseen and directed by a Selection Panel ('the Panel'), supported by a Secretariat. The Panel and Secretariat are independent of the General Council of the Bar, the Law Society and the Government. The Panel is made up of a retired senior judge, senior lawyers (including both barristers and solicitors) and distinguished lay (not legally qualified) people who share its work.

   The Panel members who will oversee the 2014–15 competition are:

   - Helen Pitcher (Chair).
   - Sir Alex Allan.
   - Sir Alistair Graham.
   - Linda Lee.
   - Martin Mann QC.
   - Sir Maurice Kay.
   - Quinton Quayle.
   - Tony King.
   - Shaun Smith QC.
   - Ranjit Sondi.

5. The process for selecting QCs is based on evidence. Two Panel members (one lay and one legally qualified) will review each application on the basis of the list of important cases, narrative description of practice and self-assessment (from the application form), and the assessments, to establish a preliminary view on the evidence. All applicants will then be considered by the full Panel. Only those applicants who appear to the Panel to demonstrate the competencies sufficiently will be invited to interview. The remaining applicants will be notified that they have been unsuccessful. All unsuccessful applicants will receive personal feedback on their application. The list of recommended candidates will be passed to the Lord Chancellor.

Equal Treatment of Applicants

6. The Panel is committed to equality of opportunity in the appointments process. Applicants who meet the standard of excellence required of Queen's Counsel will be recommended for appointment on merit, regardless of age, disability (including mental health), gender reassignment, marriage and civil partnership, pregnancy and maternity, race (including ethnic or national origins, colour and nationality) religion or belief (including lack of belief), gender, or sexual orientation (in accordance with the principles set out in the Equality Act 2010) or any other extraneous factor such as educational background, political affiliation, carer responsibilities, career breaks, part-time working or earnings. Any information which provided for purposes of monitoring data (Section J) will not be provided to the Panel and will only be used for statistical purposes in evaluating the process as a whole.

7. The Panel is particularly committed to ensuring that potential applicants who have a disability are not disadvantaged in the application process. Any applicant with particular needs should contact the Secretariat, who will make every effort to assist. QCA will on request fund the assistance of a reader, or make the application form available in Braille, for visually impaired applicants.

8. There are no quotas of any kind. All applicants are judged individually against a standard of excellence.

9. Applications from suitably qualified applicants from currently under-represented groups are welcome, including from women, members of ethnic minorities, from advocates who have a disability, from solicitor advocates and from employed advocates. QCA is committed to making appropriate adjustments where needed, to assist applicants with a disability to apply.

Demonstration of the Competencies

10. The Panel will be looking for evidence of your demonstration of the competencies in cases of substance, complexity, or particular difficulty or sensitivity, in relation to the law and courts of England and Wales (or in international courts or tribunals in respect of law applicable in this country). The application form is intended to help you present this effectively and succinctly. It does this by inviting you to provide:

- a list of your 12 most important recent cases;
- a narrative description of your practice;
- your self-assessment of your demonstration of each of the competencies in such cases;
- the names of assessors we can approach who have seen you in action in such cases.

11. Applicants should note that Panel members consider it inappropriate to have personal contact with applicants in relation to a competition for Silk.

Submitting an Application using the Electronic Application Form

12. All applications and the application fee must be received by QCA **by 5pm on 15 April 2014**. The Panel will not consider applications received after this time. Guidance relating to the application form is on Part 2 of this guidance.

Previous Applications and Outstanding Complaints

13. Each competition is separate. Any previous applicant for Silk may re-apply. Panel members will not be informed that an applicant has applied previously (although this may become apparent through, for example, comment by an assessor). The Panel will not refer back to your application, assessments or interview record from a previous competition. All assessments will be sought anew, although exceptionally an assessor may direct the Panel to their assessment in the last (2013–14) competition. However, in the case of an issue of serious concern to the Panel arising from an earlier application (relating to a matter of character or integrity), which has previously been put to the applicant in writing, the Panel may also have recourse to the earlier documentation in relation to that issue.

14. Any applicant who makes a complaint in relation to the previous (2013–14) competition may apply on the same basis as any other applicant. Panel members are not informed of the names of applicants with outstanding complaints during the competition (unless that arises from thus Complaints Committee's consideration of the complaint) to the Chairman. Where an outstanding complaint relates to the action or decision of a Panel member, the Secretariat will ensure that so far as possible that that Panel member is not directly involved in the new application.

Confidentiality

15. We will not disclose that you made an application without your agreement, except so far as is necessary for your application to be processed. If you need to contact us about your application once it has been received, you may be asked to verify your identity. We will not use the information you give us except in connection with the processing and consideration of applications.

16. To assist the processing of applications and recommendations we may disclose information from your application form to the Ministry of Justice, but not your self-assessment, summary description of practice or the names of your assessors. If you are successful we may disclose on request basic professional information such as your Inn, chambers, firm or other employer.

Handling of Information

17. We will process applicants' details, and other information provided about them, in a fair and lawful manner. However, applications for appointment to QC are exempt from the subject information provisions of the Data Protection Act 1998. Queen's Counsel Appointments (QCA) is not subject to the provisions of the Freedom of Information Act 2000.

18. Information supplied by applicants, assessors or others may be held in electronic and paper form and will be used in relation to the QC competition and for quality control, training, review or audit purposes only. Our IT consultants may also have access to data in electronic form in the course of their work. Once the selection process has been completed, the application form, assessments and other paper records will generally be retained until after the subsequent competition and then destroyed.

Timetable

19. There is no set date on which results of the competition will be announced. It is expected that an announcement will be made in early 2015, in line with previous competitions. We will inform you of the outcome of your application before the announcement.

Professional assistance with application and interview

20. The Panel is aware that some applicants seek professional help in preparing their application form and/or for interview. The application procedure, including interview, is intended to allow the excellent applicant to be identified without the need for further assistance.

21. The Panel seeks an authentic and nuanced picture of the applicant. At interview (if applicable), it does not necessarily expect a 'word perfect' performance, but wishes the applicant to show the same skills as they display in their day-to-day work, but in a different forum. 'Standard answers' (to provide what it is thought the Panel may want to hear) give a poor impression and may obscure the more positive evidence the applicant has to give.

Problems or Complaints

22. In the first instance, a problem should be referred to the QCA Secretariat or, if appropriate, to the Head of the Secretariat. In the event that the problem or concern relates to the Head of Secretariat or cannot be resolved by them, the problem may be addressed to the Chairman of the Panel. In the event that a problem cannot be resolved, and a complaint becomes appropriate, the complaint may be referred to the Complaints Committee.

23. The Complaints Committee is independent of the Queen's Counsel appointment process. Its role is to consider complaints raised by an applicant about the way in which the Panel and the Secretariat have handled his or her application, or concerns that the Panel has not applied its procedures properly. Its purpose is not to re-open or re-consider the application, nor to substitute its opinion or judgement for that of the Panel. The Complaints Committee will consider complaints after the end of the competition. Complaints must be raised in writing no later than 60 calendar days following the announcement of the outcome of the competition. A copy of the Complaints Committee Procedure is on the QCA website.

Improving the Process

24. Regardless of the outcome of your application, we value feedback on the application form, this Guidance, and on the operation of the process. We welcome feedback in any convenient form at any time and will use it to improve our performance. It will be provided to the Panel only in anonymous form and will not have a bearing on the outcome of your application. There is a facility on our website to provide feedback directly. We may also conduct a voluntary survey of applicants at the end of the competition.

The Secretariat and further assistance

25. If, having carefully read both parts of this guidance and appendices, you need further information on anything regarding the application form or the appointments process, please contact:

Queen's Counsel Appointments Secretariat
3rd Floor
Totara Park House
34–36 Gray's Inn Road
London WC1X 8HR

Telephone: 0207 831 0020

Email: enquiries@qcapplications.org.uk

QC Appointments also has a DX address:

QC Appointments
DX 387
London Chancery Ln

26. Further information is also available on our website www.qcapplications.org.uk

Please feel free to contact us at any time if you have any questions about your application. The website will be updated as necessary and as the competition progresses.

Part Two of the Guidance follows. It contains information about the application form and Guidance Notes which relate to the numbers in the right-hand column of the electronic application form.

QC Secretariat
March 2014

Part Two

[8.3]

27. The application form can be accessed and saved from the QCA website or a link emailed to an applicant. To be able to use and view the application form correctly you will need to have the latest version of Adobe reader. This can be accessed on the QCA website. For ease, a link is provided http://get.adobe.com/uk/reader/

28. In the right hand margin of the application form, there are numbered references to the detailed Guidance Notes for applicants (set out below).

29. This form is accessible offline. Once downloaded, you will need to have saved a copy to your computer or laptop, to access offline. Full instructions for using the application form will be found on the 'HELP' button in the top right hand corner. Please note you will need to have internet connection to be able to use this function. This function will also give you access to an online support facility. If you having any queries regarding the information you wish to supply in your application, contact QCA Secretariat for assistance.

30. To be aware of the fields that are required before submission, ensure that the 'Highlight Existing Fields' button is selected. You will see the field boxes are highlighted light blue and those that are mandatory will have a red box around them. Please be aware there are character limits for the size of each text box and that no further limit can be given so as to ensure fairness to all applicants.

Submitting Your Form

31. We recommend that you submit your application via the link on page 65 of the application form. Please be aware that you will need internet connectivity to access the submission page. You will also be able to make payment for your application via this page. Alternatively, you may submit your form via email, with a supporting electronic transfer or cheque payment. Please note that your payment must be received before the close of applications, otherwise your application will not be accepted. The email should be sent to enquiries@qcapplications.org.uk. Please put 'applications 2014–15' with your name in the subject box. If you do not receive a reply within 15 minutes, please contact the Secretariat. If you cannot submit by either the two methods above please contact the Secretariat at QCA who will assist you further.

Notes to the Application Form

The numbers below refer to the Guidance Notes in the right-hand column of the application form.

1. **Letters Patent** are issued by The Queen to successful applicants. Please note that (unless you advise the Secretariat otherwise using Section G (ii) – *Other Information*) the surname and forename(s) which you provide will be the names which will appear on your Letters Patent if you are successful. For example, your professional surname will appear if you are a female advocate using your professional surname on your application form. If you have middle names which you omit from the application form, these will not appear on the Letters Patent.

2. To prevent confusion with other applicants, we will use an **ID number** as well as your name. This is your Bar Council Reference or Law Society Roll number. It will help us if you are able to quote it if you telephone or write to us. If you do not know your Roll or Reference number, contact the records section of your professional body.

3. When we contact you, we will use the **forename(s) and surname** you supply in Section A. We will always use your preferred email address. If any of these details change during the course of the competition, please inform the Secretariat immediately.

4. Please ensure the **email address** you wish to use is regularly monitored. We will use this when we need to contact you, for example to arrange an interview. We may also use this address to give information from time to time on the progress of the competition.

5. You are invited to indicate your **preferred location for any interview** (if applicable). Please note that while your wishes will be taken into account, we cannot guarantee your preferred location. We expect to be holding interviews in London and Manchester. We currently expect interviews to take place in late September, October and November 2014. We will contact you in due course to give you more information about any interview.

   The interview (if applicable) will be conducted by two members of the Panel (one lay and one legally qualified). The interview will seek further evidence as to the competencies to add to, or to help the Panel assess, the information already available from your application form and assessments. The Panel will probe for examples of excellence. The interview provides applicants with a further opportunity to 'shine'. It is not determinative, but one part of the evidence which will then be considered as a whole before the Panel reaches a decision.

   Applicants who are interviewed but are unsuccessful will receive written feedback at the conclusion of the competition.

Eligibility

6. To be eligible to apply for Queen's Counsel, you must either:

   (a) have been called to the Bar of England and Wales and hold a current practising certificate; or

   (b) be a solicitor of the Senior Courts of England and Wales, and hold higher court rights of audience and a current practising certificate.

   Note that if you take up appointment to a full-time judicial post during the competition you are expected to withdraw your application for Silk.

7. Your **date of call or admission** will be used in determining your place on the order of seniority (if appointed to Silk). If you cannot provide the exact date, you will be regarded as being called or admitted on the last day of the month or year given.

8. We will inform all interviewed applicants of the decision after The Queen has approved the names of those to be appointed. In addition, the names of all successful applicants will be published, along with the broad field(s) of law in which they practise. Publication of this information is not intended to restrict the fields in which the applicant appointed as QC may practise.

Character issues

9. Before completing Section C, you should read Appendix B, which sets out the Panel's approach to handling issues of character and conduct.

Those appointed QC are expected to conduct themselves at all times in their personal and professional lives in a manner which will maintain public confidence. Section C requires you to declare any findings or pending matters relating to criminal convictions, complaints of professional misconduct, or other character issues. The Panel may take any such matters into account as part of the evidence available to it on the competencies. You should inform the Secretariat as soon as the prospect of a complaint, criminal proceedings or other issue arises. The Panel has indicated that (among other things) it takes very seriously matters relating to the following:

(a) dishonesty;

(b) sexual harassment or intimidation;

(c) drink driving;

(d) the use or handling of illegal drugs;

(e) suspension from practice.

As regards, **criminal convictions**, the Panel has agreed the following:

(a) Minor motoring offences where the applicant was not obliged to appear in court should be disregarded. However, any motoring offence resulting in disqualification, including under totting up, should be disclosed.

(b) Any conviction or caution for an offence of dishonesty or resulting in a term of imprisonment will be of serious concern and is likely to preclude appointment.

(c) Any other unspent conviction, caution or bind over will be considered on its individual merits.

10. The Panel will only consider **findings of fault or cases of professional negligence** where an applicant has admitted being at fault. Where a claim against you has been dismissed, it should not be disclosed. Where a claim has been settled, you should disclose it, but indicate clearly whether and to what extent you have accepted liability.

Findings of negligence and cases where the applicant admits to being at fault will be assessed taking into account the degree of loss and the importance of the matter to the client, along with any other relevant factors.

11. **Findings of professional disciplinary fault** will be relevant to Competency E (Integrity), as showing prima facie a failure to honour professional codes. In other respects they will be treated on a case-by-case basis having regard to factors such as the penalty imposed; whether the client or any other person suffered loss or harm, and whether the applicant accepted his or her fault, may also be relevant.

12. **Wasted costs orders** will be considered with regard to the reason given for the order being made, the amount involved and the length of time since the order was made.

13. ***If you are unsure whether or not to include a possible character issue, please contact the QCA Secretariat.***

14. A complaint which has been referred to the Office of Legal Complaints or Legal Ombudsman will be considered with regard to all the circumstances.

15. **A bankruptcy order**, debt relief order or an individual or partnership voluntary arrangement (see Note 16).

A director's disqualification order

16. **A current or recent (ie within 5 years of discharge) Individual Voluntary Arrangement (IVA) or bankruptcy or other order** will be of serious concern. An undischarged order is likely to preclude appointment. However, such cases will be considered with regard to all the circumstances.

17. You should disclose **any matter not covered by the above** categories but which a reasonable person would regard as material to your application, having regard to the general criteria mentioned above. An example would be a foreign criminal conviction or an order of a court or tribunal outside of the UK.

18. You should **disclose anything else** whether related to your professional or personal life, which could affect your standing or reputation, or could affect your suitability for appointment as QC.

Panel member recusals

19. You should complete Section D and mark the box if you wish to recuse a member of the Panel from considering your application. Reasons given will be carefully considered but are not determinative of recusal. We will determine the extent to which the matters should affect the handling of the application. If a matter arises in the course of the competition which might prompt a recusal, please contact the Secretariat quickly.

Section E: Summary description of Practice

20. In this section, you should provide a concise overview of your practice. It is split into two aspects:

    (i) a Case List of the 12 most important cases that you have dealt with, generally in the **past two years** (i.e. in 2012 or more recently), together with a note of your role as an advocate in the case and the assessors whom you would expect to comment on them;

    (ii) a narrative description of your practice.

    These will not be shown to assessors.

    The award of Silk is for advocacy in the higher courts. To merit recommendation for appointment, the competencies must be demonstrated to a standard of excellence in the applicant's professional life in cases of substance, complexity, or particular difficulty or sensitivity ("cases of substance").

    If you wish to mention a case, but its name or details are not in the public domain (e.g. because of security issues) or is confidential for other reasons, refer to the case details in such a way that it may be identified by your assessors, and so that the Panel can be clear when you are referring to that case.

    The Panel is looking for your demonstration of the competencies in cases of substance. The Panel will have regard to the case, and your role in it, and the degree of challenge and how you dealt with it. The Panel sees a distinction between 'run of the mill' cases (which may have important consequences for the immediate client, but may present limited legal or other professional challenge) from those cases which present unusual, novel or unforeseen complexities or have consequences beyond the case.

Moreover, it does not follow that all hearings in self-evidently important or substantial cases will themselves raise the same challenge or substance as the case as a whole.

Examples of the types of case which may present the characteristics of a case of substance are listed below:

- a substantive appeal before the Court of Appeal;
- a case that has been reported in a series of law reports;
- a case involving alleged historical indecent assault or rape on a child by a family member;
- other serious, demanding or sensitive criminal cases involving, for example, a fatality or complex forensic evidence. These are likely to be in Class 1, 2 or 3;
- a commercial, civil or family case involving more than £1 million;
- a test case on a point of law, or one that sets a precedent;
- a case determining the removal of a child from one or both parents;
- a case on which the employment of a workforce of more than 50 depends;
- a planning or other public inquiry of national importance or raising complex issues of law;
- a case involving serious issues of reputation;
- a case that has attracted detailed press interest;
- a case that the judge or arbitrator described as important or complex, or as involving matters of substance, difficulty or sensitivity.

It is important for the Selection Panel to gain a rounded picture of your practice as a whole. It is therefore important that you should list 12, rather than fewer, of the most important cases you have dealt with over the last two years. It is important that you should explain fully if you are unable to list 12 cases. Such reasons might include having been wholly engaged on a small number of extraordinarily time-consuming cases, or having had a career break for all or part of the period concerned. If no satisfactory explanation is given for any shortfall in cases, the Panel may conclude that the applicant prefers the Panel not to see a rounded picture of their practice.

In the case list and narrative description of practice, the Panel would expect to see mention of the 12 most important cases that you have dealt with in the past two years (i.e. in 2012 or more recently). These may include cases which settle or are otherwise resolved without a court determination. If you have fewer than 12 cases in that period, you should set out the most important cases in the past three years. 'Important' means the weight you attach to the cases, bearing in mind their significance, how recent or substantial they were, the extent of your involvement, and the degree to which others involved in the case will be able to comment effectively on your demonstration of the competencies.

The Panel recognises that where applicants have recently had a career break, for example for child care or to care for aged relatives, they may not be able to list 12 cases of importance over the last two years. The Panel will seek to avoid disadvantaging applicants in that position, subject to the need to ensure that there is sufficient evidence of applicants' current ability to make a proper decision.

If you need to go back further than the last two years, provide an explanation in your narrative description of practice (Section E (ii)). However, there is inevitably a risk that the evidence from assessors who saw you in older cases may be less useful, not least because assessors may have more difficulty recalling the detail to provide an assessment the Panel can rely on.

In addition to the names of your cases, please give the month and year of <u>your</u> involvement and indicate the role you played. A drop down menu provides for three options: 'was led', 'case leader' or 'alone' (ie sole advocate). Select the description that best matches the role you predominantly played. The Panel accepts that it is often difficult to reflect the complexities of the conduct of litigation in such brief terms. You can elaborate on your role if necessary in the narrative description of practice.

The Panel expects that the assessors you name will in general be those who can speak to your demonstration of the competencies in the cases you have named in the list. Indicate the relevant assessor using the assessor reference numbers in relation to that case. For example:

No	Name of Case	Role as advocate	Dates (mm/yy)	Assessors
			Start/end	J, P, C
3.	*Rose v Thorn*	08/13	01/14	9 2, 4 5

Section E (ii): Narrative description of practice

21. This should set out your recent practice so that the Panel can understand the context in which it is considering your readiness for Silk. The narrative description of practice, with the accompanying case list, and the self-assessment will be assessed by the Panel, together with up to nine written assessments. They are your opportunity to 'speak' directly to the Panel members to ensure that they have a clear picture of your practice and to show how well you consider that you meet each of the competencies. Please ensure the information is factual (and not evaluative).

<u>**Do**</u> include:

- What you consider are your specialism(s) and what proportion of your professional time these represent.
- What is your practice area and in which jurisdiction and/or court(s) you most regularly appear.
- If your practice extends outside England and Wales, please provide detail.

- An overview of the main types of cases you have been involved with in the last two years.
- The pattern of written and oral advocacy in your practice.
- The frequency with which you attend court as an advocate.
- Why you consider the 12 cases you have named to be particularly important or noteworthy, with an indication of their outcome.
- How often you lead or are led, and in particular in your 12 named cases, the degree to which you were the case leader, or were led or acted alone.
- Any explanation as to why you need to go back further than the last two years (i.e. before 2012) to name your 12 important cases.
- Any reasons why you are only able to name fewer than 12 cases. In the absence of such explanations the Panel may well draw adverse conclusions.
- Whether you normally appear for a particular party e.g. Prosecution/Defence.
- Indicate if appropriate your typical client e.g. Oil company, child etc.
- If you have identified fewer than 12 judicial or 6 practitioner and or 6 client assessors, please explain why. The Panel may draw conclusions from the numbers you have named, having regard to any explanation you provide.
- Any points relevant to the relative weight to be attached to assessments made by judicial, practitioner or client assessors; e.g. if the great majority of your advocacy is performed otherwise than in court.
- Any reasons why your practice in the last few years may have been atypical.
- Any other relevant factual information.

Do not include in your narrative summary:

- References to you in legal directories or elsewhere.
- Assertions about your standing or reputation in the profession.
- Any reference to sitting as an arbitrator or in a judicial capacity.
- Details of your earnings.
- Any issues of character. (These should be identified in Section C.)

To be fair to all applicants, you should be aware that each text box provided has a capped character limit to the size of the box shown, and this cannot be exceeded. **The Panel will not consider information continued on a separate sheet or elsewhere in the form.**

If you consider the Panel should be aware of personal circumstances in order fairly to consider your application, outline all relevant circumstances here in Section E (ii) **or** at Section G (ii).

Competencies

General

22. The Competency Framework for the 2014–15 competition is at Appendix A. This provides a full description of each of the competencies, which are: A (Understanding and using the law); B (Written and oral advocacy); C (Working with others); D (Diversity); and E (Integrity). In order to be recommended for appointment, you must demonstrate strong and consistent evidence of excellence across all of the competencies. The Panel reaches its conclusions on the *evidence* of the degree to which excellence in each competency is demonstrated.

Any concern expressed by an assessor amounting to an allegation of professional misconduct will not be taken into account by the Panel unless, with the consent of the assessor (if necessary), it has been put to you in writing, to be given the opportunity to provide the Panel with an explanation in writing.

Advocacy may be in written or oral form but must relate to developing or advancing a client's or employer's case to secure the best outcome in the dispute. That outcome may, for example, be secured through arbitration, court determination or a settlement agreement. Oral advocacy includes advocacy in a court or tribunal, mediation, arbitration or in negotiation.

The Panel looks both at the written (Competency B1) and oral (Competency B2) aspects of advocacy at the level of the higher courts in deciding its view of the competency overall. The outcome for Competency B overall is not reached through aggregating or averaging the B1 and B2 scores, but reflects the Panel's judgement on the applicant's written and oral advocacy taken together.

The Panel recognises that not all applicants will have had the opportunity to undertake significant oral advocacy in court and takes into account the type of practice in coming to its decision, but there needs to be some evidence of excellence demonstrated in oral advocacy.

Subject to that, there is no specific requirement as to the amount of written or of in-court advocacy so long as there is sufficient evidence for the Panel to reach a conclusion as to the extent to which an applicant demonstrates excellence in each of the competencies.

The Panel require your own assessment of how you demonstrate the competencies and requests your evidence for this. Your self-assessment forms part of the evidence the Panel will consider in determining the outcome of your application.

The Panel will in general only consider examples drawn from your professional life, not in any other capacity, including sitting as a judge or arbitrator, or work on behalf of your professional body or similar. In respect of Competency D (Diversity), you may draw on the wider aspects of your professional life, including work in chambers or your firm, but evidence should still come primarily from your professional life.

It is important that you do not just re-state the competencies and the corresponding examples. Specific instances are required, not generalities. Merely asserting that you are always good at something or making reference to your reputation or the opinion of others is not of assistance. Instead give examples that demonstrate your abilities, and explain how you did something and with what result.

The space in respect of each competency (and in respect of each of the written and oral advocacy aspects of Competency B) is restricted. To be fair to all applicants, you should be aware that each text box provided has a capped character limit to the size of the box shown, and this cannot be exceeded. **The Panel will not consider information continued on a separate sheet or elsewhere in the form.**

The self-assessment will not be shown to assessors.

Competency A. Understanding and using the law – The Competency Framework says: Has expert, up-to-date legal knowledge and uses it accurately and relevantly, and becomes familiar with new areas of law quickly and reliably.

See the Competency Framework for examples.

Competency B. Written and oral advocacy

23. The Competency Framework says: Develops and advances client's case to secure the best outcome for the client by gaining a rapid, incisive overview of complex material, identifying the best course of action, communicating the case persuasively, and rapidly assimilating the implications of new evidence and argument and responding appropriately.

The Panel will be looking both at the written and oral aspects of advocacy. Oral advocacy includes advocacy in a court or tribunal, mediation, arbitration or negotiation.

See the Competency Framework for examples of **Written advocacy**.

24. See the Competency Framework for examples of **Oral advocacy**.

Competency C. Working with others

25. *The Competency Framework says:* Establishes productive working relationships with all, including professional and lay clients, the judge and other parties' representatives and members of own team; is involved in the preparation of the case and leads the team before the court or other tribunal.

See the Competency Framework for examples.

Competency D. Diversity

26. The Competency Framework says: Demonstrates an understanding of diversity and cultural issues, and is proactive in addressing the needs of people from all backgrounds and promoting diversity and equality of opportunity.

See the Competency Framework for examples.

Competency E. Integrity

27. The highest standards of integrity are expected of all advocates. Whether or not seeking appointment as Queen's Counsel, all advocates should meet

these standards, and should expect to do so as a matter of course as part of their professional life. There is normally no need to set out examples of how you meet this competency. If, however you have reported a matter under Section C (Character Issues), you may wish to use this space to indicate why you nevertheless consider that you meet the requirements of this competency.

Experience of discrimination

28. If you consider that you have been discriminated against for any reason or at any stage in the course of your professional life, there is an opportunity to indicate this in Section G (i).

Other information

29. Any applicant who believes the Panel should be aware of their personal circumstances in order fairly to consider their application should outline all relevant circumstances in Section E (ii) or Section G (ii).

30. Applicants with a **disability** who wish the Panel to make adjustments in considering their application should include with the information at Section G (ii) the nature of their disability, its impact on their practice and the adjustment they are seeking.

Section H Judicial, Practitioner and Client Assessors

General

31. The Process requires you to provide the names of assessors in three categories: judge or arbitrator, practitioner, and professional client, client or client proxy. (The meanings of these terms are discussed below). In all we will be seeking nine assessments; four from judges/arbitrators, three from practitioners and two from clients, all in writing.

Your assessors will generally be selected in connection with your 12 major cases, as set out in your list of cases (Section E (i)). You may not subsequently put forward the names of additional assessors who were not named in your application form.

In deciding whom to name as your assessors, you need to consider whether, by virtue of their experience of Queen's Counsel, and of you, the persons you propose to name can give a sufficiently authoritative assessment on which the Panel can place weight. When considering an application, the Panel will use its own judgement to determine what weight to give to any one assessor's evidence.

If any of your assessors informs us he or she is unable to give an assessment, another assessor from the same category will be approached, where appropriate and practicable.

Please ensure that, taken together, the cases in relation to which you identify your judicial, practitioner and client assessors give a fair reflection of your practice.

If there are likely to be practical difficulties in getting in touch with a particular assessor, then you may wish to consider whether to name someone else.

Assessments will only be accepted in English.

Number of assessors

Applicants are expected to name at least eight judicial assessors, six practitioner assessors and four client assessors. The Panel may draw conclusions from the numbers of assessors you have named in any category, having regard to any explanation you provide. Applicants may if they wish name up to 12 judicial assessors, and up to six client assessors.

The Panel recognises that in some fields of practice advocates may rarely appear in court, or only appear before a limited number of specialist or local judges. The Panel welcomes applications from advocates in any area of practice in accordance with this guidance. The Panel accepts applications with fewer than eight judicial assessors, but will expect a full explanation of why it was not possible to list more.

As noted above, the Panel will be seeking nine assessments in all on each applicant; four from judges/arbitrators, three from practitioners and two from clients. Where for any reason the Panel is not able to obtain suitable assessments the applicant is likely to be at a significant disadvantage. In considering the evidence available in relation to any application it is for the Panel to decide how much weight to accord to any one assessment or assessments more generally.

Naming of Assessors

Assessors are not asked to be supporters of an applicant, but to give evidence as to how the applicant demonstrates the competencies. Assessments are an important component of the evidence to inform the Panel's decision.

You are asked to provide the names of judges/arbitrators, practitioners and clients who are connected to the cases named in your list of cases (Section E (i)), who have recent experience of your work as an advocate, and who are able to provide evidence in the form of examples to help the Panel decide whether you have demonstrated the competencies to a standard of excellence.

The assessors taken together should be able to give a fair reflection of your practice, as described in your application form. However, no one assessor is expected to be able to comment on all the competencies (although they will have the opportunity to do so).

There are no automatic consultations. Assessors will be selected from among the list of names provided by you, on the basis of their personal experience of you and the cases you name.

The Panel will expect to see in the assessor pages (Section H) the names (and contact details) of the judges or arbitrators and practitioners who had substantial involvement with you in the cases you have named in your list of cases (Section E (i)). If you have not named judicial or practitioner assessors from your major recent cases you may be asked to explain why at your interview (if called).

If, having named relevant assessors from the cases mentioned in your list of cases (Section E (i)), you have not been able to give a full complement of assessors you should if possible name further assessors from other cases of substance, complexity, or particular difficulty or sensitivity who have recent experience of you and can provide further evidence as to your demonstration of the competencies.

All assessments will be taken on the basis that they are confidential to the assessor, the Panel, the Secretariat, and, if appropriate, the Complaints Committee. Assessments are given in confidence and therefore no applicant will be entitled to see any assessment, or be informed of the names of those who provided assessments, whether the application is successful or not.

Informing your Assessors

You do not have to tell any of your assessors that you have named them. However, it is recommended that you ask any assessor whom you propose to *nominate* (please see Note 34 re Nominated Assessors) whether he or she is prepared to give an assessment. Although there is no need to do so, if you inform any of those listed in your application form that they have been included in your lists, you should explain to them that, except in the case of first nominated assessors, it will be for the Panel to decide the assessors from whom assessments will be sought.

Applicants should not solicit support. QCA will provide assessors with all the information that they need, extracted from your application form. Although there is no objection to providing potential assessors with a copy of a skeleton argument as an aide-memoire, you should not provide further material or otherwise seek to influence assessors' views. However, it is recognised that applicants may have occasion to seek advice on whether they are yet ready to apply for Silk, and that those best placed to provide such advice may well be potential assessors.

Assessors Selected by the Panel

Other assessors (i e not nominated ones) will be chosen by the Panel or on its behalf from among those listed on your form. The Panel will be looking for assessors who can speak to your demonstration of the competencies in particular in the important cases set out in your summary description of practice.

Other Considerations in relation to Assessors

You should not list as an assessor:

(a) Any member of the Panel for this competition (the Panel has agreed that it would not be appropriate for any of them to act as an assessor in respect of any application for Silk). The Panel members are listed in paragraph 4 of Part One of this Guidance and at Section D of the application form.

(b) Any current or former family member or sexual partner.

(c) The Attorney General and the Solicitor General for England and Wales, as they have indicated that it would not be appropriate for them to give assessments.

(d) Any person whom you know to be unable to give an assessment for any reason, including ill health.

It is preferable not to list as an assessor any person with whom you have a close personal or professional relationship. However, if you feel it necessary to do so, you must state the nature of the relationship. The Panel will use this information to help decide whether to seek an assessment from that person and, if it does so, what weight to give to the evidence in the assessment. Examples of relationships that must be disclosed include any relationship with:

(a) Someone who has been in the same chambers or firm at the same time as you.

(b) A partner, employee or associate of your firm, or any organisation that employs you.

(c) Your former pupil master, pupil supervisor or training principal.

For special remarks regarding judicial assessors see Note 36; for practitioner assessors, see Note 38; and for client assessors, see Note 39.

32. We normally **contact assessors** by post or DX. We therefore need their current postal addresses, including DX (but in relation to certain judges see Note 35). However, where known, email addresses and telephone numbers are also helpful. If we cannot contact an assessor we cannot obtain an assessment.

33. You do not need to give the **addresses** of serving High Court and more senior judges in England and Wales, who will be written to at their normal court, Royal Courts of Justice or the Supreme Court, as appropriate. You do not need to give the addresses of retired full time judges of England and Wales. We will contact them via the Ministry of Justice. Similarly, we will contact planning inspectors directly through the Planning Inspectorate in England or in Wales.

In the case of part-time judicial office holders, please give their chambers or other professional address in the contact details, if known.

Nominated Assessors

34. You are asked to nominate two assessors in each category of assessor (judicial, practitioner and client). The form asks you to give priority between nominated assessors. Your first choice of nominated assessor in each category will be invited by the Secretariat on behalf of the Panel to provide an assessment. If it is not possible to obtain an assessment from your first nominated assessor, then your second choice will be approached instead. We will not inform you if we have to do this. If neither your first nor your second nominated assessor provides an assessment then we will not ask you to nominate a third assessor, but will seek to ensure that you have sufficient assessments from among the assessors you have named in that category. It is important that those you nominate are in a position, through recent experience of you, to comment on your demonstration of competencies and suitability for the award, by reference to the Competency Framework.

Please note that we will not approach a nominated assessor who is not eligible (for example, your spouse or someone who has not seen you in action in a relevant case).

Your nominated and selected assessors will be asked to provide a confidential written assessment including examples in relation to each of the competencies. A copy of an assessment form and the guidance to assessors will be available on the QCA website in due course. Assessments will be accepted only in response to a request from us; unsolicited references and testimonials will not be accepted. For advice about contacting assessors yourself see Note 31 (re informing your assessors).

Information for Assessor

35. The pages in Section H entitled *Information for Judge/Arbitrator*, or *Practitioner*, or *Client*, contain the information that will be sent to the assessor about your application. This page will also be considered by the Panel along with any assessment received. The Panel will use it to understand your role in relation to the assessor and the case, and the assessor will use it to understand the context in which you have named him or her and to help recall his or her experiences of your advocacy. This is the only information about you or your case that the assessor will see. For this reason you are asked to give details of each case of substance referred to and (if more than one assessor is named in relation to any case) to set out the details in full for each assessor. Each assessor's page should be self-contained. Any cross references to other pages or other assessors may not be intelligible to an assessor.

Please give the dates on which **your** involvement in each case began and ended. Approximate dates (month and year) are sufficient.

Your description should:

- Explain briefly the nature of the case, including in what way it was a case of substance, complexity or particular difficulty or sensitivity, any especially difficult or challenging aspects, the specialist area of law to which it most closely relates (unless self-evident), and any special considerations, for example if the law applied by the court or tribunal in the case was not English law.
- Indicate to what extent you were led, were alone (ie sole advocate) or were the case leader.
- Give the role of your assessor (unless obvious eg trial judge).
- Set out the nature of your role (including the extent of your written and oral advocacy, or contribution to documentation).
- Say how long you were observed in this role.;
- Say how frequently this assessor sees you "in action".
- Mention any relationship you have with this assessor.

The explanation of your role should clearly show what you did in the case in relation to the assessor. For example in the case of a judge, whether he or she would have read your written submissions or heard oral argument from you, or observed your cross-examination, and over what period. Also indicate how frequently this assessor has experience of your work and over what period (if more than in the named case).

You should also use this field to disclose any relationship, either professional or personal, that you may have with the assessor.

Please keep to the space provided on the page. To be fair to all applicants, you should be aware that each text box provided has a capped character limit to the size of the box shown, and this cannot be exceeded. **The Panel will not consider information continued on a separate sheet or elsewhere in the form.**

The assessors' names, and judicial office (if any) (for judicial and practitioner assessors), and the firm or organisation for client assessors, on the *Information for Assessor* pages in Section H will be completed automatically for you, based on information you have entered on the *Contact Details* page for that assessor (although they may only appear when the form is printed or in 'print preview' document view.). You will not be able to overwrite or alter the information in these fields, except by amending the original entry on the previous page.

Judicial Assessors

36. You are asked to list at least eight, and up to 12, judicial assessors.

The award of Queen's Counsel is made for excellence in advocacy in the higher courts in England and Wales. It follows that the assessors to whom the Panel can attach most weight are those with best experience of advocacy in cases of substance or complexity in those courts. For that reason, although eligibility to provide judicial assessments is not confined to the judges of the higher courts in England and Wales, the Panel may well give assessments provided by judges from the higher courts in England and Wales more weight than those provided by judges from lower courts, from tribunals, or from other jurisdictions.

For most applicants, judicial assessors will be a High Court or more senior Judge, Circuit Judge, Deputy High Court Judge, Tribunal Judge or Chair, Planning Inspector, Recorder or arbitrator. In considering the evidence available in relation to any application, it is for the Panel to decide how much weight to accord to any assessment. The Panel has found that assessments from High Court Judges or more senior judges can be particularly helpful, but these are not essential. The Panel recognises that not all applicants regularly appear before such judges and so for some applicants, an assessment from the most senior judicial post-holder before whom they regularly appear in cases of substance or complexity may be more useful.

Where possible, applicants are expected to name amongst their judicial assessors a leading judge in their specialism or local area before whom they have appeared.

The Panel is looking for assessments which can reflect your demonstration of the competencies in a number of cases and circumstances. You should therefore avoid listing more than one judicial assessor from amongst those hearing the same case (e.g. in the Supreme Court or the Court of Appeal) unless he or she has other, unique, experience of you. In cases where more than one judge (or arbitrator) heard the case at the same time, the remaining judges should be identified in the case information included in the application form (Section H – *Information for Assessors*).

Please also bear in mind that senior judges in particular are unlikely to recall brief hearings, especially if some time ago.

Judicial assessments need to come from those exercising a judicial function. Accordingly, assessments from a mediator are not acceptable as judicial assessments, but the Panel will accept an assessment from a mediator as a practitioner assessor.

Practitioner Assessors

38. You are asked to list six practitioners (i.e. fellow advocates, who may be barristers or solicitors who are advocating in that case) by whom you have been led (or, if applicable, whom you have led) or against whom you have appeared or with whom you have co-defended, or otherwise been professionally involved, in cases of substance, complexity or particular difficulty or sensitivity over the last two years (i.e. in the cases you identified in Section E). Depending upon the nature of your practice, you should seek to include a mix of practitioners made up of your leading opponents, leading co-defending advocates and your own leaders. Even if your practitioner has since been appointed to full–time judicial office, please still list him or her as a practitioner, not a judicial, assessor since that is the capacity in which he or she has had experience of your work.

The Panel has indicated that, subject to the nature of the practice, it would normally expect practitioner assessments to come from QCs, or from other practitioners who are at least as senior as the applicant. As noted above, practitioner assessments may include assessments from a legal assessor in a tribunal or from a mediator.

In general terms, the broader the range of assessors the better the quality of evidence available to the Panel. It is considered helpful to the Panel for assessors to be drawn from a number of chambers. In deciding how much weight to give to a practitioner assessment, amongst other things, the Panel may have regard to the fact that an assessor is currently in the same chambers or firm as the applicant or has previously been in the same chambers or firm. The Panel may be concerned where an applicant has named several assessors from his or her own chambers or firm, although it understands that in some specialised practice areas this may be unavoidable.

Unless a suitable explanation is given in the summary description of practice, the Panel may draw adverse conclusions if fewer than six practitioner assessors are named. In any event, an applicant may be at a disadvantage if there are fewer than six practitioners from whom assessments can be sought.

Client Assessors

39. You are asked to list at least four, and up to six, professional clients, clients or client proxies in cases of substance, complexity or particular difficulty or sensitivity over the last two years (ie from the cases named in Section E (i)). In many cases the 'client' will be the instructing solicitor. However, it may include a senior legal officer in a company or other body. A 'client proxy' is an experienced professional person who is in a position of authority in connection with a client and who is able to comment with authority on the applicant's abilities. Examples might include guardians *ad litem*, police officers, medical professionals, certain expert witnesses, and professionals from social services departments.

Each individual listed will count as a separate professional client, client or client proxy, even if the individuals are from the same firm, institution or organisation. However, it is likely to be more helpful to your application if your assessors come from different firms or organisations.

The Director of Public Prosecutions has advised that individual Crown Prosecution Service (CPS) lawyers (not paralegal officers) may be listed so that they may be asked to be assessors. However, the assessment will be given by the Chief Crown Prosecutor (or equivalent) to whom the assessor reports, in consultation with his or her colleagues. Please do not name more than one CPS lawyer in any one CPS Area.

It has been agreed with the Treasury Solicitor's Department that assessments will be considered by the relevant Head of Division (or equivalent) to whom the assessor reports. This is to ensure balance and consistency in the assessments provided by Government Lawyers. The assessment may be prepared by the named Government Lawyer, in consultation with his or her colleagues, and, after consideration by the Head of Division, signed by that Government Lawyer. In some cases the assessment may actually be given by the Head of Division, in consultation with his or her colleagues. You should therefore try to avoid naming more than one Government lawyer in the same team or Division as that could result in a single potential assessment.

Employed advocates should expect to include among their client assessors at least one partner or representative from their employing firm, company or institution. If this is not possible you should provide an explanation.

Client assessors, like other assessors, need to be in a good position to give an informed view of your demonstration of the competencies required of a Queen's Counsel in England and Wales. Depending on the nature of your practice, only rarely is it likely that a client in person will have the requisite knowledge or standing to provide an assessment of assistance to your application. As with all assessments, it is for the Panel to judge the weight to be given to each assessor's evidence. Applicants can approach the Secretariat if they are unsure about naming of suitable client assessors.

Client assessors may be based in any locality and be of any national background, so long as the assessment is given in English. However, please bear in mind that the Secretariat needs to be able to contact each of your assessors.

40. By **submitting the form** you are declaring that the cases you have named in your case list are ones of substance, complexity or particular difficulty or sensitivity.

41. We also ask you to say whether there is anything in your personal or professional background which, if brought into the public domain, could affect your **suitability for appointment** or bring the legal profession or Queen's Counsel into disrepute.

You should also be aware that if you fail to declare something which later comes to light, and could have had a bearing on its decision, the Panel may then need to consider whether to recommend the removal of Silk to the Lord Chancellor.

42. In accordance with the Process, the Secretariat will send lists of all applicants to senior members of the judiciary and to the relevant professional body with

responsibility for professional conduct. For this reason we **seek your authority to check your disciplinary record** with your professional regulator or other body.

43. **The Panel expects that the information you provide in your submitted application will be complete, true and factually accurate.** It is your responsibility to ensure that the information in the form is both correct and complete. Please check carefully that all parts of the form are fully complete and accurate before you submit your application. **You will not be allowed to add to or amend your application form once the closing date has passed.** However, if you subsequently become aware of any factual inaccuracies or changes to contact details please notify the Secretariat as soon as possible and provide the revised details.

In all cases you must ensure you have added your name to the signature box at Section I of the application form. This is your 'electronic signature' and acts as your declaration and authority.

Your application must be accompanied by a fee of £2,160 (£1,800 plus VAT) payable in full by the application deadline. The preferred option for payment is to be made online after you have uploaded your application form to the submission page. Please follow the steps provided to pay by direct debit or credit card. If for any reason the Panel declines to accept your application your fee will be returned, but may be subject to a deduction to cover administrative costs.

There are no fees for payment by personal and corporate debit cards.

Credit cards will incur a £35.00 transaction fee for each application, levied by the supplier.

You may also pay by electronic payment direct to our account

Bank: Royal Bank of Scotland, Child & Co Branch,

1 Fleet Street, London EC4Y 1BD

Sort Code: 15-80-00

Account: Queen's Counsel Appointments

Account No: 10578135

Please quote your surname and ID number as the reference for your payment. You may wish to ask your bank for confirmation of payment.

OR

By means of a cheque made payable to *Queen's Counsel Appointments*. The cheque must be in pounds sterling and drawn on a UK bank or Building Society.

Any application which is made without the payment of the fee will be treated as invalid.

You should receive by email a VAT receipt for your fee once payment is confirmed online. If payment is by cheque or electronic transfer it will take around 21 working days from receipt of both your application and the payment.

In the event that the application is successful, a further appointment fee of £3,000 plus VAT will become payable, in addition to the cost of Letters Patent.

44. At Section J, all applicants are invited to provide the **monitoring information** requested. Promoting equality of opportunity and diversity in the legal professions is important to the Panel; Section J will be retained in the office and will not be provided to the Panel. The information you enter on it will only be used for statistical purposes, on an anonymised basis, and for evaluating the process as a whole. It will not be used when considering your suitability for the award of Queen's Counsel.

Disability

45. Any applicant who has particular needs participating in the application process, including those arising from a disability, should contact the Secretariat, and we will endeavour to make arrangements to meet your needs. The application form can be provided in Braille on request.

All applicants who are invited to interview (irrespective of whether they have indicated that they have a disability) will be asked to let us know of any particular arrangements which they wish us to make to enable them to participate fully in the interview (such as seating arrangements, access etc.). However, you are under no obligation to disclose details of a disability at any stage in the selection process.

46. Please ensure you tick yes or no.

47. Please ensure you tick yes or no.

Appendix A – The Competency Framework

[8.4]

The Panel will judge how far an applicant meets the competencies as described by the passage in italics. The examples provided are intended to assist applicants, assessors and others. Consideration of the demonstration of the competency is not limited to the examples quoted. To merit recommendation for appointment all competencies must be demonstrated to a standard of excellence in the applicant's professional life. In general the Selection Panel will be looking for the demonstration of the competencies in cases of substance, complexity, or particular difficulty or sensitivity. Competency B (Written and oral advocacy) *must* be demonstrated in such cases.

A. Understanding and using the law

Has expert, up-to-date legal knowledge and uses it accurately and relevantly, and becomes familiar with new areas of law quickly and reliably.

Examples:

- Is up to date with law and precedent relevant to each case dealt with, or will quickly and reliably make self familiar with new areas of law.

- Draws on law accurately for case points and applies relevant legal principles to particular facts of case.

B. Written and oral advocacy

Develops and advances client's case to secure the best outcome for the client by gaining a rapid, incisive overview of complex material, identifying the best course of action, communicating the case persuasively, and rapidly assimilating the implications of new evidence and argument and responding appropriately.

The Panel will be looking both at the written and oral aspects of advocacy. Oral advocacy includes advocacy in a court or tribunal, mediation, arbitration or negotiation.

Examples (Written advocacy):

- Writes arguments accurately, coherently and simply, and in an accessible style.
- Presents facts and structures arguments in a coherent, balanced and focused manner.
- Deals effectively with necessary preliminary stages of legal disputes.
- Gains and gives an accurate understanding of complex and voluminous case material.
- Appreciates aspects of the case that are particularly important, sensitive or difficult and appreciates the relative importance of each item of evidence.
- Prepares thoroughly for the case by identifying the best arguments to pursue and preparing alternative strategies.
- Anticipates points that will challenge an argument.

Examples (Oral advocacy):

- Deals responsibly with difficult points of case management and disclosure.
- Presents facts and structures arguments in a coherent, balanced and focused manner.
- Assimilates new information and arguments rapidly and accurately.
- Immediately sees implications of answers by witness and responds appropriately.
- Listens attentively to what is said paying keen attention to others' understanding and reactions.
- Accurately sees the point of questions from the tribunal and answers effectively.
- Gives priority to non-court resolution throughout the case where appropriate, identifies possible bases for settlement and takes effective action.
- Prepared and able to change tack or to persist, as appropriate.
- Deals effectively with points which challenge an argument.

C. Working with others

Establishes productive working relationships with all, including professional and lay clients, the judge and other parties' representatives and members of own team; is involved in the preparation of the case and leads the team before the court or other tribunal.

Examples:

- Behaves in a consistent and open way in all professional dealings.
- Establishes an appropriate rapport with all others in court and in conference.
- Advances arguments in way that reflects appropriate consideration of perspective of everyone involved in the case.
- Helps the client focus on relevant points and is candid with the client.
- Explains law and court procedure to client and ensures the client understands and can decide the best action.
- Keeps lay and professional clients informed of progress.
- Is prepared to advance an argument that might not be popular and to stand up to the judge.
- Responds to the needs and circumstances of client (including client's means and importance of case to client and bearing in mind duty to legal aid fund) and advises client accordingly.
- Meets commitments and appointments.
- Accepts ultimate responsibility for case when leading the team.
- Motivates, listens to and works with other members of own team.
- Aware of own limitations and seeks to ensure that they are compensated for by others in team.
- Able to take key decisions with authority and after listening to views.
- Identifies priorities and allocates tasks and roles when leading the team.

D. Diversity

Demonstrates an understanding of diversity and cultural issues, and is proactive in addressing the needs of people from all backgrounds and promoting diversity and equality of opportunity.

Examples:

- Is aware of the diverse needs of individuals resulting from differences in gender, sexual orientation, ethnic origin, age and educational attainment and physical or mental disability or other reason, and responds appropriately and sensitively.
- Is aware of the impact of diversity and cultural issues on witnesses, parties to proceedings and others as well as on own client, and adjusts own behaviour accordingly.
- Takes positive action to promote diversity and equality of opportunity.

- Understands needs and circumstances of others and acts accordingly.
- Confronts discrimination and prejudice when observed in others; does not let it pass unchecked.
- Acts as a role model for others in handling diversity and cultural issues.

E. Integrity

Is honest and straightforward in professional dealings, including with the court and all parties.

Examples:

- Does not mislead, conceal or create a false impression.
- Honours professional codes of conduct.
- Where appropriate refers to authorities adverse to the client's case.
- Always behaves so as to command the confidence of the tribunal and others involved in the case, as well as client.
- Acts in professional life in such a way as to maintain the high reputation of advocates and Queen's Counsel.

QC Secretariat

Appendix B – Guidance on Handling Issues of Character and Conduct

Introduction

[8.5]

A1 This Appendix gives guidance as to how the matters referred to in Section C of the application form (*Character*) will be handled by the Panel. You should read this before completing that section. It will help you to decide whether an issue is material to your application and needs to be disclosed.

A2 If, having read this Appendix, you are still in doubt as to whether to disclose a matter, then you should do so, so that the Panel can make the appropriate decision. You should be aware that if you fail to declare something which later comes to light, and could have had a bearing on its decision, the Panel may then need to consider whether to recommend the removal of Silk.

A3 The Panel expects to be notified immediately of any change of circumstances in relation to matters of character in the course of the competition. This includes:

- where any complaint against you is dismissed;
- where a finding is made against you;
- where a new issue arises (eg a complaint);

- where other action is in prospect (such as criminal proceedings, a wasted costs order, bankruptcy or voluntary arrangement, or any kind of investigation by any professional, regulatory or complaints handling authority).

Handling of issues of character

A4 The Panel has said that it will consider an issue of character only where it could affect the decision whether or not to recommend an applicant for appointment. In other words, the Panel will generally assess your application based on the self-assessment, summary description of practice, assessments and (where applicable) interview alone, without regard to any matter disclosed by you in Section C of the application form or otherwise, or in response to the professional conduct check. Only if it appears that a character issue is of sufficient seriousness to affect any eventual decision as to recommendation for appointment will the Panel be made aware of an issue of character in relation to a named applicant. If you are invited for interview, the interviewers will not generally be aware of a character issue and you should therefore not mention such a matter during the interview, unless raised by the interviewers.

Professional conduct and integrity checks

A5 In accordance with the Process, the Secretariat will send lists of all applicants to senior members of the judiciary and to the relevant professional body with responsibility for professional conduct. For this reason we seek your authority to check your disciplinary record with your professional regulator or other body.

A6 If any of the senior judges who has received the list has reason to believe that an issue concerning integrity as it relates to the Competency Framework is known to another judge, he may invite the Panel to seek comments from the judge concerned. If comments are sought from the judge concerned, the comments will be directed at the integrity element of the Competency Framework. Concerns will have to be fully particularised. If any concerns about integrity are identified in this way they will be put to you, so that you have an opportunity to provide an explanation to the Panel.

A7 Where checks with the professional bodies reveal that an applicant is or has been subject to a disciplinary finding or pending complaint, the Secretariat will contact the applicant for a full explanation, unless such explanation has already been given in the application form or volunteered by the applicant. If any matters of concern are identified in this way they will be put to you in writing by the Secretariat on behalf of the Panel, so that you have an opportunity to provide an explanation. If a finding or complaint is reported which you have not disclosed in your application form, the Secretariat will write to you to give you an opportunity to address in writing (a) the question of non-disclosure and (b) the materiality of the finding or complaint to your application.

Consideration by the sub Panel

A8 If a character issue is disclosed then the relevant part of the application form and/or correspondence (with any details identifying the applicant removed) will be placed before a sub Panel made up of members of the Panel. The sub Panel, reporting to the full Panel, will form a view as to whether the issue is serious enough potentially to affect any eventual decision to recommend an applicant if he or she otherwise appears suitable for appointment. If the sub Panel requires further information or clarification from the applicant, it will ask the Secretariat to write to him or her. The sub Panel will reach its conclusions independently of the Panel's consideration of the other evidence relating to each applicant.

A9 Only issues which the sub Panel considers to be of such seriousness as potentially to affect any eventual recommendation will be brought to the full Panel's attention in relation to a named applicant. This will normally be at the point at which the Panel decides the applicant has demonstrated the competencies sufficiently to be invited to interview. Where it is agreed that an issue is not sufficiently serious to impact on any eventual decision on an application, the Panel will not be made aware of it when considering that application. The sub Panel's role is to advise whether or not the issue is of sufficient concern that it needs to be considered by the full Panel. Final decisions as to whether or not to interview or recommend an applicant rest with the full Panel.

Considerations in determining issues of character

A10 The following considerations will be borne in mind by the sub Panel in making its decisions.

A11 Applications are assessed against the Competency Framework. All advocates, whether QCs or not, are expected to maintain the high standards of their professions.

A12 Character is considered as a whole. If more than one issue is presented by an applicant, then the sub Panel will consider:

- Whether any one issue by itself is or may be of concern; or if not
- Whether all issues taken together are or may be of concern, disregarding any that may not be taken into account (see paragraph A16 below).

A13 In other words, one relatively minor instance may not be considered serious enough to be a bar to recommendation, but the sub Panel will consider whether there is evidence of a pattern of behaviour that the Panel needs to take into account.

A14 In the case of pending criminal proceedings, complaints and professional negligence claims, or other pending matters, the sub Panel will consider whether the complaint or claim, if substantiated, would be of sufficient seriousness to provide grounds for the Panel to wish to defer any recommendation.

A15 Unless the applicant has provided a satisfactory explanation in correspondence, any question of non-disclosure of an issue by an applicant may be treated as being of sufficient seriousness to require consideration by the full Panel.

A16 The following need not be disclosed:

- Criminal convictions or cautions that are 'spent' under the Rehabilitation of Offenders Act 1974. The Panel takes the view that under the Rehabilitation of Offenders Act 1974 a candidate need not disclose a spent conviction and the Panel will not take a spent conviction into account when considering an applicant.
- Complaints, professional negligence claims and other proceedings against an applicant that have been dismissed.
- Cases of alleged negligence where liability is not admitted and has not yet been settled and where there is as yet no finding by a court or tribunal, or other resolution. (The Panel would, however, expect the applicant to inform the Secretariat of the outcome once it is reached).

A17 Subject to other factors described in this Appendix, character issues will be assessed by the Panel in the light of the following criteria:

- Seriousness.
- Time elapsed since the incident occurred.
- Experience at the time of the incident, in the sense that 'youthful indiscretions' are to be disregarded. In particular, matters predating the applicant's first Call or Admission to one of the professions will normally be ignored (although they should still be disclosed, except as specified above).
- Relevance of the incident to the Competency Framework.
- Any other feature that might cause concern, e.g. as potentially bringing the position of QC into disrepute, having an adverse impact on the client, or failure to disclose a finding or pending complaint of professional disciplinary fault.

A18 The Panel has indicated that (among other things) it takes very seriously matters relating to:

- dishonesty;
- sexual harassment or intimidation;
- drink driving;
- the use or handling of illegal drugs
- suspension from practice.

Criminal convictions (other than 'spent' convictions etc.)

A19 Particular considerations apply in the following cases:

- Minor motoring offences where the applicant was not obliged to appear in court should be disregarded. However, any motoring offence resulting in disqualification, including under totting up, should be disclosed.

- Any conviction or caution for an offence of dishonesty or resulting in a term of imprisonment will be of serious concern and is likely to be a bar to appointment.
- Any other unspent conviction, caution or bindover will be considered on its individual merits.

Findings of Professional Negligence

A20 The sub Panel will only consider findings of fault or cases where an applicant has admitted being at fault. Where a claim against you has been dismissed, it should not be disclosed. Where a claim against you has been settled, you should disclose it, but indicate clearly whether and to what extent you have accepted liability.

A21 Findings of negligence and cases where the applicant admits to being at fault will be assessed taking into account the degree of loss and the importance of the matter to the client along with any other relevant factors.

Professional disciplinary fault

A22 Findings of professional disciplinary fault will be relevant to Competency E – Integrity, as showing prima facie a failure to honour professional codes. In other respects they will be treated on a case-by-case basis having regard to factors such as the penalty imposed. Generally, a penalty such as a fine, suspension from practice or order to pay compensation is likely to be treated as indicating that the profession regarded the offence as serious, while admonishment or a reprimand may suggest that it was less serious, but this is not to be regarded as an absolute rule. Whether the client or any other person suffered loss or harm as a result, and whether the applicant accepted his or her fault, may also be relevant.

A wasted costs order

A23 Wasted costs orders will be considered with regard to the reason given for the order's being made, the amount involved and the length of time since the order was made.

An intervention by the Law Society, the Solicitors Regulation Authority, Office for the Supervision of Solicitors or the Solicitors' Complaints Bureau

A complaint which has been referred to the Office of Legal Complaints or Legal Ombudsman

A24 Such cases will be considered with regard to all the circumstances, but the sub Panel will take account of any suggestion of dishonesty, lack of openness or failure to honour professional codes or obligations to clients, or actually or potentially jeopardising clients' interests.

A bankruptcy order, debt relief order or an individual or partnership voluntary arrangement

A director's disqualification order

A25 A current or recent (ie within 5 years of discharge) Individual Voluntary Arrangement (IVA) or bankruptcy or other order will be of serious concern and is likely to be a bar to appointment. However, such cases will be considered with regard to all the circumstances.

Any other form of order or proceeding that may be material to the Panel in considering your application to be appointed Queen's Counsel

A26 You should disclose any matter not covered by the above categories but which a reasonable person would regard as material to your application, having regard to the general criteria mentioned above. An example of such a matter would be a foreign criminal conviction or an order of a court or tribunal outside of the United Kingdom.

Anything else in your personal or professional background which (if brought to into the public domain) could affect your suitability for appointment or bring the legal profession or Queen's Counsel into disrepute

A 27 You should disclose anything else at all, whether related to your professional or personal life, which could affect your standing or reputation, or could affect your suitability for appointment as Queen's Counsel or bring the legal profession or Queen's Counsel into disrepute.

Further assistance

A28 If you have any doubts about the application of this guidance to your own circumstances you may discuss the matter in confidence with a senior member of the QC Secretariat staff.

Index